Kaupang in Skiringssal

Kaupang in Skiringssal

Edited by Dagfinn Skre

Kaupang Excavation Project
Publication Series, Volume 1

Norske Oldfunn XXII

Kaupang in Skiringssal
Kaupang Excavation Project Publication Series, Volume 1
Norske Oldfunn XXII

© Aarhus University Press
& the Kaupang Excavation Project, University of Oslo 2007
Published as part of the series *Norske Oldfunn,*
Museum of Cultural History, University of Oslo
English translation: John Hines
Language revision: Frank Azevedo, John Hines
Technical editing: Frank Azevedo, Dagfinn Skre
Map production: Julie K. Øhre Askjem, Anne Engesveen
Illustration editing: Elise Naumann, Julie K. Øhre Askjem
Cover illustration: Johannes Flintoe:
"A Duel. Norwegian Depiction" c. 1835. Nasjonalgalleriet, Oslo.
Graphic design, typesetting and cover: Jørgen Sparre
Type: Minion and Linotype Syntax
Paper: PhoeniXmotion Xantur, 135 g
Printed by Narayana Press, Denmark
Printed in Denmark 2007

ISBN 978-87-7934-259-0

Copyright maps:
Contour distances 1 meter: The Muncipality of Larvik
Contour distances 5 metres: Norwegian Mapping and Cadastre Authority Scandinavia
Europe: ESRI

The University of Oslo wishes to thank the financial contributors to the Kaupang Excavation Project:

Ministry of the Environment

The Anders Jahre Humanitarian Foundation

Ministry of Education and Research

Vestfold County Council

Ministry of Culture and Church Affairs

The Municipality of Larvik

The Research Council of Norway

Arts Council Norway

Preface

As the work on this first volume from The Kaupang Excavation Project reaches an end, two feelings dominate: gratitude and humility. Above all, I wish to express my sincere gratitude towards the late Principal Inspector Charlotte Blindheim for the great confidence she placed in me by asking me to take over the direction of the archaeological investigations at Kaupang. I also wish to express my gratitude to the institutions named on the previous page that have believed in and financially supported this project. A special thanks is given to The Anders Jahre Humanitarian Foundation which gave its strong early support to the project, as a result of which I gained confidence that our aims could indeed be reached.

The Municipality of Larvik has been a crucial partner in the practical work of the excavation phase. Vestfold County Council has proved a dynamic force in protecting and developing Kaupang after the excavation period. I thank both of them. A number of individuals in Larvik were both very helpful and hospitable during the excavations, amongst whom I wish particularly to thank Marit Kaupang Aspaas, the landowner of Kaupang, for her fair approach and excellent cooperation.

The Kaupang Excavation Project Council, which is composed of representatives of key sponsors and distinguished archaeologists from Scandinavia, Britain and Ireland, has had the responsibility of ensuring that the project proceeded according to its plan. The Council has also provided advice, and undertaken crucial discussions that have helped shape the development of the project. It also played a decisive role when the final funding of the project was put in place in 2003. I wish to thank all of the members of the Council – a list can be found on p. 501 – and especially its President, Kaare Reidar Norum, for his unfailing enthusiasm and supportiveness.

For the excavation period, the project had an Advisory Committee, which advised on excavation strategy and methods. I wish to thank the members of this Committee, who are listed on p. 502, for their solid and constructive contributions. In working on this book I, as its editor, have been in touch with many specialists in most of Northern Europe who have read and commented on drafts tirelessly and patiently. My profound thanks goes to them all. Within the University of Oslo there has been multifaceted cooperation from the Museum of Cultural History.

I have had the very good fortune to be surrounded by loyal and dedicated colleagues and staff in the project's preliminary stages, during the excavations, and in the project's analysis and publication stages. My thanks to them all. The two who have been there throughout, Unn Pedersen and Lars Pilø, merit special thanks. They have been indispensable.

Humility, as was mentioned above, may not strike the reader as a virtue obviously present in my contributions to this book, e.g. in the statement in Chapter 1 of my high ambitions for the project. But someone who has the opportunity to work with such rich and important archaeological sites as Kaupang and Skiringssal must have high ambitions – anything less would undervalue the site. Excavating such sites is therefore a great responsibility. This book is published with full awareness of that responsibility. I hope that readers of the book will feel that we have lived up to it.

Oslo, November 2006

Dagfinn Skre
Leader of the Kaupang Excavation Project
University of Oslo

Contents

1   *Dagfinn Skre*
Introduction   13
   1.1   The ambitions of the Kaupang Excavation Project   15
      About the current volume   18
      Future publications   18
   1.2   Kaupang and Skiringssal in the archaeology of the Viking Period   18
   1.3   Exploring the distant past   22

Part I: **Background**   25

2   *Dagfinn Skre*
Exploring Skiringssal 1771-1999   27
   2.1   The literati and the antiquarians 1771–1850   28
   2.2   The historian and the archaeologist 1850–1867   31
   2.3   A modest revival 1901–1902   36
   2.4   Advances in Skiringssal research 1909–1950   38
   2.5   The breakthrough: Charlotte Blindheim's excavations 1950–1974   38
      and publications 1960–1999

3   *Dagfinn Skre*
Preparing the New Campaign   43
   3.1   Scandinavian urban sites prior to AD 1000: the central issues   44
      Defining the town   45
      Research on the early urban sites of Scandinavia   46
      New excavations at Kaupang   47
   3.2   Skiringssal: a central place   48
   3.3   A wider scope of questions   50

4   *Stefan Brink*
Skiringssal, Kaupang, Tjølling – the Toponymic Evidence   53
   4.1   The Early Iron-age names   54
   4.2   The Late Iron-age and Viking-age names   59
   4.3   Summary   63

5   *Frans-Arne Stylegar*
The Kaupang Cemeteries Revisited   65
   5.1   The cemeteries   68
      Søndre Kaupang (Ka. 150–166)   69

		Nordre Kaupang (Ka. 1–73)	69
		Hagejordet (Ka. 125–134)	70
		Bikjholberget (Ka. 250–323)	72
		Lamøya (Ka. 200–230)	74
		Bjønnes	74
		Vikingholmen	75
	5.2	Number of burials	75
	5.3	The dated burials	78
		The problematic 8th century	79
		The 9th and 10th centuries	80
		The late 10th century	81
	5.4	The dead	82
		The gendered burials	82
		Weapon combinations	83
		The chronology of the imported finds	84
		Population estimate	85
	5.5	Horizontal stratigraphy	86
	5.6	Mortuary customs	87
		The treatment of the body	87
		The external structure of the graves	87
		The alignment of the graves	88
		The internal structure of the graves	88
	5.7	A horseman and a falconer? Ka. 157	93
	5.8	The horseshoe from Ka. 250	95
	5.9	A couple and their sorceress? Ka. 294–296	96
		The bronze bowl	98
	5.10	Concluding remarks – Birka and Kaupang	99
		Comprehensive catalogue of grave-finds from Kaupang	102
		Concordance table	126
6		*Lars Pilø*	
		Evidence from the Settlement Area 1956-1984	127
	6.1	Introduction	127
	6.2	The methodology of the excavation of 1956–1984	131
	6.3	The interpretation of the documented structures	134
	6.4	Evidence from other parts of the settlement area	136
	6.5	The platform for the new fieldwork	137
Part II:		**Excavations and Surveys 1998-2003**	141
7		*Lars Pilø*	
		The Fieldwork 1998-2003: Overview and Methods	143
	7.1	Introduction	143
	7.2	Surveys	144
		7.2.1 Introduction	144
		7.2.2 Field surveys	144
		Method	145
		Results	148
		7.2.3 Geophysical prospection	149
		Magnetometer	149
		Ground Penetrating Radar	151
		Augering	151
	7.3	Excavations	152
		7.3.1 The main research excavation 2000–2002	153
		7.3.2 Cultural resource management excavations 2000–2003	153
		7.3.3 Minor excavations and surveillance	154
		7.3.4 Method of excavation	155

Artefact recovery from the ploughsoil   156
Water-sieving of the intact deposits   157
Environmental archaeology and geoarchaeology   158
Dendrochronology   158
Intrasis   158
Context sheets   160
7.4 Summary   160

8   Lars Pilø
The Settlement: Extent and Dating   161
8.1 Introduction   161
8.2 Topography   162
8.3 The extent of the settlement area   164
The southern settlement area   164
The central plateau   167
The northern settlement area   168
The peripheral area to the north   169
Conclusion   172
8.4 Dating   172
The establishment of the site   172
Activities pre-dating the settlement   172
The start date for the settlement   175
The end date of the settlement   177
Kaupang after the Viking-age settlement   178
8.5 Summary   178

9   Lars Pilø, Unn Pedersen
The Settlement: Artefacts and Site Periods   179
9.1 Introduction   179
9.2 A quantitative overview of the artefacts   180
9.3 Site Periods in the main research excavation of 2000–2002   184
9.4 Site Periods and artefacts   186
9.5 Summary   189

10   Lars Pilø
The Settlement: Character, Structures and Features   191
10.1 Introduction   191
10.2 The character   192
The initial seasonal settlement – Site Period I   192
The permanent settlement: the stratified deposits – Site Period II   195
The later settlement – Site Period III   200
10.3 Building constructions   203
Building A200   204
Building A406   206
Building A304   207
Building A302   207
Building A303   208
Building A301   209
A89947 – an animal pen?   211
Building on Plot "Hus III" of the 1956–1974 excavations   211
Building on Plot "Hus V" of the 1956–1974 excavations?   213
A discussion of the buildings   214
10.4 Pits   218
10.5 Jetties   220
10.6 Summary   222

11   *Dagfinn Skre*
        Excavations of the Hall at Huseby   223
        11.1 The discovery of the building platform at Huseby   223
        11.2 Trial excavation, 1999   225
        11.3 Excavation and method, 2000–2001   225
        11.4 The history of the platform site   227
              The barrow   227
              The building platform   228
              The hall   231
              The assemblage, distribution and date of finds from the hall   234
              The corner-timbered building or stofa   243

Part III: Scientific Analyses   249

12   *Rolf Sørensen, Kari E. Henningsmoen, Helge I. Høeg, Bjørg Stabell*
        and Kristine M. Bukholm
        Geology, Soils, Vegetation and Sea-levels in the Kaupang Area   251
        12.1 Introduction   251
        12.2 Soils and sediments in the Kaupang area   254
              12.2.1 Distribution and properties of the soil types   257
        12.3 Vegetation development during the late holocene   258
              12.3.1 Description of the Kaupangmyra bog, 18.5 m a.s.l.   260
              The vegetation history   260
              12.3.2 Description of the Kaupangkilen bay   265
              The vegetation history   266
        12.4 Sea-level changes during late holocene   267
              12.4.1 Sea-level AD 800   268
              12.4.2 The development of the Kaupang harbour   269
        12.5 Discussion and Conclusions   270
              12.5.1 Landscape development   270
              12.5.2 Soils and sediments   270
              12.5.3 Vegetation history   271
              12.5.4 Sea-level change   271

13   *Niels Bonde*
        Dendrochronological Dates from Kaupang   273
        13.1 Introduction   273
        13.2 Samples taken from timber found during the excavations in 1967   276
        13.3 Samples taken from timber found during the excavations in 1970   276
        13.4 Samples taken from timber found during the excavations in 2000–02   277
        13.5 Summary of the dates

14   *James Barrett, Allan Hall, Cluny Johnstone, Harry Kenward,*
        Terry O'Connor and Steve Ashby
        Interpreting the Plant and Animal Remains from Viking-age Kaupang   283
        14.1 Introduction   283
        14.2 Methods   284
        14.3 The material: an overview   287
        14.4 The features: hearths, occupation deposits, dumps, pit fills
              and harbour deposits   296
        14.5 Seasonality and permanence   301
        14.6 Provisioning and relationships with the hinterland   303
        14.7 Long-range trade   307
        14.8 Regional dietary practices and "identity"   310
        14.9 Conclusions   310

Appendix 14.1   311
Appendix 14.2   316
Appendix 14.3   317
Appendix 14.4   319

15   *Karen B. Milek, Charles A.I. French*
     Soils and Sediments in the Settlement and Harbour at Kaupang   321
     15.1 Introduction   321
     15.2 Methodology   323
     15.3 Post-depositional processes affecting the archaeological record
           at Kaupang   324
               Leaching and eluviation of elements and fine material   324
               Redistribution of iron   325
               Bioturbation   326
     15.4 Soils pre-dating the urban settlement   328
     15.5 Sediments from the earliest activity phase at Kaupang   328
     15.6 Sediments in the pathway between plots 1A and 2A   331
     15.7 Sediments on building plots 3A and 3B   333
               Plot 3B   335
               SP II, sub-phase 1: building A303   335
               The gravel layer between buildings A303 and A301   337
               SP II, sub-phase 2: building A301   337
               Plot 3A   344
               SP II, sub-phase 1: building A304   344
               The sand layer between buildings A304 and A302   346
               SP II, sub-phase 2: building A302   347
     15.8 Sediments in the midden area   352
     15.9 Sediments in the harbour area   354
     15.10 Summary and conclusion   358

Part IV: **Skiringssal**   361

16   *Dagfinn Skre*
     The Skiringssal Cemetery   363
     16.1 The extent of the cemetery   363
               Barrows on the Larvik County map of 1811   367
               Flintoe's painting and sketches of the 1830s   367
               Zeuthen's plan of 1845   370
               Aerial photography 1977–1994   373
               The original size of the cemetery   375
     16.2 The Skiringssal cemetery   377

17   *Dagfinn Skre*
     The Skiringssal *Thing* site *Þjoðalyng*   385
     17.1 Things and laws c. 800–1250   386
     17.2 Thing site and church site   389
               The large basilica at þjóðalyng   390
               þjóðalyng church – a minster   392
               þjóðalyng church – a fylkiskirkja?   394
               þjóðalyng church – a thing-site church   395
               þjóðalyng in the Viking Age   396
     17.3 The assembly place by the sacred lake   397
               The specialised cooking-pit sites   397
               The assembly place and the sacred   400
     17.4 Assembly place and *thing* site   403

18   *Dagfinn Skre*
        The Dating of *Ynglingatal*   407
        18.1 *Ynglingatal* – a poem of the late 12th century?   409
                Krag's anachronisms   409
                Krag's "Vestfold viewpoint"   410
                Krag's problematic redating   412

        18.2 *Ynglingatal* from Ari to Snorri   413
                The whereabouts of the Yngling petty kings   415
                The Oppland viewpoint and the Vestfold viewpoint   419
        18.3 Anachronisms?   422
        18.4 Emulatio Uppsaliensis   424
        18.5 The date of *Ynglingatal*   428

19   *Dagfinn Skre*
        The Emergence of a Central Place: 431
        Skiringssal in the 8th Century
        19.1 Halfdan Whiteleg's burial place – *Skereið*   432
        19.2 Halfdan Whiteleg – *þjóðkonung* and *þingmaðr*   435
        19.3 Eystein Fart – *blótmaðr*   437
        19.4 Skiringssal before AD 800   440
        19.5 The Skiringssal domain   442

20   *Dagfinn Skre*
        Towns and Markets, Kings and Central Places   445
        in South-western Scandinavia c. AD 800–950
        20.1 Trade at the central place   446
                Trade and the sacred   446
                Commercial exchange in the 1st millennium   448
                Threatening trade   450
        20.2 Towns in the king's realm   452
                Markets and towns   452
                Markets and central places   455
                Towns, kings and frontiers   458
        20.3 The Ynglings and the Danes in Viken and Skiringssal c. AD 750–950 463
                The evidence of Ynglingatal   463
                Kaupang and Skiringssal AD 800–900: between the Ynglings
                and the Danes   466
                Kaupang and Skiringssal after AD 900   468

Abbreviations   471

References   473

List of Authors   499

Members of the Kaupang Excavation Project Council 2000-2006   501

Members of the Kaupang Excavation Project Advisory Committee 2000-2002   502

Introduction

DAGFINN SKRE

The urban site of Kaupang, and the central-place complex of Skiringssal of which it was part, are key sites for the study of the Viking Period in Scandinavia. Research into these sites began more than 200 years ago, the last major project before the current one being Charlotte Blindheim's excavations between 1950 and 1974. Great advances in the understanding of urban sites and central places in Scandinavia, and much improved methods of field archaeology led to *The Kaupang Excavation Project* being planned in the late 1990s and carried out from 2000 onwards.

The principal ambitions of this project are: to produce new empirical evidence and develop a new understanding of Kaupang and Skiringssal; to develop new ways of approaching the culture and society of the Viking Age; and, to contribute new elements to the comprehensive image of the Scandinavian Viking Period. We are attempting to achieve these ambitions through high standards of fieldwork and analysis during the project, detailed dialogue with other relevant disciplines in the natural sciences and humanities, and a quite deliberate investment in extensive communication between the authors contributing to the project.

An overview of the most relevant archaeological sources for the Viking Period in Scandinavia forms the basis for an assessment of the importance of Kaupang and Skiringssal in research. To conclude, an outline is given of the understanding of the scholarly study of the past that is the basis for the design of both the project and this book.

Everyone familiar with the Viking Age in Scandinavia will have read or heard of *Kaupang*. At the farm of Kaupang in Vestfold, near the mouth of the Oslofjord, lie the remains of one of the earliest urban sites in Scandinavia, founded around AD 800 and abandoned in the mid-10th century (Fig. 1.3). The average Viking-age scholar will be less familiar with *Skiringssal*, the name by which Kaupang was referred to in the first extant source relating to the site, the travelogue of the Norwegian Ohthere (*Óttarr*) from the late 9th century (Skre, this vol. Ch. 2:29). Until the urban settlement at Kaupang was discovered by Principal Inspector (*førstekonservator*) Charlotte Blindheim in 1956, it was in fact Skiringssal that lay at the centre of archaeological and historical research attention. Documentary sources from the period c. AD 890–1300 refer to Skiringssal several times, and provide an image of the place not only as comprising an urban site but also as an important royal seat that was at the same time a cult centre and assembly place for a large

territory (Fig. 1.2) – possibly the whole of Viken, the lands surrounding the Oslofjord (Fig. 1.1).

Research into Skiringssal and Kaupang has a history of more than two centuries, within which Blindheim's excavations of 1950–1974 represented a real breakthrough. Earlier, Gerhard Schøning (1771), Jens Kraft (1822), Gerhard Munthe (comments in the 1838–1839 edition of Snorri Sturluson's *Heimskringla*), Peter Andreas Munch (1850, 1852), Nicolay Nicolaysen (1868) and Gustav Storm (1901) had each made crucial contributions to the understanding of the site (Skre, this vol. Ch. 2).

Major advances in the study of the early urban sites and central places in Scandinavia, and not least in the methods of field archaeology, meant that by the late 1990s the time was ripe to take a new step forward in research into Kaupang and Skiringssal (Skre, this vol. Ch. 3). A research project was organized at the Institute of Archaeology, Conservation and Historical Studies of the University of Oslo, and the field-

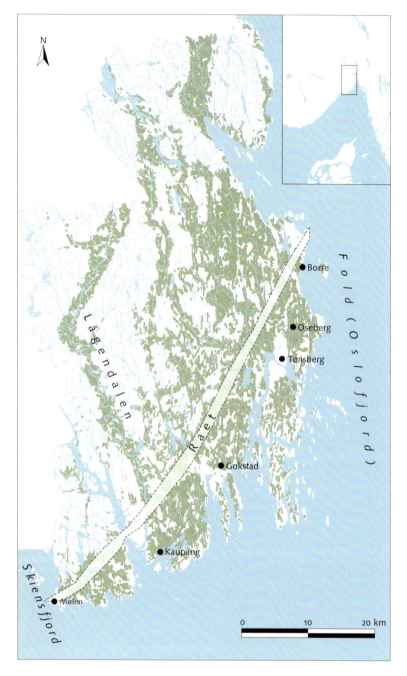

Figure 1.1 *Vestfold means "West of the Fold", and* Fold *is the ancient name of the Oslofjord. Vestfold is the richest region of Norway in Viking-period archaeology. Some of the most important sites are shown here. Areas under cultivation in modern times are shaded green, largely reflecting the situation in the Viking Age.*

There were three principal routeways in Vestfold. The first was the sailing route along the coast, *which all maritime traffic followed. The second was* Raet *(The Ridge), the great morainic belt that runs SSW to NNE a little way in from the coast. The well-drained soil of the moraine was favourable to agriculture; for land travel in coastal areas of Vestfold, Raet was the natural route. The third routeway was that from the south into the interior along* Lågendalen *(the Låg Valley). This valley, which is also well-suited to agriculture and could in parts support substantial settlement, leads up to Numedal, which in turn adjoins the mountain plateau of Hardangervidda, which one can cross to reach the western coastal regions. It is also easy to descend from Numedal into the Drammen River system or north to Ringerike, Hadeland and the remaining "Opplands" (Skre, this vol. Ch. 18:Fig. 18.2). The western boundary of modern Vestfold is the fjord now known as Skiensfjord which leads into the mouth of the Telemark River valley. This valley branches into several smaller valleys that lead into the various parts of Grenland and Telemark, and further up to the southern part of Hardangervidda. Map, Julie K. Øhre Askjem.*

Figure 1.2 *The most important elements in the Skiringssal central-place complex as they are identified in various chapters in this volume.* Kaupang *is the urban settlement (green outline; Pilø, this vol. Chs. 6–10) surrounded by cemeteries (red outline; Stylegar, this vol. Ch. 5) (cf. Fig. 1.3). The large northernmost cemetery was located by the main road which led to and from Kaupang. This cemetery was probably where the petty kings of Skiringssal and their followers were buried (Skre, this vol. Ch. 16). One kilometre along this road from Kaupang, at the farm of* Huseby, *the remains of a Viking-period hall have been excavated, probably the hall that gave Skiringssal its name (Skre, this vol. Chs. 11 and 19). The road is likely to have continued further north to the thing site of* Þjóðalyng *(black outline; Skre, this vol. Ch. 17). Just north of the assembly site was the lake* Vítrir/Vettrir *whose name indicates that it was considered sacred. On the south-eastern shore of the lake lies the small but distinct hill called* Helgefjell. *This name also denotes a sacred location (Brink, this vol. Ch. 4). The level shown for the lake is its assumed original level. The sea-level shown has been raised 3.5 m from today's level to show its level in the early Viking Age (Sørensen et al., this vol. Ch. 12:271). Illustration, Anne Engesveen.*

work of this project was undertaken in the years 1998–2003. The most important element within this fieldwork was a major excavation in the settlement area of Kaupang in the years 2000–2002 (Pilø, this vol. Ch. 7).

This volume is the first in a series where the results from this research project are published. It is appropriate, consequently, to first explain the background of the project and the objectives that have shaped both the project and the present book (1.1). Especially readers who are not specialists in archaeology, and readers with little previous knowledge of archaeology in Scandinavia, might benefit from the general sketch offered in this chapter of the significance of Kaupang and Skiringssal in the archaeology of the Scandinavian Viking Period (1.2; Figs. 1.1–1.3).

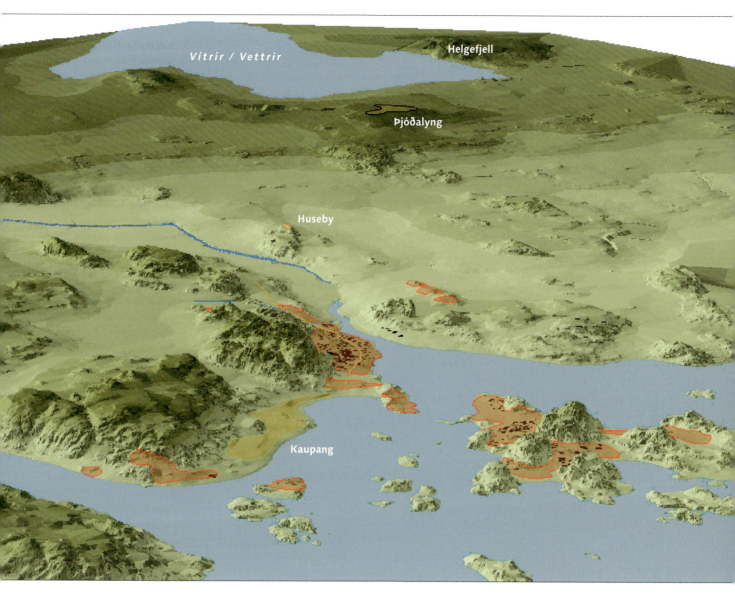

Vítrir / Vettrir

Helgefjell

Þjóðalyng

Huseby

Kaupang

Finally, the design of the project and of the current volume has been guided by specific ambitions for the scholarly study of the past, of which an account is also given (1.3).

1.1 The ambitions of the Kaupang Excavation Project

The urban centres of the Viking Period in Scandinavia are once more the targets of major research efforts. The results of the extensive excavations at Birka in the 1990s are being published (Ambrosiani 2001a, 2004; Ambrosiani and Clarke 1992, 1995b; Miller and Clarke 1997; Wigh 2001); the results from numerous excavations at Ribe and the related studies of recent decades are being brought together and published (Feveile and Jensen 2000; Feveile 2006a, 2006b); and a new campaign with fresh reviews of the vast body of evidence from earlier excavations at Hedeby has begun (e.g. Schultze 2005), and sophisticated geophysical surveys have been carried out over the whole of the settlement area (von Carnap-Bornheim and Hilberg, in press).

At the same time, there has been a great flourishing in general scholarship concerning the Viking Period and the centuries immediately preceding it, with important excavations and research work on rural central places (e.g. Larsson and Hårdh 1998, 2002, 2003; Jørgensen 2003; Larsson 2004; Lundqvist 2003; Munch et al. 2003; Söderberg 2005) and research work on the social structures of the Viking Age (e.g. Brink 1996b; Iversen 1997; Mortensen and Rasmussen 1991; Skre 1998b; Sundqvist 2002).

The new empirical evidence that has emerged has challenged many long-accepted truths, and therefore new research questions have been put on the scholarly agenda. To produce further new, concrete evidence was also one of the principal objectives of the Kaupang project when, at the end of the 1990s, new excavations were planned. We had produced for our own use overviews of the state of scholarship on Kaupang and Skiringssal and of the archaeological evidence then available. During this work, it soon became evident that it would be essential to carry out further excavations because the research questions with which we were concerned could simply not be answered with the existing evidence (Skre, this vol. Ch. 3:43–4; Pilø, this vol. Ch. 6).

In addition to the desire to produce new evidence, we recognized the need to develop new ways of approaching the Scandinavian Viking Period and to produce new elements to the overall picture of that era. New evidence will produce little additional insight if it is simply "more of the same". To justify major excavation projects, the new evidence has to be produced from deliberate and strategically designed research interventions that are directed by pertinent and central scholarly questions of wider relevance than merely to the site under excavation and the immediate fields of academic specialization to which it relates.

A research project at a site like Kaupang should therefore be concerned with topics beyond those directly concerned with the archaeology of towns. Like all fields of specialization within the multifaceted realm of archaeology, the archaeology of urban settlement must endeavour to link up with other fields within the discipline and to connect with universal research questions concerning the period under study. The study of the towns has to make itself relevant to other aspects of the subject-area by speaking clearly and audibly within the wide academic common room to which all archaeologists and historians who work on the Scandinavian Viking Age relate.

The multidisciplinary character of Viking Period studies complicates matters when it comes to realizing these general ambitions. Amongst the many disciplines interested in the Viking Period, archaeology has a distinct identity in that its primary domain is the material remains, and because new material is constantly being discovered. However another characteristic of archaeology is that in attempting to interpret this evidence, archaeologists must try to maintain adequate links with two really quite different, yet at the same time equally vital, fields of scholarship, the natural sciences and the humanities.

Close collaboration with natural scientists is indispensable because the scientists' contributions go well beyond the analysis of remains. Through detailed discussions between archaeologists and scientists we develop strategies and methods for sampling and analysis that fundamentally affect the research questions, strategy and methodology, not only during excavation but also during post-excavation work.

Furthermore, these wider links also connect archaeology with the many other disciplines concerned with the culture and society of the Viking Age: philology, toponymy, runology, textual and literary criticism, history, religious studies, art history, social anthropology, and more. As soon as the archaeologist of the Viking Period extends his or her interest beyond purely archaeological research issues such as the

chronology of arrowheads or the level of production at an iron-smelting site, it is necessary to establish and develop a dialogue with those academic disciplines. One's work would rapidly degenerate into dilettantism if, for instance, one were content to use Old Norse literature as a source without fully engaging with what historians and Norse philologists have to say about the use of such sources. Still, in our enthusiasm for interdisciplinarity, archaeologists must not ignore the discipline-specific problems which lie at the very heart of the discipline. That is where much of its creative potential resides (Skre 1999).

The rather high-flown ambition of this project has been to sort out all of this, i.e. to make a contribution to Viking-period scholarship on all three levels identified here: to produce new empirical data; to develop new methods and approaches; and to provide new details within the overall understanding of the Viking Period in Scandinavia. It has been our aim to achieve this by entering into a close collaboration with the relevant scientific fields (Sørensen et al., this vol. Ch. 12; Bonde, this vol. Ch. 13; Barrett et al., this vol. Ch. 14; Milek and French, this vol. Ch. 15; Baug, in prep.; Gaut, in prep. a; Pedersen, in prep. a and b; Pilø, in prep.; Resi, in prep. a and b). We have also consciously sought to apply the highest standards in both the fieldwork and the analytical work of this project, and to use advanced techniques of digital recording and geophysical survey (Pilø, this vol. Ch. 7:149–51, 158-60). We have simultaneously taken up major issues and basic data that have required detailed discussions with colleagues in other fields of the humanities concerned with the Viking Age (Brink, this vol. Ch. 4; Skre, this vol. Chs. 17–20; Blackburn, in prep.; Gaut, in prep. a and b; Kilger, in prep. a and b; Rispling et al., in prep.; Skre, in prep.).

These ambitions formed the basis for the planning of the project's analytical and publication stages. To create a dynamic and stimulating atmosphere within the project, a group of contributors has been put together including both distinguished and experienced scholars and talented younger researchers. Great importance has also been attached to maintaining a high level of communication between the contributors by arranging project seminars, meetings, text-based symposia, and excursions. These occasions have also helped to create a scholarly network amongst the contributors, which has proved exceptionally valuable for the younger recruits. It has also been a quite deliberate policy to create an open project circle so that the contributors can use relevant skills both within and outside the team, and use pertinent information as other scholars within the group discover it.

In a following chapter, a detailed account will be found of the principal research questions tackled by this project (Skre, this vol. Ch. 3). Immediately below is an overview of how the research tasks taken up by

Figure 1.3 *This landscape model shows the settlement area of Kaupang as far as it can be plotted from the fieldwork of 1998–2003 (Pilø, this vol. Ch. 8.3:164–72). It is possible to distinguish an area with plot-divisions and permanent buildings, shown here (yellow), from an outer zone lacking such features and with fewer artefactual finds or stratified layers (cf. Pilø, this vol. Ch. 8:Fig.8.18). This surrounding zone may have been used by visiting craftsmen and the like for temporary occupation, perhaps in tents, during periods of major influxes of people to the town.*

The town was surrounded by several cemeteries (red), some large, some small. Some of these had burials in barrows (black), others in flat graves, while yet others had a combination of these burial forms. There is also evidence of both cremation and inhumation (Stylegar, this vol. Ch. 5). The large cemetery along the road (orange) out of the town was probably not meant for the inhabitants of Kaupang but for the local petty king and his followers (Skre, this vol. Chs. 16 and 19).

The place-name Kaupang *is first recorded in a document of 1401 (DN V:290), where it is given as the name of a farm by the Viksfjord in Tjølling. However, the word itself is much older. From the period immediately after the Viking Age,* kaupangr *is known as the term meaning 'market site' and 'town'. How long this word had been current in Old Norse cannot be securely established, but there seems no doubt that it was in use in the Viking Age (Schmidt 2000b; Brink, this vol. Ch. 4:63). Its etymology is a matter of debate, but the most plausible interpretation is "trade-bay". This term was probably used for the town by the Viksfjord in its own time, but it is not clear that it would have served as a*

place-name. It is possible that the site was first referred to as Kaupang after the town had been abandoned but was still remembered.

We do not know, therefore, what the town at Skiringssal was called in the Viking Period. The view put forward by P. A. Munch in 1850 (105–6; cf. Schmidt 2000b:84–92) seems most plausible. He noted that in Ohthere's travelogue of c. 890, Skiringssal was called ān port, *"a certain port". Munch drew a comparison with the way the town of Trondheim, Norway was referred to a few centuries later. Þrándheimr was originally the name of the region, and the population of the region referred to the town simply as* kaupangr. *To people outside the region it was known as* kaupangrinn í Þrándheimi, *subsequently shortened to Þrándheimr, i.e. Trondheim. In the same way, the Viking-age population of southern Vestfold may have referred to the local town merely as* kaupangr. *It was obvious which "kaupang" they meant. In this case, this form of reference was preserved in the name of the farmstead that was later established on the site of the town. People outside that region may have referred to the site as* kaupangr í Skíringssal, *or just Skíringssal. It seems likely that Ohthere used one of those forms of reference, and that his term was re-interpreted by the Anglo-Saxon scribe who translated and wrote down his account as* ān port … þone man hæt Sciringes heal: *"a certain port … which is called Skiringssal".*

On this model of the landscape, the sea-level shown has been raised 3.5 m from today's level to show its level in the early Viking Age (Sørensen et al., this vol. Ch. 12:271). Illustration, Anne Engesveen.

the various contributors have been assigned to this and the future publications of this project.

About the current volume

At the centre of the Kaupang Excavation Project is the urban settlement that was situated on the Viksfjord at the southern end of Vestfold in the period c. AD 800–960/980, at the site where today the farm of Kaupang stands (Figs. 1.1–1.3). Since Blindheim's excavations the urban site has been called *Kaupang* after the farm, but its Viking-age name is actually uncertain (cf. Fig. 1.3). In this and the future publication from the project the name Kaupang will be used.

It is principally that site which the project has been focussed upon, and it is from there that we have obtained by far the greatest quantity of archaeological evidence from Skiringssal. In this volume the *urban site* Kaupang and its *local context* in Skiringssal are the centre of attention, and the chapters will, to varying degrees and from various angles, concern themselves with those two primary topics. The comparative ambitions are limited at this stage, but will be met to a greater degree in later volumes of this series. The objectives of this volume, each of which is fulfilled in a specific section of the book, are as follows:

- *Section I: Background.* To present the principal research questions and strategy of the project. To publish summaries and assessments of earlier research at Kaupang and in Skiringssal, and to undertake new analyses of specific categories of material previously gathered.
- *Section II: Excavations and Surveys 1998–2003.* To publish the key results of the excavations and recording undertaken during the project in 1998–2003. Only an overview is given of the arte-factual finds (Pilø and Pedersen, this vol. Ch. 9), while particular objects that are of importance in respect of, say, dating or the interpretations of buildings will be highlighted in other chapters. We have decided not to go into great detail in respect of individual layers, pits, ditches and other features. The relatively few scholars who are interested in exploring the excavation records to this level of detail are referred to the reports that are archived at KHM.
- *Section III: Scientific Analysis.* To publish the most important natural scientific analyses that have been carried out on material from Kaupang. (Scientific analysis of artefacts will be published in later volumes.)
- *Section IV: Skiringssal.* To publish investigations of the other elements within the central-place complex of Skiringssal, to examine the connexions and chronological relationships between these elements, and to attempt to reach an understanding of the emergence of the complex, its development, and its demise.

Future publications

A number of specialist studies are in preparation, which will in some cases relate directly to the principal research questions of the project and in others prepare the ground for further work on those questions. Most of these studies are concerned with one or more categories of the artefactual finds from the excavations. The classes of finds that are being worked on now include scales and weights (Pedersen, in prep. a), hacksilver and ingots (Hårdh, in prep. a), coins (Blackburn, in prep.; Rispling, et al., in prep.), Scandinavian metalwork (Hårdh, in prep. b), Continental and Insular metalwork (Wamers, in prep.), ring-pins and penannular brooches (Graham-Campbell, in prep.), soapstone (Baug, in prep.), textile tools (Øye, in prep.), whetstones (Resi, in prep. a), objects of jet, amber and precious stones (Resi, in prep. b), glass vessels (Gaut, in prep. a) and, finally, pottery (Pilø, in prep.). Some studies have a more theoretical orientation and deal with several classes of material and with different sources of evidence. This is the case with studies by Kilger (in prep. a and b), Gaut (in prep. b), Pedersen (in prep. b) and Skre (in prep.).

The project has never presumed to exploit the full scope of research possibilities that resides in the large collection of evidence from the fieldwork at Kaupang. Nor, indeed, within the relatively broad topics that are addressed in the project (Skre, this vol. Ch. 3) will the many research questions be dealt with exhaustively. We have picked out those major problems that we consider it most urgent to examine given the current state of scholarship. These have undergone adaptation in the course of the project work according to the resources available, and as opportunities provided by the evidence are recognized. Other than this, the full material is available to anyone who might wish to explore amongst the wide range of possible research questions that emerge from the analysis of the vast archaeological material from Kaupang and Skiringssal.

1.2 Kaupang and Skiringssal in the archaeology of the Viking Period

What is the place of Kaupang and Skiringssal in our understanding of the Viking Period in Scandinavia? That depends, of course, upon what sort of research issues one is interested in, and thus there is no simple answer to this question. To assess the significance and interpretative potential of the finds that are published in this and the successive volumes, it is necessary to locate them within the general context of the sources for this period in Scandinavia. The following outline emphasizes the archaeological evidence in particular.

In Norway and Sweden the great majority of archaeological finds in the museum collections have come from graves. The number of grave finds is very high, and the number of artefacts per grave is also generally high. Similarly in Denmark, burial archaeology has produced a large corpus of material, although graves are fewer there and the number of artefacts per grave is lower. However the settlement evidence there is richer than in Norway and Sweden. In most regions of Scandinavia we find both cremations and inhumations, although the ratio between the two is extremely variable. In broad terms, inhumations are most common in Denmark whereas cremations are dominant in Norway and Sweden. The graves were usually placed in barrows, but burials in stone features, stone settings, and under the level ground, are found too, especially in Denmark. Graves may be isolated, but it is more common for them to be in groups, which in Norway usually comprise up to fifteen graves. Large cemeteries are also found in most regions, but these are rare. In most cases the cemeteries can be associated with a farmstead, but in Sweden and Denmark also with a village. In the farmstead cemeteries it seems likely that just one barrow was raised for each generation, probably when the farm was inherited by the next generation.

There is no comprehensive survey of the number of unexcavated graves of the Viking Period, but there must be tens of thousands in Sweden and Norway together. The obstacle to estimating a figure is the fact that without excavation it is difficult to distinguish Viking-period funerary monuments from those of earlier periods. In Denmark the number of graves is much lower. Here it is the practice of burying under the level ground that is the biggest obstacle to estimating the number of graves.

Nor, indeed, do we have accurate figures for the number of grave finds in museum collections: in the case of Norway, estimates vary between 6,000 (Solberg 2000:222) and 12,000 (Stylegar, pers. comm.). Best known are the incredible ship graves from Oseberg and Gokstad, but these are utterly exceptional. To begin with, the state of preservation was very special in these two cases, as the barrows had been constructed of clay and turf, which meant that a great deal of the wood survived. The burials were also uncremated. However, as ship graves they are by no means unique (e.g. Opedal 1998); indeed, graves containing ships and boats are found in considerable numbers all over Scandinavia (Müller-Wille 1970).

The majority of the grave finds that are now in the museums were unearthed before c. 1900, some as a result of campaigns of excavation but most during the intensive cultivation of land that started in the early and mid 19th century (Pedersen 1989). Before 1905 Norway had no laws protecting ancient monuments, and barrows were destroyed in dreadful numbers. But the museums pursued an active policy of collection, and consequently obtained a large number of finds for their collections. The way in which the finds were made, though, meant that the information available about them varies greatly, and is usually poor. Often the only information is that the objects were found in the course of farm work. Whether they are from a single grave has frequently to be determined by the type and dating of the objects, and it often looks as if only the largest and best preserved artefacts were collected and sent to the museums.

The documentation of finds from early archaeological excavations is also of rather inconsistent quality, ranging from Hjalmar Stolpe's outstanding drawings and written records of the excavation of 1,100 graves at Birka in 1873–1895 (Gräslund 1980) to Nicolay Nicolaysen's rather meagre written reports of his excavation of some 1,400 graves in south-eastern Norway from 1867 to 1900. While Stolpe was interested in both the construction of the grave and the position of the objects within it, Nicolaysen was most concerned with collecting objects for the museum. His excavations at Kaupang are amongst the very few cases in which he produced a plan of a cemetery (Skre, this vol. Chs. 2:34–6 and 16:Fig. 16.1, 365); there are no drawings of a burial itself from his work at any site.

Hoards constitute another category of finds typical of the Viking Period in Scandinavia. From the two centuries preceding this period they are rare, while at the end of the Viking Period in particular they are very numerous. Silver is the most common metal in these hoards. Jewellery is predominant in the earlier finds, but coins appear increasingly towards the end of the period (Hårdh 1996).

Settlement finds of the Viking Period are, by contrast, much less numerous than one might expect given the large number of burial finds. The number of excavated settlements from the 1st to 6th centuries AD is far higher all over Scandinavia. This must primarily be due to the fact that the building-types and hearths of the Viking Period have not left such clear traces as those of earlier periods, making the Viking-period settlements themselves harder to recognize. The number of excavated settlements of the Viking Period has, however, grown in recent years, especially in Denmark and Sweden. These excavations provide information on buildings, settlement patterns and the like, but the quantity of artefactual finds from them is generally quite low. However systematic metal-detecting has, in recent years, produced numerous metal finds from some settlements.

Closer investigations of this kind of metal-rich settlement have shown a number of them also to have had other special features, such as halls that reveal the settlements to have been aristocratic residences. Some of these, such as Slöinge in Halland (Lundqvist 1996, 2003) are essentially a magnate farmstead and probably little else. But other settlements had a variety of functions for the surrounding community, and it has become the practice to call these "central places" (Fig. 1.4; Skre, this vol. Ch. 3.2). Most of these

N

Borg in Lofoten

Åker

Valsgärde • Vendel
Uppsala
Fornsigtuna
Adelsö • Helgö
Birka

Tune

Skiringssal • Kaupang

Spangereid

Paviken

Sebbersund • Slöinge

Løddekøpinge • Åhus
Uppåkra
Tissø • Lejre • Järrestad
Dankirke • Ribe • Toftegård
Gudme • Lundeborg

Hedeby

Reric

● Central places and magnate farmsteads
● Market places
● Towns

0   100   200 km

Figure 1.4 *Scandinavian towns, market places, central places and magnate farmsteads of the first millennium AD referred to in this volume. Map, Julie K. Øhre Askjem.*

sites have origins several centuries before the Viking Age. Some of them lost significance in the course of the Scandinavian Iron Age, and all of those that survived were abandoned towards the end of the Viking Period. At those sites which have been most thoroughly examined, it looks as if an aristocratic household was at the core of the complex. Skiringssal is one of the relatively few obvious central places of the Viking Period in Norway (Skre, this vol. Chs. 19 and 20).

Central places had functions that other settlements did not have. At Skiringssal the most important elements of the central place were the assembly place, the sacred lake, the hall, the enormous cemeteries, and the town. As later chapters will show (Skre, this vol. Chs. 11, 16, 17, 19 and 20), the scope for comparative studies of this range of phenomena is quite limited due to the paucity of such sites; indeed, in Norway, other such central-place sites are virtually non-existent. Only in southern and central Scandinavia are there comparable central-place sites, but even they are few in number.

Two categories of activity that we expect to find traces of at a central place are trade and craft production. These activities are of course in evidence at a number of sites that specialized in them; these are normally referred to as trading sites, market sites or the like. Such sites are known in Scandinavia from as early as c. AD 200 (Lundeborg on Fyn), and they increase sharply in number from the 8th century onwards (Callmer 1984; Clarke and Ambrosiani 1995:46–89; Sindbæk 2005; Skre, this vol. Chs. 3.1 and 20). Kaupang is one of these sites.

The rise in the number of such specialized sites represents an intensification of trade and craft production. But the rise is also due to the fact that before the 8th century those activities were normally performed on a limited scale in settlements, probably mainly addressing the needs of the settlement's own

inhabitants. But from the 8th century onwards those activities were less often located at farmsteads or in villages and more frequently in the specialized sites. There was thus a change in the contexts of these activities. A parallel and probably related development can be seen: at the start of the Viking Period there were changes in production and trade, with shifts from the production of individually crafted items to the serial production of identical items and from the primarily local or regional distribution of goods to trade over long distances (Callmer 1995).

The number of specialized trading and production sites in Sweden and Denmark is quite high (Callmer 1994). Very few have been found in Norway. From the period before c. AD 1000, Kaupang is the only proven example in Norway. Stray finds and place-names indicate that such sites existed at a number of other locations, but their dating is uncertain; most are probably of the 11th century or later.

The majority of the specialized trade and production sites of Scandinavia appear to have been of only local importance; most were fairly small. Just a few were large; they produce huge quantities of finds, a major proportion of which represent long-distance trade (Sindbæk 2005:80–7). Kaupang is one of these; the others are Ribe (c. AD 710–850), Birka (c. 750/780–970) and Hedeby (c. 808–1070). The character of these four sites is discussed in detail in a later chapter (Skre, this vol. Ch. 20.2).

The archaeological material from Kaupang is therefore at once unique and yet also typical of the archaeological picture drawn by Viking-age finds from elsewhere. What is typical is that much of the material was deposited as grave goods. This group of archaeological finds from Kaupang is consequently that which can most easily be correlated with other collections of Viking-age archaeological material (Stylegar, this vol. Ch. 5).

The finds from the settlement area at Kaupang

are, conversely, harder to contextualize in such a way. Some of the classes of artefacts, for instance glass beads and weights, are also found in graves, which helps to form a picture of the distribution and social context of these items. Other types of objects, such as hacksilver and coins, are very rare in graves, but do appear in large quantities in hoards. The latter category of deposits has a range of intrinsic interpretative problems, as have the graves, and the settlement finds constitute an important comparative control for both of them. Other categories of artefacts, such as loomweights and crucibles, are practically only found in settlement contexts, and in these cases the Norwegian comparative material outside of Kaupang itself is very sparse. This is also the case with the buildings and a large number of other types of finds, for which we have to turn to other market sites and towns to find any large comparable assemblages.

Characteristic of settlements is that, with few exceptions, only small items will be found complete. Large objects would usually have been picked up had they been lying on the ground, and would only have been discarded had they been broken. Many objects were also crushed by being trodden on or by other activities. Therefore, complete large artefacts have usually to be sought in the graves or the hoards. There were other processes and factors too, both during and following the period of settlement, which mean that the artefactual assemblage from settlement sites is not representative in the composition of the material culture of the once living society. Examples of such processes and factors are the value assigned to different types of artefacts by their owners, the pattern of garbage disposal in the settlement, the conditions for the preservations of organic material in the settlement deposits, the types and degree of post-depositional disturbance to the deposits etc.

The finds from the graves also have a range of inherent interpretative problems which make it difficult to make direct comparisons with the settlement assemblages. Pottery, for instance, is a common category of find in the settlement area at Kaupang, and also occurs in graves at this site. But pottery is practically completely absent from burials everywhere else in Norway. It appears, indeed, as if ceramic cooking pots and containers were rare in Viking-period Norway; soapstone cauldrons and wooden vessels were preferred. But was pottery really so rarely used in Norway outside of Kaupang as the burial record would seem to imply? Or is the absence of pottery from the graves due rather to the fact that it was simply not the practice to deposit such material in them? In contrast to the settlement assemblages, the choice of artefacts for graves was indeed based on a conscious choice of material culture, and it is quite apparent that there were conventions governing what was deposited and what was not. If we had more finds from rural settlements, it would be possible to form a

clearer idea of the use of pottery in the Viking Age in Norway. But given the present find-situation, it is not clear *how* unusual the extensive use of pottery at Kaupang was.

Altogether, one can say that in several ways Kaupang and Skiringssal are very important sites in the archaeology of the Viking Period in Scandinavia. To begin with, the urban settlement has a large number of objects in a range of types that are otherwise unusual or simply unknown in Viking-period assemblages from elsewhere in Norway. As such artefactual finds from settlements are unusual everywhere in Norway except Kaupang, the site is therefore also important to anyone working on the material from the hoards and graves. All three types of find-context pose particular difficulties of interpretation; these difficulties can more easily be delimited and checked when artefact-types occur in more than one of them.

If we look beyond the physical artefact-types themselves to types of activity, it is clear that Kaupang provides rich evidence of certain forms of activity that are otherwise very rarely seen. In particular the scope for finding evidence of trade and craft production is high in urban settlements. The crafts produced and the goods traded can be found both in graves and in hoards, but the remains of the craftsman's work and the conduct of trade are found primarily at the urban sites. The quantity of goods from long-distance trade is quite enormous at urban sites compared to what one sees at other types of sites. The assemblages from Kaupang and the other urban settlements are therefore key sources for Viking-period trade and craft. Looking beyond the urban site, the other elements of the central place Skiringssal, which are the vast cemeteries, the royal hall and the *thing* site, are also only rarely found at other sites.

If we raise the horizons yet further and look at combinations of activities, Kaupang and Skiringssal appear even more special. Only a few central places of the Viking Period with a similar activity range are known, and the number of urban settlements is even lower (Skre, this vol. Chs. 19 and 20). Research into such sites is therefore significant, not only because of their rich artefactual material and diverse and unusual activities, but also because these were the most important centres of power during the Viking Age. The study of their emergence, their elements, their development, and their demise is consequently quite fundamental to any understanding of Viking-age culture and society, and particularly for an understanding of the profound transformation from the tribes and petty kingships of the Iron Age to the kingdoms which emerged in the Viking Age and which grew, in due course, into modern nation-states.

1.3 Exploring the distant past
A few words are needed on the views of historical and archaeological scholarship that underlie the editor's

design of this volume. The individual authors answer only for their own chapters, of course; they are not to be held to account for these views. However the unity of the volume, and particularly the editor's own chapters, are informed by certain views which will be explained briefly here.

It is a basic condition of all historical disciplines that they are practised in a different period from that with which they are concerned. History has to be meaningful and relevant to readers of the historian's own time. Meaning and relevance are phenomena that are historically dependent, and what constitutes meaningful history today is different from that of fifty, five hundred or a thousand years ago.

This becomes particularly evident when reading Viking-age literary sources. For a modern reader, the sense of these is difficult to grasp not simply because of the usually dense formulae of the poetry or the runic inscriptions, but because it would have to be read in its past cultural context to convey its proper meaning. This is illustrated by the fact that the longest and most compendious of Viking-period runic inscriptions, the Rök inscription, is probably that on which opinions concerning the reading and interpretation of the text are most divided. This is not due to damaged runes or ambiguously written words, but rather arises because comprehension of the references, the context, and the meaning of the formulations, presupposes a knowledge that has largely been lost. Similar insights can be obtained by studying archaeological sources which have meaning in the form of pictures and decorations, such as the Gotlandic picture-stones (e.g. Andrén 1989) and Scandinavian animal art (e.g. Hedeager 2004).

Equally alien in form are the ancient concepts that underlay the very acts of recounting history or writing it down. In the poems, which are the only surviving literary works that can be dated with any certainty to the Viking Period itself, the principal objective was not to recount factual events. These poems operated within a symbolic and mythical reality in which events, places and individuals were linked first and foremost to what Meulengracht Sørensen (2003:267) calls "the Viking Age's perception of life and the world, its myths and concepts". This does not make it impossible to use the poetry as historical source-material, but the symbolic and literary functions of its passages have to be carefully assessed before they are pressed into service as sources for the events, places and persons mentioned (cf. Skre, this vol. Chs. 18, 19 and 20.3).

Such contextualized readings of archaeological and written sources are now effectively taken for granted in scholarly circles. But it is just as significant that we who are writing history nowadays are also subjects of our own age, and that our texts too are only meaningful within a particular set of cultural and intellectual conditions. The texts that we write are thus subject to the same preconditions as the texts and objects we treat as sources. Our texts have no objective or neutral status that enables us to reveal the "true reality" of the distant past. They are created within the universe of meaning that we belong to ourselves.

What is the consequence of this realization? For some scholars, such a realization has resulted in what I would call a sort of academic resignation, whereby they accept that all understanding is governed by its immediate historical circumstances, and therefore that no contact with past reality can ever be validated – and that such contact therefore is not worth striving for. This produces a style of historical writing that relates only to the present, with an agenda that is solely and thoroughly contemporary – involved in the political and cultural issues of here and now, and deriving its premises and objectives from that only.

What is needed in this respect is the ability to have two ideas in one's head simultaneously. Why should one system of meaning not be capable of being *recognized* and *understood* within another? It is important to appreciate that the meaningful world of the past cannot be *experienced* in exactly the same way as it was originally. If that were possible, we should feel the same real physical fear and the urge to hide indoors when we read about giants and other evil spirits *(meinvættir)* threatening human life. And when we read about Viking-age justice and honour, we should feel their inflexible and determined aggression towards anyone subject to vengeance for some offence or misdeed. These emotions are barely sensible to us, and any engagement with the past in those terms would lie outside the bounds of scholarship. But we can *recognize* both evil powers and feuds, and we can *describe* and *understand* their respective cultural significance and social role. Sometimes we may even think that we understand them empathetically. But what we write has to be meaningful for ourselves too, and for others who live in our contemporary reality, and that fear and aggression have, therefore, to be described and explained using our era's frames of reference, which in those cases would normally be psychological or anthropological. One must not, as a result, suppose that there is any coincidence between *us* and *past peoples,* or between *our* history of them and *their own* history of themselves. Yet equally, our history of them is no more right or wrong than their own; it is just more meaningful to us through our modern frames of reference.

In a scene from the film *Indiana Jones and the Last Crusade,* "Professor of Archaeology" Indiana Jones tells a student: "Archaeology is about Facts. If you want the Truth, go next door to the Philosophy Department" (Bintliff 1993:100). It is easy to agree that archaeology is stuffed with facts; that is reflected by most of the chapters in this volume. In them one can also see how important those facts are to scholarly argument. But Jones is mistaken if he thinks that facts have any value *in themselves*. Facts have no interest or meaning until they are interpreted – a state of affairs that should become equally clear as one reads this book. Facts begin to take on scholarly meaning when they are linked up with other facts, involved in some line of argument, and used to form a basis for conclusions. For instance, the pure fact observed by Milek and French (this vol. Ch. 15.5:330), visible only in their microscopes, that the earliest deposits in one of the plots at Kaupang comprised seven layers of charcoal-rich material separated by thin layers of sand, is merely a detail in itself. But the observation became extremely interesting when they noted the contrast between those deposits and the later deposits at the same location and used their scholarly competence to interpret the facts. Together with comparison of equivalent deposits at Ribe, Jutland, and Gásir, Iceland, their judgment of the Kaupang deposits leads them to interpret the seven layers as possibly representing seasonal activity, perhaps in seven successive years, on this plot – in turn a crucial factor in the view of the initial development of the settlement at Kaupang that is proposed here (Pilø, this vol. Ch. 10:193).

It is not possible to draw a really sharp distinction between facts and interpretation, because all observations of "facts" are made within particular circumstances and on the basis of certain premises that influence the observations themselves. If we take this into consideration, only the source itself remains as entirely objective – not anything we may say about it, not even what we might regard as "factual" about it. All the same, the difference between fact and interpretation is a fruitful distinction, because it makes clear that anything interesting we might have to say about the past is always a matter of interpretation and never purely or simply a matter of "fact".

The purpose of these interpretations is to render the past comprehensible and meaningful to us; to turn it into *history*. It is not meaningful as long as it remains simply a collection of facts. Contemporary interpretations create context and meaning of a kind that is accessible to contemporary people. Those who are committed to the source-critical school that has emerged within archaeology, Old Norse philology and history alike, are therefore mistaken when they believe that they can strip a source bare of all ambiguities and expose a reliable core. There is no such core, because its unveiling, and these scholars' subsequent use of the source, will always depend upon certain premises that involve elements of interpretation and which are consequently ambiguous in themselves.

Of course, this does not mean that source-criticism can be neglected. It is absolutely essential; however, one simply must not believe that it can remove all doubt. Source-criticism can only produce *degrees of reliability* for a source being used in particular ways or to support particular conclusions. This applies to interpretation too. No interpretation is ever conclusive; it is only more or less probable. In this book, particular attention is given to the degree of probability that the respective contributor considers the interpretations to have.

The view of the relationship between facts and interpretation set out here does not, thus, lead to a downgrading of source-criticism. On the contrary, it leads to a greater concern with interpretation, and with how it is presented and supported by facts and arguments. It also draws attention to the general perception of the Viking Age, the *history*, which these interpretations are intended to merge into. Finally, it emphasizes the fact that the individual interpretations and the overall *history* have qualities and elements that are *not* rooted, one and all, in the available facts.

The *history* rendered here has, therefore, to be examined minutely, because it is not only formed from the available facts but also is involved in and governs the selection and interpretation of those facts. It thus has an important and prominent position in the research process. This situation is justified, however, because the *history* is the whole justification for the scholarly study of the past, because the *history* renders the past meaningful and turns it into more than a collection of uninterpreted sources and fragmented understandings.

Published in the present book are a large number of facts concerning Kaupang and Skiringssal that have not been available before. These facts have stimulated the contributors to produce new interpretations, and to re-interpret facts known before. Out of these building blocks it has proved possible to suggest new and more comprehensive views on many issues, alongside something that is ambitiously regarded as a history of Kaupang and Skiringssal. But one has to admit that Indiana Jones was right in that neither the history nor the interpretations of archaeology can be granted the status of "Truth". What we present here are conclusions of varying degrees of probability, which are supported by the observations and arguments that are published along with them.

As noted, the interpretations that are offered here are not directionless. They find their places in one way or another within a *history* that to some extent has itself been developed in the course of the work on these chapters. And our efforts to develop this history also have a direction – an ambition that could never be fully realized, but which all the same is utterly fundamental to all research into the past – namely, to get in touch with the reality of the past as best and as fully as we can, and to present an understanding of that reality in a way that makes it meaningful for ourselves and our contemporaries.

Part I:

Background

Exploring Skiringssal 1771–1999

2

In confesso est Historiam, sine Geographia iter referre inter tenebras noctis; quod nusquam, manifestius credimus, quam in veteris patriæ nostræ Historia.
NEIKTER 1802:1

D A G F I N N   S K R E

It is a matter of fact that the writing of History without the aid of Geography is like showing someone a path in the darkness of the night. This is nowhere more evident than in the case of the History of our ancient fatherland.

The scholarly study of Skiringssal over nearly 230 years can be divided into five periods that correlate with different phases in the development of the disciplines of archaeology and history, from the pre-academic practice of these disciplines by literati and antiquarians in the 18th and early 19th centuries to the more developed and critical research methods of the 20th century.

The earlier phase is characterized by the gradual adoption and examination of new sources. The antiquarian and textual sources were first collected by Gerhard Munthe in 1838, and the location of Skiringssal, in Tjølling, Vestfold, can be said to have been established by his work. In 1850, P. A. Munch put these sources into a wider Dano-Norwegian context, and went further in linking the site to the legendary royal dynasty of Norway, the Ynglings.

The plea for archaeological work at Skiringssal made by Munthe and Munch was taken up by Nicolay Nicolaysen in 1867 when he made Skiringssal his first major archaeological project. However, the excavations of burial mounds at Kaupang did not produce the rich finds he hoped for, and for many years after his work there, archaeological exploration of Skiringssal was exiguous.

Not until Charlotte Blindheim's excavations of burials and settlement remains at Kaupang from 1950 to 1974 was there a new surge in Skiringssal research. It was Blindheim who revealed the remains of the urban site at Kaupang and retrieved a significant collection of archaeological finds which provided a basis for dating the site and for assessing the craft, trade and connexions evident there.

Research into the Viking Period in Norway is to a considerable degree based on topographic studies, and work on Skiringssal is no exception. The Old Norse literature that is concerned with the Viking Period, the sagas and poetry, includes a mass of names of farms, settlements, locations, fjords and regions. Many of these could still be found under the same names, leading those who were interested in antiquity out into the countryside. There, they found remains from this period: burial mounds, rune-stones, and settlements. The early literati and antiquarians attempted to reconcile these sources with one another and to build up an understanding of antiquity that was supported by all of the categories of evidence they had at their disposal.

In the second half of the 19th century, those antiquarian and literary traditions evolved into academic disciplines. The separate disciplines of history, archaeology, and Old Norse philology turned most of their attention inwards upon their own particular fields. Efforts were made to develop discipline-specific methods and to create a systematization and full overview of their own source-material. Over the past century the degree of interdisciplinarity has varied from discipline to discipline, largely reflecting the temperament, interest and influence of individual scholars.

Vestfold has been at the centre of the study of the Viking Period in all of these academic disciplines. Old Norse literature indicates that Vestfold was highly significant in the early historical period, and the archaeological sources there are exceptionally rich. In his history of the Norwegian kings, the Icelander Snorri Sturluson presented the Yngling dynasty as that from which the first kings of Norway emerged at the end of the 9th century. According to his account, Vestfold was the homeland of this dynasty from the 8th century onwards. Snorri's principal source was the poem *Ynglingatal,* composed, according to Snorri, by the skaldic poet Þjóðólfr of Hvini, probably around 900 or slightly earlier (Skre, this vol. Ch. 18, 19 and 20.3). The sources appear to associate the Ynglings particularly with two parts of Vestfold: Skiringssal in the south and Borre to the north.

There is a great density of ancient monuments in Vestfold, of which the ten huge burial mounds at Borre, the twelve large cairns at Mølen, and the two ship burials at Gokstad and Oseberg are the most prominent. In this, the very smallest of the 18 Norwegian rural counties, about 900 out of the total of c. 12,000 known grave finds of the Viking Period in Norway have been found (Stylegar, pers. comm.). The numerous and prominent finds and monuments makes Vestfold one of the leading areas of Viking-age research in Scandinavia (Fig. 1.1).

Consequently, a real interest in Vestfold is evident in Viking scholarship from the very beginning, where Skiringssal is referred to on a par with the other important sites in the region. Towards the end of the 19th century, however, Skiringssal began to slip into the background. The reason would appear to have been that the archaeological work there in 1867 failed to fulfil the great expectations of spectacular finds from this important site. The rich ship burials that were excavated at Gokstad (1880) and Oseberg (1904), further to the north in Vestfold, contributed to the overshadowing of Skiringssal. Not until Charlotte Blindheim's extensive excavations 1950–1974 did Kaupang and Skiringssal return to a place amongst the major sites of Viking-period studies.

There are two main questions which stand out in the work on Skiringssal: *Where* was Skiringssal? *What* was it? While the first question was definitively answered as early as the antiquarian period, in the 1820s and 30s, we are still working on the second. In this respect, there has been a massive expansion of the themes and objectives concerned. Nowadays these include discussions of the dating, structure and activities in the urban site which Blindheim located at the farm Kaupang in Skiringssal, the character and extent of the chieftainly domain of Skiringssal, and the role of Skiringssal in the northern European trade network and the cultural, social and political dynamics of the early Viking Period.

In this chapter, the principal emphasis is put upon research on the urban site at Kaupang and on the Skiringssal complex. It is the history of the course, themes and results of this research that is related here. (On this topic, see also Blindheim et al. 1981:11–16.) Research on super-regional issues involving Kaupang and Skiringssal will be discussed in later volumes in this series.

2.1 The literati and the antiquarians 1771–1850

As early as the 16th century, educated Scandinavians began to take an interest in the Old Norse literature of the Middle Ages. But it was not until the 18th century that we found anything that could be regarded as a critical assessment of these works as historical sources. At that time, historians were also starting to use other sources, in particular deeds and charters, and information from the various sources was combined and studied together. At this stage, genealogical and antiquarian issues were the centre of attention. The associations of people and events with places were investigated, the sites sought out, and names, topography and monuments were brought in as further sources.

Gerhard Schøning (1722–1780) was the first to discuss a variety of sources that referred to Skiringssal. In the first volume of his trilogy *Norges Riiges Historie (The History of the Kingdom of Norway)*, he reproduced the information in the saga *Fagrskinna* concerning the burial at "Scirisdal" in Vestfold of the head of Halfdan the Black, the father of Harald Fairhair who became the first king of Norway (Schøning 1771:437). He found that Snorri's *Ynglinga saga* also referred to Skiringssal as being in Vestfold. Snorri also provided a copy of *Ynglingatal*, whence Schøning obtained an account of how Halfdan Whiteleg, Halfdan the Black's great-great-grandfather, died at Toten in Oppland and was buried "at a Place, called Skæreid in Skirissal, or more correctly Skirisdal" ("paa et Sted, kaldet Skæreid i Skirissal, eller maatte [*sic*] rettere Skirisdal") (Schøning 1771:366–7). In a footnote he discussed the name in more detail. He refers to Jonas Ramus's assumption (1719) that the name should have been "Skierings-Aa", in other words a river, and concluded that those who knew the site should decide which was correct.

He goes on in the footnote:

Et haandskrevet Exemplar af Sogubrot giver ellers Anledning til at troe, at Sciris-sal, eller som det der heeder Skirings-Sal, har i de ældre Tiider været et meget stort og berømt Offersteed for hele Viigen … Der har mueligt staaet et af de fornemste Templer i Norge, saadant, som de paa Mære, Hlade, i Gudbrandsdalen, og fleere vare.

A manuscript Copy of *Sögubrot* [a fragmentary history], however, gives Reason to believe that Sciris-sal, or, as it is called there, Skirings-Sal, was a very large and famous Place of Sacrifice for the whole Vik area in ancient Times … It is possible, that there stood here one of the most outstanding Temples in Norway, of the same kind as those at Mære, Lade, in Gudbrandsdal, and several others.

It is the source's explicit reference to Skiringssal as the burial site of kings and as a "Temple" that interested him. Through the name, he attempted to locate this manifestly important site more precisely. But even though he was one of the most widely travelled of the early antiquarians, he could not identify its location.

The Swedish historian Jakob Fredrik Neikter discussed the name in his small thesis *Observationum historico-geographicum particula*, published in Uppsala in 1802. He was the first to link the Skiringssal of the Norse literary sources with another important source, known as "The report of Ohthere", which is found as a supplement to the Old English translation of Orosius' World History made in the lifetime of King Alfred the Great of Wessex (Neikter 1802:1–3). This report must have been committed to writing at some stage during the reign of Alfred (871–c. 900). Ohthere, *alias* Óttar in Old Norse, who lived in Hålogaland in North Norway, described some of his journeys, including one that went south to "Sciringesheal", which is described using the Old English word *port,* meaning a harbour or trading place on the coast.

Neikter's identification would not appear to have been known to the Danish man of letters Nikolai Grundtvig (1783–1872); whatever the case, he expressed himself as if he had personally discovered that Ohthere's Sciringesheal was the same as the Skiringssal of the Norse sources (Grundtvig 1819). In the meantime, the Danish language scholar Rasmus K. Rask (1815) had supposed that Ohthere's Sciringesheal was to be identified with Konghelle in Bohuslän, Sweden.

There is, however, no indication that these works were known to Norwegian antiquarians at that time. Jens Kraft, who published *Topographisk-Statistisk Beskrivelse over Kongeriget Norge (A Topographical-Statistical Account of the Kingdom of Norway),* makes no reference to them, or to Ohthere's report. On the other hand he did have access to other important sources. In addition to references to the same sources as Schøning knew, he wrote (Kraft 1822:879):

Det i Historien nævnte Skirissal eller Skiringssal synes at have været det nuværende Tjølling Sogn eller en Deel deraf og maaskee af Sandeherred; thi i et Skøde i Rigsarchivet, udstædt paa Brunlaug i Aaret 1419 paa Gaarden Gudrima, som maae være Gaarden Guren No. 16 i Tjølling Sogn, siges denne at ligge i Skirikx Saal, og i en Fortegnelse over Tønsbergs Hospitals Gods fra samme Aarhundre anføres Skirisall som et særkilt District, hvori Hospitalet eiede Gaardene Klepager, Brekke, Namfnesale (Nomesal), foruden Monom og Vestre Nesiu, der formodentlig findes i Sandeherred.

What is referred to in History as Skirissal or Skiringssal seems to have been what is now the Parish of Tjølling or some Part thereof and perhaps of Sandeherred; for, on a Document in the National Archive, issued at Brunlaug in the Year 1419 at the Farm of Gudrima, which must be the Farm Guren No. 16 in Tjølling Parish, it is stated that this is situated in Skirikx Saal, and in an account of the Estate of Tønsberg Hospital from the same Century, Skirisall is included as a distinct District, in which the Hospital held the Farms of Klepager, Brekke, Namfnesale (Nomesal), in addition to Monom and Vestre Nesiu, which presumably are in Sandeherred.

The discovery of these two 15th-century sources (DN I:46, IX:274) brought the efforts to locate Skiringssal many steps forward. It might have been Kraft himself who combined the deeds with the information in the sagas. But it is possible that in doing so he based himself on information from the knowledgeable and educated amateur Jens Christian Berg (1775–1852), as he did regarding several other historical questions. Berg was a District Judge in northern Vestfold for many years, and consequently knew the area very well.

Kraft made another crucial observation. Referring to the farm of Kaupang in Tjølling (Fig. 2.1), he wrote (1822:863) that the farm's "Name seems to show that there was formerly a Trading or Unloading Place here" ("Navn synes at vise, at her forhen har været en Handels- eller Udskibningsplads"). Otherwise, there are not many interpretations of place names in Kraft's work, so he must have considered this important. However he made no connexion between Kaupang and Skiringssal.

The first antiquarian known to have visited Skiringssal was the officer, cartographer and historian Gerhard Munthe (1795–1876) (Fig. 2.2). In 1825 he had commenced work upon a map of medieval Norway, and he undertook a huge amount of preparatory work by ploughing through the sagas, cartularies and deeds. This proved useful when in the 1830s he was drawn into Jacob Aall's plans for a three-volume edition of Snorri's *Heimskringla* (Sturluson [1838–1839]). Munthe accepted the job of writing the geographical notes for the work. This was a task he carried out with great thoroughness and scholarship. In places in the publication, Munthe's comments at the bottom of the page take up more space than the saga text itself above it. His notes form the first comprehensive discussion of the sites and landscapes of *Heimskringla,* and they mark a huge step forward in antiquarian scholarship. His study of early spellings and the etymology of Norwegian farm names was published in the public land register of 1837. On the basis of the same study, he published his map of medieval Norway in 1840, and in 1847 a catalogue of the most important place names and their etymologies. These works provided the foundations for a series of crucial studies by other scholars, including P. A. Munch.

Munthe (in Sturluson [1838–1839]:I:35) combined Ohthere's account with the Norse sources, but still did not appear to have realized that Danish and Swedish antiquaries had already successfully done so: whatever the case, he referred only to the erroneous identifications that some others had made. Munthe linked Ohthere's report to the details Kraft had assembled and wrote that the site which Ohthere visited lay doubtless in Tjølling. He discussed the tradition of Skiringssal and concluded by restricting it to the parish of Tjølling (Fig. 2.1). He mentioned the royal farmstead which he (in Sturluson [1838–1839]

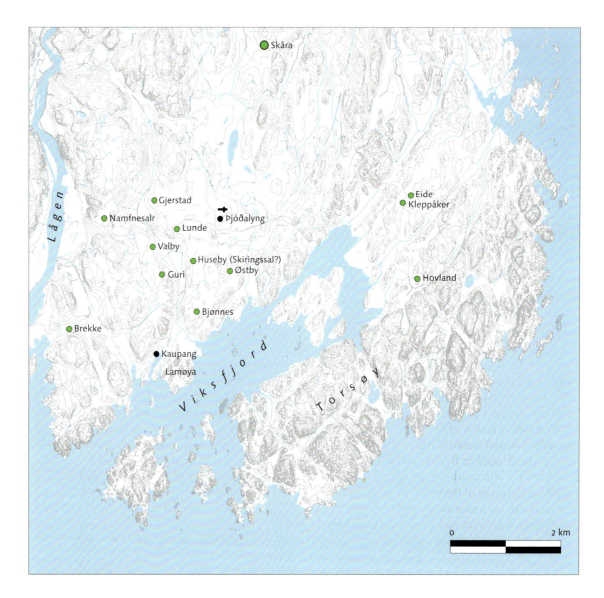

Skåra

Gjerstad

Eide
Kleppåker

Namfnesalr

Þjóðalyng

Lågen

Lunde

Valby

Huseby (Skiringssal?)

Guri

Østby

Hovland

Bjønnes

Brekke

Kaupang

Lamøya

V i k s f j o r d

T o r s ø y

0   2 km

:I:40) understood to be the farm of Gjerstad in Tjølling on the basis of *Ynglingatal*. And he mentioned "the temple", and assumed that this must have stood on the same spot as Tjølling church.

He continued thus:

... her var en besøgt Havn og uden Tvivl Markeds- og Handelsplads ved Gaardene Kaupángr (d.e. Kjøbing eller Kjøbstad, hvilket Navn endnu afgiver paalideligt Vidnesbyrd derom) ved Vigs-Fjorden ... Ved den nysnævnte Gaard Kaupang have vore Forfædre fundet en skjøn Havn for deres ikke meget dybtgaaende Skibe, med fortrinlig Anledning til at drage dem paa Land. Sammesteds sees et særdeles mærkeligt antiquarisk Feldt, opfyldt af en fast utallig Mængde Gravhøie – Stedets hedenske Begravelsesplads (?). I det Hele taget er denne Egn, de Gamles Skiringssal, saa opfyldt af Minder fra Hedenold af alle Slags, at den vel fortjente en nøiere af Kyndighet ledet antiqvarisk Undersøgelse, end den, der hidindtil er bleven den til Deel.

... here there was a much frequented Harbour and without Doubt a Market and Trading Place beside the Farms of Kaupángr (i.e. Chipping or town, a name which yields further reliable Evidence of this Point) by the Vigs-Fjord ... By the Farm of Kaupang, our Ancestors found a good Haven for their relatively shallow Ships, with ideal Scope for dragging them onto the Land. At the same Place can be seen a quite remarkable antiquarian Landscape, filled with an almost innumerable Quantity of Barrows – the Site's pagan Cemetery (?). Taken as a Whole, this Area, the Skiringssalr of the Ancients, is so replete with Monuments of Pagan Times of all Kinds, that it merits a more detailed antiquarian Examination directed by Scholarship than it has yet enjoyed.

From this text it is clear that Munthe himself had been to the site – he knew, for instance, that the harbour was shallow. It was, indeed, his usual practice to travel around and visit historic places himself. On many of his journeys he was accompanied by the painter Johannes Flintoe (1786–1870), who made drawings of important historical sites. Six of his

Figure 2.1 *The most important sites associated with the discussion of Skiringssal are marked on this map. Contour interval 5 metres. Map, Julie K. Øhre Askjem.*

drawings were printed in the edition of Snorri. The pair must have visited Kaupang sometime in the middle of the 1830s. No drawing of this site was included in the book, but Flintoe was active there all the same. There are two known sketches from this visit, and one painting (Figs. 16.3–16.4).

With the inclusion of Ohthere's report, the two lines of Skiringssal research, the textual and the antiquarian, came together. By combining them, Munthe concluded the discussion about where Skriringssal lay. Munthe's survey of the evidence was also of great importance to the understanding of *what* Skiringssal was. Ohthere's account had provided a basis for adding the trading place into the complex. Munthe could consequently link the interpretation of the farm name, Kaupang, and the good harbour and huge burial grounds he found there, to the other sources concerning Skiringssal.

The final episode in the antiquarian study of Skiringssal has remained unrecognized until now (Skre 2005). One of the first generation of academically trained Norwegian historians, Christian C. Lange (1810–1861), was a teacher at the naval school in Fredriksvern 1834–1846. After that he became the State Archivist, and moved to the capital, Christiania, now Oslo. The naval base of Fredriksvern, now Stavern, lies only 13 km west of Kaupang along the main road. In long summer vacations from school, Lange undertook antiquarian tours, including Tjølling and Brunlanes, the countryside around Fredriksvern. He might have been in contact with Munthe and Flintoe when they were in the area. In any event, he assisted Jens Kraft in his work on the revised edition of his Topographical-Statistical Description. In the summer of 1839 Kraft and Lange toured the area to look at the ancient monuments there. Later, Kraft sent his manuscript of the historical and antiquarian "Notices" for Jarlsberg Region to Lange for correction. This is no doubt the reason that Kraft's informa-

tion about Skiringssal in the revised edition that appeared in 1840 is much more detailed. However he had nothing new to say about Skiringssal; Munthe had done a thorough job.

After 1839, Lange was in close contact with Carl C. Rafn (1795–1864), secretary of Det Kongelige Nordiske Oldskriftselskab (The Royal Nordic Ancient Text Society) in Copenhagen. In 1845 this connexion led to the painter Christian O. Zeuthen's (1812–1890) being sent from Copenhagen to Brunlanes and Tjølling to draw ancient monuments. Eleven drawings are now known from this expedition. These had been thought lost, but were retrieved in two stages, first six drawings in 1968 (Larsen 1986), then five in 2003 (Skre 2005). Two of the latter group to be rediscovered are of Kaupang, comprising a map of parts of the cemeteries at Nordre Kaupang and on Lamøya. These drawings constitute the earliest antiquarian documentation from Kaupang (Skre, this vol. Ch. 16:370–2, Fig. 16.5; Stylegar, this vol. Ch. 5:Fig. 5.8).

2.2 The historian and the archaeologist 1850–1867

The second major stage in Skiringssal research began when the first generation of academically qualified scholars came onto the scene: The distinguished historian Peter Andreas Munch (1810–1863) wrote a major article that summed up the studies of Skiringssal of the preceding decades and placed the results in a wider context. The archaeologist Nicolay Nicolaysen undertook excavations at Skiringssal in 1867 which came to play a key role in archaeologists' later interest in this area.

Munch grew up in the vicarage of Gjerpen near Skien, only some 45 km northwest of Kaupang. This gave him familiarity with the area which he made use of in his first scholarly article, 'On the Position of the ancient Grenmar and other Sites that are linked to it in ancient Texts', printed in *Annaler for Nordisk Oldkyndighed,* 1836–1837. When he (1837:62) wrote, "I

Figure 2.2 *Gerhard Munthe, officer, cartographer and historian, was the first connoisseur of prehistory known to have visited (mid-1830s) Kaupang and Skiringssal. Photo, Riksantikvaren.*

have myself spent much of my Time in and around these Areas, have travelled around the whole District" ("jeg selv har henlevet min meste Tid i og ved disse Egne, har bereist hele Districtet"), he probably included Tjølling. In the article he mentioned Skiringssal and the farm of Gjerstad, both in Tjølling (Munch 1837:70).

If not before, he was certainly there in the middle of July 1850. On 11 July he wrote in a letter to C. C. Lange from the steam ship "one-half mile from Christiania" (Indrebø and Kolsrud 1924:450):

De seer mig her tiltrædende min Bergens-Reise, hvilken jeg lægger omkring Laurvig, for ved samme Leilighed at kunne bese mig lidt i Skiringssal.

Here you see me embarking upon my Bergen-Tour, which I am taking via Laurvig, in order to have a quick Look at Skiringssal at the same Time.

He wrote about the results of this visit the following summer in a letter to his friend Georg Petrie, an antiquarian scholar and tax inspector in the Orkneys (Knudsen and Andersen 1971:368):

Last summer I made a little antiquarian excursion in my own country, visiting especially a classical spot in the south, where there has been a kind of town or seaport in heathen times, mentioned among others by King Alfred in his extracts from the relations of Ohthere and Wulfstan. There I found what I must call the whole burial place of the town, being clusters of almost an immense number of barrows, large and small, many of them containing iron-swords, glass beads, and remnants of boats.

Munch's article on Skiringssal appeared in the 1850 issue of the journal that Christian Lange edited and published, *Norsk Tidsskrift for Videnskab og Litteratur.* In the autumn of that year Munch sent offprints of

this article to his colleagues, so he must already have devoted some time to this study when he visited Skiringssal.

All of the significant sources he made use of in the article were known through Munthe's work. Munch argued that Skiringssal, with a royal farm, a trading site, a temple and a cemetery, was the home of the Yngling kings. And he placed the Skiringssal complex, as it appears in the sources and ancient monuments, into a context comprising Vestfold, Denmark and Sweden. This wider context will not be discussed here, only what he said about Skiringssal and Vestfold.

The first important explanation that Munch offered (1850:105–6) concerns the reference to Skiringssal as a "port" in Ohthere's description. How could this be reconciled with the clear use of Skiringssal to refer to a district in the Norse sources? He found an answer in the common Norse practice of naming the trading place of a district. What was done was indeed to use the name of the district and to combine it with the Norse word for a trading place, *kaupangr.* The town that was located in the district of *Þrándheimr* was thus known as *kaupangrinn í Þrándheimi,* subsequently shortened to *Þrándheimr,* i.e. Trondheim. Both of these names were, according to Munch, probably used by people outside the district, while people who lived there were likely just to call the town "Kaupangr". He concluded:

I Skiringssal havde Indbyggerne selv paa samme Viis kaldet deres Kjøbstad *kaupangr,* medens fremmede kaldte den *kaupangr í Skíringssal* eller kort og godt *Skíringssalr.*

At Skiringssal, the Inhabitants in the same way called their Town *kaupangr,* while outsiders called it *kaupangr í Skíringssal* or quite simply *Skíringssal.*

Munch also discussed where the "Temple" might have been. He noted a number of place names referring to cult sites in the area, such as Hovland *(hof* = "temple")* and Torsøy (the island of the Norse god Thor), but came to no firm conclusion on this matter.

Munch thus studied the later parts of *Ynglingatal* and *Ynglinga saga,* from Halfdan Whiteleg, who was the first Yngling to settle in Vestfold, onwards. He pointed out that in so far as the burial places of these Yngling kings are recorded, as is the case for four of the six, they are either at Skiringssal (Halfdan Whiteleg at Skereid, and Olaf Geirstad's Elf at Geirstad, which Munch believed was Gjerstad in Tjølling), or at Borre (Halfdan's son Eystein Fret at *raðar broddi,* which Munch believed was Borre, and Fret's son Halfdan the Mild). He wrote (1850:108–9):

Dette viser at Skiringssal og Borro maa have været de fornemste Punkter af Vestfold i den Tid, da dette Landskab endnu havde sine egne Konger, men at det første dog har været det, hvor Kongerne stadigt opholdt sig. ... I Omegnen af *Kaupangr,* eller Skiringssals gamle Handelsplads, have vi saaledes flere højst mærkelige Punkter, der alle tyde hen paa, at Egnen i hine fjerne Tider var den fornemste, eller en af de fornemste, paa Vestfold og Hovedsædet for Ynglinge-kongerne. Endog navnet *Skíringssalr,):* Renselsens eller Opklarelsens Sal, synes at vidne om den Hellighed og Glands, der hvilede over et Sted, til hvilken etter Søgubrots udtrykkelige udsagn Indbyggerne af hele Viken søgte for at deeltage i Offringerne. Ogsaa findes her mærkelige Old-tidslevninger, der vel fortjene en nærmere Undersøgelse. Førend dette er skeet, vil det blive umuligt at sige noget med Vished om Beliggenheden af det ovennævnte *Særeið, Skæreið eller Skereið,* hvor Halfdan Kvitbein blev begraven.

This shows that Skiringssal and Borro must have been the outstanding Places in Vestfold in the Age when this Territory still had its own Kings, but that the foremost of them was that at which the Kings were normally resident … In the Vicinity of Kaupangr, or the ancient Trading Place of Skiringssal, we thus have several extremely conspicuous Features, all of which indicate that this Area, in those distant Times, was the most important, or at least one of the most important, in Vestfold, and the Principal Seat of the Yngling Kings. Further, the name *Skiringssalr,):* Hall of the Purification or the Clarification, seems to bear Witness to the Holiness and Aura that lay upon a Site, to which, according to the explicit Testimony of the Saga fragment, the Inhabitants of the whole Vik area came in order to participate in the Sacrifices. Here too are to be found remarkable Ancient Monuments, which certainly deserve more detailed Examination. Until that has been done, it will remain impossible to say anything with Certainty about the Position of the above-mentioned *Særeið, Skæreið or Skereið,* where Halfdan Whiteleg was buried.

Munch was sceptical about the historicity of the earlier generations of the royal genealogy in *Ynglingatal* and *Ynglinga saga,* and believed that this part of the poem was put together out of several different and to

some degree fictional sources. But the last six generations that were located in Vestfold and at Skiringssal, he trusted (1850:124–5). He went on to conclude:

Vi vide altsaa egentlig kun, at den Æt, der i slutningen af det 8de Aarhundrede herskede paa Vestfold, og hvorfra Harald Haarfagre stammede, hørte til Ynglingernes Slægt, var maaskee kommen fra Vermeland over Raumarike, men indstiftede etslags Familie-Helligdom i Skiringssal.

We therefore know, indeed, only that the Dynasty that at the end of the 8th Century was ruling over Vestfold, and from which Harald Fairhair was descended, belonged to the Yngling kindred, might have come from Värmland via Raumarike, but established a form of Family Cult Centre at Skiringssal.

A couple of years later, Munch (1852:380) wrote that at Kaupang, "there is such a profusion of burial mounds, that it is obvious that many Families must have lived here together" ("vrimler der saaledes af Gravhøje, at man tydelig kan see at mange Familier her maa have boet tilsammen"). And he offered the following florid depiction of life in the town (1852: 381–2):

Vi kunde heraf nogenledes danne os en Forestilling om det brogede Liv, som i hine fjerne Tider maa have fundet Sted ved Vigsfjordens Bred. ... Skibene fra Slesvig bragte vel saaledes ej alene tydske, vendiske, preussiske, russiske, græske og østerlandske Varer til Skiringssal, men ogsaa ofte Kjøbmænd og Æventyrere fra de fleste af de nysnævnte Lande. I Skiringssal kunde man saaledes vistnok see Helge-lænderen kjøbslaa med Preusseren, Thrønderen med Sax-eren og Vænderen, Søndmøringen med Danen og Svæn-sken; ved Siden af Tougværk af Hvalroshud og Pelsverk fra Nordland, kunde man vistnok see Ravsmykker fra Preus-sen, kostbare Tøjer fra Græenland og Orienten, og byzan-tinske og arabiske Mynter ved Siden af de nordiske Bauge, medens Havnen laa fuld af store og smaa Skibe af forskjel-lig Bygningsmaade, af hvilke dog især de kongelige Lang-skibe maa have tildraget sig Opmærksomhed ej alene ved deres Størrelse, men ogsaa ved Deres Pragt.

From this, we might to some degree form an Idea of the multi-coloured Life that must have been experienced in these distant Times on the Shore of the Viksfjord. ... The ships from Slesvik thus did not only bring German, Ven-dish, Prussian, Russian, Greek and Oriental Goods to Ski-ringssal, but also often Merchants and Adventurers from the majority of the Lands just mentioned. In Skiringssal, as a result, one might well see a man from Helgeland strike a deal with a Prussian, a Trøndelagman do so with a Saxon or a Slav, one from Sunnmøre with a Dane or a Swede; along-side ropes of Walrus-hide and Furs from Nordland one could surely see Amber Jewellery from Prussia, precious Fabrics from Greece and the Orient, and Byzantine and Arabic Coins alongside Scandinavian Ring-money, while the Harbour lay full of Ships both large and small, built in

Figure 2.3 *Nicolay Nicolaysen was the first archaeologist to undertake excavations at Skiringssal. He excavated 79 burial mounds at Kaupang in 1867. Photo, KHM.*

different ways, of which, however, the royal Longships would have attracted especial Attention, not only for their Size, but also for their Splendour.

Munch added (1852:382, n. 1):

Foruden den store Steensætning ved Thjodalyng findes her nede ved Havnen ogsaa en mindre. Eftergravninger vilde her vistnok give merkelige Resultater.

In addition to the great Stone-setting at Thjodalyng, there is another smaller one to be found down by the Harbour here. Excavations here will certainly yield noteworthy Results.

As Munthe before him, Munch suggested an examination of the ancient remains at Skiringssal. This was realized 15 years later by the first field archaeologist in this part of Norway, Nicolay Nicolaysen (1817–1911) (Fig. 2.3). As we shall see, it is clear that Munthe's and Munch's appeals inspired him.

Nicolaysen, the eldest son of one of the wealthiest families in Bergen, scraped a very meagre pass in a Civil Service examination in Law in 1841. It is not known if his poor result was due to lack of interest or of skill; whatever the case, neither the law nor business turned out to be his sphere of action (Lidén 2005:27). From the year of its inception in 1844, he was a member of the *Foreningen til Norske Fortidsminnesmerkers Bevaring (The Society for the Preservation of the Ancient Monuments of Norway)*, and became its chairman in 1851. In 1860 the Society became his full-time occupation. In that year, an annual grant from the state established him as the Society's employed Antiquary. He held that post until 1899, when he retired as the chairman of the Society. In this half-century he put enormous energy into work on ancient monuments in Norway. Archaeology was only one aspect of this. He was also an art and architecture historian, and was involved in restoration projects and the politics of art (Lidén 2005).

To begin with, he toed the Society's line meticulously: ancient monuments should be preserved, not excavated. This was clearly stated in his report from the excavation of the ship-mound at Borre in 1852 (Nicolaysen 1853). He was called to the site because the removal of sand from the mound in connexion with roadmaking had brought interesting artefacts to light. Nicolaysen saved the fragments that were left. He wrote (1853:4) that, had it not been the case that this mound "had attracted the particular attention of the roadmakers, it would have been able to survive in peace and quiet for a long time yet. Our society would have been the last to have involved itself in its disturbance" ("havde tiltrukket sig vejvæsenets særdeles opmerksomhed, vilde den vel endnu i lang tid kunnet blive liggende i fred og ro. Allermindst vilde vor forening have bidraget til at forstyrre den").

A decade later, Nicolaysen's attitude had undergone a radical change. He wrote (1863:3–4), "We still lack ... a rich and reliable scholarly basis, in respect of the earliest period" ("Der mangler ... hos oss forsaavidt endnu et rigeligt og sikkert videnskabeligt grundlag, hvad den ældste tid angaar"). Both the prehistoric remains themselves and the artefacts would be able to yield much information about this period, he wrote, and continued:

Men til alt dette kræves først og fremst udgravninger under opsyn af mænd med fornøden sagkundskab. Især herved er det, at fortidsvidenskaben i de seneste aar har gjort saa store fremskridt i flere andre lande og navnlig i Danmark

But for all of this, we need, first and foremost, excavations under the supervision of men with the necessary understanding. This is the means by which the understanding of the past has made such great progress in several other countries in recent years, not least in Denmark.

What was it that transformed Nicolaysen's view of excavations in this way? There can be no doubt that the widespread destruction of burial mounds that this period saw left a great impression upon him. At this time, agriculture in Norway was being modernized, and large areas were being cleared for arable fields, often at the expense of ancient monuments. Furthermore, Nicolaysen's stay in Denmark in 1855–56 must have played a significant role. There he met the Inspector of the National Museum, Jens J. A. Worsaae (1821–1885), who had recently been appointed Professor in Scandinavian Prehistory. Worsaae was in the vanguard of Danish field archaeology, and placed systematic excavations at the centre of his academic programme. In the ten years after Nicolaysen's stay in Copenhagen, Worsaae supported several initiatives to build up similar activity in Norway (Lidén 2005: 102–3).

Collaboration with Oluf Rygh must also have had significant influence on Nicolaysen. Rygh joined the directorate of the Society as early as 1859. From that year onwards, he took over Munch's position as lecturer in history at the university, and was Professor from 1866. In 1862 he took over the responsibility for the University's Archaeological Museum (Oldsaksamlingen), and in 1875 became the first Professor of Archaeology in Scandinavia.

The principal contribution to archaeology made by both Nicolaysen and Rygh was to establish systematic and detailed overviews of the material itself: Nicolaysen regarding the in situ monuments; Rygh regarding the collections of finds. The key to both of these contributions was the methodical campaigns of recording and excavation that Nicolaysen undertook. These yielded a thorough overview of the distribution of surviving monuments and their forms in different ages of the past, and provided Rygh with the large numbers of finds he needed in order to construct classified overviews of the types of artefacts and their chronologies.

Nicolaysen's yearly reports on this work, printed in the annual journal of the Society, revealed that his work as Antiquary was, in the early years, rendered difficult by lack of funds for the necessary antiquarian expeditions. In the reports for 1861, 1862 and 1863 he deplored the fact that there was no money for excavations either. These complaints did not lead to any improvement in the situation, which came only when Nicolaysen threatened to resign his post if he were not granted adequate funds for excavations. In 1866 the Parliament decided to grant an annual sum for this purpose (Nicolaysen 1894b:7). After digging a few mounds in Rakkestad, Østfold that year, Nicolaysen was ready to start the methodical excavation of the burial mounds of the country. But where should he begin? He already knew.

Seven years previously, in 1859, Nicolaysen had made a major antiquarian tour. He began at Eidfjord

at the inner end of the Hardangerfjord and travelled eastwards across the mountains to Numedal. This valley route led him south to the mouth of the river Låg at Larvik. From there, he followed the road five kilometres eastwards to Tjølling and Kaupang, which was the final place that he visited. In his travelogue, Nicolaysen wrote (1861:35–6):

Paa Kaupanggaardene i den sydligste del af prestegjeldet ved Viggfjorden, ligesom og paa Lamøen, er der en hel mængde gravhauger, som dog aar for aar forsvinde. ... Disse samlinger ... høre udentvivl til de største som finnes i vort land. Da det nu maa ansees for vist, at det gamle Skiringssal laa i denne egn, og den derværende kjøbstad *(kaupang)* endog er bevaret i gaardens navn, vilde det være af stor interesse at kunne faa haugene udgravne under sagkynnig ledning. ... Ved samme lejlighed vilde man kunne faa undersøgt de forandringer, som strøget heromkring udentvil har undergaaet siden hedendommens tid, og muligens ogsaa fastsætte, hvor de i sagaerne omtalet Skæreid og Stiflusund ere at søge.

At the farms of Kaupang in the southernmost part of the parish, alongside the Vikfjord, and also on the island of Lamø, there is a large number of burial mounds which, however, are disappearing year by year ... These clusters ... are doubtless amongst the largest to be found in our country. Since it can now be regarded as certain that the ancient Skiringssal was situated in this area, and the associated market place *(kaupang)* is still preserved in the name of the farm, it would be of great interest to be able to excavate the barrows under scholarly direction ... At the same time it would be possible to make an investigation of the changes which the stretch of land around here has evidently undergone since the Pagan Era, and perhaps also to determine where the Skæreid and Stiflusund referred to in the sagas may be found.

Skjæreid is, according to *Ynglingatal*, the burial place of Halfdan Whiteleg, and Stivlesund is the place at which the Yngling king Gudrød the Hunter-King, the great-grandson of Halfdan, was killed. Gudrød's burial place is not specified in the poem, but Nicolaysen clearly hoped that he had been buried in the same place as he was killed, and that this burial place was to be found at Skiringssal, and thus in the vicinity of Kaupang.

With expectations of this kind, it is no surprise that Nicolaysen's first target for systematic excavations of burial mounds in Norway was Skiringssal, and in particular the cemeteries at Kaupang (Blindheim 1977:17–18). Preparations were begun in 1866. In this year's annual report (pp. 104–5) we read: "For the Society's Assessment a Map has been drawn of the great Gathering of Burial Mounds that lie by Nordre Kaupang in Tjølding Parish (the ancient Skiringssal) and which it is intended to have excavated in the very near Future" ("For Foreningens Regning er optaget et

Kort over den store Samling av Gravhauger, som findes ved Nordre Kaupang i Tjødling Prestegjeld (det gamle Skiringssal) og som det er Hensigten at lade udgrave i den nærmeste Fremtid"). The map was drawn by the architect C. Christie, who undertook a number of commissions for the Society. The excavation was carried out the following year, and the map was printed, together with the report of the investigation and lithographs of several of the finds, in the Society's annual report for 1867 (Nicolaysen 1868; Skre, this vol. Ch. 16:363–5).

Nicolaysen wrote that there were 115 barrows at Nordre [northern] Kaupang (1868:77), but:

... oprinnelig var der vist endnu flere, som ere ødelagte ved markarbeide og de veje, som krysse strøget. ... Av de omtalte hauger ere 44 ... mere eller mindre udjevnede eller bevoxede med træer. De øvrige 71 bleve udgravne i August 1867 under mit tilsyn.

... originally there were certainly yet more, which have been destroyed by farming and by the roads that cross this area ... Of the barrows described, 44 have been ... more or less levelled or overgrown with trees. The remaining 71 were excavated in August 1867 under my supervision.

In eight of the 71 barrows no finds were made. The remaining 63 had greater or lesser quantities of charcoal in the centre and on the base. Thirty-nine of these also contained ashes and bone, and only 36 barrows contained any artefacts. At Søndre [southern] Kaupang he excavated eight barrows, seven of which produced artefactual finds (Stylegar, this vol. Ch. 5:69).

But this was not the end of Nicolaysen's work on Skiringssal. He took a look at the neighbouring farms to Kaupang, to the east and north. He mapped burial mounds on these farms, and found six barrows at Søndre Huseby. He excavated three of these, and two yielded finds from the Early Iron Age (Migration Period). After that, he moved over to the course of the River Låg west of Kaupang, to the farm of Rauan. What attracted him there was presumably Munthe's implication that Stiflesund was sited at the mouth of the Låg (in Snorri Sturluson [1838–1839]:I:40). Munthe thought that Olaf Geirstad's Álf was buried there too, as the site is not far from Gjerstad. At Rauan, Nicolaysen found some 20–30 barrows but did not excavate any of them. At Skåra, to the north-east of this district, he found Kongshaugen, the largest cairn in Tjølling. He believed that its size was the reason for its name, and knew that Kraft (1840:33) believed that Skjæreid was to be found there. Consequently, he also examined the eastern part of Tjølling where Munthe (in Sturluson [1838–1839]: I:5) believed that Skjæreid could have been situated, but Nicolaysen failed to find any evidence to support this.

Nicolaysen was rather disappointed by the results of his work at Skiringssal. Only one of the burial mounds at Søndre Kaupang produced finds that stood out as special. Nine of the eleven objects he considered worth reproducing on plates came from this burial. The find here was a very richly furnished equestrian grave of the first half of the 9th century, the oldest of its kind in Norway (Stylegar, this vol. Ch. 5:Fig. 5.3, Ka. 157). However he could not claim to have found any regally furnished graves. His discussion of the finds includes nothing of this kind, only observations concerning the forms of the graves and of specific artefact types (Nicolaysen 1868:90–1). Further investigations took him no closer to the goal he had set for the research at Skiringssal in 1861. That the finds were generally judged disappointing is revealed by the following footnote that the publisher, Gustav Storm, added to the 1874 reprint of Munch's article on Skiringssal (Munch 1874:360 n. 1): "The area by the Viksfjord was examined by the Antiquary Nicolaysen in 1867 but little was found" ("Egnen ved Viksfjord blev undersøgt af Antikvar Nicolaysen Aar 1867, men lidet blev fundet").

After this, his first season of excavation, we never again find Nicolaysen working with questions that were directly concerned with places and persons that were named in Old Norse literature. Not even in the publication of the Gokstad find, which is the only major archaeological study he published, does he venture into such matters (Nicolaysen 1882), despite the fact that the rich furnishing of the burial could be taken as a strong basis for linking it to the great figures of the sagas. Only a few years later the idea was propounded that the farm of Gjekstad at this find-place was the farm Geirstad of the Yngling king Olaf, and that it was he who lay in the ship (Sørensen 1902).

One may speculate that it was the disappointment at Skiringssal that led Nicolaysen to turn his attention away from historical topics and towards general cultural historical issues and simply obtaining and ordering empirical data to which he subsequently devoted himself. Likewise, Nicolaysen's close colleague Oluf Rygh did not concern himself with historical questions in his archaeological studies.

2.3 A modest revival 1901–1902

After some decades in which little scholarly attention was paid to Skiringssal, with the start of the new century a new impetus emerged. Once more both an archaeologist, Gabriel Gustafson (1853–1915), and a historian, Gustav Storm (1845–1903), were involved. Whether either one was inspired by the other, we cannot tell. But it is not improbable. Storm's highly polemical article of 1901 was a response to an article by the local historian S. Sørensen, who asserted that not only Skiringssal, but also Geirstad and Ohthere's "port", lay in the parish immediately northeast of Tjølling, Sandefjord. Sørensen (1902) subsequently defended his position, and this dispute might have led Gustafson to excavate at Kaupang in 1902.

Gustav Storm was working in the same period as Rygh and Nicolaysen, and in many respects his contribution to scholarship was similar to theirs: the evaluation and systematization of the sources lay at its heart. But unlike them, Storm was also interested in and given to tackle larger and more broadly overarching historical questions.

In his article (1901), Storm reviewed all the issues that had been at the forefront of work on Skiringssal, and introduced one more: the assembly place *Þjóðalyng* (Fig. 2.1). Here he relied upon one of the most learned Norse philologist of the time, Johan Fritzner. It was Fritzner (1883) who first proposed an interpretation of the name Tjølling, where in fact he was himself the parish priest 1862–1877. Thus a great deal of local knowledge lay behind his argument (Fritzner 1883:31):

Deraf, at det var Stedet, hvor saadant Bygdeting eller *Þjóðarmál* i ældgamle Dage holdtes, har sandsynligvis ogsaa *Þjóðalyng* faaet sit Navn. *Þjóðalyng* ... heder nemlig Kirkestedet i den Bygd, som fordum kaldtes Skiringssalr, og har oprindeligen ikke betegnet andet, end en Lynghede inden Østbygaardenes Skov, hvor Prestebolet indtil Aaret 1367 var indskrænket til de Jordstykker, som Presten havde opdyrket i Kirkens nærmeste Omgivelse. Men Anledningen til, at det blev Kirkested, gav vistnok den Omstændighed, at det tidligere havde været det Sted, hvor Bygdens Mænd samledes til *almenniligt þing.*

From the fact that this was the Place where such a local assembly or *þjóðarmál* was held in the ancient Days, it is likely that *Þjóðalyng* derived its name. *Þjóðalyng ...* is actually the name of the Location of the Church in the District that was formerly called Skiringssalr, but this originally did not refer to anything more than the Heath within the Forest of the Østby farm where, until the Year 1367, the Priest's Land was limited to those Pieces of Ground that the Priest himself cultivated immediately around the Church. But the Background for this to become a Parish Centre lay surely in the Circumstance that this had formerly been the Place where the Men of the District gathered for a general Assembly.

Alongside the church there is a dry sand and gravel area that is ideally suited to serving as a place of assembly, and Storm added good reasons for regarding this not merely as the meeting place for the district but indeed for the whole of Vestfold. The name Tjølling, or *Þjóðalyng,* meant, in Storm's view (1901: 227), "the heath on which the main assembly is held", and he believed that the name had to be very old (Brink, this vol. Ch. 4:63; Skre, this vol. Ch. 17).

Storm (1901:228–30) also undertook a re-evaluation of the account in *Sögubrot* of how, in the time of the Yngling king Eystein, sacrificial feasts were held at Skiringssal. According to *Ynglingatal,* Eystein was the son of Halfdan Whiteleg and probably, according to the

chronology of the poem, died around the middle of the 8th century. Storm traced the information about the sacrificial feasts back to the lost *Skjöldunga saga,* which he dated to around 1200 and he considered this information about events at Skiringssal more than four centuries earlier as part of the dim historical background to the saga (1901:229):

Efterretningen om, at dette Blotsted "i Skiringssal" vare oprettet samtidig med, at Ynglingekongerne vandt Herredømmet i Vestfold, stemmer paa en mærkelig Maade med Ynglingasaga uden at være afhengig af denne. ... Men om jeg end tviler om dette fælles vikværske Tempel i Skiringssal, det saakalte "Hovedtempel i Viken", har det dog vistnok sin Rigtighed, at der paa eller ved Thingstedet Thjodarlyng har været et Gude-Tempel under offentlig Ledelse.

The Account of how this Place of Sacrifice "at Skiringssal" was established at the same time as the Yngling kings won Control in Vestfold agrees in a remarkable Way with the *Ynglinga saga,* without being dependent upon it ... But although I have doubts about this common Vik-region Temple at Skiringssal, the so-called "Chief Temple of the Vik", it must surely be right that either at or near the Assembly Place of Thjodarlyng there was a Pagan Temple under public Leadership.

On the other hand, Storm (1901:228–9) placed no trust in the story involving Skiringssal in Arngrímur Jónsson's *Ad catalogum regum Sveciæ annotanda* written in 1596, although it was also based on *Skjöldunga saga.* This is an airy account of King Sigurd Ring's wooing of the gorgeous Alfsol and her two brothers' heroic battle for her virtue. Storm regarded this as creative poetic composition with a semi-historical basis.

Finally, Storm assessed the possibility that the farmstead of Geirstad, of the Yngling king Olaf, might not be at Gjerstad in Tjølling as presumed by Munch and others, but rather at Gjekstad in Sandefjord. He found no sources which stated that Olaf's farm was situated at Skiringssal, and on purely linguistic grounds Gjekstad had to be accepted as a possibility. This view was subsequently confirmed by Albert Kjær (1909a) who also, through a thorough analysis of the names and cadastres, disproved Sørensen's thesis that Skiringssal might have encompassed an area larger than the parish of Tjølling.

The Swedish-born Gabriel Gustafson was appointed professor and director of Universitetets Oldsaksamling in Oslo in the year 1900; he was a highly experienced field archaeologist who had worked on the recording and excavation of ancient monuments both in Sweden and in western Norway. After his arrival in Oslo he continued to initiate and direct comprehensive field projects. The greatest of these was the excavation of the Oseberg ship in 1904, an extremely complicated excavation that he carried out at an admirable standard for those times.

Considerably less complicated was his excavation of three or four barrows on Lamøya beside Kaupang in 1902. According to his diary, this work took only two days. There is no surviving report, and he did not publish the results. But using his diary and a sketch map he drew himself, Blindheim and Heyerdahl-Larsen (Blindheim et al. 1981:61–4, 85–8 and 213–15; Stylegar, this vol. Ch. 5:74) described the work and the finds.

Gustafson excavated three or four barrows. In one, he found two unburnt boat burials interred at different dates, one with a woman and the other with a man, and both with quite a large number of grave goods (Ka. 203–205). The next barrow, however, contained only one uncremated skeleton, and the last nothing at all (Ka. 230). A fourth barrow is numbered on his sketch map, but there are no notes to suggest that it was excavated.

It is uncertain whether it was the limited results, or the discovery of the Oseberg ship, that prevented Gustafson from continuing his investigations in the following years. But once more we find that archaeological endeavours to carry out work on Skiringssal failed to yield the results that the excavators themselves had hoped for.

2.4 Advances in Skiringssal research 1909–1950

After Storm's article and Gustafson's minor excavation, several decades passed before Skiringssal returned to the focus of scholarly research interest. Quite simply there was no basis in the existing evidence for new, specialized studies concerning this site, and the archaeologists seemed to have given up hope of finding anything more. On the other hand, great progress was being made in the study of the other early towns in Scandinavia, and Skiringssal was referred to in this context by several authors.

Concerning Kaupang, Storm had put forward the conclusion that all the sites which had this name lay in those parts of eastern Norway that were ruled by the Ynglings in the 9th century. He believed that these trading places were organized by the kings and functioned under their protection. He also suggested that the Kaupang at Skiringssal might have been the earliest of these sites (1901:232–4). On this point, he was supported by the toponymist Karl Gustav Ljunggren (1937). Ljunggren wrote that the place name Kaupang, meaning a trading place in a coastal inlet (Brink, this vol. Ch. 4:63), might have lost its descriptive sense rapidly, to become a term describing any sites at which *kaup,* meaning trade, was carried out. Many of the sites which subsequently were given this name, eight in total in Norway, are not associated with a coastal inlet of any kind.

The question of what sort of community the Skiringssal trading place had, was also discussed. Some referred to the site as a town (e.g. Brøgger 1915:24–8), while others considered it to have been a site for seasonal markets (e.g. Bugge 1915:46). Oscar Albert Johnsen (1929:18) adopted a compromise position, while Edvard Bull (1933:73) was categorical that Ohthere's Skiringssal, in contrast to Birka and Hedeby, was a harbour and not a town. At those two other sites, excavations had already by then revealed extensive settlement with specializations in craft and trade, and a quantity of written sources bore witness to the character and organization of their urban communities. The absence of comparable sources for the Skiringssal trading place would appear to have been the reason for Bull's judgment.

Concerning the demise of the Skiringssal trading place, there was a general consensus among these scholars that it was abandoned and its functions moved further north in Vestfold to Tønsberg. Several scholars, including Halvdan Koht (1921:22) linked the relocation of the trading place with the transfer of the royal residence from Skiringssal to Seim alongside Tønsberg, which he believed took place some time in the 10th century.

The royal seat that was believed to have been sited at Skiringssal in the 8th and 9th centuries attracted further scholarly attention. While attention had previously been concentrated around Gjerstad, which Munch and others believed to have been the farmstead of Olaf Geirstad's Elf, now Huseby, about 1 km to the south, became the focus of greater attention. Alexander Bugge (1915:41) was the first to draw attention to Huseby. He was of the opinion that the farmsteads of Gjerstad, Lunde, Huseby, Østby, Bjønnes and Kaupang (Fig. 2.1) must at one time have formed a single farm estate, and pointed out that several old royal farmsteads in Norway and Sweden bore the name Huseby. This thread was taken up again by Asgaut Steinnes in his dissertation "Husebyar" (1955: 21–2 and 160). He based himself on Bugge's arguments, and likewise argued that the farmstead of Huseby was at the centre of this larger estate.

Although a number of important issues were discussed, and interesting hypotheses put forward, work concerning Skiringssal manifestly suffered in this period from a lack of new source material. No one could get much more out of the available source material. But things soon changed; significant new material was soon to be found.

2.5 The breakthrough: Charlotte Blindheim's excavations 1950–1974 and publications 1960–1999

Although the archaeologists were not paying much attention to Skiringssal, locally there was considerable interest. In the years immediately after the Second World War, the sister and brother Astri and Hans Christian Jahnsen, who lived at Nordre Kaupang, collected several finds that were unearthed during agricultural work. In 1947 a trench was dug for the winter storage of turnip in a small flat patch on the rocky ridge Bikjholberget immediately adjacent to the farm buildings (Stylegar, this vol. Ch. 5:72–3). Out of the trench came a total of 15 objects from two graves. These finds included five brooches and part of a sword (Ka. 250–251). The material was sent to Oldsaksamlingen in Oslo.

In the autumn of 1949 an even richer find was unearthed during the digging of a ditch at the same place. First a man's grave was found that contained a sword, spear, axe, shield and arrows, alongside fishing equipment, the remains of a box, beads of amber and glass, a soapstone cooking vessel, and a number of minor items (Ka. 252). One hundred twenty-five clench-nails retrieved showed that the dead man had probably been interred in a boat.

This rich find attracted attention when it arrived at the museum, and the deputy director Bjørn Hougen immediately travelled down to inspect the find place. He judged that the grave had been fully excavated and permitted further digging of the ditch. But he had not even gotten back to the museum before a message came about a new find in the ditch (Ka. 253). This time Hougen decided to send the 32-year old keeper *(konservator)* Charlotte Blindheim (1917–2005) (Fig. 2.4) to Kaupang to investigate the find place. It was an obvious choice. In the eleven years since she came to the museum as a student, she had worked mostly on the Viking Period, and took her masters degree in 1946 with a study of Viking-Period women's costume. In the same year she was appointed keeper at the museum, and was given Vestfold as part of her area of responsibility.

Blindheim immediately determined that a woman's grave had been uncovered, and she completed its excavation. While cleaning the site, Blindheim found a third grave, and the richest of the three (Ka. 254). When she returned to the museum with these rich finds, it was decided that further excavations had to be conducted on Bikjholberget. The excavations, under Blindheim's direction, began the following spring, and by 1957 a total of 74 graves were uncovered on this barren ridge (Blindheim et al. 1995, 1999; Stylegar, this vol. Ch. 5:72–3). Nevertheless, perhaps only half of the graves at Bikjholberget were excavated by 1957 (Blindheim et al. 1995:153).

Blindheim's principal aim in her excavations was to find out whether Ohthere's "port" at Skiringssal had been located at the farms of Kaupang (Blindheim et al. 1995:10). The burials on Bikjholberget provided grounds to believe so: the large number and density of the graves from a period of only around 150 years indicated that a substantial population had buried its dead there; the quality of grave goods was consistently exceptional; and there were many imported articles, which was evidence of trading. The burials that Nicolaysen and Gustafson had previously excavated were also furnished at a level above the average for the region. What was new about Blindheim's discoveries

was the greater quantity of imported goods and the peculiar burial rite at Bikjholberget (Stylegar, this vol. Ch. 5:87–93, 95–101). Blindheim argued, on this basis, that Bikjholberget was the "merchants'" cemetery (Blindheim 1960:60–1; Blindheim and Tollnes 1972: 49–53). She estimated the original number of burials made at all the Kaupang cemeteries to have been "towards a thousand" ("bortimot tusen") (Blindheim et al. 1981:65).

All of this implied that Blindheim had found the burial ground of a community specializing in trade. But to achieve a more certain answer she had to locate the settlement itself and prove its character (Blindheim et al. 1981:16). To this end, Blindheim dug the first trial trenches in the most promising looking area in the summer of 1956. Here, the ploughsoil was particularly dark, a phenomenon that was familiar from the settlement area of Birka. Very soon, artefacts and culture layers were found that showed that the excavation was taking place in the base sediments of the harbour of the trading place. In the course of the following four seasons of excavation they moved up to what in the Viking Period had been dry land, and by 1967, had excavated 1,375 sq m. By 1974, minor excavations of a further 100 sq m had been undertaken in the settlement area (Blindheim 1969; Tollnes 1998; Pilø, this vol. Ch. 6).

Blindheim uncovered what were interpreted as the remains of five buildings and parts of a sixth, two jetties, six wells and pits, and two roads (Tollnes 1969, 1998). In the reconstruction drawing that was first published in 1972, the buildings stand with their long walls facing the shore. Some have bowed walls, others have straight walls built of stone or upright planks. The roofs were covered in straw (Blindheim and Tollnes 1972:63; Pilø, this vol. Ch. 6:134–6, Fig. 6.10). The full extent of the settlement area was estimated as having been 38,500 sq m.

Blindheim (1969:24–32; Blindheim et al. 1999:153–64) concluded, essentially on the basis of the artefact assemblage, that the remains of a community for which trade and craft was of central importance had been excavated, but that hunting, fishing and some agriculture had also been carried out there. From the construction of the buildings and differences in the distribution of the finds, she judged that Building I might have been a permanent, year-round dwelling house while the others were workshops. She found it possible that Building I, with the large Jetty II below it, might have been the centre of a complex. Regarding the question of whether the settlers had alone determined the site's evolution or whether the royal power had played a role, Blindheim found the latter possibility most convincing.

Blindheim dated the burials on Bikjholberget to the period 760–930/940. The other cemeteries were also created during this time span, with the exception of Lamøya, where burial might have continued

through 950 (Blindheim et al. 1999:153,162). The finds from the settlement also were dated from the end of the 8th century and some way into the 10th century (Blindheim et al. 1999:147), but very few of them were from the 10th century. Concerning the end of settlement activity at the trading place, she believed that there had been a gradual move to Tønsberg, "as a result of both political and practical/topographical conditions" ("forårsaket av både politiske og praktisk/topografiske forhold") (Blindheim et al. 1999: 163). The end of urban expansion at Kaupang was probably due to a lack of suitable space (Blindheim and Tollnes 1972:100).

In her last publication on Kaupang, Blindheim produced the following summary view of Skiringssal (Blindheim et al. 1999:153–64): Drawing upon work by Stefan Brink (1996b) and Kaare Hoel (1986), she wrote that the farm of Huseby, which probably was once called Skiringssal, was also the centre of the Skiringssal complex consisting of trading place, assembly place and cult centre. A number of neighbouring farmsteads were part of this complex too: Blindheim (Blindheim et al. 1999:156–9) specifies Guri, Lunde and Gjerstad as crucial ones, in addition to Valby, Østby and Bjønnes. It was the occupants of these farmsteads who managed the trade at the "kaupang". She supposed that the people on these farms were highly intermarried, and that they thus constituted a more complex kin-group than any that would normally be found in more straightforwardly agrarian districts. She also believed that such a community would have given women "a significant degree both of freedom and of authority" ("en betydelig grad av både frihet og myndighet" (Blindheim et al. 1999: 159).

In several works, Blindheim explored the political and trading connexions of Skiringssal. In these publi-

Figure 2.4 *Charlotte Blindheim in her study around 1950. As a result of her excavations at Kaupang 1950–1974 the trading place at Skiringssal was finally identified at the farm of Kaupang in Tjølling, Vestfold. Photo, KHM.*

cations, one consistently finds the view that the burial practices and the range of finds indicate that the site had a marked Norwegian connexion (e.g. 1997:90–1). The external links were essentially to the east and west, and only to a minor degree to the south. In an article in 1984, she discussed the impulses that led to the establishment of the trading place. On the basis of the archaeology, she found that these could be traced to Uppland in Sweden, and she associated this connexion with the Yngling dynasty, which *Ynglingatal* claims came from that area (Blindheim 1984:54–5).

She also claimed (Blindheim et al. 1999:162) – particularly on the basis of parallels in both dating and characteristic features between the equestrian grave at Kaupang and the Balladoole grave on the Isle of Man – that there had been especially close political and economic connexions between the Skiringssal complex and the British Isles and Ireland. The remainder of the finds implied such connexions as well, she wrote. Thus, Blindheim returned to the idea she had at the conclusion of the excavations at Bikjholberget, but which she had abandoned after the excavations in the Kaupang settlement area. At that time she had proposed (1969:31–2) that the settlement finds more clearly displayed connexions with Jutland and the Rhineland.

Ellen Karine Hougen (1993), who was on Blindheim's excavation and publication teams, has published a study of the pottery from the settlement excavation. As part of this work, she undertook a provisional survey of most of the dated artefact types and some of the graves from the settlement area, and included available radiocarbon dates (Hougen 1993: 49–63). She found that the activity around the harbour began perhaps even before the early 8th century, but that the settlement and the cemeteries were not established until the very end of the 8th century. The activity both in the burial ground and in the settled area appeared to cease around the middle of the 10th

century, but there had been a change of character around the year 900. Contact with the Continent is clear in the earliest phase, but the 10th century almost exclusively shows contacts with the British Isles and Ireland. The grave finds produce the same picture, both in terms of chronology and of contacts. The only difference is that there would appear to be some 9th-century finds from Britain and Ireland at Bikjholberget.

Unlike Blindheim, Hougen (1993:61–3) associated the foundation of the trading place with the Danish royal power and the king's men in Vestfold, who probably were the local kings of the Yngling dynasty. After about AD 900, the trading place lost its trade links with the Continent, probably due to the recession that the Continental towns, including Dorestad, suffered in this period. At the same time the Yngling kings moved to western Norway, which may be the reason for the more prominent Insular element amongst the finds, Hougen suggested.

Besides Hougen, Blindheim's two close colleagues, the architect Roar L. Tollnes and the archaeologist Birgit Heyerdahl-Larsen, were involved in the project. Heyerdahl-Larsen joined the project shortly after the excavations had been concluded, and became Blindheim's co-author in the publication of the grave finds (Blindheim et al. 1981, 1995, 1999). Tollnes became a member of the excavation team in 1959 and was responsible for the drawing and photography during the excavations in the settlement area. He was also given the job of publishing the finds of the remains of buildings and other structures (Tollnes 1998; Pilø, this vol. Ch. 6). Tollnes was also interested in the communication routes in the hinterland of Kaupang, and published an important discussion of these (in Blindheim et al. 1981:17–37).

Blindheim's excavations, publications and analyses of her own finds and of the archaeological material that had been retrieved from Kaupang up to her time, brought scholarship concerning Skiringssal many decisive steps forward. For the first time, the trading place at Skiringssal had been securely identified. The material from the excavations, especially the artefacts from the cemeteries and the settlement area, made it possible for the first time to explore many aspects of the site – its character, chronology, activities, settlement structure, trade goods, and range of contacts – in addition to a series of more specialized matters. Through the efforts of Blindheim and her colleagues, Kaupang was established for international scholarship as one of the earliest urban sites of Scandinavia.

Blindheim's results had consequences for the perception of the Early Viking Period. Whereas Norwegian historians had previously explained the Viking expeditions by population growth and related social and political circumstances, more emphasis was now placed upon the significance of trade (e.g. Andersen 1969:32–45, 1977:226–30). From the 1970s onwards, studies of early urbanization in Scandinavia underwent a surge, and Blindheim's discoveries were frequently referred to (e.g. Helle and Nedkvitne 1977; Christophersen 1991).

It is obvious that Blindheim had a political agenda concerning women in archaeology which she brought to her project. When she was a young student, she was one of a very few women working in Norwegian archaeology. When she herself reached a position in which she was able to do so, she strove to provide work opportunities and support for young female archaeologists. This was a clear priority of hers, and both the excavation and publication teams had a high proportion of women. Blindheim was also the first woman archaeologist in Norway to combine a scholarly career with family life.

To understand Blindheim's approach it is essential to recognize the difficult conditions under which she worked. The excavations were carried out under extremely poor economic conditions. For instance, the large number of summer houses in the Kaupang area was the only available accommodation for the work team. In the summer holiday period it was much too expensive to hire any of these; therefore, excavations took place only in the spring and autumn, when most of the summer houses were empty. Furthermore, until her retirement in 1987, Blindheim worked on this project while continuing to work full-time at Universitetets Oldsaksamling. Hence, the excavation, analysis and publication process required a full fifty years. In 1969 Blindheim and her colleagues quickly produced a provisional publication of their finds in *Viking*. She also published a number of articles both while the excavations were underway and subsequently, but the fundamental publications concerning her excavations did not appear until the years 1995–1999. Until then colleagues both in Norway and abroad had to rely on the provisional publications and could not make use of the full results.

Blindheim belonged to the generation that was young during the Second World War, and she was powerfully affected by the war. Furthermore, the strong re-orientation during the post-war period away from Central European and towards Anglo-American culture and scholarship left its mark on both her range of contacts and her research output. Even though the finds could have supported a different view, one notes a great emphasis on the British and Irish links and a correspondingly limited emphasis on the Continental links. Within Scandinavia, she would much more often draw parallels with Birka than with Hedeby. Her settlement excavations were carried out at the same time as Kurt Schietzel's major excavations in the settlement area at Hedeby, but there was no direct contact between them regarding either excavation methods or the results.

The excavations at both Bikjholberget and in the settlement area posed massive challenges to Blindheim in terms of excavation methods. In order to be able to tabulate the finds chronologically, she needed at both sites a rigorously stratigraphical approach to excavation. At that time, excavations were being carried out in Norway in which such methods were being developed, such as Anders Hagen's excavations in the cemeteries at Hunn in Østfold in the early 1950s and Asbjørn Herteig's excavations at Bryggen in Bergen and the urban site Borgund from the mid-1950s onwards. But these advances had little influence on Blindheim's methods. In fairness, one should stress that stratigraphic excavation methods were embryonic at that time; the great breakthrough in stratigraphic excavation did not take place in urban archaeology until the 1970s. Therefore, Blindheim's excavations at Kaupang were unable to deliver a comprehensive picture of the chronological development of the settlement (Pilø, this vol. Ch. 6:133–4).

At the time of Blindheim's excavations, what we now see as the crucial questions concerning early urban societies had not been formulated. Little was known about the building types or about the organization of such settlements; this lack of information deeply affected the principle questions and answers of Blindheim's project. When such information became available, especially from the excavations in Hedeby (1959–1969), Dublin (1974–1981), York (1976–1981) and Birka (1990–1995), it was difficult to make use of the results from the settlement excavations at Kaupang. Therefore, even though Kaupang continued to figure in general studies as one of the urban sites of the Viking Period, its evidence and the interpretations of it were infrequently discussed or referred to. Still, perhaps only the present author fully appreciates how crucial Blindheim's contribution was to the initiation and execution of the new excavations which were begun in 2000.

Preparing the New Campaign

3

DAGFINN SKRE

Preparations began in the spring of 1998 for the excavations that would eventually take place from 2000 to 2003. In this chapter, the research context of that planning is outlined, and the background is given to the primary research questions that were defined as the basis for fieldwork under the project. The essential research questions tackled by the research project of which that fieldwork was a part are also explained.

The principal questions for fieldwork relate to two key topics: the debate over the *first urban sites* in Scandinavia – of which Kaupang appears to be an example, and the debate surrounding the *central places* of Scandinavia in the first millennium AD – of which Skiringssal appears to be an example. A starting point is outlined from which these two topics can be investigated.

The study of the earliest urban sites in Scandinavia has been frustrated by institutional factors. For example, the great emphasis on the study of High-medieval urbanization has meant that the earliest towns have been written off as pre-, proto- or semi-urban. Recent scholarship on urban studies argues that the early urban sites have to be regarded as real towns, albeit with particular characteristics that distinguish them from the towns that developed in Scandinavia from c. AD 1000. In this chapter, some of the characteristics of the early towns are sketched, which introduces a cluster of questions to be tackled by the archaeological work at Kaupang.

In the 1st millennium AD a series of sites emerged in southern Scandinavia that are usually referred to as *central places* and which were evidently crucial in fundamental social organization, particularly juridical and cultic, within territories of various sizes. In each case, at the heart of the central place there seems to have been an aristocratic household. Several such sites also produce evidence of trade and craft. The two objectives in the study of Skiringssal are to understand this site better and to enhance the understanding of such central places in general, of their functions, and of their social and cultural significance in the second half of the 1st millennium.

The research questions specified are the basis of the discussions in the present volume. At the end of this chapter, a number of key problems that will be fully examined in future volumes of this series are outlined. Several of these are concerned with the development of a deeper understanding of the urban community of Kaupang. Other contributors will, starting from the Kaupang evidence, take up general and essential topics within Viking-period scholarship, such as trade, production, and the historical and cultural context of urban sites.

In the winter of 1996–1997 the present author succeeded Charlotte Blindheim, then in her 80th year, as leader of the Kaupang Research Project. The first year was employed in gaining an overview of the material and the state of publication, with a view to contribute to the completion of Blindheim's project. At the same time my work began to explore the possibilities of new research campaigns with the material that was available from Kaupang and the rest of Skiringssal.

Particular attention was paid to gaining a full view of the evidence and its unexploited potential, and to define the most critical research questions.

It soon became clear that the evidence available had not been fully exploited, but it was equally clear that a series of fundamental scholarly issues could not be investigated using this evidence. There were also certain problematic aspects concerning the interpretation of the remains that were unearthed in the settlement area during Blindheim's work (Pilø, this vol. Ch. 6). As a result, a strategy with three components was devised:

- To contribute to the completion of the two publications that were nearly completed (Tollnes 1998; Blindheim et al. 1999).
- To encourage graduate students to select topics for their dissertations that were either wholly or partly based on Blindheim's finds (Pedersen 2000; Tansøy 2001; Lia 2001; Melsom 2003; Johansen 2004; Andersen 2004; Østmo 2005; Engesveen 2005).
- To plan and carry out a new research project concerning Kaupang and Skiringssal.

In the spring of 1998 Lars Pilø and I began to plan new investigations at Skiringssal. That same spring, a field survey in the settlement area of Kaupang produced an unexpectedly large and interesting range of finds, and this was a major stimulus to the planning. A preliminary project involving further survey and trial excavation was carried out in 1999, and the excavations under this project took place in the years 2000–2003 (Pilø, this vol. Ch. 7; Skre, this vol. Ch. 11).

In this chapter (3.1 and 3.2) a detailed account of the research questions that lie directly behind the fieldwork and which the subsequent chapters in this volume relate to can be found. Finally (3.3) there is a summary of the other general issues considered under the project that will be discussed further in succeeding volumes. At the beginning of this volume (Skre, this vol. Ch. 1:18) there is a review of the chapters and monographs in preparation by the project team.

The research questions themselves fall into two principal areas of research. Given the character of the site, the study of *early urban sites* in Scandinavia was an obvious topic. This approach to Skiringssal was boosted when Blindheim discovered the urban settlement at Kaupang, but it can be traced in the history of Skiringssal scholarship right back to the mid-19th century (Skre, this vol. Ch. 2.2–2.5). We recognized a need to review the whole subject in light of the great advances made in relation to this topic both in excavation methods and in academic questions since Blindheim's excavations took place.

The second principal area of research is the *local context of Kaupang,* in particular aspects of settlement, culture and political structure such as the site-hierarchy and the concentration of important social functions. This has been a leading issue in Skiringssal scholarship from the start, with persistent interest in the royal residence and its connexions with the trading site, the *thing* site and the cult centre. These issues, however, have fallen into the background over the last century, largely because of the lack of new empirical evidence (Skre, this vol. Ch. 2.4). Regarding settle-

ment structure and social structure, the last two decades have seen extensive research activity in Scandinavia. We are now more conscious of a hierarchical element in settlement in certain areas, especially the principal agricultural regions. It has become standard practice to refer to the head places of these hierarchies as *central places* (e.g. Brink 1996b:238; Larsson and Hårdh 1998), a term that has come to cover a wide range of very different sites. We recognized the opportunity to advance the understanding of both central places in general, and Skiringssal in particular, by approaching Skiringssal as a central place.

Of course, an account of what we understood then, seven to nine years past, cannot be totally accurate. What follows is quite rightly shaded by how our understanding has developed in the meantime, and particularly by the revision of the project's principal research questions which were undertaken i 2002–2003 in preparation for the analysis and publication stages.

3.1 Scandinavian urban sites prior to AD 1000: the central issues

In Scandinavia, the Viking Age is a transition period from a pre-state to a state society. At the beginning of the period, power lay in the hands of chieftains and petty kings whose power-bases and residences were rural and who had varying types of authority over territories. The core of a territory was the land owned by the ruler himself. Outside of that, the ruler's area of authority was defined by where his military followers, kinsmen and allies were living and by the extent of the areas which he and they dominated. During the Viking Age, in contrast to the period that followed, the territories of petty kings and chieftains were socially rather than geographically constituted. Their areas of authority were also less stable. Altogether, the type of power and the way it was exercised was characterized by its dependence on social connexions and by the structure of a rural society.

In the course of the Viking Age, this was to change. At its end, the three Scandinavian kingdoms were created and they were governed according to rather different kinds of power structures than those of the earlier societies. Kings claimed control over a definite coherent territory with generally well-defined frontiers. They also built up an administrative and military apparatus intended to control this territory and to defend it from external enemies. One of the means of internal control was the making of new laws which meant that the king and also the Church were obliged to receive fines for certain crimes. In this way, the power apparatus of the state and the Church entered into what until then had been considered a relation between the two parties to a crime – the offender and the victim.

These are some of the numerous aspects of the development of the Scandinavian states; in addition there is urbanization. From the start, towns were closely connected to kings, but their role in the kings' government changed, as did the internal life of the towns themselves. In the first wave of urbanization in Scandinavia, which began around AD 800, trade and craft production, including a considerable level of long-distance trade, seems to have been the fundamental urban activities. As noted, the towns were closely associated with kings, although the towns themselves do not seem to have been the seats of power in the form of residences of kings or petty kings. Nor does it appear as if there was any apparatus in the towns that exercised administrative functions over the immediate hinterland of the town, as was the case in Scandinavia from the 11th/12th centuries onwards.

The close connexion between the towns of the Early Viking Period and men of power can be seen from the towns' proximity to royal farmsteads or by their location in areas of importance to kings. The introduction of urban sites to Scandinavia seems to have taken place as a royal initiative, and the emergence and continuation of the towns can be linked with kingship. The military power of the kings guaranteed secure trading in the towns (Skre, this vol. Ch. 20.1:451). The focal social functions of the region or the kingdom appear, all the same, not to have been located *within* the towns. It would seem, for instance, as far as sources can reveal, that assemblies in towns dealt with only matters concerning the town itself (Ansgar, ch. 27; Odelman 1986:105 n. 393). The *thing-moots* that dealt with cases concerning the surrounding countryside were apparently not held in the towns but in the rural areas, sometimes close to the towns (Skre, this vol. Chs. 17 and 19). Moreover the kings had their feast-halls on their rural properties rather than in the town, although again they could be close by (Skre, this vol. Chs. 11 and 19).

It was not until the second wave of urbanization in Scandinavia that the town itself – as the location of residences and a centre of administration and governmental control over a hinterland – became a place of interest for those in power. This second wave began around AD 1000 and over the following two centuries towns gradually assumed more and more functions relating to social power. Kings and bishops built their residences there and, in the course of the 12th century in particular, they became the fixed centres of the royal and ecclesiastic administrative apparatus for the towns themselves as well as for their hinterlands.

This change in the relationship between the ruling powers and the town had profound consequences for the town and the character of urban life. A town's demographic constitution, its economy, the balance between the production of goods and services, its economic and political relationship with the surrounding countryside, and the social and geographical range of the areas of distribution of the goods produced there, were all changes that occurred between the lifetime of the towns founded in the early Viking Age and that of the towns founded at the end of the Viking Period. The second wave of urbanization is not the subject of this research project, and serves here principally by contrast to highlight characteristics of the initial wave (Skre, this vol. Chs. 20.2 and 20.3).

When one approaches so fundamental and complicated a topic within history as the town, it is vital to establish a point of departure that provides room to look at the dynamism and variability of the phenomenon. It is clear that the *definition* of the town cannot be based upon variable features such as the social composition of the urban population or the possible function of the town in relation to the surrounding area; rather, it must be based upon more general and chronologically independent characteristics.

Just as important as defining the characteristics and identifying changes of the town is the identification of differences and similarities with the rural community. In this respect, it has been usual to focus on the typical urban activities of trade and craft production and to use their mass presence to identify towns. However, although trade and craft production were primary activities within the towns in this period, they were not exclusively urban undertakings. These occupations were found in thoroughly rural contexts before the Viking Period, and evidence for them is known from a diverse range of sites from the Viking Period itself, some of which are of a completely rural character. To find the towns, therefore, it is necessary not just to identify and examine the evidence of trade and craft production but also to investigate the settlement and social contexts in which they are found, whether rural or urban.

Defining the town

The debate on how to define the town is widespread over many different disciplines. Several quite distinct definitions have been produced, many of which are characterized by a strict relevance only to specific areas and periods, and a dependency upon the sources available in those contexts (e.g. Biddle 1976:100).

There are, however, other approaches to defining the town that do not incorporate the variable aspects of the town in the core definition. This sort of approach to the problem of defining the town has a long history, although it has been particularly in the foreground of international scholarship for the last thirty years. Despite the fact that the elements of this approach can be found in earlier scholarship, a comprehensive definition was not formulated until Susan Reynolds did so (1977:ix–x, 1992:49–50). It has since been used and developed by several authors who have worked on early urbanism in northern Europe, some of whom make direct reference to Reynolds (e.g. Clarke and Ambrosiani 1995:3; Pallister 2000:5);

others take more independent approaches which are nevertheless still very close to her very pragmatic approach (e.g. Helle and Nedkvitne 1977; Helle 1980).

Reynolds's approach is based upon the idea that "town" is a loose conceptual category with fuzzy boundaries. It is consequently unrealistic to aim at defining all the conceivable marginal cases; one should rather aim at identifying certain core characteristics. In work investigating towns in a given area at a given date, one has therefore to distinguish between *definition* and *description*. The *definition* must aim to represent all towns at all periods, therefore has to be quite broad and intended to describe the essential characteristics of the town. The *description,* by contrast, may be more precise about what is typical of towns in that given area and particular period.

On the basis of Reynolds' discussions the following timeless characteristics of the town can be identified, which consequently constitute the definition of the category. Towns are *relatively densely populated, permanently occupied units* of a *particular size,* in which *the principal part* of the inhabitants make their *principal livelihood from non food-producing activities.* Towns are *quite clearly delimited from their surroundings.*

This way of defining towns has certain specific constituents, some of which will be considered in what follows. An important aspect of this definition is the fact that a crucial characteristic of the town is that it is a *community.* The relatively dense, permanent occupation of a place by a relatively large group of people produces a more intense social life than that found in rural communities. Moreover, a large number of the residents make their living from work that, for the most part, requires a high degree of interaction with other inhabitants, and with visitors. All of this produces a social and cultural dynamism that will in most cases be more intense than anything that can arise in rural society.

It is also worth noting that there are a number of types of dense settlement that do not fall within the framework of this definition and which must, therefore, be considered rural. This will include sites that either are not permanently occupied or do not last very long. Settlements where subsistence activities such as agriculture, hunting or fishing are the primary economic occupations of the inhabitants also fall outside the framework of this definition. By contrast, settlements where a large part of the economic life is based upon the products of a primary occupation, such as fishing, will fall within it. The majority of the inhabitants there will be engaged in the processing of the fish, the provision of supplies for the fishing fleet and for fish processing, and trade or service activities.

An essential quality of this approach is the fact that it distinguishes between definition and description. This allows for what one might regard as the rather obvious possibility of towns' in the same area and period being different in character. With this dual approach, characteristics of towns in the second wave of urbanization in Scandinavia should be identified as *historically specific* urban traits and not as definitive characteristics of towns in general. This will apply, for instance, to such a prominent aspect of the High-medieval towns as their administrative functions relating to the surrounding areas. This has to be part of the description of the towns of this period, and must therefore not be included in the definition as a supposedly timeless characteristic of all towns – as some scholars have indeed done.

Research on the early urban sites of Scandinavia

Despite the fact that during the period c. AD 700–1300 Scandinavia had towns with a wide range of characteristics, an approach that can distinguish universal aspects of the town from chronologically specific ones has not been widely applied. Rather, the characteristics of the towns of the 13th and 14th centuries have been used in constructing a definition of *town* which has been applied to research on much earlier urban sites. What is the reason for this?

The last fifty years have seen tremendous growth in research into urbanization in Scandinavia pre–1500 AD. Extensive excavations in Norwegian and Swedish towns of that period have produced a wide range of studies. In Denmark the excavations have not been as extensive, but there has been just as significant a level of research. One can confidently declare that these three countries have led the way during the last fifty years in respect of methods of excavation, new approaches, and new insights into early urbanization in northern Europe.

Remarkably, though, the scholarship during this surge has shown relatively little interest in the first wave of urbanization in Scandinavia, that which began around 800 AD. Mostly examined have been towns of the second wave, which began around 1000 AD and rolled across Scandinavia for several centuries, resulting in towns that for the most part still exist. Insofar as excavations and research have been carried out on Early Viking-period towns, they have been primarily within scholarly circles working otherwise on rural society and with little if any contact with the scholarly circles working on the later wave of urbanization. Some of the reasons for this are quite trivial; for example, excavations of sites dating from the 11th century and later in Norway were the responsibility of *Riksantikvaren* (the Directorate for Cultural Heritage), while excavations of earlier sites were assigned to the appropriate museum from amongst the five regional museums of archaeology.

This sort of institutional division has played a role in Denmark and Sweden too. In this 50-year period Medieval Archaeology was established as an independent discipline at the Universities of Århus and Lund. The discipline was given a somewhat different profile at these two seats of learning: in Århus, Denmark emphasis was placed on the monuments, while in Lund, Sweden emphasis was placed on society. Urban archaeology was on the agenda in both universities, but more so in Lund. In this field of Scandinavian medieval archaeology the huge amounts of evidence from the High-medieval towns drew the lion's share of attention. The Viking-period towns lay on the margin of the period that scholars were supposed to be concerned with, and interest in them was consequently lower.

As a result of both the institutional division and the limited interaction between scholars, exacerbated by the research focus on the later towns, the reference point in Scandinavian scholarship for the definition of medieval towns became the towns of the 13th and 14th centuries. Consequently, the key methodological point outlined above – that towns change in character over time, so that the Early Viking-period towns might have had different functions and characteristics than the later medieval ones – has been largely overlooked.

As a result, the early towns of the Viking Period have not been identified as a group *per se,* but rather grouped and analysed together with a quite heterogeneous collection of sites, primarily in relation to the sort of activities that were undertaken at all of them, i.e. trade and craft production. From c. 700 to 1000 AD there are a number of sites, such as magnate residences, market sites and landing places, with archaeological inventories reflecting trade and craft production, and for many scholars the presence of this evidence has been reason enough to group them together as similar types of settlements (e.g. Andersson 1979:7–8; Lindquist 1985). Most sites with evidence for trade and craft production have been named using the same term, e.g. *trading site.* The result has been that the first wave of urbanization, which took place within this period, became an invisible phenomenon, hidden inside a heterogeneous collection of sites that reflect the growing economy of trade and craft production from the 8th century and throughout the Viking Age.

One can, however, find other directions in the scholarship on Viking-period urbanization. Several scholars have argued that it is not possible to make a definitive distinction between the towns of the early Viking Period and the later ones. Most prominent amongst them have been Knut Helle (e.g. Helle 1980; Helle and Nedkvitne 1977) and Björn Ambrosiani (Ambrosiani and Erikson 1996:58–63; Clarke and Ambrosiani 1995). Helle, for instance (1980:17–18), has written with reference to Hedeby and Birka that "To distinguish the most important of these trading and production centres from towns poses major conceptual problems, although that has nonetheless been usual practice." ("Å skille de viktigste av disse han-

dels- og håndverkssentrene fra byer volder store tankemessige vanskeligheter, men det har likevel vært vanlig å gjøre det.")

Some scholars have also attempted to clarify the distinctive features of the earliest wave of urbanization from those of the later wave. Johan Callmer, for instance (1994), has pointed out specific characteristics of the first wave. It is quite clear, though, that there is a need for further research on this matter. There is also a need to separate the early towns from the many other kinds of sites with evidence of trade and craft production that flourished in this period. Finally we need an examination of the relationship between towns and the power structures of the old society and of the new emerging kingdoms. These topics are taken up in this volume (Skre, this vol. Ch. 20) and in a later publication (Skre, in prep.).

New excavations at Kaupang

The principal objective of the excavations planned at Kaupang was to place the site in relation to the various types of sites with evidence of trade and craft production established in the early Viking Period. Were the settlement traces found at Kaupang the remains of one of the many seasonal market sites of this time, or were they evidence that Kaupang was one of the very few towns established in the early Viking Period? We also took account of the fact that relatively few sites, towns primarily but also market sites, had been extensively excavated. Our knowledge of the majority of sites with evidence of trade and craft production was therefore limited; consequently, we had to allow for the possibility that Kaupang could be of a character that would disrupt the categories we believed to have existed in the early Viking Age.

With reference to the general objectives, we defined the following five concrete research questions as those that the fieldwork aimed to investigate:

1. The character of the settlement – seasonal or year-round
2. The layout of the settlement – possible plots, lanes, grouped buildings, open spaces
3. Building types
4. The location and character of various forms of activity – trade, craft production, etc.
5. The dating of the settlement, and possible changes in its activities and character

Of these, especially 1, 2 and 3 are connected directly to the question of whether Kaupang was a market site or a town. When one excavates this sort of site, however, one is subject to a number of general scholarly responsibilities. In research on market sites and early towns one can find a range of different topics and issues, such as the study of buildings, ships, and of economic and cognitive history. Not all pieces of research in these fields are equally firmly linked to the towns *per se,* but rather have the character of general Viking Period studies. Their association with towns is primarily due to the fact that excavations in these contexts produce such a very rich and peculiar range of artefactual finds. A major excavation in one of the early sites was so rare an event that we could not carry it out with strict reference to only a few basic research questions. It was legitimate to allow those objectives to determine, for instance, the location and size of the excavated areas, but the excavation itself had then to be carried out in such a way that the various categories of archaeological evidence and their contextual information would be fully recorded. We had to attempt to produce a body of material that was retrieved and documented in such a way that, as far as possible, it would be amenable and available for research on most other possible issues currently known.

These considerations had certain clear consequences for the fieldwork planned for Kaupang. The first question to be resolved was whether to excavate in the settlement area or in the cemeteries. From the settlement area we would obtain material that was best suited to shed light upon the character of the settlement, e.g. whether it was urban, and how it developed. The likelihood of producing a precise chronology of both the artefactual finds and other remains that might reveal its development was also much greater with fieldwork in the settlement area than in the cemeteries. Further reasons for not excavating the cemeteries were that there is already a large collection of material from the cemeteries of Kaupang (Stylegar, this vol. Ch. 5), and that the developments in cemetery excavation methods since this material had been retrieved were not as great as those of settlement excavation. The potential for achieving new insights would therefore be much higher in an excavation in the settlement than in the cemeteries.

For these reasons, we decided to undertake a major excavation in the settlement area of Kaupang. The fieldwork had to satisfy the following requirements:

- The main excavation had to take place where the likelihood of finding stratified deposits was high, including the remains of buildings if there were any.
- The main excavation had to cover a sufficiently large, continuous area so that it could reasonably be expected to reveal the layout of the settlement – namely the presence of plot-divisions, lanes, and so on.
- In order to be able to grasp the character and development of the settlement in the greatest possible detail, and to secure the contextual and other relevant information relating to the artefactual finds, the main excavation had to be con-

ducted according to the stratigraphic method of excavation, in this case what is known as "single-context recording".
- The fieldwork had to make use of a record system that would be capable of receiving, systematizing and analysing the great quantities of data on objects and contexts that such an excavation would produce.
- The fieldwork had to produce sufficient material from outside the main area of excavation so that conclusions could be drawn about the dating, activities and possible plot-division over considerable parts of the settlement area.

The consequences of these requirements in terms of methods and excavation strategy are discussed in a following chapter (Pilø, this vol. Ch. 7).

3.2 Skiringssal: a central place

It has long been recognized that certain settlement sites in southern Scandinavia have a quite distinct character which is reflected in various ways. Typically one or more of the following features are present at these sites (cf. Brink 1996b:237–9):

- Farms that have recorded connexions with petty kings, kings or chieftains in Old Norse sources; usually the farms are also associated with churches and estates of the 11th–13th centuries.
- Specific types of farm- and place-names, usually sacral names or names which indicate that the site had important secular functions.
- *Thing* sites that are known from place-names and written sources, and which show that the place had central juridical functions.
- Rich archaeological finds, usually large barrows, richly furnished graves, hoards, or rich settlement-site finds.
- Halls which not only served as a residence for a king, petty king or chieftain but were also the locus of cult feasts and other important rituals.

The first such settlement site known through major excavations (1954–1978) and detailed publication was Helgö close to the mouth of Lake Mälaren, west of Stockholm. Since then, a number of others have received attention, including Sorte Muld on Bornholm (Watt 1991), Lejre near Roskilde (Christensen 1991), Gudme/Lundeborg on Fyn (Nielsen et al. 1994), Tissø on Sjælland (Jørgensen 2003) and Uppåkra near Lund (Hårdh and Larsson 2002; Larsson 2004) (cf. Skre, this vol. Ch. 1:Fig. 1.4). The earliest of these sites was established in the first two centuries AD and some of them, like Uppåkra, remained in being right through to the end of the Viking Period. Others, for instance Gudme/Lundeborg, ceased to function in the 6th/7th centuries. At that time new places of this kind were being established, as at Tissø. Those that were still in existence from the Viking Period all lost their focal social role sometime around AD 1000.

Since the 1980s, major excavation projects at several of these sites, accompanied by growing interest in the topic of social elites, has led to much wider work on these sites (e.g. Mortensen and Rasmussen 1988, 1991; Brink 1996b; Callmer and Rosengren 1997; Larsson and Hårdh 1998; Hårdh and Larsson 2002; Andrén et al. 2004). In the 1980s it became normal practice to use the term *central place* for such sites, borrowed from social geography.

Central-place theory was originally developed by the German geographer Walther Christaller and first introduced to archaeology by David Clarke (1972). The term refers to settlements that are distinguished from other surrounding settlements by their having essential social functions relating to the area around them. In order to participate in certain activities or to have a wide range of their needs satisfied – typically economic, juridical, cultic and administrative – the inhabitants of the area usually have to go to the central place.

The central places will themselves form their own hierarchy, from the small and local to the principal super-regional central place. The number and complexity of functions will increase as one moves up this hierarchy, and the site at the top will not only have a large number of functions but also activities with a character exclusive to it. In addition, Christaller's central-place theory is concerned with the geographical distribution of these sites, and with the pattern of communications that forms in an area with a hierarchy of central places. The further up the hierarchy one goes, the greater will be the distance from another centre at the same level. This geographical aspect of his theory has not been much used in archaeology.

Some aspects of Christaller's central-place theory are thus of limited relevance to archaeological research, but the term itself appears very apt for characterizing the sites at which one can see a grouping of social functions. It is, however, also vital to realize that merely naming a site "central place" does not on its own help to understand it. The characterization of a site as a central place is only a preliminary identification which has first to be justified, and then to be detailed and deepened. The special features of the site and what it has in common with other central places have to be understood and then used as a basis for locating it more precisely within the different categories of central places. Beyond this, it is necessary to strive towards a synthesis that will lay out the categories and characteristic features of Scandinavian central places of the first millennium AD and investigate how they change over time.

There is a lot of research of this kind now at our disposal. It shows, as noted, that central places of the first millennium AD had a wide range of functions. One common feature appears to have been that a core element was an aristocratic residence, a cultic and feast hall (Näsman 1991:169–72). It also appears that trade and craft production were found in some measure at or near many of these halls. Cult functions can be identified to varying degrees at most sites. Central juridical functions have, however, only been identified at a few, probably because these leave few traces in the available sources.

There is great variance amongst central places in terms of the size of the territory they serve. Some were used only by locals while others were used by people from several regions. The examples of central places given above are all of ones that were used by people from a wide area. The position of each central place in the conceived hierarchy can be inferred from the various types of evidence e.g.: types of place-names; the number, size and types of buildings; and the amount and exclusivity of the artefactual material.

In addition to these, there is great variance among central places of the first millennium AD, for instance in terms of how closely placed or scattered various functions are in the landscape. At some sites, such as Uppåkra, they are gathered inside an area of 1 sq km, whereas the outermost limits of the Gudme/Lundeborg complex lie 6 km apart. Some scholars have, as a result, distinguished central places from central-place complexes, central areas etc. (e.g. Brink 1996b:238; Andersson 2003:316 with refs.). In what follows we do not pay great attention to such distinctions, because the unifying force at the central place, the power and influence of the petty king or chieftain, seems to be of the same kind irrespective of the geographical layout of the site. Because the various functions and the coherent forces of the central place will be the main areas of interests here, the size of the area geographically is consequently of less importance. The term "central-place complex" is, however, used when it is appropriate to focus on the composition and disposition of different functions within the central place.

Individual scholars have concentrated on different aspects of the central places. Some put most emphasis on their political, economic and societal significance (e.g. Callmer 1998; Näsman 1991). Others, by studying archaeological and written sources, have succeeded in demonstrating that the settlement hierarchy reflects patterns of property-holding, in which the central farmstead had the right to govern and extract a proportion of the produce of the surrounding and subordinate farmsteads (Iversen 1997; Skre 1998b; Iversen 2004). Cosmological structures in these contexts have also been explored by a number of scholars (e.g. Brink 1996b; Hedeager 2001; Andrén et al. 2004).

The term "central place" has also been applied to sites which scarcely merit it. At many other sites, settlements have been found where grave finds, the size of buildings, etc., show that the occupants were of higher status than their neighbours. Such sites cannot be considered central places unless it can be shown that they fulfilled central functions for the neighbourhood.

Central places are composite and extensive complexes which pose a real challenge to archaeological investigation. Their extensive character and the meagreness of traces left by some types of functions make it difficult to be sure one has located all of the components of the central place. At some sites, as at Upp-åkra, the material remains may be so copious that a major excavation seems no more than a pin prick, while in other places they are so few that only good luck brings them to light – as was the case with our discovery of the hall at Huseby (Skre, this vol. Ch. 11:224–5). Consequently, we must anticipate that future investigations of central places, most of which are as yet poorly explored, will show them to have had greater significance than is currently thought; furthermore, central places that are at present completely unknown will surely be discovered. In Norway, sites of the same sort of wealth and size as those found in Denmark and Sweden have not been securely identified. But there are several places where there are strong hints that comparable central places may be found, for instance at Tune in Østfold county (Stylegar and Norseng 2003:325–30), Spangereid between Mandal and Farsund in Vest-Agder county (Stylegar and Grimm 2003), and Åker near Hamar in Hedemark county (Pilø 2005).

As we assessed the situation in 1997–1999, there were persuasive indications that the Skiringssal complex could justifiably be classified as a central place. Simultaneously however, as noted, this category comprises sites that are extremely varied in respect of date, activities and character. The broad application that the term has been given in archaeology has left us with a need to define it more precisely. Our intention was to deepen the understanding of the phenomenon called "central place" through an empirical analysis of each of the elements of the central place, of their role within the central place, and in Scandinavian societies of the first millennium. Such a study of Skiringssal is found in the later chapters of this volume (Skre, this vol. Chs. 16–20), but a more comprehensive discussion of Scandinavian central places will have to wait until a later volume in this series (Skre, in prep.).

In order to carry out an analysis of the central place Skiringssal, it was necessary to collect more concrete evidence about the various elements of the complex, especially regarding their dating and character. We opted to concentrate archaeological fieldwork on the two elements that offered the best chance of obtaining archaeological results: the excavations at Kaupang (Pilø, this vol. Chs. 6–10) and the identification and examination of the heart of the complex, the hall (Skre, this vol. Ch. 11). We also aimed at finding

sources of information on the landscape history of the area, and at having botanical, geological and zoological evidence from the settlement area of Kaupang analysed (Sørensen et al., this vol. Ch. 12; Bonde, this vol. Ch. 13; Barrett et al., this vol. Ch. 14; Milek and French, this vol. Ch. 15).

Beyond that, it was our wish to assemble and analyse other sources which might illuminate the other elements of the Skiringssal complex. These included the place-name evidence (Brink, this vol. Ch. 4), the cemeteries and burial practices (Stylegar, this vol. Ch. 5; Skre, this vol. Ch. 16), the *thing* site (Skre, this vol. Ch. 17), and the written sources (Skre, this vol. Chs. 2 and 18). Particular attention was paid to clarifying the dating and character of the various components so that, in a comprehensive discussion of the complex, it would be possible to consider its emergence, the changes that occurred over time, and its demise (Skre, this vol. Chs. 19–20). It is probably fair to say that it has been our ambition to re-establish and revitalize the holistic view of Skiringssal that characterized the scholarship of the mid-19th century, in particular the work of Munthe and Munch (Skre, this vol. Ch. 2:29–34).

Since the goal in Chapters 16–20 is to study one particular central place rather than to discuss such places as a class, the organization of this study is particular rather than general. With just a few exceptions (e.g. Ch. 20.1), the discussions and explanatory models are therefore more particularistic and historical than general and structural.

3.3 A wider scope of questions

In addition to the principal research questions explained so far, in planning the project we defined both a number of relatively specific questions concerning Kaupang and a series of more general questions involving crucial topics in Viking-period scholarship, particularly in respect of towns. Only certain aspects of these questions are pursued in the present volume, but in anticipation of the future publications (cf. Skre, this vol. Ch. 1.1:18) a brief account of these two sets of questions shall nevertheless be give here.

The specific questions concerning Kaupang are intended to deepen the understanding of the Kaupang community. The ambitions of the project go beyond assigning the site to one of the two categories, market site or town – which, by the way, we believe to have resolved in favour of the latter in the current volume (Skre, this vol. Ch. 20.2:452–4). We wish also to go into the specific character of the town. Because of the huge resources required to excavate such towns, our knowledge of any of them, and of the shared features or variations between them, is fairly limited. Each town is unique; therefore, we wish to reveal the peculiarities, variations, and irregularities in the structure and spatial organization of the settlement and activities at Kaupang. We also hope to investigate the social, economic, material and structural relationships within the town, together with the population's productive activities and those activities' social and cultural connexions. These studies will lay the foundation, amongst other things, for hypotheses concerning the urban lifestyle and urban identity. These studies will make use of comparisons with the hinterland and with other towns in Scandinavia, and possibly also urban sites around the Baltic and North Sea areas.

The general research questions concerning Viking-period towns take up the role and significance of Kaupang in the culture and society of the Viking Age. These matters will be studied within three principal areas: trade, craft production, and the historical/cultural context. The studies that are concerned with these areas will involve comparative perspectives that vary in scope.

Several aspects of craft production at Kaupang will be examined, including the technological, product-related, and qualitative changes that occurred in craft production following the increase in production volume and the improvement in raw material supply. Those changes also led to changes in the social situation of craftsmen, for instance in their network of contacts and the degree to which they were tied to a particular site. The targeting of production towards different social groups and different domains of consumption will also be studied.

Trade, involving both goods produced in the town and goods brought in for exchange, was a key activity in Viking-period towns. Trade and craft production were the most fundamental activities in the economic life of the town, and trade was also the most vital dynamic activity within the town's communications with its surrounding areas and more distant places. The character and development of trade, the methods of payment and the tools, are consequently key matters for study by the project. These studies will concern themselves with the distribution both of the craft products that were produced in Kaupang and of the goods that were imported to the town for sale, and where they came from and the context of their production. It is quite evident that commercial exchange became increasingly important in Scandinavia from the 8th century onwards; in this project it is particularly the cultural, economic and social aspects of this development that will be investigated.

The historical context of the development of trade, craft production and the urban settlement and its community will also be studied. Key inter-related processes such as these must be assessed in light of the formation of the kingdoms of western Scandinavia (Skre, this vol. Ch.20.2–20.3) and the Scandinavian expansion into the Baltic area, the Continent and the British Isles. The Scandinavians' appropriation of goods in these areas through trade and looting is also essential to the understanding of developments in urbanism and economic life in Scandinavia. In this regard production and economic life in the areas of colonization are also of relevance as is trading from these areas to Scandinavia.

On the basis of the detailed studies of Kaupang and Skiringssal outlined above (3.1–3.2) and the work on the more general research questions identified by the project (3.3), we shall undertake a discussion of the earliest phase of urbanization in Scandinavia as a cultural, social, economic and political phenomenon (Skre, in prep.).

Skiringssal, Kaupang, Tjølling – the Toponymic Evidence

4

STEFAN BRINK

This article deals with the toponymic evidence – the place-names – in the Tjølling area, and the historical evidence they may reflect. In the settlement district *(bygd)* of Tjølling we find a few, probably very old, settlement-names, in *-vin* and *-heimr,* presumably to be dated to the first half or the middle of the first millennium. These are grouped around a lake whose name is probably to be found as the first element of one of these names, namely *Vittersen.* This name may be interpreted as denoting a sacral lake, probably of importance in some cultic activity here, containing a word related to the ON noun *vítr, véttr, vettr, vættr* 'supernatural being, spirit, god'. Other settlement-names portray the settlement district as a large archipelago during the Iron Age, with several large and small islands, the names of some of which have been preserved. Finally the names *Huseby (< Skíringssalr), Tjølling (< Þjóðalyng)* and *Kaupang* are interpreted and discussed. These names are to be seen as evidence of the socio-economic importance of this district, with an aristocratic chieftain's or royal farmstead controlling a major harbour/market-place *(Kaupangr).*

The Tjølling settlement district has enjoyed a lot of attention in archaeological and historical research for centuries, for obvious reasons. The toponymic evidence, which also is very interesting, has not been scrutinized and discussed to the same extent, and that is a pity. Here we find some illuminating place-names together with some really obscure ones. One of the challenges to the analysis of these names is to establish some kind of chronology in the toponymic milieu, a common problem when working with the place-name material in Scandinavia.[1]

The Tjølling area received a lot of attention from early historians, who constructed their narratives on the basis of the sagas in particular, and declared this region the "cradle of Norway" (see Skre, this vol. Ch. 2; Munch 1850; Sørensen 1900, 1909a, 1909b; Storm 1901; Bugge 1909, 1915; Kjær 1909a, 1909b). This scholarship was later discredited, especially from the 1950s onwards, mainly for its insufficient evaluation of the sources and over-reliance on sagas, which shifted focus away from the Tjølling area. Instead Charlotte Blindheim's sensational archaeological excavation at Kaupang, coupled with the new interest in Borre amongst other sites (see, e.g., Myhre and Gansum 2003), changed the disciplinary standpoint from history to archaeology in respect of Tjølling, with a new focus on Kaupang. The shift can in broad outlines also be said to be one from the area being seen as a major political site, one of the significant royal strongholds important in state-formation in Norway *(rikssamlingen),* to it being regarded as perhaps the most important port and market site in early Norway, vital for trade and mercantile contact with Europe.

So what is the evidence that the place-names of the Tjølling area can bring us? Do they underline or reduce the political and mercantile importance of Tjølling? Although not so easy to interpret, coupled with the chronological uncertainties, they seem to

---

1   Normally phonetic notations from the dialect are used when analyzing names, together with early name-forms from (preferably medieval) documents. In this case, dialect name-forms are to be found in Rygh 1897–1936:VI and in the Place-Name Archive in the University of Oslo *(Seksjon for Namnegransking).* Since dialect forms have not been of decisive importance for the interpretations presented in this article, I have chosen to omit them. Anyone interested is referred to Rygh 1897–1936 or *Seksjon for Namnegransking.* Older forms of the names here cited are from Rygh 1897–1936; as for the sources, see Rygh 1897–1936.

Figure 4.1 *The settlement district of Tjølling with a reconstructed shore line towards the end of the Early Iron Age, c. 500 AD (c. 5 meter higher sea level than today). During this time there where several more straits, inlets and islands than today. These are possible to identify and couple with place names. Contour interval 5 meter. Map, Julie K. Øhre Askjem, Anne Engesveen.*

hint at the Tjølling district as one of the most interesting areas in Norway, with indications of social and political significance in prehistory and the early Christian Middle Ages.[2]

4.1 The Early Iron-age names

To give some chronological framework for the area, we can establish that Roman Iron-age finds are known from the places where today we find the settlements Slottet, Auby, Klåstad, Valby, Huseby, Håkestad, Grønneberg and Vestad, and Migration-period finds from Roligheten, Amundrød, Vik, Skalleberg, Eide, Istre and Skåra, plus finds from either the Roman Iron Age or the Migration Period from Hosle (Blindheim 1974).[3] To place these finds topographically, it seems important to note that in the very centre of the Tjølling district there is nowadays a small lake, *Vittersentjørn*, surrounded by quite a large marsh. This seems, most probably, to represent a fairly large lake, c. 1 km x 0.5, of the Iron Age, which like several other lakes in Scandinavia has been lowered and partly drained in the 19th century (Skre, this vol. Ch. 17:Fig.17.2). It is notable that this lake has a central – maybe even focal – location in relation to the distribution of the Roman Iron-age and Migration-period finds.

If we look for the earliest settlement-names in Tjølling, four names stand out: *Guri, Lauve, Vittersen* and *Lingum*. The first three are to be identified as *-vin* names, while the latter is clearly a *-heimr* name. Both the *-vin* and the *-heimr* names are, in my opinion, mainly to be dated to the Roman Iron Age or the Migration Period in Norway, although both types continued in use into the Late Iron Age.[4] In the latter period, however, it would appear that they occur as developed and stereotyped forms, such as several instances of *Askim, Solheim* etc., and *-vin* names showing no *i*-umlaut (cf. Olsen 1926:154 and 158; Jansson 1951; Ståhl 1976:75; Pamp 1974:34; Brink

1988:73, 1991). The names that may be from the Early Iron Age are of course only a mere fraction of the names once in use during this early period, a point that it may be necessary to call attention to when addressing scholars other than toponymists. As for the *-vin* name-element we have also the complication that the word **vin* originally denoted a kind of meadow (cf. Gothic *winja* 'pasture, fodder; meadow'), and

2 Normally, in an analysis of this kind of a settlement district, one would have to be much more minute and penetrating, analyzing early cadastral registers and survey maps from the 17th, 18th and 19th centuries, analysing dialect forms, collecting and analysing natural-feature and field-names and other minor names, together with a topographic analysis in the field. This has been impossible for me when writing this article. For the potential for a more minute analysis, see (below) the information from maps and the document from 1439 regarding the boundary between Østby, Huseby, Lauve etc., and the mention of a name *Helgefjell* in the vicinity, which probably has wide and important implications for understanding the early landscape here. This article is hence to be looked upon as preparatory for a more minute analysis of the Tjølling *bygd*.

3 It may be important to stress from the outset for non-toponymic specialists that these finds do not, of course, date the historical farms and hamlets in the vicinity here mentioned. The question of if and when archaeological finds can be used for dating a prehistoric settlement whose name seems to have survived into modern time is a wide and complicated one (see, e.g., Brink 1984), which I will touch upon in passing later on.

4 I here use Early Iron Age for the Roman Iron Age and the Migration Period combined (c. AD 1–600) and Late Iron Age for the Merovingian and Viking Periods together (c. AD 600–1050); roughly, because it is so difficult to be precise on chronology for place-names.

5 All early name-forms here and below are from NG.

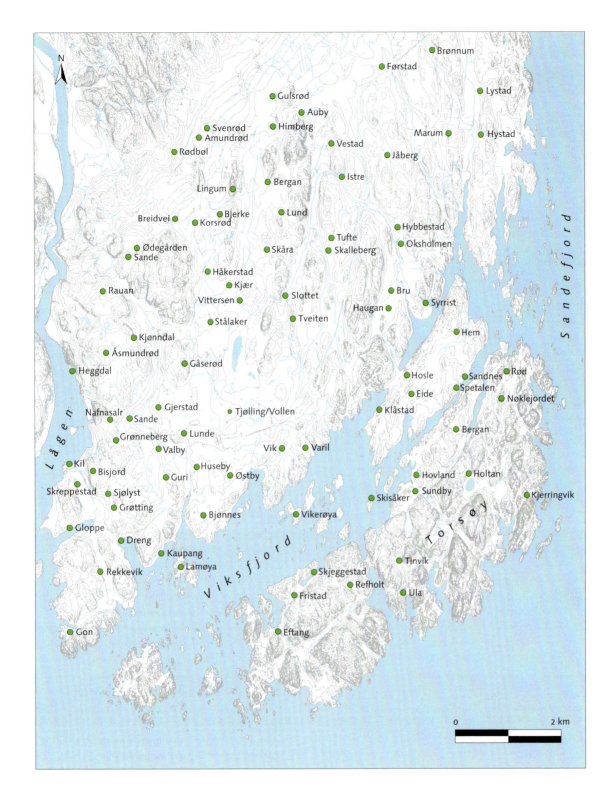

a semantic development during the Iron Age to the sense of 'settlement' seems very likely (Brink 1988: 74). The problem is, then, to decide if we can identify an original sense of 'meadow' or a later one of 'settlement' for -*vin* names.

All three -*vin* names in Tjølling are problematic in respect of their qualifiers. This, in its own right, is an indication that they are ancient. Only *Lauve* seems to be fairly uncomplicated. In 1370 it was written *a Laufuini*, in 1391 *a Laufuine*, and in 1397 *a Lauuine* and *i Laufvine* (Rygh 1897–1936:V:295),[5] which seems to indicate an older *Laufvin*, containing the ON noun *lauf* n. 'leaf, leaves', here probably indicating deciduous forest. Maybe this *vin*, 'meadow (of some kind)', was used for the harvest of leaves, cf. ON *laufadráttr* m., *laufhǫgg* n., *laufhǫgstr* m. If this interpretation is correct, it is also evidence of the age of this name, according to the criteria noted. *Lauve* is thus to be looked upon as a really old name, probably to be dated to the Early Iron Age. The other two are more difficult to interpret. *Guri* was written *Gudrina* (in acc.) in 1419 and in 1444 *Gudrine* (in nom.). As Rygh (1897–1936:VI:292–3) assumes, it looks as if the first element could contain the word *guð* n. 'god(s)', but the *-r-* is a problem that has to be addressed. Different attempts to solve this question have been proposed, but all are very intricate and rather dubious. It is, however, difficult to ignore the possibility that the first element in the name contains the word for 'god(s)'. As Guri is in the centre of the Tjølling district, interesting perspectives open up when this name is considered in conjunction with the following one, *Vittersen*. Nevertheless, the distance between Guri and the lake has to be recognized as a potential obstacle to connecting them.

Vittersen is a most interesting name. In Røde Bog (RB) it is written *i Vittrixsyni;* in 1440 *i … Vittrissinne;* in 1512 *Vittersøn;* and in a translation from 1555 of a letter from 1320 we have the form *Wettersiø* (Rygh 1897–1936:VI:295). It is notable that in the 16th century the name has transformed and wrongly (?, cf. below) been identified with the lake *(-siø)*. The oldest forms indicate that this name is an old *-vin* name, but what the first element may be is more obscure. Here, it is tempting to see an older name for the lake, a possibility already proposed by Oluf Rygh (1897–1936: VI:295), but what this name may have been is uncertain. The problem relates to how we understand the *-xs-* in the name-form in Røde Bog, a cadastral register of estates under the Bishop of Oslo prepared by Bishop Eystein in Oslo c. 1400. Normally *-xs-* stands for *-ks-* (or *-gs-*), which gives a first element **Vittiks-* which is most difficult to explain. However, there are known cases of *-x-* in 15th-century Norwegian documents being used for *-s-*, such as Gerixstad*hom* (ON *Giristaðum)*, Aurixstade (ON *Øyristaðum)*, Høixstad*hom* (ON *Heiðistaðum)* etc. (ABJ:xxx–xxxi) in Aslak Bolts *jordebok* (cadastral register) from the 1430s, and several other sources. A possible interpretation of the first element in the name *Vittersen* could therefore be as an old name of the lake, **Vítrir/Vettrir,* producing a compound **Vítrisvin/Vettrisvin.* Such a qualifier would fit very well with a possible ancient lake-name, Pr.-Germ. **Wehtr-iaʀ,* which would plausibly be identified with ON *vítr, véttr, vettr, vættr* f. 'supernatural being, spirit, god', Sw *vittra* 'fairy (of the forest)';[6] cf. OE *with* 'being, demon', OHG *with* 'spirit, being' *(< *wehti-/wehta-)* (NO:507; SEO: 1402; AEW:672). This etymology makes it possible to interpret the lake-name **Vehtriaʀ > *Vítrir/Vettrir* as 'the lake where supernatural being dwell', or perhaps 'the lake dedicated to gods and super naturals". Hence, such a name of the lake is semantically to be connected to Scandinavian lake-names such as *Guðsiōr, Tissø* ('Týr's lake'), *Odensjö* etc. A plausible assumption may thus be that here, in the very central part of Tjølling district, there was a sacral lake during the Iron Age, dedicated to gods and natural beings, per-

haps a lake where offerings were made to the deities, a well-known practice during prehistoric time in Scandinavia.[7] This old lake has today only two remnants in the form of *Vittersø-tjønna* and the small *Lille-tjønna* in the south-east (see Skre, this vol. Ch. 17: Fig.17.2). It would be interesting to see if there are any votive deposits to be found in this marsh and lake, as have been found at Tissø on Sjælland, Kärringsjön in Halland, Skedemosse on Öland and more. Vittersen-tjørn would therefore qualify for a potential successor to Kaupang for furture archaeological surveys.

In this connexion it is extremely interesting to note a natural-feature name, *Helgefjell,* for a small but very distinct hill immediately to the east of *Lille-tjønna* (Skre, this vol. Ch. 17:Fig. 17.2), a hill with a very steep side to the west, which must have fallen steeply into the former lake. This is obviously an old name, mentioned, for instance, by Alexander Bugge in *Tjølling bygdebog* (1915:41),[8] but found already in a document from 1439, cited in a judicial survey document from 1703, dealing with the boundary between the farms Austby, Huseby, Lauve etc. in Tjølling parish.[9]

In this letter six men in the local law court announce that they have walked the boundary between Austby, Huseby, Lauve etc., and in the letter the different boundary marks, in the form of bedrocks by the sea, a stone by a gate, a pine with a cross cut in it, the flat rock in the road, "og saa ouster i Helgafield", i.e. and then Helgefjell to the east, etc. are mentioned. Boundary-marks were normally noticeable and easily identified natural features, and Helgefjell seems to qualify for this purpose.

The name *Helgafjell* has many counterparts in Scandinavia and Iceland. The most famous is perhaps the *Helgafjell* in western Iceland mentioned in the often cited passage in the *Eyrbyggja Saga* when the settler Thorolf took land in *Breiðafjörð* and there built a hall with a high seat and a small cult house

---

6   The etymology for *vittra* f., proposed by Elof Hellquist (SEO:1363–4 and 1402), that the *-r* is analogously introduced from the nominative singular *vætter* of the word Sw *vätte* 'supernatural being', is probably wrong. It seems more satisfactory to connect the word to the group ON *vítr, véttr, vættr,* with the same or similar meaning of 'a spirit, a supernatural being', and hence to derive the word from a stem **wehtr-,* with a radical *-r.*

7   See e.g. Brink 2001:96–8 with refs.

8   "I skillet mellom Østby og Vittersen, som er en av de ældste gaardene i Tjølling og i gamle dager maa ha været meget større end nu, laa Helgefjeld ('det hellige fjeld'), sikkert et ældgammelt kultsted" ("At the boundary between Østby og Vittersen, which is one of the oldest farms in Tjølling and which in earlier days ought to have been much larger than now, was Helgefjeld ('The Holy Mountain'), certainly an ancient cult site").

with an altar on which he placed an oath ring. The saga continues to relate that (*Eyrbyggja saga* pp. 9–10):

Þórólfr kallaði Þórsnes milli Vigrafjarðar og Hofsvágs. Í því nesi stendr eitt fjall; á því fjalli hafði Þórólfr svá mikinn átrúnað, at þangat skyldi enginn maðr óþveginn líta og engu skyldi tortíma í fjallinu, hvárki fé né mǫnnum, nema sjálft gengi í brott. Þat fjall kallaði hann Helgafell og trúði, at hann myndi þangat fara, þá er hann dœi, og allir á nesinu hans frændr. Þar sem Þórr hafdi á land komit, á tanganum nessins, lét hann hafa dóma alla og setti þar heraðsþing; þar var og svá mikill helgistaðr, at hann vildi með engu móti láta saurga vǫllinn, hvárki í heiptarblóði, og eigi skyldi þar álfrek ganga, og var haft til þess sker eitt, er Dritsker var kallat.

Thorolf called the headland between Vigrafjord and Hofsvag Thorsnes. The headland is in the form of a mountain, and Thorolf invested so much reverence in it that no one was allowed to look towards it without having washed and nothing was allowed to be killed on the mountain, neither man nor animal, unless it died of natural causes. He called this mountain Helgafell and believed that he and all his family on the family on the headland would go there when they died. At the place where Thor had come ashore, on the point of the headland, Thorolf held all court sessions and he established a district assembly there. He considered the ground there so sacred that he would not allow it to be defiled in any way, either by blood spilt in rage, or by anybody doing their "elf-tremblers" there – there was a skerry called Dritsker [Shit-Rock] for that purpose. (Hreinsson 1997:134)

Here on *Þórsness*, 'the headland dedicated to Thor', Thorolf named the mountain *Helgafjell*, 'Holy Mountain', into which he then believed he would enter when he died, and he created a cult site for cult practices and a *thing* site for legal matters. How much truth there may be in this story is very uncertain. However, there are several other *Helgafjell* etc. in Scandinavia, and we may conclude that many of these must have had a cultic-legal background (cf. Brink 2001).

Since this name here in Tjølling is evidenced as early as 1439, and in the letter it is said that 70- to 80-year-old men could verify the boundary marks 50 years before, hence c. 1390, this name may well qualify as an old name, most probably of pre-Christian origin. The situation of this *Helgefjell* in the immediate vicinity of a lake to which it may be possible to assign a name *Vítrir/Vettrir* with its own cultic-religious background inevitably makes this a most intriguing place. If the interpretations are valid, *Helgefjell* seems to strengthen the hypothesis of previous cultic-religious activity at this former lake, and it would be extremely interesting, as mentioned above, to have an archaeological survey of the area.

North of the lake and the settlement of Vittersen we find *Lingum*. The name is written *Limaemsbygdh* in 1495; in 1496 *Lingemsbygd*; in 1512 *Limgemsbygd*; later on in the 16th century the *-bygd* is dropped and we find *Lindem, Lingem* etc. (Rygh 1897–1936:VI: 297). Rygh (loc. cit.) assumes that this name goes back to ON *Lindheimr*. However, the medieval name-forms point in different directions; the qualifier could be interpreted as: 1) *ling* 'heather' or perhaps 'moor, heath, sandy land',[10] going back to ON *lyng* n. 'heather' (< *lengwa-) (AEW:370), or a word *ling* (< *lingwa-), a cognate with *lyng*, found in Swedish place-names and in Sw *lingon* 'lingonberry' (SEO: xxx); 2) *lím* n. 'lime' (cf. Henningsmoen 1974:25–6); or 3) *lind* f. 'lime (tree)' or 'well, water' (AEW:357). This place-name is most definitely to be understood as a name in *-heimr*, but the settlement has evidently been looked upon as a habitative isolate and therefore as a separate *bygd*, 'settlement district', or perhaps it had a wider spatial denotation. Since the Tjølling settlement district probably bore the name of its central occupied area, the *bygd*, during the Early Iron Age and in the middle of the first millennium, this name, ON *Limheimsbygd*, could be a candidate for this.

There may be another early place-name in the Tjølling district, namely *Hem*, situated on a small former island between the mainland and a larger island *Þossey* (to all appearances < *Þórsøy*). This name seems to be a *-heimr* name. In Røde Bog it is written *i Hæme i Þossøynne;* in 1393 we have *a Hæme;* in 1374 *a Hæm;* and in 1427 *i Hææm* (Rygh 1897– 1936:VI:300). Rygh (loc. cit.) interprets the name as an older *Háheimr*, with the first element *hár* 'high', but notes that the hill, which might be the reason for the name, is small ("Den Høide, som her kan have givet Anledning til Navnet, er liden."). An alternative interpretation, perhaps more plausible, could be that the first element is to be connected to the homonym *há* 'bay', found in several Swedish place-names (Zetterholm 1936), cf. ON *hár* m. 'the fork on a boat to have the oar; shark (a name given the fish from its sharp, triangular fin)' (SEO:327; DEO:144). In the Early Iron Age and still during the Late Iron Age, a small but

---

9   "... byriadæ mer ta ganga og siuna klippenom, [...] og saa i fieldenden, som ligger ved Vichgarstæden, og i grindestædet, og saa ouster i Helgefield, schillrissa (dvs -rika) merchæ Ousby og Wittersyn schieret, og hellen j vejen, end merchestejnen som ligger i vejen schil Ousby og Lyfinæ, end Ryfnestejnen schil adt Vich og Ousby. var dissæ dælæ gangen for 50 aar af 70 og 80 aar gamble mannum, til sandingæ sette vj vore insigle for dette bref som giort var aar og degj som for siger." (DN 12:201, also published in Berg 1915:182 and Krohn-Holm 1970:298).

10 Cf. the cognate Sw *lung*, which denotes 'a sandy ridge, an esker' (Bucht 1951; Brink 1979:29–31). For Sw *ling*, see Melefors 1984.

conspicuous bay reached up to the settlement site of Hem from the east (Fig. 4.1). This could explain the name.

It is possible that the Early Roman Iron-age (c. AD 100–200) finds, in the form of a set of jewellery, a knife and a gold finger-ring which were excavated by Slottet in 1888 in the burial mound (12 m in diameter) of a woman interred in a small chamber (Blindheim 1974:72), may be connected to *Vittersen.* This hypothesis finds support in the fact that Early Iron-age names in -*heimr* and -*vin* seem to have denoted not so much settlements but rather larger home territories, as I have suggested and discussed elsewhere (Brink 1991, 2002b:688–9). The archaeological finds here at Slottet may well qualify as being within the home territory of an Early Iron-age *Vittersen,* although this is, of course, merely a hypothesis to be tested. Two Roman Iron-age burials at Huseby excavated by Nicolaysen in 1867 (Blindheim 1974:76) may be connected in the same way to an Early Iron-age *Guri* settlement immediately to the west of Huseby. The risk of circular argumentation is naturally – as often in the interface between archaeology and toponymy – a direct problem in cases like this, but observations of these kinds must be noted and eventually applied systematically in more extensive investigations in the future.

Thus the earliest settlement-names in Tjølling are interestingly grouped around the lake (**Vítrir/ Vettrir),* with Guri to the south, Lauve to the east and both Vittersen and Lingum to the north of the lake. When comparing this settlement situation, which I assume to represent the Early Iron Age, with the Late Iron-age settlement situation in Tjølling, one gets the impression that the focus has moved from around and north of this lake to the area south of the lake, between the lake and the sea at Viksfjorden, with Huseby at the centre. This shift in settlement structure may partly be due to the shore displacement (land upheaval), with new, dry land to cultivate, and partly to the draw of the sea for seafaring, fishing and trade.

This leads us to the question of landscape change over time, and here the place-names can provide interesting evidences for an earlier maritime landscape and help us to reconstruct an Iron-age situation. The Tjølling area has been affected by the shore displacement (Sørensen et al., this vol. Ch. 12:267–72). When Kaupang was established the sea-level was c. 3.5 m higher than it is today, and during the Early Iron Age it is possible that it was 5–6 m higher. During the Late Iron Age, with a shoreline c. 3–4 m higher up the land, there was a long, narrow bay, pointing up towards Grøtting, to the west. This bay must have been narrow and maybe quite long. It would therefore be plausible to connect the place-name *Dreng,* a settlement immediately to the west, with this former bay. The name *Dreng (i Drængh* RB; *i Drængh* 1440)

could be interpreted as containing the ON *drengr* m. 'thick log' (Rygh 1897–1936:VI:290; cf. AEW:82), originally used in a figurative sense for the long and narrow bay.

Another, smaller, bay was at Kaupang, pointing to the north, towards Guri. Malmøya and Lamøya were present, but smaller than today, and the large Vikerøya, at the end of Viksfjorden, then consisted of several smaller islands. A significant bay went from Viksfjorden to the north-east, up to Vik. This Iron-age bay is evidently the explanation of this name, *Vík* 'bay'. Next to Vik, by the ancient shoreline, we find the settlement *Varil (a Varareldi* 1376; *Vararelli* 1378; *i Varello* 1385; *i Warelli* 1391). The name probably originally denoted a landing place for ships. It contains the word *vǫr* f. 'landing place' *(varar* in the gen. sing.) and *hellir* m. 'rock, flat rock': hence ON *Vararhellir.*

To the east, west of Sandefjorden, there was a long and narrow peninsula stretching to the south. The delimitation of this elongated peninsula at the western side was a long and narrow inlet, a bay that opened out at the landward end (Fig. 4.1). This kind of small bay, with a lake-like end, was called a *mar,* ON *marr* m., or a **marm,* a word found, inter alia, in some Swedish place-names (Moberg 1988:7– 8). This word is to be found in the place-name *Marum (< Marheimar)* on the Tjølling side of the fjord, in 1341 written as *Maræimar* and *a Maræimum,* and in Røde Bog *Mareimar.*

East and south of Viksfjorden there were three islands in the Iron Age, which became connected towards the end of this period, creating the large, crooked peninsula we still have today. Thus Viksfjorden was in contact with Sandefjorden to the east for some or all of the Iron Age through two channels or sounds (cf. Blindheim 1976b:76). For the outermost of these islands, with the settlements Eftang, Fristad and Skjeggestad, the name seems to be lost. The name of the largest island is, however, known from medieval documents. In Røde Bog we find *i Sandakre i Þossøynne (Sandakr* being a now lost settlement), *i Klæpakre i Þossøy; Sannæs i Þossøynæ; i Hæmæ i Þossøynne; Sannæsrud i Þorsøy* and *Sannesrud i Þossøy;* and finally *i Holtom i Þossøy.* The name of this large island during the Middle Ages was therefore *Þossøy,* which Rygh (1897–1936:VI:304) derives from *Þórsøy,* an interpretation that may find support in the form *Þorsøy* in Røde Bog. This island name is then to be placed in the typological group of theophoric island names such as *Frösö* and *Norderö (< Njærðarøy).* It is notable that on this old island we find the place-names *Hovland (Hofland* RB) and, nearby, *Skisåker (Skesager* NRJ), both of which can be given a pagan, cultic interpretation, and so perhaps represent a cult site on the island.

Between the mainland of Tjølling and the large island of *Þossøy* during the Iron Age there was a smaller island. We may find its name in the settlement-name *Hosle,* which in 1401 was written *a Hoslu* (Rygh 1897–1936:VI:299). Rygh (loc. cit.) attempted to derive the name from a river-name, but had to admit that no potential river or stream is to be found here. Instead, this name inflected as a feminine noun, could be the older name of the island: hence **Hasla* 'the island known for hazel'. When the shore displacement had proceeded to the point that this small island was joined together with the mainland via a small passage of land, a small isthmus, this became a site in the waterway where one had to haul the ship or boat over the small isthmus between the inlet from the east and the Viksfjorden, which may be reflected in the settlement-name *Eide.* The name is the dative singular form of the word *eið* 'portage; isthmus where one has to haul the boat between areas of water'.

That the sea once formed a passage, and later on a bay, north of the former island with the assumed name of **Hasla* is corroborated by the name *Syrrist (i Siaugharystrw, i Siagharystrv* RB), which goes back to a *Sjóvaristra,* containing in its second element the name of a river, **Istra* (also found in the neighbouring name *Skallist,* in RB found as *i Skalistrw),* and the word *sjór* 'sea' as the qualifier, giving the meaning that here, at this site, the river **Istra* flowed into the sea.

This river-name, **Istra,* is also found in the settlement-name *Istre,* upstream. The name of the settlement was written *a Istru* in 1390 and in 1439 as *Istre.* This river-name has parallels in Scandinavia, but its etymology is quite obscure. Per Hovda (1971:141) thinks the river-name is a derivative with an ancient *-str*-suffix to a stem in the word ON *íss* m. 'ice', because this calm-flowing river froze unusually early.[11] The obvious connection would otherwise be with ON *ístr* n. 'fat', but why this river would be blessed with such a name (ON **Istra,* Pr.-Germ. **Istrõn)* is uncertain. Perhaps the quality of the water was likened to the white and glossy *ister* 'fat'. The more adventurous and daring toponymist would note that a hydronymic stem *ístr-* is found in river-names in Europe, for example in the old name of the Danube, *Istros* (Krahe 1964:71), and try to connect our Norwegian name with those. In this case I am more cautious, and prefer a local explanation.

Finally, we must comment on the name of the large bay of *Viksfjorden.* This name is secondary, probably formed from the settlement with the name of *Vik* into which the fjord led. Scholars have discussed the older name of this bay. One interpretation is that the old name of the bay was simply **Vík* 'bay' (Holm 1991:50); another, which has found several adherents, is that the first element in the name *Skíringssalr* (see below), a former name of the Tjølling settlement district during the Middle Ages, **Skíringr,* could have been the original name of this bay. This **Skíringr* would contain the ON adjective *skírr* 'clear', giving the name the meaning of 'clear bay' or 'bay with the clear water' (Fries 1980). This option – which I

myself once recommended (Brink 1996b: 272) – can be questioned. The older name of this bay may instead be found in the settlement-name of *Eftang,* in RB known as *Ælftangr,* an interpretation already mentioned by Oluf Rygh (1896:7; cf. NSL:96).[12] This bay thus had a typical name in *-angr,* meaning 'bay', as in *Stavanger, Levanger* etc. The first element is the word *alpt* 'swan', here in the plural, *elptr.*

After this excursus on place-names as evidence of landscape development, we can go back to the settlement-names, but turn now to the names that probably had their origin in the Late Iron Age.

4.2 The Late Iron-age and Viking-age names

In all probability, settlement-names containing *-stad* (< *-staðir)* in Norway are to be placed in the Late Iron Age or the middle of the first millennium AD (Sandnes 1973:24; NSL:294–5.; cf. Brink 1983:8–9). This holds also for place-names in *-bý* with a first element – in stem-composition – containing a word relating to some topographical or vegetational feature rather than a personal name (Hellberg 1967:407–9). For example *Valby* (: *vǫllr* 'bank, pasture, levelled field') and *Sundby* (: *sund* 'sound, strait').

The *-stad* names are *Skreppestad (i Skræippistad-hom* RB), probably containing a man's name *Skræppir,* and the much noticed and discussed *Gjerstad (a Gærirstoðum* in *Flateyjarbók; á Geirstǫðum* in *Ynglingatal; Gerestadt* NRJ), where the identification with this *Gjerstad* and the names found in *Flateyjarbók* and *Ynglingatal* is uncertain. In *Ynglingatal,* King Olaf, called *Geirstaðaálfr* "Geirstad-elf", is said to have been buried at this place. The first element seems to contain a man's name *Geirr* or *Geiri* (Rygh 1901:85). *Vestad,* in the north of Tjølling, is a very interesting name. In RB it is written *i Vestadhum,* and the first element could be interpreted as the word *vé* 'pagan cult site', or, if an adjective, 'holy, sacred'. *Hybbestad* by the river **Istra* is written *i Hyppistadom* in 1398, in 1422 *a Høyppestadom,* and in 1472 *a Hyppestadom.* The qualifier in this name may be a deprecatory nickname of a man, **Hyppir,* containing the word *hupp* 'lump' (cf. the name of a female slave in *Rígsþula: Tǫtrughypja).* *Klåstad (i Klastadom* 1372; *Klastadæ* 1426) has not been interpreted and the first element is uncertain. *Skjeggestad (i Skæggiastadum* RB) seems to contain a man's name *Skeggi* (Rygh 1901:221), and finally *Fristad (i Fristadum* RB) may be a reduction of an older **Friðreksstaðir* or something similar.

---

11 For a discussion of a Pr.-Scand. hydronymic suffix *-str,* see Andersson 1975.

12 Another possibility, which cannot be ruled out, is that *Eftang* could be an older name for a narrow, small inlet, separating Eftang from Fristad during the Late Iron Age, as has been proposed by Gösta Holm (1991:50).

Together with the -stad names, and Valby and Sundby, there are a couple of other settlement-names that might be assigned to the Late Iron Age, such as Stålåker, with no reliable older written form, Bergan (i Berghum RB), an older Bergar, and others. Valby (af Valbø RB) is a -bý/-bø name containing the word vall/voll 'flat grassland'. The name is perhaps to be seen in conjunction with the place-name Vollen found at Tjølling church to the east. This name Vollen might be old, as old as the name Þjóðalyng, and the word is often found in place-names for assembly sites, as, for instance, Vall in central locations in the old parishes in the province of Gästrikland in Sweden and in names such as Tingvalla, Þingvellir (Brink 1990:355–7, 2003, 2004). Tom Schmidt (2000a:448) has suggested that Valby is a detachment from the old Skíringssalr (→Huseby), which also seems to be the background to Østby 'the (detached) farm to the east', east of Huseby.

Medieval names, or more correctly, place-names that were established during a colonisation phase of the early Christian Middle Ages that may already have begun in the Viking Period, are settlement-names in -tveit, -rud, -rød and -bøl. Åsmundrød is an older Ásmundarruð (or -rauð), containing the man's name Ásmundr; Kolsrød (Koolsrud 1398), a man's name Kolr; Ommundrød (Amunderød 1320), which Rygh (1897–1936:VI:296) interprets as Ǫgmundarruð, hence a man's name Ǫgmundr; Svenerød, probably an older *Sveinaruð to a man's name Sveini, or a Svína-ruð, to svín n. 'pig'; Mosserød, probably an older Mosaruð to mosi m. 'bog'. A couple of names indicate deserted settlements, perhaps deserted during the late medieval agrarian crisis, such as Ødegården, Auby (Audeby 1458) and Tufte (< Tuptir), denoting the foundations of a deserted house or farm.

Finally we come to the intricate but most interesting place-names in the centre of the Late Iron-age settlement district of Tjølling, the obvious foci of which were Huseby and Tjølling church. The discussion over the years has been focused on the place-name Skíringssalr, a name lost today, but known from medieval sources. The big question has been where to locate Skíringssalr, and also what kind of denotatum the name had. Before we refer the different opinions, let us review the occasions on which the name occurs in medieval texts and documents:

In the famous poem Ynglingatal (st. 30) we read in the stanza dealing with Halfdan Whiteleg (Jónsson 1912b:12; transl. Brink):

ok Skereið
í Skíringssal
of brynjalfs
beinum drúpir

And Skereið
in Skíringssalr
leans [droops] over
the bones of the mailshirt-hero

In Snorri's Ynglinga saga (Jónsson 1922:ch. 44), in his Heimskringla, which has the poem Ynglingatal as its source, we read: *[Hálfdan hvítbeinn] varð gamall maðr; hann varð sóttdauðr á Þótni ok var síðan fluttr út á Vestfold ok heygðr þar, sem hét Skereið í Skíringssalr* ("Halfdan became an old man; he died of illness at Toten and was then carried out to Vestfold and buried in a barrow in a place called Skereid in Skíringssalr").

In chapter 10 in Sögubrot af nokkrum fornko-nungum í Dana ok Svía veldi ("A fragment of the history of some ancient kings in the Dana and Svea realms") we read: *Þá er Sigurðr Hríngr var gamall, var þat á einu hausti [...] at þá komu ímóti honom Gan-dálfs synir, mágar hans, ok báðu, at hann mundi veita þeim lið at ríða á hendr þeim konúngi, er Eysteinn hét, er því ríki réð, er þá hétu Vestmarar, en nú heitir Vestfold. Þá voru höfð blót í Skíríngssal, er til var sótt um alla vikina...* ("One autumn, when Sigurd Ring was old, the sons of Gandalf, his sons-in-law, approached him and asked if he could provide them with a force of men so they could ride to the King, who was called Eystein, and who ruled the kingdom that was called Vestmarr and which is now called Vestfold. At that time there was a major sacrifice [blót] in Skiringssal, which was visited by the whole of Vikinn…").

In Fagrskinna (Ms. A, ch. 4) we can read of Half-dan the Black: *licamr hans var iarðaðr a Steini a Ringariki enn hofuð hans var flutt i Skírns sal a Vestfold oc var þar iarðat* ("his body was buried at Steini in Ringerike, but his head was taken to Skiringssal in Vestfold and was buried there").

In a document from 1419 (DN 1:661) a Thorald Kane pawned to Sir Markvard Buk "alt Gudrina, sæm ligger i Skirix saal", and the same pledge was again in 1444 (DN 1:788): "... er Gudrino hether er ligger i Þiodlings sokn a Vestfollene". In an enumeration of landed estates belonging to St Stephan's and St Georg's Hospital in Tønsberg from 1445 (DN 9:295), we have the heading "Skirisall", under which we have the names: "Monom, Namfnesale, Brækko, Klæpakre, Næsium", some names lost today or difficult to identify, the rest to be located in Tjølling parish. Finally we have to take into account the name-form Sciringes heal found in the famous report of Ohthere's journey from Hålogaland down to Hedeby in the late 9th century.

The lively discussion on the identification of the locus of Skiringssal has been very extensive, and sometimes rather polemic, especially during the 19th century. It was probable from the documents that the name denoted not a single farm but some kind of area or district, but the question was whether the name was to be identified with the parish, which is intimated by the letters of 1419 and 1444; or with a manorial estate, consisting of some farms, as could be hinted at by the register from 1445; or as alluding to a district larger than the Tjølling parish, including Sandeherred etc. (see e.g. Munch 1850; Sørensen 1900; Kjær 1909a, 1909b; Sørensen 1909a, 1909b; Bugge 1909, 1915). Today this question seems rather academic.

What is important – an issue that was not addressed in the previous discussion in the 19th century and around 1900 – is to ask oneself what the term *salr* denoted. We also have new foundations to stand on when discussing the usage of names for parishes and settlement districts *(bygder)* during the Middle Ages (see Brink 1990).

A *salr* was originally not a district or something spatial: it was used for a building, a hall. The word *salr* was the old word for such a hall building, and we find it in some – but not many – very interesting place-names in Scandinavia, such as *(Gamla) Uppsala, Skíringssalr,* a couple of *Oðinssalr, "Tesal",* several *Sala,* and some more (Brink 1996b:255–7). These names were hence originally the names of actual halls, but must early on have been transferred to the settlement that the hall related to. Such an imposing hall, owned by a king or a chieftain, inevitably made an impression and was well known, so that from an early date the area around the hall must have been identified with the hall-name, giving then the area the meaning "the area/district under the influence of *N*-hall". This must be the explanation of why, during the Middle Ages, we find the name *Skíringssalr* as denoting an area or a district. The same is the case with, amongst others, *"Tesal",* which, during the Middle Ages, denoted the west part of Råde parish in Østfold (Rygh 1897–1936:VI:I:337). We can see that *Skíringssalr* was sometimes equal to the parish of *Tjølling,* which is not surprising. The name of the parish was probably originally *Tjølling,* but the *bygd*-name *Skíringssalr* could also be used as a geographical identifier for farms in this parish, and indeed during early Christian Middle Ages the parish could have been identified as either *Tjølling* or *Skíringssalr.* This kind of instability in the early parish-names is well known (Brink 1990:130). The fact that *Skíringssalr* is sometimes used as a synonym for Tjølling parish is not a problem, therefore; it is to be expected, with a parish name *(Tjølling)* and a name *(Skíringssalr)* that had evolved into a settlement district name for a *bygd.* We can therefore conclude this discussion by stating that *Skíringssalr* ought originally to have denoted a hall.

So what about the qualifier within the name? Several practically impossible interpretations have been proposed. The first sober suggestion is given by Rygh (1897–1936:VI:306), who concludes that the first element must be a masculine *skíring* in the genitive, a derivation with an *-ing* suffix on the adjective ON *skírr* 'clear, pure, bright, light'. And Rygh continues to state that since other names in *-salr* have a theophoric denominator, *Oðinn* in *Oðinssalr* and probably *Týr* [sic] in *Tésalr,* it would seem plausible to interpret *Skíringr* as a kind of god's name as well. Gustav Storm (1909) suggested that *Skíringr* was another name for

Freyr, since in *Grímnismál* this god is given the epithet *skírr* and one of his servants is named *Skírnir.* Sophus Bugge (in Rygh 1897–1936:VI:306) partly follows Storm's interpretation, that this *Skíringr* could contain a god's name, but doubts that a god *(Freyr)* could have been given such a name. Instead he suggests that the qualifier contains a compound **Skír-Ing,* where *Ing* is to be identified with the "god" or hero *Ing* (Pr.-Germ. **Ingwaz),* the *heros eponymos* of the early Germanic **ingwianiz,* the *ingaevones/ingvaeones* in Tacitus' *Germania* (Lund 1988:ch. 2), and the *ynglingar, inglingar:* a rather clever interpretation that links *Skíringssalr* and Vestfold to the poem *Ynglingatal* and to *Uppsala* and the *Svear* in Sweden. I doubt, however, if this is a plausible argument. It seems incomprehensible that the hero *Ing* should in this case have been called "the bright or shining Ing". No such appellative is ever recorded to my knowledge.[13] Sigurd Fries (1980) later argued a case that *Skíringr* be seen as an older name for Viksfjorden. This is more acceptable from a toponymic viewpoint; with this interpretation we could abandon the alternative with an unknown god's name **Skíringr.* The suffix *-ing* is used in many fjord- and bay-names, and the name for a bay could easily contain the word *skírr,* denoting clear water etc. However, the bay alternative is – in my view – also to be questioned; the older name for Viksfjorden is probably to be found in the settlement-name *Eftang,* which thus goes back to an ON *Elptangr.*

Andreas Nordberg (2003:268) has recently proposed an interesting interpretation of *Skíringssalr.* He argues that **Skíring-* could be a qualifier for the *salr,* the hall itself, meaning "the bright, shining hall", and gives several parallels of early descriptions of famous banqueting halls with similar epithets. The problem with this interpretation is rather on the linguistic side, since a word **skíring-* or a similar construction – a kind of extension of an adjective with the suffix *-ing* and with the same or a similar meaning – is unknown.

Today, to be on the safe side, it seems most probable that *Skíringssalr* is to be interpreted as the name of a hall, situated in Huseby, whose first element is a **Skíring* of unknown meaning and denotation. It is furthermore most likely that the name *Skíringssalr* for the hall and later on the settlement here was superseded by *Húsabýr,* a change which might have its background in the fact that in the Middle Ages *Skíringssalr* came to be used as a territorial name for the *bygd* or the parish. It is well known, when one name is "elevated" and given a new and wider denotation, for a new name to be used for the original deno-

---

13   However, one can note that the name *Ing* is connected to *Freyr* in the compound *Ingunarfreyr* (AEW:286; see also Hellberg 1986).

tatum. This is the case when, for example, a name for a settlement with a church is used for the parish and the settlement gets the new name *Kyrkbyn* 'the church village'.

There has also been some discussion over how to understand the form of the name *Skíringssalr* found in the famous report of Ohthere's voyage, namely OE *Sciringes heal*. Was this a translation of an Old Norse name, or was it a misunderstanding or misinterpretation by the Old English writer? In my opinion the easiest way to explain OE *Sciringes heal* is to see it as a corrupt form of *Skíringssalr*, where the second element *-salr* has been wrongly identified with OE *healh* m. 'bend (perhaps also bay)' by an Anglo-Saxon notetaker or interpreter, but several other possibilities seem plausible.[14]

To make a complicated case even more complicated we have probably to face another name in *-salr* in this parish, namely the aforementioned "Nafnesale" mentioned in the Tønsberg register from 1445. This name was noticed by Rygh (1897–1936:VI:292), and the following older forms where known by then: *Namfnesale* 1445; *Nummesall* 1664; *Nommesal* 1723. In the latter cases "Nafnesal" was a dependent farm under Brekke. According to Rygh (loc. cit.) this name is to be identified with the farm *Haugen* in Tjølling, and I have no reason to doubt this identification. The word *name* as a qualifier in a place-name seems a very rare bird. One scholar once made the following reflection (Rygh 1897–1936:I:358): "Nafn (Navn) findes ellers ikke som Stedsnavn og synes ikke meget skikket dertil" ("Name is otherwise never found as a place-name and does not seem very well suited as one") – a view onc can entirely concur with. A compound *Namnlösen* is, however, most common in Sweden for different kinds of topographical objects, such as small lakes, boggy land, skerries etc., and the name seems to have been bestowed upon the object by the fact that it had no name, so it was called *Namnlösen* "without name" instead. But apart from this special case, place-names in *Namn-* are extremely rare, to my knowledge. For Norway Rygh (loc. cit.) was only aware of a couple of names, which seem to go back to a rivername **Navn* or **Navná*. In these cases the element *nafn/namn* may be looked upon as a "noa"-designation, a general, "safe" word used instead of an element that was "dangerous" in some way, in the same vein as the wolf was called *Greybone/Greylegs* so as not to make some wolf attentive in the vicinity, or using an unproblematic word, such as e.g. ON *freyr* 'Lord', OHG *hêrro* 'Lord' or English *Lord*, instead of a god's name that is too holy and sacred to utter. One case, *Nantveit* in Manger (Namfnaþuæit BK), is appealingly interpreted as containing a man's name ON *Nafni* (Rygh, loc. cit.). The only other name to be considered in Norway is a lost ON *Myklunafn* (Rygh 1897–1936:I:358, 393) with the following medieval name-forms: *af Myllenamffne* 1320

in transcript 1409; *i Myklunamfne* 1445; *i Myklæ-Namfne* RB. Such a name is – as far as I am aware – totally unique. It seems to mean "the Big Name". Was it a name for a grand site that craved a grand name?

In our case we must rely on the medieval form of the name, which seems to represent an ON *Nafnasalr*, although Rygh (loc. cit.) has some doubts about the authenticity of this form. It does not fit with the later forms. Those may be valid, but if we check the source, the 1445 register, we find good, credible name-forms in the Late Old Norwegian. Thus the form *Namfnesale* should seem accurate and trustworthy. I exclude the possibility of the name containing the man's name ON *Nafni*, because place-names in *-salr* seem never to contain a man's name. To try to explain this rare name one has to speculate. A first possibility is that the first element in the name is the word *nafn* n. in the same usage as assumed in the river-names, as a "noa"-designation, perhaps for a god's name too holy to utter. The other possible explanation is that the first element is the word *nafni*, a derivation of the word *nafn*, with the meaning 'namesake'. In that case *Nafnasalr* should be seen linked with *Skíringssalr*, which seems possible with the occurrence of two *-salr* in the same settlement district. Where both *salir* dedicated to a god **Skíringr*, so that the minor *salr* had to change its name to *Nafnasalr*? I have to rest my case with presenting these suggestions. We end up with the conclusion that the Tjølling district seems to have had two place-names in *-salr*. The only other case I know of where we have two *-salr* in the same settlement district (more or less), is in Gamla Uppsala in Sweden, with *Sala* and *Uppsala*. *Nafnasalr* is something of a mystery (cf. Skre, this vol. Ch.19:439–40).

The next problem relates to *Huseby*. This name has been energetically discussed, and Asgaut Steinnes highlighted it in his book *Husebyar* of 1955. From the Swedish evidence, where the *husabyar* seem to have been royal farms constituting the great bulk of the *bona regalia*, Steinnes formed the hypothesis that the Norwegian *husebyar* were also old royal farms. Sometimes this hypothesis lead Steinnes to quite startling conclusions, as for Huseby in Tjølling, which during the Middle Ages is known to have been in seigneurial possession, owned by the nobility, and one of the biggest farms in the parish. From this evidence, Steinnes concludes: "Det kan ikkje vera stor tvil om at vi her har å gjera med ein gamal kongsgard." ("There can be no doubt that here we have to do with an old royal farm.") This may seem a poorly grounded and risky statement, but could actually agree with some evidence (Skre, this vol. Ch. 11:246–7).

As with the Swedish *husaby* names and those found in Østfold, it now seems clear that these settlements had an older name (Hoel 1986; Brink 1999b, 2000). *Húsabýr* started as a kind of appellative that replaced an older name – similar to *kyrkbyn* > *Kyrkbyn*, *prestgården* > *Prestgården* etc. – in our case here in Tjølling most certainly superseding *Skíringssalr*.

We then come to *Tjølling*, the name of the actual parish. The name is well documented in the Middle Ages *(a Þiodalyngi, Þiodalyngs sokn* 1367; *Þiodalyngs sokn* 1403; *a Þiodalynge* 1422 etc.: see Rygh 1897–1936:VI:287–8) evidencing an ON *Þjóðalyng*. This compound is transparent, containing ON *þjóð* f. 'people' and *lyng* n. 'heath'; the older forms can indicate a genitive singular first element *(þjóðar-)* as well as a genitive plural *(þjóða-)*. Fritzner connected this name with, *inter alia,* the ON *þjóðstefna* 'public, general or common meeting', whereas Gustav Storm preferred here to see *þjóð* with a meaning 'main', as in a compound ON *þjóðá* 'main river', implying that this *thing*-moot was a main, public *thing* (see Rygh 1897–1936:VI:288). It is notable here at Tjølling that *things* were held for the inhabitants of the whole of Brunla Len as late as 1557 (DN I:820). On linguistic grounds it is difficult to decide whether the name should be interpreted as the (assembly) heath for a people *(þjóðar-)* or for several peoples *(þjóða-),* and both meanings of 'people' and 'main' are possible in our case. However, if *Tjølling* is an ancient name, the latter possibility would seem less probable, since a meaning 'main' (as in ON *þjóðá* 'main river') must be secondary. Etymologically *þjóð* had the primary meaning of 'people' in all Germanic languages.

Notable are the three evidently interrelated place-names *Tjølling*, *Vollen* (no early written form) and *Lunde (a Lunde* 1451). *Vollen* indicates a flat grassland, ON *vǫllr*. The word is common in names of *thing* sites, such as *Þingvellir*, *Tingvalla* etc., and the word is also used as simplex *Vall*, *Voll* or in compounds such as *kyrkvall*. All these examples demonstrate that a *voll*, *vall* was preferred for communal meetings (cf. Brink 1990:355–7). In our case the *voll* probably was a heath, the *Þjóðalyng*. The latter name has an interesting counterpart in the *thing* and meeting place for the East Gautar in Östergötland, Sweden. They met at a place called *Lionga thing* (mentioned, for instance, in the Östgöta Law), 'the *thing* on the heath', a predecessor to the modern city of Linköping (Wessén 1921). The name *Lund* is more difficult to pin down semantically. The name denotes a grove, that much seems certain; but was it a cultic grove or some ordinary, profane grove? That we cannot say. The toponymic context of *Lund,* with neighbours *Guri,* **Skíringssalr* and *Tjølling,* makes a cultic interpretation at least an attractive possibility – perhaps even a probability.

It is an intriguing question why the church for this parish was erected at Tjølling. Normally, in a case such as this settlement district, we would have found the church in Huseby, built by the chieftain or king residing there. Instead the church was built on what was probably the communal assembly place. Over much of northern Sweden, this was a common practice. As I showed in my doctoral dissertation, many churches in Norrland must have been built on an assembly place, which may have been some kind of common for the district, and in these cases it seems probable that (more or less) the whole district was engaged in the building of the church (Brink 1990: 173–5). With Tjølling, with the notable occurrence of a noble, perhaps royal, presence at least at Huseby, this seems rather odd. One would assume that the church-builder would be the central figure at Huseby. Maybe this was the case here too, but for some reason the church was placed at the assembly place rather than at Huseby. One cannot, however, disregard the possibility that Tjølling church was built as a communal undertaking by the farmers and noblemen of the whole district (Skre, this vol. Ch. 17:394–6).

Finally we come to *Kaupang*. The name goes back on an appellative, ON *kaupangr* 'market, trading place' etc.[15] The *kaupangr* in this case denoted the harbour and probably the trading site at *Kaupang,* which, according to the archaeological surveys that have been carried out here, were of considerable extent. It seems very plausible that this *kaupangr* was under the control of the person in power, resident at, or in control of Huseby (Hoel 1986:132; Brink 1996b: 273). We do not know how old the word *kaupangr* is in the Nordic languages; the answer depends on how to understand the etymology of the word, and the possibility that the word is a loan from some other language (possibly West Germanic). It is clear that the word was used in the Viking Period, according to our sources, and the place-names in *kaupangr* etc. in Scandinavia seem to be prehistoric in many cases. Therefore the most probable assumption is that *Kaupang* is "organic" in our case, and was not given to the site in a later phase of history.

4.3 Summary

We end up with a most interesting toponymic picture for Tjølling. During the Early Iron Age the area saw agrarian activity and several settlements, according to the archaeological finds and place-names. From the surviving Early Iron-age place-names it would appear that the settlement was grouped around a lake in the central part of Tjølling, a lake with the possible name **Vítrir/Vettrir*, perhaps embodying a perception of the lake as a kind of a sacred lake. During the Iron Age, the landscape of Tjølling was different from that of today. Several large or small bays and inlets existed, and also probably three islands, of which we know the name of one *(Þossøy < Þórsøy),* a probable name for a second *(*Hasla)* but for the third island,

---

14 Another alternative is favoured by Janet Bately (2007; cf. *Orosius*), who argues for an older, lost name for Kaupang.

15 This word ON *kaupangr*, OSw *køpunger*, ODa *køping* is actually rather tricky to understand etymologically. I hope I can come back to the problem on a later occasion. For the moment, see, *inter alia,* AEW:304.

by Eftang, the name has been lost. Settlement expanded during the Late Iron Age, with several new farms, such as *Hyggestad, Klåstad, Fristad, Skjeggestad, Skreppestad, Håkestad* etc., and the focus of the district moved, from the settlement around the lake *Vítrir/Vettrir* to the area south of the lake and towards the sea, to *Huseby–Kaupang–Guri–Østby–Tjølling*. The central settlement here must have been *Skíringssalr,* denoting a feasting hall, a name later replaced by *Huseby.* It is possible to see all of these settlements as a kind of a complex (cf. Brink 1996b:238), with interdependent settlements, or rather, the main resident at *Skiringssal/Huseby having been in control over the harbour and trading-place Kaupang, and perhaps also the assembly site at Tjølling. The case discussed here is, at least for Norway, a unique case in respect of the historical information provided by place-names.

The Kaupang Cemeteries Revisited 5

FRANS-ARNE STYLEGAR

The cemeteries at Kaupang are discussed in this chapter. An overview of the different cemeteries is presented. In contrast to earlier studies, it is shown that there were several cemeteries and grave clusters at Kaupang – two extensive barrow cemeteries at Nordre Kaupang and Lamøya and a flat-grave cemetery at Bikjholberget as the major ones, plus at least five additional, lesser burial areas. There are 204 known grave-finds from a minimum of c. 700 monuments from the different cemeteries. The original number of monuments must have been considerably higher, perhaps as many as 1000.

Source-critical problems concerned in the dating of the graves are discussed. There were 116 graves which contained closely datable artefacts. The first burials seem to have taken place around AD 800. Overall, there is a slight preponderance of burials of the 10th century. The barrow cemetery at Nordre Kaupang stands out for having a clear majority of graves from late in the period under consideration. The general lack of burials with artefact-types dated to after c. 950 probably indicates that the cemeteries at Kaupang stopped being used regularly for burials somewhat before this time. Thus the apparently equal numbers of 9th- and 10th-century graves really conceal a much higher burial frequency in the later period.

When it comes to population size, different estimates are proposed here, based on the total number of graves. It is estimated that a minimum of about 200 people were living at Kaupang on average, but that the number may have been as high as about 500. In the early 10th century, the number may have been as high as about 800. As for the gender-specific burials, the female ones constitute 58% of the gendered graves in the 9th century but only 24% in the 10th. Both these numbers exceed the numbers for Vestfold as a whole, but it is argued that this in part reflects the greater number of professionally excavated graves at Kaupang. Since most of the graves at Kaupang have not been sex-attributed, it is difficult to compare what are in fact gendered graves at Kaupang (and in SE Norway) with sexed graves from southern Scandinavian cemeteries. Furthermore, it is suggested that the apparent decrease in female gendered burials from the 9th to the 10th century might in part be a reflection of changes in women's costume. Looking at the gendered male graves, there is a general increase in the number of weapons that accompany each burial from the 9th to the 10th century. When it comes to imported objects in the graves, a pattern seems to emerge whereby imports from the Continent are predominant in the 9th-century graves, with Insular and Eastern objects falling behind, while Insular, Eastern, and Continental imports are of equal importance in the 10th century.

Settlement finds in the area covered by the Hagejordet cemetery show that this burial ground was established some time during the lifespan of the settlement, but not at the beginning. The same may be true for the southernmost part of the Nordre Kaupang cemetery, where ploughmarks were observed below a cremation layer excavated in 1965. It seems likely that four very large, but undated barrows at Nordre Kaupang are among the earliest in this cemetery, since this cluster of large barrows was obviously built at a time when a large open space was available in the cemetery. Besides, they seem to have acted as a focal point for a number of less substantial barrows around them. At Lamøya, too, the occurrence of ploughmarks below one of the barrows in the SE area of the cemetery indicates that this part of the cemetery post-dates the establishment of the settlement. At Lamøya, it seems that the main cemetery originally consisted of several distinct grave clusters which grew together into one more or less continuous cemetery during the lifetime of the settlement.

Moving on to grave-types, a total of 62 burials in 46 different boats have been excavated at Kaupang. Other interesting grave-types include one possible chamber grave, a burial in a storage chest, two burials in

5. STYLEGAR: THE CEMETERIES REVISITED **65**

toboggans or trough-sleds, and two burials in log coffins. The most spectacular burial structure at Kaupang is a triple boat grave from Bikjholberget, where three adult individuals, two women and a man, were inhumed in a boat nearly 9 m long. An iron staff was associated with the woman in the stern which, together with some other special objects, suggests that she might have been a sorceress.

Finally, the question is posed concerning whether there are any parallels to the cemetery complex at Kaupang elsewhere in Scandinavia. The Kaupang cemeteries cover a wide spectrum of the myriad of rituals that we associate with Viking-age burial in Scandinavia, but the characteristic mixture of practices that produced the boat graves, chamber graves and coffin graves in one cemetery at Kaupang, namely at Bikjholberget, is hard to match. Only at Birka, or to a lesser degree at Hedeby, do we have the same mixture of rites: boat graves, chamber graves, and coffin graves, as well as relatively balanced numbers of cremations and inhumations.

To avoid the confusion resulting from the many different numbering systems that different excavators applied to the Kaupang graves, a new series of numbers has been given in the attached complete catalogue of excavated graves at Kaupang. This catalogue provides references to all earlier numbering systems.

Figure 5.1 *Excavation work at Bikjholberget in 1951. Photo, C. Blindheim.*

Figure 5.2 *Cemeteries in the Kaupang area. Green shaded areas represent the suggested, former extent of the various cemeteries mentioned in the text. Excavated barrows with a known location are white, while non-excavated ones are black-coloured. The numbers refer to grave numbers (Ka.) in the catalogue at the end of this chapter. Map, Anne Engesveen.*

Approaching Kaupang from the north, over land, a traveller would have to pass through a veritable "city of the dead" – the extensive barrow cemetery at Nordre Kaupang. Likewise, anyone arriving by ship would have had to pass the barrows at Søndre Kaupang on the south-western outskirts of the town, the substantial cemeteries on the islet of Lamøya, the lesser clusters of graves at Bjønnes, or even the flat graves in Bikjholberget, marked with low stone settings or perhaps wooden posts and with the stems of the buried boats visible above ground. In the 9th and 10th centuries the Kaupang cemeteries were an integral part of the Viking-age town. Since the 1830s, the burials have played an important part, in a long-term perspective no doubt the most important part, in the quest to tease out some of the secrets of this very first town-like settlement in what is now Norway.

In the present article, the Kaupang cemeteries are presented and discussed. One may ask why, since all of the graves were published by Charlotte Blindheim and Birgitte Heyerdahl-Larsen from 1981 onwards (Fig. 5.1; Blindheim et al. 1981, 1995, 1999). The reasons are twofold. Firstly, there is some deficiency of system and order in previous publications, making it difficult to take full advantage of them. There are a few instances where references to the same set of data contradict one another. In a small number of cases, the information supplied is misleading. Secondly and more importantly, however, I believe that the material still has much to offer. When used carefully, the burials may supply us with important information about the communities that buried their dead in the Kaupang cemeteries. In some respects, the conclusions in this article differ from those reached by earlier authors; however, this is so mostly because of the types of questions asked in this article.

In what follows, an overview of the Kaupang cemeteries is presented. The number of burials in each of them is estimated and the dating of the ceme-

N

Excavated area

Non-excavated barrow

Excavated barrow

Cemetery

Settlement area

Bjønnes

70
7
8
6
35
10
9
10 6
71
34
2
73
45 36
44 15
14
54 26
53 16
23 52 24 25
48 51 13
50 21 69
45 68
43 67 66
42 61 65
59 62 64
60 57
30 58 18
31 32
41 63
29 40 56 57
55 28 39
46 19 27

Nordre
Kaupang

37

127
126   Hagejordet

Bikjholberget
290

ndre
upang   Lamøya
Vikingholmen   203-204 229
205

230
218
217

0   200 m

teries considered. Gender and population size are investigated, as are mortuary customs and horizontal stratigraphy in the cemeteries. In every case, the material is compared not only with material from other early towns and emporia, but also with the whole corpus from Vestfold and, indeed, south-eastern Norway (in the latter cases, where references are lacking, the comparisons are based on my own, as yet unpublished studies). Some particularly interesting graves are described in more detail. *To avoid the confusion resulting from the many different numbering systems that different excavators applied to the Kaupang graves, a new series of numbers has been given in the attached complete catalogue of excavated graves at Kaupang. This catalogue provides references to all earlier numbering systems.*

There are – or rather were – a number of cemeteries in the Kaupang area (Fig. 5.2). The northernmost

of these, aligned upon the road leading to Kaupang from the main "Ra road" further north (i.e. the old transport corridor located on the Late-Glacial Ra moraine and leading through Vestfold from Borre on the Oslofjord in the east to the River Lågen in the west), was the most extensive one (Skre, this vol. Ch. 1:Fig. 1.1). A little further south was another cemetery. The flat graves at Bikjholberget, a hilly outcrop that in the Viking Age would in fact have been a headland stretching out into the town's harbour, constituted the southernmost part of this other cemetery. At Lamøya, then a small island situated in the Viksfjord immediately to the east of the settlement area, there was another extensive cemetery, including both barrows and flat graves. Yet more graves were to be found on another small islet, the aptly named Vikingholmen (a recent place-name). There were several barrows at Søndre Kaupang, as well as a substantial number of flat graves; these burials probably constituted one large cemetery before they were destroyed as a result of agricultural improvements in the 19th and 20th centuries. Smaller cemeteries were located at Bjønnes on the northern side of the northern inlet.

5.1 The cemeteries

The first artefacts from the Kaupang cemeteries are known to have reached a museum in 1842, in this case the museum in Arendal (catalogue nos. 406–407 = Ka. 406–407). The first professional excavations of the Kaupang cemeteries took place in 1867. This campaign was directed by the antiquarian Nicolay Nicolaysen (Nicolaysen 1868; Blindheim 1977). Later campaigns were led by the archaeologists Gabriel Gustafson in 1902 (Petersen 1920:182; Blindheim et al. 1981: 61–3) and Charlotte Blindheim in 1950–1957 (Blindheim 1951, 1960, 1969; Blindheim et al. 1981, 1995, 1999; Skre, this vol. Ch. 2). In addition several finds made during cultivation and contruction work over the years have been brought to the museum in Oslo.

Figure 5.3 *The horseman's grave Ka. 157. Photo, Eirik Irgens Johnsen, KHM.*

Figure 5.4 *Aerial photograph of Søndre Kaupang showing a crop-mark from a ploughed out barrow in the middle of the picture. The barrows excavated by Nicolaysen at Søndre Kaupang were on average considerably smaller than the ones at Nordre Kaupang. As this one is larger than the ones Nicolaysen recorded in 1867, the pictured barrow was probably destroyed before Nicolaysen performed his excavations. Photo, Vestfold County Council.*

Søndre Kaupang (Ka. 150–166)

Nicolaysen noted 20 barrows at Søndre Kaupang during a short visit in 1859 (Nicolaysen 1862–1866:200). Eight barrows, probably belonging to the group of 20, were excavated in 1867 (Nicolaysen 1868). Five of these were round, while three were long barrows.

The largest barrow, Nicolaysen's barrow 6, housing a cremated equestrian grave (Ka. 157; Fig. 5.3; see Ch. 5.7:93–5), perhaps in a boat, was 9.5 m across and 1.25 m high. The smaller barrows (Nicolaysen's barrows 7–9) were about 5 m in diameter and just over 50 cm high. In Blindheim's (re-)publication of the cemetery, she misunderstood Nicolaysen's measurements, believing that his *feet* (31.3 cm) were actually *ells* (62.8 cm), and thus mistakenly going on to claim that the Søndre Kaupang barrows were substantially bigger than those at Nordre Kaupang (Blindheim et al. 1981:75; cf. Fig. 5.4).

Another group of barrows was at one time located to the south of Nicolaysen's barrows, and there is also information about a substantial flat-grave cemetery in the area (Blindheim et al. 1981:60). Now, just eight barrows remain at Søndre Kaupang (Kristensen 2005:23–4).

Other graves have been discovered by chance over the years and finds from them have reached the museum in Oslo, so that in total 17 grave-finds are known from Søndre Kaupang. All of these graves are cremation burials. This probably reflects the find-circumstances, i.e. the graves' being discovered during the removal of barrows rather than during the excavation of a complete section of the cemetery. There is little information to reveal the presence of dug-down inhumation burials in this area (see below). Likewise, there is no way to determine whether the graves at Søndre Kaupang originally constituted one extensive cemetery or several smaller grave clusters.

Nordre Kaupang (Ka. 1–73)

This is the most extensive of the Kaupang cemeteries. Nicolaysen noted "hundreds of barrows" here in 1859 (Nicolaysen 1862–1866:200, my translation). According to him, the cemeteries at Kaupang and Lamøya "count without doubt among the largest in the whole of our country" (Nicolaysen 1861:35, my translation). Earlier sources reveal that there were also other kinds of monuments in this cemetery, for instance a small ship-setting (Skre, this vol. Ch. 16:371, Fig.16.5). In 1867, Nicolaysen counted 111 barrows at Nordre Kaupang – 25 long barrows, the rest of them round. That same year he excavated 71 barrows, 63 of which contained layers or concentrations of charcoal. Cremated bone was observed in only 39 of the 63, and in 36 of those, artefacts were also recovered. Eight barrows yielded no artefacts, cremation remains or charcoal.

The largest barrows, Nicolaysen's Barrows 53 and 66 (the numbers refer to Christie's plan, made in 1866 and published as an appendix to Nicolaysen 1868; Skre, this vol. Ch. 16:Fig. 16.1), were c. 25 m in diameter; the former was 2.7, the latter 2.2 m high. Nos. 50 and 51 were c. 23 m in diameter. Ten barrows were only 4–4.5 m across, while the smallest one, number 61, was only about 3 m across and 30 cm high.

In 1965 another grave was excavated at Nordre Kaupang (Ka. 37). Together with some stray finds, this brings the total number of recorded grave-finds from the main cemetery at Nordre Kaupang to 74.

One problem, that of representativity, needs to be considered regarding Nicolaysen's excavation of 1867. Thirty-nine of the barrows at Nordre Kaupang contained cremation burials. Almost as many (32) revealed no evidence of a burial at all. Eight of the latter were completely empty, while 24 contained only layers or patches of charcoal. Barrows containing layers of charcoal but which were otherwise empty have been documented elsewhere in Vestfold (cf. Gansum 2004:242–5; Gansum and Østigård 1999). It has re-

cently been argued that these "empty" barrows were never meant to be burial mounds; rather, the monumentality of the barrows and the transformative character of charcoal in ritual contexts might have led to the building of barrows during periods of social stress (Gansum 2004:242–5).

However, layers of charcoal sometimes occur in barrows containing inhumation graves (Opedal 1998: 43–4). One has to ask therefore whether some of Nicolaysen's "empty" barrows had really been erected over sub-surface inhumation graves. In fact, the majority of excavated inhumation graves from the Viking Age in Vestfold were in grave-pits beneath barrows (Sjøvold 1944:66). Richly furnished graves of this type, a number of which have yielded artefacts with clear affinities to the Kaupang finds, have been excavated both in Hedrum and at Gulli, a fact that calls for some caution (Stylegar 2005a; Gjerpe 2005c). In the latter case, a cemetery consisting of some 25 barrows was discovered by aerial photography in 1993. Nicolaysen noted a barrow cemetery at Gulli but did not excavate it (Nicolaysen 1862–1866:181). No artefacts reached any museum following the destruction of the barrows. Twenty-six circular quarry ditches – all that remained of the barrows – were excavated on the site in 2003–2004. In 15 of these, inhumation grave-pits from the 9th and 10th centuries were found (Gjerpe 2005c).

It is noteworthy that Barrows 50, 51, 53 and 56, by far the largest in the Nordre Kaupang cemetery and also larger than the barrows at Søndre Kaupang and Lamøya, were amongst the "empty" barrows. Were these four giants in the southern part of the cemetery built to cover sub-surface inhumation burials, or were they erected by people intending to put down roots in this area by such ritual means? These questions are difficult to answer without new excavations in the area where Nicolaysen's barrows were located (but see Skre, this vol. Ch. 16:380–1, 19:434–5).

A total of 140 barrows can be shown to have existed at Nordre Kaupang (Skre, this vol. Ch. 16:Tab. 16.1). The extent of the main cemetery is considered elsewhere in this volume (ibid.). Several barrows were destroyed prior to 1866. Of the 111 barrows documented by Nicolaysen in 1867, none remains today.

Hagejordet (Ka. 125–134)

This cemetery was treated as the southernmost part of the Nordre Kaupang cemetery by Blindheim (e.g. Blindheim et al. 1981:47–56). On Christie's 1866 map, four barrows (nos. 1–4) are located some 200 ells (125 m) to the south of the main cemetery. In the vicinity of barrows 1–4, and also in the area between these barrows and the cemetery at Nordre Kaupang to the north but separated from the latter by c. 85 m, a number of other finds have been made, some of them pos-

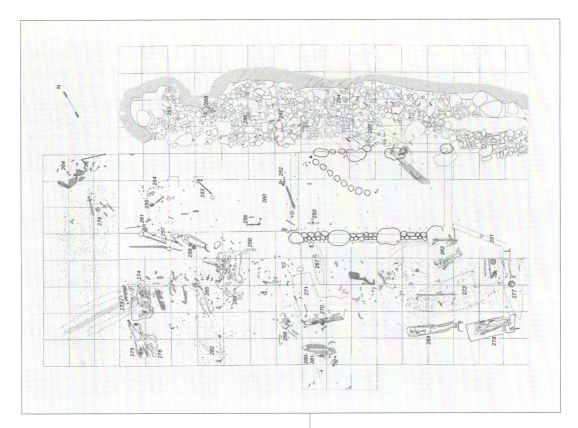

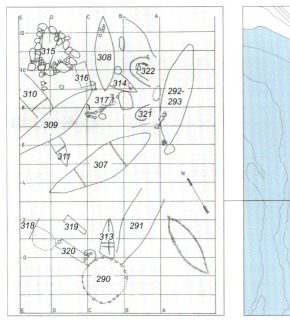

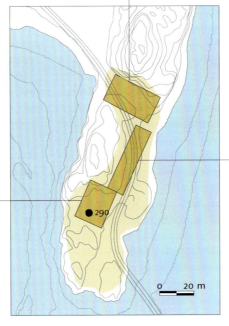

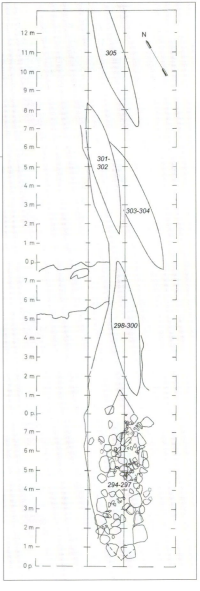

Figure 5.5 *Excavations at Bikjholberget in 1955, with the boat grave Ka. 308 clearly visible in the centre of the picture. Photo, Bertil Almgren, KHM.*

Figure 5.6 *Excavated structures at Bikjholberget (adapted from Blindheim et al. 1995). Illustration compiled by Anne Engesveen and Julie K. Øhre Askjem.*

sibly stemming from flat graves, and at least a couple of them possibly marked by a horizontal stone slab. Viking-age flat graves covered by slabs are known from elsewhere in southern Vestfold (Sjøvold 1944: 55–6). Furthermore, one grave-find from this area is said to derive from a barrow (Ka. 125). One of the sketches of Kaupang made by the artist Johannes Flintoe in the 1830s (printed in Blindheim et al. 1999: 154; Skre, this vol. Ch. 16:Fig. 16.3), shows a vertical stone in this same area, although the legend explicitly states that the cemetery, by which the artist must have meant the barrows, begins further to the north.

It is therefore most likely that the barrows and possible flat graves at Hagejordet constitute a cemetery separate from the one at Nordre Kaupang (see also Skre, this vol. Ch. 16:368–9).

Between 1999 and 2003 a number of cultural resource management trenches were excavated in this area (Pilø, this vol. Chs. 7:154 and 8:169–72, Fig 8.14). Viking-age settlement deposits were recovered from several trenches, indicating that both Hagejordet and the area between Hagejordet and the Nordre Kaupang cemetery had been used for settlement activities before a cemetery was established at Hagejordet.

Nicolaysen's barrows 1 and 2, which he did not excavate, were excavated by Blindheim in 1974 (Ka. 126 and 127). Another grave was excavated in 1958 (Ka. 130).

Bikjholberget (Ka. 250–323)
Adjoining the Hagejordet cemetery is the hilly outcrop of Bikjholberget to the south. Seventy-four graves were excavated by Blindheim in 1950–57 at two separate sites at Bikjholberget (Fig. 5.5). These two sites at Bikjholberget are part of one continuous cemetery (Fig. 5.6).

The graves at the southern site of Bikjholberget seem to have been undisturbed at the time of excavation, unlike the graves at the northern site. Apart from two low barrows (Ka. 290 and 292) and one

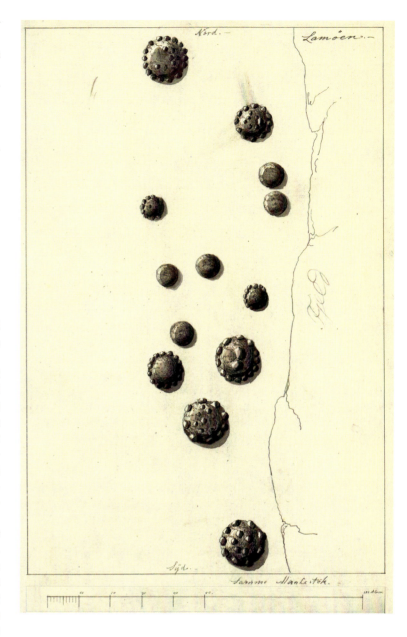

Figure 5.7 *The coffin graves Ka. 315 and 316 during excavation. In the latter grave, a chest of Oseberg type was used as a coffin. Photo, Bertil Almgren, KHM.*

Figure 5.8 *Zeuthen's 1845 plan of the northern part of the Lamøya cemetery. Original in the National Museum* (Nationalmuseet), *Copenhagen.*

four-sided stone setting (Ka. 294), all 34 individual graves from the southern site of Bikjholberget were flat graves covered by stone packings.

One of the two low barrows contained a stone cist (Ka. 290). In the flat graves, 12 boats were discovered with a total of 20 burials (Ka. 291 and 292, 294–296 and 298–312). In one of the boat graves (Ka. 307), the deceased had been placed in a wooden coffin or chamber (see below). Furthermore, in the lower-lying part of the site there were five burials in wooden coffins (Ka. 315 and 318–322), one in a chest of Oseberg type (Ka. 316), and two in toboggans or trough-sleds (Ka. 313 and 314) (Fig. 5.7).

The graves at Nordre Bikjholberget were partly destroyed by modern disturbances before the excavations began. In total 40 individual graves are known from this part of the Bikjholberget cemetery, but due to the difficult excavating conditions caused by prior disturbances and a complex stratigraphy, not all the artefacts and skeletal remains could be ascribed to specific burials. Consequently, the excavators noted that there were very probably several burials that went unobserved at Nordre Bikjholberget (Blindheim et al. 1995:55).

There are no barrows in Nordre Bikjholberget, and all known burials are flat graves. As in southern Bikjholberget, they were covered by stone packings. Different grave-types were used for the flat graves. Twenty-one(?) boats contained a total of 28 burials (Ka. 250–259, 262–268, 272 and 273, 277, 279, 282–287 and 289). There was one burial in a wooden coffin (Ka. 271) and two in log coffins (Ka. 269 and 278). One grave was a chamber grave (Ka. 270). Three burials did not reveal any grave structure (Ka. 274–276), while five of the flat graves did not reveal any grave structure (Ka. 260 and 261, 280 and 281 and 288).

The cemetery at Bikjholberget has certainly not been fully excavated. The southern part extends further in all directions (Blindheim et al. 1995:16). Pos-

sible boat graves have been discovered at a couple of spots on the northern slope, close by the cemetery at Hagejordet (Blindheim et al. 1981:56, 1995:60; Kristensen 2005:39–40).

It is possible to estimate the number of graves remaining at Bikjholberget. In total, an area covering 540 sq m was excavated by Blindheim in 1950–1957; thus there were 140 graves per 1,000 sq m. The remaining area covers c. 1,200 sq m, approximately half of which would have been suitable for burial. It can thus be estimated that around 85 graves still await excavation at Bikjholberget.

All the known burials at Bikjholberget are inhumations, which gives us a representative view of the burial custom there, as Blindheim conducted a total excavation of the graves which she encountered, not a partial trenching as Nicolaysen did at Nordre Kaupang.

Figure 5.9 *Broch's 1811 map, the so called Larvik County map* (Grevskapskartet), *showing Søndre Kaupang with fences and recent "intakes", indicating that the transformation of the traditional cultural landscape was fully under way at that time. National Map Office* (Statens Kartverk), *Hønefoss* (Grevskapskart 9B9 blad 7).

Lamøya (Ka. 200–230)

The Lamøya of today is a peninsula, but it was surrounded by the sea in the Viking Age. There are now 94 barrows and three stone settings at Lamøya (Gansum 1995; Kristensen 2005). Three barrows are long, the remaining 91 circular. Of the stone settings, two are round, while the third is possibly boat-shaped.

A plan made by C. O. Zeuthen in 1845 (see Skre, this vol. Ch. 16:370–1, Fig. 16.5; Skre 2005) shows 13 barrows at Lamøya. These can be correlated with the two southernmost of the four still existing barrows that are located to the north of the present farm buildings (Fig. 5.8). Other sources testify that there were once also barrows in the area between Zeuthen's barrows and the main cluster of barrows to the south of the Lamøya farm, as well as in the area covered by today's farm buildings (sketch by Gustafson, in Blindheim et al. 1981:62). If, for this area, we assume a density of barrows comparable to that in the main cluster further south, the number of barrows destroyed can be estimated at around 50. In the vicinity of Kongehaugen (the largest of the remaining barrows at Kaupang, with a diameteter of c. 15 m, and smaller only than Nicolaysen's Barrows 50, 51, 53 and 56), there used to be "many barrows", according to one informant (Blindheim et al. 1981:65). These must be the "more than 20 barrows" noted by Nicolaysen "in the woods to the west of the farm houses" (Nicolaysen 1868:91; cf. Blindheim et al. 1981:64). On Broch's 1811 map, the so called Larvik County map *(Grevskapskartet)*, only Kongehaugen is shown in this area, but it seems to be located in the NW corner of a cultivated area. Before cultivation therefore, there might have been more monuments to the south and east of Kongehaugen. There is also evidence of destroyed barrows in the vicinity of the possible flat grave Ka. 206 (Blindheim et al. 1981:64). Thus, in total c. 200 barrows are likely for Lamøya.

Gabriel Gustafson excavated three or four barrows at Lamøya in 1902 (Ka. 203–205, 230). Simultaneously with the excavations at Bikjholberget, two barrows (Ka. 217 and 218) and one flat grave (Ka. 219) were excavated at Lamøya in 1956. Ka. 217 was completely empty (Blindheim et al. 1995:51–2).

Apart from the barrows, there is a cluster of flat graves at Guristranda, and the majority of the 23 recorded finds from Lamøya (Ka.200–222) are in fact either from flat graves or, more likely, are from destroyed barrows. The latter case does not, however, seem likely for the graves Ka. 201–202 and 207–210, for reasons that have to do with local topography, and is certainly not so for the professionally excavated Ka. 219.

Both cremations and inhumations are known from Lamøya. One of the barrows excavated by Gustafson contained two boats (Ka. 203–204) – in one of them, Ka. 204, a male individual had been interred with a collection of cremated animal bones *(bos, ovis?* and *sus* – Blindheim et al. 1981:85).

The graves at Lamøya lie in a number of more or less distinct clusters. It is difficult to decide to what degree this reflects the original situation. But at least the cluster that includes Kongehaugen must have been distinct in the Viking Age too (although see Kristensen 2005:57). This cluster is separated by about 100 m from the nearest barrow to the south-west. It is a matter of definition whether we count the Kongehaugen complex as a grave cluster or as a separate cemetery.

Bjønnes

Nicolaysen noted five barrows at Bjønnes, just opposite the main cemetery at Nordre Kaupang. He did not excavate any of these barrows, which are no longer preserved, and we do not have any reported grave-finds from Bjønnes. Further south there is a circular stone setting. It is most likely the stone setting that Nicolaysen mentioned in 1893 (1894a:177).

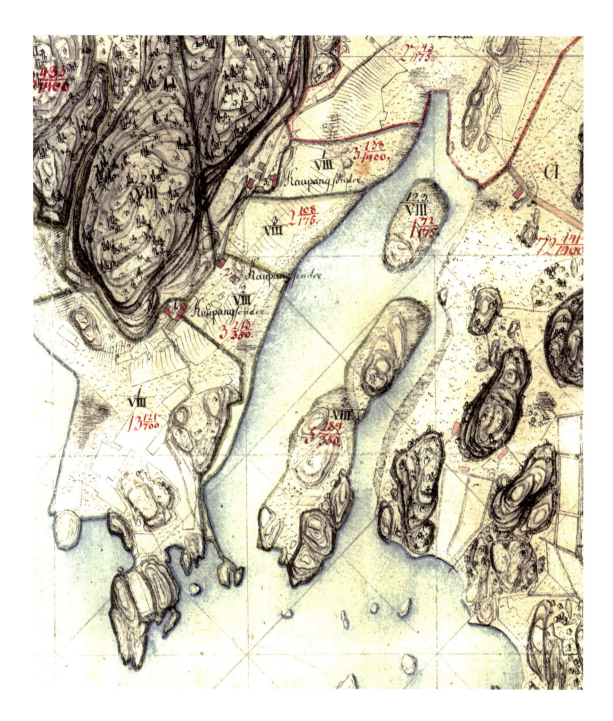

Close by is a cemetery with four or five small, boat-shaped stone settings. There are 13 known barrows left at Bjønnes, including a cluster of five to the north of the present farm buildings.

As they are clearly open to the northern inlet to the harbour, these graves must belong to the Kaupang complex.

Vikingholmen

At this site – in the Viking Age a small islet just off the Kaupang settlement – there is one comparatively large barrow and seven smaller ones, all showing clear signs of having been excavated. There are, however, no known finds from any of these barrows.

5.2 Number of burials

A total number of 204 graves and stray finds that probably derive from graves are known from the Kaupang cemeteries. If one counts the empty graves, and the graves containing nothing but layers or patches of charcoal, the number is 237. But how many burials were there originally? Based on the number of graves and unexcavated burial mounds, the following minimum figures for each cemetery can be inferred:

- At *Søndre Kaupang*, about 36 barrows and a couple of additional finds that cannot be attributed to any of these graves. Total: 38. (Ka. 150–167 = 18 recovered finds.)

0   200 m

- At *Nordre Kaupang,* 111 barrows, including the "empty" ones excavated by Nicolaysen. Skre's archival studies have proved the existence of another 29 barrows, bringing the number to 140. Skre estimates that there were a total of 263 barrows here. Total: c. 263. (Ka. 1–73)
- At *Hagejordet,* five barrows and five finds that may derive from graves. Total: 11. (Ka. 125–134)
- At *Bikjholberget,* two barrows and 72 flat graves. A further 85 as yet unexcavated graves inferred. Total: c. 160. (Ka. 250–323)
- At *Lamøya,* 108 barrows and at least 29 finds that derive either from flat graves or destroyed barrows (some of the latter finds may derive from any of the 13 barrows recorded by Zeuthen in 1845; these barrows are nonetheless included in the total number of barrows known at Lamøya). Also the more than 20 barrows noted by Nicolaysen, and around 50 destroyed barrows. Total: c. 200. (Ka. 200–228)
- At *Bjønnes,* 18 barrows, one circular stone setting and four or five boat-shaped stone settings. Total: 23. No finds.
- At *Vikingholmen,* eight barrows. No finds.

This yields a minimum of 407 documented graves (buried individuals), and 700 estimated ones. However, there is no doubt that this number is still an underestimate. Many flat graves are probably still undetected, and a large number of graves have been removed over the centuries without any finds from them having been brought to any museum. One also has to add the graves in the flat-grave cemetery at Søndre Kaupang, the extent of which we simply do not know (above). In respect of the barrow cemeteries at Søndre Kaupang, Hagejordet and Bjønnes, there is no available information on the original number of monuments. Even with the well-studied cemetery at Nordre Kaupang there is little information as to how many individuals may have been buried in each barrow. Based on the available sources, 700 graves is simply as close as one can get.

Blindheim suggested that there could have been as many as 1,000 graves in the area (Blindheim et al. 1981:65, cf. 1999:153–4). This calculation incorporates a large number of barrows believed to have been destroyed before 1867. The difference between Nicolaysen's reference to "hundreds of barrows" in 1859 (or indeed his suggestion referred to above, that the Kaupang cemeteries were amongst the very largest in Norway), and his counting of only 115 barrows eight years later, would seem to imply that a considerable number of graves were destroyed in the period 1859–1867. (Munthe's statement in 1838, that there were "an almost innumerable number of barrows" at Kaupang, seems to imply this too; see Munthe in Sturluson [1838–1839]:I:35 and Skre, this vol. Chs. 2:29–31, 16:363–5.) The earliest information we have about barrows being destroyed at Kaupang dates to 1842, when Ka. 406–407 reached the museum in Arendal. P. A. Munch visited Kaupang in 1850, and could later reveal – probably he had been given this information by the farmers – that swords, glass beads and boat remains had been found in the barrows (Skre, this vol. Ch. 2:32).

According to Skre's calculations, the number of barrows at Nordre Kaupang declined from 140 to 111 in the decades before 1866.

One reason for this massive destruction was that the tenants at Kaupang became freeholders in this period and began cultivating their new holdings. At Søndre Kaupang they bought their farms in 1858, and seem to have begun cultivating immediately; consequently, the first known grave-finds from a barrow in this area (Ka. 150–151) reached the museum in Christiania (Oslo) the following year. Destruction had begun even earlier at Nordre Kaupang, where the tenants had become freeholders during the 17th century.

However, there is reason to believe that the destruction of the cemeteries at Søndre Kaupang may have begun many years before 1858. Two related circumstances indicate this. Firstly, agricultural improvement started in Tjølling by the late 18th century. Between 1750 and 1814 the arable land used for grain alone in this area increased by 125 acres (Krohn-Holm 1974:255–7). Secondly and most significantly, although it has been estimated by one source that nobody in Tjølling planted more than half a barrel of potatoes per season around 1800, in 1812 an average family harvested 20 barrels of potatoes. In these years, too, the draining of land by means of ditches and the building of stone walls began. The initiative for many of these changes came from the Count of Laurvigen. Søndre Kaupang was part of the comital estate, and the Count's tenants were bound by their leasing contracts to build stone walls, amongst other things. This is, for example, shown very clearly at Søndre Kaupang in particular where Broch's cadastral map of 1811 shows a number of walls, garden plots, and what seems to be a current process of transforming grassland into arable land. Thus we are reminded that this excellent and detailed map does not provide us with a glimpse of a cultural landscape untouched by modern improvements (Fig. 5.9). It is highly likely that the building of walls, the increase in arable land and the establishment of potato fields in the outlands, led to the destruction of burial barrows long before 1858.

However, it is difficult (to say the least) to estimate just how many graves might have been destroyed before survey work began at Kaupang. The actual number of graves within the Kaupang complex could have been about a thousand, as suggested by Blindheim. By comparison, Birka has about 2,300–3,400 graves (Gräslund 1980:4, 82; Holmquist Olausson 1993), while Hedeby has about 7,000–12,000 (Jankuhn 1986:108; Eisenschmidt 1994:99).

5.3 The dated burials

Of the 204 burials from Kaupang, 116 contain closely datable artefacts, as opposed to burials that can only generally be dated to either the Late Iron Age (c. AD 550–1050) or even the Iron Age in general (c. 500 BC–AD 1050) (Fig. 5.10). Regrettably, no charcoal from the barrows excavated by Nicolaysen is preserved, ruling out any radiocarbon dating.

Dating the graves is not without inherent problems. Petersen (1919) established a typology for swords and other types of weaponry which, with several minor amendments (Paulsen 1956; Müller-Wille 1972; Solberg 1984; Geibig 1991; Moberg 1992), is still essentially unchanged. He likewise established a chronology for artefacts commonly found in men's graves. On the basis of both weapon-finds and women's jewellery, Petersen (1919, 1928) divided the Viking Age into three sequential phases: the Early Viking Age (9th century), the Middle Viking Age

(10th century), and the Late Viking Age (11th century).

In the case of swords, this tripartite scheme was followed by Müller-Wille (1972). For other artefactgroups, however, more refined divisions have been suggested (beads: Callmer 1977; pennanular brooches: Carlsson 1988). With reference to the oval (tortoise) brooches from Birka, Jansson (1985) argued that Petersen's chronology was in need of revision. Jansson (1985:181) suggested that the location of the transition between the Early and the Middle Viking Age (in his terminology the Early and Late Birka Period) to c. AD 900 is often based on little more than Petersen's denominations "9th century" and "10th century" as conventional labels for what are basically periods in a relative chronology. Jansson's work indicated that the transition from Early to Late "Birka Period" actually fell sometime during the second half of the 9th century (cf. Maixner 2004). More recently, the whole edifice of Viking Age chronology has been refined through the work of Skibsted Klæsøe (1999). Based on jewellery and art styles, this revised chronology brings a number of recent dendrochronological datings (Christensen and Krog 1987; Andersen 1991; Bonde 1994; Bonde and Christensen 1993b; Schou Jørgensen 1998; see also Müller-Wille 2001) into the picture. Skibsted Klæsøe (1999) divides the Viking Age into three major periods – per. 1 (AD 750/775–825/830); per. 2 (AD 825/830–960); and per. 3 (AD 960–1050/1066), with per. 2 further subdivided into three shorter phases (2a1: 825/830–860; 2a2: 860–900/910; and 2b: 900/910–960).

The revisions being made by Jansson and Skibsted Klæsøe have implicit consequences for the weapon chrononology too. Although Petersen's typological system probably covers most of the material in a satisfactory way, his chronology no longer holds. The weapon chronology has to be correlated with the chronology based on art styles and jewellery (for the earliest part of the period, this problem is discussed by Rundkvist 2003:68–9). Until this work has been done, there are effectively two chronologies available – one for men's graves and one for women's graves. The former is to a large extent a relative chronology. Nevertheless, stylistic evidence and coin datings from Danish burials indicate that the tentative relative weapon chronology is not completely erroneous. In a relative sense, however, the "10th century" may begin slightly earlier than 900 as an absolute date.

This procedural problem must be kept in mind when comparisons are made between early and late graves at Kaupang (below). The division into "early" and "late" graves is real, but it is not so certain that all the "early" graves belong to the 9th century and all the "late" graves to the 10th. The same applies when comparing the chronological distribution of female graves and male graves.

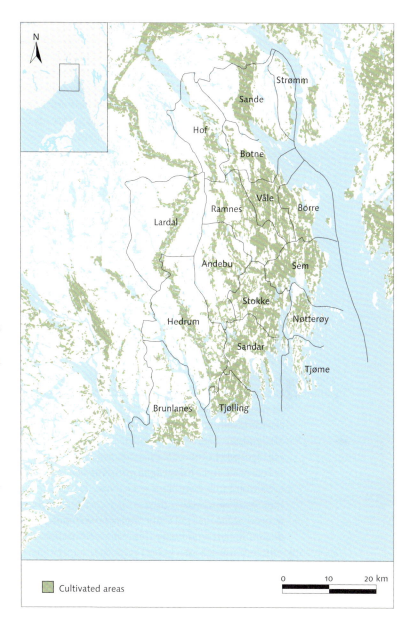

Figure 5.11 *Tjølling and neighbouring districts in southern Vestfold, with the pre-1960s boundaries. Map, Anne Engesveen.*

N

Strømm

Sande

Hof

Botne

Våle

Ramnes

Lardal

Borre

Andebu

Sem

Stokke

Hedrum

Nøtterøy

Sandar

Brunlanes

Tjølling

Tjøme

☐ Cultivated areas

0   10   20 km

The problematic 8th century

The Kaupang cemeteries include a couple of graves that have been interpreted as dating to the 8th century (Gudesen 1980:217). The most important finds in question are:

- *Ka. 150–151:* A badly preserved grave-find from a small cairn at Søndre Kaupang, recovered in 1859 or earlier (C2270–80). The find is obviously mixed, and it has tentatively been assigned two different graves by the present author – Ka. 150–151 (cf. Blindheim et al. 1981:152–4). The latter belongs to the 10th century, while Ka. 150 exhibits some weapon-types supposed by Gudesen and Blindheim (Gudesen 1980:42 and 53; Blindheim et al. 1981:153) to pre-date the Viking Age.
- *Ka. 403:* A single-edged sword without hilt and guard, found beneath a flat stone at some distance above the farm Nordre Kaupang. This find was not archaeologically investigated. Nicolaysen brought it to the museum in Christiania in 1867.

The pre-800 date for the find complex Ka. 150–151 rests upon a single-edged sword, a shield-boss and an artefact that has been interpreted as a weapon knife or sax (Blindheim et al. 1981:153).

The sword has a type H hilt. Jan Petersen's type H hilt is the most common of his types, represented by no less than 213 specimens at the time of publication in 1919; of these, 27% occurred on single-edged swords (Petersen 1919:74). This hilt-type is in need of chronological re-assessment. In northern Germany, the type is known from the late 8th century (Stein 1967). However, it is probably significant that, in her study of the Scandinavian weapon graves, Anne Nørgård Jørgensen was unable to find type H hilts in her Nordic Phase VI (c. 800–830/840), while it does occur in her Phase VII (c. 830/840–c. 900) (Nørgård Jørgensen 1999:190). Thus the sword from Ka. 150–151 probably belongs to the mid- or late 9th century.

The shield-boss is of the Galgenberg type, Nørgård Jørgensen's type SBD (cf. Nørgård Jørgensen 1999:86). While these bosses mostly occur in graves from the late 7th and 8th centuries on the Continent, they are also known from pictorial sources from the 9th century, for instance in the picture of Louis the Pious in the poem *Laus Sanctae Crucis* from Fulda (dated to 826) where the emperor holds a shield with a Galgenberg-type boss. Further examples are found in the Stuttgarter Bilderpsalter, made in Saint-Germain-des-Prés near Paris in the same period (Nørgård Jørgensen 1999:87). The date-range of this type must therefore be extended into the early decades of the 9th century.

The single-edged sax or weapon knife is badly preserved. What is left is a 12-cm long piece with the upper part of the blade and the lower part of the grip. Its greatest width is c. 3.5 cm. Blindheim (et al. 1981:153) compared this artefact to an undated single find of a sax from Gran, Vang, Hedmark (C33979).

The Gran knife is reminiscent of a single-edged sword from Torsdal, Bamble, Telemark (C4516; Gjessing 1934:pl. XI b), although it is much smaller and has, like the specimen from Kaupang, a "broken" or angled back blade-shape (the Torsdal sword, of type SAX3, dates from c. 680 right through the 8th century: cf. Nørgård Jørgensen 1999:135, fig. 116). Helgen (1975:4) dates the Gran knife to the Late Migration/Early Merovingian Periods, i.e. the late 6th and early 7th centuries, and Blindheim (et al. 1981:153) argues for a similar date for the knife from Kaupang. The basis for Helgen's suggested dating is the general observation that saxes shorter than c. 50 cm are older than the longer, single-edged swords (Helgen 1975:4).

The angled back blade-shape is the really distinctive feature of these two knives, however. In the Norwegian material, there is only one other example of a sax with a similar blade-shape. This somewhat longer specimen (blade length: 38 cm) of type R496 from Myklebost, Fjaler, Sogn og Fjordane (B7678) is from a grave-find dated by Nørgård Jørgensen (1999:227) to her Nordic Phase VII, c. 830/840–c. 900. Nørgård Jørgensen (1999:62–3) includes the Myklebost sword in her SAX5 group. This particular weapon is presumably an Anglo-Saxon import, however, which is probably the reason that it seems to stand apart from Nørgård Jørgensen's other SAX5 specimens (Gjessing 1934:100; cf. Grieg 1923:34, who argues for Anglo-Saxon influences behind the whole group of R496 swords).

The blade-shape indicates that an Anglo-Saxon origin cannot be ruled out for the Kaupang knife, either. The principal distinctive characteristic of the Anglo-Saxon weapon knife or *sax* is its angled-back blade. The average blade-length of these weapons is around 15–25 cm, although single specimens can range from 7.5 to 75 cm. The *sax* is divided into two general size-ranges, and the Kaupang specimen would seem to sit well with the smaller size range, 7.5–35 cm (Underwood 1999:68–70). In England, the *sax* was still in use in the late 10th century (Gjessing 1934:85). The badly preserved Kaupang knife is difficult to date precisely. But it cannot be ruled out that the object reached Kaupang as part of the wave of Western imports of the 9th or early 10th century (cf. Blindheim et al. 1999:55).

As for the single-edged sword in Ka. 403, it is of type SAX8, a type peculiar to Norway. Nørgård Jørgensen's (1999:190) dating of SAX8-swords is to the Early Viking Age, i.e. her Nordic Phase VII, c. 830/840–c. 900.

Blindheim's dating of the other graves to the period preceding c. AD 800 is even less convincing. They consist either of single artefacts (or the dating rests on single artefacts), or they derive from disturbed graves (Ka. 400, Ka. 283, Ka. 293, Ka. 302 and Ka. 322). Among the latter, the most promising candidate for a grave pre-dating AD 800 seems to be Ka. 293, where

both the spearhead and the arrowheads suggest an early date. But altogether, there is no grave from Kaupang with a definite 8th-century date.

In Vestfold, cemeteries established in the Viking Age are very rare, if they occur at all (Gulli in Sem/Tønsberg might be an exception: see Gjerpe 2005c). Viking-age burials are regularly found in cemeteries already established in the Late Roman and Migration Periods (c. AD 200–550). The fact that none of the cemeteries at Kaupang seems to have roots in the pre-Viking period strongly suggests that all of them are indeed intimately connected with the establishment of the town around AD 800.

Even if there were earlier burials, as at other sites, it would have to be asked whether they constitute evidence of continuity over a long time-span. Overlap between Iron-age and Viking-age cemeteries is seen elsewhere in Scandinavia, for instance in Denmark. Direct continuity, however, is less certain, and one may speculate on whether the overlap reflects the coincidental choice of a similar topographical situation or a return to a site "known" to be the cemetery of ancient ancestors or holding other significance (see also Gjerpe 2005c).

The 9th and 10th centuries

Of the 116 datable burials, 98 of them can with more or less certainty (and subject to the qualifications outlined above, respecting relative versus absolute chronology and the correlation of the chronologies for dress-accessories and weaponry), be dated to either the 9th or the 10th century – 43 to the 9th and 55 to the 10th. The remaining 18 graves cannot be dated to either of these periods because many of them contain only one datable object with a suggested dating to 850–950 (for instance shield-bosses of type R562) or a dating based purely on style (for example metalwork with symmetric animal style, or Borre Style, from <850–950).

In ten cases the dating to the 10th century rests partly or mainly upon the occurrence of soapstone vessels in the grave in question. This calls for an explanation. Jan Petersen showed that the bowl-shaped vessels belonged mainly to the 10th and 11th centuries. He knew of 157 more closely datable finds, 132 of which he dated to this period. Only 16% belonged to the 9th century (Petersen 1951:362). As for the material from Vestfold (except Kaupang), there are 57 graves with soapstone vessels, 26 of which can be dated to the 10th century, and only 3 to the 9th (10%). At Kaupang, soapstone vessels have been found in 35 graves. On the basis of other artefacts in the graves, 16 of those can be dated to the 10th century and four to the 9th. The four earliest examples are mainly from graves with uncertain datings. Well-dated 9th-century burials do not have soapstone vessels (even if soapstone vessels are plentiful in the settlement area from the early 9th century: see Baug, in prep.). On this basis, the remaining ten graves with no datable artefacts, other than a soapstone vessel, have been dated to the 10th century (for a discussion of the chronology of Viking-age soapstone vessels, see also Risbøl 1994:121–3).

Over all, there seems to be a slight preponderance of burials dating to the 10th century at Kaupang. There are, however, discrepancies between the different cemeteries. At Bikjholberget, 28 burials date to the 9th century, and an equal number to the 10th. At Søndre Kaupang there are three 9th-century graves and three 10th-century graves, while at Hagejordet there are three graves dating to the 9th century and two dating to the 10th. However, for Nordre Kaupang the numbers are three and 13, and for Lamøya they are four and 9 for the 9th and 10th century, respectively. If, for the sake of argument, we exclude the graves dated only by the occurrence of soapstone vessels, the picture is only slightly different, i.e. the 10th century is still predominant at both Nordre Kaupang and Lamøya, but less markedly so. At Bikjholberget, as mentioned above, the 9th and 10th century burials are equal in number. These differences between the cemeteries at Kaupang are striking, with Lamøya and Nordre Kaupang in particular standing out from the others in the sense that these two cemeteries have a clear predominance of 10th-century graves. In the case of Lamøya, an explanation could be that this erstwhile island was not regularly used for burial until the later phase of the Kaupang settlement's existence, as seems to have been the case with the Hagejordet cemetery further north too (see below, on horizontal stratigraphy). As for Nordre Kaupang, this particular cemetery may only have been indirectly connected to the settlement (see Skre, this vol. Ch. 16:377–83), although a gradual expansion from a rather modest beginning in the 9th century is a reasonable hypothesis in this case too.

The main point, however, is that there are almost as many Early– as Middle–Viking-age graves at Kaupang, but with a slight preponderance of 10th-century graves (noting, however, that the 116 datable burials amount to only about 20% of the estimated number of burials).

This relationship between Early– and Middle–Viking-age graves at Kaupang is similar to what Thorleif Sjøvold (1944:83) found for Vestfold as a whole. However, there are major contrasts between different districts of Vestfold. By and large, the coastal districts have a clear majority of Early–Viking-age graves. For Tjølling (except Kaupang) the ratio is 14:5, while for the neighbouring districts of Brunlanes and Sandeherred the ratios are 15:4 and 24:13, respectively. We find the opposite pattern in some of the inland districts in Vestfold. Thus, Andebu has no graves dating to the 9th century, and six dating to the 10th. The numbers for Lardal are five and fourteen, respectively. Only Hedrum (38:44) and Stokke (13:15) fit the pattern of a slight preponderance of 10th-century graves proposed by Sjøvold, as does Kaupang (Fig. 5.11).

The difference between Kaupang and the surrounding district of Tjølling is quite remarkable, and it underlines the fact that Kaupang was no ordinary settlement in the Viking Age. In respect of the mortuary customs too, it differed from the farming areas nearby.

The large percentage of recorded graves dating to the 10th century at Kaupang cannot, therefore, be explained as being simply the result of a general increase in the number of (archaeologically recognizable) burials in the region in the 10th century. Considering also the fact that the finds from the settlement seem to indicate that it was abandoned sometime between 950 and 1000, one is struck even more by the difference. We have more graves from what might amount to not much more than the first half of the 10th century than from the whole of the 9th century. It is hard to avoid the inference that this was caused by more people living at Kaupang in its late phase than in its early phase. This inference is supported by the fact that the gender ratio in the graves changes radically during this period as well (below).

The late 10th century

Viking-period graves securely dated to the period after c. 950 are rare in Vestfold, with only 16 examples outside Kaupang (and none of them from Tjølling). At the recently excavated cemetery at Gulli, for instance, none of the graves seems to post-date c. 950 (Gjerpe 2005c). A maximum of four Vestfold graves can be dated to the 11th century (three of which are single finds of one axehead). Seven of the 16 graves post-dating 950 are from the inland district of Hedrum, illustrating a more general pattern for eastern Norway, i.e. that the latest furnished Viking-age graves are to be found in the interior (Larsen 1984; Stylegar 2005c).

Two of the graves from Kaupang seem to date to the period post-dating c. 950 (not counting the undatable graves Ka. 319–320 in wooden coffins, which could be late). Ka. 211 from Lamøya contained an axehead of Petersen's type L (M), dating from c. 950 into the 11th century. In the other grave, Ka. 277 from Bikjholberget, a shield-boss of type R563 implies a date after c. 950.

Neither of these datings is beyond question, however, since we owe both chronologies (axeheads and shield-bosses) to Petersen's 1919 work, and both are probably inexact in respect of absolute date. Furthermore, single axeheads are often considered unreliable for precise dating (Blindheim et al. 1999:103). Also to be considered are the 20 graves that can only be dated to the 10th century in general. Any of those graves could, of course, belong to the period 950–1000, so that the real number of graves apparently post-dating c. 950 could be higher.

Percentage of female graves in	the 9th century	the 10th century
Kaupang	58	24
Hedrum	47	13
Sem	39	13
Stokke	38	24
Brunlanes	38	25
Sandar	20	11
Lardal/Hof	31	5
Borre/Botne/Våle/ Ramnes/Andebu	25	20

Figure 5.12 *Table of the gender ratio in the Kaupang cemeteries as compared with other areas of Vestfold.*

Nevertheless, the general lack of burials having artefact-types with a definitive dating to after c. 950 probably indicates that the cemeteries at Kaupang stopped being used regularly for burials around this time. In this, the Kaupang cemeteries are not very different from the majority of cemeteries in the coastal districts in Vestfold. In this light, Blindheim's suggested end-date for the cemeteries of around c. 950 seems reasonable (Blindheim et al. 1999:162). One must bear in mind, however, that she based (1999:153) this on the axehead found at Lamøya, and suggested an end-date for Bikjholberget of c. 930/940 – despite the late shield-boss there.

5.4 The dead

The gendered burials

Ellen Høigård Hofseth (1999) has drawn attention to the relatively high number of female graves at Kaupang. Indeed, at first sight, the proportion of female graves at Kaupang seems extraordinary compared to that in most regions of Norway; however, there are some chronological and interpretative issues worth exploring.

In Vestfold as a whole, female graves account for a quarter of the gendered graves – similar to many other coastal districts (cf. Dommasnes 1982; Hofseth 1999). But female graves are much more common in the region in the 9th century than in the 10th – 34% of the total number of gendered graves against 13%, respectively. This pattern is repeated in a number of other coastal districts (Dommasnes 1982:81–2).

The numbers for Kaupang exceed these figures in both the 9th and the 10th centuries. Of the 41 datable female graves, 22 can be dated to the 9th century, and 12 to the 10th. As for the 62 datable male graves from the Kaupang cemeteries, there are 16 from the 9th century and 38 from the 10th. Thus, the female graves comprise 58% (22 of 38) of the gendered graves in the 9th century, against 24% (12 of 50) in the 10th (the

graves dated to the period 850–950 cannot account for the difference; of the 15 graves in question, eight are male and seven are female). Even if these are median values for all the Kaupang cemeteries, at Bikjholberget, the only cemetery with a significant number of datable, gendered graves seem to conform to this pattern. Thus, of 53 gendered and datable graves at Bikjholberget, female graves comprise 50% of the graves in the 9th century, and 25% in the 10th century. It is clear from this that the Kaupang cemeteries seem to have a substantially higher proportion of female burials both in the 9th and the 10th century than cemeteries in the rest of Vestfold, although there are considerable local differences in this respect, and some areas show a rather similar pattern as Kaupang (Fig. 5.12).

How can one account for these differences? There are really four different questions to be answered. First, why is it that male burials apparently outnumber female ones in the Vestfold material – and even more so in the Norwegian material as a whole – even though Vestfold and the coastal districts of Østfold, just across the Oslofjord, have a higher proportion of female graves than the rest of the country throughout the Viking Age? Second, where are the women? Third, why is it that the number of female graves relative to male graves decreases from the 9th century to the 10th? Fourth and finally, why are there more female graves at Kaupang than in the rest of Vestfold?

The gender ratios from Kaupang and Vestfold are at odds with results from other areas of Scandinavia. Starting with Birka, Gräslund (1980:82) finds that 58% of the inhumations are female, against 61% of the cremations, although she suggests that the real distribution might be closer to 50:50. Of 113 10th- and 11th-century graves at Barshalder in Gotland, 37% were female, 49% male and 14% gender neutral (Rundkvist 2003:79). A study of a sample of 76 sexed skeletons from Hedeby concluded that 62% were male (Sellevold et al. 1984:214). Other southern Scandinavian cemeteries also show a predominance of men: Stengade II (53%), Kaagaarden (63%) and Bogø-vej (61%), while there are relatively more women at Lejre (61%) and Hesselbjerg (58%) (Sellevold et al. 1984:214–15; Bennike 1994:169). With the exception of Birka and Barshalder, these studies are based on skeletal material – what we have here, therefore, are *sexed* burials, not gendered ones. Not just the Kaupang material and the rest of the material from Vestfold, but all the Norwegian material – based as it is on the presence of gender-specific artefacts in the graves – is biased relative to the southern Scandinavian evidence, and therefore the two cannot really be compared on equal terms. It is a telling fact that Per Holck's physical anthropological analysis of Late Iron-age cremations in south-eastern Norway, although it could ascribe only 42 burials from the period to either sex, concluded that 62% of the cremation burials were actually female (Holck 1986:catalogue).

At Kaupang, the gendered burials account for only some of the dated burials, while, more importantly, the dated burials themselves account only for a minor part of the total number of burials. Thus, the gendered burials form a rather small exclusive category, and therefore one must be careful when assuming that gendered burials are the same as sexed graves. Herein lies the answer to the first and third questions asked above. In principle, one would expect a more or less equal distribution of male and female sexed graves. The reason we do not find an equal distribution in Vestfold probably has to do with the difference betwen sexed and gendered graves, i.e. more males than females were buried with gender-specific artefacts, or, more likely, more males than females were buried with gender-specific artefacts that are preserved and can be recovered by archaeologists.

There is a clear correlation between areas with a substantial number of professionally excavated graves and those with a relatively high proportion of graves gendered (identified) as graves of females. This is evident in those parts of Vestfold where only a few professional excavations have taken place, and the proportion of male graves is very high. A corroded sword or axe is easier to notice when ploughing than the remains of an copper-alloy oval brooch or a few beads. So, when we find that 58% (9th century) and 24% (10th century), respectively, of the dated graves at Kaupang are graves of females, these relatively high figures are due mainly to the substantial number of graves archaeologically investigated at Kaupang. As for the relative decrease in the gendered female graves in the 10th century, it would be tempting to attribute this to an influx of males at Kaupang in the late period. However, the decrease can be matched in Vestfold as a whole, as indeed in most of Norway (Dommasnes 1982:81–3). A more likely explanation would seem to be either a real decrease in gendered female burials compared to male, or a change in the way female graves were gendered; the latter could result, for instance, from the partial and gradual abandonment of oval brooches as part of the female dress in the 10th century, under influence from Frankish and/or Byzantine single-brooch costumes (Hedeager Krag 1994; cf. Ingstad 1999:243–4). It is also a distinct possibility that, at any point through the Viking Age, female dress customs were rather more varied than is often assumed (Martens 1969:88; see also Blindheim 1947:117–18). A survey of the Viking-age evidence from Denmark indicates that the poorest and the richest women, as implied by their grave furnishings, did not wear oval brooches (Hedeager Madsen 1990:104).

Weapon combinations

The weapon combinations show some interesting patterns. A total of 79 graves at Kaupang contained weapons (hereafter referred to as weapon graves). Of these graves, 55 could be dated, 17 (31%) to the 9th century and 38 (69%) to the 10th; the remaining 24 graves could not with any certainty be dated to either of these two periods. In other words, 69% of the dated weapon graves at Kaupang date to the 10th century. The percentages for the rest of Vestfold are very different; of 240 datable weapon graves in the rest of Vestfold, 121 (50.4%) date to the 9th century and 119 (49.6%) to the 10th, virtually an equal distribution between the two periods.

In the 9th-century weapon graves from Kaupang, granted that the number (17) is low, there is an apparently even distribution of the various weapon combinations. The full combination sword/spear/axe occurs in four (23.5%) graves. Another four graves contain a spear only, while three (17.6%) graves contain the sword/spear combination. Two (11.7%) graves contain the sword/axe combination, and one (5.9%) grave contains the spear/axe combination.

The situation of the 38 weapon graves dated to the 10th century is very different; a total of 13 (34%) of these weapon graves contained the full range of offensive weapons,. The other combinations range from three to six instances. On the other hand, a total of nine (24%) of the 9th century weapon graves contained the full weapon combination. Both these numbers (24% and 34%) are above the average for Vestfold (12 and 24%, respectively), but the 10th century percentage more so. In fact, the relative number of graves with the three types of offensive weapons at Kaupang in the 10th century is, to the best of my knowledge, unsurpassed in Norway. The single axe, so common in most of Norway, barely registers in the Kaupang cemeteries (Stylegar 2005b). This is a trait (or rather a lack thereof) found in other areas bordering at the Oslofjord too. Ka. 6 from Nordre Kaupang has three shield-bosses (Grieg 1947:20), but we cannot exclude the possibility that more than one cremated individual was buried in this barrow. Nevertheless, the 10th-century male Kaupang graves are extremely rich in weaponry.

The total number of burials is too low to draw any conclusions regarding possible differences between the cemeteries at Kaupang, but my impression is that the general observations made above hold true for each of the cemeteries. This is certainly the case for the three cemeteries with the vast majority of the weapon graves, i.e. Nordre Kaupang, Søndre Kaupang and Bikjholberget.

The increase in the number of weapons that accompany each burial from the 9th to the 10th century cannot be ascribed to a general increase in the volume of grave furnishings. The NAT (Number of Artefact-types), at least, is the same for the two periods: with a median value of seven.

Single weapons were found in a number of female gendered graves as well. Four of Nicolaysen's graves at Nordre Kaupang contained an axehead combined with oval brooches. This is also the case with five graves in Bikjholberget. While the former cremations might be double graves, the latter are certainly women's graves. Furthermore, at least two gendered female graves each contained a spear, and in two instances a shield-boss was found. The axes might of course have a double function as weapons and every-day tools, and the latter may account for their presence in female graves. For the spearheads and shield-bosses in female graves, an interpretation along the line suggested by Guttman, i.e. a connection with Valkyrie symbolism, seems possible (Guttman 2004). One grave from south-eastern Norway may be mentioned in this respect: C22541 from Åsnes, Hedmark – a sexed female grave with a "full" range of weapons (Hernæs and Holck 1984). In western Norway a small number of otherwise female gendered graves contain "male" artefacts (Dommasnes 1982:77), and the same phenomenon is known from other areas too (see, e.g., Rygh 1910:16–18).

The chronology of the imported finds

Chronological aspects of the imported finds in the Kaupang graves, especially the Insular artefacts, were dealt with at length by the original excavators (Blindheim 1976a; Blindheim et al. 1981:175–80, 1999:47–57).

In total, objects with a western Continental (including Ribe) provenance have been found in 27 datable graves (Ka. 4, 14, 37, 125, 126, 150, 157, 203, 210, 254–255, 257, 259, 277, 283–284, 287, 290, 293, 301, 304–306, 310, 316, 322, 400). Insular objects have been found in 18 datable graves (Ka. 6, 8, 157, 210, 219, 250, 253, 263, 264, 268, 279, 283, 295, 298, 300–301, 304. 306), and Eastern (i.e. including Finnish and Slavonic) in 14 datable graves (Ka. 4, 5, 6, 8, 126, 203, 254, 277, 280, 282, 286, 290, 299, 301, 307). In earlier publications, the importance and quantity of the Insular imports in the graves was sometimes overstated, as pointed out by Blindheim (et al. 1999:57). The fact is that Continental objects dominate the range of imported material in the graves, followed by Insular and Eastern objects. The numerical differences seem significant.

Thirty-eight finds with foreign objects can be dated to the 9th century. They derive from altogether 29 graves. The numbers for the 10th century are 21 items in 16 graves. The chronology of the graves is not precise enough to study the chronological distribution of the imported finds in any great detail. It is, for instance, difficult to establish whether there was an increase in imports between the early and later phase of the settlement's life-span. This could be the case, given that the 10th-century graves cover a much shorter time span than the 9th-century ones. The possible increase in imports deposited in the graves in the 10th century in comparison with the 9th cannot be attributed to a general increase in the number of objects deposited in the graves, as the NAT is constant over time (above).

However, the origin of the imported finds seems to change over time, and this fact is significant in that it reflects chronological variation in the external contacts of the settlement. The dominance of Continental finds is actually a 9th-century phenomenon. Twenty-one of the Continental imports were in 9th-century graves, as against seven of the Eastern objects and 10 Insular. In the 10th-century graves, the numbers are six, seven, and eight. A pattern seems to emerge, with imports from the Continent being predominant in the 9th-century graves, with Insular and Eastern objects falling some way behind, while Insular, Eastern, and Continental imports are of equal importance in the 10th century.

Objects made of amber are not considered in these numbers. The raw material for these objects is definitely from the Baltic area, but it is not clear from exactly where. It could be present-day Denmark or it

could be areas further east. There are 12 graves with objects of amber in them (beads in all cases but one: the spindle-whorl in Ka. 285). The amber finds are equally distributed between the 9th and the 10th centuries.

Only in a few cases do we have any indication that individuals buried at Kaupang were of foreign origin. This might be the case with the gendered female graves Ka. 126, 259 and 280, as none of those contained a pair of oval brooches (Blindheim et al. 1999:45–6). But the absence of oval brooches is no sure sign of "foreignness" in these parts. As noted above, oval brooches were not necessarily worn by all: for instance, some 25% of the gendered female graves in southern Vestfold have *beads* as the only pieces of jewellery (Stylegar, in prep. a). These three graves, however, do stand out from the Vestfold material generally in terms of their furnishings, and may well represent foreigners. This holds for Ka. 254 as well, as this grave has a quite obvious Eastern character, but does include a pair of oval brooches too (Fig. 5.13).

Population estimate

How many people might have lived at Kaupang in the Viking Age? The formula P = a x b/c, alternatively P = (a x b/c) x 1.1, where *a* is total the number of graves, *b* is the average life expectancy at birth, and *c* is the number of years the cemetery was used (Acsádi and Nemeskéri 1957, 1970), has recently been put to use in Scandinavian archaeology to estimate the size of the population burying their dead in particular cemeteries (Ravn 2003:48–49; Rundkvist 2003:79–80). Similar calculations have been made for Birka (Gräslund 1980:82–83) and Hedeby (Randsborg 1980:80).

A particular difficulty encountered when trying to estimate the population of Kaupang and other early towns is the question of seasonal variation (Gräslund 1980:83). Gräslund is probably right to argue that what she refers to as "casual visitors" are actually under-represented in the burial archaeology. Thus, the cemeteries at Kaupang to all practical purposes reflect the permanent population in the town, and there can be no satisfactory basis for an estimate of Kaupang's population during its primary season.

However, the churchyard with about a thousand burials, of which almost half have been excavated at the seasonal trading site of Sebbersund, might inspire considerable caution, even if this might have been a churchyard for a parish of unknown size, and not (only) a cemetery for people visiting the market (Christensen and Johansen 1992; Birkedahl and Johansen 1995:161). But there really is a question whether seasonal market-places had cemeteries at all in the Viking Age proper. Sebbersund apparently did not; while the site seems to gain a regional significance from about AD 700, there are no known graves pre-dating the establishment of the Christian churchyard around AD 1000 (Christensen and Johansen 1992). No cemetery has been discovered at Åhus in Skåne, nor at the non-urban trading site of Löddeköpinge, or at Paviken in Gotland (Clarke and Ambrosiani 1995:54, 64 and 85). Only Fröjel and some of the other harbours in Gotland with limited craft and trade activity in the Viking Age seem to have had cemeteries (Clarke and Ambrosiani 1995:85).

A problem specific to Kaupang is that no precise total number of graves is known. There are 407 documented graves, while estimates for the orginal number of graves range from c. 700 to c. 1,000 (above). Furthermore, while the total life-span of the cemeteries is c. AD 800–950, there is arguably some room for alternative possibilities in this respect, and the real answer may be a few years before or after 800 and a few years before or after 950, perhaps as early as 930/940 (above). Still, it is useful to make some estimates based on these numbers. A third problem springs from the fact that we cannot know for certain if all the cemeteries were used exclusively – or at all – by the people living in the settlement. Doubt has for instance been cast on whether the major barrow cemetery at Nordre Kaupang "belonged" to the settlement in a strict sense (Skre, this vol. Ch. 16:377–83; cf. Ambrosiani 1986). I would argue that similar considerations apply to other Early Viking-age urban settlements, as well – they are not specific to Kaupang. Since no one has really doubted the connection between the Nordre Kaupang cemetery and the Kaupang *complex* as such (Skre, this vol. Ch. 19:432–5), it seems reasonable to include all the cemeteries in the population estimates.

Working from a minimum estimate of a total of c. 700 graves, an average life-expectancy of 30 years, and a life-span of the cemeteries that equals 150 years, we get a population of c. 155 persons living at Kaupang.

To this, however, we must add an estimated number of "missing" children's graves. Nine graves of a total of 74 at Bikjholberget were either children's graves or double graves with a child (Ka. 262, 269, 272, 294, 298, 315, 316, 321, 322). This means that only 12% of the excavated graves at Bikjholberget contained children. This number is probably much too low as a representation of child mortality, although by no means unprecedented in the Scandinavian material. Thus, Holck only lists three children (0–14 years old) in his catalogue of Iron-age cremation burials from south-eastern Norway, while stating that children's graves of 0–7-year-olds alone ought to comprise at least 35% of the material (Holck 1986:108–9, catalogue). At Birka, Gräslund (1980:82) notes 17% children's graves amongst the inhumations. Acsádi and Nemeskéri (1970:236–51) find that children comprised 40% of the population in the period, on the basis of skeletal material from European cemeteries from the Iron Age and Middle Ages. Since children

are underrepresented at the Danish cemetery of Hjemsted, Mads Ravn adds 40% to the calculated population in his study (2003:49). Martin Rundkvist (2003:79–80) assumes a child mortality of 45%, and so adds 45% to the number of dead (adult) individuals in his calculation for Barshalder in Gotland.

Following up on our minimum proposal, then, let us add 30% to our 700 graves/dead individuals. This gives us c. 200 people living at Kaupang. Holck's analysis (1986:104), however, indicates that the average life-expectancy actually was closer to 40 years, i.e. 37.2 for men and 33.5 for women. Using 35 years, the estimated minimum population increases to c. 235.

The number could be considerably higher. A thousand graves, a life-expectancy of 40 years, and a 130-year life-span for the cemeteries give us c. 440 people, and this retains the modest estimate of child mortality at 30%. If child mortality was at 45%, the population estimate rises to c. 490 people. But the number of 10th-century graves compared with the number of graves from the whole of the preceding century calls for some caution in this respect, even if there are some unresolved matters regarding absolute chronology (above). If we apply the parameters of the earlier calculations to the 10th century alone (an average life-expectancy of 35 years and child mortality at 30%), and assume that the total number of graves belonging to the first three decades of the 10th century is 500, we get a total population in the heyday of Kaupang of c. 830 people. Again, this does not seem an improbable figure.

Under any circumstances, the population at Kaupang seems to have been considerably larger in the early 10th century (i.e. in the Middle Viking Age) than a century before. It is probably not too wild a guess that the number of people staying at Kaupang in the early 10th century could at times reach over a thousand.

Furthermore, there is every reason to believe that a substantial proportion of the adult population were unfree individuals, who were probably not given any burial at all (cf. Skre 1998b:228–30; Rundkvist 2003:80). To the town's total free population should thus, very probably, be added a considerable number of slaves.

5.5 Horizontal stratigraphy

There is little to say about the horizontal stratigraphy of the cemeteries – in the case of the cemetery at Søndre Kaupang, nothing at all, in fact. Concerning the cemetery at Hagejordet, the only certain thing one can say is that it was not established at the beginning of the settlement; the dated burials there, however, do not indicate precisely when it was established, but it was probably during the 9th century. A number of observations can be made in respect of the other three cemeteries, however.

At Nordre Kaupang, only three of the datable

graves from Nicolaysen's campaign derive from the 9th century; all the others from his campaign are from the 10th (Fig. 5.10). Two of the three 9th-century graves are located in the middle part of the cemetery (Ka. 5 and 14). Another grave (Ka. 37) was excavated in 1965 and dates to the second half of the 9th century. This is the southernmost grave in the cemetery. When it was excavated in 1965, ploughmarks were observed below the cremation layer (Blindheim et al. 1981:54, fig. 5, 55), indicating that the southernmost part of Nordre Kaupang was not established until well into the lifespan of the settlement. However, most of the excavated graves in the southern part of the cemetery cannot be precisely dated. There is a clustering of possibly late (i.e. 10th-century) graves in the northern part of the cemetery. Also, it seems likely that the four very large, but undated barrows at Nordre Kaupang, Nicolaysen's nos. 50, 51, 53 and 61, are among the oldest in the cemetery, since this cluster of large barrows was obviously built at a time when there was a large open space available in the cemetery. Several smaller barrows have been built around them. When Ka. 37 was excavated in 1965, plough-marks were observed below the cremation layer (Blindheim et al. 1981:54, fig. 5, 55), indicating that the southernmost part of the major barrow cemetery at Nordre Kaupang was not established until well into the lifespan of the settlement.

At Bikjholberget, there seems to be a discernible horizontal stratigraphy in the more southerly of the two excavated areas, which is dominated by 10th-century graves. The exception is barrow burial Ka. 200 which may date to the 9th century. This barrow seems to have been a focal point for the more recent graves Ka. 291 and Ka. 313, as well as for the undated wooden coffin burials Ka. 319. and 320 (Blindheim et al. 1995:15, fig. 3). It seems that while the 9th-century graves are concentrated in certain areas of this part of the cemetery, the later graves are found all over the cemetery. In the excavated area to the north, there is a preponderance of 9th-century graves in the western part of the excavated area while graves dating to the 10th century are predominant in the eastern part (Blindheim et al. 1999:146). There is, however, no clear-cut distribution pattern.

At Lamøya, there is a clear preponderance of 10th-century graves. There are only three 9th century graves which were found in two different find-spots located at a considerable distance from one another. One find-spot, a barrow, contained two of these three graves. As the 10th-century graves at Lamøya clearly outnumber the 9th century graves, the pattern could very well be similar to that suggested for Bikjhol-berget immediately above.

Thus the limited number of cemeteries recogniz-able at Kaupang in modern times may originally – although this cannot yet be proven – have consisted of many smaller grave clusters that only gradually merged into the later, continuous spread (cf. Gräs-lund 1980:73).

5.6 Mortuary customs

The treatment of the body

As pointed out in the preceding pages, all the known burials at Bikjholberget are inhumations. At both Nordre and Søndre Kaupang, all the burials are cre-mations. At Hagejordet, three of the burials are cre-mations, against one inhumation. Of the four graves that can only be attributed to Nordre Kaupang (i.e. either Nordre Kaupang, Hagejordet, or Bikjhol-berget), three are inhumations. It is likely, but we can-not know for certain, that these three inhumations were recovered from either Hagejordet or Bikjhol-berget. At Lamøya the picture is more mixed: four of the burials are cremations, and six inhumations.

The preponderance of one type of body treat-ment over the other (i.e. cremation or inhumation) varies considerably between the many ritual systems of Viking-age Scandinavia (Svanberg 2003). In Vest-fold, as in southern and eastern Norway as a whole, and in Sweden, cremation is clearly preponderant. For example, according to one estimate, only one in five burials in Vestfold is an inhumation (Sjøvold 1944); other researchers have suggested one in every four burials (Larsen 1982:105; see also Forseth 1993). On the other hand, further west, inhumations are as common as cremations (Schetelig 1912). In northern Norway things change again; there, inhumations are very preponderant, i.e. there are almost no crema-tions (Sjøvold 1974). In most of Denmark too, inhu-mation is almost universal, but in northern Jutland, particularly, there is a significant level of cremation (Brøndsted 1936; Ramskou 1950).

The external structure of the graves

Barrows and flat graves are unevenly distributed at the Kaupang cemeteries. Barrows are predominant in Nordre Kaupang, and flat graves at Bikjholberget, while there is no way at this stage to decide the rela-tive distribution of barrows and flat graves at Søndre Kaupang and Lamøya. So far, we know of no flat graves at either Vikingholmen or Bjønnes (the possi-ble examples in Bjønnes mentioned in Blindheim et al. 1981:51 are probably cooking pits).

Amongst the barrows, the round type predomi-nates. Of 115 barrows at Nordre Kaupang and Hage-jordet in 1867, 90 were round. Three of the eight bar-rows excavated by Nicolaysen at Søndre Kaupang were long barrows. Three of the 94 remaining burial mounds at Lamøya are long barrows. A quite remark-able fact is that all of the excavated long barrows at Nordre Kaupang that contained gendered graves, contained *female* graves (Ka. 3, 10, 14, 16 and 22). This was the case at Søndre Kaupang as well (Ka. 155: dis-cussed in Blindheim et al. 1981:57). The same pattern is known from other areas in Norway in both the Viking and pre–Viking Age (Gustafson 1993).

The flat graves at Bikjholberget were covered by stone packings. The flat graves at Søndre Kaupang, and possibly some at Hagejordet, seem to have been covered by horizontal stone slabs.

There was one four-sided stone setting at southern Bikjholberget. At Lamøya two circular stone settings are known, and one at Bjønnes. As pointed out above, the latter is probably the monument mentioned by Nicolaysen in 1893 (1894a:177). As early as 1852, P. A. Munch mentioned a small stone setting "down at the harbour" in the Kaupang area (Munch 1852:382, n. 1). This could be the circular stone setting at Bjønnes, or it might have been a now lost monument or the small ship-setting documented by Zeuthen in 1845 (above). Contrary to what was once believed (Blindheim et al. 1981:91), there actually was a ship-setting at Kaupang. It was drawn by Zeuthen in 1845 but was gone when Christie made his plan of the main cemetery at Nordre Kaupang in 1866. Furthermore, there are also four or five boat-shaped stone settings (in Norwegian *båtformede steinlegninger)* at Bjønnes. A third stone setting at Lamøya could be boat-shaped, too. Of all the stone settings at Kaupang, only the four-sided one at southern Bikjholberget has been excavated. It contained a boat grave (Ka. 294–296).

Both the ship-settings and the boat-shaped stone settings in present-day Norway have a clear and strong southeasterly distribution. With only a few exceptions they are found in the districts bordering on the Oslofjord – most of them in Vestfold, where the 45 m long ship-setting at Elgesem in Sandefjord is the largest one remaining. Ship-settings are quite common in southern Scandinavia outside of Norway, as at Blomsholm in western Sweden, Lindholm Høje in Jutland, and Lejre on Sjælland (Andersen 1995; Artelius 1996). More than 2,000 examples are known (Capelle 2004). Several such monuments have been excavated at Birka (Gräslund 1980:70). In Jutland, 138 of the 589 excavated graves at Lindholm Høje were ship-settings (Ramskou 1976). They are also known from the Baltic area, for instance in the Slavonic settlement of Menzlin by the Oderhaff in Mecklenburg (Herrmann 1982:101). As for the four-sided stone settings (in Norwegian *firkantede steinlegninger),* these are not common in Norway (although not entirely absent: see Martens 1969), but quite widespread in Sweden, especially in the western parts of southern Sweden, where they tend to be associated with circular stone settings and raised stones (Burenhult 2000:256). There are several four-sided stone settings at Birka (Gräslund 1980:68).

The alignment of the graves

Only in the inhumation cemetery at Bikjholberget, which is still being systematically excavated, is it pos-

sible to study the alignment of the graves in any detail.

The vast majority of the graves at Bikjholberget are aligned NNE–SSW or N–S. Of the 22 datable graves, this is the case with 17 (Ka. 252, 257–259, 267, 277, 282, 291, 292, 294–296, 298–300, 301 and 302, 303 and 304, 305, 308, 310 and 311, 315 and 316 – six of these are boats with more than one grave). A N–S alignment is more common in the 9th century graves amongst these (six out of nine graves), while a NNE.–SSW. alignment dominates in the 10th (seven out of 11 graves). Only four graves have an E.–W. orientation (Ka. 269, 270, 278, 309). Ka. 269 probably dates to the 9th century, the three others to the 10th. Among the E.–W. oriented graves there is only one "ordinary" boat grave (Ka. 309); the other graves in question are two log coffins (Ka. 269 and 278), and a possible chamber grave (Ka. 270). The boat grave, Ka. 307, which has a chamber, is also oriented E.–W.; this grave, however, is of the late 9th or the early 10th century.

An N.–S. alignment of the grave/body is found in the overwhelming majority of inhumation graves in Vestfold. Sjøvold (1944:71) does not know any oriented (E.–W.) Viking-period graves at all in the region.

There does not seem to be any system in the alignment of differently gendered burials at Bikjholberget; only a (minor) chronological difference. However, there is no obvious chronological system to the alignment of the other types of grave at Bikjholberget.

The internal structure of the graves

The cremation burials at Kaupang belong to two types: urned and unurned. Only two graves are of the former type. In Ka. 1, a soapstone vessel served as an urn, while an oval brooch was put to the same use in Ka. 16. Both graves are from the main cemetery at Nordre Kaupang. All the other cremation burials at Kaupang, then, are unurned cremation deposits. Such cremation deposits are the most common of all the Viking-age grave-forms in Scandinavia. Urned deposits are very rare in Vestfold, as, indeed, in Norway as a whole (such burials only occur with any regularity in Østfold and Akershus: Stylegar, in prep. b). There are only three examples in Vestfold other than at Kaupang: a soapstone vessel from an equestrian grave from Skatveit, Andebu (C8877–78) and iron cauldrons from Lille Gullkronen, Sem (C22441; see Grieg 1923:5–6, 34), and Tanum, Lardal (C2708–23).

All the cremations at Kaupang are in barrows, while inhumations occur both in barrows and as flat graves. In comparison with the cremations, the inhumation burials at Kaupang exhibit much greater variation. A large number of different forms can be discerned.

The stone cist Ka. 290

Ka. 290 was found inside a stone cist in a barrow at

Bikjholberget. Although a form first and foremost associated with Late Roman- and Migration-period graves in Vestfold, Viking-age cist burials are known in the region, but only in exceptional cases, and then only in the districts bordering on Kaupang. They are more common further west, however, and particularly in northern Norway, where in some areas burials with cists are as common as burials without (Sjøvold 1974).

The wooden coffins Ka. 271, 315, 318–320 and 322
Six wooden coffins were recovered from the excavated parts of the cemetery at Bikjholberget, one from the northern part (Ka. 271), and five from the southern part (Ka. 315, 318–320, 322). Three of these can be dated; two are of the 9th century (Ka. 315, 322), and one of the 10th (Ka. 271).

The coffins were mostly in a poor state of preservation, but it seems that rectangular coffins were predominant. One coffin may have originally been square (Ka. 322).

Four of the five coffins from Bikjholberget were found relatively close together in the southern part of the site. In exactly the same area two other rather special grave-forms were also represented (Ka. 313–314, 316, below).

The chest Ka. 316
In the case of Ka. 316 from Bikjholberget, a domestic storage chest (type Oseberg 149) was used as a coffin (Fig 16). Only two iron hinges, two iron hasps, 12 iron nails, and a lock fitting with tin-coated nails attached were left of the chest, which had had a length of 125–140 cm, a width of 65–75 cm and a height of 20–30 cm (Blindheim et al. 1999:101–2). From the shape of the hasps, the lid must have been vaulted (ibid.).

Ka. 316 dates to the 9th century, probably to the second half of that century. One adult, a gendered male to judge by the grave goods, was buried in the chest together with a child. Chests were used primarily as furniture for storage or for travelling throughout the Viking Age and later. In some instances they could have a secondary function as coffins. Besides Ka. 316 from Kaupang, domestic storage chests were used in this way at Fyrkat, Lejre and Forlev in Denmark (Brøndsted 1936; Roesdahl 1977:130), as well as in at least four cases at York (Richards et al. 1995). Similar instances are known from Råga Hörstad in Skåne and Oldenburg in Schleswig-Holstein (Strömberg 1968: 20; Kleiminger 1993:116).

The chests found at Lejre and Fyrkat had both been broken in order to facilitate the insertion of extended adult corpses. The body in the Forlev chest was laid out with knees bent, and this was most likely the case in Ka. 316 as well.

The horse burial Ka. 317, found in a separate pit to the south of Ka. 316, should probably be associated with this grave. Similar offerings associated with human burials are known from Hedrum (Stylegar 2005a, 2006).

An axe was found embedded in the grave Ka. 316, chopped into the ground outside the chest. Other examples of this rite are known from Kaupang, all of them involving axes, and all from southern Bikjholberget: Ka. 298, Ka. 299 and Ka. 305. Spearheads were found embedded in the side walls of some of the inhumation graves at Birka, while in some cases a weapon had been thrust into unurned cremation patches (Gräslund 1980:30–31, 76). A phenomenon similar to the latter, and involving swords as well as spears, was observed in the cemetery at Kvarnbacken, Åland (Kivikoski 1963:68). An example involving an axe was found at Birka (Gräslund 1980:76). In Bogøvej Grave P, Langeland, a knife was found embedded in the bottom of the grave-pit (Grøn et al. 1994:15). A similar phenomenon, but involving a sword, is known from Husby-Långhundra in Sweden (Sundqvist 1993:156). It has recently been argued that embedded weapons in Viking-age graves may be the remains of a rite designed to commit the deceased to Odin, and thereby to convey him or her to a favourable existence in the Other World (Nordberg 2002).

The trough-sleds Ka. 313–314
In two other graves from southern Bikjholberget, Ka. 313–314, what have been described as boats cut in half functioned as coffins (Blindheim et al. 1995:41–2). The boat-shaped structure in Ka. 313 was c. 2 m long (it could have been closer to 3 m), and up to 70–80 cm wide. There were traces of two ribs, but the concentration of nails at the stem characteristic of clinker-built boats is conspiciously absent. Ka. 314 was somewhat shorter than Ka. 313, and c. 65 cm wide. There was no obvious system to the distribution of nails.

Burials in half-boats are known from the Viking-age archaeological record, as at Tømmerby and Gammelby in Denmark (Müller-Wille 1970:26). However, in connexion with the "half-boats" from Birka, Anne-Sofie Gräslund (1980:25) suggests that these were in fact "single-runner sleds" or *akjas*. Blindheim considered it unlikely that anyone would have been buried in a Saami sled-type at Kaupang (Blindheim et al. 1995:98). While the latter viewpoint is probably unjustified, based, as it was, on the modern-day distribution of the Saami, it is nonetheless very probable that the boat-shaped sledge was employed by other peoples in Scandinavia besides the Saami (Berg 1935:24).

However, the absence of any obvious system to the distribution of nails in Ka. 314, and the generally small number of nails and rivets in both graves (23 in Ka. 313, 9 in Ka. 314), do point to an alternative interpretation to Blindheim's. Indeed, the form of the structures in Ka. 313–314 is very similar to the so-called trough-sleds (Berg 1935:pl II, 1–2). This type of

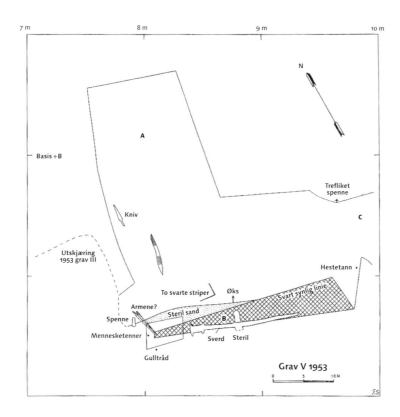

7 m   8 m   9 m   10 m

N

A

Basis ÷ B

Trefliket
spenne

Kniv

C

Utskjæring
1953 grav III

Hestetann

To svarte striper   Øks

Svart synlig linie

Armene?

Spenne   Steril sand

B

Mennesketenner   Steril

Gulltråd   Sverd

Grav V 1953

0   5   10 M

sled is known from western Norway from comparatively recent times (Berg 1935:25; regarding the use of sleds for burial, see Sindbæk 2003).

The log coffins Ka. 269 and 278

In two graves at Nordre Bikjholberget, hollowed-out logs were used for coffins. The coffin in Ka. 269 measured c. 2 m x 0.3, while that in Ka. 278 was c. 1.9 m x 0.6. Four nails were found in Ka. 269. Log coffins are known from a few southern Scandinavian cemeteries – Råga Hörstad in Skåne, and Stengade in Langeland (Strömberg 1968:29; Skaarup 1976:164), to name but two. The dimensions of the coffins in Råga Hörstad are comparable to those from Kaupang: 1.7–1.8 m x 0.56–0.6 (Strömberg 1968:29). One might also refer to a small group of trough-like coffins at Sebbersund (Nielsen 2004:110).

A type of coffin very similar to the ones from Kaupang has been found at Gulli in Tønsberg, Vestfold. Like the coffin in Ka. 269, this grave contained a row of nails, and the excavator has interpreted the find as a burial in a log boat, with the nails having been used for repairs (Gjerpe 2005c:21). Log-boat coffins are otherwise very rare in the Scandinavian material; however, a couple of instances where log boats were indeed used as coffins are known from Rösta in Ås, Jämtland (Kjellmark 1906:354–5; the Rösta cemetery is possibly a Saami one, see Zachrisson 2006), and from Sala in Västmanland (Müller-Wille 1970:no. 141–2).

Graves without coffins

Three inhumations at Nordre Bikjholberget (Ka. 274–276) were without any kind of coffin – and without any furnishings. The skeletons were found in twisted positions. The bodies had been placed directly in pits, and their feet may have been tied together (Blindheim et al. 1995:130).

Comparable graves are known: for instance Grave 363 in Fjälkinge, Skåne (Svanberg 2003:303); Bogøvej Grave P on Langeland (Grøn et al. 1994:14–15), Kalmargården in Sjælland and the southern cemetery at Fröjel, Gotland (Carlsson 1999:109–10). One might compare them to the "deviant" burials of Anglo-Saxon archaeology (Geake 1992:87–9).

At least one, perhaps two, of the skeletons is that of a male (Blindheim et al. 1995:130). Blindheim (et al. 1995:130–2) suggested that the skeletons in the graves without coffins could have been thralls. It may be significant that the presumed decapitated thralls in the graves from Lejre and Stengade II both were male (Andersen 1960:26; Skaarup 1976:56–8). For Langeland, it has been suggested that the dominance of male individuals in the graves without coffins is due to the fact that these were thralls' burials, and that the local community was importing male thralls to make up for the considerable number of men who were absent due to Viking activities (Grøn et al. 1994:151). On the other hand, Dan Carlsson suggests in the case of his material from Fröjel that the burials in the southern cemetery – which includes both burials where the dead had been placed face down in the

90   KAUPANG IN SKIRINGSSAL · PART I

Figure 5.14 *Blindheim's drawing of the chamber grave Ka. 270. From Blindheim et al. 1995.*

Figure 5.15 *Chamber graves in Vestfold. Map, Anne Engesveen.*

Cultivated areas

0   10   20 km

grave, and decapitated burials – are actually indicative of this and other similar sites' judicial functions, an interpretation that would seem to fit the situation at Kaupang as well (Carlsson 1999:158). A slightly later parallel, possibly also reflecting judicial authority, is known from the Danish site of Tissø, where two decapitated individuals were buried to the south of the manor site, near a river crossing (Jørgensen 2002:244).

The chamber grave Ka. 270

Ka. 270 from Nordre Bikjholberget was described alternately as a "chamber grave" and a "coffin grave" by Blindheim, with reference to Gräslund's terminology (Blindheim et al. 1995:76, 110–11; cf. Gräslund 1980). Here, we are dealing with a rectangular, c. 2 m x 1.2 pit cut deep into the ground, i.e. c. 1.2 m (Fig. 5.14). This shaft is oriented E.–W. To the north, from the western end of the main pit, there is a rectangular extension, measuring c. 0.8 m x 1.2. Lots of rivets and nails were found at the southern end of the pit; a number of others, although fewer, were noted all over the structure. The nails indicate that the walls of the pit were originally lined with planks, as suggested by Blindheim (et al. 1995:72).

Blindheim did not know of any parallel to this grave-form (et al. 1995:110–11). However, assuming that the description of the grave is accurate, we have an obvious parallel in the material from Nordre Farmen in Hedrum, excavated by Nicolaysen in 1887 (Nicolaysen 1888; cf. Sjøvold 1944:47; Stylegar 2005a).

The latter is an undated grave with a horse skeleton. I would, however, like to suggest an alternative interpretation of Ka. 270.

Viking-age chamber graves have recently been shown to be more common in Norway than previously believed (Stylegar 2005a). Of the 40 or so recognised chamber graves in the Norwegian record, only 16 have been found outside southern Vestfold, i.e. outside the districts bordering on Kaupang (Fig. 5.15). There are 15 in Hedrum alone (op. cit.). This suggests the interesting possibility that Ka. 270 might actually be a chamber grave.

The suggested wooden wall linings (and possible roof construction) support this, as does the size of the cut. Silke Eisenschmidt draws a boundary line between large coffins and chambers at a width of 1.2 m, as in our case (Eisenschmidt 1994). Two features, however, complicate this interpretation. Along the southern end of the grave was a structure interpreted by Blindheim as a separate "chamber", broadly rectangular and measuring 1.8 m x 0.4. It was covered by a wooden structure interpreted by Blindheim as a steering oar (Blindheim et al. 1995:72). Stratigraphically, however, it cannot be ruled out – indeed, it is likely – that this rectangular structure is actually part of the bigger chamber. It seems obvious that a body was placed in this structure with its head towards the west, as attested by the presence of textiles and furnishings. The stratigraphy in this end of the chamber suggests that there was indeed a body lying in a wooden coffin here. Chamber graves with coffins are common in Denmark and northern Germany (Eisenschmidt 1994), but are unknown not only in the large number of chamber graves from Birka, but also from the Norwegian material – with one exception, the grave from Haugen in Rolvsøy, Østfold (Stylegar 2003a:358–61).

In southern Scandinavia, the chamber graves are mostly oriented E.–W. As in our case, the head is placed to the west. In Viking-age inhumation graves in Vestfold, and in areas such as Skåne and Bornholm, the head is usually placed to the north. There is, however, one detail distinguishing the Bikjholberget chamber from the Danish ones. In the latter, the coffins are almost without exception placed in the northern part of the chamber; sometimes in the middle of it. The only other case where the coffin has been placed by the southern chamber wall is the Haugen grave. Thus, we may here have a regional feature of the Oslofjord area.

What about the rectangular extension to the north, then? In Birka, the horses were usually placed on a platform, 1 or 2 feet above the bottom of the grave, and always outside the actual grave chamber. In one case the roof of the chamber extended over the horse. The horse platforms are usually of the same length as the width of the grave: the measurements vary between 1.2 and 2.1 m. There is, however, a number of exceptions where the length of the horse platform exceeds the width of the grave, in some instances substantially so. Horse platforms occur regularly in connection with the chamber graves in Vestfold, and they are always located to the north of the chamber (Stylegar 2005a). At Bikjholberget, horse teeth were indeed found both inside the chamber and in the extension, and what we have here may be an unusual horse platform (cf. Birka graves Bj 560, 946–8: Arbman 1940–1943).

Another interpretation seems more likely, though. The artefacts inside the chamber were found at different levels, indicating disturbance prior to excavation. Furthermore, traces of what could be the gable end of another coffin were observed a short way north of the head-end of the coffin by the southern wall. I would suggest that the "extension" to the north is actually a coffin grave aligned N.–S. that cut into the chamber later.

The grave in Ka. 270 was a lavishly furnished one. A gold thread found where the head was supposed to be, indicating the presence of luxurious textiles (Ingstad 1999:240; cf. Hägg 1984:65). The burial is dated to the early 10th century.

The excavators did not exclude the possibility that there may have been other plank-lined pits that went unnoticed at Bikjholberget (Blindheim et al. 1995: 111). This could, for instance, be the case with Ka. 280 and 281.

Chamber graves seem, along with ship burials, to represent a supra-regional burial ritual of an obviously aristocratic character. That this ritual was reflected in southern Vestfold in the Viking Age should come as no surprise. Hedeby and, to some degree, Birka seem to have been centres for the introduction of the chamber-grave custom in their respective hinterlands. It is credible that Kaupang should have played a similar role in Vestfold.

The boat graves
Altogether 62 burials in 46 different boats have been excavated at Kaupang. This makes Kaupang the largest concentration of boat graves in Scandinavia. These numbers are more or less in agreement with Blindheim et al. 1981. Only one (Ka. 40) of the graves excavated by Nicolaysen, however, qualifies as a boat grave according to Müller-Wille's criteria (1970), according to which a total of 51 boat graves would be identified at Kaupang. The dubious boat graves from Nicolaysen's 1867 campaign are marked as "boat grave?" in the catalogue. Of the 62 certain or possible boat graves, 12 are cremations and 50 inhumations. Most of the boat graves are gendered – 32 male, and 23 female. There are about as many from the 9th century as from the 10th – 22 and 23, respectively; and the relative distribution of the gendered graves is similar to the graves in general. There are eight male graves dating to the 9th century, against thirteen female. In the 10th century the situation is reversed and we have seventeen male graves against only six female.

The boats in the graves at Kaupang were from 4–5 to 12 m long. Wood fibres from five of the boats in southern Bikjholberget show that the vessels were made of oak (Blindheim et al. 1995:95).

Double burials occur in about 7% of the boat graves in Norway (Müller-Wille 1970:78). It is all the more remarkable that 10 of the 46 boats (i.e. more than 21%) at Kaupang contained more than one individual. In four of the cases, three adult individuals had been buried in the same boat (Ka. 294–296, Ka. 298–300, Ka. 257–259, Ka. 285–287). Moreover, Ka. 294 and 298 contained two individuals, one of them an infant in both cases. The only parallels to these graves are a boat grave at Sebbersund, where a 3.8 m long boat contained three buried individuals, other ones at Scar, Orkney and at Olavsklosteret/Tønsberg, Vestfold, also with three individuals, and a further example at Nabberör, Öland, with at least four individuals. The latter dates to the 8th century (Müller-Wille 1970:160). Double burials in boat are Ka. 301–302, Ka. 303–304, Ka. 310–311, Ka. 254–255, Ka. 263–264 and Ka. 265–266.

The boat grave Ka. 307 at southern Bikjholberget is peculiar in that it has a *chamber*. The chamber or coffin was c. 2.8 m long, considerably longer than the wooden coffins from Kaupang. Its width is not recorded. It was erected between two of the ribs of the c. 7 m long boat. Due to the poor state of preservation, nothing is known about the method of construction.

While occurring regularly in ship graves (Tune, Gokstad, Oseberg, Storhaug, Grønhaug, Hedeby and Sutton Hoo), burial chambers are very seldom found in the smaller boat graves. Haakon Shetelig did not list a single example in his 1917 survey (Schetelig 1917:237). Michael Müller-Wille (1970:77) does, however, note three examples from western Norway: at Holmedal (Sogn og Fjordane), and Osnes and Røyrvik (both Møre og Romsdal).

The furnishings – a sword of type M with an hourglass-shaped inlay in the upper part of the blade and a copper-alloy belt buckle, to name but two – date the grave to c. 900. The artefacts were found inside the chamber.

5.7 A horseman and a falconer? Ka. 157

The furnishings in Ka. 157 from Søndre Kaupang included a matching pair of stirrups (Fig 3). While horse equipment is relatively common in Viking-age graves from Norway, especially in the eastern districts, graves with specialised riding equipment, i.e. spurs and stirrups, form a relatively small and distinct group (Braathen 1989; Sørheim 1997). The so-called horseman's graves, of which there are c. 120 in Norway, and many in both Denmark and Sweden, have been dealt with in detail elsewhere, and are often seen as evidence of a particular political and/or military structure, or of specific religious beliefs (Botond 2002; Braathen 1989; Lyngstrøm 1995; Pedersen 1997b; Roesdahl 1983; Simonsson 1969; Wallin 1995; Ziefwert 1992).

The "horizon" of horseman's graves in Scandinavia falls in the 10th century. However, some of the finds from Norway are older. Ka. 157 dates to the first part of the 9th century, as does a grave from Ophus in Vang, Hedmark. Two other finds, from Farmen in Vang, Hedmark, and Særheim in Klepp, Rogaland, both belong to the period 800–900. These early finds could be indicative of influences from the Continent, where horseman's graves are known from the Merovingian period (Braathen 1989; Müller-Wille 1977; Stein 1967).

Ka. 157 is a very richly furnished grave in Kaupang respects. It contained an assorted assemblage of horse equipment, tools, weapons, and furniture. Also, it is one of the possible boat graves from Nicolaysen's 1867 excavations. Besides the stirrups, another object from the grave might point towards the adoption of Continental practices.

The object in question is a small bell made of copper alloy (Fig. 5.16, top). While this bell might be part of the rather lavish horse harness featured in the grave, another interpretation is worth exploring, namely the use of small bronze bells in *hawking*. In Scandinavian contexts, iron bells of various types are known to have been part of the horse equipment (Petersen 1951:56–5). For bells made of copper alloy, however, the interpretation differs – and varies. Small bells or rattles of type R 593 were found in 11 different graves in Birka. In five of these the bells seem to have been associated with the clothes of the deceased (Gräslund 1984:122). Gräslund interprets the bells as resulting from East Baltic influences, but she also mentions parallells from Frisian burial finds (ibid.). Among the Latvian tribes, small bells could be hung from the copper alloy chains attached to the women's costume (Sedov 1982:236). Copper alloy bells of similar types have also been used as part of the horse harness in the Baltic area (Sedov 1982:237; incidentally, a small copper alloy bell of type R 593 in the Borre ship burial seems to have been associated with a horse's head gear).

Reconstructing the original function from grave finds is one thing. Recently, however, small copper alloy bells have been found in settlement contexts in Scandinavia. The finds in question, from Uppåkra and Järrestad, both in Scania, seem to suggest a link between the bells made of copper alloy and hall buildings (af Rosenschöld 2005, who, by the way, interprets these objects as musical instruments). This link points towards some kind of connection between the bells and aristocratic life. One possible connection is found in aristocratic hunting practices.

Some copper alloy bells known from the archaeological record have been interpreted as hawking bells, i.e. bells attached to one foot of a falcon or a hawk used for hunting purposes, and designed to make it easier to find the bird if it is tangled up in a bush etc. during the hunt. For instance, it has been suggested that the small copper alloy bell from the Sutton Hoo ship burial was worn by a falcon or hawk (Carver 1998:136). The bell finds from Fröjel have been discussed in a similar way (Carlsson 2000), while Maria Vretemark (1983) discusses the possible link between small bells and falconry in a more general way.

Nicholas Orme, writing of the education of the medieval English kings and aristocracy, says that hunting came second only to fighting as the most prestigious physical activity (Orme 1984:191, cited after Almond 2003:39). The earliest record of falconry in Anglo-Saxon England was the dispatch by St Boniface of a hawk and two falcons from the Continent to King Æþelbald of Mercia in 745–6. Hawking as a highly developed form of hunting was established in continental Europe around AD 500 already,

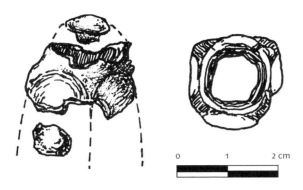

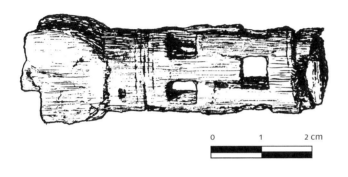

as evidenced by various Germanic laws (Lindner 1973:165–6). It was no different in Viking Age Scandinavia, where written sources record hawking in several instances. Thus, according to Frankish sources, Godfred, the early 9th century king of the Danes, was killed by his own son while out hunting, just as he was about to release his falcon from its prey. According to the Norse sagas, earl Håkon had to pay 100 "marks" of gold and 60 hawks or falcons as tribute to Harald Bluetooth. Olav Tryggvason, on the other hand, is said to have plucked the feathers off his sister's hawk in a fit of fury (Bø 1962:9–11). The latter examples are from the 10th century. By the mid-11th century at the latest hunting falcons were being exported from Norway to England (Oggins 2004: 64–5).

Judging from finds of bones from birds of prey in cremation graves, however, hawking seems to have been practiced in Scandinavia almost as early as on the Continent. Lavishly furnished graves like Vendel III and Valsgärde 6 contains birds of prey, as do at least 14 other Swedish graves, dating from the late 6th to the 10th century (Vretemark 1983; Gräslund 2004; cf. Ljungkvist 2005 for a revised dating of the supposed oldest finds, from Gamla Uppsala). There are also a number of Continental finds of birds of prey in graves. In a cremation grave dating to c. 800 from Hedehusum/Süderende on Föhr, bones from a man,

his dog and his falcon was salvaged (Jankuhn 1960: 36). In a somewhat earlier grave from Staufen in Dillingen, a man had been inhumed along with rich furnishings, including a hawk or a falcon placed at his right hand (Stein 1967:138–9).

Pictorial evidence for hawking in Scandinavia includes the 11th century picture stones from Alstad, Toten (Norway), and Böksta, Uppland (Sweden), both of which show a mounted man with dog(s) and bird(s) of prey. The tapestries from the Oseberg ship burial (dated dendrochronologically to AD 834) also include a scene with a mounted man and two birds of prey, interpreted as either falcons or hawks (Hougen 1940; Åkerström-Hougen 1981; Ingstad 1992:234). The birds' pointed wings suggest that they are indeed falcons.

Thus, hawking as an aristocratic and royal hunting technique is an established fact in the Viking Age (see also Stalsberg 1982; Ambrosiani 2001b). But is the bell in Ka. 157 indicative of hawking? The burial itself is obviously that of a prominent person, and the presence of a hunting falcon or hawk does not seem out of context in this social milieu. The hypothesis is strengthened by the possibility of there being one or more dogs in the grave. The presence of these dogs was suggested by Blindheim and Heyerdahl-Larsen on the basis of a copper alloy swivel rescued from the cremation remains by Nicolaysen (Fig. 5.16, bottom). This swivel seems to be similar to a Danish specimen which is interpreted as a strap distributor from a dog lead (Blindheim et al. 1981:208; cf. Thorvildsen 1957:fig. 34, from Lille Lime, Jutland). This is important, because dogs were used to assist in the hunt in all varieties of hawking and falconry (Oggins 2004:32), as suggested by the grave from Hedehusum, as well. The rest of the falconer's equipment, his gloves and the bird's foot leashes, would have been made of organic material and left no traces in a cremation grave. Even if the presence of dogs (?) and a riding horse in Ka. 157 is not in itself evidence of hawking, it is strongly indicative of hunting, and thus lends credibility to the idea that the copper alloy bell was in fact a foot bell for a hunting bird, and that hawking was the kind of hunting practiced.

5.8 The horseshoe from Ka. 250

A horseshoe was found with the artefacts associated with the double boat grave Ka. 250 from Bikjholberget. Near the shoe was a collection of horse bones. Ka. 250 dates to the 9th century. In the Scandinavian Viking-age assemblage horseshoes are not otherwise known, their function presumably being filled by crampons or frostnails.

In other parts of Europe, however, horseshoes are known in the Viking Age. Both Byzantine and Frankish sources mention shoes for horses in the the 9th and 10th centuries; emperor Leo's Strategicon (886–912), for instance, puts horseshoes together with stirrups among the horsemen's equipment (Steuer 2000:194). The oldest Continental finds are also from the 9th and 10th centuries (Steuer 2000:193). For a long time to come, though, horseshoes were expensive and relatively rare; a source from the 11th century tells that a shod horse at that time was worth twice the amount of an unshod one (Steuer 2000:195)

The shoe from Ka. 250 has a width of 10,4 cm and is 9,6 cm high (Fig. 5.17). It is rounded and broad, and it has a set of shallow calkins. There are three holes to each branch. The holes have separate countersunk slots for the nail-heads, similar to Clark's (1995) types 1 through 3. The shoe is so heavily worn at the toe that the hoof itself would have been eroded.

The Kaupang specimen lacks the wavy edge typical of early medieval shoes. The large rectangular countersunk slots, the generally crude appearance of the shoe, its rounded and broad shape, as well as the wide-webbed but thin metal suggest that the Kaupang shoe is of Clark's type 1 (Clark 1995:85).

British finds confirm a "pre-Conquest" date for this type (Clark 1995:93). Finds from the 10th century and early/mid-11th century are confirmed from a number of sites (Clark 1995:93). A single 9th century specimen has been found in Winchester (Clark 1995:94). Horseshoes of type 1 seem to have persisted in use into the 12th century (Clark 1995:95). The presence of calkins on the Kaupang specimen may indicate a late date (Clark 1995:85).

Thus, the horseshoe from Ka. 250 seems to be of either Late Viking Age or Early Medieval date. The find context, however, is difficult. The artefacts belonging to Ka. 250 were found during construction works, and while the find assemblage was salvaged and brought to the museum in 1947, the detailed find circumstances were not recorded until three years later (Blindheim et al. 1981:217). One cannot rule out the possibility that the horseshoe represents a secondary intrusion.

There are a number of horseshoes presumably associated with grave finds in the museum's collections. All of the associated find assemblages belong to the Viking Age. Most of these finds reached the museum at an early date; in the late 19th century in most cases. With just a few exceptions, the horseshoes are not found in professionally excavated graves. None of these finds are convincing, as the stratigraphy is either unclear in some cases, or the horseshoes are of late, even modern types in others. In the majority of cases only one shoe was salvaged. It was probably for these reasons that Jan Petersen did not include horseshoes in his survey of Viking Age artefacts (Petersen 1951).

One probable cause for a possible later intrusion might be the road that today passes over Bikjholberget on its way from Kaupang to Lamøya. The Lamøya road was most likely built between 1805 and 1811, since it is shown on Broch's 1811 map but not on a six year older map (Blindheim et al. 1981:66, n. 11). But for topographical reasons there was probably a simpler road here long before this, since the sound between Lamøya and the mainland was at its narrowest at this place. In principle, it is not unlikely that a road or a path existed here at some time after the cemetery went out of use. As soon as the sound between Lamøya and the mainland dried up, this would have been the obvious place to cross over to the island.

To sum up, then, it is possible that the horseshoe actually belongs to Ka. 250. But source-critical considerations make it more likely that is represents a secondary intrusion, related to the Lamøya road established at some time after the Bikjholberget cemetery was abandoned.

5.9 A couple and their sorceress? Ka. 294–296

The most spectacular burial arrangement at Kaupang is the triple boat grave Ka. 294–296 from Bikjholberget, where three adult individuals were inhumed in a boat nearly 9 m long (Fig. 5.18). The boat was aligned SW.–NE. In the stem, and with her head facing away from it, lay a woman (Ka. 294). She probably had an infant (or possibly a small animal) at her pelvis. On her northern side was a man with his head close to hers (Ka. 295). Then followed a horse with a bronze-decorated harness, and then a dog. By the dog lay (see below) another woman with her head facing the stern (Ka. 296). Yet another man was lying beneath the boat (Ka. 297). His burial dates to the 9th century, all the others most likely to the early 10th.

The two women's graves in particular were lavishly furnished. Ka. 294 contained, for instance, a pair of gilded oval brooches, a silver arm ring, and a silver ring that seems to have been part of a bead necklace. Silver arm rings or bracelets are commonly found in Middle Viking-age treasure hoards, but are also known from a number of particularly rich women's

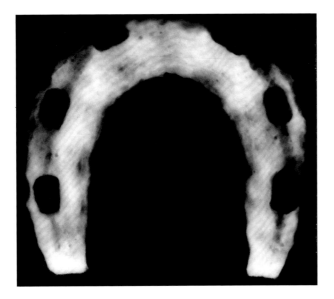

Figure 5.17 *The horseshoe from Ka. 250. The type is early medieval, but the shoe is most likely a later intrusion in the grave. The road to Lamøya, which post-dates the use of Bikjholberget for burials, passed right over this grave. X-ray, KHM.*

Figure 5.18 *Ka. 294–296 during excavation. This four-sided stone setting (left) marked one of the most intriguing graves at Kaupang. Photo, Charlotte Blindheim, KHM.*

graves. There is only one other example from Vestfold: Haugen/Hedrum (C5305–06, 5357–59), but there are a few others from western Norway – in Rogaland, Gausel/Hetland (B4233, S11640) and Bore, Klepp (S8506); in Hordaland, Veka/Voss (B6228); in Sogn og Fjordane, Dale/Fjaler (B5919); and in Møre og Romsdal, Heime-Giske/Giske (B675–683).

The woman in Ka. 296 had been inhumed with a number of peculiar artefacts. Foremost amongst these is an Insular bronze cauldron of Trotzig's group C (Trotzig 1984), with a runic inscription: *i muntlauku* (Liestøl 1953, 1960:189–91). Inside this cauldron were a gilt copper-alloy rod and a "tweezer-shaped" copper-alloy artefact with only one arm, looped (for suspension?) at one end and with three small nails and traces of iron at the other, as well as a copper-alloy ring that might have been used for the suspension of the bowl. Near the bowl was found a small egg-shaped stone. To this find-complex also belongs a spit or, rather, iron *staff* (Price 2002:192, with reference to Bøgh-Andersen 1999:47–8). Ka. 296 also contained two objects usually associated with men's graves: an axehead and a shield-boss.

In their totality, the burials Ka. 294–296 are hard to interpret, but were clearly very special. An interpretation of this grave complex will be suggested here.

The staff in Ka. 296 is of a type suggested by Neil Price (2002) to be a sorceress's staff, and, indeed, there are some indications that the woman in Ka. 296 was a person of special status. It is noteworthy that two of the above-mentioned graves with silver arm ring(s), those at Gausel and Veka, also had an iron staff each. The staff in Ka. 296 lay at the bottom of the boat, under a large stone.

Apart from the inscribed cauldron and the staff, there is the dog. The dog, an adult male specimen, had been butchered and carved; in general, dogs in graves are typically intact, i.e. not butchered (A.S.

Gräslund, pers. comm.). The head was found on top of the bronze cauldron. Only one other grave at Kaupang contain dogs: Ka. 218 on Lamøya (the swivel in Ka. 157 from Søndre Kaupang seems to belong to a dog lead, thus pointing towards the presence of one or more dogs in this grave, as well). There may have been more dogs in the graves at Nordre Kaupang, but since Nicolaysen did not collect bones we will never know. Suffice it to say that dogs are not common in the inhumation graves at Kaupang, and it is significant that one occurs in a grave that is also "special" in several other respects (cf. Gräslund 2004 on dogs in Scandinavian Late Iron-age graves in general).

Fragments of leather(?) found near one of the oval brooches suggest that the woman in Ka. 296 could have been wearing a costume somewhat out of the ordinary. Judging from the position of the preserved parts of the skeleton and the position of the pair of oval brooches in the grave (both of them lying face-down in the boat), she may have been buried sitting up.

Seated burial is one of the characteristics of Price's *völva* graves (2002:127–40). It is known primarily at Birka (Gräslund 1980:37–40), but there are examples from other places in central Sweden, Iceland and Russia, as well as at a number of sites in what is now Norway: Sandvik, Nord-Trøndelag; Tjøtta, Nordland; Hov, Nordland; and possibly Olavsklosteret/Tønsberg, Vestfold (Rygh 1877; Marstrander 1973; Nordman 1989). We have two more possible examples at Kaupang: Ka. 267 and Ka. 284, both gendered female graves.

The deposition of "male" objects in the grave of a woman corresponds to a pattern found in a small number of Scandinavian graves singled out by Price as "special". Most prominent amongst these is the extraordinary double burial of a man and a woman at Klinta, Köpingsvik, Öland (Price 2002:142–9). The couple's bodies had been cremated in a boat, and the

burnt bones of the woman interred along with a number of grave goods, including an iron staff and a bronze bowl as well as a "male" axe.

Could we possibly have here, then, the grave of a sorceress? It seems certain at least that this grave belongs to the same class of burials as those discussed by Price. The woman's seated position, the iron staff, and the transgression of gender roles implied by the presence of a shield-boss and an axehead, strongly suggest that the woman in Ka. 296 was indeed a *völva*.

The bronze bowl

The bronze bowl in this grave has sometimes been placed in a very different context. The runic inscription *i muntlauku* means literally "In (or into) the hand basin" (Fig. 5.19). Aslak Liestøl suggested that the bowl had originally, i.e. in the Insular context, been used for the ritual washing of hands in connection with the Christian mass (1953). He suggests that it had been used as a hand basin in Scandinavia as well (1960:191). This is supported by a later find from Bråtorpsjön in Södermanland, Sweden, of a bronze bowl with the runic inscription *mudlög*, i.e. "hand basin". The latter find is dated to the 12th or 13th century (Voss 1991:200). Egil Mikkelsen has suggested that the Kaupang bowl, together with some other Insular artefacts from Kaupang, are relics from missionary activities in the Oslofjord area emanating from the British Isles in the early 9th century (Mikkelsen 1999).

Be that as it may, the bowl must have been put to a different, non-Christian, use in the local context. It is

of similar type to Bj. 544 from Birka and Ts 8334 from
Borg in Lofoten (Trotzig 1984:230; Munch 2003:244).
Inside the former were found two drinking horns and
a silver rim-mount from a glass bowl, suggesting that
at least this specimen may have been part of a set of
drinking equipment (Trotzig 1984:227–8, who argues
for a wider range of interpretations than Liestøl when
it comes to the functions of the bronze vessels).
Archaeological support for an interpretation along
the lines suggested by Liestøl derives from a woman's
chamber grave at Hørning, Denmark, where a bronze
bowl was found along with a small side-table thought
to be a wash-stand. In another case, from Ballyholm,
Co. Down, Northern Ireland, a woman was buried on
a raised beach near the sea with a pair of oval
brooches and a bronze bowl with wool in it (Bøe
1940:73–5). In a recently excavated woman's grave at
Adwick-le-Street in South Yorkshire, England, plant
tissue and fragments of wood, probably hazel, were
found associated with a bronze basin. In the latter
case, however, the plant remains are thought to be
part of the earth matrix of the burial, rather than the
contents of the basin itself (Speed and Walton Rogers
2004:80). Linen associated with several of the Danish
basins may have served to protect their contents or
the valuable basin itself (Pedersen 1997a:88). In
Norway, Insular bronze vessels are in most cases,

although not exclusively, found in women's graves
(Wamers 1985:113–15).

Both the (ritual) washing, the possible association with drinking, and the fact that these vessels are
usually found in women's graves, suggest a connexion
with the symbolism of the hall, but also (and the two
are not mutually exclusive) with the remedies of a
"cunning woman". The basin could have been used for
the ritual cleansing of the woman or her "patient".
Ritual purposes have been suggested for the presumably antique cauldron deposited in the burial at
Bjerringhøj; in this case that was a deep cauldron
(Iversen and Näsman 1991:59). It is possible that the
runic inscription is a spell, or part of a spell. The
inscription was probably never finished (Liestøl
1960:190).

This interpretation is congruent with some of the
other items in this particular grave, first and foremost
the iron staff. Taken together with the unusual position of the body and the presence of the butchered
dog, this might indeed be the burial of a woman with
a very special status, possibly that of a sorceress (cf.,
e.g., the mid-10th-century "sorceress" in Fyrkat grave
4, also with an iron staff: Price 2002; Roesdahl 1977).

Although precise datings are lacking, all three
graves inside the boat seem to belong to the early 10th
century (cf. Blindheim et al. 1999:142–3). Indeed, it is

Figure 5.19 *The bronze bowl with the runic inscription* i
muntlauku *(drawing) on the inside. Photo and drawing,*
KHM.

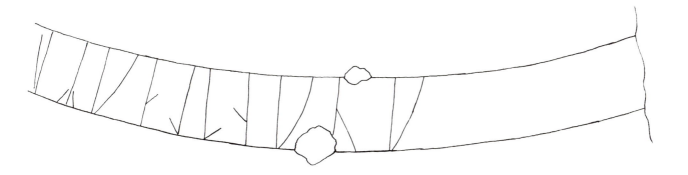

quite possible that all three are more or less contemporary. It is possible that Ka. 294 and Ka. 295 represent a married couple of high social standing, while
the seated woman in the stern is a sorceress with a
particular relationship with the couple, for whom she
had been been performing her services while still
alive – as well as in death, judging from her position
at the rudder, steering the little family towards the
realm of the Dead (Fig. 5.20).

5.10 Concluding remarks – Birka and Kaupang

Even if we have only 204 recorded grave-finds available to study from a total of more than 600 grave
monuments, we can draw some conclusions about
the Kaupang cemeteries. The cemeteries are quite
outstanding in a number of different ways, some of
which have been discussed in this chapter. There are
features that bind the Kaupang graves to southern
Vestfold, and others that do not. I consider it an open
question whether the Kaupang cemeteries to some
extent conform to a southern Vestfold ritual system,
or if, in Tjølling and the neighbouring districts, we
are rather faced with areas *influenced* by Kaupang as
the latter's sphere of influence (compare the role of
Birka in central Sweden in this respect). There are
indeed some peculiarities distinguishing southern
Vestfold from the surrounding areas when it comes to
burial rituals, and this might indicate that the latter is
in fact the case.

There are several cemeteries at Kaupang. While
the picture is clearest at Lamøya, I have suggested that
even the most extensive cemeteries, Bikjholberget
and Nordre Kaupang, might have consisted of lesser,
distinct grave clusters in the 9th century, the early
phase of the settlement, when the first burials took
place there. The growing together of these putative
grave groups is probably due to the growing number
of people being buried at Kaupang in the later part of
the settlement's existence.

As for Christianity, there is nothing particularly
"Christian" about the graves in any cemetery at
Kaupang. In general, I think it is nigh impossible to
identify graves as belonging to converted individuals
unless those graves occur in churchyards or at least in
cemeteries of their own. No such separate cemetery
has been discovered at Kaupang.

The Kaupang cemeteries cover a wide range of the
myriad of rituals that are associated with Viking-age
burial in Scandinavia. Most of these have parallels
elsewhere in the Norse world. The specific mixture of
rituals that leads to boat graves, chamber graves and
coffin graves occuring in the same cemetery at Kaupang, namely at Bikjholberget, is harder to match. But
there are a number of parallels in the coastal regions
of Norway, at cemeteries that this author would interpret as aristocratic: Olavsklosteret/Tønsberg (Nordman 1989); several sites in Hedrum (Stylegar 2005a);
and Gulli/ Tønsberg (Gjerpe 2005c), all in Vestfold,
come to mind, but also, *inter alios,* Revheim/
Stavanger (Sørheim et al. 2004), or the possibly royal
cemetery at Visterflo in Østfold for that matter
(Brøgger 1922; Stylegar 2003b). There are also similarities between these southern Norwegian cemeteries and a number of aristocratic burial grounds in
southern Scandinavia, in particular those in Denmark and northern Germany discussed by Müller-
Wille (1987:69–90).

But is there anywhere else where a considerable
number of aristocratic burial rites occurs in a context
that also includes more "ordinary" types of grave, and
indeed is spread across several distinct cemeteries or
groups of graves? In other words, is there a parallel to
the general pattern that we have at Kaupang, i.e. to
the Kaupang burial complex as a whole (Fig. 5.20)?

Birka is really the obvious answer. Here we have
the same typical mixture of rites: boat graves, chamber graves and coffin graves, as well as quite an even
ratio of cremations and inhumations. The Birka

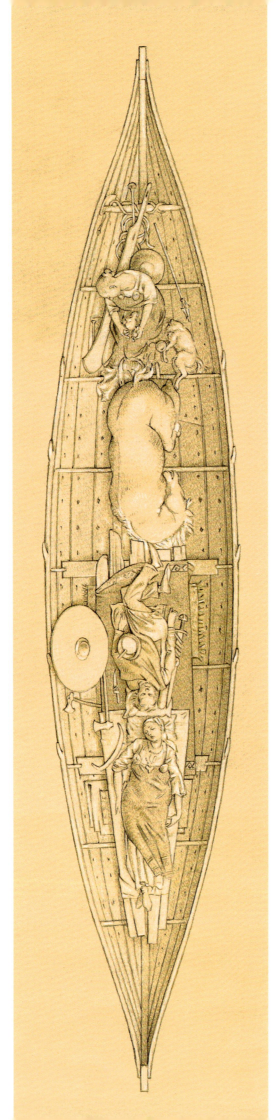

Figure 5.20 *A grave of a special kind: Suggested reconstruction of the boat grave Ka. 294–296. Illustration, Þorhallur Þráinsson.*

Figure 5.21 *Participants at the Viking Congress in Bergen visiting the excavation at Bikjholberget in September 1953. Photo, KHM.*

graves are spread across six separate and at least partly contemporaneous cemeteries. At the major one at Hemlanden, immediately to the north-east of the settlement area, at least 1,600 graves can be seen. Most of these are round barrows, often very substantial ones. Both cremations and inhumations are known from Hemlanden. Most of the inhumations are in the area to the west, while the cremations dominate the remaining, much larger area (Gräslund 1980:5–6). There is also a smaller cemetery immediately to the south of the settlement area, with almost exclusively flat graves, known in the literature as the cemetery north of Borg. This is where many of the chamber and coffin graves are concentrated (Gräslund 1980:5–6; Ambrosiani 1992:18–19).

Of the other Early Viking-age towns in Scandinavia, Hedeby shows a similar complexity to a certain extent (Arents 1992), but Ribe does not (Feveile 2003).

The extent of the cemeteries and the number of graves is of course different between Birka and Kaupang, but there seem to be very clear similarities between Hemlanden and Nordre Kaupang on the one hand and between the cemetery immediately to the south of the settlement area and Bikjholberget on the other – the first two dominated by barrows and cremations, the latter two by different kinds of richly furnished inhumations.

The distribution of burial customs across the Birka cemeteries suggested to Björn Ambrosiani that "different groups of people were buried in different cemeteries" (1992:20, cf. Gräslund 1980:77–8). This is of course a possible interpretation of the situation at Kaupang, too. It is difficult to compare the different cemeteries at Kaupang – the state of excavations is too different to make this a fruitful undertaking. Only Nordre Kaupang and Bikjholberget can really be compared. What is the reason for the differences between the cremation barrow cemetery at Nordre

Kaupang and the flat-grave inhumation cemetery at Bikjholberget? This is of course a question with general implications and interest. It can be put differently. Who was buried at Nordre Kaupang and Bikjholberget, respectively? Were they different categories of people? We really cannot say. In the case of Birka, there have been several attempts to pin down what exactly distinguished the people using either of the cemeteries. Those inhumed in chambers or coffins are alternatively interpreted as craftsmen and merchants who had travelled to the town from afar, or as local people who had converted to Christianity (Ambrosiani 1992:20). Steuer, discussing the early 10th-century chamber graves at Hedeby, attributes them to a leading social stratum, a "Kaufleute-Krieger-Gruppe" (Steuer 1984:360).

The one thing that can be stated with any certainty in this regard, is that this pattern, as found at Nordre Kaupang contra Bikjholberget and Hemlanden, contra the cemetery to the south of the settlement area, must correspond to the ritual reality of Scandinavian towns in the 9th and early 10th centuries. Whether the explanation for it is social, religious, or ethnic remains to be seen.

Comprehensive catalogue
of grave-finds from Kaupang

Abbreviations

Birka I   Arbman 1940–1943
BS   Solberg 1984
Redskaper   Petersen 1951
JP (number)   Petersen 1928
JP type   Petersen 1919
R (number)   Rygh 1885
SK   Skibsted Klæsøe 1999
Valsgärde   Arwidsson 1954

Cat. no.	Museum no.	Location	Name	Monument type	Grave-type	Body treatment
Ka. 1	C4198–4203	N. Kaupang	Nicolaysen's Barrow 47	Barrow	Boat grave?	Cremation
Ka. 2	C4204–4205	N. Kaupang	Nicolaysen's Barrow 109	Barrow		Cremation
Ka. 3	C4206–4215	N. Kaupang	Nicolaysen's Barrow 113	Barrow		Cremation
Ka. 4	C4216–4224	N. Kaupang	Nicolaysen's Barrow 112	Barrow	Boat grave?	Cremation
Ka. 5	C4225	N. Kaupang	Nicolaysen's Barrow 10	Barrow		Cremation
Ka. 6	C4226–4234	N. Kaupang	Nicolaysen's Barrow 90	Barrow		Cremation
Ka. 7	C4235–4236	N. Kaupang	Nicolaysen's Barrow 92	Barrow		Cremation
Ka. 8	C4237–4243	N. Kaupang	Nicolaysen's Barrow 91	Barrow		Cremation
Ka. 9	C4244	N. Kaupang	Nicolaysen's Barrow 84	Barrow		Cremation
Ka. 10	C4245–4251	N. Kaupang	Nicolaysen's Barrow 85	Barrow		Cremation
Ka. 11	C4252–4253	N. Kaupang	Nicolaysen's Barrow 18	Barrow		Cremation
Ka. 12	C4254	N. Kaupang	Nicolaysen's Barrow 19	Barrow	Boat grave?	Cremation
Ka. 13	C4255	N. Kaupang	Nicolaysen's Barrow 26	Barrow		Cremation
Ka. 14	C4256–4259	N. Kaupang	Nicolasyens Haug 94	Barrow		Cremation
Ka. 15	C4260	N. Kaupang	Nicolaysen's Barrow 100	Barrow		Cremation

Finds	Date	Literature
Double-edged sword (JP type M), spearhead (JP type K), axe (JP type H), boss (R562), soapstone vessel, copper alloy ring-pin, hone, textiles, stone, 20 rivets	*900–950* Sword: 825–950 Spearhead: 900–950 Axe: 900–950 Boss: 850–950	Blindheim et al. 1981:200
Sword (JP type M), sword?, axe (JP type E/F)	*850–950* Sword: 825–950 Axe: 850–950	Blindheim et al. 1981:200
2 oval brooches (JP 51), 2 beads (1 cornelian?), iron saucepan, iron frying pan, iron spit?, spindle-whorl, looped hone, 2 sickles, axe (JP type H), horse bit, rivet, iron rod, iron cauldron?, iron rattle	*900–950* Oval brooch: <850–950 Axe: 900–950	Blindheim et al. 1981:200–1
Double-edged sword (JP type N, ULFBEHRT-blade), double-edged sword, spearhead (BS VII.2A), axe (JP type H?), boss (R562), sickle, weight (spherical), weight (cubooctaedric), copper alloy key (symmetric animal style), soapstone vessel, 2 hones, egg-shaped stone, 4 flints, c. 20 rivets	*900–950* Sword: 850–900 Spearhead: 900–950 Axe: 900–950 Boss: 850–950 Weight: 860–>1000 Symmetric animal style: <850–950 Soapstone vessel: 900–1000?	Blindheim et al. 1981:201
Pottery (Slavonic), 1 bolt, 6 rivets	*800–900?* Pottery: 800–900?	Blindheim et al. 1981:201–2
Double-edged sword (JP type X), iron rattle, spearhead (BS VII.2A), axe (JP type H), 3 bosses (R562), copper alloy scales, weight (cubooctaedric), sickle, at least 2 soapstone vessels, several hones, flints, scissors, horse bit, 2 rivets, axe, iron handle attachment, knife?, iron mount, iron plate (from cauldron?), pieces of iron	*900–950* Sword: 900–1050 Spearhead: 900–950 Axe: 900–950 Bosses: 850–950 Soapstone vessel: 900–1000?	Blindheim et al. 1981:202–3
Boss (R562), horse bit, cruciform mount of iron, iron fragments, soapstone vessel, double-edged sword?, arrowhead?, sickle?	*900–950?* Boss: 850–950 Soapstone vessel: 900–1000?	Blindheim et al. 1981:203
Sword (JP type H), spearhead (BS VII.1B), axe, boss (R562), arrowhead (R535?), copper alloy scales, 3 weights (spherical), weight (unknown type), copper alloy ring-pin, copper alloy bell, soapstone vessel, several hones, flints, iron handle, horse bit, knife?, sickle?	*900–950* Sword: 800–950 Spearhead: 900–950 Boss: 850–950 Weight: 860–>1000 Soapstone vessel: 900–1000?	Blindheim et al. 1981:203–4
Pieces of iron frying pan or cauldron, rivet, horse bit, egg-shaped stone, iron socket, pieces of iron		Blindheim et al. 1981:204
2 oval brooches (JP 51), 2 beads (glass), spindle-whorl of soapstone, axe (JP type K), sickle, soapstone vessel, iron sword-beater, horse bit, iron hook, casket handle, iron rod, rectangular iron mount, hone, 2–3 rivets	*900–1000* Oval brooches: <850–950 Axe: 900–1000 Soapstone vessel: 900–1000?	Blindheim et al. 1981:204
Axe (JP type G/H), 2 soapstone vessels, fragmentary iron cauldron, rivets, sickle, scissors	*900–950?* Axe: 850–950 Soapstone vessel: 900–1000?	Blindheim et al. 1981:204
4 rivets		Blindheim et al. 1981:204–5
Sickle, iron rod, 11 rivets, iron rod (tang for arrowhead?), fragmentary iron cauldron, spearhead?		Blindheim et al. 1981:205
Iron sword-beater, iron handle, sherds of pottery (tatinger ware), sherds of pottery, rivets, horse bit, sickle	*800–900?* Pottery: 800–900?	Blindheim et al. 1981:205
Hone, iron rivet		Blindheim et al. 1981:205

Cat. no.	Museum no.	Location	Name	Monument type	Grave-type	Body treatment
Ka. 16	C4261–4265	N. Kaupang	Nicolaysen's Barrow 77	Barrow		Cremation
Ka. 17	C4266	N. Kaupang	Nicolaysen's Barrow 11	Barrow		Cremation
Ka. 18	C4267	N. Kaupang	Nicolaysen's Barrow 57	Barrow		Cremation
Ka. 19	C4268	N. Kaupang	Nicolaysen's Barrow 35	Barrow		Cremation
Ka. 20	C4269	N. Kaupang	Nicolaysen's Barrow 70	Barrow		Cremation
Ka. 21	C4270	N. Kaupang	Nicolaysen's Barrow 69	Barrow	Boat grave?	Cremation
Ka. 22	C4271–4275	N. Kaupang	Nicolaysen's Barrow 60	Barrow		Cremation
Ka. 23		N. Kaupang	Nicolaysen's Barrow 16	Barrow		Cremation
Ka. 24		N. Kaupang	Nicolaysen's Barrow 28	Barrow		Cremation
Ka. 25		N. Kaupang	Nicolaysen's Barrow 32	Barrow		Cremation
Ka. 26		N. Kaupang	Nicolaysen's Barrow 33	Barrow		Cremation
Ka. 27		N. Kaupang	Nicolaysen's Barrow 36	Barrow		Cremation
Ka. 28		N. Kaupang	Nicolaysen's Barrow 41	Barrow		Cremation
Ka. 29		N. Kaupang	Nicolaysen's Barrow 45	Barrow		Cremation
Ka. 30		N. Kaupang	Nicolaysen's Barrow 48	Barrow		Cremation
Ka. 31		N. Kaupang	Nicolaysen's Barrow 52	Barrow		Cremation
Ka. 32		N. Kaupang	Nicolaysen's Barrow 59	Barrow		Cremation
Ka. 33		N. Kaupang	Nicolaysen's Barrow 64	Barrow		Cremation
Ka. 34		N. Kaupang	Nicolaysen's Barrow 83	Barrow		Cremation
Ka. 35		N. Kaupang	Nicolaysen's Barrow 86	Barrow		Cremation
Ka. 36		N. Kaupang	Nicolaysen's Barrow 114	Barrow	Boat grave	Cremation
Ka. 37	K/XXIII, K/XXIVd	N. Kaupang		Barrow?	Boat grave	Cremation
Ka. 38		N. Kaupang	Nicolaysen's Barrow 25	Barrow		
Ka. 39		N. Kaupang	Nicolaysen's Barrow 37	Barrow		

Finds	Date	Literature
2 oval brooches (JP 51), textiles, iron sword-beater, scissors, spindle-whorl of burnt clay, axe (JP type H), sickle, horse bit, (harness) mount	*900–950* Oval brooches: <850–950 Axe: 900–950	Blindheim et al. 1981:205
Fragment of natural stone		Blindheim et al. 1981:206
Rivet, pieces of iron		Blindheim et al. 1981:206
Spearhead (JP type M/K), iron fragment	*900–1000* Spearhead: 900–1000	Blindheim et al. 1981:205
Adze, 2 rivets		Blindheim et al. 1981:206
Fragmentary iron cauldron, arrowhead, 1 or 2 iron socket, iron ring, iron file?, fragmentary iron mount, hone, several rivets		Blindheim et al. 1981:206
Bead (glass), iron sword-beater, soapstone vessel, sickle, horse bit, iron escutcheon , rim mount for iron cauldron?, rivet or bolt, iron fragment, iron brace, spearhead?, spherical stone	*900–1000?* Soapstone vessel: 900–1000?	Blindheim et al. 1981:206–7
Soapstone vessel	*900–1000?* Soapstone vessel: 900–1000?	Ab. 1867:78
Rivets		Ab. 1867:78
Rivet		Ab. 1867:79
2 rivets		Ab. 1867:79
Sword		Ab 1867:79
Iron fragments		Ab. 1867:79
Pottery		Ab. 1867:79
Rivets		Ab. 1867:79
Rivets		Ab. 1867:79
Rivet, iron fragment		Ab. 1867:79
Rivets		Ab. 1867:80
Soapstone vessel	*900–1000?* Soapstone vessel: 900–1000?	Ab. 1867:80
Rivets		Ab. 1867:81
C. 50 rivets		Ab. 1867:86
Double-edged sword (JP type H), adze, iron cauldron, boss (R562), at least 6 arrowheads (5 similar to R539, 1 similar to R535), 2 sickles, 2–3 iron keys, 2 iron hooks, pottery (Tating Ware), pottery (Badorf Ware), mosaic tesserae, 4 beads, hone, iron slag, pieces of iron, rivets, nails, axe (JP type G)	*850–900* Pottery: 800–900? Sword: 800–950 Axe: 850–>900	Blindheim et al. 1981:221–2
Empty barrow		Ab. 1867:78
Empty barrow		Ab. 1867:78

Cat. no.	Museum no.	Location	Name	Monument type	Grave-type	Body treatment
Ka. 40		N. Kaupang	Nicolaysen's Barrow 43	Barrow		
Ka. 41		N. Kaupang	Nicolaysen's Barrow 51	Barrow		
Ka. 42		N. Kaupang	Nicolaysen's Barrow 54	Barrow		
Ka. 43		N. Kaupang	Nicolaysen's Barrow 66	Barrow		
Ka. 44		N. Kaupang	Nicolaysen's Barrow 99	Barrow		
Ka. 45		N. Kaupang	Nicolaysen's Barrow 110	Barrow		
Ka. 46		N. Kaupang	Nicolaysen's Barrow 5	Barrow		
Ka. 47		N. Kaupang	Nicolaysen's Barrow 9	Barrow		
Ka. 48		N. Kaupang	Nicolaysen's Barrow 12	Barrow		
Ka. 49		N. Kaupang	Nicolaysen's Barrow 13	Barrow		
Ka. 50		N. Kaupang	Nicolaysen's Barrow 14	Barrow		
Ka. 51		N. Kaupang	Nicolaysen's Barrow 15	Barrow		
Ka. 52		N. Kaupang	Nicolaysen's Barrow 17	Barrow		
Ka. 53		N. Kaupang	Nicolaysen's Barrow 27	Barrow		
Ka. 54		N. Kaupang	Nicolaysen's Barrow 30	Barrow		
Ka. 55		N. Kaupang	Nicolaysen's Barrow 34	Barrow		
Ka. 56		N. Kaupang	Nicolaysen's Barrow 38	Barrow		
Ka. 57		N. Kaupang	Nicolaysen's Barrow 40	Barrow		
Ka. 58		N. Kaupang	Nicolaysen's Barrow 49	Barrow		
Ka. 59		N. Kaupang	Nicolaysen's Barrow 50	Barrow		
Ka. 60		N. Kaupang	Nicolaysen's Barrow 53	Barrow		
Ka. 61		N. Kaupang	Nicolaysen's Barrow 55	Barrow		
Ka. 62		N. Kaupang	Nicolaysen's Barrow 56	Barrow		
Ka. 63		N. Kaupang	Nicolaysen's Barrow 58	Barrow		
Ka. 64		N. Kaupang	Nicolaysen's Barrow 65	Barrow		
Ka. 65		N. Kaupang	Nicolaysen's Barrow 72	Barrow		
Ka. 66		N. Kaupang	Nicolaysen's Barrow 73	Barrow		

Finds	Date	Literature
Empty barrow		Ab. 1867:78
Empty barrow		Ab. 1867:78
Empty barrow		Ab. 1867:78
Empty barrow		Ab. 1867:78
Empty barrow		Ab. 1867:78
Empty barrow		Ab. 1867:78
Layers or patches of charcoal		Ab. 1867:78
Layers or patches of charcoal		Ab. 1867:78
Layers or patches of charcoal		Ab. 1867:78
Layers or patches of charcoal		Ab. 1867:78
Layers or patches of charcoal		Ab. 1867:78
Layers or patches of charcoal		Ab. 1867:78
Layers or patches of charcoal		Ab. 1867:78
Layers or patches of charcoal		Ab. 1867:78
Layers or patches of charcoal		Ab. 1867:78
Layers or patches of charcoal		Ab. 1867:78
Layers or patches of charcoal		Ab. 1867:78
Layers or patches of charcoal		Ab. 1867:78
Layers or patches of charcoal		Ab. 1867:78
Layers or patches of charcoal		Ab. 1867:78
Layers or patches of charcoal		Ab. 1867:78
Layers or patches of charcoal		Ab. 1867:78
Layers or patches of charcoal		Ab. 1867:78
Layers or patches of charcoal		Ab. 1867:78
Layers or patches of charcoal		Ab. 1867:78
Layers or patches of charcoal		Ab. 1867:78

Cat. no.	Museum no.	Location	Name	Monument type	Grave-type	Body treatment
Ka. 67		N. Kaupang	Nicolaysen's Barrow 74	Barrow		
Ka. 68		N. Kaupang	Nicolaysen's Barrow 75	Barrow		
Ka. 69		N. Kaupang	Nicolaysen's Barrow 76	Barrow		
Ka. 70		N. Kaupang	Nicolaysen's Barrow 93	Barrow		
Ka. 71		N. Kaupang	Nicolaysen's Barrow 105	Barrow		
Ka. 72		N. Kaupang	Nicolaysen's Barrow 106	Barrow		
Ka. 73		N. Kaupang	Nicolaysen's Barrow 115	Barrow		
Ka. 125	C4317	Hagejordet		Barrow		Inhumation?
Ka. 126	K/XXXV	Hagejordet	Nicolaysen's Barrow 1?	Barrow	Boat grave	Cremation
Ka. 127	K/XXXVI	Hagejordet	Nicolaysen's Barrow 2?	Barrow	Boat grave	Cremation
Ka. 128	K/XXIVa	Hagejordet		Casual find		
Ka. 129	K/XXIVb	Hagejordet		Casual find		
Ka. 130	K/XXII	Hagejordet		Flat grave?	Boat grave	Cremation
Ka. 131	C22309a	Hagejordet		Casual find		
Ka. 132	C22309b	Hagejordet		Casual find		
Ka. 133	Lost find	Hagejordet		Casual find		
Ka. 134	C54272	Hagejordet		Casual find		
Ka. 150	C2270–2280 I	S. Kaupang		Barrow		Cremation
Ka. 151	C2270–2280 II					Cremation
Ka. 152		S. Kaupang	Nicolaysen's Barrow 1	Barrow		Cremation
Ka. 153	C4286	S. Kaupang	Nicolaysen's Barrow 2	Barrow		Cremation
Ka. 154	C4287–4288	S. Kaupang	Nicolaysen's Barrow 4	Barrow		Cremation
Ka. 155	C4289–4290	S. Kaupang	Nicolaysen's Barrow 5	Barrow		Cremation

Finds	Date	Literature
Layers or patches of charcoal		Ab. 1867:78
Layers or patches of charcoal		Ab. 1867:78
Layers or patches of charcoal		Ab. 1867:78
Layers or patches of charcoal		Ab. 1867:78
Layers or patches of charcoal		Ab. 1867:78
Layers or patches of charcoal		Ab. 1867:78
Layers or patches of charcoal		Ab. 1867:78
Glass pseudo-cameo inlay, axe	*800–900* Pseudo cameo: 775–825	Blindheim et al. 1981:211–12
Equal-armed silver brooch (unica?), c. 20 beads, copper alloy tweezers, weight (spherical), sheet copper alloy, 3–4 bone combs, iron hinge, rivets, slag	*900–1000* Tweezers: 900–1000 Weight: 860–>1000	Blindheim et al. 1981:222–3
Bead (glass), spherical lead object, knife, iron point, rectangular iron mount, iron fragments, iron strike-a-light?, rivets, nails, slag, cremated animal bone		Blindheim et al. 1981:223
Copper alloy thistle brooch		Blindheim et al. 1981:221–2
Copper alloy arm ring, textiles (wool)	*800–850* Arm ring: 800–850	Blindheim et al. 1981:221–2
2 horse bits, sickle, 2–3 beads (glass), rivets, nails		Blindheim et al. 1981:221
Axe (JP type F)	*900–1000* Axe: 900–1000	Blindheim et al. 1981:215–6
Copper alloy bracelet	*800–850* Arm ring: 800–850	Blindheim et al. 1981:215–6
Rivets		
Iron ring		
Single-edged sword (JP type H), axe (JP type B), boss (type Galgenberg), spearhead (BS V.3)	*800–850* Sword: 800–950 (H) Axe: 700–850 Boss: 650–>800 Spearhead: 750–800	Blindheim et al. 1981:211
Sword (JP type O), copper alloy thistle brooch – symmetric animal style, 2 soapstone vessels (weapon knife?, bead (glass), scythe, adze, hone, rivets, nails, iron file?, piece of iron – these objects derive from either of the two graves)	*900–950* Sword: 875–950 Symmetric animal style: <850–950 Soapstone vessel: 900–1000?	Blindheim et al. 1981:211
Rivets		Ab. 1867:87
Spearhead (JP type K?), arrowhead, 3–4 rivets	*900–950?* Spear: 900–950?	Blindheim et al. 1981:207
Bead (glass), spindle-whorl of stone, rivet		Blindheim et al. 1981:207
Copper alloy key, sherds of pottery (Rhinish)		Blindheim et al. 1981:207

Cat. no.	Museum no.	Location	Name	Monument type	Grave-type	Body treatment
Ka. 156	C4291–4292	S. Kaupang	Nicolaysen's Barrow 7	Barrow		Cremation
Ka. 157	C4293–4315	S. Kaupang	Nicolaysen's Barrow 6	Barrow	Boat grave?	Cremation
Ka. 158		S. Kaupang	Nicolaysen's Barrow 8	Barrow		Cremation
Ka. 159		S. Kaupang	Nicolaysen's Barrow 9	Barrow		Cremation
Ka. 160	C15214–15218	S. Kaupang		Barrow	Boat grave	Cremation
Ka. 161	C15219	S. Kaupang		Barrow		
Ka. 162		S. Kaupang		Barrow		
Ka. 163		S. Kaupang		Barrow		
Ka. 164		S. Kaupang		Barrow		
Ka. 165	C33255	S. Kaupang		Barrow (the object may or may not derive from Ka. 163 or Ka. 164)		
Ka. 166	Lost find	S. Kaupang		Flat grave?		Cremation
Ka. 167	Lost find	S. Kaupang	Kristensen's A390	Barrow		
Ka. 200	C5508–5509	Lamøya		Flat grave?		
Ka. 201	C15010–15011	Lamøya		Flat grave		Cremation
Ka. 202	C17719–17722	Lamøya		Flat grave		Cremation
Ka. 203	C21843, 21960	Lamøya	Gustafson's Barrow 1	Barrow	Boat grave	Inhumation
Ka. 204	C21960 I				Boat grave (with cremated animal bones)	Cremation

Finds	Date	Literature
Iron forging hammer, hone, rivets, sword?		Blindheim et al. 1981:207
Double-edged sword (JP type H, ULFBEHRT-blade), spearhead (BS VI.3A), axe (JP type D), boss, 2 arrowheads (1 similar to R540?, 1 similar to R545), iron rattle (R462), 2 stirrups, copper alloy horse bit, copper alloy swivel (from a dog lead?), copper alloy bell, copper alloy button from a horse harness?, copper alloy animal head from a horse harness?, sickle, 2 knives, iron rasp, iron spoon auger, iron tool (indeterminable type), 2 iron hasps for a chest (Oseberg type), fragmentary iron mount for a chest (Oseberg type), 2 pieces of sheet iron, iron lock spring, iron rod, iron key?, iron mount, iron hinge, iron clamp, fragmentary iron cauldron, at least 12 rivets, object of whalebone (cord tightener?), hone, ornated iron mount (from a sword scabbard?), 4 curved iron pieces, iron ring with clamp, scythe?, 2 fishing hooks?, spearhead, fragmentary shield-grip?, iron handle, iron rod, several iron pieces	*800–850* Sword: 800–950 Spearhead: 800–900 Axe: 800–850 Rattle: 800–>900	Blindheim et al. 1981:207–9
Rivets		Ab. 1867:90
Rivets		Ab. 1867:90
Double-edged sword, knife, strike-a-light with copper alloy mount (symmetric animal style), sickle, hasp, key, fragmentary iron cauldron, lock mount, mount for chest (type Oseberg), handle for iron cauldron, scutcheon, key?, hook-shaped iron object, iron bolt, rivets	*850–950* Symmetric animal style: <850–950	Blindheim et al. 1981:212
Fragments of 1 or 2 oval brooches (JP 37)	*800–850* Oval brooches: 800–850	Blindheim et al. 1981:212
Empty barrow		Ab. 1890:78
Indeterminable iron objects, rivets		Ab. 1890:78
Indeterminable iron objects, rivets		Ab. 1890:78
Axe (JP type H)	*900–950* Axe: 900–950	Blindheim et al. 1981:220
Scissors		Blindheim et al. 1981:66
Iron fragments, soapstone fragments, hone		Kristensen 2005:24
Soapstone vessel, spearhead?, flint?	*900–1000?* Soapstone vessel: 900–1000?	Blindheim et al. 1981:212
Double-edged sword (JP type Q), soapstone vessel	*900–1000* Sword: 900–1000 Soapstone vessel: 900–1000?	Blindheim et al. 1981:212
Spearhead (BS VII.2B), axe (JP type G), axe (JP type E), soapstone vessel, rivet	*900–950* Spearhead: 900–1000 Axes: 850–>900	Blindheim et al. 1981:212
2 oval brooches (JP 42), textiles (wool), Equal-armed silver brooch, strike-a-light, Thor's hammer?, strap buckle, scutcheon, knife, rivets, nails, fishing hook, 8 beads (7 glass, 1 cornelian)	*800–900* Equal-armed brooch: 750–850? Oval brooches: 825–850	Blindheim et al. 1981:213
Spearhead (JP type B/C), 2 arrowheads (1 similar to R539), knife, iron spoon-auger, sickle, scissors?, file, iron fragments, arrowhead?, handle attachment for wooden bucket, iron hook, arrowhead?, sherds of pottery, 4 beads (glass), stave from wooden bucket, fragmentary oak keel-plank from a boat, c. 240 rivets, 2 oval hammer-stones, flint nodule, iron fragments	*800–900* Spearhead: 800–950 Stratigraphy: predating Ka. 203	Blindheim et al. 1981:214–5

Cat. no.	Museum no.	Location	Name	Monument type	Grave-type	Body treatment
Ka. 205	C21960 II	Lamøya	Gustafson's Barrow 2	Barrow		Cremation
Ka. 206	C27148	Lamøya		Flat grave?		Inhumation?
Ka. 207		Lamøya		Flat grave		
Ka. 208	C27220 (Grave I)	Lamøya		Flat grave		Inhumation?
Ka. 209	C27220 (Grave II)	Lamøya		Flat grave		
Ka. 210	C27220 (Grave III)	Lamøya		Flat grave		Inhumation?
Ka. 211	C31482	Lamøya		Casual find		
Ka. 212		Lamøya		Casual find		
Ka. 213		Lamøya		Casual find		
Ka. 214		Lamøya		Casual find		
Ka. 215		Lamøya		Casual find		
Ka. 216	K/XXVIII	Lamøya		Casual find		
Ka. 217	K/XXXIX	Lamøya	Gyrihaugen	Barrow		
Ka. 218	K/X	Lamøya	Dortehaugen	Barrow		Inhumation?
Ka. 219	K/XXVII	Lamøya		Flat grave		Inhumation
Ka. 220	Lost find	Lamøya		Casual find		
Ka. 221	C54296/1	Lamøya		Casual find		
Ka. 222	C54290/1	Lamøya		Casual find		
Ka. 223	Lost find	Lamøya		Casual find		
Ka. 224	Lost find	Lamøya		Casual find		
Ka. 225	C54290/2	Lamøya		Casual find		
Ka. 226	C54290/3	Lamøya		Casual find		
Ka. 227		Lamøya		Casual find		
Ka. 228	C54292/1	Lamøya		Casual find		

Finds	Date	Literature
Piece of iron, horse bit, rivets, glass stave, 5 beads		Blindheim et al. 1981:215
Soapstone vessel, 3 beads (3 glass), iron cauldron	*900–1000?* Soapstone vessel: 900–1000?	Blindheim et al. 1981:216
Lost find: Sword, 2 axes, several "brooches", 3 hones		Blindheim et al. 1981:65
Sword (JP type H), sword, axe (JP type E), axe (JP type F), boss (R562), copper alloy penannular brooch (symmetric animal style), 2 hones	*900–950* Sword: 800–950 Axe: 850–> 900 (E) Axe: 900–1000 (F) Boss: 850–950 Symmetric animal style: før 850–950	Blindheim et al. 1981:216
Axe (JP type G/H)	*850–950* Axe. 850–950	Blindheim et al. 1981:216
2 oval brooches (JP 37), textiles (linen, wool), horse-shaped copper alloy brooch (assymetric animal style), copper alloy needle case	*800–850* Oval brooches: 800–850 Assymetric animal style: 775–850	Blindheim et al. 1981:216
Axe (JP type L/M), textiles	*950–>1000* Axe: 950–>1000	Blindheim et al. 1981:220
Soapstone vessel	*900–1000?* Soapstone vessel: 900–1000?	Grieg 1943:483
Spearhead		Grieg 1943:483
Sword, spearhead, 2 axes, soapstone vessel	*900–1000?* Soapstone vessel: 900–1000?	Grieg 1943:483
Soapstone vessel, rivets	*900–1000?* Soapstone vessel: 900–1000?	Grieg 1943:483
Sword (JP type H)	*800–950* Sword: 800–950	Blindheim et al. 1981:222
Empty barrow		Blindheim et al. 1995:51–3
Jet ring, bead (glass), bone gaming-piece, spindle-whorl, iron needle, sickle-shaped cutting tool, tongue-shaped strike-a-light (symmetric animal style – Birka I, Taf. 145:6), 2 iron rings, rivet, clamp, hook, wooden remains of floorboard, dog rib, c. 180 rivets	*<850–900?* Tongue-shaped strike-a-light: 800–900? Symmetric animal style: <850–950	Blindheim et al. 1995:51–2
2 oval brooches (JP 51), cruciform Insular copper alloy mount, 8 beads (glass), soapstone vessel, iron frying pan (R430), iron key (R459), sickle, small iron ball, one or more knives, rivet, undeterminable iron fragments, iron slag, wooden cask, textiles (linen, wool)	*<850–950* Oval brooches: <850–950	Blindheim et al. 1995:52–3
Sword		
Insular mount		
Silver dirham		
Soapstone vessel		Kristensen 2005:61
Sword		Kristensen 2005:60
Sword		Kristensen 2005:61
Sword		Kristensen 2005:61
3 beads (glass)		Kristensen 2005:62
Sword		

Cat. no.	Museum no.	Location	Name	Monument type	Grave-type	Body treatment
Ka. 229		Lamøya		Lost find from barrow		
Ka. 230		Lamøya	Gustafson's Barrow 3	Barrow		
Ka. 250	C27740A, K/XXIVe-g?	Bikjholberget		Flat grave	Boat grave, double grave	Inhumation
Ka. 251	C27740B	Bikjholberget		Flat grave	Boat grave	
Ka. 252	C27997 grave A	Bikjholberget		Flat grave	Boat grave	Inhumation?
Ka. 253	C27997 grave B	Bikjholberget		Flat grave	Boat grave	Inhumation
Ka. 254	C27997 grave C	Bikjholberget		Flat grave	Boat grave	Inhumation
Ka. 255	K/1950 grave I				Boat grave, possibly in same boat as Ka. 254	Inhumation
Ka. 256	K/1950 grave II	Bikjholberget		Flat grave	Boat grave?	Inhumation?
Ka. 257	K/1950 grave III	Bikjholberget		Flat grave	Boat grave?	Inhumation
Ka. 258	K/1950 grave IV				Boat grave?	Inhumation
Ka. 259	K/1950 grave V				Boat grave? Probably in same boat as Ka. 257–258	Inhumation
Ka. 260	K/1950 grave VI	Bikjholberget		Flat grave	?	Inhumation?
Ka. 261	K/1950 grave VII	Bikjholberget		Flat grave	?	Inhumation?
Ka. 262	K/1952 grave I	Bikjholberget		Flat grave,	Boat grave, double grave (infant)	Inhumation

Finds	Date	Literature
Rivets, etc.		Blindheim et al. 1981:63
Rivets, etc.		Blindheim et al. 1981:63
2 oval brooches (JP 37), textiles (wool, linen?), Equal-armed brooch (assymetric animal style), Insular strap buckle with copper alloy mount, double-edged sword, spearhead, scythe, spindle-whorl of soapstone, horseshoe (Clark 1995 type 1?, probably later intrusion), c. 160 rivets, scissors, knife, iron key, animal bone (*equus*) (copper alloy key), (hone), (copper alloy trefoil brooch – SK type 1)	*800–900* Strap buckle: 850–900? Oval brooches: 800–850 Assymetric animal style: 775–850 Trefoil brooch: 750–825	Blindheim et al. 1981:216–7
Oval brooch (JP 37)	*800–850* Oval brooch: 800–850	Blindheim et al. 1981:217
Double-edged sword (JP type X), sword?, spearhead (BS VII.2C), axe (JP type E), boss (R 562), 8 arrowheads, knife, knife?, sickle?, strike-a-light, scissors, knife, knife, lock, 2 knives?, fishing hook, pieces of iron, soapstone sinker, 5 beads (4 glass, 1 amber), 7 flints pieces of coal blend, c. 135 nails and rivets, animal teeth (*equus*), soapstone vessel	*900–950* Sword: 900–1050 Spearhead: 900–1000 Boss: 850–950	Blindheim et al. 1981:217–8
2 oval brooches (JP 37), oval brooch (JP 27), textiles (wool), iron sword-beater, soapstone vessel, boss (R562), arrowhead (R540?), soapstone vessel, hone, rivets, (Insular mount of gilt copper alloy?)	*800–900* Oval brooches: 800–850 (JP 37) Oval brooch: 775–825 (JP 27) Boss: 850–950	Blindheim et al. 1981:219
2 oval brooches (JP 37), copper alloy equal-armed brooch (SK type 3), copper alloy rectangular brooch (symmetric animal style), 4 copper alloy arm rings (bracelets) (3 JP 185, 1 R 709), copper alloy chain from necklace, copper alloy spiral from necklace, copper alloy cord, textiles (wool), copper alloyring, 18 beads (13 glass, 4 amber, 1 silver), sickle, arrowhead?, knife	*800–850* Arm rings: 800–850 Oval brooches: 800–850 Symmetric animal style: <850–950 Equal-armed brooch: 875–950	Blindheim et al. 1981:219
Double-edged sword (JP type H), spearhead, iron sword-beater?, boss (R564), iron handle, boss?	*800–850* Sword: 800–950 Boss: 800–850	Blindheim et al. 1995:61
Double-edged sword (JP type M), spearhead (BS VII.2B), Kesselgabel (Valsgärde 8 Taf. 31 nr 556), boss (R562), boss?, crampon?, hone	*900–950* Sword: 825–950 Spearhead: 900–1000 Boss: 850–950	Blindheim et al. 1995:61–2
Double-edged sword (JP type H), spearhead (BS VII.2C), boss (R562), knife/arrowhead, 2 scissors, lock with scutcheon, iron hinge, looped needle case, tweezers, strike-a-light (R462), needle hone, sword?, spearhead?, scythe	*900–950* Sword: 800–950 Spearhead: 900–1000 Boss: 850–950 Tweezers: 900–1000	Blindheim et al. 1995:62–3
Sword (JP type E), spearhead (BS VII.2B)	*900–1000* Sword: 800–tall Spearhead: 900–1000	Blindheim et al. 1995:63–4
Copper alloy coin brooch, copper alloy fragments (oval brooch?), knife (Redskaper fig. 110), needle hone, iron cauldron/bowl (Redskaper fig. 198), soapstone vessel (R729), sickle, textiles (wool)	*900–1000?* Soapstone vessel: 900–1000?	Blindheim et al. 1995:63
Sword (JP type X), (knife?), (fishing hook?)	*900–1000* Sword: 900–1050	Blindheim et al. 1995:64
Axe (JP type D/E), boss (R562), tang, cork, iron fragments	*850–950* Axe: 800–>900 Boss: 850–950	Blindheim et al. 1995:64–5
Double-edged sword (JP type M), axe (JP type K), knife, boss, leather purse?, rivets, weight?	*900–950* Sword: 825–950 Axe: 900–1000	Blindheim et al. 1995:66–7

Cat. no.	Museum no.	Location	Name	Monument type	Grave-type	Body treatment
Ka. 263	K/1952 grave II	Bikjholberget		Flat grave	Boat grave	
Ka. 264	K/1954 grave IV				Boat grave, possibly in same boat as Ka. 263	
Ka. 265	K/1953 grave I	Bikjholberget		Flat grave	Boat grave	Inhumation
Ka. 266	K/1953 grave VIII				Boat grave, possibly in same boat as Ka. 265	Inhumation
Ka. 267	K/1953 grave II	Bikjholberget		Flat grave	Boat grave, seated burial?	Inhumation
Ka. 268	K/1953 grave III	Bikjholberget		Flat grave	Boat grave	Inhumation
Ka. 269	K/1953 grave IV	Bikjholberget		Flat grave	Log coffin	Inhumation
Ka. 270	K/1953 grave V	Bikjholberget		Flat grave	Chamber with coffin?	Inhumation
Ka. 271					Wooden coffin?	Inhumation
Ka. 272	K/1953 grave VI	Bikjholberget	Constantia	Flat grave	Boat grave	Inhumation
Ka. 273	K/1953 grave VII	Bikjholberget		Flat grave	Boat grave?	Inhumation?
Ka. 274		Bikjholberget		Flat grave	Grave without coffin	Inhumation
Ka. 275		Bikjholberget		Flat grave	Grave without coffin	Inhumation
Ka. 276		Bikjholberget		Flat grave	Grave without coffin	Inhumation
Ka. 277	K/1954 grave I	Bikjholberget	Felt Veien, Albertina	Flat grave	Boat grave	Inhumation
Ka. 278	K/1954 grave II	Bikjholberget	Felt Veien	Flat grave	Log coffin	Inhumation

Finds	Date	Literature
Sword (JP type L), (spearhead – JP type K?), (axe?), (2 beads?)	*900–950* Sword: 850–950 Spearhead: 900–950	Blindheim et al. 1995:67
Sword (JP type H), spearhead (JP type E?), axe (JP type G/H), knife, sickle, mount for casket?, strike-a-light, copper alloy ring-pin, 2 small Insular copper alloy objects (manuscript turners?), copper alloy button, ornament of copper alloy or silver, 3 pieces of silver (Hacksilver?), 2 tongue-shaped mounts of sheet copper alloy (strap ends?), 2 soapstone vessels, (axe – JP type A?), (forging hammer?), (needle hone?)	*800–900* Spearhead: 800–900 Axe (G/H): 850–950 Axe (A): 700–850 Sword: 800–950	Blindheim et al. 1995:79
2 oval brooches (JP 37), 2 beads (rock chrystal), spindle-whorl, knife, slag?, iron fragment?, textiles (wool, linen)	*800–850* Oval brooches: 800–850	Blindheim et al. 1995:67–8
Sword (JP type H)	*800–950* Sword: 800–950	Blindheim et al. 1995:74
2 oval brooches (JP 37), feathers/down, Equal-armed brooch (SK type 1), 10 beads (glass), 37 rivets, textiles (wool)	*800–850* Oval brooches: 800–850 Equal-armed brooch: 800–850	Blindheim et al. 1995:68–9
2 oval brooches (JP 37), copper alloy rectangular strap buckle, rectangular Insular book mount of copper alloy, copper alloy needle, 19 beads (glass), spindle-whorl, 2 knives, 14 rivets, textiles (wool)	*800–850* Oval brooches: 800–850	Blindheim et al. 1995:69–70
Axe (JP type A), knife, pottery, 4 nails	*800–850?* Axe: 700–850	Blindheim et al. 1995:70
Sword (JP type M), axe (JP type G/H), sickle/scythe, hone, brooch, 4 beads (glass), spearhead (JP type K?), hone, bolt, lock mount, knife, hand-made pottery (North-sea type), rivets, smoothing stone?, textiles (gold thread), animal teeth *(equus)*, (trefoil brooch – SK 3)	*900–950* Sword: 825–950 Axe: 850–950 Spearhead: 900–950 Trefoil brooch: <850–>900	Blindheim et al. 1995:70–2
Axe (JP type H), knife (Redskaper fig. 104), knife, animal teeth *(equus)*	*900–950* Axe: 900–950	
Axe (JP type G), knife (Redskaper fig. 107?), oval brooch?, fragment of pottery, needle hone, bead (glass), penannular copper alloy brooch (JP 231), tongue-shaped strike-a-light with copper alloy mount (JP 146/147 – symmetric animal style)	*850–900?* Axe: 850–>900 Tongue-shaped strike-a-light: 800–900? Symmetric animal style: <850–950	Blindheim et al. 1995:72–3
Sword (JP type H)	*800–950* Sword: 800–950	Blindheim et al. 1995:73–4
Skeleton		Blindheim et al. 1995:74
Skeleton		Blindheim et al. 1995:75, nr 1
Skeleton		Blindheim et al. 1995:75, nr 2
Sword (JP type M), spearhead (JP type E?), boss (R563), knife (Redskaper fig. 107), spearhead, sickle, Penannular iron brooch, clamp, rivets, soapstone vessel (R724), glass sherd (from beaker?), rivets and nails	*950–1000* Sword: 825–950 Spearhead: 800–900 Boss: >950	Blindheim et al. 1995:76–7
Sword (JP type M), spearhead, axe (JP type G), knife (Redskaper fig. 106), penannular copper alloy brooch (Birka I Taf. 52, 3, 5 and 6), hone	*850–950* Sword: 825–950 Axe: 850–>900	Blindheim et al. 1995:77–8

Cat. no.	Museum no.	Location	Name	Monument type	Grave-type	Body treatment
Ka. 279	K/1954 grave III	Bikjholberget	Felt Fjellet	Flat grave	Boat grave	Inhumation
Ka. 280	K/1954 grave V	Bikjholberget	Felt Veien	Flat grave	Chamber grave?	Inhumation
Ka. 281	K/1954 grave VI				Chamber grave? Ka. 280 and 281 may or may not consitute one grave	Inhumation
Ka. 282	K/1954 grave VII	Bikjholberget	Felt Veien	Flat grave	Boat grave	Inhumation
Ka. 283	K/1954 grave VIII	Bikjholberget	Felt Fjellet	Flat grave	Boat grave	Inhumation
Ka. 284	K/1954 grave IX	Bikjholberget	Felt Fjellet	Flat grave	Boat grave, seated burial?	Inhumation
Ka. 285	K/1954 grave X	Bikjholberget	Felt Fjellet	Flat grave	Boat grave	Inhumation
Ka. 286	K/1954 grave XI				Boat grave	Inhumation
Ka. 287	K/1954 grave XII				Boat grave	Inhumation
Ka. 288	K/1954 grave XIII	Bikjholberget	Felt Veien	Flat grave	?	
Ka. 289		Bikjholberget	Felt Veien	Flat grave	Boat grave, heavily disturbed	Inhumation
Ka. 290	K/I	Bikjholberget	Maihaugen	Barrow	Stone cist	Inhumation
Ka. 291	K/II	Bikjholberget	Kosmos	Flat grave	Boat grave	Inhumation
Ka. 292	K/III grave I	Bikjholberget	Ormen Lange	Barrow	Boat grave	Inhumation
Ka. 293	K/III grave II	Bikjholberget	Ormen Lange	Lower than grave I, below the boat		Inhumation

Finds	Date	Literature
Sword (JP type O), spearhead (BS VII.2C), boss (R562), knife, copper alloy buckle-tongue (Birka I fig. 458), hone, flint, 2 long nails, rivets, bead (glass), indeterminable iron pieces	*900–950* Sword: 875–950 Spearhead: 900–1000 Boss: 850–950	Blindheim et al. 1995:78–9
Cruciform silver pendant, 7 beads (5 glass, 2 amber), knife, arrowhead, iron object, silver coin?	*900–1000?* Silver pendant: 900–1000?	Blindheim et al. 1995:81
Axe (JP type K?), scythe, knife (Redskaper fig. 107), handle, flint, 2 beads (1 glass), needle hone, soapstone vessel (R729), mount for a casket, hone, rivets and nails	*900–1000?* Axe: 900–1000? Soapstone vessel: 900–1000?	Blindheim et al. 1995:81
Spearhead, axe (JP type I), knife (Redskaper fig. 107), crampon (Birka I Taf. 39, 1–2), 2 mounts shaped like miniatyre axes, hook, flint, hook and mount for casket, spindle-whorl (Redskaper fig. 164), lock (Birka I Taf. 273, 1a-c), burnt wood, 2 beads (1 glass, 1 rock chrystal), 2 weight (spherical), rivets, (knife?), (bone spindle-whorl?), (soapstone spindle-whorl?)	*900–1000* Axe: 900–1000 Weight: 860–>1000	Blindheim et al. 1995:82
Oval brooch (JP 51), oval brooch (Berdal), oval brooch (Style III/E), copper alloy drinking horn mount, soapstone vessel, loom weight, textiles (wool)	*850–950?* Blindheim: 900–950 Oval brooch: <850–950 (JP 51) Oval brooch: 775–850 (Berdal) Oval brooch: 750–800 (style III/E) Soapstone vessel: 900–1000?	Blindheim et al. 1995:82–3
2 oval brooches (JP 51), axe (JP type K), axe (JP type K), knife (Redskaper fig. 104?), spindle-whorl, 3 beads (1 glass, 2 amber), spindle-whorl, fragmentary glass beaker, textiles, animal teeth *(equus)*	*900–950* Oval brooches: <850–950 Axe: 900–1000	Blindheim et al. 1995:83
2 oval brooches (JP 51), axe (JP type H), iron cauldron (R731), soapstone vessel (R729), key (Birka I Taf. 270 2Bg3), small ring, mount from casket, knife, scissors, needle hone, soapstone vessel, knife, knife, handle, knife, indeterminable piece of iron, 2 beads (glass), spindle-whorl of amber, mount, heckle?, textiles (wool)	*900–950* Oval brooches: <850–950 Axe: 900–950	Blindheim et al. 1995:83–4
2 oval brooches (JP 37), trefoil brooch (symmetric animal style), trefoil brooch (SK type 3), 2 beads (1 cornelian, 1 amber), belt buckle (Redskaper fig. 272), belt buckle, 2 hones, 3 soapstone fragments, rivet, textiles (wool)	*850–900* Oval brooches: 800–850 Trefoil brooch: <850–>900	Blindheim et al. 1995:85
Spearhead (JP type E?), axe (JP type D), 2 iron gaffs (Redskaper fig. 152), knife, knife, lead sinker (Redskaper fig. 146), hone, bead (amber or cornelian), soapstone vessel, (sword JP type H possibly from this grave)	*800–850* Spearhead: 800–900 Axe: 800–850	Blindheim et al. 1995:85–6
Rivets		Blindheim et al. 1995:96
Skeleton		Blindheim et al. 1995:77
Hand-made pottery (North sea type), arrowhead (Birka I, Taf. 10:5), iron tool, socket for arrowhead/javelin, rivet, nails, 2 iron rods, piece of amber, flint	*800–900?* Pottery: 800–900?	Blindheim et al. 1995:18–19
Oval brooch, textiles (wool), trefoil brooch (SK type 3), sickle, knife, 2 keys (R459), iron mount, 2 animal teeth *(equus)*, c. 240 rivets and nails	*c. 900?* Trefoil brooch: c. 900	Blindheim et al. 1995:19–21
2 spearheads (JP type K), axe (JP type F), boss (R562), sickle (R358), knife (Redskaper fig. 107), plane tool, 2 iron awls (?), scraper tool of iron, iron shaft, iron handle for wooden bucket, soapstone vessel (R729), iron fragments, 2 hones, bead (glass), piece of clay, flint, pottery sherds	*900–950* Spearhead: 900–950 Axe: 900–tall Boss: 850–950	Blindheim et al. 1995:21–2
Spearhead (Stein 1967 Taf. 60, nr 5), 4 arrowheads (R540), knife (Redskaper fig. 105), lead capsule (reliquary?), copper alloy belt buckle (Birka I, Taf. 86, nr 15), c. 500 rivets and nails, 3 iron brackets, horse skeleton	*c. 800?* Spearhead: 700–800	Blindheim et al. 1995:21–2

Cat. no.	Museum no.	Location	Name	Monument type	Grave-type	Body treatment
Ka. 294	K/IV grave I	Bikjholberget	Forargelsens Hus	Flat grave/four-sided stone setting	Boat grave, double grave (infant)	Inhumation
Ka. 295	K/IV grave II				Boat grave	Inhumation
Ka. 296	K/IV grave III				Boat grave, seated burial?	Inhumation
Ka. 297	K/IV grave IV	Bikjholberget	Forargelsens Hus	Below the boat		Inhumation
Ka. 298	K/V grave I	Bikjholberget	Forargelsens Hus II	Flat grave	Boat grave, double grave (child)	Inhumation
Ka. 299	K/V grave II				Boat grave	Inhumation
Ka. 300	K/V grave III				Boat grave	Inhumation
Ka. 301	K/VI grave I	Bikjholberget	Najaden	Flat grave	Boat grave	Inhumation
Ka. 302	K/VI grave II				Boat grave	Inhumation
Ka. 303	K/VII grave I	Bikjholberget	Rosshavet	Flat grave	Boat grave	Inhumation
Ka. 304	K/VII grave II				Boat grave	Inhumation

Finds	Date	Literature
2 gilded oval brooches (JP 51), textiles (wool), trefoil brooch (JP 98 – symmetric animal style), silver ring, 29 beads (glass), silver bracelet, iron handle (Birka I, Taf. 212, fig. 7), 2 iron rods, iron sword-beater, key (Redskaper fig. 257–58), knife, ring (horse bit?), animal teeth	900–950 Oval brooches: <850–950 Trefoil brooch: <850–>900	Blindheim et al. 1995:22–4
Sword (JP type X), axe (JP type K), axe (JP type B), javelin/arrowhead, at least 4 arrowheads (R539), boss (R562), scythe (R386?), iron frying pan/saucepan, soapstone vessel (Redskaper fig. 191), arrowhead, hone, iron object (horse-/dog collar?), 2 spindle-whorls, pottery, 3 beads (glass), 2 knives, 2 nails, rivet, horse skeleton: strap end, strap plate, plate with pin through, 32 small copper alloy coated iron rivets, horse bit (R566)	900–1000? Sword: 900–1050 Axe: 900–1000 (K) Axe: 700–850 (B) Boss: 850–950	Blindheim et al. 1995:22–4
2 oval brooches (JP 51), copper alloy basin with runic inscription (Trotzig group C), copper alloy ring with clamp, tweezer-shaped copper alloy object with one arm, gilt copper alloy rod, iron sword-beater, iron staff, axe (JP type G/H), horse bit (R567), iron rod, 5 beads (glass), egg-shaped stone, hone, hand-made pottery, boss (R562), sheet iron, fragments of wood and bark, 2 iron brackets, dog skeleton	850–950 Oval brooches: <850–950 Axe: 850–950 Boss: 850–950	Blindheim et al. 1995:22–4
Spearhead(BS VI.1A), penannular brooch of lead/iron/tin, strike-a-light (R426), 2 flints, iron objects (tool?), 2 knives, egg-shaped stone, sherds of soapstone vessel, hone	800–850 Spearhead: 750–850	Blindheim et al. 1995:22–4
Sword (JP type M), forging hammer, forging tong, sickle (R348), spearhead (BS VII2B), axe (JP type F), boss (R562), knife, copper alloy ring-pin (JP 237), ring-pin of copper alloy, round Insular mount of gilt copper alloy with spiral ornaments, Insular mount of gilt copper alloy, 4 beads (2 glass, 2 amber), soapstone vessel (Redskaper fig. 190), iron gaff (Redskaper fig. 151), looped hone, flint, knife, textiles	900–1000 Sword: 825–950 Spearhead: 900–1000 Boss: 850–950 Axe: 900–1000	Blindheim et al. 1995:26–8
Equal-armed brooch of copper alloy (SK type 2), copper alloy arm ring (JP 195), copper alloy ring from necklace?, 22 beads (18 glass, 1 rock chrystal, 1 cornelian?, 2 amber), miniature spearhead, axe (JP type A), key (Redskaper fig. 254–55), 2 knives, spindle-whorl, iron fragments	800–850 Axe: 700–850 Equal-armed brooch: 800–850 Arm ring: 800–850	Blindheim et al. 1995:26–8
Single-edged sword (JP type H), axe (JP type E/F/G), Insular mount of gilt copper alloy, knife, 2 rivets, nails, knife?, hone, strike-a-light, indeterminable iron fragments, c. 850 rivets and nails	850–950 Sword: 800–950 Axe: 850–1000	Blindheim et al. 1995:26–8
Double-edged sword (JP type C), spearhead (BS VI.3A), knife, weight (spherical), ring-pin of copper alloy, 3 beads (2 amber, 1 jet), spindle-whorl, hand-made pottery, glass sherd – (the weight, the jetbead, and the pottery possibly from Ka. 303–304)	860–900 Sword: 775–850 Spearhead: 800–900 Pottery: 800–900 Weight. 860–>1000	Blindheim et al. 1995:29–30
Spearhead (JP type F?), axe (JP type K), sickle, scissors (Redskaper fig. 168), 3? knives, casket?mount, iron object (sword-beater?), looped hone, crampon?, indeterminable iron fragments, c. 240 rivets and nails, one piece of cremated bone (found in the boat)	c. 900 Spearhed: 850–>900 Axe: 900–1000	Blindheim et al. 1995:29–31
Oval brooch (JP 30), Equal-armed brooch (SK type 3), axe (JP type G), sickle (Redskaper fig. 82), 7–8 beads (4 glass, 1 amber), 5 knives, lead sinker (Redskaper fig. 146), arrowhead (R545?), hone, spindle-whorl, iron fragments (2 knives?)	875–900 Oval brooch: 800–850 Equal–armed brooch: 875–950 Axe: 850–>900	Blindheim et al. 1995:30–2
2 oval brooches (JP 37), Insular mount of gilt copper alloy, 3 beads (glass), 2 copper alloy fragments, 5 sherds of glass (Trichterbecher), hand-made pottery, knife, flint nodule with bent nail, flint nodule with iron ring, egg-shaped stone, textiles (wool, linen?). The following objects derive from any of the graves in Ka. 303–304: Iron fragments, 2 egg-shaped stones, 2 slags, flint, c. 500 rivets and nails The following objects found under Ka. 301 may or may not derive from Ka. 303–304: weight, jet bead, pottery, glass sherd	800–850 Oval brooches: 800–850 Pottery: 800–900	Blindheim et al. 1995:30–2

Cat. no.	Museum no.	Location	Name	Monument type	Grave-type	Body treatment
Ka. 305	K/VIII	Bikjholberget	Skibladner	Flat grave	Boat grave	Inhumation
Ka. 306		Bikjholberget	Martine	Flat grave	Boat grave	
Ka. 307	K/IX	Bikjholberget	Sistemann	Flat grave	Boat grave with chamber	Inhumation
Ka. 308	K/XI	Bikjholberget	Thorshøvdi	Flat grave	Boat grave	Inhumation
Ka. 309	K/XII grave II	Bikjholberget	Smertensbarnet	Flat grave	Boat grave	Inhumation
Ka. 310	K/XIII grave I	Bikjholberget	Britannia	Flat grave	Boat grave	Inhumation
Ka. 311	K/XIII grave II				Boat grave	Inhumation
Ka. 312	K/XXV	Bikjholberget		Flat grave	Boat grave	Inhumation?
Ka. 313	K/XVI	Bikjholberget	Astrids Kiste	Flat grave	Toboggan/ trough-sled	Inhumation
Ka. 314	K/XVIII	Bikjholberget		Flat grave	Toboggan/ trough-sled	Inhumation
Ka. 315	K/XIV	Bikjholberget	Ringen	Flat grave	Wooden coffin	Inhumation
Ka. 316	K/XV	Bikjholberget	Pulterkammeret	Flat grave	Chest (type Oseberg), double grave (child)	Inhumation
Ka. 317	K/XXI			Flat grave		Horse grave
Ka. 318	K/XVII	Bikjholberget	Charlottes kiste	Flat grave	Wooden coffin	
Ka. 319	K/XXXVII	Bikjholberget	Wenckes kiste	Flat grave	Wooden coffin	Inhumation
Ka. 320	K/XXXVIII	Bikjholberget	Randis kiste	Flat grave	Wooden coffin	Inhumation

Finds	Date	Literature
Double-edged sword (JP type K, HLITER-blade?), spearhead (JP type E), axe (JP type D/E), axe (JP type I), boss, 16? arrowheads (R539), 7 beads (6 glass, 1 stone), sickle, knife, hand-made pottery, 3 glass sherds (Trichterbecher etc), 2 boat rivets, nails, 2 flints, silver coin?, pumice, animal skeleton *(ursus)*, animal horn and bone *(bos)*, animal teeth *(equus)*, c. 450 rivets and nails	*c. 900* Sword: 800–875 Spearhead: 800–900 Axe: 800–>900 (D/E) Axe: 900–1000 Pottery: 800–900	Blindheim et al. 1995:32–4
Pottery (Tating Ware), round Insular copper alloy mount, silver ring (JP 194), fragments of amber (bead?), spindle-whorl	*800–900?* Pottery: 800–900?	Blindheim et al. 1995:32–4
Sword (JP type M, inlay on blade), copper alloy belt buckle, bead (cornelian), strap buckle of iron, mount piece of iron (for belt/sword? – possibly symmetric animal style), indeterminable iron fragments, knife, looped hone, smoothing stone?, c. 250 rivets	*850–950* Sword: 825–950 Symmetric animal style: <850–950	Blindheim et al. 1995:34–5
Spearhead (BS VII.2C), boss (R562), copper alloy needle, 7 beads (glass), sickle, file?, knife, iron cauldron (Redskaper fig. 198), hone, knife?, silver coin?, indeterminable iron fragments, c. 250 rivets and nails, button, textiles (wool)	*900–950* Spearhead: 900–1000 Boss: 850–950	Blindheim et al. 1995:35–6
Double-edged sword (JP type M), spearhead (JP type K), spearhead (JP type I), axe (JP type I), bronxe ring-pin, forging tong (Redskaper fig. 62), file?, hammer, 3 knives, soapstone vessel, handle, strap buckle of iron for horse harness, bead (glass), horse bit, arrowheads, 2 bolts, c. 200 rivets and nails, c. 40 g of cremated human and animal bones, weapon knife, boss?, pieces of wood from the boat, textiles (wool)	*900–950* Sword: 825–950 Spearheads: 900–950 Axe: 900–1000	Blindheim et al. 1995:36–8
2 oval brooches (JP 37), horse-shaped copper alloy brooch, 57 beads (56 glass, 1 amber), rectangular mount, iron rod, pottery (bar lip pottery), spindle-whorl, fragmentary sickle, scutcheon, wooden bucket	*800–900* Oval brooches: 800–850	Blindheim et al. 1995:36–8 and 39–41
9? arrowheads (R539), knife, iron chain, bark, flint, burnt stone, c. 130 rivets and nails, double-edged sword, knife, axe (JP type D), copper alloy ring-pin, wooden cup (type Gokstad)	*800–900* Axe: 800–850	Blindheim et al. 1995:39–41
Double-edged sword (JP type V, pattern-welded blade), round brooch of gilt copper alloy (JP 129–30, profile animal style), rivet, indeterminable iron fragments, bead (glass)	*900–950* Sword: 900–1000 Round brooch: 900–950	Blindheim et al. 1995:40–1
Sickle, knife, key (Redskaper fig. 258), 23 nails and rivets		Blindheim et al. 1995:41–2
Knife, 9 rivets		Blindheim et al. 1995:42
Spearhead (BS IV.3), 2 beads (amber), soapstone vessel, glass stave, soapstone sinker, c. 50 nails and rivets, mount piece of iron/scutcheon, copper alloy needle, textiles	*800–900?* Spearhead: 610/20–740/50 Soapstone vessel: 900–1000?	Blindheim et al. 1995:42–44
Spearhead (BS VI.4B), axe (JP type A), boss, boss (R562), iron cauldron, scutcheon (type Oseberg), hinges from casket, file?, knife, 12 rivets and nails, hone. Objects found in secondary position: Trefoil brooch (geometric style), sickle, iron hook/ fishing hook, knife, indeterminable iron fragments, 2 hinges?, bead (glass), a piece of cremated bone	*850–900?* Spearhead: 800–900 Axe: 700–850 Boss: 850–950	Blindheim et al. 1995:44–5
The horse grave Ka. 317 probably belongs to Ka. 316: Carved horse skeleton, horse bit (Redskaper fig. 18), 1 iron nail with gilt copper alloy coated head, 5 iron nails, cruciform iron mount (R621), adze, flint, arrowhead, 2 rectangular iron plates		Blindheim et al. 1995:49
Bead (glass), iron nails, flint		Blindheim et al. 1995:46
2 nails		Blindheim et al. 1995:46–7
Wooden cup, 2 nails		Blindheim et al. 1995:47–8

Cat. no.	Museum no.	Location	Name	Monument type	Grave-type	Body treatment
Ka. 321	K/XIX	Bikjholberget		Flat grave		Inhumation
Ka. 322	K/XX	Bikjholberget		Flat grave	Wooden coffin	Inhumation
Ka. 323	K/XXVI	Bikjholberget		Flat grave	?	Inhumation
Ka. 400	C2317 I	'N. Kaupang'		Barrow		Cremation
Ka. 401	C2317 II	'N. Kaupang'		Barrow		Inhumation?
Ka. 402	C2317 III	'N. Kaupang'		Barrow		Inhumation?
Ka. 403	C4070	'N. Kaupang'		Flat grave		Inhumation
Ka. 404	C4316	'N. Kaupang'		Casual find		
Ka. 405	C14678	'Kaupang'		Barrow		
Ka. 406	C30264	'Kaupang'		Flat grave?		Cremation
Ka. 407	C30265	'Kaupang'		Barrow		Inhumation
	1950	Bikjholberget		Collection of casual finds		
	1951	Bikjholberget		Collection of casual finds		
	1952	Bikjholberget		Collection of casual finds		
	1953	Bikjholberget		Collection of casual finds		
	1954	N. Bikjholberget		Collection of casual finds		

Finds	Date	Literature
Spearhead (BS VII.2B), axe (JP type G/H), 2 beads (1 amber, 1 stone), knife, indeterminable iron fragments	*900–950* Spearhead: 900–1000 Axe: 850–950	Blindheim et al. 1995:49
Double-edged sword (type Mannheim), knife, c. 10 nails	*800–850?* Sword: 800–850?	Blindheim et al. 1995:48
Rivets, flint, animal teeth (equus), cremated bone		Blindheim et al. 1995:50
Oval brooch (Berdal type)	*800–850?* Oval brooch: 775–850	Blindheim et al. 1981:211
Two oval brooches (JP 51), axe	*850–950* Oval brooches: <850–950	Blindheim et al. 1981:211
Axe		Blindheim et al. 1981:211
Single-edged sword (R498)	*830/840–900?* Sword: 830/840–900	Blindheim et al. 1981:211
Stone sinker		
Spearhead (JP type B/C?)		Blindheim et al. 1981:211
2 oval brooches (JP 51), trefoil copper alloy brooch (SK type 4), conical copper alloy button, 12 beads (11 glass, 1 cornelian), spindle-whorl, soapstone vessel	*850–950* Oval brooches: 850–950 Trefoil brooch:850–925?	Blindheim et al. 1981:220
Axe (JP type E?), sword pommel (JP type O)	*850–950* Axe: 850–> 900 Sword: 850–950	Blindheim et al. 1981:220
2 beads (glass), round stone, spindle-whorl of soapstone, spindle-whorl of stone, 2 spindle-whorl of fired clay, ring, triangular clamp, needle case? of iron, copper alloy ring, hinge?, rod		Blindheim et al. 1995:65
Fragments of soapstone, hone, spindle-whorl/bead of jet, spindle-whorl/bead of amber, loom weight of fired clay, flint, horse bit, c. 60 rivets and nails, piece of bone (modern?)		Blindheim et al. 1995:66
Thorn from Insular ring-pin, 6 beads (3 glass, 2 amber, 1 rock chrystal), flywheel of soapstone, knife, arrowhead, slag, flint, loom weight? of fired clay		Blindheim et al. 1995:67
Axe (JP type K), knife, sickle, boundle of sowing needles?, iron fragment, round copper alloy pendant, knife, slag, knife/sickle, bead (glass), scissors?, knife?, 2 ring-pins		Blindheim et al. 1995:75
Sword (JP type H), sword (JP type M?), axe (JP type I?), sickle, spearhead?, iron object, oval brooch?, spindle-whorl of fired clay, spindle-whorl of stone, hone, 2 soapstone vessels		Blindheim et al. 1995:86

Concordance table

C2270–2280 I	Ka. 150	C27997 grave C	Ka. 254	K/VI grave II	Ka. 302
C2270–2280 II	Ka. 151	C30264	Ka. 406	K/VII grave I	Ka. 303
C2317 I	Ka. 400	C30265	Ka. 407	K/VII grave II	Ka. 304
C2317 II	Ka. 401	C54272	Ka. 134	K/VIII	Ka. 305
C2317 III	Ka. 402	C31482	Ka. 211	K/IX	Ka. 307
C4070	Ka. 403	C33255	Ka. 165	K/X	Ka. 218
C4198–4203	Ka. 1	C54290/1	Ka. 222	K/XI	Ka. 308
C4204–4205	Ka. 2	C54290/2	Ka. 225	K/XII grave II	Ka. 309
C4206–4215	Ka. 3	C54290/3	Ka. 226	K/XIII grave I	Ka. 310
C4216–4224	Ka. 4	C54292/1	Ka. 228	K/XIII grave II	Ka. 311
C4225	Ka. 5	C54296/1	Ka. 221	K/XIV	Ka. 315
C4226–4234	Ka. 6			K/XV	Ka. 316
C4235–4236	Ka. 7	K/1950 grave I	Ka. 255	K/XVI	Ka. 313
C4237–4243	Ka. 8	K/1950 grave II	Ka. 256	K/XVII	Ka. 318
C4244	Ka. 9	K/1950 grave III	Ka. 257	K/XVIII	Ka. 314
C4245–4251	Ka. 10	K/1950 grave IV	Ka. 258	K/XIX	Ka. 321
C4252–4253	Ka. 11	K/1950 grave V	Ka. 259	K/XX	Ka. 322
C4254	Ka. 12	K/1950 grave VI	Ka. 260	K/XXI	Ka. 317
C4255	Ka. 13	K/1950 grave VII	Ka. 261	K/XXII	Ka. 130
C4256–4259	Ka. 14	K/1952 grave I	Ka. 262	K/XXIII	Ka. 37
C4260	Ka. 15	K/1952 grave II	Ka. 263	K/XXIVa	Ka. 128
C4261–4265	Ka. 16	K/1953 grave I	Ka. 265	K/XXIVb	Ka. 129
C4266	Ka. 17	K/1953 grave II	Ka. 267	K/XXIVd	Ka. 37
C4267	Ka. 18	K/1953 grave III	Ka. 268	K/XXIVe–g	Ka. 250
C4268	Ka. 19	K/1953 grave IV	Ka. 269	K/XXV	Ka. 312
C4269	Ka. 20	K/1953 grave V	Ka. 270	K/XXVI	Ka. 323
C4270	Ka. 21	K/1953 grave VI	Ka. 272	K/XXVII	Ka. 219
C4271–4275	Ka. 22	K/1953 grave VII	Ka. 273	K/XXVIII	Ka. 216
C4286	Ka. 153	K/1953 grave VIII	Ka. 266	K/XXXV	Ka. 126
C4287–4288	Ka. 154	K/1954 grave I	Ka. 277	K/XXXVI	Ka. 127
C4289–4290	Ka. 155	K/1954 grave II	Ka. 278	K/XXXVII	Ka. 319
C4291–4292	Ka. 156	K/1954 grave III	Ka. 279	K/XXXVIII	Ka. 320
C4293–4315	Ka. 157	K/1954 grave IV	Ka. 264	K/XXXIX	Ka. 217
C4316	Ka. 404	K/1954 grave V	Ka. 280		
C4317	Ka. 125	K/1954 grave VI	Ka. 281		
C5508–5509	Ka. 200	K/1954 grave VII	Ka. 282		
C14678	Ka. 405	K/1954 grave VIII	Ka. 283		
C15010–15011	Ka. 201	K/1954 grave IX	Ka. 284		
C15214–15218	Ka. 160	K/1954 grave X	Ka. 285		
C15219	Ka. 161	K/1954 grave XI	Ka. 286		
C17719–17722	Ka. 202	K/1954 grave XII	Ka. 287		
C21843, 21960	Ka. 203	K/1954 grave XIII	Ka. 288		
C21960 I	Ka. 204	K/I	Ka. 290		
C21960 II	Ka. 205	K/II	Ka. 291		
C22309a	Ka. 131	K/III grave I	Ka. 292		
C22309b	Ka. 132	K/III grave II	Ka. 293		
C27148	Ka. 206	K/IV grave I	Ka. 294		
C27220 (Grave I)	Ka. 208	K/IV grave II	Ka. 295		
C27220 (Grave II)	Ka. 209	K/IV grave III	Ka. 296		
C27220 (Grave III)	Ka. 210	K/IV grave IV	Ka. 297		
C27740A	Ka. 250	K/V grave I	Ka. 298		
C27740B	Ka. 251	K/V grave II	Ka. 299		
C27997 grave A	Ka. 252	K/V grave III	Ka. 300		
C27997 grave B	Ka. 253	K/VI grave I	Ka. 301		

Evidence from the Settlement Area 1956–1984

6

LARS PILØ

The collection and evaluation of the available evidence from the settlement area were important tasks prior to the renewal of fieldwork at Kaupang. The evaluation, which was undertaken in 1998–1999, included a critical assessment of Tollnes's interpretations of the evidence from Blindheim's excavations of 1956–1984. The evaluation influenced the strategy for the 2000–2002 excavations.

There had been one large and several minor excavations in the settlement area during the period 1956–1984. No overall site surveys were undertaken, however. The data from these excavations yielded important information on the dating, international trading contacts, craft activities and daily life of the settlement.

In this paper the results of the assessments of the documentation and interpretations from the excavations of 1956–1984 are presented. The methods of data collection and the quality of the data are examined. The interpretations of certain structures as the remains of buildings and jetties are questioned and alternative interpretations suggested. Traces of plot-divisions are identified and an adjustment of the northern extent of the settlement area is suggested.

In section II of this volume a full re-interpretation of the evidence from the Blindheim excavations is presented, which draws on the results from the excavations of 2000–2002.

6.1 Introduction

Three important tasks prior to the renewal of fieldwork at Kaupang were the collection and assessment of the available evidence from earlier excavations in the settlement area, and the assessment of the interpretations based upon this evidence. The evidence had been partially published in preliminary papers (Tollnes 1969, 1976) and then had been published in full by Roar L. Tollnes in a 1998 publication. The assessment is based on the 1998 publication and on the complete excavation archive, which is kept in the Museum of Cultural History, University of Oslo. The present paper discusses the assessment, which provided an important platform for the renewed fieldwork.

Prior to 1956 there had been no reported finds from the settlement area. In fact, the existence of a settlement was not known because previous excavations had concentrated on the cemeteries (Skre, this vol. Ch. 2:39). During her excavations at the cemetery at Bikjholberget 1950–1957 (Stylegar, this vol. Ch. 5:72–3)

Charlotte Blindheim suspected the existence of a settlement area in the field to the west of the cemetery due to the presence of dark coloured topsoil.

In 1956 she started excavations in this area (Figs. 6.1 and 6.2). A trial trench, measuring 9 x 2 m, was sunk in what was believed to be the former harbour area (Tollnes 1998:15). Excavations were started here because wooden chips had been noticed in this particular area during coring and the digging of drainage ditches (Tollnes 1998:95). Below a 0.5 m thick marine deposit of post–Viking-age date, a waterlogged deposit of wooden chips appeared (Fig. 6.3). A ceramic sherd of Badorf ware was recovered from this layer, the first such sherd found at Kaupang (Tollnes 1998:95). In 1958 an excavation area was opened to the west of the 1956 trial trench (Tollnes 1998:17) (Fig. 6.2).

A trench for a water pipe was dug in the settlement area in the autumn of 1958 (Figs. 6.1 and 6.2). Blindheim recorded most of the section of this trench; only the northernmost part was less well doc-

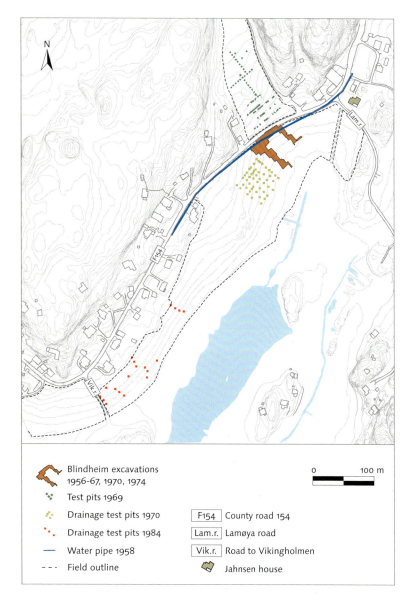

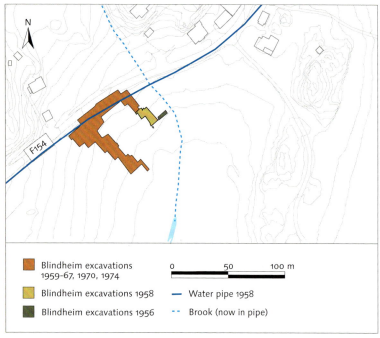

Blindheim excavations
1956-67, 1970, 1974

Test pits 1969

Drainage test pits 1970

Drainage test pits 1984

Water pipe 1958

Field outline

F154	County road 154
Lam.r.	Lamøya road
Vik.r.	Road to Vikingholmen
	Jahnsen house

0   100 m

Blindheim excavations
1959-67, 1970, 1974

Blindheim excavations 1958

Blindheim excavations 1956

Water pipe 1958

Brook (now in pipe)

0   50   100 m

Figure 6.1 *Areas investigated in the settlement area 1956–1984. Contour interval 1 meter. Map, Julie K. Øhre Askjem.*

Figure 6.2 *The main excavation area 1956–1974. Contour interval 1 meter. Map, Julie K. Øhre Askjem.*

umented, being only sporadically observed by a local amateur archaeologist (Astri Jahnsen) under extremely difficult weather conditions. A continuous and thick culture layer was seen in the section of the water-pipe trench a little to the northwest of the 1956 trial trench and the 1958 excavation area. The combined evidence from these three initial excavations, which were closely linked spatially, pointed consistently to the presence of thick cultural deposits in one specific area, and this evidence governed the choice of excavation area for the coming years (Figs. 6.1 and 6.2).

From 1958 onwards there were excavations in this area each year until 1967, with the exception of 1961 (Figs. 6.1 and 6.2). Due to problems in finding housing during the summer, excavations took place in the spring and/or the autumn. Funding was limited, and the excavation crew, usually 10–15 members, consisted of a mixture of archaeology students and local people. The excavation periods in the autumn were on average 6–7 weeks long. Given these conditions Blindheim received remarkable results, uncovering a total of 1,350 sq m, and documenting important structures, which at the time were interpreted as the remains of houses, wells and jetties (Figs. 6.4 and 6.10). Thousands of artefacts were recovered. Even though the interpretation of the excavated structures may now be questioned (see below), Blindheim's excavation in the settlement area was a milestone in the investigation of Kaupang. Any doubt that Kaupang was the site of *Sciringes heal* was dispelled, and at the same time important information on dating, craft and trade networks was collected.

The large-scale excavation was followed by a few smaller excavations (Fig. 6.1). A series of test pits and narrow trenches was dug in 1969 in the slope to the north of the main excavation area in order to shed light on the nature of the deposits there. A small area adjacent to the excavation area of 1956–1967 was dug

Figure 6.3 *The 1956 trench in Viking-age harbour sediments during different stages of excavation. The picture of the early stages of the excavation is taken facing northeast, the other one facing southwest. Photo in KHM Archive.*

in 1970, and a similar area was dug in 1974. All the excavations of 1956–1974 totalled 1,475 sq m (Tollnes 1998:15).

In 1964 a house was built for the Jahnsen family just north of the Lamøya road, outside what was then believed to be the boundaries of the settlement area (Fig. 6.1). In 1978 this house was extended. No real excavation work took place during the construction periods but the site was visited and the presence of scorched stone, charcoal and burnt bone was noted (Blindheim et al. 1981:77–8).

Two sets of drainage ditches were dug after the main excavation was concluded (Fig. 6.1). The northern slope of the central ridge was trenched by the farmer in 1969, and small test pits were dug in these trenches in 1970. The same happened on the southernmost slope of the central ridge in 1984 (Tollnes 1998:21–2).

6.2 The methodology of the excavations of 1956–1984

For the times, the excavations of 1956–1984 were well done methodologically. The quality of documentation also benefited a great deal from the inclusion of the trained architect Roar L. Tollnes in the excavation crew from 1959 onwards (Fig. 6.6). He became responsible for the plan drawings and photography, and later went on to publish the excavations of 1956–1984 (Tollnes 1998).

The ploughsoil covering the main excavation site was removed both mechanically and manually, and in both cases without sieving (Tollnes 1998:17). The topsoil is likely to have contained artefacts from the most recent, destroyed phases. These artefacts were not recovered more than occasionally, and the artefactual record is therefore likely to be chronologically incomplete.

Initially, in 1956 and 1958, the excavations took place in the harbour where stratification was easy to

Figure 6.4 *An aerial photo from 1966 showing Blindheim's main excavation area with the stone construction of the so-called houses and Jetty 2 visible. Photo in KHM Archive.*

Figure 6.5 *Charlotte Blindheim, Sigrid Kaland and Ellen-Karine Hougen (from left to right), photographed during a break in the 1969 excavation at Kaupang. Photo in KHM Archive.*

Figure 6.6 *Roar L. Tollnes during documentation work. Photo in KHM Archive.*

see. The deposits were removed stratigraphically. The precise co-ordinates of the location of each artefact were noted.

This system was changed as the excavations approached areas with a higher density of artefacts and more complex stratification. Stratigraphic excavation was abandoned, and the deposits were removed in spits and squares. An overall system of 2x2 m squares was employed at Kaupang. Spits were 10 cm thick. While most artefacts were only recorded according to their respective square and spit, the precise co-ordinates of the location of special artefacts were still noted (Tollnes 1998:17).

According to Tollnes no or very little sieving took place (Tollnes 1998:17); however, notes in the excavation diaries indicate that occasional small-scale sieving took place. Even though the large number of small finds in the artefact assemblage from this excavation bears witness to a well-trained crew, the lack of sieving inevitably led to a bias in the record towards larger objects. Large-scale sieving was, of course, seldom implemented on excavations in Scandinavia at the time.

The cultural deposits were generally termed "black earth", even though their colour and composition varied. Little emphasis was put on stratigraphy after the 1958 excavation season. It is stated that there was generally no stratification (Tollnes 1998:13), only some areas with clearly redeposited material: mostly sand, gravel, clay and stone. It is also mentioned that it was impossible to separate stratigraphic levels in the deposits during excavation (Tollnes 1998:17, 41). However, looking at the published section drawings and the photos in the archive, one can have little doubt that stratification was generally present in the deeper deposits where lighter coloured lenses of sand separated darker coloured layers (Fig. 6.8). However, since the deposits were removed in spits, it is impossible now, except in a few cases, to relate with certainty

specific artefacts to specific stratigraphic layers that are documented in section drawings or photos.

Features were seldom recognized in the dark-coloured deposits until the light-coloured sandy layers were uncovered towards the bottom of the excavation. Thus, there is little recorded information on the relation of such features to the surrounding deposits. Furthermore, the 1998 publication makes it clear that most of the excavated features (especially post- and stake-holes) were interpreted as being contemporary, even though there is no stratigraphic information to support this. The clearest example of this interpretation is the so-called House 1, where all elements belonging to standing structures are combined into the same reconstructed building, together with the stone structures present.

Even when there was stratigraphic information present to illuminate possible phasing, on the whole little emphasis was placed on this information. An example of this is the line of three posts which were

Figure 6.7 *Blindheim's main excavation in progress. Photo in KHM Archive.*

Figure 6.8 *Stratification in the Blindheim excavations, shown in one of the sections from the House V area. From Tollnes 1998:Pl. 27.*

supposed to mark the eastern wall of House II. They were covered by stones in an irregular line. These stones were believed to be part of the wall construction of House II. The position of the stones on top of the post-holes was explained by later displacement of the stones (Tollnes 1998:28–9). The question of whether the stones' position on top of the post-holes could be the result of the stone line and the post line belonging to two different phases was not discussed.

During many large-scale excavations of areas with preserved cultural deposits, it is quite common that the lowest layer containing cultural deposits is not reached everywhere in the area excavated due to a lack of time and resources. This was the case in the main Blindheim's excavation. However, the extent to which the lowest layer containing cultural deposits was reached in the different parts of the excavation is not quite clear. Based on the published evidence, archival information and comments by Tollnes, only the areas around Houses 1 and 2 and Jetty 2, and the harbour areas associated with Jetty 1 and 2, would appear to have been excavated completely (Fig. 6.9). Furthermore, houses 1, 2 and 6 were the only areas where features cut into the subsoil were documented (Tollnes 1998:Pl. 7, 12A, 12B). The area to the north-west of the 1958 water-pipe trench was only partially excavated. This area contained parts of what were then interpreted as Houses 1, 3 and 4. The House 5 area was only partially excavated also. Thus detailed information about features cut into the subsoil is not available for these areas.

6.3 The interpretation of the documented structures

When the excavations in the settlement area at Kaupang were undertaken there was very little material from sites of this kind with which to compare what was found. Plot-division on Viking-age urban sites was as yet unknown. There was also very little comparative regional material illuminating Viking-age building techniques in this part of Scandinavia. Therefore the excavators had to rely exclusively on the data itself for the reconstruction of the excavated structures. The lack of stratigraphic sequencing made their task even more difficult.

Prior to our own excavations begun in 2000, our evaluation in 1998–1999 raised questions and doubts concerning Blindheim's and Tollnes's findings, and these questions and doubts caused us to reinterpret their findings, *provisionally,* during our evaluation. Furthermore, our provisional reinterpretation shaped elements of our excavation strategy for the following years. A *fuller* reinterpretation of Blindheim's and Tollnes's findings, in light of our own excavations of 2000–2002, is presented elsewhere (Pilø, this vol. Ch. 10).

The Tollnes reconstruction, first published in 1972, and upheld unaltered by its author in his 1998 publication, showed a group of houses, erected along the beach, with one of the long sides of each house facing the shore (Fig. 6.10). Except for the rectangular House 5, these houses had an egg-shaped ground plan with an asymmetric roof-carrying construction. Their construction included rows of stones together with a variety of post-holes, stake-holes and large hammered posts as part of their walls and the roof-bearing structures. In front of the buildings were two stone jetties, one of which was of quite substantial size – 28 m long in its shortest phase.

Excavations have taken place at a number of Viking-age urban sites since the 1960s, most notably

Hus V: Profil y 4,5 (NØ)

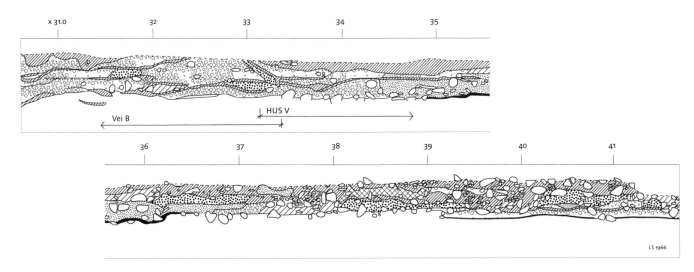

at Birka, Hedeby, Ribe, York and Dublin (Ambrosiani and Clarke 1992; Bencard and Jørgensen 1990; Feveile and Jensen 2000; Hall 1984, 1994; Jensen 1991a; Schietzel 1981; Wallace 1992). All of these urban sites show a similar pattern: The settled area had been laid out in plots. The houses, when found, invariably lay with their gable end facing the shore or a street. The houses were built symmetrically, either with pairs of inner roof-bearing posts or with the roofs resting on the walls. However, at other types of sites involved in trading which have been excavated, there is no evidence of plot-division, and sunken huts are the most prominent feature (Christensen and Johansen 1992). The question facing us in 1999 was: What kind of settlement was Kaupang?

When the empirical evidence from the Blindheim excavations was evaluated by us prior to the renewal of fieldwork, it became clear that the original interpretation of the evidence was no longer tenable. There is a striking absence of any wall remains whatsoever on the sides of the supposed houses that face away from the shore. This absence was explained by a combination of the walls' being destroyed by the construction of the 1958 water pipe, and the walls' being situated outside the excavated area (Tollnes 1998:25). However, evaluation of the empirical evidence suggested that such walls had never in fact existed, thus making it unlikely that the excavated remains were derived from buildings. Furthermore, the combination of most of the features in one area into only one building, without consideration of stratigraphical information, also seemed doubtful.

Wattle constructions along the shore were a regular feature of Blindheim's main excavation area, and were interpreted as parts of the walls of buildings. These structures, however, had much in common with the wooden fences marking the borders of plots found in Ribe (Bencard and Jørgensen 1990; Jensen 1991a:6), and to some degree also with such wooden

fences found in Trondheim (Christophersen and Nordeide 1994:275). A reinterpretation of the presumed walls as plot-division fences would make Kaupang more similar to sites like Ribe, Dublin, York and Birka. Furthermore, tentative remains of buildings other than those reconstructed by Tollnes could be discerned inside the supposed plots, as a number of post-holes could be seen there.

The large stone structure to the east (Fig. 6.11) was interpreted by both Blindheim and Tollnes as a stone jetty. Their interpretations were questioned in our evaluation of the excavation data, especially regarding the structure's seaward end, which extended to a point where it was 1 m above present sea-level. Tollnes estimated that the Viking-age sea-level was 2.5 m above the present sea-level (Blindheim et al. 1981), but this height would have left the lower end of the jetty 1.5 m below the water level. In addition, new evidence suggested that Tollnes's estimate of the Viking-age sea-level was too low, by as much as 0.5–1 m. It is not likely that compaction of the underlying clay layers, after they became dry land as a result of isostatic uplift, would have had any significant influence on these levels (Sørensen et al., this vol. Ch. 12:270). Thus, the lower end of the stone structure could hardly have been built in the Viking Age unless the remains are only the bottom of a large stone jetty which had been more than 2.0 m higher (with an overall height of more than 2.5m), which is not very likely.

However, the stones were covered with a dark, homogeneous "black-earth" deposit, generally believed to be of the Viking Age. If the stones had not belonged to a jetty, but rather to a stone structure of a later date, then the black-earth deposit would also have had to have been of a date which was later than the Viking Age. We could not solve this problem during the preparation phase of 1998–1999, but it was solved during the main excavation in 2000–2002 (see Pilø, this vol. Ch. 7:10:220–2).

Figure 6.9 *Fully excavated areas in Blindheim's main excavation marked in dark colour. Light colored areas were not fully excavated. Illustration, Julie K. Øhre Askjem.*

Figure 6.10 *Reconstruction drawing by Tollnes, first published in Blindheim and Tollnes 1972:63.*

A more detailed reinterpretation of the documented structures in the Blindheim excavations, using the additional evidence from our new excavations, is presented elsewhere (Pilø, this vol. Ch. 10).

6.4 Evidence from other parts of the settlement area

When the first map of the settlement area was produced after the Blindheim excavations (in Blindheim et al. 1981), the settlement itself was not thought to have extended much further than the brook just north of Blindheim's main excavation area. In his 1998 publication, however, the possibility of a more northerly limit to the settlement area was raised by

Tollnes (Tollnes 1998:20). The data from the area north of the main Blindheim excavation was derived partly from observations made of sections in the 1958 water-pipe trench (see above). The supposed limit of the settlement area on the 1981 map coincided with the limit of Blindheim's observations; observations beyond this point were carried out by an amateur archaeologist, under extremely difficult weather conditions, and the low quality of those observations probably led to the original conclusion that there was no settlement in this area, even though cultural deposits were noted.

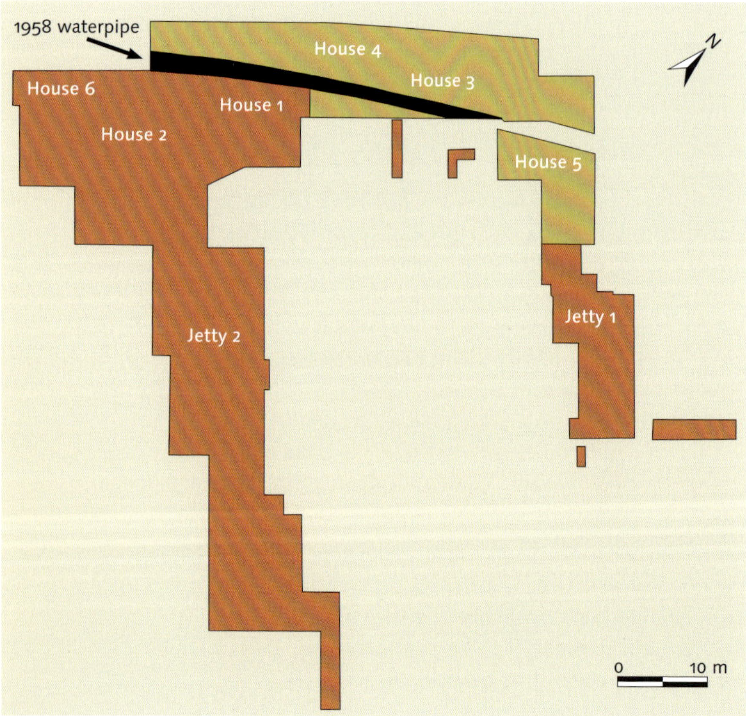

Published material and archive reports suggested the presence of settlement remains even further to the north than the end of the water pipe (Fig. 6.12). During the excavation of an extension to the Jahnsen house there in 1964, a layer of scorched stones and charcoal was uncovered, along with burnt bones. This layer was tentatively interpreted by Blindheim as being from an *ustrina*, a common ground for cremation (Blindheim et al. 1981:77-81). However, a more recent investigation of additional bone material from this area, following another excavation of an extension to the house in 1978, failed to produce evidence of human bone; it produced only what were identified as animal bones among the remains (Blindheim et al. 1981:79). The artefacts recovered from this area along with the bones include glass beads, crucible fragments, ceramics, slag, iron rivets and a spindle-whorl (Blindheim et al. 1981:55–6 and archive information). Thus an interpretation of deposits from the area around the Jahnsen house as settlement deposits seems more consistent with the data than does the original interpretation.

During the clearance of a building destroyed by fire further north in 1942, seven shallow pits containing burnt bone, charcoal and ash were uncovered (Fig. 6.12). A further three pits were found in the vicinity, one of which contained three glass beads.

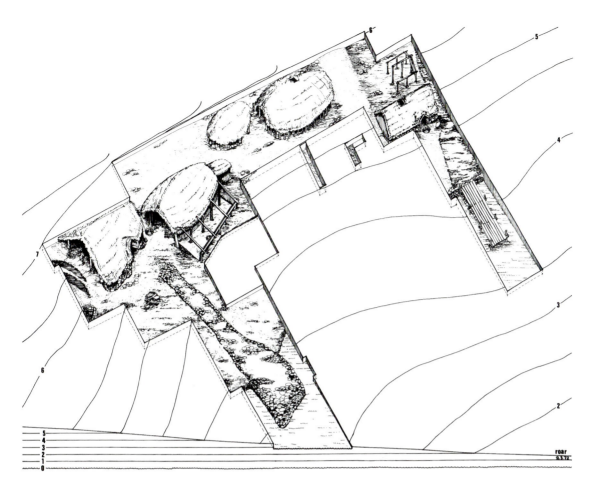

These pits have been interpreted as cremation pits due to these contents (Blindheim et al. 1981:55). In view of what is known about Viking-age burial customs at Kaupang and in the region, this interpretation seems doubtful, and these pits may represent settlement features.

However, it was noted that graves were found in this area as well. During an observation of the water-pipe trench in 1958, the amateur archaeologist Jahnsen recorded a cremation grave there (Fig. 6.12), containing iron rivets and nails, presumably from a boat (Blindheim et al. 1981:55). A fragment of a bronze bracelet with textile remains, which was found just north of this grave, probably also derives from a grave. Four barrows just to the north of Bikjholberget also bear witness to burial in this area (marked in Fig. 6.12). Two of these mounds were excavated by Blindheim in 1974 (Blindheim 1977; Blindheim et al. 1981: 55–6). Of importance is the presence of iron slag which was noted in the fill of one of the barrows; iron slag had frequently been reported from this area (Blindheim et al. 1981:56, and reports in the Kaupang archive).

In conclusion, there is substantial evidence to allow for an interpretation that the settlement area extended to the north, beyond the border shown on Blindheim's 1981 map. The size of the extension, the character, and the dating of the settlement here could not be determined on the basis of the data which

were available before 2000. The presence of both settlement traces and burials in the same area suggested that this area had changed its function during the lifespan of the settlement. The presence of slag in one of the barrows in this area suggested that a settlement area was later used as a cemetery (cf. Skre, this vol. Ch. 16:368–9, 382).

In general it can be said that before the initiation of renewed fieldwork in 1998 there was very little evidence of either the character or the extent of the settlement in the southern and central parts of the estimated settlement area. Only a few small test pits dug in 1970 and 1984, mainly in connection with drainage ditches, indicated the presence of cultural deposits there, but their character and precise dating were uncertain (Tollnes 1998:21–2). How far south the settlement extended was also unclear. The estimated limit at the time here was based on topography, the colour of the topsoil and the presence of graves (Tollnes 1998:12).

6.5 The platform for the new fieldwork

After the available evidence from the settlement area was collected and assessed, some important conclusions could be drawn. The extent of the settlement area seemed to be somewhat unclear to both the north and the south. In the north the evidence suggested possible settlement which had later been covered up by an extension of the cemeteries; in the

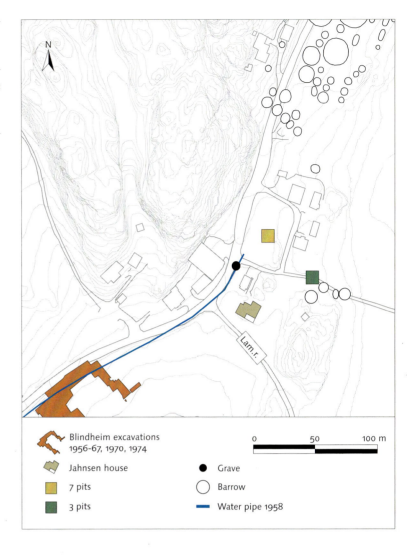

Figure 6.11 *The stone structure, interpreted as a jetty, during excavation. Photo in KHM Archive.*

Figure 6.12 *The northernmost area. Barrows are taken from Skre, this vol. Ch. 16:Fig. 16.10. Contour interval 1 meter. Map, Julie K. Øhre Askjem.*

Blindheim excavations 1956–67, 1970, 1974	
Jahnsen house	Grave
7 pits	Barrow
3 pits	Water pipe 1958

south there was hardly any evidence available. To determine more precisely the extent of the settlement area it would be necessary to conduct excavations in the parts of the settlement area concerned. Such excavations became possible as part of the cultural resource management projects in 2000–2003 (Pilø, this vol. Ch. 7:153–4, Fig. 7.14). In addition there was the question of the Viking-age sea-level, the answer to which would have direct influence on determining the width of the settlement area. A joint project was initiated to elucidate this issue (Sørensen et al., this vol. Ch. 12:267–70).

The possible presence of plots in the area of the Blindheim excavations makes Kaupang more like a number of other Viking-age urban sites. Tentative remains of houses on the same plots also hinted at a settlement pattern more alike that at other urban sites. However, the question of the permanence of the settlement remained unsolved after the Blindheim excavations. To investigate the validity of these tentative reinterpretations and to supply new and independent information it was of vital importance to undertake a further large-scale excavation in the

settlement area. This excavation was undertaken in 2000–2002 (Pilø, this vol. Ch. 7:153).

Thus the collection and assessment of the available data from the settlement area at Kaupang provided an important element in the preparations for the renewed fieldwork there: the quality of the old data, especially from the main excavation 1956–1974, allowed them to be put into a new context. However, the limitations of the old data showed the necessity of renewed fieldwork at Kaupang to collect new data on the character, dating and extent of the site.

Part II:

Excavations and Surveys 1998–2003

The Fieldwork 1998–2003: Overview and Methods

7

LARS PILØ

Surveys and excavations undertaken at Kaupang between 1998 and 2003 are described. The surveys consisted of fieldwalking, metal detecting, geophysical mapping and auger probing. Methodological issues concerning fieldwalking and metal detecting are discussed in some detail. The field surveys have yielded the first information on the dating, extent and settlement density of the site as a whole. The excavations consisted of both research excavations and cultural resource management (CRM) excavations. The research excavations covered a large central area and gave information on site dating and the settlement structure. The CRM excavations consisted of narrow trenches in nearly all parts of the settlement area and provided data from areas which had until then been untouched by archaeological excavations. The excavation methods, especially the use of single context documentation, digital documentation (Intrasis) and sieving strategies, are described. The excavations included geoarchaeological sampling and the implementation of environmental sampling according to the York protocol. Dendrochronology is also an important source of information. The quality and limitations of the collected data is discussed.

7.1 Introduction

The fieldwork at Kaupang was designed to provide information about the date, extent, structure, character and building types of the settlement. Since these objectives were at the same time of both a general and a more detailed nature, both surveys and excavations were conducted. Today the Viking-age settlement at Kaupang is situated in a rural landscape with some suburban housing. This has facilitated the large-scale implementation of field surveys, and also allowed for a relatively free choice of location for the main research excavations (MRE).

The fieldwork at Kaupang from 1998 to 2003 was in two parts, with 1998–1999 being the pilot project period which included surveys and limited trial trenching, and 2000–2003 being the main project period, which included a series of excavations, in addition to continuing surveys. The surveys began with systematic fieldwalking in 1998. Three further major fieldwalks were conducted, with the last taking place in the spring of 2000. The latter coincided with the first metal detector survey; three more surveys were conducted by 2002. Generally the conditions for fieldwalking and metal detection were excellent, and large numbers of artefacts were recovered.

Geophysical mapping was also undertaken: fluxgate-gradiometer mapping of the central settlement area in 2000 and georadar mapping in the former harbour area in 2003. Auger probing for cultural deposits took place in 1999.

There were several excavations during the fieldwork programme of 1998–2003, the most important being the MRE conducted in the central settlement area during 2000–2002. In 2003 there was limited excavation in the former harbour area. The other excavations were related to cultural resource management (CRM) and included a series of trenches for a pipeline, and a pedestrian path, mostly excavated during 2000, but with additional smaller trenches in 1999, 2001, 2002 and 2003. The excavations uncovered settlement remains consisting of a combination of various layers of soil, stones, hearths, postholes and large pits. Only the large pits had waterlogged preservation conditions in the lower part; otherwise, preservation of organic material was poor. Agricultural activities had led to the destruction of the more recent layers belonging to the Viking-age settlement, and in some areas to the total destruction of deposits, leaving behind only features cut into the sub-soil.

Besides a description of the individual parts of

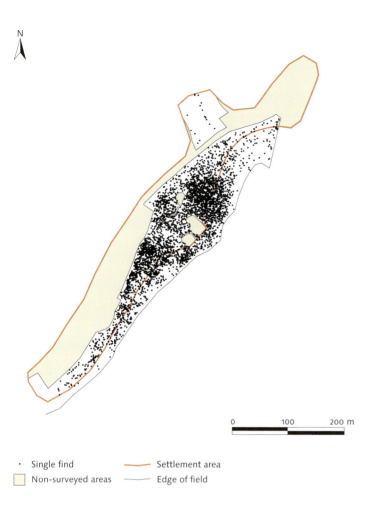

N

Single find
Non-surveyed areas
Settlement area
Edge of field

0   100   200 m

Figure 7.1 *Aggregated artefact recovery during field surveys 1998–2002. Illustration, Julie K. Øhre Askjem, Lars Pilø.*

Figure 7.2 *The settlement area at Kaupang, seen from the north. Surveyed areas and modern features. Photo, Dagfinn Skre. Illustration, Elise Naumann.*

the fieldwork, this chapter contains information on methods of survey and excavation, and a discussion of the quality of the recorded data. Detailed technical information on the fieldwork can be found in the archive reports, KHM (Baug 2003, 2004; Gaut 2001a, 2001b; Kristensen 2001a, 2001b, 2003a, 2003b, 2003c, 2003d; Pilø 1999a, 1999b, 1999c, 2001; Pilø et al. 2000, 2003; Skre 1998c; Tonning 2001; Wiker 2000, 2001).

7.2 Surveys

7.2.1 Introduction

As described elsewhere (Pilø, this vol. Ch. 6:136–7), Blindheim's excavations had taken place only in the northern part of the settlement area, and no systematic surveys had been undertaken. Very little was known about other parts of the settlement area prior to the excavation campaign of 2000–2003. The surveys were designed to collect archaeological data over large parts of the settlement area. Three types of surveys were conducted: field surveys, geophysical mapping and auger probing.

7.2.2 Field surveys

The field surveys at Kaupang were designed to provide basic information on three main issues: the dating of the settlement, its extent, and areas with special activities, such as crafts. The surveys were also meant to provide information to be used during the selection of the location of the MRE. Both traditional fieldwalking and metal detection were employed as survey methods at Kaupang. The field surveys have led to the collection of 4,336 artefacts from the settlement area: 1,940 from fieldwalking and 2,396 from metal detection (Fig. 7.1).

The settlement is situated on a slope along a former strait which once separated Kaupang from the island of Lamøya. Some parts of the settlement area are inaccessible for fieldwalking due to the presence

Modern housing

Central plateau

Surveyed areas

Modern farms (Nordre Kaupang)

of modern housing with gardens and a road (Fig. 7.2). In the central settlement area there is an elevated plateau with quite steep slopes to the north, east and south. The rest of the area generally slopes towards the southeast. The problem of displacement of artefacts due to ploughing and erosion in these slopes was obvious even before the surveys started. For this reason no light could really be shed on the location of various activities, since the large-scale displacement of artefacts had led to a blurring of whatever patterns might have been present. The situation may be different on the central plateau, where little displacement has taken place. Apart from the central plateau here, the intra-site character of the deposits which have been subjected to modern agricultural activity has very probably been completely or at least partly lost. Even so, the artefacts recovered have yielded important new evidence on the dating and the extent of the site.

Method

Field survey is normally used to detect sites in large areas. Thus most publications on this survey method tend to concentrate on how to discover sites, and how to delimit and date them. In recent years the focus has been on the methodological weaknesses of field surveys, especially on the concept of 'site' and on collection bias (e.g. Banning 2002; Frankovich et al. 2000; Haselgrove et al. 1985; Hinchliffe and Schadla-Hall 1980; Schofield 1991).

Even though there are more problems involved with the field survey method than previously recognized, it is still a valuable method of survey. In recent years the introduction of metal detectors to the surveying process has led to a marked increase in the number of artefacts recovered (e.g. Henriksen 2000). Metal detecting provides a picture of artefact distribution in the ploughsoil which has a complementary bias to that gained from traditional fieldwalking, thus leading to a more complete picture of the sites surveyed.

Today, many sites are so disturbed by modern agriculture that all the remaining evidence is scattered in the ploughsoil. In many cases some lithics and the occasional pottery sherd are all that can be observed. Field surveys of early urban settlements and central places are, however, at the opposite end of the scale. Here surveys are often undertaken on tilled soil covering intact cultural deposits. The number of recorded artefacts is very high. Metal detectors are often used, in addition to traditional fieldwalking. Water-sieving of the ploughsoil can be applied too, both as a control on collection bias and as an independent collection method.

The methodology of intra-site field survey is less well developed than that of regional field survey. While these two methodologies share some common problems (for instance delimitation and collection

bias), there are some problems which are specific to intra-site surveys, such as the uneven frequency of survey of different parts of the site, and the geo-referencing of large numbers of artefacts.

Five major variables influence the process of artefact collection:

- It is of great importance to the record whether the survey is done by visual inspection or with metal detectors. Obviously, detectors do not react to non-metal objects, leading to a clear bias in the collected material, even though metal detectorists do recover some non-metal artefacts which they happen to see. Conversely, only artefacts on the surface are recorded during visual survey, whereas artefacts up to 10 cm deep in the soil (and sometimes deeper) are recorded during detector survey.
- Survey intensity is another obvious variable. The shorter the distance between individual surveyors, the larger the number of artefacts recovered. Speed, however, is also influential here. Since many of the artefacts are very small (e.g. beads or fragmented dirhems) they may be overlooked if the walking speed is too high. Also the intensity of survey tends to increase (i.e. the walking speed decreases) when many artefacts are encountered, whereas the intensity decreases (i.e. the walking speed increases) when few or no artefacts are recovered. The combination of these two effects may create an overemphasis (on distribution maps) of artefact concentrations in the ploughsoil (Wandsnider and Camilli 1992).
- Collection bias is another variable (e.g. Shott 1995:477–8 and references cited there). The quality of survey depends greatly on the skill of the individual surveyor. Sites like Kaupang contain many different artefact types. Some artefacts are easily seen by all surveyors, while others are seen only by some. The same principle applies to metal-detector survey. In addition, the sheer quantity of artefacts will often lead to pragmatic decisions to leave behind some artefact types.
- The state of the ground surface is a very important factor during artefact collection. During fieldwalking a ploughed and then washed-out surface is preferable, whereas an even surface is ideal for metal detecting; the degree of surface washout is of no importance in metal-detector survey.
- The quality of visual survey is highly dependent on weather conditions (Bowden 1999:125). A low sun creates many contrasts on the surface, causing some artefacts to become difficult to see. The best condition is a slight drizzle which eliminates shadows on the surface and allows the artefacts to keep their colour. Weather is of little importance during metal-detector survey.

Figure 7.3 *Systematic fieldwalking at Kaupang, March 1999. Photo was taken towards the southwest of the area with the highest density of artefacts, which was in the slope northeast of the central plateau.*

Figure 7.4 *Metal detecting at Kaupang, March 2000. Photo was taken facing northeast towards the gentle slope south of the central plateau.*

There are some factors which influence only metal-detector survey, such as the type of detector, the level of ground effect (the background noise from the soil), the types of metals present, the size and shape of the metal artefacts, and the distance from the surface that the search coil is held. However, since metal detectors have found their way into the archaeological toolbox only quite recently, there is still a general lack of publications on the metal-detector survey method. This lack of publications has been exacerbated, to a degree, by the fact that metal detecting has been sub-contracted to non-archaeological specialists; neither they nor the archaeologists they have worked with have written about their experiences (with a few exceptions, e.g. Paulsson 1999).

In addition to these methodological problems during the actual collection of artefacts, there are a number of post-depositional factors which influence the ploughsoil record:

- The degree of the damage to or the destruction (from agriculture, etc.) of the cultural deposits is, of course, a major factor. Sometimes only the most recent layers are damaged or destroyed on sites with cultural deposits, leading to a dating bias in the ploughsoil assemblage. If more recent, artefactually barren, deposits have covered the artefact-carrying layers, there will be few if any artefacts in the ploughsoil in such areas, thus giving a false negative impression.
- Once the artefacts end up in the ploughsoil several factors – mechanical breakage, changes in temperature and humidity – lead to a rapid deterioration of the artefactual record. Only lithics, slag and other objects of hard material survive for long. Whether metals survive is very much influenced by the local soil chemistry. Thus the ploughsoil assemblages are biased compared to the original assemblages in the intact deposits.

- Movement of artefacts in the ploughsoil, leading to displacement or pattern blurring, is also a common problem. The most common cause of general displacement is down-slope soil erosion (Rick 1976). Individual artefacts may of course be displaced due to a number of other causes.

There are also depositional processes, which may give a picture of activities on the site, which could prove difficult to interpret. These are mainly connected to the use of middens and to artefact-specific discard patterns.

All of these factors influence the archaeological record, and thus the reliability of the interpretations. Therefore it is very important that they be discussed. However, it should be kept in mind that the goal must be to assess the real information value of these assemblages, not to disqualify them. In any case, ploughsoil assemblages cannot be used to illuminate the underlying intact deposits, any more than artefacts from different phases can be used to illuminate one another. They are assemblages which have their own special character and status. Ploughsoil assemblages are best studied by intensive water-sieving sampling, but because this is often not feasible, sampling is normally undertaken by field surveys, often in connection with small-scale sieving.

Most early urban settlements are not accessible to field surveys, Kaupang is; therefore, it is an important site in this respect. The main reason for the inaccessibility of the other sites – besides the obvious case of settlement continuity into modern times – is that no ploughing is taking place, and thus no deposits are exposed. There is, however, one notable exception in addition to Kaupang – Hedeby. Extensive surveys over many years have yielded important artefactual evidence and insight into the structure of the Hedeby site (Schietzel 1981). In addition, a number of sites loosely grouped together as 'central places' (e.g.

Uppåkra and Slöinge in Sweden, and Gudme in Denmark: Hårdh 2001; Lundqvist 2003; Nielsen et al. 1994, respectively) have similarities in finds and cultural deposits to those at Hedeby and Kaupang.

Surveys at Kaupang, both fieldwalking and metal-detecting, have been conducted with a short distance (2 m) between individual surveyors, thus aiming for a full coverage of the area surveyed. Survey walking speed has been lower than normal walking speed. Therefore, the surveys at Kaupang must be considered as very intensive in nature. The total area covered by the field surveys at Kaupang is approximately 62,500 sq m, most of which has been surveyed several times, both through fieldwalking and metal detecting. The total fieldwalked area is 60,000 sq m, while the total metal-detected area is 46,500 sq m. In general the survey conditions were excellent. Most fieldwalking was undertaken in the spring on washed-out surfaces which had been ploughed the previous autumn. Most metal detecting was undertaken in the spring, and only on more or less even surfaces.

During the fieldwalking the surveyors walked in a line (Fig. 7.3) and the field supervisor criss-crossed in the tracks behind to check whether certain artefact-types were missed by the surveyors. In contrast the metal detectorists walked individually. Because the field was harrowed just prior to the metal-detector surveys, the surveyors could use their own very visible footprints to ensure that all areas were covered by the survey (Fig. 7.4). No control of metal-detector survey quality was undertaken. If the number of artefact recoveries decreased, the walking speed of the detectorists would increase, a phenomenon also noted at Uppåkra (Paulsson 1999). This methodological problem is also well known from fieldwalking (see above) but was more pronounced in the case of the metal detecting.

Each artefact was geo-referenced individually by EDM, and assigned an ID during this process, using the Intrasis documentation system (see below). The area investigated during each survey was also mapped.

Conservation of material collected during metal-detector survey demands considerable resources. In addition there is the problem of distinguishing between Viking-age artefacts and objects which stem from farming activities in more recent times. The problem concerning the latter applies mostly to distinguishing artefacts of iron from more recent objects of iron. After the first metal-detector survey there were therefore thorough discussions on whether to leave behind groups of material – for instance unspecified lead waste from casting. However, because most artefacts had to be cleaned to determine what they were, large-scale in-field artefact discrimination was not practical. Only iron objects were not recorded during metal detecting – unless they could be identified by the archaeologists as dating to the Viking Age. During fieldwalking all materials were collected except non-tool flint, bone and iron (unless dating to the Viking Age). The ploughsoil was sieved in a small number of one-metre squares in the autumn of 1999 to check whether some groups of artefacts were being systematically overlooked during fieldwalking. This was found not to be the case, and this result was later confirmed by the large-scale sieving of the ploughsoil covering the MRE.

Modern agriculture has affected the site at Kaupang very directly. In large parts of the settlement area there are no longer any intact deposits beneath the ploughsoil. Based on auger probing, however, three main areas with deposits have been identified (Fig. 7.5). One is situated in the slope south of the excavation area of 1956–74, northeast of the central plateau. The second is in an area just south of the central plateau, where the MRE took place in 2000–2002. The third area with deposits is just outside the Viking-age beach area. The deposits in this area are

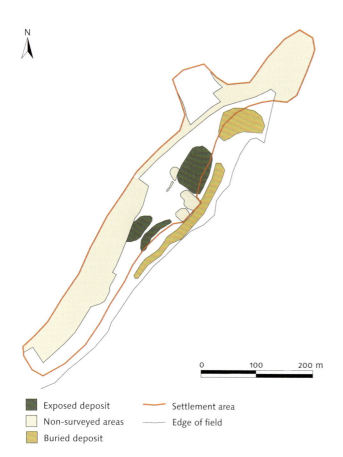

N

Exposed deposit
Non-surveyed areas
Buried deposit
Settlement area
Edge of field

0   100   200 m

Figure 7.5 *Known areas with deposits, some of them exposed just beneath the ploughsoil, while others are covered by marine sediments in the former harbour basin. Illustration, Julie K. Øhre Askjem, Lars Pilø.*

Figure 7.6 *Artefact recoveries from fieldwalking (left) and metal detecting (right) plotted on map showing the frequency of survey. Illustration, Julie K. Øhre Askjem, Lars Pilø.*

now buried beneath marine sediment. There are problems involved with auger probing as a method of identifying deposits (see below). Therefore, there may be more areas (with deposits) yet to be found, but unfortunately the extent of the preserved cultural deposits at Kaupang is not yet known precisely. This is particularly the case in the modern gardens to the southwest. This further complicates the evaluation of the connection between the ploughsoil assemblage and the intact deposits.

During the excavation of 1956–1974 the topsoil covering the excavation area was removed without sieving, and later put back into place, thus leading to only a minor distortion of the artefact record in this area.

Kaupang is missing what is commonly referred to as 'background noise' of earlier human activities in the settlement area. Because of its location very close to the sea, and the general land uplift taking place, most of the settlement area was not suitable for settlement prior to c. AD 400–600 (Sørensen et al., this vol. Ch. 12:267–70). Farming activities in more recent times have led to only small-scale deposition of modern artefacts, mostly concentrated in specific areas.

Results

Extent

The distribution plot of the material collected from the ploughsoil shows that Viking-age artefacts are found along the slope, all the way from the northern end of the survey area to the southern end. The number of artefact recoveries diminishes towards the edges of the settlement area (Figs. 7.1 and 7.6).

There are two clear clusters of material, both of which are associated with areas having preserved cultural deposits. These clusters appear on plots produced both by fieldwalking and metal detecting. Both clusters are situated in areas with a high number of survey passes, making survey intensity an issue here. However, another map (Fig. 7.7), with plotting based on the average number of artefact recoveries per survey, shows that these are genuine clusters. They are, however, probably somewhat overemphasized compared to the ploughsoil assemblage clusters, because more effort was made in areas with many finds. Furthermore, the original clusters have been extended to a larger area by ploughing and erosion. This is particularly the case with the northeastern cluster, which lies upon quite a steep slope.

Generally the intact deposits in the harbour area have made only a limited contribution of artefacts to the ploughsoil assemblage. These deposits are only marginally affected by ploughing, as they are mostly buried under later marine sediments. The consequences of this are not so visible in the central and southern part of the settlement area because erosion and agriculture have displaced artefacts from the slopes into the former harbour basin, leading to artefact recoveries there. In the northernmost sector the situation is different. Most of the surveyed area is sit-

Non-surveyed areas — Settlement area
Surveyed once · Single find
Surveyed twice
Surveyed 3 times
Surveyed 4 times

Non-surveyed areas — Settlement area
Surveyed once · Single find
Surveyed twice
Surveyed 3 times

0   100   200 m

uated in the former harbour basin, and erosion from higher areas plays no part here, since the settled area is largely covered by a road and a modern farmstead. Thus the few finds in the northern part do not necessarily imply less settlement. The lack of consistent data on the extent of the cultural deposits, both in and outside the surveyed area, makes it difficult to discuss this in greater detail at the present time.

Dating

The metal-detector survey produced by far the greatest quantity of datable artefacts, yielding a large number of coins, brooches and hacksilver. The ploughsoil assemblage points to a dating of the site to between c. AD 800 and c. AD 960/80. Important in this respect is that intact deposits are preserved in only a minor part of the settlement area. This means that artefacts from the earliest deposits are also found in the ploughsoil, and the ploughsoil assemblage does not have a clear bias towards the later part of the settlement period. The lack of a bias for the later settlement period is supported by the fact that the majority of the artefacts date from the 9th century. A handful of objects are clearly earlier than AD 800, some of them even from the 4th century, but these are so few that they are best regarded as having remained in circulation in the Viking Age. A more detailed discussion of dating is found elsewhere in this volume (Pilø, this vol. Ch. 8:172–8).

Late-medieval pottery was also recovered from the fields at Kaupang. It probably derives from the medieval farm of Kaupang, known through written sources from the early 15th century onwards. Pollen analysis hints that the farm was established at that time (Sørensen et al., this vol. Ch. 12:263–5).

Based on the results from surveys and sieving, the number of artefacts still lying in the ploughsoil in the settlement area is well above 100,000, maybe as high as 200,000–300,000.

7.2.3 Geophysical prospection

Magnetometer

A magnetometer survey was undertaken in March–April 2000, covering approximately 20,000 sq m centrally placed in the settlement area and the former harbour basin (Binns 2000). The survey was conducted by Richard Binns, M.Sc., Trondheim, using a fluxgate gradiometer *(Geoscan FM36)*. The grid system was based on 20 m squares. The measurements were conducted with a 0.5 m interval on the north-south axis and a 1.0 m interval on the east-west axis (Fig. 7.8). On the basis of the results from the first phase of mapping, three smaller areas in the south, centre and north were chosen for a more detailed survey in which the measurements were conducted with a 0.25 m interval north-south and a 0.5 m interval east-west.

The purpose was twofold. Firstly, this was an experiment to see whether fluxgate gradiometer map-

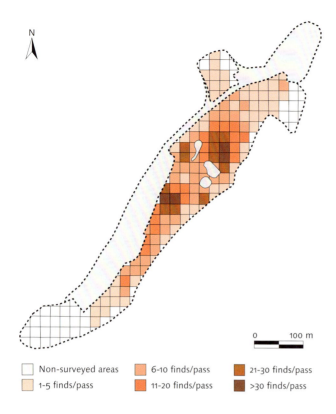

Figure 7.7 *Plotting of artefacts based on the average number of artefact recoveries per survey, both fieldwalking and metal detecting, in 20 x 20 m squares. Illustration, Julie K. Øhre Askjem, Lars Pilø.*

Figure 7.8 *Map of the area surveyed by fluxgate gradiometer (left) and a more detailed view of the results (right). In the lowest lying part of the mapped area (southeast) a speckled zone can be seen. This cultural deposit containing wooden chips, bone and other material was deposited on the bottom of the Viking Age harbour (see Fig. 7.5). Above this zone is a light grey area with parallel darker curved lines. These are beach ridges from the time of the Viking-age settlement (Sørensen et al., this vol. Ch. 12:255). Contour interval 1 meter. Map, Julie K. Øhre Askjem. Plot from fluxgate gradiometer, Richard Binns.*

Figure 7.9 *Map of the areas surveyed by Ground Penetrating Radar. Contour interval 1 meter. Map, Julie K. Øhre Askjem. Plot from GPR, Allied Associates.*

ping would provide meaningful results in the settlement area at Kaupang. Secondly, if that were the case, work would be done on the interpretation of the results of the fluxgate gradiometer survey as the results from the research excavation appeared. If the survey map corresponded with certain types of structures and deposits this might have meant that it would have been possible to gather evidence from other unexcavated parts of the site covered by the geophysical survey.

However, the results of the fluxgate gradiometer survey were not as informative as had been hoped. For example, the presence of magnetic bedrock (gab-

bro) made interpretation difficult because large areas were heavily influenced by the magnetic bedrock, showing up as black, in part white, areas on the map, because the magnetism made the calibration of the instrument difficult (Fig. 7.8). In areas with less magnetic background noise a number of concentrated dark dots (suggesting the presence of pits) could be discerned. Excavations later showed that some of these concentrated dark dots were indeed pits. In other cases, however, test excavations for possible pits revealed no such features. In these cases the high magnetic value was probably due to the presence of large boulders just below the subsoil. In one case, two

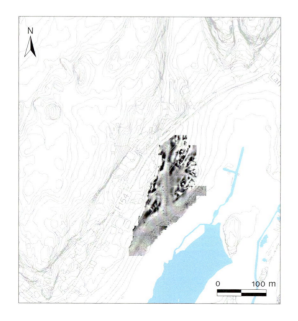

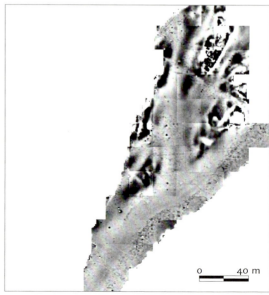

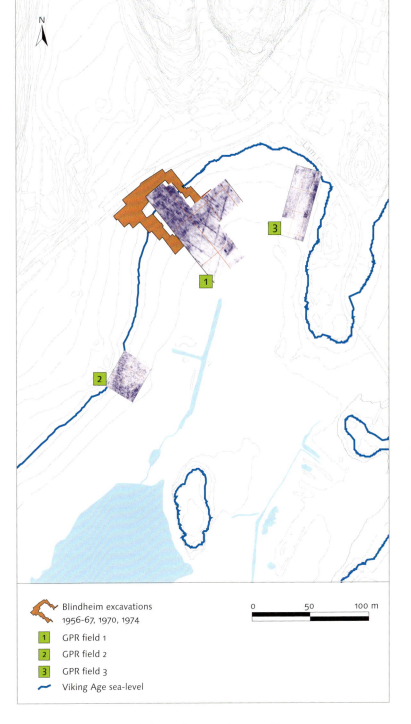

intersecting drainage ditches caused high magnetic values.

Nevertheless, excavations showed that some of the very high magnetic values were not caused by the bedrock or large boulders but rather, at least in one case, possibly by slag and the presence of several large pits. We concluded it was difficult to use the results from the fluxgate gradiometer survey as an independent source of information on the settlement area, and that excavation was necessary to verify the results. Therefore, fluxgate gradiometer surveys were discontinued.

However, one clear result is that the Viking-age beach zone can be identified on the survey map as parallel, curved, thin lines along the former strait (Sørensen et al., this vol. Ch. 12:255).

Ground Penetrating Radar

Investigations in the harbour in 2003 included a partial survey using Ground Penetrating Radar (GPR). The survey was conducted by Dr. Susanne Lorra and Dr. Andreas Karthage of Allied Associates, Borken, Germany (Lorra and Karthage 2003). The main purpose of the survey was to determine if GPR could provide information on whether intact cultural deposits were present. The GPR survey was undertaken using a *GSSI model SIR-3000 terraSIRch* as a control unit, and a 400 MHz GSSI antenna.

Three areas were surveyed (Fig. 7.9), covering a total of 6,100 sq m. Only one (Field I) yielded good results. It is situated partly in the unexcavated area surrounded on three sides by the excavation area of 1956–1974 and extending further into the former harbour. The GPR showed anomalies over a large area, between "Brygge I" and "Brygge II" and to the east of the excavation area of 1956–1974, and it was suspected that these were caused by intact cultural deposits. An evaluation trench in the summer of 2003 confirmed this. Thus it is likely that further GPR surveys at

Kaupang, combined with limited excavation, could lead to more detailed information on the extent of cultural deposits.

Augering

It was considered important to obtain an overview of the in situ deposits in the settlement area during the pilot project 1998–1999. Therefore, information was collected both by archive studies and hand-auger testing, conducted in the spring of 1999.

A hand auger was used to measure the extent of cultural deposits in different parts of the site. The

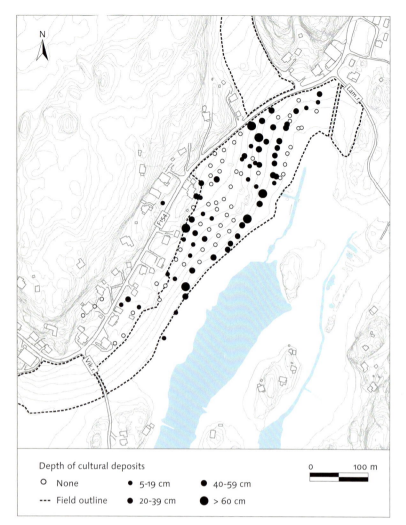

Depth of cultural deposits

○ None   ● 5-19 cm   ● 40-59 cm

--- Field outline   ● 20-39 cm   ● > 60 cm

0   100 m

Figure 7.10 *Map of auger sample points. Contour interval 1 meter. Map, Julie K. Øhre Askjem.*

Figure 7.11 *The main excavations 2000–2003. Contour interval 1 meter. Map, Julie K. Øhre Askjem.*

areas with preserved deposits, but measurements concerning the depth of the deposits were not precise. It could also be seen that Viking-age clay layers, caused by the digging of large pits, had been mistaken for subsoil, thus leading to an underestimation of the depth of some cultural deposits. In other cases the thickness of deposits, as estimated by auger testing, could not be confirmed during excavation, which was probably caused by the auger hitting large features, such as pits or more recent drainage ditches. Auger measurements in the harbour confirmed the presence of waterlogged deposits; for example, several of the deepest measurements there showed fragments of wood chips and other organic material in the lower part of the soil profiles.

Fig. 7.5 shows the main areas with preserved deposits, based on evidence from archive studies, auger testing and excavation. There are several smaller pockets with preserved deposits elsewhere in the settlement area, for instance on the central plateau and in the vicinity of the excavation area of 1956–1974. Testing in the gardens of the modern housing at Kaupang was not very intensive, and therefore little is known about the extent of deposits there.

7.3 Excavations

Initially only research excavation was planned in the years 2000–2002 at Kaupang. However, because of a long overdue refurbishment of local modern infrastructure inside the Viking Age settlement area, a number of CRM excavations were added to the excavation programme in 2000, and continued in 2001–2003. Limited trial trenching for this CRM plan was undertaken in 1999. A brief summary of each element of the fieldwork is presented here. A more detailed description of the results and a more integrated approach to their interpretation can be found elsewhere in this volume (Pilø, this vol. Chs. 8, 10; Pilø and Pedersen, Ch. 9).

hand auger contained a narrow furrow (c. 1 cm) on one side, which collected a soil profile. Measurements could be taken down to a depth of 100–110 cm. A total of 114 sample points were measured (Fig. 7.10). In addition some information was collected from four test pits, dug in connection with a geological investigation in the area (Sørensen et al., this vol. Ch. 12:269, Fig.12.11).

Even before the results were evaluated we were conscious of the fact that this kind of soil-depth mapping was of limited value compared to core drillings. However, augering is much simpler and quicker than core drilling and the low stratigraphic information value of the auger samples can be compensated for by simply taking more samples. We anticipated that some stratification would show in the auger soil profiles, but little such stratification was recorded except in the former harbour basin. Excavations in 2000–2002 demonstrated that this was not due to the absence of stratified deposits but rather to the low quality of the soil profiles supplied by the auger.

Generally, excavations in areas where auger testing had been done showed that the auger measurements were of an even lower information value than we had suspected. To some degree they could point to

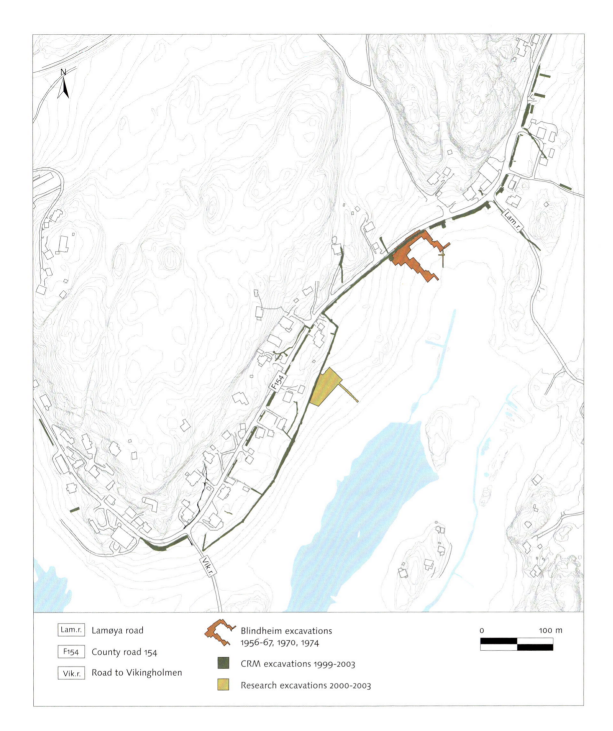

Lam.r.	Lamøya road
F154	County road 154
Vik.r.	Road to Vikingholmen

Blindheim excavations
1956-67, 1970, 1974

CRM excavations 1999-2003

Research excavations 2000-2003

0   100 m

7.3.1 The main research excavation 2000–2002

The MRE was the key part of this fieldwork campaign at Kaupang (Fig. 7.12). The excavation was planned to yield information on the start date of the settlement, on the settlement structure (especially plot division), building types, crafts and environmental issues. The excavation site was chosen because it was centrally located in the settlement area, but at the same time distant from the site of the 1956–1974 excavations. In addition it had relatively well-preserved cultural deposits and a high density of surface finds.

The excavation site covered 1,100 sq m, of which 400 sq m were excavated down to the original beach deposit (Fig. 7.13). It was situated between 3.5 and 6 m above present sea level, and thus included areas suitable for settlement. It also included the Viking-age shoreline in front of the settled area. Compared to the excavation area of 1956–1974, situated between 1.0 and 4.5 m above present sea level, it was situated on somewhat higher ground; hence, there was a greater chance of finding building remains.

7.3.2 Cultural resource management excavations 1999–2003

A large-scale excavation in areas affected by a new water and sewage system and a footpath was conducted in 2000 (Fig. 7.14), in advance of the MRE.

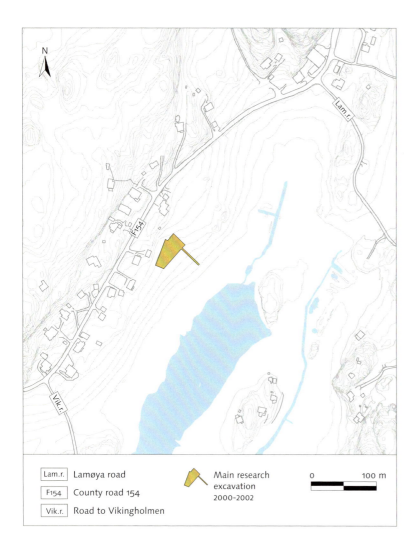

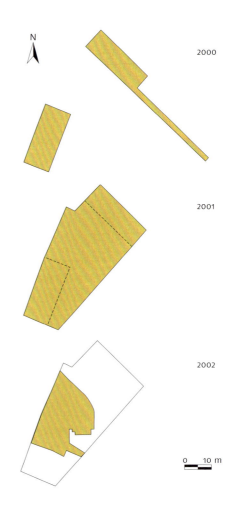

2000

2001

2002

N

Lam.r.	Lamøya road
F154	County road 154
Vik.r.	Road to Vikingholmen

Main research
excavation
2000-2002

0   100 m

0   10 m

This excavation was preceded by trial trenching in the autumn of 1999, covering 240 sq m within the site. The 2000 CRM excavations consisted of a series of trenches with a total length of 800 m. The trenches were normally 2–3 m wide, and the total excavation area covered 2,250 sq m. In 2000–2003 a number of additional shorter and narrower trenches had to be opened to allow for connections to be made between modern buildings and the new sewage system. These trenches had a total length of 650 m and covered an additional 610 sq m, bringing the total area excavated for CRM purposes at Kaupang during 1999–2003 to 3,100 sq m.

In effect these trenches constituted a series of exploratory trenches all the way from the northern barrow cemetery to the southern barrow cemetery (on the cemeteries, see Stylegar, this vol. Ch. 5). The CRM excavations allowed new evidence to be gathered from parts of the settlement area which had previously seen very little archaeological activity. However, due to the narrowness of the trenches and extensive disturbance in the areas along the modern road, the information collected is of limited value.

7.3.3 Minor excavations and surveillance

In addition to these large-scale interventions a few, more limited, excavations were undertaken.

A test excavation, which had three goals, was undertaken in the harbour area in 2003 (Fig. 7.11). These three goals were: firstly, to collect environmental evidence from the better preserved deposits in the harbour area because they were thought to contain evidence from more recent phases that were no longer preserved in the settlement area; secondly, to shed light on the quality of the GPR survey by investigating some of the deposits mapped; and thirdly, to collect evidence on the state of preservation of the deposits in the harbour. The excavation achieved all three goals. Deposits, which dated to the 9th century and possibly the early 10th century, were found, and appropriate sampling was undertaken. The extent of the cultural deposits in the harbour was seen to match GPR findings, encouraging the use of GPR as a future survey tool at Kaupang. Since the 2003 trench was close to the excavation areas of 1956 and 1958, it could clearly be seen that the state of preservation of deposits had deteriorated substantially during the last 50 years.

Figure 7.12 *The main research excavation. Contour interval 1 meter. Map, Julie K. Øhre Askjem.*

Figure 7.13 *The main research excavation year-by-year. Illustration, Elise Naumann.*

Figure 7.14 *The CRM excavations 1999–2003. Contour interval 1 meter. Map, Julie K. Øhre Askjem.*

Figure 7.15 *The ploughsoil sieving machine.*

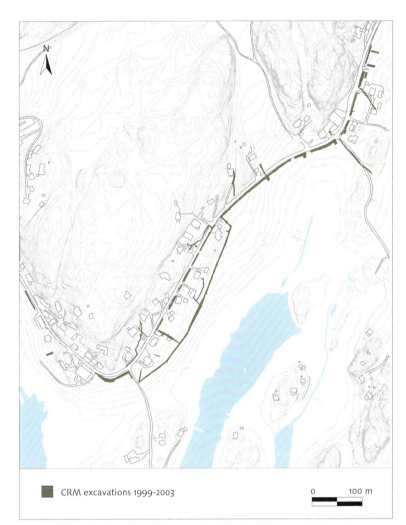

CRM excavations 1999-2003   0   100 m

Four small test pits were dug in the northern beach area in 2001 with the goal of gaining more geological information on the layers with beach sand and water-rolled Viking-age artefacts discovered during the CRM excavation in 2000 (Sørensen et al., this vol. Ch. 12:269,Fig.12.11).

7.3.4 Method of excavation

The earlier excavations in the settlement area had uncovered what were described as thick unstratified deposits (Tollnes 1998:13). However, studies of the original documentation and the published empirical evidence led us to believe that while the uppermost levels may be without stratification, the lower levels could well be stratified (Pilø, this vol. Ch. 6:133–4), as is indeed the case in comparable Viking-age urban sites (Ambrosiani and Clarke 1992; Bencard and Jørgensen 1990; Hall 1984; Jensen 1991a; Schietzel 1981; Wallace 1992). Therefore preparations were made for both mechanical and stratigraphical excavation of the deposits.

Stratified deposits were not expected in the area investigated for CRM reasons, because extensive testing with augers showed only a dark homogeneous deposit below the ploughsoil. However, as the excavation quickly proved, stratified deposits were indeed present in the area next to the MRE, even though auger testing had failed to identify them (see above). These deposits had to be excavated to a tight deadline, and full-scale stratigraphical excavation was not possible. This was unfortunate, and has made it difficult to correlate this excavation fully with the later MRE which was conducted in the adjacent area with full regard to the stratification. Nonetheless, the experience gained from this CRM excavation proved very useful when conducting the MRE. In addition, vital geoarchaeological information was collected from the longitudinal section of the trench (Milek and French, this vol. Ch. 15:328–31).

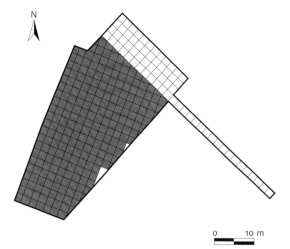

N

0   10 m

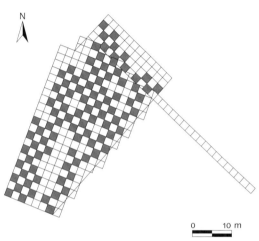

N

0   10 m

Figure 7.16 *Removal of topsoil covering the main excavation area in 2x2 m squares. Dark green areas were metal detected during topsoil removal. Illustration, Elise Naumann.*

Figure 7.17 *Sieving of ploughsoil covering the main excavation area. Soil from the dark green squares was sieved. Illustration, Elise Naumann.*

Figure 7.18 *Screen shot of Intrasis.*

fined, but their interpretations were not at all clear. During the later stages of the excavations a greater variety of effort was put into documenting individual contexts, instead of allotting the same time and effort to each individual visible layer. Some areas, like the midden area, contained very heterogeneous, deep deposits, consisting of a mass of small interleaved deposits of little archaeological value or significance. Here 5 cm spits of deposits were defined as representing a particular stratigraphic horizon and a single context, even though stratigraphy showed that there were many separate incidents of dumping here. This approach permitted more resources to be put into excavating the occupation deposits very carefully. The method worked well, and it also stressed the importance of on-site interpretation.

Because of the implementation of *single context* recording, most features were emptied rather than cross-sectioned. Exceptions to this rule were post-holes, the fills of which were cross-sectioned. If the section revealed nothing of importance (which was usually the case), the rest of the fill was removed. To enable micromorphological sampling, however, some cross-sections were established on the plots during the 2002 field season by leaving 25 cm wide sections. At an early stage the modern drainage ditches crossing the site were emptied to allow for studies of the sections they produced through the deposits. Some of these sections were documented by drawing.

To enable the sufficiently precise location of artefacts retrieved from the water sieving of excavated deposits, layers greater than 1 sq m were separated into smaller units during excavation and recording, using 1 x 1 m squares, aligned with the national geographical grid system of Norway.

Artefact recovery from the ploughsoil

It was known from the field surveys that the plough-soil covering the MRE area contained a high number

The documentation method employed during the MRE was *single context* recording which was developed in England during the 1970s in connection with urban excavations (Harris 1989; Lucas 2001). Each layer and feature is recorded as a discrete individual context; contexts are excavated in the reverse order to that in which they were deposited.

Applying *single context* recording at Kaupang was a demanding process. The cultural deposits in the settlement area are compressed and dry, and consist of humus, sand, silt and clay – except for the water-logged deposits in some of the pits, which contain a broader selection of organic material. Many of the deposits were difficult to delimit, as they had been the object of intense bioturbation and leaching (Milek and French, this vol. Ch. 15:324–8). This created a number of problems which had to be solved *en route*.

In the initial phases of the MRE much time was spent on defining each single context in order to document each one as precisely as possible, prior to moving on to their interpretation. To achieve some degree of consistency in the description of layers, a standardized layer description form was used *(The Archaeological Soils Recording Chart,* developed by Artacorn: http://www.artacorn.com). This approach did not work in practice. A high number of contexts were de-

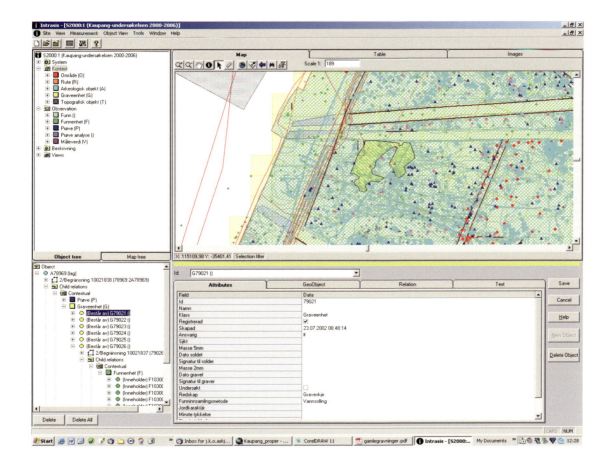

of artefacts. Full-scale sieving of the ploughsoil was not possible, but measures were taken to recover a proportion of the artefacts during topsoil removal. The excavation area was divided into 2x2 m squares (Fig. 7.16). A grid system on a different alignment was used in the northern part of the excavation. Every second square in a checker board pattern was selected for sieving, and the soil from each of these squares was stored.

The soil in the remaining squares was not sieved, but during the removal of the ploughsoil a metal detector was employed on most squares (Fig. 7.16). The soil was removed in 10-cm spits, thus facilitating metal detecting, and yielding at least some metal artefacts from unsieved squares as well.

Ploughsoil sieving was undertaken using a specially developed dry-sieving machine (based on an idea in Hunt and Brandon 1990), which in fact was a re-built cement mixer (Fig. 7.15). Under good conditions this machine reduced the soil for water-sieving by two thirds. Tests showed that it did not harm the artefacts if operated properly, even though it tumbled the soil together with small stones; in fact dirhems and other fragile objects passed undamaged through the machine. In addition to saving time during the water-sieving process, the dry-sieving also saved the ploughsoil from being washed out during water-sieving.

The original plan was to sieve the ploughsoil from every second square, but this proved too costly and not worthwhile. In the end, 35% of the ploughsoil – or c. 95 cu m – was sieved (see Fig. 7.17). No bone or other material of uncertain or post-medieval date was collected from the ploughsoil. In spite of this, more than 1,400 finds units were recovered from the ploughsoil covering the MRE area, including slightly over 2 kg of ceramics, and 19.5 kg of flint.

The distinction between the ploughsoil and the culture layers below was easily visible during this work. It was mostly the later medieval plough layer that appeared below the modern ploughsoil. In some areas modern ploughing had removed all cultural deposits, so that removal of the topsoil exposed the original beach deposit.

Water-sieving of the intact deposits

All excavated deposits from intact contexts and from the later medieval plough layer were water-sieved. The basic mesh width used was 5 mm. In addition, part of each intact context, never less than 20% of the total, was sieved through a 2 mm mesh. The first bucket of soil from a new context was always sieved in the 2 mm mesh. If interesting remains appeared, such as debris from glass-bead production or concentrations of fishbone, the remainder of the deposit was also sieved to 2 mm. A record was kept of the volume of soil excavated from each context and of the amount sieved through the 2 mm and 5 mm meshes respectively. Only beads and zooarchaeological material recovered from the 2 mm mesh have been catalogued separately; other material from the 2 mm mesh has been catalogued together with that from the 5 mm mesh. In all, about 120 cu m of cultural deposits was sieved.

Environmental archaeology and geoarchaeology

Samples for environmental analysis were taken during the MRE, in cooperation with *The Centre for Human Palaeoecology* at the University of York. The samples for environmental archaeology were GBA samples *(General Biological Analysis)* and BS samples *(Bulk Sieving Samples)* (Dobney et al. 1992). By far the most important specific results were derived from the GBA samples, while the BS samples yielded only meagre remains of seeds, which had limited general information value. The results of the environmental archaeological analysis are described at length elsewhere (Barrett et al., this vol. Ch. 14), including an analysis of the zooarchaeological assemblage from Kaupang.

The difficulty in separating layers at Kaupang presented many problems to the excavation crew. To gain more information on how the deposits were formed, and what kind of processes had affected them, an extensive programme of soil and sediment sampling was launched in 2002. This was done in cooperation with the *Charles McBurney Laboratory for Geoarchaeology* at the University of Cambridge. The geoarchaeological samples were analysed by a variety of analytical methods, of which thin-section soil and sediment micromorphology proved the most valuable. The results from the geoarchaeological analysis are presented at length elsewhere (Milek and French, this vol. Ch. 15).

Dendrochronology

Dendrochronological dating of wooden planks and timbers from Kaupang has been undertaken by Niels Bonde at the National Museum of Denmark. The results from the dendrochronological analysis are described elsewhere (Bonde, this vol. Ch. 13).

Intrasis

The basic tool for field documentation at Kaupang was *Intrasis* (short for *Intra-site Information System)*. Here only a brief outline of what Intrasis is and what it can do will be given. More information can be gained at http://www.intrasis.com. Intrasis is an archaeological information system for recording and managing field data, developed by the Swedish National Heritage Board *(Riksantikvarieämbetet).* The system is based on Geographic Information System (GIS) technology and runs on software based on Windows standards.

This software is used to register, import, edit and manage data derived from a special type of Electronic Distance Measurer (EDM) called Geodimeter (Fig. 7.19).

The data are stored in a database (an MS-SQL server database), and Intrasis works as the interface for the user to this database. It is possible to adapt the structure of the database to a current excavation which allows, for instance, the addition of new types of artefacts, features, samples etc. The computer system is thus quite flexible.

Intrasis also consists of an extension for ESRI ArcView GIS. The Intrasis GIS extension is used for downloading data from the excavation database to ArcView. At the Kaupang Excavation Project, Intrasis was normally used only for entering and editing data, while ArcView was used for analysis and presentation of data.

An important part of Intrasis is its capability to map and at the same time encode the archaeological layers and features. This enables measurements of layers, features, samples etc. to be imported and placed in the correct table in the database. The coding gives features, layers, samples etc. unique identities and can also be used to create relations between them. When, for example, the outline of a posthole or the location of an environmental sample is measured, it is automatically given a unique number by the Geodimeter. At the same time the 3D measurements are encoded, making it possible for the system to recognize what the object is (for instance an environmental sample), and also to which context it belongs (a specific hearth for instance). When measurement data are imported from the Geodimeter, the system registers information on the ID number of the environmental sample, which context it belongs to and its exact geographical location. The creation of relationships between for instance, features and layers, can also be achieved manually during data entry and noted on context sheets (see below).

Intrasis is not perfect, but it works well and is stable. It crashed seriously only a couple of times during the period 2000–2004, which is not a bad track record considering that it was bombarded with data for three years, and that it was still under development at the time. More than 100,000 individual points were measured. Support was received from the developers by phone and e-mail when trouble occurred. Even if data was lost due to a crash, it could be restored from a backup. The Kaupang Excavation Project cooperated closely with the developers of Intrasis, including an annual meeting where experiences from the preceding excavation season were discussed; these experiences were taken into account in further development of the programme.

When Intrasis handles a lot of data, as was the case at Kaupang, its performance suffers because the structure of the programme is complex and because

Figure 7.19 *Georeferencing during field survey.*

the data have to pass through a network. There are ways around these problems, such as using a specific view in the programme and using a faster network connection , but they are not full solutions; hence, the editing of objects in particular is slowed down. Furthermore, Intrasis does not yet handle section drawings.

Using computer programmes for the storage of archaeological data always raises the question of how accessible these data will be in the future. This is also a concern of the Kaupang Excavation Project. Since Intrasis is used on a large scale in Sweden the accessibility problem will not be only a local problem for the Kaupang Excavation Project alone, but will have to be dealt with centrally by the National Heritage Board. This emphasises the advantages of using internationally developed computer systems; the file formats used by Intrasis are based on international standards, which offers a sense of security of sorts (safety in numbers) because it ensures that if these formats are no longer used for some reason, the problem will be international rather than local in nature.

There are several problems concerning digital documentation, three of which will be addressed here. One problem concerns the definition of the geographical limits of layers and features and the question of doubt/uncertainty. The Intrasis system does not accept dotted lines. So the archaeologist documenting the limits of a context, if uncertain as to where its limits are, will have to make a decision on the spot instead of resorting to the normal dotted line. The dotted line can be a good thing because it represents the uncertainty of the excavator. It can also, however, be an excuse to postpone (indefinitely) a decision about the extent of a context, which often results in problems during the post-excavation phase. If the excavator is uncertain about the extent of a layer, this uncertainty should be noted in the 'free text' field available on the context sheets. Adjusting the

extent of a layer during the excavation process is easily done, either by editing the existing polygon or by mapping and importing a new polygon (coined 'Geo-object' by Intrasis) and deleting the previous one.

A second problem is that the system allows extremely precise documentation of layers and features, a problem already touched upon. Instead of letting interpretation guide decisions as to what are considered meaningful contexts, the system allows for each thin layer, each little seemingly insignificant feature, to be recorded and excavated individually. In principle then, interpretation can occur at a second stage. This is potentially a good idea, especially because it facilitates the re-interpretation of the recorded data. However, the idea of excavating and recording objectively first and interpreting subjectively later is a problematic concept (Andrews et al. 2000; Hodder 1997), and has its roots in the excavation methodology of the 1970s and 1980s, and its links to New Archaeology (Chadwick 1997). Moreover, what archaeologists perceive as meaningful contexts (and interpret as occupation layers, middens, dumps etc.) may however be undermined by micromorphological analysis of how these contexts were formed. Furthermore, there is the problem that in the real world, excavations do not have infinite economic resources. Attempts have to be made to answer specific research questions within time and money budgets. From this perspective documenting every single context, just because it is now easier to do so, is not necessarily sensible. It could lead to the excavation of a better documented but smaller area, and lead to a failure to answer the key research questions that inspired the excavation. The focus must remain on the research questions and upon field interpretation. Sometimes it will be sensible to excavate very carefully (for instance with primary deposits in buildings), while at other times it will be more sensible to disregard small layers and patches in the stratigraphical sequence and instead excavate in thicker contexts (for instance in re-deposited layers), guided by field interpretation, as was done in Ribe (Feveile and Jensen 2000).

A third, more technical problem is that it is difficult to refer to contexts by their numerical IDs. There are simply too many numbers to keep track of. At Kaupang this has led to the continuation of the traditional field method of nicknaming contexts (often sniggered at today), a method also used in Blindheim's excavations at Kaupang. At the new Kaupang excavation objects have been nicknamed *Christer's latrine, The corner-timbered well* or even *The super-gravel* during the excavation process. As Intrasis provides the option of naming objects *in addition* to giving them an ID number, these names can be recorded in the system. The function of the names should, however, be limited to the excavation and interpretation process.

Despite these three problems, using Intrasite-GIS has been a great help for the Kaupang Excavation Project. When implementing this kind of GIS technology in fieldwork, archaeologists (including us) have learned that the technology involved requires that they undergo extensive preparation and education, which in turn implies the need for permanent excavation staff. Furthermore, the technology does not make the excavation phase either faster or less expensive; rather, the opposite is rather the case. The benefit is that the technology eases the management of large amounts of data. The system allows each individual archaeologist to participate in the documentation process and it facilitates their access to all available field data. It also makes it possible to analyse the data in greater detail during the excavation, increasing the level of on-site interpretation and thus the quality of excavation. In addition it cuts down dramatically on post-excavation and post-survey work. All these benefits make the extra work before and during the excavation more than worthwhile.

Context sheets

Context sheets were an important part of the documentation process for the Kaupang excavation. It is now possible to record data electronically in the field, but because no fully satisfactory electronic system was available at the time, information was written down on context sheets and then entered into the system manually indoors. There were different context sheets for layers and features, and there were also sheets that were used to keep track of the subdivisions within archaeological layers.

All basic documentation was done by the individual excavators. The forms they used contained compulsory fields where certain types of data had to be entered. This secured a consistency in what was recorded about each context. Alongside the standard fields the forms also contained a free text field, where the excavator could add information on the basis for the interpretation, further descriptive details, doubts and queries, etc.

7.4 Summary

The fieldwork at Kaupang was designed to provide information on certain aspects of the settlement: dating, extent, structure, character and building types. Both surveys and excavations were conducted to recover data which could illuminate these aspects. Because the fieldwork took place in a rural landscape, it was largely up to project managers to decide which areas would be the target for investigations. Only modern housing with gardens in the southwestern part of the settlement provided some obstacles to the collection of data.

The settlement area at Kaupang provided excellent opportunities for field-survey, because large parts of the site had been cultivated until recently. In addition, much of the Viking-age deposits have been destroyed by ploughing, yielding a ploughsoil assemblage that is not too distorted chronologically. The collected material has given the site a wider chronological span than the excavations have revealed, but the core still lies in the 9th century. The surveys have also provided evidence from parts of the settlement where very little archaeological activity had previously taken place.

Sufficient intact deposits remain in limited areas to allow for stratigraphic excavation to provide chronological sequences and permit studies of settlement remains. The MRE was centrally located in an area with intact stratification. The CRM excavations yielded evidence from areas which had seen very little archaeological activity prior to 1998. The more recent phases of the urban site have not been revealed by the excavations (with the exception for the harbour excavation of 2003), because of destruction of the more recent deposits by ploughing.

The MRE was conducted using single-context recording, which proved very challenging due to the bad preservation of the deposits. The implementation of micromorphological analysis became a valuable tool in the interpretation of the deposits. Environmental sampling was undertaken according to the York protocol. Dendrochronology provided important dating information.

Nevertheless, it must be remembered that the quality of the evidence at Kaupang does not allow for definitive and detailed answers to all the questions asked about the settlement because the evidence has been altered or destroyed, both by depositional and post-depositional processes. Therefore, the evidence comes in bits and pieces, which have to be fitted together as well as possible. Much of the picture is missing because it has been destroyed by post-depositional processes, as is commonly the case in archaeological excavations.

The Settlement: Extent and Dating

8

LARS PILØ

The available evidence for the extent and dating of the settlement at Kaupang is analysed in this chapter. The sources used are mainly archaeological, and derive from both settlement and cemetery contexts. Particular emphasis is attached to the settlement evidence; data from both earlier (1956–1974) and more recent excavations (2000–2003) are considered. Furthermore, information on sea-level changes is also important when considering the extent of the settlement.

Plot-division has been found in three widely separate areas: in the excavation area of 1956–1974 to the north, in the cultural resource management (CRM) trench of 2000 on the central plateau and in the main research excavation (MRE) area of 2000–2002, just south of the plateau.

It is suggested that the settlement extended further north than previously believed, perhaps by as much as 200 m. The character of the northernmost settlement, however, is not well illuminated by excavations, and no traces of plot-divisions or building remains have yet been found there. The evidence in the settlement area south of the MRE is sparse, but there are some indications of more permanent settlement in part of the area. Due to a new, higher estimate of the Viking-age sea-level, the available strip of land suitable for settlement is now thought to have been narrower than previously believed.

The combined evidence from dendrochronology and artefacts points to the establishment of the settlement around AD 800. The earliest dendrochronological date, AD 803, is for a wooden jetty. The stratigraphical evidence in the settlement area comes to an end c. AD 840/50, for some intrusive pits possibly as late as AD 900. Dating information from the more recent phases is based on artefacts from the modern ploughsoil and on deposits in the harbour. These suggest that the settlement at Kaupang ended some time between 960 and 980.

8.1 Introduction

The Viking-age town of Kaupang was once a large specialized settlement for production and trade, which left a very definite imprint on the landscape in which it was situated. Its central area, divided into plots with houses, was continuously used; peripheral areas were probably used only temporarily. Surrounding the settlement were several large cemeteries (see Stylegar, this vol. Ch. 5:Fig.5.2). However, during the thousand years or so since the settlement was abandoned, farming has obliterated most of the visible traces of the settlement and its cemeteries. This has led to uncertainty concerning the extent and dating of the settlement, and the size of its cemeteries.

Today, Kaupang is a quiet setting for farming and suburban housing (Fig. 8.1, left). Due to land upheaval the sea-level has fallen by c. 3.5 m, transform-

ing the landscape (Sørensen et al., this vol. Ch. 12: 271–2). The former sound, along the edge of which the settlement was once situated, has dwindled to a shallow inlet, no longer navigable. Most of the former harbour-basin is now dry land.

The precise location of the settlement area was not known before Blindheim's excavation in 1956. However, the cultivated soil along the western side of the Kaupang inlet had a very dark colour, which bore witness to its origin as disturbed settlement deposits. This led Blindheim to start excavations here (see Pilø, this vol. Ch. 6:129). Blindheim's excavations of 1956–1974 provided new information on settlement remains in one particular area of the settlement, but overall knowledge of the settlement area remained sketchy. When the map of the settlement was published by Blindheim (et al. 1981), the extent of the set-

area (Hougen 1993:50-53). They highlighted the ambiguous evidence concerning the settlement in the 10th century – a recurrent theme in the investigation of Kaupang.

In this chapter the extent and dating of the settlement area will be examined in more detail than has previously been possible, based on new data collected during the fieldwork of 1998–2003 (Pilø, this vol. Ch. 7) and on studies of archival material (Pilø, this vol. Ch. 6). Other information on the settlement – character, plots, buildings and activities – will be discussed elsewhere (Pilø, this vol. Ch. 10).

8.2 Topography

Even though it might be difficult to picture in light of today's lower sea-level, the settlement at Kaupang was originally situated along the western side of a sound (Figs. 8.1 right and 8.2). From the north, small boats from the inner Oslofjord area could reach Kaupang through a waterway protected by islands. Larger boats would have had to follow an outer route because of the shallowness of the sound at the northern end of the Viksfjord (see Blindheim et al. 1981:23–32 for a description of waterways around Kaupang). To the south, however, all passage had to take place on the open sea. In addition a major regional waterway – the *Lågen* River – flows into the sea close by (Fig. 8.3). Therefore, from a logistical point of view the location of the settlement was well chosen, although other

tlement area was estimated on the basis of four main criteria: an assessment of the local topography, the presence of dark-coloured topsoil, the absence of graves, and a Viking-age sea-level estimated at 2.5 m above present sea-level (Blindheim et al. 1981:19; Tollnes 1998:11-12). The dating of the settlement area to the late 8th and the 9th centuries was based on the dating of artefacts collected during the excavations of 1956–1974 (Blindheim et al. 1981:181-6). The cemeteries, however, continued in use until the middle of the 10th century. A few metal artefacts, dated to the 10th century, had also been collected from the settlement

Figure 8.1 *Left: Kaupang today. Right: Kaupang with a sea-level 3.5 m higher, as it was in the Viking Age. Photo, Dagfinn Skre, edited by Lars Pilø.*

Figure 8.2 *A 3D map of the Kaupang area with a sea-level of 3.5 m. Estimated settlement area with plot-division marked with a black contour. Illustration, Lars Forseth and Lars Pilø.*

Figure 8.3 *Map of the Kaupang region today. Double arrow with "?" marks a shallow sound which may have been passable in smaller boats in the Viking Age, cf. Brink, this vol. Ch. 4:Fig. 4.1. Illustration, Julie K. Øhre Askjem.*

issues, such as politics and agricultural resources in the vicinity, also played a major role in the choice of this location.

The borders of the settlement appear quite well defined. To the north the settlement was delimited by a mound cemetery, to the west by rock outcrops (which rise quite steeply up to 32 m above present sea-level) and to the south by another mound cemetery and the sea. The eastern border was defined by the sea.

New evidence from studies of sea-level changes indicates that the sea-level around AD 800 was c. 3.5 m above present level, not 2.5 m as previously estimated (Sørensen et al., this vol. Ch. 12:271–2). Thus the area suitable for settlement was more limited than previously believed, especially in the north where land suitable for building was already scarce. The Viking Age building remains in the main research excavation (MRE) were situated no lower than 4.5 m above present sea-level, i.e. 1 m above the Viking Age sea-level. The reason for this buffer-zone between the sea and the settlement is very likely to be the regular occurrence of high tides. Because of the local topography Kaupang would have been vulnerable to high tides, especially in connection with storms from the southeast, which are now (and were probably then) common during autumn and winter (Sørensen et al., this vol. Ch. 12:268).

There is a beach deposit of coarse sand overlying marine clay along the Viking-age shoreline in the settlement area. In higher areas the subsoil is moraine with a high frequency of stones; on the slopes from the central plateau clay is the predominant subsoil. Evidence suggests that the inhabitants of Kaupang avoided settling in areas with clay, i.e. only pits are found in such areas. They preferred to settle in the areas with coarse sand.

When the area was settled around AD 800, the first inhabitants would have had an easy time of

clearing it. The area was covered with a typical coastal vegetation of grass, small bushes and alder near the sea, and a forest of pine and oak further inland (Sørensen et al., this vol. Ch. 12:260–6). The vegetation along the shore was removed during the initial phase of the settlement. Little other clearance was necessary, as the area did not contain many large stones and boulders (Sørensen et al., this vol. Ch. 12:254, and observations during excavations). In the areas closer to the sea, only a thin layer of soil had formed on top of the beach deposit (Milek and French, this vol. Ch. 15:328), and here settlement took place more or less immediately on the beach sand.

A small brook (marked on Fig. 8.10) through the northern part of the settlement area provided the only supply of running fresh water on the site. Otherwise fresh water must have been drawn from wells; it is abundant a metre down in the subsoil in most of the settlement area.

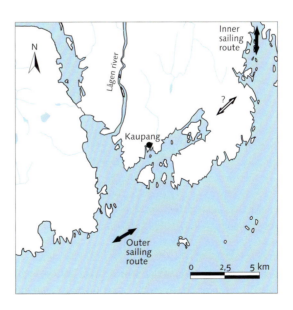

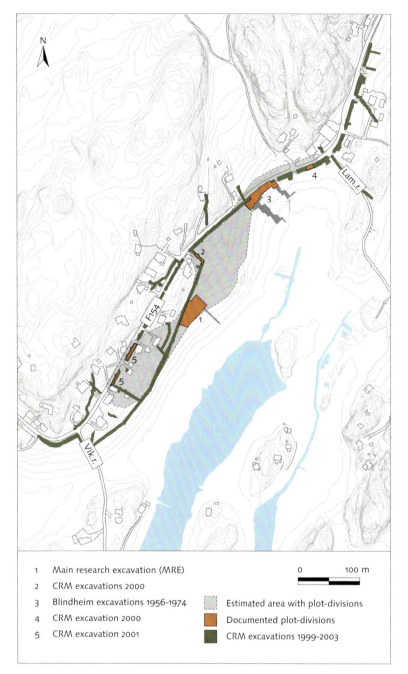

1   Main research excavation (MRE)
2   CRM excavations 2000
3   Blindheim excavations 1956-1974
4   CRM excavation 2000
5   CRM excavation 2001

0   100 m

         Estimated area with plot-divisions
         Documented plot-divisions
         CRM excavations 1999-2003

8.3 The extent of the settlement area

The settlement area at Kaupang can be divided into two parts: a central area with plot-divisions or indications of plot-divisions, and peripheral areas without plot-divisions or indications thereof. While the presence of settlement deposits may be demonstrated quite effectively through coring, test pitting or small-scale excavations, plot-division is best documented through large-scale excavation. Therefore our knowledge of the presence of plot-divisions is limited by the extent of excavated areas, which are arguably quite small compared to the total size of the settlement area. In addition, major parts of the settlement area have seen only trenching, which has yielded little more than indirect evidence of plot-division.

Figure 8.4 *Estimated area with plot-divisions (in grey). Documented plot-divisions in brown. Contour interval 1 meter. Map, Julie K. Øhre Askjem.*

Figure 8.5 *The southern settlement area. Contour interval 1 meter. Map, Julie K. Øhre Askjem.*

Figure 8.6 *Plot-divisions in the MRE.*

Figure 8.7 *Photo of possible path or small road at the western end of plot 4B in the CRM trench of 2000. The measuring rod is 2 m long in 25 cm divisions. View facing north.*

The southern settlement area

Plot-division is best documented in the (MRE) (Figs. 8.4, no. 1 and 8.6). Three plots (1A, 2A, 3A) were completely excavated and three other plots further west (1B, 2B, 3B) were partially excavated. Two other plots (4A, 4B) were clearly visible to the north of plots 3A and 3B. In addition, more plots could be discerned in areas which were cleaned but not excavated. In the Cultural Resource Management (CRM) trench adjoining the MRE a possible path or small road was found. It consisted of a double row of stones situated at the edge of the slope, at the western end of plot 4B (Fig. 8.7).

Even with plot-divisions so well documented in the central part of the site, only 40 m further west the situation is quite different. A rock outcrop limits the available area for settlement a few metres east of the MRE. On the western side of this exposed bedrock there is a distinct layer of fire-cracked stones (Fig. 8.5, no. 1) and pockets of deposits similar to the later medieval plough layer in the MRE. The latter was also noted during Blindheim's 1958 observation of a trench in this area (Tollnes 1998:19-20). Extensive layers with fire-cracked stones are generally dated to the period c. AD 600–1400 in Scandinavia, with a main concentration in c. 800–1200 (Pilø 2005:136-40). This layer of fire-cracked stones contained a glass mosaic bead of Viking-age dating, and thus in all likelihood is contemporary with the Viking-age settlement. However, the area above the rock outcrop seems to have had a character quite distinct from that of the plot-divided settlement area below.

The area south of the MRE has yielded only sketchy information on the settlement, as it has been seen only in trenching (Fig. 8.5). In addition there is no preserved stratigraphy in the cultivated fields, only pits and other features cut into the subsoil. The southernmost part, just north of the Vikingholmen road, is partly disturbed due to modern building

activities. The evidence for plot-division is thus meagre and indirect.

Artefacts recovered from the ploughsoil in the cultivated southeastern part of the settlement area point to activity all the way south, ending close to the modern road to Vikingholmen (Fig. 8.5), but artefact finds are far fewer than further north (see Pilø, this vol. Ch. 7:Fig.7.2). The ploughsoil in the cultivated southeastern part shows little trace of disturbed cultural deposits, being light in colour and containing only a few fragments of burnt bone and the occasional fire-cracked stone. However, a large part of the sur-

veyed area is in the former harbour-basin, which could explain the low frequency of artefact finds. Most of the southern area that might have been part of the Viking-age settlement contains modern houses and gardens today; it is therefore inaccessible to surface surveys.

Several pits were found in the cultivated field during CRM trenching. Two pits (A1625, A1635; Fig. 8.5, no.2), immediately to the south of the main excavation area of 2000–2002, were of much the same character as the pits in the main excavation area, containing preserved wattle in their waterlogged, lower parts.

Figure 8.8 *Excavated settlement remains on the plateau. View facing west. Sketch, Lars Pilø.*

Figure 8.9 *Excavated settlement remains on the plateau. Contour interval 1 meter. Map, Julie K. Øhre Askjem.*

Figure 8.10 *The northern, plot-divided settlement area. Contour interval 1 meter. Map, Julie K. Øhre Askjem.*

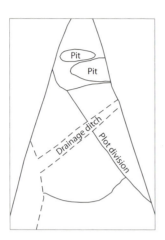

A series of six radiocarbon dates of the wattle has confirmed their Viking-age date. Further south another pit appeared (A14204; Fig. 8.5, no.3); this feature seemed to have been backfilled shortly after being dug and no artefacts were recovered. Some 10 m north of this pit a shallow ditch (A12714) ran at right angles to the shoreline. It was 1.5–2 m wide, c. 0.2 m deep at the most; the excavated length was just over 4 m, and it lay between 4.3 and 4.7m above sea-level. Associated artefacts indicate a Viking-age date. This structure may well be the remains of a plot-boundary or a lane/alley.

Even further south another area with pits appeared (Fig. 8.5, no. 5); these pits were more irregular in shape, and not waterlogged, so that no wood was preserved. They yielded only a few datable artefacts, such as ceramics, but generally the artefacts appear to be of Viking-age date. There were also some traces of settlement features in the same area as these pits, like shallow ditches. However, due to the narrowness of the trench it was not possible to determine precisely the character of the remains here. The natural beach deposit in the trench in this area lies at only 4.1–4.4 m above present sea-level. This is maybe too low to allow for building remains to be found – in the MRE, the building remains were at least 4.5 m over sea-level.

However, in the gardens to the west of the CRM trench, away from the Viking-age shore-line, two small areas with intact archaeological deposits were uncovered (Fig. 8.5, no. 4). The deposits contained hearths and several artefacts (including crucible frag-

ments, ceramics, slag and a lead spindle-whorl). The narrow excavation trenches, of which large parts were disturbed, did not permit detailed information on the character of the settlement here. No clear plot-division has been documented in this area so far, but it cannot be ruled out, given the limitations of the available data. The presence of hearths, apparently of the same type as those found in the buildings in the MRE, does suggest that houses and maybe also plot-division were present here.

The CRM trench in the field contained no cultural remains to the south of the area marked no. 5 on Figure 8.5, where the height of the natural beach deposit continues at the same level (4.1–4.4 m above present sea-level). Only at the very end of the trench, close to the Vikingholmen road, does the terrain rise to 4.8 m above sea-level, but still no cultural activity was detected.

Based on the evidence from the trenches, the settlement area with plot-divisions did not extend all the way to the southern barrow cemetery. The exact limit of the plot-divided area is difficult to estimate, but it probably ended just south of the area with pits in the CRM trench in the field (marked "5" on Figure 8.5), and also just south of the area with hearths and settlement finds, (marked "4" on Figure 8.5). However, there is little to indicate that an extensive dumping layer – like that found in the MRE – was present in the southernmost part of the estimated area with plot-divisions. This absence of an extensive dumping layer could indicate that this area saw less intensive settlement activity than the central area.

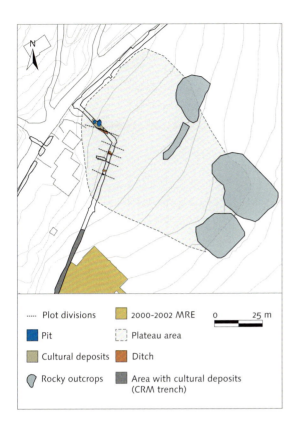

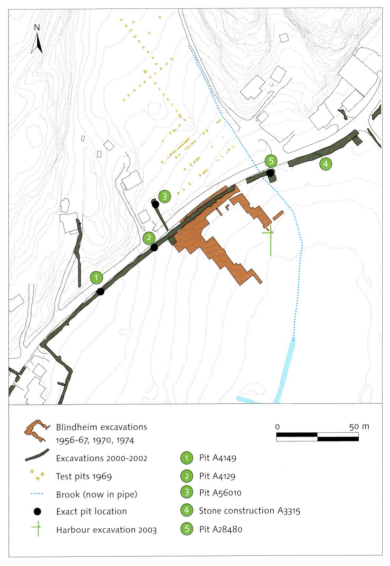

Blindheim excavations
1956-67, 1970, 1974

Excavations 2000-2002

Test pits 1969

Brook (now in pipe)

Exact pit location

Harbour excavation 2003

1 Pit A4149

2 Pit A4129

3 Pit A56010

4 Stone construction A3315

5 Pit A28480

..... Plot divisions

Pit

Cultural deposits

Rocky outcrops

2000-2002 MRE

Plateau area

Ditch

Area with cultural deposits (CRM trench)

0   25 m

0   50 m

There is little to indicate the character of the settlement further to the south, beyond the limit of the estimated plot-divided area. It may only have been used temporarily or seasonally. The low number of artefact recovered from the ploughsoil suggests only limited activity, and no artefacts were recovered south of the modern road to Vikingholmen. In this southernmost area settlement was delimited by a barrow cemetery to the south (see Stylegar, this vol. Ch. 5:Fig.52), and by the bedrock of Kaupangåsen to the west.

The central plateau

No traces of plot-division or cultural deposits were found in the CRM trench in the slope between the area of the MRE and the central plateau. This may be the result of destruction of remains by ploughing, but it is also possible that the slope was not settled. On the plateau itself no preserved deposits and only a few features were encountered in the southernmost 25 m of the trench, and the evidence for the presence of plot-division is meagre. However, in the central western part of the plateau, deposits, features and clear evidence for plot-division were encountered (Fig. 8.4, no. 2).

Settlement deposits, several small ditches, a number of post-holes, and two large pits were discovered (Fig. 8.8). These remains are interpreted as representing plots with buildings and associated wells. The alignment of the ditches and the limits of the cultural deposits, which probably indicate plot-boundaries, provide some structural information about the lay-

out and orientation of the settlement on the central plateau (Fig. 8.9). The ploughsoil has a dark colour in the western part of the plateau, also indicating the presence of a disturbed settlement deposit.

The eastern part of the plateau has not seen any excavation, and there is little to suggest that there are cultural deposits preserved here today. Fewer artefacts have been recovered here than further west on the plateau, and the light colour of the ploughsoil suggests that cultural deposits of the same character as further west on the plateau are not present. As the area in question is quite flat and bounded on two sides by outcrops, it does not seem at all likely that the light colour of the ploughsoil is a result of the destruction and subsequent down-slope erosion of Viking-age deposits. The fluxgate-gradiometer map does not show any clear anomalies here, except for what could be some large pits. The lack of information allows a number of different interpretations. The eastern part of the plateau could have been without permanent settlement, and left open for a number of different purposes (assembly area, market, seasonal

Figure 8.11 *Deep narrow pit (A4149), excavated in the northern slope of the central plateau. Scale to the left is 2 m in 25 cm divisions.*

Figure 8.12 *A stone construction (A3315) found 2000 north of the excavations of 1956–1974. It was covered by modern road fill, and therefore had not been as much affected by modern ploughing as other remains in the area.*

Figure 8.13 *The excavation area of 1956–1974, with plot-divisions indicated. Sketch, Lars Pilø.*

The northern settlement area

The northern settlement area is quite well defined by the topography (Figs. 8.1 and 8.2). A large rocky hill *(Kaupangåsen)* rises steeply in the west, effectively blocking any extension of the settlement in this direction. To the northwest the topographical situation is the same, with another rocky hill *(Kuleåsen)*. Between the two hills, however, there is a area with moraine deposits. At the top of the slope, some 100 m from the Viking-age shoreline, a flat area extends towards the north. A settlement area with traces of post-holes and cooking pits was uncovered just north of the slope in 2005, during CRM trenching (Vandrup Martens, pers. comm.). This settlement area may be centuries older than the Viking-age settlement (see below). Further north this area turns boggy, and eventually becomes a real bog, the Kau*pangmyra,* from which the pollen samples described by Sørensen et al. (this vol. Ch. 12:260–5) were taken.

No traces of cultural deposits or plot-divisions were found in the CRM trench in the northern part of the central plateau. Between the central plateau and the excavation area of 1956–1974 there is a slope which lies along the modern main road. It is badly disturbed by recent ploughing; therefore, no cultural deposits are preserved in its upper part. Three deep pits were uncovered in this area (Fig. 8.10, nos. 1 (A4149), 2 (A4129) and 3 (A56010); Fig. 8.11). Two of these, A4149 and A4129, contained a number of Viking-age artefacts; A4149 also contained wood which could be dated by dendrochronology to post–AD 793 (Bonde, this vol. Ch. 13:279). The third pit, which contained a wooden barrel, did not yield datable artefacts in the fill. A radiocarbon date from the barrel was 1380+50 BP, cal AD 620–770 (Beta 206202). As the dated barrel was made of spruce, a tree species which may reach an age of over 100 years, this date could well be indicative of Viking-age construction.

Artefacts have been recovered from the upper

settlement with tents). Or it could have been used for a different kind of settlement, which did not leave behind the usual deposits so typical of the settlement at Kaupang, for instance a high-status building (or buildings). Without any hard evidence, however, this all remains speculation.

Apparently there was only permanent settlement and plot division at the western end of the plateau. The reason for this may be that a main road ran through the length of the settlement here. No such road has been found during the excavations on the plateau, but its existence is inherently likely; otherwise all movement along the settlement would have had to take place in the beach zone, where the loose sand would not have been at all convenient for carts etc. In addition, movement along the beach zone would have been disrupted by the rock outcrops at the eastern end of the central plateau.

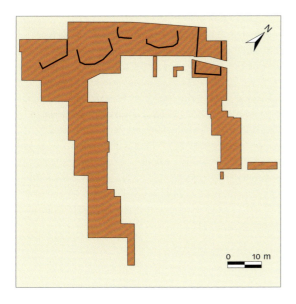

part of the slope during field surveys, albeit in lower numbers than further down slope. The evidence suggests that there was settlement activity here in the Viking Age, but damage to the evidence by ploughing and erosion makes it hard to reach definitive conclusions. The subsoil here is mainly poorly drained moraine and some clay, which may have been considered less suitable for settlement than the better drained beach sands further down slope.

In fact, intact cultural deposits are preserved further down slope, closer to the Viking-age shoreline, and this area had the highest frequency of artefact recovery during the field surveys. The ploughsoil here is very dark, which also suggests the presence of disturbed cultural deposits. However, this area has seen only limited test pitting and augering (Pilø, this vol. Ch. 7:Figs.7.6, 7.7, 7.10), and little is known about the character of the remains here.

The excavation site of 1956–1974 was situated in a shallow depression to the southeast of the slope. Based on the reinterpretation of the structural remains, which are quite similar to the remains found in the MRE, plot-division is present here (Fig. 8.13; see Pilø, this vol. Ch. 10:194 for more detailed information on plot-division).

Indications of plot-division were found even further north than the excavations of 1956–1974. The CRM excavations in 2000 showed the presence of a stone construction similar to those seen in the excavations of 1956–1974 and 2000–2002 (Fig. 8.10, no. 4; Fig. 8.12: A3315). A pit (Fig. 8.10, no. 5:A28480) was found between the excavation area of 1956–1974 and feature A3315.

Much of the Viking-age deposits to the immediate north of A3315 were destroyed by foundations for 19th-century farmhouses. There are artefacts in the ploughsoil in the tilled part of the area south of the Lamøya road, but they are not as abundant as the artefacts in the ploughsoil in the central area. Most of

the area just south of the Lamøya road would have been below Viking-age sea-level; therefore, the low frequency of finds could simply reflect that. There is, however, no evidence for plot-division north of the stone construction A3315.

The slope between Kaupangåsen and Kuleåsen was investigated by Blindheim through a series of test pits and trenches in 1969 (Fig. 8.10; Tollnes 1998:20-21), and field surveys took place here during 1998–2002 (Pilø, this vol. Ch. 7:144–9). There are few artefacts in the ploughsoil on the slope, and to judge from its colour the ploughsoil does not appear to contain disturbed cultural deposits, except in the lowermost few metres. However, artefacts and disturbed cultural deposits could have moved down the slope due to ploughing and erosion. The test pits and trial trenches in the slope revealed a few small features, and some artefacts, including a weight, were recovered from the ploughsoil at the same time.

Above the slope there is a flat area which was also test pitted by Blindheim, but no artefacts were recovered. The field surveys barely touched upon this area, and likewise did not produce artefacts. This flat area is most likely outside the Viking-age settlement area, but what may be earlier settlement remains are located here.

Due to the absence of the characteristic dark-coloured ploughsoil caused by disturbed cultural deposits, this area was interpreted by Tollnes as having been an open area that may have seen sporadic settlement. With the newly collected information on post-depositional processes on the site in mind, it now seems reasonable to interpret it as a part of the settlement site that was not divided into plots, and which did not see permanent settlement in the Viking Age.

The peripheral area to the north

When the first map of the settlement area was produced following the excavations of 1956–1974, the set-

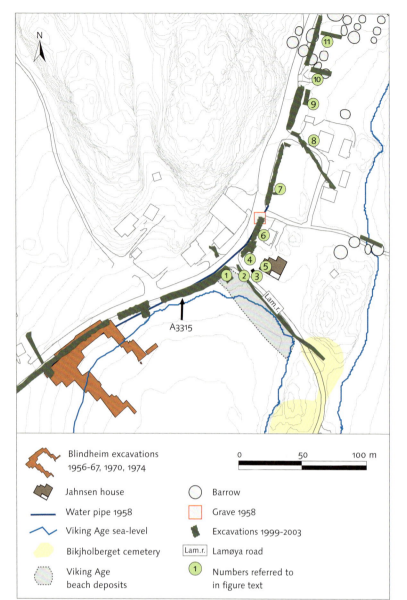

Figure 8.14 *Evidence from the northernmost settlement area. Green areas are excavation trenches from 1999–2003. 1: Test pits in beach deposit. 2: Old sewer trench 3: Test pit. 4: CRM trench. 5: Extension of Jahnsen house. 6–7: CRM trenches. 8: CRM trench, with the encircled "8" marking the location of a large pit (A94901). 9–11: CRM trenches. Contour interval 1 meter. Map, Julie K. Øhre Askjem.*

Figure 8.15 *Stratified occupation deposits in a section of the trench along the Lamøya road. A series of thin black occupation deposits, intersected by lenses of sand, can be observed below a thick, more recent plough layer. Length of folding rule c. 20 cm.*

beach-deposit are of the Viking Age. The beach stopped approximately where the Lamøya road runs today. On the spot marked "1" on Figure 8.14, three 1 sq m test pits were dug into the beach-deposit, which at its highest point was 3.8 m above present sea-level.

A typical stratified occupation deposit was observed in the northwestern part of a trench along the Lamøya road (see Fig. 8.14, no. 2 and Fig. 8.15). It appeared to be of much the same character as the earliest deposits in the MRE, i.e. thin, black occupation deposits, intersected by lenses of sand, and lay c. 3.8 m above present sea-level. It was truncated by a more recent plough layer, which had presumably removed the upper parts of the Viking-age deposit here. As this part of the fieldwork was only a watching brief (the re-excavation of an old sewer trench), no excavation of deposits took place, and there is no information on the date of the lowermost, black deposits.

Viking-age settlement deposits were also documented less than 10 m further to the northeast, and slightly further away from the beach. A test pit (Fig. 8.14, no. 3 and Fig. 8.16) showed the presence of stratification which yielded information both on settlement and beach formation. The sandy layers in the section which are situated up to 4.05 m above present sea-level did not contain artefacts. They are presumably of pre–Viking-age date, and associated with the beach which was present in the area prior to the establishment of settlement here. The layer marked "6" on the section (as in the archive report) contained a sherd of Badorf pottery, as well as a high frequency of both zooarchaeological material and fire-cracked stones. The layer above ("5") likewise contained much zooarchaeological material and fire-cracked stones. Fire-cracked stones were also reported from the layer above "5". The Viking-age deposits had apparently been truncated here by a more recent plough layer, visible in the upper part of the section. The findings in this test pit were similar to previously

Legend

Blindheim excavations 1956-67, 1970, 1974

Jahnsen house

Water pipe 1958

Viking Age sea-level

Bikjholberget cemetery

Viking Age beach deposits

Barrow

Grave 1958

Excavations 1999-2003

Lam.r. Lamøya road

1 Numbers referred to in figure text

0   50   100 m

tlement itself was not thought to extend much further than just north of the area then excavated. Before the excavations resumed in 2000 the basis for this assumption was questioned, as the available evidence pointed to the presence of both settlement remains and graves to the north of the Lamøya road (Pilø, this vol. Ch. 6:136–7).

As can be seen from Figure 8.14, a number of CRM trenches were excavated in the northern peripheral area between 1999 and 2003. These trenches were quite narrow and in addition heavily disturbed by modern trenching for pipes, cables etc., so the information gathered is often meagre and difficult to interpret.

Between the Bikjholberget cemetery and the stone structure A3315 (Fig. 8.14), there was a small bay in the Viking Age, with a beach of fine-grained sand. The sand here contains numerous artefacts (slag, beads, pottery, whetstones, etc.) and many bones, mostly water-rolled. All the datable artefacts from the

Figure 8.16 *Photo taken in test pit (Fig. 8.14, no. 3). Layer marked "6" contained Badorf pottery and slag, in addition to a high frequency of both zooarchaeological material and fire-cracked stones, which were also present in the layer marked "5". The sandy layers beneath "6" did not contain artefacts and are presumably pre–Viking-age beach-deposits. The length of the section is about 1 m.*

reported findings from this area (Blindheim et al. 1981:77–8 and reports in the project archive).

Archive studies have pointed to the presence of iron slag to the north of the Lamøya road (Pilø, this vol. Ch. 6:136–7). The excavations of 2000–2003 also led to the recovery of iron slag both north and south of this road, including slag from intact Viking-age deposits, as described above. In addition, slag was present in the fill of one of the grave mounds here. An earlier date for some of the slag is not very likely as palynological analysis has shown that there was very little activity at Kaupang prior to the establishment of the settlement (Sørensen et al., this vol. Ch. 12:270–2). It is most likely that the iron slag is associated with the Viking-age settlement.

The CRM trench marked "4" on Figure 8.14 contained a layer of fire-cracked stones, and a number of artefacts were recovered from this deposit – glass beads, soapstone, iron and bone. A high frequency of fire-cracked stones was also noted when the Jahnsen house was extended in 1978 (Fig. 8.14, no. 5; report in the project archive).

The CRM trench marked "6" on Figure 8.14 contained a modern plough layer. A number of artefacts were recovered from this layer – a weight, ceramics, amber, glass, iron, slag, burnt clay and bone. A small pit was also uncovered.

The CRM trench marked "7" on Figure 8.14 contained three pits, but only one of these contained intact deposits, which included a glass rod, glass beads, glass, iron, slag and bone.

As one moves further north and enters one of the Kaupang farmsteads, evidence of settlement becomes scarcer. Archive studies had indicated that this area had also seen settlement in the Viking Age (Pilø, this vol. Ch. 6:136–7,Fig.6.12), but few remains were found during the excavations of 1999–2003. Two CRM trenches along the modern main road were devoid of Viking-age settlement remains but were quite dis-

turbed by modern trenches. One large pit (A94901) with a wooden construction of standing planks was documented during the CRM excavations in 2002 (Fig. 8.14, no. 8). A wooden plank in this pit was dendrochronologically dated to the winter of AD 806/807 (Bonde, this vol. Ch. 13:279). Further north still a cultural deposit was discovered during test excavations in 1999 (Fig. 8.14, no. 9). No datable artefacts were recovered and therefore it is possible that the layer may not be connected to the Viking-age settlement.

Only a few graves and barrows are known from the area on and around the farmstead close to the pit A94901 (Blindheim et al. 1981:55–7). However, keeping in mind that this area has been the location of a farmstead since at least the early 19th century, it is remarkable that there were preserved grave mounds here that could be recorded at all. It is likely that most graves in this area – belonging to the southernmost part of the barrow cemetery at Nordre Kaupang – were removed before the first map of these monuments was produced in 1866. A ring ditch associated with one such mound, situated 20–30 m south of the mapped cemetery, was found during test trenching in 1999 (Fig. 8.14, no. 10 and Fig. 8.17). This area is discussed in detail by Skre (this vol. Ch. 16:368–9,381–2).

Further north still, in another test trench, a small number of features was documented within the known limits of the mound cemetery (Fig. 8.14, no. 11). These appeared to be possible settlement remains, but no dating evidence was recovered.

The most plausible interpretation of the data described above, especially the structures and artefactual evidence, is that the settlement area extended well to the north of what was previously believed to be its limit. However, no evidence has so far been produced for plot-divisions or building remains this far north, which suggests that the character of the settlement here differed from that in the settlement's central areas. Possibly this northern, peripheral area was

used only temporarily during summer seasons. The high frequency of slag suggests that smithing took place here, an activity which is dangerous to conduct inside a dense settlement because of the fire risk involved. The high frequency of fire-cracked stones in the area close to the beach is also noteworthy. At some point during the life-span of the settlement the northernmost part was abandoned and some of it was later used as a cemetery (see Skre, this vol. Ch. 16:381–2). As neither the settlement finds nor the graves in this area are very precisely dated, it is impossible to know whether this change from settlement area to cemetery was a quick or a gradual process, or when it happened.

Conclusion

From the above discussion, it is possible to conclude that the settlement area was longer and somewhat narrower than estimated in Blindheim et al. 1981 (Fig. 8.18). The central part of the settlement was divided into plots, but it is uncertain whether the peripheral parts were plot-divided. The northernmost part of the settlement area does not appear to have been divided into plots.

The total length of the settled area would have been 750 m at the most. Its width varied. It could have been as narrow as 20 m in the northern part but as wide as 90 m in the central part. The settled area was a maximum of 54,000 sq m, of which around 20,000 sq

m had plot-divisions. The northernmost part was converted into a cemetery in the later part of the 9th or early 10th century. The presence of these more recent graves in an earlier settlement area would suggest that the settlement area contracted over time; this process may have started in the 9th century.

8.4 Dating

The establishment of the site

Based on artefacts recovered during the settlement excavations of 1956–1974 and on the inferred dates of the earliest graves, the date of the establishment of the Kaupang settlement was believed to be the late 8th century, but that there were probably activities of various sorts at the site as early as the beginning of the 8th century (Hougen 1993:49–52, 54-5). However, new information from the excavations of 2000–2003, and a re-examination of the earliest grave finds (see Stylegar, this vol. Ch. 5:79–80), have shown that there is no firm evidence for 8th-century settlement at Kaupang.

Activities pre-dating the settlement

The earliest traces of activity which can be associated with an urban settlement are now dated to c. AD 800, on the evidence of dendrochronology, and artefacts from the settlement and graves (see below). However, this area – which proved well suited for settlement in the Viking Age – could have been in use as a landing place or harbour for some time before the settlement was established. The hall at Huseby pre-dates the settlement at Kaupang (Skre, this vol. Ch. 11:242–3). It would be reasonable to suggest that the Huseby hall needed a nearby harbour – and the closest well-suited harbour was the bay where the town was established. However, there is little evidence to support such a hypothesis at present (Skre, this vol. Ch. 16:381–2).

So far no settlement deposits immediately pre-

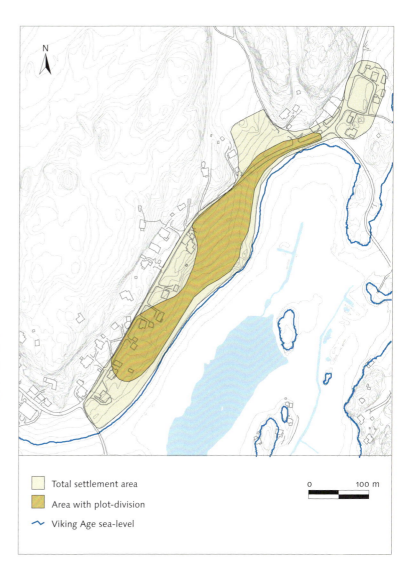

dating the Viking Age have been found at Kaupang. Occasionally artefacts earlier than c. AD 800 have been found in the settlement area, but most of these (if not all) can be dismissed as later introductions. Artefacts earlier than the Viking Age can be divided into several categories based on their context:

- Artefacts from disturbed contexts, found above the Viking-age shoreline. These artefacts may have found their way into the settlement area before the Viking Age, but could also have arrived as introductions in the Viking Age (or later). This cannot now be determined because of the lack of a secure context.
- Artefacts from disturbed contexts, found below the Viking-age shoreline. These artefacts are likely to have arrived at the site in the Viking Age or later.
- Artefacts from stratified deposits. These artefacts are found in Viking-age deposits and most likely derive from re-use, re-cycling or continuous circulation.

Of all the artefacts, the one which most likely came to Kaupang before AD 800 is a Merovingian gold tremissis found in the modern ploughsoil during metal-detector survey (Fig. 8.19). It is dated to c. AD 650 (Blackburn, in prep.). This coin was recovered in an area that would have been dry land when the coin was struck. It shows little sign of wear, and could be evidence for earlier activity in the Kaupang area or, perhaps less likely, might have been removed from its primary context during the Viking Age and redeposited at Kaupang. In any case, this is a very rare artefact in a Scandinavian context. Only five other tremisses have been found in Scandinavia, all of them along the western coast of Jutland, and all believed to derive from 7th-century deposits (Blackburn, in prep.).

A number of dirhems, recovered as single finds

Figure 8.20 *Four dendrochronologically dated wooden posts in the excavation of 1956–1974, indicated by arrows and squares. Plan from Tollnes 1998:plate 12A, with additions. Illustration, Roar L. Tollnes, edited by Lars Pilø.*

from the ploughsoil, predate AD 800; many of these were found above the Viking-age shoreline. However, 8th-century dirhems are regularly included in late 9th- and 10th-century hoards in Scandinavia, and thus their presence at Kaupang is no indicator of pre–AD 800 activities here (Blackburn, in prep.).

A fragment of an equal-armed brooch of copper alloy (C52519/14481), of probable 8th-century date (Hårdh, in prep. b), was recovered from the later medieval plough layer in the MRE area. However because, stratigraphically, it overlay deposits from the early Viking-age, it cannot point to pre–AD 800 activities on the site. This is probably a piece of scrap metal.

Other pre–Viking-age artefacts from disturbed or uncertain contexts were found at or below the Viking-age shoreline:

Two Roman coins have been collected from the settlement area (Blackburn, in prep.). One is from the MRE, but from the later medieval plough layer (C52519/1014067: Constantine 1, AD 307–337) and the other is from the excavations of 1956–1974, but with uncertain stratification (B1022a: Valentinianus 1, AD 364–375). Both find spots would have been in the water or at the water's edge if the coins were deposited within 100 years or so after they were struck, thus making it more likely that they arrived at the site as later introductions. Roman coins are well known from other Viking-age sites, such as Ribe and Birka (Bendixen 1981:97; Feveile 2006a: 284–5; Jensen 1991a:19; Rispling 2004:27-8).

Two strike-a-lights of a Migration-period type have been recovered from the modern ploughsoil near the excavations of 1956–1974 (C32106 and C33585a: the latter erroneously ascribed to Søndre Kaupang in the catalogue of the Museum of Cultural History, University of Oslo). Their find spots would have been under water in the Migration Period, and therefore they were most likely deposited here at a later date. Curiously, these are the only strike-a-lights from the Tjølling parish and two of only eight such artefacts from Vestfold. It is possible that they should be linked to the settlement remains on the flat area, just north of the slope (mentioned above). This type of artefact is normally recovered from graves, and the find spot (at the bottom of the slope) means that they could originally have been deposited in graves, located on the upper part of the slope, that were destroyed in the Viking Age or later.

Re-use of older artefacts is also a possible reason for the presence of three pieces of flint with invasive retouch, one of which is part of a handle for a flint dagger of Late Neolithic/Early Bronze-age date. The three pieces of flint were recovered from the modern ploughsoil in the settlement area. These artefacts must have been deposited in the settlement area at a far later date than their date of production, as their find spots would have been covered by at least 10 m of water in the Late Neolithic; however, these three artefacts show no signs of water rolling. Therefore, they probably arrived at the site in the Viking Age, either for re-use as strike-a-lights or simply because their peculiar retouch and shape led to their collection as curiosities.

One artefact of pre–Viking-age date was recovered from an intact deposit in the MRE, i.e. a fragment of a cruciform brooch of Migration-period date (C 52519/16453: Hårdh, in prep. b). However, the date of the context is definitely early Viking-age, and therefore this artefact should probably be regarded as a piece of scrap metal.

Excavation in the beach deposits below the earliest layers associated with the settlement yielded a few examples of small lenses of humus, sometimes with a few fragments of bone. There were no artefacts associated with these lenses. They are probably the result of sporadic human activity on the beach, but a natural origin cannot be excluded.

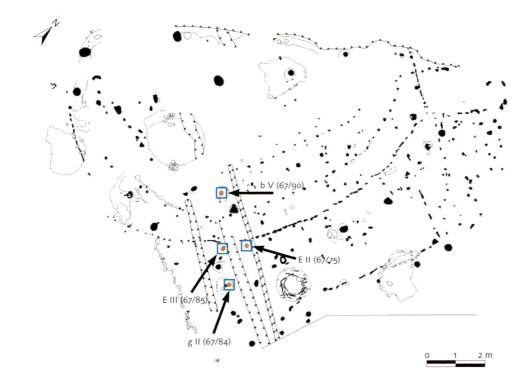

b V (67/90)

E II (67/75)

E III (67/85)

g II (67/84)

0   1   2 m

There is no palynological evidence for farming in the area prior to the establishment of the settlement. This is not very surprising because the area suitable for farming would have been very limited in the centuries preceding the settlement. The higher sea-level would have left only the central plateau available for farming, and even this would have been exposed to a salty environment. However, traces of ploughing with an ard have been found underneath two grave mounds (situated 8–9 m above present sea-level) at Lamøya (Blindheim and Heyerdahl-Larsen 1995:51-2), so agriculture was practised in the vicinity. It cannot, however, be excluded that this cultivation was contemporary with the settlement, as the graves, which are later than the agricultural traces, cannot be more precisely dated than to the Viking Age in general.

Some clearance of pine seems to have taken place in the area from the beginning of the 8th century, and birch clearance even earlier (Sørensen et al. this vol. Ch. 12:263). This could simply indicate the exploitation of wood in the area by nearby farms, as there is little evidence for grazing.

The conclusion is that so far there is little evidence for settlement activity in the centuries immediately preceding the establishment of the urban site. There are only faint traces of agricultural activities in the Kaupang area. Thus, as far as we know, the settlement was founded on "virgin" land, on a beach in an area which had seen little or no prior settlement in the immediately preceding centuries. However, it is possible that in the 8th century the area may have been used as a harbour for the nearby settlement at Huseby.

The start date for the settlement

The evidence for the dating of the earliest settlement at Kaupang is threefold: dendrochronological dates, dates of artefacts in the earliest layers (especially glass beads), and the dating of the earliest graves from the cemeteries.

The earliest dendrochronological dates derive from three wooden posts (EII, EIII, gII), which had been hammered down into the beach, just outside a plot ("Hus I") uncovered in the excavations of 1956–1974 (Fig. 8.20). The sapwood was fully preserved, and thus the felling date for all three posts could be precisely identified as the summer of AD 803 (Bonde, this vol. Ch. 13:276, Tab.13.2 nos. 67/84, 67/85, 67/75). There are no traces of earlier use on these posts. They may be from the northwestern end of a wooden jetty. In addition there is another sample, with the sapwood nearly intact but without the bark, which is dated to AD 797–802 (Bonde, this vol. Ch. 13:276, Tab. 13.2, no. 67/90). This derives from one of the planks around a post in the b-series (bV). Two other structures (A94901 and A10135), from the CRM excavations in locations distant from the excavations of 1956–1974, are dated to AD 806/ 807 and AD 808, respectively. Together with the AD 803 dates they indicate increased construction activity at Kaupang from AD 803 onwards. However, it is important to note that the dendrochronologically dated timbers are not associated with the Site Periods of the MRE and cannot be related with certainty to the earliest structural remains from the excavations of 1956–1974. The dendrochronology thus provides an absolute dating of when the settlement at Kaupang must have existed, but it does not necessarily provide a start date *per se*.

Figure 8.21 *Wasp beads from the MRE. Upper left bead is 15 mm long. Photo, Eirik I. Johnsen, KHM.*

Figure 8.22 *Calibrated radiocarbon date from the excavations of 1956–1974. Original date was given as 1120+ 90 BP. A new calibration was done in 2003. Illustration produced in Oxcal by Lars Pilø.*

Figure 8.23 *10th-century glass bead (C52517/2686), recovered during field survey. Diameter of bead 15 mm. Photo, Eirik I. Johnsen, KHM.*

The dendrochronological dates may indicate the establishment of the market place, but could as well indicate the beginning of the permanent settlement – a phase during which the construction of more elaborate structures probably became more common.

Datable artefacts from the stratified deposits of Site Period (SP) I in the MRE provide an independent dating of the earliest settlement. In essence this means analysing the glass beads and the composition of the different types (Wiker, rep. in proj. archive) as the other artefact types available do not have the same chronological information value. A comparison with the detailed bead chronology of Ribe (Feveile and Jensen 2000) is important in this respect, but not without problems: some bead types present in Ribe c. AD 800 and before are not present until SP II at Kaupang. However, the bead types present in the SP I deposits, such as segmented metal-foil beads and small, drawn beads, fit well with a dating of SP I to c. AD 800. The so-called "wasp beads" (Fig. 8.21), of which there are six from stratified deposits in the MRE (but only one from SP I deposits), are common in Ribe in the last decades of the 8th century, but also appear occasionally in layers dated to the very early 9th century (Feveile and Jensen 2000). The blue polyhedral beads which are common in Ribe in the 8th

century but disappear before c. AD 790 are not found at Kaupang. In summary, beads did *not* appear at Kaupang before c. AD 790 and perhaps not until c. AD 800.

One sherd of supposed Mayen pottery has previously been used to support a dating of Kaupang to the 8th century (Hougen 1993:28, 54). However, recent finds of Mayen pottery in mid–9th-century deposits at Birka suggest that this dating is too narrow and that similar pottery could have reached Kaupang after AD 800 (Bäck, pers. comm.).

The radiocarbon dating of samples from the Blindheim excavation has previously yielded dates ranging from the 5th to the 9th centuries (Hougen 1993:49 and archive information). However, as was usual at the time, the dated wood was not identified by species. Consequently little value can be attached to the datings, as the samples may derive from long-lived trees like oak or pine. Only one sample, from two thin wooden stakes in the harbour, has an acceptable context, and its dating is 1200+90 BP (T-132) which, if calibrated, covers the entire Viking Age (Fig. 8.22).

The cemeteries at Kaupang were believed to contain a few graves of possibly late 8th-century date, but doubt has been cast on these early datings (see Stylegar, this vol. Ch. 5:79–80). The lack of evidence for farming in the area in the centuries immediately preceding the establishment of the settlement makes it less likely that these graves, if of late 8th-century date, can be connected to pre-existing settlements in the area. However, graves may have been situated in the area for other reasons, prior to the establishment of Kaupang settlement, perhaps because of harbour activities connected with the hall at Huseby (Skre, this vol. Chs. 16 and 19).

According to dendrochronology, the settlement was in use by AD 803. The glass beads found indicate a date for the earliest deposits of c. AD 800, and not before c. AD 790. Altogether, the evidence available

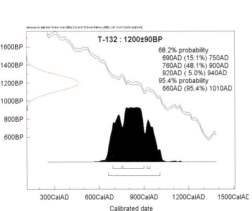

T-132 : 1200±90BP

68.2% probability
690AD (15.1%) 750AD
760AD (48.1%) 900AD
920AD (5.0%) 940AD
95.4% probability
660AD (95.4%) 1010AD

points to quite a narrow time span for the start of the settlement, i.e. within a decade prior to AD 803.

The end date of the settlement

While the start date of the Kaupang settlement is relatively precisely defined, the end date is more elusive, and some of the evidence seems contradictory. The main problem is that the cultural deposits from the most recent phase of the settlement (SP III) have been destroyed by ploughing. The dating evidence in the settlement area is thus mostly in the form of stray finds in the ploughsoil.

The surviving features from the most recent settlement phase are the intrusive pits with preserved wood that can be dated dendrochronologically. However, the number of features that can be dated this way is small. The dendrochronological dates from Kaupang's most recent settlement phase derive from the CRM trench beside the main excavation area of 2000–2002, i.e. the construction dates of two large, intrusive pits (A15175 and A9422). The dates are the winter of AD 849/850 and AD 850, respectively; a piece of wood dumped into the latter feature was dated to AD 863 (Bonde, this vol. Ch. 13:280, A14098).

However, there can be no question that the settlement, or at least activity at Kaupang, extended much later. Most of the Islamic coins probably arrived at the site in the second half of the 9th century. However, nine coins date to the 10th century, and four of them, recovered from different parts of the settlement area, were struck in the mid-10th century (945/946, 945–951, 952–954, 951–955; Blackburn, in prep.). They might have been deposited as early as the 950s, but probably no later than 980 – in that case one would expect Western coins and other artefact types from that period to be represented.

Two of the weight types (cubo-octaedral and spherical) which were frequently recovered from the ploughsoil are normally dated post-AD 860/880, and

appear in graves at Kaupang dated to AD 900–950 (Pedersen, in prep. a).

Some 200 of the approximately 4,000 glass beads recovered from Kaupang during the fieldwork of 1998–2003 can be dated to the 10th-century, according to the glass bead chronology published by Callmer (1977). However, some of the less diagnostic or common types supposedly of 10th-century date have also been found in intact stratigraphic deposits at Kaupang dated to the first half of the 9th century, implying that their date-range was set too narrowly by Callmer. The better defined types assumed to be of 10th-century date are found almost exclusively in the late-medieval or modern plough layer, and therefore are more reliable indicators (e.g. Fig. 8.23). Twenty-five of these are dated as late as c. AD 950–980 according to Callmer (Wiker, report in project archive).

There are also only a very few pieces of 10th-century metalwork from the excavations and surveys of 1998–2003. The excavations of 1956–1974 revealed four or five metal artefacts which could possibly be of 10th-century date (Hougen 1993:50–3). However, they are not diagnostically 10th-century types, but could also be dated to around AD 900 or slightly before. Two pieces from the fieldwork of 1998–2003 are, however, likely to be of a 10th-century date. Two fragments of a trefoil brooch with late–Jellinge-/ early–Mammen-style decoration were recovered from the modern ploughsoil above plot 1A in the MRE. The brooch can be dated to the middle of the 10th century (Signe Horn Fuglesang, pers. comm.). There are also a few pieces of metalwork in the Borre Style, but as this style developed in the second half of the 9th century these pieces cannot be used to prove 10th-century activity at Kaupang.

Remarkably, in view of the marked presence of Badorf ware at Kaupang, there is a complete absence of the succeeding pottery-type, the readily recognizable Pingsdorf ware. This is a very common type of pottery in the 10th century, which began to appear from the very beginning of that century (Sanke 2001). It is, however, doubtful whether much chronological weight can be attached to the absence from Kaupang of a specific 10th-century Continental pottery type. To date, English pottery has not been recovered at Kaupang either, probably because of the nature of the contact between Kaupang and England, i.e. the pottery-using people of England did not travel to Kaupang. That is hardly surprising given the historical context. Likewise, the heavy increase in Viking raids on the Continent following the death of Louis the Pious in AD 840 could be an important factor in the change of contact patterns, which may be demonstrated by the absence of 10th-century Continental pottery-types at Kaupang.

The cemeteries were used unabated until the middle of the 10th century, at which time most pre-Christian graves disappear from the region (Stylegar, this vol. Ch. 5:81–2). The types of graves remained the same, and the frequency of burial in the cemeteries apparently saw no diminution.

Based on the available evidence discussed above, it can be stated that there was 10th-century settlement activity at Kaupang and that it ended some time between 960 and 980. There is thus no longer a dating discrepancy between the settlement area and the cemeteries. However, it is still an open question as to what kind of settlement activity took place at Kaupang after AD 840/850, as there are no preserved settlement deposits from this period, only fill in pits and re-deposited material in the harbour. This question of the character of the site post–AD 840/850 is discussed further in Chapter 10 of this volume.

Kaupang after the Viking-age settlement

Evidence from palynology suggests that there was a phase of forest regeneration after the site had been abandoned (Sørensen et al., this vol. Ch. 12:266).

Soon, however, agriculture started in the settlement area, and has continued until the present day. The areas close to the shore were most likely left for grazing, until land upheaval made them a less salty environment. This means, for instance, that both of the major excavation sites probably remained untilled down to the late Middle Ages. This fits well with artefactual evidence recovered from both the late-medieval plough-layer and the modern ploughsoil here, consisting of late-medieval pottery and baking stones (bakstehelle). A farm at Kaupang is mentioned for the first time in 1401 (DN V:290), and again in 1402 (DN I:419).

8.5 Summary

The Viking-age settlement at Kaupang was established around AD 800. It was situated on the western shore of a sound that was connected to the inner Oslofjord region at its northern end and to the open ocean to the south. At its zenith the settlement extended for 750 m along the shore, while in width it varied between 20 and 90 m. The settled area covered 54,000 sq m. Approximately 20,000 sq m of the area was divided into plots. The peripheral areas to the north, west and south were probably used in a different way than the central, plot-divided areas. These peripheral areas may have been occupied only seasonally, or used for special purposes. Some of the northernmost settlement area was converted into a cemetery in the later part of the 9th or first half of the 10th century.

The available evidence suggests that settlement activity continued well into the second half of the 10th century when, after the settlement activity came to a halt, the forest started to regenerate in the area. By the end of the Middle Ages farming gained a foothold in the area, and has played a major role since then in the transformation and destruction of the Viking-age remains.

The Settlement: Artefacts and Site Periods

9

UNN PEDERSEN, LARS PILØ

A quantitative overview is given of the artefacts recovered during the surveys and excavations in the settlement area 1998–2003. A stratigraphic sequence based on the main research excavation of 2000–2002 is presented. The excavated deposits are divided into three main Site Periods. Site Period I is identified as the initial seasonal settlement, which probably lasted less than 10 years. Plots were demarcated from the beginning of this settlement. Site Period II starts when houses were built on the plots. This period can be divided into two sub-phases on some of the plots. The end of Site Period II is created by the disturbance to the deposits by ploughing. The transition to Site Period III, which covers the remaining period of settlement, is therefore not contemporaneous within and between plots. The only remaining intact deposits from Site Period III are from pits dug into the earlier deposits. Two plough-layers cover the intact, stratified deposits; a later medieval plough-layer and the modern ploughsoil.

The distribution of the artefactual evidence from the main research excavation of 2000–2002 is analysed according to the different Site Periods to provide a sequence of both chronological and functional character. Several types of artefacts, present from Site Period II onwards, are not represented in Site Period I. There is little change in the artefactual record between Site Period II and III. There is, however, a clear distinction between the artefacts from intact deposits from Site Periods I–III (covering c. AD 800–900) and the artefacts in the plough-layers (covering c. AD 800–960/980). In addition to early 9th century material, the latter contain dirhams and weight types of late 9th- and 10th-century origin, 10th-century metal artefacts and the majority of the rock-crystal beads, though in a disturbed context.

9.1 Introduction

The artefacts from Kaupang provide valuable information on the following issues: the dating of the site (coins, decorated metalwork, beads and pottery), craft activities (waste and tools from metal casting, blacksmithing, glass-bead production, amberworking and textile production), exchange (coins, hacksilver, weights, pottery, soapstone, whetstones, glass beads and gemstones), daily life (pottery, soapstone vessels, knives and strike-a-lights), and a number of other important issues.

Thorough discussions of these artefacts – including their dating, place of origin, function and distribution in the settlement – will be found in a series of forthcoming studies. This paper presents a quantitative overview of the artefactual record from the fieldwork at Kaupang 1998–2003 and discusses some general chronological developments in the record. The overview is based on the preliminary cataloguing.

Modifications can be expected during the publication process as a result of the completion of the conservation process and the specialists' final evaluations. The discussion of chronology is based on the material from the main research excavation (MRE) of 2000–2002 because it combines stratified deposits excavated using single-context recording and a high number of artefactual finds.

The artefacts from the fieldwork at Kaupang 1998–2003 derive from both surface surveys in different parts of the settlement area and excavation of specific sites within it. As an artefactual assemblage from a Viking-age town, it is matched only by the record from Hedeby (Schietzel 1981). Other sites – like Ribe, York and Dublin (Feveile 2006a; Hall 1984; Wallace 1992) – were not both surveyed and excavated, because these towns have seen continuous urban settlement since the Viking Age, making overall surveys impossible. Birka (Ambrosiani and Clarke 1992)

Table 9.1 *Artefacts and bone material from the 1998–2003 surveys and excavations presented by material (wood excluded), with some selected types of each presented by weight or number. Note that changes are anticipated in the course of the publication process as this overview precedes most specialists' final evaluations and the completion of the conservation process.*

+ *Includes heavily corroded iron discarded after x-ray evaluation.*

has not been readily available for field survey as no ploughing has taken place since c. 1930.

The artefacts from the MRE were retrieved by water-sieving all the excavated deposits (including the plough-layers) which were documented using *single-context* recording. This makes the record comparable to the records from the Birka Excavations 1990–1995, which also covered a settlement area from the Viking Age, excavated in *single contexts*. The 1990–1991 *Posthus* excavation at Ribe (Feveile 2006a, 2006b) was conducted in much the same way, and also provides a useful comparison, even though most of the material is somewhat older than that found at Kaupang.

9.2 A quantitative overview of the artefacts

The excavations and surveys at Kaupang have yielded a large and heterogeneous artefact assemblage, ranging from large amounts of mass materials such as slag, bones and clay to rare artefacts such as a Merovingian gold coin and a cornelian stone inlay. Amongst the metal artefacts of gold, silver, copper alloy and lead, there are coins (Blackburn, in prep.; Kilger, in prep. a, b; Rispling et al. in prep.), hacksilver (Hårdh, in prep. a), weights (Pedersen, in prep. a), Scandinavian, Continental and Insular metalwork (Hårdh, in prep. b; Wamers, in prep.; Graham-Campbell, in prep.) and waste from metalworking (Pedersen, in prep. b). The iron artefacts range from a few sword-hilt fragments and a large axe to knives, a pair of shears and a wide range of nails. Glass is represented by a wide variety of imported and locally produced glass beads (Wiker, in prep.), waste from glass-bead production, and imported vessel glass (Gaut, in prep. a). The heterogeneous stone material covers a wide variety of artefacts of amethyst, cornelian, rock-crystal, jet, garnet, amber and slate (Resi, in prep. a, b), soapstone (Baug, in prep.), sandstone, basalt from the Rhineland and more. There is a wide variety of

pottery wares (Pilø, in prep.) and a large group of clay objects including loomweights and spindle-whorls for textile production (Øye, in prep.), and moulds and crucibles for non-ferrous metalworking. There are also large amounts of iron slag from blacksmithing and sintered clay from high-temperature working. Finally, there is the animal bone material (Barrett et al., this vol. Ch. 14:Tab.14.4). A minor group of worked bone fragments includes comb fragments and gaming pieces.

In total, more than a tonne of artefact and bone material was collected during all of the excavations and surveys 1998–2003 (Tab. 9.1). The proportion of broken and fragmented objects is high – as expected of settlement material largely consisting of discarded objects and waste. The bone material is highly fragmented. Not a single complete glass, ceramic or soapstone vessel was recovered, and only seven crucibles were retrieved more or less complete. Even 30% of the generally quite small glass beads are fragmented, although many of the beads are probably accidental losses.

With a few exceptions, the datable artefacts belong to the Viking Age – with an emphasis on the 9th century, but continuing into the second half of the 10th (see Pilø, this vol. Ch. 8:172–8). There is a handful of objects pre-dating the Viking Age and a small collection of pottery sherds dated to the 12th–16th centuries. Fifteen fragments of baking plates and ten fragments of styli are most likely from the post–Viking Period as well. Moreover an indeterminable proportion of the undatable artefacts from disturbed deposits may post-date the Viking Age.

The artefacts derive from both field surveys and excavations (Tab. 9.1). The ploughsoil assemblage is dominated by artefacts made of hard and durable materials, as artefacts made of softer materials are highly susceptible to destruction in the ploughsoil. Neither flint nor bone, and only complete and imme-

Material	All surveys and excavations 1998-2003 Selected types (incl. fragments)			Field surveys/ test excavation 1998-2002[1]		CRM excavations 1999-2003[2]		Main research excavation 2000-2002[3]		Harbour excavation 2003[4]	
	Total weight in kg	Kg	No	Kg	No	Kg	No	Kg	No	Kg	No
Gold	0.01			0.002		0.002		0.006		0	
Silver	0.6			0.5		0.008		0.1		0	
Coins			70		55		2		13		
Hacksilver		0.3		0.2		0.003		0.06			
Others		0.2		0.2		0.003		0.03			
Copper alloy	4.5			3.2		0.3		1.0		0.01	
Weights			46		34		2		9		1
Ingots			82		58		5		18		1
Spillage		1.3		1.0		0.04		0.3			
Others		2.1		1.4		0.2		0.5		0.002	
Lead	23.5			19.4		0.3		3.8		0.001	
Weights			317		239		11		67		
Ingots			99		84		2		13		
Spillage		5.6		4.6		0.08		0.9			
Others		8.0		6.1		0.2		1.7		0.001	
Iron+	71.4			2.1		21.3		48.0		0.04	
Nails			3 744		4		1 063		2 677		
Weights			14		7		1		6		
Knives			50		2		27		21		
Others		46.3		1.8		13.4		31.1		0.04	
Glass	2.3			0.6		0.4		1.3		0.02	
Beads			3 825		542		597		2 644		42
Production waste		0.4		0.2		0.03		0.2		0.002	
Vessels			339		64		54		218		3
Others		0.5		0.2		0.08		0.2		0.002	
Amber	0.3			0.007		0.04		0.3		0.01	
Beads			75		2		11		61		1
Production waste		0.1				0.02		0.1			
Others		0.2		0.005		0.01		0.2		0.01	
Amethyst	0.005			0.001		0		0.004		0	
Beads			4		1				3		
Others											
Cornelian	0.02			0.006		0.004		0.012		0	
Beads			22		6		4		12		
Others		0.002		0.002							
Rock-crystal	0.5			0.02		0.02		0.5		0.001	
Beads			30		1		5		23		1
Others		0.47		0.019		0.015		0.47			
Jet	0.04			0.005		0.006		0.026		0	
Armrings			10		2		1		7		
Others		0.01		0.001				0.009			
Worked bone/antler	0.3			0.015		0.02		0.3		0	
Pottery	35.2			1.5		10.4		23.3		0.03	
Badorf		10.7		0.6		4.0		6.1		0.002	
Tating		0.5		0.04		0.1		0.4			
Others		24.0		0.9		6.3		16.8		0.028	
Clay	126.3			3.9		17.1		104.7		0.6	
Spindle-whorls			41		3		8		30		
Loom-weights		47.6		2.3		9.1		36.0		0.2	
Moulds		6.0				0.7		5.3		0.01	
Crucibles		4.5		0.07		1.5		2.9		0.003	
Others		67.7		1.5		5.7		60.1		0.4	
Soapstone	36.3			3.1		10.8		22.4		0.02	
Spindle-whorls			33		5		8		20		
Vessel fragments			453		32		82		339		
Others		12.5		1.5		5.6		5.4		0.02	
Slate	28.3			4.6		4.8		18.9		0.03	
Whetstones			1 023		132		156		728		7
Others		12.5		1.3		2.7		8.5		0.01	
Various stones	130.9			3.3		31.3		96.3		0.005	
Flint	77.6			0.08		16.1		60.8		0.6	
Slag/ sintered clay	298.5			9.5		70.6		218.0		0.4	
Bones	187.5			0.002		45.9		138.8		2.8	
Other	1.6			0.3		0.3		0.8		0.2	
All	1 025.6			52.1		229.7		739.3		4.8	

1 C52003, C52263, C52264, C52265, C52517
2 C52516
3 C52519
4 C53160

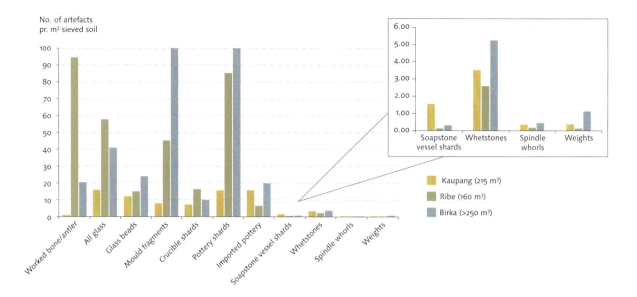

No. of artefacts
pr. m³ sieved soil

Kaupang (215 m³)
Ribe (160 m³)
Birka (>250 m³)

diately identifiable objects of iron of probable Viking-age types, were collected during the field surveys (see Pilø, this vol. Ch. 7:145). Other metals are strongly overrepresented within the material from the field surveys due to the extensive use of metal detectors. This bias can clearly be seen in the evidence for lead, which comprises 37% of the total amount of material by weight from the surveys. Lead gives a strong signal to detectors compared to gold, silver and copper alloys.

The overview in Tab. 9.1 shows how the general picture is dominated by the finds from the MRE, which make up more than 70% of the total, reflecting the considerable extent of this excavation as well as the extensive sieving regime (see Pilø, this vol. Ch. 7:155). Sieving led to the near total collection of what was present in the deposits at the time of excavation, limited only by the mesh width used in the sieves. In the case of the MRE only very small items (below 5 mm) may have escaped, but the sampling of a specific percentage of soil sieved to 2 mm mesh width (a minimum of 20% of stratified deposits) allows for an estimate of these very small items too. But of course, some objects would have been overlooked in the sieving process due to the human factor. Water-sieving was implemented on a more limited scale during the cultural resource management (CRM) excavations, and thus the artefactual records from these excavations are less complete.

The local preservation conditions at Kaupang significantly affect what is found. The unfavourable conditions for organic material in the dry cultural deposits are illustrated by the very limited amount of worked bone and antler found. Even the more substantial amount of 188 kg of unworked animal bones falls way below the 5.9 tonnes of animal bones found during the Birka excavations of 1990–1995 (Wigh 2001:37). On the other hand, the small-scale harbour excavation of 2003 in the lower lying, more humid part of the site, yielded a higher proportion of organic material such as bones, due to better preservation conditions for such material there.

Due to very poor preservation conditions for metals, much of the iron at Kaupang is corroded beyond recognition. X-ray studies have in many cases not produced any further information about the original shape of the iron objects. Hence, the total of 71 kg of iron includes 31 kg of heavily corroded iron that was disposed of after x-ray evaluation. Likewise, heavily corroded remnant traces of silver and copper-alloy objects were repeatedly observed during the excavations, but these objects could not be recovered.

Qualitatively the artefact assemblage from Kaupang has a strong resemblance to those from Birka, Ribe and Hedeby. The presence of material from crafts such as metal- and amberworking, glass-bead and textile production, and exchange-related artefacts like coins, weights, imported beads and pottery, stand out as shared characteristics of these sites. Even if it were judged by the artefact assemblage alone, Kaupang could be grouped among the few Viking-age towns, characterized by long distance trade and import demanding crafts as opposed to the regional market places of this date (r.e. Sindbæk 2005). Compared to other Norwegian Viking-age finds, the artefact assemblage at Kaupang is outstanding. Amongst the few Viking-age settlement sites surveyed hitherto, none are comparable to Kaupang with respect to either the quality or quantity of their artefact assemblages. The chieftain's farm at Borg in Lofoten has some comparable imports and craft, but far fewer artefact types and lower amounts (Munch et al. 2003). Whilst some of the imports do find counterparts in the Norwegian grave finds, both the production waste and the imported pottery are unparalleled in the graves.

The 1990–1995 excavations at Birka (Ambrosiani and Clarke 1992), and the 1990–1991 *Posthus* excava-

Figure 9.1 *A comparison of number or weight of some selec-ted artefacts types per cubic metre of sieved soil from the MRE at Kaupang, the Birka Excavations 1990–1995 and the Posthus excavation at Ribe of 1990–1991 (based on Andersson 2003; Feveile and Jensen 2000; Gustin 2004; personal communications from Björn Ambrosiani, Mathias Bäck, Claus Feveile and Torbjörn Jakobsson Holback). Illustration, Jørgen Sparre.*

tion at Ribe (Feveile 2006a, 2006b) are comparable to the MRE at Kaupang in respect of methods of artefact recovery. Thus quantitative comparison is possible. At Birka, however, the rather longer time span (from about AD 750 until about AD 970, starting c. 50 years earlier than Kaupang) and the slightly more than 250 cubic metre of sieved soil compared to Kaupang's total of 215 cubic metre, have to be taken into account. With Ribe too, an earlier date (preserved layers from about AD 700 down to about AD 850) and 160 cubic metre of sieved soil must be taken into account, as well as the absence of ploughsoil covering the stratified deposits.

A comparison of the amount per cubic metre of some selected artefact types at Kaupang, Ribe and Birka illustrates that most artefact types are less abundant at Kaupang (Fig. 9.1). Some striking differences, especially the much lower amounts of worked bone/ antler, are very likely to be a direct reflection of the poor preservation conditions at Kaupang. Other differences may be more significant, particularly when seen in relation to materials relatively unaffected by post-depositional processes. For example, the amount of glass per cubic metre at Birka and Ribe is 2.5 and 3.5 times more than at Kaupang, respectively. Comparing the more limited amount of waste from glass-bead production at Kaupang, for example the handful of tesserae against the thousands found during the *Posthus* excavation at Ribe (Feveile and Jensen 2000:fig. 5), it seems evident that a different intensity of craft activity lies behind the observed dissimilarities. These differences may also reflect more general trends in bead production in Scandinavia as the main bead-producing period at Ribe lay in the 8th century. The more equal amount of glass beads per cubic metre, especially at Kaupang and Ribe, suggests that the total amount of glass beads circulating at the sites was nevertheless more similar.

The remarkably lower amount of clay moulds at Kaupang in comparison with Birka and Ribe reflects the poor preservation conditions for moulds at Kaupang, but probably also the fact that metalcasters' workshops were not encountered in the MRE, as they were in the Birka and Ribe excavations. The absence of such workshops would also explain the lower frequency of crucibles per cubic metre at Kaupang.

Scant pottery finds at Kaupang probably reflect that pottery was imported. Birka and Ribe within pottery producing regions have much more pottery. The amount of imported pottery per cubic metre at the three sites is comparable, while the use of alternative vessels at Kaupang is reflected by the much greater frequency of soapstone vessel fragments. However, the very limited amount of soapstone per cubic metre from the Posthus excavation at Ribe is a chronological feature too, as all the soapstone objects are found in layers post-dating AD 800 (Feveile and Jensen 2000:fig. 11).

The amount of spindle-whorls per cubic metre is more level at the three sites. Several marked concentrations of loomweight fragments in the plot-division ditches at Kaupang are remains from upright looms, most likely originally located in the nearby buildings. The 470 database entries from the MRE at Kaupang often comprise several fragments each, while the 563 fragments of loomweights found during the Posthus excavation at Ribe (Feveile and Jensen 2000:fig. 5) is a total. Thus, when comparing the two sites, the quantity of fragments per cubic metre is higher at Kaupang. This might reflect a higher intensity of textile production in the excavated area at Kaupang, or merely that loomweights were dumped in the excavated area adjacent to the plots.

Whetstone is another artefact type with a higher frequency per cubic metre at Kaupang. The difference between the frequency of whetstone at Ribe and that at Kaupang is even larger than shown in Fig. 9.1, as all possible fragments of whetstones are included

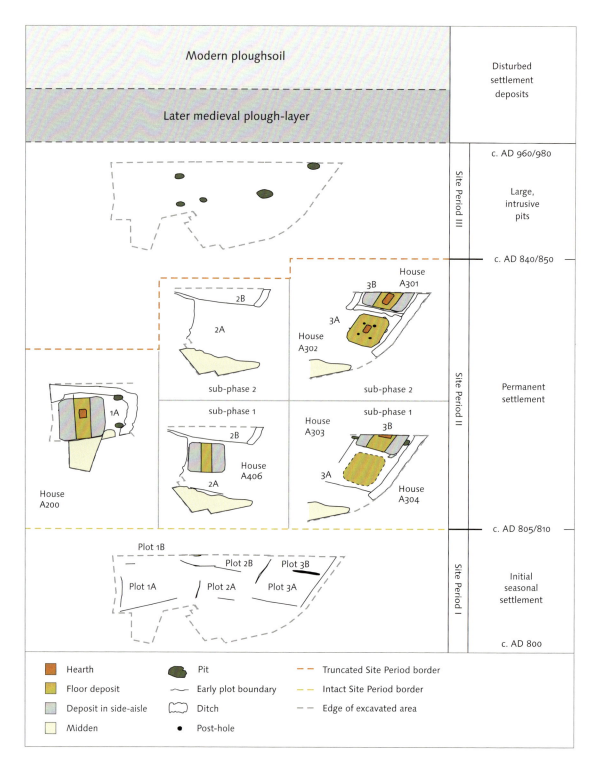

Hearth		Pit		Truncated Site Period border
Floor deposit		Early plot boundary		Intact Site Period border
Deposit in side-aisle		Ditch		Edge of excavated area
Midden		Post-hole		

in the numbers from Ribe, while 6 kg and 2 kg of slate fragments and unworked pieces can be added to the identified whetstones at Kaupang and Birka respectively (personal communications from Björn Ambrosiani and Claus Feveile).

The number of weights per cubic metre is also higher at Kaupang than at Ribe, but considerably lower than at Birka. The high number of weights at Birka is probably partly due to the concentration of weights found in the metalcasting workshop, but the generally late chronological distribution of weights at Kaupang (see below) suggests that chronological factors may also be important.

The forthcoming studies will address all of these complex questions in more detail – evaluating factors of chronology, the degree of fragmentation and the scale of intensity.

9.3 Site Periods in the main research excavation of 2000–2002

Overall site phasing is always a difficult task in excavations with complex stratigraphy and even more so in

Figure 9.2 *A schematic overview in perspective of the Site Periods of the MRE (see Pilø, this vol. Ch. 10:192–203 for details). The date range of the preserved deposits from Site Period III (fill in pits) is c. AD 840/850–900. Illustration, Lars Pilø.*

excavations of sites with plot-divisions. The phasing of the individual plots takes place during the post-excavation work and is facilitated by the implementation of single-context recording in the field. It is often a more tedious than difficult task, i.e. the main problem is deciding what constitutes an event important enough to signify a new phase. However, inter-plot phasing regularly proves more difficult as stratification seldom can be followed across plot boundaries (see for example Schietzel 1981:51). This is due to the constant re-digging of ditches, renewal of fences, trampling and other activities that took place in the divisions between the plots. This was also the case at Kaupang, and inter-plot phasing was thus impossible. Even so it can be seen that the same sequences are represented on most of the six excavated plots – a development from a seasonal (Site Period [SP] I) to a permanent settlement (SP II and probably much of SP III), and a later truncation of the stratified deposits by ploughing (the later medieval plough-layer and the modern ploughsoil: see Fig. 9.2).

In general it can be said that the deposits were best preserved on Plot 3B and least well preserved on Plot 1A, i.e. that the deposits were at their deepest (up to 25 cm) in the northern part of the excavation area and absent or nearly absent in the southern part. This is a direct consequence of a combination of ploughing and local topography. The northern part of the excavation area is at the lower end of a slope; hence, eroded soil from further up the slope washed into this area. This is also where the later medieval plough-layer was at its deepest (c. 15 cm). Modern ploughing has removed the later medieval plough-layer and most of the stratified deposits in the south, to the extent that fresh straw was found directly on the top of the occupation deposits of House A200.

Most deposits have been intensively bioturbated (disturbed by faunal activity, mainly earthworms), which has probably led to a vertical displacement of some small artefacts (< 5 mm), like beads and small pieces of bone (Milek and French, this vol. Ch. 15: 326–8). Thus single artefacts of small size cannot be used as dating evidence. In addition, the difficulty of discerning features in the deposits may have caused some small intrusive pits, post-holes or other features to be overlooked during the excavation process. As a consequence, later material may have been assigned to an earlier level than it should have been. Large intrusive features would most likely have been visible in the naturally deposited beach sand below the archaeological deposits as the intact archaeological strata seldom exceeded 15–20 cm in depth. Few such undetected intrusive features were recorded, only a few small post-holes. Thus the problem of undetected intrusive features is probably limited.

The dating range of the stratified deposits is c. AD 800–840/50 for SP I–II and post AD 840/850 for SP III, probably no later than AD 900. The dating of the earliest layers is based on two sources. The first is dendrochronological dates from the excavation of 1956–1974 (Bonde, this vol. Ch. 13:276–7), where the earliest constructional details are very similar to those uncovered in SP I. The second is a comparison of the composition of the bead assemblage in the earliest layers with the well-dated Ribe material (see Pilø, this vol. Ch. 8:176). This second dating method must be kept in mind when using the bead material for dating purposes in future, to avoid circular arguments.

Site Period I, which comprises the earliest, seasonal part of the settlement, appears to have been quite short-lived, probably less than 10 years, from around AD 800 until AD 805/810 (see Pilø, this vol. Chs. 8: 175–7 and 10:192–5). It is very likely that the plots were laid out simultaneously, and therefore that the start date of this Site Period is the same on each individual plot. However, the length of this initial Site Period may vary from plot-to-plot, as some plots may have seen earlier permanent occupation than others. The main artefact-carrying deposits from this period are a number of outdoor occupation deposits. There was no settlement on the beach prior to the establishment of the seasonal settlement, and the artefactual material should be chronologically "clean", with the few exceptions stated above.

Site Period II contains deposits from the earlier part of the permanent settlement. The upper parts of the deposits from this period were truncated by ploughing. Based on artefacts from the deposits belonging to this site period, and on dendrochronological evidence from intrusive pits from SP III, the end date of the preserved deposits should be c. AD 840/850 (Pilø, this vol. Chs. 8:177–8 and 10:192). The deposits from SP II are very varied, and include occupation deposits in houses, midden layers, levelling layers, hearths, pits and ditches. SP II can be divided into sub-phases 1 and 2 on Plots 3A and 3B, as these plots contained evidence of consecutive buildings. The same subdivision has been made on Plot 2A, where a building erected in sub-phase 1 was demolished in sub-phase 2, when the plot was left open. Plot 2B could also be subdivided, but only an animal shed was found there. There has been too much damage by ploughing on Plots 1A and 1B to support this subdivision there, even though the presence of intrusive post holes suggests that consecutive buildings were erected there as well. The digging of large pits began in SP II and it is thus likely that at least some residual material is present amongst the artefacts attributed to this period, especially in secondary deposits.

As mentioned above, the deposits from SP II were truncated by later ploughing, and therefore the later settlement activity at Kaupang is assigned as a whole to *Site Period III*. Thus the transition from SP II to SP III is created by post-depositional processes, not by a functional change as was the case in the transition from SP I to SP II. The transition from SP II to SP III is not contemporaneous within and between plots, because of the different degree of plough damage to the deposits on the different plots. Except for intrusive pits and deposits in the harbour, there are very few preserved deposits from SP III. The stratified material from this period derives mostly from the secondary fill of pits, which also suggests that at least some of the material attributed to this period is residual. Only a few of the pits can be dated dendrochronologically. The latest date is from a loose piece of wood in the backfill of pit A9422 dated to AD 863, but the fills in some of the pits may be later than this date. There are no indications that the fill in the pits postdate AD 900 and this is therefore set as the end date of the stratified settlement deposits from SP III. For a discussion of the character of the settlement during SP III, see Pilø (this vol. Ch. 10:200–3).

The stratified deposits were covered by two plough-layers. A *later medieval plough-layer* covered part of the excavation area. Associated with this layer was a post-Viking-age road (A407). The later medieval plough-layer contained artefacts from disturbed Viking-age deposits and some with a late-medieval date. The *modern ploughsoil* covered all of the excavation area. The two plough-layers, even though they were both disturbed, were separated during phasing. It was assumed that the displacement of artefacts was less pronounced in the later medieval plough-layer than in the modern ploughsoil, and that the later medieval plough-layer is devoid of modern material. The artefactual material in the later medieval plough-layer is a mixture of artefacts from different contexts – from disturbed deposits from SP I–III, and from the Late Medieval farming activities. The number of post-Viking-age artefacts is very limited, and most artefacts associated with the later medieval plough-layer (with the exception of iron slag) may be said with confidence to belong to the Viking-age settlement.

9.4 Site Periods and artefacts

Table 9.2 presents the artefacts from the MRE in relation to the Site Periods, based on the preliminary cataloguing. The table contains two additional categories "SP I–III" and "Without SP". "SP I–III" denotes artefacts which derive from intact deposits, but which have been impossible to relate to specific Site Periods. This is usually caused by the artefacts belonging to a part of the excavation area where excavation was discontinued in 2002. The date range for the artefacts from intact deposits from SP I–III is c. AD 800–900. "Without SP" contains the remaining finds, derived from cleaning layers, of other disturbed deposits or artefacts which for various reasons have no context recorded. The date range for artefacts without SP is c. AD 800–960/980.

In each case, the total weight of all the artefacts/bones ascribed to SP I and III constitutes minor proportions (3%) of the total weight of all the material from the MRE. This reflects respectively the short-lived nature of SP I and the few intact deposits of SP III. The total weight of all the material from SP II, the later medieval plough-layer and the modern ploughsoil is distributed more evenly (Tab. 9.2). About 28% of the total is ascribed to SP II, while the later medieval plough-layer and the modern ploughsoil each have about 20% of the total. The high percentage in the two disturbed plough-layers illustrates the importance of including this material when discussing the activity at Kaupang. Thirteen percent of the total could be related no more specifically than to SP I–III and 12% is not related to a specific Site Period.

Comparing the artefact types in the stratified deposits (SP I–III) with the later medieval and modern ploughsoil is not straightforward. As mentioned above, the continual disturbance of the late-medieval and modern plough-layers has led to the degradation or destruction of many of the artefacts contained in these. As a result, differences in artefact types between SP I–III compared to the plough-layers may be the products of differential preservation rather than of chronological relationships. The chronological value of the various artefact-groups must therefore be assessed case-by-case.

Some artefact types are less susceptible to post-depositional processes than others and comparison between Site Periods should therefore be relatively unproblematic. Soapstone sherds and whetstones are good examples; beads of glass and gemstones are others. Metal artefacts, like coins, weights, hacksilver, jewellery, models, etc. carry valuable chronological information, but the conditions for the preservation of silver, copper-alloy and iron at Kaupang are generally poor. Silver was of central importance in the Viking Age, but this metal is unfortunately the most affected by the poor and differential preservation conditions at Kaupang, making it hard to conduct a straightforward comparison of the silver artefacts present in different Site Periods. Differences in soil chemistry may have played a part in addition to chronological variation. For example, the site of the MRE was close to the Viking-age sea-level, and consequently the level of salt in the soil is quite high. A high level of salt has a direct negative impact on the preservation of metals, especially silver. Consequently silver may be better preserved in the ploughsoils, as the salt in this soil matrix was presumably leached to the deposits below. Judging from the state of preservation of silver, with relatively well preserved silver in the ploughsoils and very poorly preserved silver in the stratified deposits, this would indeed seem to be the case at Kaupang. However, a pilot study could not confirm higher levels of salt in the stratified deposits compared to the later medieval plough-layer (Milek, rep. in project archive), so we are probably only looking at a small part of a much larger complex of preservation issues. The case of pottery is rather more ambiguous, as the degree to which ceramic sherds are affected by ploughing depends on the fabric and how hard the ceramic pieces have been fired. Thus it is hardly surprising to find the hard-fired, fine-tempered, wheel-thrown Badorf Ware increasing its total percentage frequency in the ploughsoils compared with softer, coarser-tempered and hand-made ceramics. Similarly the low percentages of shelly-ware pottery (3–5%) and clay loomweights (4–6%) in the ploughsoils are more likely to reflect post-depositional destruction than chronological changes.

Craft activities and exchange, main characteristics of the artefact assemblage at Kaupang, appear from SP I onwards. The craft activities are represented from SP I by production waste such as slag, crucibles, loomweights and rods from glass-bead production. Exchange is represented by imported objects like Shelly Ware and Badorf pottery and the characteristic black and yellow wasp beads. Their early appearance corresponds with observations from Ribe. All the wasp beads from the *Posthus* excavation at Ribe and the 1990–1995 excavation at Birka were deposited before 820 (Feveile and Jensen 2000:fig.11; Björn Ambrosiani, pers. comm.). Three of the six wasp beads from the MRE at Kaupang belong to SP I and SP II and all but one fall within SP I to SP III. Hence the wasp beads seem to have an early chronological distribution at Kaupang. In the *Posthus* excavation at Ribe, Badorf Ware is found from AD 790 to 800 and Shelly Ware from 760 to 780, both being found throughout the preserved settlement phases until 850 (Feveile and Jensen 2000:fig 6).

There is a marked difference between the artefact assemblage of SP I and that from the later Site Periods and ploughsoils. Several types of artefacts present from SP II onwards are not found in SP I. The total absence of cornelian beads, rock-crystal beads, mosaic eye-beads, soapstone vessels and slate whetstones of the Eidsborg type in SP I cannot be explained by factors of preservation and is hence significant. The total lack of dirhams and weights in SP I is unlikely to be the result of post-depositional processes. Judged from the very faint traces of silver in SP I and the marked increase in silver in the later part of SP II, it seems likely that SP I lacked hacksilver as well.

During SP II a series of new artefact types were introduced – some in the earliest deposits of the period, like Eidsborg whetstones, mosaic eye-beads and soapstone vessels. In the *Posthus* excavation at Ribe no Eidsborg whetstones are found in stratified deposits dated before AD 850 (Feveile and Jensen 2000:fig. 11), and the type thus makes a pronouncedly earlier appearance at Kaupang – perhaps not so surprisingly, considering the short distance from the quarry in Telemark. In contrast, mosaic eye-beads are found somewhat earlier at Ribe, by the end of the 8th century (Sode and Feveile 2002:5–6). The first few fragments of soapstone appear c. AD 800–820 in the *Posthus* excavation at Ribe and this material first becomes quite copious from c. AD 820 onwards (Feveile and Jensen 2000:fig. 11). Soapstone vessels are absent from the archaeological record in Norway in the centuries prior to the Viking Age (Pilø 1989) but are a typical artefact type in Norwegian Viking-age graves. Soapstone vessels appear at Kaupang from the start of SP II, but are absent from the very short-lived SP I. It is not likely that their introduction at Kaupang should coincide exactly with the start-date of the production of soapstone vessels in the Viking Age in general. It is more likely that the introduction of soapstone vessels from the beginning of SP II reflects a change in the activity at the site. Future studies of the origin of the pottery present in SP I at Kaupang may shed light on this question.

Later in SP II cornelian beads and exchange-relat-

Table 9.2 *The distribution of the material from the MRE by Site Period, the grand total and some selected artefacts. Note that changes are anticipated in the course of the publication process as this distribution precedes most specialists' final evaluations and the completion of the conservation process.*

	Site Period I			Site Perio[d]	
	No:	Kg:	%	No:	Kg:
Grand total all artefacts/bones		21.9	3%		206.4
Hacksilver	0		0%	5	
Dirhams	0		0%	0	
Weights	0		0%	8	
Glass rods	48		23%	66	
Mosaic eye-beads	0		0%	10	
Wasp beads	2		33%	1	
Amber		0.02	8%		0.09
Cornelian beads	0		0%	2	
Rock-crystal beads	0		0%	0	
Jet		0.005	19%		0.002
Badorf pottery		0.4	7%		1.6
Shelly-ware pottery		0.1	15%		0.3
Tating pottery		0	0%		0.1
Spindle-whorls	1		2%	15	
Loomweights, clay		2.3	6%		16.5
Crucibles		0.1	3%		0.7
Soapstone vessels		0	0%		1.3
All whetstones, slate		0.2	2%		2.8
Eidsborg whetstones, slate	0		0%	7	
Slag/sintered clay		3.3	2%		25.9
Flint		1.8	3%		11.1

ed items in the form of weights and hacksilver are introduced. With the exception of one weight on plot 1A (which is not sub-phased) these all belong to sub-phase 2. All three artefact types have a generally late distribution in the Kaupang settlement. Eighty per-cent of the weights and more than 50% of the cor-nelian beads and hacksilver belong to the plough-lay-ers. The late appearance of the cornelian beads is con-gruent with their general dating in Scandinavia. According to Callmer (1977:tab. 1) these beads appear only sporadically before AD 860. In the *Posthus* exca-vations at Ribe cornelian beads are found for the first time c. 820–850 (Feveile 2006b, personal communica-tions).

There are few changes in the artefact material from SP II to intact deposits from SP III, though rock-crystal beads are represented for the first time. The late chronological distribution of this type is strengthened by the fact that more than 70% are from the plough-layers. In the *Posthus* excavation at Ribe rock-crystal beads are found earlier, from 780–800 onwards (Feveile 2006b, personal communications).

A more marked difference is observed between intact deposits from SP I–III compared to the plough-layers. Although dirhams minted in the late 8th and early 9th century are found at Kaupang, their distribution in the MRE points towards a rather later appearance as none are represented in the stratified deposits. Two special weight types (cubo-octahedral and oblate spherical) that make a general appearance in Scandinavia after c. AD 860/870 and AD 870/880, respectively (Gustin 2004:314; Steuer 1987:460) also belong mainly to the plough-layers. The presence of these artefact-types in the plough-layers suggests a chronologically diagnostic introduction of Oriental material after c. AD 860/870, although it should therefore be noted that the mosaic eye-beads are present earlier. Furthermore, a few objects in the Borre and Jelling Styles, dated to respectively AD 875–950 and AD 900–950 (Fuglesang 1993), are like-

wise all found in the plough-layers.

Although the datable later medieval material is limited, it is possible that some of the artefacts with a wide date range, deriving from the plough-layers, are actually of post-Viking-age date. This is especially the case with the iron slag, as this material was used as fill in the post-Viking-age road (A407). Some of the

Site Period III			Site Period I-III			L.m. plough-layer			Mod. ploughsoil			Without SP			Total		
No:	Kg:	%	No:	Kg:	%	No:	Kg:	%	No:	Kg:	%	No:	Kg:	%	No:	Kg:	%
	25.4	3%		99.7	13%		169.0	23%		129.6	18%		87.3	12%		739.3	100%
0		0%	4		13%	6		20%	10		33%	5		17%	30		100%
0		0%	0		0%	6		50%	4		33%	3		17%	12		100%
1		1%	2		2%	19		23%	44		54%	8		10%	82		100%
2		1%	14		7%	19		9%	33		16%	29		14%	211		100%
0		0%	3		9%	3		9%	12		36%	5		15%	33		100%
1		17%	1		17%	0		0%	1		17%	0		0%	6		100%
	0.01	4%		0.03	12%		0.02	8%		0.03	12%		0.06	23%		0.26	100%
1		8%	1		8%	6		50%	1		8%	1		8%	12		100%
1		4%	2		9%	6		26%	11		48%	3		13%	23		100%
	0.001	4%		0.004	15%		0.002	8%		0.005	19%		0.007	27%		0.026	100%
	0.2	3%		1.3	21%		1.0	16%		0.9	15%		0.7	11%		6.1	100%
	0.01	2%		0.1	15%		0.03	5%		0.02	3%		0.1	15%		0.66	100%
	0	0%		0.2	45%		0.06	14%		0.04	9%		0.04	9%		0.44	100%
3		5%	9		14%	11		17%	12		19%	12		19%	63		100%
	1.8	5%		8.7	24%		2.1	6%		1.3	4%		3.3	9%		36.0	100%
	0.1	3%		0.3	10%		0.8	28%		0.5	17%		0.4	14%		2.9	100%
	0.8	5%		0.6	4%		5.6	33%		2.8	17%		5.7	34%		16.8	100%
	0.2	2%		0.8	8%		1.4	13%		2.6	25%		2.4	23%		10.4	100%
2		2%	5		6%	18		22%	32		39%	18		22%	82		100%
	5.4	2%		10.0	5%		68.1	31%		78.0	36%		27.3	13%		218.0	100%
	1.8	3%		3.9	6%		10.9	18%		22.5	37%		8.8	14%		60.8	100%

soapstone sherds and whetstones may also be associated with the late-medieval farm or even pre-modern farming activity.

9.5 Summary

The fieldwork at Kaupang 1998–2003 led to the recovery of a large and diverse collection of artefacts related to a wide variety of crafts, exchange and household activities. However, the conditions for the preservation of bone, antler and metals were generally poor. The assemblage collected from the ploughsoil is dominated by artefacts of durable materials and the large number of lead artefacts from the ploughsoil is partly due to the strong signal given by this metal during metal detector surveys. The assemblage from the MRE was recovered using water sieving, and therefore has a clearer emphasis on smaller objects than the ploughsoil assemblage. Qualitatively, the material is only matched by material from other Viking-age towns such as Ribe, Birka and Hedeby. Comparison of this material with the record from Birka and Ribe shows a broad similarity in artefact types, but a generally lower frequency of individual pieces of the artefact groups per excavated unit of soil at Kaupang. Some, but not all of this, may be due to poor preservation conditions.

An overview of the Site Periods of the MRE and the distribution of the most important artefact groups have yielded important results, namely that materials related to craft production and exchange are found throughout the sequence. However, the artefact assemblage from the first seasonal settlement, SP I, is rather different from the assemblages from SP II and later. Eidsborg whetstones, soapstone vessels and mosaic eye-beads were introduced with the permanent settlement, SP II, around AD 805/810. Hacksilver occurs for the first time in the later part of SP II, c. AD 820–840/850, and likewise cornelian beads. Dirhams, certain types of weights, and rock-crystal beads appear late in the sequence, probably after AD 840/850.

The Settlement: Character, Structures and Features

10

LARS PILØ

This chapter discusses the character and structural remains of the Viking-age settlement at Kaupang. The main topics discussed are: whether the settlement was seasonal or permanent, the development of plot-divisions within the site and the different types of construction present.

The evidence to illuminate these topics derives from a number of archaeological sources. The structural remains themselves, albeit often poorly preserved, are an important source of information on plot-divisions, buildings and other constructions. Earlier data from the 1956–1974 excavation is also a source. Micromorphological analysis provided valuable information on the initial seasonal settlement phase, Site Period I (SP I, c. AD 800–805/810), and on layer formation in the harbour, where the only intact deposits from the whole settlement period are preserved. Micromorphological evidence from occupation deposits inside the buildings (SP II, c. AD 805/810–840/850) also contributed significantly to the interpretation of the structural remains. Environmental archaeology provided insights into the economy and living conditions on the site, and to the question of permanence of settlement.

The available evidence suggests that the laying out of plots coincided with the establishment of the settlement. In the initial phase (SP I) there was only seasonal activity on the site, but within the first decade a more permanent settlement developed (SP II) which involved the construction of buildings, more elaborate plot-divisions and the establishment of lanes. The character and structure of the settlement post AD 840/850 are more elusive as most of the structural remains have been destroyed by ploughing. Evidence from the harbour and the cemeteries suggests that the permanent settlement continued at least into the first decades of the 10th century. Artefacts point to activity at Kaupang until AD 960/980, but the character of this activity is not known.

The buildings at Kaupang are poorly preserved. In general they seem to have had pairs of interior roof-bearing posts. In some of the buildings there was a central aisle containing a floor area with a central hearth. Few remains of the outer walls were found. Some of the Kaupang buildings appear to be similar to the Type 1 buildings from Dublin, but the poor preservation of the buildings at Kaupang makes a closer comparison difficult. A number of large pits have been excavated at Kaupang, many of which had excellent conditions for preservation in their lower levels and therefore yielded detailed information on construction in wattle, plank and corner-timbering (Norwegian: "lafting"). However, the function of the pits remains largely undetermined.

The presence of jetties at Kaupang is discussed, and it is suggested that there were no long stone jetties on the site as previously believed, but rather stone deposited to create stable ground in and just above the tidal zone. The presence of wooden jetties is indicated by posts hammered deep into the beach deposits.

10.1 Introduction

The excavations at Kaupang in 2000–2003 yielded important new data on the establishment and character of the Viking-age settlement, as well as information on buildings and other structures. This evidence is presented and discussed here, together with a reassessment of the data from the excavations of 1956–1974. Among the most important issues are the questions of the permanence of settlement, the development of plot-divisions and the character of the buildings. Due to the generally poor conditions of preservation at Kaupang, the details of the building

Figure 10.1 *The earliest settlement deposit (AL100381) on Plots 3A and 3B of the MRE, intersected by numerous small pits and stake-holes from later settlement phases. Scale bar 1 m. Facing east.*

Figure 10.2 *Main research excavation of 2000–2002, Site Period I. Illustration, Lars Pilø.*

words, it is defined by post-depositional site formation processes, rather than functional/artefactual changes – in contrast to the transition from SP I to SP II. From SP III only sunken features, such as pits, and harbour deposits are known.

10.2 The character

The initial seasonal settlement – Site Period I

The best evidence for the earliest settlement period (SP I) derives from the main research excavation (MRE) of 2000–2002, since this excavation was conducted using single-context recording. However, some information can also be derived from the excavations of 1956–1974 (which were excavated in 10-cm spits), due to the structural similarity of the remains in the two excavation areas. Additional information was derived from the 2000–2003 Cultural Resource Management (CRM) excavations as well.

The initial settlement at Kaupang took place along the western shore of a sound. There is no evidence of prior trading or craft activities in the area. An agrarian settlement has been found just outside the settlement area, but this may pre-date the Viking-age settlement by several centuries (Pilø, this volume, Ch. 8). In contrast to Ribe (Feveile 2006a:24–7), there is no solid evidence to support a hypothesis that trading and production took place on the beach before the actual laying out of plots was undertaken. A few small artefacts and some bone fragments were recovered from the upper level of the beach sand, but they are likely to be intrusive to the beach sand due to bioturbation (Milek and French, this vol. Ch. 15:326–8) or trampling.

The earliest settlement at Kaupang was seasonal, leaving behind thin occupation deposits (Fig. 10.1), traces of fences and a large number of stake-holes visible in the beach sand, but no buildings, more elaborate plot-divisions or lanes. The stake-holes may

constructions remain elusive, and therefore different interpretations of the building remains are possible. In sharp contrast to the poor preservation of buildings, the preservation of wooden linings in pits was very good; for example, a number of wooden structural elements in wattle, planking and corner-timbering ("lap-jointing" or Norw.: "lafting") were preserved because of the anaerobic conditions in the lower levels of most of the pits.

Judging from the combined dating evidence from artefacts and dendrochronology (Pilø, this vol. Ch. 8:172–8) the preserved plots, buildings and other construction remains appear to derive from the period AD 800–840/850 (Site Periods (SP) I–II). Except for a few sunken features, deposits from the following century or so (SP III) have been disturbed by ploughing. The end of SP II is thus defined by the appearance of the destruction horizons of the later medieval plough-layer or the modern ploughsoil (where the older plough-layer is no longer preserved); in other

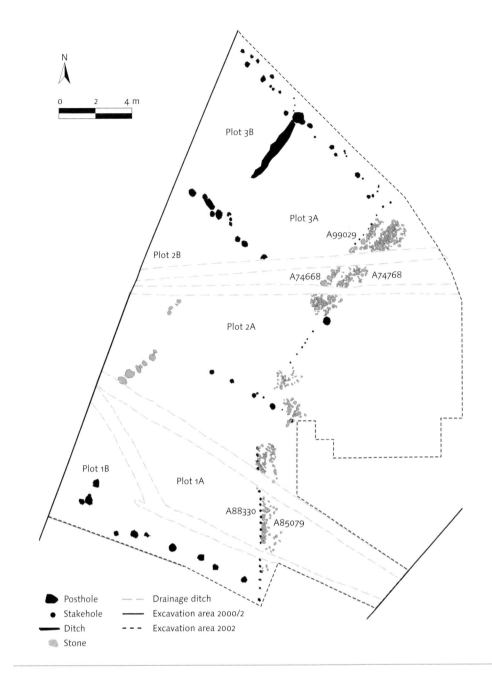

Posthole
Stakehole
Ditch
Stone

Drainage ditch
Excavation area 2000/2
Excavation area 2002

derive from windbreaks, but as most of the stake-holes cannot be linked securely to SP I, this remains only a possibility. The occupation layers which were investigated through micromorphology likewise indicated outdoor deposition (Milek and French, this vol. Ch. 15:328–31). Due to the absence of buildings, it is unlikely that Kaupang was occupied during winter. In addition there was only limited dumping connected to the earliest settlement, which also points to its temporary character. The earliest layers on Plot 3B consisted of thin occupation horizons interrupted by lenses of sand-deposition, also suggesting seasonal or at least intermittent settlement (Milek and French, this vol. Ch. 15:328–30).

The duration of the seasonal settlement (SP I) varied on the individual plots. Evidence suggests that some plots (like Plot 3B) were permanently occupied (i.e. they had buildings raised upon them) relatively early compared to others (like Plot 2A). Micro-morphological evidence indicates that the SP I settlement deposits on Plot 3B exhibited seven occupation layers, each of which may represent a separate occupation event (Milek and French, this vol. Ch. 15:329–30); therefore, it is possible that these layers represent seven years of seasonal settlement.

The plots were quite small. Only the three easternmost SP I plots were fully uncovered (Fig. 10.2). Plot 1A measured 9 x 8.5 m, Plot 2A 6.5 x 6 m and Plot 3A 7.5 x 6.5 m, with their shorter sides parallel to the shore. In their small size they differ from plots at Ribe, where the plot width is similar but the estimated plot length is much longer (Feveile 2006a). However, a shorter plot length cannot be ruled out in Ribe; the excavations in the 8th- and 9th-century settlement area were generally quite small, and may have missed the subdivision of the plots. The width of the

This combined phenomenon of piles of fire-cracked stone and rows of larger, unburned stones was also observed during the excavations of 1956–1974 (Fig. 10.4, bottom). These jumbled rows of stones were then interpreted as the remains of the walls of buildings. As discussed elsewhere (Pilø, this vol. Ch. 6:134–5) this is not very likely, and it is now evident that the fire-cracked stones and rows of larger, unburned stones represent the edges of plots. The fire-cracked stones in the excavations of 1956–1974 are most clearly present in connection with Plot "Hus I", where they represent one of the very earliest features, separated only by a thin sandy layer from the natural beach-deposit (Fig. 10.4; Tollnes 1998:32).

Information from the excavations of 1956–1974 suggests that wooden fences were also an integral part of the earliest settlement in this part of the site. In two or three cases – Plots "Hus II", "Hus III" (Fig. 10.6) and possibly "Hus V" – fences, delimiting the lower part of the plots, can now be seen to be stratigraphically older than the lines of stones. In a fourth case – Plot "Hus I" – there were several fences, but one of these (the b-series in Tollnes's terminology: 1998:65–7) appears to be associated with the long pile of fire-cracked stones mentioned above, and therefore to belong to the earliest phase of the settlement.

The similarity of the evidence from two clearly spatially separated excavation areas does point to the definition of plots by fences in the earliest phase being a shared phenomenon over large parts of the settlement area. In fact the excavated structures are so similar that it makes sense to correlate the Site Periods of the MRE with the available stratigraphic information from the excavations of 1956–1974. However, information on the activities on the plots in SP I can only be gathered from the MRE, as the earliest finds in the excavations of 1956–1974 are mixed with SP II finds, due to the non-stratigraphical excavation method then employed.

Kaupang plots is quite varied, and as such they are more similar to Dublin (Wallace 1992) than the more regular plots at Ribe.

Fences, delimiting the plots from the beach, are typical features of the plots in SP I (Fig. 10.3). Fire-cracked stones were dumped outside the fences, leaving a long pile of stones adjacent to them (Fig. 10.4). These fire-cracked stone piles belong to the very earliest part of SP I and were in some cases (Plot 3A of the MRE and Plot "Hus I" in the excavations of 1956–1974 – see below) succeeded by lines/low walls of unburned stones in SP II. The two features differ in that the piles were simply dumped, whilst the lines/low walls were constructions which were built to contain the soil on the plots, and therefore were probably linked to more permanent settlement.

The most common waste product during SP I was fire-cracked stones, which seem to have been carefully removed from the plots and deposited outside the fences marking the eastern edge of the plots. These fire-cracked stones were probably associated with the heating of water for cooking or other purposes. Plot 1A was the only plot with clear evidence for the activity which took place there in SP I. An occupation deposit (AL79606) located centrally on the plot contained 61 glass beads; most were white, but blue beads were also present. A wasp bead and some gold-foil beads were also present, as were 43 glass rods and additional pieces of glass waste. Of special interest is a fragment of a thin iron rod with a half-finished white glass bead attached to it (Fig. 10.5). No furnace fragments were recovered. The deposits were water-sieved using a 2-mm mesh, and the material should thus represent a near total collection of what was in the deposit at the time of excavation. However, the southern part of the deposit was damaged by recent ploughing, and by modern drainage ditches, as a result of which some material had been removed. The quantity of beads and beadmaking debris is rather small (a total of 36 g), and therefore we may be looking at the remains of only a short episode of beadmaking on Plot 1A.

The permanent settlement: the stratified deposits – Site Period II

After a short-lived initial phase of seasonal occupation, a permanent settlement developed – SP II. Evidence from the MRE suggests that this change was a gradual process. On some plots buildings appeared early, while on others they were raised later; on some plots no buildings were raised. The period of permanent occupation is best known from the MRE, but evidence from the excavations of 1956–1974 is also important.

The start of SP II is defined by the construction of buildings on most of the plots (Fig. 10.7). The plots'

limits were to a large degree based on the plot-boundaries from SP I.

One major change was the construction of a lane (A70369, Fig. 10.8) between Plots 1A and 2A, which was made by taking about a metre along the northern side of Plot 1A, and setting up a wattle fence to separate the plot from the lane. There was also a wattle fence on the side of Plot 2A. Later in SP II, however, this lane seems to have fallen into disuse, as midden deposits from Plot 1A lay over the fence, spilling out into the lane area.

Figure 10.5 *A selection of remains from beadmaking on Plot 1A, SP I. On the lower right-hand side: a melted bead with an iron rod (C52529/21706, length of iron rod 8 mm). Photo, Eirik Irgens Johnsen, KHM.*

Figure 10.6 *The preserved lower part of wooden stakes, constituting a fence separating the Plot "Hus III" from the shore. The trench is a product of the method of excavation, not a Viking-age feature. Photo, Tollnes 1998:fig. 3.18.*

Figure 10.7 *The MRE area in SP II. The buildings shown may not be contemporary, as there is no stratigraphic contact across the plot-divisions. Illustration, Julie K. Øhre Askjem.*

The lane itself contained a thick sandy layer (AL70370) which had been dumped there (Milek and French, this vol. Ch. 15:331–3), presumably as a foundation for a wooden pavement. The ground in the lane had been quite soggy, as was evidenced by the presence of a silty layer (AL71495/AL77852, Fig. 10.8) below the sand. This deposit contained imprints of human feet and animal hooves, proof of walking in the lane when it was moist (Fig. 10.9). The imprints were preserved when the sand deposit filled the lane, and thus appeared after removal of this layer during excavation. The silty layer contained c. 2 kg of bone, evidence of waste-disposal in the lane.

A similar lane was uncovered in the excavations of 1956–1974, the so-called "Road B" (Tollnes 1998:104), which was a gravelly area between the Plots "Hus III" and "Hus V".

The plot-division to the north of Plots 3A and 3B (A63192, Fig. 10.10) developed into a ditch in SP II. This ditch may also have served more practical purposes, for instance, to redirect rainwater which would otherwise have been running down the slope into the

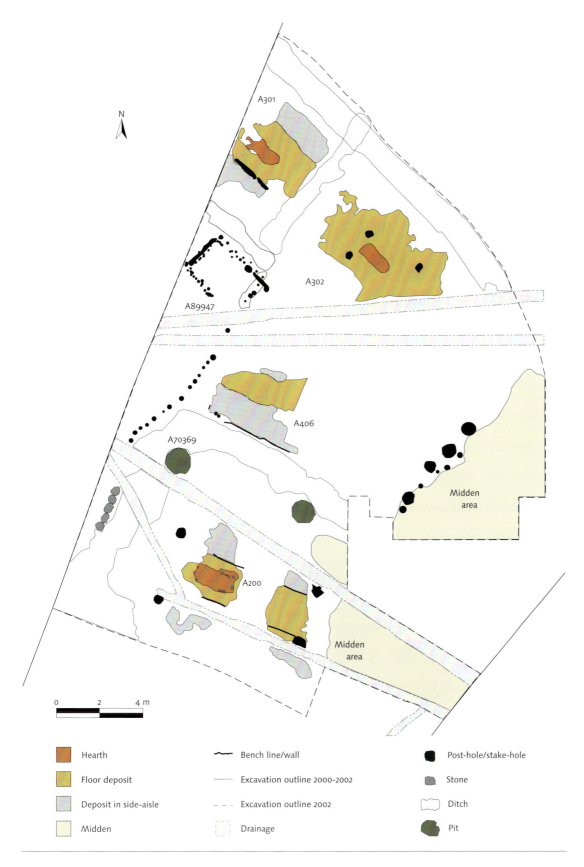

N

A302

A89947

A406

A70369

Midden
area

A200

Midden
area

🟧 Hearth	〜 Bench line/wall	⬛ Post-hole/stake-hole
🟨 Floor deposit	— Excavation outline 2000-2002	⬜ Stone
⬜ Deposit in side-aisle	--- Excavation outline 2002	⬜ Ditch
🟨 Midden	⬝⬝⬝ Drainage	🟢 Pit

0   2   4 m

plots, as witnessed several times during the excavations of 2000–2002. However, there was a large number of post-holes in the ditch as well, evidence that
fences were also erected in this plot-division. There
would seem to be no practical reason for a fence at
the bottom of this ditch. Probably the ditch was filled
in by waste and water-transported material and a
fence was built on top of it. Later the ditch was emp-

tied again. This process may have been repeated several times. The combination of a ditch and post-holes
can also be seen in the northern part of the MRE area
(ditch A20665).

A similar ditch was uncovered in the excavation
area of 1956–1974, between Plots "Hus I" and "Hus II"
(Tollnes 1998:25–6). It is interesting to note that both
this plot-division ditch and A63192 stopped at the

Figure 10.8 *The darker deposits running vertically represent lane A70369. Plot 1A is on the right; Plot 2A is on the left; Plot 2B is in the lower part of the picture. Facing southeast. Scale bar 1 m.*

Figure 10.9 *Imprints in layers AL71495/AL77852 in the lane between Plots 1A and 2A, from both humans (some marked with a black outline) and animals. Illustration, Charlotte Melsom.*

Figure 10.10 *The plot-division ditch A63192. Scale is 1 m. View facing northwest.*

eastern end of the plots, while the excavated lanes continued beyond these points and into the beach area. This suggests that the lanes functioned as a means of communication beyond the plot-divided area, maybe as access routes to wooden jetties (see below).

As mentioned above, some of the plots that were situated in the outer, eastern row had small-to-large stones along their edges. The larger stones were

invariably placed along the lower edge of the plots, and it seems likely that they were deliberately placed there to prevent downhill erosion of the soil on the plots. The smaller stones were found on the edges of plots in both the outer and inner rows. These stones were placed more randomly along all the edges, probably simply as the result of clearing waste from the plots, rather than as a deliberate structural feature. Clay loomweight fragments were frequently found together with the stones.

The first large pits appeared at approximately the same time as the first buildings were built. Even though the deposits in these pits were better preserved because of waterlogging, and have been intensively sampled and analysed, it has not been possible to determine the function of the pits with certainty (Barrett et al., this vol. Ch. 14:297–300). Analysis of the large pits in the MRE area show brackish conditions in the Viking Age, so they are not likely to have been wells for drinking water. Other pits, situated in higher-lying areas, could have been used as wells (see below).

Buildings were constructed on most of the plots, and as the plots were quite small, the buildings left little vacant space (Fig. 10.7). Some of the buildings contained a central hearth, a floor in the central aisle and areas for sitting and/or sleeping in the side aisles, but several building-types were present. The buildings with a central hearth were of a type which permitted year-round settlement (see below), and there is other evidence which indicates occupation or activity at Kaupang outside the summer months. A bone from a Little Auk *(Alle alle)*, which is likely to be a winter catch (Barrett et al., this vol. Ch. 14:301), was recovered from one of the earliest deposits of SP II in the ditch between Plots 1A and 1B. A bone from a Brent Goose *(Branta bernicla)* – a species which is to-day present in the Oslofjord area only during spring and autumn – was collected from the floor layer of

Building A302: Plot 3A, SP II, sub-phase 2 (Barrett et al., this vol. Ch. 14:301). One of the earliest dendrochronological dates also points to activity at Kaupang outside the growth season for trees: C52516/A94901, which was felled in the winter between AD 806/807 (Bonde, this vol. Ch. 13:279). This sample derives from a large pit at the northern end of the settlement area (see Pilø, this vol. Ch. 8:171, Fig. 8.14 no.8). Artefacts which point to permanent settlement are a few quernstones, of both Rhenish basalt and local rock. Also the presence of a large number of clay loomweights could be an indication of a permanent settlement, as looms are not very likely to have been brought in for operation at a seasonal market.

In SP II substantial dumping took place on the beach zone in front of the plots, and also on the plots themselves. This was, of course, a natural consequence of the development from seasonal to permanent settlement. Much of the material dumped in front of the buildings was domestic refuse, mainly from the cleaning of the hearths (Milek and French, this vol. Ch. 15:352–4).

There is, however, one piece of evidence which may cast some doubt on the permanence of settlement – the insect assemblage (Barrett et al., this vol. Ch. 14:302–3). If Kaupang was a permanently occupied site, the absence of an obligate synanthrope insect-fauna (wholly dependent on human settlement), as at other Viking-age urban sites, calls for an explanation. The difference between the insect fauna at Kaupang and that at other Viking-age urban sites may have been caused by several factors. Kaupang was founded in an area with no prior urban settlement. Transportation to Kaupang would often have involved long journeys by sea, hindering the introduction of obligate synanthrope species. The climate at Kaupang is much colder during the winter than at many of the other Viking-age sites which have had their insect fauna analysed. It may be that buildings were – for various reasons – left unheated during periods of the winter, and this would have made survival of the obligate synanthrope species difficult. The insect evidence does not on its own disprove permanent occupation of the site.

A total of seven buildings belonging to SP II were investigated in the MRE. Six are believed to have had a mainly domestic function (see below). The last building was probably an animal shed. However, outside the Plot 1A–3B area, remains from two possible workshops for metal casting were uncovered. One workshop was found on Plot 1B in the CRM trench, where the outer edge of an occupation deposit was uncovered which contained mould fragments, slag, a piece of gold and drops of silver. The deposits at the northern end of the MRE area also showed a concentration of mould fragments, silver and gold, but this area was not excavated further.

The later settlement – Site Period III

One of the main interpretational problems at Kaupang is the character of the settlement after c. AD 840/850 (SP III), as the more recent deposits in the settlement area are disturbed by ploughing, a destruction which started in the later medieval period. Even though artefacts in the ploughsoil, such as glass beads and metal artefacts, point to continuing activities into the 960s and 970s (Pilø, this vol. Ch. 8:177–8), they yield little information on the character of the settlement. Other artefact groups (like casting moulds) which could have shed light on precisely dated activity patterns are badly affected by the post-depositional processes in the plough-layers, or are impossible to date more precisely in relation to the whole settlement period (e.g. crucibles and loom-weights). Thus, even though there is solid evidence for the settlement's start date and the dating of the remaining stratified deposits, it is difficult to determine if there was permanent settlement throughout SP III, if there were periods of abandonment, or if parts of SP III saw only seasonal settlement.

There is little evidence from the cemeteries to suggest a major change in settlement character at Kaupang during the second half of the 9th century and the first half of the 10th century. Burials took place unabated in the later phases of the settlement (see Stylegar, this vol. Ch. 5), and there is thus nothing to suggest declining settlement activity or any change in settlement pattern. The cemeteries show continuity in burial customs, and the most likely explanation for this phenomenon is that the burial grounds were used by the same population throughout, from around 800 to the mid-10th century.

The only preserved deposits from SP III (apart from fill in intrusive pits) are in the sediments in the harbour area. The main deposit is a layer interpreted as a marine deposit, containing waste swept off the beach, or in some cases, dropped from boats. This marine deposit was sandy and contained wood chips, bones and a small number of artefacts. Environmental analysis indicates that the material in this marine deposit derived at least in part from buildings (Barrett et al., this vol. Ch. 14:299–300). The deposit was excavated in spits, and a cubo-octahedral weight was recovered from the second (from the top) of four 5-cm spits. The weight is likely to be an accidental loss, dated to no earlier then AD 860/880 (Pedersen, in prep. a). Micromorphological analysis of the deposit strongly indicates that the weight is unlikely to be intrusive (Milek and French, this vol. Ch. 15:355). As the upper part of the deposit was truncated by wave activity, it seems likely that waste from the settlement continued to be dumped for a period post–AD 860/880. If the weight in question from spit 2 is early (i.e. AD 860/880), this would imply that deposits were continuing to build up for at least an additional 20–30 years, assuming that the rate of deposition in the harbour remained constant. Bearing in mind that the upper part of this deposit is truncated and that the weight may also be later than AD 860/880, it seems likely that settlement waste continued to be dumped on the beach and re-deposited in the harbour in the early 10th century, possibly even later. It is noteworthy that the amount of wood in the deposit increased around and after the time of deposition of the weight, which again does not imply any decrease in activities on the site.

There are only a few intrusive features besides the pits in the MRE. The lack of intrusive post-holes could be taken as an indication of a cessation in the construction of buildings on the plots, but other, and perhaps more plausible, explanations may be put forward to explain this phenomenon. Buildings like A301 and A303 yielded no or very few features related to standing structures cut into the deposits below; only the hearth was cut into the underlying deposits by c. 15 cm (see below). Other buildings, like A302, yielded only very shallow post-holes, or none – like A304. Therefore, the low number of intrusive features (again excepting pits), is hardly a strong argument for a change in settlement character on the plots.

Some of the pits (like A65132 and A64891 on Plot 1A) are contemporary with the buildings in SP II and continued to be in use into SP III, others (like A43852 (Plot 3B) and A65446 (Plot 3A)) are positioned in a way which makes it unlikely that buildings could have been built on the plots if the plot-divisions remained the same during SP III. Unfortunately none of these pits could be dated by dendrochronology. However, the fill in A43852 was interpreted to consist of re-deposited material from within buildings (Barrett et al., this vol. Ch. 15:298–9), indicating the presence of buildings in SP III. There is little positive evidence for the stability of the plot-divisions in SP III. However, the ditches between Plots 3A/3B on one side, and 4A/4B on the other appear to have been functioning

	3B, SP I	3B, SP II, s 1	3B, SP II, s 2	Later medieval plough-layer	Modern ploughsoil	Influence by ploughing
Excavated area/volume	20 sq m	20 sq m	20 sq m/ 1.17 cu m	20 sq m/ 0.59 cu m	c. 20 sq m/ 4 cu m	
Pottery	0 g	22 g	429.5 g	51.8 g	49.5 g	Very high
Soapstone sherds	0 g	0g	20.3 g	34.8 g	34.8 g	
Crucible-fragments	0 g	2.3 g	24.6 g	4.4 g	3.0 g	Some
Glass sherds	0 g	0 g	1.5 g	0.9 g	0.4 g	Some
Beads	0 pieces	10 pieces	63 pieces	25 pieces	12 pieces	
Loomweight-fragments	0 g	136.8 g	282.9 g	99.4 g	0 g	Very high

Table 10.1 *A comparison of selected artefact-types from Site Periods I and II and the plough-layers.*

beyond SP II. In fact the only other stratified deposit from the settlement area in SP III (except pit-fill) derives from the ditch. In situ carbonized material and ash were uncovered here, suggesting that a fire had taken place in this area, in the early part of SP III. However, the scale of this fire is not known, as remains of it were not preserved on the neighboring plots due to plough damage.

Information on the settlement's character in the later phases can also be gathered by looking at the artefact assemblage in the later medieval plough-layer which consists largely of disturbed deposits from the latest phase of the settlement (SP III). However, it also contains some material from SP II, and even in some cases – where destruction has been extensive – from SP I. The medieval tillage may have led to some horizontal displacement of artefacts, but not nearly to the extent caused by modern agriculture.

One way of addressing this problem of mixture is to look at a selected portion of the assemblage from the part of the MRE area where the underlying deposits have been least damaged. This involved testing the later medieval plough-layer covering Plot 3B. This choice was also supported by the later medieval plough-layer being at its deepest here (c. 10 cm). Unfortunately, this plot is situated close to a slope (to the north, leading to the central plateau), which could imply that some eroding soil from the slope had come down into the test area, potentially adding more material from Site Periods I–II. However, this problem is probably not significant. The most likely result of the creation of the later medieval plough-layer in the test area would be an initial disturbance of the more recent deposits. Then, as ploughing continued, cutting steadily into older deposits in the slope, soil would erode from the slope, leading to a

gradual build-up of the plough-layer covering Plot 3B. Since ploughing in medieval times was quite shallow (perhaps 10–15 cm), the deeper parts of the later medieval plough-layer would soon have been left untouched by the plough. Only with the advent of modern machinery did ploughing down into the lower parts of the later medieval plough-layer begin, leaving behind the lowest part of the deposit, which is likely to contain only very limited amounts of non-local material eroded from the slope.

The later medieval plough-layer was excavated in the same way as the underlying stratified deposits, i.e. in 1 m squares with water-sieving of all excavated deposits. Thus the comparison between these assemblages should not be influenced by the excavation method. The modern ploughsoil was water-sieved in a selection of 2 m squares with a different orientation.

When considering the impact of ploughing on the artefactual record and the different soil volumes sieved, one finds that the later medieval plough-layer assemblage appears quite similar to what was found in the stratified deposits of Building 301 below. This similarity could be taken as an indication that the settlement did not undergo a substantial change in character for some time post-c. AD 840/850, but it does not indicate anything definite about how long the settlement's character remained unchanged. None of the artefacts recovered from the later medieval plough-layer above Plot 3B are of clear 10th-century types.

Artefact recovery from the modern ploughsoil is low considering the volume of sieved ploughsoil compared with the stratified deposits. This probably implies that soil with a low frequency of artefacts was added to the modern ploughsoil covering Plot 3B.

The only two artefact groups believed to be relatively unaffected by ploughing are beads and soap-

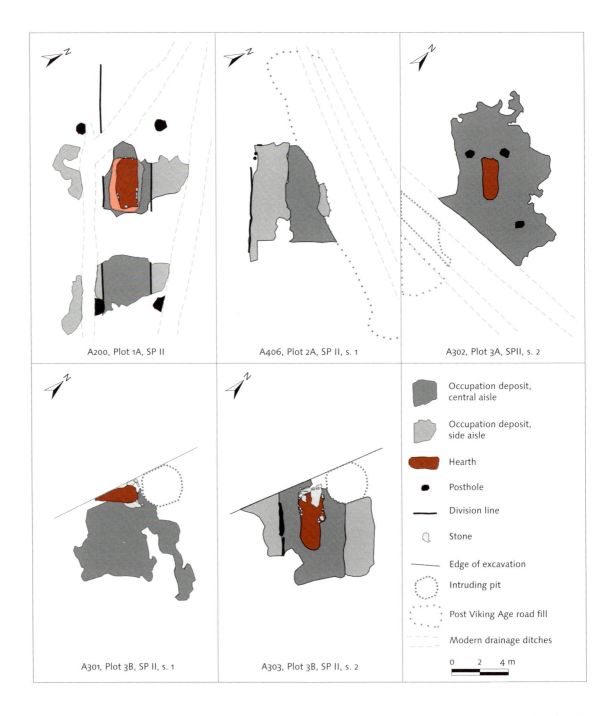

A200, Plot 1A, SP II

A406, Plot 2A, SP II, s. 1

A302, Plot 3A, SPII, s. 2

A301, Plot 3B, SP II, s. 1

A303, Plot 3B, SP II, s. 2

▪	Occupation deposit, central aisle
▪	Occupation deposit, side aisle
▪	Hearth
●	Posthole
—	Division line
⬠	Stone
—	Edge of excavation
⬭	Intruding pit
⬭	Post Viking Age road fill
- -	Modern drainage ditches

0   2   4 m

stone sherds. A comparison of the weights of artefact groups shows that there are 20.3 g of soapstone sherds from SP II compared to 69.6 g from the ploughsoil. The beads give the opposite picture: 63 pieces were recovered from SP II, while only 37 pieces where recovered from the ploughsoil, even though the ploughsoil covers a period of c. 100 years whereas the stratified deposits cover only c. 50 years. The beads are probably the better indicator of the two, as the production of soapstone vessels increased throughout the Viking Age, and the sherds themselves are so heavy that just a single sherd may disrupt the picture. The beads could indicate that settlement activity declined after SP II, but the low number of beads could also be a product of other factors, such as fewer

beads in circulation, or destruction in the ploughsoil. In any case this way of approaching the information value of ploughsoil assemblages has inherent problems, and for this reason not too much significance should be attached to the results.

The second half of the 9th century most likely saw continued permanent settlement at Kaupang. This is evidenced by the presence of building waste in the intrusive pits of SP III, by the composition of the artefact assemblage in the later medieval ploughlayer, by the continual build-up of deposits in the harbour, and by the cemeteries. Looking at the evidence from the cemeteries and the harbour, one can conclude that it seems likely that the permanent settlement at Kaupang continued into the first decades

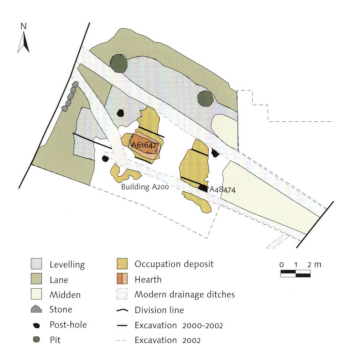

Figure 10.11 *An overview of the most important Viking-age building remains uncovered during the main research excavation, 2000–2002. Illustration, Lars Pilø.*

Figure 10.12 *Plan of important elements on Plot 1A, Site Period II. Illustration, Julie K. Øhre Askjem.*

Figure 10.13 *Remains of the central parts of building A200. The earthen floor, the central hearth and the two parallel lines, one on each side of the hearth are visible. The light coloured beach sand below the remains is also visible. Facing northwest.*

Legend:
- Levelling
- Lane
- Midden
- Stone
- Post-hole
- Pit
- Occupation deposit
- Hearth
- Modern drainage ditches
- Division line
- Excavation 2000–2002
- Excavation 2002

0 1 2 m

of the 10th century. The artefactual evidence from the settlement area even indicates some activity at Kaupang until AD 960/980. However, the details of this final settlement period remain elusive, as there are only two graves which may possibly post-date AD 950 (Stylegar, this vol. Ch. 5:81). The lack of cemetery evidence may not, however, be directly linked to the absence of a permanent population, as burials are generally quite rare in this region after c. AD 950.

10.3 Building constructions

The remains of seven buildings (five of which are depicted on Fig. 10.11) were uncovered during the MRE. In addition, the remains of two buildings can be discerned amongst the features documented in the 1956–1974 excavations. They are presented below, by order of plot and Site Period/sub-phase. They are all dated to the first half of the 9th century.

Before describing the individual buildings, it is necessary once again to note the very poor preservation conditions on the site. This led to the blurring of layers, which in turn made the interpretation of the structural remains very difficult at times. In addition, some of the buildings extended beyond the edge of the excavation area, or were affected by ploughing. The near absence of wall remains and the low number of symmetrically placed interior roof supports added to the problems. The use of single-context recording in combination with thin-section analysis of sections cut along the axes of some of the buildings has yielded some information on the size and lay-out of the buildings and on their function. Constructional details above ground remain, however, largely conjectural.

Building remains in the MRE were typically defined by the presence of a central hearth and dark occupation deposits. In some cases two parallel lines could be discerned in the occupation deposits on

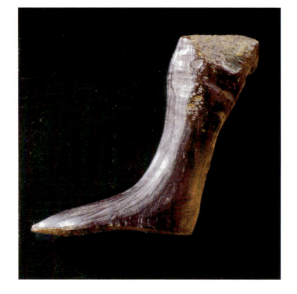

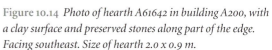
Figure 10.14 *Photo of hearth A61642 in building A200, with a clay surface and preserved stones along part of the edge. Facing southeast. Size of hearth 2.0 x 0.9 m.*

Figure 10.15 *Amber foot (C52519/15942) recovered during the cleaning of the earthen floor of building A200. Length from heel to toe 23 mm. Photo, Eirik Irgens Johnsen, KHM.*

Figure 10.16 *Building A406 on Plot 2A, Site Period II, subphase 1. Illustration, Julie K. Øhre Askjem.*

either side of the hearth. These lines signify a division – most likely formed by a plank standing on edge – between the actual earthen floor in the central aisle and areas for sitting/sleeping in the side aisles. Remains of the outer walls were rarely found. Some post-holes were recorded, which may be linked to roof support, but not in all buildings. If some buildings were constructed without a hearth or any interior division of the floor area, they would have been very hard to recognize during excavation. Only thin section analysis would be able to indicate if the occupation deposits were formed indoors. One such example is discussed below (A304). The buildings invariably had their short end facing the shore.

Building A200

Building A200 was uncovered on Plot 1A, in SP II (Fig. 10.12). This was the only building recognized on this plot, which had only a thin layer of cultural deposits preserved above the beach sand because of later ploughing. The presence of post-holes later than building A200 suggests that buildings were built on the plot at a later stage. The environmental evidence from the fill of two later pits on the plots suggests likewise (Barrett et al., this vol. Ch. 14:298–9).

The remains of the building had been damaged by both medieval and more recent ploughing. In addition two modern drainage ditches cut through the remains (Fig. 10.13). Only the central part of the building was comparatively well preserved – by Kaupang standards at least. The rest of the occupation deposits had been ploughed away, and ploughing had also split the preserved occupation deposits in two, with beach gravel appearing in between. No traces were found of the outer walls. The preserved elements of the building comprised a hearth, occupation deposits, two parallel markings for planks (one on either side of the hearth), and four post-holes, one of them with the remains of a wooden post. The

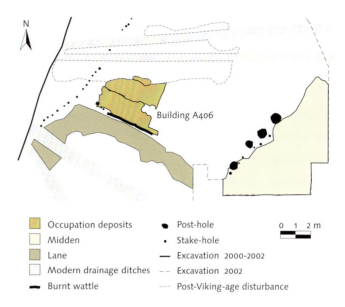

Building A406

▨ Occupation deposits	● Post-hole	0 1 2 m	
□ Midden	• Stake-hole		
▨ Lane	─ Excavation 2000-2002		
□ Modern drainage ditches	– – Excavation 2002		
━ Burnt wattle	--- Post-Viking-age disturbance		

building had its gable end towards the shore, and was aligned WNW–ESE.

The hearth (A61642, Fig. 10.14) was rectangular in outline, measuring c. 2.0 x 0.9 m. Stones had probably extended along the entire edge originally, but ploughing had removed most of them. It was filled with ash and had a layer of burnt clay on the surface. Like some of the other hearths at Kaupang it contained a relatively large amount of bone (c. 0.5 kg), probably because the presence of ash had raised the pH-value inside the hearth, benefiting the preservation of bone. The hearth also contained a number of artefacts, some of which (like glass bead production waste) seems to be residual material deposited on the same plot in SP I.

Two parallel lines in the occupation deposits were recorded, one on each side of the hearth, with a distance between the lines of 1.95 m. This indicates the width of the floor area quite precisely (see below). The southern line was preserved in three parts to a maximum length of 9.2 m, extending well to the west of the preserved occupation deposits. This line extended into the passage between Plots 1A and 1B, indicating that the building may have been extended towards the west during its lifetime – or that this lane had already been filled in before the erection of building A200.

The occupation deposit inside the parallel lines was a dark-coloured sandy layer, mixed with charcoal and a little humus. It was very similar to the occupation deposits in the side aisles. In all likelihood the occupation deposit inside the lines constitutes the earthen floor of the building and the artefacts found embedded in it are therefore of primary importance for the interpretation of the function of the building. However, as a general rule, large objects would have been removed from the floor when broken and only small objects would have remained on or in the earthen floor (Schiffer 1996:58–60). In addition there

is the problem that while some of the objects may be primary refuse, others might have been residual objects that were re-deposited in connection with the digging of pits for the hearth and the post-holes.

Most of what has been recovered from the earthen floor is typical settlement material such as bone, flint, slag, burnt clay, beads, ceramics, whetstones, iron and crucible fragments. A spindle-whorl may point to domestic activities, but only one fragment of a loomweight was recovered. However, loomweights, even in fragments, are large objects that would usually be removed when broken, so their near absence from the earthen floor may be of little importance. More than 400 g of loomweight fragments have been recovered from the midden layer east of the building. Twenty small pieces of amber (total weight 1.8 g) were recovered from the earthen floor; together with an amber foot (Fig. 10.15) recovered during the initial cleaning of the earthen floor, this could point to amber working going on in building A200, albeit hardly on a large scale (see Resi, in prep. b). Ten iron nails were recovered from the earthen floor; they might have belonged to some part of the structure.

The occupation deposits in the side aisles contained lower amounts of artefacts, which is quite natural as these deposits were both more limited in extent and thinner than the earthen floor in the central aisle. The only exception to this is the ceramics. While 26 g of ceramics were recovered from the earthen floor, 167 g were recovered from the occupation layers in the side aisles. Interestingly, and in contrast to other buildings in the MRE area, none of the ceramics are of the Badorf Ware types, even though Badorf-type pottery constitutes c. 30% by weight of the pottery recovered from the stratified deposits (Pilø, in prep.), and is present on the site already in SP I. Badorf Ware also occurs only infrequently in the midden layer (A68495) to the east of building A200. This layer consists mainly of hearth waste, which

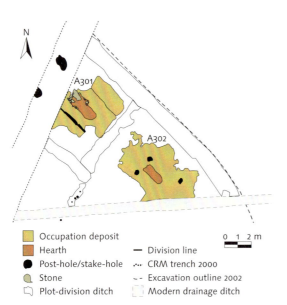

Figure 10.17 *Buildings A301 and 302 (phase b). Illustration, Julie K. Øhre Askjem.*

Occupation deposit
Hearth
Post-hole/stake-hole
Stone
Plot-division ditch

— Division line
··· CRM trench 2000
-- Excavation outline 2002
Modern drainage ditch

0 1 2 m

probably originated from the hearth in building A200. Of the c. 117 g of pottery recovered here, only about 4 g (two sherds) are of Badorf Ware types. (For a discussion on the presence and absence of wares, and possible reasons for this, see Pilø, in prep.).

The intact occupation deposits in the northern side aisles extend 1.5 m from the markings for the plank, but their northernmost part may have been disturbed by a drainage ditch. In the southern aisle they extend for 2.0 m, which is probably a better estimate of the width of the side aisles. Together with the width of the central earthen floor of 2.0 m, the total width of the building would have been 6.0 m. The length of the building was more than 9 m, but probably less than 11 m.

Four post-holes – in two pairs, marked on Fig. 10.12 – may belong to building A200, as part of its internal roof-bearing supports. However, the stratigraphy can relate only the eastern pair directly to the building, while the western pair is known only to be later than SP I. The distance between the pairs of post-holes is 6.9 m. The distance between the eastern pair of post-holes is 2.6 m, while the western pair of post-holes is 3.1 m apart. The southeastern post-hole preserved the lower part of a post. It was made of oak, rectangular in shape and measured 15 x 10 cm in cross-section, with its longer side perpendicular to the longest axis of the building. It was dendro-dated, but the sapwood was not preserved, and the date could not be set more precisely than post-c. AD 714 (Bonde, this vol. Ch. 13:279, no. F1016957). If this post-hole belongs to the building, the small size of the roof-bearing post indicates a light roof construction, which means that a turf roof is not likely.

The northwestern post-hole (A61953) contained a netsinker (C52519/22677), re-used as a grinding stone, and also a stone of the same shape but without the furrows characteristic of netsinkers (C52519/22769). These may represent some kind of offering in con-

nection with the raising of the building. Interestingly, three other post-holes on this plot also contained re-used netsinkers or presumed netsinkers. Although these features cannot be assigned to SP II with certainty, this peculiar phenomenon was only noticed on Plot 1A.

This building, like the other buildings at Kaupang, had no certain traces of any entrances. Presumably one entrance was situated at the eastern, gable end of the building, towards the shore. That would explain the dumping of hearth and floor materials just outside this part of the building. There could also have been an entrance in the western end.

There is little evidence to illuminate the function of the building. Most of the artefacts point to domestic activities, but as mentioned above, amberworking probably took place too, albeit on a limited scale. The deposits in the midden area in front of the building contained a concentration of debris from whetstone production that could possibly be linked to this building. These deposits also contained a fair amount of amber (5.3 g). However, traces of specialized activities are generally few, and a mainly domestic function may be surmised.

Building A406

Building A406, which stood on Plot 2A in SP II, sub-phase 1 (Fig. 10.16), was very poorly preserved, even by Kaupang standards. Its northern part had been cut by a post-Viking-age road, and the eastern part was probably severely affected by post-depositional processes, leaving no identifiable traces behind (the straight-lined limit of the deposits here were caused by a section). Only part of an earthen floor and the southern side aisle survived. No hearth or post-holes could be identified. Interestingly though, a thin dark line in the deposits seems to represent the southern wall of the building – the only instance of a preserved wall-line at Kaupang. It appears to have been a wattle wall, but no identifiable pieces of daub were encountered. There was also a short, thin line of charcoal at the western end of the deposit in the southern side aisle, which may be the final remains of the western wall.

The preserved central earthen floor measured 1.5 m in width, as did the southern side aisle. If the entire width of the central earthen floor is preserved, then the building would have had a width of c. 4.5 m.

The building did not have a preserved hearth, and since this is normally a well constructed feature, cut into the underlying layers, there is reason to believe that there never was one. Only a few artefacts were recovered from the deposits associated with the building. No loomweight fragments were found, and only about 10 g of ceramics and trace amounts of amber were recovered. There is therefore no indication of the function of this building. It may not even have been a dwelling.

Building A304

Even though occupation deposits were noted on Plot 3A during SP II, sub-phase 1, no remains of buildings were observed during excavation, and therefore the plot was believed to have seen only temporary settlement between the seasonal settlement of SP I and the construction of building A302 in SP II, sub-phase 2. However, the micromorphological analysis strongly indicates that the occupation deposit in SP II, sub-phase 1, had accumulated on a floor surface, i.e. indoors, and thus that there was a building present on the plot in this sub-phase (Milek and French, this vol. Ch. 15:344–6). This building (A304) did not have a preserved hearth, and showed no traces of the outer walls – it is indicated, in other words, only through the occupation deposits.

According to the micromorphological evidence the occupation deposit contained indications of bark and wood tissue in the northwestern part of the building. Sand had been sprinkled on the occupation deposit there to keep it dry. The micromorphological evidence also suggests that there was a functional difference between the northwestern and southeastern parts of A304, as the deposits in the southeastern part had a higher quantity of wood and bark chips, whereas the deposits in the northwestern part contained more dumped hearth waste (Milek and French, this vol. Ch. 15:344–6).

Based on the recorded occupation deposits on Plot 3A, SP II, sub-phase 1, the building measured c. 6.2 x 4.4 m. It is difficult to say anything specific about its layout, except that it was different from the layouts of buildings like A200, A302 (phase b) and A303, as there were no traces of a central hearth and no clear divisions between a central area and side aisles. The central and southeastern parts of the occupation deposits were recorded as one layer during the excavation process, while the northwestern and northeastern parts were recorded separately and as several

different contexts. Presumably this signifies a difference in the deposits in these two areas which is also indicated by the micromorphology of the deposits in the northwestern part, and implies some sort of internal division in the building.

The occupation deposits contained a little debris from glass-bead production, including glass rods and other pieces of production waste. A few glass sherds, some glass beads and trace amounts of amber were also recovered. In addition the occupation deposits contained the usual settlement waste, such as bones, burnt clay, flint, slag, iron, whetstones, loomweight fragments and ceramics. There were no clear differences in the artefactual assemblages between the different contexts. The amount of waste from glass bead production is somewhat higher than in other excavated buildings, and may indicate that such production took place in this building. It is worth noting that production waste was recovered from two different stratigraphic levels inside the building, which may indicate that production was not a one-off incident. However, the small amount of production waste, in combination with the presence of the usual settlement waste, including loomweight fragments, points to the function of the building being mainly domestic, a conclusion which is supported by the micromorphological evidence.

Building A302

Building 302 stood on Plot 3A in Site Period II, sub-phase 2 (Fig. 10.17). The eastern end of the building was destroyed by drainage ditches, and a later pit (A65446, SP III) cut through the southwestern side aisle, in the vicinity of the hearth. The occupation could be divided into two phases: an early phase (a) with a central hearth and a marked side aisle to the northeast, and a late phase (b) where the same occupation deposits covered both the central floor area and the side aisles. The hearth served both phases.

The occupation deposit situated in the central aisle of *phase a* contained c. 700 g of slag and 300 g of burnt clay, plus some fragments of furnaces, in addition to small amounts of crucible fragments and a piece of a clay mould. In addition it contained typical settlement waste such as glass beads, pottery, flint and bone. The northeastern side aisle contained markedly less slag (34 g) and burnt clay (52 g). The later occupation deposit *(phase b)* contained more than 2.2 kg of slag and c. 650 g of burnt clay, in addition to more than 200 g of furnace fragments and tuyères. Small amounts of crucible and mould fragments were also recovered, in addition to the usual settlement finds. Two shallow pits in the northeastern part of the building, belonging to phase b, also contained substantial amounts of slag (total c. 300 g), furnace fragments (total c. 450 g) and burnt clay (total c. 100 g), in addition to small amounts of crucible and mould fragments.

The generally large amount of slag in the occupation deposits indicates that iron smithing took place in building A302 in both phases. However, it seems unlikely that this was a workshop *per se* as other artefacts more typical of a dwelling, such as pottery, soapstone sherds, glass beads and bone are also present. The micromorphological analysis of the occupation deposits also indicates a domestic function for the building (Milek and French, this vol. Ch. 15:347–52). It is unlikely that the slag derives from earlier activities on the plot as building A304 below A302 did not contain nearly the same amount of slag as building A302.

The hearth A64768 was sited centrally in A302. It was rectangular in shape, measured c. 1.5 x 0.6 m, and was sunk to a depth of 10 cm. It was in use in both phases of the building. The hearth was covered by a clay coating including some stones. It was not framed by stones, as was usual at Kaupang, but may have had another kind of surround, as indicated by the presence of negative features at the edges of the hearth. The hearth had been made with clay mixed with silt, sand and small amounts of plant matter (Milek and French, this vol. Ch. 15:347–8). The hearth contained a relatively large number of finds, including slag, furnace fragments, pottery, a crucible fragment and waste from glass bead production.

The structural elements of building A302 are not well defined. Three small post-holes may belong to the building (see Fig. 10.17), and a fourth would, if symmetrically placed, have been removed by a modern drainage ditch. The post-holes were, however, first documented when they became visible in the beach sand. It is therefore possible that they belong to

building A304 (see above). However, the posts seem to be symmetrically placed around the hearth of A302. There are no traces of walls or entrances. Based on the extent of the occupation deposits, the building would have measured c. 6.3 x 4.3 m in both phases.

A layer of compacted grass phytoliths was uncovered in the occupation deposit in the central aisle (Milek and French, this vol. Ch. 15:348). This is probably another indication that grass was used as floor material in the buildings. This interpretation is supported by the recovery of well-preserved grass from pit A65132 on Plot 1A, which has been interpreted as deriving from a building floor based on the environmental evidence (see Barrett et al., this vol. Ch. 14: 298).

Micromorphological analysis indicates that the northwestern end of the building may have seen different use. The deposit here contains less charcoal and burnt bone, and does not appear to have been a trampled surface (Milek and French, this vol. Ch. 15:348–50). The area in question would have been quite restricted, only about 1 m, and therefore could have been used for storage.

Building A303

Building A303 stood on Plot 3B, in SP II, sub-phase 1 (Fig. 10.11). It was probably the earliest building to be built on any of the six excavated plots. Building A303 was stratigraphically earlier than Building A301. A layer of beach gravel was spread on top of A303 to consolidate the ground before the erection of the next building on this plot. The remains of the building were poorly preserved, even by Kaupang standards. It had a central hearth, which was surrounded by occupation deposits. These deposits also contained patches of clay, probably not the remains of a floor proper, but more likely material added to the earthen floor when considered necessary. No postholes could be linked to this building and no remains of the outer walls were found. The northwestern end of the building lay outside the area of the MRE. No structures or deposits from the adjacent CRM trench can be linked securely to building A303. Due to the poor preservation of the building remains nothing further can be said about its layout and size.

The hearth (A79070) was rectangular and measured 2.0 x 0.5 m (Fig. 10.18). Remarkably, the longer axis of the hearth ran across the building, not along its main axis as with other hearths at Kaupang. The hearth was cut into the ground by as much as c. 30 cm to the northwest, but only by a few centimetres to the southeast. A large stone slab was positioned at the base of the southeast end. The hearth contained relatively few artefacts and bones.

The occupation deposit (AL81762) contained the usual settlement finds such as glass beads, pottery sherds, small fragments of amber, a fragment of a loomweight, slag, burnt clay and bones. Micromorphological analysis indicated that this layer was likely to represent a gradual accumulation on the floor of the building (Milek and French, this vol. Ch. 15:335–7). It contained several thin layers of sand, which are likely to have been sprinkled on top of the deposit. Artefacts were also recovered from the patches of clay on top of the occupation deposit. The finds from the clay patches were very similar to the finds from the occupation deposit.

Building A301

Building A301 stood on Plot 3B in SP II, sub-phase 2 (Fig. 10.17). It was only partly uncovered as the western part of the building lay outside the MRE. A 2 m wide segment of the western end was excavated during CRM excavations in 2000, but this excavation was mainly conducted using spits (see Pilø, this vol. Ch. 7:155), and little information on the building could be collected, except for what may be two associated post-holes (see below). In addition, an intrusive pit (A43852) cut through the northern part of the building. As was the case with the other buildings on Plots 3A and 3B, the deposits were investigated using micromorphological analysis (Milek and French, this vol. Ch. 15:337–43), which has added considerably to our knowledge of the layout and function of this building.

The building remains consist of a rectangular hearth, a central earthen floor and side aisles. The hearth (A47445) measured 1.7 x 0.8 m and was surrounded by stones. It was only shallowly cut into the deposits below. It had a stone slab in the lower part. The surface of the hearth was covered by a thin layer of clay mixed with small amounts of organic matter and coarse sand (Milek and French, this vol. Ch. 15:338). The hearth itself contained mainly ash, clay and silt in addition to a few artefacts. It was situated only c. 1.5 m from the eastern end of the building, which suggests that the hearth, while placed upon the central axis of the building, was not positioned at the centre of the floor area.

The central floor was 2.4 m wide. The occupation deposits, which in some places exceeded 10 cm in depth, consisted mainly of debris from the hearth, intermixed with sandy/silty lenses. Micromorphological analysis demonstrated that the upper horizon of this occupation deposit had been truncated, probably several times. Amongst the finds recovered from the deposit were a piece of hacksilver, as well as the usual settlement finds such as loomweight fragments, a few sherds of pottery, glass beads and bits of amber. Although there are few loomweight fragments in the occupation deposit in the central aisle, a large num-

ber of such fragments (and complete loomweights) could be observed in contemporary contexts along the edges of the plot, and in the plot-division ditch to the north. Obviously, broken loomweights, large pieces of pottery and the like were removed from the floor of the building and dumped outside.

The micromorphological evidence suggests that the central floor area saw considerable walking activity, and thus that it was the central artery for communication through the building. During excavation, the deposits in the side aisles looked very similar to the deposit in the central aisle. However, subsequent analyses of thin sections (Milek and French, this vol. Ch. 15:339–43) and of the BS (bulk-sieving) samples and their residue (Barrett et al., this vol. Ch. 14:296–7) have revealed some nuances, which indicate that the side aisles were mainly intended for sitting/sleeping, rather than walking. There were indications that organic bedding materials were located in the side aisles. The northeast side aisle, which was the better preserved, appeared to be c. 1.2 m wide. This width has been confirmed by micromorphological analysis of both the northeast and southwest side aisles.

A narrow line of sand between the central floor area and the southern side aisle probably derives from a wooden plank, which was set on its edge. Its function was probably to contain organic bedding materials in the side aisle, to prevent them from coming into contact with the hearth.

No traces of the outer walls were uncovered during excavation, but results from the micromorphological analysis strongly suggest that the building did extend all the way to the edge of the plot (Milek and French, this vol. Ch. 15:337–46). It is most likely that the northeastern limit of the occupation deposit in the northeast aisle also indicates the location of the outer wall.

As mentioned above, the central floor area was c. 2.4 m wide and the side aisles c. 1.2 m. This would mean a total building width of c. 4.8 m. The length of the building is unknown; only 4 m of its length were encountered in the excavation site of the MRE. If the two post-holes of the CRM trench of 2000 belong to this building, its length must have exceeded 6 m.

No post-holes for interior roof-bearing posts definitely associated with building A301 were encountered during the MRE. However, two large post-holes were discovered in the CRM trench of 2000. They are

Figure 10.19 *A89947, facing southeast. Scale is 1 m.*

Figure 10.20 *A89947, an animal pen? Drawing, Elise Naumann.*

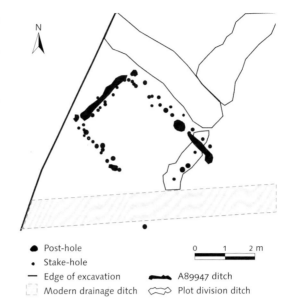

- ● Post-hole
- · Stake-hole
- — Edge of excavation   ▬ A89947 ditch
- ⌐ Modern drainage ditch   ⌣ Plot division ditch

0   1   2 m

positioned in a way which makes it possible, or maybe even likely, that they belong to this building (see Fig. 10.17).

It is of interest to note that a number of iron nails were uncovered from the central occupation deposit and the side aisles, just as in building A200. They may be linked to the building's construction.

The abundance of loomweight fragments on the edges of Plot 3B suggests that textile production took place in building A301. There are no other traces with a clear indication of craft activity. The micromorphological analysis indicates that building A301 was used for domestic purposes, and the remains from textile production fit well into this picture.

A89947 – an animal pen?

Remains of a construction of a different character than the buildings were uncovered on Plot 2B – A89947 (Figs. 10.19 and 10.20). This plot had no other traces from buildings. It also contained a high density of artefacts and bones, indicative of waste disposal. A89947 was first noted in the field, when it appeared as a construction cut into layer AL88965, a quite extensive SP I deposit. The construction is thus likely to belong to SP II or III. However the exact level from which the construction was dug down cannot be determined. The eastern end of the construction crossed the division between Plots 2A and 2B. This indicates that the construction was built after this plot-division was no longer in use, i.e. in SP II, sub-phase 2 or later.

The construction consisted of a line of densely set stake-holes and two narrow ditches. The ditch at the short, northwest end was the most marked. The construction was probably originally rectangular in shape, but the southern part was not well preserved. This part lay against the plot-division fence, and in addition part of it may have been destroyed by a modern drainage ditch. At the time of excavation, it

measured 3.5 x 2 m, but it may originally have been somewhat longer. The construction contains a large number of small post-holes/stake-holes, which indicate that the standing structure had to be repaired a number of times. There were no traces of interior roof-bearing posts; indeed, there is little evidence of whether this construction had a roof. The clear traces of densely set stake-holes in the wall-line suggest that the construction had a wattle wall.

Remarkably, there was a clear difference in the colour of the beach gravel on the inside and the outside of the construction, with the inside being more brown. This phenomenon probably corresponds to what is known as organic staining – a dark brown pigmentation of the fine soil matrix by humic acids (Milek, pers. comm.). This phenomenon must result from the activities inside the construction. The small size of the construction, the repeated repairs, and the difference in soil chemistry, strongly indicate that this is a construction with a function quite different from the buildings. The most likely interpretation is that it was an animal pen, maybe a pig sty; this would correspond nicely with the high level of waste on this plot.

Building on Plot "Hus III" of the 1956–1974 excavations

The discovery, using new knowledge, of previously unrecognized structures on old site plans is a well-known exercise but one fraught with difficulties. Of course, the problem is that if – as in this case – the structures had been easily visible to start with, they would also have been spotted by the original excavators. Thus such exercises can only be performed with some difficulty and with somewhat ambiguous results. In addition, all settlement archaeologists know that to gather the most information on structures, they are best interpreted in the field so that additional detail can be looked for and documented. This is, of course, impossible when using only old site plans. As

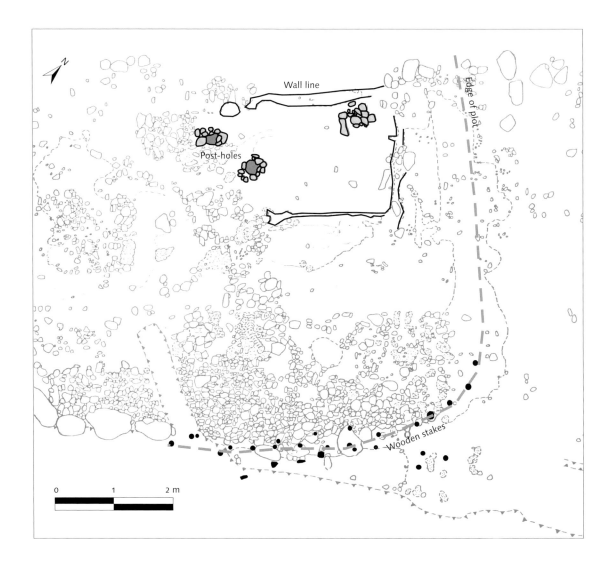

Figure 10.21 *Part of a building construction on Plot "Hus III" of the 1956–1974 excavations. Based on a simplified version of pl. 23 in Tollnes 1998. Redrawing, Lars Pilø.*

Figure 10.22 *Wall-lines of the building construction on Plot "Hus III". Notice that the western wall-line (on the right) is broader than the eastern wall-line (on the left). Facing south. Tollnes 1998:fig. 3.16.*

a consequence, looking at old site plans normally only allows for the detection of possible or probable structures. Little detail can be expected from such plans. At Kaupang there is also the problem that the excavations of 1956–1974 were conducted in 10-cm spits, which makes it hard to see if deposits and features belong to the same stratigraphic level. Thus, while it is possible to see two further structures in the excavation areas of 1956–1974, little can be said about their construction.

The clearest building construction in the excavation area of 1956–1974 was found on the plot which was believed by the excavators to be "Hus III" (Tollnes 1998:40–2). All the structures situated there were interpreted as belonging to a single building lying with its long side towards the shore. However, based on the information on plots and buildings collected during the MRE, this discovery can now be given a different interpretation.

The earliest structure on this plot is a wooden fence separating the plot from the shore (Figs. 10.21 and 10.22). In this case the lower parts of the stakes were preserved, as the conditions on this part of the site were quite moist. Mention was made of deeply

lying "burnt layers" *("brannlag")* covered by deposits of sand (Tollnes 1998:43). These deposits are quite likely to correspond with the earliest outdoor occupation deposits of the MRE. Thus, this phase of the plot probably coincides with SP I of the MRE.

Covering the stakes was a line of a large stones, visible in the lower part of Fig. 10.21. They are likely to have been placed here as a revetment for soil that was dumped into the lower, eastern part of the plot. The plot itself was situated on a slope, with a rather marked drop towards the shore at its lower end, and such infilling served to level the ground. After this

infilling had taken place a structure was built on the plot; its wall-ditches and possibly also post-holes can now be discerned. Unfortunately, time did not allow for the excavation of the post-holes, and their stratigraphic association with the wall-line is not known. The building itself should probably be associated with SP II of the MRE.

Part of the wall-line was visible as three clear dark lines in the sand deposit (Figs. 10.21 and 10.22). These are probably the remains of a wall of vertical planks. The eastern and northern wall-lines were very narrow and hardly allowed for more than a row of standing planks set quite simply into the ground. The western wall-line was broader, and might have contained a sill-beam or had a similar construction to the other wall-lines.

There were no remains of a hearth, nor were any occupation deposits belonging to this building preserved or recognised. We are probably looking at only the cut features of this building – and then, only at some of those. Thus the layout and the size of the building are not known with any accuracy. The building must have been at least 3 m wide. The two parallel wall-lines were 2 m apart, but the area to the east had

few stones, and the building may have continued into this area. However, the well-defined edge of the stony area, visible in Fig. 10.21, which might be taken as an indication of the limit of the building's construction, is in fact the result of the excavation method – a section was placed here. The limit of the structure to the west is not known. Essentially, we may be looking at either a small building or part of a larger structure only partially preserved.

Building on Plot "Hus V" of the 1956–1974 excavations?

Whilst a lack of post-holes is normal for most structures at Kaupang, the case of the possible building on Plot "Hus V" is quite the opposite. This structure is represented by a number of clay-lined post-holes, with imprints of the posts.

The plot itself, previously interpreted as a building (Tollnes 1998:47–9), is of much the same type as the other plots on the site. There seems to have been an early fence separating the plot from the shore, but information on this fence is vague. There is a very early settlement deposit lying immediately above the beach sand and this corresponds well with SP I of the

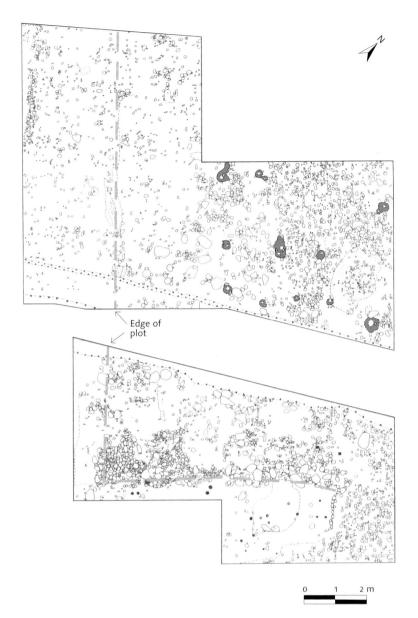

Edge of
plot

0   1   2 m

Figure 10.23 *Clay-lined post-holes on Plot "Hus V" marked in grey. Redrawn by Lars Pilø after Tollnes 1998:pl. 26.*

Figure 10.24 *Two clay-lined post-holes belonging to the building on Plot "Hus V". Tollnes 1998:fig. 6.3.*

Figure 10.25 *Dublin building FS 88 (Wallace 1992:pl. Xb). Size of building c. 8.5 x 6 m.*

deposits or features. Clay-lined post-holes in a plot-division ditch were uncovered during the MRE, serving as a reminder that the post-holes on Plot "Hus V" do not necessarily derive from a building.

A discussion of the buildings

The very poor preservation conditions severely limit our knowledge of the building techniques at Kaupang. The excavated buildings were a heterogeneous group. Thus, even though it is easy to let our impression of the buildings at Kaupang be dominated by building A200 and other buildings with similar layouts – with their striking similarity to the Dublin Type-1 buildings (Fig. 10.25) – this would oversimplify the picture. The buildings varied in size, different construction techniques were used, hearths were present only in some of the buildings, and their layouts differed.

Building no.	Length	Width
A200	9–11 m	6.0 m
A301	> 4 m	4.8 m
A302	6.3 m	4.3 m
A304	6.2 m	4.4 m
A406	–	4.5 m

Table 10.2 *Sizes of buildings excavated at Kaupang during the MRE.*

Generally it can be said that the buildings were quite small, and well suited to the conditions of urban settlement, including the small plots. The largest building (A200) measured c. 10 x 6m, but the other buildings were smaller in size (Tab. 10.2). Many of the plots were quite small, and this directly influenced the size of the buildings on them.

MRE. Overlying this deposit was a stone construction, built as a revetment for soil within the plot. It was less well built than the similar construction on Plot "Hus III". This construction is probably to be associated with SP II of the MRE.

The features marked on Fig. 10.23 were described by Tollnes as being clay-lined post-holes, with imprints of the posts. Some of them were double posts (Fig. 10.24). The imprints of the posts were round, with a diameter of 8–13 cm.

Some post-holes may be missing in the eastern, lower part, which was not uncovered. Tollnes stated that the post-holes were positioned high up in the cultural deposits. Interpretation is made more difficult by the presence of concentrations of clay in many places on this plot. Only the features with imprints of posts have been marked on Fig. 10.23. They may belong to a structure, but its character cannot be determined now. There were no other associated

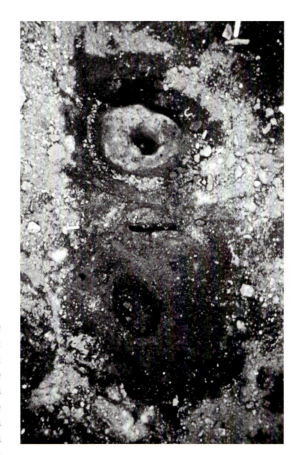

The evidence for constructional detail is meagre at best. The presence of post-holes associated with some of the buildings indicates that interior wooden posts, dug into the ground, were used to support the roof in at least some of the buildings. Other posts may have stood on sill-stones. The character of the roof is little known. Evidence for turf which was recovered from the environmental material in pits (Barrett et al., this vol. Ch. 14:287) may be related to roofing material for the buildings excavated during the MRE. However if turf had been used for roofing material in these buildings it would be expected in demolition levels, as in Dublin. This is not the case for Buildings A303 and A304, which are the only buildings with preserved demolition levels. It might have been the case with other buildings, but a turf roof is quite heavy and would have demanded substantial timber for the roof-bearing posts, of which there is little evidence – compared to the preserved,

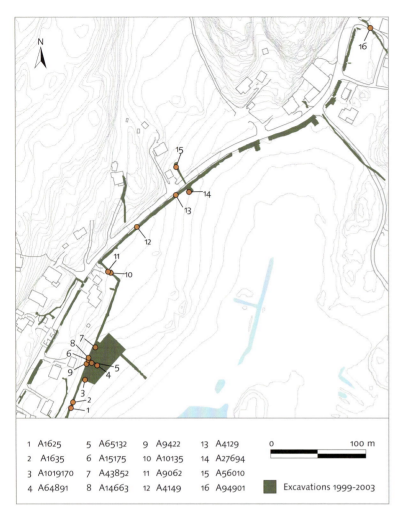

1	A1625	5	A65132	9	A9422	13	A4129
2	A1635	6	A15175	10	A10135	14	A27694
3	A1019170	7	A43852	11	A9062	15	A56010
4	A64891	8	A14663	12	A4149	16	A94901

0   100 m

Excavations 1999-2003

Figure 10.26 *Plan of location of all pits with preserved wood, from the 2000–2003 excavations. Drawing, Julie K. Øhre Askjem.*

Figure 10.27 *Photo of wattle-lined pit A9422. The yellow plastic sticks were used for geo-referencing. Facing southwest.*

but rather slight roof bearing post in building A200. On the other hand, turf roofs have been interpreted for the Dublin buildings on the basis of the presence of sods in the demolition levels (see above), and these buildings had only relatively slight roof-bearing posts.

The traces of the outer walls of the buildings were very scarce. The building on Blindheim's Plot "Hus III" seems to have had a wall-line of planks set in a foundation trench. The badly preserved building on Plot 2B exhibited faint traces of what could have been a wattle wall. As the buildings on Plot 3B were constructed on a layer of light-coloured gravel which had been introduced to the site before building began, it is unlikely that cut or intrusive features belonging to the outer wall of these buildings would have been overlooked – especially since the animal shed A89947 had substantial traces of this type of wall construction. Thus, in these cases, the wall was probably not sunk into the ground, but rested upon it, on a sill. This sill seems to have stood directly upon the ground surface, as there were no traces of sill-stones or their imprints.

The use of a sill-beam for the outer walls implies that the buildings had rectangular ground plans, not curved walls. The walls themselves could have been constructed either of wattle or with planks (vertical or horizontal). Different building techniques for walls might have been used in different buildings. Remarkably, no remains have been found of daub which would have been expected to have covered any wattle walls. However, this is also the case in Dublin, where the well-preserved remains of wattle walls show no signs of having been daubed. The reasons for the absence of daub are yet to be understood in Dublin, but it has been suggested that the walls might have been covered internally with textiles (Wallace 1992:13). The climate at Kaupang is considerably harsher than in Dublin. If wattle was used for the outer walls, winter settlement in the buildings would not have been possible without some kind of insulation. Clay was readily available below the beach sand, a fact which was well known to the inhabitants from their digging of pits. Even though daub is best preserved when structures have burned down, the absence of lumps of clay in the intact deposits is a sign that the insulation of walls with clay was not done. Clay was not visible in the thin sections of the occupation deposits either, except for hearths (Milek and French, this vol. Ch. 15:324–5). In Blindheim's excavations a large number of unburnt loomweights of clay were recovered, and such loomweights were also recovered from the MRE. This shows that the clay would not always have disappeared as a result of post-depositional processes. There were also no signs of dumped daub in the midden area between the plots and the sea.

Other material might have been used for insulating wattle walls, for instance animal dung, which would not have survived to the present. On the other hand, there is little to suggest that animal dung was readily available for this purpose in Kaupang, where pigs were the only animals that might possibly have been reared (Barrett et al., this vol. Ch. 14:305). The absence of insulating materials for wattle walls indi-

cates that wattlework was not utilised, and this in turn suggests that walls were made of planks, placed either vertically or horizontally. Corner timbering was probably not used for the structural walls on a regular basis at Kaupang (even if this technique was known – see below), as this would preclude the interior roof-bearing posts present in some of the buildings.

Four buildings had a hearth positioned along their central axis, albeit not always centrally placed within the building. Four buildings (A200, A302, A303 and A406) showed a separation of the central floor area from the side aisles. The evidence indicates that the central floor area was an activity area for walking and cooking, while the side aisles were used for sitting and sleeping. Other buildings did not show this type of layout. One building (Blindheim, Plot "Hus III") showed what may be interior partitioning. The presence of such a partition was also indicated by micromorphological evidence in two other instances (Buildings A302 and A304), which demonstrated that trampling had not taken place in a small part of the northwestern segment of the buildings, possibly because these areas were used for storage.

There is no structural evidence to show where the entrances to the buildings were placed, as these were not fastened into the ground. Functionally speaking, though, they are likely to have been placed in the gables of the buildings, as there was very little room between the presumed position of the outer building walls and the edges of the plots. Entrances in the gables are rare on contemporary sites in northern Europe, both urban and rural, but are known from the Sognefjorden area in western Norway (see for instance Larsen 1995, on the Ytre Moa site).

The buildings excavated during the MRE seem to have had a mainly domestic function. There are some traces from craft activities, like amberworking in building A200 and blacksmithing in building A302,

but only in the latter case was this of any substantial character. However, the other artefacts recovered from building A302 indicated a domestic function.

Kaupang buildings, such as A200, may provide important background material for understanding the context in which buildings such as Dublin Type-1 developed, but it should be noted that the Kaupang buildings pre-date those in Dublin by at least a century. It could be proposed that what we are seeing at Kaupang is simply a section of a typical rural longhouse (as it is known in Scandinavia) – the dwelling part with the hearth – and that the Kaupang buildings may therefore not differ greatly from rural longhouses as they appear to do. On the other hand, the small size of the buildings and the slight interior posts indicate that the Kaupang buildings would have appeared very different from the more solid rural longhouses, even if their internal layout had its origin in that type of building. It should also be noted that little is known at present about Viking-age rural longhouses in southeastern Norway.

What was uncovered in the MRE was not so much the physical remains of the buildings themselves as traces of their use, i.e. their hearths and occupation deposits. The buildings were not fastened into the ground – most of the walls must have rested upon sill-beams and many posts must have stood on sill-stones. The post-holes that were found were mostly quite shallow. This also distinguishes the Kaupang buildings from contemporary buildings of the region, which were to all appearances built in a much more solid manner, with roof-carrying posts dug deeply into the ground, entrances clearly defined, and sometimes visible remains of the outer walls. The "light" construction technique at Kaupang could be mirroring the urban context, in that these buildings might not have been built for the same kind of long-term permanent occupation as the more solidly constructed rural buildings.

Figure 10.28 *Corner-timbered well A10135.*
Bottom: detail of corner-timbering technique.

Figure 10.29 *"Brygge I" during excavation in 1958.*
Facing east. Photo, Tollnes 1998:fig. 5.4.

	Number	In combination with wattle
Wattle	7	
Plank lining	6	2
Re-used barrels	4	1
Corner timbering	1	1
Total	18	

Table 10.3 *Pits with preserved wooden lining, from the 1956–74 and 2000–2003 excavations.*

A total of 18 pits had some preserved wooden lining (Fig. 10.26); a smaller number of pits had no lining. In some cases the lining's presence was clearly a function of preservation, while in others wattle seemed to have been removed and only small stakes and some branches remained. Most large pits, especially those which were intended to remain as open structures, probably had some kind of lining to prevent the collapse of their sides.

Four types of lining are present in the pits: wattle, planks, re-used barrels and corner timbering (Tab. 10.3). A combination of wattle with the other types is seen in four cases, either functioning simultaneously or one type substituting another during repair. Wattle is the most common material for lining the pits (Fig. 10.27).

The wattle (and the stakes) were usually made from hazel, juniper or sallow (Tollnes 1998:87, 90; Høeg, report in the project archive). Wattle was used in both large and small pits.

Wooden planks were used to line six pits. Most of these planks were identified as oak. As a rule the planks had been hammered or pushed into the soft clay in a vertical position, but sometimes they were

10.4 Pits

A number of large pits have been recorded at Kaupang, both during the excavations of 1956–1974 and during the fieldwork of 2000–2003. Only waterlogged pits with preserved wooden elements (mainly wattle or planks) are treated here. The excavation and recording of the pits have provided important information on a number of issues, most importantly environmental information and construction techniques, the latter of which is considered here. Some of the wood found its primary use in the pits, while other wood was only secondarily placed there. The construction of the lining of the pits sheds light on the use of different construction techniques at Kaupang.

placed horizontally. It seems that the main concern was that the lining be a stable casing for the pit; the construction technique and materials seem to have been of secondary importance. In pit A15175, the largest one excavated at Kaupang, re-used planks from a number of different sources were used.

The use of wooden barrels for lining pits is well known from most urban settlements, and Kaupang is no exception. However, a barrel (of spruce) was well preserved in only one instance, in pit A56010, which was probably backfilled quite quickly. In other cases only the very lowest part of the barrel was preserved. In one instance the staves of the barrel were made of maple and the hoops of hazel and birch (Tollnes 1998:89).

One pit, A10135, had the lower part of its wall lining constructed in corner-timbering (Fig. 10.28). The upper part was probably made in wattle, judging from the wooden stakes preserved on the outside of the corner-timbered box. The corner-timbering was well executed. Thick planks, with notches on both their upper and lower sides, were used for the box.

The dated timber in this construction was felled during the summer of AD 808 (Bonde, this vol. Ch. 13: 277–8, nos. A14257, A13719, A15835, A15847). This construction is remarkable, both for its early date and its advanced technique. It pre-dates by slightly more than a century the earliest previously known example of corner-timbering in Norway – the lower part of the burial chamber in the Gokstad ship burial (Bonde and Christensen 1993) – and its craftsmanship is quite superior to the corner-timbering in the Gokstad find.

The use of corner-timbering in wells is well known from the Continent, going far back into prehistoric times (Zimmermann 1998:70–6). In most regions this technique was used exclusively for the construction of wells. There are no documented wells with corner-timbering in Norway prior to the High Middle Ages (c. AD 1050–1500), but this absence may be due to the small number of excavations of rural settlements from the Viking Age.

The function of the pits is still an open question, even after the examination of the environmental evidence. Some of them on higher ground might have

Hard

Tollnes'
stone jetty
Phase 1

Possible
hard

Tollnes'
stone jetty
Phase 2

Clearance
cairn

Figure 10.30 *Stone construction ("Brygge II"), previously interpreted as a stone jetty, with the original interpretation and phasing on the left, and the new interpretation on the right. Redrawn by Elise Naumann after Tollnes 1998:fig. 5.7.*

Figure 10.31 *Driven posts from the excavations of 1956– 1974. Features marked in red denote possible posts for a wooden jetty. Blue squares denote posts dendro-dated to AD 803. Redrawn by Lars Pilø after Tollnes 1998:pl. 12A, 16 and 18.*

been used as wells for drinking water, but those closer to the shore contained brackish water, and were thus unsuitable for use as drinking water wells. There is no evidence that they were used as cesspits (Barrett et al., this vol. Ch. 14:297–9).

Some pits have vertical cuts while the cuts of others are rather funnel-shaped, with a wide opening and steepening sides deeper down in the pit. However, perhaps no great weight should be attached to the shape of the pits when interpreting their function, as their shape may simply be a product of erosion and/or backfilling (Schiffer 1996:218–20).

10.5 Jetties

The question of how the traders landed their ships at Kaupang has also been discussed, mainly by Tollnes (1998:95–7). Previously it was believed that Kaupang had stone jetties. This belief was based on the so-called "Brygge I" and "Brygge II" from the excava-

tions of 1956–1974. Very little of the beach zone was investigated during the MRE and therefore no new information on jetties was collected. Likewise the 2003 excavation in the harbour was situated outside the beach zone and jetties were not encountered. Consequently, the re-interpretation of these stone constructions has to rely mainly on a re-examination of the previously collected evidence. However, new evidence on the sea-level in the Viking Age (Sørensen et al., this vol. Ch. 12:267–70), and on the source of the "black earth" deposit have contributed valuable information to this re-interpretation.

The supposed northern jetty ("Brygge I", Fig. 10.29) was uncovered below stratified deposits, and there can hardly be any doubt as to its Viking-age date. However, the documentation does not justify the term "jetty" or "pier" *("brygge")* ascribed to it by Tollnes. It is rather a layer of large, unburned stones interspersed with a large number of small fire-cracked stones, which were probably deposited here in order to facilitate walking and transport in the soggy beach area. This type of structure is now recognised as a common feature on early landing sites (McGrail 1985), and is known as a "hard". Several wooden stakes (lying parallel to the shoreline) and bundles of twigs were found underneath the stone. They probably represent an earlier attempt at consolidating the landing place. The stone structures in the tidal zone at Kaupang have been interpreted as hards by Ellmers (1985:28).

The function of "Brygge II" is less clear-cut (Fig. 10.30). The concentration of stones started on the shore just outside two plots ("Hus I" and "Hus II"), and extended well into the former harbour basin. The construction was divided into two phases by Tollnes. Phase 2, which is the lower, eastern end of the feature, was separated from the upper part by an area with few stones. This lower end is situated at what is now known to be c. 2.5 m below the Viking-age sea-level;

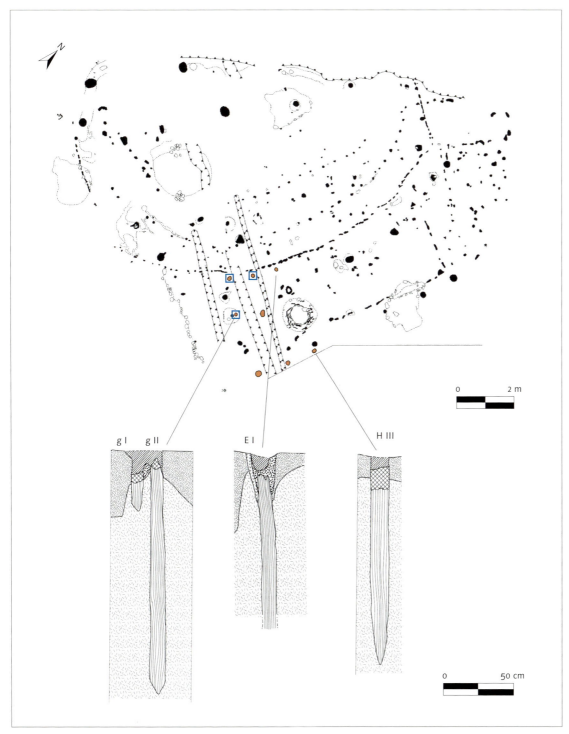

g I g II   E I   H III

0   2 m

0   50 cm

therefore, the construction would have had to have been significantly higher than its preserved height in order to have had any function in the Viking Age. Tollnes reported that the lower end was later partly covered with stones from clearance, mixed with earth. The presence of "black earth" *("svartjord")* covering the stones was noted but, as is now known, this layer is likely to be a post-Viking-age agricultural layer, and thus does not date the stone construction to the Viking Age. Tollnes also pointed to the fact that a field boundary is situated here on a map from 1811. Few artefacts were recovered and no fire-cracked

stone were documented from the lower, eastern end of "Brygge II". It seems most likely that the lower end of the stone structure relates to post-Viking-age agricultural activities and consists of stones cleared in cairns or dumped at the edge of a field. Furthermore, part of a similar stone feature was uncovered during the harbour excavations in 2003; it is situated c. 1.3 m above present sea-level. In this case, no finds were recovered, but it was also interpreted as a structure which post-dated the Viking Age and which was related to agricultural activities.

The higher end of the feature (phase 1) belongs at

least partly to the Viking-age settlement period. In the part closest to the plots the construction was seen to contain a sequence of deposition – unburned stones directly on the beach sand, then fire-cracked stones above them, and finally more unburned stones on the top (Tollnes 1998:98).

However, there is a discrepancy between Tollnes' description of this stone construction as being "one" construction, and the written records and photographs which seem to show that it consisted of at least two parts (Fig. 10.30). Tollnes describes the part closest to the plots as being "made up of patches of larger and smallish stones on the surface, all tightly packed" ("partivis av store og mer småfallen stein i overflaten, alt i tett pakning"). Many of the small stones were scorched. Further away from the plots (at grid point −16y) the small fire-cracked stones disappeared, and the construction widened gradually. Also, the stones there were placed with more care and intermixed with sand and black earth. As can be seen from Fig. 10.30, this part of the construction was not directly linked to the higher part. It may be that these stones were placed there in the Viking Age as a more elaborate "hard" to facilitate transport in the soggy tidal zone, but it is also possible that the stones were placed there at a later date.

Much of the confusion concerning these stone constructions derives from Tollnes' use of the term "black earth" ("svartjord") to designate most cultural deposits, whether they are intact Viking-age deposits or disturbed later medieval plough-layers. Of course this distinction only became clear as a consequence of the excavation in 2000–2003. However, this lack of separation of intact and disturbed deposits makes it difficult to judge whether the structures can be linked stratigraphically to the Viking-age settlement.

However, even with the problematic documentation in mind, there is no evidence to support the interpretation of these features at Kaupang as Viking-age stone piers or jetties. The stone features "Brygge I" and "Brygge II, phase 1" are probably simply layers of stone formed by dumping in the soggy tidal zone; such features are known from similar urban sites such as 11th-century Bergen (Herteig 1969:75–7).

However, other types of jetties might well have been present at Kaupang. In the beach zone of the excavation area in 1956–1974 a number of driven posts were discovered, some of which seem to be related to the earliest phase of settlement (Fig. 10.31). Most of these posts were in a vertical position, but there were also some placed at an angle. They give the impression of deriving from wooden jetties. They had been ascribed to the so-called "Hus I" but, as noted above, the previous interpretation of the structures excavated in 1956–1974 cannot be maintained in light of the new evidence. Also, the use of deeply driven posts is not known in Viking-age house-building traditions but is well evidenced in the context of Viking-age bridges and jetties (for instance in Hedeby: Schietzel 1984c). The width of the wooden jetty east of Plot "Hus I" would have been c. 1.7 m.

10.6 Summary

The Viking-age settlement at Kaupang was founded c. AD 800 on a formerly unoccupied beach along a small sea strait, with ample access to the major waterways. Its founding is clearly represented by the plot-division fences, which are the stratigraphically earliest activity on the site. Settlement was seasonal in the initial phase, but within the first decade it became permanent. During the transition, buildings were constructed on the plots, pits were dug, and extensive dumping of waste took place. The buildings investigated in the main research excavation of 2000–2002 appear to have had a mainly domestic function, but the remains of workshops were also located (although not excavated to any degree). Few cultural deposits post–c. AD 840/850 were preserved in the settlement area, but evidence from the harbour and the cemeteries indicates that permanent settlement continued at least into the first decades of the 10th century. Artefacts recovered from the modern ploughsoil, dating to the second half of the 10th century, indicate that there was activity on the site as late as that date, but the character of that activity remains obscure.

Judging from the buildings uncovered in the MRE, the typical Kaupang building would have had two pairs of interior roof-bearing posts, a central hearth surrounded by an earthen floor, and side aisles physically separated from that floor. The earthen floor was mainly a walking area, while the side aisles appear to have been for sitting and sleeping. Some of the buildings had indications of a room with a different function at one end of the building. The buildings were invariably placed with their gable end towards the beach. The outer walls, of planks or wattle, presumably rested on sill-beams, while the door(s) might have been placed in the gable(s). In their general layout, some of the Kaupang buildings appear very similar to the Type-1 buildings from Dublin, but the generally poor preservation conditions on the site make a closer comparison difficult.

The waterlogged pits preserved wood that sheds light on the building techniques used in Kaupang in the Viking Age. The pits were lined with wattle, planks, re-used barrels or corner-timbering. There is no clear evidence of their function.

Jetties at Kaupang were probably made of wood. The stone constructions "Brygge I" and "Brygge II" (upper part of phase 1) are now interpreted to be stone introduced to the tidal zone to facilitate transport in the soggy beach zone. "Brygge II" phase 2 is now interpreted to be a post-Viking-age clearance cairn, while the dating and function of the lower part of "Brygge II" phase 1 remains uncertain.

Excavations of the Hall at Huseby 11

DAGFINN SKRE

In 1999 the surveyors for the Kaupang project discovered a building platform at the farm of Huseby, about 1 km north of the settlement area at Kaupang. The platform was some 36 m long and 13 m wide, and had bowed long sides. It was situated on the crest of a rocky hillock and was widely visible. On comparable platforms in the area around lake Mälaren, Sweden, halls built in the 8th century and standing until the end of the Viking Period have been found.

A trial excavation was undertaken in 1999 and the platform gradually excavated in 2000 and 2001. When the platform was constructed, a barrow of the 4th or 5th century AD had been laid flat. Between 200 and 300 cu m of soil and stone had also been brought up then onto the hillock to build the platform.

Because of the very difficult ground conditions, no definite post-holes were identified, although there were several likely candidates. It is possible, nevertheless, with particular reference to the foundations of long walls and two probable post-holes, to propose what the ground-plan of the building was like. Activities in the centuries following the Viking Period have disturbed the soil so that stratified layers from the functioning period of the platform are virtually entirely lost. Artefacts from the Viking Period to modern times have been found together in the soil covering the platform.

A range of finds from the Viking Period can be linked to an aristocratic context. Alongside the form of the platform and the building these clearly point to a hall having been placed on the spot. The finds show that the building was raised some time in the mid or second half of the 8th century. It most probably went out of use at the beginning of the 10th century. The foundations and an oven from a corner-timbered (lafted) type of building (a *stofa*) were also found. This may have been constructed by the 11th century, and could have played a part in the role of the farmstead as a royal administrative farm.

Farms with the name Huseby have long occupied a special position in Scandinavian historical research, especially in Sweden and Norway (for a review of research, see Olausson 2000). These farms are normally large and centrally placed and several sources indicate that they played a role in the government of the early kingdom. Most scholars nowadays believe that the farms were given the name Huseby at the end of the Viking Period, some time in the 11th century or a little earlier. In Norway, the majority of the 54 Huseby farms are found around the Oslofjord: i.e. in Østfold, Vestfold, and northwards up to Romerike. In Sweden, the great majority of Husebys are found around lake Mälaren. In Denmark and Schleswig-Holstein, there are 10 Huseby farmsteads (Westerdal and Stylegar 2004:101). Like most of its namesakes, Huseby in Tjølling is also a large farmstead. It is centrally locat-ed in the best agricultural area of Tjølling (Fig. 11.1).

Since the name Huseby is manifestly younger than the farmsteads which bear it, they must have had other names previously. The place-name specialist Kåre Hoel (1986) has proposed that this Huseby in Tjølling was formerly called Skiringssal (Brink, this vol. Ch. 4). The association of two such significant names with one and the same farmstead was the reason why The Kaupang Excavation Project chose to examine the farm more closely (Skre, this vol. Ch. 3).

11.1 The discovery of the building platform at Huseby

At Huseby a peculiar formation – in modern archaeology called a building platform – has attracted the attention of archaeologists on several occasions during the last century. In 1918, divinity student Ballestad

was recording ancient monuments in Tjølling, commissioned by Universitetets Oldsaksamling and in his report from Huseby (gnr. 32 bnr. 20), he wrote:

Like søndenfor samme gaard skal der ifølge traditionen ha været et tingsted. Ved undersøkelse fandt jeg at her engang i tiden var kjørt jord op og jevnet ut mellem bergrabberne, saa der var fremkommet et firkantet slet stykke 35 m x 5 m. I stykkets utkant fandt jeg etslags fotkjæde.

Immediately south of the same farmstead there is traditionally claimed to have been a *thing*-place. On investigation I found that at some date earth had been carted up here and spread out evenly between the ridges of rock to produce a four-sided platform measuring 35 m x 5 m. At the outer edge of the platform I found a sort of kerb-ring.

This site is located on *Husebyhaugen* (the Huseby Hillock), which protrudes about 4 m above the surrounding terrain. West of this hillock the land falls away quite steeply towards the Guri Brook, while to the east there is a much more gentle slope, and to the north and south the land is quite flat. The hillock measures about 220 m N–S and 70 m E–W, and its highest point, at its northern end, is c. 22 m above sea-level. The northern part of the hillock is mostly naked rock, but the southern end has some pockets of soil here and there. The building platform is situated at the northernmost and highest point on the hillock (Fig. 11.2).

The next report of the site is from 1955, when Bertil Almgren from the University of Uppsala visited his friend and colleague Charlotte Blindheim's excavations at Bikjholberget. We do not know if it was Ballestad's account that led them to Husebyhaugen, or Almgren's familiarity with the Swedish building terraces which were then being excavated, as at Helgö (Holmqvist 1961). In any event, the Kaupang project archive, KHM, includes three photographs by Almgren of Husebyhaugen and the building platform. In 1999, Charlotte Blindheim told me that Almgren had then been sure that an ancient building had stood on this spot, but that she never had the means to investigate the matter.

In the spring of 1999 the Kaupang Excavation Project began its field-recording in Tjølling (Skre, this vol. Ch. 3:50) which was undertaken while working through the archival material. Ballestad's report and Almgren's photographs had not yet come to light. The fieldwork was focussed particularly upon the recording of the fields east, west and north of the modern farmstead at Huseby (Pilø 1999d). There, several finds turned up including a bead and an axe of the Viking Period (KHM Aks. 99/64). The returns were otherwise meagre, except for those from two relatively recently cultivated field-edges that abut Husebyhaugen on the northern and eastern sides. There were found ploughed-out hearths, a post-hole, a whetstone, burnt bone, and a spindle-whorl – altogether, evidence that this was the site of a settlement from some time in the first millennium AD (Fig. 11.2).

During a lunch-break two of the survey team took a short walk in order to look at the barrow on the southern end of the hillock. They came back with

Figure 11.1 *The central part of Tjølling, facing south. 1: the building platform at the farmstead at Huseby. 2: the settlement area of Kaupang (behind the wooded ridge). Photo, D. Skre, Kaupang Excavation Project.*

Figure 11.2 *Plan of Husebyhaugen and its surroundings with the platform and the finds from the ploughed fields in the immediate vicinity of the hillock marked. On the south-western edge of the hillock lies a barrow from some time in the first millennium AD. Contour interval 1 meter. Map, Julie K. Øhre Askjem.*

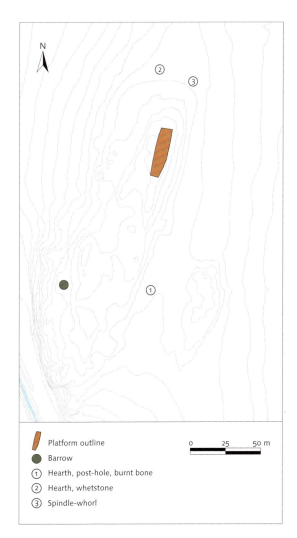

/ Platform outline
● Barrow
① Hearth, post-hole, burnt bone
② Hearth, whetstone
③ Spindle-whorl

0   25   50 m

quite other things than burial mounds on their minds. Up on the highest point of the hillock they had found what could only be a man-made platform; to judge from its form it was meant for a building. In the days that followed the platform was surveyed and the visible elements recorded.

The platform is almost perfectly flat and has bowed long sides which measure at maximum c. 36 m N–S. It is 13 m wide E–W in the middle, narrowing to c. 8.5 m at either end. It was constructed in a hollow in the rock, the edges of which protrude slightly beyond the upper surface of the platform at its southern end and along its western edge. To the north, the rock reaches up to the same level as the platform, and continues north of it as a smooth rock slope that falls steadily down to the field and the roadway to the north and north-west (Fig. 11.2). To the east, the platform's flat top reaches a sharp edge, and east of this the built-up construction slopes down towards the natural rock surface below. In several places along the sides of the platform's flat top, especially clearly on the west, there are stones sticking up which describe the bowed outline (Fig. 11.5).

The platform appeared to be undisturbed except for one rectangular pit measuring c. 1.5 x 3 m and 0.4 m deep. This was dug a little to the north of the centre of the platform around 1960. The present owner of the farm, Clas Huseby, took part in that excavation. He reports that a large piece of soapstone with a hole in it was found. The description is clearly that of a loomweight (see below). This has since been lost.

11.2 Trial excavation, 1999

The discovery of the building platform was quite a surprise, as no such feature had until then been found in Norway. Such platforms are, however, known in the region around lake Mälaren, Sweden (see below).

In order to determine whether there had been a building on the platform in the Iron Age, it was

decided to undertake a trial excavation in September 1999. It was conducted by Dr. Svante Norr (1999).

The nearly vertical sides of the existing pit on the platform were cleaned so that the sections could be studied. In addition, a small trench on the eastern edge of the platform was dug, slightly north of its north-south midway point. Stones were found that were interpreted as the possible foundation of an external wall. 162 fragments of burnt clay were found, several of them with the impressions of withies showing that they had formed part of a wattle-and-daub construction; these were therefore interpreted as the remains of a burnt building of Iron-age type. Also found were burnt bone and scorched stone. The discovery of a faceted cornelian bead indicated that the platform, probably also the building, existed in the Viking Period (Fig. 11.13).

11.3 Excavation and method, 2000–2001

In 2000, the south-eastern quarter of the platform was stripped of turf using a digging machine and the area excavated. In 2001, the remainder of the platform was de-turfed, and the majority of the area excavated. All of the soil below the turf was wet-sieved. At the beginning of the excavation in 2001, the whole platform was surveyed with metal detectors. Areas which returned signals were marked. Soil and charcoal samples were collected from several contexts. Both burnt and unburnt bone were collected. Norr was the site director. The excavation report was written by Øysten Lia (2005).

Excavation was carried out in one-metre squares. As it was effectively impossible to identify intact stratigraphical deposits, the excavation was done in spits 5 cm deep. The lack of undisturbed stratigraphy was probably the result of both natural decomposition and disturbance resulting from human activities post-dating the Viking Period. As a result, it was not possible to see any distinct differences between the

constructional fill of the platform itself and the layers that had built up during the various phases of activity upon it. This interpretation of the stratigraphy is supported by the fact that the quantity of scorched stone, probably originally deposited within the building on the platform, decreased the deeper we got.

In the deposits a quantity of coarse domestic pottery was found that probably derives from the Early Iron Age, and which, to judge by the degree of fragmentation and wear, would appear to have lain for some time at a settlement site. This indicates that some of the material used to build the platform was taken from a settlement site, and that some of the artefacts may have been re-deposited in this way.

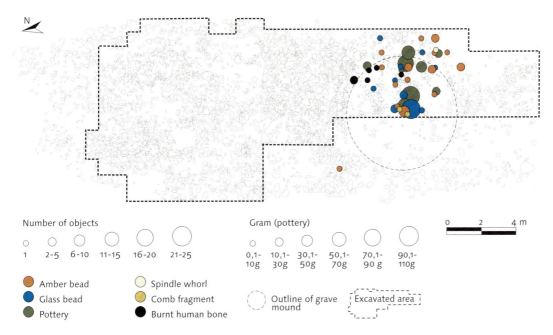

However the finds from the Viking Period and later can with great confidence be associated with activities up on the platform.

As a rule, foundations, post-holes and the like were extremely difficult to identify. The platform was built principally of stone, some pieces of which were nearly a metre across. The great quantity of stone made it hard to distinguish between stones that formed part of the fill of the platform and stones that had had some function in buildings on top of the platform. A few post-holes could be identified with varying degrees of certainty because the stones around the presumed post-holes formed a reasonably clear ring – probably packing stones that surrounded the post. But since it was very hard to see any difference between the soil that filled the presumed post-hole and the soil surrounding the ring of stones, all such interpretations are somewhat doubtful.

When the turf had been stripped off, at the southern end of the platform it was possible to discern a circular zone with a slightly lighter fill and less stones. This proved to be the remains of a burial mound of the Early Iron Age (see below). There it was easier to identify features. Nevertheless the fills were so uniform that it was decided not to section the post-holes. The likelihood of finding the edges of the features was considered minimal. Instead, the holes used for the posts themselves, the post-shadows, were emptied so that the packing stones and any foundation stones could be seen.

The deposits overlying the massive stone packing of the platform was not excavated in its entirety. After the removal of the turf, priority was given to identifying post-holes and foundations, and to disentangling, excavating and recording them. Beyond that, the deposits were excavated as far as was necessary to reveal structures, to clarify their nature, and to collect a sufficient quantity of artefactual finds to be able to assess the character and date of the structures and other activities. Over most of the platform only two spits were excavated, i.e. to a depth of about 10 cm below the turf. The excavations were focussed on the south-eastern and northern parts of the platform. An area of around 40 sq m at the very northern end and about 150 sq m in the south-western corner were left unexcavated. All that was done there was to record the stones that protruded after the turf had been removed. Finds that appeared at this stage were also recorded. The area excavated is shown in Figure 11.6.

11.4 The history of the platform site

Three main periods in the history of this site can be distinguished. The first phase of activity was the building of a burial mound there in the 4th or 5th century AD. Several centuries later, in the second half of the 8th century, this barrow was partially flattened, and the building platform constructed. On top of the platform a building was raised, to all appearances a hall. It is difficult to tell how long this use of the platform continued. It certainly lasted through the 9th century. Several finds could be attributable to the 10th century although none can be assigned to that period with certainty. Two coins from the second and fourth quarters of the 11th century, respectively, show that there was activity of a character that could most reasonably be associated with a building at that date too. But they need not have anything to do with the hall; indeed, maybe they should be linked to a *stofa*, i.e. a lafted or log-cabin type of house with a corner oven, of which traces were also found on the platform. Two coins of the 15th and 16th centuries should probably also be connected to this building.

The barrow

Several barrows with graves of the Early Iron Age have been found at Huseby (Blindheim 1974), and after the excavations on Husebyhaugen one more can be added to the list. At the southern end of the plat-

Figure 11.5 *The platform after excavation, facing south. Photo, D. Skre, Kaupang Excavation Project.*

Figure 11.6 *Stones that were visible after cleaning and excavation. That the quantity of stones in the plan appears lower at the northern end and in the south-western quarter is due to the fact that these areas were only cleaned, not excavated any deeper after the removal of the turf. This revealed fewer stones from the fill. Map, Julie K. Øhre Askjem.*

Object	Number or Weight (g)
Amber beads	24
Glass beads	33
Spindle-whorl	1
Pottery	345.2 g
Comb fragments, burnt	2
Human bone fragments, burnt	6

Table 11.1. *Finds that are associated with the burial of the 4th or 5th century AD.*

form a circular feature was found with a slightly lighter fill and much smaller stones than on the rest of the platform. A number of finds dating to the 4th or 5th centuries were made in and just outside this area (Figs. 11.3, and 11.4). These were finds of the type that are typically found in burials of this period. There was also a considerable quantity of burnt bone in the area. Six fragments could be identified with certainty as human, three of them skull fragments. The finds indicate that this was a woman's grave. The absence of bucket-shaped pottery makes a dating to the 4th century most probable.

In the circumference of the remaining base of the barrow it could be seen that stone had been laid against the face of the barrow when the platform was constructed. At the level to which it was reduced the barrow had a diameter of c. 7.5 m. Since the burial itself has been disturbed, this level cannot be far from the natural rock on which the barrow was built. In one place, a little to the north-west of the centre of the barrow, the natural rock was found at about a depth of 25 cm, but its depth varied. The maximum possible diameter of the barrow would have been 8.5 m.

The building platform

There is not any real secure information about the rock formation below the building platform. As a result, the exact quantity of the platform's fill cannot be calculated. The surface of the platform measures over 300 sq m, and a sloping edge down to the rock on the eastern side is up to a metre high. To judge from the formation of the rock as it appears around the platform and at the bottom of the pit within the platform, the average depth of the fill is around 0.7 m. The total mass of fill should therefore be something over 200 cu m. The fill would appear to be earth and stone taken from the surrounding fields. If the average transport distance is set at 75 m, moving this amount of fill would have required 300 man-days of work using the means available at that time (based upon the guidelines described in Skre 1998b:320 n. 328). The uncertainties in the calculations are considerable, and the figure should probably lie somewhere between 200 and 400 man-days. Some filling material was already available in the barrow that stood on the site, but this is of little significance in relation to the margins of error we are dealing with here.

The selection of the site for this construction

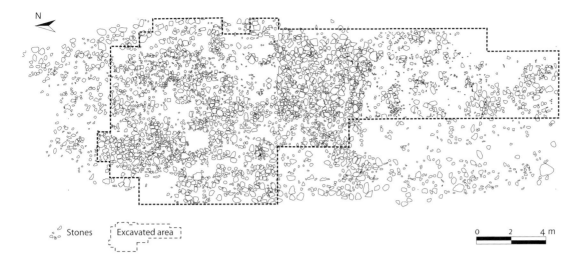

Stones | Excavated area

0   2   4 m

would appear to have an obvious purpose – the building on the platform was to be as conspicuous as possible from the surrounding areas. A great deal of work was invested in achieving this objective. It is probably no coincidence that there was already a burial mound there. It is known that houses were sometimes built over graves in Scandinavia. One example is the longhouse from the Late Iron Age at Borg in Lofoten, which had, amongst other things, a central hallchamber. This building was raised over two graves of the Early Iron Age (Holand and Hood 2003).

After the removal of the turf, it was possible to survey the platform in more detail. It measured 36 m from the protruding rock at the southern end to the corresponding rock at the northern end. At the southern end, the platform abuts a straight rock edge, and terminates along a fairly straight E–W line. To the north, the boundary against the edge of the rock is less even, with the result that one small tongue of the platform sticks out about 2 m further to the north-east (Figs. 11.5 and 11.6).

At the northern end the surface of the platform is 8.4 m across. At the southern end the width is c. 8.6 m. These figures probably represent the original dimensions there. Otherwise, the width varies somewhat. At the widest point, about 10 m from the northern end, the surface of the platform is 13 m E–W. At the same distance from the southern end it is 12.1 m across. It is clear that the eastern edge has slipped away a bit, probably from a point about 16–17 m from the northern end southwards. This impression is corroborated by the absence along this section of the eastern edge of the stones that elsewhere follow the edge of the platform to the east and west. With the exception of a few stones to the north, the eastern row has rolled down in its entirety. The last stone that can be attributed to this row lies c. 15.5 m from the northern end of the platform. Further south, there are no stones along the eastern edge (Fig 11.8). Ballestad's

report indicates that in 1918 there were stones there too; they have probably since slipped down. It would therefore appear that the platform was originally of very regular form, with symmetrically bowed long sides and stones along all of its edges.

Buildings that dominate the local topography are known at a number of high-status settlement sites from the Viking Period and the preceding centuries in Scandinavia – e.g. at Borg in Lofoten (Munch et al. 2003) and Slöinge (Lundqvist 1996, 2003). But the practice of constructing a platform to further highlight a building is of very limited chronological and geographical occurrence. Building platforms of this character are as yet known first and foremost from the area around lake Mälaren, Sweden, and are mostly dated to AD 700–1000.

The first of these was excavated in 1985–1988 at Sighildsberg in Håtuna, also known as Old Sigtuna (*Fornsigtuna*). This farmstead is referred to in a number of documentary sources that relate to the Viking Period or even earlier, including Snorri's *Ynglinga saga* (Ch. 5). There one can read that when Odin settled in Scandinavia, it was "in the place which is now called Old Sigtuna" ("þar sem nú eru kallaðar fornu Sigtúnir"). Texts from the early Christian Middle Ages show this farmstead to have been royal property in the 11th century (Damell 1991b). That was probably also the case in the Viking Period (Hedmann 1991: 96). Here there were two platforms, measuring 30 m x 14 and 43 m x 17 respectively, the former about one metre high and the latter about two. Both had bowed long sides and were placed upon natural ridges and positioned so that they were clearly visible from the surrounding landscape, especially from the navigation channel immediately alongside (Hedman 1991: 58). On each of the platforms evidence of a large building was found, measuring 28 m x 9.5 and 40 m x 11 respectively. From the finds, the type of building, and their size and position, the small building was interpreted as the hall of the royal farmstead and the large one as the barrack-building for the retainers. From the artefactual finds and thermoluminescence, the functioning period of the buildings was interpreted to have begun in the 8th century and continued into the second half of the 10th (Hedman 1991: 67–71; Damell 1991a:123).

A similar platform has been found at Granby-Hyppinge in Vallentuna, again on a dominant high-point. The major farmstead complex of Granby-Hyppinge was the main residence of a cheiftainly kingroup in the Viking Period (Carlsson 1989). The platform was constructed in the same way as those at Old Sigtuna, measuring 40 m x 10 and having bowed long sides. A brooch found at the platform can be dated to the end of the Viking Period (Hedman 1989:97).

At Karsvik in Bromma, there is a building platform, also in a dominant position on the crest of a morainic ridge (Ringsted 2005). The surface of this platform measured 26 m x 10 and the platform had gently curving long sides. It was around one metre high. No excavations have been carried out there as yet, and so there is no dating evidence. The platform is situated in an area with a concentration of archaeological sites, including building terraces and stone-settings. Ringsted has not published any details of the size and significance of the farm.

At Valsgärde, 3 km north of Gamla Uppsala, a building platform measuring 45 m x 10 at its base was found in 1994. A small trial excavation was carried out that year; two further trenches were dug in 1996. These excavations uncovered indications that there had been a hall upon the platform. No datable finds were made, but in the well-known cemetery immediately alongside the platform there are burials of the Vendel and Viking Periods (Norr and Sundkvist 1995, 1997).

Both Hedman (1991:73) and Brunsted (1996:29–30) assume that the platform that was partially excavated at the royal farmstead of Adelsö in the years 1916–1920 may have been a building platform of the same type (Thordeman 1920:15–21). This farm is located on the island next to Björkö, where Birka was situated. A runic inscription from the farm is addressed to the king. This inscription, which was commissioned by the king's champion, is dated to the end of the 11th century (Brundsted 1996:10–11). Adelsö is recorded as a royal farmstead in a letter of 1200, and at the end of the 13th century became a royal summer palace built in brick on the platform (Thordeman 1920:1–14). The platform measured around 40 m x 15 and has slightly bowed long sides. Limited excavations of building terraces on the slope to the east and north of the platform in 1991–1994 revealed the remains of buildings and finds that date construction to the mid- or late 8th century. The buildings on the terraces remained in use to the end of the 10th century. Midden layers that probably came from the plat-

form have the same date-range. Amongst other things, a silver coin was found, fragments of gold, amber, glass beads, and objects that display a high level of craftsmanship (Brundsted 1996:28–30). This dating evidence is thus congruent with the chronology of the town of Birka on the neighbouring island.

North of the church at Gamla Uppsala there are two artificial platforms on which buildings once stood. One of these has been excavated, and traces of two halls were found (Duczko 1997:78; see Skre, this vol. Ch. 18:424–5, Fig. 18.3 G–H). The dating of these halls is not without problems. It seems clear that the elder one was constructed in the 7th century. Duczko (1997:76) dates the construction of the more recent one to the late 8th century and its burning down to the beginning of the 9th. Three of the object-types found could be dated: a brooch (8th century), a cornelian bead (850–1000 AD; Callmer 1977:type T007), and several iron spirals. The latter belong to a broad chronological span from the end of the 7th century through to the middle of the 10th; although, according to Hedlund (1993:68), their closest parallels appear right at the very end of this period. Of the four radiocarbon datings, one is too far off to be taken into consideration, but the other three lie in the period from the second half of the 7th century through to the end of the 9th (cal AD 640–765, 670–795, 710–875; Hedlund 1993:68). On the evidence of the radiocarbon datings it would appear rational to date the building of this hall to the middle of the 8th century. The bead and the iron spirals imply that the hall remained in use to the end of the 9th century or some way into the 10th, when it burnt down (Ljungkvist 2000:151).

Recently, Alkarp and Price (2005) have carried out a georadar investigation of the area east of these two platforms, where the church now stands (Skre, this vol. Ch. 18:425, Fig. 18.4). They found traces of a wooden church that must be the predecessor of the stone church which was built in the 1030s. According to Adam of Bremen, the first church at this site was constructed over the remains of the pagan temple. The georadar investigation also revealed remains which Alkarp and Price suggest are to be interpreted as a very large hall, about 14 m wide. This would appear to have stood upon a building platform fully 60 m long with the same alignment as the platform on which the other hall stood, i.e. NNW–SSE. This building may be the hall that Adam referred to, and therefore may fill the interval between the hall on the terrace further north and the earliest timber church . If that is so, this third hall would have been constructed late in the 9th century or at some time in the 10th.

A common feature of all of these platform sites is the fact that the platform was constructed over a natural high-point in the terrain, and thus made the buildings particularly conspicuous in the landscape. The platforms were built of large quantities of stone,

Figure 11.7 *Feature An6, which is interpreted as a post-hole for a roof-bearing post in the southern half of the building. Photo, D. Skre, Kaupang Excavation Project.*

and had bowed long sides in the same style as the side walls of the buildings that stood on top of them. All the examples that have been examined had halls, and those that can be dated with some degree of accuracy were constructed in the 8th century, several of them towards the end of that century. Their functioning lives continued in a number of cases up to some point in the 10th century, and in Uppsala possibly into the 11th. All of the platforms are found at sites of manifestly high status. Uppsala, Adelsö and Fornsigtuna have royal associations, Valsgärde is connected with the cream of the military aristocracy, and Granby and Karsvik belonged to a landowning social elite. It is also striking that two of the royal farmsteads with building platforms are situated alongside the two earliest urban sites in Sweden, Birka and Sigtuna. These parallels will be explored further in a later chapter (Skre, this vol. Ch. 18.4).

The hall

There are not very many definite traces now of the building that stood on the platform at Husebyhaugen. What we have consists principally of a row of stones along the eastern and western edge of the platform. Beyond those, the size and shape of the platform provides a certain amount of information. Finally, there are a number of more or less definite post-holes, although as noted, none of these can be regarded as entirely certain. The interpretation of the building's remains must therefore depend primarily upon the most reliable remains, and upon a comparison with corresponding traces of hall buildings of the same period. Based on these considerations, a selection has been made from the possible post-holes that were recorded during excavation.

In most buildings of the Early Iron Age in Scandinavia, the weight of the roof was borne by pairs of posts that stood at quite regular intervals along the full length of the structure. In the Late Iron Age, from

the 7th century onwards, there was an architectural development that led to the roof's weight being transferred from free-standing pairs of posts of that kind to posts within the walls. This meant that the number of internal post-pairs could be reduced, if not entirely done away with as is the case in several buildings of the 11th and 12th centuries.

What was evidently wanted in a hall was an open, central space with no posts, and this must be the reason why the solution of transferring the weight to the wall posts was chosen in several halls from the end of the 7th century onwards. There are, for instance, 10–11 pairs of posts in the three halls at Lejre that were in use between the end of the 7th century and the 10th. The central chamber of the halls, some 10 m long, however, was kept free of internal posts. The halls were around 48 m long and 11.5 m wide (Christensen 1991). The two halls at Slöinge were 30 m long and 8.5 m wide, and were in use from early in the 8th century to the first half of the 9th (Lundqvist 1996, 2003: 50–60). The positioning of the posts was more or less the same as that in the Lejre halls.

In some halls from the same period the number of internal post-pairs was reduced even further. For instance there were only three pairs of roof-bearing posts in the 35 m long and 8 m wide hall at Tissø constructed in the 8th century. In the fourth hall that was constructed at this site in the 10th century, the dimensions grew to 48 m x 12.5 but the number of internal post-pairs fell to two (Jørgensen 1998, 2001). In the hall measuring c. 40 m x 10 at Uppsala there were three pairs of roof-bearing posts placed approximately in the same relative positions as the three pairs in the Tissø hall (Duczko 1993; Jørgensen 2001). Both at Tissø and Uppsala the halls had closely spaced posts in the walls (Fig. 11.9).

The Huseby hall would appear to have had most in common with the halls at Tissø and Uppsala. There are possible post-holes in two areas within the

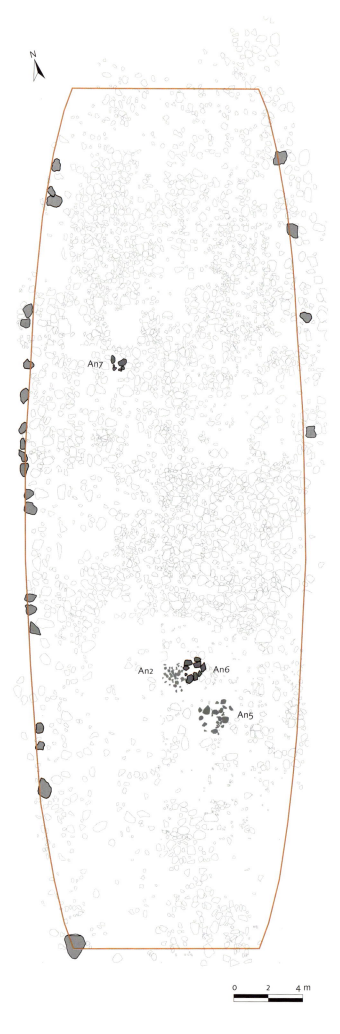

Figure 11.8 *On the basis of foundations and probable post-holes that can be assigned to a hall, this is the most plausible ground-plan. An6 and An7 are probable post-holes; they lie equidistant from the mid-axis of the platform, on opposite sides. From features An2, probably a worn hollow in a doorway, and An5, a hollow of unknown function, charcoal for radiocarbon dating was taken. Plan, D. Skre, Kaupang Excavation Project.*

Figure 11.9 *Comparable plans of the 8th-century halls at Tissø (top) and Uppsala. The latter has only been partially excavated (southern part); the reconstruction of the northern segment (to the right) is based upon that partial excavation. Both halls have three pairs of roof-bearing posts. In the Uppsala hall only one of the post-holes from the central pair is visible. The other lies beneath the stone-packing. Figure from Jørgensen 2001:fig. 12.*

platform, one in the southern half of the platform and one in the northern. In the southern half, only the eastern segment was excavated, and this explains why possible post-holes have only been identified on the eastern side of the long axis of the platform. This is where the probable post-hole An6 is situated (Figs. 11.7 and 11.8). The diameter of this feature is about 1 m. The seven packing stones were placed around a post of 0.4–0.5 m in diameter. Here there was a depth of only 0.25 m down to the rock on which the post must have rested. The post-shadow contained a great deal of burnt daub.

At a corresponding distance from the northern end of the platform the probable post-hole An7 was situated (Fig. 11.8). This went much deeper down, presumably because the depth of the platform was much greater. This is the point at which the only modern intervention into the platform had been made, so that only the very bottom of the post-hole survived. Around a flat basal stone lay seven large packing stones. The post would appear to have had a diameter of 0.4 m. The fill of the post-shadow contained a great deal of charcoal. No matching post on the other side of the central axis was identified, but the open area in the stone packing there could have accommodated a post.

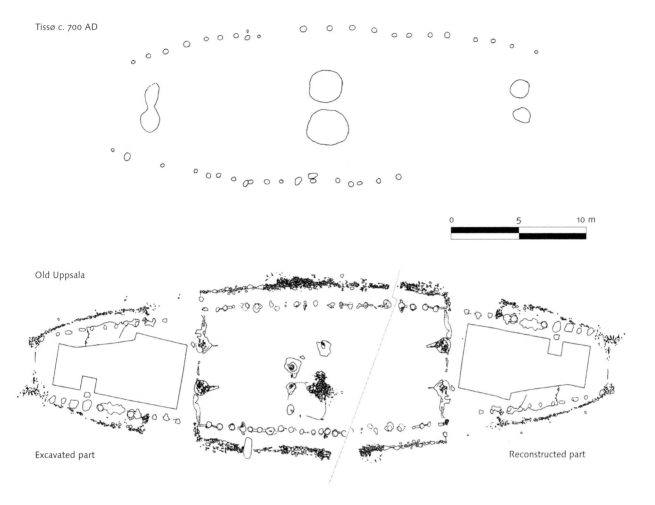

Tissø c. 700 AD

Old Uppsala

0   5   10 m

Excavated part

Reconstructed part

No evidence of posts in the middle of the building was found, as was the case in the halls at Uppsala and Tissø (Fig. 11.9); but the possibility of there having been more pairs of posts both here and elsewhere cannot be excluded. The likelihood of finding definite post-holes on the building platform was, as noted, low. Posts could, moreover, have been supported by flat stones that have since been removed. At a building site that consists of such large quantities of large stones, this is far from unlikely. However no finds have been made of such flat stones that might have provided foundations for roof-bearing posts. It is therefore probable that the weight of the roof was borne principally by the posts in the walls.

No post-holes that can be attributed to the walls were located. However there were, as noted, rows of stones along the long sides of the platform. These must have been the foundation stones for the walls of the structure (Fig. 11.8). It was noted that the stones in the north-west and east had rolled down, in some cases since Ballestad's visit in 1918. The most likely wall construction is that the wall posts rested on sills that again rested on the rows of stones.

Because of the erosion of the platform's eastern edge, the distance between the eastern and western walls is not entirely certain. If we assume only slight

erosion to the north-east, the building would have a central axis around which the post-holes described were symmetrically arranged. This central axis agrees perfectly with the central axis through the best-preserved areas of the platform at the northern and southern ends. There is no sign of the northern end wall of the building, but it probably stood near the edge of the platform, like the south-western corner stone of the structure.

With all of these uncertainties, we are left with a building with a maximum width of 11.7 m, narrowing to 7.9 at the ends (Fig. 11.8). The length would have been about 35 m. The presumptively roof-bearing posts An6 and An7 were positioned 11 m from their respective ends of the building.

A building of these dimensions would have needed a strong internal structure to bear the weight of the roof and resist the powerful pressure of the wind that its exposed position implied. Since there appear to be so few internal roof-bearing posts, much of the weight must have been carried by the wall posts. Since there are no post-holes for such posts, only rows of foundation stones, these posts must have stood upon a sill which in turn lay upon the foundation stones. This technical solution is known in Northern Europe throughout the first millennium

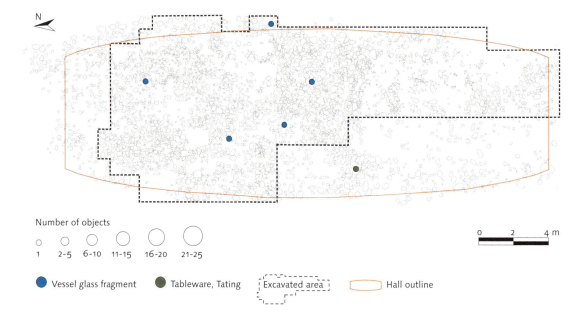

Number of objects

○ ○ ○ ○ ○ ○
1 2–5 6–10 11–15 16–20 21–25

● Vessel glass fragment   ● Tableware, Tating   [Excavated area]   ⬭ Hall outline

0   2   4 m

AD, usually in combination with a few internal roof-bearing posts, as in this case (Zimmermann 1998).

There is no definite evidence of a hearth within the building. This is most probably because of work on the ground in connexion with the construction of the later timber building which stood on the platform (see below). The hearth of the hall ought to have been in the area where this building was placed (Fig. 11.24).

The relatively large amount of burnt daub, a total of 192 g, three fragments of which had marks of withies, shows that the wall panels between the wall posts were filled with wattle and daub. This type of wall is entirely consistent with the method of construction that has been proposed above. The fact that the daub was burnt shows that the building burnt down.

The hall probably had a central chamber with entrance chambers at both the northern and southern ends of that chamber. There may also have been smaller chambers at each end of the building. The partition wall between the main chamber and the entrance chambers would most logically have run where the pairs of roof-bearing posts stood. This would produce a central chamber that was about 13 m long and a good 150 sq m in area.

As the discussion above implies, the proposed reconstruction of the hall is highly uncertain. Even though they were not referred to in the course of fieldwork, the interpretations of the building evidence have subsequently been illuminated by the excavations of halls at Uppsala and Tissø. If one ignores the parallels to those two halls, the most convincing arguments for the suggested ground-plan are the form and position of the platform itself, and the rows of stones that must be foundations for the bowed exterior walls of the structure. I regard the post-holes as too uncertain to be made to carry any particular weight in the discussion about the form of the building.

The assemblage, distribution and date of finds from the hall

The find-assemblage and its distribution have, as we shall see, several significant features in common with what is found at other halls. First and foremost, there are relatively few finds – halls would appear to have been regularly cleaned out (Jørgensen 2002:238; Söderberg 2005:84–5). But those objects that were found are usually of specific types.

Figure 11.10 *The distribution of tableware (Tating) and of certain or probable sherds of Viking-period beakers. Map, Julie K. Øhre Askjem.*

Figure 11.11 *Tableware (Tating Ware, to the right, c. 2 cm long) and certain or probable sherds of Viking-period beakers. Photo, Eirik I. Johnsen, KHM.*

Typical is the presence of sherds of high-status drinking vessels, such as glass beakers and Tating-ware pottery (Herschend 1993:190), which have been found, for instance, in the hall-chamber at Borg (Holand 2003a, 2003b) and in the Slöinge hall (Lundqvist 1996:13–24, 2003:108–14). Sherds of such vessels have also been found on the Huseby platform (Fig. 11.11). All of the other types of pottery found in the settlement area of Kaupang are either transport vessels or cooking pots. The exclusive Tating-ware only occurs as jugs and bowls (Hougen 1993:25). The finds of sherds from drinking beakers and tableware are concentrated around the centre of the building (Fig. 11.10). The sherd of Tating Ware and four of the five sherds of glass were located in this area, one of them just outside the presumed line of the wall.

Typically weaponry and fragments of weaponry are found in halls. In the hall at Borg, for instance, two arrowheads and four sword-fragments were found (Arrhenius and Muyingo 2003:171), and in one of the halls at Old Sigtuna an arrowhead of Wegraeus' type D (Wegraeus 1986) was found, which was used for warfare (Hedman 1991:64). From the Huseby hall there are two arrowheads, one definite, the other not so (Fig. 11.18). The find C52518/357 appears to be an arrowhead of Wegraeus' type D. These are long, thin arrowheads intended to penetrate chainmail or other forms of armour (Wegraeus 1986:29). The more common sub-type D1 (Rygh 1885:no. 546) is triangular in cross-section while our specimen, which is of sub-type D2, is quadratic in cross-section. The former type has been found in graves at Kaupang but not the latter. Peter Lindbom, who identified both the arrowheads from Huseby, writes (pers. comm.) that our arrowhead is atypical in that it lacks the ledge normally found on the tang of such arrowheads. This is presumably either an unfinished specimen or a clumsily made one. It can be dated to the Viking Period.

The other arrowhead, C52518/3 (Fig. 11.18), is of a Viking-period type, closest to Wegraeus' type A2. It has close parallels in several graves at Kaupang, including Ka. 37 from Nordre Kaupang, which dates to the second half of the 9th century, and Ka. 252 from the first half of the 10th. According to Lindbom this type is particularly frequent in 10th-century equestrian and weapon graves, and can therefore be regarded as having been produced for warfare rather than for hunting. Both of the arrowheads from the Huseby hall would therefore appear to have been made for this purpose. One of them was found in the central chamber of the hall while the other lay in the far southern end of the building (Fig. 11.19).

In many halls, silver objects of various kinds have been found. At Borg, three pieces of plain hacksilver were found (Munch 2003:245), in the hall at Strøby Toftegård, Sjælland, many such fragments (Söderberg 2005:155), and at Slöinge four pieces (Lundqvist 1996:21–2, 2003:70–1). Silver jewellery or fragments of silver jewellery are also usual.

On the Huseby platform one fragment of a silver spiral was found (Figs. 11.18 and 11.19). This weighs 1.65 g and is of a Viking-period type. To judge by its thickness, it is probably from an armring. The fragment has been broken off at both ends, not cut off, so it is uncertain whether this was used for currency or broken up for some other reason. Another small piece of silver was also found. It was broken off from a larger piece and had triangular punchmarks along its three original edges (Fig. 11.18). It has not been possible to identify this for certain, but it may be the lower part of a so-called "Valkyrie" figure: a female figure, as is known from several sites, such as Birka (Arwidsson 1989:58–9) and Uppåkra (Bergqvist 1999: 119). The Valkyrie relates to a warrior society and military activities. Both pieces of silver were found in the central chamber of the hall, the spiral in the northwestern corner and the possible Valkyrie fragment in the south-eastern.

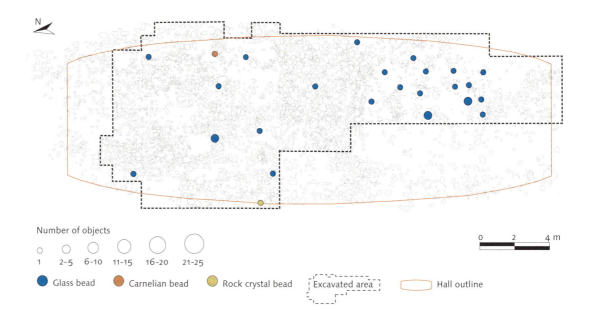

Number of objects

○ ○ ○ ○ ○ ○
1   2-5 6-10 11-15 16-20 21-25

● Glass bead   ● Carnelian bead   ● Rock crystal bead   ⌐ ¬ Excavated area   ⬭ Hall outline

0   2   4 m

Figure 11.12 *The distribution of beads of glass, cornelian and rock crystal. Glass beads of uncertain date are not included. Map, Julie K. Øhre Askjem.*

Figure 11.14 *The distribution of artefacts associable with textile production. Map, Julie K. Øhre Askjem.*

Figure 11.13 *Beads of glass, cornelian and rock crystal from the 8th–10th centuries. The beads were found spread out over the whole area and their original arrangement is unknown. Photo, Eirik I. Johnsen, KHM.*

Figure 11.15 *Artefacts that can be associated with textile production: spindle-whorls of lead and soapstone (lower left), a selection of loomweight-fragments of burnt clay, and a large soapstone weight. Photo, Eirik I. Johnsen, KHM.*

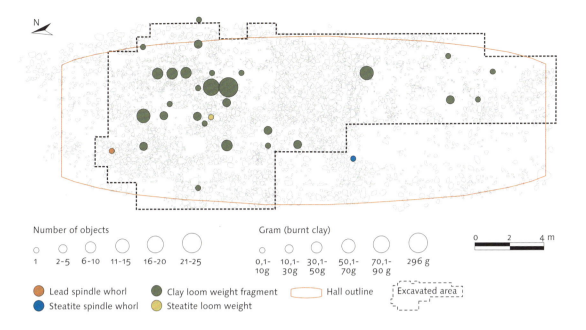

Number of objects						Gram (burnt clay)								
○	○	○	○	○	○		○	○	○	○	○	○		
1	2-5	6-10	11-15	16-20	21-25		0,1-10g	10,1-30g	30,1-50g	50,1-70g	70,1-90 g	296 g		

0   2   4 m

● Lead spindle whorl   ● Clay loom weight fragment   ▭ Hall outline   ⌐ Excavated area ⌐

● Steatite spindle whorl   ● Steatite loom weight

From the Huseby hall we also have 31 glass beads, one cornelian bead and one bead of rock crystal, all of them securely datable to the 8th–10th centuries, (Fig. 11.13). The glass beads were found over the whole area excavated, but the majority were found in the south. The cornelian and rock-crystal beads were at the northern end of the central chamber (Fig. 11.12). The materials, quantities and distribution of beads at Borg are practically identical to those from Huseby (Borg: 30 glass; 1 amber; 1 cornelian; 1 rock crystal; 1 jet; 1 of unidentified stone). Many of those at Borg came from the hall-chamber, but most were from the midden area outside the building (Näsman 2003). At Slöinge, 74 beads were found, spread over much of the settlement area (Lundqvist 2003:81, 114–17).

In halls, there are usually limited numbers of sherds from cooking vessels (Herschend 1993). At Slöinge, there were both soapstone sherds and Slavic pottery in the hall-chamber, but far fewer of them than in other parts of the settlement site (Lundqvist 1996:13, 20, 2003:75). Sherds of soapstone cauldrons were also found at Borg, 59 in all, with a marked concentration around the hall-chamber (Johansen et al. 2003). None of the fragments of cooking vessels from

Figure 11.16 *The distribution of artefacts that can be linked to crafts other than textile production. Map, Julie K. Øhre Askjem.*

Figure 11.17 *Artefacts that can be associated with various crafts: small chips of amber (lower left), yellow-green raw glass and a blue glass cane from beadmaking (lower middle and right), sherds of crucibles (upper right and middle) and a mould for metal-casting (upper left). Photo, Eirik I. Johnsen, KHM.*

the Huseby platform can be securely connected to the hall. Six fragments of soapstone (steatite) vessels were found, but none of these are definitely from Viking-period types; moreover, one of them can be dated to the Christian Middle Ages. There are also sherds of coarse, plain pottery which are most probably from the Early Iron Age. As was noted, these sherds were probably redeposited in the soil when the platform was constructed. Some of the sherds could be Slavic pottery of the Viking Period; only fabric analysis can determine whether or not that is the case.

Normally, the majority of evidence of productive activity at principal farmsteads is found elsewhere than in the hall (Herschend 1993:182, Jørgensen 2002: 218). Traces of certain crafts do nonetheless appear in some halls (e.g. Herschend 1995:225–7, Jørgensen 2002:241). In the halls at Slöinge, evidence of amber-working, textile production, beadmaking, metalcasting and the preparation of garnets for jewellery production was found (Lundqvist 1996:18–23, 2003:72–4). Exactly the same crafts are represented in the Huseby hall. Most in evidence are finds representing textile production (Fig. 11.15).

At Slöinge, both loomweights and spindle-whorls were concentrated in the area with the halls (Lundqvist 2003:74). At Borg there was a concentration of spindle-whorls in the hall-chamber, and a concentration of fired clay loomweight-fragments just inside one of the long walls of that chamber. There was probably a loom standing there when the hall was abandoned. None of the five soapstone weights was found in the hall-chamber but these are not necessarily loomweights, they may have been weights for yarn or fishing lines (Johansen et al. 2003:144–5). In the Huseby hall, 49 fragments of fired clay loomweights were found. Most of these lay in the northern part of the hall site, both along the northern wall of the main chamber and in what is assumed to have been the northern entrance chamber (Fig. 11.14). There may

have been looms in both rooms. Two spindle-whorls, of lead and soapstone respectively, were lying in the main chamber.

Manifestly associated with the production of glass beads in the Viking Age is a drawn glass cane with tong-marks found on the Huseby platform (Fig. 11.17). The glass corresponds both in colour and in type to ten of the blue beads that were also found (Fig. 11.13). This is the most numerous group of beads; they may have been produced on the spot. There are also a number of other fragments of glass that may be waste from beadmaking. Two molten drops of light green and transparent red glass were found alongside the cane, and nine hammered pieces of green and yellow-green glass are of the kind that is commonly found among the remains of Viking-period beadmaking, as indeed within Kaupang (Fig. 11.17; Gaut 2004). At Borg there was no definite evidence of glass-beadmaking (Näsman 2003:239). But at Slöinge there is the detritus of glass-beadmaking at several places in the settlement site, and in profusion in the post-holes from the two hall buildings (Lundqvist 1996:Tab. 1, 18–24, 2003:118). Consequently there can be little doubt that beads were made in the hall there.

In addition to the evidence for glass-beadmaking at Slöinge, a total of 107 fragments of garnet were found. This red, crystalline mineral was used as an abrasive in the Viking Period, and for settings in jewellery (Arrhenius 1997). Modest remains from garnetworking are known from several settlements. The large quantity at Slöinge is probably due to the site being located only two kilometres from a natural outcrop containing this mineral. It is likely that garnet was collected there for wider distribution.

One of the 107 pieces of garnet from Slöinge shows clear signs of working; the majority of the remaining pieces are probably waste from garnetworking (Lundqvist 1996:20, 2003:73). The single piece that was found at Huseby also shows signs of

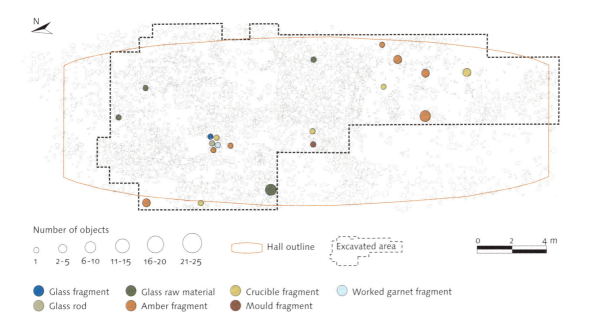

Number of objects

○ ○ ○ ◯ ◯ ◯
1 2-5 6-10 11-15 16-20 21-25

▭ Hall outline   ⌐Excavated area⌐

0   2   4 m

● Glass fragment   ● Glass raw material   ● Crucible fragment   ○ Worked garnet fragment
● Glass rod   ● Amber fragment   ● Mould fragment

working. This piece is barely a millimetre long, and was found by filtering a soil sample through a fine-meshed net. It must represent production waste. Garnets were inlaid, inter alia, in basket-shaped pendants made of interwoven, thin gold wire in a sort of knitting technique (see Fig. 11.18; Larsson 2005). A crushed gold-wire pendant of this kind was found in the Huseby hall (Figs. 11.18 and 11.19). Pendants of the same type have been found in rich graves at Birka (Graves 557, 559, 581; Geijer 1938:113–14, Taf. 31:3–5 and 31:13) and Valsgärde (Grave 10). The type belongs to the 9th and 10th centuries (Larsson 2005). Ours has nothing inside it; the content presumably was taken out through a hole that can be seen in the pendant.

This kind of gold wire was also used for brocading narrow tablet-woven braids of silk. For this sort of weaving, two large weights were required, each of them weighing almost 2 kg (Larsson 2005). At Huseby, one soapstone weight of a good 1.9 kg was found (Fig. 11.15). About 40 years ago, as noted, the present owner of the farm was digging the pit that can be seen on the platform. He tells how he then came across a very similar weight of the same size, which unfortunately is now lost. Our soapstone weight was found 1 or 2 m from where the previous example was reportedly found. The fragment of garnet was also found in this area, while the gold-wire pendant was found 4–5 m further east. All of these finds are from the northern end of the central chamber (Figs. 11.14, 11.16 and 11.19).

Larsson (2005) writes that, in order to work with wires of this kind, it was necessary to keep them

Figure 11.18 *Various metal objects from the hall. From upper left, a bronze ring-pin, an Irish bronze brooch with remains of amber inlay, an iron frostnail, and two iron weights; from mid left, a gilt bronze mount, probably Frankish, a silver spiral fragment, probably armring, two iron arrowheads of types D2 (left) and A2. The gold-wire pendant (lower middle; detail below) has parallels in Birka and Valsgärde in Uppland. A small silver fragment (lower middle) with punchmarks may come from a so-called "Valkyrie" figure. The two silver coins from the mid- and late 11th century (lower left) should probably be associated with the* stofa *building that was built after the hall was demolished (Fig. 11.24). Photo, Eirik I. Johnsen, KHM.*

Figure 11.19 *The distribution of the various metal objects. Map, Julie K. Øhre Askjem.*

warm; therefore, the work had to be done beside the hearth. As reported, we have not succeeded in pinpointing the hearth's location in the Huseby hall. In Larsson's judgment, weaving and embroidery with gold threads were women's jobs that were performed within halls. This conclusion is based, to some extent, on the finds from Huseby. The garnet could have been associated with these craft activities.

Several tiny fragments of amber are very probably the detritus from amberworking (Figs. 11.16 and 11.17). Most of these were found in the southern end of the hall, although some were at the northern end of the central chamber. There was also a smelting crucible of a Viking-period type and four crucible-fragments of the same type. One of these fragments has green corrosion products that imply the casting of a copper alloy. There was also a mould fragment of fired clay. Most of these finds were lying in the central

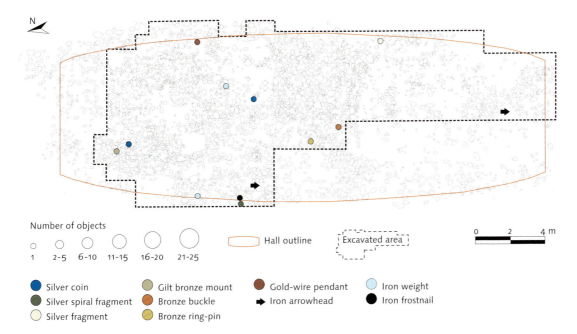

Number of objects

○ ○ ○ ○ ○ ○
1   2-5 6-10 11-15 16-20 21-25

▭ Hall outline   ▭ Excavated area

0   2   4 m

● Silver coin   ● Gilt bronze mount   ● Gold-wire pendant   ○ Iron weight
● Silver spiral fragment ● Bronze buckle   ➤ Iron arrowhead   ● Iron frostnail
○ Silver fragment   ● Bronze ring-pin

chamber. At Slöinge too, evidence of casting and other work with precious metals was found in the hall area (Lundqvist 1996:20, Tab. 3, 2003:73). In a wall trench from one of the halls at Järrestad slag from goldworking and a mould-fragment were found (Söderberg 2005:89, 92, 229). At Tissø as well, there was a great deal of casting waste in the hall area (Jørgensen 2002:fig. 13).

Looking at the evidence of craftwork altogether (Figs. 11.14 and 11.16), there is a fairly definite pattern. There is most evidence for amberworking in the south, and many of the loomweight-fragments in what is assumed to be the northern entrance chamber. Weaving needed more light, which may explain the placing of a loom there just inside the door. Otherwise the majority of the evidence for craftwork in the Huseby hall is found in the northern end of the hall-chamber.

It may cause some surprise that several of these crafts, especially those that required high temperatures, were carried out in halls. However, at Järrestad and Slöinge, where the excavations included the settlement areas outside the halls, remains of craft activities were found not only in the halls. Söderberg (2005:221–6) summarizes these results and discusses two alternative interpretations of the material evidence. On the one hand, craftwork in the hall may have had a more ritual character whereby the lord's role as the bringer of wealth and the character of craft as the transformation of raw materials into valuable artefacts were conjoined at a metaphorical level concerned with the creation of values (Hed Jakobsson 2003:171; Söderberg 2005:223). On the other hand, Söderberg discusses the possibility that the traces of craft activity were not the result of activity within the hall but were deposited in a votive manner, especially when they are found in post-holes (2005:224–6). Both of these explanations have to be regarded as feasible, either together or separately.

A number of metal objects that can be dated to the Viking Age were found on the Huseby platform (Fig. 11.18), such as an Irish buckle which has remains of amber inlay, and a presumably Frankish gilt bronze mount. Neither of these has any known definite parallels (Wamers, in prep.). Together with a ring-pin and two weights, these are entirely congruent with a high-status, hall context. The majority of these artefacts lay in the central chamber of the hall (Fig. 11.19).

Both the composition and the distribution of the finds' assemblage point in exactly the same direction as the platform itself and the building traces – they are typical of what is found in halls. Nearly the full range of find-types typical for hall sites has been encountered. However, one typical find which we lack is gold-foil figures (*gullgubber*). Several halls have produced these, but there are places where they were not found, including Tissø. One possible explanation for their absence at Huseby is that they seem to belong to the two centuries preceding the Viking Period. The latest dated context of which I am aware is at Slöinge. Two posts in Building III are dendrochronologically dated to the decade AD 710–720. The posthole for one of them contained 48 gold-foil figures. In total, 54 foil figures were found in this building. This building was replaced by Building II which has only three gold-foil figures (Lundqvist 2003:58, 66). Lundqvist (2003:60) believes that Building II was constructed in the second half of the 8th century and remained standing into the first half of the 9th. The difference in the number of gold-foil figures may imply that these figures went out of use towards the end of the 8th century.

The evidence allows two ways of dating the platform and the hall, radiocarbon dating and artefactual finds. Radiocarbon samples were taken from two features, An2 and An5. Feature An2, which was in the southern part of the building (Fig. 11.8), was a hollow in the surrounding fill immediately west of the post-

Find no.	Object	Description	650	700	750	800	850	900	950	1000	1050	1100
	Radiocarbon date	Charcoal from An2										
1012	Bead	Glass: red, yellow and blue. Callmer B416										
85	Blown glass fragment	Rimsherd										
1495	Blown glass fragment	Sherd of yellow-green beaker, three horizonal ribs										
1	Mount	Gilt copper alloy										
711	Bead	Glass: blue and white. Callmer B381										
1021	Bead	Glass: blue. Callmer A172										
130, 1014, 1015, 1019, 1045	Beads, 5	Glass: blue translucent. Callmer A171										
610, 253	Frostnails, 2	R591 Petersen's Type 1										
618	Bead	Glass: black and yellow. Callmer B092										
922	Potsherd	Tating										
1497, 1501	Blown glass fragments, 2	Sherds of drinking glass, possibly funnel-shaped beaker										
48	Brooch	Copper alloy with amber inlay. Irish										
903	Bead	Glass: segmented, gold foil in glass. Callmer E140										
	Radiocarbon date	Charcoal from An5										
670	Gold pendant	Woven gold wire										
1018, 1027, 1046, 1483	Beads, 4	Glass: yellow. Callmer A060										
1545	Blown glass fragment	Sherd of light green-blue thin-walled beaker										
357	Arrowhead	Wegraeus' Type ?D2										
498	Spiral fragment	Silver. Armring?										
255	Ring pin	Copper alloy, type R862										
252	Bead	Rock crystal, polyhedrical. Callmer S012										
1	Bead	Cornelian, faceted. Callmer T007										
3	Arrowhead	Wegraeus' Type A2										
927	Weight	Iron with copper-alloy cap, spherical										
434	Weight	Iron with copper-alloy cap, spherical										
920	Coin	Silver. Danish. Lund. Hörda-Knut/Magnus 1035-1047										
258	Coin	Silver. German. Lower Lorraine, Cologne 1079-1089										

■ Secure date   ■ Unsecure date   ■ Radiocarbon date

hole An6. The hollow was filled with densely packed humus containing scorched stones, burnt bone, fragments of charcoal, and pieces of burnt daub. A small piece of amber was found in this fill. The finds and the composition of the fill indicate that this is a preserved culture-layer that can be associated with the building. The reason why this layer had not been disturbed by later interventions on the platform is probably that it lay protected in the hollow. This hollow might have been worn down in the southern entrance area between the entrance chamber in the south and the central main chamber. Dated charcoal-fragments from this feature are from the period AD 655–770 (1σ, T-15238, birch).

Feature An5 lay a couple of metres south-east of An2 and was deeper. It stood out from the surrounding soil with its fill of scorched stone, fragments of charcoal, burnt bone and daub. This fill contained a glass bead, small pieces of amber, a sherd of Viking-period pottery and a whetstone-fragment. This layer too is probably what is left of a culture-layer which survives from the building because it lay in a hollow. The charcoal-fragments were dated to the period AD 790–995 (1σ, T-15325, oak).

All of the datable artefact-finds are from disturbed layers. In what follows, those objects that are later than the grave in the flattened barrow but earlier than the 15th century are discussed (Fig. 11.20).

None of the artefacts can be dated to earlier than AD 700, and therefore this is in all probability the earliest possible dating for the platform and the hall. It also fits the radiocarbon datings. There are several artefacts that may be from the 8th century, but the date-range of most of these continues into the 9th century. A blue bead with red and yellow decoration has the earliest *terminus ante quem,* c. AD 760. A black glass bead with yellow decoration is earlier than c. AD 800, while a sherd of Tating Ware must be earlier than c. AD 850. The five blue translucent beads occur most frequently in the early 8th century, more sporadically in the following two centuries. Set in the context of the earliest of the radiocarbon datings, this indicates that the hall on the platform came into being in the mid or second half of the 8th century.

Regarding the end of the hall, there are five artefacts in particular that may help in dating. The five items – three beads and two weights – cannot have been deposited before the second half of the 9th cen-

Figure 11.20 *Datable artefacts that are later than the burial of the 4th or 5th century and earlier than the 15th- and 16th-century coins. The numbers in the left column are sub-numbers to KHM number C52518, except for the number of the cornelian bead found in 1999, which is sub-number to C52285. Illustration, Jørgen Sparre.*

Figure 11.21 *The remains of the medieval oven. The severely burnt quadrilateral stone that remains from the oven's fire-surface can be seen in the middle of the picture. Photo, facing west, D. Skre, Kaupang Excavation Project.*

tury, the beads sometime after c. AD 860 and the weights after c. AD 875. There is also a sixth object, an arrowhead, that was probably deposited in the final phase of the hall, but a definite *terminus post quem* cannot be given for this artefact.

The earliest possible date of the end of the hall and platform is, therefore, the final quarter of the 9th century. All in all, six objects were deposited before c. 925. Many other artefacts *could* have been deposited after the first quarter of the 10th century, but none *had* to have been, because in some cases their date-ranges stretch right back to the beginning of the 9th century, and even back into the 8th. A probable end-date for the hall, which is also consistent with the latest radiocarbon date, is thus around the year 900 or sometime in the first half of the 10th century.

All the same, we cannot exclude the possibility that the hall remained in use throughout the 10th and 11th centuries because the two coins belong to the end of that period (Figs. 11.18 and 11.19). The absence of securely dated evidence from the period c. 950-1050 nonetheless suggests that there was no activity on the platform in that period, and that therefore the coins should be associated with the corner-timbered building which, to judge by its oven-type, may have been constructed in the 11th century (see below).

The corner-timbered building or *stofa*

Approximately in the middle of the western half of the platform, stones were encountered that had been part of the fire-surface of an oven. The largest stone was a flat, quadrilateral piece that had been shattered into several fragments. Before fragmentation the stone's fours sides measured about 50 cm. The stone had been severely burnt. The small stones around it to the south and west had also been affected by heat and should be counted as parts of the fire-surface. This fire-surface apparently continued to the west, towards the unburnt stones protruding there (Fig.

11.21). The stones sticking out around the fire-surface had not been scorched. The intense impact of the heat on the stones in the fire-surface and the total lack of traces of fire on the stones standing around it, shows that those standing around it must have been screened in some way.

This type of oven-base is familiar from excavations in the medieval towns of Trondheim and Oslo, where the fire-surface was screened by stones standing on edge or by a thick hood built of clay and stones. The large stones protruding to the south-east, south, west and north were part of the structure surrounding the fire-surface, in this case obviously a hood of clay and stone (Sørheim 1989:figs. 6, 16, 25;

Figure 11.22 *Interior of Innsteinstadstova at Jølster, Sogn og Fjordane, now at Sunnfjord Museum. Note the oven in the corner and the two doors, the right door leading into the fore-room, the left leading into the* kleve, *a bedroom. There was no chimney on this type of oven, so the smoke came out into the room and then escaped through the* ljore, *the opening in the roof. This* stofa *was built around 1500. Photo, Birger Lindstad.*

Figure 11.23 *Lafted* stofa *from about 1300 which originally stood on the farm of Rauland in Numedal, now at the Norsk Folkemuseum (Norwegian Folk Museum), Oslo. The* stofa *on Husebyhaugen may have been 2 m longer and 0.5 m wider than this example. Photo, Norsk Folkemuseum.*

Berg 1992:figs. 1, 5; Christophersen and Nordeide 1994:fig. 167). Judging from the size of the fire-surface and its position on the platform, the oven must have been a corner oven of a type that is known to have existed from the 11th century into the late Middle Ages (Sørheim 1989). The open side of the oven must have faced east. The oven must be from a building that succeeded the hall.

Ovens of this kind were constructed in corner-timbered, *alias* lafted, buildings of the type known as a *stofa* (Christie 2001; Sørheim 2005). This type of building would appear to have been introduced at the same time as the corner oven, namely in the 11th century. There were also examples of *stofa* buildings with a hearth in the centre of the floor, but the corner oven was clearly most common. The corner oven in the *stofa* always had its open side facing the long wall of

the building, opposite the corner where the oven was located. Ovens like this are known in surviving buildings of the Middle Ages, for instance the well-preserved *stofa* Innsteinstadstova at Jølster, Sogn og Fjordane, which was built around 1500 (Fig. 11.22).

A *stofa* could have one, two or three rooms. In Oslo there is a chronological change from the one-room *stofa* as the dominant type in the 11th century to the virtually complete predominance of the two-room type from around 1100 (Fet 1989:81–2). The second room was a narrow fore-chamber extending the building at the end at which the oven was situated. A door in the wall beside the oven led into this fore-chamber (Fig. 11.22). The entrance to the building, located on one of its long walls, close to a corner, led into this fore-chamber (Fig. 11.23). The fore-chamber itself could be divided in two by a wall, so that the innermost part, furthest from the entrance to the building, became a room on its own, known as the *kleve,* which was used as a bedroom. Normally, this room had an entrance from the main chamber (Fig. 11.22). A *stofa* with two or three rooms and a corner oven was the most common type of building in some country districts in Norway right up to around 1800 (Visted and Stigum 1971:75–9).

Buildings of this type in 11th–15th century Oslo had a main chamber which measured up to 6.6 m x 6.8 (building K139 of c. 1200, Schia 1987:71; Fet 1989: 29, fig. 21), but larger chambers are known too. The main chamber in a *stofa* at the farm of Rauland in Numedal, constructed sometime between 1250 and 1350 (Berg 1990:118–20), measured c. 8 m square (Fig. 11.23).

The position of the oven-remains at the Huseby platform shows that the oven was positioned in the corner of a *stofa* the long axis of which ran N–S. The foundations of the *stofa* are also preserved on the

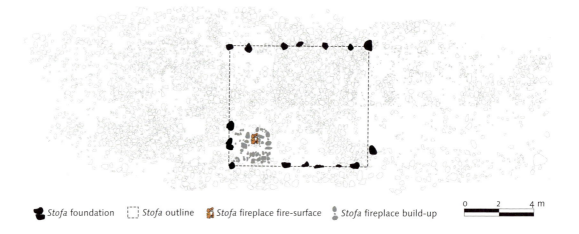

Stofa foundation   Stofa outline   Stofa fireplace fire-surface   Stofa fireplace build-up

    0   2   4 m

platform (Fig. 11.24). Two parallel rows of stones run N–S, one about 1.5 m west and the other about 6.5 m east of the fire-surface. These stones stood out a little higher than the surrounding stone fills, and many of them were larger than those around them. These two rows of stones are probably the foundations of the western and eastern exterior walls of the structure. To the south, they both end on approximately the same line. The eastern row terminates in a large stone which is probably a corner-stone. As the oven stood in one corner, the north wall of the *stofa* must have stood slightly to the north of that. Here there are individual stones that could be the remains of the foundation of that wall.

As can be seen from the plan (Fig. 11.24), the positions of the eastern and the western walls are the best documented. The distance between them is about 8.5 m, which makes out the breadth of the building (E–W) The length (N–S) is more uncertain, but given the assumptions above it would be 10.2 m. Both are measured from the assumed centre-lines of the walls. There is no evidence that this *stofa* had more than one room.

At the earliest, this *stofa* could have been constructed in the 11th century, when ovens and buildings of this kind first came into use. Therefore, the two coins from the middle and end of the 11th century could be related to this building. What is more certain is that this building was standing when two coins dated to 1448–1481 (Denmark, Christian I) and 1559 (Lübeck, Sechsling) were lost, at the northern edge of the building and a few metres north, respectively. Several other objects, including some copper-alloy buckles, may also derive from the 15th–16th century, but they cannot be any more precisely dated.

Buildings of this type were used as dwelling houses for farms, and this may have been the case here. In any event, it is certainly one of the largest of its kind. Bjørkvik (1998:206) described the Rauland *stofa* as

having been built for a prosperous farmer with a large household. The same must have been the case with the Huseby *stofa*, where the main room was even larger. Buildings of this type, some of them on royal farmsteads, are known to have been used for what must be described as public purposes. While those that are known from rural areas and average town-houses have a nearly square ground-plan (Fet 1989:82; Christie 2001:132), these public *stofa* buildings are oblong. In the fortified royal court at Bergen, excavations revealed the remains of a building measuring 7–8 m x 13, probably from the middle of the 13th century. Its position and size indicate that it served some public functions (Christie 2001:133–4). In the royal court at Oslo a similar building of the same period measuring 11 m x 17 was found (Christie 2001: 135). At Kirkjubø on the Faroes the remains of a *stofa* measuring 8 m x 11 are still standing. This building, which probably served some public purposes at the bishop's court, was probably constructed in Norway, dismantled and transported to the Faroes around 1300 (Christie 2001:135–9). At the Norwegian royal farmstead at Papa Stour, Shetland, the remains of a *stofa* from the middle of the 13th century, 5 m across and at least 8 m long, have been excavated. This too was probably freighted from Norway (Crawford 2001).

If the Huseby *stofa* was just a normal farmhouse, it belonged to a well-off household that needed a lot of space. However, it might have served other purposes too, perhaps for public meetings or as a night-shelter for large numbers. If it dates back as far as the 11th century, as the one-room plan could indicate, it could have been built because the farm was then conceivably a royal administrative farmstead, whereby this building was one of the "houses" the farmstead was named after. The name Huseby is usually explained as "a farmstead with many, fine or splendid buildings" ("en Gaard der har mange, gode eller prægtige Huse") (Rygh 1898:57). The two coins of the

Figure 11.24 *The inferred ground-plan of the lafted build-ing with a corner oven, the* stofa. *Plan, D. Skre, Kaupang Excavation Project.*

11th century are both foreign, and the later one in particular is from a period in which the king was severe in enforcing a ban on foreign coins in his realm. Foreign coins of this date are consequently extremely rare finds in Norway (Gullbekk 2003). It is possible that its presence in the *stofa* on Husebyhaugen is due to the fact that royal administrative farmsteads served as collection points for such coins.

Part III:

Scientific Analyses

Geology, Soils, Vegetation and Sea-levels in the Kaupang Area

12

ROLF SØRENSEN, KARI E. HENNINGSMOEN,
HELGE I. HØEG, BJØRG STABELL AND KRISTINE M. BUKHOLM

The main aim of this chapter is to provide as much environmental background information as possible for the new archaeological excavation projects at the Viking-age settlement at Kaupang. The geological history, based on previous publications and a new mapping of the site and the surroundings, is described in detail. Emphasis has been placed on the distribution and characteristics of the soils. The anthropogenic soil material (cultural deposits) deposited during the occupation of the settlement is described, and the erosion history after the settlement was abandoned is quantified. Pollen analysis of a nearby peat-bog describes natural and man-made vegetation changes before, during, and after the occupation of the settlement. Pollen and diatom analyses of the present embayment sediments give supplementary information on the local vegetation development, as well as circulation-pattern changes in the fjord system. Emphasis has been placed on changes in the agricultural activities at and around the settlement. Previous and new data on sea-level changes, adjusted to the Kaupang area and supplemented with sediment studies at the settlement, indicate a slightly higher Viking-age sea-level than earlier reported. It also gives information on changes in Viking-age maritime communication during the occupation of the settlement. Instrumental and historical data on tidal variation indicate that occasional extreme spring tides, up to c. 1.5 m above mean sea-level, might have had some impact on the shore constructions and the lower areas of the Viking-age settlement.

12.1 Introduction

The landscape and soils in the region are influenced by the underlying bedrock, which consists of varieties of the monzonitic Larvikite Complex of the southern Permian Oslo Graben (Petersen 1978). A detailed map of the bedrock at Kaupang and the surroundings (made by H. Th. Arnestad Bjærke) has been published by Henningsmoen (1974).

The light grey Larvikite is coarse-grained and has minerals that release plant nutrients easily and therefore contribute to the distribution of the luxuriant natural vegetation in the region. The rocks have high levels of the phosphate mineral apatite (Låg 1945), which is reflected in the chemical composition of the soils.

Major landscape forms, such as Viksfjord and the lowland further to the NE, have developed at boundaries between the different large semi-circular Larvikite intrusions. The higher grounds towards the NNW and on the Eftang peninsula south of Viksfjord are a result of more resistant rocks (Larvikites with different mineralogy and texture, cf. Petersen 1978).

The palaeo maps with sea-levels of 40, 20 and 5 m higher than today, show this very clearly (Figs. 12.1 and 12.2). On a detailed scale, the Rhombeporphyry dyke that crosses the western outlet of the Kaupangkilen bay (Henningsmoen 1974:fig. 1) is the natural threshold of the bay, and functions today as the local 'ox-ford' (where the cattle wade over the bay from one pasture to another).

The area was deglaciated around 12,000 BC,[1] and during the retreat of the glacier front a number of ice-marginal deposits were formed. Many of these have been covered by younger sediments, but the largest ones can be seen as wide, NE–SW ridges in the landscape. One such ridge system occurs on the Eftang Peninsula, and another major ridge is located where the community church is built, i.e. *The Tjølling Moraine* (Olsen and Løwe 1984).

---

1 Generally all the ages given are in calibrated radiocarbon years, BC or AD (cf. Stuiver et al. 1998), if not otherwise stated. See also Tab. 12.2 and the text on p.268.

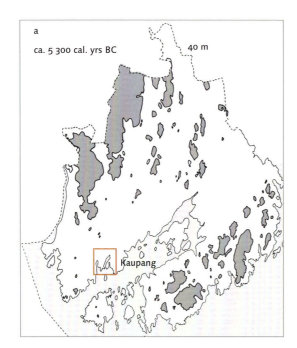

a
ca. 5 300 cal. yrs BC   40 m

Kaupang

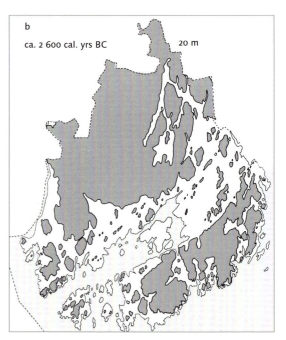

b
ca. 2 600 cal. yrs BC   20 m

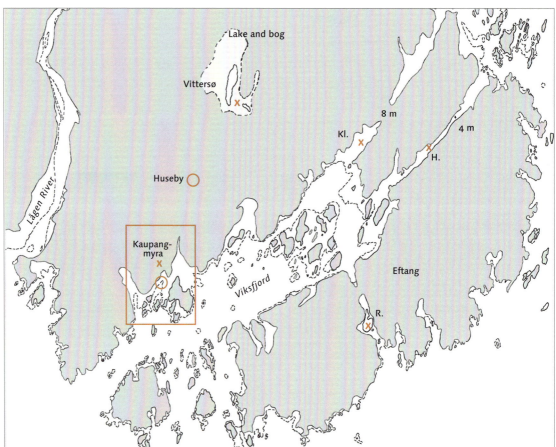

Lake and bog

Vittersø

8 m

Kl.

4 m

H.

Huseby

Lågen River

Kaupang-
myra

Viksfjord

Eftang

R.

During deglaciation, the sea-level was just below 158 m a.s.l. (Henningsmoen 1979), and the whole region was covered by an arctic sea under which large volumes of glacial and marine clay were deposited.

During the subsequent regression, much of the ice-marginal deposits and the marine clay were reworked by waves and shore currents. In particular, the bedrock hills were washed free of loose deposits, and

beach sand and gravel, locally several metres thick, can now be found at the foot of the rounded Larvikite hills, gradually thinning out towards the depressions in the landscape. The beach sands normally overlie marine clay. The ice-marginal ridges are also covered by beach sand and gravel, but they also have numerous glacial erratics (stones and boulders) concentrated on the crests of the ridges. On agricultural land

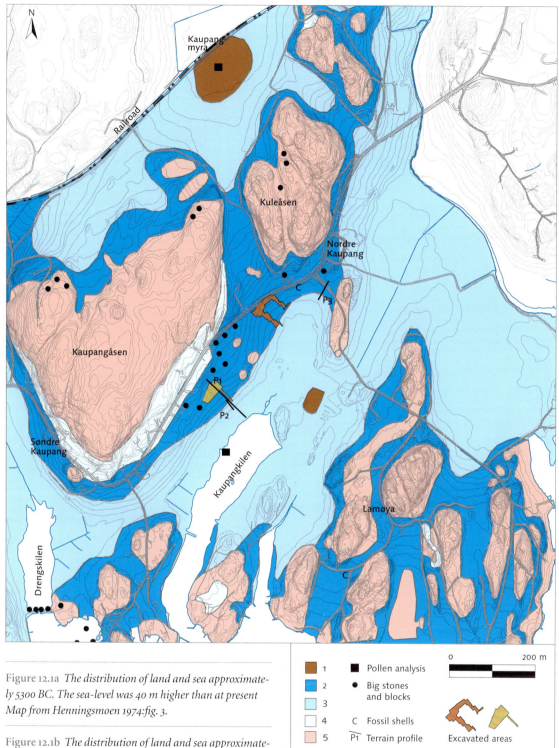

Figure 12.1a *The distribution of land and sea approximately 5300 BC. The sea-level was 40 m higher than at present Map from Henningsmoen 1974:fig. 3.*

Figure 12.1b *The distribution of land and sea approximately 2600 BC. The sea-level was 20 m higher than at present (Henningsmoen 1974:fig. 3).*

Figure 12.2 *The distribution of land and sea approximately AD 500. The sea-level was 5 m higher than at present. The Kaupang area is framed. The archaeological sites Kaupang and Huseby are marked with circles. Other radiocarbon-dated sites: R. Refsholttjern (tarn); Kl. Location of the Klåstad Viking shipwreck; H. Holkekilmyra (bog). Map, Rolf Sørensen.*

Figure 12.3 *Map of loose deposits with sample points and terrain profiles. Modified from Bukholm (2001). Legend: 1. Organic deposits (peat bog); 2. Beach sediments (sand with granules); 3. Fine-grained marine sediments; 4. Thin and discontinuous coarse-grained beach sediments; 5. Mainly bare rock. Illustration, Anne Engesveen and Julie K. Øhre Askjem.*

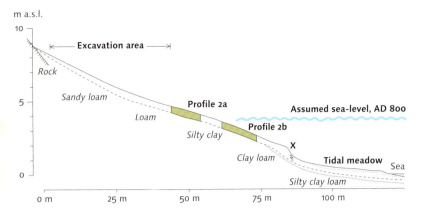

m a.s.l.

Excavation area

Rock

Sandy loam

Loam

Profile 2a

Silty clay

Profile 2b

Assumed sea-level, AD 800

X

Clay loam

Tidal meadow

Sea

Silty clay loam

0 m   25 m   50 m   75 m   100 m

Figure 12.4 *Terrain profile 1. Transect over the excavation area 2000-2002 down to sea-level, with generalised thickness of cultural deposits (ploughsoil included). Location on Fig. 12.3. Illustration, Jørgen Sparre.*

Figure 12.5 *Terrain profile 2. Detailed description of soil and sediment stratigraphy in two transects, a and b. Location shown on inset map, and on Figs. 12.3 and 12.4. Illustration, Jørgen Sparre.*

these stones and boulders have been cleared away, and used to make either stone walls or clearance cairns, which can be observed in the area today.

12.2 Soils and sediments in the Kaupang area

The regional distribution of Quaternary sediments is shown on the map by Olsen and Løwe (1984). Locally the sediments were mapped in detail by Bukholm (2001), as shown in Fig. 12.3.

A minor ice-marginal zone is located on the southern foot-slopes of the hills Kaupangåsen and Kuleåsen, and the large quantity of stones and boulders uncovered during excavations along the road and in the main excavation area reflects this. Just outside, south of the ice-margin, boulder clay was deposited. The primary till material has been reworked by the sea during the lowering of the sea-level, and gravelly beach sand is washed out over the marine boulder clay and surrounds the hills.

Nearly all of the area occupied by the former Viking-age settlement is located on beach sediments overlying marine clay (recent mapping of the cultivated soils in the region by the Norwegian Institute of Land Inventory, NIJOS 1993, and by Bukholm 2001). The beach deposits (medium to coarse sand) are moderately to imperfectly well drained. The thickness of sand decreases down-slope, and on the lower part of the formerly occupied (and now partly excavated) area, the underlying marine clay (silty clay loam) occurs just under the plough layer (see Figs. 12.4 and 12.5), producing a poorly drained soil. Today the area with cultural deposits is found on both the sandy and clayey sediment units.

Some of the marine clayey sediments have become sensitive (unstable), and small 'quick-clay' slides (Rosenqvist 1960; Bjerrum 1971) have been observed just south of the main excavation area 2000-2002 (Fig. 12.5: profile 2b; Pilø, this vol. Ch. 7:153, Fig. 7.12), and near Søndre Kaupang (Fig. 12.3), a farm

further to the west. However, the clay sediments have become sensitive or 'quick' after the abandonment of the settlement because the sea-level and groundwater levels have fallen, causing dilution of the original marine salt. At the time of settlement the ground was stable enough for constructing buildings and other constructions.

To map the extent and thickness of the cultural deposits, augering at 25 m intervals was carried out along seven terrain profiles over the 1956–74 and 2000-2002 excavation areas, and where the black cultural deposits were seen between the farms Søndre and Nordre Kaupang (Bukholm 2001). One of these profiles, traversing the 2000-2002 excavation area, is shown in Fig. 12.4. The subsoil variation on the slope reflects depositional processes during land upheaval combined with sediment distribution during deglaciation.

The cultural deposits are thin (20–30 cm) on the upper slope (most likely due to erosion, see below), increasing to 50 cm or more on the middle slope. At the lower end of the cultivated field the cultural deposits may be up to 90 cm thick (X in Fig. 12.4). At this point the stratigraphy is as follows: marine silty clay loam occurs below 110 cm, deposited before the settlement occupation; then follows c. 5 cm of black silt with frequent pieces of fragmented wood deposited below the Viking-age sea-level at the time of settlement occupation. About 15 cm of dark grey sand that lies on top of the silt is interpreted as beach sediment formed at the time the sea-level was about 1 m higher than today (i.e. around AD 1670: see Fig. 12.10b). Above the beach sand lies 90 cm of fairly homogeneous black cultural deposits. They show no sign of wave-washing, and consequently must have accumulated when the sea-level was 1 m or less above the present level, i.e. during approximately the last 330 years.

In the embayment, just outside the tidal meadow (Fig. 12.4: SE end of profile), a 160 cm long sediment

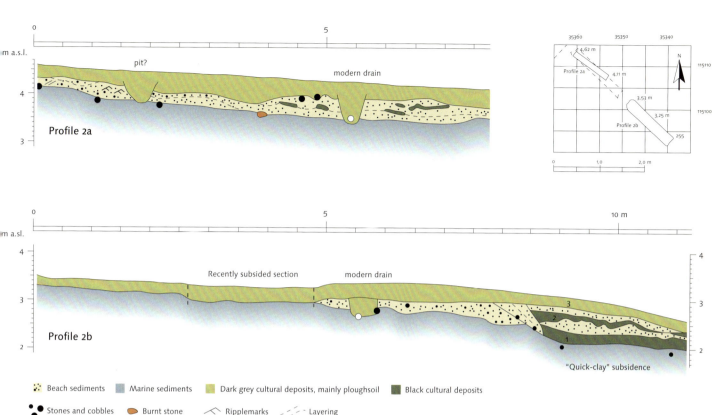

pit?

modern drain

Profile 2a

4.62 m

Profile 2a

4.11 m

3.53 m

3.25 m

Profile 2b

N

255

m a.sl.

Recently subsided section   modern drain

3

2

1

Profile 2b

"Quick-clay" subsidence

Beach sediments   Marine sediments   Dark grey cultural deposits, mainly ploughsoil   Black cultural deposits

Stones and cobbles   Burnt stone   Ripplemarks   Layering

core was collected for pollen and diatom analyses. From a depth of c. 65 cm up to c. 35 cm below the sediment surface, the marine mud shows clear influence of eroded material transported from the area covered with anthropogenic soil material. The upper part is less dark, and this is evidence that erosion from the land areas must have decreased. A layer of gravelly sand occurs between a depth of 10 and 15 cm, and this layer is also observed over most of the tidal flat. Applying an average sedimentation rate in the embayment sediments of 0.65 mm per year (see below), would suggest that this may reflect an extreme storm event that occurred about 150 years ago (Sørensen 2002).

Two transects in Profile 1 were described in more detail (Fig. 12.5), and the upper one (Profile 2a) shows varying thickness in the cultural deposits, overlying beach gravel and sand with lenses of anthropogenic soil material incorporated, particularly between 4 and 8 m in the lower part of profile 2a where the beach sediments are thickest. The underlying marine silty clay shows sign of weathering in the upper 10 cm ('white clay'), indicating weak soil development before the settlement was established (cf. Milek and French, this vol. Ch. 15:328).

In the upper part of Profile 2a (between 1 and 2.5 m) the beach sediments show wave-washed structures and layering. This unit is also a mixture of pure sand and gravel and thin horizons of dark-coloured anthropogenic soil material. Both units are interpreted as beach ridges, formed at high tide or by storm waves at the time the settlement was occupied. The tops of the two beach ridges are respectively 4.2 and 4.0 m above present sea-level (Fig. 12.5). The assumed sea-level in AD 800 was c. 3.5 m (Figs. 12.4 and 12.10b) and high tides or storm waves 0.5–0.7 m above mean sea-level must be considered to have been normal in a moderately sheltered embayment such as this was during the Viking Age.

The mapping of the area by Flux-gate magnetometer shows a series of features sub-parallel to the contour lines, up to c. 4.2 m above sea-level (a.s.l.), just S of the main excavation area of 2000-2002 (cf. Pilø, this vol. Ch. 7:150, Fig.7.8). We suggest that the Flux-gate recordings and the observed beach ridges in Profile 2a are related, although the Flux-gate map is more diffuse at the profile position.

Profile 2b (Fig. 12.5) was described from features in the N wall of the "washing pit" used during the 2000–2002 excavation. The upper end of the profile is 3.53 m a.s.l., and this is approximately at the sea-level of AD 800 (Figs. 12.4 and 12.10b). Notably, the beach sediments are absent below the cultural deposits between 0 and 5 m in the profile, possibly due to erosion when the sea was at this level. From 5 m down to the end of the profile, coarse beach sediments are present below the cultural deposits. When the supporting construction in the washing pit was removed, the side-walls caved in because of unstable silty clay in the subsoil. The described soil profiles lay at least half a metre in from the originally dug pit, and showed one small subsidence between 2.5 and 5 m in

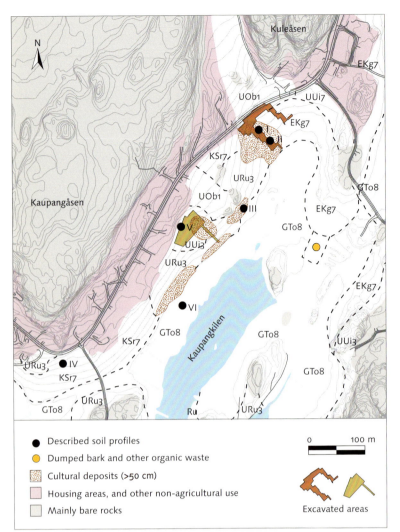

Figure 12.6 *Simplified soil map of the Kaupang area (compiled and modified from maps by NIJOS 1993, Bukholm 2001). The mapping unit code: The first letter indicates the WRB soil group; the next two letters give the Soil Series name (see Tab. 12.1); the number following them indicates topsoil texture (0 = gravel, 9 = heavy clay). The location of the six soil profiles described (I–VI) is marked on this map. A brief description of the major soil types is given in Table 12.1. Illustration, Anne Engesveen and Julie K. Øhre Askjem.*

Legend (map):

- ● Described soil profiles
- ○ Dumped bark and other organic waste
- ▦ Cultural deposits (>50 cm)
- ▨ Housing areas, and other non-agricultural use
- ▨ Mainly bare rocks
- 0 — 100 m
- Excavated areas

of a mixture of dark coloured cultural deposits and light coloured lenses of sorted sediments, probably because the topsoil was disturbed by excess use of water at and near the washing pit.

As described above, there are clear signs of soil movement from the upper sandy slopes over the whole area with cultural deposits. Some erosion took place during the Viking-age occupation of the area, registered in soil and sediment profiles below Viking-age sea-level, but a considerable amount of erosion must have occurred after the abandonment of the settlement.

Using erosion models adapted to Norwegian conditions, i.e. mainly the length of snow-cover and frost in the soil (Jordforsk 1997), it has been estimated that 5–10 cm of surface materials might have been eroded from the settlement area during the last 400 years (Bukholm 2001).

The thick accumulation of cultural deposits at the lower end of the field (Profile 1, point X, Fig. 12.4) is estimated to have an average thickness of 50 cm over a 10 m slope-length. If this soil volume were distributed over the 55 m slope-length of the settlement area above the Viking-age sea-level, it would represent approximately 10 cm of eroded surface soil. As mentioned above, this erosion must have occurred during the last 350–400 years. The observed accumulation of soil material below the Viking-age sea-level is deposited over a large area, and represents roughly another 10 cm of surface of erosion from the land area when the settlement was occupied.

On an average one may expect that approximately a total of 20 cm topsoil has been removed from the settlement area since the Viking Age, especially from the upper slopes. However there was also an accumulation of waste-products in and around the buildings in the settlement area, and these were incorporated in the original soils and sediments (cf. Milek and French, this vol. Ch. 15:333–54).

Profile 2b (Fig. 12.5), which is interpreted as contemporaneous with the 2000-2002 excavation.

At the lower end of the profile an older subsidence appears. A small landslide has characteristically occurred on the slope-break (with an increase from c. 10% to more than 20% of slope). The lower layer of anthropogenic soil material (layer No. 1 in Profile 2b, Fig. 12.5) has sunk c. 50 cm and moved down-slope 70–80 cm in one event. This layer is pitch black, is different from the recent dark grey ploughsoil, and does not show any sign of wave washing. Since it must obviously have formed as a surface layer by erosion of anthropogenic soil material from the settlement area, the sea-level must have been less than 2.5 m above present, i.e. at about AD 1200 or later (Fig. 12.10b).

The next irregular layer (No. 2) is deformed and partially disrupted. This indicates that the subsidence occurred while the soil was saturated with water (such as after heavy rain: cf. Rosenqvist 1960). The dark coloured anthropogenic soil material in this layer must have been transported from up-slope surface soils as a mud-flow, presumably at the same time as layer No. 1 sank in.

Layer No. 3 is the modern ploughsoil, consisting

Soil series	Map symbol symbol	WRB* classification	Texture– Topsoil	Texture– Subsoil	Drainage properties	Parent material
Kaupang	E Kg	Stagnic Albeluvisol (E)	Gravelly, silty loam	Gravelly, silty clay loam	Poor	Boulder clay
Øberg	U Ob	Endogleyic Umbrisol (U)	Sandy loam	Sandy loam	Moderate	Gravely beach sand
Uranienborg	U Ui	Stagnic Umbrisol (U)	Loamy sand	Sandy loam	Poor	Beach sand / marine mud
Rud	U Ru	Arenic Umbrisol (U)	Sandy loam	Loam	Imperfect	Beach sand / marine mud
Snapsrød	K Sr	Stagnic Cambisol (K)	Sandy loam	Silty clay loam	Poor	Marine mud
Torpedalen	G To	Mollic Gleysol (G)	Loamy sand	Silty clay loam	Very poor	Marine mud
Cultural deposits	W Ah	Hortic Anthrosol (W)	Sandy loam	Sandy loam /var.	Moderate– poor	Variable

*WRB = World Reference Base for Soil Resources (Deckers et al. 1998; Driessen et al. 2001).

Table 12.1 *Selected average characteristics of soil-types at and around the excavation area 2000-2002. See soil map with unit symbols (Fig. 12.6).*

A more advanced erosion model (ERONOR: Lundekvam 2002) confirms that this amount of erosion is reasonable, although a number of factors are unknown, particularly the variation in rainfall and the frequency of extreme rainfall events in the actual time-interval.

12.2.1 Distribution and properties of the soil types

The classification of *anthropogenic soils (Anthrosols)* in the current Norwegian system (Greve et al. 1999) requires the presence of at least a 50 cm thickness of *anthropogenic soil materials* (the term is used synonymously with *cultural deposits* throughout the paper). The primary distribution of the cultural deposits was most probably irregular and the subsequent erosion was most probably also irregular (see above). The present distribution of anthropogenic soil and other soil types is shown in Fig. 12.6, but the map gives only an indication of where the thickest cultural deposits occur. The various soil-types in the area are defined by textural variations and drainage properties, as well as slope and stoniness in the topsoil. The main characteristics of the soils are presented in Tab. 12.1.

The soil development in the profiles from outside the settlement area is weak, due to the area's late emergence from the sea. The settlement area extends

up to c. 10 m a.s.l. and this level emerged from the sea approximately 700 BC (Fig. 12.10a), whereas the lower part of the settlement area is c. 4 m above present sea-level, and thus emerged approximately 750 AD (Fig. 12.10b).

The upper and better drained areas with thick gravelly beach sand might possibly have been cultivated before the establishment of the settlement, whereas the areas closer to the sea-level at the time had high groundwater levels and might only have been utilised for cattle grazing; see the vegetation history for Kaupangkilen bay (Fig. 12.9a–b).

The parent material for the soil-type Kaupang (**EKg**), consisting of a marine silty clay loam with gravels and "drop-stones" and boulders dumped from ice bergs, was formed when the glacier front was located near the Kaupang area. Some of the other soil-types (**UOb, KSr** and **UUi**) also contain "drop-stones" and boulders which are numerous in the 2000-2002 excavation area. The Kaupang soil series is the only one defined in this area. All the other soil-types are defined elsewhere in south-eastern Norway (Nyborg and Solbakken 2003).

Soil-type **UOb** is found on the upper slopes, close to the hill at the northern boundary of the main excavation area of 2000-2002. This soil-type is classified

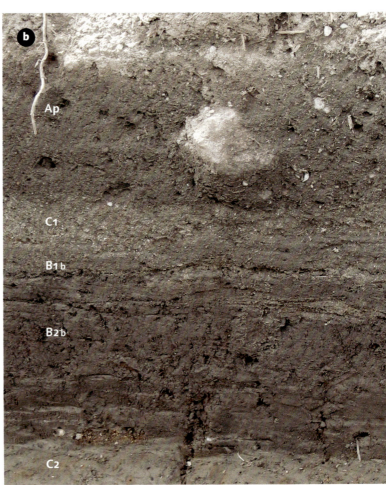

as *Umbrisol* due to the high content of organic material (and dark colours) in the topsoil, and because the anthropogenic soil material is generally too thin to qualify for classification as Anthrosol. One soil-profile (V) is described in this unit (Sørensen, unpubl.).

The soil-types **UUi** and **URu** are found on the middle slopes, where most of the former Viking-age settlement was located. All of the 2000-2002 excavation lies within unit **UUi** which has poorer drainage properties than unit **URu** (Tab. 12.1 and Fig. 12.6). Both units are classified as *Umbrisols* due to the present distribution of anthropogenic soil material in the topsoil. Two small areas with >50 cm thick anthropogenic materials are mapped in unit **UUi,** in the settlement area (Bukholm 2001).

Before settlement times, these soils were most probably *Stagnic Cambisols* (cf. type **KSr,** Tab. 12.1). The mapping unit **KSr** occurs in the same position as unit **URu** and is probably found as a complex with **URu.** One soil-profile (IV) was described in the **KSr** unit, well outside the settlement area, and it is therefore used as a reference profile for comparison with soils developed in the cultural deposits (Bukholm 2001).

From approximately the 2 m contour-line down to present sea-level, the soil-type **GTo** is predominant. Thin horizons with anthropogenic soil material are common in the subsoils of this unit (Fig. 12.7b). Two soil-profiles (III and VI) are described (Bukholm 2001; Sørensen, unpubl.).

On the original soil maps (NIJOS 1993), only one area was mapped as Anthrosol (**WAh**) around the excavation area 1956–74 (Pilø, this vol. Ch. 6). Two soil-profiles (I and II) have been described in this unit. However, new mapping revealed four other small areas with anthrosols (Bukholm 2001; see Fig. 12.6). Details of the six soil-profiles will be published elsewhere.

12.3 Vegetation development during the Late Holocene

The land near the Kaupang site (within a radius of 5 km) first rose above sea-level early in the Atlantic period (*sensu* Mangerud et al. 1974), and the first vegetation was established on rocky islands (Fig. 12.1). The full vegetation history of the region is described by Henningsmoen (1974, 1980), and the general development from the Atlantic period onwards is only briefly recapitulated here.

The Atlantic period (8,000–5,000 ^{14}C years BP)[2] was warm and moist and climatically the most favourable period for vegetation growth during the Holocene. The most warmth-demanding vegetation first appeared in this period. Elm (*Ulmus glabra)* and

Figure 12.7a *Anthrosol profile 5.6 m a.s.l., from the southern edge of the 1956–74 excavation area. Described by Bukholm (2001). The layers from bottom: BC, gravelly beach sand; Bw, c. 15 cm of slightly developed B-horizon; Antr., c. 35 cm of anthropogenic materials; Ap, 25 cm recent plough layer. Photo by Dagfinn Skre 1999.*

Figure 12.7b *Anthropogenic soil material deposited below the Viking-age sea-level (located c. 1 m above present sea-level). The layers from bottom: C2, primary marine silty clay loam with rusty mottles (due to fluctuating water-table); B2, massive, fine-grained anthropogenic material (c. 20 cm thick); B1, mixed layered younger sediments and anthropogenic material; C1, mineral soil deposited after the abandonment of the Kaupang settlement (c. 10 cm thick); Ap, the recent, 25 cm thick plough layer. Photo by Rolf Sørensen 2002.*

lime *(Tilia cordata)* had maxima, and based on the occurrence of even more demanding taxa, the summer temperature is calculated to have been at least 2°C higher, and the winter temperature even 3–4°C higher than at present (Iversen 1944; Hafsten 1956).

The Sub-Boreal period (5,000–2,500 ^{14}C years BP) was climatically slightly less favourable and more variable than the Atlantic period. The warmth-demanding trees were still present, but generally in lesser quantities. The regression of the sea had by then produced large areas of dry land, some of which had well-drained sandy soils favourable for early agriculture. The site of the Kaupangmyra bog was a shallow and sheltered bay by 2600 BC (Figs. 12.1 and 12.2).

The climatic cooling continued in the subsequent Sub-Atlantic period (500 BC to the present), and the humidity increased. The warmth-demanding trees declined or disappeared. Two new forest trees colonized the area, i.e. beech *(Fagus silvatica)* and spruce *(Picea abies)*. The climate was rather variable. The latter part of the Viking Age was for instance favourable (start of the Medieval Warm Period), whereas the later Little Ice Age represents a noticeable deterioration (Grove 2002) that had an effect on agriculture, but mainly in marginal areas. It cannot be detected in our pollen diagrams (Figs. 12.8 and 12.9).

Two locations have been sampled for pollen ana-

lysis, the Kaupangmyra bog and Kaupangkilen bay (Fig. 12.3). The sediments from Kaupangkilen bay were sampled with a 75 cm long and 7.5 cm diameter "Russian" corer in June 2002, in very shallow water just outside the reed-belt. Samples for pollen and diatom analyses were taken at intervals of 5 and 10 cm respectively, with exact volume (1 cu cm), from the upper 1 m of sediments.

The Kaupangmyra bog was sampled with a "Hiller" corer at the site where the small remnant of the former bog was undisturbed and the peat was thickest in 1951. Most of the bog was already cultivated at that time. We have later tried to resample the site, but it has been impossible to find undisturbed peat or other suitable localities in the vicinity. We have therefore used samples that have been stored for more than 50 years in sealed and air-tight glass tubes for AMS radiocarbon dating. The samples for pollen analyses were cut from the Hiller chamber at intervals of 5 or 2.5 cm (Fig. 12.8), but not to exact volume. The samples from both sites have been prepared according to standard techniques (Fægri and Iversen 1950; 1989). Between 200 and 1,000 pollen grains were

---

2   The subdivision of the Holocene (Mangerud et al. 1974) is based on radiocarbon years (^{14}C years BP).

Figure 12.8 *The vegetation history from the Kaupangmyra bog. Percentage pollen diagram. The normal percentage scale is shown in solid colours, and the 10x enhanced one is vertically hatched with a lighter hue. The vertical lines also show analysed levels. The vertical lines running through the diagram represent zone boundaries. Radiocarbon-dated levels are marked with black bars on the top of the diagram (Tab. 12.2). The zone boundaries can be identified in the lower column. Analysed by Kari E. Henningsmoen. Illustration, Jørgen Sparre.*

counted in each sample (in most cases c. 500 pollen grains), varying according to pollen concentration, and the results are presented in pollen diagrams, constructed by the computer program TILIA (Vers. 1.1). The diagrams (Figs. 12.8 and 12.9) were drawn by TILIA.GRAPH (by Grimm & Graphic Software System), and the boundaries for the local pollen-assemblage zones (LPAZ) were drawn manually (full vertical lines in the diagrams). Ecologically indifferent pollen-types represented by only a few grains have not been included in the diagrams. The complete dataset can be obtained from Kari E. Henningsmoen and Helge I. Høeg.

To each sample from the Kaupangkilen bay, two *Lycopodium* tablets were added (Stockmarr 1971) (each tablet contains 12,542 ± 415 spores). Although these sediments were rich in fine silt and clay, hydrofluoric acid was not used, but the fine mud fraction was carefully decanted. Charcoal particles have been counted in the Kaupangkilen bay section, and presented as percentages of the total number of pollen grains plus charcoal. The sample from Kaupangmyra bog was analysed before the Stockmarr method had been introduced, and it has not been possible to carry out a new analysis (as mentioned above).

12.3.1 Description of the Kaupangmyra bog, 18.5 m a.s.l.

At the request of Charlotte Blindheim the Kaupangmyra bog was sampled in 1951, with helpful assistance from the landowner, Astri Jahnsen. The percentage pollen diagram (Fig. 12.8) from Kaupangmyra bog (**Km**) is constructed from the basic data analysed in 1951–1952. A somewhat simplified diagram from the site was published by Henningsmoen (1974). The present diagram is subdivided into four local pollen-assemblage zones (LPAZ). The recently obtained AMS radiocarbon dates (Tab. 12.2) provide a depth-scale in *calibrated years Before Present* (BP) because

the TILIA program cannot handle BC and AD at the same time. In addition to the traditional pollen curves in the Kaupangmyra bog diagram, there is a corrosion curve, showing corroded pollen from deciduous trees as a percentage of the total quantity of the same category.

Although the bog lies approximately 700 m from the settlement we regard the analysis from this site as the most reliable due to the site's sediment characteristics (particularly for the terrestrial peat, i.e. the upper three pollen-assemblage zones) and the well dated upper 125 cm of the peat. The group CULT. (cultural indicators) in the pollen diagram includes only cerealia, *Plantago lanceolata* and *P. major*. Other anthropogenic indicators in this diagram (for instance *Rumex*, *Artemisia* and Chenopodiaceae) are not specified, since they obviously occur in nearshore vegetation (in the lower part of the diagram) as well as in connection with agricultural activity.

The vegetation history

LPAZ – **Km 1:** *Ulmus – Quercus – Tilia* (390–130 cm) The zone represents marine conditions with silty clay sediments. Diatom analyses show exclusively marine and brackish taxa, corroborated by the presence of foraminiferae tests and marine dinoflagellate cysts. Elm, oak *(Quercus robur)* and lime are well represented, but not so amply as in the Atlantic times, corroborated by other pollen diagrams from the Vestfold area (Henningsmoen 1974; 1980). The high percentage of pine *(Pinus silvestris)* in this zone is obviously due to marine over-representation (Fægri and Iversen 1989).

The clay sediments contain no datable material and on the basis of the pollen assemblage, the bottom layer is assumed to be younger than 3800 BC. The sea-level curve (Fig. 12.10a) indicates that the site became dry land around 2300 BC. The actual isolation from the sea is not represented in the diagram (see zone

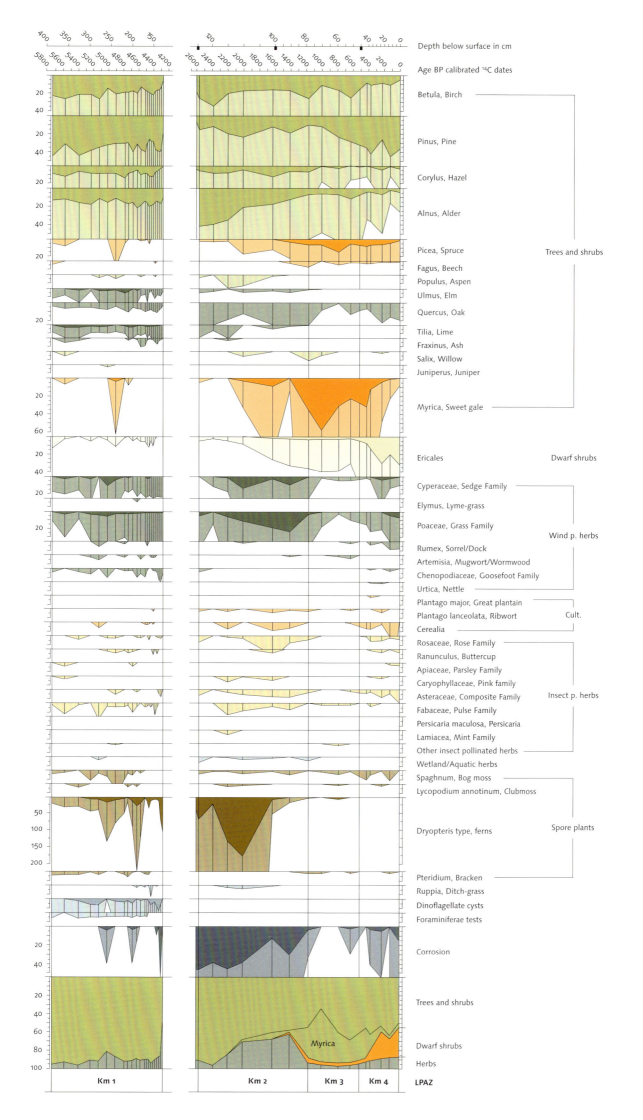

| Depth below surface in cm |
| Age BP calibrated ¹⁴C dates |

Betula, Birch

Pinus, Pine

Corylus, Hazel

Alnus, Alder

Picea, Spruce

Fagus, Beech

Populus, Aspen

Ulmus, Elm

Quercus, Oak

Tilia, Lime

Fraxinus, Ash

Salix, Willow

Juniperus, Juniper

Myrica, Sweet gale

Trees and shrubs

Ericales — Dwarf shrubs

Cyperaceae, Sedge Family

Elymus, Lyme-grass

Poaceae, Grass Family

Rumex, Sorrel/Dock

Artemisia, Mugwort/Wormwood

Chenopodiaceae, Goosefoot Family

Urtica, Nettle

Wind p. herbs

Plantago major, Great plantain

Plantago lanceolata, Ribwort

Cerealia

Cult.

Rosaceae, Rose Family

Ranunculus, Buttercup

Apiaceae, Parsley Family

Caryophyllaceae, Pink family

Asteraceae, Composite Family

Fabaceae, Pulse Family

Persicaria maculosa, Persicaria

Lamiacea, Mint Family

Other insect pollinated herbs

Insect p. herbs

Wetland/Aquatic herbs

Spaghnum, Bog moss

Lycopodium annotinum, Clubmoss

Dryopteris type, ferns

Spore plants

Pteridium, Bracken

Ruppia, Ditch-grass

Dinoflagellate cysts

Foraminiferae tests

Corrosion

Trees and shrubs

Myrica

Dwarf shrubs

Herbs

Km 1

Km 2

Km 3

Km 4

LPAZ

261

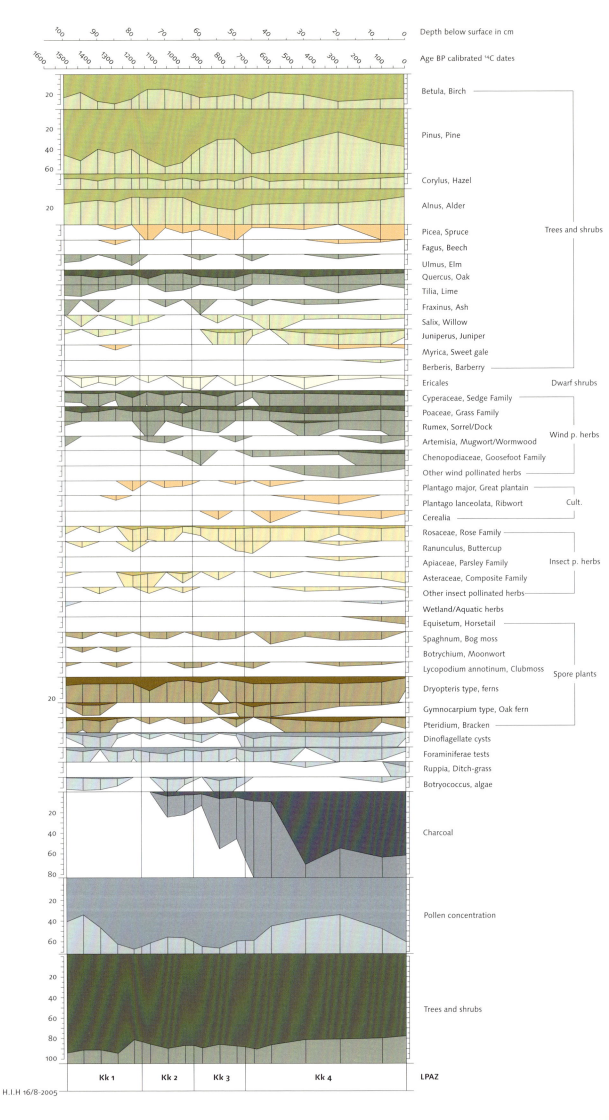

Depth below surface in cm

Age BP calibrated ¹⁴C dates

Betula, Birch

Pinus, Pine

Corylus, Hazel

Alnus, Alder

Picea, Spruce   Trees and shrubs

Fagus, Beech

Ulmus, Elm

Quercus, Oak

Tilia, Lime

Fraxinus, Ash

Salix, Willow

Juniperus, Juniper

Myrica, Sweet gale

Berberis, Barberry

Ericales   Dwarf shrubs

Cyperaceae, Sedge Family

Poaceae, Grass Family

Rumex, Sorrel/Dock

Artemisia, Mugwort/Wormwood   Wind p. herbs

Chenopodiaceae, Goosefoot Family

Other wind pollinated herbs

Plantago major, Great plantain

Plantago lanceolata, Ribwort   Cult.

Cerealia

Rosaceae, Rose Family

Ranunculus, Buttercup

Apiaceae, Parsley Family   Insect p. herbs

Asteraceae, Composite Family

Other insect pollinated herbs

Wetland/Aquatic herbs

Equisetum, Horsetail

Spaghnum, Bog moss

Botrychium, Moonwort

Lycopodium annotinum, Clubmoss   Spore plants

Dryopteris type, ferns

Gymnocarpium type, Oak fern

Pteridium, Bracken

Dinoflagellate cysts

Foraminiferae tests

Ruppia, Ditch-grass

Botryococcus, algae

Charcoal

Pollen concentration

Trees and shrubs

Kk 1   Kk 2   Kk 3   Kk 4   LPAZ

262

H.I.H 16/8-2005

Figure 12.9a *The vegetation history of Kaupangkilen bay – Percentage pollen diagram. The normal percentage scale is shown in solid colours, and the 10x enhanced one is vertically hatched with a lighter hue. The vertical lines also show analysed levels. The zone boundaries can be identified at the bottom. Analysed by Helge I. Høeg. Illustration, Jørgen Sparre.*

Km 2 below). The zone therefore represents the first half of the Sub-Boreal chronozone (*sensu* Mangerud et al. 1974).

LPAZ – **Km 2:** *Alnus – Betula – agricultural indicators* (130–78 cm)
The sediments are terrestrial and consist of a brushwood peat. Two levels are radiocarbon dated (at 125 and 100 cm: see Tab. 12.2). The diatoms in these terrestrial layers were almost disintegrated and only a very few minute fragments were found.

The site was isolated from the sea at about 2300 BC (4,300 years BP calibrated). The calibrated age scale in Fig. 12.8 indicates that the lowest part of the terrestrial peat (at a depth of 130 cm) is 2,600 years old (c. 600 BC). Accordingly there is a hiatus of approximately 1,700 years. The abrupt changes in the type of deposits, in diatom conditions, and in many of the pollen diagram curves between 125 and 130 cm all indicate a noticeable hiatus. The cause for this might have been some slight erosion on the tidal flats just before isolation, and/or that the site dried out and the organic matter was decomposed (oxidized) and no accumulation took place until a change in climate occurred. The corrosion column in Fig. 12.8 shows relatively poor pollen preservation in this zone, worst in the lower part, but improving higher up. This implies the presence of oxygen in a peat-forming environment that was dry in the lower part, slowly changing to more moist conditions with less oxygen over time.

The pollen zone shows a deciduous forest in the lower part of which alder is dominant, together with a considerable amount of fern in the field layer. The most demanding trees (elm, oak and lime) have decreased from zone **Km 1,** in accordance with the climatic deterioration from the Sub-Boreal to the Sub-Atlantic period represented in this and subsequent zones.

The pine representation is moderate, considering the very ample pollen production of the species.

There are clear indications of human influence in zone **Km 2.** The forest declines gradually, first birch *(Betula verrucosa)* and then alder *(Alnus incana/ glutinosa),* probably due to clearance for agricultural purposes. Maxima of grass and other graminids together with insect-pollinated herbs corroborate the open landscape interpretation. *Plantago lanceolata* is present in almost all samples, indicating pasturing, and the presence of cereals indicates agriculture. These human activities probably took place somewhere in the near vicinity of the bog. At both of two levels (100 and 70 cm deep) more than 1,000 pollen grains have been counted, to corroborate the peak and decline of agricultural influence, respectively. According to the radiocarbon dates, this agricultural phase took place before the establishment of the Kaupang settlement, as the zone ends about AD 800.

LPAZ – **Km 3:** *Pinus – Picea – Myrica* (78–45 cm)
The sediments in the whole zone consist of brushwood peat, and there is an increasing element of *Sphagnum* moss from 60 cm upwards. *Picea* is established about the zone boundary between **Km 2** and **3,** which accords well with the date of AD 830 (cf. discussion below – Kaupangkilen bay). *Fagus* occurs here at the same time. The zone represents the time from about AD 800–1500, thus including the Kaupang settlement period.

There is a temporary cessation in agricultural activity near the bog. *Plantago lanceolata,* cereals, graminids and insect pollinators decrease or disappear. The zone boundary is defined by these indicators, as well as by the *Picea* expansion. However, some of the deciduous trees seem to have been utilized because birch, hazel *(Corylus avellana),* elm and oak decreased while the conifers increased. Sweet gale *(Myrica gale)* had obviously taken over most of the

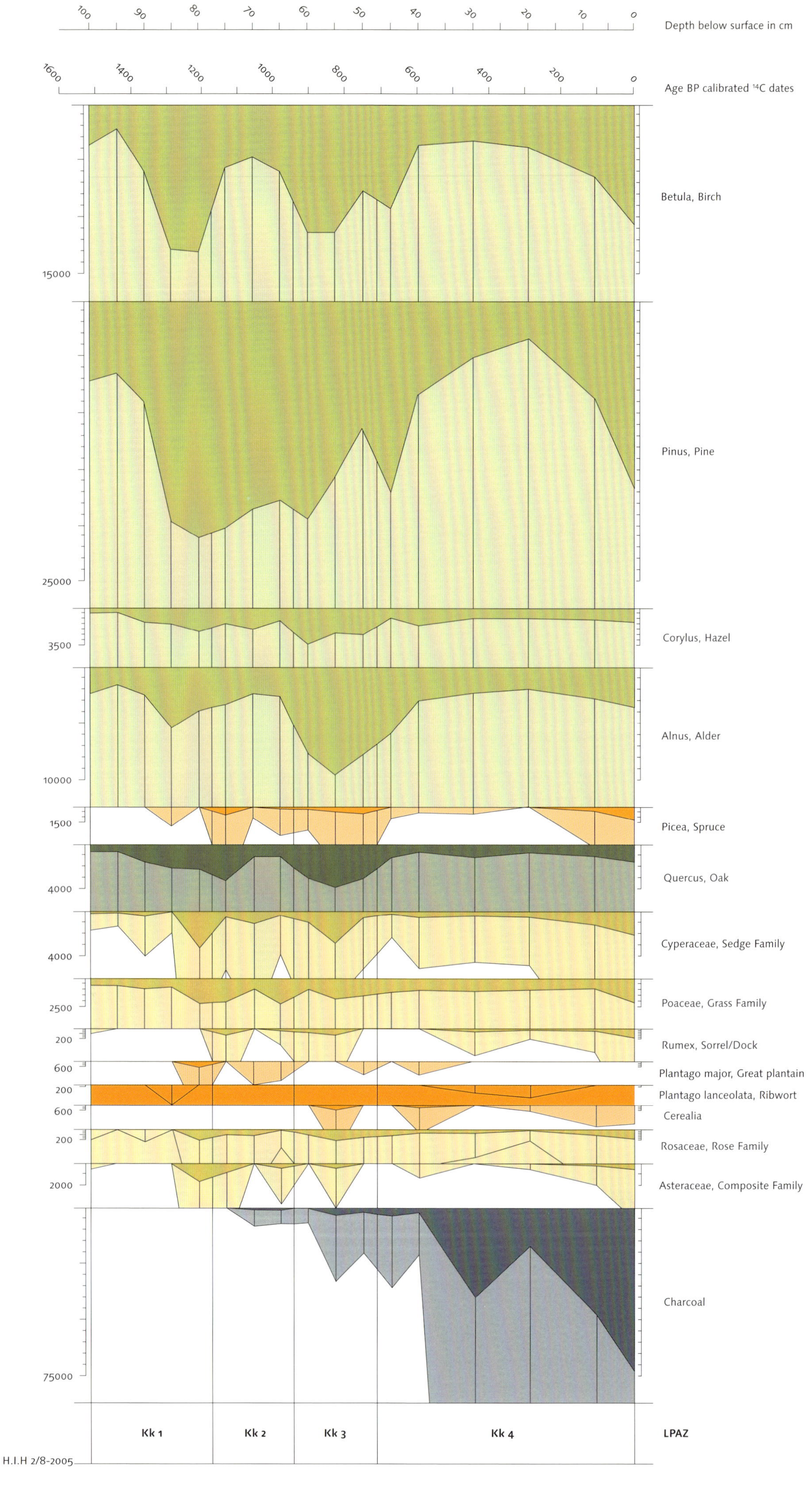

Depth below surface in cm

100 90 80 70 60 50 40 30 20 10 0

Age BP calibrated ¹⁴C dates

1600 1400 1200 1000 800 600 400 200 0

Betula, Birch

15000

Pinus, Pine

25000

Corylus, Hazel

3500

Alnus, Alder

10000

Picea, Spruce

1500

Quercus, Oak

4000

Cyperaceae, Sedge Family

4000

Poaceae, Grass Family

2500

Rumex, Sorrel/Dock

200

Plantago major, Great plantain

600

Plantago lanceolata, Ribwort

200

Cerealia

600

Rosaceae, Rose Family

200

Asteraceae, Composite Family

2000

Charcoal

75000

Kk 1   Kk 2   Kk 3   Kk 4   LPAZ

264

H.I.H 2/8-2005

Figure 12.9b *The vegetation history of Kaupangkilen bay – Pollen-concentration diagram. The left-hand scale with numbers shows the content of pollengrains per cu. cm, in solid colours. The curves with low numbers are enhanced by a factor of 10 and vertically hatched. The vertical lines also show analysed levels. The zone boundaries can be identified at the bottom. Analysed by Helge I. Høeg. Illustration, Jørgen Sparre.*

wet ground at the expense of other wetland taxa, such as the sedges (Cyperaceae) and perhaps some of the grass (Poaceae) taxa. The spread of *Myrica* might also to some extent have played a part in the decrease of alder and some birch, but both alder and birch might also have been utilized by the Kaupang inhabitants. Towards the end of the zone – about AD 1400 – and after the Black Death, *Plantago lanceolata* and cereals start to reappear, indicating a new expansion of agricultural activities in the area.

LPAZ – **Km 4:** *Pinus – Picea – Ericales* (45–0 cm)
The zone covers the time from about AD 1500 up to the present. Cerealia and the other indicators of human activity continue and increase upwards, and some of the tree species decrease. Ericales – mostly heather *(Calluna vulgaris)* – replace *Myrica,* and corrosion increases again, probably a result of drying out due to drainage and cultivation of the bog area.

12.3.2 Description of the Kaupangkilen bay

The whole section consists of marine sediments, with marine and brackish diatoms, foraminiferae tests and marine dinoflagellate cysts (Fig. 12.9a). The embayment is now in the process of being isolated from the sea, and the whole section has therefore developed in an environment that is similar to the lowest zone in Kaupangmyra bog (LPAZ – **Km 1;** Fig. 12.8). Some small mollusc fragments occurred at a depth of 63 cm in the sediments, but the radiocarbon dating gave unreasonable results (far too old) and therefore is not considered here. Other means of dating the section rely on the expansion of *Picea*, which is well dated in this region. Averaging six datings gives an age of about AD 830 for the expansion of *Picea* (Henningsmoen in Hafsten et al. 1979; Fig. 12.10). A similar age is given by the Kaupangmyra bog diagram (Fig. 12.8). *Picea* occurs at 85 cm and from between 80 and 75 cm

deep (Fig. 12.9a). We assume an age of AD 830 for the material at a depth of 77 cm in the sediment. This gives an average rate of sedimentation of 0.65 mm per year, which is slightly higher than that estimated further east in this fjord system (Ormåsen 1977).

However, the variability in the pollen-concentration curve (Fig. 12.9b) indicates changes in pollen influx and some variability in sedimentation rates in the bay. The sedimentation rates were governed by the erosion from the nearest land areas (bare soil on cultivated land and from the settlement area when it was in use, and after the abandonment). Another factor (even today) is the sediment transported by the River Lågen during flood events, combined with westerly winds that bring fine mud into the bay.

In a shallow bay like this, one must allow for a certain amount of re-suspension of sediments by waves as well as the re-deposition of pollen grains, some of which might have been eroded from the surrounding land areas. With the exception of the high percentage of pine in most of the section (Fig. 12.9a and 12.9b) which is due to marine over-representation of pine (Fægri and Iversen 1989), we believe that the pollen distribution gives a fairly reliable picture of the vegetation changes at and around the settlement.

The percentage pollen diagram (Fig. 12.9a) and the concentration diagram (Fig. 12.9b) from the Kaupangkilen bay (**Kk**) are subdivided into four local pollen-assemblage zones (LPAZ). The following interpretation is mainly based on the concentration diagram, and must therefore be considered as tentative. Despite the uncertainties of timescale in the concentration diagram, we believe that it gives a more reliable picture of the vegetation changes, than the percentage diagram.

There are clear similarities in the vegetation development of the last 1,500 years at the two sites, but the Kaupangkilen bay diagrams give a more localized history of the settlement environment.

Locality, and height a.s.l. (m)	Lab.no.	¹⁴C age	Calibrated age	Correction, cm (km)*	Adjusted height, m
Napperødtjern II, 31.5	T-2433	5570 ± 200	4605–4235 BC	- 249 (17.2)	29
-- „ -- I	T-2432	5460 ± 230	4515–4020 BC	-- „ --	„
Tjønna, Vittersø, 26.1	T-2140	5280 ± 110	4245–3975 BC	- 53 (3.8)	25.6
Bekketjern myr II, 26,1	T-2435	4340 ± 130	3105–2875 BC	- 389 (33.2)	22.1
-- „ -- I	T-2434	4120 ± 150	2895–2475 BC	-- „ --	„
Tjønna, Sundene, 13.0	T-2141	2920 ± 100	1280–965 BC	- 110 (18.4)	11.9
Holtantjern, 11.4	T-89 B	2400 ± 150	785–380 BC	- 16 (3.2)	11.2
Båsmyr I, 7.7	T-29	2425 ± 85	760–400 BC	- 64 (12.8	7.1
-- „ -- II	T-30	2260 ± 145	630–205 BC	-- „ --	„
Mørjetjern, 3.4	T-2144	1200 ± 110	AD 685–975	+ 3.8 (2.4)	3.5
Holkekilmyra, 3.2	T-1380	1140 ± 140	AD 760–1020	- 6.0 (4.0)	3.2
Refsholttjern, 2.1	Tua-4218A	800 ± 30	AD 1225–1265	0 (0)	2.3
Kaupangmyra bog, 18.5					
Depth 45 cm	Tua-4204	390 ± 35	AD 1460–1510	0	18.5
" 100 cm	Tua-4205	1725 ± 40	AD 270–390	0	- " -
" 125 cm	Tua-4206	2495 ± 50	775–500 BC	0	- " -

* *Correction of threshold height in cm (±), depending on the distance between Kaupang and the various locations along the isobase projection line. Distance in km, from Kaupang to the dated locality, along the isobase projection line.*

Table 12.2 *New radiocarbon calibration and isobase correction of dated localities from southern Vestfold (Henningsmoen 1974, 1979), adjusted to the Kaupang area.*

The vegetation history

LPAZ – **Kk 1**: *Pinus – Betula – Alnus* (100–77.5 cm)
The lower part (100–90 cm) has a very low pollen concentration. In this zone c. 200 pollen grains have been counted per sample. The sediments are clayey, and iron sulphide concretions become common in the upper part. The vegetation was most likely a coastal forest with pine and oak on the drier locations and alder in waterlogged areas and near the coastline. In the upper part of the zone there are indications of forest clearing, first alder and then birch. The increase in grasses and sedges may also indicate more open land areas. A few pollen grains of *Plantago lanceolata* and *P. major* may indicate some cattle grazing, trampling and minor agricultural activities before the establishment of the settlement.

LPAZ – **Kk 2**: *Pinus – Picea* (77.5–62.5 cm)
The pollen concentration is moderately high. In this zone 300–400 pollen grains have been counted per sample. The sediments are clayey and iron sulphide concretions are common. The appearance of spruce at the boundary between the zones **Kk 1** and **Kk 2** is dated to AD 830 (see above). The amount of *Picea* pollen is low and the age of the zone boundary is therefore uncertain. There is a marked reduction in birch and oak pollen and some reduction in alder and pine in this zone, indicating more forest clearing,

possibly for building materials and/or firewood (Fig. 12.9b). The absence of agricultural indicators is apparent, whereas the presence of *Plantago major* indicates some trampling either by cattle or humans. We believe that zone **Kk 2** represents the time of settlement at Kaupang.

LPAZ – **Kk 3**: *Betula – Alnus – Corylus* (62.5–47.5 cm)
In this zone 400–600 pollen grains have been counted per sample. There is a noticeable change in sediment properties (increasing water content and LOI from a depth of c. 63 cm and upwards). The clay content is increasing and iron sulphide concretions are common. Some charcoal is present in the sediment. Alder and birch increase rapidly, and also oak and hazel recover at the middle part of the zone. Pollen of *Hordeum* and *Secale* indicate some agriculture in the vicinity. Deforestation starts in the upper part of the zone.

LPAZ – **Kk 4**: *Betula – Alnus – Cerealia* (47.5–1 cm)
In this zone 200–400 pollen grains have been counted per sample. The clay content reaches a maximum in the lower part of the zone, and iron sulphides are no longer observed. Part of this zone (from 40 to 8 cm deep) has a very low pollen concentration. There is a marked increase in charcoal in the sediments, and the most likely source of this must be erosion from open

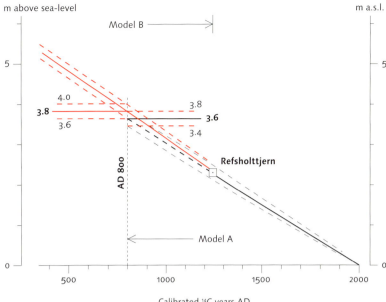

m above sea-level

Figure 12.10a *Sea-level change for the last 6,500 years in the Kaupang area. The sites: Tjønna-Vittersø lake, Kaupangmyra bog, Holkekilmyra bog and Refsholttjern tarn are shown in Fig. 12.2. Illustration, Jørgen Sparre.*

Figure 12.10b *Detailed sea-level curve for the last 1,500 years, with two alternative values for the Viking-age sea-level (AD 800). The Refsholttjern tarn is shown in Fig. 12.2. Illustration, Jørgen Sparre.*

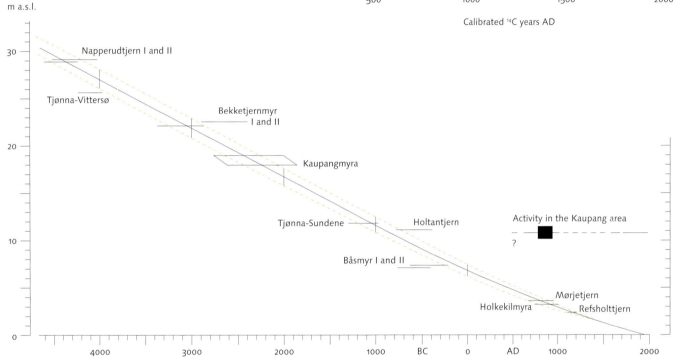

fields in the former settlement area, as well as from new clearance. The cereal pollen (mainly *Hordeum*, and with *Triticum* in the upper part) and grazing indicators such as *Plantago* are present throughout the zone, implying that the area around the embayment was utilized for pasture, with some cultivated fields, more or less continuously up to the present.

12.4 Sea-level changes during Late Holocene

The calibrated sea-level curve (Henningsmoen 1979: fig. 5) originally adjusted to a small lake, Fossanetjern, north of the Ra at Larvik, has been re-adjusted to the Kaupang area (Tab. 12.2). An isobase projection line with orientation 22°N, and with a gradient of c. 0.12 m km^{-1} at 3800 BC has been applied (cf. Sørensen

1999). At present, the gradient is c. 0.015 mm km^{-1}, in the same direction (Olesen et al. 2000). The rate of sea-level change in this region has decreased gradually from c. 5.0 mm yr^{-1} at the end of the Bronze Age to c. 3.5 mm yr^{-1} during the Viking Age (Fig. 12.10a). For the last 800 years the average rate of sea-level change has been 3.0 mm yr^{-1} (Fig. 12.10b), and this value agrees with those reported for the last 100 years by Sørensen et al. (1987; 3.0 mm yr^{-1}). The more recently modelled and slightly lower rate of relative sea-level change for this region (Olesen et al. 2000; 2.0 mm yr^{-1}) most likely reflects the global rise in sea-level during the last 10 years (www.grida.no/climate/ipcc_tar/wg1/424.htm).

The sea-level investigation method we have ap-

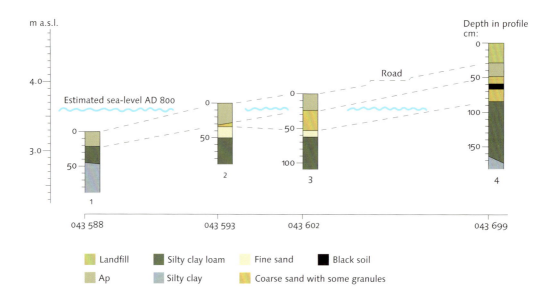

| Landfill | Silty clay loam | Fine sand | Black soil |
| Ap | Silty clay | Coarse sand with some granules |

plied (pollen and diatom analysis and radiocarbon dating of isolation sediments) register the *mean high (MHW)* or *mean spring high tide (MHWS)* levels (Stabell 1982; Behre 2002) – in this case 11 and 14 cm, respectively, above mean sea-level, which again is 50 cm above 'Chart Datum' for this region (Sjøkartverket 2000). A new calibration of the radiocarbon dates for the curve mentioned was carried out by Steinar Gulliksen, Trondheim Radiocarbon Laboratory, using OxCal v. 3.8 (Stuiver et al. 1998; Bronk Ramsey 1995, 2001).

Several factors contribute to uncertainties in sea-level curves (Figs. 12.10a and 12.10b). The standard deviation in the radiocarbon datings varies between ± 30 and ± 230 (Tab. 12.2). Some of the analysed basins lie in areas with thick marine sediments (Olsen and Løwe 1984), and a postglacial compaction of the clays is estimated to 0.4 m for the Båsmyr area (Rosenqvist 1958). The Tjønna-Vittersø lake (Tab. 12.2) lies in a similar environment, and even larger values of postglacial compaction can be expected.

At the nearest tidal gauge, Helgeroa (some 15 km to the west, in a fjord system similar to the Kaupangkilen bay) the highest astronomical tide (HAT) is 30 cm above mean sea-level (MSL). Measured tide levels at Helgeroa for the last 75 years (http://vann-stand.statkart.no/) show that extreme spring tides (meteorological factors included) of c. 90 cm above MSL occur once a year, and spring tides of + 50 cm over MSL are measured regularly each year. The extreme high tides occur mainly in late autumn and winter. We assume that the tidal variation was fairly similar during the Viking Age. An estimate of these uncertainties is indicated in the sea-level curves (Figs. 12.10a and 12.10b).

To get a better overview of the sea-level changes during the last 1,500 years a detailed sea-level curve has been drawn (Fig. 12.10b). For the last c. 800 years the curve is based on one location, Refsholttjern tarn

(Fig. 12.2). The radiocarbon dating of this site is the most precise of all the sites presented in Fig. 12.10a (Tab. 12.2). The isolation of the lake from the sea is well documented by both pollen and diatom analysis. The basin threshold is sheltered from wave action, but formed of sandy sediments, and we assume a threshold erosion of c. 20 cm after isolation.

The radiocarbon dating of the isolation level (cf. Hafsten 1959; Kjemperud 1981) in these lake sediments gives an average rate of sea-level change of 3.0 mm yr^{-1} (model A in Fig. 12.10b) for the last 800 years. The rate is identical with that reported for the last hundred years by Sørensen et al. (1987).

The next part of the curve (model B in Fig. 12.10b) is based on the average rate of sea-level change between AD 800 and 900, calculated from Fig. 12.10a to be 3.5 mm yr^{-1} (red lines in Fig. 12.10b). Although most of the radiocarbon dates forming the basis for Fig. 12.10a have large standard deviations (cf. Tab. 12.2) there is a change in the relative sea-level regime between the birth of Christ and the Viking Age. The older part of the curve is almost linear, whereas the younger part is slightly curved and gives reduced rates of relative sea-level change. Exactly when the change in the relative sea-level regime occurs cannot be determined from our data, but a change from 3.5 to 3.0 mm yr^{-1} between AD 800 and 1250 seems reasonable to us.

12.4.1 Sea-level AD 800

Model A has been linearly extrapolated from the Refsholttjern tarn date backwards to AD 800. This gives a mean high (MHW) sea-level of 3.6 ± 0.2 m. By applying model B where the red line has been linearly extrapolated from the Refsholttjern tarn date backwards to about AD 500, the mean high sea-level becomes 3.8 ± 0.2 m. The uncertainty (± 0.2 m) in both models includes one standard deviation in the radiocarbon date of the isolation of Refsholttjern

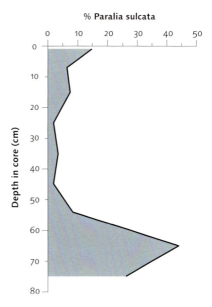

% Paralia sulcata

Figure 12.11 *Terrain profile 3. Detailed description of sediment stratigraphy in four pits. The two uppermost ones are also analysed by archaeologists (Tonning 2001). Location on Fig. 12.3. Illustration, Jørgen Sparre.*

Figure 12.12 *Distribution of the diatom Paralia sulcata in the Kaupangkilen bay sediments, expressed as a percentage of all diatoms in each sample. Location on Fig. 12.3. Illustration, Jørgen Sparre.*

tarn, and the normal tidal variation. The mean sea-level (MSL) will be c. 10 cm lower than the numbers given above. In the discussion which follows we will use an average value adjusted to MSL 3.6 ± 0.2 m as the sea-level AD 800.

To test the validity of our sea-level determination, we investigated a transect just south of the farm Nordre Kaupang (Fig. 12.3) which was located on a line that would have traversed the assumed Viking-age sea-level (Fig. 12.10b). Four pits were dug and the sediments were sampled and described in detail (Sørensen 2002). In the two uppermost pits archaeological investigations were carried out (Tonning 2001). In Pit. 1 the ploughsoil (**Ap**) rested directly on silty clay loam. Pit. 2 had a thin wedge of dark stratified deposits between the ploughsoil and the underlying 10 cm thick layer of fine sand (near-shore sediments). Pit. 3 and the two lowermost ones contained beach sediments with maximum grain size in the pebble fraction (< 3.5 cm in diameter). This indicates a moderate energy level of the wave action, and we assume that this represents the ordinary high tide wave zone.

In Pit. 3, which has a land surface 3.84 m above present sea-level, the c. 30 cm of beach sediments contained much wave-washed burnt bone. In the highest situated pit (no. 4) the top of the ploughsoil is 4.26 m above present sea-level. The underlying c. 20 cm of beach sediments contained large amounts of washed burnt and unburnt bone, many fire-cracked stones, as well as two fragments of Badorf pottery, connecting the layer to the time of the Kaupang settlement. The beach deposits situated at 4.05m above present sea-level and lower in the section did not contain artefacts (Tonning 2001).

In Fig. 12.11 the sea-level at AD 800 (3.6 m) is drawn, and the top of the beach sediments (below 25 cm of **Ap**) in Pit. 3 coincide with this level. The top of the beach sediment (cultural deposit) in Pit. 4 lies

only 50 cm above this level. The ploughsoil is very dark and we assume that this is due to erosion of cultural deposits on higher grounds during the settlement time and also due to cultivation of the fields in historical times. The land surface might therefore have been slightly lower (c. 10 cm) during settlement time.

The sediment studies along profile 3 confirm therefore that the sea-level at AD 800 was approximately 3.6 m above present sea-level. The reworked cultural deposits in Pit. 4 may reflect the wave action of an ordinary storm or one of the monthly occurring spring tides (http://vannstand.statkart.no/).

12.4.2 The development of the Kaupang harbour

When the settlement was in use, the inner part of the Kaupangkilen bay was a sheltered harbour, with good protection from northerly and north-westerly winds, but the fjord system was open to wind and storms from the SW. However, the south-westerly storms occur mainly during late autumn and winter. These are often accompanied by extreme high tides (http://vannstand.statkart.no/). The form of the harbour and its orientation would favour extra high spring tides, because the south-westerly wind would push water into the embayment. This happens regularly also in recent times.

The sediment core taken in the present-day bay showed marked changes in the sediments at a depth of c. 63 cm. An increase in LOI, water content, and darker mud, occurred between 63 and 35 cm. Pollen (see above) and diatom analyses were also carried out on these sediments. No full diatom analysis was undertaken, but the number of the diatom *Paralia sulcata* was counted against the number of "other" diatoms. The total number of diatoms counted in each sample varied between 204 and 358. The diatoms grouped as "others" are mainly benthic marine, but planktonic marine diatoms are also present.

Paralia sulcata is considered to be thycoplanktonic (it survives in the water column but derives from elsewhere) due to the fact that it is primarily characterized as a benthic species (Round et al. 1990; Hasle and Syvertsen 1996), but is also found in large numbers in the plankton. It is also considered to prefer a minimum water depth of 1 m and fine-grained and organic-rich sediment (Zong 1997). The percentage distribution of *Paralia sulcata* in Kaupangkilen bay core (Fig. 12.12) shows high percentages (> 25%) in the bottom (75–65 cm) samples, while the samples above vary between 15 and 2 %. The samples with high percentages of *Paralia sulcata* coincide with low water content in the sediment, low loss on ignition (and slightly higher contents of coarse material than above).

The seaway through Holkekilen was closed due to the post-glacial sea-level regression (see Fig. 12.2) at about AD 750 (Fig. 12.10b). We believe that the marked change in the diatom flora (i.e. percentage of *Paralia sulcata)* was caused by a change in the circulation pattern of the larger fjord system, i.e. the closing of the Holkekilen strait. The change in the diatom flora occurs between 65 and 55 cm, and this may indicate that the closing of the strait took place around the time of abandonment of the settlement, estimated from pollen analysis to occur at around 63 cm in the core (see above, and Fig. 12.9b). The critical height in the Holkekilen strait (measured to 4 m a.s.l.) may be slightly higher today than it was in AD 800, due to sediment build-up on the bottom of the narrow valley by erosion from the steep sides after the Viking Age.

12.5 Discussion and Conclusions

12.5.1 Landscape development

The palaeo-maps in Figs. 12.1 and 12.2 show the enormous landscape changes that occurred from c. 5000 BC to AD 500. Up to around 200 BC two passages formed an inland seaway between Kaupang and Sandefjord, and further north towards Tønsberg. At that time the first passage, the Klåstad strait (with a critical height at c. 8 m above present sea-level; Fig. 12.2; Kl) was closed. The Holkekilen strait (Fig. 12.2; H) was probably open for smaller boats up to c. AD 750, but boats could easily be hauled a short distance over land for another 100 years. The closing of the eastern end of Viksfjord changed the marine circulation, and the fjord became a brackish estuary.

The higher lying areas where the settlement was established emerged from the sea at the transition between the Bronze Age and Iron Age. At approximately AD 750 the sea-level was c. 4 m above its present level (Fig. 12.10b). Even before that time the Kaupangkilen bay was a sheltered harbour (Fig. 12.2).

The local passage between the mainland and Lamøya (Fig. 12.3) closed at around AD 1300 and the present-day Kaupangkilen bay was then formed.

12.5.2 Soils and sediments

The higher lying part of the Kaupang settlement was established on an area of land that had been above sea-level for several hundred years and vegetation was well-established, which is indicated in the pollen diagram Fig. 12.9b. But there had not been enough time for any clear soil-profile development. Even today the soils outside the settlement area are classified as weakly developed soils, i.e. Cambisols (e.g. **KSr:** Fig. 12.6 and Tab. 12.1). Weak soil formation can also be observed in the lower part of the settlement area, in the clay below the cultural deposits in profile 2a (Fig. 12.5), and below the investigated midden (cf. Milek and French, this vol. Ch. 15:252–4).

Before clearance, the land probably had many large stones and blocks on the surface due to a short halt in the movement of the ice front during deglaciation. During the 2000-2002 excavation a considerable number of such blocks were uncovered, most of which were probably lodged in the sediment during deglaciation.

Both the 1956–74 and the 2000-2002 excavations have been made in gravelly beach sands, which have a current thicknesses of up to 50 cm, below cultural deposits (Fig. 12.5). The dark-coloured cultural deposits are a mixture of gravelly beach sands and anthropogenic soil material, and are mostly classified as Umbrisol (Fig. 12.6; Tab. 12.1). Silty marine clay below most of these beach sands prevents drainage, and most of the area is characterized by poorly drained subsoils (Tab. 12.1). The area of the 1956–74 excavation just south of the tarmac road must have been a rather wet place during the Viking Age because this depression collects drainage water from a fairly large sediment-covered area up-slope. The 2000-2002 excavation area is also located on beach sand over marine silty clay, but the actual moisture conditions are (and most probably were) better. Between the 1956–74 and the 2000-2002 excavation there is an area with clay soil on the surface (**KSr 7;** Fig. 12.6), and similar soils occur further to the west.

Surface erosion in the settlement area, amounting to about 20 cm (Bukholm 2001), has occurred since the settlement was established. At least 50% of this has occurred since the abandonment of the settlement. A marked bench with thick anthropogenic soil material in the lower part of the present-day fields confirms considerable soil movement on these slopes. Erosion from the settlement areas is also reflected in soil profiles below the Viking-age sea-level (Fig. 12.4b) as well as in the bay sediments.

Some postglacial compaction in areas underlain by clay can be expected (cf. Rosenqvist 1958), but because the total thickness of sediments over bedrock is moderate (generally <5 m) the compaction is estimated to be less than 10 cm in the settlement area.

The pollen diagrams from the bay (Fig. 12.9) show a marked increase in charcoal for about the last 500 years. This reflects the most recent phase of agriculture, when there were more open fields, and the very light charcoal and ash material was washed into the shallow bay. However, both the soil profile III (Bukholm 2001) and the profile in Fig. 12.7b show a phase with deposition of marine mud (lighter coloured silty sediments) on top of the anthropogeogenic material, but below the modern plough-layer. These observations are not contradictory, because a short phase of reforestation is recorded in the pollen analysis of the bay sediments (first half of zone **Kk 3**; Fig. 12.9b). The settlement was most likely overgrown some time after abandonment (AD 1050–1250: Fig. 12.9b), i.e. for a period of c. 200 years, and this might have resulted in a brief period with less erosion to the lower slopes and the embayment. In addition the bay became more sheltered from wave action as the sea retreated. The latter half of zone **Kk 3** shows a new phase of deforestation, and the first appearance of cerealia (Fig. 12.9b). The youngest phase of erosion is expressed in the dark-coloured modern ploughsoil on land, and the final phase of charcoal deposition in the bay sediments.

12.5.3 Vegetation history

The Kaupangmyra bog site gives reliable information on the regional vegetation development, particularly for the last 2,600 years (Fig. 12.8) where the terrestrial peat layers are well dated. The radiocarbon datings seem to be reliable in spite of the prolonged storage of the samples. The establishment of *Picea* in the area was previously found to have taken place at about AD 830 (cf. above, p. 263). The present datings (Tab. 12.2) agree well with this.

The start of the peat-producing phase in the Kaupangmyra bog appears at about 600 BC, and this agrees well with the climatic deterioration around the Sub-Boreal–Sub-Atlantic transition. The local plant succession around the site seems clear. The oldest, rather oxidized peat shows an *Alnus* carr with ferns dominating in the field layer. The decrease in both taxa may partly be due to natural succession, but probably also to some forest clearance, in view of the increase in cereals, weeds, grasses and other herbs. Sedges and some *Myrica* probably grew in the wettest parts: cf. the decreasing oxidation in the peat (indicated by the corrosion curve). As human influence (agricultural activity) decreased and the climate became more humid, wetness increased at the site and oxidation/pollen corrosion decreased. This is shown by a dominance of *Myrica* in the field layer, followed by a dominance of Ericales with some *Sphagnum* in the dryer and oxidized upper peat, where the pollen assemblage indicates the re-establishment of agriculture around the bog. The pollen diagram (Fig. 12.8) therefore indicates that there has been agricultural activity near the bog from at least c. 600 BC to about AD 800. From AD 800 to 1500, including the time of the Kaupang settlement and the Black Death event, there were few, if any, agricultural activities near the bog, but some of the forest trees were evidently utilized. From about AD 1500 agricultural activity has increased, and at present the whole bog is cultivated.

Soils favourable for early agriculture near the Kaupangmyra bog occur on the northern foot-slopes of both Kaupangåsen and Kuleåsen hills and in the depression between these hills. This depression is less than 500 m from the settlement area.

Although the dating of the Kaupangkilen bay section is uncertain, we offer a concentration diagram (Fig. 12.9b) and believe that this shows a fairly realistic picture of land use around the bay from approximately AD 500 to the present. We assume that the forest clearing took place before the settlement was established, and that zone **Kk 2** represents the period of activity at Kaupang. Some of the better drained areas might have been cultivated, but more likely were used as partly cleared pastures, prior to the establishment of the settlement.

After the abandonment of the settlement, new forest was established fairly rapidly and remained for approximately 200 years. The final clearing of land started c. AD 1150, but was most likely intensified after The Plague (AD 1349–50) (which is not shown in the pollen distribution). The charcoal curve and the low but continuous cerealia curve (Fig. 12.9a or 12.9b) indicate continuous agricultural activities around the bay for the last 400–500 years.

It is possible to relate the erosion history to the different phases of deforestation, re-forestation, and urban and agricultural activities at and around the settlement. However, the uncertainty in the dating of the events described above is at least ± 100 years.

12.5.4 Sea-level change

The sea-level curve (Fig. 12.10a) shows that the Kaupangmyra bog was isolated from the sea about 2300 BC. During the Viking Age the rate of sea-level change was about 3.5 mm per year (Fig. 12.10b), and this implies that the mean sea-level (MSL) changed from c. 3.6 m at AD 800 to c. 3.2 m above present sea-level by AD 900. We assume an uncertainty of approximately ± 20 cm for these numbers, and this includes ordinary tidal variations. We have registered wave-washed sediments containing artefacts of the Viking Age up to 4.2 m above present sea-level, i.e. 60 cm above MSL at AD 800. This may reflect wave action of an ordinary storm or one of the monthly spring tides. Small tidal variations are currently measured for the spring and summer months (Sjøkartverket 2003), and we assume that such variations also occurred during the Viking Age. At present, extreme spring tides of 140 cm above MSL occur statistically every 20 years, and c. 90 cm above MSL every year, but only in the late autumn and winter months (Sjøkartverket 2003). Assuming similar conditions during the Viking Age, such extreme events must have had some impact on the harbour structures and the lower parts of the settlement.

Acknowledgements

Most of the fieldwork has been financed by the Kaupang Excavation Project. Helge Lundekvam has calculated soil erosion over the settlement area. Figs. 12.2 and 12.10a have been drawn and digitised by Åslaug Borgan and Berit Hopland. We are very grateful to the persons and institutions mentioned.

Dendrochronological Dates from Kaupang

13

NIELS BONDE

In Norway, tree-ring analyses aimed at constructing long reference chronologies, which can be used to date wood samples from archaeological excavations, have primarily focussed on Norway spruce *(Picea abies* [L.] Karsten) and Scots pine *(Pinus sylvestris* L.). Unfortunately, the reference curves for southern Norway do not cover the period we term the Viking Age. Dendrochronological investigations of living oak trees from southern Norway have, however, shown that it is possible to date samples of oak with the aid of the large reference curves for oak that have been constructed in Sweden and Denmark. These curves do cover the Viking Age. The dendrochronological analyses from Kaupang relate to three campaigns of archaeological excavation: 1967, 1970 and 2000–02. The material is composed entirely of timber found preserved in waterlogged deposits, such as in the harbour and in pits. The analysis of 45 samples of oak *(Quercus* sp.) shows that the samples originate from trees which were felled between AD 800 and AD 870. In all, 41 samples were dated and a site chronology of 345 years has been produced, covering the period from AD 518–862.

13.1 Introduction

In recent decades dendrochronology has become one of the most important scientific dating methods for archaeology in northern Europe. It is independent of all other dating methods, historical, archaeological and scientific, such as radiocarbon dating, and it offers the historian and the archaeologist the answer to one of the most important questions relating to the investigation of an archaeological find: How old is it? And the result is often of such a quality that existing theories must be discredited if they conflict with the date obtained.

In order to carry out dendrochronological dating investigations of timber found in an archaeological context, it is a pre-condition that a well-founded master chronology of the specific species has been constructed for the area from which the samples originate. In northern Europe oak is the preferred wood species for dendrochronological investigations. Several large master chronologies for oak have been constructed for southern Sweden that are suitable for dating material from the Viking Age. For south-western Sweden – Västergötland – a master chronology has been produced for oak covering the period AD 753–1975 (Bråthen 1982), and further south in Sweden several master chronologies have been constructed

for Skåne/Blekinge covering the period from AD 578 to the present (Bartholin 1993). In Denmark, similarly, several large chronologies have been produced for oak that cover the period from around the birth of Christ up to the present day. The curve for western Denmark thus covers the period from 109 BC to the present, while the curves for eastern Denmark go back to the beginning of the 5th century AD.

In Norway, by contrast, Norway spruce and Scots pine were until recently the two tree species on which most tree-ring research had been carried out (Høeg 1956; Kirchhefer 1999; Thun 2002, 2005). Sharpening the contrast, no master chronologies that cover the Viking Age have been constructed with these species for central and southern Scandinavia (Bartholin, pers. comm.; Thun 2002).

The reason for this discrepancy can be found in the history of the use of oak in southern Norway. In prehistory and medieval times oak was one of the dominant trees in the coastal woodlands of southern Norway (Fig. 13.1). The quantity of structural timber found during the archaeological investigations at Kaupang shows oak to have been the preferred species, which is not surprising considering its hardness, solidity, strength, elasticity and durability: oak is by far the best raw material provided by nature for a

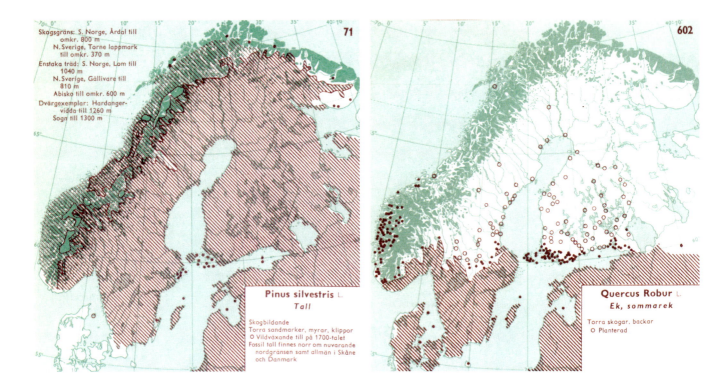

71

Skogsgräns: S. Norge, Årdal till
    omkr. 800 m
N. Sverige, Torne lappmark
    till omkr. 370 m
Enstaka träd: S. Norge, Lom till
    1040 m
N. Sverige, Gällivare till
    810 m
Abisko till omkr. 600 m
Dvärgexemplar: Hardanger-
    vidda till 1260 m
Sogn till 1300 m

Pinus silvestris L.
Tall

Skogbildande
Torra sandmarker, myrar, klippor
O Vildväxande till på 1700-talet
Fossil tall finnes norr om nuvarande
    nordgränsen samt allmän i Skåne
    och Danmark

602

Quercus Robur L.
Ek, sommarek

Torra skogar, backar
O Planterad

wide variety of purposes. However, severe over-exploitation – especially in the 17th century – virtually exterminated Norwegian oak. Consequently, up until now, it has not been possible to construct a continuous master chronology for oak from southern Norway because the majority of the oak trees that now grow in the area germinated in the first half of the 18th century, and also because it is very rare to find oak timber preserved in great quantity in old Norwegian buildings or any huge structure like waterfront constructions (e.g. timber revetments), or bridges and road constructions and the like.

A solution to this problem appeared in 1991, when, in a paper given at a seminar at The Norwegian Academy of Science and Letters in Oslo, Kjeld Christensen (1993:57) concluded that:

The investigations have shown that modern oak chronologies from Norway, northern Jutland and western Sweden contain a rather strong common growth signal …[and] … it will be possible to date well-replicated oak chronologies from the whole area of natural oak growth in Norway, as well as many curves for single Norwegian oak trees, correctly and securely by synchronization with existing oak chronologies for northern Jutland and western Sweden.

On the basis of Christensen's findings, the finds from Tune, Gokstad and Oseberg were investigated at the beginning of the 1990s with the aim of dendrochronological dating. These finds originate from the area around Oslofjord. From investigations of samples taken from timber in the burial chambers at the three sites, a curve was constructed for the

Oslofjord area covering the period AD 537–891, a total of 355 years. This curve was subsequently used to date the ships from the three sites (Bonde 1997).

A dendrochronological study can give information on when the annual rings in a tree were formed as well as when the tree was felled. The possibility of arriving at a precise determination of the felling date for samples originating from oak trees is dependent upon there being bark or sapwood preserved on the sample. The sapwood lies just beneath the bark and comprises the outer layers of xylem, which, in the growing tree, contain living parenchymatic cells with stored food reserves (the tree's most recently formed annual rings). It is later transformed into heartwood when all the physiological functions in the sapwood cease (Kaennel and Schweingruber 1995). In timber from an oak tree – which is a ring-porous wood species – sapwood is easy to detect because the large spring vessels in the tree rings (Fig. 13.2) are not filled with tyloses, causing the vessels to stand out as "open holes". There is also a distinct colour difference between heartwood (dark) and sapwood (light). Under normal conditions both of these indicators (vessels and colour) can be seen with the naked eye. If bark or sapwood is preserved on the sample, the date can be determined with remarkable precision, in ideal cases to within a few months as, for example, in the dendrochronological investigations of the burial chamber in the Oseberg ship. Here it has been possible, in collaboration with archaeobotanists, to establish that the burial took place in August or September AD 834 (Bonde and Christensen 1993) as several dendrosamples taken from the burial chamber have the

Figure 13.1 a+b *Natural distribution of Scots pine* (Pinus sylvestris L.) *and oak* (Quercus *sp.*). *Hultén 1971.*

Figure 13.2 *Cross-section of oak* (Quercus *sp.*) *tree rings.* Photo, National Museum of Denmark.

waney edge preserved. The waney edge is "the curved cambial surface exposed by removing the bark, i.e. the last-formed tree ring before felling, sampling, or death of the cambium. In dendrochronology, its presence implies that the sample is complete to the last year of growth" (Kaennel and Schweingruber 1995).

If we have the date for when the trees that provided timber for a structure were felled, we have, as a rule, also a date for the structure's construction. In the past – namely, prior to industrialisation – timber was not stored and seasoned for any appreciable time as it was normally worked and used "green", which is when it is easiest to work using hand tools – axes, wedges etc. (Hollstein 1980:35–37). If there was any storage/seasoning time at all, it would only be the time it took to transport the wood from place of felling to place of use. This means that if the felling date can be established, the date of utilisation is normally the same. In this way it is possible to date a structure, house, bridge, well etc. However, account must of course be taken of later repairs and the possible re-utilisation of timber. Therefore, as many samples as possible are normally taken. If there are many samples available from the same structure, and the dendrochronological studies show that they originate from trees that were felled in the same year, there is a great probability that the trees were felled *ad hoc* and used immediately. Similarly, it will be possible to judge whether timber has been re-utilised, whether repairs have been carried out, and to identify building phases, and so on.

When it is decided to carry out a dendrochronological investigation on material from an archaeological excavation there are two decisive factors that must be taken into account. Firstly, the choice of *wood species* for investigation: is there a master chronology for the species of wood to be investigated? Secondly, does this chronology cover the period from which the archaeological find originates?

Obviously, it is not possible to date wooden artefacts or timber from the Viking Age if the master chronology does not cover this period.

Consequently, only oak was included in the study concerning the archaeological investigations at Kaupang. Fortunately there was sufficient material to allow many samples to be taken for analysis. Forty-five samples of oak *(Quercus* sp.) were obtained from the excavation. In addition, six samples of Scots pine *(Pinus sylvestris* L.), three of ash *(Fraxinus excelsior* L.), two of beech *(Fagus sylvatica* L.) and finally, one of poplar *(Populus* sp.) were sampled. As no chronologies have been constructed for ash, beech and poplar extending back to the Viking Age in southern Scandinavia, the samples from these species are not dated.

All the samples were taken as cross-sections by sawing through the timber pieces. All samples were processed in the dendrochronological laboratory in

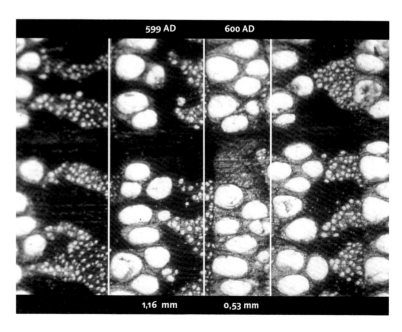

the Environmental Archaeology Unit at the National Museum of Denmark (Fig. 13.3), after which they were returned to the University of Oslo. There are those who consider it too brutal an action to saw through old timber in this way. From an antiquarian point of view it is certainly necessary to weigh up each investigation very carefully in order to ascertain whether such an operation is justifiable in relation to the information that will be forthcoming from a dendrochronological study. There is, however, no doubt that a cross-section gives the best sample. It ensures that the material does not disintegrate and produces individual samples containing the maximum number of tree rings and with any sapwood intact.

The samples of oak are from three excavation campaigns: 1967 (12 samples), 1970 (5 samples) and 2000–02 (28 samples). In choosing the samples, purely dendrochronological criteria were employed: 1) Does the sample contain an adequate number of annual rings for a dendrochronological investigation? 2) Is there sapwood or possibly bark preserved on the sample?

13.2 Samples taken from timber found during the excavations in 1967

Eleven samples out of twelve have been dated. Seven of the samples have sapwood preserved, of which four have the waney edge. One of the samples, with sapwood and waney edge, has only 16 tree rings and is not dated. The majority of the samples originate from material which can be ascribed to a construction (a jetty?) in the area "Hus I" ("House I") (Tollnes 1998:64–80; Pilø this vol. Ch. 8:175, Fig. 8.20). The three dated samples with the waney edge preserved are from posts hammered into the ground. The investigation shows that they all come from trees felled in the summer of AD 803. A total of eight samples can be assigned to this particular date (see Fig. 13.6).

A further sample comes from a tree for which the

felling date can be estimated to lie between AD 808 and AD 814. This sample can possibly be assigned to a "pit" in the area around "Hus I". There is, however, some doubt as to whether the timber from which it is taken is securely identified.

The last two samples originate from fill in "Grop B" ("Pit B"). One of these has sapwood preserved and originates from a tree estimated to have been felled between AD 794 and AD 807. The other sample originates from a tree which has an estimated felling date of *after* AD 809. The tree-ring curves for the two samples do *not* cross-date. In general in this investigation, the term "does not cross-date" means that the *t*-value, which denotes the degree of cross-dating (synchronisation) between the curves, is *below* 3.50. The two samples do, however, cross-date with the Oslofjord chronology *(t=4.80* and *t=6.82)* and with some of the individual tree-ring curves, as well as with the chronologies based on samples from the individual constructions (wells, pits, etc.) produced in the course of the Kaupang investigation (for *t*-value see Baillie and Pilcher 1973). This means that the two trees from which the samples originate do belong to the greater area around Oslofjord and that it is justified to use the curves from them in the making of *a master site chronology that can be used for dating purposes in the future.* Since both pieces were found as fill in the pit "Grop B", the felling date for the two trees does not date the filling up of the pit, but relates to other and earlier activities.

13.3 Samples taken from timber found during the excavations in 1970

Four of the five samples have been dated (see also Fig. 13.6), of which three have sapwood preserved. All five samples come from timber found in a pit called "Brønn 4" ("Well 4") (Tollnes 1998:90–2; Pilø, this vol. Ch. 10:218:20). The function of the pit is unknown.

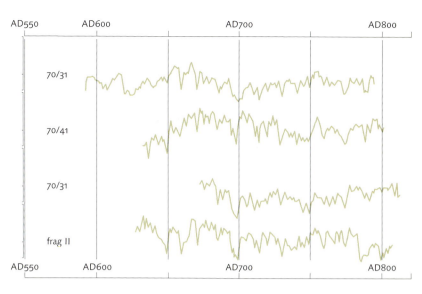

AD550	AD600		AD700		AD800

70/31

70/41

70/31

frag II

AD550	AD600		AD700		AD800

Figure 13.3 *Measuring a sample. The sample is mounted on a travelling stage and the tree-ring widths are entered directly into a computer. Photo, National Museum of Denmark.*

Figure 13.4 *Tree-ring measurements plotted as a function of time. The measurements are from four samples taken as cross-sections from timbers found in a well ("Brønn 4") during the 1970 excavations. The curves show a high degree of similarity. Graphics: Claudia Baittinger, revised by Jørgen Sparre.*

The tree-ring curves (Fig. 13.4) from the four dated samples cross-date with high *t*-values (min. 7.27, max. 9.61) (Baillie and Pilcher 1973), indicating that the timber from which the samples originate "belongs together". An examination of the investigated timber shows, furthermore, that it represents structural timber with no visible traces of working to indicate previous use. Given the very short period within which the trees from which the samples originate were felled, the study shows that the construction of *"Brønn 4"* can be dated to about AD 814.

In Tollnes's description of the find it is observed that "Several of the planks show signs of having been used in other circumstances and have clearly found secondary use in the well" ("Flere av plankerne har spor av bruk i annen sammenheng, og har tydeligvis fått sekundær anvendelse i brønnen"). Four figures are also presented (Tollnes 1998:fig. 4:5) which show five pieces of timber found in the well. It is clear from these illustrations that all the pieces of timber show signs of having been used for something other than "normal" well timbers. This also applies to the plank which is described as "the immediately most interesting plank from Well 4" ("den umiddelbart mest interessante planken fra Brønn 4") where a circular hole in the plank is interpreted as a possible window (Tollnes 1998:fig. 6:6). None of the pieces of timber illustrated has, however, been studied as part of the present dendrochronological investigation.

13.4 Samples taken from timber found during the excavations in 2000–02

Of the 28 samples, 26 have been dated. The samples were taken primarily from timber belonging to six structures, first and foremost pits, where the water-logged conditions have had a preservative effect on the wood.

Pit *"A10135: Laftet trekasse"* ("Logbox"), is probably a well. Six samples were investigated, and all were dated. Four samples have sapwood preserved, of which one sample (A15835 with 16 sapwood rings) comes from a tree with an estimated felling date of AD 804–808. The other three samples all have a number of sapwood rings preserved which lies above the upper limit given in the sapwood statistics – min. 7 and max. 21 sapwood rings (Christensen and Havemann 1992) – used in this investigation. In the case of two of the samples (A13719 with 22 sapwood rings and A14257 with 32 sapwood rings) the latest annual ring in each sample was formed in AD 805, but it is not possible to determine whether this represents the waney edge. In the third sample (A15847 with 25 sapwood rings), it can be established that the waney edge is present, and that it was formed in AD 808. It was also possible to ascertain that the last-formed tree ring is not fully formed. This means that the tree from which the sample originates was felled during the growing season, i.e. May–September AD 808. On the basis of the dendrochronological investigations it can be concluded that the construction of *"A10135: Laftet trekasse"*, can be dated to the summer of AD 808.

The reason that such a definite conclusion can be drawn is because the investigation shows that the tree-ring curves (see Fig. 13.5) from three of the samples (A14639, A15835 and A15847) cross-date perfectly with very high *t*-values (min. 15.10 and max. 17.40) (Baillie and Pilcher 1973). This means that they originate from one and the same tree, felled in AD 808, and that the pieces of timber from which they originate must have been split from the trunk and used immediately in a working process that happened within a very short time span: the felling of the tree, the cleaving of the trunk, the shaping of the timber and the assembly of the well casing. If there had been re-use of timber it is very probable that the pieces of timber would have been "mixed up" with timber from other structures. The result of the dendrochronological research would then show a much

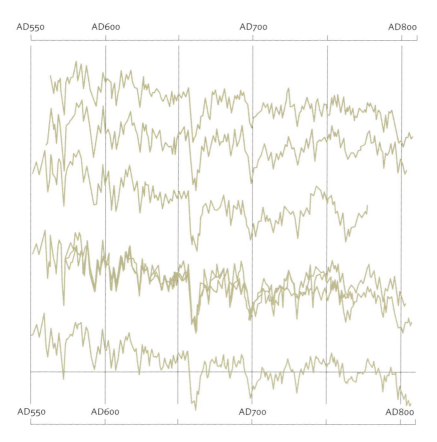

greater scatter in the felling dates for the trees from which the samples originate. The tree-ring curves for the two other samples (A13719 and A14257), which also come from trees that were felled around AD 808, also cross-date well with the samples A14639, A15835 and A15847. All five pieces of timber from which the samples are taken are described as "solid board placed on edge" ("Solid kanstilt bord", note by Unn Pedersen 2000) and the research demonstrate that they all come from trees that most likely were felled in the same year. Furthermore the similarities between the tree-ring curves indicate that the samples originate from trees that grew in the same woodland. Experience gained from hundreds of investigations indicates that if there is great coincidence between the tree-ring curves and if the felling dates are more-or-less the same, then the felling dates for the trees from which the investigated samples originate also give the date for the construction of the structure under investigation.

It should be noted that the tree-ring curve for sample A14376, which Unn Pedersen terms "narrow trimmed board" ("Smalt tilhugget bord"), does not cross-date with the tree-ring curves from the other samples from this structure but fits in perfectly with the rest of the material from Kaupang and the Oslofjord chronology. From a dendrochronological point of view the sample clearly belongs in another context, which *could* mean that it originates from a piece of timber from a fill layer or from a piece of re-utilised timber originating from a tree felled 15–20 years be-

fore the well was constructed (earliest at the beginning of the AD 780s).

The dates for the samples taken from timber pieces A13719, A14257, A14639, A15835 and A15847 give, therefore, the construction date for the well, whereas the piece of timber numbered A14376 *could* have been re-used.

Included in the well-construction are several large pieces of timber that quite clearly show traces of working, revealing that these had been used previously for another purpose. *None* of these pieces of timber was, however, investigated as part of this dendrochronological study, as in the selection of samples emphasis was placed on choosing samples *which would give a date for the construction of the well casing,* not dates from re-utilised timber which must originally have belonged in another context.

Pit *"A13561"*. Two samples (P9/1? and P9/6) were investigated, and both were dated. Sapwood is not preserved on either sample. The tree-ring curves for the two samples cross-date. The felling dates for the trees from which the samples originate are estimated to *after* AD 779 (P9/6) and *after* AD 813 (P9/1?).

Pit *"A15175"*. Thirteen samples were investigated, of which 12 have been dated, and all tree-ring curves from the 12 samples cross-date. The circumstances for the excavation of this structure were very complicated and literally made it impossible to differentiate between structural timber (well) and timber pieces belonging to the fill of the well. On the other hand, the tree-ring investigation does not reveal any differ-

Figure 13.5 *Tree-ring measurements plotted as a function of time. The measurements are from three samples – A14639, A15835 and A15847 – taken as cross-sections from timbers found in a well (A10135) during the excavations in 2000. The curves show such a high degree of similarity that it is very likely that the three samples derive from the same tree. Upper: the three individual measurements. Middle: the three measurements superimposed. Bottom: the result averaging the three measurements to produce a curve representing one tree. Graphics: Claudia Baittinger, revised by Jørgen Sparre.*

Figure 13.5 *Tree-ring measurements plotted as a function of time. The measurements are from three samples – A14639, A15835 and A15847 – taken as cross-sections from timbers found in a well (A10135) during the excavations in 2000. The curves show such a high degree of similarity that it is very likely that the three samples derive from the same tree. Upper: the three individual measurements. Middle: the three measurements superimposed. Bottom: the result averaging the three measurements to produce a curve representing one tree. Graphics: Claudia Baittinger, revised by Jørgen Sparre.*

Figure 13.6 *Bar diagram of dated samples from excavations at Kaupang in 1967, 1970 and 2000, showing the number of tree rings per sample. Illustration, Niels Bonde, revised by Jørgen Sparre.*

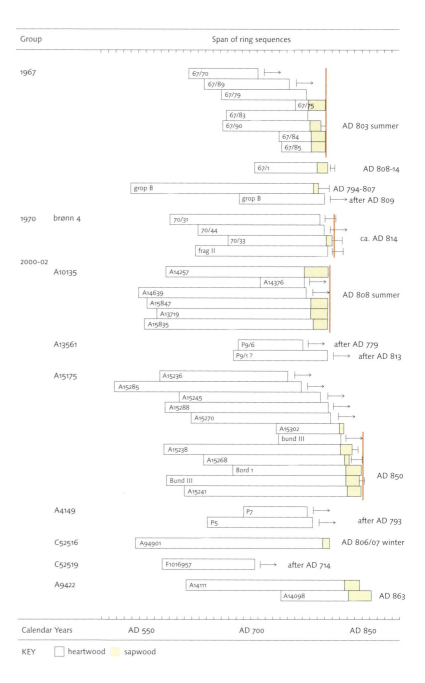

ences in the samples examined with respect to origin and time. On the contrary, the synchronisation values (*t*-values) that were obtained in the cross-dating of the tree-ring curves from the samples within this structure, clearly show that this material can be termed homogeneous, which could indicate that all the samples originate from one and the same structure. A clear distinction between structural timber and timber in the fill is not possible based on tree ring analysis alone, but six of the samples have preserved sapwood and the estimated felling dates for the trees from which the samples originate all fall within the decade AD 840–850. The interpretation is that the well was constructed in AD 850–51.

Pit *"A4149".* Two samples (P5 and P7) were investigated, and both were dated. Neither of the samples

has sapwood preserved. The tree-ring curves from the two samples do not cross-date. Like the instance with the material from 1967, as well as the sample (A14376) from structure A10135 discussed earlier, the two curves cross-date with the Oslofjord chronology and the chronologies for the individual constructions from the Kaupang site. The felling dates for the trees from which the samples originate are estimated to *after* AD 786 (P7) and *after* AD 793 (P5).

Two samples from the campaigns in 2001 and 2002 – one with waney edge – come from trees that were felled in the winter AD 806–807 and *after* AD 714, respectively.

Pit *"A9422".* Three samples were investigated, of which two have been dated; both have preserved sapwood. The tree-ring curves from the two dated sam-

Master chronologies	Oslo Fjord Norway	Västergötland Sweden	Scania Sweden	Denmark east	Denmark west
Kaupang site chronology	10,59	2,81	2,06	3,38	6,82

Table 13.1 *Results – t-values – of cross-dating the Kaupang site chronology. For t-values see Baillie and Pilcher 1973.*

ples do not cross-date. The two samples were dated in the same way as the three previously mentioned instances (see material from 1967 "Grop B", Pit A10135 sample A14376 and Pit A4149 samples P5 and P7). It can be estimated that the trees from which the dated samples originate were felled in AD 849–850 (A14111) and about AD 863 (A14098 re-utilised timber found as fill in the well).

13.5 Summary of the dates

After thorough analysis the tree-ring curves from all the dated samples have been combined to give an averaged site chronology to be used for dating purposes. It has a length of 345 years and covers the period AD 518–862 (see Tab. 13.3). This curve has been compared with master chronologies for oak from southern Scandinavia and, as is apparent from Tab. 13.1, good synchronization values are obtained with two of the useable references, the Oslofjord curve and the Danish curve for Jutland. The high t-value for the Oslofjord chronology, $t = 10.57$, confirms that the oak timber used at the Kaupang site – not surprisingly – originates from trees that grew in the area around the town. No "exotic" material from Denmark, Sweden, northern Germany, or even England for that matter, has been found.

On the basis of the dating diagram (Fig. 13.6) it can be concluded that in the parts of the Kaupang settlement from which the samples originate there was (great?) building activity in the first half of the 9th century: The wooden jetty in the Hus I area was built in AD 803, and two pits/wells were constructed

in AD 808 *("A10135 – Laftet trekasse")* and about AD 814 *("Brønn 4")*. For the dated material as a whole, the dating of oak from the different structures reveals activity extending up until c. AD 863. The material from the excavations in 1967 and 2000–2002 comes from two distinct parts of the living quarters in the settlement. In the northern part we have the 1967 material and in the southern part the material from 2000–2002 (Skre and Stylegar 2004). The result of the dendrochronological study clearly demonstrates that the building activity in the two parts was more or less contemporary in the first decades of the 9th century.

The results of the dendrochronological research open a narrow "time window" to the activities at the Viking town at Kaupang. It is based on material sampled in the parts of the settlement where there are good conditions for the preservation of organic material, such as in the waterlogged soil close to the waterfront and deep holes such as pits and wells where the fill remains wet and so significantly reduces the rate at which the wood decays. In archaeological excavations on dry land no organic material is preserved except that which is carbonised and, under favourable circumstances, perhaps bone. Here we normally find only inorganic material such as stone, metal, pottery etc.

It should be emphasised that the above conclusions are, with respect to dating, based exclusively on the dendrochronological results and are completely independent of any observations which may have been made in connexion with the excavation itself, or later.

Dendro number	Excavation year	Excavation number	Number of rings	Start year	End year	Sapwood	Felling
n0630019	2000	A15847	245	AD563	AD807	yes	AD808 spring/summer
n0630029	2000	A15835	244	AD560	AD803	yes	AD804-8
n0630039	2000	A14639	227	AD551	AD777	no	after AD785
n0630049	2000	A14376	61	AD714	AD774	no	after AD782
n0630059	2000	A14257	219	AD586	AD804	yes	AD804-8
n0630079	2000	A13719	231	AD574	AD804	yes	AD804-8
n0631039	2000	A14098	121	AD742	AD862	yes	AD863
n0631049	2000	A14107	162			no	Not dated
n0631059	2000	A14111	235	AD614	AD848	yes	AD849-50
n0632019	2000	A15238	254	AD584	AD837	yes	AD838-44
n0632029	2000	A15241	238	AD612	AD849	yes	AD849
n0632039	2000	A15245	192	AD605	AD796	no	after AD804
n0632069	2000	A15253	41			yes	Not dated
n0632079	2000	A15268	197	AD638	AD834	yes	AD835-49
n0632089	2000	A15270	190	AD622	AD811	no	after AD819
n0632099	2000	A15285	253	AD518	AD770	no	after AD778
n0632109	2000	A15288	221	AD586	AD806	no	after AD814
n0632119	2000	A15302	90	AD737	AD826	yes	AD828-42
n0632129	2000	A15175 III	259	AD588	AD846	yes	AD847-52
n0632139	2000	A15175 III bn	83	AD740	AD822	no	after AD830
n0632149	2000	A15175 I	172	AD678	AD849	yes	AD850
n0632159	2000	A15236	175	AD579	AD753	no	after AD761
n0633019	2000	P5	143	AD643	AD785	no	after AD793
n0633029	2000	P7	89	AD690	AD778	no	after AD786
n0634019	2000	P9/1 el 3	129	AD678	AD806	no	after AD813
n0634049	2000	P9/6	89	AD683	AD771	no	after AD779
n0636019	2001	F1016957	126	AD581	AD706	no	after AD714
n0636029	2002	A94901	261	AD546	AD806	yes	AD806/07 winter
n0638019	1967	grop B	254	AD540	AD793	yes	AD794-807
n0638029	1967	grop B	114	AD688	AD801	no	after AD809
n0638039	1967	67/1	101	AD707	AD807	yes	AD808-14
n0638049	1967	67/70	95	AD619	AD713	no	after AD721
n0638059	1967	67/71	16			yes	Not dated
n0638069	1967	67/75	42	AD761	AD802	yes	AD803 spring/summer
n0638079	1967	67/79	114	AD663	AD776	no	after AD784
n0638089	1967	67/83	111	AD669	AD779	no	after AD787
n0638099	1967	67/84	63	AD740	AD802	yes	AD803 spring/summer
n0638109	1967	67/85	59	AD744	AD802	yes	AD803 spring/summer
n0638119	1967	67/89	116	AD640	AD755	no	after AD763
n0638129	1967	67/90	132	AD665	AD796	yes	AD797-802
n0639039	1970	70/31	203	AD592	AD794	yes	AD801-15
n0639049	1970	70/33	141	AD672	AD812	yes	AD814-24
n0639059	1970	70/44	170	AD632	AD801	no	after AD809
n0639069	1970	70/45	80			no	Not dated
n0639079	1970	frag II	181	AD627	AD807	yes	AD811-25

Table 13.2 *Survey of the oak* (Quercus *sp.) samples examined.*

AD518								103	112	90
-	99	94	95	113	87	100	118	72	118	90
-	109	113	70	95	125	84	98	112	91	102
-	98	97	103	99	96	91	121	86	87	117
AD551	90	100	107	100	99	102	89	91	121	96
-	85	88	116	101	86	99	98	102	106	104
-	87	74	103	112	99	98	94	95	101	105
-	91	103	113	99	85	103	102	106	104	90
-	92	96	100	87	110	96	87	113	99	88
AD601	105	107	100	87	102	104	90	94	95	100
-	112	87	94	107	98	103	104	90	98	102
-	106	105	84	88	103	97	104	104	105	84
-	94	109	97	103	102	96	105	100	87	97
-	109	97	100	100	102	95	106	90	86	104
AD651	110	92	104	104	96	104	110	91	77	99
-	109	95	101	92	98	107	102	106	105	80
-	83	107	109	101	88	109	100	95	95	104
-	107	95	105	105	78	90	111	103	91	101
-	99	101	113	99	91	98	98	97	88	94
AD701	100	104	103	103	99	86	111	106	100	96
-	93	103	105	85	91	105	107	107	93	83
-	105	103	99	107	98	96	110	103	90	81
-	95	114	102	97	102	101	93	98	109	94
-	93	108	100	101	92	98	101	105	96	94
AD751	103	95	110	98	103	99	101	101	90	94
-	107	102	95	99	106	99	89	103	105	94
-	107	105	90	94	95	89	114	105	94	94
-	100	109	97	95	103	105	92	88	108	96
-	96	101	109	96	98	110	97	93	93	101
AD801	102	101	102	98	98	99	107	99	89	99
-	108	95	105	100	81	94	107	105	99	102
-	104	96	101	105	89	95	106	109	91	90
-	101	110	97	101	95	101	107	94	82	98
-	114	105	100	99	88	105	99	99	91	101
AD851	114	83	68	124	106	105	93	102	104	106
-	94	90								

Table 13.3 *The Kaupang site chronology for oak* (Quercus *sp.*) *based on data from tree-ring sequences from 41 samples. The data are filtered with a five-year running mean. The chronology is 345 years in length and covers the period AD 518 to AD 862.*

Interpreting the Plant and Animal Remains from Viking-age Kaupang   14

JAMES BARRETT, ALLAN HALL, CLUNY JOHNSTONE,
HARRY KENWARD, TERRY O'CONNOR AND STEVE ASHBY

This chapter outlines the results of analyses of the plant remains, insect remains and animal bones recovered from the main research excavation of 2002 at Kaupang (with some comparative treatment of material from the cultural resource management (CRM) excavation in 2000 and the harbour excavation in 2003). Both surface-laid deposits (such as house floors and occupation deposits) and waterlogged pit fills have been examined, but only the latter produced well-preserved material. The survival of animal bone at Kaupang was particularly poor. Despite these limitations, it proved possible to illuminate a number of the Kaupang Project's research questions. The formation of individual features and feature types has been clarified, with pit fills interpreted as redeposited house floor sweepings, for example. The seasonality and permanence of the site has been explored – Kaupang was probably occupied year-round, at least occasionally, but it also produced evidence of either periodic abandonment or a relatively short overall lifespan. It has been possible to demonstrate that the settlement drew on a range of agricultural and forest resources from its local hinterland, implying that it either controlled or was controlled by a regional polity. Conversely, the ecofactual evidence of long-range trade was very limited. There is, however, a slight possibility that skins (furs?) were stored indoors at the site prior to transhipment. Be it evidence of trade connections or culturally prescribed dietary preferences, the ecofactual evidence from Kaupang also showed associations with both the Baltic region to the east and the North Atlantic region to the west.

14.1 Introduction

This chapter surveys the recovery, analysis and interpretation of plant remains, insect remains and animal bones from the main research excavations of 2002 and the harbour excavation of 2003 at Kaupang. Almost all of the material is from Site Periods I–III (SP I-III) and thus dates to the early 9th century (Pilø, this vol. Ch. 9). Most of it, excavated in 2002, is from Plots 1A, 1B, 2A, 2B, 3A and 3B (henceforth referred to as "1A–3B") but small-scale study has also been made of material originally deposited in the settlement's harbour, which was excavated in 2003. Cross-reference will be made to work on plant remains, insect remains and animal bones recovered during cultural resource management (CRM) excavations conducted in 2000 (Hufthammer and Bratbak 2000; Buckland et al. 2001).

The ecofactual material from Kaupang can inform interpretation of the settlement in a variety of ways. It is possible to characterise the nature of specific deposits, such as occupation deposits and pit fills, to shed some light on the seasonality and permanence of the settlement, to evaluate the local economy and the site's articulation with its hinterland, to illuminate the character of long-range trade and to place the occupation of Kaupang within a wider comparative context. The range of interpretations possible is enhanced by the survival of some deposits preserved by anoxic waterlogging, principally pit fills. Unfortunately, however, the breadth and depth of interpretation is also severely limited by the small number of deposits preserved in this way, particularly in comparison with some other Viking-age and later medieval urban sites (e.g. Schia 1988; Kenward and Hall 1995). Moreover, bone preservation at Kaupang is extremely poor. Most of what survives has been burnt and highly fragmented. Were it not for the critical importance of Kaupang to the history of Viking-age Europe, a bone assemblage of this kind might go unanalysed. In sum, analysis of the ecofactual material from Kaupang has presented both opportunities and challenges. The work has sometimes been an

Table 14.1 *Charred plant remains and other components of the light (floating) fractions from 54 selected BS samples. Charcoal abundance: material included A – alder* (Alnus); C – *hazel* (Corylus); Con – *Coniferae; F – ash* (Fraxinus); Q – *oak* (Quercus); ?P – *?rose family, pro parte (Pomoideae); S/P – willow/aspen/poplar* (Salix/Populus). *Numbers represent the three-point semi-quantitative scale of abundance outlined in the methods section (14.2).*

exercise in wringing limited information from very poorly preserved material. Nevertheless, the overall results have proven informative regarding a number of the Kaupang Project's research questions, and thus worthwhile.

14.2 Methods

The ecofacts considered here were recovered in three main ways (cf. Dobney et al. 1992): as 'bulk sieved' samples, as 'general biological assemblage' samples or as 'site riddled' bone. Sediments from deposits that were not waterlogged, but seemed likely to yield charred botanical material, were typically collected as bulk sieved (BS) samples of c. 10 litres and processed in the field by flotation (in which the heavy fraction was retained by a 1 mm mesh and the floating light fraction by a 0.5 mm mesh). High priority was given to hearths, occupation deposits, dumps and other potentially informative layers. These samples proved to be rather homogeneous and the material they contained was very poorly preserved. Thus only a selection of heavy fractions and light fractions were chosen for post-excavation analysis (see section 14.3 below). Materials from the heavy fraction were quantified by weight and all plant taxa and other components of the light fractions were recorded using a three-point semi-quantitative scale: from 1 (one or a few specimens or fragments) to 3 (abundant, or a major component of the sample).

Waterlogged deposits were typically collected as whole earth general biological assemblage (GBA) samples of c. 10 litres each. Subsamples of these (usually constituting a minimum of 3 kg of sediment) were later sieved to 300 μm in the laboratory, with invertebrate macrofossils recovered using procedures broadly following the paraffin (kerosene) flotation method described by Kenward et al. (1980, 1986). A tally of plant remains and other components of the GBAs was recorded together with notes on the gener-

al nature of the material. All plant taxa and other components were recorded using a four-point semi-quantitative scale: from 1 (one or a few specimens or fragments) to 4 (abundant, or a major component of the sample). Invertebrate remains were identified in the flot (for familiar species) or placed on damp filter paper for more careful inspection where necessary. The remains of adult beetles and bugs from a selection of the best preserved samples from the 2002 excavation were 'detail' recorded in the terminology of Kenward (1992). Adult beetles and bugs, other than aphids and scale insects, were recorded fully quantitatively and a minimum number of individuals estimated on the basis of the fragments present. Other invertebrate macrofossils were usually recorded semi-quantitatively using the scale described by Kenward et al. (1986) and Kenward (1992), again using estimates for extremely abundant taxa. Quality of insect preservation was recorded using the scales of Kenward and Large (1998). GBA samples from the 2003 harbour excavation were qualitatively assessed as an adjunct to the present work. The interpretative methods employed for insect and botanical remains were essentially the same as those employed in work on a variety of sites by Hall, Kenward and co-workers (see Kenward 1978, with modifications outlined by, for example, Kenward and Hall 1995).

Site riddled bone was recovered by on-site sieving (to 2 mm or 5mm) of excavated sediment from layers that were not otherwise sampled. Approximately 50% of this material was later selected for identification and recording, to which bone from the BS and GBA samples was added. Regardless of the method of field recovery, in the laboratory all mammal and bird bone retained by a 4 mm sieve and all fish bone retained by a 2 mm sieve was analysed. Moreover, mammal- or bird-bone fragments that passed through the 4 mm sieve were scanned for identifiable specimens, virtually none of which were found.

Feature Type	Site Period	Plot	Context	Intrasis sample	Charcoal abundance	Charcoal dim. mm	Barley	Other plant and non-plant components
Hearth, House 200	II	1	61643	63190	1	10		bark, herbaceous detritus
Hearth?	II	2	61359	61410	2	15		*Carex*, bone (burnt and unburnt), plant fuel ash
Hearth, House 302	II	3	76910	78141	2	20	1	bark
Hearth, House 302	II	3	77718	78274	2	15	1	*Carex, Chenopodium album, Potentilla* cf. *erecta*, unburnt bone
Hearth, House 303	II	3	84844	84895	1	10		
Floor, House 301	II	3	66085	66400	1 Q	10		plant fuel ash, *Corylus avellana* nutshell
Floor, House 303	II	3	64713	78923	1 F Q	10		
Floor, House 303	II	3	64713	81537	1	5	1	
Floor, House 406	II	2	69242	69305	2 C F Q	15	1	plant fuel ash, *Carex, Potentilla* cf. *erecta*, uncharred wood
Floor, House 406	II	2	69242	69306	2	10	1	plant fuel ash, *Corylus avellana* nutshell, cf. *Juniperus communis* (seed)
Floor, House 406	II	2	69242	69307	1	10	1	plant fuel ash (2), *Carex, Corylus avellana* nutshell, *Potentilla* cf. *erecta*
Floor, House 406	II	2	69242	69308	1 F Q	15		plant fuel ash (2), *Rubus fruticosus* agg.
Occupation	I	2	75167	75215	2	10	1	plant fuel ash
Occupation	I	2	75579	75679	1	15		plant fuel ash
Occupation, House 200	II	1	61670	62377	1	15	1	Gramineae, *Stellaria media*, unburnt bark, unburnt bone, plant fuel ash
Occupation, House 301	II	3	62023	63610	2	15	1	*Avena, Rosa*, bark, charred organic material
Occupation, House 301	II	3	62023	63865	1 A C F Q S/P	10	1	plant fuel ash, *Carex, Corylus avellana* nutshell, charred organic material
Occupation, House 301	II	3	62068	63864	2 A/C Q	10		plant fuel ash, *Corylus avellana* nutshell
Occupation, House 302	II	3	67217	71214	2	30	1	*Carex*, charred organic material
Occupation, House 302	II	3	76555	76884	2	15		*Carex, Galium aparine*, unburnt fish bone, plant fuel ash
Occupation, House 303	II	3	81762	82228	1 ?P Q			*Corylus* avellana nutshell
Occupation, House 303	II	3	81762	82229	2	15		*Corylus avellana* nutshell, *Rubus fruticosus* agg.
Occupation, House 303	II	3	81762	82227	1 Q S/P	20	1	cf. *Juniperus communis* (seed)
Occupation	I-III	2A-2B	78587	78680	2	15		plant fuel ash
Occupation	II	3A	82178	82311	2	15		plant fuel ash
Occupation	II	3A	85299	86599	2	10	1	*Chenopodium album, Galium aparine*, unburnt bark
Side Aisle, House 301	II	3	65556	66061	1	15	1	plant fuel ash, *Carex, Corylus avellana* nutshell, *Polygonum persicaria, Stellaria media*, charred organic material
Side Aisle, House 301	II	3	70806	71121	1 F Q S/P	20	1	plant fuel ash, *Corylus avellana* nutshell
Side Aisle, House 302	II	3	78497	78572	2	20	1	*Carex, Potentilla* cf. *erecta*, plant fuel ash
Side Aisle, House 406	II	2	68378	68451	1 F Q	25	1	plant fuel ash
Dumping	II	1	64612	64667	2	10		*Triticum/Hordeum*, plant fuel ash
Dumping	II	3	65597	66007	2	30		
Dumping	II	3	68717	68753	2	30	1	*Carex, Chenopodium album, Galium aparine*, charred organic material, plant fuel ash
Dumping	II	3	74121	74138	1	5		Cerealia indet., plant fuel ash
Dumping	II	3	74188	74292	2	30	1	bark, plant fuel ash
Dumping	II	3B	70602	73307	2	15	1	charred organic material, plant fuel ash
Dumping	II	3A-4B	71826	79086	2	15	1	cf. *Linum usitatissimum*, unburnt bark, unburnt cancellous bone and fish bone, plant fuel ash
Dumping	II	3A	83246	87783	1	10	1	*Carex, Polygonum persicaria*, unburnt bone, burnt fish bone, plant fuel ash
Dumping	II	3A	84296	84672	2	15	1	*Carex*, plant fuel ash

Feature Type	Site Period	Plot	Context	Intrasis sample	Charcoal abundance	Charcoal dim. mm	Barley	Other plant and non-plant components
Ditch	II	3	76697	77600	2	25	1	uncharred bark, plant fuel ash
Pit A82649	II	3	83319	83825	1	10	2	*Atriplex, Avena, Carex, Chenopodium album, Galium, Polygonum persicaria*, cf. *Secale cereale*, unburnt bark and cancellous bone, charred organic material (2), herbaceous detritus, plant fuel ash
Pit A43852	III	3	61237	83550	1	10		*Carex, Galium aparine*, charred organic material, fuel plant ash
Pit A65132	III	1	84282	84730	1	25		cf. *Secale cereale*, charred organic material, unburnt fish bone
Pit A74095	I-III	3	73950	74003	2	20		*Chenopodium album*, uncharred Rubus idaeus
Pit fill	II	3A	84615	84937	1	15	1	*Carex*, plant fuel ash
Layer	I	2	75001	75134	2	25		*Carex*, plant fuel ash
Layer	II	2	64458	64550	2	15	1	*Carex* (2), *Chenopodium album, Gramineae, Rumex*, bark, bone, plant fuel ash
Layer	II	2	74037	74111	2	25		*Carex, Potentilla* cf. *erecta, Scirpus lacustris* sl, *Stellaria media, S. palustris/graminea*, uncharred bark, plant fuel ash (2)
Layer	II	3	70696	71949	1	15		*Carex*, Chenopodiaceae, *Corylus avellana* nutshell, *Eleocharis palustris sl*, charred organic material, plant fuel ash
Layer	II	3	73520	78273	2	15	1	*Carex, Chenopodium album, Galium, Polygonum hydropiper*, cf. *Triticum*, bark, charred organic material, plant fuel ash
Layer	II	3	75751	75820	1	20	1	*Bilderdykia convolvulus, Carex*, cf. *Eleocharis* sp., *Secale cereale*, charred organic material, plant fuel ash
Layer	II	3	78143	78190	1	10	1	*Carex*, charred organic material, plant fuel ash
Layer	II	3A	76661	78003	2	20	1	*Carex*, Gramineae, *Plantago media, Ranunculus* Section *Ranunculus, R. flammula*, cf. *Triticum*, plant fuel ash
Layer	II	3	78393	78456	1	10	1	*Carex*, cf. *Secale cereale*, cf. *Triticum*, charred organic material, plant fuel ash

The bone assemblage was recorded following the York protocol, which is described by Harland et al. (2003). It entails the detailed recording of diagnostic elements, 17 for mammals, c. 20 for fish (dependent on species) and 8 for birds. These elements are identified to the finest possible taxonomic group and recorded in detail – typically including, as appropriate, element, side, count, measurements, weight, epiphyseal fusion, tooth wear, modifications (including burning and butchery), fragmentation, texture and estimates of fish size. Although identified as diagnostic elements, fish vertebrae are recorded in slightly less detail (measurements are not taken and texture is not scored, for example). 'Non-diagnostic' elements are only identified beyond class for special reasons. Examples include butchered specimens, birds (which are represented by only a few bones at this site), and other taxa that would otherwise not be recorded.

These are indicated as presence data only in quantitative tables. For mammals and birds, the principle elements in the 'non-diagnostic' category are ribs and vertebrae.

The bones have been quantified by number of identified specimens (NISP), including all bones or only the diagnostic elements as indicated. Toothwear has been recorded using the methods of Grant (1982) for pigs and cattle, and Payne (1987) for caprines (sheep and goats). A detailed technical report and a digital archive have been submitted to the Kaupang Excavation Project and will be kept on file at the University of York. The small number of measurements in this archive follow von den Driesch (1976) and Harland et al. (2003), but they have not been analysed due to the shrinkage associated with burning (Shipman et al. 1984).

14.3 The material: an overview

Tables 14.1, 14.2 and 14.3 summarise the contents of a selection of BS light fractions, BS heavy fractions and GBA samples. A complete list of plant taxa recorded from the site is included in Appendix 14.1, and a list of 'useful' taxa along with their English and Norwegian common names is included in Appendix 14.2. A complete list of insect and other macro-invertebrate taxa is included in Appendix 14.3. The contents of the animal bone assemblage are summarised in Tables 14.4 and 14.5. A complete list of the mammals, birds and fish identified, with their Latin, English and Norwegian names, is included in Appendix 14.4. More detailed quantitative data regarding all of the ecofacts considered can be found in Barrett et al. (2004a).

In comparison with the preservation of plant material at some other sites of broadly comparable date – such as parts of York, Dublin and Hedeby – the preservation of plant material in the deposits from Kaupang examined for this study was rather limited, at least in terms of the range of taxa present, although those deposits with anoxic waterlogging generally yielded material of good quality. Such deposits were invariably the fills of pits. Surface-laid occupation layers, however, generally contained only small amounts of charred material, mainly charcoal, with a little charred hazel nutshell and some charred cereals (mainly barley) and weeds likely to have been growing with the cereal crop, and perhaps a few remains originating in burnt peat or turves. Other evidence of burning consisted of material variously recorded as 'ash beads', 'glassy ash' and 'ash concretions' – plant ash in small subspherical clasts or larger, more amorphous, whitish fragments – all no doubt originating in plant material. The few uncharred remains from surface-laid deposits are thought for the most part to be of recent origin. This is not surprising given the micromorphological evidence of extensive bioturbation by earthworms (Milek and French, this vol. Ch. 15:326–8).

Insect remains in the waterlogged deposits were usually diluted, so some of the groups recorded were small, but some of these small groups were useful for interpretation at the context level, and they contributed to the body of data for site-level analysis. The average concentration of insect remains in the recorded samples was low and none of the assemblages were very large, even after processing of quite large subsamples in some cases (the largest group was of 178 individuals from 7.0 kg of sediment from context AL88226, sample P88241). The concentration of adult beetle and bug remains, at 24 per kg (based on MNI) in the subsamples recorded quantitatively, was very low by comparison with beetle and bug remains in broadly similar deposits (Kenward and Hall 1995; Kenward 1988; Allison et al. 1999). However, for the Søndersø site at Viborg, Denmark, the value was 27 per kg (Kenward 2005). Whether these low concen-

trations are indicative of how the sites were used will depend on the taphonomy of the deposits in question (how long pits were open before being filled, for example), but it may be relevant that the Søndersø site was probably not intensively urbanised. In neither of these cases does post-depositional decay seem to have been responsible for the low concentrations: the deposits on which the estimates of concentrations are based were those with fossils, and almost none gave even hints that an appreciable proportion of the beetles at least had been completely lost by decay (the more delicate remains such as lice might have been, however). Overall, the most plausible explanation for the low concentrations of remains is that insect populations were quite restricted and that their remains were diluted by abundant plant debris. The implications of the insect remains for the intensity and permanence of occupation are discussed further in section 14.5 below.

Most of the botanical evidence from these deposits at Kaupang is of woody taxa, probably mostly originating from brushwood or other 'twiggy' litter – this might well be the source of, for example, juniper, and some heathland plants (especially various of the mosses). Wood chips from wood-working and/or construction might well have been used for litter in the first instance, too, rather than just being thrown away, though presumably their presence in pit fills indicates that their eventual fate was to be discarded (see section 14.4 below). Wood chips were a primary constituent of house foundations and floor layers in Viking-age Dublin, where preservation was better (Geraghty 1996). Grassland is represented in some deposits, with some freshwater marsh and saltmarsh taxa perhaps from cut vegetation or dung, but perhaps just arriving by natural dispersal from the nearby waterside of the fjord. There was perhaps also some imported turf, especially in the case of one sample (from pit A99030, Plot 2B, SP I) with waterlogged rhizome/culm fragments bearing a very characteristic "dried-unrewetted" appearance. Several other pit fills might have contained smaller components of rather similar material. It is tempting to see this as originating in turves used in roofing; the use of turves in roofing was a practice also known from the Dublin excavations (Geraghty 1996).

The insect remains were predominantly of species associated with, or at least often found in, decaying matter ranging from dryish mouldering plant debris to dung and animal remains. Species found primarily in natural or semi-natural habitats were rare and often typically associated with herbaceous vegetation. Insects associated with trees, whether living or dead, were uncommon. This ecological group was mainly represented by *Rhinosimus planirostris* and *Dromius quadrimaculatus* and *D. quadrinotatus,* the first associated at least as often with small dead twigs as with substantial timber, the last two living on trees,

Feature Type	Site Period	Plot	Context	Sample	Original Sample Volume (l)	Density Gravel	Density Bone	Density Charcoal	Density Hazelnut
							(g/l, >4mm)		
Floor, House 303	II	3	64713	78923	10	118,28	0,16	0,44	0,00
Floor, House 303	II	3	64713	81537	10	100,91	0,06	0,05	0,00
Occupation, House 303	II	3	81762	82227	10	71,30	1,13	0,33	0,00
Occupation, House 303	II	3	81762	82228	10	76,48	2,41	0,33	0,01
Occupation, House 303	II	3	81762	82229	10	101,63	1,78	0,22	0,00
Occupation, House 406	II	2	69242	69305	10	38,84	3,16	4,45	0,00
Occupation, House 406	II	2	69242	69306	10	31,16	4,75	3,90	0,00
Occupation, House 406	II	2	69242	69307	5	49,52	8,60	6,48	0,00
Occupation, House 406	II	2	69242	69308	9	57,17	3,28	2,01	0,00
Occupation, House 301	II	3	62068	63864	7,5	29,45	7,29	0,19	0,03
Occupation, House 301	II	3	62023	63865	9	42,35	1,94	0,26	0,01
Occupation, House 301	II	3	66085	66400	11	26,08	0,20	0,29	0,02
Side Aisle, House 406	II	2	68378	68451	10	68,64	2,30	3,58	0,00
Side Aisle, House 301	II	3	65556	66061	10	35,80	2,30	0,82	0,03
Side Aisle, House 301	II	3	79806	71121	10	34,24	2,85	0,84	0,05

Feature Type	Site Period	Context	Intrasis sample	Gravel	Charcoal abundance	Charcoal maximum dim.(mm)	Wood or twig fragments	Bark	Wood chips	Hazel nut
Hearth (House 200)	II	61643	62381	3	1	10				1
Hearth (House 301)	II	47045		2	1	10				1
Dumping	II	68495	68512	2	3	10	1			
Pit A99030	I	99879	99948	2	3	20	3	2	2	1
Pit A65132	II	86018	86040	2	2	10	2	1	1	1
Pit A65132	II	86018	86385	1	1	5	1	1	1	1
Pit A65132	II	86018	86386	1	1	10	3	1	1	1
Pit A65132	II	86018	86387	2	1	15	1	2	1	1
Pit A65132	II	86018	87731	2	1	10	3	2	1	2
Pit A65132	II	86018	87732	2	1	20	3	2	2	1
Pit A43852	III	61411	87216	2	1	10	1 (ch)			
Pit A43852	III	87427	87447	1	2	20	1	1		1
Pit A43852	III	87626	87649	2	2	20	2	2	1	1
Pit A43852	III	87669	87679	2	2	20	2	1	1	2
Pit A43852	III	88226	88241	3	3	20	3	3	1	2
Pit A64891	III	65189	87792	2	2	20	1			1
Pit A64891	III	87793	87806	3	2	10	2	1	1	1
Pit (Heritage Management)	I-II	94901	94864	2	1	15	2	1		1
Harbour Spit 2	I-III	4453	4758	+			+	+	+	+
Harbour Spit 4	I-III	4453	4900		+	10	+	+	+	+
Harbour Spit 5	I-III	4453	4933S		+	10	+	+	+	+
Harbour Spit 6	I-III	4453	4950		+	10	+	+	+	+

Table 14.2 *Principal contents of the heavy fractions from 15 selected BS samples from building 'floor', 'side aisle' and 'occupation' deposits.*

Table 14.3 *Summary of the contents of 22 selected GBA samples (Numbers represent the four-point semi-quantitative scale of abundance outlined in the methods section (14.2); + indicates presence data only).*

Strawy material	Barley	Burnt bone	Unburnt bone	*Omosita*	Human fleas	Other notable inclusions	Comments
		1	1				
		1	1				
		1					very poor preservation, mostly charcoal & ash
+		1	1	+		rye, hemp, strawberry, hop, woad, raspberry, rose	some turf input; clean water & outdoor insects
+		1	1			raspberry, blackberry	very few insects
+					+	bee	compressed strawy material, some probably cereal but mixed, no parasite eggs, no insect evidence for use as animal bedding, small 'outdoor' insect component
+				+			compressed strawy material, *Apion* weevil implies hay
+	1			+		hop, strawberry, blackberry	compressed strawy material, insects are a typical range of occupation site decomposers
		1	1			flax, hop, hemp,	insects may imply waste from a building
+	1	1	1	+	+	flax, hemp, hop, woad, honey bee	plants and insects may imply redeposited floor material
		2	1				no insects observed
	1	1	1				poor preservation
		1	1	+		blackberry	insects imply dry animal matter, some possible indoor fauna
	1	1	1	+		hemp, raspberry, blackberry	insects imply dry animal matter
+	1	1	1	+		blackberry	insects imply dry animal matter
		1	1			raspberry	poor preservation
		1	1			flax, hop, raspberry, strawberry, blackberry	poor preservation
			1			raspberry	no identifiable insects
						blackberry	insects are decomposers & feeders of hay-like vegetation
						hop, woad, blackberry, flea (? species)	insects hint at decomposing floor litter, conceivably from a stable/byre
						blackberry, strawberry, rose, apple core	insects imply foul matter
	+				+	blackberry, rose, evidence of turf	one flea, but no unambiguous 'house fauna'

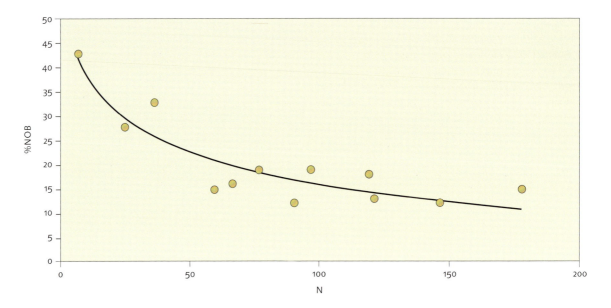

sheltering in bark crevices, but ranging onto twigs in search of prey (Lindroth 1986). There were a few bark beetles, probably imported with timber, but not enough to provide evidence of the relative importance of tree species. Even woodworm beetles *(Anobium)* were rare.

It has proved difficult to identify the specific uses of pits or the nature of conditions in the buildings from these deposits, in stark contrast to the evidence from sites such as 16–22 Coppergate, York (Kenward and Hall 1995), where many of the pit fills proved to be rich in faecal material, whilst another important component of the deposits in general was an abundance of remains of plants used in textile dyeing. Neither of these characteristics can be attributed to the Kaupang sediments based on the samples under consideration.

Nevertheless, many of the deposits at Kaupang contain an appreciable component of fauna presumed to have originated from within buildings ('house fauna'). It seems very possible that most of the deposits analysed here included material cleared from floors, perhaps predominantly waste from indoor processes rather than the debris of long-term domestic life (a contrast with many of the deposits at the Coppergate site in York). There were some records of human fleas *(Pulex irritans)* from two deposits, five being recovered from one of these, and three records of 'Siphonaptera', which were probably human fleas but which lacked easily identifiable parts (heads and genitalia). These were probably brought from within buildings in which they bred, but human fleas can also occur in stable manure deposits where the larvae could breed (and indeed the adults feed on livestock), and so are apparently not exclusively confined to human dwellings. No lice were found, though this might have been a result of the preservational regime rather than their absence when the deposits formed.

There was no coherent evidence for the presence of stable manure in the samples analysed (cf. Kenward and Hall 1997). Pale, soft, and apparently newly-emerged remains of *Apion* weevils were found in a number of the samples. Such remains are very typical of stable manure assemblages, in which they are frequently accompanied by a range of weevils and other insects found on herbaceous plants. In the context of Kaupang, however, they are likely to represent imported hay or turf rather than manure.

There were three assemblages with appreciable numbers of the beetle *Omosita colon,* together with a range of other species likely to have been attracted to dryish animal matter (including skins and bones). The possible significance of these samples is discussed in sections 14.4 and 14.7 below.

While imported plant resources demonstrate the presence of various kinds of vegetation within the catchment of Kaupang, the biota cast rather little light on semi-natural habitats on or immediately adjacent to the site, except for the consistent component of weed taxa, most of which might well have been growing around the settlement. Their numbers were much smaller than those in occupation deposits at some other sites of the period, however, and weed-associated insects were quite rare (cf. Kenward and Hall 1995). Indeed, outdoor insect fauna was remarkably limited in most cases, considering that the analysed waterlogged layers were all external deposits. The number of outdoor individuals is not proportional to assemblage size across the samples, the regression line showing a reduction in the importance of the outdoor component with increasing assemblage size (Fig. 14.1). This probably means that the larger assemblages included substantial autochthonous or imported communities, while the smaller assemblages were dominated by background fauna. This offers support to the argument that the more richly organic deposits consisted mainly of waste which either came from

Figure 14.1 *Plot of number of adult beetles and bugs (N) against percentage assigned to the 'outdoor' category (% NOB) for the assemblages from the Kaupang site. Logarithmic trend line added. R² = 0.83. Illustration by the authors.*

buildings or was very rapidly deposited and buried, so that insects could not breed in large numbers.

Fully aquatic invertebrates were present but were rare, with the exception of water-flea resting eggs (mostly *Daphnia):* overall, aquatic beetles and bugs accounted for only 1% of the fauna, far less than at many other sites. Fully aquatic plants were absent. Waterside insects were also rare (2% of site fauna), though some plants typically found by water sometimes occurred in quantity – especially celery-leaved crowfoot *(Ranunculus sceleratus),* and also several marsh/swamp taxa. There are three likely sources for aquatic and waterside remains in deposits formed as a result of intensive occupation: imported water, imported waterside resources, and flooding (occasionally, aquatics might have lived in pits, wells and ditches at many sites, but this seems to have been the exception in intensively used, urban or semi-urban areas). Given the quantity of evidence and the proximity of the site to the fjord, and the relative fall in the water level since the Viking Age, any or all of these mechanisms could have operated. There is a good chance that the "compressed straw" in one of the samples from context AL86018 included cut wetland vegetation, given the nature of some of the taxa present as fruits and seeds and perhaps also given some of the epidermis material which might well have come from culms (stems) of large sedges or emergent plants such as bulrush or sea club-rush *(Scirpus* spp.), although it could not be identified with certainty (see section 14.4 below).

The presence of quite large numbers of water-flea eggs and the absence of other aquatics perhaps would support an argument for imported water rather than flooding (a much richer fauna being expected from the latter). Flooding does seem to be a possibility, however, from the rather abundant (but small) fragments of colonial coelenterate stems noted during botanical analysis. It may be more likely, however,

that these arrived with seaweed (of which there is some evidence from the charred plant remains) or shellfish (of which the only evidence from these samples was traces of bivalve periostracum, any calcareous shell components probably having dissolved) (cf. Buckland et al. 1993). There were small quantities of salt-tolerant plants such as sea arrow-grass *(Triglochin maritima)* in the deposits, probably no more than casual arrivals from nearby fjord-edge communities.

A very modest range of food taxa was represented amongst the plant remains. As far as 'staples' are concerned, there were low concentrations of cereals (as charred grains), mainly barley (the most frequently recorded plant taxon, though only twice present at more than very low concentrations), with a little rye and oats, but with no certainly identified wheat. This is entirely consistent with what might be expected in the Kaupang area at this period; furthermore, a low concentration of charred cereals was also found in Viking-age Dublin (Geraghty 1996). Wild foods included rose, blackberry, raspberry, strawberry, apple and perhaps rowan. There were no clearly cultivated fruits and no evidence of importation of exotic fruits.

Hemp and hop were both recorded in pit fills. Hemp is likely to have been a fibre crop, though its use as food for human or animal consumption and as an oil-seed, like flax, cannot be discounted. Hop might have been used for flavouring beer (see section 14.6 below). Amongst the plants recorded at Kaupang, only woad stands out as being likely to have been used for dyeing textiles (although many of the wild plants could conceivably have served this purpose). Flax (linseed) was also identified.

Although first introduced to Norway in prehistory, woad, hemp, flax and the cereals would all have been locally available in the Viking Age. All of the other plants recorded from Kaupang are native to Norway and all might have grown in the vicinity of

Type	Site Period I	II	III	I-III	Disturbed	Unphased	Total
Bird							
Side aisle		3					3
Ditch		3		1			4
Dumping		1					1
Floor		1					1
Hearth		1					1
Layer	1	6					7
Occupation		2					2
Pit			5				5
?					3		3
Fish							
Agricultural horizon					5		5
Animal burrow					1		1
Side aisle		163	1				164
Ditch		58	11	82			151
Dumping		120					120
Feature		6					6
Floor		66					66
Hearth		20					20
Layer	40	214		2	2		258
Occupation	1	19					20
Passage		37					37
Pit	8	22	540	1			571
Posthole				1			1
Road					1		1
Stakehole				1			1
?					71	4	75
Mammal							
Agricultural horizon					1516		1516
Animal burrow					17		17
Side aisle		1641	252				1893
Ditch		4815	804	4163			9782
Dumping		7753					7753
Feature		615					615
Floor		1533					1533
Hearth		829					829
Layer	2376	21607		834	53		24870
Occupation	881	6842					7723
Passage		2951					2951
Pit	153	29	5248	235			5665
Posthole			100	115			215
Road					102		102
Stakehole				25			25
Stonepacking				27			27
?					3616	189	3805
Total	3460	49357	6961	5487	5387	193	70845

Table 14.4 *Distribution of all bone by phase and context type.*

the site. A single positive identification was made of a honey bee, *Apis mellifera,* and there were two tentative identifications, but these are not enough to demonstrate bee-keeping (compared with the abundant bees from Oslo (Kenward 1988), York (Kenward and Hall 1995) and Aberdeen, Scotland (Hall et al. 2004).

These results are broadly comparable with those of Buckland et al. (2001) regarding samples collected during the CRM excavation at Kaupang in 2000. For example, a "superabundance" of *Omosita colon* beetles was also noted in pit A28375 and, to a lesser degree, pit A9422. However, minor differences do occur. Finds from the CRM excavation of 2000 which were not represented in the 2002 material include wheat, from pit A5190, and lice *(Damalinia* sp.), probably sheep lice *(D. ovis),* from pit A1625. Dung beetles also occurred in this well, and in pit A1635, possibly suggesting that these features served in part as watering holes for livestock (Buckland et al. 2001).

Turning to the faunal evidence, in total, 70,845 animal bone specimens were examined from Plots 1A-3B. All site periods and context types were dominated by mammal bone (69321), followed by fish (1497) and bird (27) (Tab. 14.4). There were, however, some differences in the relative abundance of fish and mammal bones across the site (see section 14.4 below). Of the large assemblage recorded, only 1506 specimens were diagnostic elements that could be attributed to taxonomic categories below class (Tab. 14.5). Of these, 855 were mammal, 639 were fish and 12 were bird. The tiny percentage of identified bone was due to extremely poor preservation.

Most of the Kaupang bone assemblage was burned. This pattern applies to both the mammal (75% burned) and bird (63% burned) assemblages. Perhaps surprisingly, however, only 27% of the fish bone was clearly burned. This last pattern is partly explained by the high proportion of fish recovered from pits, the fills of which were waterlogged and

exhibited better preservation conditions. For example, whereas only 21% of fish bones from pits were burned, 62% of the fish bones from ditches were burned. The predominance of burned mammal and bird bones is almost certainly due to poor preservation conditions. For complex chemical and mechanical reasons they have been found to survive in acidic soil conditions (e.g. Nicholson 1996).

The poor preservation at Kaupang is also evident from the high level of fragmentation of the bones. Based only on the identified diagnostic elements (the bones which were measured), among the largest specimens in the collection, the mean fragment size for mammal bones was only 27.2mm. This is extraordinarily small in an assemblage dominated by large species such as pigs, cattle and caprines (sheep or goats). Moreover, the vast majority of identified specimens represented less than c. 20% of a complete element and the unidentified bone typically consisted of very tiny fragments. The preservation of the unburned bones can also be assessed based on their texture (Harland et al. 2003). It is consistently poor, with the exception of fish bone from pits, where a few "good" and one "excellent" texture states were noted.

The very poor preservation conditions would have reduced the absolute quantity of bone at Kaupang to a large, but unmeasurable, degree. They have also reduced the identifiable component of the assemblage to a tiny fraction of the total. More importantly, however, they would have had a major impact on the relative representation of taxa and elements which therefore cannot be accurately modelled (Lyman 1994; Costamagno et al. 2005). From what is known about bone survival, the combination of excellent recovery methods, high fragmentation, poor bone-tissue preservation (texture) and preservation by burning is likely to produce unusual patterns where, for example, small robust bones survive to a greater degree than large ones (e.g. Nicholson

| | Site Period | | | | | | |
Type	I	II	III	I-III	Disturbed	Unphased	Total
Bird							
Barnacle goose		present	1				1
Brent Goose		1					1
Eider		present					
Shelduck		1					1
Domestic Fowl		3	3		1		7
Great Black-backed Gull					1		1
Little Auk		1					1
Subtotal		6	4		2		12
Fish							
Shark, Skate & Ray Orders		1	3				4
Dogfish Families			1				1
Eel		1					1
Atlantic Herring	1	66	177	12	7		263
Salmon & Trout Family		8					8
Trout		1					1
Cod Family	5	74	27	13	8	2	129
Cod		70	26	9	8		113
Ling		14	2	1	2		19
Pollack	1						1
Saithe	2	48	13	4	6		73
Hake		16	1	6	1		24
Gurnard Family		1					1
Wrasse Family			1				1
Subtotal	9	300	251	45	32	2	639
Mammal							
Large mammal	3	33	17	7	5		65
Medium mammal 1	6	47	18	10	10		91
Medium mammal 2		8		1			9
Shrew species			1				1
Dog family		1	present		3		4
Cat		26	2	5			33
Cat?		2		1			3
Horse		2		1			3
Pig	9	228	41	23	33	1	335
Pig?	1			1	1		3
Deer			1				1
Red deer			1				1
Cattle	10	116	22	17	16		181
Sheep/goat	5	84	13	7	11	1	121
Sheep		2					2
Hare		2					2
Subtotal	34	551	116	73	79	2	855
Total	43	857	371	118	113	4	1506

Table 14.5 *Number of identified bone specimens (NISP) by site period of all species based on diagnostic elements (other records noted as present only).*

1995; Bond 1996). As discussed below, this is in fact what emerges from the Kaupang assemblage.

The very small mammal assemblage identified is dominated by four domestic taxa: pigs (NISP = 338), cattle (181), caprines (123, probably including both sheep and goats, although only the former were definitively recognised) and cats (36). Moreover, 91 pig- or sheep-sized (medium mammal 1) specimens can probably be divided disproportionately between these two taxa, and 65 large mammal identifications are almost certainly cattle given the virtual absence of deer (represented only by one red deer antler tine and a worked antler comb tooth) and horse (represented by only three specimens). In sum, therefore, these common domestic taxa constitute approximately 98% of the mammal assemblage. The remaining trace species include the deer and horse just mentioned, four dog or wolf (probably large dog) specimens, two hare bones and one shrew bone (which can probably be considered a natural introduction to the site). Particular attention was paid to the possible inclusion of other wild taxa, such as the fur-bearing species recovered at Birka (Wigh 2001), but it is clear that they were not present in the material analysed from Kaupang. All of these patterns are consistent with the smaller assemblage from the CRM excavation at the site in 2000 (Hufthammer and Bratbak 2000).

The 639 identified fish bones were dominated by marine species, with eel and salmonids being the only possible prey of fresh water (although they can also be caught in the sea). Eleven main taxa were identified, but five species constitute most of the assemblage: herring (NISP = 263), cod (113), saithe (73), hake (24) and ling (19). Moreover, another 129 cod family specimens can probably be divided between cod, saithe and ling. These five taxa are thus likely to constitute c. 97% of the fish assemblage. However, five mineralised vertebral centra from cartilaginous fish, perhaps dogfish, may under-represent the im-

portance of this group as they produce few other ossified structures. The remaining taxa include the above-mentioned salmonids (nine specimens, of which one was probably trout), and one specimen each of eel, pollack, gurnard and wrasse. This assemblage is broadly similar to the collection from the CRM excavation (Hufthammer and Bratbak 2000), but it has a higher proportion of herring and exhibits minor differences in the representation of trace taxa. Flatfish were not represented in the 2002 material for example, although they were present in the 2003 harbour assemblage.

Although the Kaupang fish bone assemblage is tiny compared to some, it is similar in scale to many from Viking-age Europe and is better recovered than most (cf. Enghoff 1999, 2000; Barrett et al. 2004b). The site riddled material will be heavily biased by the poor preservation discussed above, but 38% of the fish assemblage was from pit fills which were at least partly waterlogged and produced some good-quality fish bone. The Kaupang material may thus be of interpretive value.

Only a few of the 27 bird bones recognised in the assemblage could be identified beyond the level of class. Twelve were diagnostic elements following the York recording protocol, but a few additional specimens were also identified (Tab. 14.5). Overall, seven bird species were identified. Nine specimens were firmly identifiable as domestic fowl ("chicken"), and many of the specimens only identifiable as "bird" were probably domestic fowl. The identifications were all made on elements on which this species can be clearly distinguished from other galliform birds such as pheasant *(Phasianus colchicus)* or black grouse *(Lyrurus tetrix)* (see Erbersdobler 1968). The other species reflect Kaupang's coastal location. Two specimens were identified as barnacle goose, one as brent goose, one as shelduck, one as eider duck, one as great black-backed gull and one as little auk.

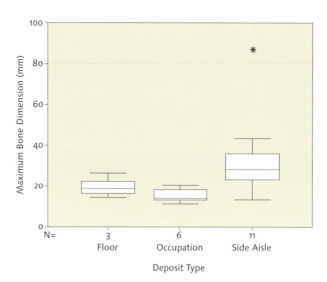

Figure 14.2 *Maximum dimension of identified mammal bones from house "floor", "occupation" and "side aisle" deposits. Illustration by the authors.*

Zooarchaeological goose bone identifications have been shown to be problematic (Barnes et al. 1998, 2000), but the small species in question are not among the taxa which can be easily confused. The little auk identification was made on the distal half of a left ulna, which was lightly charred. However, the morphology of the ulna is distinctive in alcids, and the specimen was closely compared with other alcid species and with other birds of a similar size. Despite the imperfections of the specimen, the identification is made with confidence.

As noted above, the poor preservation and small sample size of the ecofactual material from Kaupang limits its interpretive potential. Nevertheless, it can contribute to our understanding of a series of thematic issues, ranging from the character of specific features to the super-regional context of the settlement. Each of these themes will now be considered in turn.

14.4 The features: hearths, occupation deposits, dumps, pit fills and harbour deposits

The main feature types sampled were hearths, floor and occupation layers, side aisle layers, dumps, pit fills, harbour deposits and undefined "layers". Based on the sediment micromorphology evidence (Milek and French, this vol. Ch. 15) one can approach the samples with several hypotheses in mind: that floor and occupation deposits were augmented by sweepings from the hearths, that side aisle deposits resembled occupation deposits in the central aisle with less evidence of trampling, that dumps were largely composed of redeposited occupation deposits and that the harbour deposits were predominately composed of woodworking debris (no micromorphology samples of pit fills were analysed). The micromorphology evidence also suggests that gravel and sand were sometimes laid as primary floor deposits and that cut vegetation (possibly as straw mats), wood chips and

bark were occasionally significant components of floor litter. These interpretations can be corroborated and augmented using the evidence under consideration in this chapter. The ecofacts also add information regarding the pit fills, and suggest that the harbour deposits were largely redeposited occupation material.

Before considering the evidence, however, it is necessary to sound a cautionary note. The interpretations drawn below regarding specific feature types rely on an assumption that the sampled material was in situ rather than being residual or intrusive. This would be a naïve hypothesis on multiperiod sites where middens overlie houses and vice versa with much mixing and disturbance. At Kaupang, however, the period of occupation appears to have been limited, and the maintenance of plot boundaries also prescribed the use of space during the lifetime of the site. Moreover, samples with relatively unambiguous field interpretations are the focus of this consideration.

To begin with the hearth samples, these produced charcoal, charred bark, charred barley grains, charred hazelnutshell and fragments of burnt and unburnt bone (Tab. 14.1). These materials were then spread onto the floor and occupation layers within the houses. Charcoal and plant fuel ash are ubiquitous in these feature types and charred hazel nutshell, charred barley grains and bone fragments are also common in small numbers. Some floor and occupation deposits were also particularly rich in gravel-sized stone (Tab. 14.2). It might have been purposefully deposited as a living surface, a practice documented in later Viking-age Dublin (Wallace 1992; cf. Milek and French, this vol. Ch. 15:337).

The few side-aisle samples examined were very similar to the material from floor and occupation layers and must also have received redeposited hearth waste. The side aisles were different, however, in that they included slightly larger fragments of bone (Fig.

Figure 14.3 *Location of pit A99030 from Site Period I. Illustration, Julie K. Øhre Askjem.*

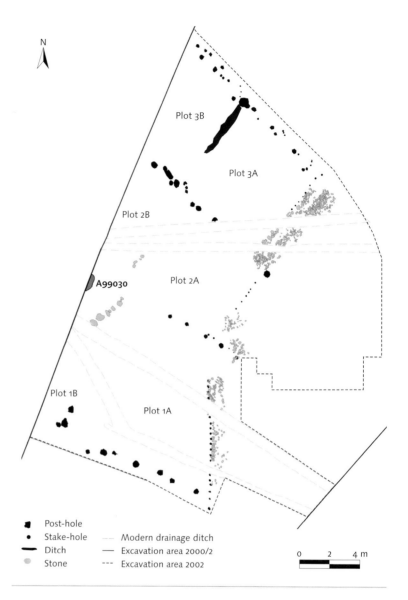

Plot 3B

Plot 3A

Plot 2B

A99030

Plot 2A

Plot 1B

Plot 1A

■	Post-hole		
●	Stake-hole	⋯	Modern drainage ditch
━	Ditch	──	Excavation area 2000/2
●	Stone	---	Excavation area 2002

0   2   4 m

14.2). This may be consistent with the interpretation, based on the micromorphology evidence, that they received less traffic and suffered less trampling. In the well-preserved houses of Viking-age Dublin, side aisles consisted of slightly raised platforms of brushwood and organic material over a base of generic floor material (the latter of which typically had a high concentration of wood chips). The objects found in the Dublin side aisles (such as hazel nutshells) were less fragmented than elsewhere in the houses, presumably because they fell down among the brushwood and were thus protected from trampling and cleaning (Geraghty 1996). Similar features might have existed in the less well-preserved buildings at Kaupang.

Like the interior deposits, the exterior dumping layers are characterised by charcoal and plant fuel ash with occasional bone fragments and charred barley grains (Tab. 14.1). This pattern is consistent with the suggestion noted above that they are largely composed of redeposited occupation deposits (Milek and French, this vol. Ch. 15:354). However, the dumps do seem to be missing the hazel nutshell characteristic of interior deposits at Kaupang. Much of this midden material might thus have come directly from its source (charcoal and ash from hearths) rather than via occupation deposits. The one "whole earth" GBA sample examined from dumping layers was composed mostly of charcoal and ash (Tab. 14.3). This is not to say that occupation layers were never redeposited on exterior middens, but it does seem likely that the latter were mainly created by the direct dumping of hearth waste.

All of the evidence discussed thus far has derived from material preserved without the benefit of waterlogging – mainly by charring. Fortunately, a few pit fills and the harbour deposits were waterlogged, leading to the preservation of both unburnt plant material and insect remains. It is therefore possible to infer

more about the formation of these features and (indirectly) about the floors and possibly roofs from which some of the material probably came.

The pits which produced waterlogged material were sufficiently small in number to make it worth treating them individually (Tab. 14.3; see Figs. 14.3–14.5). Starting with SP I, one GBA sample from pit A99030 on Plot 2B was studied. It included much charcoal, but also gravel and uncharred wood fragments, bark, wood chips and strawy material. Hazel nutshell was represented, along with woad, raspberry and plant remains characteristic of turf. Burnt and unburnt bone fragments were present along with the remains of insects characteristic of clean water and outdoor environments. This feature was not used as a cesspit, but its original function is unclear. It seems possible, however, that it received some redeposited floor litter. Many of the charred inclusions match what was found in the BS samples from internal deposits, and both wood chips and strawy material were identified as probable flooring by sediment micromorphology (Milek and French, this vol. Ch.

A82649

House A301

House
A302

Plot 2B

House
A406

Plot 2A

A65132

Midden
area

Plot 1A

House
A200

Midden
area

Hearth	Midden
Floor deposit	Drainage
Bench deposit	Pit
Bench line/wall	Stone
Ditch	Excavation outline 2000-2002
Post-hole/stake-hole	Excavation outline 2002

0   2   4 m

Figure 14.4 *Location of pits A65132 and A82649 from Site Period II. Illustration, Julie K. Øhre Askjem.*

Figure 14.5 *Location of pits A43852, A65132 and A64891 from Site Period III. Illustration, Julie K. Øhre Askjem.*

Figure 14.6 *Compressed strawy material from context AL86018 of pit A65132, Site Period II. Illustration by the authors.*

recognisable suite of house-floor inclusions: gravel, charcoal, wood fragments, bark, wood chips, occasional barley grains and burned and unburned bone. Traces of useful plants – flax, hemp, hop, woad, strawberry, raspberry and blackberry – were present. The insects, including two human fleas, also suggested waste from inside a building. In sum, whatever its initial function, this pit was probably filled with house-floor sweepings once it went out of use, possibly from house A200 on Plot 1A, SP II.

The possible use of strawy material as house-floor litter requires brief elaboration in light of the micromorphology evidence. Milek and French (this vol. Ch. 15:348, 354) note the presence of wavy lenses of phytoliths in layers interpreted as in situ or redeposited occupation surfaces. These were interpreted as possible evidence of woven grass mats. Such mats might have existed at Kaupang, but no fragments have been preserved in the waterlogged GBA samples and the compressed straw from pit A65132 suggests that cut vegetation was also simply spread on the floor.

The fills of pit A43852 from Plot 3B, SP III, may also represent material redeposited from inside a building. Five samples from five separate contexts were studied. These were all very similar, with the caveat that two exhibited poor preservation. Overall, the fills were characterised by the now familiar combination of charcoal, gravel, wood fragments, bark, wood chips, hazel nutshell, occasional barley grains and both burnt and unburnt bone fragments. One sample also produced strawy material and the pit included evidence of hemp, raspberry and blackberry. No human fleas were identified, but one sample produced some possible indoor fauna.

The fills of this pit resembled others from the site in many ways, but the pit was also distinctive in producing an insect assemblage dominated by two taxa: *Omosita colon* and a *Ptinus* sp. *O. colon* is found in

15:345, 348). The evidence of imported turf could also represent roofing material. As has been noted in passing above, these interpretations find parallels in the buildings of Viking-age Dublin (Geraghty 1996).

A clearer picture emerges from pit A65132, of Plot 1A, SP II, for which six samples from context AL86018 were analysed (poorly preserved upper fills of pit A65132 from SP III are not considered here). This pit was characterised by well-preserved compressed strawy material which was probably a mix of true cereal straw and other plants such as grasses, sedges and moss shoots (Fig. 14.6). The material was not finely comminuted as would typify herbivore dung and no parasite eggs were identified. Moreover, there was no insect evidence to suggest the material's use as animal bedding. Instead, the samples produced a

decaying matter, typically bones, dry carrion or old skins. *Omosita* and perhaps also the *Ptinus* sp. might have been exploiting a variety of materials at the Kaupang site; one hypothesis is that the *Omosita* and perhaps also the *Ptinus* sp. had invaded stored skins before they (and/or detritus from them) were discarded in the pit. This line of argument is supported by the record of an adult (?identification) and two larvae of the hide beetle *Dermestes lardarius,* found in decaying animal matter, sometimes in houses and birds' nests. Elements of the remaining fauna might have come from indoors (notably *?Tenebrio obscurus),* and many might have been attracted to hides or bones, but are not necessarily characteristic of skins or decaying animal matter. Smaller numbers of *Omosita* were also recorded in pits A99030 and A65132, which could be taken to imply that similar habitats existed at the site in periods I and II. As noted above, a "superabundance" of *Omosita colon* beetles was also found in pit A28375 and, to a lesser degree, pit A9422 from the CRM excavation in 2000 (Buckland et al. 2001).

The presence or absence of stored skins, conceivably furs, at Kaupang is highly relevant to the interpretation of the site's long-range trade connections (see section 14.7 below). It is also possible, however, that the insects described above were simply attracted to dry bones which might originally have been discarded in the pits at Kaupang in great numbers. Only fragments of bone survive at Kaupang, but pits were explicitly used for animal bone disposal at other broadly comparable sites such as Melbourne Street from Middle Anglo-Saxon Hamwic (Southampton) in England (Bourdillon and Coy 1980). Pit A43852, with its abundant *Omosita,* also produced a rich bone assemblage for this site (some of it from the samples yielding these distinctive insects).

The pit produced a total of 3,403 bones. Most were small fragments and only 328 specimens (236 fish, 87 mammal and 4 bird) were identified beyond the level of class. Nevertheless, this is a significant proportion of the total identified bone from the site, particularly in the case of fish. The main fish taxa represented were herring, cod, saithe, ling, dogfish, hake, and shark or ray. The mammal taxa were cattle, pig, caprine, cat, deer (one red deer antler tine and a comb tooth of unidentified antler) and shrew. The only identified bird specimens were of domestic fowl. These bones are not consistent with waste from fur preparation or skinning.

The fills of pit A64891, from Plot 1A, SP III, were more poorly preserved. Nothing can be inferred from the insects, but sample 87806 produced charcoal, gravel, wood fragments, bark, wood chips, hazel nutshell, burnt and unburnt bone, flax, hop, raspberry, strawberry and blackberry – typical occupation-deposit refuse.

Waterlogged deposits from the Viking-age har-

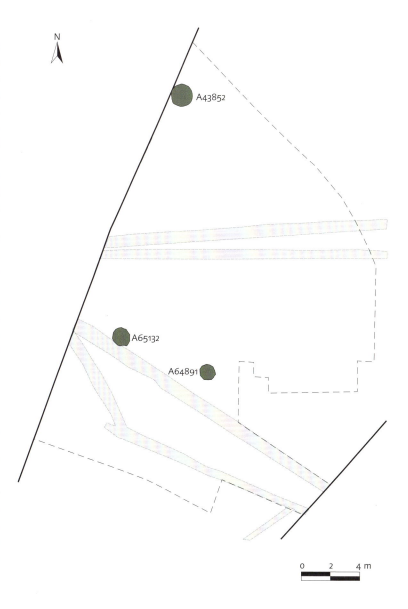

bour sediments were similar to the pit fills in many ways, but they lacked gravel and strawy material. Wood fragments, twigs, bark and wood chips dominated the matrix of all four samples examined. They also contained charcoal, hazel nutshell, barley, hop, woad, apple core, blackberry, strawberry and (in one sample) evidence of turf. Bone was not recorded during the GBA assessment, but it was collected by hand from the harbour deposits so the absence of this category from Table 14.3 should not be taken as significant. The insects were only assessed qualitatively, but hinted at decomposing floor litter (probably from a house, but conceivably a byre or stable). A single human flea was identified.

Based on intra-site micromorphological comparisons, the harbour deposits have been interpreted as waste from woodworking activity (Milek and French, this vol. Ch. 15:355). Assessment of the GBA samples, which represent a larger volume of material than the soil thin sections, may qualify this conclusion. The layers exhibit a number of inclusions – from charcoal and hazel nutshell to a human flea – which are consistent with occupation deposits on house floors. As discussed above, the wood chips and other woody debris are also consistent with floor litter – if perhaps incidentally as a by-product of woodworking. The discrepancy between the micromorphology and GBA evidence may be due to a combination of two factors. The first of these is the above-mentioned difference in the volume of material examined using the two methods. The second is that interpretation of the micromorphology samples is necessarily based on comparing waterlogged harbour sediments (where inclusions are very diluted by abundant preserved organic material) with freely drained floor deposits (where inclusions are concentrated by decay of most of the organic component).

Having suggested that the harbour samples may partly derive from floor litter, the paucity of gravel and the lack of strawy material must be revisited. These materials were common in deposits interpreted as floor litter above (principally pit fills). Their paucity in harbour samples may be due to sorting by wave-action or a discrepancy in chronology between the harbour layers and the pits of Plots 1A-3B. Alternatively, the harbour deposits may be a mixture of occupation and woodworking waste, the latter possibly from the construction of jetties or similar structures in the harbour itself.

In the discussion thus far, animal bone has only occasionally played a part in the interpretation of specific feature-types. This is to be expected given the poor preservation at Kaupang, but a few general patterns are worth noting. Firstly, only 14 fish bones (11 herring, 2 cod and 1 cod family) from the site were crushed, conceivably by mastication. Crushed herring bones have been interpreted as evidence of human cess in other contexts (cf. Wheeler and Jones

1989), but none of the Kaupang fish bones exhibited the complementary signs of partial digestion. The crushed bones may thus indicate trampling rather than ingestion. Along with the insect and plant remains, this evidence suggests that cesspits were not among the features sampled in the 2002 excavation.

The small sample of identified bone makes it difficult to evaluate intra-site patterning by feature type. Only a few observations are likely to be meaningful, and even these sometimes relate to preservation conditions rather than structured deposition. Pits and side aisles are particularly rich in fish bone – with ratios of fish:mammal of 0.1 and 0.09 respectively, compared to the site average of 0.02. In the case of pits, this probably relates to anoxic preservation conditions, but the same cannot be said of side-aisle deposits. In the latter case, more fish bone may have survived due to lower levels of trampling during the formation of the deposits. Within the pits, it is particular contexts rather than all pit-fills that are rich in fish bone. In pit A43852, for example, it is only contexts AL61411, AL87427, AL87626 and AL87669 that produced high ratios of fish:mammal. Similarly, in pit A65132 only context AL86018 was unusually rich in fish. It may be relevant that in pit A43852 the largest fish assemblages came from layers relatively low in the pit stratigraphy and therefore presumably most consistently waterlogged. Among the pits, it is A43852 which stands out as unusually rich in fish bone (with 517 specimens and a fish:mammal ratio of 0.18). By building, house 406 (Plot 2A) has a slightly elevated concentration of fish bone (210 specimens from floor and side aisle layers, producing a fish:mammal ratio of 0.12).

At the species level, with the exception of some patterning in the cat data discussed below, the broad characteristics of the mammal assemblage are repeated across those phases and context types for which sample sizes justify comparison. Structured or ritual deposition of animal bones is a characteristic of some European contexts of the first millennium AD (e.g. Campbell 2000; Wigh 2001), but there is no evidence that particular mammal taxa or elements were assigned to specific pits or other features at Kaupang. Overall, the rank order of pigs>cattle>caprines is repeated in most context types, including pits, with cattle and caprines occasionally reversing their order of abundance in cases where sample sizes were small (dumps, for example). As discussed below in section 14.6, however, the importance of pigs may be exaggerated by preservation conditions favouring small robust foot bones. Cattle were more abundant in the better preserved harbour deposits, but in all cases sample sizes are very small.

Most of the cat specimens derive from ditch fills (e.g. contexts AL68122, AL68504 and AL75386), predominately from SP II. One small group of cat bones from context AL68122 (the fill of a ditch dividing

Plots 3A and 3B in SP II) probably represents skinning (see section 14.7).

The sample size of the fish assemblage is too small to subdivide by feature-type and phase, but it is notable that the rank order of herring and cod (the two most abundant taxa) does differ across space and time. In particular, cod is the more abundant of the two in SP II, whereas herring is more common in SP III (Tab. 14.5). These differences can be explained in spatial terms. Most of the herring bones are from pit A43852, belonging to SP III.

14.5 Seasonality and permanence

Despite poor preservation, the ecofactual evidence from Kaupang can shed some tentative light on the question of the settlement's seasons of occupation and degree of permanence. If summer occupation is taken as given, the critical question is whether the settlement was occupied continuously throughout the year – particularly in winter. This issue can be addressed by consideration of migratory bird species and, in an indirect way, the representation of synanthropic insects in the waterlogged deposits.

As noted above in section 14.3, only 27 bird bones were recognised in the assemblage and few of these could be identified beyond class. These records are important, however, as the only possible indicators of year-round occupation at Kaupang in the zooarchaeological assemblage. After domestic fowl ("chickens", nine specimens), coastal and marine birds predominate. Of the latter, two specimens were identified as barnacle goose and one as brent goose. Both species breed in the Arctic and disperse around the coasts of northwestern Europe for the winter. One specimen of little auk was also identified. This species also breeds in the Arctic, dispersing to sea at high latitudes during the winter.

All three species are likely to have been caught outside the summer months, but before drawing conclusions it is necessary to consider the migratory behaviour of each species in detail and to recognise that breeding and wintering distributions can undergo changes through time. It must also be kept in mind that birds can be preserved for later consumption (Serjeantson 1998).

Of the three species under consideration, the little auk provides the strongest evidence. It breeds in the high Arctic and disperses at high latitudes (particularly among broken pack ice) during winter, principally from October to April. During this period, small numbers are sometimes found as far south as Skagerrak, and wrecks of little auks can also be blown south by prolonged gales (Snow and Perrins 1998). The single specimen of this species was found in context AL70553, a deposit in the ditch between Plots 1A and 1B in SP II.

The brent and barnacle geese are probably indicative of spring or autumn occupation rather than mid-winter. Two populations of brent geese are potentially relevant to Kaupang. One breeds in the Russian tundra and winters in the Netherlands, southeastern England and western France. A second breeds in Spitsbergen and Franz Josef Land and winters in northeastern England (Snow and Perrins 1998). The Russian tundra breeders migrate through the Baltic in mid-September to early October, typically passing through southern Scandinavia in October-November. During their return migration they leave southern Scandinavia in May-June. The Spitsbergen and Franz Josef Land breeders migrate down Norway's west coast, gathering in southern Scandinavia in early October before moving on to England. On their return, they pass through northwestern Denmark in April-May. If these migration patterns were similar in the Viking Age, the brent goose specimen from Kaupang is thus likely to represent a spring or autumn catch. It was from context AL67217, an occupation layer in house 302 of Plot 3A, SP II, sub-phase 2.

There are three main migratory populations of barnacle geese (Snow and Perrins 1998). One breeds in Greenland and winters in Ireland and western Scotland, one breeds in Spitsbergen and winters in the Solway Firth (on the Anglo-Scottish border) and one breeds in northern Russia and mainly winters in the Netherlands. The Greenland population was unlikely to have come within the range of Kaupang's inhabitants. The Spitsbergen population presently migrates down the west coast of Norway (conceivably bringing it within range of the settlement's economic catchment) in September, returning in April/May. More realistically, the northern Russian population migrates over southern Scandinavia in August/September and March/April. In sum, the barnacle geese from Kaupang were most likely to have been caught during their migrations in late summer/early autumn or late winter/early spring. However, a few pairs of this species (c. 40 in 1996) have actually started breeding in Norway in recent decades (Snow and Perrins 1998), suggesting that they might also have done so in the distant past. Thus they are less convincing indicators of year-round settlement than the little auk and (to a lesser degree) the brent goose specimens. One of the barnacle goose bones was found in context AL74188, a dumping deposit of SP II, sub-phase 2 on Plot 3A. The other was from context AL60829, a pit deposit of SP III on Plot 3B.

Although many of the plant remains found are indicative of summer and autum, there is no botanical evidence from Kaupang that can be said to corroborate or refute year-round occupation. The same applies to the insect remains, with the caveat that the synanthropic component of the fauna may have implications regarding the degree of permanence of the settlement.

	Kaupang	Viborg	Copper-gate	Oslo	Deer Park Farms	Buiston
% SA	48	33	55	62	54	36
% SF	33	21	24	33	9	26
% ST	14	13	24	28	12	10
% SS	0	0	7	1	33	0

Table 14.6 *Percentages of categories of synanthropic fauna in the amalgamated insect assemblages from Kaupang and other sites (see text). SA – all synanthropes; SF – facultative synanthropes; ST – species which are typically synanthropic; SS – strong synanthropes.*

	Kaupang	Viborg	Copper-gate	Oslo	Deer Park Farms	Buiston
SF as % SA	70	62	44	53	18	71
ST as % SA	30	37	43	46	21	29
SS as % SA	1	0	14	2	61	1

Table 14.7 *Internal structure of the synanthropic fauna in the amalgamated assemblages from Kaupang and other sites (see text). SA – all synanthropes; SF – facultative synanthropes; ST – species which are typically synanthropic; SS – strong synanthropes. Data for Deer Park Farms are strongly skewed by the abundant* Aglenus brunneus: *see Table 14.8.*

It has been suggested (Kenward 1997) that analysis of the synanthropic insects (those species favoured by human activity) from archaeological deposits can provide a range of information about the character and use of sites. This has indirect implications for seasonality. Where the favourable habitats created by humans are missing for part of each year, a synanthropic insect fauna will be prevented from developing to the same degree as in a settlement continuously occupied for many years. This relationship is not, however, a straightforward one. The abundance, diversity and character of the synanthropic insect fauna would also have been influenced by: the ultimate length of occupation (years, decades or centuries), the character and density of settlement (how urban it was), and the intensity of external contacts through which the insect populations were introduced (and/or augmented).

The synanthropic component at Kaupang was distinctive, with a large proportion of facultative synanthropes (common in natural as well as artificial habitats), few typical synanthropes (typically associated with humans, but able to live in nature) and almost no obligate or strong synanthropes (absent from or very rare in natural habitats in the relevant

geographical area) (Tab. 14.6). While this evaluation is based on analysis of a limited number of deposits of a restricted range of types (no floors, for example), and the whole-site assemblage is fairly small (1,024 adult beetles and bugs), it is hard to believe that it differed greatly from the fauna of the site as a whole. Many of the assemblages had high diversity and are almost certainly rich in background fauna, which should mean that they represent an "averaged" fauna for the site, and others appeared to contain material dumped from within buildings; so it is clear that "house fauna" has been sampled.

The statistics for the site fauna as a whole thus show that synanthropes were not as strongly represented as in some other occupation sites. However, the comparative figures are sometimes substantially affected by the presence of other components, for example the strength of the outdoor fauna, and at two of the comparative sites by *Aglenus brunneus*, which can be extremely abundant. The first problem is easily overcome by examining the internal structure of the synanthropic fauna (Tab. 14.7). This shows that species designated as facultative synanthropes (likely to have colonised from natural habitats as well as artificial ones, though it should be remembered that the classification is inevitably somewhat arbitrary) were far more important at Kaupang than at the broadly contemporaneous site of Coppergate, York, or at the small isolated rural site of Deer Park Farms, County Antrim, Northern Ireland (Allison et al. 1999; Kenward 1997; Kenward and Allison 1994; Kenward and Hall 1995). Indeed, this component gives a value closest to that of the isolated lake-dwelling at Buiston, Ayrshire, Scotland (Kenward 1997; Kenward et al. 2000) and of the essentially rural workshops at Viborg, Denmark (Kenward 2005). Facultative synanthropes were important in occupation deposits at the medieval "Søndre Felt" site in Oslo (Tab. 14.7), suggesting the possibility of regional differences. However, the large proportion of facultative synanthropes at Søndre Felt was the result of the abundance of a small number of species in a few samples, and the synanthrope fauna of the site as a whole was rich and well developed. This simply serves as a reminder that species composition must be examined, rather than relying simply on summary statistics.

The proportion of facultative synanthropes probably reflects the degree to which more specialised synanthropes – much less likely to have been abundant in the wild locally, and therefore relying on trade and the passage of time – had been able to colonise and survive. Although a few species thought to be more specialised had arrived, presumably as a result of trade (e.g. *Aglenus brunneus* and *Tenebrio obscurus)*, the data for the Kaupang site appear to suggest relative isolation, a new and short-lived settlement, or intermittent occupation.

These comparative figures are somewhat skewed by the presence of abundant *Aglenus brunneus*, which probably bred in the deposits post-depositionally, at Coppergate and Deer Park Farms. Removing *A. brunneus* (Tab. 14.8) emphasises the similarity between Deer Park Farms and Coppergate, and between Kaupang, Viborg and Buiston, with Søndre Felt somewhat intermediate. The values for the typical synanthropes emphasise the similarity between the intensively occupied sites at Coppergate and Oslo.

There was a slight, but statistically insignificant, increase in the proportion of synanthropes in the assemblages through time, but no pattern in the variation of the internal structure of the synanthrope component. Unfortunately, It was thus not possible to address the question as to whether the site was permanently or seasonally occupied in the various site periods – there were too few deposits containing appreciable numbers of insects in each phase to provide an objective assessment. Nevertheless, the extremely limited synanthrope fauna, and the predominance of facultative forms, may be indicators of seasonal or intermittent occupation for at least part of the settlement's lifetime, large populations of typical or strong synanthropes being unable to develop in a short period of occupation, and (if occupation was in summer) not having artificially warmed places for wintering. Seasonal occupation could also account for the rather limited abundance of annual nitrophile weeds in comparison with other occupation sites. Alternatively, the poorly developed synanthropic fauna may imply a relatively short overall lifespan for the intensive occupation at Kaupang (if one assumes, based on the artefactual evidence, that external contacts were frequent and widespread).

	Kaupang	Viborg	Copper-gate	Oslo	Deer Park Farms	Buiston
SF as % SA	70	62	48	53	44	71
ST as % SA	30	37	47	46	53	29
SS as % SA	0	0	5	1	3	1

Table 14.8 *Internal structure of the synanthropic fauna in the amalgamated assemblages from Kaupang and other sites (see text), after removal of* Aglenus brunneus. *SA – all synanthropes; SF – facultative synanthropes; ST – species which are typically synanthropic; SS – strong synanthropes.*

14.6 Provisioning and relationships with the hinterland

A major role of ecofact studies in urban archaeology is to study how towns and their precursors were provisioned (e.g. Prummel 1983; Crabtree 1996; Wigh 2001; O'Connor 2004; Enghoff, in prep. a). Did Kaupang's occupants produce their own food (as has been argued for Dorestad for example (Prummel 1983)) or rely on an extensive hinterland (as suggested for Fishergate in York for example (O'Connor 1991))? Moreover, if the town was provisioned by a hinterland, can the structure of the ecofact evidence shed any light on how this exchange was organised (cf. O'Connor 2001)?

To begin with arable agriculture, the pollen evidence from Kaupang suggests local cereal cultivation until the time of Kaupang's occupation, followed by cessation of this activity until late in the Middle Ages (Sørensen et al., this vol. Ch. 12:271). Sørensen et al. thus tentatively suggest that local cultivation stopped when the settlement was founded, which would have necessitated significant provisioning from distant sources. Barley grain is ubiquitous in the samples we have studied from the site and oats and rye have also been recorded. Wheat has been found in one sample from the CRM excavation in 2000 (Buckland et al. 2001).

Given the imprecision of radiocarbon dating (on which the pollen evidence relies), and the relatively short (c. 150-year) occupation of Kaupang, one could alternatively argue that agriculture dwindled in the region only after the settlement was abandoned. One scenario that could have accounted for this pattern would have been that the land had remained owned by elite patrons (and had thus been unavailable for use) despite the decline of the urban site. The interpretation that agricultural activity declined around Viking-age Kaupang does require a specific explanation. It runs counter to the widespread expansion of farming observed in northwestern Europe in the centuries leading up to the end of the first millennium AD (e.g. Karlsson and Robertsson 1997; Fossier 1999; Macklin et al. 2000).

In light of the above, it is difficult to say if the barley, oats, rye and (to a lesser degree) wheat consumed at Kaupang were locally produced or imported. Possible imported rye was recognised by measuring grains from the 10th-century fortress of Fyrkat in Denmark (Robinson 1991 and references therein), but early Viking-age evidence of the large-scale shipment of grain is not known to the authors. No large concentrations of grain suitable for metrical analysis were recovered from Kaupang. There is, however, evidence of cereal straw, so some local production can be assumed. Moreover, the absence of grain pest insects argues against the presence of large quantities of stored imported grain on the site (Kenward and Williams 1979; Buckland et al. 2001). It is conceivable that small quantities of wheat, for example, were traded over long distances, but in sum it seems probable that most or all of the cereals used at Kaupang were produced in its hinterland.

The sparse remains of flax (linseed, mostly from pit A65132, but with a record of capsule fragments from A64891) represent a plant useable for fibre, as food or a source of oil. There is no reason to think that it represents imported material, so this crop might also have been grown in Kaupang's hinterland.

Local cultivation of hemp is also probable given the remains of this plant found in some of the pit-fill samples. It was recorded at Kaupang in small amounts from two pits and more frequently in two of the fills of a third (A65132). This is most likely to have been a fibre crop, though its use as food for human or animal consumption and as an oil-seed is also possible. Almost all of the material from Kaupang comprised achene fragments, which may indicate breakage during processing for food or oil extraction. In the hinterland of Birka in the region around lake Mälaren, Sweden, hemp was probably introduced early in the first millennium AD and was increasingly cultivated during the Viking Age (Karlsson and Robertsson 1997).

Although a native plant, hop may also have been grown or purposefully collected. It was present in trace amounts in two pits, but rather frequent through the fills of pit A65132, reaching an abundance of 3 (on the 4-point scale used) in two samples from context AL86018. Behre (1983, 1984) has described the finds of hops from Hedeby, and put them in the context of early medieval use of plants as flavourings for beer. This plant was frequent at Coppergate (Kenward and Hall 1995), and has also been recorded at Birka, Sweden (Hansson and Dickson 1997), and Novgorod (M. Monk, pers. comm.), whilst Aalto and Heinäjoki-Majander (1997) have demonstrated its importance in 9th-/10th-century deposits at the Viking-age town of Staraja Ladoga in western Russia. The use to which the hops were put does seem most likely to have been related to flavouring beer, though the plant is credited with other uses such as in dyeing.

In contrast to the rich evidence for dye plants in York (Kenward and Hall 1995, and a more recent synthesis by Hall and Kenward 2004), only woad stands out amongst the plants recorded at Kaupang as being likely to have had this purpose (although certainly many of the wild plants might have furnished colour for textiles). It is difficult to see why woad remains were present in the Kaupang deposits (in single fills in each of two pits, but also recorded from a sample from the "harbour area" recovered during the 2003 excavation) unless it had been brought for use in dyeing – though it is a successful coloniser of certain kinds of disturbed soils (having, for example, become a pernicious weed in parts of North America following introduction by European settlers). Woad is well known from the Viking Age in southern Norway from its presence in the Oseberg ship-burial (Holmboe 1927).

A variety of other plant resources must also have been collected from the settlement's hinterland. A variety of tree species provided building material, firewood and (perhaps incidentally) twig and wood-chip floor litter. Cut strawy vegetation was also collected for this purpose and turf may have been cut (conceivably for roofing). Hazelnuts were a ubiquitous snack food and the seeds of a variety of berries made their way into the settlement's deposits. Apples were also eaten. The limited waterlogged preservation at Kaupang made the study of possible coppicing practices impossible, but some level of woodland management seems probable given the vast amount of fuel that the settlement must have required. Many of the deposits studied in this chapter and by micromorphology (Milek and French, this vol. Ch. 15), were at least partly composed of wood ash and charcoal. However, the necessary forested land must have been some distance from the settlement given the paucity of insects associated with trees (see section 14.3, above).

The plant (and indirectly also the insect) remains thus imply the existence of a substantial hinterland around Kaupang, which one can speculate either controlled or was controlled by the settlement's inhabitants or patrons. Without such an inalienable link it is difficult to envisage how the settlement could have functioned.

The animal bone both corroborates and modifies this interpretation. The relevant evidence includes the species represented, the ages at which they were (or were not) killed and the ways in which they were butchered. In large, well-preserved, faunal assemblages these and other variables (e.g. bone measurements) can shed detailed light on hunting, fishing, husbandry and provisioning practices (e.g. Prummel 1983; O'Connor 1989; Wigh 2001; Schmölcke 2004). Given the extremely poor bone preservation at Kaupang, however, one's objectives must be modest and one's interpretations tentative.

The first observation to make is that there was a virtual absence of wild mammal remains (with the exception of one red deer antler tine, a worked antler comb tooth, two hare bones and one shrew bone). As noted in section 14.3 above, this pattern is clear despite carefully examining all 70,845 specimens for evidence of other wild taxa.

The paucity of remains of wild mammals (many of which would be forest dwellers in a Norwegian context) is also consistent with the virtual absence of freshwater fish remains and the complete absence of "inland" wild bird remains from the site. It would seem that the wild resources of the settlement's terrestrial hinterland were not exploited. The fish assemblage is dominated by marine species, with eel (one specimen) and salmonids (salmon or trout, nine specimens), which inhabit both marine and freshwater environments, being the only possible prey from rivers, lakes or streams. After domestic fowl ("chickens", which were presumably kept in the settlement), coastal and marine birds predominate, with no taxa indicative of fowling undertaken inland from the site.

This pattern is consistent with some other proto-urban settlements of broadly comparable date, such as Fishergate in York (O'Connor 1991) and Melbourne Street ("Hamwic") in Southampton (Bourdillon and Coy 1980). However, it differs from others, such as Ribe (where fish caught in fresh water were more abundant: Enghoff, in prep. b) and Birka (where furbearers were common: Wigh 2001). At Fishergate in York, this limited species diversity has been interpreted as evidence that the settlement's food supply was provided (and thus controlled) by an elite patron (O'Connor 1991). A semi-autonomous urban population might be expected to exert a greater level of consumer choice and thus produce a more diverse faunal assemblage – as is evident in later sites from York such as 16–22 Coppergate (O'Connor 1989). A similar interpretation may be relevant to Kaupang (although use was made of coastal birds and a number of marine fish species). Later medieval towns in Norway, which were fully urban, produced slightly more remains of wild mammals and inland birds (e.g. Lie 1988, 1989; Hufthammer 2000, 2003). The lack of remains of furbearers is discussed further in section 14.7 below.

The domestic mammals identified were mostly pigs, cattle and caprines (sheep or goats) – with smaller numbers of cats (36 specimens), dogs (probably 4 specimens) and horses (3 specimens). The main body of material, from Plots 1A–3B, was notable in producing a rank order of pig>cattle>caprines. A relatively high proportion (or occasionally dominance) of pig bones is consistent with broadly Viking-age centres in the Baltic region and western Jutland such as Birka, Hedeby, Groß Strömkendorf, Menzlin and Ribe (e.g. Reichstein and Tiessen 1974; Hatting 1991; Wigh 2001 and references therein; Schmölcke 2004). Moreover, the earliest (11th- to 12th-century) phase of medieval Oslo also produced a relatively high proportion of pig bones (Lie 1988; see also Hufthammer 2003). Thus this pattern could be interpreted as an extreme expression of an "eastward-looking" husbandry and provisioning system – possibly with an element of environmental determinism given the evidence of forest in Kaupang's hinterland and thus availability of local pannage.

This hypothesis is weakened, however, by the observation that pigs were also very abundant in late Viking-age Irish towns, particularly Dublin (e.g. McCormick 1997, 2005). In these instances, the pigs are thought to have been stall-raised "in town". The pattern is therefore interpreted as evidence of strained political relations between Hiberno-Norse centres and their Irish hinterlands – which might otherwise have been expected to provision the towns (McCormick 2005). A similar interpretation could conceivably apply to Kaupang, given the tentative identification of a pigsty at the site (Pilø, pers. comm.). It seems more likely, however, that pigs were

abundant at Kaupang and other "eastern" centres because of the availability of extensive tracts of forest for pannage within their hinterlands.

It is also possible that the species representation at Kaupang might simply have been very biased by the unusual preservation and recovery conditions of the site. If it is correct that small robust elements have been favoured, the high proportion of pigs is partly due to taphonomy and the fact that they have four developed digits, compared with the two of cattle and sheep.

The finds from the Kaupang harbour excavation in 2003 may shed additional light on the relative importance of pigs. Here they were less abundant than cattle. This difference may simply reflect the tiny sample size of the harbour assemblage, patterned refuse-disposal practices or sorting by wave-action. However, given that preservation was better in the harbour the dominance of pigs in the rest of the site may well be a taphonomic bias, at least in part.

The aging evidence for pigs (and all species) is poor due to tiny sample sizes and the taphonomic impact on the elements that are best represented (making epiphyseal fusion data of limited value). Nevertheless, it is worth noting that no pig deciduous fourth premolars were recovered and that almost all permanent fourth premolars and first to third molars were unworn or in early stages of wear (Barrett et al. 2004a). This may imply that the pigs were killed between their first and second year based on Silver's (1969) tooth-eruption data.

Pigs are typically killed young because most are kept for meat rather than for breeding stock. However, the complete absence of piglets is notable. It is probably due to the poor preservation conditions (immature bone is particularly susceptible to destruction), but could alternatively imply that pigs were not usually raised within the settlement. Instead, Kaupang might have been provisioned with forest-herded pigs from farms in the countryside as discussed above (cf. Crabtree 1994; Verhulst 2002). Theoretically, this hypothesis could be tested by studying the diet of the pigs using stable isotope analysis. Unfortunately, however, there was insufficient collagen preserved in the bones from Kaupang (Richards, pers. comm.).

The pigs consumed were probably all domestic even if they were herded in a forest hinterland. The material was not conducive to osteometric analysis (due to fragmentation and burning), but where it could be observed tooth-size and -morphology were entirely consistent with domestic pigs (Payne and Bull 1988; Rowley-Conwy 1995). The pigs would presumably have been herded "into town" given that most parts of the skeleton are represented (with a quantitative bias towards small robust elements such as the metapodials, tarsals and phalanges consistent with preservation by burning). Cut marks on the pig bones, including a scapula, humerus, pelvis and femur, are most consistent with disarticulating whole skeletons on site.

Notable exceptions to the otherwise complete skeletal representation of pigs are the upper and lower canines. They are missing from the Plot 1A–3B collection despite their distinctive appearance and the preservation of other pig teeth. They have not been separated from the assemblage as artefacts (Pilø, pers. comm.), leaving curation in the Viking Age or anomalous preservation as possible explanations. Given their recovery from the Kaupang harbour deposits, where preservation was slightly better, the latter interpretation seems most likely.

Like the pigs, the cattle from Kaupang are represented by all parts of the skeleton, with a bias towards teeth and the small robust elements of the feet. Cut marks on a radius, two femora and three metapodials are consistent with disarticulating the skeleton (probably during primary butchery) and (in the case of the metapodials) hide removal. A single horn core indicates the presence of a horned "breed", but it was too fragmentary to yield statistics regarding size or shape. The aging evidence suffers from the problems noted above regarding pigs, but once again it may be meaningful that no deciduous fourth premolars were recovered (Barrett et al. 2004a). If this is not due to the poor preservation of juvenile teeth, it implies that the cattle were butchered at some point after approximately 2 years of age (although a very few unfused early-fusing elements, such as proximal phalanges, were present in this collection and a few juvenile cattle bones were also noted in the harbour assemblage). The wear stages of the permanent teeth imply that the Kaupang cattle were not kept into old age either. For example, at least some were killed between approximately 24 and 30 months based on unworn third molars. The one complete mandible from the site, found in pit A65132 of Plot 1A, included teeth with the most advanced wear states in the collection. Its third molar was in Grant's (1982) stage G, probably indicating an age of greater than 5 years (Grigson 1982).

The paucity of calves at Kaupang could be due to the tiny sample size or poor preservation of juvenile bone. Alternatively, it could imply that the settlement was not raising cattle. In the latter case it would have been provisioned from hinterland farms. In at least some cases (the individuals with unworn third molars) the cattle were killed as prime meat animals of nearly adult size. The Kaupang evidence is too incomplete to read much into this observation, but a focus on beef consumption (rather than the local production of dairy products, for example) has been observed at comparable settlements. Examples include Dorestad (Prummel 1983) and 16–22 Coppergate, York (O'Connor 1989). Annalistic references regarding medieval Dublin can be employed to bring

this practice to life. In the 12th century thousands of cattle were driven into town from neighbouring kingdoms to pay for mercenary services (Holm 1986).

Two of the caprine specimens, a skull fragment with horn core and a distal tibia, were identified as sheep (the former more definitively than the latter). The rest were undifferentiated, so it is not possible to indicate whether goats were present at Kaupang. Goats were very common however, at later medieval urban sites in Norway (Lie 1988; see Hufthammer 2003), so it is probable that both species were present. As with the pigs and cattle, a range of skeletal elements was recovered implying the presence of complete caprine carcases at the site. The familiar bias towards robust foot bones and teeth is also observable. No cut marks were noted on specimens identified as sheep or goat. Tooth wear could only be assessed on five isolated specimens, all of which are consistent with adult "sheep" rather than old individuals or "lambs". Most of the observable epiphyses were also fused, indicating mature animals. Although these aging indicators are superficially consistent with meat and perhaps wool rather than milk production, the problem of small sample size is particularly acute for this group of animals. Some comparable settlements (e.g. Ribe, see Hatting 1991) have produced significant numbers of old caprines interpreted as evidence of wool production. Others, such as Birka (Wigh 2001) and 16–22 Coppergate, York, (O'Connor 1989) have produced mostly sub-adult and young adult caprines (younger than approximately four years) interpreted as multi-purpose meat and wool producers. In any case, at Kaupang they were presumably brought "to town" to be slaughtered for their meat. Alternatively, the putative goats among the material may have been kept in the settlement as multi-purpose milk, meat, horn and hide producers (cf. Lie 1988).

Little can be said about the tiny numbers of horse and dog bones identified, except to note that horse is typically uncommon at comparable proto-urban sites (Wigh 2001) and that dogs might have been more numerous at Kaupang than the four identified specimens imply. Thirty-two mammal and three fish bones exhibited clear carnivore tooth impressions consistent with dog gnawing. Cats are discussed in section 14.7 below.

As noted above, most of the identified fish and bird bones are from coastal or fully maritime species. The cod, saithe, ling and hake were probably caught from boats using traditional hand lines in relatively deep water (cf. Vollan 1974; Sørheim 2004; Olsen 2004). Ling and hake prefer particularly deep water, but can sometimes be found relatively close to shore – during summer in the case of hake (Whitehead et al. 1986). These four taxa represent a fishery distinct from the herring, which were probably caught by net (Sørheim 2004), although coastal traps can also be effective (von Brandt 1984). Nets are indirectly evidenced at Kaupang, due to the numerous recoveries of netsinkers (Pilø, pers. comm.). As noted above, the nine salmonid specimens identified (one of which may have been a trout based on the criteria of Feltham and Marquiss 1989) could have been caught in either fresh or salt water – probably by hook, spear or net (von Brandt 1984). The Lågen River, which is renowned for its salmon fisheries, meets the sea close to the Kaupang site.

Little can be said of the cartilaginous fish, as their mineralised vertebral centra could not be identified to species. If dogfish however, as suspected, they could have provided both food and oil (cf. Lie 1988). The remaining trace taxa probably represent incidental catches. The wrasse specimen (a vertebra which could only be identified to family) is interesting insofar as it may imply some fishing in the inter-tidal zone (Whitehead et al. 1986). The single gurnard, a common food of large gadids such as ling (Muus and Dahlstrøm 1974), may be the only indication of gut contents in the assemblage. In the site riddled material this lacuna could be a recovery bias, but this seems unlikely in the pit fills where tiny herring bones were well represented (unless some of the herring themselves were gut contents from the large gadids). Fish might thus have been partly prepared off-site. As discussed below in section 14.7, however, there is no evidence of the long-range trade of dried or salted fish to or from this site.

Domestic fowl aside, the bird bones also represent exploitation of the coast or sea, possibly at some distance from the settlement. The barnacle goose, brent goose and little auk specimens have already been discussed in section 14.5 above. Two other waterfowl were identified: one specimen each of shelduck and of eider duck. Eider duck were numerous in the assemblages from Hedeby (Reichstein and Pieper 1986:53–4) and Birka (Ericson 1987). Ericson (1987) has suggested that the eider from Birka had been hunted along the coast of central Sweden using air nets (typically strung between two islets) and transported over considerable distances to the town. A single specimen of great black-backed gull, also a coastal bird, may represent an opportunistic scavenger, but gulls do seem to have been eaten in some regions of northern Europe during the Viking Period and Middle Ages (cf. Serjeantson 1988; Hufthammer 2003).

In sum, the ecofactual evidence suggests that Kaupang must have controlled or drawn on a productive hinterland stretching well beyond the settlement's immediate environment. Inland, it relied on an extensive (but probably local) agricultural and wooded hinterland. To seaward, its occupants might have utilised an equally (or perhaps more) extensive maritime hinterland.

14.7 Long-range trade

Although the artefacts from Kaupang are clearly indicative of long-range trade, the same cannot be said of most of the ecofacts. To begin with the plant remains, with the exception of woad, hemp, flax and the cereals, all of the plants recorded from Kaupang are native to Norway and all might have grown in the vicinity of the site. Moreover, the crop plants would all have been introduced first before the 9th century. Thus none is significant in terms of possible trade connections. There were no clearly cultivated fruits and no evidence of importation of exotic fruits – in contrast to the figs and grape pips from medieval Oslo, for example (Griffin 1988).

In the same vein, the poorly developed synanthropic insect fauna at Kaupang could also imply modest levels of trade. It is equally possible, however, that this pattern was a result of the limited overall life-span of the settlement or periodic (at times possibly seasonal?) abandonment (see section 14.5).

As noted in section 14.3 above, during analysis of the bone assemblage particular attention was paid to the possible inclusion of fur-bearing species, such as the squirrel, fox, brown bear, pine marten, polecat, wolverine, badger, otter and lynx recovered at Birka (Wigh 2001). It is clear, however, that they were not present. This observation is considered to be conclusive, given the fine level of recovery at Kaupang, the bias towards preservation of small bones at this site and the fact that 70,845 specimens were examined. The pattern is also consistent with the smaller assemblages recovered during the CRM work in 2000 (Hufthammer and Bratbak 2000) and the harbour excavations in 2003.

The only convincing evidence of skinning of any species at Kaupang is one group of cat bones from context AL68122 (the fill of a plot division ditch between Plots 3A and 3B, SP II). It included tarsals, metatarsals, phalanges and a caudal vertebra – presumably deposited while processing (or disposing of) a cat pelt. Cat remains are relatively common finds at broadly contemporary sites in Europe (e.g. Crabtree 1989; Hatting 1990; Wigh 2001; O'Connor 2004); cats often served as a source of fur, and also acted as predators of commensal pests, and presumably as pets (the wild cat, *Felis silvestris*, is not recorded in the fauna of Norway). Cats were particularly common in medieval Oslo (Lie 1988; Hufthammer 2000). Two hare bones from Kaupang, a metatarsal and a phalanx, could conceivably also relate to skinning, but in the absence of characteristic cut marks other explanations are equally plausible.

Unlike such evidence from Birka (Wigh 2001), the zooarchaeological evidence from Kaupang does not imply that the settlement was involved in the processing and trade of fur. However, this observation conflicts with what would be expected based on the 9th century account of Ohthere's trading expedition (Fell

1984). If both sources are combined in a general way (they differ slightly in date), it is possible that most furs entered Kaupang in an entirely pre-processed state and/or that they were re-exported rather than used to serve local needs.

The presence of processed furs at Kaupang is one way that the insect evidence could be explained. As noted in sections 14.3 and 14.4 above, fills of pit A43852, and to a lesser degree other deposits from the site, included unusually large numbers of *Omosita colon* beetles, together with a range of other species likely to have been attracted to dryish animal matter (including skins and bones): *Saprinus* sp., *Creophilus maxillosus, Trox scaber, Dermestes lardarius* adults and larvae, *Necrobia violacea, Necrobia* sp. indet. and *Tenebrio obscurus* (Tab. 14.9). The abundance of the genus *Omosita* in particular is exceptionally high in these deposits, in comparison with 3,069 comparative assemblages recorded at least semi-quantitatively that are known to one of the authors (Harry Kenward). This beetle was also described as "superabundant" in pit A28375 from the 2000 CRM excavation (Buckland et al. 2001). As discussed in section 14.4 above, the pit fills were probably composed at least in part of redeposited floor litter, so these finds may imply the storage of furs in buildings. Unfortunately, however, no animal hair itself was observed to corroborate this hypothesis. Another alternative is that these insects were simply attracted to dry bones in the deposits, but bones occur in pits at broadly comparable sites (e.g. Kenward and Hall 1995), and none of those pits exhibit the same abundance of *Omosita* beetles. Further possibilities are that the insects were attracted to dried fish or hides (rather than furs). Thus, in sum, due to the weakness of the ecofactual evidence, the possibility of fur trade at Kaupang remains a hypothesis rather than a conclusion.

Stockfish (dried cod and related species) were widely traded from Arctic and northwestern Norway in the Middle Ages (Nedkvitne 1976, 1993; Perdikaris 1999; Sørheim 2004). There are remains of stockfish in early post–Viking-age deposits from Trondheim (Hufthammer 2003) and evidence from areas of Norse settlement in Scotland imply that this commerce may have been active as early as the 11th century (Barrett 1997; Barrett et al. 1999, 2000). However, there is not yet convincing evidence that this trade existed on any scale earlier in the Viking Age (Barrett et al. 2004b). Most importantly, the elements present at Kaupang suggest that whole fish were consumed (Tab. 14.10). All parts of the skeletons of cod, saithe, ling and hake are represented; there is no *predominance* of cleithra, supracleithra and caudal vertebrae, which would be indicative of imported stockfish (Barrett 1997). The paucity of cleithra at Kaupang could be interpreted as indicating that stockfish were exported from the site, but is more likely to be a taphonomic pattern given the fragility of this ele-

ment and the presence of some supracleithra (identifiable as cod family only and thus not shown in Table 14.10) and caudal vertebrae.

Herring from broadly contemporary settlements may occasionally represent cured trade goods, at inland Dorestad for example (Prummel 1983; Enghoff 1999), but they could derive from local fishing in most cases. The Kaupang assemblage is too small to detect whether the specialised butchery sometimes indicative of herring curing was employed (Enghoff 1996). Thus it is not possible to tell whether the herring were locally caught or imported as cured fish, but the former seems probable.

The status of domestic fowl ("chickens") in Viking-age Norway is slightly ambiguous due to the paucity of bone assemblages of this date from the region. However, hen bones were recovered from a possible Iron Age settlement at Viklem in Trøndelag (Hufthammer, pers. comm.). Moreover, a number of Viking-age and earlier records of domestic fowl are known from Sweden (Tyrberg 2002, pers. comm.), including the Viking-age trading settlement of Birka (Wigh 2001). Thus it is likely that they were locally available (Hufthammer, pers. comm.). Nevertheless, the slight possibility remains that they were introduced to Kaupang by long-range transport or trade, presumably from Denmark or Sweden. The other bird species from Kaupang could have been acquired locally, although one cannot rule out the possibility that some of the seabirds were cured and traded over considerable distances (cf. Serjeantson 2001).

Taxon	n
Saprinus sp.	1
Creophilus maxillosus	2
Omosita colon	97
Trox scaber	3
Dermestes lardarius adults	? 3
do. larvae	6
Necrobia violacea	1
Necrobia sp. indet.	1
Tenebrio obscurus	1 ? 1

Table 14.9 *Numbers of individuals (n) of beetles from pit A43852 which may have been attracted to stored skins.*

Table 14.10 *Element distribution of cod and herring (diagnostic elements only). See Barrett (1997) for definitions of vertebrae groups.*

Table 14.11 *Estimated total length of the main fish species from Kaupang based on a comparison of diagnostic elements with reference specimens of known size.*

Element	I	II	III	I-III	Disturbed	Total
Cod						
Abdominal Vertebra Group 1		9	3	1		13
Abdominal Vertebra Group 2		9	3	1	3	16
Abdominal Vertebra Group 3		11	7	2	1	21
Articular				1		1
Caudal Vertebra Group 1		13	8	1		22
Caudal Vertebra Group 2		6		1	2	9
Dentary		3		1	2	6
First Vertebra		1				1
Maxilla		4		1		5
Parasphenoid		1				1
Posttemporal		1				1
Premaxilla		8	2			10
Quadrate		2	2			4
Vomer		2	1			3
Atlantic Herring						
Abdominal Vertebra	1	30	78	6	4	119
Articular			1			1
Caudal Vertebra		26	85	4	3	118
First Vertebra		7	6	1		14
Opercular			1			1
Penultimate Vertebra			1			1
Quadrate			2			2
Ultimate Vertebra				1		1
Vertebra		3	3			6

Total Length	I	II	III	I-III	Disturbed	Total
Cod						
301-500mm		7	1	2		10
501-800mm		5	3	1	2	11
801-1000mm		4	1			5
>1000mm		3				3
Ling						
801-1000mm		5				5
>1000mm		1			2	3
Saithe						
501-800mm	1	1	2	1		5
801-1000mm		10	2		3	15
>1000mm		10		1	1	12
Hake						
501-800mm		2		2		4
801-1000mm		4		1	1	6
>1000mm		1				1

14.8 Regional dietary practices and "identity"

Dietary practices differed through space and time in northern Europe during the Viking Age. These differences were probably due to a combination of factors, ranging from local environmental conditions to emblematic expressions of identity (e.g. Barrett and Richards 2004; Schmölcke 2004). Within this mosaic of cultural food ways, Kaupang sits between "east" and "west".

If not just a product of unusual preservation and recovery conditions, the abundance of pigs at Kaupang is characteristic of proto-urban settlements in the Baltic region such as Birka, Hedeby and Groß Strömkendorf rather than comparable North Sea sites such as York and Hamwic (Southampton) (O' Connor 2004 and references therein; Schmölcke 2004). The abundance of herring also has echoes of Baltic dietary preferences (Enghoff 1999), although this species does occur in North Sea emporia as well (Barrett et al. 2004b).

In contrast, the trio of cod, saithe and ling (particularly of large sizes: Tab. 14.11), occasionally joined by hake or haddock, is very characteristic of Viking-age and later medieval assemblages from elsewhere in Norway (Lie 1988; Lindh 1991; Perdikaris 1999; Hufthammer 2000, 2003; Sørheim 2004) and from the North Atlantic region (Amorosi 1991; Barrett et al. 1999; Cerón-Carrasco 2005; Krivogorskaya et al. 2005). If not purely a matter of local availability, the dominance of these species in the fish-bone assemblage implies dietary choices with northwestern rather than eastern connections (cf. Schmölcke 2004).

Unfortunately, the bird-bone assemblage is too small to show meaningful patterns. With the exception of the slight possibility that domestic fowl were introduced from southern Scandinavia or eastern Sweden (as discussed in section 14.7 above), the species represented are not indicative of specific regional or cultural dietary practices.

14.9 Conclusions

Compared with the preservation at some Viking-age "towns", the preservation of ecofactual material at Kaupang was very limited. Nevertheless, analysis of what does survive has provided a wide range of evidence regarding the character and function of this important settlement. The site was probably occupied year-round, at least occasionally, but it also produced evidence of either periodic abandonment or a relatively short overall lifespan. Kaupang drew on a range of agricultural and forest resources from its local hinterland, implying that it either controlled or was controlled by a regional polity. The ecofactual evidence of long-range trade was very limited, but there is a slight possibility that skins (furs?) were stored indoors at the site prior to transhipment. Lastly, the subsistence practices at Kaupang implied associations with both the Baltic region to the east and the North Atlantic region to the west.

Acknowledgements

Lars Pilø provided frequent and timely advice regarding the archaeological context of the assemblage and supplied information for Figures 14.3–14.5. The on-site sampling was directed by Cluny Johnstone of the University of York and the lab processing of the GBAs was conducted by Suzi Richer and Cath Neal. Jamie Andrews took on the onerous burden of sorting, counting and weighing the unidentified bone. Allan Hall thanks Joanna Bending, University of Sheffield, for indirectly bringing the presence of remains of juniper in the samples to his attention. The stable isotope samples were analysed in Michael Richards' laboratory at the University of Bradford. Anne Karin Hufthammer, Julie Askjem and Even Andersen assisted with finding Norwegian zooarchaeological reports, which Eva Sköld and Marcus Smith kindly helped translate. Bjarne Gaut also assisted with translation. Inge Enghoff generously provided information regarding her analysis of bone from Ribe in advance of publication. Anne Karin Hufthammer and Tommy Tyrberg kindly provided advice regarding the presence of domestic fowl in Viking-age Norway and Sweden. Paul Buckland, Peter Rowley-Conwy, Lars Pilø and Dagfinn Skre provided helpful comments on an early version of this paper. The support of the Department of Archaeology, University of York, is also gratefully acknowledged.

Appendix 14.1

Complete list of plant taxa recorded from deposits at Kaupang. For vascular plants, nomenclature and taxonomic order follow Tutin et al. (1964–1980), for mosses Smith (1978). Preservation of plant material was by anoxic waterlogging except where noted. Plant taxa marked * were certainly or probably of recent origin in all cases where they were recorded. C – number of contexts, S – number of samples, in which remains were recorded (where both recent and ancient materials were recorded, only those contexts with ancient material are included in this count).

Taxon	Common name	Parts recorded	C	S
cf. Selaginella selaginoides (L.) Link	?lesser clubmoss	megaspores	-	-
Pteridium aquilinum (L.) Kuhn	bracken	stalk fragments	1	1
Juniperus communis L.	juniper	seeds	1	1
		leaves	2	2
		shoot fragments	1	3
cf. *J. communis*	?juniper	charred seeds	2	2
Coniferae	conifer	charcoal fragments	2	2
		leaf/leaves	1	1
		part-charred wood fragments	1	1
		twig fragments	1	1
		wood chips	4	5
		wood fragments	1	1
Salix sp(p).	willow	buds	2	2
		fruits	2	2
		leaf fragments	1	1
		twig epidermis fragments	1	1
		twig fragments	1	1
cf. *Salix* sp(p).	?willow	wood fragments	4	4
Salix/Populus sp(p).	willow/aspen	charcoal fragments	4	4
		wood fragments	1	1
Populus sp(p).	aspen	buds and/or bud-scales	5	7
Betula pendula Roth	silver birch	bark fragments	1+?1	1+?1
Betula sp(p).	birch	fruits	4	4
		buds and/or bud-scales	2	2
Alnus sp(p).	alder	charcoal fragments	1	1
		buds and/or bud-scales	1	3
		female cones/cone-axes	1	1
Alnus/Corylus	alder/hazel	charcoal fragments	2	2
Corylus avellana L.	hazel	buds and/or bud-scales	1+?1	1+?1
		charcoal fragments	3	3
		nuts and/or nutshell fragments	9	14
		charred nuts and/or nutshell fragments	18	22
		roundwood fragments	1	1
Quercus sp(p).	oak	buds and/or bud-scales	3	6
		charcoal fragments	11	15
		wood chips	1	1
		wood fragments	2	2
Humulus lupulus L.	hop	achenes	3	5
		bracts	1	1
Cannabis sativa L.	hemp	achenes	3	4
Urtica dioica L.	stinging nettle	achenes	8	11

Taxon	Common name	Parts recorded	C	S
U. urens L.	annual nettle	achenes	6	10
Polygonum aviculare agg.	knotgrass	fruits	5	8
P. hydropiper L.	water-pepper	fruits	3	4
		charred fruits	2	2
P. persicaria L.	persicaria/red shank	fruits	5	6
		charred fruits	4	4
P. lapathifolium L.	pale persicaria	fruits	4	5
		charred fruits	2	2
Polygonum sp(p).	knotweeds, etc.	fruits	1	1
Bilderdykia convolvulus (L.) Dumort.	black bindweed	fruits	1	1
		charred fruits	1	1
Rumex acetosella agg.	sheep's sorrel	fruits	3	3
Rumex sp(p).	docks	fruits	3	5
		charred fruits	1	1
		perianths/perianth segments	1	1
Chenopodium album L.	fat hen	seeds	9	14
		charred seeds	12	12
Atriplex sp(p).	oraches	seeds	7	12
		charred seeds	1	1
Chenopodiaceae	goosefoot family	charred seeds	3	3
Montia fontana ssp. *fontana* (Fenzl) Walters	blinks	seeds	1	1
*Caryophyllaceae	pink/campion family	seeds	-	-
Stellaria media (L.) Vill.	chickweed	seeds	5	7
		charred seeds	5	5
S. palustris Retz./*S. graminea* L.	marsh/lesser stitchwort	seeds	2	6
		charred seeds	1	1
Sagina sp(p).	pearlworts	seeds	1	1
Scleranthus annuus L.	annual knawel	fruits	2	2
Spergula arvensis L.	corn spurrey	seeds	1	1
		charred seeds	2	2
Agrostemma githago L.	corncockle	seeds	1	1
Silene vulgaris (Moench) Garcke	bladder campion	seeds	1	1
Silene sp(p).	campions, etc.	seeds	2	2
Ranunculus Section Ranunculus	meadow/creeping/bulbous buttercup	achenes	7	11
		charred achenes	1	1
R. cf. *sardous* Crantz	?hairy buttercup	charred achenes	1	1
R. sceleratus L.	celery-leaved crowfoot	achenes	8	12
R. flammula L.	lesser spearwort	achenes	3	5
		charred achenes	1	1
Fumaria sp(p).	fumitories	seeds	5	5
Descurainia sophia (L.) Webb ex Prantl	flixweed	seeds	1	1
Isatis tinctoria L.	woad	pod fragments	2	2
Rorippa palustris (L.) Besser	marsh yellow-cress	seeds	2	2
Rorippa sp(p).	yellow-cress	seeds	1	1
Capsella bursa-pastoris (L.) Medicus	shepherd's purse	seeds	1	1
Thlaspi arvense L.	field penny-cress	seed fragments	2	2
Raphanus raphanistrum L.	wild radish	pod segments and/or fragments	2	2
Filipendula ulmaria (L.) Maxim.	meadowsweet	achenes	3	4

Taxon	Common name	Parts recorded	C	S
Rubus idaeus L.	raspberry	seeds	9	9
R. fruticosus agg.	blackberry/bramble	seeds	8	13
		charred seeds	4	4
Rosa sp(p).	roses	achenes	2	2
		charred achenes	1	1
Potentilla palustris (L.) Scop.	marsh cinquefoil	achenes	2	2
P. anserina L.	silverweed	achenes	4	5
P. cf. *crantzii* (Crantz) Beck ex Fritsch	?alpine cinquefoil	achenes	1	1
P. cf. *erecta* (L.) Räuschel	?tormentil	achenes	6	11
		charred achenes	4	5
Potentilla sp(p).	cinquefoils, etc.	achenes	2	4
Fragaria cf. *vesca* L.	?wild strawberry	achenes	3	3
cf. Alchemilla sp(p).	?lady's mantles	achenes	-	-
Alchemilla/Aphanes sp(p).	lady's-mantle/ parsley-piert	achenes	-	-
cf. Pomoideae	?*Crataegus/Malus/ Pyrus/Sorbus*	charcoal fragments	1	1
Malus sylvestris Miller	crab apple	endocarp	2	1
Sorbus aucuparia L.	rowan, mountain ash	seeds	1	1
Sorbus sp(p).	rowan/whitebeams	seeds	1	1
Trifolium pratense L.	red clover	calyx/calyces and/or pods	1	1
		pods and/or pod lids	1	1
Leguminosae	pea family	calyx/calyces or flowers	1	4
		flowers and/or petals	2	4
		immature seeds (waterlogged)	1	1
		pods and/or pod fragments	1	3
*Leguminosae	pea family	waterlogged seeds	-	-
Linum usitatissimum L.	cultivated flax	seeds	3	2
		capsule fragments	1	1
cf. *L. usitatissimum* L.	?cultivated flax	charred seeds	1	1
L. catharticum L.	purging flax	seeds	1	1
Euphorbia helioscopia L.	sun spurge	seeds	-	-
cf. *Acer* sp(p).	?maple, etc.	charcoal fragments	1	1
Malva sylvestris L.	common mallow	nutlets	2	2
Hypericum sp(p).	St John's worts	seeds	2	2
Viola sp(p).	violets/pansies, etc.	seeds	7	11
		charred seeds	1	1
		capsule segments	1	3
Heracleum sphondylium L.	hogweed	mericarps	1	1
Umbelliferae	carrot family	mericarps	1	1
Calluna vulgaris (L.) Hull	heather, ling	capsules	1	1
		flowers	1	1
Empetrum sp(p).	crowberry	seeds	1	1
Fraxinus excelsior L.	ash	charcoal fragments	12	12
Galium aparine L.	goosegrass, cleavers	charred fruits	6	6
Galium sp(p).	bedstraws, etc.	charred fruits	2	2
Galeopsis Subgenus *Ladanum*	hemp-nettles	charred nutlets	1	1
G. Subgenus *Galeopsis*	hemp-nettles	nutlets	2	5
Galeopsis sp(p).	hemp-nettles	nutlets	1	1
Lamium Section *Lamiopsis*	annual dead-nettles	nutlets	-	-
Lamium sp(p).	dead-nettles, etc.	nutlets	1	1
Stachys sp(p).	woundworts	nutlets	2+?1	2+?1

Taxon	Common name	Parts recorded	C	S
cf. *Glechoma hederacea* L.	ground-ivy	nutlets	1	1
Prunella vulgaris L.	selfheal	nutlets	2	4
Lycopus europaeus L.	gipsywort	nutlets	3	5
Labiatae	mint family	calyces	1	1
Hyoscyamus niger L.	henbane	seeds	1	2
Solanum nigrum L.	black nightshade	seeds	3+?1	4+?1
S. dulcamara L.	woody nightshade	seeds	1	1
Veronica sp(p).	speedwells, etc.	seeds	1	1
Rhinanthus sp(p).	yellow rattles	seeds	1	5
Plantago major L.	greater plantain	seeds	1	1
P. media L.	hoary plantain	charred seeds	1	1
P. lanceolata L.	ribwort plantain	seeds	1	1
Campanula rotundifolia L.	harebell, bluebell	seeds	2+?1	2+?2
Eupatorium cannabinum L.	hemp agrimony	achenes	1	1
Bidens sp(p).	bur-marigolds	achenes	2	3
Achillea millefolium L.	yarrow	capitulum fragments	1	1
*Matricaria maritima L./	sea/scentless			
M. *perforata* Mérat	mayweed	achenes	-	-
Senecio sp(p).	groundsels/rag-			
	worts	achenes	1	1
Carduus/Cirsium sp(p).	thistles	achenes	6	8
Centaurea cf. *nigra* L.	?lesser knapweed	involucral bracts	1	1
Centaurea sp(p).	knapweeds, etc.	achenes	3	3
		immature achenes	1	1
		involucral bracts	1	1
Leontodon sp(p).	hawkbits	achenes	3	3
*Sonchus asper (L.) Hill	prickly sow-thistle	achenes	-	-
*S. oleraceus L.	sow-thistle	achenes	-	-
*Taraxacum sp(p).	dandelions	achenes	-	-
Lapsana communis L.	nipplewort	achenes	3	3
Hieracium sp(p).	hawkweeds	achenes	1	2
Compositae	daisy family	achenes	1	1
		involucres/fragments	1	1
Triglochin maritima L.	sea arrowgrass	carpels	1	2
Juncus cf. *maritimus* Lam.	?sea rush	seeds	2	3
J. inflexus L./J. *effusus* L./	hard/soft/compact			
J. *conglomeratus* L.	rush	seeds	5	6
J. cf. *gerardi* Loisel.	?mud rush	seeds	3	3
J. *bufonius* L.	toad rush	seeds	10	15
Juncus sp(p).	rushes	seeds	3	5
Luzula sp(p).	woodrushes	seeds	2	5
Gramineae	grasses	waterlogged caryopses	3	7
		charred caryopses	4	4
		waterlogged culm bases/		
		rhizome fragments	1	1
		waterlogged spikelets/		
		spikelet fragments	1	1
Gramineae/Cerealia	grasses/cereals	waterlogged culm nodes	3	4
		waterlogged culm frag	1	4
Cerealia indet.	cereals	charred caryopses	1	1
		waterlogged culm frag.	1	1
cf. *Triticum* sp(p).	?wheats	charred caryopses	3	3
Triticum/Hordeum sp(p).	wheat and/or barley	charred caryopses	1	1
Secale cereale L.	rye	charred caryopses	3+?4	3+?4

Taxon	Common name	Parts recorded	C	S
Hordeum sp(p).	barley	charred caryopses (inc. some hulled specimens)	41	45
Avena sp(p).	oats	charred caryopses	2	2
Agrostis sp(p).	bent grasses, etc.	waterlogged caryopses	1	1
Danthonia decumbens (L.) DC. in Lam. & DC.	heath grass	caryopses	2	5
		waterlogged spikelets/ spikelet fragments	2	4
		waterlogged chaff	1	2
Scirpus cf. *maritimus* L.	?sea club-rush	nutlets	4	7
S. *lacustris* sensu lato	bulrush	nutlets	1+?2	1+?2
		charred nutlets	1	1
Eleocharis palustris sensu lato	common spike-rush	nutlets	7	12
		charred nutlets	2	2
cf. *Eleocharis* sp(p).	?spike-rushes	nutlets	1	1
Carex sp(p).	sedges	nutlets	9	14
		charred nutlets	30	33
Musci (remains were leaves and/or shoot fragments unless otherwise indicated)				
Sphagnum squarrosum Crome			1	2
Sphagnum sp(p).		leaves	3	3
		leaves and shoot tips	3	3
		leaves and shoot fragments	1	1
Polytrichum commune Hedw.			1	2
Polytrichum commune var. *commune* Hedw.			1	1
Polytrichum/Pogonatum sp(p).		leaf-bases	2	2
		shoot fragments	1	1
Polytrichum sp(p).		leaves/leaf-bases and/ or shoot fragments	2	4
		shoot fragments	1	4
Dicranum scoparium Hedw.			1	1
Dicranum sp(p).			1	3
Leucobryum glaucum (Hedw.) Ångstr.			1	1
Racomitrium sp(p).			2	4
Plagiomnium undulatum (Hedw.) Kop.			1+?1	1+?1
cf. *Plagiomnium* sp(p).			1	1
Pseudobruym cinclidioides (Hüb.) Kop.			1	1
Aulacomnium palustre (Hedw.) Schwaegr.			1	2
Climacium dendroides (Hedw.) Web. & Mohr			1	2
Leucodon sciuroides (Hedw.) Schwaegr.			2	2
Antitrichia curtipendula (Hedw.) Brid.			1	1
Thamnobryum alopecurum (Hedw.) Nieuwl.			1	1
Thuidium tamariscinum (Hedw.) Br. Eur.			1+?1	2+?3
cf. *Cratoneuron commutatum* (Hedw.) Roth			1	1
Calliergon cuspidatum (Hedw.) Kindb.			1	3
Isothecium myosuroides Brid.			1	1
Homalothecium sericeum (Hedw.) Br. Eur. / H. *lutescens* (Hedw.) Robins.			1	1
Hypnum cf. *cupressiforme* Hedw.			1	1
Rhytidiadelphus cf. *squarrosus* (Hedw.) Warnst.			1	3
Rhytidiadelphus sp(p).			1	1
Pleurozium schreberi (Brid.) Mitt.			1	2
Hylocomium splendens (Hedw.) Br. Eur.			5	7

Appendix 14.2

'Useful' plant taxa recorded from deposits at Kaupang, with their Norwegian vernacular names (courtesy of Den virtuella Floran, http://linnaeus.nrm.se/flora).

Taxon	Parts used	Norwegian name	English name
Pteridium aquilinum	Fronds	Einstape	Bracken
Juniperus communis	Shoots, Berries	Einer	Juniper
Salix	Wood, Twigs	Vier	Willow
Populus	Wood	Osp	Poplar/aspen
Betula	Wood, Bark	Bjørk	Birch
Alnus	Wood	Svartor	Alder
Corylus avellana	Wood, Nuts	Hassel	Hazel
Quercus	Wood, Acorns	Eik	Oak
Humulus lupulus	Fruits	Humle	Hop
Cannabis sativa	Fruits	Hamp	Hemp
Isatis tinctoria	Leaves	Waid	Woad
Rubus idaeus	Fruits	Bringbær	Raspberry
Rubus fruticosus agg.	Fruits	Bjønnbær	Blackberry
Rosa	Fruits	Nype	Rose
Fragaria cf. *vesca*	Fruits	Markjordbær	Strawberry
Malus sylvestris	Fruits	Villapal	Wild Apple
Sorbus aucuparia	Fruits	Rogn	Rowan
Linum usitatissimum	Seeds, Stem Fibres	Lin	Flax, Linseed
Empetrum	Fruit	Krekling	Crowberry
Calluna vulgaris	Whole Plant	Røsslyng	Heather, Ling
Fraxinus excelsior	Wood	Ask	Ash
Secale cereale	Grains, Straw	Rug	Rye
Hordeum	Grains, Straw	Bygg	Barley
Avena	Grains, Straw	Havre	Oats

Appendix 14.3

Complete list of invertebrate remains recorded from samples from the Kaupang site. Order and nomenclature follow Kloet and Hincks (1964–1977) for insects. Where both secure and tentative identifications of a given taxon were recorded, only the former is listed here. The remains were of adults unless stated. 'sp.' indicates that record was probably an additional taxon, 'sp. indet.' that the material may have been of a taxon listed above it.

Coelenterata
*Coelenterata sp. (hydroid stem or theca)

Nematoda
*?Heterodera sp. (cyst)

Annelida: Oligochaeta
*Oligochaeta sp. (egg capsule)

Crustacea
*Daphnia sp. (ephippium)
*Cladocera sp. (ephippium)

Insecta
Hemiptera
Lygaeidae sp.
Cimicidae sp.
Corixidae sp.
Philaenus spumarius (Linnaeus)
Cicadellidae sp.
?Euconomelus lepidus (Boheman)
Delphacidae sp.
*Auchenorhyncha sp. (nymph)
*Psylloidea sp. (nymph)
*Aphidoidea sp.

Diptera
*Chironomidae sp. (larva)
*Diptera sp. (adult)
*Diptera sp. (pupa)
*Diptera sp. (puparium)

Siphonaptera
*Pulex irritans Linnaeus
*Siphonaptera sp.

Trichoptera
*Trichoptera sp.

Coleoptera
Dyschirius globosus (Herbst)
Clivina fossor (Linnaeus)
Patrobus ?atrorufus (Strom)
Patrobus sp. indet.
Trechus ?micros (Herbst)
?Trechus sp.
Pterostichus melanarius (Illiger)
Pterostichus ?nigrita (Paykull)

Pterostichus (Poecilus) sp.
Pterostichus spp.
Calathus sp.
Amara sp.
Dromius quadrimaculatus (Linnaeus)
Dromius quadrinotatus (Zenker)
Metabletus sp.
Carabidae spp. and spp. indet.
Helophorus spp.
Cercyon analis (Paykull)
Cercyon atricapillus (Marsham)
Cercyon haemorrhoidalis (Fabricius)
Cercyon quisquilius (Linnaeus)
Cercyon ?tristis (Illiger)
Cercyon spp. indet.
Cryptopleurum minutum (Fabricius)
?Hydrobius fuscipes (Linnaeus)
Chaetarthria seminulum (Herbst)
Hydrophilinae sp.
Acritus nigricornis (Hoffmann)
Saprinus sp.
Histerinae sp.
Ochthebius sp.
Ptenidium spp.
Acrotrichis sp.
Ptiliidae sp.
Catops sp.
Micropeplus porcatus (Paykull)
Micropeplus tesserula Curtis
Megarthrus sp.
Acidota cruentata Mannerheim
Phyllodrepoidea crenata (Gravenhorst)
Eusphalerum ?minutum (Fabricius)
Phyllodrepa ?floralis (Paykull)
Omalium ? italicum Bernhauer
Omalium caesum or italicum
Omalium ?rivulare (Paykull)
Omalium sp. indet.
Xylodromus concinnus (Marsham)
Omaliinae spp.
Carpelimus bilineatus Stephens
Carpelimus elongatulus (Erichson)
Carpelimus sp.
Platystethus arenarius (Fourcroy)
Platystethus nodifrons (Mannerheim)
Anotylus nitidulus (Gravenhorst)
Anotylus rugosus (Fabricius)
Oxytelus sculptus Gravenhorst

Stenus spp.

Lathrobium sp.

?Rugilus sp.

Leptacinus ?intermedius Donisthorpe

Leptacinus sp.

Gyrohypnus angustatus Stephens

Gyrohypnus fracticornis (Müller)

Gyrohypnus sp. indet.

Xantholinus sp.

Neobisnius sp.

Philonthus spp.

Creophilus maxillosus (Linnaeus)

?Ontholestes sp.

Quedius spp.

Staphylininae spp. indet.

Tachyporus sp.

Tachinus sp.

Cypha sp.

Cordalia obscura (Gravenhorst)

Falagria caesa or sulcatula

Crataraea suturalis (Mannerheim)

Aleochara sp.

Aleocharinae spp.

Euplectini sp.

Pselaphidae sp.

Trox scaber (Linnaeus)

Geotrupes sp.

Aphodius ?fimetarius (Linnaeus)

Aphodius granarius (Linnaeus)

Aphodius ?rufipes (Linnaeus)

Aphodius ?sphacelatus (Panzer)

Aphodius spp. and spp. indet.

Clambus sp.

*Melanotus erythropus (Gmelin) (larva)

Dermestes ?lardarius Linnaeus

*Dermestes lardarius (larva)

?Dermestes sp. indet.

Anobium sp.

Ptinus fur (Linnaeus)

Ptinus raptor Sturm

Ptinus sp. and spp. indet.

Lyctus linearis (Goeze)

Necrobia violacea (Linnaeus)

Necrobia sp. indet.

Malachius sp.

Brachypterus sp.

?Meligethes sp.

Omosita colon (Linnaeus)

Glischrochilus quadripunctatus (Linnaeus)

Monotoma longicollis (Gyllenhall)

Cryptophagus ?scutellatus Newman

Cryptophagus spp.

Atomaria spp.

Ephistemus globulus (Paykull)

Orthoperus spp.

Coccidula ?scutellata (Herbst)

?Scymnus sp. s. lat.

Coccinellidae sp.

Lathridius minutus group

Enicmus sp.

Corticaria spp.

Corticarina sp.

Corticarina or Cortinicara sp. indet.

Cisidae sp.

Aglenus brunneus (Gyllenhal)

Tenebrio obscurus Fabricius

Rhinosimus planirostris (Fabricius)

Anthicus sp.

Chrysomelinae sp.

Galerucella sp.

Longitarsus sp.

Crepidodera sp.

Chaetocnema arida group

Chaetocnema concinna (Marsham)

Chaetocnema sp. indet.

Cassida sp.

Apion spp.

Sitona sp.

Notaris acridulus (Linnaeus)

Cidnorhinus quadrimaculatus (Linnaeus)

Ceuthorhynchinae sp.

Curculionidae spp. and spp. indet.

Scolytus ?intricatus (Ratzeburg)

Leperisinus varius (Fabricius)

Scolytidae sp.

Coleoptera spp. and spp. indet.

*Coleoptera spp. (larva)

Hymenoptera

*Chalcidoidea spp.

*Proctotrupoidea spp.

*Hymenoptera Parasitica spp.

*Apis mellifera Linnaeus

*Apoidea sp. indet.

*Formicidae spp.

*Hymenoptera spp.

*Insecta sp. (larva)

Arachnida

*Pseudoscorpiones sp.

*Aranae spp.

*Acarina spp.

Appendix 14.4

English, Latin and Norwegian names of birds, fish and mammals identified at Kaupang. Nomenclature follows Harland et al. (2003) and references therein.

	Common name	Latin name	Norwegian name
Bird	Brent Goose	*Branta bernicla*	Ringgås
	Barnacle Goose	*Branta leucopsis*	Hvitkinngås
	Eider	*Somateria mollissima*	Ærfugl
	Shelduck	*Tadorna tadorna*	Gravand
	Swan, Goose & Duck Family	Anatidae	Andefamilien
	Domestic Fowl ('Chicken')	*Gallus gallus*	Høne
	Great Black-backed Gull	*Larus marinus*	Svartbak
	Little Auk	*Alle alle*	Alkekonge
Fish	Shark, Skate & Ray Orders	Pleurotremata/Hypotremata	Hai/Skate/Rokke
	Dogfish Families	Scyliorhinidae/Squalidae	Rødhai/Håfamilien
	Eel	*Anguilla anguilla*	Ål
	Atlantic Herring	*Clupea harengus*	Sild
	Salmon & Trout Family	Salmonidae	Laksefamilien
	Trout?	cf. *Salmo trutta*	Ørret
	Cod Family	Gadidae	Torskefamilien
	Cod	*Gadus morhua*	Torsk
	Ling	*Molva molva*	Lange
	Pollack	*Pollachius pollachius*	Lyr
	Saithe	*Pollachius virens*	Sei
	Hake	*Merluccius merluccius*	Lysing
	Gurnard Family	Triglidae	Knurrfamilien
	Wrasse Family	Labridae	Leppefiskfamilien
	?Halibut	cf. *Hippoglossus hippoglossus*	?Kveite
Mammal	Shrew Species	*Sorex*	Spissmus
	Dog Family	Canidae	?Hund
	Cat	*Felis catus*	Katt
	Horse	*Equus caballus*	Hest
	Pig	*Sus domesticus*	Gris
	Deer	Cervidae	Hjortedyr
	Red Deer	*Cervus elaphus*	Hjort
	Cattle	*Bos taurus*	Storfe
	Sheep	*Ovis aries*	Sau
	Sheep/Goat	*Ovis aries* or *Capra hircus*	Småfe, Sau/Geit
	Hare	*Lepus*	Hare

Soils and Sediments in the Settlement and Harbour at Kaupang

15

KAREN B. MILEK AND CHARLES A. I. FRENCH

Soils and sediments from the settlement and harbour areas at Kaupang were sampled and analysed in order to enhance the understanding of site stratigraphy, and to help solve a range of interpretive problems encountered during the excavation. The samples were taken from the main research excavation of 2000–2002, the cultural resource management (CRM) trench of 2000 (close to the main research excavation) and the harbour excavation of 2003. They were analysed using a broad suite of geochemical techniques as well as the micromorphological analysis of thin sections, but this paper focuses primarily on the results of micromorphological analysis, which provided the most useful information about the original composition and mode of formation of the sediments prior to their alteration by post-depositional processes.

Immature, gleyed soils were identified below the archaeological sediments on the site, indicating the presence of a young, but stable land-surface prior to the establishment of the urban settlement. The study of sediments associated with the initial, seasonal settlement showed that in the area of the CRM trench, this phase was characterised by around seven short-term activity events. On plots 3A and 3B, micromorphology samples taken from transects through the main axes of the buildings helped to delimit and characterise the occupation surfaces and the different activity areas within them. A study of the sediments in the pathway between plots 1A and 2A, and the sediments in the midden area east of plot 1A, provided information about their composition and possible origin, and the environmental conditions under which they had accumulated. Finally, the sediment sequence in the harbour area was examined in order to determine the composition of the different layers and their depositional environments.

15.1 Introduction

The Viking-age urban settlement at Kaupang is situated on the shores of the Viksfjord, at the southern end of Vestfold, in southern Norway (Fig. 15.1a). As the first urban settlement in Norway, and as a regional centre for craft production and trade in the 9th and 10th centuries, the site is of unique importance for the understanding of the social and economic history of early Viking-age Scandinavia (Skre, this vol. Ch. 1). The most recent archaeological investigations at this site focussed on two areas (Fig. 15.1b). In 2000–2002, excavations took place on part of the urban settlement area, which contained building plots, streets, and middens (Fig. 15.1c). Some of the key research issues in this area included how the urban settlement had developed, and how different activities related to craft production, trade, and urban living had been organised (Skre this vol. Ch. 3:47; Pilø, this vol. Ch. 7,

8, 10). In order to shed further light on the development of the settlement, excavations were also conducted in 2003 in an area that had formerly been part of the Viking-age harbour in Kaupang Bay (Fig. 15.1d). An important issue that emerged from this excavation was whether the harbour contained deposits that could provide information about the later life of the town, the uppermost phases of which had been truncated by later medieval ploughing activity. In consideration of the social and economic importance of the site in the 9th and 10th centuries, every effort was made to extract as much information as possible from the surviving archaeological record in both the settlement and the harbour areas (Pilø, this vol. Ch. 7).

As the excavations proceeded, the archaeological sediments at Kaupang posed many challenges. Differences in the colour, texture, and composition of the

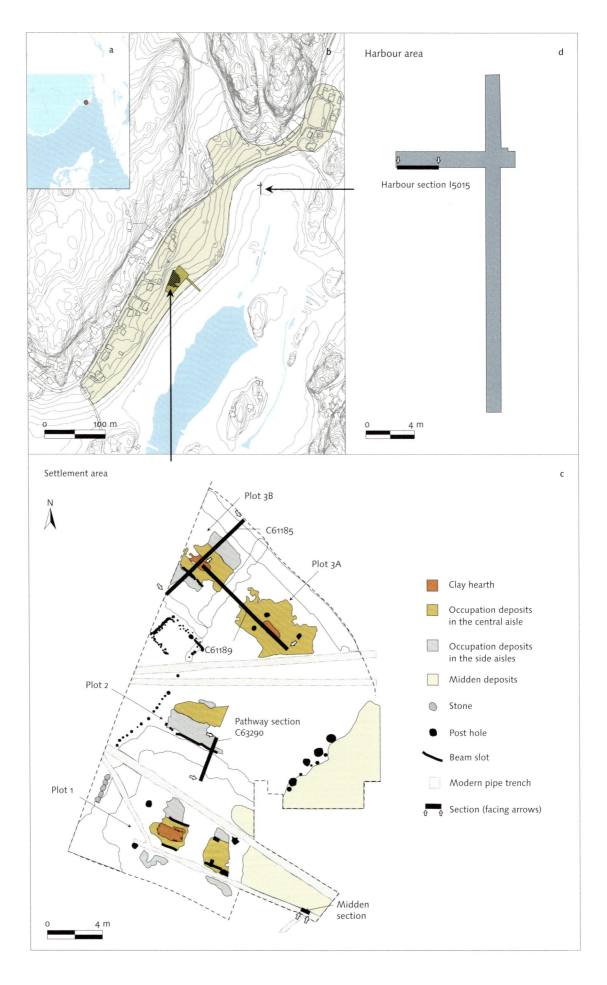

a

b

Harbour area   d

Harbour section I5015

0   100 m

0   4 m

Settlement area   c

N

Plot 3B

C61185

Plot 3A

C61189

Plot 2

Pathway section
C63290

Plot 1

Midden
section

Clay hearth

Occupation deposits
in the central aisle

Occupation deposits
in the side aisles

Midden deposits

Stone

Post hole

Beam slot

Modern pipe trench

Section (facing arrows)

0   4 m

Figure 15.1 *Map of Kaupang, showing the location of the site (a), an overview of the site with the locations of the excavation areas (b), and the locations of the sections in the settlement area (c) and the harbour area (d), from which micromorphology samples were taken. Illustration, Julie K. Øhre Askjem.*

layers were often extremely subtle, and the ability of the excavators to detect compacted surfaces was inhibited by the coarse, sandy texture of the deposits. On building plots 3A and 3B, these subtle differences and diffuse boundaries between layers made it difficult to delimit floor areas, and to interpret the precise forms and functions of the buildings. Elsewhere on the site, such as the midden, the pathway between plots 1A and 2A, and the harbour area, there was some uncertainty about how the sediments had been deposited, and the extent to which they had been affected by the sea. In addition, no soils were visible in the field below the Viking-age occupation deposits, which raised questions about the environmental conditions on the site prior to the establishment of the urban settlement, and the nature of the earliest settlement phase. Variability in the preservation of artefacts and archaeological stratigraphy also raised many concerns about the complex post-depositional processes that had clearly affected the site. It was obviously vital to understand these processes, and to pay them due consideration when drawing archaeological interpretations.

In order to tackle the many questions and interpretive problems that surfaced during the excavation at Kaupang, a programme of soil and sediment analysis was integrated into the project research design. This geoarchaeological programme targeted five main areas: building plots 3A and 3B, the pathway between plots 1A and 2A, the midden east of plot 1A, the harbour area, and the extensive sequence of soils and sediments dating from the Iron Age to the present, which were observed in the CRM trench (Fig. 15.1c–d). A broad suite of analytical techniques was applied, especially in the early, assessment phase of the geoarchaeology programme, when the widest possible data set was needed to characterise the depositional and post-depositional processes that had been prevalent on the site. Soils and sediments from

building plots 3A and 3B and from the CRM trench northwest of plot 3B were sampled and analysed for pH, electrical conductivity, magnetic susceptibility, loss on ignition, elemental composition, and micromorphology (Milek and French, forthcoming). Subsequent, more detailed analyses of the buildings in plots 3A and 3B, the midden, the pathway, and the harbour area concentrated on the use of micromorphology – the analysis of undisturbed soils and sediments in thin section – because of the unique ability of this technique to provide information about the original composition and mode of formation of the sediments prior to their alteration by post-depositional processes.

15.2 Methodology

The micromorphology samples discussed here were taken from soil and sediment profiles exposed in the CRM trench, the pipe-trench that had sectioned the midden stratigraphy, the trench excavated in the harbour area, and from baulks that had been positioned to form transects across the buildings and pathways on the site (Fig. 15.1c–d). After written and photographic records of cleaned sections were made, samples were taken following the method outlined in Courty et al. (1989). Rectangular aluminium tins (c. 5 x 6 x 10 cm) were inserted into the sections, the undisturbed blocks were cut free with a sharp knife or trowel, and the samples were tightly wrapped in plastic to prevent the loss of water and structural integrity during storage and transport.

Thin sections were manufactured from the undisturbed blocks at the McBurney Geoarchaeology Laboratory at the University of Cambridge. Since the soils and sediments at Kaupang were extremely sandy, and were already rather dry when sampled, the blocks were air dried for three months rather than being dried by the acetone replacement method. The dried blocks were then impregnated with crystic polyester resin and thin sectioned following the method described by Murphy (1986). Thin sections were first studied at a scale of 1/1 and then analysed with petrological microscopes at magnifications ranging from x4 to x400 with plane-polarized light (PPL), cross-polarized light (XPL), oblique-incident light (OIL), and ultra-violet light (UVL). This permitted the identification of the mineral, organic, and anthropogenic components in the soils and sediments, including ash, charcoal, organic matter in various stages of decomposition, minute artefacts, and bones. Since charcoal identification was conducted by Barrett et al. (this vol. Ch. 14:284), this analysis was not carried out on the thin sections. However, fish bones were distinguished from mammal or bird bones based on their shape and internal structure; all references to bone in the text refer to mammal or bird bone (which cannot be differentiated in thin section), unless specifically identified as fish. Thin-section analysis also made it possible to observe the physical organisation of these components, the microscopic structure of soils and sediments, and the sequences of sedimentary and pedological processes that had affected their development and preservation (Courty et al. 1989).

Micromorphological analysis produces visual data, which are normally presented in the form of photographs and written descriptions of the components and features observed under the microscope. The interpretation of micromorphological data is based on an understanding of sedimentary, pedological, and biological processes, as well as intercomparisons with data from reference samples and other micromorphological studies (e.g. Canti 2003; Courty et al. 1989; FitzPatrick 1993). The intercomparison of visual data requires that written descriptions follow international, standardised descriptive terminology, such as that provided in guides by Bullock et al. (1985) and Stoops (2003). In the text that follows, specialised micromorphology terms are explained briefly the first time they are mentioned, but more detailed explanations may be found in these international guides.

15.3 Post-depositional processes affecting the archaeological record at Kaupang

The geoarchaeology study found that the generally poor preservation of the artefacts, bones, and sediments at Kaupang was due to the effects of a range of post-depositional processes, including leaching, eluviation of fine material, bioturbation, and the redistribution of iron. These natural pedogenic processes had altered the original composition, chemistry, colour, and structure of the soils and archaeological sediments, dramatically reducing the varieties of textures, consistencies, and colours that would have been inherent in the original layers, and making them harder to distinguish. The occupation deposits on

plots 3A and 3B, for example, were rendered almost uniformly sandy and black, with only subtle differences in the proportions of sand, charcoal, and organic matter. Bioturbation by soil fauna contributed to the problem by disturbing and mixing layers, and blurring the boundaries between them.

Leaching and eluviation of elements and fine material

The sandy soils and sediments at Kaupang were highly susceptible to leaching and eluviation, processes that remove clay, silt, fine organic matter, and certain elements, and that therefore had an enormous impact on the final composition of the archaeological deposits. For example, the occupation deposits in the settlement area at Kaupang are now slightly acidic (pH 5.0 to 6.0), commonly contain 20–50% fine charcoal fragments, and are black in colour, but the charcoal component indicates that they originally contained large quantities of white to grey, alkaline wood ash. Wood ash is normally composed of fine-grained calcium carbonate and small fragments of incompletely combusted, carbonised wood (Brochier 2002; Canti 2003), but percolating rainwater and acidic conditions can dissolve the calcitic component and wash it down the profile, so that only the charcoal is left behind. The leaching of calcium carbonate from the sediments at Kaupang has removed a significant component of the ash, and it is therefore likely that they used to resemble the ash-rich sediments at Viking-age Birka and York (Ambrosiani 1995; Ambrosiani and Clarke 1995a; Hall 1994).

Bones that had been deposited on outdoor surfaces, and that were exposed for some time prior to burial, were also very vulnerable to leaching. Significant differences in bone preservation were noted, with bones in the pathway and the midden exhibiting more severe alteration than bones in the occupation deposits in the houses. Evidence of bone degradation (diagenesis) in the outdoor deposits included the development of orange-brown rims on the surfaces of bones (pellicular alteration) and around internal cracks (irregular alteration). Many bones also lost their birefringence – the colours caused by the refraction of light by crystalline minerals when placed between crossed polars – and lost their ability to autofluoresce in UV light – an ability common to phosphatic materials such as bone, coprolites, and fresh organic matter (Courty et al. 1989). The physical alteration of bone, the loss of birefringence, and the loss of ability to autofluoresce, indicate that the bones were subject to dissolution by slightly acidic rainwater and/or microbial attack, the breakdown of collagen, and the leaching of calcium and phosphorus (Hedges 2002). The better preservation of bone in the indoor occupation deposits, presumably because of their more rapid burial, helped to differentiate between indoor and outdoor occupation deposits on the settlement when this interpretation was in doubt.

Acidic conditions also promoted the post-depositional dispersion of fine organo-mineral material from many of the archaeological sediments and underlying soils. This material was carried down the soil profile in suspension by percolating rainwater, a process that left behind eluviated soil and sediment fabrics characterised by sand grains surrounded by smooth coatings and bridges of fine mineral material (Fig. 15.2). Many of the less organic layers and pit fills on plots 3A and 3B, as well as the soils buried below the earliest archaeological deposits on the settlement, had been post-depositionally eluviated. This loss of fine material was partly responsible for the very coarse texture of many of the archaeological sediments and soils, which would originally have contained slightly more silt and clay.

Some of the leached and eluviated elements and fine organo-mineral material that were carried down the profile were re-deposited in the beach sands underlying the site. In the CRM trench, just 1–2 cm below the earliest occupation deposits, micromorphological analysis identified a horizon where sand grains were coated and bridged by a series of compound coatings made up of the calcium, iron, phosphorus, and other materials that had been leached from the overlying archaeological layers (Tab. 15.1, layer 8.2; Fig. 15.3). The formation of each coating was a separate depositional event (known as an illuvial event), and is a reflection of the changing chemistry of the archaeological sediments higher up the profile.

The first coatings to form were yellow to orange-brown, and were either amorphous, or in the form of fan-shaped crystals that exhibited pale yellow to orange birefringence. Although the precise composition of these coatings can only be confirmed by sub-microscopic analyses such as scanning electron microscopy or electron microprobe analysis, the optical properties of these features closely resembled the calcium-iron-phosphate coatings that have been identified at other bone-rich archaeological sites in moist, temperate, and subboreal areas with acidic soil conditions (e.g. Adderley et al. 2004; Simpson et al. 2000; Jenkins 1994). While the source of calcium and phosphate at these other sites was attributed to the decomposition of bone, at Kaupang both wood ash and bone in the archaeological sediments higher up the profile could potentially have been the source of the calcium and phosphate in these distinctive coatings.

Overlying these yellow to orange-brown coatings were red-brown coatings composed of oxidized iron, possibly complexed with organic matter. Finally, a series of non-laminated, impure and dusty clay coatings were deposited. These were red-brown or brown in PPL, and had birefringence fabrics in XPL that were either granostriated (with domains of colour oriented around sand grains) or stipple-speckled (with small, discrete domains of colour). This

sequence of coatings indicates that calcium was among the first elements to be leached from the overlying archaeological sediments. The loss of calcium reduced the pH of the sediments and promoted the leaching and down-profile deposition of iron and organic matter. Finally, the deposition of dusty clay coatings is probably related to the later disturbance of the surface of the site, possibly by ploughing in the later medieval period (Lewis 1998; Macphail et al. 1990).

Redistribution of iron

The soils and sediments at Kaupang contained a wide range of iron pedofeatures, including nodules, coatings, and pans. These features formed when percolating rainwater or a fluctuating water table created localised reducing conditions, picked up iron ions in solution (e.g. from clay or decomposing plant matter), and later re-deposited them under oxidizing conditions, where they formed bonds with other materials, such as clay, organic matter, or phosphorus. The ways in which iron is redistributed is therefore related to the composition of the sediments and soils, past environmental conditions, and environmental conditions up to the present day.

Amorphous nodules of iron oxide were observed in low quantities throughout the archaeological sediments at Kaupang (0.5–3%), where they were frequently associated with charcoal fragments. This common association is probably due to the ability of the microscopic pores in carbonized wood to adsorb the organic compounds and phosphates that have washed downwards through the stratigraphy – literally filtering them out of percolating water. Charcoal is therefore likely to contain a concentration of organic and phosphatic compounds, with which iron tends to bond under oxidizing conditions.

Iron pans, where oxidized iron reached concentrations of c. 30%, sometimes formed post-depositionally at the boundaries between the archaeological sediments and the beach sands, where they also tended to be associated with charcoal and organic matter lying on the surface of the sand (Fig. 15.4). Such features were found, for example, at the base of the earliest archaeological horizon at Kaupang (sample KPG02-2, layer 7.2; Figs. 15.4, 15.7; Tab. 15.1), at the base of the pathway between plots 1A and 2A (KPG02-60; Figs. 15.9 and 15.14), and at the base of a post-hole in house A302 (KPG02-68; Fig. 15.16). In the case of these iron pans, iron precipitation was also promoted by the abrupt textural boundary between the finer archaeological sediments and the coarser, more porous sands, which stopped the advancing wetting front that was carrying the iron in solution.

The soils and sediments that had experienced waterlogging displayed the most dramatic iron pedofeatures. The soil buried below the midden deposit (KPG02-16, layer 7; Fig. 15.8; Tab. 15.6) had been gleyed

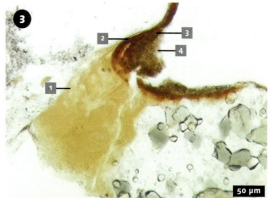

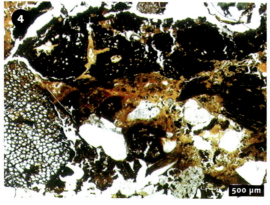

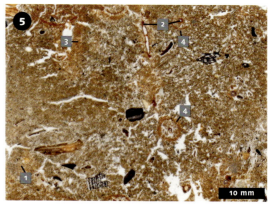

due to its proximity to the water table and the poor drainage of the underlying marine clay (Sørensen et al., this vol. Ch. 12:354). Iron had impregnated 5–10% of the soil, and because the iron nodules had bonded with clay, they had helped to prevent the eluviation of fine mineral material, and had preserved the original soil fabric (Fig. 15.10). In the harbour area, formerly waterlogged marine sediments that contained organic matter and charcoal dried out (oxidized) when isostatic uplift eventually raised them above sea-level (KPG03-7, layer 17; Fig. 15.38; Tab. 15.7). This resulted in the formation of amorphous iron pedofeatures covering 2–5% of the sediment, including plant cell structures replaced by iron (plant pseudomorphs), and various types of coatings around voids where organic matter had oxidized (Fig. 15.5).

Subrounded red-brown nodules with sharp boundaries were found in the midden sediments, the pathway, and other outdoor areas on the Kaupang settlement. Although clearly related to iron precipitation, the precise origin of these unusual features remained uncertain until their progressive stages of development were observed in the thin sections from the midden sediments (KPG02-15, 16; Fig. 15.8; Tab. 15.6). In midden layers 1–5/6.1, where bone was abundant, it was possible to observe the progressive stages of bone decomposition, and to see that these red-brown nodules were formed by the bonding of iron to bone weathering products. In the early stages of diagenesis, the bone fragments exhibited a halo of

amorphous red-brown material, where weathering by dissolution and/or microbial attack had caused the breakdown of collagen (Hedges 2002) (Fig. 15.6a). Although the precise elemental composition of the red-brown halos will have to be confirmed by submicroscopic analyses (Lewis and Milek, forthcoming), their optical characteristics strongly suggest that they were composed of iron bonded with elements that had been liberated from the weathered bones – most likely phosphorus and calcium. As the diagenesis of the bones progressed, they gradually lost all of the structure afforded by the collagen, and became amorphous compounds of iron and phosphorus, possibly also with a calcium component (Fig. 15.6a–b). As mentioned above, the bonding of iron with bone decomposition products (specifically the calcium and phosphate derived from hydroxyapatite, $Ca_5(PO_4)_3(OH)$), and the neoformation of Ca-Fe-phosphate features, are phenomena that have previously been observed in bone-rich archaeological sediments (Adderley et al. 2004; Jenkins 1994; Simpson et al. 2000).

Bioturbation

Besides being affected by the post-depositional movements of fine mineral material and soluble elements, the archaeological deposits had been severely altered by the activity of soil fauna. Worms and mites attracted by palatable organic matter had worked through the sediments, disturbing their original

Figure 15.2 *Eluviated soil fabric, in wich sand grains (1) are coated and bridged by fine mineral materials (2), in sample KPG02-2, layer 8.1, from the CRM trench (see Fig. 15.7) (partial XPL). Illustration by the authors.*

Figure 15.3 *Compound coatings of Ca-Fe-phosphate (1), Fe (2), silty clay with Fe (3), and silty clay with organic pigmentation (4) in sample KPG02-2, layer 8.2, from the CRM trench (PPL). Illustration by the authors.*

Figure 15.4 *Iron pan cementing charcoal in sample KPG02-2, layer 7.2, from the CRM trench (PPL). Illustration by the authors.*

Figure 15.5 *Iron nodules (1), coatings (2), hypocoatings (3), and quasicoatings (4) in sample KPG03-7, layer 17, from the harbour area (PPL). Illustration by the authors.*

Figure 15.6 *Progressive stages of bone diagenesis. Early stage: class 1 pellicular alteration on a bone in sample KPG02-16, layer 5/6.1 (a). Intermediate stage: class 2–3 pellicular alteration and reddening due to precipitation of Fe on a bone in sample KPG02-15, layer 3.2 (b). Advanced stage: amorphous Fe-P feature in sample KPG02-16, layer 5/6.1 (c). (PPL). Illustration by the authors.*

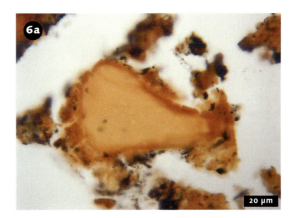

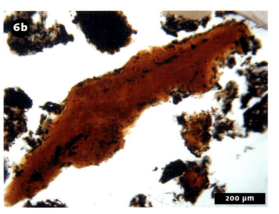

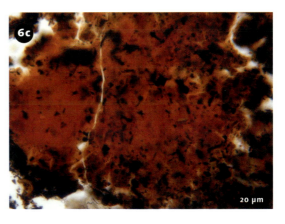

structure, mixing their contents, and blurring the boundaries between them. Their paths created channels and irregularly shaped voids, which were then filled with a sandy, disturbed matrix and soil fauna excrement in the form of minute aggregates of fine mineral material (Fig. 15.25). When the archaeological deposits were examined in thin section, it was possible to distinguish between the excremental fabrics created by soil fauna, and the undisturbed fabrics of the original sediment.

Because of the severity of bioturbation at Kaupang, and because there was a clear relationship between the severity of bioturbation and the nature of the original sediments, the ratio of original to excremental fabric (described as the o/e ratio) was calculated for each layer. The best preserved deposits on plots 3A and 3B – the charcoal-rich, compacted occupation surfaces in the buildings – had been 50% reworked by soil fauna, while more organic deposits were 80–90% reworked, and the fine mineral material in the sandiest layers had been 100% reworked (Tabs. 15.2–15.5). In comparison, the midden sediments were better preserved, with ratios of original to excremental fabrics being 70/30 or better. This is probably due to the high proportion of unpalatable charcoal relative to palatable organic matter in the midden sediments.

Because soil fauna channels cut across sediment boundaries, and these channels could potentially be filled with intrusive material from higher or lower layers, they had the effect of blurring the boundaries between layers, and inhibiting the ability of archaeologists to determine the composition, structure, internal organisation, and compaction of the original sediments. The same problems applied to the recovery of small artefacts and macrofossils (especially those under 5 mm in diameter), and to the sediment analyses that were conducted on bulk samples, since these presented an averaged picture of the sediment composition, in which the material infilling the faunal channels was mixed with the original sediments. In thin section, however, it was possible to distinguish between the original sediment fabric and areas that had been disturbed by soil fauna, allowing a more accurate characterisation of the original sediments. During micromorphological analysis, care was taken to record the composition, compaction, and internal

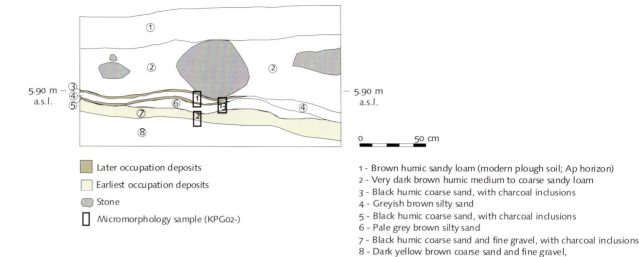

Later occupation deposits

Earliest occupation deposits

Stone

Micromorphology sample (KPG02-)

1 - Brown humic sandy loam (modern plough soil; Ap horizon)
2 - Very dark brown humic medium to coarse sandy loam
3 - Black humic coarse sand, with charcoal inclusions
4 - Greyish brown silty sand
5 - Black humic coarse sand, with charcoal inclusions
6 - Pale grey brown silty sand
7 - Black humic coarse sand and fine gravel, with charcoal inclusions
8 - Dark yellow brown coarse sand and fine gravel,
     apparently cemented by iron oxides

organisation of the preserved aggregates of original sediment, and to exclude the material that infilled the faunal channels. This distinction is reflected in the micromorphology descriptions of the occupation deposits on plots 3A and 3B, where most space is devoted to the preserved aggregates of original sediment, even if these represented only 15–50% of the layer being examined (Tabs. 15.2–15.5). Because thin section analysis made it possible to filter out the effects of post-depositional processes, and to interpret archaeological deposits based on their original characteristics, this technique became the most important tool of the geoarchaeology programme.

15.4 Soils pre-dating the urban settlement

One of the goals of the geoarchaeological programme was to establish whether any soils were buried below the archaeological deposits in order to understand the environmental conditions at Kaupang prior to the establishment of the urban settlement. In micromorphology samples from the CRM trench and the midden area east of plot 1A, an immature (weakly developed) brown earth was found below the earliest archaeological deposits (Fig. 15.7, layer 8; Fig. 15.8, layer 7). In the CRM trench, eluviation had depleted much of the fine mineral material from this soil, leaving behind a skeletal fabric of sand grains coated and bridged with fine organo-mineral material (Fig. 15.2). However, the soil buried beneath the midden was better preserved, allowing the identification of an immature and gleyed soil that had developed on imperfectly drained beach sands (Aurousseau et al. 1985; Bridges 1997).

The texture of the soil beneath the midden varied from sandy silt loam, where the coarse sands and silts were embedded in the fine mineral material, to loamy sand, where fine mineral material coated and bridged the sand grains (Tab. 15.6). The micromass consisted of pale brown to red-brown silty clay, which was speckled to dotted with black, silt-sized particles, and contained <2% amorphous organic matter and <2% fine charcoal. The clay was moderately well oriented, showing birefringence fabrics (b-fabrics) in cross-polarized light that were stipple-speckled (small domains of oriented clay) to mosaic-speckled (large domains of oriented clay), and exhibited some granostriation (clay oriented around sand grains) (Figs. 15.10–15.11). The orientation of the clay was the result of repeated cycles of wetting and drying and the weathering of sands. This soil horizon, which can be classified as a cambic B horizon (or Bw horizon) exhibited the iron mottling typical of groundwater gley soils. Groundwater gleys occur in the lowest parts of the landscape, and typically form on permeable parent materials, such as sands, that overlie a poorly drained substratum – in this case, marine mud (Bridges 1997).

The identification of a soil, albeit an immature one, below the midden indicates that there had been a stable land-surface at c. 4.10 m above present sea-level for several decades – perhaps as long as 100 years – prior to establishment of the urban settlement. Although this land-surface may have been within the range of extreme high tides (Sørensen et al., this vol. Ch. 12:269), this does not appear to have impeded soil development in the area.

15.5 Sediments from the earliest activity
phase at Kaupang

Archaeological deposits from the initial settlement phase at Kaupang (site period I) were examined in section in the CRM trench, where they rested directly on top of the incipient soil discussed above (Fig. 15.7, layer 7). These deposits consisted of 1–3 mm thick sub-horizontal lenses of charcoal, which alternated with 3–10 mm thick lenses of loamy medium to coarse sand (Fig. 15.12). In thin section KPG02-2, only the three lowermost charcoal lenses were well pre-

Figure 15.7 *East-facing section from the CRM trench north-west of plot 3B, showing the locations of the micromorphology samples. Illustration by the authors.*

Figure 15.8 *South-facing section from the midden area east of plot 1A, showing the locations of the micromorphology samples. Illustration by the authors.*

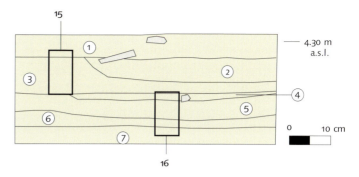

1 - Very dark greyish brown silt loam
2 - Black silt loam
3 - Dark greyish brown coarse sandy loam containing organic matter
4 - Black coarse sandy loam
5 - Black silt loam
6 - Dark greyish brown coarse sandy loam containing organic matter
7 - Grey fine sandy silt containing concretions of oxidised iron

served, while the others had been disturbed by soil fauna, but it was possible to distinguish up to four other lenses. The best preserved charcoal lens was the lowermost one, which had post-depositionally been incorporated into an iron pan (Fig. 15.12, layer 7.2). Since the uppermost charcoal layers had been partially reworked, they are described together, as layer 7.1 (see Tab. 15.1; Fig. 15.12).

Like all of the other archaeological deposits that developed on the beach sand at Kaupang, the coarse component of these deposits consisted mainly of quartz, feldspar, sandstones, and several types of igneous rocks, including granite and monzonite. These minerals were mainly in the form of subrounded to subangular grains of medium to coarse sand, but 2–5% was gravel-sized. Layer 7.1 also contained a substantial component of coarse charcoal up to 6 mm in diameter (5–10%), which was distributed in a series of 3–7 lenses (Fig. 15.12). Elongated pieces of charcoal were horizontally or sub-horizontally oriented except in areas where there had been obvious disturbance by soil fauna. Both coarse and fine charcoal fragments were also embedded in iron nodules that had a similar fabric to that of the iron pan at the base of the layer. These iron nodules had sharp boundaries, and were subrounded, which strongly suggests that they had originally formed part of a thin iron pan that had been disrupted by soil fauna. A few other iron nodules, which were "cleaner" and had bone fragments in them, bore the characteristics of bone in an advanced stage of diagenesis.

The micromass, which had been partially eluviated, consisted of an intimate mixture of amorphous organic matter, clay, silt, very fine sand, and fine charcoal. It was very dark brown, heavily dotted by silt-sized particles, and had a mosaic-speckled b-fabric that was often masked by organic pigmentation and dark brown amorphous organic matter. Unfortunately, very few plant cell fragments and no tissue frag-

ments had survived decomposition, making it impossible to identify the type of organic matter that had originally been deposited. Phytoliths were present, but it was not possible to quantify them, since they too were frequently masked by amorphous organic matter. Trace amounts of minute bone fragments were also embedded in the micromass (Tab. 15.1). These were subrounded in shape, and sometimes heavily weathered; they reached a maximum length of 1 mm, but most were under 300 μm.

The lower boundary of layer 7 was very sharp, and was marked by an iron pan (7.2). This was a 2–3 mm thick, wavy horizon, with a sharp upper boundary and a diffuse lower boundary. It consisted largely of fine and coarse charcoal fragments up to 7 mm in diameter (40–50%), and a mixture of silt loam and amorphous organic matter that had been impregnated by oxidized iron (Tab. 15.1). There were trace amounts of plant tissue residues that had been impregnated by iron, but most organic matter appears to have achieved an advanced state of decomposition before it was impregnated. Many phytoliths were present, in localised areas reaching concentrations of c. 10%. Most of the voids had been filled with a red-brown, limpid, isotropic material, which reflected orange and red colours in OIL (Fig. 15.4). Although it is possible that other colloids had also been deposited in this horizon, the strong orange and red colours exhibited by the dark red-brown, isotropic material in OIL indicate that the horizon was cemented mainly by oxidized iron.

Layer 7 differed both from the occupation deposits that accumulated within the buildings in later phases of the site, and from the midden deposit that accumulated on the eastern edge of the site. The near-horizontal charcoal lenses, which contained horizontally-oriented charcoal fragments, are interpreted as activity surfaces. However, they were very fine compared to the occupation deposits in the houses, and

Layer and microstratigraphic unit	Groundmass						Micromass	Organic and Anthropogenic Components			Pedofeatures			
	Texture class and sorting	Orientation of components	Microstructure	Porosity	C/F100 µm ratio	C/F related distribution	Nature of fine mineral material	Amorphous organic matter	Charcoal	Bone	Silty clay loam coatings	Subrounded Fe nodules with bone	Diffuse Fe nodules, coatings	Yellow to orange coatings
7.1	Poorly sorted organic loamy medium/coarse sand	Sub-horizontal lenses of sand and oriented charcoal	Complex: bridged grain, intergrain micro-aggregate, local subangular blocky	■■■■■	30/70	Enaulic, gefuric, local porphyric	Grey-brown to very dark brown; dotted; mosaic-speckled	■■■■	■■■■	+		+	■■	+
7.2	Poorly sorted loamy medium/coarse sand	Horizontal orientation of elongated charcoal	Subangular blocky; local crack structure	■■■	65/35	Porphyric	Red-brown; speckled; mosaic-speckled		■■■■■■■				■■■■■	
8.1	Well sorted medium/coarse sand	Random	Bridged grain	■■■■■■	90/10	Gefuric	Brown, red-brown; dotted; stipple-speckled to mosaic-speckled	■	+				■■	
8.2	Well sorted medium/coarse sand	Random	Bridged grain	■■■■■	85/15	Chitonic, gefuric	Brown, red-brown; dotted; stipple-speckled to mosaic-speckled	+	+		■		■■■	■■

+ Present in trace amounts, ■ <2%, ■■ 2–5%, ■■■ 5–10%, ■■■■ 10–20%, ■■■■■ 20–30%, ■■■■■■ 30–40%, ■■■■■■■ 40–50% (of visible area)

were separated by fine lenses of sand or loamy sand. They therefore appear to have been the result of short-term, periodic occupation events, rather than long-term occupation on the same spot. Unfortunately, because the minute sand layers between the activity horizons had not been clear in the field, and their full extent is not known, it is impossible to say whether they were deposited by storms or whether they were intentionally sprinkled.

It is notable that these deposits bore a close resemblance to the multi-laminated occupation deposits at other Viking-age and medieval seasonal market places, such as Ribe, in Denmark, and Gásir, in Iceland. At Ribe, deposits associated with the phase 3 seasonal market place were also characterised by relatively thin, alternately dark and light layers. The dark layers contained more humus, charcoal, and artefacts, and were interpreted as seasonal activity surfaces, while the light layers were composed of purer sand that appeared to have been spread over the surface of the plots between periods of trading activity (Bencard and Jørgensen 1990). Similarly, at Gásir, the seasonal occupation of "booths" resulted in the accumulation of extremely thin, alternately black and brown layers – the black ones rich in charcoal, and the brown ones consisting of relatively clean silt (Roberts 2003). Considering these parallels, it is possible that the earliest archaeological deposits at Kaupang, which also seem to have been formed by short-term, periodic activity events, are representative of seasonal craft and trading activity. If this is the case – and it cannot be proven – it is also possible that the seven charcoal lenses visible in thin section KPG02-2 represent seven seasons of activity on this plot. However, since the horizontal extent of each of these lenses is not known, it is difficult to know whether this number – even as an estimate – can be applied to other plots in the vicinity or elsewhere in the settlement area.

The material that was deposited in this early phase bears some resemblance to the material deposited in the later occupation deposits in the houses,

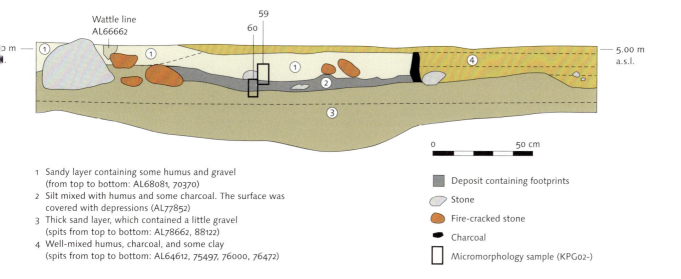

Wattle line
AL66662

59
60

5.00 m
a.s.l.

0   50 cm

1 Sandy layer containing some humus and gravel
   (from top to bottom: AL68081, 70370)
2 Silt mixed with humus and some charcoal. The surface was
   covered with depressions (AL77852)
3 Thick sand layer, which contained a little gravel
   (spits from top to bottom: AL78662, 88122)
4 Well-mixed humus, charcoal, and some clay
   (spits from top to bottom: AL64612, 75497, 76000, 76472)

■ Deposit containing footprints
◓ Stone
● Fire-cracked stone
◆ Charcoal
▢ Micromorphology sample (KPG02-)

Table 15.1 *Micromorphology descriptions of the earliest occupation layer at Kaupang (layer 7) and the underlying beach sand (layer 8) in sample KPG02-2.*

Figure 15.9 *Northwest-facing section C63290, showing the profile across the pathway between plots 1A and 2A and the locations of the micromorphology samples. Illustration by the authors.*

---

where organic matter and wood ash were also the main anthropogenic constituents. The organic matter had completely decomposed, and unfortunately the absence of plant tissues or coprolites makes it impossible to determine the nature of the original organic material. As in the later occupation deposits, the wood ash had been severely affected by post-depositional leaching of the calcitic ash component, and only carbonised wood fragments were preserved. Compared to the later occupation deposits, there was significantly less bone in the early activity layers: no trace of burnt bone and only trace amounts of unburnt bone were found in thin section (Tab. 15.1). The bone fragments that were present in the early activity layers were also smaller than the bone fragments in the house floors, subrounded in shape, and appeared to be heavily trampled. The high degree of weathering evident in the bone fragments deposited in this early activity phase also suggests that they had been exposed on the surface of the ground before being buried.

15.6 Sediments in the pathway between plots 1A and 2A

An unusual set of environmental conditions resulted in the preservation of human footprints and animal hoof marks in the pathway that ran between plots 1A and 2A (Pilø, this vol. Ch. 10:196, Fig. 10.9). In the field, these impressions seemed to have been made in soft, moist mud that had dried hard, and had then been covered with a thick layer of sand (Fig. 15.9). The goal of the geoarchaeology programme was to provide more detail about the composition of the sediment in which the footprints were found, the environmental conditions under which they had formed, and the origins and formation of the sand layer that had covered them.

The sediment in which the footprints had been preserved (Fig. 15.9, layer 2; AL77852) contained a mixture of two fabrics. The dominant fabric was a sandy silt loam with an average coarse/fine ratio of 60/40, and this contained pockets and irregular bands of coarse sand with a coarse/fine ratio of 95/5. Both of these sediment fabrics must have derived from local soils and beach sands that had been trampled onto the pathway. This layer contained several features that were likely to have been products of trampling under moist conditions, including a clear, undulating upper boundary, and two thin (1–3 mm) zones of compacted fine mineral material (Fig. 15.14). One of these thin compacted zones also contained horizontal planar voids (Fig. 15.13), which are typically produced by downwards compression in silty and loamy sediments, and have frequently been associated with trampled surfaces (Bresson and Zambaux 1990; Davidson et al. 1992; Gé et al. 1993; Rentzel and Narten 2000).

The fine mineral material in layer 2 was brown, with a dotted limpidity and a stipple-speckled b-fabric. The clay component of this fine mineral material, which was responsible for the birefringence fabric,

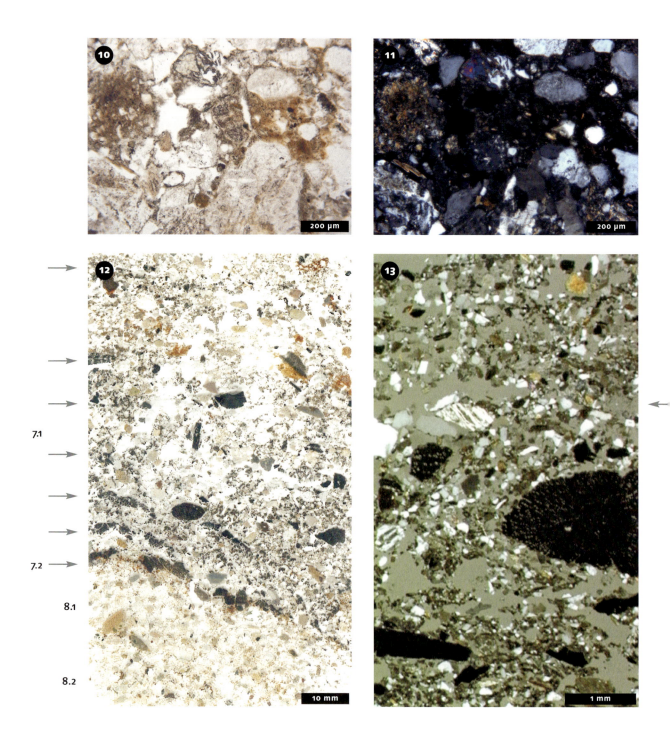

was also responsible for the ability of the sediment to dry hard after the footprints had been made. The fine material also contained some minute anthropogenic inclusions, such as charred organic remains up to 4 mm in size (5–10%), dark brown amorphous organic matter (2–5%), bone (<2%), and burnt bone up to 2 mm in size (<2%). The small size of these anthropogenic remains might have been a result of fragmentation by trampling (Nielsen 1991). In addition, the low frequency and random distribution of anthropogenic inclusions compared to the activity surfaces, indoor occupation deposits, and midden deposits on the site suggest that this material had not been dumped on this spot, but instead had been carried there on the soles of trampling hooves and feet.

The bones in the pathway were highly weathered, exhibiting darkening on surfaces and along internal cracks, weak or no birefringence in XPL, weak fluorescence under UV light, and yellow or red-brown halos in PPL. The poor preservation of the bones in the pathway relative to the bones in the indoor occupation deposits on plots 3A and 3B suggests that the exposure of the bones on the outdoor surface had promoted the breakdown of collagen and the leaching of calcium and phosphorus.

In the field, iron oxide features had been visible in the muddy layer containing the footprints. In thin section, it was observed that 2–5% of the layer had

Figure 15.10 *Incipient soil buried below the midden sediments, in sample KPG02-16, layer 7 (PPL). Illustration by the authors.*

Figure 15.11 *Incipient soil buried below the midden sediments, in sample KPG02-16, layer 7 (XPL). Illustration by the authors.*

Figure 15.12 *Sample KPG02-2, showing multiple charcoal lenses (arrows) associated with the initial phase of the urban settlement. Illustration by the authors.*

Figure 15.13 *Compacted surface and horizontal planar void created by trampling in the pathway (KPG02-59, partial XPL). Illustration by the authors.*

Figure 15.14 *Samples KPG02-59 and 60, showing the sediments in a pathway that had preserved human and animal footprints. Illustration by the authors.*

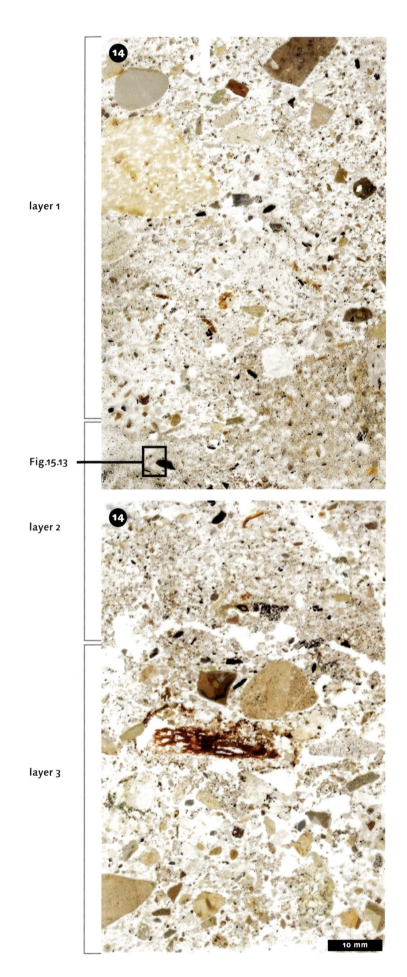

been moderately to strongly impregnated by iron oxides, and some of these nodules were clearly fragments of former iron pans that had been disturbed by soil fauna. At the lower boundary of the sandy silt loam, an 8 mm thick iron pan had formed, which was associated with a large, iron-impregnated plant tissue. This plant tissue had been only partially decomposed when it was impregnated with iron, which suggests that the impregnation process began soon after it was deposited. The precipitation of iron at this boundary was likely to have been due to the finer texture and lower porosity of the sandy silt loam compared to the poorly sorted sand and gravel layer below (Fig. 15.9, layer 3; AL78662), which would have halted the downward-moving wetting front and caused the oxidation of iron in this location.

The layer containing the footprints was covered and preserved by a c. 15 cm thick layer of poorly sorted sand, gravel, and small pebbles (Fig. 15.9, layer 1; AL70370). This layer also contained charcoal fragments (c. 2%) and burnt and unburnt bone fragments up to 4 mm in length (c. 2%). The poor sorting and anthropogenic inclusions in this deposit support the view that it was an intentionally dumped levelling layer rather than a water-lain deposit.

15.7 Sediments on building plots 3A and 3B

On plots 3A and 3B, most of the occupation deposits from the period of permanent settlement were black, organic, and charcoal-rich sandy loams, and the similarities in their colour and texture made them difficult to distinguish and interpret in the field. The role of the geoarchaeology programme was to clarify the limits of their boundaries, their mode of formation,

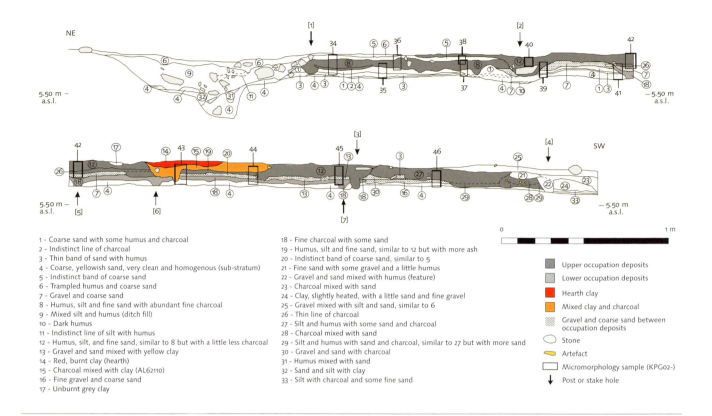

NE

5.50 m —
a.s.l.

[5]   [6]   [7]

SW

5.50 m —
a.s.l.

1 - Coarse sand with some humus and charcoal
2 - Indistinct line of charcoal
3 - Thin band of sand with humus
4 - Coarse, yellowish sand, very clean and homogenous (sub-stratum)
5 - Indistinct band of coarse sand
6 - Trampled humus and coarse sand
7 - Gravel and coarse sand
8 - Humus, silt and fine sand with abundant fine charcoal
9 - Mixed silt and humus (ditch fill)
10 - Dark humus
11 - Indistinct line of silt with humus
12 - Humus, silt, and fine sand, similar to 8 but with a little less charcoal
13 - Gravel and sand mixed with yellow clay
14 - Red, burnt clay (hearth)
15 - Charcoal mixed with clay (AL62110)
16 - Fine gravel and coarse sand
17 - Unburnt grey clay

18 - Fine charcoal with some sand
19 - Humus, silt and fine sand, similar to 12 but with more ash
20 - Indistinct band of coarse sand, similar to 5
21 - Fine sand with some gravel and a little humus
22 - Gravel and sand mixed with humus (feature)
23 - Charcoal mixed with sand
24 - Clay, slightly heated, with a little sand and fine gravel
25 - Gravel mixed with silt and sand, similar to 6
26 - Thin line of charcoal
27 - Silt and humus with some sand and charcoal
28 - Charcoal mixed with sand
29 - Silt and humus with sand and charcoal, similar to 27 but with more sand
30 - Gravel and sand with charcoal
31 - Humus mixed with sand
32 - Sand and silt with clay
33 - Silt with charcoal and some fine sand

Upper occupation deposits
Lower occupation deposits
Hearth clay
Mixed clay and charcoal
Gravel and coarse sand between occupation deposits
Stone
Artefact
Micromorphology sample (KPG02-)
Post or stake hole

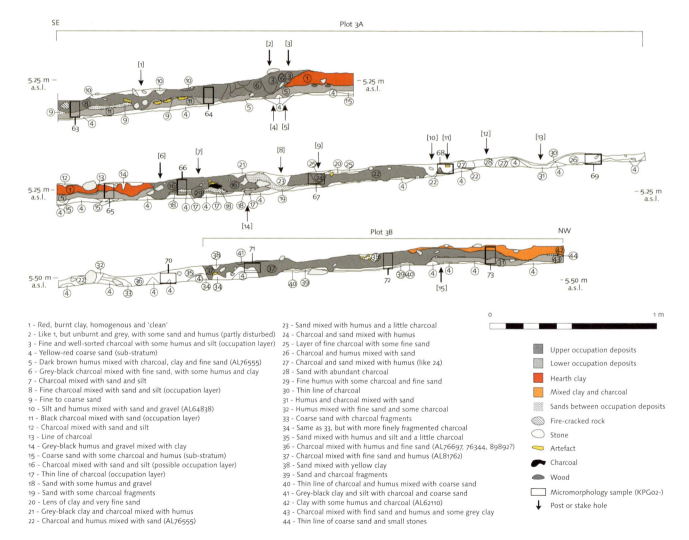

SE   Plot 3A

5.25 m —
a.s.l.

Plot 3B   NW

5.50 m —
a.s.l.

1 - Red, burnt clay, homogenous and 'clean'
2 - Like 1, but unburnt and grey, with some sand and humus (partly disturbed)
3 - Fine and well-sorted charcoal with some humus and silt (occupation layer)
4 - Yellow-red coarse sand (sub-stratum)
5 - Dark brown humus mixed with charcoal, clay and fine sand (AL76555)
6 - Grey-black charcoal mixed with fine sand, with some humus and clay
7 - Charcoal mixed with sand and silt
8 - Fine charcoal mixed with sand and silt (occupation layer)
9 - Fine to coarse sand
10 - Silt and humus mixed with sand and gravel (AL64838)
11 - Black charcoal mixed with sand (occupation layer)
12 - Charcoal mixed with sand and silt
13 - Line of charcoal
14 - Grey-black humus and gravel mixed with clay
15 - Coarse sand with some charcoal and humus (sub-stratum)
16 - Charcoal mixed with sand and silt (possible occupation layer)
17 - Thin line of charcoal (occupation layer)
18 - Sand with some humus and gravel
19 - Sand with some charcoal fragments
20 - Lens of clay and very fine sand
21 - Grey-black clay and charcoal mixed with humus
22 - Charcoal and humus mixed with sand (AL76555)

23 - Sand mixed with humus and a little charcoal
24 - Charcoal and sand mixed with humus
25 - Layer of fine charcoal with some fine sand
26 - Charcoal and humus mixed with sand
27 - Charcoal and sand mixed with humus (like 24)
28 - Sand with abundant charcoal
29 - Fine humus with some charcoal and fine sand
30 - Thin line of charcoal
31 - Humus and charcoal mixed with sand
32 - Humus mixed with fine sand and some charcoal
33 - Coarse sand with charcoal fragments
34 - Same as 33, but with more finely fragmented charcoal
35 - Sand mixed with humus and silt and a little charcoal
36 - Charcoal mixed with humus and fine sand (AL76697, 76344, 89892?)
37 - Charcoal mixed with fine sand and humus (AL81762)
38 - Humus mixed with yellow clay
39 - Sand and charcoal fragments
40 - Thin line of charcoal and humus mixed with coarse sand
41 - Grey-black clay and charcoal mixed with coarse sand
42 - Clay with some humus and charcoal (AL62110)
43 - Charcoal mixed with find sand and humus and some grey clay
44 - Thin line of coarse sand and small stones

Upper occupation deposits
Lower occupation deposits
Hearth clay
Mixed clay and charcoal
Sands between occupation deposits
Fire-cracked rock
Stone
Artefact
Charcoal
Wood
Micromorphology sample (KPG02-)
Post or stake hole

Figure 15.15 *Northwest-facing section C61185, showing the profile across plot 3B and the locations of the micromorphology samples. Illustration by the authors.*

Figure 15.16 *Northeast-facing section C61189, showing the profile across plots 3A and 3B and the locations of the micromorphology samples. Illustration by the authors.*

and their composition, in order to refine interpretations of the forms and functions of the buildings. Twenty-four micromorphology samples were analysed from sections placed along the main axes of the buildings on plots 3A and 3B, 13 from the NE–SW transect through plot 3B (Fig. 15.15, section C61185), and 11 from the SE–NW transect through plots 3A and 3B (Fig. 15.16, section C61189). These samples captured the full depth of the period II stratigraphy on the building plots at approximately 0.5 m intervals.

Site period II on plots 3A and 3B consisted of a complex series of archaeological deposits and negative features that were associated with two main building sites (Pilø, this vol. Ch. 10:207–11). In the southeastern plot, 3A, there was a building with two occupation phases (A302 and A304), which were separated by a thin, discontinuous, moderately sorted sand layer. In the northwestern plot, 3B, there were two superimposed buildings (A301 and A303) separated by a layer of coarse gravel. Buildings A301, A302, and A303 had central hearths, but the hearth of A303, the earlier of the two buildings on plot 3B, did not appear in section C61185 because it was slightly northwest of this profile. In the field, it was extremely difficult to differentiate activity areas within the buildings, and to delimit their outer walls. Interpretations of the size and organisation of the buildings based on context plans differed slightly from interpretations that could be drawn from the sections. Micromorphological analysis permitted these interpretations to be slightly refined, and facilitated their integration.

Plot 3B

SP II, sub-phase 1: building A303

The main occupation deposit associated with building A303 was represented in section C61185 by layer 18

(Fig. 15.15) and in section C61189 by layers 31 and 43 (Fig. 15.16). It was 2–5 cm thick, and its composition was described in the field as fine charcoal and humus, mixed with some sand. A number of small negative features were associated with this layer, all of which appeared to be 3–6 cm wide in the section drawings (they had not been visible in plan) and might have been stake-holes (Fig. 15.15, [5]–[7]; Fig. 15.16, [15]). At least three of these putative stake-holes ([5], [7], [15]) were positioned on the outer edges of the main occupation deposit, suggesting that the stakes were the structural supports of a small building that was c. 2 m wide. Alternatively, building A303 could have been a three-aisled structure, with the stakes dividing space between the central aisle and the side aisles. In this case, the side aisles would be represented by layers 1 and 3 (on the northeast side of the central aisle) and layer 16 (on the southwest side of the central aisle) (Fig. 15.15). These sandy layers contained some charcoal, amorphous organic matter, and minute bone fragments, but were so heavily bioturbated (c. 90% or more), that little evidence remained of their original microstructure or composition. In general, these layers were much sandier and contained less organic and anthropogenic material than the side aisles of the later building, A301, and they resemble much more closely the outdoor deposits between buildings A301 and A302 (e.g. section C61189, Fig. 15.16, layer 26).

Layer 18, the main occupation deposit in building A303, was captured in micromorphology samples KPG02-41, -43, -44, and -45, but was so badly preserved in KGP02-43 that this sample will not be included in the discussion (Tab. 15.2; Fig. 15.15). This layer was best preserved in samples KPG02-44 and -45, where approximately 30% of the original sediment fabric had been left undisturbed by soil fauna. In thin section, the preserved aggregates of original sediment were composed of organic sandy loams, in which the fine material appeared to consist entirely of charcoal,

Thin Section	KPG02-41	KPG02-44	KPG02-45
O/E ratio *	10/90	30/70	30/70
Overall porosity	■■■■■■■	■■■■■■■	■■■■■■■
Overall microstructure	Intergrain microaggregate; local subangular blocky with channels	Complex: intergrain microaggregate, subangular blocky, channel	Complex: intergrain microaggregate, subangular blocky, channel
Microstructure	Subangular blocky with channels	Subangular blocky, with channels	Subangular blocky, with channels
Porosity	■■■■■	■■■■	■■■
Orientation of constituents	Random	Horizontal	Random; localised horizontal; localised horizontal lenses of medium to coarse sand
Texture class	Organic sandy loam	Organic sandy loam	Organic sandy loam
C/F100 µm ratio	60/40	60/40	60/40
Nature of fine material	Brown, dotted; undifferentiated b-fabric; mainly charcoal, amorphous organic matter and silt-sized mineral grains	Brown, dotted; undifferentiated b-fabric; mainly charcoal, amorphous organic matter and silt-sized mineral grains	Brown, dotted; undifferentiated b-fabric; mainly charcoal, amorphous organic matter and silt-sized mineral grains
Fe nodules	■	■	■
Bone	■■	■■	■
Burnt bone	■	■	■
Bone alteration	Pits, cracks, Fe/Mn staining	Pits, cracks, Fe/Mn staining	Pits and cracks
Max. bone size	0.5 mm	1.7 mm	2 mm
Leather		+	
Dark brown to black amorphous organic matter	■■■■	■■■	■■■
Fe-replaced organic matter			+
Fungal hyphae/sclerotia	+		
Charred organic matter	■■■■	■■■■■■■	■■■■■■
Max. charcoal size	2.0 mm	7.0 mm	2.3 mm
Identifiable charcoal	Deciduous wood	Deciduous wood	Deciduous wood
Calcareous ash			+
Non-metallurgical slag		+	
Interpretation	Difficult to interpret due to amount of disturbance by soil fauna	Occupation deposit	Occupation deposit

Description of preserved aggregates with original sediment fabric

* Ratio of original, undisturbed fabric to excremental fabric. E is characterised by an intergrain microaggregate structure and high porosity due to reworking by soil fauna.
\+ Present in trace amounts, ■ <2%, ■■ 2–5%, ■■■ 5–10%, ■■■■ 10–20%, ■■■■■ 20–30%, ■■■■■■ 30–40%, ■■■■■■■ 40–50% (of visible area)

amorphous organic matter and silt-sized mineral grains. The birefringence fabric was undifferentiated, and very little clay could be observed in thin section. The deposit had consisted predominantly of charcoal (20–50%) and dark brown to black amorphous organic matter (c. 10–20%), which was why the layer had appeared black in the field. Unfortunately, the organic matter was in an advanced state of decomposition, without any cell structures preserved, and was therefore no longer identifiable. The charcoal, on the other hand, was quite highly fragmented (mainly silt-sized), but still reached sizes of up to 7 mm, making it possible to identify a range of deciduous woods. The deposit also contained highly fragmented bones (2–5%), and burnt bones (c. 1%), all of which were under 2 mm in length. These were not significantly weathered, but exhibited some pitting and cracking as a result of the slightly acidic conditions in these sedi-ments. Some bone fragments also showed some amorphous, dark brown staining from the precipitation of iron and/or manganese oxides.

The coarse component of layer 18 was randomly oriented in sample KPG02-41, possibly because the sediment aggregates had been turned over by soil fauna, but in samples 44 and 45, it could be observed that a significant proportion of elongated bone fragments, charcoal, strands of amorphous organic matter, and elongated mineral grains was horizontally oriented. In addition, in sample 45, several horizontal lenses of medium to coarse sand were embedded within the finer matrix (Fig. 15.18). Such horizontal orientation would normally result from the gradual accumulation of material on a relatively compact surface, and for this reason, layer 18 is interpreted as an occupation surface. Although it is difficult to be certain about the agent of deposition of the well-sorted

Table 15.2 *Micromorphology descriptions of layer 18, the occupation deposit in building A303.*

sand layers, a couple of scenarios are possible. If the small structure had been periodically abandoned, and had been partially open to the elements, it is possible that the sand had been carried by wind and deposited in the building during stormy weather. It is also possible that sand had been occasionally sprinkled over the floor area in order to help keep it drier and more salubrious. Since some of the sand layers were not perfectly sorted, and elongated sand grains were often sub-horizontally or obliquely oriented, it is quite likely that the sand layers had been deposited deliberately.

The gravel layer between buildings A303 and A301

Sealing this occupation deposit from SP II, sub-phase 1 was a 1–2 cm thick, extensive layer of sand and gravel, which was represented in section C61185 by layers 7, 20, 13, and 30 (Fig. 15.15), and in section C61189 by layer 44 (Fig. 15.16). This layer was poorly sorted, consisting of 30–40% gravel and pebbles (2 mm–18 mm), about 50% medium and coarse sand (200 μm–2 mm), and 10–20% fine mineral material. The fine mineral material was in the form of coatings around sand and gravel grains, and intergrain microaggregates (soil fauna excrement). There were also a few larger aggregates of fine mineral material that contained <2% minute bone, burnt bone, and charcoal fragments. These appeared to be intrusive, and had probably been dragged into the gravel layer by soil fauna from the occupation layers above or below. The original sand and gravel layer therefore appears to have contained little fine material, and was mainly composed of subrounded grains of granite, monzonite, sandstone, quartz, and feldspar. In the part of the layer labelled "layer 13" on section C61185, there was also a large, gravel-sized aggregate of sandy clay that was heavily mottled with oxidized iron as a result of repeated cycles of saturation and oxidation. The orientation of this aggregate of sandy clay and other

elongated mineral grains was predominantly horizontal or oblique.

The fact that this gravel layer was 5.65 m above sea-level (a.s.l.) and was poorly sorted eliminates the possibility that it had been deposited by the sea. Instead, the dominant oblique orientation of the mineral material, the thinness of the layer, and the fact that its extent was closely associated with the occupation deposit below it, all suggest that it had been intentionally deposited. After the earlier structure had been abandoned and the stakes associated with it had been removed, a layer of gravel extracted from elsewhere on the beach had been spread over the muddy, organic occupation layer – perhaps to consolidate the ground surface and to prepare the plot for the construction of a new building. This was quite a common technique, and was practiced, for example, in later Viking-age Dublin (Wallace 1992).

SP II, sub-phase 2: building A301

Above the gravel layer was another series of occupation deposits and negative features, which belonged to a three-aisled building (Fig. 15.17). In the centre of the building was a rectangular clay hearth (Fig. 15.15, layer 14), which was surrounded by heterogeneous deposits containing mixed clay, ash, and charcoal (Fig. 15.15, layer 15; Fig. 15.16, layer 42). The central aisle of the structure contained black layers, c. 4–8 cm thick, which were described in the field as being composed of humus, silt, fine sand, and finely fragmented charcoal (Fig. 15.15, layers 12, 19 and 26; Fig. 15.16, layer 37). In section C61185, it is possible to see that the layers in the central floor area were physically separated from the building's side aisles by negative features (Fig. 15.15, [2]–[3]).

Both of the side aisles contained 4–7 cm thick, black occupation layers that appeared very similar to the sediments in the central floor area, and were described in the field as being composed of silt,

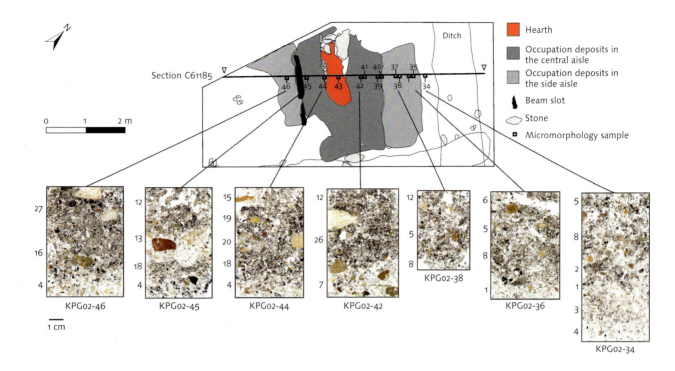

humus, sand and charcoal (Fig. 15.15, section C61185, layers 8 and 27). In plan (Fig. 15.17), the northeast side aisle (layer 8) appeared to be slightly narrower than the southwest side aisle (layer 27). However, in section (Fig. 15.15), the side aisles appeared to be the same width, with layer 8 extending as far as a small post depression on the edge of the plot boundary ditch (Fig. 15.15, [1]). As will be discussed below, micromorphological analysis of samples KPG02-34, -36, and -38 supported the interpretation that layer 8 did extend as far as indicated in the section drawing. Another small post-hole or post depression (Fig. 15.15, [4]) was located on the outer edge of the southwest side aisle, making both of the side aisles c. 1.2 m wide.

The micromorphology samples that were taken from section C61185 (Fig. 15.15) provided valuable information about the organisation and use of space inside building A301. In thin section KPG02-44, the aggregates of clay that had once formed part of the hearth were easily identified, although they themselves had not been reddened by heat and could not have been from the upper surface of the hearth. The hearth had been plastered using wet clay tempered with 5–10% herbaceous plant matter and c. 5% coarse sand. During the construction of the hearth, this clay mixture had been smeared over a flat surface with horizontal strokes, which had resulted in the horizontal orientation of both the plant matter and the clay (Fig. 15.20). Although the original size and shape of the plant tissues had left planar voids in the hardened clay, the tissues themselves were in an advanced state of decomposition – they did not have identifiable cell structures, but were in the form of yellow,

Figure 15.17 *Plan of building A301, showing the locations of the micromorphology samples. Illustration by the authors.*

Figure 15.18 *Lenses of sand (arrows) in sample KPG02-45, layer 18 (PPL). Illustration by the authors.*

Figure 15.19 *Wood ash (1) and burnt bone (2) in sample KPG02-43, layer 15 (PPL). Illustration by the authors.*

Figure 15.20 *Aggregate of clay from the hearth in building A301; sample KPG02-44, layer 15 (XPL). Illustration by the authors.*

Figure 15.21 *Aggregate of clay from the hearth in building A302; sample KPG02-65, layer 1 (partial XPL). Illustration by the authors.*

amorphous masses or red-brown humus-iron complexes. The yellow, amorphous, organic masses contained low frequencies of phytoliths.

Besides containing aggregates of clay from the hearth itself, the mixed deposits associated with the hearth (Fig. 15.15, layer 15) contained an abundance of pale brown and grey aggregates of microcrystalline calcium carbonate (Fig. 15.19). Optically, these aggregates closely resemble wood ash, which is produced when calcium in wood cells is released during combustion, absorbs moisture and carbon dioxide from the air, and recrystallises as fine-grained calcium carbonate (Canti 2003:347–8). As previously mentioned, it was very unusual for calcareous ash to be preserved

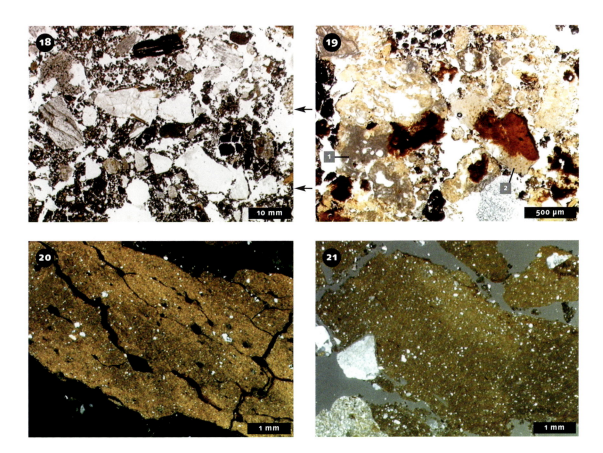

at Kaupang, and the presence of wood ash around the hearth of building A301 must be due to the high quantities of ash in the original deposit. In thin sections KPG02-43 and -44, this pale, ashy material was associated with high concentrations of charcoal, burnt bone, and a material known as "non-metallurgical slag" – glassy, vesicular granules formed by the melting of siliceous sands and ashes at high temperature. Similar types of hearth residues were also found in lower concentrations in the occupation deposits in the central aisle (layers 12 and 19, Tab. 15.3), and in still lower concentrations in the side aisles (layers 8 and 27, Tab. 15.3). This indicates that ash residues had spilled over the edge of the hearth and had been trampled around the structure, and/or that they had been deliberately sprinkled in order to "sweeten" the occupation surfaces and to keep them dry.

All of the black occupation deposits in the building had been given very similar field descriptions (see Fig. 15.15). Close examination in thin section confirmed that they did indeed have a very similar composition: dark brown humus, finely fragmented charcoal, sand, and silt in subtly different concentrations that would have been extremely difficult to distinguish in the field (Tab. 15.3). In addition, all of the deposits in the building had been severely disturbed by bioturbation, which had had the effect of mixing layers and blurring the boundaries between them. In thin section, it was possible to see that the best-preserved occupation deposits in building A301 were in

the central aisle, where the ratio of original, undisturbed sediment to sediment that had been reworked by soil fauna (the o/e ratio) was about 50/50, and the overall porosity was 20–40%. In contrast, the occupation deposits in the side aisles were relatively poorly preserved. They contained as little as 15% undisturbed sediment, and were characterised by a more open, porous microstructure (40–50% void space) containing abundant soil fauna excrements (intergrain microaggregates).

The preserved aggregates of undisturbed sediment in the occupation deposits in building A301 were mainly composed of charred organic matter and dark brown to black uncharred organic matter in an advanced stage of decomposition. This material dominated the fine fraction, and created the black colours that had been visible in the field. Very little clay was visible in thin section, but silt-sized mineral grains were present and sand was ubiquitous, particularly in the side aisles, where the coarse/fine ratio was 60/40. Among the charred materials, deciduous wood tissue was dominant, but seeds were also present in low frequencies throughout the structure. In the occupation deposits in the central aisle southwest of the hearth (Fig. 15.15, layer 12), and in the southwest side aisle (Fig. 15.15, layer 27), charred and uncharred organic matter were present in relatively equal concentrations (20–30%, Tab. 15.3). However, northeast of the hearth, the occupation deposits in the central aisle contained a slightly higher concentration of charred organic matter (mean of 35%) relative to uncharred, amorphous organic matter (mean of 15%) and included the only charred nutshell fragment found in thin section (Fig. 15.15, layers 12, 26, sample KPG02-42; Fig. 15.22). In contrast, the northeast side aisle (Fig. 15.15, Tab. 15.3, layer 8) contained higher concentrations of uncharred organic matter (mean of 25%) relative to charred organic matter (mean of 12%). The composition of the central floor area and the side aisles differed subtly in other ways as well, including a slightly higher concentration of burnt bone fragments (up to 2–5%) and non-metallurgical slag (up to 2%) in the central floor area (Tab. 15.3, layers 12, 19, and 26).

The porosity of the preserved aggregates of undisturbed sediment was similar throughout most of the building, with void space usually in the range of 10–20%, except in the slightly more compacted occupation deposits in the central aisle northeast of the hearth (5–10% void space). Although this suggests that the central aisle had experienced heavier foot traffic than the side aisles, it is unfortunately no longer possible to determine if the sediments once had a microstructure related to trampling/compaction (e.g. massive, platy, or prismatic) since all of the aggregates of original, undisturbed sediment now have a subangular blocky microstructure that is likely to have developed post-depositionally as a result of repeated cycles of wetting and drying, and freezing and thawing.

The distribution and orientation of components such as mineral grains, charcoal, and bone fragments offer more useful information about the formation processes of the occupation deposits, because although they are predominantly randomly organised, there were localised lenses where elongated bone, charcoal, and mineral grains exhibited a preferential horizontal orientation (Figs. 15.22–15.23). Fine lenses of horizontally oriented components were clearest in

the central aisle in samples KPG02-42 and -44, but this might have been due to the fact that the deposits in the central floor area had been less disturbed by soil fauna. Although less frequent, horizontally oriented bone and charcoal fragments were also found in the side aisles, suggesting that the occupation layers throughout the building had built up to thicknesses of up to 8 cm through the gradual deposition of debris on a sequence of accruing surfaces. Where such surfaces appear particularly well defined and continuous in thin section, such as at the boundary between layers 12 and 26, this is likely to represent a truncated surface – the point at which an occupation surface had been swept, scraped, or spaded. That cultural practices could result in the net accumulation of debris on the floors, and that this build-up could be handled by the periodic truncation of the accumulated deposits, was also suggested for 10th-century Anglo-Scandinavian houses at York, where insects specific to dry, indoor environments ("house fauna") were found in pit fills and backyards of tenements (Hall and Kenward 2004; Kenward and Hall 1995). Such practices continued until the mid-20th century in traditional houses with earthen floors in the Outer Hebrides and Iceland, where organic and ash-rich occupation deposits were periodically cleared out and used to fertilise the fields (Milek 2006).

Since the materials that accumulated in the occupation deposits included organic litter, hearth waste, and food remains such as bone fragments and charred nutshell, it is likely that the functions of the building included cooking and eating. Micromorphological analysis produced no evidence of metalworking or any other type of craft-production in the building, although craftwork involving organic materials that have subsequently decayed cannot be ruled out. Overall, although the occupation deposits throughout the building were very similar, the central aisle contained slightly more hearth waste, was more

Thin section	KPG02-46	KPG02-45	KPG02-44	KPG02-42	KPG02-38	KPG02-36	KPG02-34
Layer described	27	12	19	12/26	8	8	8
O/E ratio *	15/85	30/70	50/50	50/50	15/85	15/85	20/80
Overall porosity	■■■■■■	■■■■■■■	■■■■■■	■■■■■	■■■■■■	■■■■■■	■■■■■■
Overall microstructure	Intergrain microaggregate, channel, local subangular blocky	Intergrain microaggregate; channel; local subangular blocky	Intergrain microaggregate, subangular blocky, channel	Intergrain microaggregate, subangular blocky, channel	Intergrain microaggregate, channel, local subangular blocky	Intergrain microaggregate, channel, local subangular blocky	Intergrain microaggregate, channel, local subangular blocky

Description of preserved aggregates with original sediment fabric

	KPG02-46	KPG02-45	KPG02-44	KPG02-42	KPG02-38	KPG02-36	KPG02-34
Microstructure	Subangular blocky with channels	Subangular blocky with channels	Subangular blocky with channels	Subangular blocky with some channels	Subangular blocky with channels	Subangular blocky with channels	Subangular blocky with channels
Porosity	■■■■	■■■■	■■■■	■■■	■■■■	■■■■	■■■■
Orientation of constituents	Random	Random; localised horizontal	Random; local horizontal in upper 1 mm	Random; local horizontal; small horizontal sand lens	Random; localised horizontal	Random; localised horizontal	Random
Texture class	Organic sandy loam	Organic sandy loam	Organic sandy silt loam	Organic sandy silt loam	Organic sandy loam	Organic sandy loam	Organic sandy loam
C/F100 μm ratio	60/40	60/40	40/60	40/60	55/45	60/40	60/40
Nature of fine material	Brown, dotted; undifferentiated b-fabric; mainly organic matter, charcoal, silt, phytoliths	Brown, dotted; undifferentiated b-fabric; mainly organic matter, charcoal, silt, phytoliths	Brown, dotted; undifferentiated b-fabric; mainly organic matter, charcoal, silt, phytoliths	Brown, dotted; undifferentiated b-fabric; mainly organic matter, charcoal, silt, phytoliths	Brown, dotted; undifferentiated b-fabric; mainly organic matter, charcoal, silt, phytoliths	Brown, dotted; undifferentiated b-fabric; mainly organic matter, charcoal, silt, phytoliths	Brown, dotted; undifferentiated b-fabric; mainly organic matter, charcoal, silt, phytoliths
Fe nodules	+	■	■	■	■	+	+
Fe infillings in charcoal pores	+				+	+	
Bone	■	■■	■	■	■■	■■	■■
Burnt bone	■	■	■■	■	■	■	■
Bone alteration	Subrounded, cracks, pits	Subrounded, cracks, pits, Fe/Mn staining	Fe/Mn staining; burnt bone cracked	Subrounded, some Fe/Mn staining	Subrounded, cracks, pits, some Fe staining	Subrounded, cracks, pits, Fe/Mn staining	Subrounded, cracks, pits, Fe/Mn staining
Max. bone size	4.5 mm	4.8 mm	3.3 mm	1.1 mm	1.3 mm	3.0 mm	3.0 mm
Dark brown to black amorphous organic matter	■■■■■	■■■■■	■■■■■	■■■■	■■■■■	■■■■■	■■■■■
Wood tissues	■						
Omnivore excrement			+				
Fe-replaced organic matter			+			+	+
Charred organic matter	■■■■■	■■■■■	■■■■■	■■■■■■	■■■■	■■■■	■■■■
Max. charcoal size	8.8 mm	6.5 mm	3.1 mm	5.0 mm	2.8 mm	4.8 mm	3.1 mm
Identifiable charred organic matter	Deciduous wood, seed	Deciduous wood	Deciduous, coniferous wood; seed	Deciduous wood; nutshell	Deciduous wood	Deciduous wood, seeds	Deciduous wood
Calcareous ash				+		+	+
Non-metallurgical slag	+	+	+	■		+	
Interpretation	Side aisle: occupation deposit with additional organic input	Centre aisle: occupation deposit with additional input of hearth waste	Centre aisle: occupation deposit with additional input of hearth waste	Centre aisle: occupation deposit with additional input of hearth waste	Side aisle: occupation deposit with additional organic input	Side aisle: occupation deposit with additional organic input	Side aisle: occupation deposit with additional organic input

* Ratio of original, undisturbed fabric to excremental fabric. E is characterised by an intergrain microaggregate structure and high porosity due to reworking by soil fauna.

+ Present in trace amounts, ■ <2%, ■■ 2–5%, ■■■ 5–10%, ■■■■ 10–20%, ■■■■■ 20–30%, ■■■■■■ 30–40%, ■■■■■■■ 40–50% (of visible area)

compacted, and was less disturbed by soil fauna than the side aisles. This would suggest that the side aisles had been subjected to more post-depositional bioturbation because they contained relatively more humified plant matter, which was more palatable to soil fauna, and were less compacted, which made it easier for soil fauna to penetrate them. The evidence therefore points to a different treatment of occupation surfaces and to a different use of space in the centre aisle and side aisles.

The centre aisle – particularly on the northeast side of the hearth – is likely to have been the main artery for foot traffic through the building. The hearth waste that accumulated in the centre aisle, including ash, charred organic remains, burnt bone, and non-metallurgical slag, could have become incorporated into the occupation deposits in several ways, such as accidental spillage from the hearth, accidental dumping, and/or intentional dumping in order to "sweeten" the floors, to absorb moisture and odours, or to act as an insecticide (cf. Hakbijl 2002). The humified plant material that accumulated in the centre aisle could also have derived from a number of sources. For example, it could have been from dumped refuse (intentional or accidental), attrition of the building (e.g. falling thatch, decomposing timbers), mats, plant material that was accidentally tracked in from the outside, or plants deliberately scattered as litter. It should be noted here that the accumulation of organic litter on the floors did not necessarily mean that conditions in the house were squalid or unpleasant. Although the complete decomposition of these plant materials makes it impossible to identify them in thin section, the types of organic materials that might have been deliberately scattered on the floor in order to provide an absorbent and dry occupation surface include straw, hay, moss, rushes, wood chips, and leaf litter (Geraghty 1996; Hall and Kenward 2004).

There was a physical barrier between the side aisles and the centre aisle, which resulted in the separation and differentiation of the deposits that accumulated in these areas. The material making up the deposits in the side aisles included a mixture of hearth waste and organic matter, though it had a slightly lower proportion of hearth waste and a slightly higher proportion of organic matter than the material in the centre aisle. It should also be noted that the deposits in the side aisles did not resemble the midden material that accumulated east of the building plots, which was characterised by larger gravel, bone, and charcoal fragments, and features resulting from severe bone diagenesis (see below, and Tab. 15.6). Instead, the type, size, organisation, and orientation of the material in the side aisles, and its similarity to the material in the central aisle, suggest that it was a domestic occupation deposit that had accumulated on a gradually accruing surface. Hearth debris could have become incorporated by either accidental deposition or intentional deposition to keep moisture, odours, and insects at bay; humified plant material, like that in the centre aisle, could have come from a wide range of sources, including food refuse, organic building materials, mats, and loose bedding materials. Since the side aisles had received an additional input of organic matter relative to the centre aisle, and this organic matter seems to have required a sill to contain it, the side aisles were quite likely to have held loose brushwood or softer bedding materials such as straw, hay, leaf litter, and/or moss. The practice of filling the side aisles with organic bedding materials is paralleled in 9th- and 10th-century Dublin, and also in some rural Viking-age houses, such as the one at Aðalstræti 14–18, Reykjavík (Geraghty 1996; Milek 2004; Simpson 1999; Wallace 1992). There is no evidence in the surviving archaeology that the side aisles in house A301 were raised substantially above the level of the central floor area, and

Thin Section	KPG02-63	KPG02-64	KPG02-65	KPG02-66
Layer described	11	11	5	17
O/E ratio *	15/85	20/80	50/50	10/90
Overall porosity	■■■■■■	■■■■■■	■■■■■■	■■■■■■
Overall microstructure	Intergrain microaggregate; localised subangular blocky	Intergrain microaggregate; localised subangular blocky	Subangular blocky; intergrain microaggregate	Intergrain microaggregate; localised subangular blocky

Description of preserved aggregates with original sediment fabric

	KPG02-63	KPG02-64	KPG02-65	KPG02-66
Microstructure	Subangular blocky with channels	Subangular blocky with channels	Subangular blocky with occasional channels	Subangular blocky, with channels
Porosity	■■■■■	■■■■	■■■■	■■■■■
Orientation of constituents	Random; localised horizontal orientation of elongated woody tissues	Random; localised horizontal orientation of constituents	Horizontal; horizontal lenses of charcoal, organic matter, and sand	Random
Texture class	Sandy silt loam	Sandy silt loam	Sandy silt loam	Sandy silt loam
C/F100 µm ratio	40/60	35/65	30/70	40/60
Nature of fine material	Brown, dotted; undifferentiated b-fabric; mainly organic matter, charcoal, silt, phytoliths	Brown, dotted; undifferentiated b-fabric; mainly organic matter, charcoal, silt, phytoliths	Brown, dotted; mosaic-speckled b-fabric; clay and silt intimately mixed with organic matter, charcoal, and phytoliths	Brown, dotted; undifferentiated b-fabric; mainly organic matter, charcoal, silt phytoliths
Clay coatings			■	
Fe nodules	+	■	■■	■
Bone	■	■	■■	■■
Burnt bone	+	+	■■	+
Bone alteration	Subrounded, cracks, irregular alteration, red-brown discolouration, loss of birefringence, Fe/Mn staining	Subrounded, pits, cracks, Fe/Mn staining	Subrounded, Fe/Mn staining	Subrounded, Fe/Mn staining
Max. bone size	1.1 mm	750 µm	5.0 mm	2.0 mm
Dark brown to black amorphous organic matter	■■■■■■	■■■■■■	■■■■■■	■■■■■
Wood tissues	■		+	+
Phlobaphene-containing tissues		■■		
Fe-replaced organic matter	■	■	■	
Fungal sclerotia		+		+
Charcoal	■■■	■■■■■	■■■■■	■■■■■
Max. charcoal size	2.0 mm	4.0 mm	4.0 mm	2.3 mm
Identifiable charcoal	Deciduous wood	Deciduous wood	Deciduous wood	Deciduous wood
Non-metallurgical slag			+	+
Interpretation	Indoor occupation deposit with predominantly organic input, including wood	Indoor occupation deposit with predominantly organic input, including wood	Indoor domestic occupation deposit	Difficult to interpret due to amount of disturbance by soilfauna

* Ratio of original, undisturbed fabric to excremental fabric . E is characterised by an intergrain microaggregate structure and high porosity due to reworking by soil fauna.

+ Present in trace amounts, ■ <2%, ■■ 2–5%, ■■■ 5–10%, ■■■■ 10–20%, ■■■■■ 20–30%, ■■■■■■ 30–40%, ■■■■■■■ 40–50% (of visible area)

it is possible that the physical barrier between them was simply a low sill, which had to be stepped over. This might have been the case at Viking-age Dublin and York as well, for although Hall (1994) and Wallace (1992) have suggested that the side aisles contained earthen benches raised as high as 0.45 m above the level of the central floor area, the surviving archaeo-logical evidence could also support the interpretation that the side aisles were raised only a few centimetres. Regardless of their original height, the side aisles in house A301 were likely to have functioned as sitting, working, eating, and sleeping areas out of the way of the main route of foot traffic through the centre of the building.

Plot 3A

SP II, sub-phase 1: building A304

Above the extensive sand layer, AL78662 (Fig. 15.16, layer 4), there was a series of 1 to 3 cm thick occupation deposits on plot 3A, which were associated with building A304 (Fig. 15.16, layers 5, 11, 17). Since one of these occupation deposits, layer 17 (sample KPG02-66), was severely disturbed by soil fauna, and only c. 10% of the original sediment fabric was preserved, the analysis of building A304 concentrated on the other two occupation deposits, layers 5 and 11 (samples KPG02-63, -64, and -65; Tab. 15.4).

Although they had not been visible in plan, a number of small negative features associated with building A304 were visible in section C61189 (Fig. 15.16). These were only 3–6 cm wide, and might have been stake-holes, or depressions made by stakes set into the sand. One of these stake-holes was located close to the northwest edge of layer 17 (Fig. 15.16, [14]). Two other stake-holes ([4]–[5]) were below post-holes associated with the later building, A302 ([2]–[3]), suggesting that successive phases of post-holes had been repeatedly re-cut in a similar location as posts were replaced, and that there was some continuity of building form from the earlier to the later building phases.

Towards the southeast end of building A304, the lower occupation deposit was represented by layer 11 (Fig. 15.16). This layer was described in the field as "charcoal-mixed black sand", but in thin sections KPG02-63 and -64 it was possible to see that it was a sandy silt loam that contained relatively little charcoal (5–20%) compared to its organic matter content (30–40%; Tab. 15.4). This organic matter was predominantly dark brown to black and amorphous – in such an advanced state of decomposition that its cell structure was no longer apparent. Some organic residues were red-brown in colour because they had been post-depositionally impregnated with iron (<2%), but these had already been in an advanced state of decomposition when they were impregnated, and therefore it was not possible to identify the tissues. The dark-coloured, amorphous organic matter, along with fine charcoal, silt-sized mineral grains, and phytoliths, formed the bulk of the fine groundmass of the sediment. The fine material had an undifferentiated b-fabric, and the sediment appeared to contain a minimal clay component.

Although the composition of layer 11 was dominated by fine organic matter, there was also a significant coarse fraction (coarse/fine ratio was 35/65 to 40/60; Tab. 15.4). This coarse fraction consisted mainly of coarse sand derived from the local beach deposits, but it also included sand-sized charcoal-fragments and plant tissue residues in various states of decomposition. There were a significant number of phlobaphene-containing plant tissues (c. 5% in

KPG02-64; Fig. 15.24), which are typical of protective tissues such as bark (Bullock et al. 1985). There were also a small number of wood tissue residues (c. 0.5%; Fig. 15.25). Since oxidizing conditions are prevalent, the survival of wood and bark tissues in layer 11 may be due to the fact that these types of plant tissues are more resistant to decay than other types of tissues – phlobaphene-containing tissues in particular are quite unpalatable to soil fauna. These plant tissues, along with other elongated constituents such as charcoal, certain minerals, and bone (c. 1%), tended to have a horizontal orientation, and appeared to have accumulated on a gradually accruing occupation surface. The concentration of wood and bark tissues in layer 11, as well as the unusually high concentration of decomposed organic matter, are unique among the occupation deposits studied at Kaupang, and indicate

Figure 15.22 Charred nutshell (1), bone fragments (yellow) (2), and charcoal (3) in sample KPG02-42, layer 26 (PPL). Illustration by the authors.

Figure 15.23 Lens of sand, containing horizontally oriented sand grains in sample KGP02-42, layer 26 (PPL). Illustration by the authors.

Figure 15.24 Fragment of phlobaphene-containing tissue (bark) (1), charcoal (2), and bone (3) in sample KPG02-64, layer 11 (PPL). Illustration by the authors.

Figure 15.25 Wood tissue surrounded by plant matter that has been reworked by soil fauna in sample KPG02-63, layer 11 (PPL). Illustration by the authors.

Figure 15.26 Clay coatings surrounding fragments of amorphous organic matter in sample KPG02-65, layer 5 (partial XPL). Illustration by the authors.

Figure 15.27 Lens of coarse sand (1) in a matrix of intimately mixed clay, silt, charcoal (2), amorphous organic matter (3), and bone (yellow) (4) in sample KPG02-54, layer 5 (PPL). Illustration by the authors.

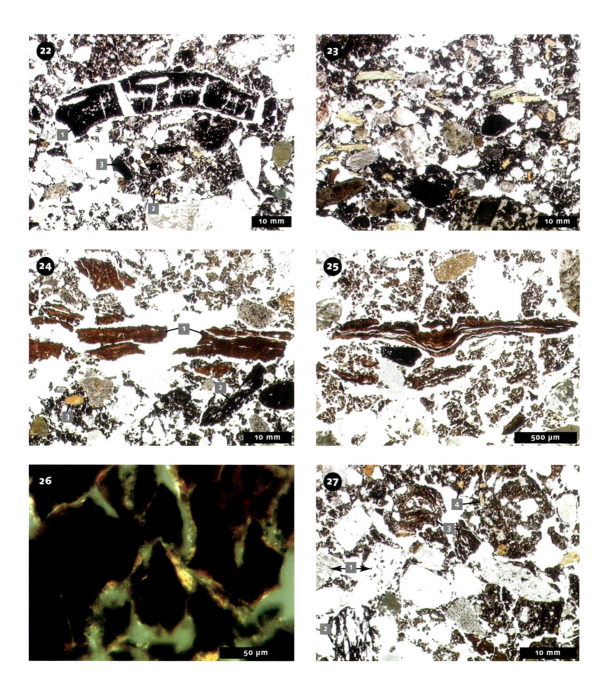

that in its earlier occupation phase, space in the southeast end of building A304 was used and/or maintained in a special way. The micromorphological evidence suggests that the area might have been covered with wood chips, such as those found in the harbour sediments (see below), and in pits A64891, A65132 and A43852 (Barrett et al., this vol. Ch. 14: 298–9). In building A304, such material could either have been dumped, spread as floor litter, or derived from *in situ* wood-working.

Northwest of layer 11, the occupation deposit in building A304 was represented by layer 5, which was described in the field as dark brown humus mixed with charcoal, clay, and fine sand (Fig. 15.16). In thin section (KPG02-65), layer 5 appeared to have many similarities to layer 11, including a very high concentration of amorphous organic matter (c. 30%) and rare wood tissues (<0.5%), but it also contained a much higher clay content (Tab. 15.4). Some of this clay was intimately mixed with the amorphous organic matter, charcoal, and silt-sized mineral grains in the fine groundmass, which resulted in a mosaic-speckled birefringence fabric. Some clay (c. 2%) was also present in the form of non-laminated dusty clay coatings that surrounded sand grains, organic matter, and other coarse constituents (Fig. 15.26). The distribution of these clay coatings was not even throughout the layer, but was related to the distribution of the clay aggregates in the layer above, which was the hearth associated with the later house, A302 (Fig. 15.16, layer 1). The clay in layer 5 was therefore a product of post-depositional illuviation of clay from the hearth above, and was not a characteristic of the original sediment.

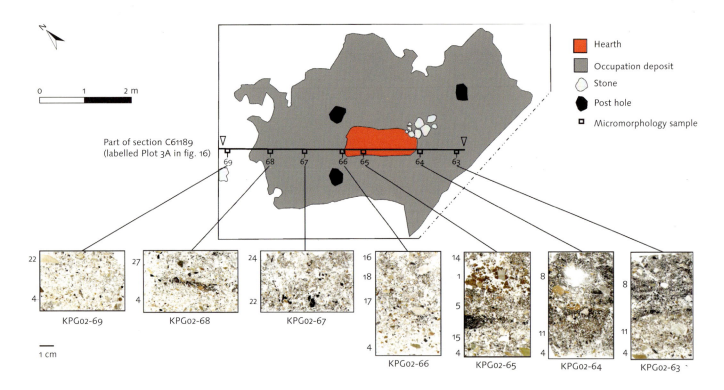

Part of section C61189
(labelled Plot 3A in fig. 16)

Hearth
Occupation deposit
Stone
Post hole
Micromorphology sample

KPG02-69
KPG02-68
KPG02-67
KPG02-66
KPG02-65
KPG02-64
KPG02-63

1 cm

Even though about half of layer 5 had been bio-turbated, several horizontal lenses of charcoal, organic matter, and coarse sand were preserved, where elongated constituents tended to be horizontally oriented (Fig. 15.27). The lower boundary of layer 5 was marked by a lens of charcoal that must originally have been a thin layer of wood ash, although the calcareous component had since been leached. A lens of coarse sand, which was similar to those that were described in building A301, layer 18 (Fig. 15.18), could have been sprinkled over the floor in order to help keep it dry. Lenses of both wood chips and coarse sand were also found in finely laminated floor deposits in 10th-century houses in Dublin, where they were interpreted as having provided clean and absorbent occupation surfaces (Geraghty 1996). The presence of fine horizontal lenses within layer 5, and the dominant horizontal orientation of constituents, suggest that the layer had formed fairly rapidly through periodic accretion on an active occupation surface.

While layer 11 was characterised by a higher proportion of wood and bark tissues, and contained only c. 1% bone and trace amounts of burnt bone, layer 5 contained c. 2% bone and c. 5% burnt bone up to 5 mm in size (Tab. 15.4). Layer 5 also contained trace amounts of non-metallurgical slag, which, along with the burnt bone and charcoal, is an indication that hearth waste had been integrated into the deposit. Building A304 did not contain a hearth, and therefore

it must be assumed that this hearth waste had been carried from elsewhere and deposited intentionally. This is supported by the presence of the lens of pure charcoal at the lower boundary of layer 5, which was clearly formed in a single dumping event. Therefore, although layers 5 and 11 had in common a very high content of amorphous organic matter, differences in the higher quantity of wood and bark chips in layer 11 and the higher quantity of dumped hearth waste in layer 5 suggest that the two areas were used and/or maintained slightly differently.

The sand layer between buildings A304 and A302

Buildings A304 and A302 were separated by a thin, discontinuous, sandy layer (Fig. 15.16, layers 9 and 18). The segment of layer 18 that was captured in sample KPG02-66 was only about 1 cm thick, had a diffuse boundary, and had been heavily reworked by soil fauna. It consisted predominantly of moderately sorted medium and coarse sand and fine gravel, and was clearly derived from a beach deposit. It also contained a small amount (c. 20%) of fine organo-mineral material in the form of intergrain microaggregates (soil fauna excrement), which had probably originated in the organic layers above and below the sand, and had been worked into the sand by soil fauna activity. This sand layer could either have been blown over the lower occupation surface during a brief period of abandonment, or it could have been intentionally sprinkled in order to prepare a clean surface prior to

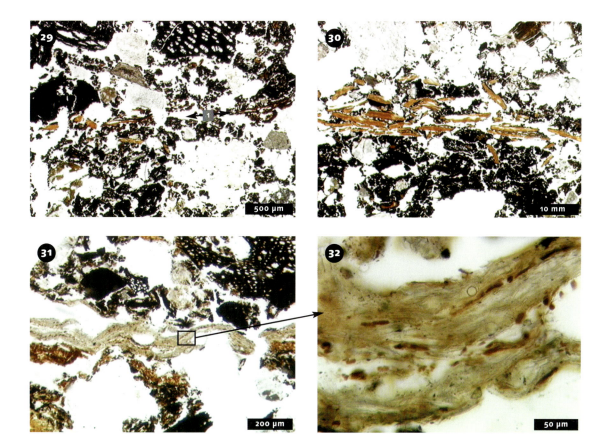

Figure 15.28 *Plan of building A302, showing the locations of the micromorphology samples. Illustration by the authors.*

Figure 15.29 *Horizontal lens of plant tissues (1) in sample KPG02-63, layer 8 (PPL). Illustration by the authors.*

Figure 15.30 *Horizontal lens of fish bone in sample KPG02-64, layer 8 (PPL). Illustration by the authors.*

Figure 15.31 *Wavy aggregate of grass phytoliths, possibly a mat fragment, in sample KPG02-63, layer 8 (PPL). Illustration by the authors.*

Figure 15.32 *Close up of phytoliths in the possible mat fragment in sample KPG02-63, layer 8 (PPL). Illustration by the authors.*

the construction of the hearth and the restructuring of the building. Since it is only moderately sorted, and contains coarse sand and gravel, it is more likely that it was spread intentionally.

SP II, sub-phase 2: building A302

Above the patchy sandy layer, building A302 contained a rectangular clay hearth and a series of associated occupation deposits and negative features (Fig. 15.28). Three large post-holes to the north, east, and west of the respective corners of the hearth might represent the three corners of a rectangle of roof-carrying posts (see Pilø, this vol. Ch. 10:208). Other negative features were not visible in plan, because their fills were very similar to the deposits that surrounded them, but they were clearly visible in section C61189 (Fig. 15.16). For example, the northwest and southeast ends of the hearth were bounded by negative features containing grey-black, charcoal-rich, sandy fills (Fig. 15.16, [2],[3],[6]) that were very similar to the adjacent occupation deposits (layers 8 and 16). It is possible that these negative features had held posts or horizontal beams that enclosed the hearth, and had been infilled with sediment from the floors when the timbers were removed.

The clay hearth in the centre of building A302 (Fig. 15.16, layer 1) had been constructed using similar materials and techniques as were used in constructing the hearth in building A301. In sample KPG02-65, it could be seen that the hearth had been made with brown, speckled clay mixed with 5–10% coarse silt, 2–5% fine to medium sand, and <1% herbaceous plant matter. The fact that the proportions of coarse mineral material and plant matter were slightly different in the two hearths suggests that they were constructed at different times using different batches or mixtures of clay. Nevertheless, the methods of construction were very similar: the clay mixture had been smeared over a flat surface, which had resulted in the distribution of some of the coarser sand in horizontal lenses, as well as the horizontal orientation of the plant matter and the clay (Fig. 15.21). The plant matter had decomposed, and had left behind fine horizontal planar voids in the clay, some of which contained post-depositional iron oxide coatings.

The best preserved occupation deposits in building A302 were located southeast of the hearth, in layer 8, a 4–7 cm thick layer described in the field as fine charcoal mixed with sand and silt (Fig. 15.16). In thin sections KPG02-63 and -64, it could be seen that the abundant charcoal component (50–60%) was not mixed in the sediment in a homogeneous way, but was concentrated in 4–5 fine lenses, each about 3 mm thick, which were separated by sandier lenses. This charcoal component consisted mainly of deciduous wood tissues, but some charred seeds were also present. The amorphous organic matter that formed c. 15% of the groundmass, the bone fragments that were present in frequencies of 1–10%, and the burnt bone fragments that were present in frequencies of 0.5–5%, were also sometimes concentrated in horizontal lenses (Fig. 15.29; Tab. 15.5). In sample KPG02-64, for example, there was a remarkably preserved, continuous lens of fish bone, including fins, vertebrae, and cranial elements up to 10 mm in length (Fig. 15.30). Other elongated constituents in layer 8, including bones, minerals, and lignified plant tissues (0.5–1%), tended to be horizontally oriented as well. The dominant horizontal orientation of constituents, and the concentration of many constituents in discrete lenses, indicate that the sediment accrued through the punctuated deposition of food preparation waste, sand, and hearth waste, the latter of which included charcoal, burnt bone, and trace amounts of calcareous ash and non-metallurgical slag. Layer 8 therefore appears to be a domestic occupation deposit, similar in composition to the sediments in the central floor area of building A301, but with a slightly higher con-

centration of charcoal and burnt bone, and more pronounced horizontal bedding.

The preservation of the horizontal bedding in layer 8 was remarkably good, considering that 70–80% of the fine mineral material in this layer had been reworked by soil fauna (Tab. 15.5). Although the sediment microstructure was mainly intergrain microaggregate due to the large number of faunal excrements, and although undisturbed aggregates of fine material were preserved in only a few localised areas, the unpalatable charcoal lenses had largely been avoided by soil fauna. There was some evidence that the pronounced horizontal bedding in layer 8 was a product of the way in which the floors had been used and maintained. For example, this layer contained trace amounts of elongated, wavy aggregates of amorphous organic matter, in which compacted, rod-shaped grass phytoliths were lying in a uniform direction – aggregates that may be residues of grass mats (Figs. 15.31–15.32). These elongated aggregates bore a close resemblance to features found in better-preserved floors in tell sites in eastern Europe and the Middle East, which have also been interpreted as woven grass mats (Kovacs, forthcoming; Matthews 1992:Figs. 98–101). If grass mats had occasionally been laid over the occupation deposits in building A302, this would have promoted the accumulation of material in the form of discrete lenses, and would have reduced the vertical mixing normally caused by trampling on an active floor surface (Gifford-Gonzalez et al. 1985; Matthews 1995; Nielsen 1991; Villa and Courtin 1983).

Northwest of the hearth, the occupation deposit was represented by layer 16 which, like layer 8, had been described in the field as charcoal mixed with sand and silt (Fig. 15.16). As observed in sample KPG02-66, the fine fraction in layer 16 bore a very close resemblance to that in layer 8: in both cases, the fine fraction had a brown-coloured, undifferentiated

Thin section	KPG02-69	KPG02-68	KPG02-67	KPG02-66	KPG02-64	KPG02-63
Layer described	26	27	22	16	8	8
O/E ratio *	3/97	5/95	10/90	30/70	30/70	20/80
Overall porosity	■■■■■■■	■■■■■■■	■■■■■■	■■■■■■	■■■■■	■■■■■■
Overall microstructure	Intergrain microaggregate	Intergrain microaggregate	Intergrain microaggregate	Intergrain microaggregate; localised subangular blocky	Intergrain microaggregate; localised subangular blocky	Intergrain microaggregate; localised subangular blocky

Description of preserved aggregates with original sediment fabric

	KPG02-69	KPG02-68	KPG02-67	KPG02-66	KPG02-64	KPG02-63
Microstructure	Subangular blocky	Subangular blocky	Subangular blocky	Subangular blocky	Subangular blocky	Subangular blocky
Porosity	■■■■	■■■■	■■■■	■■■■■	■■■■	■■■■■
Orientation of constituents	Random	Random; horizontal within lenses of charcoal and gravel	Random	Random	Horizontal; horizontal lenses of charcoal, organic matter, bone, sand	Horizontal; horizontal lenses of charcoal, organic matter, sand
Texture class	Loamy sand	Organic sandy loam	Organic sandy loam	Organic sandy loam	Sandy organic loam	Sandy organic loam
C/F100 μm ratio	70/30	60/40	60/40	50/50	40/60	40/60
Nature of fine material	Brown, dotted; undifferentiated b-fabric; mainly organic matter, charcoal, silt-sized minerals, phytoliths	Brown, dotted; undifferentiated b-fabric; mainly organic matter, charcoal, silt-sized minerals, phytoliths	Brown, dotted; undifferentiated b-fabric; mainly charcoal, organic matter, silt-sized minerals, phytoliths	Brown, dotted; undifferentiated b-fabric; mainly organic matter, charcoal, silt-sized minerals, phytoliths	Brown, dotted; undifferentiated b-fabric; mainly charcoal and organic matter	Brown, dotted; undifferentiated b-fabric; mainly charcoal, organic matter, silt-sized minerals, phytoliths
Fe nodules	■	■	■	■	+	■
Bone	+	■	■	■■■	■■■	■
Burnt bone	■	■	+	■	■■■	■
Bone alteration	Subrounded, irregular alteration, pits, cracks, Fe/Mn staining	Subrounded, pits, cracks, Fe/Mn staining, some loss of birefringence	Fe/Mn staining	Subrounded, pits, cracks, Fe/Mn staining	Generally well preserved; some loss of birefringence	Subrounded, pits, cracks
Max. bone size	1.8 mm	5.0 mm	1.1 mm	4.0 mm	10.0 mm	1.3 mm
Dark brown to black amorphous organic matter	■■■■	■■■■	■■■■	■■■■■	■■■■	■■■■
Lignified plant tissues	+		+		■	■
Fe-replaced organic matter	+			+	+	■
Charred organic matter	■■■	■■■■	■■■■■	■■■■	■■■■■■■	■■■■■■■
Max. charcoal size	2.6 mm	3.5 mm	2.3 mm	3.5 mm	10.0 mm	5.0 mm
Identifiable charred organics	Deciduous wood, seeds	Deciduous wood	Deciduous wood	Deciduous and coniferous wood	Deciduous wood, seeds	Deciduous wood, seeds
Calcareous ash					+	
Non-metallurgical slag		+			+	+
Other notes of interest	Relic fragments of Fe pans consolidating siliceous ash, charcoal, burnt bone	Lower boundary marked by a 5 mm-thick lens of charcoal, woody tissues, and burnt bone, consolidated by Fe and Ca-Fe phosphate infillings			Lowermost charcoal lens is capped by a continuous lens of fish bones	Charcoal is concentrated in five separate lenses; Fe-replaced plant tissues had been decomposed when impregnated
Interpretation	Outdoor activity area	Outdoor activity area	Indoor activity area	Indoor activity area	Indoor domestic occupation deposit	Indoor domestic occupation deposit

* Ratio of original, undisturbed fabric to excremental fabric . E is characterised by an intergrain microaggregate structure and high porosity due to reworking by soil fauna.

+ Present in trace amounts, ■ <2%, ■■ 2–5%, ■■■ 5–10%, ■■■■ 10–20%, ■■■■■ 20–30%, ■■■■■■ 30–40%, ■■■■■■■ 40–50% (of visible area)

b-fabric, consisting mainly of organic matter, charcoal, silt-sized minerals, and phytoliths, with a minimum of clay (Tab. 15.5). Layer 16 also contained a similar quantity of bone as layer 8 (c. 5%), but it contained significantly less burnt bone (c. 1%), and no traces of non-metallurgical slag. In addition, the overall charcoal component in layer 16 was significantly less than in the occupation deposits southeast of the hearth – only c. 15% – and the proportion of amorphous organic matter was somewhat higher – c. 25%. Overall, the differences in composition between layers 8 and 16 suggest that space had been used and/or maintained differently in these two areas, with layer 8 receiving significantly more hearth waste, and layer 16 receiving more organic matter.

The texture and organisation of the material in layer 16 were also different from those in layer 8. It contained more sand, for example, and the horizontal lenses and common horizontal orientation of constituents that characterised layer 8 were not observed in the segment of layer 16 captured in sample KPG02-66. Layer 16 had been severely reworked by soil fauna, perhaps because of its light, sandy texture and abundance of palatable organic matter, so that only about 30% of its original fabric was preserved. However, if there had originally been a tendency for constituents to be horizontally oriented, some evidence for this would presumably have been preserved, as they had been in other layers. Therefore, it is likely that the formation processes that produced layer 16 were different from those that produced layer 8; layer 16 might in fact have never been a heavily trampled floor-surface.

Northwest of layer 16, and separated from it by some stones and a small post-hole (Fig. 15.16, [8]), was layer 22 (AL76555), which had been described in the field as charcoal and humus mixed with sand (Fig. 15.16). Unfortunately, only a small portion of this layer was captured in thin section KPG02-67, and

it had been so severely reworked by soil fauna that only about 10% of its original sediment fabric survived. Due to this substantial reworking, the microstructure of this sediment was predominantly intergrain microaggregate – that is, the fine mineral material was almost entirely in the form of faunal excrement. From the portion that could be observed in thin section, layer 22 was an organic sandy loam with a coarse/fine ratio of 60/40 (Tab. 15.5). Its fine fraction, like those in layers 8 and 16, contained very little clay, and was dominated instead by organic matter, charcoal, silt-sized mineral grains, and phytoliths. Compared to the occupation deposits described above, it contained relatively low quantities of charcoal (c. 25%), amorphous organic matter (c. 10%), bone (c. 1%) and burnt bone (c. 0.5%), and none of these constituents were horizontally oriented (Tab. 15.5). Layer 22 does not appear to have been a trampled floor surface and does not appear to have received much input from the domestic hearth. It is therefore possible that building A302 had contained two separate activity areas – a large room that contained the hearth, and a smaller area, c. 1 m long, that might have functioned as a storage area.

Layer 22 was bounded on its northwest edge by a series of intercutting negative features – probably post-holes – which had not been seen in plan (Fig. 15.16, [10]–[13]). Northwest of these features was layer 26, which had appeared similar to layer 22 in the field, but which appeared very different from layer 22 where it was captured by thin section KPG02-69. Layer 26 was a loamy sand that contained only about 30% fine mineral material mixed with c. 10% charcoal, and c. 10% amorphous organic matter (Tab. 15.5). This layer had been so severely bioturbated that 97% of its fine mineral material was in the form of faunal excrements. Reworking by soil fauna had also disturbed iron pedofeatures, producing subrounded iron nodules. The bone in this layer was severely

Layer and microstratigraphic unit	Groundmass			Micromass	Organic and Anthropogenic Components									Pedofeatures			
	Texture class and sorting	Orientation of components	Microstructure	Nature of fine mineral material	Dark brown to black amorphous organic matter	Lignified tissues	Phlobaphene-containing tissues	Maximum plant size (mm)	Charcoal	Maximum charcoal size (mm)	Bone	Burnt bone	Maximum bone size (mm)	Silty clay loam coatings	Subrounded Fe nodules with fine Charcoal, silt grains, and/or bone	Diffuse Fe nodules, coatings, hypocoatings, quasicoatings	Faunal excrement
1	Sandy silt loam	Horizontal lens of phytoliths and non-metallurgical slag	Strongly developed very fine subangular blocky; crumb	Medium brown, dotted; undifferentiated b-fabric; mainly organic matter, charcoal, silt-sized minerals, phytoliths	■	■		2.1	■■■■■■	12	■	■	0.8	+	■	■	■■
3.1	Organic sandy silt loam	Horizontal orientation of elongated bone	Strongly developed very fine subangular blocky; crumb	Medium brown; dotted; undifferentiated b-fabric; mainly organic matter, charcoal, silt-sized minerals, phytoliths, diatoms	■■	+		2.0	■■■■	4.5	■■■	■	10	+	■■	■	■■
3.2	Organic sandy silt loam	Horizontal orientation of elongated bone; lens of gravel, charcoal, fish bone	Strongly developed very fine subangular blocky; crumb	Medium to dark brown; dotted; undifferentiated b-fabric; mainly organic matter, charcoal, silt-sized minerals	■■■			0.7	■■■■■	15	■■	■	10	+	■■	■■	■■■
4	Very coarse sandy silt loam	Horizontal orientation of elongated charcoal; horizontal lens of coarse sand	Strongly developed very fine subangular blocky; intergrain micro-aggregate	Medium to dark brown; dotted; undifferentiated b-fabric; mainly organic matter, charcoal, and silt-sized minerals	■■■			0.6	■■■■	4.0	■	+	0.6	+	+	■	■■
5/6.1	Organic sandy silt loam	Horizontal orientation of elongated charcoal and plant; lenses of charcoal	Strongly developed very fine subangular blocky	Medium to dark brown; dotted; undifferentiated b-fabric; mainly organic matter, charcoal, and silt-sized minerals	■■■■■ ■	+		12	■■■■■	10	■	+	5	+	+	■	■■
6.2	Silty clay loam	Horizontal orientation of silt-sized charcoal and organic matter	Strongly developed very fine subangular blocky	Pale to medium brown; speckled to dotted; stipple-speckled b-fabric	■■■			0.7	■■■■	0.9						■■	■
7	Mixed sandy silt loam and loamy sand	Random	Moderately developed subangular blocky and bridged grain	Pale brown to pale grey-brown; speckled to dotted; stipple-speckled to mosaic-speckled b-fabric with some granostriation	■			0.1	■	0.2				■		■■■	+

+ Present in trace amounts, ■ <2%, ■■ 2–5%, ■■■ 5–10%, ■■■■ 10–20%, ■■■■■ 20–30%, ■■■■■■ 30–40%, ■■■■■■■ 40–50% (of visible area)

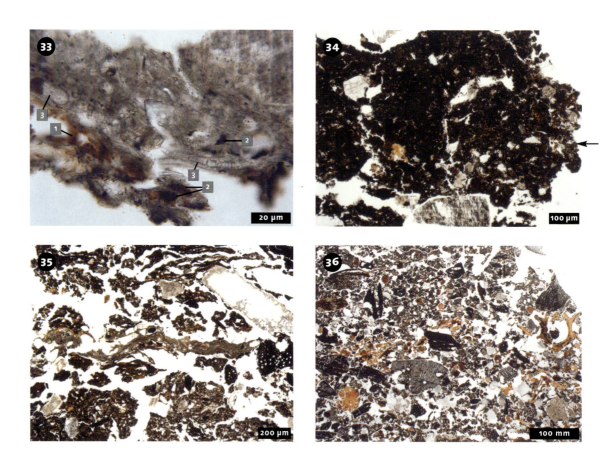

weathered, exhibiting the same advanced, irregular alteration that was also observed in the pathway between plots 1A and 2A (described above), and in the midden sediments (described below). The poor state of the bones, the relatively low quantity of anthropogenic material and the random organisation of constituents suggest that sample KPG02-69 had been taken outside of building A302 (Fig. 15.28). It is likely that the intercutting, putative post-holes (Fig. 15.16, [10]–[13]) represent the northwest wall of building A302.

15.8 Sediments in the midden area

Associated with site period II on the eastern edge of plot 1A, there was an extensive midden made up of small dumps of very dark greyish brown to black silt loam and the occasional lens of coarser sand (Fig. 15.1). The goal of the geoarchaeology programme was to provide more information about the composition and organisation of these sediments, in order to help determine their origin, and to confirm that they were secondary rather than primary deposits. There was also some question about whether this material might have accumulated on an active shoreline, or a shoreline that was affected by periodic flooding, and whether some of it might have been reworked by waves.

Where they were sampled for micromorphological analysis, the midden deposits were situated at 4.10–4.35 m above present sea-level (Fig. 15.8). As dis-

cussed above, they had accumulated on top of an incipient soil horizon. There was no evidence in the field or in thin sections KPG02-15 and -16 (Fig. 15.37) that the sediments had ever been affected by wave action; for example, there were no visible discontinuities, layers of sands or gravels, or water-reworked layers. The midden sediments in this area therefore appear to have been deposited above the high-tide wave-zone, and even though they might have been within the range of extreme high tides (Sørensen et al., this vol. Ch. 12:268), there was no apparent flooding event during the time they were accumulating. If there were any harbour constructions east of the midden area, it is possible that these could have sheltered the midden deposits from wave action in the case of an extreme high tide event.

The boundary between the immature soil and the earliest midden sediments (layer 6) was very abrupt, marking a sudden change in land-use. At this boundary there was a 2–4 mm thick layer of dense silty clay loam that had not been observed in the field and the extent of which is therefore not known (layer 6.2, Tab. 15.6). This silty clay contained silt-sized charcoal fragments, organic matter, and diatoms with the dominant horizontal orientation and good sorting typical of water-lain sediment (Fig. 15.33). It is likely that this material washed off the adjacent midden, and was re-mixed and deposited by rainwater, possibly in a small depression.

The midden deposits on top of this thin layer of

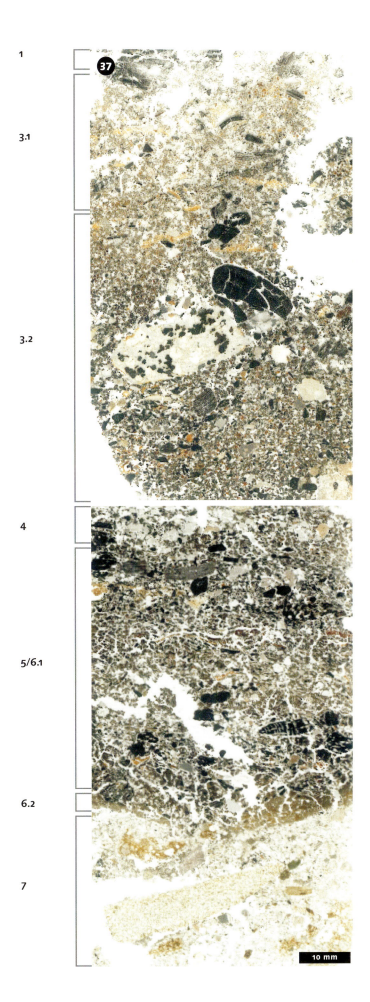

Figure 15.33 *Silty clay loam, containing water-lain organic matter (red-brown) (1), charcoal (black) (2), and diatoms (colourless) (3), in sample KPG02-16, layer 6.2 (PPL). Illustration by the authors.*

Figure 15.34 *Lens of very fine sand (arrow) embedded in fine organo-mineral material in sample KPG02-16, layer 5/6.1 (PPL). Illustration by the authors.*

Figure 15.35 *Elongated aggregate containing compacted, horizontally bedded phytoliths in sample KPG02-16, layer 5/6.1 (PPL). Illustration by the authors.*

Figure 15.36 *Lens of charcoal and fish bone (orange) in sample KPG02-15, layer 3.2 (PPL). Illustration by the authors.*

Figure 15.37 *Micromorphology samples from the midden area: samples KPG02-15 (top) and KPG02-16 (bottom). Illustration by the authors.*

silty clay loam consisted of sandy silt loams with different proportions of anthropogenic materials and organic matter (layers 1–6.1, Tab. 15.6). In thin section, these layers appeared to be discrete, with clear and often abrupt boundaries, indicating that each one represented a separate dumping event. No periods of stand-still were visible within the midden sequence in this particular location (e.g. wind-blown sand layers, incipient soil development), suggesting that it formed fairly rapidly.

In thin section, it was clear that many of the layers observed in the field contained finer layers within them. The upper and lower portions of layer 3, for example, differed enough in composition, and had a sufficiently sharp boundary between them, to warrant separate micromorphological descriptions. However, layers 3.1 and 3.2 were themselves far from homogeneous: 3.2 contained a lens of gravel- and pebble-sized stones and charcoal, and another lens with a high density of bone. The gross distinctions between layers 5 and 6 were not sufficient in thin section to justify separate micromorphology descriptions, but within layer 5/6.1, there were two lenses of larger charcoal fragments, each of which must have represented a separate dumping event. The macroscopic stratigraphy should therefore be viewed only as a coarse level of description. Like most middens, the dumping area east of plots 1A–3A contained a complex sequence of numerous small, discrete deposits. The two micromorphology samples described

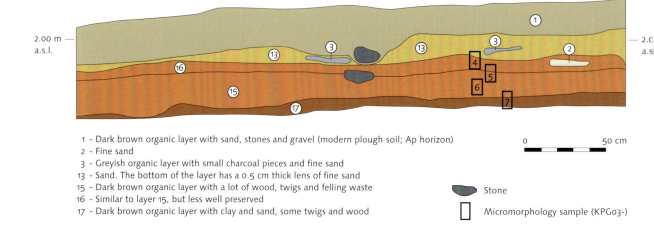

2.00 m — a.s.l.

2.0 a.s

1 - Dark brown organic layer with sand, stones and gravel (modern plough soil; Ap horizon)
2 - Fine sand
3 - Greyish organic layer with small charcoal pieces and fine sand
13 - Sand. The bottom of the layer has a 0.5 cm thick lens of fine sand
15 - Dark brown organic layer with a lot of wood, twigs and felling waste
16 - Similar to layer 15, but less well preserved
17 - Dark brown organic layer with clay and sand, some twigs and wood

0   50 cm

Stone

Micromorphology sample (KPG03-)

here cannot provide information about the horizontal extent of each of these small deposits, and it is therefore not possible to know how representative they are of the midden as a whole.

Like the occupation deposits in plots 3A and 3B, the midden deposits contained little in the way of soil material, but seemed to be primarily comprised of anthropogenic materials – in particular charcoal, decomposed organic matter, bone, and burnt bone – mixed with the sand that was so ubiquitous on the settlement (Tab. 15.6). Clay was not evident in thin section (note the undifferentiated b-fabric), and the fine material was largely composed of silt-sized charcoal, amorphous organic matter, silt-sized mineral grains, and phytoliths. Layers 3.2 and 5/6.1, which contained c. 10–30% amorphous organic matter, 20–30% charcoal, 2–5% bone, and up to 2% burnt bone, had a similar composition to the occupation deposits on plots 3A and 3B. Some of the aggregates in the midden even contained lenses of fine sand, which had also been present in the undisturbed aggregates in the house floor sediments (e.g. Fig. 15.34). In addition, layer 5/6.1 contained trace amounts of elongated, wavy, grey aggregates of amorphous organic matter containing compacted, horizontally bedded phytoliths (Fig. 15.35). These grass residues were identical to the putative grass mat residues found in layer 8 of building A302, which were discussed above. The evidence therefore suggests that layers 3.2 and 5/6.1 were partially composed of occupation deposits that had been cleaned out from buildings on the settlement and discarded in the midden.

The midden also contained other waste materials, including hearth waste and food refuse. The thin sections contained several lenses of large charcoal fragments, sometimes up to 15 mm in diameter, which probably represented dumped hearth waste (Tab. 15.6). One of the charcoal lenses in layer 3.2 also contained a high concentration of fish bones, including

vertebrae and other elements, suggesting that food waste and hearth waste were mixed and then dumped together (Fig. 15.36). The composition of layer 1 was unusual, for it was dominated not only by large charcoal fragments, but also by a high concentration of silica phytoliths and droplets of melted silica, all of different sizes and orientations. This layer was therefore probably ash residue from burnt grass or dung (Courty et al. 1989).

Layer 3.1 and the upper 1 cm of layer 3.2 contained up to 6% bone, an unusually high concentration that was only rarely found in the house-floor sediments on the settlement (e.g. layer 8, building A302). The bone fragments in the midden were also larger than in the indoor occupation deposits, reaching lengths of up to 10 mm. This suggests that the bone might have come straight to the midden as food waste, and might not have been subjected to the severe processes of fragmentation and size reduction that normally occurs on trampled occupation surfaces (Nielsen 1991). The bone in the midden was generally not well preserved, but like the bone in other exposed, outdoor deposits on the settlement, was often highly weathered, or in advanced stages of diagenesis (Fig. 15.6). Although the size, preservation, and organisation of the material in the midden are consistent with the characteristics of dumped, outdoor deposits rather than trampled indoor deposits, it is of course not possible to know how far the material was transported before it was dumped in this location. Although there was no evidence for activity surfaces in the thin sections examined here, it remains possible that there were activity surfaces elsewhere in the midden area.

15.9 Sediments in the harbour area

The excavations in the former Kaupang Bay area uncovered sediments at elevations of 1.60–2.00 m above present sea-level, which had accumulated just off

Figure 15.38 *North-facing section I5015, from the E–W profile through the harbour sediments, showing the locations of micromorphology samples. Illustration by the authors.*

shore during the Viking Age (Fig. 15.1). These sediments contained Viking-age artefacts, including a cubo-octahedral weight dated to AD 860/870 or later (Pilø, this vol. Ch. 10:200). This particular find was significant because it post-dated the intact archaeological layers that had been excavated in the settlement area, and its presence implied that the harbour sediments contained preserved archaeological deposits from the late 9th or early 10th century. It therefore became a priority to understand as much as possible about the harbour sediments, particularly their composition and origin, the environmental conditions under which they had been deposited, and the extent to which they might have been disturbed by post-depositional processes. The geoarchaeology programme aimed to answer these questions, and paid particular attention to the integrity of layer 15 (AL4453) in order to evaluate whether the cubo-octahedral weight was *in situ,* or whether it might have originally been deposited higher up the sequence.

The sediment profile in the former Kaupang Bay (Fig. 15.38) revealed a sequence of marine sediments, beach sediments, and plough soils that had been produced as isostatic uplift gradually changed the depositional environment. Layers 15 and 17 were fine sandy silt loams that were deposited by bottom currents in a foreshore environment, c. 1–2 m below sea-level. As the sea-level dropped, this part of the bay became shallower and the influence of waves and tides gradually became stronger, producing the alternate sand and mud laminae in layer 16. When the sea-level dropped still further, the land emerged into the active beach zone, producing wave-washed sand layer 13. Both layers 13 and 16 had abrupt lower boundaries, or discontinuities, indicating that earlier sediments had been scoured (Fig. 15.42). It is not possible to know how much of sediment was lost in each of these erosion episodes, or how many episodes of deposition and erosion occurred in this dynamic environment,

but it is clear that the Viking-age marine deposits in this area (layers 15 and 17) are incomplete.

The earlier Viking-age marine deposits, layers 15 and 17, contained similar fine organo-mineral matrices: intimate mixtures of amorphous organic matter, clay, fine to medium sand, and silt, including an abundance of phytoliths and diatoms (Tab. 15.7). Their coarse fraction consisted mainly of anthropogenic inclusions such as uncarbonised wood fragments (deciduous and coniferous), seeds and charcoal. While the charcoal reached sizes of up to 5 mm in diameter, and was present in concentrations of c. 5% in both of these layers, the size and concentration of the wood and barkfragments increased dramatically over time, from a maximum size of 10 mm, and frequencies of <2% in layer 17, to a maximum size of over 50 mm, and frequencies of 20–30% in layer 15. The boundary between layers 15 and 17 was in fact diffuse, and was not a product of different depositional environments, but rather of an increase in the rate of wood deposition. The cubo-octahedral weight, which was found in the lower part of layer 15, was therefore associated with the start of this increase in wood-deposition.

Where layers 15 and 17 were sampled for micromorphological analysis, only limited types of anthropogenic material appear to have been deposited in the harbour area. The large pieces of wood and bark that dominated the anthropogenic component in layer 15 (AL4453), and which also dominated the GBA samples (Barrett et al., this vol. Ch. 14:300), suggest that some of this material might have been wood chips derived from wood-working debris. It is possible that this waste is representative of the activities that were taking place on the nearby beach – boat-building, for example. Although small quantities of bone had been recovered fro the harbour sediments (Barrett et al., this vol. Ch. 14:300), no bone was observed in thin section in layers 15 or 17, possibly because of the small

Layer and microstratigraphic unit	Groundmass			Micromass	Organic and Anthropogenic Components								Pedofeatures			
	Texture class and sorting	Orientation of components	Microstructure	Nature of fine mineral material	Amorphous organic matter	Woody tissues	Phlobaphene-containing tissues	Maximum plant size (mm)	Charcoal	Maximum charcoal size (mm)	Bone	Maximum bone size (mm)	Pyrite	Silty clay loam coatings	Diffuse Fe nodules, coatings, hypocoatings, quasicoatings	Faunal excrement
13.1	Water-reworked lenses of well-sorted medium-fine sand, moderately sorted coarse sand, and silt loam (mud)	Horizontal to sub-horizontal lenses	Pellicular; localised subangular blocky (mud lenses) and intergrain microaggregate (excrement)	Mud lenses: grey to red-brown; dotted; stipple-speckled b-fabric; contains phytoliths	▪▪		+	1.0	▪	3.0				▪		▪
13.2	Well-sorted medium-fine sand; water-reworked plant tissues are visible at the lower boundary; contains <5% reworked aggregates of sandy silt loam	Horizontal orientation of elongated plant tissues at the lower boundary	Single grain	Silt loam aggregates: grey; speckled to dotted; stipple-speckled b-fabric	▪▪	+	+	3.5	▪	2.0				▪		+
16.1	Water-reworked fine sandy silt loam, with lenses of better-sorted fine sand and finer-grained silt loam	Horizontal lenses	Strongly developed very fine subangular blocky; localised platy (where plant matter is dominant) and single grain (sand lenses)	Red-brown; dotted; stipple-speckled b-fabric; contains phytoliths	▪▪▪▪	▪		▪	1.0	▪	1.0				+	+	▪
16.2	As above, but sandier; more lenses of well-sorted fine-medium sand, poorly sorted coarse sand, gravel	Sub-horizontal lenses	Strongly developed very fine subangular blocky; localised platy (plant matter) single grain (sand lenses), and crumb (faunal excrement)	Red-brown; dotted; stipple-speckled b-fabric; contains phytoliths	▪▪▪▪	▪▪▪▪	▪▪	10	▪▪	8.0	+	4.5		▪	+	▪▪
16.3	Water-reworked fine sandy silt loam, with a few lenses of better-sorted fine sand and finer-grained silt loam, similar to 16.1, above	Sub-horizontal lenses	Strongly developed very fine subangular blocky; localised platy (where plant matter is dominant) and single grain (sand lenses)	Red-brown; dotted; stipple-speckled b-fabric; contains phytoliths	▪▪▪▪	▪	+	3.0	▪▪	5.0	+	0.1		+	+	▪
15	Unsorted; fine-medium sandy silt loam, with indistinct lenses where coarse sand and large lignified tissues are concentrated	Coarse horizontal lenses; horizontal orientation of elongated plant	Moderately-weakly developed medium-fine subangular blocky, with localised platy (where plant matter is dominant)	Red-brown; dotted; stipple-speckled b-fabric; contains phytoliths and diatoms	▪▪▪▪▪	▪▪▪▪▪	▪▪	50+	▪▪	5.0			+	+	+	▪
17	Unsorted; fine sandy silt loam	Random	Moderately developed medium-coarse subangular blocky	Red-brown; dotted; stipple-speckled b-fabric; contains phytoliths and diatoms	▪▪▪▪▪	▪	▪	10	▪▪	5.0			▪	+	▪▪	+

+ Present in trace amounts, ▪ <2%, ▪▪ 2–5%, ▪▪▪ 5–10%, ▪▪▪▪ 10–20%, ▪▪▪▪▪ 20–30%, ▪▪▪▪▪▪ 30–40%, ▪▪▪▪▪▪▪ 40–50% (of visible area)

sizes of the micromorphology samples and the overall low concentration of bone. The charcoal present in layers 15 and 17 was derived from wood ash residues, and must represent episodes of hearth cleaning, but this component was neither as large in size nor as common as in the midden area east of the settlement (discussed above). In addition, the sediments in the harbour differed in composition from the occupation deposits on plots 3A and 3B, which contained much less clay, much more coarse sand and gravel, more charcoal, and more bone. This was true even of the occupation deposits in building A304, which contained evidence for the presence of wood chips. In contrast to the midden area east of the settlement, the micromorphology samples from the former harbour area do not provide direct evidence that the harbour was used as a disposal area for general household rubbish such as food waste or cleaned-out indoor occupation deposits. However, it remains possible that household rubbish was one of the sources of the anthropogenic material in the harbour area; if so, it was re-mixed and sorted by waves before some of the light material was carried out and deposited in the foreshore sediments by bottom currents.

In layer 15, it was possible to distinguish at least five major depositional events, in which larger wood fragments appeared to be concentrated in rough layers and were sometimes associated with short, discontinuous lenses of coarse sand. Although it is impossible to put a timescale on these layers, they could represent either storm events, in which waves on the shore-face and bottom currents varied in intensity, or periodic dumping episodes, in which heavier materials such as sand settled first, followed eventually by the wood once it became waterlogged. The wood, bark, and charcoal fragments, as well as the bone and amber pieces found during the excavation (Pedersen and Pilø, this vol. Ch. 9), could have been swept off the beach by waves, and were light enough to be car-

ried out into the bay by shore and bottom currents and deposited on the foreshore. However, artefacts such as the cubo-octahedral weight, which was 10 mm wide and 3.5 g, were too heavy to have been deposited by currents in the foreshore environment; if the weight had been swept off the beach in a storm, sorting by water would have caused it to be deposited with other gravel-sized materials. Instead, it must represent an accidental loss or a dumping event. The weight was heavy enough to have settled immediately on the bottom of the bay, where it was buried by more marine silt. The density of the silt loam matrices in layers 15 and 16 make it unlikely that the weight originated higher up the sequence, and sank through the sediments before coming to rest in layer 15. Although some bioturbation by marine organisms cannot be ruled out, subsequent bioturbation by soil fauna was consistently low throughout the harbour sequence. The evidence therefore supports the view that the weight did not move since it was deposited in layer 15, and therefore, that it can be used to date this layer.

Layers 15 and 17 were so rich in organic matter – most of it anthropogenic in origin – that they proved to be the ideal environment for the development of pyrite (FeS_2): rounded, crystalline framboids that are black in plane-polarized light, and have a metallic lustre under oblique incident light (Fig. 15.39). Pyrite framboids form through the interaction of sulphate in water and iron in soil and plants, and are common in marsh soils and peat (FitzPatrick 1993). The fact that pyrite was found in the lower part of layer 15 (trace amounts), and was relatively abundant in layer 17 (<2%; Tab. 15.7), especially in association with organic matter, indicates that the sediments in the harbour area had certain chemical similarities to marsh soils due to the fact that human activity in the area had artificially enriched their organic matter content.

Because isostatic uplift caused the sea-level to drop at a minimum rate of 3.5 mm per year (Sørensen

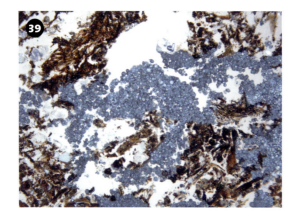

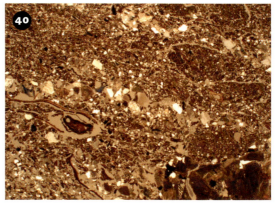

et al., this vol. Ch. 12:267), approximately 200 years after the abandonment of the urban settlement the sediments that had been accumulating in the harbour area became increasingly affected by waves and tides. As has already been mentioned, this transition was marked by a discontinuity in the sediment sequence – a very sharp boundary between layers 15 and 16, indicating an erosion face (Fig. 15.42). The basic matrix of layer 16 consisted of fine sandy silt loam with 10–20% amorphous organic matter – a muddy deposit that would have accumulated in a low-energy marine environment (Tab. 15.7). However, layer 16 also contained well-sorted lenses of fine silt or fine sand, evidence of occasional water-reworking and influence by tides. Sandwiched between finer layers 16.1 and 16.3 was layer 16.2, which had a similar micromass, but was sandier, and contained more lenses of well-sorted fine to medium sand, as well as the occasional lens of poorly sorted coarse sand and gravel (Fig. 15.40). Layer 16.2 also contained more anthropogenic material than either layers 16.1 or 16.3, including some wood fragments (10–20%; up to 10 mm in length), charcoal fragments (2–5%; up to 8 mm in length), and a single bone fragment (4.5 mm). These anthropogenic inclusions were re-deposited materials derived either from the erosion of layer 15, below, or from the erosion of the settlement area.

As the sea-level dropped still further, the sediments in the harbour area eventually emerged above the intertidal zone, where they encountered a new,

higher energy depositional environment on the wave-washed beach. Once again, the transition from layer 16 to layer 13 was marked by a discontinuity in the sediment sequence. The abrupt boundary between layers 13 and 16 contained water-reworked plant tissues that had been eroded from the top of layer 16 (Fig. 15.41). As had been observed in the field, the bottom 1.5–2.0 cm of layer 13 (designated here as 13.2), consisted of well-sorted medium to find sand. Above this, layer 13.1 contained multiple, water-reworked lenses of well-sorted medium to fine sand, moderately sorted coarse sand, and well-mixed, homogenous silt loam. The inclusions of charcoal, wood, and bark tissues in these layers were low in frequency (<2%) and small in size (1–3.5 mm), and there is little doubt that they were re-deposited.

15.10 Summary and conclusion

Although the excavation and interpretation of the settlement at Kaupang presented many challenges to the excavators due to the subtle differences in the colour, texture, composition, and compaction of the archaeological layers, a close study of the sediments resolved many of these problems. Chemical and micromorphological analyses identified a whole range of site-formation processes, which made it easier to understand why the boundaries between layers had often been difficult to see in the field, and why the anthropogenic sediments had come to have such similar colours and textures. Of the many post-depo-

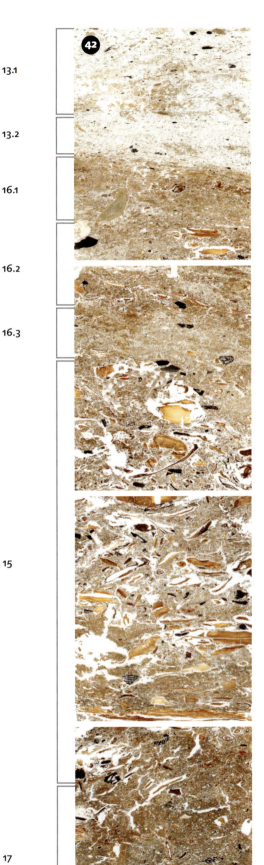

13.1

13.2

16.1

16.2

16.3

15

17

Figure 15.39 *Pyrite framboids (blue-grey) in sample KPG03-7, layer 17 (PPL and OIL). Illustration by the authors.*

Figure 15.40 *Lenses of medium sand and silt loam in sample KPG03-5, layer 16.2 (partial XPL). Illustration by the authors.*

Figure 15.41 *Water-reworked organic remains in sample KPG03-4, at the boundary between layers 3.2 (top) and 16.1 (bottom) (PPL). Illustration by the authors.*

Figure 15.42 *Micromorphology samples from the harbour area; samples KPG03-4 (top) to KPG03-7 (bottom). Illustration by the authors.*

sitional processes identified, the leaching of elements such as calcium and phosphorus, and the bioturbation by soil fauna had the most potent effect on the preservation of the archaeological sediments. Nevertheless, when they were analysed in thin section, it was often still possible to gain an understanding of the original composition and organisation of the sediments prior to their alteration by post-depositional processes. For example, although the calcareous component of wood ash had largely been leached away, it was still possible to identify those sediments that were originally composed of hearth waste because in thin section it was possible to observe concentrations of minute fragments of wood charcoal, burnt bone, non-metallurgical slag, and rare aggregates of preserved calcareous ash. Also, by studying the soils and sediments in thin section, it was possible to filter out the material that was infilling faunal channels, and to focus analysis on the aggregates of undisturbed sediment. In this way, it was possible to obtain a better understanding of the composition of the original archaeological sediments prior to their disturbance by soil fauna.

Although in the field it had not been possible to identify buried soils underlying the settlement, the analysis of micromorphology samples from the CRM trench and the midden trench revealed that the landsurface on which Kaupang was situated had been stable enough to develop a very thin, immature, gleyed cambisol that had developed on imperfectly drained beach sands. Above this soil in the CRM trench, there were archaeological deposits associated with the initial, seasonal period of settlement at Kaupang. These deposits took the form of alternating lenses of charcoal and sand, which appeared to be the result of short-term, periodic activity events. Seven different occupation surfaces could be counted in thin section, and while it is possible that these represent repeated, perhaps seasonal, trading activity in the vicinity of the CRM trench, it is not possible to know if this number can be applied to other plots in the vicinity.

Each of the buildings on plots 3A and 3B had two occupation phases in which the size and/or function of the structures were different. This development was clearest in plot 3B, where buildings A301 and A303 were separated by a dumped gravel layer. Both of these buildings contained occupation deposits rich in hearth waste and organic matter, and appeared to have had a function that included cooking and food-consumption. Space in the later, larger building (A301) had been divided into three aisles: a centre aisle that contained a clay hearth and an occupation surface that was especially rich in hearth waste, and two side aisles that contained deposits especially rich in decomposed plant matter. The micromorphological evidence showed that each of the side aisles was about 1.2 m wide. While the centre aisle appeared to have been the main artery for foot traffic through the building, the side aisles had been less trampled, and were more likely to have functioned as sitting, working, eating and sleeping areas.

On plot 3A, buildings A304 and A302 were separated by a thin, patchy sand layer that was probably intentionally deposited. The lower occupation phase was not associated with a hearth, and it contained low quantities of hearth waste and an exceptionally high concentration of plant matter. It also contained identifiable wood and bark tissues, suggesting that part of the occupation surface might have been covered with wood chips. In comparison, the later building was larger, had a central hearth, and appeared to contain two separate rooms. Around the central clay hearth and in the southeast end of the building, the floor surface might occasionally have been covered with grass mats, and might have accumulated through the punctuated input of hearth refuse, food waste, organic matter, and sand. At the northwestern end of the building, in a space about 1 m wide, the occupation deposit had been less trampled, and had received little input of hearth waste. It is possible that this small space had functioned as a storage area.

The pathway between plots 1A and 2A contained thin, compacted lenses of mud and irregular bands of coarse sand. Anthropogenic inclusions, such as charcoal, bone and burnt bone, were randomly distributed and low in frequency, suggesting that they had not been dumped but rather had been transported and worked into the sediment by trampling hooves and feet. In contrast, the midden area was used for the dumping of artefact-production waste, such as whetstones, as well as cleaned-out indoor occupation deposits, hearth waste (e.g. wood and grass/dung ash), and food waste (e.g. fish bones). However, it should be noted that the midden deposit to the east of the

settlement area was extensive and contained a complex sequence of deposits, so it would be unwise to generalise about the entire deposit based on the study of a single section and two micromorphology samples. The part of the midden observed here had accumulated fairly rapidly, without any evident stand-still periods, and it had not been affected by wave action or floods.

The harbour area contained a well-preserved sequence of sediments and soils dating from the Viking Age to the present day, which had developed as isostatic uplift caused gradual changes to the depositional environment. The 9th- and 10th-century sediments, including the layer with the cubo-octahedral weight, had accumulated c. 1–2 m below sea-level, in a foreshore environment relatively unaffected by waves. In thin section, these sediments contained large quantities of wood and bark fragments, and small charcoal fragments, material that was probably derived from wood-working debris, possibly mixed with household rubbish such as food waste or cleaned-out floors. This light, organic material could either have been dumped or swept by waves off the beach before being carried out and deposited in the bay by bottom currents. However, if the weight had been carried by water it would have been deposited with gravels of similar size and weight, and its presence in the fine foreshore sediments indicates that it must have been dumped or accidentally lost from above.

The rate of wood deposition in the foreshore of the harbour area increased in the late 9th or early 10th century. The upper part of Viking-age marine sediment was eroded a couple of hundred years later when it was succeeded by a new, higher energy depositional environment that was increasingly under the influence of tides. The sediment that accumulated in this tidal environment contained some wood fragments and small pieces of charcoal, which could have been eroded from the sediment below, or from the settlement area on land. The upper part of this layer was truncated by wave action as it emerged above the intertidal zone, and subsequent deposits were wave-washed sands. Gradually these sands emerged above the ambient high tide, and formed a stable land-surface that was eventually ploughed.

Acknowledgements
The authors are grateful to the Kaupang Excavation Project for funding this study. Thin sections were made by Julie Miller at the McBurney Geoarchaeology Laboratory, University of Cambridge. This paper benefited from comments by Lars Pilø, Dagfinn Skre, Rolf Sørensen, James Barrett, Ian Simpson, Helen Lewis, Marco Madella and anonymous referees.

Part IV:

Skiringssal

The Skiringssal Cemetery

16

DAGFINN SKRE

The size and significance of the most important cemetery at Kaupang, the main burial ground at Nordre Kaupang, are assessed here on the basis of maps and depictions from the 19th century and aerial photographs from 1994. A total of 140 barrows can be located, but it is evident that there were formerly many more. Based on the same sources the original number is estimated to have been 200–300 barrows.

While the other cemeteries at Kaupang are manifestly connected to the town and the harbour, the cemetery at Nordre Kaupang must be regarded as a "road-cemetery"; it lies along the route between Kaupang harbour and the central settlement zone of Skiringssal with its royal hall and assembly place. This route is also the main road to and from Kaupang. Such road-cemeteries are well known in Vestfold and elsewhere. As in this case, they usually lie in constricted passages in the landscape along the principal approaches to major farmsteads. The purpose of placing the cemeteries thus might have been to stage the approach of travellers by presenting the position and importance of the site and the petty king's seat.

Because of its position and the burial practices, this cemetery is linked to the royal farmstead of Skiringssal, and it is proposed that it was the burial place of the Skiringssal petty kings and their supporters in the surrounding farmsteads. Arguments are put forward that the four most prominent barrows at the site – all of which were void of finds – were amongst the earliest. They may therefore be earlier than the first datable finds from the cemetery, which are of the early 9th century.

In 1867, when Nicolay Nicolaysen was to launch the first archaeological excavations at Kaupang, he decided to focus principally upon the cemetery at Nordre (Northern) Kaupang, where he excavated 71 barrows. At Lamøya there was at least the same number of barrows, but he must have considered the site at Nordre Kaupang to stand out as the most important in the area. Here the largest burial mounds were to be found, occupying a dominant place in the landscape. The fact that Nicolaysen was hunting for the graves of the Yngling petty kings (Skre, this vol. Ch. 2:35–6) would certainly have influenced his decision.

Nowadays a great deal more is known about the various cemeteries at Kaupang, and particularly the large flat-grave cemetery at Bikjholberget, than in Nicolaysen's time (Blindheim et al. 1981, 1995, 1999; Stylegar, this vol. Ch. 5). Although the results of Nicolaysen's excavations were a disappointment for both himself and his contemporaries, the cemetery at Nordre Kaupang does still stand out as a special and significant one. The more precise explication of this importance is a vital element in the examination of the Skiringssal complex. New evidence has emerged since Blindheim (et al. 1981) wrote about this site. All of the evidence will be used to carry this work forward, in the first place with a view to estimating the extent of the cemetery and the number of barrows. Upon this foundation, and with reference both to the position of the cemetery in the landscape and to other sources, an attempt shall be made to summarize its role and connexions.

16.1 The extent of the cemetery

The first antiquarian map of the full extent of the cemetery was undertaken by the architect Chr. Christie in 1866, in preparation for Nicolaysen's excavation the following year (Fig. 16.1; Skre, this vol. Ch. 2:35–6). At that time, the cemetery had already been severely damaged. The earliest report of the removal of barrows at Kaupang is from 1842, when finds that resulted were delivered to Arendal Museum (Ka. 406–7). When P.A. Munch visited in 1850 he could see

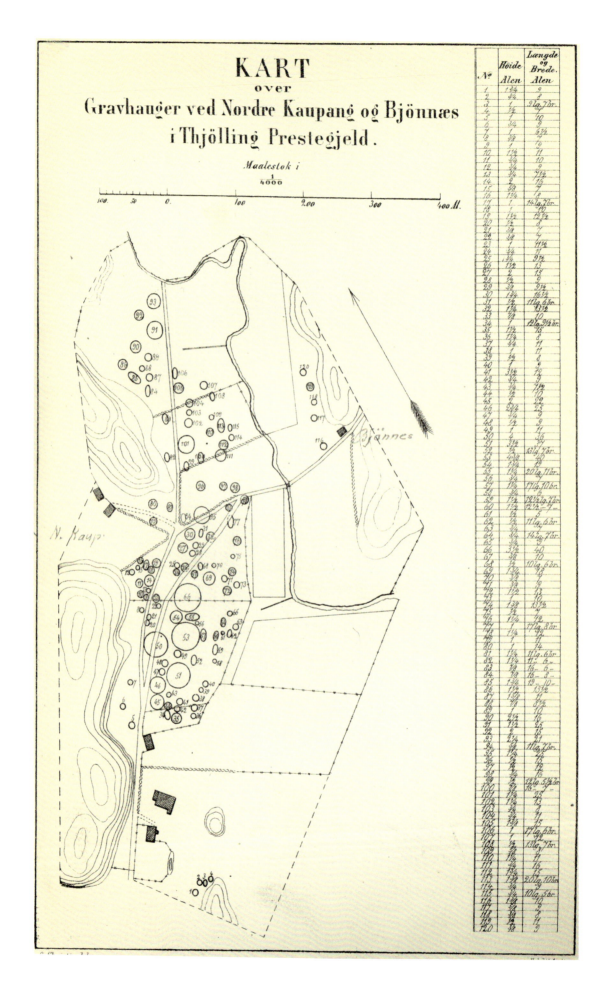

Figure 16.1 *Architect Chr. Christie's map of 1866 showing the barrows at Nordre Kaupang and Bjønnes. The height and diameter of the barrows, and the length and breadth of the long barrows, are given in ells. The barrows numbered 116–120 lie on the neighbouring farm to Kaupang, Bjønnes. In the era of Kaupang these were separated from the others by a channel about 30 m wide (cf. Fig. 16.10). In terms of the zoning of the cemetery followed here, barrows 1–4 belong to the cemetery of Hagejordet (Stylegar, this vol. Ch. 5:70–2). The large and coherent cemetery that Christie mapped thus consisted of barrows Nos. 5–115, a total of 111 mounds. The map is reproduced after Nicolaysen 1868.*

that swords, glass beads, and the remains of boats had been found in the barrows (Skre, this vol. Ch. 2:32). He must have seen these objects on the site, and they must have come from barrows that had been destroyed during his visit or before it. It is possible that Munch himself organized for barrows to be dug out when he visited. None of these finds can now be attributed to specific cemeteries at Kaupang.

In 1859 Nicolaysen was at Kaupang and Lamøya, and reported that barrows were disappearing yearly. On this occasion he collected some of the grave goods and took them back to the museum in Christiania (Ka. 150–1, 400–3). He gave the number of barrows at Nordre Kaupang as "hundreds, round and oblong intermixed" ("hundrevis, runde og avlange om hverandre") (Nicolaysen 1862–1866:199). In connexion with the excavation of 1867 he wrote (1868:77) that there were then 115 barrows at Nordre Kaupang but "…originally there had certainly been more, which have been destroyed through agriculture and by the roads which cross the site" ("… oprinnelig var der vist endnu flere, som ere ødelagt ved markarbeide og de veje, som krysse strøget"). He left 44 of the 115 barrows unexcavated because they were more or less destroyed or overgrown by trees.

Christie mapped a total of 120 barrows at Nordre Kaupang and the neighbouring farm of Bjønnes (Fig. 16.1). Five of these (Nos. 116–20) lay at Bjønnes, east of the stream. Four barrows (Nos. 1–4) lay at the very southern end of the map, 85 m from the main site. As will be demonstrated, there is no secure basis for counting these nine barrows as belonging to the cemetery, which consequently, in 1866, consisted of 111 barrows. Barrows 1–4 are counted here as belonging to the cemetery of Hagejordet, while the five at Bjønnes make out one of several small groups of barrows there (Stylegar, this vol. Ch. 5:70–2, Fig. 5.2).

Nicolaysen reported that after his excavation the barrows were reconstituted. In the decades that fol-

lowed, the cemetery site was under cultivation, and barrows disappeared. In 1918 a divinity student, Ballestad, who was recording ancient monuments in the area on behalf of Universitetets Oldsaksamling, reported that there were then only six or eight barrows left (KHM TopArk). When the Inspector Grieg from Universitetets Oldsaksamling visited in 1931 these had also gone (Grieg 1943:475). The four small barrows at the very south on Christie's map (Fig. 16.1:Nos.1–4) must have escaped the notice of both of these men as they were still there in 1974 when Blindheim had two of them excavated (Ka. 126–7). Now there is no sign of any of these.

From the sources on the cemetery, it is clear that there were more barrows there than shown on Christie's map of 1866. How many could there have been? It is impossible to give a precise answer, but fortunately there are some sources that can be used to make an estimate. In what follows these sources are analysed with a view to answering three complementary questions. How many barrows can be registered for certain? With reference to evidence for yet more barrows, how dense may the placement of barrows in various parts of the site be inferred to have been? And finally, how wide were the limits of the cemetery originally? The relevant sources are as follows:

- The Larvik County map of 1811 (Fig. 16.2; Blindheim et al. 1981:18).
- Johannes Flintoe's painting "A Duel. Norwegian Form" ("En holmgang. Norsk fremstilling") from the mid-1830s (Fig. 16.4; Blindheim et al. 1999: 169; Skre and Stylegar 2004:4. Kept in the National Gallery, Oslo), and two sketches by Flintoe from the same year (Fig. 16.3; Blindheim et al. 1999:154).
- A plan of a section of the Nordre Kaupang cemetery drawn by the artist C.O. Zeuthen in 1845. This plan was recently discovered in the National

Figure 16.2 *This section of what is known as the Larvik County map (Grevskapskartet) of 1811 shows the same area as Figure 16.1, together with an area further north in which there had also been burial mounds before Christie mapped the site. On the map, which was drawn to the scale of 1:4000, tracks are marked with a double or single brown line, according to the size of the track. The cartographic guidelines have been preserved (here cited after Engesveen 2002). They prescribe that cultivated fields are to be mapped accurately, as should the unploughed pieces of land between the fields. For all enclosed fields, meadows and pastures, the boundaries are to be recorded. Each matriculated piece of land was to be defined by a red boundary line, and the matriculation number and the size of the landholding, measured in tønner of land, were to be added to the map in black and red figures, respectively. Levels were to be recorded so that one could assess steepness, the degree of slope, and altitude. The map shows that the major heights are represented by contours and shadowing. Lesser peaks and slopes are represented by hachuring in the direction of the fall.*

Through such lines, one can find several barrows marked on the map. This was not an antiquarian mapping exercise, so there would have been no aim to include all of these. The barrows are marked in the same way as other raised areas of the same size and shape, such as knolls. After eliminating the relatively few raised areas which coincide with knolls, we are left with thirteen signatures that must be burial mounds. Seven of these coincide with barrows on Christie's map (Nos. 46, 50, 51, 53, 91, 97 and 105) while a further three are barrows that must have been removed before 1866 (Nos. 122, 124 and 125). There are also three circles marked in the northern part of the cemetery. Two of these (Nos. 87 and 121) agree with barrows that can be found on Christie's map and aerial photographs respectively, and the third (No. 123) is therefore also counted as a secure barrow. The seven of the thirteen that reappear on Christie's map have been given a number from that map. The six that are not shown there have been numbered in series with his sequence of numbers: cf. Figure 16.10.

This map is preserved in the archive of the National Map Office (Statens Kartverk), Hønefoss (Grevskapskart 9B9 blad 7); reworked by Anne Engesveen.

Museum in Copenhagen (Skre 2005) and is published here for the first time (Fig. 16.5).

- Christie's map of the site of 1866 (Fig. 16.1), and Nicolaysen's description from the following year, are the best reports on the site. These two sources were published together (Nicolaysen 1868).
- Several aerial photographs which were taken for archaeological recording in the past few decades. On these photographs traces of levelled barrows can be seen as crop-marks (Figs. 16.7–16.9).
- Finally, traces of graves and barrows were found in the course of archaeological work in 1965 (Blindheim et al. 1981:50 fig. 3 No. VIII, 55, 78 fig. 3) and in 1999 (Pilø, this vol. Ch. 8:171, Fig. 8.17).

In what follows, the sources listed above are evaluated side-by-side, and especially with reference to Christie's map, which offers the most thorough documentation of the site. For the sake of clarity I have divided the site into the zones shown on Figure 16.6. All of the barrows that can be identified in addition to the 111 recorded by Christie have been given a number continuous with his series. These numbers have been put on the barrows on the maps and photographs on which they can be identified, and in the final reconstruction map of the cemetery (Fig. 16.10).

The analysis of the maps and aerial photographs was carried out by cand. philol. Anne Engesveen using the mapping programme MapInfo. The maps

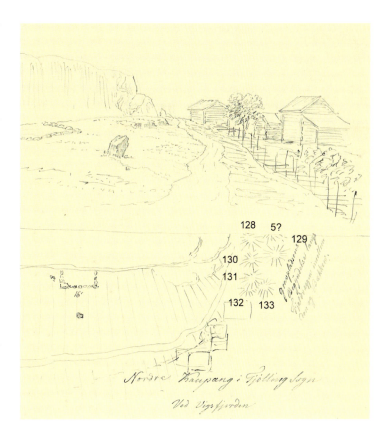

Figure 16.3 *Johannes Flintoe's two sketches of Nordre Kaup-ang from the mid-1830s. These sketches, which are a map and an outline of the same area, seem to have been prepared as documentation of the southern end of the cemetery, which he needed for the painting he was subsequently to produce (Fig. 16.4). The text beside the barrows reads "The Beginning of the Cemetery along the Cliff, between that and the Stream" ("Gravpladsens Begyndelse langs Fjeldvæggen imellem den og Bækken"). In addition to the burial mounds, one can see a raised stone approximately 60–70 m to the left of them. It cannot be determined whether this is one of the Viking-period megaliths or a boundary stone from more recent times.*

The sketch shows seven barrows. One of these (No. 5) can be identified on Christie's map. In the case of the re-maining six (Nos. 128–133), this sketch is the only preserved record. Original in the the Directorate for Cultural Heri-tage's archive (Riksantikvarens arkiv), *Oslo; reworked by Anne Engesveen.*

and photographs have been rectified using the Larvik Municipality's digital area map with a contour inter-val of 1 meter. The various items of information from the separate maps and photographs were compared by superimposing them in MapInfo. With reference to the precision of the sources, and to the diameter and position of the barrows, an assessment was made of which barrows may be one and the same feature. Finally all of the recorded barrows were added to a general map (Fig. 16.10). From that, a map to illus-trate the estimated total number of barrows was pro-duced (Fig. 16.11).

Barrows on the Larvik County map of 1811

In 1805, when Norway was part of the Kingdom of Denmark and Norway, King Christian VII required that the domain of the region of Larvik, which was the king's personal property, be mapped, just as the whole of Denmark was at that time. This was done in the years 1807–1818. Several different officers carried out the task, and the quality of what was produced varies greatly. Fortunately, the map of Kaupang was drawn by Lieutenant Broch, who produced the best maps in the whole series.

The instructions for the mapping project have been preserved, meaning that the various symbols are known and a total of thirteen barrows can be identi-fied on the map (Fig. 16.2). Several of these barrows are, as will be demonstrated, also known from other sources. Eight of them are on Christie's map (nos. 46, 50, 51, 53, 87, 91, 97 and 105) and another one on the

earlier map has been identified through aerial pho-tography (No. 121, cf. Figs. 16.7–16.9). This leaves four mounds (Nos. 122, 123, 124 and 125) that are not attest-ed to in any other sources. These four must have been removed between 1811 and the production of the next map that covers these parts of the cemetery, i.e. Christie's map of 1866.

Flintoe's painting and sketches of the 1830s

In the 1830s the antiquary Gerhard Munthe and the painter Johannes Flintoe visited Kaupang (Skre, this vol. Ch. 2:30–1). From Flintoe's hand, two sketches have been preserved from this expedition (Fig. 16.3) and one painting (Fig. 16.4). While the sketches por-tray the site just as Flintoe saw it, the painting is clear-ly historicized, and presents the landscape as he imagined it would have been in the Viking Age.

The two sketches present, respectively, an outline sketch and a map of one and the same area – the farmyard that then stood on one of the farms at Nordre Kaupang. Just north of the farm buildings the sketch map has the southernmost end of the ceme-tery, with a total of seven barrows included in the drawing. Alongside these Flintoe wrote "The Begin-ning of the Cemetery along the Cliff, between that and the Stream" ("Gravpladsens Begyndelse langs Fjeldvæggen imellem den og Bækken").

With reference to the topographical details in the drawing, the cliff and the road, it is possible to posi-tion these quite precisely. Between the 1811 mapping and Flintoe's visit, the farmyard had moved south-

Figure 16.4 *Johannes Flintoe's painting "A Duel. Norwegian Depiction" ("En Holmgang. Norsk Fremstilling") was produced after his visit to Kaupang in the mid-1830s. In the background one can see the cemetery from around Barrow 66 (right) southwards (towards the two houses). He places the southern boundary of the cemetery where the sketch (Fig. 16.3) puts it. The painting is manifestly historicizing, and one cannot, consequently, attach any weight to every detail in the cemeteries it portrays. When Christie surveyed the site thirty years later, none of the barrows had standing stones or kerbrings as is the case with several in this picture. However such features were recorded further north in the cemetery by C.O. Zeuthen in 1845 (Fig. 16.5), and it is not improbable that they were to be found in the southern part of the cemetery too. Photo, The National Gallery* (Nasjonalgalleriet), *Oslo.*

wards to the spot upon which it lay at the time of Christies visit in 1866. Sometime between Flintoe's and Christie's visits the road north of the farmyard had also been repositioned, probably in connexion with the relocation of the farmyard. On both the Larvik County map of 1811 and in Flintoe's sketches, the road passes on the western side of barrow No. 5. The re-routing of the road was probably an element within the comprehensive reorganization of properties and relocation of buildings at Kaupang in the 1840s and 50s (Krohn-Holm 1970:215–22).

Although Flintoe's map is only a sketch, it is possible to compare it with Christie's map. Of the seven barrows on the sketch, one can be identified on Christie's map (No. 5). The other six (Figs. 16.3 and 16.10, Nos. 128–33) must have been removed between the 1830s and 1866, probably as a consequence of the relocation of the farmyard and re-positioning of roads.

Here, at the very southern end of the cemetery, two further barrows are known that are absent from Christie's map. A little further to the east, the ring ditch of a barrow with a diameter of about 6 m was found in 1999 (Pilø, this vol. Ch. 8:Fig. 8.17; Fig. 16.10 No. 126). Someway to the south-east of Flintoe's barrows, a grave was excavated in 1965 (Fig. 16.10 No. 127; Ka. 37; Blindheim et al. 1981:50 fig. 3 No. VIII, 55, 78 fig. 3, 221–2).

The earliest information about the assaults on the Kaupang cemetery comes, as noted, from 1842, but one cannot conclude that the destruction started then. Consequently one cannot rely upon the position of the southern limit of the cemetery as implied by Flintoe's sketch of the 1830s. In Norway, a comprehensive re-organization of agriculture began in the middle of the 19th century, including the drainage of bogs and the bringing of new areas under cultivation. In Norway thousands of barrows were destroyed as a consequence of this development. Furthermore, such

changes on some properties and areas occurred well in advance of the 19th century reorganization, including the many farms in southern Vestfold that were in the possession of the Count (Stylegar, this vol. Ch. 5:78). Nordre Kaupang, however, unlike Søndre Kaupang, was owned by its farmers from the 17th century onwards, and one might consider the possibility that this farm was not affected by agricultural reorganization. All the same, the new methods of agriculture that were adopted by neighbours may have influenced how independent farmers, like the ones at Nordre Kaupang, ran their farms.

As noted, Christie's map includes four barrows positioned 85 m beyond the southern edge of the main cemetery (Nos. 1–4). It may appear reasonable to assume that the cemetery may have stretched all the way down to these, but there is little positive evidence to support such an assumption. Immediately west of these four southernmost barrows, Blindheim observed traces of a fifth (Blindheim et al. 1981:55), and a grave was discovered about 50 m west of the four in 1958 (Ka. 130; Pilø, this vol. Ch 8:Fig. 8.14). Immediately to the east of the four barrows a thistle brooch has been found, probably once part of a grave deposit (Ka. 128). The evidence from Blindheim's excavation and the state of the artefacts found in the area indicate that there were both inhumations and cremations in this group. In the Nordre Kaupang barrow cemetery only cremation graves have been found. This indicates that this southern group of barrows should be considered a separate cemetery from the Nordre Kaupang cemetery.

In the 85 m stretch between these burials (Nos. 1–4 etc.) and the southern end of the Nordre Kaupang cemetery no grave finds have been made. Nor are there any barrows marked in this area on the Larvik County map from 1811. But since that map only shows large barrows, one cannot exclude the possibility that smaller barrows were there. The map shows the area

between the southernmost barrows and the southern edge of the cemetery as pasture and meadow, i.e. in other words, as unploughed land. This land-use would not have removed any barrows, although the area could, of course, have been ploughed either in earlier times or subsequently, and therefore barrows might have been destroyed before Flintoe's visit. There was a farmstead at the southern end of the cemetery in 1811, and it had been moved a short way south when Flintoe made his sketch about 25 years later. This building activity may have removed a number of barrows. But even though that possibility cannot be excluded, there is really no basis upon which to extend the cemetery further south than Flintoe documents it. Barrows 1–4 and the total of ten

grave finds from this area (Ka. 125–34) are therefore catalogued separately as a distinct cemetery, Hage-jordet (Stylegar, this vol. Ch. 5:70–2).

Flintoe's historicized painting, which portrays a duel on the hilltop east of the cemetery on the other side of the stream, shows the southern part of the burial ground, approximately from Barrow 66 south-wards (Fig. 16.4). Although the information in the picture is supported by other sources, the picture cannot be treated as a reliable source, as the artist indulged his artistic licence to shape the dramatic scene that is the principal motif of the painting. The features of the landscape are exaggerated, and one has to allow for the fact that the same may have been done with those of the cemetery.

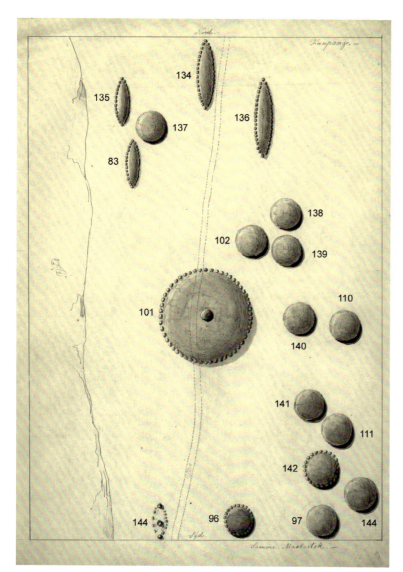

Figure 16.5 *Christian Olavius Zeuthen's plan from the summer of 1845 showing 13 round barrows, 4 long barrows, and a small ship-setting at Kaupang. Zeuthen was then drawing burial mounds, megaliths and stone-settings in Tjølling and Brunlanes as commissioned by Det Nordiske Oldskriftselskab of Copenhagen (Skre 2005). Original in the National Museum* (Nationalmuseet), *Copenhagen; reworked by Anne Engesveen.*

top and four also had kerb-rings. None of the barrows on Christie's map have any such features, nor are they mentioned in Nicolaysen's account of the excavation in 1867. One can almost certainly take it that Nicolaysen would have included these details if they had been there (Blindheim et al. 1981:75). It appears, therefore, appropriate to regard these features as the products of Flintoe's imagination. However a newly discovered source of evidence, Zeuthen's plan, gives one reason to reconsider this matter.

Zeuthen's plan of 1845

In the summer of 1845, the Danish architect and artist C.O. Zeuthen came to Tjølling and Brunlanes, where he drew several cemeteries and megaliths. Altogether eleven drawings are known from this excursion, five of them are plans (Larsen 1986; Skre 2005). One of the plans has "Kaupang" written on it (Fig. 16.5), and is from the cemetery at Nordre Kaupang; another is inscribed "Lamøen" (Stylegar, this vol. Ch. 5:Fig. 5.8).

Zeuthen's plans of the monuments in Brunlanes and Tjølling were drawn to a common scale and in two standard forms. When he was faced with a large cemetery, as at Nordre Kaupang and on Lamøya, he could consequently only include part of the sites. He probably chose a portion that displayed the variation in grave-forms at the sites – this is what his commissioning patron would have been interested in (Skre 2005).

What part of the cemetery at Nordre Kaupang is mapped by Zeuthen? The large barrow in the centre of the plan, together with the road, and the cliff to the west, makes it easy to orientate oneself. The barrow is Christie's No. 101. Zeuthen depicted the barrow with a diameter of 25 ells (15.7 m), which matches Christie's measurement exactly. In 1867 Nicolaysen referred to this barrow as amongst those which were "…more or less flattened, or overgrown with trees",

On the other hand, the picture is most certainly not utterly devoid of scholarly value. From the scale of the figures in the cemetery, the largest of the barrows are about 12–14 m in diameter – this holds for some four or five mounds. On Christie's map there are only four barrows of this order of size in the southern part of the cemetery, and most are smaller. However there are four measuring 22.6–25.1 m. Thus Flintoe did not exaggerate the diameter of the barrows; quite the opposite. The height of the barrows in the picture appears to have been between 2 and 3 m at most. This agrees well with the largest barrows on Christie's map. What one cannot do, though, is link particular barrows in the picture directly with examples on the map. Nor can one confidently assess the extent of the cemetery from the picture except insofar as the southern boundary does appear to agree with Flintoe's sketch.

Slightly more reliable observations can be made in respect of a couple of other features of the barrows in the picture. Four barrows in the picture were furnished with standing stones some 1–2 m high at the

("... mere eller mindre udjevnede eller bevoxede med træer") and which, in consequence, he did not excavate. Christie gave the height as only one and a quarter ells (c. 0.8 m). The road which runs over the barrow in Zeuthen's drawing and which was moved to the western edge in 1866 no doubt contributed to the destruction of the feature.

Considered as archaeological evidence, all of Zeuthen's five plans are of high quality, but they were drawn on the basis of particular premises. Three of the cemeteries he drew on his Vestfold excursion are known, one through an excavation report and two because they are still there. A comparison of his plans and those sources shows that the location of the barrows and their diameter – or length and breadth in the case of long barrows – are quite accurately recorded. But no premium was placed upon bringing out irregularities in the form of the barrows, which are drawn as rather idealized geometric figures. Also idealized are the kerb-rings, which are presented, in effect, as a signature on the plan. On the other hand, one can be confident that the kerb-rings on the plans really were there. The megaliths appear to have been given individual features on the plans (Skre 2005:182).

What appears to be special in the case of the plan of the Nordre Kaupang cemetery is that here Zeuthen's idealization appears to have gone a step beyond that in his other plans. All of the small round barrows are drawn as of the same diameter, 7–8 ells (4.5–5 m). True enough, Christie's map does also show barrows of this size in the cemetery, but one cannot believe that this level of regularity corresponded to the facts. As can be seen on Zeuthen's Lamøya plan (Stylegar, this vol. Ch. 5:Fig. 5.8), the diameter of the barrows normally varies considerably. Zeuthen's approach was to survey in the centre of the barrow and to measure the diameter of each individual example. On his Kaupang visit, Zeuthen conceivably took inadequate field-notes on the diameters of the barrows, except for mound 101, and so had to construct a plan that lacked this information. The long barrows on the Kaupang plan, however, appear to be portrayed in accurate, precise detail, with the length and breadth varying from case to case.

As a result, one can rely upon Zeuthen's plan of Kaupang when he portrays kerb-rings with several barrows and a megalith on one of them. The plan thus confirms that the peculiarities Flintoe painted a decade or so previously really were to be found in the cemetery. Whether or not they were present in the southern part of the site, or were as numerous as Flintoe's painting shows, is not certain. It is easy to imagine that Flintoe artistically imposed a megalith here and a kerb-ring there. But even then, his inspiration would have come from barrows in the same cemetery. In Vestfold, megaliths on Viking-period burial mounds are otherwise unknown, but kerb-rings are not uncommon (Sjøvold 1944:50–2). On the

other hand there are a lot of megaliths from the Early Iron Age, some free-standing, some in the kerb-rings of the barrows, and others on the tops of barrows – including examples close to Kaupang (Hougen 1924). These could have stimulated the raising of megaliths on the barrows at Kaupang. Zeuthen's drawing also shows a small ship-setting, a form of grave that has not formerly been identified at Kaupang (Stylegar, this vol. Ch. 5:88).

Why, then, had the megaliths, kerb-rings and ship-setting been removed at Kaupang by 1866? There was considerable re-location of farmsteads and building of houses in the 1840s and 50s. Stone was therefore needed for foundation walls, and it is far from unlikely that much was obtained from the funerary monuments close by.

If one compares the positions of the barrows, there are only two or three examples that show a perfect agreement with Christie's map. Evidently there were inaccuracies in the plotting of the barrows on one of the maps if not both. As noted, the quality of surveying is good on Zeuthen's other plans which can be checked, but his field notes from the Nordre Kaupang cemetery seem to have been of a poorer quality and his plan of Kaupang may therefore be less accurate than the others. Christie's map cannot have been bad; if that had been the case, one should expect Nicolaysen to have corrected or supplemented the information it contained.

In the present circumstances, there are two ways of checking the accuracy of Christies maps. The accuracy of Christie's map can be studied by comparing the placement of barrows on the map and on aerial photographs. In addition, Blindheim made a remark concerning the four southernmost barrows on the map, which were still there in 1974. Blindheim (et al. 1981:56; Blindheim 1977:22) reported that the position of the barrows was not entirely in agreement with Christie's map, but that these must be the same features all the same. In the case of the aerial photographs, it is the four barrows Nos. 90–93 which offer real control evidence. In general terms, the agreement with Christie's map is good. The distance between the barrows varies by up to 5 metres, and their diameter by 1–2 metres, but only in one case by as much as 3 metres. For a map at the scale of 1:4000 this can be regarded as very good. Some of this precision was lost in H.C. Jahnsen's redrawing of Christie's map (Blindheim et al. 1981:74 fig. 1).

As none of the maps is perfectly precise in respect of the size and placement of the barrows, in the following comparison of Zeuthen's plan and Christie's map I have been generous to a degree. Barrows which only partly overlap and which do not differ too dramatically in size are reckoned to be the same. Zeuthen's six barrows which, apart from No. 101, can be identified on Christie's map with relatively high confidence are No. 83, which must be the southernmost of the four long barrows to the north, and Nos. 96 and 97, which must be the two southernmost round barrows. Further, No. 111 must be the northernmost of Zeuthen's south-eastern group of five; No. 110 must one of the two barrows immediately to the east of the large central barrow; and No. 102 must be the one that is located nearest to the great barrow in the north-east (Figs. 16.1 and 16.5).

The other barrows shown by Zeuthen lie in areas which are void of such features on Christie's map. These barrows must have been removed before 1866. In the case of long barrow No. 83, which as noted would appear to be the only one of these that was drawn in a reasonably naturalistic manner, the dimensions agree exactly with those given by Christie. Moreover Christie recorded the diameter of the five small round barrows as from 11 to 16 ells, while Zeuthen, as noted, drew them all as 7–8 ells in diameter.

A comparison of Zeuthen's and Christie's plans thus shows that each includes a number of barrows that cannot be found on the other. The explanation of why some are absent from Christie's map is straightforward enough, i.e. they were removed in the years between 1845 and 1866. But how can it be that nine of Christie's barrows are missing from Zeuthen's records (Nos. 82, 99, 100, 103, 104, 105, 107, 109 and 112)? It was noted above that Nicolaysen recorded that a number of barrows were nearly flattened, or overgrown with trees. These include several of those that are missing from Zeuthen's plan (Nos. 82, 103, 104 and 107). They may already have been damaged in Zeuthen's time, and omitted by him for that reason. Two of the others that Zeuthen did not record (Nos. 105 and 112) are only partly within the limits of the plan, and may have been left out for that reason. On none of his plans did Zeuthen include barrows that only intrude into the edges of the area drawn (Stylegar, this vol. Ch. 5:Fig. 5.8; Skre 2005:figs. 1–3). Christie also noted Nos. 99 and 100 to be 0.3 and 0.5 m high respectively, while No. 109 is 0.4 m high. It is possible that Zeuthen either overlooked these, or chose to omit them because they were so small and low.

Consequently there are 11 grave monuments on Zeuthen's plan, seven round barrows (Nos. 137–43), three long barrows (Nos. 134–6), and a small ship-setting (No. 144) that are absent from Christie's map. Christie has 15 barrows inside the area covered by Zeuthen. It may, therefore, appear that in fact there were something like 26 barrows here in 1845. As this conclusion is the product of a number of assumptions, the figure cannot be regarded as exact. All the same, it gives a clear indication of the rate of destruction of the site in the two decades following Zeuthen's visit. This is also the period in which Munch and Nicolaysen were reporting destruction. Within the zone of the cemetery that Zeuthen's plan covers, it would appear that around 40% of the barrows were lost between 1845 and 1866. Furthermore, barrows would probably have been removed before then as well. The segment of the cemetery that is covered in Zeuthen's plan measures around 4,600 sq m, and the density of barrows in 1845 can thus be calculated to a little under 6 barrows per 1,000 sq m. In 1866 that figure had fallen to around 3.5.

It would seem that the rate of loss of barrows preceding Christie's visit was much greater in the central and northern sections of the cemetery than further south. Of the six barrows that were included in the Larvik County map from 1811 but were absent from Christie's, all lay in central and northern zones. Three of these were sited on the piece of land which Christie has lying immediately north-east of the central crossroads, and thus at the extreme southern edge of the central zone. Of the six barrows which are either fully or partially within this area on Christie's map (Nos. 94–8 and 111), five were recorded by Nicolaysen as having been damaged or overgrown. The sixth is right in the corner of this area and thus apparently enjoyed greater protection. This piece of land was probably under cultivation and the barrows were therefore probably gradually ploughed down in this period. It seems reasonable to believe that the destruction of the barrows here was just as intense as in the area that is covered by Zeuthen's plan. The estimate of 6 barrows per 1,000 sq m can therefore be assumed for the whole of the area that is called the central zone of the cemetery in Figure 16.6. In this part of the site there are 25 barrows on Christie's map. To be added are the 11 that are recorded on Zeuthen's plan and the 3 from the Larvik County map of 1811. The total number of barrows recorded in this part of the cemetery is therefore 39.

In the southern area of the cemetery the barrows are much more densely sited in Christie's map, with a total of 74 in all. To be added are the 6 barrows shown in Flintoe's sketch and the 2 that have been discovered by excavation. The recorded total is therefore 82 barrows. One can be sure of the edges of the site to the east and west since the boundaries here were the shore-line and the cliff. But to the south and the north-west the extent of the cemetery has been quite severely reduced. To the north-west, immediately west of the central crossroads, cultivation had probably removed a number of barrows before Christie's visit. His map shows a tongue of cultivated land intruding between barrows 12 and 16 in the south and 79 in the north. This area was already under cultivation in 1811, and therefore any barrows here could have been lost at an early date.

Within the southern zone of the cemetery too there was a degree of destruction of the barrows, but it was probably less severe than further north. Some places here appear completely undisturbed, for instance, because they are so densely packed with barrows that there can hardly ever have been any more.

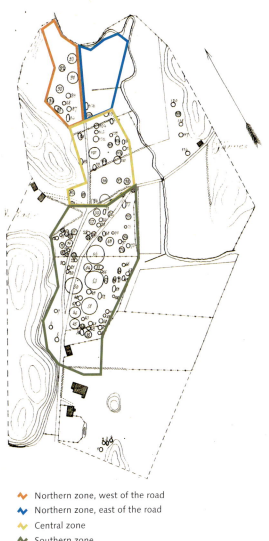

Figure 16.6 *Map showing the zoning of the cemetery as referred to in the text. After Nicolaysen 1868; reworked by Anne Engesveen.*

◆ Northern zone, west of the road
◆ Northern zone, east of the road
◆ Central zone
◆ Southern zone

This is the case, for example, in the area with the eleven barrows numbered 9–19, the density of which is as great as 14 barrows per 1,000 sq m. One may cautiously postulate that the density of barrows in the southern zone of the cemetery as a whole was around 7 barrows per 1,000 sq m.

Aerial photography 1977–1994

In 1977 Norway's first systematic aerial photographic search for ancient monuments that had been ploughed down was undertaken. It was the then student of Archaeology, Per Haavaldsen, who flew over the area he was working on for his master's dissertation on the Early Iron Age in southern Vestfold (Haavaldsen 1980). He took several photographs at Kaupang and other sites (Haavaldsen 1977). New photographs were taken in 1994 in connexion with the so-called Vestfold Route Project (Vestfoldbaneprosjektet) by Vestfold County Council, which recorded the ancient monuments in an area where a new railway line was planned to run through southern Vestfold. Both of these campaigns revealed cropmarks from ploughed-down burial mounds in the northernmost part of the Nordre Kaupang Cemetery – the area that lies north of Zeuthen's plan. A selection of the photos is reproduced her (Figs. 16.7–16.9). In what follows, this area is divided into three segments, of which the very northernmost is referred to as *north of the stream*, while the southern zone is divided into *west of the road* and *east of the road* (Fig. 16.6).

West of the road the traces left by barrows 90, 91 and 93 on Christie's map can be recognised (Fig. 16.7), and in Figures 16.8 and 16.9, No. 92 can also be seen. These four barrows were all excavated by Nicolaysen in 1867. No. 91 can also be found on the Larvik County map of 1811 (Fig. 16.2). Furthermore, in Figure 16.7 one can also see traces of yet another barrow north-west of No. 93. This barrow (No. 145) must have been levelled before 1866.

The first four of these barrows (Nos. 90–93) were relatively large, with diameters, according to Christie, of 15–25 ells (9.5–16 m). From the aerial photograph, the fifth (No. 145) can be calculated as having been about 6 m in diameter. Except for this one, there is no trace in the aerial photographs of the small barrows in this area (Nos. 84–89 in Christie's map). The round barrows amongst these were of 8.5–13.5 ells (5.5–8.5 m) in diameter. The fact that they do not appear on the aerial photographs is probably attributable to their not having had ring-ditches, or any such ditches' having been shallow. Crop-marks are visible because the fill of the ring-ditches provides better conditions for growth, while the conditions inside of the ditch, where the barrow itself stood, are sometimes poor. There is some indication that ring-ditches of significant depth tend to accompany the larger barrows. As a result, one has to reckon that there might have been more small barrows in this area than appear either in the aerial photographs or on Christie's map, but probably no more large ones. Altogether 11 barrows have been recorded west of the road.

The destruction of barrows west of the road had begun before 1866. The north-westernmost (No. 145)

may have been removed even before 1811, when the area in which it had lain was noted as under cultivation. We have assigned the southernmost part of this field to the central area of the cemetery, and here Zeuthen's plan shows three barrows that had been lost by 1866 (Nos. 134, 135 and 137). In 1867, Nicolaysen described four barrows (Nos. 86–89) west of the road as damaged or overgrown with trees. Since all of these were small barrows that would be most vulnerable to damage through cultivation, the most likely explanation is plough-damage rather than tree-damage.

The density of barrows west of the road was probably higher than is shown by aerial photography and Christie's map combined. The 11 barrows recorded provide 2.2 barrows per 1,000 sq m, but in the southern, least damaged section, the density is around 4. One can cautiously assume that the density throughout this area was originally somewhat lower than that inferred for the adjacent area to the south, possibly at 5 barrows per 1,000 sq m.

In the area east of the road, Christie's map has two barrows at the very south (Nos. 105 and 106). One of these (No. 105) can also be identified on the Larvik County map of 1811. Further to the north, that map has three barrows marked (Nos. 121–123). One of these (No. 121) can also be seen on the aerial photographs (Figs. 16.7–16.9). North, north-east and south of this crop-mark there are traces of a further three smaller barrows (Figs. 16.7 and 16.8, Nos. 146–148)

which are not recorded in any other source. Consequently 8 barrows have been recorded east of the road. There is no evidence that the destruction of barrows was underway here before 1811, but in the years between then and 1866 a large number of barrows must have been lost in this area.

In Figure 16.8 in particular, one can see that in addition to the features definitely identified as barrows , there is very irregular growth in the northern half of the field east of the road, as also along the road in the southern half. In several places there may be arcs of rings, but none of these can be identified as barrows with complete confidence. The clarity with which a refilled ring-ditch stands out is dependent not only upon the growth-conditions in the year of the aerial photography but also upon the size of the barrow and the ring-ditch, the state of the soil, and the degree to which the barrow and the ring-ditch has been ploughed down. On the Larvik County map from 1811 one can find several marks in this area that could well be barrows. Together with the high density of demonstrable barrows in the northern part of this area, the presence of indistinct crop-marks and possible indications of mounds on the 1811 map imply that the density of barrows might have been more or less the same as on the west side of the road, i.e. at around 5 barrows per 1,000 sq m.

North of the stream there is no evidence for barrows other than that which is provided by aerial pho-

Figure 16.7 *Crop-marks of barrows east and west of the road. Looking west. Photo, Vestfold County Council; reworked by Anne Engesveen and Elise Naumann.*

tography (Figs. 16.8 and 16.9). To the north there is a clear sign of one barrow, 6.5 m in diameter. Barely 20 m south of this ring there is a c. 15 m long boat-shaped crop-mark. It is difficult to determine whether this represents a grave, and it is therefore not included in what follows. Around the barrow to the north and southwards right down the slope to the stream there are further crop-marks. Some of these are probably segments of ring-ditches, but no definite barrows can be identified. On all of the available aerial photographs large parts of this area are in shadow, and it is difficult to read clear formations on the pictures. However there is little doubt that there were barrows in the whole of this area. The direction in which the cemetery expanded here was quite evidently towards the north, and the clear, ring-shaped crop-mark probably shows one of the most northerly barrows. Tentatively a density of 4 barrows per 1,000 sq m can be suggested in this area.

In the Larvik County map of 1811 the area west of the road was under cultivation, and a minor track ran between the fields and on to the north-west. This cultivation may have removed barrows even before 1811. Otherwise the area east of the road and north of the stream is marked as lightly wooded, possibly pasture, and the remaining barrows here must have been removed in the years between 1811 and 1866.

The original size of the cemetery

Aerial photography has shown that the cemetery once extended further to the north-east and the north than is revealed by Christie's map. In this northern zone of the cemetery, one may assume that the aerial photographs give a reliable basis for determining the original limits of the cemetery to the north, east and west. Along the eastern edge of the site the sea came into a Viking-period bay. This ran north past the mouth of the stream (Fig. 16.10). Towards the shore, the lowest barrows mapped by Christie have

their lower edges between the modern 4 and 5 m contours. This is so consistent throughout the cemetery that one can trust that Christie's map here shows the original eastern boundary of the site from barrows Nos. 114 and 115 southwards. In the distinctly sloping terrain this would produce a strip from 5 to 15 m wide between the barrows and the sea-shore. To the west the boundary follows the cliff, except for one place where, as noted, a number of barrows may have disappeared. However, as noted, the southern limit is less certain although there is no definite reason to extend the cemetery further to the south than indicated by Flintoe's sketch and the graves identified. This burial area is shown in Figure 16.10.

As Table 16.1 reveals, 140 burial mounds have been identified at the site, namely 1 ship-setting (No. 144), 29 long barrows, 109 round barrows, and one of undetermined form (No. 127). It is clear that the total was once a great deal higher. The destruction of barrows on the site had probably begun even before 1811, and accelerated in the final couple of decades preceding the map drawn by Christie in 1866. The records for the situation prior to 1866 are haphazard and incomplete, but still yield a basis for an estimation of the original density of barrows in different zones of the cemetery. The records are best in the central area of the site, weaker in the south and weakest at the northern extremity.

As one can see in Table 16.1, the estimated total number of barrows is 263, a figure which of course is highly uncertain. The original number of barrows must in any case have been more than 200, possibly closer to 300. An attempt to visualize the original number of barrows of the cemetery is presented in Figure 16.11.

There are other major cemeteries in Vestfold besides Kaupang and Lamøya, but most of these represent the Early Iron Age too. The largest of these is situated on the farms of Brunla and Agnes in

Figure 16.8 *Crop-marks of barrows north of the stream, and east and west of the road. Looking north. Photo, Vestfold County Council; reworked by Anne Engesveen and Elise Naumann.*

Figure 16.9 *Crop-marks of barrows north of the stream, and east and west of the road. Looking east. Photo, Vestfold County Council; reworked by Anne Engesveen and Elise Naumann.*

Brunlanes, where there is a cemetery of 89 barrows (Askeladden ID 3671). This cemetery must be of the Iron Age. There are most probably also barrows of the Viking Period at the site, but there is no basis on which to suggest a specific number of Viking-period burials there. The largest cemetery that is securely dated to the Viking Period is Gulli near Tønsberg, which at the time of excavation contained 42 graves, originally possibly 60 (Gjerpe 2005a:14–15).

16.2 The Skiringssal cemetery

Having reached an estimate of the original size of the Nordre Kaupang cemetery, it is time to discuss its connection and meaning in the context of the other elements in the Skiringssal central place complex. As will be shown, the cemetery's location along a Viking-age trackway is of significance.

The cemetery is located on the strip of land that runs between Kaupang and the lands to the north where the other components of the Skiringssal complex, the hall and the assembly place, can be found (Skre, this vol. Chs. 11, 17, 19). Due to the topography of the area, this must have been the main route on land to and from Kaupang. To the west of the Kaupang settlement, the steep cliffs and the Kaupangmyra bog are obstacles to movement, and on the south-western side of the settlement area the sea washed right up against the sheer mountain face (Skre, this vol. Ch. 1:Fig. 1.3).

On the Larvik County map of 1811, the main road from the Kaupang farms to the north runs through the cemetery site. Approximately in the middle of the cemetery there is a side-road that runs towards Bjønnes in the east (Fig. 16.2). This side-road cannot date back to the Viking Period. On Christie's map it disturbs several barrows, and in the 9th century, with a sea-level 3.5 m above the present, the road would have to have crossed a bay about 30 m across and more than 1 m deep (Fig. 16.10). Viking-period traffic must have run through the cemetery from its southern to its northern end and vice versa.

As the N–S route on Christie's map interferes with the burial mounds only to a minor degree, Tollnes (Blindheim et al. 1981:21) inferred that the line of this route is as old as the town. However, as demonstrated, particularly the central and northern zones of the cemetery were already severely damaged when Christie's map was drawn. Nicolaysen reports that this damage was caused by roads amongst other things. Zeuthen's plan, for instance, shows that 21 years before Christie's visit the roadway followed a rather different line, and ran across a large barrow. This plan also reveals that there were barrows at that date on the line of the road that Christie drew 21 years later. It is, consequently, difficult to infer from the courses of routes on Christie's map and the County map where the Viking-period trackway lay.

More confidence can probably be attached to the fact that in the eastern part of the cemetery, immediately above the barrows that border on to the shoreline, there is a corridor between the mounds on the site (Figs. 16.10 and 16.11). This begins between Barrows 35 and 36, and continues along the western side of Barrows 37–40, 58–60, 72, 71, 76, 77, 33, 97, 141, 110, 109 and 107. To the north of here the cemetery is more severely damaged, and it is not so easy to determine the further course of this corridor with certainty. The most reliable point may be where the road crosses the Guri stream on Christie's map. The crossing place was the same on the Larvik County map of 1811. Normally, ancient trackways ran by preference along a particular contour. The corridor identified follows more or less the present 7 m contour, which was 3.5 m above sea-level in the Viking Period, from the far southern end of the site right the way up to the crossing of the Guri stream (Fig. 16.11).

North of the stream there are no secure points showing the course of this corridor, although from

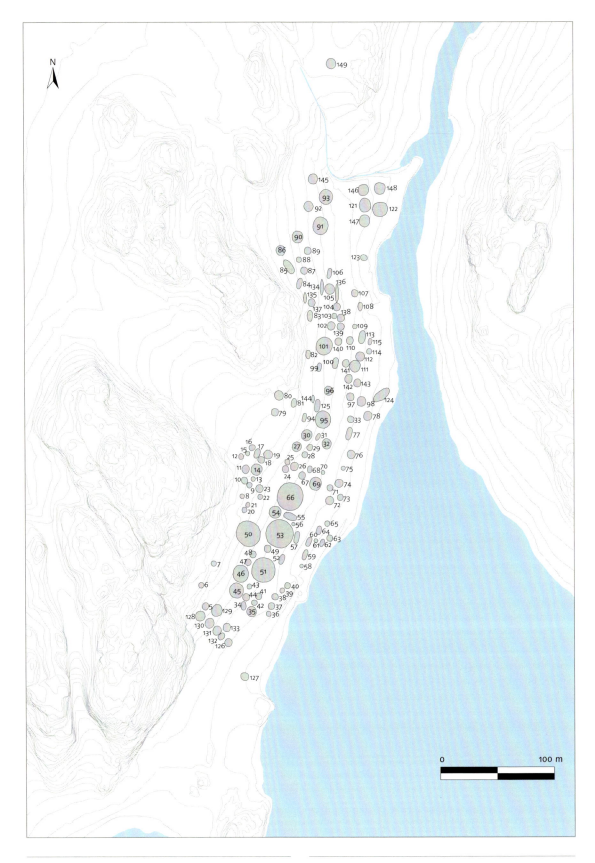

Figure 16.10 *The cemetery at Nordre Kaupang, as it can be reconstructed on the basis of the available sources. The barrows recorded are numbered in accordance with Figs. 16.1–16.3, 16.5 and 16.7–16.9. Contour interval 1 meter. As the sea level is raised 3.5 m to the Viking-age level, the lowest contour interval is 0.5 meters. Map, Anne Engesveen.*

Figure 16.11 *Map with visual representation of the recorded and estimated number of barrows, totalling 263. In the case of the 123 estimated barrows, there is no evidence for their position, form or size. Amongst the recorded barrows, long barrows constitute 23%, and 28 of the 123 signatures have consequently been drawn as long barrows. No less than 55 of Christie's 86 round barrows were 5.0–8.7 m in diameter, and*

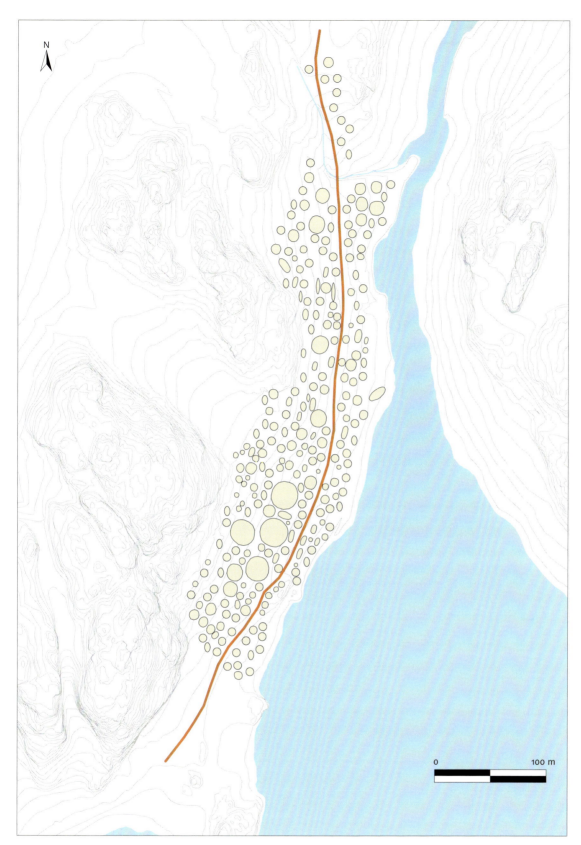

the signature for round barrows has therefore been standardized at 7 m. This is close to the norm for Vestfold (Sjøvold 1944:49). Most of the long barrows were 7–10 m long and 4–6 m wide, and these signatures have consequently been set at 8 m long and 5 m wide. Most of the long barrows are also aligned more or less N–S, and this has been standardized as well. In respect of location, the signature has been mechanically distributed in every part of the cemetery.

The probable trackway has been added. At the southern end of the site the route is well attested, but to the north there are alternatives to what is suggested on this map. Contour interval 1 meter. As the sea level is raised 3.5 m to the Viking-age level, the lowest contour interval is 0.5 meters. Map., Anne Engesveen.

the terrain it would appear most likely that a track-way would have continued through the cemetery northwards approximately where the road was on the map of 1811. The alternative, to go further east, on the flat area beneath the rocky knolls, would have been a poor one, as the ground was fairly wet there. The most plausible route for the corridor through the cemetery has been drawn in on Figure 16.11.

In the southern part of the site, in particular, this corridor is very clear. It can also be seen that the bar-rows along this section of the corridor, and especially along its eastern side, lie practically in a row as if they were constructed along a specific line. Such a line can hardly have been anything other than an extant track-way that was in use when the mounds were raised. Since this is the best preserved part of the cemetery, the whole corridor appears quite firm, and it is likely that it genuinely marks a trackway that was being used while the cemetery built up around it, and that ran through the whole burial ground.

This routeway appears to have been the primary reference point for the siting of the cemetery. A con-nexion with the town is not followed to its greatest possible degree, as the cemetery terminates nearly 200 m north of the northern end of the marked-out plots of the settlement. Furthermore it terminates about 85 m north of the northernmost of the burials that securely can be connected to the town, the ceme-tery at Hagejordet. In the strip of land north of Hagejordet no further finds that could derive from graves have been made. Therefore, the cemetery does not seem to have had its primary connection to the town and its population.

The people that buried their dead in the Nordre Kaupang cemetery seem to have preferred the areas along the road and to have avoided the areas further from it. In the area called "west of the road" (Fig. 16.6), the cemetery could have extended westwards and up the slope, but there is no evidence of burials here. Instead, the barrows of the cemetery lie close to the road, never more than 75 m away from it.

The distribution of graves from the 9th and 10th centuries does not reveal any convincing horizontal stratigraphy in the site. There is a certain clustering of 10th-century burials in the centre of the cemetery (Nos. 83, 112 and 113; Ka. 34, 4 and 3) and in the north-ern zone (Nos. 85, 90, 91 and 92; Ka. 10, 6, 7 and 8), but there is nearly the same number in the southern zone (Nos. 16, 18, 35, 47, 60 and 77; Ka. 1, 11, 16, 19, 22 and 23). The only two definite 9th-century burials lie in the southern zone (Nos. 94 and 126; Ka. 14 and 37). It is possible that one can detect a tendency for the ear-liest barrows in the cemetery to have been construct-ed in the southern part, and that there was a subse-quent expansion towards the north, at the same time as there was an increase in the density of barrows in the southern zone.

Such a chronological pattern is rendered more credible by the marked concentration of the largest barrows of the cemetery in the southern zone. The four largest barrows on Christie's map measure 22.6–25.1 m in diameter (Nos. 50, 51, 53 and 66) and are 2.2–2.7 m high. All of these burial mounds were exca-vated by Nicolaysen, but none of them contained any finds. Two (Nos. 50 and 53) were completely empty, while the other two produced charcoal and ash, possi-bly also burnt bone. Such a group of four large bar-rows must have been constructed while there was still plenty of space in the cemetery; in other words, early in its history. Three of these barrows were also raised along the line of the routeway through the cemetery described above. As noted, that routeway was proba-bly a primary feature of alignment for the cemetery, and the proximity of the large mounds to it empha-sizes yet again that the area must have been relatively void of barrows when they were placed there. As well as lying alongside the routeway, these four large bar-rows are sited where they are most conspicuous from the harbour basin to the south and from the entrance to the harbour from the sea, which lies to the east of them.

Thus there are a number of factors that indicate that some, if not all, of the four largest barrows in the cemetery are amongst the earliest. Since none of them contained any finds it is conceivable that some of them pre-date the 9th century, the horizon from which the earliest grave finds date (Stylegar, this vol. Ch. 5:79–80). It is typical of the great barrows of east-ern Norway of the 8th century that they cover crema-tion burials with few or no grave goods (Myhre 1992:164–5). Empty barrows and barrows with noth-ing more than burnt bone are, however, not uncom-mon in the Viking Age, although at Kaupang the pro-portion of these is higher than usual. In all, 31 of the 71 barrows Nicolaysen excavated at Nordre Kaupang were void of finds and even of cremated bone. Thus 43% of the mounds did not even have the remains of the bodies of the dead.

Why are so many barrows empty? The principal symbolic significance of the burial mound was to serve as a memorial to the deceased. People remem-bered who lay in the mounds, and through the barrow their memory was physically present to the living. The construction of the barrow was probably an intimate part of both the funeral and the process of inheri-tance, and the provision of a physical memorial also linked the memory of the deceased to a specific place (Skre 1997). From the rich burial archaeology of the Viking Period, it is known that rituals and customs associated with burial had many forms which led to diverse forms of funerary memorials and combina-tions of grave goods, and to considerable variation in the treatment of the dead body (Stylegar, this vol. Ch. 5:82-5, 87–93). Not placing the deceased's body in the burial mound should be regarded as one of these options. The placing of the deceased's body in the

Area	Number of barrows recorded	Estimated number of barrows per 1,000 sq m	Area in sq m	Total estimated number of barrows
Southern zone	82*	7	21,800	152
Central zone	38**	6	8,500	51
Northern zone, west of the road	11***	5	5,000	25
Northern zone, east of the road	8****	5	4,900	25
North of the stream	1*****	4	2,500	10
Total	140		42,700	263

Table 16.1. *A summary of the results of the analysis of the various zones within the cemetery (Fig. 16.6) in respect of the number of barrows recorded and the estimated number of barrows per 1,000 sq m. On the basis of the estimated density of barrows and the actual area of the different zones, an original number of barrows in the cemetery is calculated. Several barrows are recorded in more than one source, and only the most certain are included in the following list of documented barrows:*

* 74 in Christie's map, 6 in Flintoe's sketch, 2 through excavations in 1965 and 1999, respectively
** 25 in Christie's map, 11 in Zeuthen's plan, 2 on the Larvik County map of 1811
*** 10 in Christie's map, 1 on an aerial photograph
**** 2 in Christie's map, 4 on aerial photographs, 2 on the Larvik County map of 1811
***** 1 on an aerial photograph

grave-monument was evidently not so crucial a part of the Norse rituals as it was in Christian burial. For example it has been demonstrated that the amount of bone in the great majority of cremation burials is less than half of what the cremation of a body would produce (Holck 1996:80–89).

It is difficult to come to a definite conclusion about what lay behind the diversity of burial practices. But it does seem reasonable to suppose that whenever the body is completely absent from the memorial that was raised to the dead, it is because the body simply was not present in the rituals. It may have been the case that death occurred in such a way that the body was elsewhere, or had to be abandoned, e.g. at sea or in enemy territory, or just because the deceased died so far away that it was not possible to transport the body. Like a large number of runestones which state that the person it was raised in the memory of died in distant lands, the empty barrows show that the raising of a memorial to the dead had to be carried out all the same, probably as an element of the funerary and inheritance rituals (see Stylegar, this vol. Ch. 5:69–70 for other views).

The other cemeteries at Kaupang have a different relationship with the landscape than that of Nordre Kaupang (Stylegar, this vol. Ch. 5:Fig. 5.2). The burial ground at Bikjholberget is situated almost right out in the harbour basin, and very close to the settlement.

That is also the case with the graves at Søndre Kaupang and Vikingholmen. The burials on Lamøya are likewise just about as far down by the harbour and the entrance channel to the north, west and south as they could possibly be. Some of the cemeteries at Bjønnes are in a location clearly visible from the northern entrance channel to the harbour, others from the routeway through the Nordre Kaupang cemetery. Only these few at Bjønnes and the vast cemetery at Nordre Kaupang have any connexion with land transport. All the other cemeteries are oriented towards seaway travellers, and towards the urban settlement itself. They stand out as cemeteries for those whose principal business was with the town, i.e. its residents and visitors. In the case of the cemetery at Nordre Kaupang, its clear association with the routeway could indicate that this was not the burial place for the people who lived in the town, but rather for those who belonged to the other parts of Skiringssal, which were located in the area where the road up from the harbour led.

There is another circumstance that points towards the same conclusion. As has been noted, there appears to have been an area with no burials to the south of the cemetery. Further south of that area, at Hagejordet, several grave finds and five barrows are known; four of those barrows were included on Christie's map (Nos. 1–4). Strikingly enough, three of

C17615–18	Valby	Barrow	2 copper-alloy mounts, 2 spindle-whorls, glass beads, bronze spiral bead, nails, boat rivet, copper-alloy mounts
C11772–74	Østby	Flat grave	12 amber gaming pieces, 5 glass beads, axe, lost beads
C16181–83	Østby N	Cairn	Glass bead, amber bead, 2 whetstones
C31483	Østby N	Flat grave?	Two-edged sword, axe (Petersen Type F, fig. 37), iron fragments (knife?, nail, arrowheads)
C3658–59	Huseby	Barrow	20 complete and 20 fragmentary glass beads, spindle-whorl
C5509	Gjerstad	Flat grave	27 glass beads

them lie pretty well in an E–W row, and also stand partly upon the rocky knolls to the south. The other securely located grave finds from this area also follow the line of this row. It is as if the area north of these had some use that prevented burial there. Earlier, 10 pits with burnt bone, charcoal and ash, probably settlement features, have been found in this area (A94901, Pilø, this vol. Ch. 6:136–7, Fig. 6.12). Today there is a farmstead and settlement in that area; the only archaeological investigation during the field-work 1998-2003 was a trench that was dug in the farmstead in 2002. The only thing of definitely Viking-age date that was found there was a well with a lining plank that is dendro-dated to the winter of 806/807 (A94901, Pilø, this vol. Ch. 8:Fig. 8.14, No. 8; Bonde, this vol. Ch. 13:279). It is difficult to reconcile this discovery with a burial ground; indeed, it does not give any clear hint at all as to what this area might have been used for. Its proximity to a sheltered and gently sloping shore may suggest a beaching place for boats or shipbuilding, and possibly a boat-house *(naust)*, something which the settlement and the cemetery otherwise left little space for in the harbour area. But there is no concrete evidence for this use of the space.

The differences in burial practices between the various cemeteries also imply that the cemetery at Nordre Kaupang did not belong to the same milieu as the others. At Lamøya there are both inhumation graves (six, although some uncertain) and cremations (four), while at Bikjholberget there are only inhumation graves. Bikjholberget also displays a wide range of variation in respect of other details of burial practice (Stylegar, this vol. Ch. 5:73, 99). At other sites in Vestfold than Kaupang, nearly three-quarters of Viking-period graves were cremations (Forseth 1993: 174), and the uniform practice of cremation at Nordre Kaupang reflects a connexion with the local rural society rather than with the culturally more heteroge-

neous population resident in or visiting the town. Amongst the seventeen graves found at Søndre Kaupang there are twelve cremations. The rite used for the other five is not known. This cemetery could have had a cultural attachment like that at Nordre Kaupang.

On the evidence of the dated graves, the cemetery was in use for some 150 years from around the year 800. But, as noted, the four large empty burial mounds could be somewhat earlier. The frequency of burial would undoubtedly have fluctuated during the 150–200 years the site was being used. The number of dated graves from the 10th century is much greater than those from the 9th century, but the proportion of dated burials that are dated is too low to yield any particularly detailed picture of the variations in burial frequency. Across the entire period that the cemetery was in use, on average one or two mounds were raised per year. In the 9th century the quantity was probably at the lower end of this range, in the 10th century at the upper end if not higher still. The number of burials is consistent with a population of 60–100 individuals, or 10–15 households, averaged over the whole period. There is nothing in the ratio of the sexes to suggest that this community had anything other than a normal number of women and men (Stylegar, this vol. Ch. 5:82–3).

At the seven farms in the central settled area of Tjølling (not including Kaupang), that is Valby, Østby, Huseby, Gjerstad, Lunde, Guri and Bjønnes (Brink, this vol. Ch. 4:Fig. 4.1), there are relatively few grave-finds from the Viking Age, only six certain cases in all (Tab. 16.2). In other areas of Tjølling 26 Viking-period burials are known. It is reasonable to surmise that the households from a number of the farmsteads in Skiringssal buried the majority of their dead in the large cemetery of Nordre Kaupang (cf. Ambrosiani 1986).

The cemetery at Nordre Kaupang is not the only

Table 16.2 *Burial finds of the Viking Period in the central settled area of Tjølling (Valby, Østby, Huseby, Gjerstad, Lunde, Guri and Bjønnes). Three stray finds have been omitted, but C31483 and C5509 are stray finds that are accepted as grave-finds because of the character of the assemblage.*

one that lies along a routeway. This phenomenon is known in many parts of Scandinavia, and in southern Vestfold there a several large burial grounds sited in this way (Gansum 2002; Engesveen 2005). Tracks crossing dry land in this period did not follow definite and fixed lines, but were rather traffic corridors. When a particular path became hard to move along, perhaps as a result of erosion, people started to travel along another path parallel to it. Several of these road cemeteries are positioned where the topography makes these corridors relatively narrow. Those who wished to travel along a corridor therefore had little choice but to pass through the cemetery (Engesveen 2005:114–15, 120–1). Engesveen's analyses of several such sites in Vestfold have demonstrated that the key objective in the siting of the cemeteries was that they be conspicuous to those who came along the routeway. Their visibility in relation to specific parts of the landscape, which is usually emphasized in landscape-archaeological analyses of the cemetery, was a much less significant factor, if indeed it were taken into consideration at all. This is no very great surprise when one remembers that only the very largest barrows would have been visible from a great distance. All one can see from far off are the relatively few great barrows that stand out on the horizon.

The cemetery at Nordre Kaupang is consistent with this characteristic feature. Everyone who had to travel to or from Kaupang over land had to make his way through the cemetery. When the cemetery had reached its maximum extent some decades into the 10th century, it was necessary to follow a route more than half a kilometre long through the barrows. This was not only the case for those who took the land route to the town, but also for anyone who came by sea and had business up in the district. Some way north of the cemetery, the road on the 1811 map div-

ides, with one track going north-westwards to Guri, Valby and Gjerstad, the other north-eastwards to Huseby, where the hall was (Skre, this vol. Ch. 11) and on to *Þjóðalyng*, where the assembly place was (Brink, this vol. Ch. 4:63; Skre, this vol. Ch. 17:Fig. 17.6, Ch. 1:Fig. 1.2). Many of those who came to the harbour and had business in the district would presumably have had to go to the assembly place or the hall. It would appear that it was the access to those locations that determined the siting of the cemetery.

What might have been the purpose of staging the visitors' approach in this way? As noted, the burial mounds had a memorial function, having been raised to commemorate the dead. In farmstead burial grounds the barrows of the ancestors, which made them physically present at the farm, were a visible declaration of the occupier's right to the land, i.e. there lay the human chain from which he had inherited it (Skre 1997). But barrows also occur in other localities besides farmstead cemeteries. In other places, different aspects of the memorial function of the barrow besides the right to inherit might have been more to the fore. Individual heirs' right to the land cannot have been the most important consideration at a place such as Skiringssal. The cemetery at Nordre Kaupang might have been used by many households, possibly 10 to 15, housed at an equivalent number of farmsteads within Tjølling. It must have been the royal seat that bound them together. This is probably the cemetery in which the Skiringssal petty kings, their households, and the people who occupied the farms around them, were interred. Those who came to the hall, the assembly place, and to the area at the centre of the petty king's power, had to be made to recognize his lordly importance and power by passing through the memorials raised to his ancestors and his people.

The Skiringssal *Thing* Site *Þjóðalyng*   17

DAGFINN SKRE

![decorative initial] An important role of a central-place such as Skiringssal was to serve as a site for juridical and cultic functions. Especially juridical affairs, but also, to varying degrees, cult activities, took place at *Þjóðalyng,* the dry sandy plain where the church was built in the 12th century. This examination of archaeological, toponymic and documentary sources concerning the assembly place is primarily aimed at elucidating the *thing* site's age and the size of the territory whose population it served. These sources are also used in an attempt to outline the changing functions and roles of such assembly places from the Early Iron Age to the beginning of the Christian Middle Ages.

The church at *Þjóðalyng* is the second largest of the five rural district basilicas of eastern Norway. It is also by far the largest Romanesque church in Vestfold outside of the town of Tønsberg. The size and expensive form of the structure probably reflect unusually extensive rights to income for this church in the 11th and 12th centuries. These rights, and perhaps the size of the building too, were presumably linked to the location of the church at the assembly place of *Þjóðalyng.* From the very beginning, it was the church of this moot. This shows that *Þjóðalyng* was still a *thing* site in the 10th and 11th centuries, to which men came from a wide area, perhaps from the whole of Vestfold or Viken. The assembly place might gradually have lost its significance after the royal foundation of Tønsberg and its *thing* site at Haugar, both of which seem to have taken place around 1100.

Cooking pits, post-holes and graves that have been found near the church site are from a much earlier period. These show that *Þjóðalyng* was an assembly place as early as the late Early Iron Age, before c. 600 AD. The proximity of the sacred lake *Vítrir/Vettrir* and the mountain *Helgefjell* immediately north of the *thing* site strengthens the impression given by other sources, namely, that at this date, assembly places were to a great extent the locations of cult activity. It was probably at such assembly places that seasonal feasts were held, to which sources relating to much of the Germanic world testify. After the changes that took place in, *inter alia,* the social context and the forms of cult in the 6th century, the halls of kings and chieftains seem to have become a more important cultic and political arena. The regular assemblies at sites such as *Þjóðalyng* might therefore have lost part of their previous cultic functions and been left with much of the juridical, and to some extent also with the administrative and political functions, which the sources show that the *thing*-moots had in the 11th and 12th centuries.

One of the fundamental institutions of Viking society was the *thing.* At the general assembly all of the free men from the *thing*-district would assemble to resolve conflicts and disputes of law, while at representative *thing*-moots only some selected individuals took part. In the 12th and 13th centuries, the *thing* had not only juridical but also what may be described as administrative functions, such as ensuring that the weapons of the *leidang*-men were in order, and determining the boundaries of the *leidang*-districts. Even what could be called political issues were dealt with at the *thing.* Besides all of these functions, the *thing* served as a forum where friendships and alliances were negotiated and confirmed, agreements concerning marriage and other important matters were entered into, and the latest news was spread. Most forms of business at the *thing* were conducted according to rituals, some of which had a cultic component.

Sources revealing the character of *thing*-moots in

the Viking Age are very scarce. But even though crucial factors, such as the religion and the nature of royal power, were different than they were in the 12th and 13th centuries, the *thing*-moots were probably the most important juridical, political and social assemblies for Viking society (Andersen 1977:247–62; Helle 1974:179–89).

As already noted, the essential social functions of Viking Age society were located at what commonly is called central places (Skre, this vol. Ch. 3.2:48–50). The significance of the *thing*-moots for the common man as well as for kings and chieftains, is the reason why several *thing* sites were situated at major farmsteads which, as indicated by archaeological finds and documentary sources were the homes of chieftains or leading men (Andersen 1977:255). At Skiringssal too, there was a *thing* site which may date from the same time as the other elements of the central place – the town, the hall and the cemetery – broadly speaking the 8th–10th century. In what follows, the sources concerning this *thing* site will be examined with a view to dating its use as precisely as possible, and to investigating the size and extent of the surrounding area from which those who attended this assembly came. The function of the *thing*-moot before and during the Viking Period will also be elucidated. But first, the system of laws and assemblies in the Viking Period and the two centuries immediately following it will be discussed.

17.1 Things and *laws* c. 800–1250

There is no very detailed information about the system of *things* in Norway, or about the laws of the different regional assemblies, before the 12th and 13th centuries. Sagas and poems, charters and annals from this period, provide information on these subjects, but the key sources are the laws for the four law-regions (Fig. 17.1). The law-codes are preserved in various redactions, which include early decrees, some of which are from the 12th century, a few possibly from the 11th. The Gulathing Law is preserved in a version of c. 1250 but contains many earlier clauses; the Frostathing Law, likewise, in a version from the 1260s (Robberstad 1969:7–11; Eithun et al. 1994:9–12; Hagland and Sandnes 1994:xxx–xliv). The laws of the Borgarthing and Eidsivathing survive only in fragments, most of which are Christian laws, in manuscripts of the 13th and 14th centuries, but both include earlier components (Rindal 1997:23–4; Halvorsen 1997:65–7). These regional laws were in force until they were revised under Magnus Hakonsson (king 1263–1280), who was given the cognomen "Law-restorer", and a single law for the whole kingdom was produced in 1274.

The principal assemblies in the four major law-regions, which would appear to have been created in the 10th and 11th centuries, were representative *things*. Within each of these regions there were *things*

at several levels, but the number, responsibilities, and meeting-places of these various *things* are relatively obscure matters. There is a range of evidence, however, that *things* were held for the *fylki*, or 'folk', for sections of the *fylki* (the *herað*, *fjórðungr* [quarter] and/or *þriðjung* [third]), and for local settlement areas (Andersen 1977:250–3). *Things* of different levels of that kind are described in the Gulathing Law. However Helle (2001:77–9) could find no evidence in High-medieval sources that the *things* on the levels between the four major *things* and the district *thing* ever actually met, and it appears as if by this date it was only at the highest (major) and the most local (*herað*) levels that the *thing*-system was really in operation. It is conceivable that *things* at intermediary levels appear in the law-codes as an anachronistic shadow of the *thing*-system from before the establishment of the four principal law-regions, and that they had no practical role by the time the laws were written down.

The first two of the four major law-regions began to take shape in the 10th century in the coastal lands of western and central Norway. Helle (2001:30–7) finds it possible to place some credence in the poems and sagas which relate that Hakon the Good, probably in the 930s, extended the area under the authority of the Gulathing and issued new laws. The *thing* site at Gulen had until then been an assembly place for a smaller area, but became the principal *thing* for the whole of western Norway and Agder. Helle also concludes that a change from general assemblies to representative *things* took place at about that time. The model for the new system was probably introduced by Hakon from the English legal system; he himself was fostered by King Athelstan in England, who developed the legal system in that kingdom. It has been suggested that an equivalent development in the Frostathing law-region occurred even earlier (Indrebø 1935; Hagland and Sandnes 1994:xiv–xv), but there is no definite evidence for this; it would be valuable to have this issue researched anew.

The legal and *thing*-systems in the two law-regions of eastern Norway, the Eidsivathing (the Opplands) with its *thing* site at Eid (Eidsvoll) and the Borgarthing (Viken) with its *thing* site at Borg (Sarpsborg) (Fig. 17.1), are less well illuminated in the surviving sources. Some scholars have been of the opinion that the whole area was unified as a single law-region, the Eidsivathing law-region, in the 11th century, and that this law-region was divided in two in respect of Christian law alone. In *Heimskringla* (Ch. 114), Snorri gives Saint Olaf the credit for having joined several earlier *thing*-districts together into the Eidsivathing law-region. According to the chronology of this saga, this would have taken place in the winter of 1021–1022. In the Legendary Olaf's Saga, which contains a great deal of material from an otherwise almost entirely lost saga of Olaf from c. 1180, it is stat-

Figure 17.1 *Law-regions of the 13th century with their main thing sites. The four law-regions of Norway were apparently founded in the 10th/11th centuries, probably as the result of a royal initiative. The Gulathing and Frostathing law-regions seem to be the earliest, whereas the two law-regions of eastern Norway probably were founded in the 11th century. While the laws of the two former law-regions are preserved in several versions, to a great extent only the Christian laws and a couple of pages of the secular law of the two eastern regions survive. In the map the approximate extent of the law-regions is indicated. Except for Borgarthing only the extent within the present Norwegian national border is given. Map, Anne Engesveen, Julie K. Øhre Askjem.*

ed that Olaf issued a single law for the Opplands and the eastern areas of Viken, which might have been done on the same occasion.

None of these sagas can be reckoned as particularly reliable sources, and the key role they attribute to Saint Olaf might have been due to the need to glorify the martyr-king and to endow social orders with his authority. There is no other evidence that Viken and the Opplands formed a single law-region (Halvorsen 1997:67; Riisøy 2003:156–7). True enough, only one fragment of a separate secular law-code for Viken is known, and this appears to be from a legal codex that contained laws for both Viken and the Opplands respectively (Seip 1957:149). But the text of this specific fragment does appear to be well adapted to the geographical division of Viken, since it refers to a sub-division into a half-*fylki thing*, a *fylki thing*, and a three-*fylki thing* (NLG II:523). And Viken did indeed consist of three *fylki*: these are listed in the region's Christian law as Ranrike (Bohuslän), Vingulmark (Østfold and the southern part of Akershus), and Vestfold (Fig. 17.1; Skre, this vol. Ch. 18:Fig. 18.2).

Other factors suggest that these two law-regions were established at different times. The history of the conversion of the two regions was rather different, as burial according to non-Christian practices virtually disappeared in Viken around 950, whereas in some parts of the Opplands it continued right up to the middle of the 11th century. The need to have Christian laws accepted was therefore evident earlier in Viken, and this must be the reason why the Christian law of this area, as compared to the Christian law of the Opplands, has several features which appear very archaic (Halvorsen 1997:67). On these grounds it seems reasonable to assume that the two eastern Norwegian law-regions, Borgarthing and Eidsivathing, were established at different times and never formed one common law-region.

The *thing* site of the Borgarthing, Borg, is first

mentioned by Snorri. In *Óláfs saga ins helga* (Heimskringla, Saint Olaf's Saga, Ch. 61), he writes that Olaf founded a stronghold, a town, a royal court, and a church, at Borg, and that thereafter this was his preferred residence when he was in Viken. The earliest information about Borg as a *thing* site comes from the same saga (Ch. 173), where it is stated that the Danish king Knut the Great (the English King Canute) held a *thing* in every *fylki* along the coast and was hailed as king. The last place at which he held such a *thing* was Borg, and the context indicates that this would have been in 1028.

But, as has been said, any individual claim made in these late sources has to be treated with some caution. There are, however, elements in the Christian law of the Borgarthing that indicate that at least some parts of it derive from the 11th century, and that the Borgarthing must thus have been functioning as the legal assembly of Viken from that time onwards. Some of the clauses in the Borgarthing's Christian law, which is preserved in three redactions, were added in the 12th century (Seip 1957:150; Halvorsen 1997:66–7). That the Borgarthing functioned as the legal assembly of Viken in both of these centuries would thus appear to be securely documented.

But what about the laws, the legal regions, the *thing*-system and *thing* sites in the period *preceding* the establishment of the four major law-regions? On the whole, one has to admit that this period lies largely in an almost impenetrable darkness. But as will be shown, a number of contemporary sources of various kinds can be compared to later evidence to shed some light on the matter.

The Germanic word *þing* itself shows that by the Viking Period, the *thing*-institution had already existed for many centuries. This word denotes a parliamentary assembly in all of the Germanic languages, which is evidence that the institution goes back to the beginning of the first millennium AD. Why this word came to denote these meetings is not clear, but probably has to do with the other meanings the word seems to have had, namely 'time' and 'meeting' (Bjorvand and Lindeman 2000:940). These meanings show that two of the fundamental characteristics of the institution, 'meeting at fixed time', were features from the beginning. In his *Germania* (Lund 1988:Chs. 11–13) of AD 98, Tacitus described a Germanic system, both of law and for the resolution of conflicts, which has much in common with the *thing*-systems of a thousand years later, including fixed meeting times and agreements marked by the thingmen's striking their weapons together. Nonetheless the institution likely underwent vast changes during this long period (cf. below).

In relation to a somewhat later period, A. W. Brøgger (1921:35–6) concluded that the compensation provisions and terminology known from the law-codes and sagas of the 12th and 13th centuries were based upon Roman weight-units. He could identify these units in weights from graves and in gold rings from hoards of the Migration Period. For this reason, he argued that the compensation system had its origin in that period, and that there was a legal system as early as the 5th or 6th century.

It has to be admitted, concerning much of the early scholarship on legal concepts and the *thing*-system in the Viking Period and before, that it was based too much upon an evolutionary perspective and on common assumptions, frequently out-of-date, concerning the nature of society in this period (Iversen 1997:37–9). For example, it has been customary to attribute the kin-group with much too prominent a role in the legal system (e.g. Andersen 1977:247–8). Similarly the "farmers", a term that occurs frequently both in the law-codes and in sagas, have been presented as a more or less uniform group which could be found at the *things* of the late Viking Age as the opposition to the power of the king. As Adolfsen (2000) points out, this image hides the fact that there was an aristocracy which used the *thing* to further its own interests, partly by holding the leadership of the other farmers, and partly by being the royal representatives (the *lendmenn* or sheriffs). Helle (2001:212) argues that when the Gulathing Law was composed, the independence of the old aristocracy had been suppressed: they had become the tame spokesmen of the king. But both before and during the earliest era of the kingdom-state, the *thing* was the forum in which the great men and chieftains flourished (Riisøy 2005:74). Amongst their methods to win their cases was the use or the threat of violence (Adolfsen 2000:101–2).

Thing sites from the Viking Age, and perhaps from earlier too, can be identified through placenames that can be dated on linguistic grounds with some degree of certainty (Andersen 1977:249). In the case of Østfold, Stylegar and Norseng (2003:506) infer that a uniform system of local assemblies, the *herredsting*, was introduced perhaps as early as the 9th century, and at the latest by the end of the 10th.

Also, before the establishment of the four principal law-regions, there must have been a legal system and legal regions (Brink 2002a:91–2). There were probably no laws as we would understand them; rather, there was legal custom. Specific cases were decided as the concrete application of this custom, not on the basis of precisely defined legal rules. This is probably the reason why several clauses in the regional law-codes have a casuistic character. In a legal tradition of this nature, the juridical frame of mind would have been formed by the actual decisions of the *thing*-moot, and the legal tradition would thus derive a regional character linked to each of the *thing*-areas. This is the sense in which the concept of *law* can be used to describe the legal system both before and during the Viking Period.

Concerning the *thing*-system in the Viking Age, it is reasonable to assume that the 12th- and 13th-century system below the principal legal assemblies, with its *things* for several *fylki*, divisions of the *fylki* and local rural districts, had its roots in the Viking Period if not earlier. Brink (2002a:98) has interpreted a runic inscription on the Forsa Ring (an iron ring preserved as a door ring in Forsa Church, Sweden) to indicate that there was a law for Hälsingland in Sweden in the 9th century. Law-regions of a similar size, in Viken more or less corresponding to a *fylki,* were probably also in existence in other parts of Scandinavia at that time.

There are very few surviving sources that reveal the legal concepts which pertained during the Viking Age; furthermore, the most serious problem in trying to use 12th- and 13th-century sources to shed light upon the previous period is that the king, and sometimes also the bishop, had a crucial role in the shaping of the law-codes which have survived. The growth of the national kingdom from the 10th century onwards, and the subsequent Conversion and introduction of a literary culture, were all major, fundamental influences in the formulation of the laws and the legal system. It has proved extremely difficult to break through this barrier caused by a paucity of sources, and therefore modern scholarship has largely – with a few exceptions (Iversen 1997; Brink 2002a) – limited itself to proposing general observations about Viking-period law.

Brink (2002a:93–9) takes the relatively small quantity of contemporary sources on Viking-period juridical ideas and legal systems on their own; specifically, these consist of two 9th-century runic inscriptions and three 10th-century treaties between Scandinavians and Greeks. These sources have a number of features that can be matched with features in the laws that were written in the 13th and 14th centuries. His research indicates that some topics in these earlier laws, such as the right of a murderer to sanctuary at specified places and his obligation to declare his crime publicly, represent a tradition that goes back to at least the early Viking Period. Concerning the size of the law-regions and the structure of the *thing* sites, Brink draws a number of conclusions (2002a; cf. below).

As Iversen declares (1997:39), it is only "subtle, specific analyses of the legal clauses that can reveal their meaning" ("nitide enkeltundersøkelser av lovbestemmelser som kan avklare deres mening"), i.e. by examining both the context of the clauses in the law itself and their social context. He himself (1997) has successfully undertaken such an analysis of *thralldom* (slavery) in Early Medieval Norway. He is able to trace some points all the way back to the Migration Period.

Comparable analyses of other topics in the laws, and of the *thing*-system, are badly needed. It would be both relevant and rewarding to analyse the laws and *thing*-systems of eastern Norway in relation to those of Denmark and western Sweden. As several scholars have noted, the division into *herred*-districts, which is documented in the Viken area as early as the 11th century through the Christian law of the Borgarthing, was probably established while this area was under the rule of the Kings of the Danes (Sogner 1961; Stylegar and Norseng 2003:482–7). Danish overlordship in Viken is first in evidence in the early 9th century, and rule over Viken and the Opplands was contested between the Danish and Norwegian kings from the 10th century down to c. 1200 (Skre, this vol. Chs. 18:412, 20:463–9). As already noted, Snorri wrote that the Danish King, Knut the Great, was hailed at the Borgarthing in 1028. Nineteen years later the Norwegian King, Harald Hard-Rule, was likewise ceremonially recognized at the same *thing* (Seip 1957:149).

17.2 *Thing* site and church site

Amongst the most striking names of *thing* sites in Scandinavia is Þjóðalyng. This name, which cannot post-date the Viking Period, reveals that a *thing* site existed there. It is paralleled by the names of other *thing* sites in Scandinavia (Brink, this vol. Ch. 4:63). The topography provided a site that was well suited to the purposes of a *thing* site. This assembly place probably went out of use before the High Middle Ages, for it is never referred to as a *thing* site in records from this period (Storm 1901:227). After the middle of the 14th century the number of surviving deeds is so large that we can assume that had there been a *thing* at Þjóðalyng the documents would have revealed it. In 1557, a *thing* was held there for the whole of Brunla County (southern Vestfold) (DN I:820), but this is so late and unique an event that we cannot suppose that it had any connexion with the use of the site for *thing*-moots more than four centuries earlier.

The name Þjóðalyng originally referred to the dry sand and gravel ridge on which the present church was built some time in the early or mid-12th century (Figs. 17.2 and 17.4: on the dating of the church, see Brendalsmo and Sørensen 1995:92). The first element in the place-name, Þjóð, has the basic sense of "troop" or "band", "people" or even something like "tribe/ nation" ("Flok, Skare", "Mennesker", "Folkeslag, Folkeferd, Nation") (Fritzner 1886–1896:3:1024–5). The second element in the place-name reveals what sort of vegetation was found there, i.e. ling/heather. The massive wash-through of the sandy ground hinders the formation of a soil cover, and when such areas are grazed, they become overgrown with heather. Such heath-vegetation is found in several parts of the coastal area of Vestfold in similar geological circumstances (pers. comm. Rolf Sørensen).

Nowadays, the morainic ridge itself is not cultivated, but the farmers who work the adjoining lands report that the soil there is extremely poor. So, indeed, it was in the Middle Ages also. In a letter that Bishop Hallvard sent on 18 August 1367 one reads (DN I:396):

Af þui at Þiodalynghs kirkiæ aa Væstfold er j store vmæghd ok fatøkt. sua at hon orkar æighi med sinum godze presbo-let þær vpbyggia ædr aftr husa. sæm vforsyniu firir ældz vada vp gæk vttan prestæns skuld. ædr glømsku. sua ok sakar þærs at fyrnæmft presboll var litit ok sua sændit at þær vox sialdan korn aa eftir þui sæm oss teet er. hafuum ver. med rade ok samðykt vars capituli. þæssa skipan aa gort at hedan j fra æuælægha skall Saxa vik ok litla Vik vera presboll till fyrnæmfdrar Þiodalynghs kirkiu. sua at fyr-næmfdar iardar skulu vera j allu þui frialse sæm annur presboll her i varo biskupsdøme ero.

Because the *Þiodalynghs* church in *Væstfold* is in great want and poverty, so that with its endowment it is not able to build up the manse there or to reconstruct the necessary buildings that were unexpectedly destroyed by fire through no fault or neglect of the priest's, and also because the aforementioned priest's farmstead was small and so sandy that rarely would any corn grow there, according to what we have been told, we have, with the counsel and consent of our chapter, determined that from henceforward and for ever *Saxa vik* and *litla Vik* will be the farmstead of the priest for the aforesaid *Þiodalynghs* church, so that these lands shall have the complete freedom from obligations that the other priests' lands in this diocese have.

If the poor sandy plain was a misfortune for the priest, it was nevertheless an ideal place for use as a *thing* site. The well-drained ground was not turned into a mess by the footsteps of the thingmen, even in rainy weather. The vegetation, heather, indicates that this was an open area that was well suited for a place of assembly. The small moraine ridge is quite flat on top, and falls away relatively steeply on all sides. It was probably this flatter top, which measures 150–200 m in diameter, that was the *thing* place itself (Figs. 17.2 and 17.4).

The priest's farmstead is bounded by Huseby to the west and Østby to the north, east and south. The extended line of the boundary shows that this property was carved out of Østby (Fig. 17.2), but when might that have taken place? The dating of the creation of priests' farmsteads in Norway is relatively uncertain, although it is usually assumed that in the earliest years of the Church, the priest was a member of the household of the founder of the church (Sandvik 1965:57; Skre 1995). The establishment of a separate holding for the priest may have been a feature of the political strategy of the Church from the end of the 12th century onwards, aimed at achieving greater economic independence (Sandvik 1965:59). The priest at *Pjóðalyng* had in any event his own land-holding at the beginning of the 1360s. It is likely that

this was taken out of Østby in the 13th or early 14th century. The priest's holding was manifestly created around a church that was already there.

In the first two centuries of Christianity in Norway, churches were usually built at major, central farmsteads, either amongst or in the immediate vicinity of the farm buildings. The place of construction reflected who the founder of the church was, i.e. the man whose farm it was built on (Skre 1988, 1998b: 93–127; Brink, this vol. Ch. 4:63). But, as has been shown, the priest's farmstead at *Pjóðalyng* was created later than the church itself, and no other farmstead is known there. As has been noted, this land is not at all well suited to farming, and no archaeological, place-name or documentary evidence indicates that there had been any farmstead in the vicinity.

It may therefore be inferred that the church of *Pjóðalyng* was linked to the *thing* site rather than to any particular farm. As was customary, the church took its name from its situation. When the parish-system was introduced at the end of the 12th century, the parish took its name from the church. This is the reason why, from the Late Middle Ages until today, *Pjóðalyng*, now Tjølling, is the name of this parish. This transfer of name was quite normal for medieval parishes in Norway. Since the majority of churches were associated with a particular farm, most parishes have a name that was originally a farm-name. Since the *Pjóðalyng* church, and subsequently the parish, bore the name of the assembly place and not a farm, the assembly probably organized the building of the first church there.

The connexion between the *thing* site *Pjóðalyng* and the church means that the church and its history can be used to shed light on the history of the assembly place, and this is what will be investigated in the following. The two key questions to answer in this section are the same ones enunciated at the very beginning of this chapter, i.e. whether the history of the church can help to date the *thing* site and to indicate the size of the area it served as an assembly place.

The large basilica at *Pjóðalyng*

The church site at *Pjóðalyng* may well be older than the existing church. As excavations at a number of medieval church sites have shown, a high proportion of 12th- and 13th-century churches were constructed on sites which already had Christian burials, and in many cases a church too (Skre 1995). We can therefore reckon with the possibility that the church site at *Pjóðalyng* had been consecrated at the beginning of the Christian period in Norway, which goes back here at least to the 11th century, probably even to the second half of the 10th. The sharp fall in the number of pagan burials in Vestfold and other coastal areas in southeastern Norway after around AD 950 may mean that a shift to Christian ritual practice took place that early (Skre 1998a; Stylegar, this vol. Ch. 5:81–2).

Figure 17.2 *The* thing *site at Þjóðalyng and its immediate surroundings. The* thing *site itself is probably the flat area on the crest of the morainic ridge, about 150–200 m in diameter. At the end of this plateau lies the church (cf. Fig. 17.4). The farm boundaries show that the priest's farmstead forms an enclave within the farm of Østby, out of which it was presumably created. Systematic drainage during the last centuries has reduced the water level of the lake north of the* thing *site substantially from the reconstructed level on this map. Contour interval 1 meter. Map, Anne Engesveen and Julie K. Øhre Askjem.*

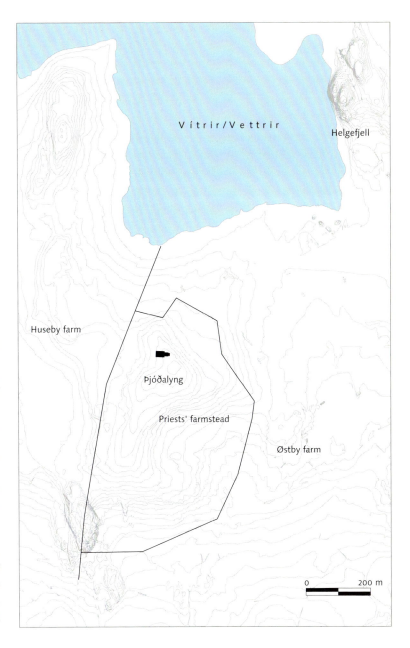

When, in the first half of the 12th century, a stone church was built at *Þjóðalyng*, it was decided to build it as a Romanesque basilica, a type of structure that was used in relatively few cases; there are eleven in Norway, of which eight are in eastern Norway. Of these eleven, six are in towns and five of those are cathedrals (in the towns of Nidaros [Trondheim], Bergen, Stavanger, Hamar and Oslo), and the sixth is one of the royal town churches (Lavrans' church in Tønsberg). Besides the church at *Þjóðalyng* , the other five in rural areas are in Aker near Oslo, Hadeland (Nicolay's Church), Hof at Toten, and Ringsaker in Hedemark (Tab. 17.1). *Þjóðalyng* church was extensively rebuilt in the 1760s after a fire and other damage, and now the church no longer has the basilican form. The ground plan and a number of features of the building are, however, known from documentary evidence from the rebuilding, and the investigations by the architect Carl Berner in 1901 (Elster and Storsletten 1989; Brendalsmo 2003).

Thus all of the Norwegian cathedrals were basilican, and this type of building was also used first and foremost for Episcopal churches in Sweden and Denmark. There are even fewer surviving Romanesque basilicas outside of towns and monasteries in those countries: just one in Sweden (Hulterstad, Öland) and two in Denmark (Skarpsalling and Tamdrup in Jutland) (Wienberg 2001:284, fig. 10). Generally, the basilican form was used for churches that were constructed at important sites (Wienberg 2001:279).

The principal advantage of the basilican form is that the two long rows of pillars in the nave allow for it to be wider, i.e. the width would otherwise be limited by the carrying capacity of the roof-timber. The five 'country basilicas' in Norway are consequently amongst the largest churches outside of towns. Very few other Romanesque churches in Norway exceed 250 sq m in the total area of the nave and the choir, and most are considerably smaller. The largest of the basilicas, Aker near Oslo, measures 434 sq m. The second, *Þjóðalyng* church in Viken, is 394 sq m. The three basilicas in the Opplands are considerably smaller (Tab. 17.1).

Compared to the other Romanesque stone churches in Vestfold (Tab. 17.2; Fig. 17.3), *Þjóðalyng* church is by far the largest outside of Tønsberg. No church in the region measures more that 240 sq m, which is just 60% of the size of *Þjóðalyng* church. What was the reason for building such a large and expensive church at *Þjóðalyng* ?

It is conceivable that the explanation for such a large church being built at *Þjóðalyng* lies in the size of the area from which its congregation would come. This sort of connexion has been demonstrated in the case of Danish Romanesque village churches (Nyborg 1986), and in several Swedish studies (Wienberg 2001:274). A large parochial territory provides a good

Region, law-region, diocese	Church	Nave+Choir = Total area, sq m
Viken, Borgarthing, Oslo		
	Aker	384+50 = 434
	Þjóðalyng	306+88 = 394
Opplands, Eidsivathing, Hamar		
	Ringsaker	236+40 = 276
	Hof	211+47 = 258
	Nicolay	206+42 = 248

Table 17.1 *The areas of the five basilicas of eastern Norway which are not in towns – the so-called 'country basilicas' – show that the two which were constructed in Viken are significantly larger than the three in the Opplands. This difference between the larger and the smaller basilicas also respects the boundaries between the dioceses of Oslo and Hamar, and those between the law-regions of the Borgarthing and Eidsivathing. Because the churches at Þjóðalyng, Ringsaker and Hof were reconstructed, the figures for them do not accurately reflect their original sizes.*

Church	Size, sq m	Population 1801	Land-tax 1905
Þjóðalyng	394	1427	1440
Borre	240	1290	860
Ramnes	237	1228	1190
Sem	204	2632	1385
Hedrum	203	1368	1240

Table 17.2 *Comparison of the size of the church, the parish population figures in 1801 (http://digitalarkivet.uib.no/) and land-tax in 1905 (Matrikkelen 1905) for five of the largest Romanesque stone churches in Vestfold. The population census from 1801 at least gives an impression of sorts concerning the demography in the Middle Ages. A basis for comparing the economic resources of the parishes is the land-tax, as this was based upon a fiscal assessment of the agricultural potential of the parish.*

income and requires a more capacious church to provide sufficient space. On the whole, it was the original parochial territories that subsequently became the parishes, and in the following little investigation the sizes of the later parishes will be compared. The figures from the 19th century cannot be reckoned as a precise reflection of the situation 700 years previously. However the consistency of the agrarian settlement and the parish boundaries justifies the comparison, although the figures have to be treated with caution.

Table 17.2, in which *Þjóðalyng* parish is compared with other parishes in Vestfold with large Romanesque stone churches, implies that population size and economic resources of the parish do not explain why *Þjóðalyng* church is so much larger than the others. Even though in terms of both population level and agricultural potential *Þjóðalyng* is the greatest (the high population figure for Sem must be due to its proximity to Tønsberg), the differences are not of a degree that can explain the great discrepancy in the size of *Þjóðalyng* church.

Þjóðalyng church – a *minster*

As Wienberg (2001:285–7) points out, the reason for the construction of large churches in the High and Late Middle Ages is known, i.e. it was manifestly economic. The Church simply had the wealth to build a large church building. It is reasonable to believe that the large churches in the rest of Scandinavia from before 1200 had a similar background. The explana-

tion for the building of the large and expensive church at *Þjóðalyng* must therefore be looked for in the church's material resources from the beginning of the 12th century.

Before the parish-system was established and the tithe was introduced, a church's main income came from the various services performed by its priest or priests, e.g. marriages, funerals, baptisms etc. Its income was therefore dependent on the number of people it served. Normally, a church was used by the population of the immediate locality. But a few churches were sought by people from larger outlying areas, and these churches consequently enjoyed a considerably higher income than others. This system could be found over a large part of Europe in this period and earlier. In England, these central or mother churches were known as *minsters;* in other places they were known as *baptismal churches* etc. (Blair 1988). These most central churches within each diocese had several priests, who took responsibility for the pastoral duties in a large parochial territory, within which there were also several smaller churches, mostly private and local chapels (Skre 1998a, 1998b).

The rights to income were retained by many of these churches when the earlier arrangements for funding were superseded by the tithe-system in the first half of the 12th century. In some places the rights to income were still retained after the establishment of the parishes. In several places, Late-medieval sources reveal that some churches kept the right to

Figure 17.3 *The surviving or recorded Medieval churches of Vestfold have been plotted on this map. The black contour shows buildings or parts of buildings that are from the Romanesque period, while the hatched contour shows those from the Gothic period. The crosses mark churches with an unknown ground plan; the black crosses indicate stone and the white crosses timber churches. The churches in the lower right margin were in the only town in Vestfold, Tønsberg when the churches were built. With its 33 examples, Vestfold has the greatest concentration of stone churches in Norway. The only preserved stave church in the* fylki, *Høyjord, is also plotted. There are 45 Medieval church sites in Vestfold. Map, Jan Brendalsmo.*

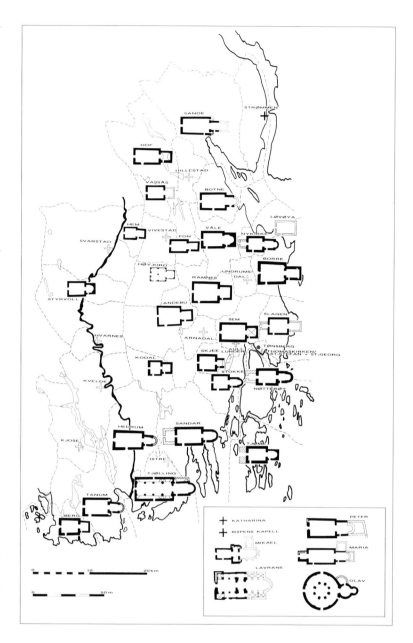

the tithe of several neighbouring parishes. This was the case, for instances, of the four main churches in Romerike in the Opplands, which held such privileges as late as the 1390s (Skre 1998b:78–89). Similar tithe-privileges for the main churches in Ringerike and Hadeland are recorded in a charter of 1560 (DN II:1163), and in the case of several of the *fylki*-churches in Trøndelag at the beginning of the 15th century (Skre 1998b:73). In several places there is strong evidence for the existence of similar arrangements, e.g. at Stange church in Hedmark (Skre 1995).

There seems to be some connexion between churches with rights to income of this kind and those churches that the laws call *fylki*-churches (*fylkiskirkja:* the Frostathing Law, the Gulathing Law, the Borgarthing Law) or main churches (*höfuðkirkja:* the Eidsivathing Law). A very high proportion of these churches were located at royal farmsteads (Sandnes 1969; Skre 1998b:93–104). In light of the king's central role in the process of Conversion, these churches were likely amongst the first to have been built. This again may be a reason why they had special income rights and were used by parishioners from a large area (Skre 1998b:78–89).

Their high incomes were probably an essential factor behind the large size of the main/*fylki*-churches in Romerike, Ringerike and Hadeland. One of these, Nicolay's Church at Gran, Hadeland, is basilican. In the case of several of the remaining basilicas, there are various reasons for arguing that they were

main/*fylki*-churches (Christie 1969:115; Müller 1971:172). Could this be an explanation for *Þjóðalyng* church's size too?

When one looks at the composition of *Þjóðalyng* church's landed property, as it is recorded in Bishop Eystein's land-book of the 1390s (RB:51–4), one notes that it has characteristics typical of churches that enjoyed the same extensive tithe-income privileges – the priest had extensive property and the church building itself relatively little (Skre 1998b:88). E-manuelsson (2005:320–1) has picked out those elements of the landed property that were acquired in the course of the 14th century, and thus has reconstructed the churches' lands c. 1300 throughout the diocese. At that date, the properties of the priest and the church in *Þjóðalyng* were very extensive, i.e. nearly 50% greater than those of any other priest and church in Vestfold. Regarding the ratio between the priest's and the church building's property at *Þjóða-*

lyng, the land-book reveals that it was all, in fact, the priest's. All of the property attached to the building (RB:53–4) was acquired during the 14th century. This means that the church as a building had no property at all in the 13th century or before, and that all of its income came from tithes. It is self-evident that not only the construction but also the maintenance and functioning of such a large church required considerable income, presumably more than would have come in as tithes from *Þjóðalyng* parish alone. Consequently, it may be inferred that *Þjóðalyng* church at the time it was built, that is the first half of the 12th century, had income from a district beyond its own parish, i.e. *Þjóðalyng* church had the type of tithe rights held by English *minsters* and southern European baptismal churches.

Þjóðalyng church – a *fylkiskirkja?*

Are there any traces of these rights to income in the surviving documentary sources? *Þjóðalyng* church is one of the churches where the value of the annual tithe around the year 1400 is given in RB; it was then equivalent to 8 Marks (RB:569; Emanuelsson 2005: 320). Compared to the relation between tithe value and parish size for other churches in Vestfold, this value fits the area of *Þjóðalyng* parish well. The tithe's value is lower in parishes with a lower population size than *Þjóðalyng*, and fairly equal in parishes of similar population size. At this time, therefore, *Þjóðalyng* church, unlike the *minsters* in Romerike, Ringerike and Hadeland, had no tithe income from any parishes other than its own, with the exception of the small subsidiary parish of Istre (DN II:139 and 606). Obviously, therefore, some time before 1400 the bishop had ensured that the churches in the deanery of Vestfold had their tithe incomes regularized; i.e. that they came to receive tithe only from their own parish. For churches which formerly had more extensive rights to tithe, this will have meant a considerable reduction in income. This reduction may be the reason why the church building at *Þjóðalyng*, possibly at the bishop's instigation, received considerable endowments of landed property in the 14th century. Therefore, the regularization of the Vestfold churches' rights to income probably took place around 1300 at the latest.

So *Þjóðalyng* church was a *minster*, but it was not a *fylki*-church. The *fylki*-churches of Vestfold were listed in the Christian laws of the Borgarthing (B I:8). They are Sem church, c. 30 km northeast of *Þjóðalyng* church, and Hedrum church, which is 7 km north (Fig. 17.3). The former was the *fylki*-church of northern Vestfold and the latter of southern Vestfold. What are referred to as *fylki*-churches in the Borgarthing Law are therefore really half *fylki*-churches; such churches are also found in Trøndelag (Sandnes 1969). The point concerning the terminology is, as will be discussed later, *not* that these were churches for the

populations of their respective parts of the *fylki*, but rather that the *fylki*-men, who represented the *fylki* at the Borgarthing, were responsible for maintaining these churches. As is shown in Table 17.2 and Figure 17.3, the Romanesque churches at Hedrum and Sem were amongst the largest in the *fylki*, even though they were much smaller than *Þjóðalyng* church.

One may draw the conclusion that not all churches that had established special rights to income were given the status of a *fylki*-church. The arrangement by which a system of *fylki*-churches, district *(herreds-)* churches, and private *(høgendes-)* churches was established, to use the terminology of the Eidsivathing Law, can be understood as an attempt to share the responsibility for the maintenance of the heterogeneous mass of churches that were in existence before the parish-system was introduced. Some of these churches were built by private individuals, others by associations of various kinds; some had several priests who also served other churches in the area that did not have their own priest; some churches were maintained by the patron who had built them or by his heirs, while others had income from tithes and from the provision of pastoral services over a greater or lesser territory (Skre 1995, 1998a, 1998b:64– 127).

The bishop was concerned that no churches should fall into disuse and decay, and with the help of the king he secured arrangements at the *thing*-moots for their maintenance. The laws stated who was responsible for maintaining which churches, but the terminology has to be regarded as fairly elastic. It most certainly does not reflect a well-ordered, hierarchical, and geographically comprehensive body of churches, as some scholars have imagined (e.g. Smedberg 1973). In the case of the selection of the *fylki*-churches, the king and the bishop may indeed have chosen churches that lay on royal farmsteads. The king thus escaped the responsibility of maintenance himself, while from the bishop's point of view it must have been advantageous for the central churches to be located at farmsteads belonging to the church's most powerful supporters. The two *fylki*-churches of Vestfold at Sem and Hedrum both have richly ornamented portals (Lidén 1981:67), which may indicate that these churches were particularly closely associated with aristocratic circles, possibly the king's own men. Sem is mentioned by Snorri as a royal farmstead as early as the reign of Harald Fairhair *(Haralds saga ins hárfagra*, Ch. 36). The earliest information on the ownership of the farmstead of Hedrum, where the church was located, is that it was, in its entirety, the priest's holding (RB:49). The transference of this large farmstead to the Church – the largest priest's holding in all of Vestfold, in fact (Emanuelsson 2005:320–1) – could only have been effected by a wealthy landowner, in this case, probably the king (cf. Krohn-Holm 1982:162).

It is reasonable to expect, therefore, that in the

Borgarthing law-region there would be more churches with special income rights than those that are listed as *fylki*-churches. This was certainly the case in the Eidsivathing law-region. That law does not identify the main churches by name, but it is evident from the code that there was a main church in each *priðjung* ("third" or "riding"), which was a secular division. At the same time, a closer analysis of the tithes due to the churches in Romerike shows that it was not only the three main churches in the three *priðjungs* of Sørum, Nes and Ullinshov that enjoyed the tithes from a large territory but also Eid church, situated at the assembly site of the Eidsivathing in the far north of Romerike (Skre 1998b:78–89). The reason for its extended rights to income must be that this was a *thing*-site church, whose primary connexion was with the assembly place rather than with a farmstead. Therefore, there was no single farmer on whom the burden of maintaining the *thing*-site church could be placed. The responsibility of maintaining the *thing*-site church was probably at an early stage shared by the thingmen living in the church's vicinity, as it probably was for the *fylki*-churches. When the tithe was introduced in the early 12th century, the responsibility for maintaining both these types of churches was probably converted into a right for each church to receive tithe from its surrounding area, although this area might have had a number of churches which at a later stage became parish churches. As long as the *thing*-site church or the *fylki*-church retained these rights, the surrounding parish churches would receive only a reduced tithe from their own parish, if any at all.

Þjóðalyng church – a *thing*-site church

Could, then, the church at *Þjóðalyng* be a *thing*-site church, like the church at Eid, the *thing* site of the Eidsivathing law-region? Could such a status explain why the church at *Þjóðalyng* held extensive rights to income in the early 12th century, probably even earlier? *Thing*-site churches were to be found not only at Eid but in other parts of Norway as well, for instance at the assembly place of the Frostathing at Logtu in Trøndelag (Christiansen 1989:104–7; Hagland and Sandnes 1994:xxvi). There was probably a church at the assembly place of the Gulathing (Helle 2001:56). In the town of Sarpsborg, the meeting place of the Borgarthing, there were several churches that no longer exist. Churches were also found at *thing* sites below the highest level, as at Gildesvollen in Ringebu in Gudbrandsdal (Skre 1983), and several other places in Scandinavia (Brink, this vol. Ch. 4:63; Lidén 1974: 211–12).

Thing-site churches such as Eid are, therefore, amongst those that drew income from more than their own parishes alone, and such privileges must be a key factor in explaining why a large and expensive basilica was raised at *Þjóðalyng* in the 12th century.

The laws that survive show that *thing*-site church-es could have particular functions in the *thing*-system. Clauses in the Frostathing Law reveal that the priest at Logtu was charged with the care of the law-book, and that he should ring the church bell when he was about to go to the assembly place with that book. These clauses date to the period 1161–1168. Somewhat later, both the law-book and the seal of the *thing* were kept in the church (Hagland and Sandnes 1994:xxvi). At both the Eidsivathing and the Gulathing, the priests of the diocese were required to meet in the presence of the bishop (E:10; G:3). In the Eidsivathing Law, the purpose of this meeting is described in more detail: the bishop was to check that the priests had the right books and that they could performe the duties expected of them (Lidén 1974).

Clauses requiring the bishop and priests to meet at the *thing* are not found in the Borgarthing Law. There are several provisions, however, that presuppose that the bishop was present. At the time at which the basilica was constructed at *Þjóðalyng*, there was just one diocese, Oslo, in eastern Norway. The see of Hamar was established in 1152/53. Before this time, the bishop who met with his priests and sang mass for the thingmen at Eid was, therefore, the same bishop who met with the thingmen in the southern half of his diocese, in the Borgarthing law-region. It is likely that the practice was the same there, and perhaps also at the *thing*-moots for each *fylki*, even though this is not recorded in the extant versions of the law. The presence of a large number of priests could explain the unusually large choir in *Þjóðalyng* church, which is fully 88 sq m, much greater than the choir in the largest basilica, Gamle Aker (Tab. 17.1). The bishop was also required to hold a mass for the thingmen (E:10), which could explain the large nave in *Þjóðalyng* church. The church at Eid also has a larger choir and nave than usual. In this unique cruciform Romanesque church the nave measures 156 sq m, the side aisles 53 sq m, and the choir 51 sq m: a total of 260 sq m – one of the largest churches in this area. Lidén (1974) connects the size and the unusual form to its function as a *thing*-site church.

This conclusion would have been better founded if it were possible to compare the church buildings at *Þjóðalyng* and Eid with churches at other major *thing* sites. But unfortunately, the grounds for such comparison are weak. The church at Logtu is not preserved in its earlier medieval form as it was demolished and rebuilt in the Late Middle Ages (Lidén 1974:211; Ekroll 1997:283–4). The churches that were built at the other two law-regions' assembly places have also been demolished: the size of the church that was at the meeting site of the Gulathing is not known (Helle 2001:56); the Borgarthing probably met at one of the churches in the town of Sarpsborg, where nearly all of the medieval town area has been washed away by the River Glomma.

Still, there is good reason to conclude that the

unusual size of the *Þjóðalyng* church was probably due to it being a *thing*-site church. It must have been this status, as well as the importance of the *Þjóðalyng thing* site, that gave the church the high income that made the building of such an extravagant church possible. The status as *thing*-site church gave the *Þjóðalyng* church the same type of rights to income as the *fylki*-churches, comparable to the English *minsters.* The status as *thing*-site church both supplied the economy for building such a large church and created the need for it. The unusual size of the choir and nave was probably to accommodate the large crowds that came to the assemblies; the priests came to meet their bishop and the thingmen came for the *thing*-moot.

Þjóðalyng in the Viking Age

What does all this say about the *thing* site of *Þjóðalyng*, our principal point of interest? As noted above, the connexion between the *thing* site and the church confirms that the *thing* site was in use when the first church at *Þjóðalyng* was constructed. Since we do not know whether the basilica was the first church here, the building of the first church at *Þjóðalyng* cannot be dated any more closely than to some time in the period 950–1150. Even if a church had been built here early in this period, the *thing* site was probably functioning for much of this period, so that the church remained in a position to build up the rights to income that would have been essential for the raising of such a large building.

Probably the *thing* site was still in service when the basilica was built. As has been noted, its functioning as a *thing*-site church could explain the church's large choir and nave, The conclusion is that the *thing* site at *Þjóðalyng* remained in use at least into the 11th century, and probably into the 12th. After the *thing* site ceased to be used, the administration of this church and its income was probably transferred to local church stewards appointed by the bishop. This became the usual arrangement from the late 12th century onwards.

That the first church at *Þjóðalyng* was built at the *thing* site and not at the royal administrative farmstead of Huseby immediately adjacent (see Brink, this vol. Ch. 4:63; Skre, this vol. Ch. 11) may indicate that the king did not participate in the enterprise. It is possible that the church was founded before Huseby became a royal manor. This independence from the king may be the reason why this church did not become a *fylki*-church.

How large was the area for which *Þjóðalyng* was the *thing* site? In his article on *thing* sites, Fritzner (1883:31) regarded *Þjóðalyng* as the site of a rural district moot, i.e. the local assembly. Storm (1901:227) was of a different view, as he emphasized a fine shade of meaning in the lexical element *þjóð*-. In certain contexts, he writes, it may mean:

... noget udmærket og fremtredende. f. Ex. *Þjoðá* Hovedelv, *Þjoðhlið* Hovedport, *Þjoðleið* Hovedvei, *Þjoðráð* ypperlig Raad, *Þjoðvegr* Hovedvei o.s.v. Jeg anser dette for rigtigere, og at altså *Þjoðalyng* nærmest betyder "Lyngen, hvor Hovedtinget holdes", og antager, at dette *Ting* har været Hovedting ikke alene for Herredet, men også for de omliggende Herreder, vistnok for hele Vestfold i den Tid, dette havde egne Konger.

… something special and pre-eminent. E.g. *Þjóðá:* major River, *Þjóðhlið:* major Gateway, *Þjóðleið:* major Road, *Þjóðráð:* first-class Counsel, *Þjóðvegr:* major Road, etc. I regard it as more correct that *Þjóðalyng* more precisely means "the Heath at which the main *Thing*-moot is held", and infer that this *Thing* was the principal Assembly not only for the District but also for the surrounding Districts, likely enough for the whole of Vestfold at the Time at which it had its own Kings.

This is not a particularly convincing line of argument. In the contexts Storm cites, *þjóð* clearly has a derived sense. There is nothing about the name *Þjóðalyng* that suggests that the first element has such a derived sense, and Fritzner's interpretation of the first element of the name as simply "of the folk" is the more plausible (cf. Rygh 1897–1936:VI:288–9; Brink, this vol. Ch. 4:63).

There is, however, the detail of the written forms of the names, which Storm did not attach any importance to, but which is of interest in this context. As Rygh (1897–1936:VI:288) pointed out, the written forms reveal that in the original forms of the names the first element might have been the genitive plural, not the genitive singular as Fritzner assumed. To get the singular form, Fritzner had to insert an *r*, so that the postulated original form of the name became **Þjóðarlyng.* But all of the written forms, from the earliest in 1367 and later in great quantity down to the end of the Middle Ages have no *r* here. It is widely attested that sounds in place-names can completely disappear in constellations like this, but in this case it remains only a hypothesis, and the name is perfectly well formed and meaningful without this emendation. If the plural form were the original one, the meaning of the name would be "the heath of the *peoples*" (Brink, this vol. Ch. 4:63), which would indicate that people from various areas, possibly from more than one *fylki,* had assembled at the *thing* here.

If we are to trust the saga sources referred to above, the Borgarthing was founded and its laws, which covered the whole of Viken, were formulated under Olaf the Saint in the 1020s. As already noted, a fragment of the Borgarthing Law shows that there were subsequently *things* at the *fylki* level. As Helle noted for the Gulathing law-region (p. 386), these *fylki thing* seem to have been a relic from the earlier *thing* system; they hardly met after the creation of the four large law-regions. Prior to this development, the *thing* for Vestfold might well have had an assembly place at *Þjóðalyng*. From the early 12th century, it appears that the main *thing* site for Vestfold was Haugar near Tønsberg. After that town was founded, probably at the end of the 11th century, it was a principal buttress of the royal power. It was at the Haugarthing that Harald Gille was hailed as king in 1130, as were several later kings.

Consequently, the Viking-age *thing* site for Vestfold could well have been at Skiringssal (Andersen 1977:251). The establishment of both the Haugarthing and the Borgarthing might have been stages in the same strategy that the kings of this era appear to have followed, i.e. establishing new centers of power, both towns and assembly places, probably with a view to weakening the old aristocracy. In Vestfold, as Johnsen (1939:24) and Andersen (1977:251) have suggested, the central functions of Skiringssal might have been transferred to royal Tønsberg, where the fortified cliff *Tunsberget*, the *thing* site at Haugar, and the royal homestead of Sem with its *fylki*-church, surrounded the town.

So, even before the establishment of the Borgarthing, there might have been a *fylki thing* in Vestfold. Maybe also this site was the assembly place for a *thing* serving a larger region, possibly the whole of Viken. This, however, is extremely uncertain; and the uncertainty is even greater as we move back in time to the 9th and 8th centuries. As has been shown, certain facts suggest that the *thing* site at *Þjóðalyng* was also used, at an early date, by the population of a larger region; but this is difficult to substantiate. It is, however, as will be shown in the following section, quite plausible that the *thing* site was in use at this early date, and even before then.

17.3 The assembly place by the sacred lake

How far back does the use of the *thing* site at *Þjóða-lyng* go? Storm (1901:227) traced the name itself back into the Early Iron Age, several centuries before the Viking Period:

"*Þjóðalyng*" er ialdfald et meget gammelt Ord, ældre end det levende oldnorske Sprog, og i en Sammensætnings-form, som peger langt tilbage i Fortiden.

"*Þjóðalyng*" is in any Event a very old Word, earlier than the living Old Norse Language, and is in a compound Form that points far back into Prehistory.

Rygh too (1897–1936:VI:289) was of the opinion that the name had to be "…extremely old" ("... meget gammelt"), by which one can infer a dating which matches Storm's. As Brink (this vol. Ch. 4:63) writes, this line of argument is not conclusive from a purely linguistic and toponymic angle. But, as we shall see, a number of finds have been made at the *thing* site which corroborate the views of Storm and Rygh.

The specialised cooking-pit sites

In connexion with the extension of the *Þjóðalyng* churchyard, an archaeological excavation in 2003 was undertaken north and northeast of the church (Skul-lerud 2003). The site, which measured a good 3,600 sq m, lay on the northern slope below the flat plateau that must have been the *thing* site itself. There had been a ploughed field here, and the ploughsoil of some 30–40 cm was first removed by machine. Beneath the plough-layer a morainic layer was found, dominated by fine sand. Within the layer a total of 15 cooking pits, 3 hearths, and 19 post-holes could be seen (Figs. 17.4, 17.5). The great majority of these features were in the southern and south-western part of the site, adjacent to the churchyard, and it looked as if the north-eastern edge of a larger area of such features had been uncovered. Ploughing had removed most of the features and only the bottommost 20 cm were left. It is consequently difficult to say anything certain about the original dimensions of the cooking pits, other than that they must have been considerably more than 1.4–1.6 m in diameter as was recorded in most cases.

Clusters of cooking pits of this kind can, in Norway, be dated to the period from around the birth of Christ to AD 600 (Gustafson 2005:105; Martens 2005: 40; Pilø 2005:138–41) and, together with the post-holes and the fireplaces, they occur commonly in settlements of this period. But these post-holes could not be sorted into any regular pattern that might indicate that they belonged to the types of buildings that are typical of the agrarian settlements of this period. It would therefore appear that the post-holes, which were also mostly quite small, were not from ordinary buildings. This could be explained by the excavation having uncovered the north-eastern limit of a settlement site, where simple or temporary buildings might have been raised, whereas the stouter houses were further to the southwest. However the area southwest of the excavation site is on a hill with a slope of 1:7, which makes it too steep to be suitable for building; furthermore, flatter, more suitable terrain for building was available on all sides (Fig. 17.4).

The post-holes and cooking pits uncovered northeast of the churchyard can hardly, therefore, be part of a settlement. What other types of sites are such clusters normally associated to? Clusters of cooking pits can in some cases be associated with pagan cemeteries, and this may be the case at *Þjóðalyng*. Niels Seierløv Stephansen, the parish priest of Tjølling from 1800 to 1833, wrote concerning Vollen, the plateau on which the church stands (1970 [1800–1825]:17):

I øvrigt har det Jordstykke her som kaldes Volden ey heller været umerkeligt i Oldtiden; thi ved mit komme [til kallet, dvs i året 1800] fandtes endnu Levninger af et Slags He-densk Offerplats af smaae Kampesteen indcirklet og broelagt og især Levning af en Kiæmpe eller mænneskelig Figur dannet paa den horisontale Flade af Kampesteen, som alt nu er bortryddet til nyttigere Brug, som og for Kiørselen og excerseringens Skyld.

Apart from this, the Piece of Land here that is called Volden was certainly not insignificant in the ancient Past; for, when I arrived [to the appointment, i.e. in the year 1800] there were still Remains of a Sort of pagan Place of Sacrifice in the form of small Boulders encircled and paved and especially the Remains of a Giant or human Figure formed on the level Surface out of Boulders, all of which have now been removed for more practical Use, some also for Ease of Transport and the Purpose of Drill.

In 1805, Stephansen had a new house built at the priest's homestead, which is still there (Krohn-Holm 1970:358). It was very likely here that he found "more practical Use" for the stones that were laying only a few metres away. Most of them probably found their way into the walled cellar of the house. But at the last moment, the antiquary Martin Friedrich Arendt happened to record the "enclosed places of sacrifice". According to his travel notes, which are among his papers kept in the National Museum in Copenhagen, he visited Tjølling church on 8th June 1804. There he made a sketch plan, and his observations formed the basis of a lecture he held five years later at L'Acadamie Celtique in Paris. The lecture was published in the Academy's proceedings, which contain a plan of five stone-built circles beside Tjølling church (Arendt 1810, pl. 26; drawing also reproduced in Blindheim 1974:122).

This plan has been the source of some uncertainty, as it does not seem to match the location. In Arendt's surviving papers the full manuscript for his lecture and a sketch plan that was the basis for the printed plan is still extant. This provides more detail than the printed version. Amongst other features, the sketch has a written note that shows that what appears on the printed version as a north point was actually directed to the east. Consequently the hill, road and fences on the sketch fit with the actual topography of the site, and on this basis the graves have been put into the plan of the *thing* site, Figure 17.4.

East of what was then the north-eastern corner of the churchyard, immediately south of the area of excavation in 2003, Arendt found five stone-built circles with a diameter of 15 to 17.5 paces according to the measurements he noted on his sketch: in other words, c. 11–13 m. On the sketch, the distance between the individual stones is less regular than it appears to be on the printed version, and the stone-built circles' similarity to a type of grave that is relatively common in the area from the Early Iron Age, the same period as the cooking pits belong to, is manifest (Hougen 1924). All of the circles appear to have a more or less

continuous row of stones at the outer edge; the number of stones within each circle varies. The two circles furthest east are the most densely packed with stones. It is presumably these that Stephansen was referring to when he used the term "paved".

It is much less clear what Stephansen was referring to as the human figure, which was supposedly formed out of boulders. One notes that he referred to the stones in the circular constructions as "small boulders" whereas he referred to the figure as made out of "boulders". In other words, the figure he referred to was presumably made of rocks that were larger than those in the circles, which Arendt notes were about a foot long. Stone-built funerary monuments of the Early Iron Age can take many different forms but these are always geometrical rather than figurative. Body-shaped monuments are quite unknown. Stephansen himself was completely indifferent to ancient monuments, as is shown in his correspondence with Jens Kraft of around 1820 (Kraft's private archive, RA). Kraft had read Arendt's manuscript and wrote to Stephansen for further information, but the latter had nothing to say on the subject. Stephansen's report on the human shape of the stone construction was most probably based on the local tradition. The local tradition might have contained references to a stone structure of the common Early Iron Age type which had a geometrical form that inspired the local imagination to believe that it looked like a man. But one cannot ignore the possibility that there might have been an ancient monument of a uniquely different and figurative form here.

Stephansen does not give any further information about where this enigmatic stone structure was located on the plateau. As far as the circles are concerned, however, it is worthwhile to note that these were situated right out on the north-eastern edge of the plateau, as indeed the church is. The location of both the circles and the church may reflect the fact that the remainder of the plateau was to be kept free for some other purpose.

Funerary monuments of the Early Iron Age are found in a great variety of places. For example, in southern Vestfold they are found both spread out and clustered in cemeteries, as at Þjóðalyng. Rather few settlements sites have been found in Vestfold, and it has not proved possible to confirm any single pattern of topographical relation between settlement and cemetery. A close proximity between a cemetery and a contemporaneous settlement has been proven in some cases. Still, this cannot be the case with all sites with graves, the number of such sites is just too high. Furthermore, as has been noted, there are no signs of a farmstead at Þjóðalyng, nor of anything to indicate that the area of cooking pits was part of a settlement.

An alternative possibility would appear equally plausible – that the location of the funerary monuments, the cooking pits, hearths and post-holes is

Figure 17.4 *A detailed plan of the* thing *site at Þjóðalyng and the most important features found there. The area of cooking pits east and northeast of the church (Fig. 17.5) and the five graves southeast of the church recorded by Martin Friedrich Arendt in 1804 are shown. As one can see, the choir of the extant church is located on top of a small ridge which falls gently away along its length towards the NNW. This could indicate that there was an earlier church on the highest point of the ridge here, where the choir and the eastern end of the nave are now found. When a new church was raised on an extant church site in the 12th and 13th centuries, it was usual to place the boundary between the nave and the choir in the same place as it had been in the earlier church. Contour interval 1 meter. Map, Julie K. Øhre Askjem.*

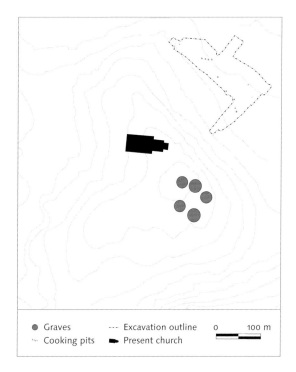

● Graves   ⋯ Excavation outline   0   100 m
⋰ Cooking pits   ◣ Present church

connected to the role of the site in the Early Iron Age as a fixed assembly place, probably related to what in the Viking Period are known as *thing* sites. There are several examples of burials found at *thing* sites (e.g. Sandnes 1974:38). The post-holes might be from the temporary shelters people constructed for spending the night here on the periphery of the assembly place itself. Booths of this kind at later *thing* sites are referred to in several sagas, and their remains have also been identified (Benediktsson 1974:382; Barnes 1974: 383). That the Iron-age booths for temporary occupation could have been built with roof-supporting posts is confirmed, *inter alia*, by the thousands of scattered post-holes at the seasonal market-place at Tissø, Sjælland (Jørgensen 2002:240).

The cooking pits at sites with no signs of permanent occupation, sometimes also associated with hearths and scattered post-holes, are a familiar phenomenon over much of Scandinavia. Martens (2005: 37) has termed them *specialized cooking-pit sites*, a term which will be used from here onwards.

The discussion of the practical function of the cooking pits has been based on Old Norse written sources and a diverse body of ethnological evidence (e.g. Heibreen 2005). The pits that are found in larger clusters, either at settlements or in the specialized sites, are identified by most scholars as evidence of the preparation of food. Cooking in a pit is certainly not the usual cooking method of a household, since a pit is first and foremost well suited to the preparation of large quantities of food, perhaps particularly meat. The number of pits at settlements also shows that the digging of a pit was not something that was done every year, but only at intervals of several years (Henriksen 1999:118–19). When the stones in a cooking pit

have been heated up and the pit is kept covered with turf or some other material, it can be used for cooking over several days. The construction of cooking pits is therefore especially appropriate for occasions when a large number of people stay at a particular site for several days.

Many authorities link the cooking pits with the word *seyðir*, which in the sagas denotes a fire or pit for cooking food, usually meat (e.g. Ólsen 1910; Myhre 1980:200–9; Narmo 1996; Vikstrand 2001:328; Gustafson et al. 2005:*passim*). Narmo (1996:92–4) refers to several sources that indicate that this mode of cooking was associated with sacrifice, and that the combination of cooking and sacrifice created and confirmed group-solidarity amongst the participants.

As can be seen from the plan (Fig. 17.4), four of the cooking-pits at Þjóðalyng, 1.3–1.6 m in diameter, lie in a straight line at intervals of 2.0–2.6 m (Fig. 17.5). Such regular rows have also been found elsewhere (Henriksen 1999; Martens 2005:38–40; Thörn 2005). In Germany, Denmark and southern Sweden there are many dozens of pits in rows of this kind, and their regular disposition is probably due to their having been constructed along a common boundary, possibly a fence or a track. Such a large number of pits cannot have been in use at one and the same time. Earlier pits were presumably visible as hollows, and the new ones were laid out to maintain the regular pattern established by their predecessors. The reason for this is difficult to conceive, but it is reasonable to believe, as Henriksen (1999:116) does, that these features were linked to ritual feasts. The location of new pits in a specific relation to old ones may have been parts of the ritual.

In terms of the number of pits, the four at Þjóða-

Figure 17.5 *Four cooking pits in a row revealed in 2003 just northeast of Tjølling church. For the position of this site, see Fig. 17.2. Photo, KHM.*

lyng can hardly be compared to the much larger, and consistently earlier, Danish, Swedish and German rows of pits, and consequently their interpretation must be different. The most plausible interpretation of the four regular cooking pits is that they were built and used at the same time. On that occasion, it is probable that food was prepared for a relatively large number of people, given that a single pit with a diameter of about a metre could be used to prepare food for at least 30 people (Pilø 2005:195 n. 526). If used to their full capacity, these four pits could have been used to prepare food for at least 200 people.

The assembly place and the sacred

Many specialized cooking-pit sites have, like this one at *Þjóðalyng*, been identified very close to medieval church sites, usually on the edge of the churchyard (e.g. Bagøien 1976; Skre 1983; Narmo 1996; Bergstøl 2005; Reitan 2005; Risbøl 2005; Stene 2005). Excavations in central agricultural zones, where the churches are usually situated, encounter cooking pits in settlements more often than specialized cooking-pit sites. But in the vicinity of the churches, the situation is different. The large number of specialized cooking-pit sites by churches is so striking that there must be a special explanation. As many of these scholars agree, it is reasonable to consider these cooking-pit sites as the traces of assembly places for the population of the area in the Early Iron Age. The chronological range of these pits through the first five to six centuries AD shows that most of these assembly places continued to be used for several hundred years.

The inferred association between these pits and cult activities, and the frequent occurrence of such sites beside medieval church sites, have inspired many of the scholars cited to theorize ritual continuity from the period of the cooking pits to that of the building of the medieval church – which means over a period of a thousand years. The problem is to main-tain the link through the second half of this period, when there are very few if any signs of cult activity at these sites. Several of the scholars mentioned have explained this gap in the material evidence by changes in cooking methods and ritual forms around AD 500/600, i.e. to new styles that left no physical traces. Other sources of evidence, for instance place-names, may indicate that cult activities and rituals of a sacral character, such as horse-fights, occurred at the same site both before and after these changes took effect (e.g. Narmo 1996:96–7; Brink 2002a:107).

In order to understand the connexion between the Early Iron-age assembly places and the churches of at least 500 years later, it is necessary to consider changes in the activities at these assembly places during that time span. The regular assemblies that appear to have been a feature of most Germanic societies in the Iron Age, i.e. the seasonal feasts (de Vries 1970:446; Andrén 2002:311–12), are of importance in this regard. Over much of the Germanic world, there were three seasonal annual feasts. Their character can only be glimpsed from the sources, but it was probably composite, i.e. not only religious, but concurrently administrative, legal, social, and political. It is reasonable to infer, along with de Vries (1970:445) that, in an early period, the seasonal feasts were of a predominantly sacral character, and that the fundamentally juridical modes and rituals of the *thing* evolved on that foundation. This development is partly inferred from the fact that in the Viking Period the *thing*-moots were held according to ritual forms that seem to have had some sort of sacral foundation and character. Because of the paucity of sources, it is only the final stage of this inferred development that can be described with some clarity,

The ritual forms of the *thing*-moot are apparent, for instance, in the way in which a *thing* site was arranged in the Viking Age. True enough, the sources that talk about this are from very different parts of

the Scandinavian Peninsula, and some of these are 12th- and 13th-century sagas. But some common features in these sources are clear enough for us to trust them. The *thing* site seems to have been enclosed with a *véband*, a fence of hazelwood stakes stuck into the ground and joined by a rope. The enclosure appears to have been circular (Schledermann 1974:374; Olsen 1975; Brink 2002a). The judges sat within the circle; furthermore, it was forbidden to carry weapons within the circle. The men of the *thing*-assembly stood outside and signalled their support for a decision by striking their weapons together (Brink 2002a:89–90).

Sites of this kind are, inevitably, difficult to identify archaeologically, and I know of only one possible example. During the excavations beneath St Mikael's Church at Slagelse in western Sjælland, Olaf Olsen (1972:148–52) found 36 holes for posts 6–10 cm in diameter that had been driven up to 1.8 m deep into the sandy ground. The posts pre-dated the first church, which was of the 11th century, and the posts in the few well-preserved areas were so numerous that Olsen judged there to have been thousands of them originally. There was a tendency for the postholes to form rows, which together with their coincidence with the church site and their location on a dominant high-spot led Olsen to suggest that they had been part of a series of *vébönd* (plural) that had been put up successively on the site.

The root of *vi* or *vé* is a Common Germanic word meaning 'holy'. In the Viking Age the word is also used for holy places within Nordic cult life (Vikstrand 2001:298–332; Brink 2002a:106). In several place names -*vi* as a final element is compounded with the names of gods such as Frey, Odin or Thor. A runic inscription from Oklunda in Östergötland shows that a murderer was protected from his pursuers when he sought refuge in a *vi* (Jesch 1998:66–7; Vikstrand 2001:323–4; Brink 2002a:93–6). Several sources also refer to another legal ritual which appears to have some cult associations, namely the practice of sacrificing an animal after a case had been decided at the *thing* (Brink 2002a:106–7).

The interweaving of juridical and cult practices that these sources bear witness to is not difficult to comprehend, as both served the same purpose – the maintenance of the community. The Christian laws, which were themselves formulated and put into effect at the *thing*, show that the connexion between the legal moot and religious matters remained after the Conversion. The chronology of the inferred evolution from seasonal feasts of he Early Iron Age to Viking-age *thing* assemblies is discussed further below.

At the *thing* site of *Þjóðalyng* there is further evidence that it was an assembly place for multifaceted meetings of this kind, possibly for seasonal feasts, in the Early Iron Age. About 300 m northeast of the church are the shores of the lake which, according to Brink (this vol. Ch. 4:56) was probably called *Vítrir* or

Vettrir (Fig. 17.2). This name derives from the word *vættr,* which is a general term for all supernatural beings (Brink, this vol. Ch. 4:56; Munch 1967[1854]: 81–6; Fritzner 1886–1896:3:982; Christiansen 1975:678; Steinsland 2005:352–3). Brink interprets the name of this lake as "the lake where supernatural beings dwell" or "the lake dedicated to gods and supernatural beings". This interpretation is not definite, but is supported by the fact that there are several names containing this element in Scandinavia, including the names of rivers and farms. Rygh (1897-1936:XII:56) refers to Magnus Olsen, who identified the name-element *vættr* in the farm-name Vetten, which occurs in Hedmark (twice, in Stange and Furnes), in Vetti in Sogn (Årdal), as well as in other places, including two cases in Iceland.

The farm north of the lake *Vítrir/Vettrir* is called *Vítrisvin* or *Vettrisvin,* and thus incorporates the name of the lake, i.e. "the plain beside *Vítrir/Vettrir".* Farm-names ending in *-vin* are usually dated to the Early Iron Age, and the name of the lake should therefore be from that period as well.

At the south-eastern end of the lake, about 850 m northeast of the *thing* site, is *Helgefjell,* "the holy mountain", a name that is attested to here as early as 1439 (Fig. 172). This name, which is found in five other places in Norway too *(www.visveg.no),* recurs elsewhere in Scandinavia and Iceland. It is referred to in *Eyrbyggja saga,* where the giving of this name is attributed to the settler Thorolfr (Brink, this vol. Ch. 4:56–7). Names which reveal that conspicuous knolls and mountains were attributed with a sacral significance in the pre-Christian era occur in many parts of Scandinavia (Vikstrand 2004b:318–24). This name is difficult to date, but this saga at least shows that such names were given in the Viking Period. It could go further back into the Iron Age too, but Vikstrand (2001:236) finds indications that names with the name-element *helg-* are mostly from the later part of the pre-Christian era. The name *Helgefjell* cannot be from the Christian period because in Christian ideology, nothing in nature can be holy in itself. Holiness was bestowed only through some consecration ritual, which took place only in respect of churchyards, church sites, and the like (Jensenius 2001:26). *Helgefjell* is a striking natural feature that rises sharply in a rounded form 25 m above the surface of the lake *Vítrir/Vettrir* (Fig. 17.2).

There are also sacral names for lakes in several other parts of Scandinavia. Brink (this vol. Ch. 4:56, 1998:313–14) notes lakes such as *Guðsior* (the gods' lake), *Tissø* (Tyr's lake), *Odensjö* (Odin's lake) and *Helgasjö* (the holy lake). The practice of associating the names of gods and other sacral name-elements with lakes must be related to a common association between cult practices and lakes, bogs, springs and rivers all over the Germanic area (Stjernquist 1998; Brink 2001:96–8; Müller-Wille 2002; Kaul 2003; Sund-

qvist 2004:152–4). In certain periods and in particular places these cult practices included the sacrifice of weaponry, pottery, jewellery, and other types of artefacts that have been preserved to the present day. The practice of the votive deposition of such items in water was widespread in southern Scandinavia, especially in the Early Iron Age (Ilkjær 2002, 2003; Fabech 1991, 1997:149, 1998), but the practice also continued through the Viking Period, up to the Christian period (Zachrisson 1998:118; Hedeager 1999; Andrén 2002: 316–17; Lund 2004). Beside the lake at Tissø in Sjælland, for example, a central-place complex from the period AD 550–1000 with an aristocratic farmstead, a seasonal market place, and a cult site, has been excavated. The farm buildings are sited by the side of the lake, and in the water immediately adjacent to them, votive depositions of large quantities of weaponry were made (Jørgensen 2002). In Norway too, we find widespread deposition of precious, Viking-period metalwork under water. Ryste (2005:56) has identified a total of 156 caches of this kind, of which 108 are from identifiable find-places. Twenty-eight of these were found either in or beside an area of water, i.e. a lake, bog, or river.

There is thus a close ideological, functional, chronological and topographical relationship between *Vítrir/Vettrir, Helgefjell* and *Þjóðalyng.* Cult activities connected with the lake must have taken place at its southern end, as that is where *Helgefjell* is found. Here the distance was shortest between the lake and the *thing* site, where people gathered regularly for moots which had a sacral component.

There is one further point indicative of a connexion between cult activities involving the lake and the assemblies at *Þjóðalyng.* The word *vættr* could be taken to mean either "evil" or "good" supernatural beings. Amongst the evil, *meinvættir,* were the giants and dwarves; amongst the good, *hollar vættir,* were the Æsir and Vanir. It is not normal for sacral names to include a general name for all supernatural beings, both good and evil, as seems to be the case with the lake *Vítrir/Vettrir.* The other lakes with sacral names are all named after *hollar vættir,* and it is to be assumed that the same should be the case in respect of the lake near *Þjóðalyng.* The only group of *hollar vættir* that have the element *vættir* itself in their names are the *landvættir.* Munch (1967[1854]:81 and 85) describes these as "the guardian spirits of the land" of all kinds, including:

... lavere, kollektive, overnaturlige vesener, som alver, huldrefolk, underjordiske osv., og ... skikkelser fra den "høyere mytologi", æser, vaner m.m.

… lower, massed, supernatural beings, such as elves, little people, subterranean beings etc., and … beings from the "higher mythology", the Æsir, Vanir and so on.

The sources from 12th- and 13th-century Iceland show that it was extremely important for the local inhabitants to stay in the good graces of the *landvættir* of the place, so that misfortune did not befall the land. It was the hostility of the *landvættir* that Egil Skalla-Grimsson sought to arouse when he wished to avenge himself on the Norwegian king Eirik Blood-axe and his queen Gunnhild. On his journey out of their kingdom, Egil landed on an island where he raised a *níðstöng,* a horse's head on a hazelwood pole, and turned it to face his enemies. Then he said *(Egils saga Skalla-Grímssonar,* Ch. 57):

…sný ek þessu níði á landvættir þær er land þetta byggva, svá at allar fari ðær villar vega engi hendi né hitti sitt inni fyrr en þær reka Eirík konung ok Gunnhildi ór landi.

… I turn this *níð* (insult) to those *landvættir* who dwell in this land, so that they should all become lost and none come to or find their proper place before they drive King Eirik and Gunnhild from the land.

This can only be a matter of speculation, but the lake *Vítrir/Vettrir* could be the local *inni* of the *landvættir,* i.e. their home or dwelling place. Here, beside a *thing* site, is precisely where one would expect to find a sacral site associated with the *vættir* who, in the same way as the *thing* did, maintained and guarded the land and its inhabitants.

17.4 Assembly place and *thing* site

In the introduction, two questions were posed: during what period was the *thing* site at *Þjóðalyng* in use, and how large an area did it serve as an assembly place? It has not been possible to answer either of these questions conclusively, but on the basis of the discussion above some opinions can nonetheless be outlined.

The name of the *thing* site (*Þjóðalyng*) must go back to the pre-Christian era, although the name does not lend itself to any closer dating than that. Sources from the early 19th century show that there were several pagan burial monuments at *Þjóðalyng* together with a paved area that would appear to have been of a quite exceptional nature. These were probably from some time in the first six centuries AD, and could indicate that this site served a special purpose in the Early Iron Age. An area of cooking pits and post-holes on the slope north of the flat *thing* site itself is from the same period. This area is of a type that is known over much of Scandinavia. They are called "specialized cooking-pit sites" and have two characteristic features:

- The post-holes are not arranged into the sort of regular pattern that we find with the post-holes of farm buildings from this period. They are therefore probably the traces of small and temporary structures.

- Four of the cooking pits lie in a regularly spaced row, which suggests that they were in contemporary use. Food for a large number of people (at least 200) could have been prepared in these pits.

Both of these features indicate that at *Þjóðalyng* relatively large numbers of people temporarily and contemporaneously occupied the site. These assemblies were probably seasonal feasts such as were typical in the Germanic world, and which had a composite sacral, juridical and social character. The proximity of the lake *Vítrir/Vettrir* ("the lake where supernatural beings dwell" or "the lake dedicated to gods and supernatural beings") and *Helgefjell* ("the holy mountain") indicates that cult activities were amongst those that were carried out at these assemblies. The name of the lake must derive from the Early Iron Age, in other words from the same period as the cooking pits and the post-holes at *Þjóðalyng*, and, considered altogether, this implies that *Þjóðalyng* was an assembly place for seasonal feasts for a fairly significant amount of time during the period AD–600 AD. The name of the mountain might go back to the same period, but it is more likely to date from the later centuries of the first millennium AD.

It seems likely that there is some connexion between these seasonal feasts and *Þjóðalyng*'s role as a *thing* site in the 11th and 12th centuries. The choice of this site for the church that was built here is best explained through the site being a *thing* site. The specific position of the church building, on the northern edge of the *thing* site, may imply that the plateau itself was still reserved for use as an assembly place. The church site could have been established as early as the second half of the 10th century, or in the 11th. The large and special church that was built here in the first half of the 12th century also shows that this church had an income that probably derived from its role as a *thing*-site church. The unusually large size of the choir may be related to the fact that the priests were to meet their bishop at the *thing* and sing mass with him. The large nave may have been built to accommodate the whole assembly of thingmen.

Sources from the Continent show that the Germanic seasonal feasts of the Early Iron Age had a clear and perhaps even predominantly sacral element to them. The juridical rituals and legal traditions were probably developed within this context. The *thing* sites and moots of the Viking Period were also conspicuously associated with rituals and concepts that had religious connotations, although their key functions appear to have been juridical, administrative and social.

Beyond these coarse chronological outlines, it is difficult to say anything definitive about the dating and the stages of development leading from the seasonal feasts of the Early Iron Age to the 11th century *thing*-moots at *Þjóðalyng*. But we shall have a go, all

Figure 17.6 *The lake* Vítrir/Vettrir *is now almost entirely overgrown, and the water level has been reduced by trenching. In the background is the assembly place* Þjóðalyng *(1), the hall site at the farm of* Huseby *(2), the urban site* Kaupang *(3), and the cemetery* Skereið *(4) (Skre, this vol. Chs. 11, 16, 19). Photo, Dagfinn Skre.*

the same. From the coincidence in position and dating between the sites with sacral names and the assembly places revealed by cooking-pit sites, we can infer that the assembly places must have been locations at which seasonal feasts were held during the period c. AD–600 AD. Cooking pits at assembly places appear to be reflections *not only* of necessary practical activities (the preparation of food while people were staying at the assembly place), *but also* of ritual activity with possibly cultic elements (communal preparation of food and feasting), *and* of a significant social event (a communal feast for some social or political grouping) (cf. Gjerpe 2001).

Around the 6th–7th centuries the ritual depositions in water appear to cease in Scandinavia, and the ending of the practice of cooking in pits shows that the forms of ritual changed too. This is the same phase during which the hall appears to have taken on greater significance as a cultic, political and social arena (Fabech 1991; Herschend 1993). This development may have left the *thing*-moots with a more distinctly juridical character, even though the other components were still there. At Skiringssal, this development is probably represented by the presence of an Early Iron-age assembly place beside a lake with a sacral name, and by the building of a hall at Huseby, about 1 km southwest of the *thing* site, at the mid or end of the 8th century (Fig. 17.6; Skre, this vol. Chs. 11 and 19:439).

But there does not appear to have been a complete change in the forms of cult and law. As we have seen, the *thing* sites retained a sacral element into the Christian Middle Ages. Furthermore, after AD 600 one can see a tendency to seek to link up with the sacral sites and practices of earlier eras. This may be the reason why votive deposition under water is taken up again in several parts of Scandinavia at the beginning of the Viking Period, and continues long into the Christian times.

It is probably these long lines of continuity and change in the position and function of the assembly places that explain why a large number of church sites are at or near farms that have sacral names (Olsen 1926:230–4). Some of these names were formed in the Early Iron Age, i.e. during the same period to which the specialized cooking-pit sites belong. Some scholars have believed that the sites' function as a holy place was continuous from the Early Iron Age to the church-building of the 11th or 12th centuries. One must, however, consider the changes that took place in the function of the assembly places during this long period, so that by the time the churches were built those had developed into more juridical and administrative fora where, inter alia, the question of the erection of the church would have been discussed. Such places were nonetheless scarcely free of connexions with the pagan gods and powers, and the bishop would certainly have been careful to perform the ritual of exorcism that was required before a church site on a former cult site was consecrated (Jensenius 2001:26). At *Þjóðalyng* it was also found appropriate to dedicate the church to Michael (RB: 51), the archangel who, with his flaming sword in hand, led the heavenly hosts in battle against the forces of darkness, and who escorted the souls of the faithful into the Kingdom of Heaven. Like the great majority of the many European medieval churches dedicated to Michael, the church at *Þjóðalyng* stands high and distinct in the landscape. This situation was also probably another reason why it was dedicated to him. The archangel was thought to prefer such high places when he set foot on Earth (Olsen 1972:131–2).

On the basis of the coincidence between its being used as an assembly place for seasonal feasts in the Early Iron Age, as a *thing* site in the Viking Period, and as a church site in the early Christian Middle Ages, one could straightforwardly infer that *Þjóða-lyng* was a meeting place for a thousand years. Do-

cumentary evidence of the 14th century and later shows that *thing* sites of this period were not permanent. That they were also moved relatively often in the Viking Period is shown by two runestones in Vallentuna, Uppland, Sweden. Here, in the 11th century, one stone was raised on the shore of a lake. The inscription on it declares that here Ulf's sons Ulfkel(?), Arnkel and Gye created a *thing* site. Some decades later Jarlabanki raised a runestone not very far away. On that stone it is written that he is establishing a *thing* site at that place. This is where Vallentuna church was built (Jansson 1984:125–6).

Consequently, we must also consider the possibility that the *thing* site in Skiringssal was moved both during the Viking Period and before. Still, the many indications of *Þjóðalyng's* being an assembly site over a very long time span make this alternative less likely. Jarlabanki was a particularly powerful local magnate and such may have been able to enhance their own prestige by suppressing smaller ones. But the major *thing* sites, whose location was founded in centuries of continuous use and in the minds of kings, chieftains and common men in a vast circumference, would be less exposed to this kind of change.

It is hard to form an estimate of the size of the territory from which people came to *Þjóðalyng*. In the case of the earliest periods, I cannot see any basis at all on which this question could be tackled. In the case of the later periods, the relevant evidence is paltry. It would, however, appear that a common law-region in Viken was founded at the beginning of the 11th century with a juridical *thing* site at Borg. Under the Borgarthing Law, in addition to the *thing* at Borg for the whole law-region, *things* were held elsewhere for *fylki* and for half-*fylki*. From the beginning of the 11th century onwards, the *thing* site at Skiringssal may have served either all or half of Vestfold. Such local *thing*-moots may have become the arenas of aristocrats that opposed the king, particularly in the so-called "civil-war period" in the century after 1130. It seems likely that the Haugathing at Tønsberg was established by the king early in the 12th century as part of his efforts to break down the power structures of the aristocracy. Probably as a consequence of this strategy, the Skiringssal *thing* site at *Þjóðalyng* may have come into disuse some time in the mid or late 12th century.

It is possible that before the establishment of the Borgarting law-region, during Skiringssal's pre-eminence in the 8th to 10th centuries, the Skiringssal *thing* site at *Þjóðalyng* was sought by people from the same area as in the 11th and 12th centuries. But one must also consider the possibility that this *thing*-site was sought also by people from outside of Vestfold, possibly from the whole of Viken. This question has to be considered within a wider frame of reference, and is taken up again in Chapter 19.

The Dating of *Ynglingatal* **18**

DAGFINN SKRE

Ynglingatal is the most extensive amongst the relatively few textual sources that refer to Skiringssal. It mentions 27 generations of Yngling petty kings. According to the poem, the first twenty of these were kings in Uppsala, Sweden; the next one moved from there; and the final six generations are associated with locations in and around Vestfold and the Opplands – the latter being the interior regions of eastern Norway. The stanzas that mention the six "Norwegian" Ynglings contain much information which is of interest for the study of Skiringssal. For that reason the poem's value as a source is discussed here.

The poem's source value is highly dependent on the time distance between its composition and the lifetime of the persons it mentions, which for the "Norwegian" Ynglings would be the 8th and the 9th century. The date of the poem is therefore a key issue. The poem is preserved only in Snorri Sturluson's *Heimskringla* written in the 1220s, and in that work Snorri claimed that the poem was composed by the late 9th/early 10th century *skáld* Thjodolf of Hvini. Therefore, based primarily on Snorri's claim, *Ynglingatal* has been dated by most scholars to the end of the 9th century or around 900.

The late 9th-century dating has recently been challenged by Claus Krag, who argues that the poem was composed much later, namely towards the end of the 12th century. However, a detailed examination of Krag's arguments reveals a number of weaknesses in respect of both his case *against* the traditional dating and that *for* a later dating. Furthermore, his revised dating raises several problems that he has either not addressed satisfactorily or at all. Krag's claim that the tradition of the Ynglings was actually created among 12th- and 13th-century Icelandic historians and that *Ynglingatal* was composed in the course of that tradition's development is critically examined below. The conclusion is reached that neither the development of the Icelandic Yngling tradition nor Krag's other arguments can be used to support his dating of the poem.

Indeed, in the end, a careful evaluation of Krag's arguments and of those that have emerged in the wake of his work, together with an investigation of the cultural context and aristocratic ideology of Skiringssal, leads to the conclusion that the traditional late 9th-century dating of *Ynglingatal* is still the most plausible one.

No piece of Norse literature has been as widely discussed as the skaldic poem *Ynglingatal*, which is a genealogy of 27 generations of Yngling petty kings mainly describing their deaths and burials. The poem's prominent position is due to its length (it comprises 37 stanzas), its great presumed age (it is traditionally dated to the late 9th century or around the year 900), and especially to the link between the Ynglings and the Norwegian royal dynasty of the following centuries. This link does not occur in the poem itself, but can be traced to the Icelandic historians of the 12th and early 13th centuries. The claim that there was a connexion between the Yngling dynasty of the 6th–9th centuries and the Norwegian royal dynasty of the 10th–12th centuries was probably first made by Ari the Wise (1067/68–1148) and was then developed by several historians until it emerged in its final shape in *Heimskringla*, written by Snorri in the 1220s. Snorri wrote that the first king of Norway, Harald Fairhair, was of the Yngling line, and that he was the son of Halfdan the Black who was paternal uncle of Rögnvald Lord of the Heaths, in whose honour the poem was composed (Fig. 18.1).

Other accounts of the genealogy of the Ynglings are found in texts written in the decade preceding Snorri's work. But except for a strophe reproduced in

Snorri: The "Norwegian" Ynglings

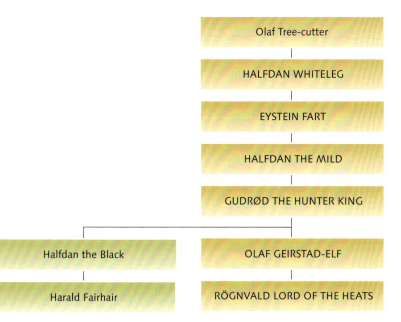

Figure 18.1 *In capitals, the sequence of the last six "Norwegian" Ynglings, as given in* Ynglingatal. *Olaf Tree-cutter is also mentioned in* Ynglingatal, *while Halfdan the Black and Harald Fairhar's connexion to the Yngling dynasty is first mentioned by Ari the Wise in the 1120s/30s and was probably concocted by him. The Ynglings' bynames do not appear in* Ynglingatal. *Illustration, Jørgen Sparre.*

the Tale of Olaf Geirstad-Elf in *Flateyjarbók* (Krag 1991:141), a manuscript of the late 14th century, *Ynglingatal* itself is preserved only in one text, the *Ynglinga saga* of Snorri Sturluson of the 1220s where, significantly, he claimed that it was the work of the late 9th-/early 10th-century skaldic poet *(skáld)* Thjodolf of Hvini. Thjodolf is referred to in a number of contexts in Snorri's *Ynglinga saga* as one of Harald Fairhair's skalds, and he must therefore have lived in Harald's reign (Krag 1991:34–6), that is c. 870–930. Walter Åkerlund's (1939) dating of the poem to the late 9th century or around AD 900 has been accepted by most scholars.

From our perspective, the connexion between the petty kings mentioned in *Ynglingatal* and the Norwegian royal dynasty of the 10th and following centuries is of little importance. What makes the poem interesting in a study of Skiringssal is that it associates the last six generations of Yngling petty kings with certain places and regions in Vestfold and other parts of the Viken area. Amongst these places is Skiringssal. If it derives from the late 9th century, as follows from Snorri's claim of its origin, *Ynglingatal* would be one of two contemporary sources that refer to events and persons in Skiringssal in the period which is studied in this volume, the other source being Ohthere's account (Skre, this vol. Ch. 2:29). The poem contains certain pieces of information which are highly relevant to the issues which are to be discussed in the two following chapters. But before *Ynglingatal* can be used as a source for 8th- and 9th-century Skiringssal, it is essential to assess whether Snorri's attribution of the poem to Thjodolf can be correct – for some scholars have alleged that it is *not,* and have further-

more alleged that the poem is not of the late 9th century but c. 300 years later.

A later dating of *Ynglingatal* would not rule out the possibility of using the poem as a source about individuals and events in 8th- and 9th-century Skiringssal, as the poem might include traditions deriving from this period. But since such a dating would increase the time span between the lifetime of these individuals and the composition of the poem by some 300 years, in which traditions would have been transformed and influenced by many individuals and circumstances, a later dating would make it even more difficult to identify reliable historical information in the poem in a convincing way. Tradition from the late 9th century is much more likely to have survived until Snorri's time in a near original shape if it had the form of a strictly metrical poem than if it was transmitted as separate small stories or as a saga. Furthermore, a late date would remove the main basis for relying on the information in the poem, namely the setting in which a poem of this kind would have been performed by its skald – in praise of Rögnvald Lord of the Heaths and with him and his men as the audience. In such a setting the skald would have had to stick quite faithfully to the common contemporary knowledge of the individuals and events mentioned in the poem. Consequently, a later dating would seriously reduce the scope for using this poem as a source for the 8th and 9th centuries.

As the historian Jørn Sandnes has written (1994: 231), no one now can discuss the provenance of *Ynglingatal* without taking account of the 1991 book by the historian Claus Krag. In this book and in a contemporary paper (Krag 1990), Krag delivers a very thorough and well argued case for a later dating of *Ynglingatal* than has been commonly accepted. Krag argues that Snorri's claim that *Ynglingatal's* author was Thjodolf is false. Instead, he argues that the poem should be dated to the end of the 12th century or around 1200. He argues too that the poem was com-posed in such a way as to appear ancient and further-more that it was composed with the twin aims of honouring the descendants of Harald Fairhair and of strengthening the Norwegian king's claim of sover-eignty over Viken by asserting that Harald's alleged royal forefathers, the Yngling dynasty, had links to Vestfold. Krag notes, in supporting his argument, that in the late 12th century this overlordship was under challenge from the Danish king (Krag 1990: 192–3).

The first section of the following study (18.1) will be a summary and discussion of Krag's positions on the origin and dating of the poem and of the debate which has followed in the wake of his works. In the following two sections, two of the main points in Krag's argument are discussed in detail. Section 18.2 discusses his perception of how the Icelandic histori-ans' view of the Ynglings developed from the early 12th century to the time when Snorri wrote his *Yng-linga saga,* the 1220s. Krag's view is that towards the end of this period of about a century there was a development, whereby Icelandic historians linked the Ynglings more closely with Vestfold. Thus the very strong link between the Ynglings and Vestfold in *Ynglingatal* becomes one of Krag's main reasons for dating the poem to the late 12th century. Section 18.3 considers the other of Krag's main reasons for claim-ing that the poem was composed in the late 12th cen-tury, namely the occurrence in the poem of elements which would be anachronistic in a poem of the late 9th century. The discussion considers whether these elements could nevertheless have appeared in a poem written in the last decades of the 9th century.

Section 18.4 assesses whether *Ynglingatal's* con-tents are consistent with certain elements of the ide-ology of lordship that can be discerned in 9th-centu-ry south-eastern Norway. Finally, section 18.5 sum-marizes the discussions and presents a conclusion on the dating of *Ynglingatal.*

Before this discussion, however, it is necessary to explain the use of the term "Yngling" in this and the following two chapters. As noted, the connexion be-tween the petty kings mentioned in *Ynglingatal* and the Norwegian royal dynasty of the 10th century on-wards is not under discussion here. In what follows, the term *Yngling* is therefore used solely in relation to individuals who are mentioned in *Ynglingatal* (Fig. 18.1). Like most studies that have grappled with this question, the linkage between Harald Fairhair and the Ynglings will be treated as a product of the Ice-landic saga-writing milieu in the early 12th century.

18.1 *Ynglingatal* – a poem of the late 12th century?

The following critical presentation of Krag's argu-ment firstly presents his two main points, the ana-chronistic elements he identifies in *Ynglingatal* and the development of the tradition amongst Icelandic

historians in the 12th and early 13th centuries. Secondly, some problematic aspects of his dating of the poem to the late 12th century are discussed.

Krag's anachronisms

One of Krag's two principal arguments for dating *Ynglingatal* later than the 9th century is that it con-tains anachronisms, namely concepts and ideas that, although they may have existed elsewhere at the time, were not known in late 9th-century Scandinavia (Krag 1991:47). He believes there are several such ana-chronisms. The most important of them is "… the doctrine of the four elements in the specific form that it took in the Christian Middle Ages" ("… læren om de fire elementer i den spesifikke form læren fikk i kris-ten middelalder"), which in Norway would be post 11th century (Krag 1990:180). If Krag succeeds in his argument that this doctrine can be identified in the poem, and if he is right in his dating of the introduc-tion of the doctrine to Norway and Iceland, *Yng-lingatal* cannot be of a late 9th-century date.

It is commonly accepted that the doctrine of the four basic elements – air, water, earth and fire – was developed quite early, starting in the 6th century, and was gradually incorporated in the Church's curricu-lum in seminaries and monasteries as is known, *inter alia,* from Bede's Biblical commentaries of the early 8th century (Krag 1991:56–7). However, Krag (1991:58) believes that this doctrine was introduced to Scandi-navia through the teachings of the Church after the general conversion of Norway in the first decades of the 11th century…

… og etterhvert blitt mer eller mindre almeneie. *Ynglingatal* må være samtidig med eller yngre enn denne lærdommen, som vel tok til å bli spredt på Island og i Norden på slutten av 1000-tallet og i de første tiårene av 1100-tallet.

… and gradually became more or less common knowledge. *Ynglingatal* must be contemporary with or later than this teaching, which undoubtedly began to be disseminated in Iceland and in Scandinavia at the end of the 11th century and the early decades of the 12th.

Krag identifies the teaching of the four elements though detailed linguistic and literary analyses and arguments that will only be discussed in general terms here. His conclusion is that the purportedly late 9th-century poem contains kennings for fire and water, the use of which, he believes, presupposes knowledge of the genealogy of the legendary charac-ter Fornjot as it was developed in post-conversion times. This character is referred to in *Flateyjarbók,* a manuscript codex of the 1380s which contains copies of earlier sagas, of which the relevant text in this case is apparently from the 12th century (Krag 1991:54). In *Ynglingatal* Fornjot's genealogy is presented fully developed, as Krag sees it, in the sense that he is ascribed three sons; between them, he and his sons each ruled one of the four elements. Krag (1991:58) concludes his discussion with the claim that…

… hele Fornjot-genealogien må forutsettes som kunnskapsbakgrunn for *Ynglingatals* dikter. *… Fornjot-genealogien er utenkelig uten mot bakgrunn av fire element-læren.*

…the entirety of the Fornjot genealogy has to be taken as a conceptual prerequisite for *Ynglingatal*'s poet. … *The genealogy of Fornjot is inconceivable independent of a foundation in the doctrine of the four elements.*

The philologist Bjarne Fidjestøl, in a review of the book, examined Krag's arguments in detail. He pointed out that several aspects of the arguments are less conclusive than Krag had suggested. He considered one of them implausible, namely Krag's interpretation of Fornjot as the character who controlled the fourth element, earth. Krag's interpretation is based upon the fact that the second part of Fornjot's name, *jótr,* can be identified with a giant, *jötunn;* therefore, Krag argues that the whole name *Fornjótr* must be interpreted as "Ancient Giant" ("urjotnen") (Krag 1991:55). Fidjestøl (1994:195) criticised this argument with the observation that "strictly speaking, it is only the *-t-* that the two words have in common" ("Strengt teke er det berre *-t-* dei to orda har felles"). Fidjestøl thus concluded that Krag's interpretation of Fornjot as the character who controlled the fourth element, earth, was erroneous. In his view, consequently, Fornjot and his three sons cover only three of the four elements, and he added (1994:195), "A four-element doctrine that has only three legs to stand upon, does not stand very securely!" ("Ei fire-elementlære som berre har tre bein å stå på, står ikkje heilt støtt!") He characterises Krag's conclusion concerning the four-element theory as "an over-interpretation" ("ei overtolking") (1994:196). Sandnes (1994:230) similarly found Krag's case to be unproven on this key issue.

Therefore, one cannot say that Krag has succeeded in overcoming all reasonable doubt about whether the doctrine of the four elements in *its fully developed 12th-century form* lies behind the construction of the relevant kennings in *Ynglingatal*. This argument for a post-11th-century dating of *Ynglingatal* is thus weakened. His dating of the introduction of the doctrine to Norway and Iceland will be discussed in chapter 18.3.

Has Krag succeeded in overcoming all reasonable doubt about his other crucial arguments concerning further anachronisms he perceives, i.e. those with a 12th-century Christian character that he believes he can identify in the poem? These are euhemerism – the idea that the pagan gods had been human beings; and possible Christian features he finds in the account of Aun and Adil (1991:58–9 and 67–72). In the case of euhemerism, Krag's interpretation of the first four petty kings in the poem as being gods is far from explicit, and therefore has to be characterized as quite unconvincing (Sundqvist 2002:44 and 162–6). Moreover, concerning the possible Christian features Krag alleges to find in the account of Aun and Adil, his view that Aun's sacrifice of his son, Adil, is influenced by the Christian model does not rely entirely on the formulations of the poem itself but rather upon his own reading of the poem in light of what Snorri wrote in *Ynglinga saga*, which expands upon several issues mentioned in the poem and adds others (Norr 1998:102; Sundqvist 2002:44–5). Finally, Krag's arguments (1991:96–9) that the poem was composed as a versified adornment to an extant, written saga of the 12th century have also been met with powerful counter-arguments (Sundqvist 2002:45).

Krag's "Vestfold viewpoint"

Having introduced his case for a later dating of *Ynglingatal* with an argument concerning supposed anachronisms he perceives in it, Krag makes his second key argument in support of a later dating by locating the composition of the poem within the evolution of what he calls the "Vestfold viewpoint" which was developed in 12th- and early 13th-century Icelandic historiography. Krag's description of this development differs from what have been the common positions in this debate, namely whether or not *Ynglingatal* provides an authentic genealogy of the Yngling petty kings from Halfdan Whiteleg onwards (Fig. 18.1), and whether or not the Icelandic historians were correct to link Harald Fairhair and his father Halfdan the Black to this line. Krag (1991:162) takes issue with these scholars on these two points, and declares that …

Ynglingegenealogien var *først* en genealogi for Harald Hårfagre og hans forfedre på Opplandene og i Sverige; og *siden* ble Vestfold-kongene knyttet til, samtidig som man så mer og mer gjorde opplandskongene til Vestfold-konger.

The genealogy of the Ynglings was *in its origin* a genealogy for Harald Fairhair and his ancestors in the Opplands and in Sweden; and the Vestfold kings were added to it *subsequently,* at the same time as and in the same process by which the Opplands kings were gradually turned into kings of Vestfold.

Krag's description of the development of the "Vestfold viewpoint" goes as follows: he points out (1990: 181) that the founding father of Icelandic historical writing, Sæmund the Wise (1056–1133), in his history of the kings of Norway, seems to have referred only to Halfdan the Black and Gudrød the Hunter-King as Harald Fairhair's ancestors – his father and paternal grandfather, respectively. Sæmund's history has been lost, but the poem *Nóregs konungatal* of c. 1190 was apparently based upon it. Krag points out that judg-

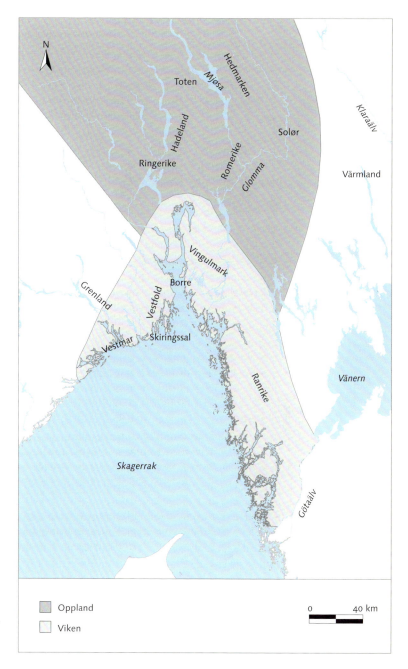

ing from *Nóregs konungatal* Sæmund did not mention the Yngling dynasty by name at all; furthermore, from the information in this poem that Halfdan was buried in a barrow in Ringerike, Krag infers (1990: 182) that Sæmund understood Halfdan to have been king over the Opplands – the interior districts of eastern Norway, including Ringerike – rather than over the coastal region of Vestfold (Fig. 18.2).

Moreover, Krag goes on to argue that the genealogy of the Ynglings was created not by either *Ynglingatal's* skjald or Sæmund but rather by another Icelandic historian, Ari the Wise (1067/68–1148), who was a near contemporary of Sæmund's. Krag's sources for Ari's perception of the Ynglings are partly Ari's *Íslendingabók* of c. 1122–1133 which contains two genealogical lists in which Ynglings appear, and also *Historia Norvegiae* (HN) by an unknown author. Krag dates HN to the second half of the 12th century, and argues (1991: 145–9) that it was based on Ari's lost history of the kings of Norway from the first half of that century. Since Krag wrote his book, two works on HN have argued for dating it to 1152/53 (Ekrem 1998) and 1160–1175 (Mortensen 2003:24) respectively, but neither of these affects Krag's argument.

In HN Halfdan Whiteleg and his descendants are called Ynglings for the first time in any surviving documentary source and they are also presented as kings of the Opplands (Krag 1990:184). Only in a later text that is known as "The Tale *(Þáttr)* of the Oppland Kings" (The Tale) are they also associated with Vestfold. The Tale states that Halfdan Whiteleg was king of Oppland (Krag 1991:133). The link with Vestfold arose when, according to The Tale, his son Eystein was married to the daughter of the king of Vestfold; furthermore, it states that the three subsequent Yngling petty kings, Halfdan the Mild, Gudrød the Hunter-King and Halfdan the Black, held power in Vestfold as well as in the Opplands (Krag 1990:191).

Krag thus finds that the Ynglings' association

with Vestfold is reinforced between HN and The Tale. He finds a further development in the same direction in Snorri's *Ynglinga saga* of the 1220s, according to which Harald Whiteleg had conquered parts of Vestfold. Thus, the Yngling petty kings' rule in Vestfold was pushed two generations back, from Halfdan the Mild to Halfdan Whiteleg. Concerning the three generations after Eystein, what is stated in *Ynglinga saga* is more or less the same as in The Tale; in *Ynglinga saga*, however, Halfdan the Black's *original* kingdom was Vestfold. He won the Opplands, according to Snorri, by conquest (Krag 1990:191).

In Krag's view, the introduction and gradual chronological expansion of the Yngling petty kings' rule in Vestfold from HN via The Tale to Snorri are explained by a desire on the part of the author of The Tale, and even more so on Snorri's part, to develop a historical association between the Ynglings and Vest-fold. Krag alleges that these two authors felt that if the Ynglings' rule in Vestfold could be historically proven to date to generations before Halfdan Fairhair, then the subsequent kings of Norway, who claimed to be descended from the Ynglings had a stronger case for claiming Vestfold as their legitimate territory. This historical validation of the Norwegian kings' claim on Vestfold was undoubtedly needed, according to Krag, after the Danish King Valdemar claimed over-lordship in Viken in the 1160s. According to both *Fagrskinna* and *Heimskringla*, King Valdemar's claim was supported, amongst other things, on the basis that several kings of Denmark since the time of Harald Bluetooth had been kings in Norway (Krag 1990:186). Krag consequently perceived attempts by Snorri and the author of The Tale to develop a histor-ical association between the Ynglings and Vestfold as part of a campaign to counter King Valdemar's claim to Viken.

Comparing *Ynglingatal* with the development described above, Krag finds in *Ynglingatal* what he calls the "developed Vestfold viewpoint". In the evolu-tion of the idea of the Ynglings' connexion with Vestfold, *Ynglingatal* lies between The Tale, which is of an uncertain date but probably from the late 12th or the 13th century, and *Ynglinga saga* of the 1220s, he claims. In *Ynglingatal*, Halfdan Whiteleg is already linked with Vestfold by being buried at Skereid in Skiringssal; however, in Ari's *Íslendingabók*, in HN and in The Tale, Halfdan is linked *only* to the Opp-lands. Furthermore, his son Eystein is supplied with a strong connexion to Vestfold in *Ynglingatal*, in that he was buried at "Raet's Edge", supposedly in Vestfold, indicating that he ruled there. This differs markedly, Krag argues, from HN (second half of 12th century) where Eystein is referred to only as king of Oppland, and from The Tale where he is only married to the daughter of the king of Vestfold. Since the stronger connexion with Vestfold, in Krag's view, developed after HN, and since Snorri manifestly considered the poem to be of an early date, *Ynglingatal* must have been composed after HN and well before Snorri's time. Krag concludes (1990:180) that *Ynglingatal* was composed in the late 12th century or around 1200.

Krag's problematic redating

Below (18.2), the "developed Vestfold viewpoint", as described by Krag on the basis of his analyses of the surviving texts, is examined critically. But even if one accepts portions of his analysis, certain major prob-lems remain, some of which must be considered quite fundamental and therefore damaging to his analysis (Fidjestøl 1994:197–8; Norr 1998:104–5): If *Ynglingatal* was composed in a context and at a time when the connexion between the Yngling dynasty and the Nor-wegian royal family from Harald Fairhair onwards was already established and recognized, and further-more if the poem was composed with the aim of fur-nishing the contemporary Norwegian royal family and its rule over Vestfold with historical legitimacy, why does the poem make absolutely no mention of Harald or his father Halfdan? Moreover, why is the main character of the poem, the man in whose hon-our it was composed, Rögnvald Lord of the Heaths rather than Harald himself?

Krag provides no convincing answers to these questions. Indeed, he even seems to weaken his own argument when he notes (1991:166) that the last stan-za in the poem, where Rögnvald is named, may be the only one composed by Thjodolf of Hvini, i.e. that it had been incorporated into *Ynglingatal*, which accor-ding to Krag was composed c. 300 years after Thjod-olf's time. In essence, this answer only further weak-ens his argument because it raises the question of why Krag's presumed late 12th-century author would include a stanza the very presence of which would undermine what is supposedly the real purpose of his poem? Indeed, the only thing that would have made sense would have been for Krag's presumed 12th-cen-tury author to compose a completely new poem that would contain absolutely nothing that might cause readers to doubt the connexion he was trying to legit-imize.

One further issue in this case remains unresolved in Krag's book (cf. Fidjestøl 1994:193–4). On several occasions Krag takes up the question of whom "the burden of proof" falls upon in the debate over the dating of *Ynglingatal*: those who propound the tradi-tional late 9th-century dating, relying on Snorri's attribution of the poem to Thjodolf, or those who argue for the much later 12th-century dating. At one point (1991:34) Krag cites Jón Helgason's dictum con-cerning the eddic poems (1953:96):

Den eneste absolut sikre kendsgerning er, at digtene er overleverede i islandske håndskrifter, hvoraf det vigtigste er fra 13 årh. Bevisbyrden påhviler den, der vil søge deres op-rindelse i ældgamle tider eller fjerne egne.

The only absolutely certain fact is that the poems have been transmitted through Icelandic manuscripts, the most im-portant of which are of the 13th century. The burden of proof falls upon those who would seek their origins in ancient times or far-off places.

Although Jón Helgason puts the case starkly, he does point out a form of evaluation that has to be under-taken for each of these texts. In the case of *Yng-lingatal*, a central issue in such an evaluation has to be an examination of the context in which the poems were written down, namely Snorri's writing chamber. To begin with, it is clear, also to Krag, that Snorri accepted *Ynglingatal* as genuinely from Thjodolf's time, the late 9th/early 10th century. The next ques-tion is, therefore, whether a re-dating of the poem such as Krag proposes is consistent with Snorri's knowledge of his sources and, most especially, with his knowledge of his Icelandic colleagues. *Ynglingatal* was composed in *kviðuháttr,* a metre that is not particularly difficult, but which nonetheless required a fairly high level of competency on the part of the skald that composed the poem. At the end of the 12th century most such skalds were Icelanders (Holtsmark 1970:389). As a major Icelandic politician intimately familiar with his country's history and literature, Snorri personally knew, or knew of, every skald of his time that could have composed such a poem and he knew the literary production of each of them. Consequently, his acceptance of it as being more than 300 years old suggests that no near contemporary of Snorri's composed *Ynglingatal.*

A recent study has developed linguistic arguments that support this point. Christopher Sapp (2000) has undertaken a linguistic analysis of four poems composed in *kviðuháttr.* He compares the occurrence and use of the expletive particle *of* in *Ynglingatal* with its occurrence and use in four other poems composed in the same metre, two of the 10th century, one of the late 12th, and one of the 13th century. A number of philological studies of other texts have demonstrated that the use of *of* changed during those 400 years. Sapp discovered that both the occurrence and the grammatical function of *of* in *Ynglingatal* have marked parallels with those in the two 10th-century poems, in contrast to the two later ones. He concludes that "…the poem was composed before expletive *of* ceased to be used productively in the eleventh century" (2000:95). Therefore, one must ask: Would it have been possible for someone writing in the late 12th century to convincingly simulate the earlier usage of *of*? If the answer is "no", Krag's argument for dating *Ynglingatal* to the end of the 12th century or around 1200 cannot be supported.

Notwithstanding the criticisms that can be levelled against Krag's works, and despite, too, the other contributions that have been made in the debate over the dating of the poem, it has to be accepted that Krag did succeed, as he said himself, in "…unhitching some of the moorings so that the Yngling tradition floats more freely" ("… å løse noen fortøyninger så ynglingetradisjonen flyter friere") (1991:73) – meaning, in respect of the chronology of the development of that tradition. He has sown seeds of fundamental doubt about the late 9th-century dating of the poem that had hitherto been accepted by most scholars. Krag himself dates the poem to a much later period of history, the late 12th century or c. 1200. However, as has been shown, there are quite fundamental problems with such a dating that are therefore damaging to Krag's analysis. In what follows, the two key points in his analysis, the development of the "Vestfold viewpoint" and the supposed anachronisms, are examined in greater detail.

18.2 *Ynglingatal* from Ari to Snorri

The absence of specific pieces of information in HN and earlier texts is a key point for Krag. He points out that some time after HN was written, which probably happened early in the second half of the 12th century, and up to Snorri's creation of *Ynglinga saga* in the 1220's, specific pieces of information, which are also present in *Ynglingatal*, first appear in the other surviving texts. This information is not present in HN or in Ari's earlier *Íslendingabók.* From what is known about the writings of the even earlier Icelandic historian Sæmund, these items of information were not present there either. The information in question mostly relates to the connexion between the Yngling petty kings and Vestfold. From the fact that HN and the earlier texts do not contain this information, and from the fact that the information is conveyed in *Ynglingatal*, Krag assumes that the authors of HN and the earlier texts did not know the poem, and that the reason for their lack of knowledge of *Ynglingatal* is that it had not yet been composed. On the basis of this assumption and on the basis of the comparison between the information conveyed in *Ynglingatal* and in the two texts written *after* HN – The Tale and Snorri's *Ynglinga saga* – Krag proposes a late 12th-century date for the creation of *Ynglingatal.*

But this is not, in reality, a persuasive argument. In the following an alternative hypothesis will be explored, namely that the poem was widely known to Icelandic historians from the beginning of the 12th century, and that these Icelandic historians from Ari to Snorri – each of them with his own particular motives – selected information from the poem and combined it with material from other sources with the principal aim, in all cases, of constructing a genealogy for the Norwegian kings of their own day. However, according to the hypothesis which will be explored in the following, they each chose different solutions which in turn determined what they included or excluded from their respective genealogies.

The hypothesis which will be explored here is thus that *Ynglingatal* was known not only to Snorri but also to all the earlier authors whose works mention the Ynglings – Ari's preserved *Íslendingabók,* HN and The Tale, the two last by unknown authors. The two main characters in this sequence are, as Krag indeed claims, Ari and Snorri. HN was probably based on lost works by Ari. The Tale will also be taken into consideration. Although the composition of this text is difficult to date, it must have been written after HN. Sæmund's lost works will not be discussed, as the assumptions about their content on the matters discussed here are too uncertain for them to bear any conclusions.

To explore this hypothesis, the geographical information in the five above-mentioned texts concerning the six final generations of the Ynglings will be compared (Tabs. 18.1–18.6). For Ari's *Íslendinga-*

bók, Finnur Jónsson's edition of 1930 is used; for HN, the edition of Ekrem and Mortensen (2003); for The Tale, the edition of *Hauksbók* that was printed in 1892–1896 (pp. 456–7); and of course, for *Ynglinga saga* and *Ynglingatal*, the editions published by Finnur Jónsson in 1911 and 1912 (a and b) respectively.

The tables will reveal both parallels and discrepancies between these texts. The discrepancies are in some cases contradictions, in others the absence in some texts of information given in others. While Krag interprets the discrepancies between the texts merely as changes in the tradition of the Ynglings itself, it will be argued here that several of the discrepancies are due to differences in the character of the texts, resulting from differences in the aims and concerns of their authors. Finally, these aims and concerns will be discussed on the basis of the patterns formed by the parallels and discrepancies between the texts.

These differences in the character of the texts will be analysed more thoroughly in due course; here, by way of introduction, three types of differences will be pointed out. Firstly, neither Ari's *Íslendingabók* nor HN contain any information whatsoever on whom the Ynglings married, while The Tale and *Ynglinga saga* both contain great amounts of such information. It may appear, then, as if the authors of the latter two systematically used – and may even have concocted – this information in order to furnish their respective histories with context, coherency and meaning. Secondly, the texts do not all contain similar amounts of geographical information. While both The Tale and *Ynglinga saga* have a lot of place-names, *Íslendingabók* and HN have remarkably little geographical information. For example, the account in HN jumps directly from Olaf Tree-cutter living in Uppsala, Sweden (Skre, this vol. Ch. 1:Fig. 1.3), to the acceptance by the Norwegians *in montanis* of his son, Halfdan Whiteleg as their king. How this move was effected, or which of them moved, is simply not mentioned. Thirdly, neither *Ynglingatal*, Ari's *Íslendingabók* nor HN say anything about which territory each king inherited from his father, or which areas each king subsequently acquired or lost – things which The Tale and *Ynglinga saga* have much to tell about.

The patterns in these discrepancies and parallels are obvious: the authors of *Ynglinga saga* and The Tale addressed a number of issues, while Ari and the author of HN had a very narrow focus. Ari tells little else than who was son of whom, while the author of HN was concerned with relating a small story about each king. As will be demonstrated, HN in many ways bridges all the texts, as the small stories related there take heed of every piece of information conveyed by Ari, and at the same time they correspond closely to stories that are included in The Tale and *Ynglinga saga* – and, indeed, to *Ynglingatal*.

As will be shown, there are marked similarities between The Tale and *Ynglinga saga* in that their authors include the same types of information. These two texts also include the information presented in HN, but in general the quantity and level of detail of that information is extended. This indicates that the differences noted between Ari's *Íslendingabók* and HN on the one hand, and The Tale and *Ynglinga saga* on the other, are principally to be understood as differences in what the authors were concerned with, and to a much lesser extent as developments in the 12th- and early 13th-century Icelandic historiography, as Krag interprets them. Following from the hypothesis posed above, a main point to be examined below is whether each specific difference would be consistent with the authors' – from Ari to Snorri – having selected their information from a common source, *Ynglingatal*, and having combined it, with some embellishment, with other material from their predecessors' writings and with oral tradition which they had gained knowledge of: and in this way composing their own versions of the Yngling tradition. What would argue against the hypothesis that *Ynglingatal* was known by all the authors in question would be items of information in the texts that might be incompatible with information in *Ynglingatal*, because they could show that the poem was not known to Ari or to the authors of HN and The Tale. Snorri certainly knew the poem, as he refers it.

Before comparing information in the various texts, it is important to clarify obvious relationships between them. The practically verbatim common passages between The Tale and *Ynglinga saga* (Krag 1991:135, 138 and 142) show that their authors had access to some of the same sources. Gjessing (1873:31) assumed that one common source was Ari's lost history of the Norwegian kings, and this is a realistic possibility. As noted, the author of HN also probably had access to this source. Furthermore, *Ynglingatal* is referred to in The Tale, which shows that the author knew, or at least knew of, the poem. But the original shape in which The Tale was written down, possibly in the late 12th or early 13th century, is unknown, since it is preserved in quite a late text, *Hauksbók*, written early in the 14th century. Therefore the reference to *Ynglingatal* in The Tale might be a later interpolation, and the author of the original version of The Tale did not necessarily know the poem.

There is no doubt that *Ynglingatal* associates several of the final six Yngling petty kings with Viken, particularly with Vestfold, but not with the Opplands. Of those place-names in the poem that can be located with certainty, only one belongs to the Opplands – the place at which Halfdan Whiteleg died, Toten (Fig. 18.2). In all of the other texts that refer to the Ynglings, including Snorri's *Ynglinga saga*, the Opplands are much more strongly represented. The challenge that the hypothesis discussed here poses is therefore not, like Krag, to explain why Vestfold

Halfdan Whiteleg	Ynglingatal	Ari's Íslendingabók	HN	The Tale	Ynglinga saga
King over		Upplendinga conungr	Accepted as king in montanis (The Opplands?)	Solør	Accepted as king in Solør
Married to				Daughter of the king in Hedmark	Daughter of the king in Hedmark
Conquers/ inherits				Romerike, Hedmark	Romerike, Hedmark, Hadeland, Toten, part of Vestfold, Vermland
Died at	Toten		Toten	Toten	Toten
Buried at	Skereid in Skiringssal			Hedmark	Skereid in Skiringssal

Table 18.1 *Geographical facts relating to Halfdan Whiteleg in the five texts examined.*

comes more strongly into the picture in The Tale and *Ynglinga saga* than in Ari's *Íslendingabók* and HN, but rather to explain why the Opplands should appear so very markedly in all the texts except in *Ynglingatal*. The explanation of this will finally be sought in the motives that the two principal characters, Ari and Snorri, might have had when they worked with the genealogy of the Yngling petty kings.

The whereabouts of the Yngling petty kings

As can be seen from the comparison of geographic information related to the first of the six "Norwegian" Ynglings, Halfdan Whiteleg (Tab. 18.1), there is essentially agreement between the five texts where they have the same type of information, but elsewhere there are discrepancies in respect of both the type of information included and the level of its detail. The general pattern is that the scope of themes and the level of detail increases from Ari/HN to The Tale and further still in *Ynglinga saga*. Ari's *Íslendingabók* and HN have few and non-specific geographical details, but as Solør is in the Opplands, there is no contradiction between them and those found in *Ynglingatal* and The Tale. The Tale and *Ynglinga saga* each give accounts of Halfdan's conquests, which Ari's *Íslendingabók* and HN do not. There are no contradictions between their accounts, although *Ynglinga saga* includes more regions than The Tale. But, significantly, there is a contradiction between The Tale and *Ynglingatal* concerning Halfdan's place of burial.

Ynglingatal only offers information on Halfdan's places of death and burial, but does not, directly, offer information on the area he ruled. Nevertheless, it is reasonable to assume that he would have been buried

in the heart of the area he ruled, which would then be in Vestfold. However all the other texts associate him exclusively, *Ynglinga saga* primarily, with the Opplands. How should these differences be understood?

The association of the Yngling petty kings with the Opplands had begun in the previous generation. On Halfdan's father, Olaf Tree-cutter, *Ynglingatal* offers the curt information that he burnt *við vág*, "by the sea/bay". In *Ynglinga saga* this is expanded by the statement that he died in a fire by Lake Vänern, after he had cleared the land of Vermland. The latter information is also recorded in The Tale. In geographical terms, Vermland is adjacent to the Opplands (Fig. 18.2); therefore, by identifying *vág* with Lake Vänern and by placing Olaf in Vermland, Snorri and the author of The Tale establish the Opplands as being the point of entry for the Ynglings to Norway. It is worth noting that the connexion between Olaf and Vermland/Vänern does not follow from the information supplied in *Ynglingatal*. In light of the other geographical information in *Ynglingatal*, like the burial place of Olaf's son Halfdan, the *vág* might just as well be the Oslofjord.

Ari's *Íslendingabók* and HN also associate Halfdan with the Opplands. Ari wrote that Halfdan was king of Oppland, while HN offers a slightly more detailed account that may provide a better idea of what had been included in Ari's lost history of the kings. The list of kings that is preserved in Ari's *Íslendingabók* is assumed to be just an abbreviated version of his lost history. What is worthy of attention is that HN does not tell us where Halfdan's power was situated; it only tells us who it was that accepted him as king when he arrived from Sweden – *Norwagensis in montanis* – which probably means the Opplanders.

This is in fact exactly what Snorri says. The omission of Halfdan's later conquests, as related in The Tale and in *Ynglinga saga,* from both Ari's *Íslendingabók* and HN is consistent with the fact that these two texts do not include that sort of information for any of the Yngling petty kings.

The absence of information on Halfdan's place of burial in Ari's *Íslendingabók* and HN is hardly to be regarded as significant. No such information is recorded for any king in those two texts. Snorri's reliance on the information about Halfdan's place of burial in *Ynglingatal* rather than in The Tale, if indeed he had access to the latter or to its sources, is also readily explicable. It is fully congruent with the principles for writing history that Snorri laid out in his introduction to *Heimskringla;* he writes that he has most confidence in poems because they are old and because wise men have regarded them as true.

Unlike Ari's *Íslendingabók,* HN and The Tale, Snorri attributed Halfdan with the acquisition of power over Vermland, which in the west borders on Solør, and thus is topographically connected to the Opplands. But he also assigns a conquest of part of Vestfold to Halfdan, information that is not found in any of the other three texts. Snorri probably inserted the conquest of Vestfold so that he could explain why, according to *Ynglingatal,* Halfdan was buried in Vestfold. He apparently thought that Halfdan must have had some association with Vestfold because that was where he was buried. It thus seems that Snorri has attempted to reconcile *Ynglingatal's* indistinct geographic information on Olaf's place of death (the *vág)* and the indisputable connexion of Halfdan to Vestfold found there, with the information in Ari's text and those of other historians that he may have had access to, all of which, as far as they are known, connect Halfdan with the Opplands.

The discrepancy between The Tale and *Ynglingatal* in respect of Halfdan's place of burial must have some other explanation. It is necessary to look at the context in which this detail is given in The Tale, and to compare that with Snorri's text. The Tale relates that Halfdan's father Olaf and his men had to flee north of Lake Vänern …

… ok ruddu þar markir ok byggðu þar stór heruð ok kölluðu þat Vermaland, ok kölluðu Svíar því Óláf trételgju, ok var hann þar konungr til elli. Kona hans hét Sölva. Hún var systir Sölva ins gamla, er fyrstr ruddi Sóleyjar. Óláfr ok Sölva áttu tvá syni, hét annarr Ingjaldr, en annarr Hálfdan. Ingjaldr var konungr í Vermalandi eptir föður sinn, en Hálfdan var fæddr upp í Sóleyjum með Sölva, móður-bróður sínum. Hann var kallaðr Hálfdan hvítbein. Hann var konungr í Sóleyjum eptir Sölva konung. Hann fékk Ásu, dóttur Eysteins konungs illráða af Heið. Sá Eysteinn lag_i undir sik Eynafylki í þrándheimi ok fekk þeim til konungs þar hund sinn, er Sórr hét; við hann er kenndr Sórshaugr. Hálfdan hvítbein eignaðist Raumaríki ok mikit

af Heiðmörk. Hann varð sóttdauðr á ðótni, ok var hann fluttr á Heiðmörk ok heygðr þar.

… and they cleared fields there and settled a great area which they called Vermland, and the Swedes gave Olaf the nickname of Tree-cutter, and he remained king there into his old age. His wife was called Sölva. She was the sister of Sölvi the Old, who first cleared Solør. Olaf and Sölva had two sons, one called Ingjald and the other Halfdan. Ingjald was king in Vermland after his father, but Halfdan was brought up in Solør by Sölvi, his mother's brother. He was known as Halfdan Whiteleg. He was king of Solør after King Sölvi. He married Asa, daughter of King Eystein Hard-ruler of Hedmark. This Eystein had conquered Øynafylke in Trøndelag and made his dog king there, whose name was Sor; Sorshaug [= Sakshaug] is named after him. Halfdan Whiteleg gained possession of Romerike and much of Hedmark. He died on his sickbed in Toten, and was carried to Hedmark and buried under a barrow there.

The author of The Tale has interpolated here the story of the Oppland king Eystein's harrying of Trøndelag and the barrow for his dog. Snorri included that story as well, but he put it into the saga of Hakon the Good (Ch. 12), so that it appears in Snorri a couple of centuries later than The Tale has it.

There is another point at which the author of The Tale and Snorri used the old traditions in a different way, and this point is more relevant to our immediate concerns. The introductions concerning Olaf's clearances in Vermland are practically identical, but the following passage in Snorri on his spouse and his kindred is different from The Tale:

Ólafr fékk konu þeirra, er Sölveig hét eða Sölva, dóttir Hálfdanar gulltannar vestan af Sóleyjum. Hálfdan var son Sölva, Sölvarssonar, Sölvasonar hins gamla, er fyrstr ruddi Sóleyjar. … Ólafr ok Sölva áttu tvá sonu, Ingjald ok Hálf-dan; Hálfdan var uppfœddr í Sóleyjum með Sölva, móður-bróður sínum; hann var kallaðr Hálfdan hvítbeinn.

Olaf married a woman who was called Solveig or Sölva, the daughter of Halfdan Goldtooth west in Solør. Halfdan was the son of Sölvi, son of Sölvi son of Sölvi the Old, who was the first to clear and settle Solør … Olaf and Sölva had two sons, Ingjald and Halfdan. Halfdan grew up in Solør in the home of his mother's brother Sölvi, and he was known as Halfdan Whiteleg.

One can see that, in The Tale, the genealogy of Olaf's wife Sölva has been cut down by four generations compared to her genealogy in *Ynglinga saga.* While The Tale has her as the sister of Sölvi the Old, she is his great-great-granddaughter according to *Ynglinga saga.* Here, her father is given as Halfdan Goldtooth. However, this Halfdan otherwise does not appear in *Ynglinga saga* either before or after, and indeed neither do his ancestors all the way back to Sölvi the Old.

Eystein Fart	*Ynglingatal Íslendingabók*	Ari's	HN	The Tale	*Ynglinga saga*
First king of				Romerike	Romerike and part of Vestfold
Married to				Daughter of the king of Vestfold	Daughter of the king of Vestfold
Conquers /inherits					The rest of Vestfold
Buried at	On the point of the ridge by the Vadla stream		Body lost		On the ridge by Vadla in Borre

Table 18.2 *Geographical facts relating to Eystein Fart in the five texts examined.*

There is therefore no reason to believe that Snorri has invented these generations; rather it was probably the author of The Tale, or of his source, who reduced the genealogy that had been laid out in an earlier and more comprehensive text.

However, a reduction of that kind causes complications: in this case, between the two Halfdans in the story. What The Tale's author presents as the burial place of Halfdan Whiteleg might in his source, which he seems to have cut substantially, have been given as the burial place of Halfdan Goldtooth. For Halfdan Goldtooth to have been buried in Hedmark would indeed be reasonable because he is not identified as having been king anywhere other than in the Opplands. It seems that the author of The Tale was responsible for a similar merging of information in the case of Gudrød the Hunter-King (Tab. 18.4) who, according to the author of The Tale, died at Stiflusund which was at Geirstad in Vestfold. However, no other text locates Stiflusund, nor refers to Geirstad except in connexion with Gudrød's son Olaf Geirstad-Elf.

It may thus appear that both the author of The Tale and Snorri were faced with a problem over Halfdan Whiteleg's place of burial, and opted for very different solutions. Snorri decided to place his trust in the information in *Ynglingatal*, and might himself have added that Halfdan conquered part of Vestfold in order to rationalize the place which was, according to *Ynglingatal*, chosen for his burial. On the other hand, the author of The Tale located Halfdan's place of burial in Hedmark based upon a source which he corrupted in the process of cutting it down, or which might have been corrupt in the first place.

In the account of Eystein Fart (Tab. 18.2), the same relationship between the texts is found as in respect of Halfdan, i.e. the scope of themes and the level of detail increases from HN to The Tale and fur-

ther still in *Ynglinga saga*. No information on Eystein's place of burial is given in The Tale but it is there in *Ynglingatal*. The detail that Eystein inherited the rest of Vestfold from his father-in-law is only to be found in *Ynglinga saga*. But this is also implied in The Tale in that it is stated there that his father-in-law had no sons. The information that Vadla is situated in Borre, Vestfold, is only found in *Ynglinga saga*.

There is less discrepancy between the texts in respect of what they have to say about Eystein than in what they have to say about Halfdan. The only point at which there might appear to be a contradiction is in HN's claim that Eystein's body disappeared, *"disparuit"*, in the sea after he was thrown overboard. Krag (1991:135) considers it important that this does not agree with *Ynglingatal* or *Ynglinga saga*, both of which say he was buried in a barrow. But the contradiction is less obvious than it may seem. Firstly, HN does not mention either the burial or burial place of any of the Ynglings. This seems to have been a deliberate and systematic omission made by the author when he selected his information from his sources. It may seem as if he chose to write that the body disappeared simply to round off appropriately the story of Eystein's drowning. Secondly, there is in fact no contradiction in the disappearance of the body of the deceased and the raising of a barrow for him. There are many such cenotaphs, empty barrows known from the Viking Period in Scandinavia (Skre, this vol. Ch. 16:380–1).

In respect of Halfdan the Mild, there is the same expansion in the scope of themes and the level of detail as observed above, but there are no contradictions between the texts (Tab. 18.3). Nor in the case of Gudrød the Hunter-King are there any contradictions between the texts (Tab. 18.4).

Ari's *Íslendingabók* and HN say nothing about Olaf Geirstad-Elf (Tab. 18.5), only about his assumed brother Halfdan the Black, who is not, however, men-

Halfdan the Mild	*Ynglingatal*	Ari's *Íslendingabók*	HN	The Tale	*Ynglinga saga*
King of				The kingdom of Eystein	The kingdom of Eystein
Married to				Daughter of the king of Vestmar	Daughter of the king of Vestmar
Place of residence	Holtan				Holtan in Vestfold
Died at				Vestfold	Vestfold
Buried at	Borre			Vestfold	Borre

Table 18.3 *Geographical facts relating to Halfdan the Mild in the five texts examined.*

tioned in *Ynglingatal*, and who is consequently not dealt with here. Between the other texts there is the usual development in scope and detail of information, but no contradictions. Still, comparing the information about Olaf's domains with that about his forefathers', there is one puzzling detail. The Tale and *Ynglinga saga* are in agreement that Olaf lost his domains in the Opplands and only retained power over areas in Viken. What is puzzling is that he *had so* much territory in the Opplands in the first place, because his kingdom there, as far as it can be traced back through his ancestors to Eystein Fart, was only supposed to have comprised Romerike. Neither The Tale nor *Ynglingatal* relate that it was extended during the two generations that lie between Eystein and Olaf. Concerning the extent of the kingdom of Olaf and his three immediate predecessors, it seems that both Snorri and the author of The Tale were unable to produce internally consistent histories.

What is more important, though, is that The Tale and *Ynglinga saga* are not entirely in agreement over which areas Olaf held in Viken, and here also both these texts disagree to some extent with *Ynglingatal*. The poem as reproduced in *Ynglinga saga* does not mention Grenland and Vestmar; these places are only mentioned in the strophe reproduced in the Tale of Olaf Geirstad-Elf in *Flateyjarbók* (Krag 1991:141). It is possible that Snorri omitted this strophe because the information there did not suit his purposes (see below). But it is also possible that Snorri did not know this strophe. Whatever the case, there is a stronger focus on Vestfold in Snorri's text than in the strophe in *Flateyjarbók,* as Grenland is definitely not a part of Vestfold and Vestmar could at most comprise the southernmost part of the area that was identified as Vestfold (Fig. 18.2).

Gudrød the Hunter king	*Ynglingatal*	Ari's *Íslendingabók*	HN	The Tale	*Ynglinga saga*
First king of					The kingdom of Halfdan
Married to					Daughter of the king of Alfheim
Conquers /inherits					Half of Vingulmark
Died at	Stiflusund			Stiflusund at Geirstad in Vestfold	Stiflusund
Buried at					

Table 18.4 *Geographical facts relating to Gudrød the Hunter-King in the five texts examined.*

Olaf Geirstad-Elf	Ynglingatal	Ari's Íslendingabók	HN	The Tale	Ynglinga saga
King of	Grenland and Vestmar			Grenland and Vestfold	Vestfold
Loses				Vingulmark, Romerike, Hedmark, Solør	Vingulmark, Romerike, Hedmark, Toten, Hadeland and Vermland
Place of residence					Geirstad
Died at	Folden beach			Geirstad	
Buried at	Geirstad			Geirstad	Geirstad

Table 18.5 *Geographical facts relating to Olaf Geirstad-Elf in the five texts examined.*

In the case of the final Yngling, Rögnvald Lord of the Heaths, there is also a contradiction between The Tale and *Ynglinga saga* in respect of where his kingdom lay (Tab. 18.6). This is discussed below.

The Oppland viewpoint and the Vestfold viewpoint

This review of the geographical information about the Ynglings in the five texts examined reveals weaknesses in Krag's argument that the texts, from Ari's *Íslendingabók* /HN to The Tale to *Ynglinga saga*, reflect a steady reinforcement of the idea that the Ynglings belonged to Vestfold. Moreover, it undermines his basis for placing *Ynglingatal* in that sequence, and his claim that this placement reveals at what time the poem was composed. As has been shown, both similarities and differences between the texts can be explained in other and simpler ways than Krag does. And at no single point is it necessary, or indeed even reasonable, to assume, as Krag infers, that *Ynglingatal* was unknown to Ari, or to the authors of HN and The Tale.

In this section, the main points of the survey just undertaken will be summarized within a sketch of how the historians from Ari to Snorri handled the information on the Ynglings they probably had available to them. Are there any patterns in their handling,

and if so, what might explain them?

As was shown above, in the highly abbreviated version of Ari's history of the Norwegian kings that we have, there is very little information on the Ynglings. The context in which such information as is given appears is nevertheless illuminating. There are two places in his text in which Ari lays out sections of varying lengths of the Yngling genealogy, first a short section on the dynasty of Harald Fairhair and then a slightly longer section on Ari's own kindred (Jónsson 1930:7 and 41). In Ari's genealogies the kings from Halfdan Whiteleg onwards have the same bynames as in Snorri's *Ynglinga saga* written a century later, but these bynames do not appear in *Ynglingatal*. These bynames indicate that in Ari's time there were already stories about each of these petty kings, probably inspired in part by *Ynglingatal*.

The *only* piece of geographic information found in Ari's *Íslendingabók* concerning the four generations of "Norwegian" Yngling petty kings mentioned by him is that he refers to Halfdan as a king of Oppland, *Upplendinga conungr*. This is indeed in agreement with the information in *Ynglingatal* that he died at Toten, but not with the poem's evidence that he was buried at Skiringssal. The place of burial has to be regarded as providing a stronger indication of where Halfdan really belonged than his place of

Rögnvald Lord of the Health	Ynglingatal	Ari's Íslendingabók	HN	The Tale	Ynglinga saga
King of				Grenland	Vestfold

Table 18.6 *Geographical facts relating to Rögnvald Lord of the Heaths in the five texts examined.*

Historia Norvegiæ	Ynglinga saga
Halfdan Whiteleg was accepted as king in the Opplands when he came from Sweden	Halfdan was *first* king over Solør, which is in the Opplands
Halfdan Whiteleg died at Toten	Halfdan Whiteleg died at Toten
Implies that Gudrød the Hunter-King had a kingdom *in montanis* (presumably the Opplands)	Implies that Gudrød the Hunter-King had a kingdom in the Opplands as well as in Vestfold

Table 18.7 *A comparison of the three geographical facts found in* Historia Norvegiæ *with their corresponding versions in* Ynglinga saga *shows that there are no discrepancies. Here it is inferred that HN's phrase* in montanis *refers in fact to the Opplands.*

death; but why then, if Ari really knew *Ynglingatal*, did he make him a king of Oppland?

The explanation must lie in an idea which was probably Ari's own – the linking of the dynasty of Harald Fairhair to the Ynglings as he knew them from *Ynglingatal* and from other sources. If he could persuasively establish such a link, he could follow Harald's ancestry right back to the legendary kings of Uppsala. Through the work of Ari's predecessor Sæmund the Wise, Harald was already associated with the Opplands by the identification of the king of Oppland, Halfdan the Black, as his father. Ari's contribution was probably that he joined the Ynglings, with such information as he had about them from *Ynglingatal* and possibly other sources, to the kindred of Halfdan the Black. But the problem was that the Ynglings, according to the place-names in *Ynglingatal*, were *only* associable with Viken – except in just one case. That exception was the information in *Ynglingatal* that Halfdan Whiteleg died at Toten. Ari picked this up, and aided by this one piece of information he managed to turn Halfdan into a king of Oppland.

This intervention, making the Ynglings kings of Oppland, can be called the *Oppland viewpoint;* Ari was probably its originator. By means of it, Ari was able not only to give Harald Fairhair a very distinguished genealogy but also to link *himself* to the then royal family of Norway. For he believed he could connect his own family to the Ynglings through Halfdan Whiteleg's second son Gudrød being his own ancestor fourteen generations back (Jónsson 1930:41).

Krag attaches particular importance to the differences in the geographical references between Ari's *Íslendingabók* /HN on the one hand and The Tale and *Ynglinga saga* on the other. But, as noted, several of the differences between them seem rather to be attributable to what the three authors were really concerned with, which in the case of the author of HN was not geography. Ari may have been concerned with

this sort of material, but that is difficult to determine because from his hand we have only the two genealogical lists with little geographical information, not the entire history he apparently wrote of the kings.

The development that Krag detects in the Ynglings' whereabouts from HN to *Ynglinga saga* is not, in fact, as obvious as he claims. If one takes the geographical information in HN on its own, which consists of only three points, direct comparison with the corresponding details in *Ynglinga saga* shows that there is complete agreement (Tab. 18.7). In respect of Halfdan, just like *Ynglinga saga*, HN says nothing more than where he was first accepted as king, not where he might subsequently have conquered. In the case of Gudrød, the fact, according to HN, that his son Halfdan the Black succeeded him in the Opplands is here taken to imply that Gudrød held power in the Opplands. Likewise, the fact, according to *Ynglinga saga*, that Gudrød succeeded to the kingdom of Halfdan the Mild, successor of Eystein Fart, who was king in Vestfold plus Romerike, which is in the Opplands, is here taken to imply that Gudrød *also* ruled in the Opplands.

Consequently, no real change can be detected from the geographical information in HN to that given by Snorri in *Ynglinga saga*. Therefore, the development of the Vestfold viewpoint as described by Krag has no foundation in these two texts. Also, in light of the lack of geographical information in HN, it seems unreasonable for Krag (1990:183–4, cf. 1991: 145) to write that the author of HN, in Krag's view basing himself on Ari's lost history of the kings, "manifestly presents the 'Norwegian' Yngling kings, both Halfdan Whiteleg and all his descendants down to and including Halfdan the Black, as kings of Oppland" ("entydig fremstiller de 'norske' ynglingekongene, både Halvdan Hvitbein og alle ettermennene hans til og med Halvdan Svarte, som opplandskonger"). One ought rather to say that HN, together with the preserved work of Ari, offers minimal information on the territories ruled by the Ynglings from Halfdan Whiteleg to Gudrød the Hunter-King.

It also seems unjustifiable for Krag (1990:145) to consider all the information in The Tale and *Ynglinga saga* that is not found in the surviving genealogies of Ari's *Íslendingabók* or in HN as new additions to the tradition from after Ari's time – for instance, information on the connexion between the Ynglings and Vestfold. All one can say for certain is that this information appeared in the surviving texts after Ari's time and after HN was written. On this issue, Krag's assessment is the drawing of a conclusion *ex silentio*. Contrary to his view, we have to reckon with the possibility that the earlier traditions and texts, possibly including Ari's lost history of the kings, contained much that was not included in his abbreviated genealogical lists and which the author of HN, with his narrower range of interest, chose to omit. There are really no discrepancies between the texts that make it necessary to infer that Ari and the author of HN had no knowledge of *Ynglingatal*.

The Tale is the text that is most difficult to place in relation to the others. As Tables 18.2–18.5 show, The Tale lacks some details that are found in *Ynglingatal* and *Ynglinga saga*. Krag apparently explains this by the *Ynglinga saga* having been composed after The Tale, the two texts representing stages in a gradual consolidation of the Ynglings' connexion with Vestfold. But the relative poverty of The Tale in respect of information on the Vestfold association of the Ynglings could be explained another way. In the first place, the dating of The Tale is uncertain. It could well be later than *Ynglinga saga*, in which case the differences between these two texts would have to have other explanations than Krag's version of their development. Regardless of the texts' dating, it is clear that the author of The Tale was not concerned with the Ynglings in the way that Ari and Snorri were, as his primary concern was with the kings of the Opplands. The overriding focus on the Opplands in The Tale is perfectly apparent in the text. For instance, it tells of the kingdom Halfdan Whiteleg's second son Gudrød held in Hedmark, and of four generations of his descendants. This is material that Snorri did not include in *Ynglinga saga*. On this matter, The Tale probably stands closer to Ari's lost history of the kings, since it was indeed from this Gudrød that Ari himself reckoned his descent.

In this way, one could say that The Tale expresses a clearer Oppland viewpoint than that which is found in *Ynglinga saga*. It is difficult, however, to see, as Krag does, The Tale as a stage in a development of the Yngling tradition leading to a Vestfold viewpoint. If nothing else, the uncertain dating of The Tale is a problem here. The Tale can reasonably be regarded as an attempt to relate the story of kings of the Opplands and to construct a genealogy for the Fairhair

dynasty by reconciling information from diverse sources for the royal lines in eastern Norway in the 8th and 9th centuries. The solutions selected by the author of The Tale in such a reconciling were probably more similar to Ari's than to Snorri's.

Snorri too must have laboured to get Harald Fairhair's genealogy to hold together. Unlike Ari in the preserved text from his hand, Snorri included all of the geographical information from *Ynglingatal*, and this faced him with an even more demanding task than that which Ari had. As a result, many of the 'facts' in *Ynglinga saga* concerning the marriages and conquests of the Yngling petty kings were probably concocted by Snorri in order to shape a consistent history.

There is, however, one feature of the rich material in *Ynglinga saga* concerning Vestfold that is so striking that it cannot be explained in this way. This concerns the items of information that are not found in any other text, not even in *Ynglingatal*, and which therefore cannot be interpreted as the sharpening up of material that in other and earlier sources was presented in more general terms:

- Snorri's statement that the burial place of Eystein Fart at Vadla is situated at Borre in Vestfold. *Ynglingatal* refers only to the Vadla stream (Tab. 18.2).
- Snorri's narrowing of Olaf Geirstad-Elf's kingdom in Viken to Vestfold alone. *Ynglingatal* gives Grenland and Vestmar; The Tale Grenland and Vestfold (Tab. 18.5).
- Snorri's information that Rögnvald Lord of the Heath's kingdom was in Vestfold. The Tale says it was in Grenland (Tab. 18.6).

What one can see from all three points is that Snorri tended to link three of the Yngling petty kings more closely to Vestfold than the authors of the other texts, including *Ynglingatal*, did. Concerning the first point, it is not certain where Vadla was. It may in fact have been a place in Østfold (Skre, this vol. Ch. 20: 465), and Snorri may have claimed a different location for Vadla at the cost of that site. In the next two points, Snorri's sharpening up of the information was at the cost of Grenland and Vestmar, the southernmost part of modern Vestfold and the areas beyond that to the west and south-west (Fig. 18.2). It thus appears reasonable to conclude, along with Krag, that Snorri did have a Vestfold viewpoint in the sense that he exaggerated the connexion between certain Ynglings and this *fylki*. It is conceivable that Snorri's understanding on each of the above three points was derived from sources he relied upon. But his tendency to exaggerate is sufficiently clear to oblige us to consider whether he may have had some specific agenda.

Snorri manifestly wished to give Harald Fairhair and his successors a long and honourable genealogy by creating a clear and solid association between them and the Yngling petty kings. He harmonized a variety of sources, and based himself principally upon those he found most reliable. It would appear as if on specific matters he wanted to connect the Ynglings more clearly to Vestfold than was the case in those of his sources that have survived. Krag (1990: 185–90) explains this tendency on the basis that Danish pressure on Viken from the mid-1160s down to Snorri's time may have rendered it desirable for him, and for those who commissioned him, to emphasize the historical right that the Norwegian royal dynasty had to one of the regions within the disputed area – the claim to Vestfold. But if one looks at the three points above, Snorri's tendency to exaggerate the Yngling petty kings' connexion with Vestfold does not represent any toning up of the significance of Viken, as Krag claims. Snorri's Vestfold viewpoint was developed at the expense of areas that lie partly *within* Viken. Vestmar was part of Viken, and Grenland is also in some contexts considered part of this region.

Snorri's Vestfold viewpoint, as it has been laid out in the three points above, thus has to have a different explanation from that which Krag proposed. Krag's main explanation, that Snorri desired to show the historical right of the Fairhair dynasty to Viken, is probably true. That he allowed Vestfold to assume a greater importance than other parts of Viken may be due to the fact that he understood this to be the most significant area within the region. His stay in the town of Tønsberg in Vestfold in 1217–1218 may be relevant here. The imposing burial mounds of Vestfold, not least the large group at Borre, may have made an impression on him (Skre, this vol. Ch. 1:Fig. 1.1). There are no equivalent groups of great barrows in Vestmar. By referring to their burial mounds, and thus linking the Ynglings all the more firmly with Viken, he may have intended to reinforce the Norwegian king's claim to this territory.

Both Ari and Snorri very probably connected the poem about the Yngling petty kings, a royal line in Viken, to the Fairhair dynasty by asserting ties of kinship between the Yngling petty kings and petty kings in the Opplands. This procedure faced both of them with problems to which they found different solutions. Ari's solution was probably governed by the fact that he was concerned above all to connect Harald Fairhair and his forefathers in the Opplands to the genealogy of *Ynglingatal*, and thus he picked up the only piece of information in *Ynglingatal* that could be used to establish such a link – that Halfdan Whiteleg died at Toten. That is probably the reason why Halfdan is the only one of the "Norwegian" Ynglings that Ari supplies with any geographical information.

Snorri had the same objective, but as he chose to take heed of all of the geographical information in *Ynglingatal* without loosening the connexion between the Ynglings and the Opplands, he had to produce a much stronger connexion between the Yngling petty kings and Oppland than is found in *Ynglingatal* and in what is preserved of Ari's writings. Snorri, or the authors of his sources, achieved this by connecting Halfdan Whiteleg to the Solør dynasty in the Opplands and by placing his father in the neighbouring district Vermland. The following generations of Yngling petty kings were, as additions to their kingdom in Vestfold and Viken as they could be inferred from *Ynglingatal*, supplied with possessions in the Opplands by Snorri or by the authors of his sources.

Compared to the author of *Ynglingatal* therefore, both Ari and Snorri have a distinct Oppland viewpoint. Snorri also wanted to strengthen the foothold of the Fairhair dynasty in Vestfold as opposed to the rest of Viken, and on two points went further in that direction than *Ynglingatal* provides any basis for. In this sense it is correct to say that Snorri's *Ynglinga saga* – in comparison with *Ynglingatal*, Ari's *Íslendingabók* and The Tale alike – had a Vestfold viewpoint.

For his part, Krag concluded, as noted, that *Ynglingatal* has a less developed Vestfold viewpoint than is found in Snorri, and consequently he placed the poem between HN and Snorri in the sequence of development he believed he could trace from Ari's Oppland viewpoint to Snorri's Vestfold position. As has been shown here though, Snorri also gave the Ynglings a much more conspicuous connexion with Oppland than appears in *Ynglingatal*. In Krag's developmental scheme of the Vestfold viewpoint, logically, the composition of *Ynglingatal* should therefore be dated *after* Snorri's *Ynglinga saga* – a state of affairs that must be taken as an indication that the course of development Krag believed he discovered fails to take account of essential elements in the relationships between the texts.

18.3 Anachronisms?

In this section and that which follows, two topics will be examined, both of which may show that the traditional dating of *Ynglingatal* to the end of the 9th century is the correct one. A literary and philological contextualization of a poem from c. AD 900 or a little earlier is inevitably difficult, considering the relatively few, fragmentary and late-copied literary works that are preserved from this period. Such a contextualization has nonetheless been explored in an exhaustive way, most recently by Walter Åkerlund (1939) and Claus Krag (1991). What is attempted in the following is rather what might be called a cultural-historical contextualization. In this first section, it is argued that a Christian frame of mind like that Krag believed he could identify in *Ynglingatal* could indeed have been introduced to Scandinavia as early as the 9th century. After that (18.4), it will be investigated whether the association with the kingdom of the Svear and Uppsala that is found in the poem could be chronologically diagnostic of the beginning of the Viking Age.

Even if one accepts Krag's conclusion that the four-element doctrine stands behind the construction of two kennings in *Ynglingatal* (18.1), it remains to evaluate his dating of its introduction to Scandinavia to the end of the 11th century and the first decades of the 12th (Krag 1991:58). To begin with, Krag supplies no evidence to support this dating; he merely asserts it. On the question of such a late dating of the introduction of the doctrine to Scandinavia, Sandnes (1994:230) concurred with Magnus Olsen's view that one "…should not underestimate the cultural level and the 'European' orientation of the poetic circle around the petty kings of Vestfold in the early Viking Age" ("…ikke bør undervurdere det kulturelle nivå og den "europeiske" orientering i skaldemiljøet omkring vestfoldkongene i tidlig vikingtid").

This early European orientation is all the more plausible when one notes that the traditional late 9th-century dating of the poem places it in a milieu with close connexions to the urban site Kaupang in Skiringssal, where ships with people and goods from the Frankish lands would anchor, and where, too, people from those areas probably resided for periods (Skre, this vol. Ch. 20:455). As Krag writes, the four-element doctrine was by then common knowledge in the Christian areas, and contact between the Scandinavians and the Christian Franks in Skiringssal and similar sites must have been sufficiently close and durable for ideas about the fundamental constitution of the world – such as we can characterize the four-element doctrine to be – to have been passed on.

The inscription on the Rök stone shows that both legendary material and ecclesiastical points of view from the Frankish Empire – along with specifically Christian philosophies – were known in Northern elite circles in the 9th century. This, the longest runic inscription in Scandinavia, consists of about 750 runes carved into a stone in the churchyard of Rök in Östergötland, Sweden. It is dated by most scholars to the beginning of the 9th century. The inscription includes a reference to the Ostrogothic King, Theoderic the Great, who died in 526, and who, at the time the inscription was made, was a popular but controversial character in Francia (Wessén 1958:38). The Church condemned him, in part because Pope John died as his prisoner. However he was very popular amongst commoners and aristocrats alike due to his renown as a wise lord and redoubtable warrior (Wessén 1958:43; Grønvik 1983:113–18, 2003:57–60). The Emperor Charlemagne's removal of his statue from Ravenna to Aachen, a very demanding project, shows the importance that was then attached to him. A knowledge of these conflicting views of Theoderic must, according to Ottar Grønvik's assessment, lie behind a passage in the inscription which Grønvik (1983:114) understands as: "… and still talked about, discussed are his [Theoderic's] affairs, i.e. the lawsuits or conflicts he was involved in" ("…og fremdeles samtales det, diskuteres det om hans [Theodoriks] saker, d.e. om de rettssaker eller stridigheter han var innblandet i") (cf. Grønvik 2003:54).

The reference to Theoderic on the Rök stone was probably the result of the flourishing of attention to him and of legends concerning him in the wake of the transhipment of his mounted statue in 801, to become the first equestrian statue north of the Alps. In a strophe in the inscription, Theoderic is described as sitting on his steed with his shield hanging on a strap over his shoulder; this description agrees with a contemporary description of the statue. Whoever composed the inscription, or a source close to him, must have seen the statue himself (Wessén 1958:44; Grønvik 1983:117, 2003:54–5 and 58–9).

The moving of the statue resulted in the wide dissemination of the idea that the origins of the Goths lay in the North. The reference to Theoderic in the Rök inscription shows that this idea and other legends about him were known in the milieu in which the inscription was composed. The reference to him on the Rök stone probably derived from a desire to create an association with Theoderic by incorporating him into the genealogy of the man in whose memory the inscription was made (Widmark 1997: 174). Grønvik's dating of the inscription to c. AD 810 is based partly on philological criteria, and partly on the number of generations which, the inscription claims, had passed since the death of Theoderic. Even if one applies Bugge's dating (1910) to 830–840 or Düwel's dating (2001:115) to the first half of the 9th century, one can nonetheless state that the inscription, and probably also the sources it was based upon, were fully up-to-date with contemporary events and currents in the Frankish realm, including the views and doctrine of the Church (Grønvik 2003:55).

Even if one were to accept Krag's argument that knowledge of the four-element doctrine is reflected in the text of *Ynglingatal*, it is nonetheless possible that this teaching and other Christian elements he believes to be reflected in the poem were known in elite Scandinavian circles in the late 9th century. For example, such knowledge could have been the result of either the extensive voyaging from Scandinavia from c. AD 800 onwards, or of people from Christian lands during this period travelling to and even taking up residence in the urban communities of Scandinavia. As Fidjestøl (1994:196–7) pointed out, the four-element doctrine was not used in the poem to highlight a specific idea involving what the doctrine itself is concerned with, namely the creation and fundamental constitution of the world. This lack of active use of the doctrine to convey its true message, is thoroughly consistent with the skald not assuming that

Figure 18.3 *Map of Gamla Uppsala, showing (B) the three great barrows of c. AD 550–625, (F) the church that includes what remains of the cathedral of the beginning of the 12th century, and (G–H) the two platforms north of the church. On the southerly platform (G) traces of two halls were excavated in 1988–1992, the earlier one from the beginning of the 7th century and the later raised in the mid-8th century and burnt to the ground at the end of the 9th or sometime in the 10th century. Georadar surveys reveal that there was a later hall on a platform 60 m long, part of which was covered by the church, while part of the platform extends north from there (Fig. 18.4). This may be the hall of the 10th and 11th centuries that was described by Adam of Bremen. Contour interval 2 m. Illustration, Duczko 1997.*

this message was familiar to all of his audience. Nor do the other anachronisms identified by Krag appear in such a fashion as to imply that the poem's public was thoroughly schooled in the Christian world-view. The way these elements are used, and the inchoate form in which they appear, is in fact consistent with these Christian concepts having been adopted, integrated, and reformed within a non-Christian world-view. Such a flexible and adaptive approach to new philosophies is typical of Norse paganism, which can be characterized as a non-dogmatic religion that readily incorporated new gods and concepts (Steinsland 2005:33–4).

Krag's attempts to cast off *Ynglingatal*'s late 9th-century moorings were thus perhaps not so successful. There is good reason to question his case for anachronisms in the poem (18.1). And even if one accepts that the relevant elements are to be found in *Ynglingatal*, it still remains to make the case that they actually *are* out of place in a poem of the late 9th century, which Krag does not do.

All the same, this is a *negative* argument in the sense that it only casts doubt on the basis of Krag's conclusion concerning the poem's date. This argument does not in itself provide any *positive* evidence that the poem does indeed come from Thjodolf's era. That would require us to identify features within *Ynglingatal* that can be accepted as typical of the early Viking Period. In the next section the association with Uppsala that appears in the poem will be examined in this regard.

18.4 Emulatio Uppsaliensis

At Gamla Uppsala in Uppland, Sweden (Skre, this vol. Ch. 1:Fig. 1.3), traces of settlement dating from as early as the Bronze Age have been found; furthermore, there are remains of what can be called an aristocratic social group (Duczko 1993; Sundqvist 2002: 94) dating from the 6th/7th century onwards

throughout the Viking Period. Here there were hundreds of grave mounds, many of them still preserved, and foremost amongst them four immense barrows. Excavations have shown that two of them contained elite graves of the 6th and 7th centuries (Ljungkvist 2006:57). The grave itself in the third mound has not been excavated, but limited excavations in the barrow have shown that it is of the same period (Gräslund 1993:191–4). The fourth mound has not been investigated. From the centuries after the huge barrows were built, several hall buildings (see below) testify to the continued aristocratic character of the site.

From the 6th to the 11th century, Uppsala was the place of residence of the uppermost social group in Uppland, referred to in some contexts as "the kings of the Svear [Swedes]". In recent times the place-name has gained the prefix Gamla (Old) because the name Uppsala was transferred in the High Middle Ages to the town that was growing at the site of the former Uppsala harbour, originally known as *Árós*, "river mouth" (Sundqvist 2002:96–7). Below, the name Uppsala is used of the site to which it originally pertained.

In the name Uppsala the element *sala* means "halls" (plural); therefore, the name must derive from more than one hall that stood at the site (Gräslund 1993:180–2; Brink 1999a:38–9, esp. n. 15; Sundqvist 2002:96–7). North of the still standing stone church, built around 1100 (see below), there are two artificial platforms, one higher than the other (Fig. 18.3, G and H). Between 1988 and 1992 parts of two consecutive halls were excavated on the higher platform which is closest to the church. The earlier of these halls, which was constructed at the beginning of the 7th century, was rectangular, 26 m long and 10 m wide. The later one, constructed in the mid-8th century and remaining in use to the end of the 9th century (or perhaps even into the 10th), was 40 m long by 10 m wide, and had bowed long walls. There was probably a hall on

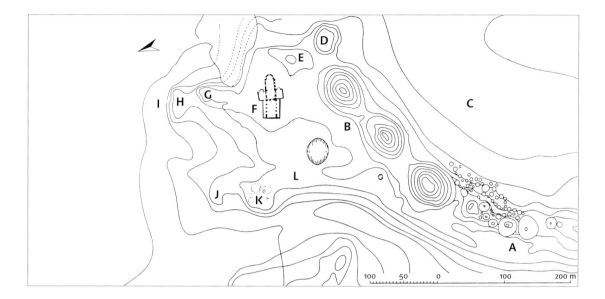

the other platform too, and the name Uppsala presumably derives from the period of these halls: from the 7th century or later (Hedlund 1993; Gräslund 1993; Gräslund 1997; on the date, see Skre, this vol. Ch. 11:230). The name Uppsala is first found recorded on a runestone from Sparlösa in Västergötland. This inscription was probably cut in the 8th century (Gräslund 1993:183).

The date of the construction of the first church at Uppsala is uncertain, but most experts believe that there would have been a wooden church before the large cathedral that was built in stone in the 1130s or a little later. Christian graves have been found that predate this stone church, and several other indications of an earlier wooden church have been uncovered (Sundqvist 2002:298–9). This wooden church, is supposed to have been built on the site of the demolished pagan temple (Sundqvist 2002:299–301; Alkarp and Price 2005).

Just north of the still standing stone church (Fig. 18.3, F) georadar investigations have recently revealed traces of an even larger hall than those excavated on the platform, about 14 m wide (Fig. 18.4, N4 and N5). In the churchyard one can see the outlines of what is thought to be an artificial platform a good 60 m long (Alkarp and Price 2005; Skre, this vol. Ch. 11:230). The supposed remains of the hall revealed by the georadar fit well on to this platform. In the georadar survey, there were also found what are thought to be traces of a wooden church which was probably the first wooden church at this site (Fig. 18.4, N3). This church seems to have been built over the southern part of the foundations of the hall. This hall probably fills the chronological gap between the most recent of the two excavated halls, which was burnt at the end of the 9th century or beginning of the 10th, and the wooden church, which was probably raised at the end of the 11th century or the beginning of the 12th.

It may be this latest hall that Adam of Bremen referred to in his history, from the 1070s, of the archbishopric of Hamburg. He referred to the Uppsala hall several times, first in relation to the period of Archbishop Unni, that is in the 920–930s (Book I, ch. 60). Adam wrote that Uppsala was the most important sacred place of Swedish paganism. As Dillmann (1997) has pointed out, in most cases Adam used a term which means "temple" to refer to the sacred site at Uppsala. But at one point in the text he used the term *triclinium,* which means "dining hall" or "feasting hall". It was evidently a hall of the Norse type, where both feasts and cultic rituals took place, that he had in mind.

Adam's account indicates that the sacred site at Uppsala had a pre-eminent position in the final century of the Viking Age in Scandinavia. Other circumstances indicate that the site had long had such a position. Brink (1996a:63) pointed out the hundreds of *Uppsalr/Uppsalir* farm names that are found in Scandinavia, and wrote:

Their base is … of course the famous *(Old) Uppsala,* the royal and ecclesiastical centre of the Swedes during (at least) the Viking Age and the early Middle Ages.

What may lie behind this name-copying? Some of the *Uppsalr/Uppsalir* farm names clearly derive from the centuries following the Viking Period when they were probably used because people liked them and found them suitable; therefore, people used them widely in those times. Brink (1996a:78) called this the "*psychological* transfer of a name". But in the cases of the earliest of these farm-names, those that date from the Viking Period or even before, he has a different explanation for the name-copying. In these cases, he argues, the farm-name was probably selected in a wish to create a link with a site, usually a highly prestigious one, that the name derived from. Brink (1996a:78) called this the "*socially conditioned* transfer of a name".

In the cases of the earliest *Uppsalr/Uppsalir* farm names, he wrote, it must have been a desire to associate with Uppsala, the royal seat of the Svear and their religious centre, which lay behind the choice of name.

Sandnes (1998), discussing and expanding on Brink's ideas, has undertaken an interesting and necessary refining of the phenomenon of name-copying. As far as the *Uppsalr/Uppsalir* names are concerned, however, he rejects the idea that these represent some copying of Uppsala of the Svear – he describes the notion as "practically absurd" ("bortimot absurd") (1998:86). Surprisingly, this strong rejection of Brink's idea is not supported by any argument, but he proposes a different explanation of the name; that the *Uppsalr/Uppsalir* names were primarily given to settlements that could be characterized by the initial element *upp*, meaning "up"; in other words, their names derived from the fact that they were located on higher ground than other settlements.

Sandnes's explanation, however, is based on some shaky arguments. For example, he explains the absence of the names with the reciprocal name element *ned*, "down", on the basis of his conviction, which is unsupported and therefore of limited value, that settlements in the Norwegian countryside usually spread upwards in the landscape (Sandnes 1998:83, n. 83). A different explanation seems more plausible. Even though no systematic studies have been carried out, one gains a very clear impression from travelling in Norway that farms with the name *Uppsalr/Uppsalir* are located higher in the landscape than the average location of farm settlements. This should be looked at in connexion with a point that Sandnes did not consider, namely the general occurrence of the name element *salr* and its plural, *salir*. In Norway, this name element appears very rarely in any combination other than *Uppsalr/Uppsalir*. That shows that the compounds *Uppsalr/Uppsalir* were a fixed pattern, and that for the most part they were the specific compounds that were used to name farms placed high in the landscape. In Sandnes's terminology (1998:83) this would be "adaptive naming" ("tilpasset oppkalling").

As Brink proposed, this fixed compound name can hardly have any other source than Uppsala in Uppland, Sweden. But the relevant adaptation that took place in the use of *Uppsalr/Uppsalir* indicates that the farm was named because of its location and not necessarily because it stood out already with any of the qualities that were associated with the Uppsala in Sweden. All the same, one cannot ignore the fact that the *Uppsalr/Uppsalir* name carried certain connotations that one would very probably wish to endow the farm with. Whatever the case, the frequent use of the name must imply that the Uppsala of the Svear was popularly known, at least within the areas in which the earliest examples of the *Uppsalr/Uppsalir* name are found.

Oluf Rygh's survey of the names of farms and settlement districts in Norway has 48 *Uppsalr/Uppsalir* farms (Rygh 1897–1936). Most of these, 33 cases, are in eastern Norway. There are also four in Agder, nine in western Norway, one in Trøndelag and one in Nordland. A small minority of these 48 names may date from after the age of the Uppsala temple, but this would not disturb the striking concentration in eastern Norway – it must reflect in which part of Norway the name *Uppsalr/Uppsalir* was most popular in the period from the 7th century to the end of the Viking Period. Consequently, the *Uppsalr/Uppsalir* names of this date are most common in the Opplands and the Viken area.

The archaeological finds from the Viking Period in Viken and the Opplands also show clear links with the rich grave finds of the Mälar region at, for instance, Vendel and Valsgärde. These links begin as early as the 7th century, are very prominent in the 8th century, and can be traced into the Early Viking Period. Blindheim (1984:54–5) interpreted this pattern as corroboration of the account in *Ynglingatal* and *Ynglinga saga* that a ruling dynasty from Uppland, Sweden conquered parts of Opplands and Viken in the late 7th or in the 8th century. This possibility cannot, of course, be excluded, although the finds can most certainly be interpreted in other ways. In the present context, it is the evidence from the archaeological finds for communication and influence between Uppland and Opplands and Viken that is significant.

An even more explicit tendency to try to associate oneself with Uppsala can be found at Skiringssal. As has already been shown (Skre, this vol. Ch. 11:229–31), the practice of constructing building platforms for halls was found at Uppsala and on other farms around Mälaren that belonged to the highest elite or to the king. The construction of the platforms can, where more accurate datings are possible, be assigned to the 8th century, with several examples from the second half of that century. The only case that is definitely older is the earlier of the two halls excavated on one of the Uppsala platforms (Fig. 18.3, G). This 26 m long rectangular hall, and thus also its platform, is from the 7th century. The hall that was built in the 8th century was far more imposing: 40 m long and with pronounced bowed sides. Given that halls on platforms occur first at Uppsala, the practice probably spread from there, and it may have been the building of the more imposing second hall that inspired the construction of similar platforms with comparable halls in elite contexts around Mälaren. The king of the Svear had such a hall built at several of his farmsteads in this region, and the model seems to have been imitated by other high-ranking men within the area of his power.

At Huseby in Tjølling is the only other known platform with a hall outside the Mälar region. The platform is of the same type as those in Sweden, not only in respect of topographical position, but also in

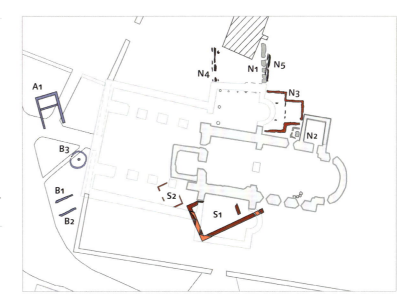

Figure 18.4 *The results of the georadar surveys at Uppsala drawn together with the existing church and post-holes uncovered by excavations in the northern transept. N3 is what are assumed to be the remains of the wooden church which preceded the existing church built in the 1130s. As is clear from the plan, these remains correspond perfectly with the post-holes uncovered in the transept. North of this supposed first church are traces of what may be the remains of the Uppsala hall from around AD 900 (N4 and N5). These traces could not be followed further north because of a bell-house and the disturbance resulting from centuries of burial. Illustration, Alkarp and Price 2005:fig. 2.*

structural form, size, and date. The outline of the hall building is also the same (Skre, this vol. Ch. 11:231–4). One should not attach too much significance to its unique character outside the Mälar area. The history of archaeology has many examples of new types of ancient monument, having once been identified, starting to turn up in many locations. It was barely 20 years ago that the first building platform was identified; eventually, such platforms may end up with a wider distribution than can be seen as yet. But enough is known nonetheless to allow us to accept some general facts about their distribution, date, and social connexions.

What possible background is there for the construction of such a platform at Huseby? The absence of any connexions with Denmark is quite striking. The halls found in Denmark are never situated on platforms and rarely in exposed locations in the landscape. It is difficult to escape the conclusion that the model must have come from Uppsala. If one considers the position of the hall in the landscape (Skre, this vol. Ch. 11:Figs. 11.1 and 11.2), there are further clear parallels between the Huseby and Uppsala sites. Both were located so that they were made conspicuous first and foremost to the surrounding settlement, and also in relation to communication routes. What seems to have been crucial was to mark local dominance, probably over both residents and travellers.

It is very unlikely that there was an intimate political relationship between the petty king of the Huseby hall and the king of the Svear – the distance between them was too great, and there is no direct evidence in the sources suggesting such a relationship. The similarity of the Huseby site to that at Uppsala probably had to do with attempts to invest the Ski-ringssal petty king, probably an Yngling at this time (Skre, this vol. Ch. 19.3), with authority by borrowing such authority from a recognized source, Uppsala. What was fundamental was the connotations the

adoption of certain elements associated with Uppsala brought with them. Rather than merely *imitation*, this is therefore probably a matter of *emulation*, and the phenomenon can therefore be described as *emulatio Uppsaliensis*.

In *Ynglingatal* the genealogy of six generations of petty kings in Vestfold and neighbouring regions from Halfdan Whiteleg to Rögnvald Lord of the Heaths is linked to the dynasty of the Uppsala kings. Rögnvald's genealogical table was thereby made to run back through fully 27 generations. Many scholars have pointed out that the linkage to the Uppsala kings appears to be constructed (Myhre 1992c:263). The establishment of kinship with the kings of the Svear and their homestead must have been an important stage in *emulatio Uppsaliensis* as it contributed to the endowment of the Ynglings with the sort of authority and lordship that the kings of Uppsala enjoyed. The fact that the composition of *Ynglingatal* is congruent with a general trend within the aristocratic ideology of the Early Viking Period in the Opplands and Viken supports the dating of the poem to the end of the 9th century.

18.5 The date of *Ynglingatal*

Krag's impressive studies of *Ynglingatal* have, in my judgment, their greatest value in their systematic and insightful analyses of earlier scholarship and of the ancient texts. His conclusion that Snorri linked the Ynglings more closely to Vestfold than was the case in Snorri's sources also seems to be well founded.

The conclusions he reached concerning the date and provenance of the poem, however, are far from secure. All the same, he has expounded several new arguments both *against* a late 9th-century dating of the poem and *for* a late 11th-century dating. Therefore, his studies have inspired a debate that pays much greater attention to the arguments *pro et contra* the two alternative datings. Consequently, while the late 9th-century dating formerly had the support of most scholars, a productive uncertainty about it has grown since Krag's works appeared. In my opinion, this uncertainty can be reduced by probing the arguments presented by Krag, of which the most important are the question of anachronisms and the developments in the Icelandic historiography. Such examination by several scholars has, as argued above, resulted in the building up of a firmer foundation for a conclusion on the dating issue. On the basis of the above discussions, the main points of which are summarized below, this conclusion will be drawn.

- Krag's case for there being anachronisms in *Ynglingatal* is inconclusive, and there are strong counter-arguments to his arguments in support of it. Most important are the philological and literary-historical arguments against his central point, the identification of the four-element doctrine in the poem.

- Even if one accepts Krag's argument that references to the relevant elements can be found in the poem, it remains to be shown that these really would be anachronistic in a poem of the late 9th century. No such case is made; moreover, there are good reasons for believing that it would *not* be anachronistic for these elements to occur in poem of this date.

- Krag's representation of the development of the Vestfold viewpoint does not appear securely founded. Some passages in the texts are over-interpreted, and little attention is paid to the fact that the texts themselves are of a different character and have different focus. Nor is it treated as significant that Ari may have had a definite motive for emphasizing the connexion between the Ynglings and Oppland and for toning down the Ynglings' Vestfold connexion, namely to strengthen the link probably created by his predecessor Sæmund between the Fairhair dynasty and the petty king of Oppland, Halfdan the Black. Oppland was the common meeting ground for the Fairhair dynasty and the Ynglings and Ari therefore focused on the two dynasty's connexions with that region.

- A detailed analysis of the texts shows that there is little or no development towards a stronger emphasis on Vestfold from Ari to Snorri. What can be found is a definite broadening scope of themes in the texts to include geographical information, marriages and conquests, and an increasing level of detail in the information. These changes seem mainly to be the result of Snorri's including more of the geographical information from *Ynglingatal* into his text than earlier authors

did, causing him to use marriages and conquests to create coherency in his story and to maintain the Ynglings' connexion with the Opplands.

- Even if one accepts Krag's representation of the development of the Vestfold viewpoint, it is a considerable jump from that position to use this development for dating the composition of *Ynglingatal*. The consistency between the poem and information that is first found in other texts in the late 12th and early 13th centuries can be explained in other ways than by arguing that the poem was composed at that time rather than the late 9th century. There is nothing in any of the texts before Snorri that is inconsistent with their authors having known *Ynglingatal*.

- There are several problems with Krag's dating of *Ynglingatal* to the end of the 12th century. Most fundamental is the lack of any explanation of why the poem was composed for Rögnvald Lord of the Heaths rather than Harald Fairhair, who, according to Krag, is the one it was really meant to honour. Furthermore, it is difficult to understand why Snorri would have accepted as genuinely of the late 9th century a poem that supposedly had been composed in Iceland in or just before his own life-time.

- Both toponymical and archaeological sources indicate that 8th- and 9th-century petty kings and chieftains in eastern Norway, and especially at Skiringssal, attempted to associate themselves with Uppsala, its kings, and their sacred sites. This phenomenon is plausibly to be understood as an *emulatio Uppsaliensis:* an attempt to reproduce the authority of the kings of Uppsala in another place and in different circumstances. *Ynglingatal* fits such a context well, and this fit supports the traditional dating of the poem to the end of the 9th century.

Therefore, the conclusion from all of this has to be that the traditional dating of the poem to the end of the 9th century or around AD 900 is more credible than Krag's alternative dating. This conclusion is taken as a starting point in the following two chapters. As we have seen (18.2), the 12th- and 13th-century historians' and saga authors' reading of the poem was heavily influenced by their desire to link the Ynglings to the Fairhair dynasty. As a result, probably starting with Sæmund, they developed what has been described above as the Oppland viewpoint. Subsequently, Ari probably linked the Ynglings to the Fairhair dynasty and thus linked them much more firmly to the Opplands than *Ynglingatal* is evidence for. Snorri inherited the Oppland viewpoint from Ari. But it would also appear as if Snorri, because of the

Danish king's claim over Viken, wanted to link the Ynglings more closely with Vestfold than with other parts of Viken, even though the link in *Ynglingatal* was not so specific. In this sense, one can say that he developed a Vestfold viewpoint.

If *Ynglingatal* is read independently of the later texts concerning the Ynglings, and so is released from the connexions with the Opplands and Vestfold that were added in by Sæmund, Ari, Snorri and possibly others, it becomes a genealogical poem concerning petty kings, of which the last six generations were associated with Viken, primarily with Vestfold. Such a reading will be explored in Chapters 19 and 20.3.

The Emergence of a Central Place: Skiringssal in the 8th Century

DAGFINN SKRE

The early development of Skiringssal is explored in this chapter through an integrated examination of archaeological, toponymic and documentary evidence. An attempt is made to assess the dating of and relationships between the elements of the Skiringssal complex, and to assess the relevance of each of them to the complex's overall development.

In the course of the 8th century it appears that the *thing* site, the hall and the cemetery were established as the core elements of the complex. The first two of six generations of Ynglings in Viken, Halfdan Whiteleg and Eystein Fart, can be linked to the development of the complex. Around AD 800, when the urban site was founded as the final component of the complex, Skiringssal already served as a central place for Vestfold and perhaps even for the whole of Viken. There are several indications that the hall was the centre of a large landed estate that comprised at least 10–15 farms around it, possibly even more.

How did a central place come to be established in Late Iron Age Scandinavia? It is certainly ambitious to try to answer this historical type of question when one considers the paucity of sources at disposal. The establishment of sites such as these must be connected in some way with long-term fundamental social and cultural processes, as well as with decisions taken by individuals and with specific events in the reality of history. While archaeological sources usually can help to reveal processes and structures, one should ideally have documentary sources in order to propose something more than uncertain hypotheses about single events, or about individuals and their choices. However, there are very few such contemporary texts that refer to places, persons and events in 8th-century Scandinavia.

Skiringssal, however, is referred to in several documentary sources from the Viking Age and the following few centuries, and therefore exploitation of the information from these texts and from archaeological and toponymic sources allows one to outline the development of this central place as a historical process. The toponymic and archaeological evidence has already been presented and assessed in previous chapters in this volume (Brink, this vol. Ch. 4; Skre, this vol. Chs. 11, 16 and 17). So too has *Ynglingatal* (Skre, this vol. Ch. 18), but the other written sources have only been touched upon (Skre, this vol. Ch. 2). Now these will be presented below in due course, and their value as evidence in answering the questions under discussion will be investigated. In the following discussion no one category of evidence has priority at the outset. The questions under consideration and the scope for making a relevant interpretation of the various forms of evidence will determine how each category of evidence is applied.

First, it is necessary to say a few words about the methodology which will be used to compare such widely differing sources of evidence. Since the archaeological and toponymic evidence has been thoroughly discussed in previous chapters, there is no need here for further discussion of it. However, the situation concerning the documentary evidence is different, i.e. this evidence must be assessed for its value both individually and within each source's relevant context. The date of composition and the character of the text will be the most important issues in determining the value of a documentary source. The written sources in question were – except for *Ynglingatal* – composed 350–550 years after the period they refer to; therefore, it is difficult to rely upon specific items of information that occur, for instance, in just one source. One can have greater confidence in them when the information they offer agrees with, or proves meaningful when one puts it together with, other sources of information – be they archaeological, toponymic, or documentary. To assess whether two written sources are consistent, it is essential to assess in turn whether one source obtained its information from the other, or whether both obtained it from a third (lost) original source. For instance, a piece of information in Snorri's *Ynglinga saga* cannot support the plausibility of the equivalent piece of information in *Ynglingatal*, because the poem is reproduced in the saga, and Snorri used the poem as one of its sources.

However, a connexion between information from two or more independent sources is still insufficient grounds for treating the information as reliable historical evidence. There are problems of interpretation with all the different types of source, and therefore these problems have to be evaluated case-by-case as part of the discussion. These assessments therefore will rarely end in unambiguous conclusions, i.e. they can only be assigned degrees of probability, which we shall attempt to define in each case.

19.1 Halfdan Whiteleg's burial place – *Skereið*

One of the questions that arose early on in the study of Skiringssal was this: Where is *Skereið* in Skiringssal? This location is recorded in *Ynglingatal* as the burial place of Halfdan Whiteleg, the first of the Yngling kings who ruled in Vestfold. The stanza (no. 30) is as follows in the original (shown below). The left-hand column has the text of the poem as edited by Finnur Jónsson (1912b:12), the middle column a nearly verbatim translation into Norwegian by Krag (1991:32), and the right-hand column an English translation in more natural order by John Hines. Below these three columns is a translation of Finnur Jónsson's somewhat freery paraphrase (1912b:12, transl. Hines).

A number of scholars, including Bugge (1871), have been of the opinion that *Skereið* is not to be understood as a place-name, but rather as a kenning.

Bugge believed *Skereið í Skíringssal* to be a kenning for "the land at Skiringssal". But as Åkerlund (1939: 112–13) has emphasized, such a reading poses linguistic problems. A reading of *Skereið* as a place-name is consistent with the poem's regular listing of the burial places of the Ynglings. Snorri would also have understood it thus.

There is no reference to a place called *Skereið* in any other source, nor has the name been in use in more recent times. But must all the place-names in *Ynglingatal* have referred to real places? In other words, was there ever a place called *Skereið*?

It is not difficult to connect many of the place-names in *Ynglingatal* with either existing or historically attested names. But it has been difficult to connect *Skereið* and some other place-names in the poem in a similar manner. An extensive body of scholarship on the place-names has been published, discussing also those that are found in the early sections of the poem, which deal with the Yngling kings in Uppsala in what is now Sweden (refs. in Åkerlund 1939; Sundqvist 2002; Vikstrand 2004a). Even though the connection of certain names to a specific place is debated, it is generally accepted that the names themselves are authentic, even those that could only have been known in the immediate locality. Vikstrand (2004a) argues, for instance, that one of the names, *Skúta* in stanza 3, was the name of a relatively minor river near Uppsala, a name that could hardly have been known or used outside the immediate area. He therefore believes that its author, Thjodolf, must have had, amongst his sources for this part of the poem, access to a Swedish tradition concerning these places and kings.

A closer examination of the stanzas that relate to Vestfold and the neighbouring areas (nos. 30–37) reveals a possible pattern which may be of use in determining which types of place-name can be identified with ease and which cannot. The recognizable names are *Þótn* (a region), *Skíringssal* (a district), *Holtar* (a

Þat frá hverr,	Det spurte enhver	All have learnt
at Halfdanar	at Halvdan	that the settlers of law-suits
sökmiðlendr	sakmeglene	had to miss
sakna skyldu,	savne skulle,	Halfdan,
ok hallvarps	og steinvarpets	and Hallvarp's
hlífinauma	vernegyger	shielding goddess (Hel),
þjóðkonung	tjodkongen	took the people's king
á Þótni tók.	på Toten tok;	at Toten.
Ok Skæreið	og Skereid	And *Skereið*
í Skíringssal	i Skiringssal	in Skiringssal
of brynjalfs	over brynjealvens	droops over the bones
beinum drúpir	bein luter	of the mail-coated warrior.

Everyone has heard that the men of peace had to miss Halfdan, and Hel took the people's king at Toten;
And Skær-eid in Skiringssal mourns over the king's bones.

farm), *Borro* (a farm), *Fold* (a fjord), *Vestmar* (a region), *Grenlands fylki* (a region) and *Geirstöðum* (a farm). Therefore, the names of settled districts, farms, a fjord and regions are here; in other words, precisely those types of names which, together with the names of major rivers and islands, are considered to be the most stable over time (Rygh 1898; NSL). More susceptible to change over time are the names of minor units such as local names within the boundaries of a farm, or the names of streams, channels, creeks, small islands, and so on.

As a result, it is not surprising that the names in the Vestfold stanzas that cannot be identified straightaway appear to be of the latter sort. *Skereið* is probably the name of a limited site. The other two are *Stíflusund*, where Gudrød Hunter-King was slain, and *Vöðlu straumr*, which is associated with the burial place of Eystein Fart. The semantics of the name elements show that *Stíflusund* was a channel with man-made navigational barriers. It is not so clear what *Vöðlu straumr* signifies. A sea current has been suggested, but most believe that this name refers instead to a river or stream (the debate is summarized by Brøgger 1916:43–6; Åkerlund 1939:113–14; Løken 1977: 79–82; Myhre 1992a:37–8; Krag 1991:134–6). The meaning of the name points towards the latter, i.e. a river or stream. *Vöðlu* is related to *vaðill*, which means a ford or fording place. Therefore, this name is perhaps most likely to have been linked to a minor watercourse or current (Skre, this vol. Ch. 20:465).

The pattern created by those names that can be connected to modern names thus indicates that the place-names in *Ynglingatal* are consistently authentic. If we trust Snorri's information that it was Thjodolf of Hvíni who composed the poem for Rögnvald Lord of the Heaths, possibly sometime around the year 900 (Skre, this vol. Ch. 18), it is difficult to see how the place-names can be anything other than authentic. Rögnvald and his men, who were the skald's audience, would know the names and places in question.

Munthe (in Sturluson [1838–1839]:I:5) suggested that *Skereið* is a place to the southeast of Tjølling, namely the isthmus *(eið)* between Viksfjord and Sandefjord. Although he offers no arguments in support of his idea, it must have been based upon the fact that this is the most conspicuous neck isthmus in the area. Munch (1849:178) guessed that the name referred to the same locality, and narrowed it down to the farm Eid which is found there (Brink, this vol. Ch. 4:Fig. 4.1). On the basis of the similarity of names, Kraft (1840:336) suggested that *Skereið* could be the farm Skåra further north in Tjølling, where moreover "…in Addition to some minor Barrows, there is in one special Place a conspicuous Grave-Mound, composed mostly of Stone". ("... foruden nogle mindre Høie er paa et udmærket Sted en anseelig meest af Stene sammenkastet Høi".) In 1867 Nicolaysen exam-

ined all of these sites without finding any corroborative evidence that any of them was *Skereið* (Skre, this vol. Ch. 2:35–6).

Finnur Jónsson (1900–1901:22) identified two elements in the name *Skereið*, *sker* and *eið*. Concerning the second element, *eið*, Rygh (1898:48) wrote that it may have two meanings: either "a narrow Strip of Land linking two wider Areas" or "a Stretch of Land, long or short, where one can take the Road over Land instead of over Water or Ice". ("et smalt Landstykke, som forbinder to bredere" eller "en Strækning, kortere eller længere, hvor man maatte tage Veien over Land istedetfor Vand- eller Isveien".) The first element, *sker,* means a piece of rock that protrudes above a surrounding plain, which could be either water or a flat area of land (Fritzner 1886–1896:3:310). The name must therefore, wrote Finnur Jónsson, be read as "the *eið* by the *sker*". ("Eidet ved skjæret".)

Finnur Jónsson (1900–1901:23) attempted to identify such a location in Skiringssal, and he concentrated on the Kaupang area:

… er der en ø, Lamø, der nu er bleven landfast, uagtet landet ved springflod endnu kan omflyde den. På dennes østside er der en lille vig, hvor der findes et skær (en stor klippe). Nordøst for den igen et lille næs, der tidligere har været meget langstrakt, da indskæringerne på bægge sider før er gået langt længere op i landet – og gør det nu -, end kortet antyder. Det er denne langstrakte landstrimmel, der før er bleven kaldet *eið* og efter skæret i vigen, nok så betegnende, *Skæreið*. … En lævning af en gravhøj har jeg dog her ikke fundet.

… there is an island, Lamø, which is now attached to the mainland, although during the spring tides the land around it may be flooded. On its eastern side there is a small inlet, in which there is a *sker* (a large rock). Northeast of this there is a small headland, which formerly would have been quite elongated as the inlets on both sides previously ran further up into the land – and indeed do so now – than the map shows. It is this long strip of land, which was first called *eið,* and then, after the rock in the inlet, so conspicuous and suggestive, *Skereið*. … I have, however, found no trace of a burial mound here.

In his book on the Vestfold kings' burials, Brøgger (1916:42) wrote that the connection between Skiringssal and Tjølling appeared certain:

... mens derimot stedsnavnet *Skereið* – naar man ikke skal gi sig ut paa dilettantens sedvanlige gjetninger, og de har hittil behersket omraadet – er helt ukjent i vore dager. Finnur Jónssons forklaring av navnet som "eidet ved skjæret" (i tilfælde ved *Lammøen*) er i virkeligheten saken like nær. Det er ikke i Tjølling i vore dager nogen gravhaug av de dimensioner at den kunde hjælpe os paavei her. Vi maa nøie os med en almindelig holdt forklaring, at Halvdan har været begravet etsteds i Tjølling, hvor hans kongsgaard har været.

... while, however, the place-name *Skereið* – if one is not to indulge the typical guesses of the dilettante which up to now have dominated this issue – is completely unknown in our days. Finnur Jónsson's explanation of the name as "the isthmus by the rock" (in fact on *Lammøen*) is in reality just as wide of the mark. Nowadays there are no grave mounds in Tjølling of the dimensions that might help us on our way in this respect. We have to be satisfied with a general explanation, that Halfdan was buried somewhere in Tjølling, where his royal farmstead was located.

Possibly, though, one can get a bit further. Concerning the name-element *sker*, Rygh (1898:75) wrote: "Skjær; in Names most often referring to bare Rocks that stick up from the Ground-surface … however sometimes also to low, isolated Peaks". ("Skjær; i Navne oftest sigtende til bare Klipper, som stikke op af Jordmark …, dog tildels vel ogsaa til lave, isolerede Fjeldhøider.") Rygh was naturally also aware of the other meaning of the word, which is given by Sandnes and Stemshaug (NSL) as "bedrock or collection of stones that reach to or slightly above the water-level". ("fast berg eller samling av steinar som når opp i eller litt over vassflata".) But this other meaning is rarely attested in early place-names, in Rygh's view. On the other hand it is common in later names, especially post-medieval formations, and then in a particular form, *Skjæret* (Rygh 1898:75; NSL).

A farm-name in Tjølling shows that *sker* in the former sense was used in name-formation in this area. Rygh writes (1897–1936:VI:290-1) of Farm No. 15 Sjyllist (Skierlosse, Schiørløs), that the first element may be *sker* in the sense of a bare rock that protrudes above the surface of the ground. He argues that the name is to be analysed as *skerløs*, in other words a farm with no *sker*, i.e. a farm with deep soil. This farm is not located by the coast nor by a lake, so that the other sense of *sker*, bedrock or stones that reach to or above water, cannot come into question.

Finnur Jónsson's suggestion that *Skereið* is to be looked for on the eastern side of Lamøya rests upon his supposition that the name refers to a rock in the sea; however, this is, from Rygh's analysis, in conflict with the patterns of name-formation in this early period. Furthermore there are no burial mounds in the place that Finnur draws attention to. However there can be no doubt that *Skereið* would be a very appropriate name for the spot where the cemetery of Nordre Kaupang is situated (Skre, this vol. Ch. 16). This narrow strip of land between sea and the ridges is manifestly an *eið* that connects the more open area in the harbour and the town with the broad and open agrarian landscape that opens up at the northern end of the area (Skre, this vol. Ch. 16:Fig. 16.10). The Germanic root of *eið* is **aida*, a derivative of the element **ei*, meaning "to go" (Falk and Torp 1903–1906:133). In addition to the topography that the name-element indicates – a narrow piece of land which links two

broader areas – it also implies that people moved here, as they indeed did where the cemetery is situated. The Nordre Kaupang cemetery is located along the main road to and from Kaupang (Skre, this vol. Ch. 16:Fig. 16.10). In this stretch there are rocks of various sizes protruding from the ground in many places. From Bikjholberget in the south to the northern limit of the cemetery there are at least ten such rocky places, which in Old Norse would be called *sker*.

The last word in the stanza, *drúpir*, has a double meaning, according to Finnur Jónsson (1900–1901: 23): "bows down" and "grieves". Åkerlund (1939:113) considered that the primary meaning of the word here was that of bowing down. One gets closest to the sense of the word with expressions such as "to bow over" or "crouch over". As Krag writes, it seems strange for a place to bow over a grave. "One would rather expect that the burial mound 'bowed'", ("Snarere skulle man vente at gravhaugen 'lutet'") he writes (1991:132–3). It sounds less odd when one takes into account the large number of burial mounds in the cemetery at Nordre Kaupang. The name of this place might gradually, as the number of mounds grew, have taken on a closer association with the barrows that were found there and with the function of the site as a cemetery than with the natural feature the name originally designated. The poem appears to have been composed in the later part of the period in which the cemetery was in use, when the number of barrows would have been great. As Krag points out, a mound can be said to crouch over or bow over the burial it hides.

The cemetery also fulfils Brøgger's expectation of major burial mounds. The site stands out from the others at Kaupang in respect of the size of the barrows. As noted (Skre, this vol. Ch. 16:380, Fig. 16.10), the four largest specimens on Christie's map measure 22.6–25.1 m in diameter (nos. 50, 51, 53 and 66) and are 2.2–2.7 m in height. Five barrows in the same site measure 13.8–15.7 m (nos. 45, 46, 101 and 91). This is markedly larger than the barrows in the other Kaupang cemeteries. Of the eight barrows that were still to be found at Søndre Kaupang when Nicolaysen visited in 1867, the largest was barely 10 m across. On Lamøya, the only large barrow measures 15 m across, and with a couple of exceptions all of the rest are less than 10 m across. There are no other large barrows of the Viking Period anywhere else in Tjølling.

Both the position of the cemetery and the size of the barrows show clearly that the burial ground at Nordre Kaupang was the most important in the Skiringssal complex. It is also big by the standards of the region, for it is one of the three largest clusters of large Viking-age barrows in Vestfold. The usual cemeteries of this period in Vestfold do not have such large barrows, even when the graves are just as well furnished as the most splendid at Nordre Kaupang. An example of this is the cemetery at Gulli near Tønsberg, which has several well-furnished graves but no barrows more than 10 m in diameter (Gjerpe 2005b: 25, fig. 9). There are larger individual barrows of the same period than the four at Nordre Kaupang, such as the Oseberg barrow 36 km to the north, which was 40 m across (Brøgger et al. 1917:134), and the Gokstad barrow, 15 km further north, which was about 50 m in diameter (Skre, this vol. Ch. 2:Fig. 2.1). But regarding clusters of large barrows, there are only two sites in Vestfold that can be compared to the cemetery at Nordre Kaupang. At Mølen, 18 km west of Kaupang, there are four cairns from 25 to 35 m in diameter (Marstrander 1976:14). At Borre, 45 km to the north, there have been nine barrows with diameters from 32 to 45 m (Myhre 1992b:159). Several of the barrows at Borre are earlier than those at Kaupang. The dating of the cairns at Mølen is uncertain, although several factors indicate that they, like at Borre, are of the Viking Period or of the two preceding centuries (Løken 1977). There are a number of indications that some of the four large barrows at Nordre Kaupang are of the 8th century (Skre, this vol. Ch. 16.2). At Kaupang, therefore, we have one of Vestfold's three largest clusters of great barrows from the later first millennium AD.

The four large barrows at Nordre Kaupang may thus be earlier than the oldest dated examples on the same cemetery, which are of the 9th century (Stylegar, this vol. Ch. 5). It is possible that they were raised in the 8th century when, according to the chronology of the poem, Halfdan Whiteleg would have been buried at *Skereið*. Myhre (1992d) has collected the various suggestions that have been made for dating the lives of the Ynglings. According to these, Halfdan probably died around AD 750. But considerable doubt has to be attached to this dating, since all of the chronologies that have been generated for the final six generations in *Ynglingatal* take it as a premiss that these generations are to be linked to the Fairhair dynasty. As discussed in an earlier chapter, this link was probably concocted by the Icelandic historian Ari the Wise in the 1120s–1130s (Skre, this vol. Ch. 18:411). Nevertheless, one comes to about the same date for Halfdan's death, or possibly somewhat later, by counting five generations back from the probable dating of *Ynglingatal*, the late 9th century or c. 900.

If we explore the possibilities further, it is of interest that, according to the poem, Halfdan died at Toten, about 200 km further north. The stanza on Halfdan reports that *Skereið* droops over *brynjalfs beinum*, "the warrior's bones". The expression is perhaps to be read literally, or it might be a kenning for the king's cenotaph. Of the four large barrows, two (nos. 51 and 66) were completely empty, while the other two (nos. 50 and 53) are amongst the total of 27 barrows that contained charcoal but no grave goods. Three of these 27 also contained burnt bone and ashes, but Nicolaysen (1868:78) does not tell us which three.

The connexion between *Ynglingatal* and Skiringssal would thus appear to be of the same character as that between the poem and Borre (Skre, this vol. Ch. 20.3:463–5). Both at Borre and at Skiringssal there are burial mounds that from their dating and the nature of the cemeteries might have housed the royal burials which the poem recounts were made there. Like Myhre (1992e:282), one could explain this by suggesting that Thodolf might have located the burial places of Rögnvald's forefathers at sites that were relevant to the realization of Rögnvald's own political ambitions, and where there were burial mounds that would fit. Certainly the skald had to glorify his lord and contribute to the enhancement of his renown and the furtherance of his ambitions, but I find it difficult to believe that there was room for the falsification of such concrete pieces of information concerning ancestors as close as Halfdan and his descendants, who lived only five generations and less earlier. Rögnvald's men would know where his forefathers were buried, and the falsification of such information would shame their king (Skre, this vol. Ch. 20.3:465–6).

There was certainly somewhat more room for creativity on the skald's part as to who was the father of whom. Here the old wisdom applies: "Only the mother knows". To connect Halfdan to the kings of Uppsala through his father Olaf, a relatively obscure figure (stanza 29), consequently appears a much simpler project. Of Olaf, neither how he died nor where he was buried is noted. The poem lacks details of the death of only one of the other 27 Ynglings, Domar (stanza 6; Krag 1991:132). And the only place mentioned in connexion with Olaf is Uppsala, which he left. The lack of detail in the poem's information about Olaf makes him look like a product of the skald's poetic powers, created in order to link Rögnvald and his forefathers to Uppsala and the renowned royal line there (cf. Skre, this vol. Ch. 18:424–8).

19.2 Halfdan Whiteleg –
Þjóðkonung and *Þingmaðr*

Who was Halfdan? Apart from the names of the Ynglings and the genealogical information, *Ynglingatal* mostly contains details of how each of the Yngling kings died and where each was buried. In some cases there is additional geographical information, such as where they came from, went to, or dwelt. In the great body of scholarly discussion of *Ynglingatal*, especially among those who have used the poem as a source to historical events and developments, it has been these geographical references that have been the subject of a particularly intense academic debate. In connexion with the final six generations, i.e. those linked to Vestfold and the Opplands, the debate has focused especially upon their places of burial (Skre, this vol. Chs. 18:413–22 and 20:463–7).

However the poem does contain another category of information that has attracted less attention, i.e.

the cursory characterizations that are offered for several of the Ynglings. Some attention has been paid to the characterization of Rögnvald Lord of the Heaths, who is called *reiðar stióri* (stanza 37), which has been interpreted as "wagon steerer", "ship-steersman", and "leader of a mounted troop" (discussion summarized in Åkerlund 1939:124).

There are in the poem, however, interesting characterizations of other Ynglings too. This is true, for instance, of the first stanza in the Vestfold series, on Halfdan Whiteleg, quoted above. This is the only stanza in the entire poem where the skald, by starting the stanza: "*Þat frá hverr...*" ("Everyone has heard..."), explicitly presupposes that the skald's audience possessed a certain knowledge. It appears that it was still, five generations after his death, an important element in people's memory of him that Halfdan was *þjóðkonung* (king of the people), that he died at Toten, had been buried at *Skereið*, and that he was a great *sökmiðlendr* (see below) and was mourned by others of that kind. The skald's introductory words about Halfdan show that he was for the first time in the poem recounting material that was widely known amongst his audience; therefore, this is one sign amongst several that the genealogy preceding Halfdan was fabricated.

According to Finnur Jónsson (1900–1901:22) *sökmiðlendr* means:

... 'sak-megler', en fredelig sindet mand; jfr. at 'miðla mál' 'udjævne en sag'. Denne betegnelse karakteriserer tillige Halfdan selv.

... 'cause-mediator', a peacefully minded man; cf. to *miðla mál,* 'to settle a dispute'. This description equally characterizes Halfdan himself.

Brøgger (1916:42) proposed the sense of "the men who come to the *thing*", and several scholars have followed this course, including Åkerlund (1939:111). In *Ynglingatal*, characterizations of this kind, which can be said to point at political and legal accomplishments, are relatively rare. Halfdan is also described in this stanza as *þjóðkonung* and *brynalfr*, king of the people and warrior, which are more in line with the most common characterizations of chieftains and kings, both in this poem and in others. The most common expressions are ones that deal with martial accomplishments and leadership, and some concerned with generosity (Norr 1998:82–3; Sundqvist 2002:141–3).

Ynglingatal is a panegyric, and the skald will therefore have expressed and undoubtedly exaggerated those characteristics that were considered honourable. But the fact that characteristics such as *sökmiðlendr* are rare, together with the skald's statement that his audience know Halfdan's capabilities as a mediator, renders this information reliable. The char-

acterizations that follow later in the stanza are likewise reliable. *Þjóðkonung* has to be regarded as a relatively imprecise description, but it shows in any event that Halfdan ruled over the population of a significant area. If we look at the three characterizations of Halfdan altogether, he was, according to *Ynglingatal*, a formidable figure with powers that were effective both for his people and for his peers, and which therefore gave him a very honourable reputation and caused people to honour his memory.

For Rögnvald, to whom the panegyric was addressed, this point in the poem was decisive. Here the account of his closest forefathers was introduced, i.e. those who over five generations back could be associated with the area in which he himself was a powerful man. His position rested, to a certain extent, on people's memory of them, which it was the poem's job to reformulate and to honour. The places, events and attributes that were associated with them were thus of significance. This was not least the case with Halfdan, who is described at the start of this section of the genealogy (Skre, this vol. Ch. 20:466).

Halfdan was associated with two areas, the Opplands and southern part of Vestfold – he died at Toten, but his place of burial was in Skiringssal. The latter point shows that it was there that he had his primary powerbase; or more precisely, that it was there that his successor, who was to lead the funerary rituals (Skre 1997), intended to have his powerbase, probably continuing that of his predecessor Halfdan.

The mediators of law-suits, those who endeavour to resolve disputes and settle strife, had the *thing* site and the moot-assembly as their most important arena. In this role, Halfdan may have operated at several *thing* sites in the two regions. But his principal connexion with Skiringssal renders it reasonable to infer that his abilities were demonstrated particularly at Skiringssal's *thing* site *Þjóðalyng* (Skre, this vol. Ch. 17).

The stanza declares that everyone has heard of Halfdan's abilities as a mediator of suits, a reputation that he must have enjoyed even in his life-time, which, according to the chronology of the poem, would have been in the first half of the 8th century or somewhat later (see above). This reputation must have led many to come to the *thing* site at Skiringssal in order to have their disputes resolved, with the result that the *thing* site in Halfdan's day became more important than it had been before. There are other indications that the *thing* site was visited from a wide territory, perhaps from the whole of Vestfold or even more, in the Viking Period (Skre, this vol. Ch.17:406). The characterization of Halfdan in the poem is a further piece of evidence pointing in the same direction. It is possible that the *thing* site achieved its position under his rule, and that his position and qualities were what led to *Þjóðalyng* becoming the principal assembly place for a greater area than it had previously been, possibly the whole of Viken.

A *thing* site of the Viking Period is normally situated by a chieftain's or petty king's seat, and *Þjóðalyng* is no exception. Runic inscriptions from the late Viking Period in Uppland also show that chieftains could establish *thing* sites (Jansson 1984:125–6; Skre, this vol. Ch. 17:405). It is possible that Halfdan founded the *thing* site at Skiringssal, but if that were the case he did so at the site of an earlier assembly place. This question is discussed further below, after the next Yngling, Eystein, has been considered.

Why should one establish a new cemetery at *Skereið*? As has already been noted (Skre, this vol. Ch. 16:382–3), the location of this cemetery is not special in any way. In the first millennium AD, both in Vestfold and elsewhere in Scandinavia, cemeteries were established along the most important access roads to major farmsteads, as this one was. The founding of a new cemetery was, all the same, a distinct event that must have had a cause. If indeed it were true that Halfdan was buried at *Skereið*, his barrow must have been one of the first, maybe even the very first, there. The cause for initiating a new cemetery on the occasion of his burial might have lain in the circumstances concerning Halfdan that have already been discussed. His renown as a king and mediator might have given the *thing* site at *Þjóðalyng* significance for the entire region. What then would have been more natural than to have built his grave-mound down by the harbour where many of the thingmen arrived, and right beside the road that they had to take up to the *thing* site? In this way the *thing* site could benefit from his prestige even long after his lifetime because in passing his mound, the thingmen would be reminded of Halfdan and of his abilities as an assemblyman. Perhaps they did indeed miss him, as the composer of *Ynglingatal* would have us believe.

19.3 Eystein Fart – *blótmaðr*

The last three sentences in the manuscript *Sögubrot* deal with a King Eystein. *Sögubrot* is the name that has been given to a surviving fragment of the otherwise lost *Skjöldunga saga,* not in the form in which it was originally written, but in a redaction of c. 1300 (Krag 1991:228; *Skjoldunge saga* [1984]:29). The original saga was composed sometime around 1200 or somewhat earlier (*Skjoldunge saga* [1984]:20). *Sögubrot* relates that Alfar and Alfarin the sons of Gandalf came to Sigurd Ring and asked for his help:

... at riða a hendr þeim konungi, er Eisteinn het, er þui riki reð, er þa hetv Vestmarar, en nv heitir Uestfolld. þa voru hofð blot i Skiringssal, er til var sott um alla Uikina...

...to ride against that king who was called Eystein, who ruled over the kingdom which was then called Vestmar but is now named Vestfold. At that time sacrifices were held in Skiringssal, which were attended from the whole of Viken...

In *Sögubrot* the two sons of Gandalf also appear in King Harald War-Tooth's army *(Danakonunga Sögur*: 18; *Skjoldunge saga* [1984]:83), according to the chronology of this saga, sometime in the mid-to-late 8th century. They are associated with the kingdom of Alfheim (Elf-home), which supposedly lay between two rivers, the Glomma in Østfold, Norway and the Göta River in what is now western Sweden. The accounts of both the kingdom and its kings and heroes appear in a number of sources, and seem to have a legendary character. The references to Alfheim must therefore be regarded as legendary material, even though this Alfarin also appears in Snorri *(Ynglinga saga*:ch. 48), who has Gudrød, Eystein's grandson, marrying Alfarin's daughter Alfhild. A number of scholars have discussed whether the accounts of Alfheim could have some historical basis, but anything of that kind is difficult to determine (Stylegar and Norseng 2003:410–13).

The information about the sacrificial feasts at Skiringssal is, however, more specific, and this cannot be said to be conventional, for information of this kind is not otherwise common in saga literature. But as long as this information is not supported by other information, it cannot be assigned value as historical evidence, for the saga was written down far too long after the period it purports to describe.

Another source for what might have been in the lost *Skjöldunga saga* is Arngrímur Jónsson's *Ad catalogum regum Sveciæ annotanda* of 1596. His main source for this early period was the *Skjöldunga saga* itself, which was still available in Copenhagen when Arngrímur was working on his text. He also had access to Snorri's *Ynglinga saga*, but *Skjöldunga saga* was his principle source for information about the legendary king Sigurd Ring, the subject of the passage in question here (*Skjoldunge saga* [1984]:22–5).

Arngrímur wrote that Sigurd Ring, in his old age, which according to the chronology of the saga would have been at the end of the 8th century, travelled to Viken in Norway in order to take part in the sacrifices that were held at Skiringssal (*Skjoldunge saga* [1984]: 91). Here he met the incredibly beautiful Alfsol, courted her, was rebuffed, but did not give up; he fought her brothers and won. But Alfsol took her own life, and Sigurd was so remorseful that he in turn took his own. This story clearly has a romantic character, probably supplied by Arngrimur. But some pegs that it could have been hung upon must have been provided by the *Skjöldunga saga*, probably the names of the principle characters and places. If nothing else, this account does seem therefore to show that the information on sacrificial practices at Skiringssal was in the *Skjöldunga saga*, and was not an addition in the redacted version of the saga that is found in *Sögubrot*.

What then of the relationship between the *Skjöldunga saga* and the rather younger *Ynglinga saga*? According to Krag (1991:183), Snorri's *Ynglinga saga* and the *Skjöldunga saga* can hardly be based on any common textual source. Krag (1991:191) also concludes that the Yngling genealogy was not known to the author of the *Skjöldunga saga*. Storm (1901:229) considered *Sögubrot* to be independent of the *Ynglinga saga*, and trusted the information about sacrificial practices in Eystein's time. On the other hand Snorri did know the *Skjöldunga saga*, as chapter 29 of the *Ynglinga saga* shows, and this adequately explains the agreements that there are between those two sagas. Any agreement that may be found between information in the *Skjöldunga saga* and in *Ynglingatal* would, however, be of greater interest, because there is no reason to think that the author of that saga knew the poem.

There is one further point to raise before the information in *Sögubrot* about sacrificial practices at Skiringssal during Eystein's reign is compared to information in other sources. As Meulengracht Sørensen (2003:266–8) has pointed out, the information in Norse literature has to be analysed in terms of the role it has in the narrative in which it is embedded before it can possibly be used as historical evidence. The narrative is a composed unity in which the author, in order to achieve his purpose, reshapes the elements it is constructed of, or even creates new ones. It is necessary therefore to assess whether the elements in the text that may be used as historical evidence could have been created or transformed in order to fulfil the author's intentions.

What, therefore, were the roles in the *Skjöldunga saga* of Skiringssal and the sacrifices there? It is difficult to form an opinion on this matter because the sources for the original text of the saga are secondary and fragmentary. *Sögubrot* breaks off just where Skiringssal is mentioned. It may appear as if Arngrímur's account of Sigurd Ring's visit to Skiringssal was an immediate continuation of the history Sögubrot begins, but this is far from certain. All the same, it looks as if the purpose of referring to Skiringssal in both texts was so that the story could be told, i.e. for the

story to work out, it was necessary that it take place where many people were assembled. The sons of Gandalf wished to fight against Eystein, and we suspect that they wished to go to the sacrifice at Skiringssal because they could reckon with his being there. The tale of Sigurd Ring also needs a considerable gathering of people in order to work out – he needed, specifically, to meet a woman he had never seen before. None of the information given appears to require this place to have been Skiringssal rather than somewhere else; it seems rather as if Skiringssal appears in the account because it was a place were the saga author and his public knew that a large crowd was assembled, possibly for a sacrifice.

As a result, it is difficult to see any reason why the author of the *Skjöldunga saga* should have invented the sacrifices at Skiringssal. Quite a different matter is the degree of accuracy that there would have been in the late 12th-century author's understanding of what was going on in Vestfold some four centuries previously. In this respect, the *Skjöldunga saga* cannot be considered as a historical source of any value unless this information is matched by some other evidence from the period in question.

Thus, is there any congruency between what we can put forward concerning the account of a sacrifice at Skiringssal in the *Skjöldunga saga* and earlier sources? Stanza 31 in *Ynglingatal* on Eystein goes as follows in the original (Krag 1991:134; Hines; Jónsson 1912b:12–13, transl. Hines) (shown below).

In the first place, we see that Eystein is referred to in two independent sources – an indication that these sources are about a genuine historical figure. Storm (1901:229) was also taken by the fact that the passage in *Sögubrot* places the sacrificial feasts at Skiringssal in the same period in which the Ynglings were establishing themselves, and therefore considered this to be in agreement with *Ynglingatal*.

But Storm did not notice another link between *Sögubrot* and *Ynglingatal*. The only epithet that characterizes Eystein as a man in stanza 31 is *rekks löðuðr*.

En Eysteinn	Men Øystein	But Eystein
fyr ási fór	for åsen fór	went before the sailyard
til Býleists	Til Byleists	to Byleist's
bróður meyjar,	brors datter,	brother's girl,
ok nú liggr	og nå ligger	and now lies
und lagar beinum	under sjøens ben	under the bones of the sea,
rekks löðuðr	helteinnbyderen	the bidder of yeoman,
á raðar broddi,	på raets kant,	on Ra's edge,
þars élkaldr	der den iskalde	where, ice-cold,
hjá jöfur gauzkum	hos den gautske fyrste	at the home of the Gautish king,
Vöðlu straumr	Vadla-straumen	the Vadla stream
at vági kømr.	til vågen kommer	meets the bay.

But Eystein came, struck by the sailyard, to Byleist's brother's daughter, and now the one who invites the heroes lies beneath the stone mound at the end of the Ra, where Vadla's ice-cold stream reaches the sea, at the home of the Gautish king.

Finnur Jónsson interpreted *rekkr,* gen. sg. *rekks,* as "hero", but it could equally well denote the more general "fighting man, warrior". This is a kenning of a fairly common type. Norr (1998:82) classifies this term amongst those that characterize a king's qualities as a military leader, but it really belongs more to the category of those terms that emphasize a king's generosity and hospitality. None of those terms are particularly frequent in *Ynglingatal* (Sundqvist 2002: 141–3), but they are nevertheless familiar within the genre.

The utterly typical character of this kenning naturally undermines its significance as evidence for anyone looking for peculiar elements in people's memory of Eystein. There is, however, another point that argues for this kenning and others in *Ynglingatal* as closely reflecting the general perception of Eystein. The selection of kennings in skaldic poetry is frequently metrically determined, but *kviðuháttr,* the metre of *Ynglingatal* (Åkerlund 1939), does not have so strict a metre that it would have limited the skald's options as much as some other verse forms might have. One can consequently reckon that the most pertinent reason for the skald's selecting this kenning was to emphasize an important characteristic of Eystein's, something he was known for, namely that he invited heroes/warriors/freemen. Finnur Jónsson (1893–1900:24) understood the expression to mean that Eystein was "…a hospitable king, who was eager to have heroes in his retinue" ("... en gæstfri konge, der gærne vil have helte i sin hird"). An alternative possibility is that he invited heroes/men at arms to feasts – or to sacrifices, such as the *Sögubrot* tells us were held at Skiringssal in Eystein's day.

With this interpretation of *rekks löðuðr* the parallelism between the *Sögubrot* and *Ynglingatal* turns out to have been closer than Storm indicated; both sources may in different ways develop the same basic events for which Eystein appears to have been renowned, i.e. sacrificial feasts, which were typically held at specific times every year. Many petty kings and chieftains issued invitations to these, but if this interpretation is correct, Eystein's feasts must have had a special character or dimension which fixed them within the memory of the people that survived him.

This connexion is uncertain, however, because the kenning *rekks löðuðr* is conventional, and because this interpretation is only one of several possibilities. It is necessary to investigate whether the information about Eystein's hosting sacrificial feasts is supported by any other source. To be able to select the relevant sources, it is necessary first to clarify in which period Eystein might have lived. Those scholars who have studied the chronology of this period put Eystein in the 8th century. Estimates of his date of birth vary from AD 695 to 730, and his date of death from 750 to 760 (Myhre 1992d:269). As has been noted, these datings are insecure, and may be too early.

In this matter, we can work with approximately the same degree of accuracy as was possible concerning the dating of the hall, the remains of which were excavated at Huseby in Tjølling (Skre, this vol. Ch. 11:243). On the basis of finds and radiocarbon datings, the construction of this hall is dated to the mid or second half of the 8th century. It appears to have stood until some time in the first half of the 10th century. From the connexion between the name Skiringssal and this hall (Brink, this vol. Ch. 4:61) it would appear, in its own time, to have been called a *salr.* This word was closely synonymous with *höll* (hall), and *rann.* These words never referred to the principal room in farmers' houses, but instead referred only to the principal room in the homesteads of kings or jarls. This room, in the Viking Age most often a separate building, was the place that the retinue gathered (Meulengracht Sørensen 2003:268–9).

It was in halls of this kind that sacrifices were celebrated (Meulengracht Sørensen 1991; Brink 1999a). And, as is clear, there is a good correspondence in the datings, i.e. the Huseby hall could have been built in Eystein's day. Was this, therefore, the hall that Eystein invited people to? Was this the hall in which sacrificial assemblies took place during his reign and subsequently, was this hall the *Skíringssalr* itself? That sacrificial feasts did take place in the hall that has been excavated is not in question; this is implicit both in the function of this type of building and in the finds. Amongst the earlier finds from the hall are sherds of Tating Ware, a type of fine tableware that was used for mugs and drinking bowls, which derives from the period 750–850. Sherds of glass beakers which were found may also be of the 8th century (Skre, this vol. Ch. 11:Figs. 11.10, 11.20).

It seems likely, therefore, that sacrificial feasts in Eystein's day were held in the very hall whose remains have been excavated at Huseby. When composing *Ynglingatal* more than a hundred years later, the skald seems to have selected a prominent feature in the people's memory of Eystein – that he was a great *blótmaðr* (master of sacrificial feasts). This characterization seems, indeed, to have survived up to the time when the *Skjöldunga saga* was composed. In that saga, as it is known from *Sögubrot,* Eystein is again associated with sacrificial feasts. The chronological correspondence between Eystein's supposed lifetime and the archaeological remains of the hall at Huseby, even though both are imprecisely dated, indicates that there was a factual historical background to the traditions recorded in *Ynglingatal* and *Skjöldunga saga,* c. 100 years and c. 400 years after the actual events.

Central-place complexes could, however, have several halls and at Skiringssal there is an indication that there was one more. Brink (this vol. Ch. 4:62) discusses the name *Nafnasalr,* which is the ancient name for the site where the small farm of Haugen came to be (Brink this vol. Ch. 4:Fig. 4.1). This is a raised ridge with a good view to the east, where one can see the neighbouring farmstead of Gjerstad and further on to the *Þjóðalyng thing* site some 2.2 km away (Skre, this vol. Ch. 17), and also to the west, where one can see the lower reaches of the Lågen River, only 600–700 m away. There has not been any excavation at *Nafnasalr*.

The name is not one of the known types of compounds with *-salr/-salir*. A rare type of name with this element has a theophoric first element, like in *Oðins-salr*. These were, as Brink notes (this vol. Ch. 4:61), names of actual halls. The only name with the element *-salr/-salir* which occurs frequently in Norway is the name *Uppsalr/Uppsalir*. The compound of the two elements in the name, *Upp* (up) and *-salr/-salir* is a fixed pattern and consequently there most likely has never been any hall at most of the farms which bear this name (Skre, this vol. Ch. 18:425-6). In contrast, the name *Nafnasalr* is unique and thus it seems likely that the name does indeed derive from an actual hall on the site.

One of the possibilities Brink notes is that the first element of *Nafnasalr* in fact means "name-brother"; in other words, it means a hall that had the same name as another hall – in this case, presumably, Skiringssal. One possible interpretation of this name and location in the Skiringssal complex is that the hall which appears to have stood there was the first Skiringssal. This yielded its name when a new one was raised on Husebyhaugen, which was more centrally located in what became the core of the Skiringssal complex after the town was founded around AD 800. The hall on Husebyhaugen was built along the main route which led from the town and the harbour through the Skiringssal cemetery and up to the *Þjóðalyng thing* site (Skre, this vol. Ch. 1:Fig. 1.2).

If it is something of this kind that the passage in *Sögubrot* and stanza 31 of *Ynglingatal* point towards – that sacrificial feasts at Skiringssal saw kings and chieftains come together from an extensive region, possibly the whole of Viken, as early as the middle or second half of the 8th century – this could be the reason that the whole complex around the hall took its name from that hall, as Brink (this vol. Ch. 4) demonstrates. The hall was closely linked to the king of the hall, who ruled over the entire central-place complex. This must be the reason that the complex was named after hall.

19.4 Skiringssal before AD 800

To sum up so far, Skiringssal emerged as an important site around the middle of the 8th century. According to *Ynglingatal*, the burial place of the first of the Yngling kings who can be considered a historical figure, Halfdan Whiteleg, was located here. There are good reasons to conclude that his barrow, which according to *Ynglingatal* was raised at a place called *Skereið*, was one of the four large barrows sited on the

isthmus where the roadway up from the harbour of Skiringssal passes.

The roadway from the harbour led up to the other two principal components of the Skiringssal complex, the hall and the *thing* site *Þjóðalyng* alongside the sacred lake *Vítrir/Vettrir*. As an assembly place, the *thing* site was older than Halfdan's day, but his qualities as a settler of lawsuits may have given it greater importance, so that people came here from a wider region, possibly the whole of Viken.

The hall, which gave its name to the entire complex, may possibly be linked to the next Yngling, Eystein Fart. In his time there were reportedly sacrifices held at Skiringssal. The fact that the hall provided the name shows that the king of the hall was the unifying and focal force within the complex, and presumably too that the activities that took place there, the sacrifices, were the most important events in Skiringssal. The excavated hall building at Huseby-haugen (Skre, this vol. Ch. 11) was raised in this period, or possibly soon after. It is possible that an earlier hall with the same name stood at the farmstead that was called *Nafnasalr* just 2 km northwest of Huseby-haugen (Skre, this vol. Ch. 1:Fig. 1.2). Eystein was probably the builder of one or both of these halls, and likewise probably the initiator of the sacrificial feasts at Skiringssal.

Skiringssal seems to have been established as a major juridical site for kings and chieftains in the Viken area in Halfdan's time and then to have become even more important by also becoming a significant cultic site during the time of Halfdan's successor, Eystein. But what happened next? According to *Ynglingatal* Eystein was buried *á raðar broddi*, which is probably not in Skiringssal, but more likely in the northern Viken area, either near Borre or across the fjord, by Mossesundet (Skre, this vol. Ch. 20:464–5, Fig. 20.1). More than anything else a king's burial site indicates where his main seat was located, and by the time of his death Eystin's seat cannot have been Skiringssal. In Eystein's time a change seems to have occurred in the Ynglinga kings' connection to Skiringssal. Contributing to this impression is the fact that no sources indicate that the next two Ynglings, Halfdan Milde and Gurdød Hunter King, had a connection to the Skiringssal area. This issue will be explored in the following chapter (Skre, this vol. Ch. 20.3).

Of the elements of the Skiringssal complex referred to here, only the *thing* site and the sacred lake appear to have had a more ancient history than Haldan's time. The question therefore arises: Do the developments of the mid-8th century onwards mark a break with the period before? Was a new level in the social hierarchy introduced in the form of kings, and a new type of central place established here, in the very south of Vestfold?

This region bears no signs of central places before

the age of Skiringssal. Further south in Scandinavia there were central places with juridical, cult and social functions for the surrounding area throughout most of the first millennium AD. Such sites were created in two periods, either early in the millennium, or in what in Norway is known as the Merovingian Period, c. AD 550–800. Skiringssal emerges in the second period, and the growth of this site thus fits into a general picture in terms of not only the type of site but also its date of development.

Rather more complicated is the question of to what extent the 8th century saw a new, upper stratum of social hierarchy in this region. This is the sort of phenomenon that can only be traced in the broadest of outlines in the archaeological evidence. It is first and foremost burial evidence that provides information on this kind of development, and such evidence is, in this case, both chronologically and materially patchy. In the burial record, the existence of social elites of the very highest level will only be reflected through a relatively small number of graves per generation. Finds from only a minor number of these graves will have made their way into archaeological collections, and we therefore cannot expect to have a coherent series of graves of this character from across the periods in which such a social elite lived. Similarly, neither can we expect to be able to see if such an elite was absent for a number of generations.

Furthermore, graves are indirect sources of evidence, affected by many problems of interpretation. The choice of things that were deposited as grave goods was dependent upon what is vaguely called "burial practice", which was influenced by myths, ideology and religion. Since the impact of each of these factors cannot easily be defined, the identification of the social circumstances of the people from the burials themselves is a problematic matter. It becomes most difficult of all in relation to periods and graves in which finds are generally scarce, such as the pre-Roman Iron Age and the Norwegian Merovingian Period. In relation to periods that are richer in finds, in which one can observe a full range from the most humble burials to the impressively richly furnished ones, the foundations are stronger. In these cases too, however, one has to be cautious, as the grave furnishings, the form of the monument and its size, and the splendour of the funeral feast, would have been determined first and foremost by the successors of the deceased. A series of factors, such as their immediate need to demonstrate their presence politically and socially, would consequently have affected the character of the grave.

As a result it is only possible to sketch out an answer by examining whether there is any sign of a social stratum in the archaeological remains from Tjølling that can be compared to what was there in the 8th and 9th centuries. From the 3rd century AD down to c. AD 500 there are rich grave finds in this area. However, these do not make this settlement area special as such grave finds are typical for this part of Vestfold. The neighbouring districts to the north, east and west, Hedrum, Sandar and Brunlanes (Stylegar, this vol. Ch. 5:Fig. 5:11), are amongst the very richest in grave finds for this period in eastern Norway (Hougen 1924; Blindheim 1974). In Tjølling there are grave finds from the whole of the area which, to judge by the farm names and grave finds, would appear to have been settled in the Viking Age. Moreover, out in the countryside there are many grave monuments of types that are usually dated to this period (Jahnsen 1974; Løken 1974).

Several of the burials in Tjølling from the period c. AD 200–500 contained splendid artefacts. Two women's graves from early in the 5th century from Amundrød (C29300) and Roligheten (C14338–50) were furnished with a large number of objects of high quality. The richest grave of all, however, is a man's grave from about the year 500 (C18892–904). This was discovered at the farm of Skåra in 1897 in the same barrow as Nicolaysen had looked at in 1867 in his hunt for *Skereið*. Regrettably, the find was made in the course of a non-scholarly excavation, and it is partly for this reason that the artefacts are in a poor state. They are nonetheless sufficient to show that this was an exceptionally rich grave. The weaponry included everything that belonged to the full weapon set of that period: a sword decorated with silver rivets, two spears, a large sax, a shield boss decorated with silver rivets, and a bundle of arrows for military use. In respect of dress accessories and jewellery, there was a large cruciform relief brooch of high quality, silver clasps, a gold ring, and two copper-alloy belt buckles. There were several further rivets and mounts of silver, a large copper-alloy bowl from some Roman area, a glass beaker, and sherds of at least four different pots. The cruciform relief brooch indicates that the grave is either a double grave with a male and a female, or that the barrow contained two separate graves which were mixed during excavation. Nevertheless, the majority of finds must stem from the male grave. Both the artefact types and the grave form itself, an inhumation in a large barrow, are familiar across southern Vestfold from this date. However none of the other graves in this area exceeds the Skåra grave in terms of quantity and quality of grave goods, and this is clearly the richest male grave of the Migration Period in Vestfold (Blindheim 1974:84).

Thus here in the settlement area of Tjølling, about 3 km north of the *thing* site, around AD 500 a man who belonged to the area's uppermost social stratum of that period was buried. There is, however, very little sign of this social elite over the next two centuries. This is in fact a period of few finds overall in eastern Norway, and considered in this context, southern Vestfold is actually relatively rich in grave finds of this period (Gudesen 1980:156). But the quantity of finds is nevertheless small, and therefore no great importance should be attached to the fact that there are only a few ordinary finds from Tjølling compared to the number and quality of finds from the neighbouring districts of Hedrum and Brunlanes (Blindheim 1974; Gudesen 1980:216–17). If we look at that area as a whole, there is evidence of a social group whose standing was on a par with that of groups found elsewhere in Scandinavia. For example, from Nes in Hedrum there are fragments of a helmet of the Vendel type and the pommel of a splendid sword (C20286), and from Brunlanes also several fine objects.

In terms of the burial evidence, therefore, there is nothing to suggest any change in the social hierarchy in the period c. 500-750, that is, between the two better-known phases of the Migration Period and the time of the Ynglings. Although there is evidence of a high social stratum from the time before the Ynglings, the account in *Ynglingatal* of them being an intrusive royal dynasty cannot be dismissed. But on this point the poem cannot be regarded as having any authority as a historical source. It would appear to be equally likely that the petty kings of Skiringssal had their roots within the local elite kin groups.

The Skiringssal complex may, therefore, have developed on the basis of local conditions; but that development would not have taken place in any sense on its own. As noted, the Merovingian Period is one of the two periods in the first millennium AD when central places with cult, juridical and social functions were founded. The establishment of Skiringssal was therefore connected to a course of social development that had common features across the whole of southern Scandinavia. This phenomenon will be discussed in a later volume in this series (Skre, in prep.).

19.5 The Skiringssal domain

If Snorri is to be believed, the six "Norwegian" generations of *Ynglingatal* exercised power over different parts of Viken and the Opplands (*Ynglinga saga*:chs. 44–50; Skre, this vol. Ch. 18). There is no information on this issue in other sources, and therefore Snorri cannot be regarded as reliable on this point. But the pattern he describes could well reflect the historical reality – unstable dominance that shifted in the course of a generation and between generations. It could also well be that he was correct in assigning a sphere of influence, that included both Viken and the Opplands, to both this and the other royal dynasties to which he refers. But, as there is no other evidence, we will never know.

It is nearly as difficult to assess the extent of the local land held directly by the king of Skiringssal. Through studies of a number of localities in southern Scandinavia it would now appear clear that the kings and chieftains of the Late Iron Age had quite exten-

sive local landholdings; some of them had several estates within the area of their power (Skre 1998b; Callmer 2001; Jørgensen 2001; Iversen 2004). Such an estate must have existed at Skiringssal too, and this is probably the basis for the hall's name becoming the name of the district.

In a number of cases, analysis of documentary sources from the later Middle Ages has made it possible to reconstruct Viking-period estates of this kind (Skre 1998; Iversen 2004). Unfortunately it is not possible to undertake any such work concerning Tjølling because in the High and Late Middle Ages a large amount of land in this area was owned by nobles (Krohn-Holm 1974:172–7). Both Krohn-Holm (1974: 155) and Berg (1909) found that in the 14th century secular landlords owned the great majority of the farms in the core zone of Tjølling. There was practically no royal property, nor any significant peasant landholding, and the Church had only limited holdings. No registers of these estates survive, and other documents that could allow one to trace the history of the estates are far too few in number.

It is, however, possible to discern a few indications of the extent of estates in the Viking Period. In the High and Late Middle Ages joint ownership was very common in Norway, i.e. many individuals or institutions held larger or smaller shares of a farm. Through inheritance, sale, pawning and the like, the number of owners of a farm could multiply, and the individual shares therefore could be extremely small. In practice, this was a matter of theoretical shares, i.e. each joint-landowner had the right to an annual portion of the income from the farm corresponding to the size of his share. This system probably emerged in the 11th and 12th centuries. In the later Middle Ages it was usual for the landowners to collect shares in a systematic manner, so that they gradually came to hold the whole farm. It could, however, be very hard to gather up all of the shares in a farm, especially for non-ecclesiastical landowners, who could find it difficult to wrest portions held by the Church from that institution's grip. As a result, when a farm appears in Late-medieval sources as entirely in the possession of a single owner, it would very probably never have been divided up. And such full ownership is usually interpreted as evidence that the farm had been owned by major landholders ever since the Viking Period, either by the king or by other major secular figures, if not by some ecclesiastical institution. The extensive noble full ownership in Tjølling at the end of the Middle Ages thus suggests that many of the farms were likewise in the hands of major landholders in the Viking Period and subsequently.

Another piece of evidence for the extent of the Skiringssal estate lies in the frequency of burial at the cemetery that was linked to the king of Skiringssal and his people. In a previous chapter (Skre, this vol. Ch. 16:382–3) it was proposed that the population of some 10–15 farmsteads buried their dead in this cemetery. There should, therefore, have been such a number of farms making up the estate. But there could well have been more farms belonging to it. It was probably the king's fighting men who had the privilege of burying their dead in his cemetery. Other farms, meanwhile, may have been worked by other classes: thralls, or people having varying degrees of freedom.

A final piece of evidence lies in the size of the area that was called Skiringssal in two 15th-century documents (DN I:146 and IX:274; Skre, this vol. Ch. 2:29). Four farms in these letters are identifiable: Guri, Namfnesale, Brekke and Kleppåker (Rygh 1897–1936. VI:304). These are located respectively 1 km west, 3 km northwest, 5 km southwest and 9 km east of Huseby. If we can use this evidence, and assume too that the estate would have comprised the farms lying between these points, that landholding would have been very large; it would have comprised most of the southern part of Tjølling (see Brink, this vol. Ch. 4:Fig. 4.1).

We cannot, therefore, say anything for certain about the extent of the estate of the king of Skiringssal, or about the chronology of the development of the estate and its subsequent history. The indications we have, however, suggest that it was a large one, comprising at least 10–15 farms, and probably a great deal more. It could also have included landholdings outside of Tjølling. And of course, when a town, Kaupang, was established in the Skiringssal harbour it became a part of the domain of the king of Skiringssal (Skre, this vol. Ch. 20:466–7)

Towns and Markets, Kings and Central Places in South-western Scandinavia c. AD 800–950

20

DAGFINN SKRE

Around AD 800 a town, Kaupang, was founded as a new component of the central place at Skiringssal. Discussed in this final chapter are some of the crucial aspects of this event and the subsequent history of the town and the cental place. Considered first are the reasons why a large number of specialized sites for trade and craft coincide with sites for cultic activities in this period. A fundamental reason appears to have been that the combination of the sacral character of the central place and the military power of the local leader guaranteed secure trading conditions.

Secondly, the specialized trading and production sites of south-western Scandinavia are examined in relation to the distinction that was drawn in chapter 3.1 between towns and market sites. The connexions between site types and various kinds of central places reveal that a close relationship between the towns and the Danish kingdom flourished in south-western Scandinavia at the end of the first millennium AD. The three towns of the Danish king's realm, Ribe, Kaupang and Hedeby, had one clear common feature – they were all positioned on the borders of his territory. It is likely that the three towns were founded by the Danish king on the model of the Frankish and Anglo-Saxon *emporia* which, *inter alia,* served to represent a strong royal presence at the frontier.

Finally, the relationship between Skiringssal, the Danish king, and the Yngling dynasty of petty kings is discussed in an attempt to shed light upon fundamental changes in the history of Kaupang and of Skiringssal, and upon the demise of Kaupang in the mid-10th century. Around the time when Kaupang was established, the Yngling petty king seem to have moved to Borre in northern Vestfold. The authority of the Danish king over Skiringssal and Viken apparently diminished at the end of the 9th century, allowing the Ynglings to recover their position in Skiringssal. The transition to Christian religious practices in Viken in the middle of the 10th century and the consequent demise of both pagan cult activities and the sacral character of Skiringssal were probably key factors in the abandonment of Kaupang at that time.

In this final chapter the discussion of Kaupang and Skiringssal is broadened both chronologically, thematically and geographically. However, no attempt is made at a conclusive summary or integration of all the research topics and results presented in the preceding 19 chapters. Those chapters stand on their own, although they are extensively inter-related and cross-referenced. Most of the analysis of the archaeological finds from Kaupang that is currently underway must be published before the synthesis anticipated in Chapters 1.1 and 3.3 can be realized. An attempt at such a synthesis will therefore appear in the final volume of this series (Skre, in prep.).

In this chapter a number of particular problems are discussed, and this discussion should be viewed as presaging some of the topics that will be at the heart of the concluding volume of this series. The first problem, discussed in section 20.1 below, is this: Why do specialized sites for trade and craft coincide with sites for cultic activities in the first millennium AD? To answer this question requires that Skiringssal and Kaupang be placed in their respective super-regional, south-western Scandinavian contexts. In section 20.2, the major specialized sites for trade and craft are discussed in light of the distinction made in an earlier chapter between two types of such sites, markets and towns (Skre, this vol. Ch. 3.1). The conclusions from this discussion lead to an analysis of the relationship between markets and towns on the one hand, and the major central places and the burgeoning Danish royal power on the other.

In the final section of this chapter, 20.3, the discussion returns to Kaupang and Skiringssal, including a discussion of the circumstances whereby power was developed and held in Skiringssal from its founding until its demise around the middle of the 10th century. An attempt is made to sketch the changing relationship between what appears to have been Viken's two most significant dynasties of that period, the Ynglings and the successive Danish kings.

20.1 Trade at the central place

What peculiar characteristics of trade could have existed in the 1st millennium in Scandinavia, such that trade was so often directed to central places where many people gathered for cult or juridical purposes? Did trade have an ideological, economic, or political character, or a combination of all three? The inter-relationships between ideology, economics and politics constitute a huge area for study which can only summarily be discussed here in the context of answering these two questions. These inter-relationships will be examined in greater breadth and depth by Christoph Kilger (in prep. b) in a future volume in this series.

The earliest description of trade and craft-production at a central place in Scandinavia comes from Snorri in *Óláfs saga ins helga* (St Olaf's saga, Ch. 77) where he wrote:

I Svíþjóðu var þat forn landzsiðr, meðan heiðni var þar, at höfuðblót skyldi vera at Upsölum at gói; skyldi þá blóta til friðar ok sigrs konungi sínum, ok skyldu menn þangat sækja um alt Svíaveldi, skyldi þar þá ok vera þing allra Svía; þar var ok þá markaðr ok kaupstefna ok stóð viku. En er kristni var i Svíþjóð, þá helzk þar þó lögðing ok markaðr.

Amongst the Swedes it was an ancient custom, throughout the heathen time, that the chief sacrifice took place in the month of Goe at Uppsala. At that time sacrifice was to be made for peace and victory to the king; and people came thither from all parts of Sweden. There would also be the *thing*-moot of the entire Swedish people; there was also a market there, and meetings for buying, which continued for a week. But after Christianity was introduced into Sweden, a juridical *thing* and market were held there.

Sundqvist (2002:99–105) has concluded that this passage reflects historical reality. Indeed, evidence of trade and craft-production from the Viking Period has been found at Uppsala, and the annual market called *Disaþing* was still being held there in 1296. The first element of the market's name derives from the plural noun *dísir*, a general name for the pre-Christian female powers such as valkyries, norns and the like, which can include goddesses (Munch 1967

[1854]:67–8). Snorri wrote that there was a *dísasalr (dísa* hall) at Uppsala, and that *dísablót (dísa* sacrifice) took place there (Sundqvist 2002:100). The second element, *þing*, indicates that the market was held in association with a *thing*-moot. This name's first element shows that the *thing* and the market were of pre-Christian origin.

The evidence of trade and craft-production covers an area of many hectares north, east and southeast of the hall platforms at Uppsala (Skre, this vol. Ch. 18:Fig. 18.3). In recent years, a few sunken huts and a large quantity of finds, the evidence of craftwork from the 8th to the early 11th century, have been retrieved (Ljungkvist 2006:50–6). Up to now, many of these finds have been made by metal-detecting; the few trenches excavated have been too small to show exactly the context of the activity represented by these finds. But it would appear plausible that these are the remains of a market place from that period.

In the present context, however, it is not critical whether Snorri's account bore any relation to what was actually going on at Uppsala in the last 300 years of the 1st millennium. What matters is that he portrayed the connexion between a cluster of activities – a connexion that is well documented over much of Europe. To examine this connexion requires a brief discussion of the complex inter-relationships between the ideological, economic and political aspects of trade.

Trade and the sacred

Evidence suggesting trade and craft production in contexts similar to that which Snorri described has been found at some of the central places that emerged in Scandinavia even as early as the early 1st millennium. Archaeological investigations of these sites vary in extent; therefore, so does the knowledge of what was going on at them. Amongst the best examined are the sites at Gudme/Lundeborg on Fyn (Skre, this vol. Ch. 1:Fig. 1.4). The central settlement of Gudme lies about 4 km inland, west of its harbour site Lundeborg; together they make out the central place Gudme/Lundeborg. Both sites originated around AD 200 and from this time onwards the harbour was a market site with extensive traces of trade and craft (Thomsen 1993; Hedeager 2001). Both Gudme and Lundeborg appear to maintain their status and their activities down to around AD 600; furthermore, a reduced level of activity at the market site appears to continue until around AD 800.

The centre of the central place was the Gudme hall. The earliest was an enormous hall of some 500 sq m, about 50 m long, built in the 3rd century. This was replaced in the mid-4th century by a somewhat smaller hall (Sørensen 1994). The surrounding area contained about 50 farmsteads which presumably belonged, in one way or another, to the lord of the hall. In the hall and the central settlement area large quantities of precious metals have been found, some in the form of treasure hoards. More such hoards were found in the surrounding area, including the largest gold hoard found in Denmark, the Broholm treasure of more than 4 kg. Most of the objects in the treasure hoards are Scandinavian, although a considerable number are of Roman or Byzantine origin. Altogether, approximately 10 kg of gold have been found in and around Gudme (Thomsen 1993:97).

Immediately to the west of the hall is a lake; the area is surrounded by three hills at a distance of 1.5–2.5 km. The lake and hills have interesting names; the lake simply takes its name from the place itself, Gudme Sø (Gudme Lake). Gudme means "the gods/gods' home"; in other words, "the place where the ancient god/gods were thought to live". West of the lake and the hall is Gudbjerg, "the hill of the god[s]". To the south lies Albjerg, "the hill of the shrine", and to the north Galbjerg, which may mean "the hill of sacrifice" (Hedeager 2001:475).

East of the hall, between it and the market site, there is a huge cemetery, Møllegårdsmarken, and there are also several minor burial sites in the area. Møllegårdsmarken is the largest known pagan cemetery in Denmark with more than 2,200 excavated burials, most of them contemporary with the hall. The size of this cemetery is quite exceptional, as cemeteries of Gudme's time usually have around a hundred graves (Michaelsen 1993:63–4). Møllegårdsmarken also stands out for having several very richly furnished graves, some with imported Roman objects (Hedeager 2001:474).

In Scandinavian terms the market site at Lundeborg is special in that no other such sites are known from this early date. The site covers some 70,000 sq m and extends 900 m along the shore (Thomsen 1993: 70). There is comprehensive evidence of craftwork, while coins and hacksilver/-gold together with weights show that the goods were being made for sale. Imported goods, especially Roman beads, glass vessels, and *terra sigillata* pottery, show that these goods were traded here too. There is some suggestion that the market site was divided into a craft area and another zone in which the imported goods were traded (Thomsen 1993:74). While craft-production took place throughout the lifetime of the site, importation was essentially limited to the 3rd and 4th centuries; no evidence of imported goods dating to after c. AD 500 has been found. The demise of the import trade is probably linked to the fall of the Roman Empire around AD 400 (Thomsen 1993:97–8).

Tools and detritus from craftwork show that a range of crafts was practised at Lundeborg, including the casting and working of silver and gold, bronze casting and ironworking. There is also evidence of carpentry, amber-, horn- and boneworking, and possibly potting and the manufacture of glass beads. A high proportion of the 8,000 iron nails found can be

associated with the building and repair of ships and boats (Thomsen 1993:72–86). The activity layer, which in most places was about 0.5 m thick, consisted of a very large quantity of charcoal, most of which must have come from the craftsmen's hearths.

Only in the southern area and in the earliest activity layer was there any evidence of buildings. This was in the form of floor-surfaces of c. 4 m x 5. The judgment of the excavators, which seems reasonable, is that these were huts for temporary occupation. Concentrated patches of evidence for particular activities indicate that there were also workshops, probably within light and temporary structures (Thomsen 1993:71, 81). From this evidence one can conclude that there were no permanent craft-activities at Lundeborg; the site was probably a seasonal market.

Gudme was a centre of the very highest level of secular power, and its kings were closely linked to the world of the gods. The king's residence, the central hall, was probably also the central cult-place for a large hinterland. The kings of Gudme must have had connexions with the Roman provinces from which trade goods arrived at the harbour for Gudme, Lundeborg. Varying amounts of the imported goods were apparently traded on the shore, where there were also craftsmen producing and selling their wares. These markets, as well as the cultic activities, were probably held for a period during the summer when sailing conditions were favourable. The remarkable size of the market must in part have been due to the large number of people who assembled for the cult activities at Gudme.

At Gudme/Lundeborg therefore, several of the elements that Snorri referred to have been located within a defined area; furthermore, excavations there better illuminate the site's activities and their contexts than was the case of Uppsala. Also, while at Uppsala the activities seem to have been quite densely concentrated, at Gudme they were spread out over an area of several square kilometres which is in fact a characteristic found at several central places from the first millennium in Scandinavia. There is no doubt, though, that there was a connexion between the elements at Gudme/Lundeborg. Most important in the present context, however, are the functional and historical relationships between the elements, not their precise geographical proximity to one another.

There is no sign at Gudme/Lundebrog of a *thing* site, while Uppsala appears to have had one. However, it is the relationship between two other features that will be focused upon here, i.e. the relationship between trade and craft production and places that were manifestly central and significant sacred sites. What sort of relationship was there between these two features? To penetrate deeper into this issue, an example from the Christian Frankish kingdom will be discussed.

In 634/5, the Frankish King Dagobert founded the

market of St-Denis just north of Paris. Here lay the monastery of St-Denis, which the king endowed with considerable income from the market. It was held under the king's protection every year starting on the feast day of St Denis, 9 October. This was a good time for trade in wine, for which this market became a centre. The combination of the market and the saint's festival was particularly powerful, according to Frans Theuws (2004). In his view, the religious framework for trading activities had a definite function. He postulates that coins were struck on such occasions, and that those coins, by portraying or naming the saint, drew their value from the realm of the sacred, which in this context was one of several forms of "imaginary world" imbued with essential qualities (Theuws 2004:128). Another sort of "imaginary world" which also gave value to objects was constituted of the special, distant sites with mythical qualities – "beyond the horizon", as Moreland (2004:147) calls them.

No coins were struck at Gudme/Lundeborg, but objects of precious metal were cast there, and these may have derived some of their value and attractiveness from the sacred character of the site (Hedeager 2001:483–7). For Scandinavians of the 3rd and 4th centuries, the Roman Empire was undoubtedly a world "beyond the horizon" with mythical qualities and one with which stories were associated. Not only the locally produced crafts but also the imported Roman crafts at Lundeborg may therefore have drawn value from these "imaginary worlds".

Hedeager (2001:500–5) believes that the sacral character of Gudme/Lundeborg was of much deeper and wider significance than just providing trade goods and crafts with added value. She argues that the cosmological world was a holistic model that explains the presence at Gudme/Lundeborg of the whole range of activities and elements. The topographical elements of lake, streams and hills, and the market site, hall and cemetery, were placed in such a way as to make Gudme/Lundeborg *Ásgarðr (Asgard) reconstructed*.

Hedeager also incorporates the imports and craftwork at Lundeborg into her model. Thereby she presents a possible answer to the question posed in the introduction to this chapter: Why do sites for trade and craft coincide with sites for cultic activities in this period? She recognizes (2001:487–90) the major methodological problems in using 13th-century literary sources concerning Asgard to hypothesize about a central place some 600 to 1,000 years older, but writes that these sources may nonetheless "give us some ideas about the beliefs that informed the construct of Gudme as a sacred site".

However the huge interval between the establishment of Gudme and the written sources (c. one millennium) does not only cast the connection between Gudme and the 13th-century myths of Asgard into doubt. It also casts doubt upon the explanatory valid-

ity of Hedeager's model. Were humanly constructed and topographical elements at Gudme/Lundeborg put together and named on the basis of a desire to recreate Asgard, as Hedeager hypothesizes? Or were the concepts of Asgard, as they were developed over a greater or lesser part of the 1st millennium AD, themselves shaped on the basis of central places such as Gudme/Lundeborg? In other words, Asgard, as it is known from the 13th-century sources, could just as well be "Gudme reconstructed" as the inverse.

In the search for an explanation as to why specialized sites for trade and craft coincide with sites for cultic activities in the first millennium AD, there is, however, good reason to go along with Hedeager and Theuws, i.e. to attribute with explanatory significance the connexion between trade and craft production and the various sorts of "imaginary world" of the central place. In Theuws' thinking, this connection supplies currency, craft products and trade goods with value; in Hedeager's thinking the activities are linked together through a reconstruction of a cosmological unity. As I see it, though, more is needed than cosmological elements alone – an economic element must also be incorporated in the explanation. This is the issue of the following discussion.

Commercial exchange in the 1st millennium

While anthropology and the historical disciplines for decades drew a sharp distinction between an economic and a social understanding of the production and exchange of objects in pre-modern societies, in recent years this distinction has become less sharp. Originally it was established in the mid-20th century in the context of social anthropological studies of pre-modern societies. Karl Polanyi (1944) developed the theory that the economy of a pre-modern society is not an independent sphere, but rather is "embedded" in the other spheres of such a society. Therefore, in such societies the exchange of objects fundamentally follows lines of social relationship, primarily in the form of gift-giving. Here too Marcel Mauss's (1954 [1925]) understanding of the position of the gift in pre-modern societies has been of great importance. In the view of both Polanyi and Mauss, it was in modern societies that buying and selling (commercial exchange) first became available as a form of transaction between independent parties without implications of a social relationship beyond the transaction itself.

Polanyi's understanding has been highly influential in both social anthropology and the historical sciences; many scholars who accept his understanding have concluded that most exchanges of goods in the Viking Period and before took the form of gift-giving, or were otherwise essentially a matter of plunder. The discussion in more recent years of material exchange in pre-modern societies has led to a blurring of the sharp distinction between gift-giving and commercial exchange. This development is part of a general trend away from model-building and towards an understanding of pre-modern economies as dynamic and complex. As Moreland has put it (2000b:69): "We destroy the distinctiveness of economic processes in the eighth century by the imposition of evolutionary and developmental models".

This does not mean that the models and their constituent concepts have to be abandoned. Mauss, Polanyi and others have provided tools that are essential to the understanding of pre-modern societies. In the concrete analyses of specific cases, however, those tools should not be applied like ideal types; rather they should be compared to and modified by the empirical observations concerning the society under investigation. The idealistic application of concepts and theories "…must give way to a deeper appreciation of the intricacies of real historical and social formations" (Moreland 2000a:31). All societies embrace a plurality of forms of transaction, and it is our job to identify the specific forms and the economic, social and ideological meanings that they have.

On the basis of archaeological evidence alone, it is difficult to identify forms of transaction. We find the objects, but they do not themselves tell us how they were exchanged. Past commercial transactions can therefore only emerge as probabilities; they can rarely be demonstrated with certainty. Indications of such transactions taking place may be forms of likely currency and other trade-related items found in appropriate contexts. Finds of silver and gold are thus not enough on their own; for them to be used as evidence of trade they have to be found in contexts and forms that render it likely that they constituted a medium of exchange.

Amongst the earliest finds of this kind in Scandinavia are the 25 purses with a total of some 200 Roman silver coins from the large deposit of early–3rd century AD weapons found in a bog, then a lake, in the valley Illerup Ådal in Jutland, Denmark (Ilkjær 2000:48 and 122). The 150 or so tinder-flints that were found within the excavated area of this lake may indicate that the equipment of 150 conquered warriors, sacrificed in the lake by the victorious army, was found there (Ilkjær 2000:136). Approximately one in six therefore seems to have carried coins in a belt-pouch type of purse. These purses also contained other small items that were probably used as currency: glass beads, a piece of cut gold, and several pieces of bronze. Similar finds were made in the large deposit of weapons found at Ejsbøl.

The earliest finds from the activity layers at Lundeborg are also from the 3rd century, and there too were located a quantity of finds of the same kind: about 150 coins, essentially Roman silver coins, and many fragments of cut gold, all of them weighing between 0.5 and 20 g. Touchstones for testing the purity of the gold have also been found; these were principally used to assess the value of metal objects, presumably in connexion with their use as mediums of exchange. Pieces of cut silver, bronze and iron were also found, many of them in small clusters. Crucial to the interpretation of these cut-metal fragments as currency rather than as metalworker's raw material is the presence of some 40 lead or bronze weights used for weighing pieces of precious metal (Thomsen 1993:77–80).

The coins were probably not used as cash, but rather as a medium of exchange in the same way as the pieces of metal and probably the glass beads too. This is what George Dalton (1977:198–9) calls "primitive money"; it can also take the form of goods such as salt, clothing, butter, and more. Dalton suggests (1977:199) that these forms of currency were used in societies that had "only small market sectors and petty or peripheral market exchange". Dalton's characterization fits very well the economy of Scandinavia through the end of the 1st millennium AD, where a market sector would appear to have been present to a limited, and fluctuating, degree throughout the period. The distinct growth in specialized trade and production sites from the 8th century onwards indicates that the market sector of the economy expanded in the Viking Period. Further expansion must have taken place at the end of the 9th century, when standardized weights and precise metrology were introduced to Scandinavia (Gustin 2004). This must have contributed to the integration of local and regional exchange systems around the Baltic Sea and the Skagerrak/Kategat (the seas between southern Norway's south coast, Sweden's west coast and Denmark) into a super-regional trading system. This development was probably also linked to the fact that as the 10th century progressed silver became a more important form of currency (Hårdh 1996), probably at the expense of, although not necessarily to the exclusion of, other forms of hackmetal and commodities such as iron, textiles and furs. There is some evidence that these commodities were used as media of exchange in this period (Naumann 1987). A runic inscription from Hedeby records that – as read by Liestøl (1973: 97–104) – "Oddulf gives Eirik a shield in return for otter pelts".

Dalton's description does not, however, accurately describe the situation in Scandinavia in the centuries following the Viking Period, when that sort of exchange system continued to exist alongside a monetary economy, and the economy as a whole included a significant volume of transactions (Pettersen 2000). This system of multiple payment methods has a number of ethnographic counterparts (Dalton 1977: 199–200). It was developed in Scandinavia even before the Viking Period. Minting began in Ribe as early as the beginning of the 8th century and at Hedeby in the early 9th century, while in the rest of Scandinavia weighed silver was a common currency from the end of the 9th century and throughout the 10th. But throughout this period it is likely that barter of goods and the use of primitive money were the two most common forms of exchange.

These lines of development cannot, as has been stressed, be understood with the aid of models and concepts alone – nor can they be understood without them. Another crucial point recognized in more recent economic anthropology is the need to focus on production and consumption as well as on the forms of transactions (Moreland 2000a). The reason that transactions attracted so much more interest than these other two activities is no doubt because anthropologists and economic historians were far more fascinated by them – which perhaps implies that they are easier to classify and identify than other economic activity.

Production, for example, is a relatively slippery phenomenon to categorize. Nonetheless Callmer (1995) has defined some essential categories, distinguishing the artisanal production of unique items from the serial production of identical items. The former can be linked to production on demand, whereby the customer gives the craftsman specifications for making the item. Serial production is, on the other hand, directed towards a market, and at the point of production the producer does not necessarily know who the customer will be. The products of both types of production might have been exchanged between craftsman and customer by way of commercial exchange, but the context of production would have been quite different. Serial production presupposes access to a considerable number of customers, ideally at sites such as a market or a town. This is probably the reason that serial production, according to Callmer (1995), was introduced in Scandinavia in the 8th century and increased markedly during the Viking Period, when sites of that kind increasingly emerged. At the same time, the products themselves became more widely distributed.

Callmer's analysis shows that the form of transaction is not necessarily the key to grasping and understanding essential socio-economic developments. At the inception of the Viking Period, those developments did not seem to involve the introduction of new forms of transaction, but rather of new forms of production, and also changes in the context and volume of both production and transactions.

Threatening trade

One provisional conclusion that can be drawn from the discussion above is that the locating of specialized trade and production sites at central places does *not* appear to have occurred because the central place's business, including trade and craftwork, had a predominantly sacred character, as Hedeager appears to suggest. Nor does Theuws's understanding – that both goods and currency derived some of their value

from the sacral context – seem to capture the essence of the relationship. Rather, it would appear as if specialized commercial production and commercial exchange were businesses in their own right throughout the 1st millennium AD. In order to explain why these economic activities were located at central places, I believe one further topic has to be introduced; it is a feature of the form of transaction (commercial exchange) that is under discussion here: namely its threatening character.

Commercial exchange represents uncertainty and potential threat for both parties to a transaction (Gustin 2004:166–74). By its very nature, a commercial exchange transaction involves the possibility of one of the two parties agreeing to pay a higher price than the other would in fact have accepted; also the goods that one obtains may be of poor quality; finally, one could quite simply be cheated. Such transactions are thus threatening in that they potentially involve the loss of face and honour. Gift-exchange may be perilous too, either because the recipient may bring shame to the giver by refusing the gift, or by giving much too large or too small a gift in return. The menace implicit in commercial exchange is nonetheless greater than that in gift-exchange. While it is a friendly gesture to invite someone to participate in a gift-exchange relationship, an invitation to buy or sell is quite simply an invitation to possible enmity, because the parties to the transaction have fundamentally conflicting interests. In the exchange of gifts it is the *person* one creates ties to, while in commercial transactions one wants to take possession of the other person's *goods:* the person who has them is in fact standing in the way. One is aware that the seller will attempt to achieve a high price, and may even hide flaws in the goods. While a gift brings with it generosity and goodwill towards the recipient, the sale goods carry the poison of suspicion.

In order to reduce the menace, commercial transactions have to be socially embedded. Polanyi drew a sharp line between modern societies where such transactions are detached from social relations and pre-modern societies where all transactions are socially embedded. But contrary to what Polanyi claims, even modern transactions are socially embedded by means of all the trade instruments used to create trust: consumer law, standardized units of weight and value, international agreements concerning banks and credit cards, and so on. For without trust, trade cannot take place. In Viking-period society, what arenas allowed commercial transactions to take place within a social framework providing both parties the security necessary to trade?

Just as Viking-age laws were applicable only to the inhabitants of the region where the laws pertained, so too were the social and moral norms of good conduct, honour and the like applicable only in encounters with others whom one knew to share such norms. Within social groups self-defined in this way as an "us", all interaction between individuals formed part of a complex mass of relationships. This was equally true of commercial exchange relationships. If one was trading with people one knew or trusted, one could trust not to be deceived, and one could likewise not allow oneself to behave dishonourably (Gustin 2004:169). Trade that took place within established social networks was as secure as any other exchange within those networks.

If strangers came into the law-region, they did not enjoy the protection of the law, nor was it necessary to behave decently towards them. It was acceptable in principle to cheat and abuse strangers, even to rob and kill them – as long as they had no protection in the form of friendship, kinship or some other alliance with inhabitants of the region.

The more extensive distribution of goods during the Viking Period, which accelerated with the integration of local and regional weight-systems at the end of the 9th century, ushered in changes in this situation. But the changes were complex, and their form and their effect upon different social groups have to be distinguished. One cannot directly transfer the character of the law-region to social networks. While the law-regions were rather well defined geographically, the various social groups' networks were of differing geographical extent. Aristocratic groups might have had kinship and friendship connexions that extended over much of Scandinavia and even beyond, while minor farmers probably had most of their friends and kindred locally.

The changes that took place in the Viking Period were thus most evident in relation to those social groups that had previously maintained networks that were essentially local or regional. Once again, it was changes in production and not in the forms of exchange that appear to have had the greatest impact. The serial production that grew massively from the 8th century onwards was most certainly not concerned with exclusive, prestigious goods, but rather with items for the average population. Recurrent in the great majority of burials of this period are glass beads, weaponry and metal jewellery, some made locally, some imported from other parts of Scandinavia, some from further afar.

The changes in production and exchange in the Viking Period consequently impacted social groups differently. While the social elite was generally able to continue obtaining drinking vessels and valuable weapons via the same lines of connexion as before, the commodity transactions for the masses were extended beyond the known local and regional contexts. Those who had goods to market were exposed to foreign purchasers from unknown places that may have had different, unfamiliar, social norms and rules. The lack of common norms and social connexions created a lack of trust in transactions with those strangers, and this was a serious obstacle in obtaining objects of desire. If one were to get hold of such objects by other means than robbery, it had to be done in some arena where even people that were strangers to one another could exchange goods in relative security.

Obviously, for an arena of that character to function required physical security; in other words, those who were trading, and their goods, had to be protected against robbery and attack. Protection could only be guaranteed by a secular leader with sufficient armed force. For people to feel that the goods and valuables they took to the trading site were secure, there had to be means for resolving disputes that might arise in the course of trade. This sort of arbitration mechanism likewise had to be guaranteed by armed force.

However a "peace" that is dependent upon military force alone is fragile. A forum for trade between strangers required, in addition to security guarantees, a context that was super-regional and that had the widest possible recognition and respect. This permitted the embedding of commercial transactions in social norms and cultural values that were shared by people over a much wider area than either the law-region or the social networks of ordinary farmers, i.e. an area which was not subject to the authority of some local chieftain or petty king.

All of these contexts were to be found at the leading central places. In addition to the fact that such places had military power and a mechanism for resolving conflicts, the archaeological evidence and above all the place-name evidence, demonstrates that they had a sacrosanct character which produced the universally recognized and inviolable quality that surrounded commercial transactions with the necessary security. However strange and unknown the craftsman or trader who offered coveted goods might be, at least a respect for and recognition of the sacred peace of the site was common currency. Thus the parties shared some common norms, connected with the site, which created a peaceful context by removing the threat from trading.

However it was not possible for sacrosanct central functions to produce a pan-cultural context. Christian craftsmen or traders had to have other forms of protection and guarantees before they could operate in the same way as others. Laws that gave these strangers special protection are found in England from the 7th century onwards (Sawyer 1986:60; Gustin 2004:179–80), and similar legal traditions probably developed at the Scandinavian trading sites.

The connexion between trade and craft production and the sacred sites that can be observed in Scandinavia from both archaeological and written evidence from c. AD 200 is, as far as I can see, sufficiently explained by the characteristics of the central place as a centre of military power, a forum for the resolution of disputes, and an inviolable sacred site. These were the essential requirements for the context that commercial transactions needed, especially for anyone who did not belong to a social network which ensured that trade with strangers would be relatively safe.

The association with the sacred did not really affect the commercial character of these transactions. The greatest relevance of the sacred to trade is that it constitutes a principal component of the context in which these menacing transactions could be embedded. There is consequently little reason to look for any fundamental relationship between the commercial value of the trade goods and the sacred character of the trading site, as Theuws seems to do. In my view, he has not evaluated, as is absolutely essential, the relative importance of the different components of the goods' commercial value, and he has generally overrated the value they might have derived from the sacral context within which they were either manufactured or obtained. Such transference of value from site to goods cannot, of course, be entirely discounted. But the crucial element of value has to be found elsewhere.

The key motive for obtaining things, indeed the reason for attributing them with value, has rather to be sought in the relatively universal human wish to obtain items that one thinks are of use, and the desirability of the beautiful and rare, of that which has coveted qualities. Amongst those qualities will be a reflection of sacred and distant mythical places, but also a reflection of other imaginary and *real* worlds, and of course the object's inherent perfection and beauty. If that period's values really were founded upon knowledge of the objects' association with imaginary worlds, and if basic human standards of worth were not also involved, how then should we, with our extremely limited knowledge of the myths and understandings of prehistory, recognize what was of value? Even though some such objects undoubtedly elude us, we are certainly not mistaken to believe that gold and silver objects of high-quality craftsmanship and exceptional beauty, or aesthetically striking and appealing objects from distant lands, were also valued by Viking-age people.

As has already been shown, the place-names *Vítrir/Vettrir* and *Helgefjell* show that the assemblies at Þjóðalyng could have had a religious character. The hall too, and the activities that went on there, must have also (Skre, this vol. Chs. 11, 17:401–4, and 19:439). In the immediate vicinity there are two other farms with names which may have a cultic background, Guri and Lunde, both of them neighbours to Huseby (Brink, this vol. Ch. 4:56, 63). The vast cemetery along the road between Kaupang and the hall, and the assembly site, created a sacred environment for all those who travelled by land to and from Kaupang. Consequently, all of the element types that represent

the sacral character of Gudme are also to be found at Skiringssal. Although founded several centuries apart, the two sites must have been of a rather similar nature, which in turn must have been one of the main reasons that Kaupang was founded at Skiringssal around AD 800.

At some point around the year 890 the Norwegian Ohthere *(Óttarr)* travelled to Skiringssal by making a voyage lasting a good month from his homestead in Hålogaland in North Norway (Bately and Englert 2007). Later in his travels, he described his home and his journeys to King Alfred of Wessex, and the account was written down. He must have sailed a fairly large ship, and have had a crew whose duty was also to protect him, themselves, the ship, and its cargo.

Even though Ohthere was protected by his crew, he must have had connexions in order for such a journey to be safe. He must have had friends and relations along the way who made it reasonably secure for him to sail along a coastline occupied by strange and martial people. Connexions of this kind had made it possible for people such as him to travel like that for centuries beforehand. While the journey to Skiringssal and on to Hedeby must thus, for Ohthere, have been of the same kind as his forefathers had undertaken for generations, the situation was probably quite different for some of his crew. They were dependent upon Ohthere's connexions for their protection. And when they reached Skiringssal, and would predictably have looked around and probably also both sold and bought, their security would have depended further upon the protection that visitors to that place enjoyed. For them, it was a matter of real significance that people at Skiringssal were protected by the king's power and the sacred character of the site. Both of those factors must have made all encounters and transactions with strangers much more secure than the meetings they had with unfamiliar ships and people during the long voyage south from their homeland.

20.2 Towns in the king's realm

Above, some of the connexions between central places and specialized sites for trade and craft-production have been described. These connexions provide much of the explanation for why these specialized sites were located at central places. But they fail to explain why two different specialized site *types* emerged at the beginning of the Viking Period – seasonal market places and permanently occupied towns. This topic and the relationship between each type and the various sorts of central place are discussed below.

Markets and towns

Even though a few specialized sites for trade and craft production are found earlier, in the 8th and 9th centuries they became many in number. A survey of the archaeological remains of these sites reveals that there are systematic differences between site types – for instance in the artefactual assemblages (Sindbæk 2005:74–98, in press). Søren Sindbæk has analysed a wide variety of specialized trade and craftwork, and it is reasonable to agree with him (2005:97) that there are only a few sites in Scandinavia – Hedeby, Birka, Ribe and Kaupang – that show a significant connexion with long-distance trade systems before the 11th century. This connexion is represented by their large quantities of goods imported from outside Scandinavia. Furthermore, the quantity of balances, weights and coins, and evidence of the use of silver as a currency, is much higher at these four sites than at the smaller sites. Similarly, these four sites have a broad range of craftwork that made use of imported raw materials, mainly metalcasting and glass-bead production. The minor sites have little if any such craftwork, but do, conversely, have craft production based upon local raw materials, such as combmaking and ironworking (Sindbæk 2005:96–7). The small quantities of silver, balances and weights at the smaller sites indicate that trade there was principally carried out by bartering goods, not by using silver as a currency.

Sindbæk has thus done a much needed classifying of the markedly diverse range of specialized trade and craft-production sites of Viking-period Scandinavia. In the present context, it is of interest to see how his classification relates to the two issues that are at the heart of this investigation, central places and urbanization. According to how urban communities have been defined previously in this volume (Skre, this vol. Ch. 3:45–6), the Early Viking Period in Scandinavia had only three specialized trade and craft-production sites, and possibly a fourth (Ribe, see below), at which the presence of all of Reynolds's criteria has been securely demonstrated: a permanent settlement of a specific size that stands out from those around it, in which the inhabitants are primarily engaged in secondary or tertiary subsistence work. At Hedeby (Schietzel 1981, 1984a, 1984b, 1984c), Birka (Ambrosiani and Erikson 1992, 1996) and Kaupang (Pilø, this vol. Chs. 8:164–72 and 10:192–203), the presence of large and densely inhabited settlement sites – 24, 7 and 5.4 ha, respectively – has been demonstrated, at which trade and craft production were the principal means of subsistence.

Year-round and continuous occupation can be demonstrated, *inter alia,* by the remains of housing constructed for year-round use. Such evidence has been identified at Birka (Ambrosiani and Erikson 1992, 1996), Hedeby (Schietzel 1984a) and Kaupang (Pilø, this vol. Ch. 10:203–17). Both the solidity of construction and the presence of permanent hearths show that these houses were not intended just for temporary occupation. In their construction and interior provisions the houses have features in common with houses found at rural settlements in the same areas, except that the houses in the towns never have byres or stalls.

Buildings for year-round housing are not found at the seasonal market sites. At some of those, such as Sebbersund (Christensen and Johansen 1992) and Åhus (Callmer 1982, 1991), there are sunken huts, such as also occur at Hedeby. But at none of the seasonal market sites do those huts appear to have functioned as long-term housing; they were workshops or housing for temporary occupation.

In addition to the houses for year-round occupation, the three sites have other finds that provide evidence of a permanent population. At a site where people were permanently settled the proportion of objects associated with household activities such as the preparation of food, the making and mending of clothing, the building and maintenance of housing, etc., will be higher than at a site where people only temporarily resided. One problem, however, is that many household artefacts can be used for a wide range of functions, for instance in craftwork; therefore, the objects used for preparing food, above all, can be used as evidence of a permanent population. A great number of those objects were made of wood, and their finding depends upon suitable conditions for the preservation of organic material. Amongst the sites in question, Hedeby, Birka and Kaupang, these conditions occur over wide areas really only at Hedeby, where indeed a very large collection of household material has been found, such as wooden ladles, spoons, bowls, jugs, containers and plates (Schietzel 1984b). At Birka and Kaupang such wooden household material is practically absent, and one has to refer to objects of stone or metal, such as cooking pots of pottery or soapstone, hand-querns, keys and spoons. Many of these have been found at Birka, although as yet these finds from the settlement area have not been published (Björn Ambrosiani, pers. comm.). From Kaupang, too, there are many such finds (Pilø and Pedersen, this vol. Ch. 9:Tab. 9.1).

The occurrence of other permanent installations besides houses may show that a site was permanently settled. At Hedeby, Birka and Kaupang the remains of wharves have been found. At Hedeby, where extensive excavation has taken place in the harbour area, very extensive and solidly built wharf-structures have been found (Crumlin-Pedersen 1997:57–68). At Birka only the earliest parts of the harbour area have been excavated. There, a large and well-built wharf was found with a stone core and timber casing (Ambrosiani and Erikson 1996:21–4). At Kaupang the probable remains of timber wharfs have been found, as well as a large area of cobbling in the shore zone intended to facilitate loading and unloading, and possibly also the drawing up of ships and boats, i.e. a "hard" (Pilø, this vol. Ch. 10:220–2). At Hedeby, wooden paving has also been found in streets, bridges, and revetments along the stream that runs through the settlement.

The extent to which the remains of structures such as these are found by excavation depends upon the conditions for the preservation of timber.

In the cases of Hedeby and Birka written sources confirm the character of these sites as permanently occupied, specialized trading and craft-production sites. Hedeby, Birka and Kaupang can be classified as towns according to Reynolds's definition (Skre, this vol. Ch. 3:45–6).

Ribe would appear also to have had urban settlement for parts of its functioning period in the 8th and 9th centuries. Here a market site was founded in the first decade of the 8th century; it was soon divided into plots along one main street. Within these plots there is comprehensive evidence of trade and craftwork down to the middle of the 9th century (Feveile 2006a). However the issue of permanent settlement is not easy to determine with certainty. The areas excavated in the zone divided into plots are relatively small, and it has therefore been difficult to identify any definite buildings. On the strength of stratigraphical information, including the presence of clay floors at several levels, Feveile (2006a:35) regards it as nonetheless probable that from Phase F onwards there were permanent houses in the zone divided into plots; in other words, from the 790s.

Immediately north and east of Ribe's plot-divided zone there were buildings of the same type as one finds in the rural settlements of this region (Feveile 2006a:38–40). These buildings appear to have been permanently occupied from the middle of the 8th century onwards, but the finds from them imply that the occupants were not involved in trade and craft production as their primary activities. The conclusion must therefore be that it is the permanent occupation of the plots which marks the unbroken presence of a population whose business was, first and foremost, trade and craft production. From the existing evidence, Ribe thus changed character in the 790s from a seasonal market place to a town.

There is one further place that merits special discussion, namely Åhus in north-eastern Skåne. Here, two separate areas with extensive evidence of trade and craft production have been excavated (Callmer 1991, 2002). The earlier site, from c. AD 700–750, was manifestly a seasonal market place. Callmer (1991:38–42) has discussed, however, whether the later site, dating to c. 750–850, could be classified as urban – which he believes, making certain allowances, would be valid. From the evidence that has been presented, those allowances appear to be rather generous. The site has sunken huts and post-built structures. There is no evidence that the sunken huts could have been used for permanent occupation. The interpretation that has been offered of one post-built structure is unpersuasive, and Callmer indeed describes it as very uncertain. From what has been published, it cannot be decided whether any buildings had a hearth. Nor

has a find-assemblage been presented that in quantity or character would imply the comprehensive domestic activity one would expect if the site were in permanent occupation for several decades. My own judgment is, therefore, that on the basis of the investigations that have been presented up to now, Åhus cannot be identified as an urban settlement. The evidence of year-round, permanent settlement is too weak.

Reynolds has established an important distinction between the period-free *definition* of urban communities and the chronologically and geographically determined *description* of the urban communities that may be found in a given area at a particular time. Such a discription of the Viking-age towns of Scandinavia is not to be discussed in any depth here, but one point of interest will be noted. In contrast to the seasonal market sites, such as Åhus (Callmer 1982, 1991), Paviken (Clarke and Ambrosiani 1995:84–5) and Sebbersund (Christensen and Johansen 1992; Birkedahl and Johansen 2000), the town areas at Hedeby, Birka, Kaupang and Ribe were divided into *plots* – defined areas which were usually separated from one another by trenches or fences. These plots were established when the settlement was founded, and their boundaries are quite stable over time. The plots usually lie with a shorter end, normally measuring 5–8 m, against a street or some open area. Their length apparently varies considerably. The plot was the area that one household or one group of people had the right to use. There was usually a house on the plot, and there could be an outhouse too.

Plot-division like this has not been discovered at any of the seasonal market places. In some cases, as in Åhus, there is some regularity in the positioning of the sunken huts and the other features that may indicate some form of spatial organization of the market site which maintained a certain stability over time (Callmer 2002:131–3). However Callmer does not refer to any marking of boundaries between sunken huts; so, it has not been shown that the user's right of control comprised an area around the building. In Ribe, division into plots has been securely demonstrated from the very beginning of the market place in the early 8th century (Feveile 2006a:27–8), several decades before the settlement took on an urban character in the last decade of that century. In the excavated plots at Kaupang too, one can see a short, preliminary period, of less than a decade, with seasonal use before houses were constructed for permanent occupation (Pilø, this vol. Chs. 9:185–6 and 10:192–5). This is such a short period that it is reasonable to infer that at Kaupang it was the *intention* from the very outset to found a permanently settled, urban community. That does not seem to have been the case at Ribe. In early Ribe therefore, the plot-division appears to have belonged to a different type of context than that of the other Scandinavian market sites and towns.

With what is known now about the specialized sites for trade and craft production in Scandinavia at the beginning of the Viking Period therefore, only Ribe, Birka, Hedeby and Kaupang can be classified as towns in accordance with the criteria defined in Chapter 3.1. One important point is that their identification as towns is based fundamentally on the towns' internal physical, economic and social circumstances; the identification is not based on any particular relationship they might have had with central-place complexes. The sacral and other social functions that different elements of Skiringssal appear to have had are consequently of no relevance to the definition of Kaupang as a town. The connexions between the founding of Kaupang and the central-place functions of Skiringssal are nonetheless obvious, and these relationships will be investigated below.

Markets and central places

The discussion above has shown there to be a number of systematic differences between seasonal market sites and permanently settled towns. The four towns are also the only sites that appear to belong to a network of trade in imported goods and that have full evidence of trade using silver as currency and of craft production using imported raw materials. A range of artefactual finds, such as the great quantities of imported pottery, including cooking vessels, shows that those who transported the goods to and from these towns also came from far away. Some of the visitors, and possibly also some of the permanent residents, would have come from Slavonic, Frisian and Frankish lands, and probably from Britain and Ireland too. At the seasonal market sites the raw materials used by craftsmen were much more of local origin, and the trading would probably, for the most part, have been conducted between local and regional agents – as well as taking the form of barter to a high degree.

In this section and the next, an assessment will be made as to whether towns and market places with these characteristic features stood in any different relation to central places, and whether those central places that had market sites differed from those that might have been associated with towns. These discussions raise the question as to what type of connexion existed between central places and the kings that, at the end of the first millennium AD, established super-regional territories in various parts of Scandinavia.

While the traces of trade and craft at most central places are of limited extent from the earlier centuries AD, there is a marked increase from the 8th century onwards. The most striking exception is, as noted, at Gudme/Lundeborg, which is the only early site that has evidence of a distinct location for trade and craft within the central-place complex. Helgö in Lake Mä-laren, Sweden, where, as at Gudme, activity began early in the first millennium AD, may be another exception (Lamm 1999). Sites such as these show that commercial exchange did exist throughout the period, but it was so limited in extent that it provided a foundation for only a very few specialized sites. The evidence for trade and craft production from other central places of the first half of the first millennium AD is so slight that it probably represents only production for and trade with the actual occupants of the central place.

This is a realistic conclusion also from the scattered evidence of trade and craft that is found at many central places in the period c. AD 600–1000. Production for and trade involving the occupants of the central places themselves is, for instance, a reasonable interpretation of the remains of craft production at the chieftainly farmstead of Järrestad in south-eastern Skåne which can be dated to c. AD 600–1000 (Söderberg 2005:74–84), and possibly also Toftegård in the south-east of Sjælland (Tornbjerg 1998) and Slöinge in Halland (Lundqvist 2003). These sites and a number of others that have been identified as central places in the literature appear to show few traces of the essential social functions that can be associated with central places. Their most vital role was probably as aristocratic farmsteads with certain central functions for the immediate neighbourhood. But at all sites referred to above, the excavations have been too limited for one to reach definitive conclusions about the sites' complexity.

Insufficient excavation is a major problem for anyone wishing to investigate the relationship between trade and craft production and central places. Amongst the market sites that emerge towards the end of the first millennium AD, there are several where more or less definite signs of central-place functions have been discovered. Several market sites have been shown, on the other hand, to have had apparently no such connexions. This latter category is, however, a very dubious one, as the stratified, find-rich deposits of market sites make such sites relatively easy to identify archaeologically. It is more difficult to locate traces of the other elements of a central-place complex, such as a *thing* site, a holy place, a hall, and other elements of the settlement. As a result, it might be that many of the apparently isolated market sites, such as Sebbersund on the Limfjord, were in fact parts of central-place complexes which have yet to be recognized as such. It is also plausible that sites such as Järrestad and Toftegård will eventually prove to have been more complex than is presently thought.

This situation means that many sites at which only limited excavation has taken place cannot be discussed in relation to the issue under consideration. The discussion that follows will, therefore, deal only with well-illustrated cases where both market sites and central-place complexes are proven to have co-existed at the same site. The four towns will also be discussed.

A very clear example is at Tissø on Sjælland, where a large aristocratic farmstead that existed from c. AD 550 to the early 11th century has been excavated (Jørgensen 2003; Jørgensen et al. 2004). In the middle of the 7th century the farmstead was moved about 600 m to the south, where it remained until the early 11th century. It is the later farmstead that is considered here. Immediately south of the principal hall was a cult building that was enclosed by a fence so that it could only be approached from the hall. The farmstead also had other buildings that have been identified as storehouses, cart-sheds, a smithy, etc.

The farmstead was surrounded by a fence; outside the farmyard, in three separate areas to the north, south and south-west, there is comprehensive evidence of trade and craft production. Especially striking are the concentrations of finds in the southern and south-western areas. The many traces of structures in these areas comprise sunken huts and a number of post-holes with no clear system such as might indicate that they belonged to permanent buildings. Jørgensen (2003:201–2) interprets them as the remains of light structures for temporary occupation and temporary workshops. Curved or crooked lines of fencing probably provided wind shelter for the workplaces of the craftsmen. From the character of the structures and the artefactual finds, Jørgensen concludes that the market place was only used seasonally. Activity here increased markedly in the Viking Period.

At Uppåkra in western Skåne there is, as will be demonstrated, a pattern in the distribution of finds that may show that trade and craft production were located within the central-place complex in a way similar to that at Tissø. At Uppåkra, thick stratified deposits have been found, in some places more than a metre deep, dating from the final centuries BC to the end of the 11th century. Striking changes in the finds indicate that a major change in the character of the site occurred at the end of the 10th century (Tegnér 1999). It appears that its functions as a central place had come to an end then; therefore, the finds from the four previous centuries will be considered here.

Within the area of c. 1,200 m x 700 in which finds have been made from throughout this period, including the Viking Age, there are three distinct concentrations of finds: one on the highest point where the church now stands, another south-west of this, and a third further south (Hårdh 1998:fig. 8). The concentrations of finds coincide with the areas having deep stratified deposits. Concentrations are 200–300 m in diameter and separated by corridors some 100–200 m wide in which the finds are fewer and the stratified deposits shallower.

From the early phases at Uppåkra finds are few, but they increase sharply after c. AD 600 (Hårdh

1998:114). The overwhelming majority of the finds have been made by metal-detecting or collection during fieldwalking. The only major excavations have been carried out in the southern part of the north-eastern find cluster. Here a cult building has been uncovered; it was reconstructed at least nine times in the same place, to the same size and in the same structural style from the 3rd century through to the beginning of the Viking Period. It may have a successor that was built on the same spot, albeit in a different style. This may have served the same cult functions right through the Viking Period (Larsson and Lenntorp 2004).

Because the excavations at Uppåkra are limited, it is difficult to form a clear judgment of the spatial distribution of functions in the find area. Therefore, one has to rely upon the topography, the depth of the stratigraphy, and above all upon the distribution of finds. In what follows, such an analysis will be attempted by comparing the distribution of specific classes of finds at Uppåkra with the distribution of corresponding material at Tissø, where more extensive excavations revealed a much clearer picture of the spatial organization of functions.

There is no published evidence that gives any impression of the focussed location of craft production within the find area at Uppåkra; but it is possible from the published evidence to gain a certain impression of the distribution of trading evidence. The Viking-period finds that are the strongest indicators of commercial exchange, weights and Islamic silver coins, occur in all three concentrations of finds. In the southern and western clusters they are evenly distributed, but in the north-eastern one, where the cult building lay, the distribution is very distinctive (Gustin 1999:figs. 13–14; Silvegren 1999:figs.17–18; Tegnér 1999:229 and fig. 1). There is a clear tendency for both coins and weights to lie in the southern part of the north-eastern concentration, around the cult building, while the middle and northern parts have fewer. There are also interesting differences between the three concentrations of finds. For example, there is a tendency for weights and Islamic coins, not only in terms of their quantity but also as a proportion of the total amount of finds, to be fewer in the north-eastern cluster than in the southern and western ones.

The distribution of Viking-period finds at Uppåkra before the changes at the end of the 10th century show the same tendency as seen at Tissø (Jørgensen 2003:190–1, figs. 15.7, 15.14 and 15.24; Jørgensen et al. 2004:56 and 61). At Tissø the Islamic coins and the weights are distributed similarly in distinct parts of the site, and this intra-site distribution correlates with the functional zoning within the complex. In relative terms, these finds are fewest in the enclosure with the hall itself, and the examples that have been found there, especially the weights, are clustered around the hall and the cult building. At both Uppåkra and Tissø the cult building is at the southern end of the north-eastern concentration of finds. Considering that the cult building and the associated concentration of finds were located at the highest point at Uppåkra, these parallels in the distribution of finds render it reasonable to infer that the northerly concentration at Uppåkra may represent the central courtyard of the site. There is one further find group that displays a distribution pattern that supports this view, namely glass vessel fragments. At both Uppåkra and Tissø these were concentrated around the principal court (Stjernqvist 1999:fig. 1; Jørgensen et al. 2004:56). The toponymic evidence from Uppåkra also suggests that there was a major farmstead on the site of the assumed central courtyard (Ridderspore 1998:175).

At Tissø, as noted, Islamic coins and weights have been found primarily in the market area, which here too, for the most part, lies to the south and south-west of the central courtyard. On the strength of the evidence that has been published so far, it is credible to hypothesize that the structure of Uppåkra was similar to that of Tissø, with a central, chieftainly residence in the area where the cult building has been excavated and the church stands today, and a market place with craft activities where the two concentrations of finds are located further to the south and south-west. An annual market at Uppåkra can be traced in documentary sources of the 15th and 16th centuries, and Andrén (1998:139–40) believes this market to have a history running back to the Viking Period, and maybe even earlier.

Therefore, it may appear that in the Viking Period down to the end of the 10th century, trade and possibly craft production as well were accommodated at Uppåkra in much the same way as at Tissø. A central farmstead with a cult building was at the heart of the complex at both sites, with a market site linked to it in the south and south-west. At both sites the large areas with comprehensive evidence of trade and craft show that such activities at these two sites were at a level that far exceeded the needs of the occupants of the central place itself. The market presumably attracted craftsmen and traders from the wider region, possibly from even further a field. The markets probably took place on the occasions when people were gathered at the site for cult festivals, and perhaps for *thing*-moots as well.

How might such a complex have been utilized by its owner? Jørgensen (2003:204–7) believes that the central court at Tissø was not permanently occupied by its aristocratic owner. He proposes the hypothesis that Tissø was one of several residences of the royal family that also held Lejre, further east on Sjælland. The basis of this hypothesis is the limited quantity of finds from the principal court, the high proportion of fragments of weaponry and horse-gear of high quality, and the lack of domestic finds and mundane func-

tional buildings for domesticated animals. He also stresses the size of the market place and its markedly seasonal appearance and finally, the absence of aristocratic burials. He infers that activity at the market site increased massively when the king was in residence in his court, and that at other times the court had a local caretaker. The model Jørgensen bases himself upon is that of the Carolingian Pfalz, and the Emperor's various residences in his realm. The most important of these, the residence at Aachen, shows real similarities to Tissø not only in its functions but also in the location of the residence and the cult building – in Aachen a church – within the complex (Jørgensen 2003:204–6).

Is there any basis for comparing Danish royalty during the Viking Period to the Frankish emperorship? The term "king", *konungr,* and the many other terms for men of power and authority that can be found in the skaldic poetry form an imprecise vocabulary, of which the constituents are not easy to distinguish from one another and which can be used for men of power having very different levels of strength and authority (Sawyer 1982:46). Central areas in all three Scandinavian countries have various archaeological finds showing that there were powerful dynasties as early as the Early Iron Age. But from the beginning of the 8th century onwards, Denmark produces evidence of the emergence of a royal power with more extensive lordship and a wider territorial authority than had been seen before. The digging of the Kanhave canal across the island of Samsø in 726, and in particular the major rebuilding of the Danevirke in 737, show that there was a king around who not only had the resources to organize major construction projects but who also had a large territory to defend. A Danish king *Ongendus* is referred to as early as the beginning of the 8th century in *Vita Willibrordi* (ch. 9). Subsequently, the king of the Danes appears in the Royal Frankish Annals from around 777 and on through the 9th century. This source makes it perfectly clear that he had an extensive area of authority and major resources (Sawyer 1991:278; Roesdahl 1992:73–4). A similar development of a central royal power can be made out in western Norway from the end of the 9th century onwards. In Sweden the development of a super-regional royal authority is less easy to follow; *Vita Anskarii* (chs. 11 and 26–30) refers to kings in the region around Lake Mälaren at the beginning of the 9th century, but how far their territory extended is uncertain (Sawyer 1982:54).

From this evidence it would seem that development towards central royal authority took place earlier in Denmark than in Norway and Sweden. The pressure of the Franks on the southern border of Denmark may have catalysed this. However, such development in the three countries might only *appear* to be different because the quantity and quality of the sources varies so much. Evidence like that of the Royal Frankish Annals does not exist for Sweden and Norway. Turning to other types of evidence, the growth in the number of central places in many parts of Scandinavia, from the 6th and 7th centuries onwards, and the contemporary establishment of significant cemeteries with princely graves – such as Borre in Vestfold, Gamla Uppsala, and Vendel and Valsgärde in Uppland – give good reason to believe that the hierarchization of the societies in all of these areas had begun by that time.

Jørgensen's hypothesis that there might have been a central royal authority on Sjælland with its seat at Lejre as early as the mid-6th century could thus be correct. His idea about how the principal courtyard and hall at Tissø were used would appear to be well grounded in the site's archaeology. Only further investigations will be able to show whether Uppåkra might have functioned similarly. Uppåkra was founded long before Tissø; therefore, one has to assume that the site's functions and the way its aristocratic owner elected to utilise it would have changed during its history of more than a thousand years. It is possible that the increase in the quantity of finds at Uppåkra around AD 600 indicates such a turning point; this was only a few decades after the establishment of Tissø. It is perfectly conceivable that a Danish king with a seat on Sjælland could at that date have controlled a territory that included the west of Skåne. However it is difficult to find positive support for any such connexion. Irrespective of whether the owner of Uppåkra permanently occupied the site or only visited it on specific occasions, he was probably the key figure in the site's juridical and religious functions.

If Jørgensen is right in his hypothesis of how Tissø was used by its owner, one has to search amongst the uppermost aristocratic rank, i.e. amongst kings with super-regional power, to find the lords of central places which have a large hinterland and which show conspicuous traces of all the social functions of a central place and extensive evidence of trade and craft production. This search needs to be carried out on a larger number of such sites, and especially on those that can be associated with the royal families of the period – although once again, the condition of the sources makes any such study difficult. No central settlement has been found at Borre, and the limited excavations of a possible market area at Uppsala have already been referred to. At the legendary royal Danish seat at Lejre on Sjælland where, as at Uppsala, major halls from post-600 AD have been excavated, the investigation of the "workshop area" (Christensen 1991:53–4) is too limited to judge whether production there was directed primarily at the occupants of the central place, or to judge to what extent trade went on there too.

Provisionally, therefore, this conclusion must stand: At a few major central places after c. AD 600

there is an observable connexion, like that at Gudme as early as the Early Iron Age, between market sites and central places with cult and other central functions. Various circumstances, described above, indicate that these sites should be associated with the emergence of super-regional royal power and authority.

Towns, kings and frontiers

The quality of the evidence is not particularly clear either for anyone who wishes to examine the local context of the four Scandinavian towns from the early Viking Period. The surroundings of Ribe have not as yet revealed clear traces of anything that could be called a central place. The market site was located in an area where there seems to have been neither settlement nor cultivation (Feveile 2006a:29–30). A connexion between Ribe and the rich site of Dankirke 7 km south-west of Ribe has been proposed (Jensen 1991b), but if that were so it could only have been of any significance at the very beginning of Ribe's history, and before Ribe became a town, as Dankirke appears to have lost its aristocratic character at the beginning of the 8th century. There are, however, a number of indications of an early royal involvement with Ribe. Sceattas were struck in or somewhere near to Ribe already in the early 8th century, and a particular type of coin from the beginning of the 9th century may also have been minted there (Jensen 1991a:11 and 53; Feveile 2006a:31).

The evidence of royal involvement at Hedeby is rather clearer. Here the location of the town, and the historical and archaeological evidence, all associate the town with the king of the Danes. The Royal Frankish Annals record that in 804 the Danish King Godfred came with his entire fleet and cavalry to *Sliesthorp*, which lay on the boundary with the Saxons (Rau 1955:78–81). The name *Sliesthorp* denotes an otherwise no more precisely located site at the end of the Schlei fjord, the very area where Hedeby was subsequently to flourish. The occasion for the king's visit was that the Frankish Emperor had conquered the land of the Saxons, moved the northernmost Saxon population to south of the Elbe, and granted the evacuated land to the Saxons' eastern neighbours, the Slavonic Obodrites, who were allies of the Franks. This created a new balance of power in the area. The threat to the kingdom of the king of the Danes was very much greater, and in 808 Godfred mounted an attack on the Obodrites' trading site of Reric. He plundered Reric and carried off the *negotiatores*, "merchants", of the site who, accompanied by his entire army, he brought to *portum, qui Sliesthorp dicitur*, "the port that is called Sliesthorp". Many scholars have considered this to mark the founding of Hedeby. Strictly speaking, it is not stated that Godfred relocated the traders there and ensured that they stayed. But one has to ask oneself why else he would have taken the trouble of taking them with him rather than just simply taking their lives and stealing their wares in Reric.

The Annals also record that Godfred remained in *Sliesthorp* for some time, and that he had a defensive wall built right across the Jutland peninsula. This is where the Danevirke rampart lies, but, despite extensive excavation, it has not proved possible to link any of the construction phases of the earthwork to Godfred's reign. In fact the rampart was already in existence by then, since its earliest dendrochronological dates are from 737. It is possible that Godfred's contribution was to renew the palisades and other defensive works on the existing rampart.

Thorough excavations in Hedeby have shown that activity in the town began early in the 9th century, although for the most part the dating evidence is not precise enough to be connected directly with what the Annals record. The exception is the dendrochronological evidence which consists of more than 3,000 datings from Hedeby. The earliest of these, a sample from a building, is from 811. A bridge over the stream that runs through the settlement is dated to 819. However there is only a small number of datings before the 830s (Schultze 2005). The great majority of the dated samples come from the wet area around the stream. It seems likely that this damp area would have been built on relatively late, and that there was earlier settlement on drier land a dozen metres or so further north and south. The building of 811 stood right on the outer edge of the excavation area (Schultze 2005:364 and abb. 5). The dendrochronological datings are therefore consistent with the Annals' date for Godfred's relocation of the merchants in 808.

From early in the 9th century coins were being struck in Hedeby, a fact that also reflects a significant royal involvement in the economy and administration of the town. Several other sources of the 9th century show that the king of the Danes had men either in or around Hedeby to look after his interests in the town and to watch over the southern border of Denmark. Into the 10th century too, runic inscriptions and other written sources indicate a strong royal connexion with Hedeby. A very rich boat chamber grave immediately outside the defensive wall of the town has been linked to the Danish royal family by several scholars (Müller-Wille 1976; Wamers 1994). Both the ostentatious burial-form and the wealth of the grave goods support such an identification. Wamers (1994: 32–42) dates the burial to the period AD 830–850, and proposes that the man buried may be the Danish king, Harald Klakk.

The diverse forms of evidence thus provide a variety of information, direct and indirect, confirming the Danish king's presence in Hedeby/Schleswig, and his likely participation in the foundation of the town. The main point in the present context is, however,

whether any central-place elements can be found around the town, and whether they can be dated to the period of its foundation. The record in the Annals that the king then came twice in four years to *Sliesthorp* with his army indicates that he had a secure base there where supplies were available, so that the army had food, and the king and his immediate retinue had accommodation. The text of the Annals for 804 refers to the site as a *portus*, a term that implies that here there were permanent harbour facilities and buildings. No such site has been identified, although a promising candidate has recently appeared at the site of Schaalby, also called Füsing, on the northern side of the fjord immediately opposite Hedeby. A river that flows into the fjord there creates an exceptionally good anchorage. On a high point by the mouth of the river a series of artefactual finds have been made that can be associated with a high-status milieu, and with craft and trade. These finds go back to the 7th century and extend towards the end of the 10th. Finds of fire-cracked stone and areas with preserved cultural deposits indicate that the site had been permanently settled (Dobat 2004, 2005a, 2005b: 73–5).

Only further work can determine whether Schaalby was an aristocratic residence and whether it had any connexion with the king of the Danes. In any event, a royal presence in and around Hedeby is well documented. It seems clear, though, that Hedeby's local context had a quite different character from the two central places that were discussed above, Tissø and Uppåkra. In and around Hedeby there is no sign of the sort of central-place functions, especially in respect of cult, that are in evidence at the other two sites. The location of Hedeby in a contested border area and its association with a defensive earthwork constitute a quite different political, ethnic and economic context. What one may ask is: To what extent did that special context influence the decision to found a town there rather than just a seasonal market like those at Tissø and Uppåkra?

Therefore, what might be the reasons for founding a town in a border zone? To begin with, in distant frontier areas such as this the king needed a base where, through his own men, he could maintain a significant and permanent royal presence. But it is doubtful whether the kings of the Viking Period could establish towns where it seemed politically convenient; there must also have been an economic basis for the town. Kings simply did not have sufficient control over the economy and individuals in their kingdom to create a town where there was no such basis. The potential for trade on the cultural, political and economic border between the Danes and the Slavs could be such a basis. Consequently, the trading that went with Hedeby's location in a border zone would have been every bit as crucial to its establishment and continued existence as royal initiative and support would have been. The Royal Frankish Annals, which are the most important documentary source for this period, are primarily concerned with political events, and say little or nothing about other aspects of social life. The acts of war, such as Godfred's raids on the Frisian coast and his plundering of Slavonic Reric and slaughter there, might give the impression that the circumstances were bad for trading contacts between the Danes and their two neighbouring peoples. But there is little in the archaeological finds to suggest any great trade barriers between these areas.

If one is to determine whether the location at the border was a reason for the king's choosing to found Hedeby there, one has to build upon a more solid foundation than the generalizations above, such as the better-recorded histories of nearby towns from the same period. Those histories show that the founding of Hedeby quite clearly falls within the pattern of the time concerning the foundation of towns along the southern North Sea coast and on both sides of the English Channel. From around AD 600 onwards, a series of new towns were founded in these areas; they are usually referred to as *emporia* in the literature, a term taken from Bede and other contemporary authors (Hodges 1982). The emporia flourished until about the middle of the 9th century, when many of them disappeared. They differ from the earlier towns in a number of ways, including in their locations. The emporia are typically located on the frontiers of the kingdoms, usually on the coast, although slightly withdrawn within a fjord or an estuary so that the town is in a sheltered position (Clarke and Ambrosiani 1995:19; Verhulst 2000:111). The later examples, particularly those founded towards the end of the 7th century or later, seem to have been closely linked to the kings of their areas.

Whether Birka was founded in a frontier zone is difficult to determine. Anders Carlsson (1997) argues that it was, and he also argues that it had a close connexion with the nearby royal *vill* on Adelsö. This complex, he believes, stood in opposition to Fornsigtuna (Old Sigtuna) and Gamla Uppsala further north. One has to say, though, that his conclusions are based on insecure premises, as the sources for political alliances and conflicts in this period and region are extremely sparse.

Ribe, by contrast, most certainly lay in a political and cultural border zone between the Danes and the Frisians. There is a marked cultural ambiguity in the character of the site. The finds, especially those of items that were produced on site, are clearly of Scandinavian character. But a quantity of imported goods and raw materials for the craftsmen at Ribe came from Frisian and Frankish lands. This is the case with basalt quernstones, glass drinking vessels, Rhenish pottery, and raw materials for the metalcasters and glass-bead makers (Feveile 2006a:30–1). The division

of the area into plots also has its closest parallels in Frisian lands. While the areas at Kaupang, Birka and Hedeby divided up in this way were clearly aligned on the harbour, activity on the plots at Ribe was focused along the street which ran past them all. This is the pattern one finds at comparable sites along the coast of Frisia, such as at Medemblik, Westenschouwen and Rijnsburg (Jensen 2004:243). Some similar sites in Frisia have the same mixture of agrarian settlement and trade and craft production that has been found at Ribe.

A number of scholars have suggested that the Frisian influence over Ribe was strong, and that the site would have been under Frisian control for some part of its history of some 150 years (Feveile 2006a: 28–30 with refs.). This view fits well with the fact that the site does not seem to form part of any local central-place complex. However the minting of coinage that began at Ribe early in the 8th century implies some royal involvement. The major change that is apparent at Ribe in the 790s – its transition from a market site to a town – might have reflected greater involvement by the Danish king who was then under military pressure from the south, and therefore might have wanted a strong and permanent presence at Ribe, the most important point of entry for seaway traffic from the south. The king could have achieved this presence at Ribe, as he did a few years later at Hedeby, by endeavouring to secure permanent occupation on the plots of the market site.

These two towns on the southern frontier of the king of the Danes thus seem to have had certain features in common. Neither of them would appear to have been part of a central-place complex with a focal cult role as was the case at the market sites of Tissø and Uppåkra. Nevertheless they do both appear to have been associated with royal authority. In the case of Hedeby, this connexion is well documented, and it seems appropriate to regard King Godfred as the founder of the town.

The southern border of the territory of the king of Denmark is quite naturally more widely referred to in contemporary sources than his territory's northern border. To the south lay the sphere of Frankish interests, which already had a developed literate culture. The Frankish authors were less concerned with the northern territorial border of the king of the Danes; the only time that frontier was referred in the Annals was in the context of something that affected the plans of the Emperor of the Franks. In the Royal Frankish Annals for 813 it is reported, amongst other things, that the two Danish kings, the brothers Harald and Reginfred, were unable to come to an agreed meeting with the Emperor because they were travelling (Rau 1955:102):

Qui tamen eo tempore domi non erant, sed at Westarfoldam cum exercitu profecti, qua regio ultima regni eorum inter septentrionem et occidentem sita, … cuius principes ac populus eis subici recusabant. Quibus perdomitis cum revertissent et fratrem ab imperatore missum recepissent…

However, at that time they [i.e. the kings] were not at home, but had set out with an army to Vestfold, the most distant part of their kingdom lying to the north-west, …where the princes and people were refusing to be subject to them. Having suppressed them, and when they had returned, and received the brother sent by the Emperor…

These two became kings in 812. They were the sons of the Godfred who became king sometime between 798 and 804 and died in 810. Given that Vestfold was already part of their kingdom by 813, it is reasonable to suppose that their overlordship there had continued from their father's time, and maybe even longer. The source shows that the Danish kings' interests in Vestfold were significant enough for both of them to lead a military expedition there.

Lordship over a town would have been one of those significant interests, and it is possible that the conflict which is referred to in 813 involved Kaupang. Even though neither this nor any other source makes any explicit connexion between the king and Kaupang, it is difficult to imagine a town having been founded in Vestfold without the knowledge of the king of the Danes or indeed without his involvement. The location of Kaupang by the border of the Danish kingdom fits the pattern of the foundation of the other two towns, Hedeby and Ribe, in south-western Scandinavia in the decades around AD 800. Similarly, regarding the border location, the parallel seems clear between Kaupang and those other two towns in the Danish king's territory and the contemporary and rather earlier Frankish and Anglo-Saxon emporia. The Frankish and Anglo-Saxon sites were connected to royal authority as can be demonstrated in the case of Hedeby and as seems probable in the cases of Ribe and Kaupang too.

It is therefore reasonable to infer that the foundation of the towns of Kaupang and Hedeby around AD 800 and the fairly contemporaneous establishment of the permanent settlement in Ribe were initiated by the king of the Danes following the model of the Frankish and Anglo-Saxon emporia. The object of these foundations was probably the same as in the Frankish and Anglo-Saxon realms: to provide secure fora for the exchange of goods from both sides of the border, and to establish an economic basis for a permanent royal presence. Such presence could not only administer the king's privileges and supervise his other interests in that region, but also scrutinize the goods and men entering and leaving the kingdom through these important border points, and report on events and individuals that might be of significance from the king's point of view (Middleton 2005).

The market sites from the same period would appear to have been of quite different character. They were of varying size and significance – some of them probably attracted people only from the immediate neighbourhood while others were of super-regional importance. The largest market sites appear to have been part of central-place complexes. These complexes had an aristocratic residence at their core, and cult, juridical and political functions were probably found here. The local figure of authority and the sacral character of the site produced secure assembly places for people who were not otherwise tied to one another by social or political links. Some of these central places in south-western Scandinavia might have belonged to the king of the Danes, while others would have had local or regional rulers as their lords. They were market places for local goods, although objects that had been imported or manufactured in the towns also found their way to them. A similar pattern of emporia on the borders and market places at secular and ecclesiastical centres within a kingdom is found in the Anglo-Saxon kingdoms of the same period and a little earlier (Palmer 2003).

The transition from locating specialized sites for trade and craft production at central places to locating them on the border of the king's territory marks a major change in the concept of royal lordship. Formerly this concept in Scandinavia was of an essentially social rather than territorial character. The king's area of power was centred on his home and landed possessions. This core was surrounded by a sphere of influence that was not precisely demarcated in territorial terms. It was dependent upon the king's military dominance, and upon whatever social ties he could establish with other kings and powerful men. Through alliances and marriages he could obtain influence over areas which, however, could be lost as soon as the alliances were broken. All in all, this sort of lordship was more socially than territorially defined. It is entirely congruent with this understanding that major market sites were established beside the leading aristocratic homesteads, as at Uppåkra and Tissø.

The establishment of towns on the borders of the kingdom shows that, in the decades around AD 800, the king of the Danes adopted a thoroughly new concept of his lordship – one that was *territorially defined*, and had *borders*. This was the Continental model of lordship that had been introduced into northern Europe early in the first millennium AD by the expansion of the Roman Empire. It was carried on by the Germanic kingdoms that were established within the limits of the former Empire. It is only with the foundation of the border towns by the Danish king that this territorial concept of lordship is first observed in Scandinavia. It was not before the final decades of the 9th century that there were signs that a king with comparable ambitions, Harald Fairhair, was setting about establishing himself in those lands that would eventually become the kingdom of Norway. Both the dating and the extent of his kingdom are a matter of debate, but it seems clear that he began his conquests sometime in the final third of the 9th century and that his kingdom was largely comprised of western Norway. There is little to suggest that he had significant lordship in Viken (Krag 1995:84–8).

The three towns in the realm of the Danish king, Hedeby, Ribe and Kaupang, are alike in that they are all located in border areas, but their local contexts are quite different. Only in the case of Kaupang would it appear that there was a central place already in being that was attended by people from a wide area (Skre, this vol. Ch. 19). In the case of Hedeby, and less certainly so with Ribe, it is possible to trace a royal presence in the area, but neither of those two sites seems to have had a central-place complex with the composite bundle of focal social functions before the foundation of the town.

This difference between Kaupang and the other two towns probably correlates with the fact that while Hedeby and Ribe were on the frontier of areas that had different linguistic groups and partially different cultures, Kaupang lay on the border of areas inhabited by Scandinavians who had no such differences. In fact the common features in culture and religion shared by the people on either side of the border may have in part determined the town's being constructed on the northern border of the Danish king within an existing central-place complex with cultic and juridical functions for a vast area. While the guarantee of safe trading at Hedeby and Ribe must have been secured first and foremost by the military power of the king, it was probably the sacral character of Skiringssal, founded in beliefs shared by people from both sides of the border, that was a significant factor in guaranteeing safe trading for people from wide areas on either side of that further northern border (cf. pp. 450–2).

At Hedeby and Ribe it was of greater moment to create pan-cultural and pan-religious fora where people of different cultural backgrounds could meet. At Ribe, a church was reportedly founded in the mid-850s (Rimbert, ch. 32, in Odelman 1986:61; Jensen 1991a:53), and a few years before the same had happened in Hedeby (Rimbert, ch. 24, in Odelman 1986:48–9, transl. Hines). There must be some truth in Rimbert's portrayal of the consequences of the church being built in Hedeby, even if his portrayal is somewhat pious:

There was great joy in the town, so that even people of our land [i.e. Francia] could go there freely without the slightest fear – such as had not been the case before; merchants from here as much as those from Dorestad. For this reason there was a wealth of all sorts of goods to be had there.

Nearly 30 years earlier, Ansgar, the main character of Rimbert's narrative, had founded a congregation and had a church built at Birka in the land of the Swedes. There is no trace in either documentary or archaeological material of any comparable missionary venture or church-building in Vestfold. Written sources do not refer to any missionary efforts in Viken before the second half of the 10th century (see below; Skre 1998a). If any such attempts had been made from Hamburg in Ansgar's time, around AD 825–865, Rimbert would probably have mentioned them. The reason the missionaries seem not to have journeyed to Kaupang might have been that this site, through its location at Skiringssal, was so manifestly pagan. In contrast, Birka was not located in such a sacral environment. From Birka it is about 70 km to Uppsala, which at that time was apparently the central cult place in the land of the Swedes.

The establishment of the three early south-western Scandinavian towns thus had a complicated background. The first precondition was the 8th-century boom in the trade and production of goods meant for a considerable proportion of the population. The other crucial precondition was the emergence of a form of royal power and authority on the model of the Continental Germanic kingdoms. The realization of this type of kingship required a strong king with power to maintain control over large areas and with sufficient resources to keep that control relatively stable over time. Such royalty in Scandinavia appears to have emerged first of all in Denmark, around AD 800. It must have been this kingship's need for unbroken and powerful representation at its most important border-points that led to a specific form of specialized trading and production sites, *towns*, being founded at Ribe, Hedeby and Kaupang. And it was probably the great potential for trade in these vital political and economic border zones that yielded adequate economic foundations for the survival of such sites.

Thus the basis for the establishment of the towns was quite different from that of the market sites, as is manifest in their respective locations and the finds they produce. While the towns are located on the borders of the kingdom, the market sites are located within the heartland of the area over which the relevant king held lordship. This is true whether it was the king of the Danes himself who was the lord of the central place, as Jørgensen believes to have been the case at Tissø, or whether one of his sub-kings was resident there, as might have been the case elsewhere, for instance at Uppåkra. The difference in finds at the two categories of site is also sharp. While the towns were clearly linked into long-distance trading connexions, the market sites were for the most part places for the exchange of goods that were produced in Scandinavia, possibly mostly at the central place or within the borders of the kingdom. These differences

Stanza	Yngling	Place	Relationship
30	Halfdan Whiteleg	*Þótni*	Place of death
		Skereið í Skíringssal	Place of burial
31	Eystein Fart	*á raðar broddi [...] Vöðlu straumr*	Place of burial
32	Halfdan the Mild	*Holtar*	Place of residence
		á Borrói	Place of burial
33–4	Gudrød Hunter-King	*Stíflusund*	Place of death
35	Olaf Geirstad-Elf	*Vestmar ok Grenlands fylki*	King of
		Foldar þröm	Place of death
		á Geirstöðum	Place of burial
36	Rögnvald Lord of the Heaths	–	–

Table 20.1 *Places with which the final six generations of Ynglings are associated in* Ynglingatal.

reflect the fundamental differences in the origins of each type of site. While the market sites had their roots in an old social order with essential local and regional networks and a central place at the heart of the petty king's authority, the towns had their roots in a new order involving kingdoms with territorial borders which the king kept under watch, and where trade was part of an international trading system.

Around the year 890 Ohthere from Hålogaland sailed along the coast of *Norðweg,* Norway, until he reached *Sciringes heal,* Skiringssal. When he sailed on from Skiringssal he had *on þæt bæcbord Denamearc,* "Denmark on the back-board [the port side]" (Lund 1983:24). Thus he sailed in Danish waterways from Skiringssal to Hedeby. Skiringssal thus lay either on or near the border between *Norðweg* and *Denamearc.* Even though on his month-long voyage from Hålogaland to the land of the Danes he would certainly have landed many times, to stop for the night and to obtain provisions, he reported no landing places before Skiringssal. That his arrival there was so significant was probably because it was the obligatory stopping place for anyone who wished to sail that route along the coasts of the Northmen and further into the territory of the king of the Danes.

20.3 The Ynglings and the Danes in Viken and Skiringssal c. AD 750–950

From the above, I conclude that the king of the Danes, around AD 800, was responsible for the foundation of the town of Kaupang at Skiringssal. In an earlier chapter in this book the case was made for the association of Skiringssal with the Ynglings in the 8th century (Skre, this vol. Ch. 19). How can these two propositions be reconciled, and what was the relationship of the Danish and the Ynglings with Kaupang and Skiringssal in the years down to the disappearance of the town and the Skiringssal complex in

the mid-10th century? These are the themes of the following discussion.

The evidence of *Ynglingatal*

Of the two Ynglings who might have been living when Kaupang was founded at Skiringssal, Eystein Fart and his successor Halfdan the Mild, *Ynglingatal* has little to say about anything except their deaths. In an earlier chapter (Skre, this vol. Ch. 19:437–40) Eystein has been linked to Skiringssal, but it is unlikely that his burial place was there (see below), and that he was associated with Skiringssal throughout his life. Of Halfdan the Mild it is stated that he *bjó Holtum,* "was settled at Holtar", and was buried at Borre. There is nothing to suggest that Halfdan the Mild had any connection with Skiringssal.

A synopsis of the place-names in the final seven stanzas of *Ynglingatal* (Tab. 20.1) shows that the final six generations of Ynglings were associated with a range of sites. It is worth considering whether these sites form any sort of pattern. In addition to Skiringssal, several of them can be securely identified (cf. Fig. 20.1): *á Þótni,* at Toten; *á Borrói,* at Borre; *Vestmar ok Grenland,* Grenland and the coastal districts around Grenland and at the southern end of Vestfold; *Foldar þröm,* the shore of the Oslofjord. There is little hope of locating *Stíflusund.* But for the other three places – *Holtar, Geirstöðum* and *Vöðlu straumr* – the most significant possibilities regarding their locations will be reviewed and assessed below.

The first place which is hard to identify is that named *Holtar* in the poem, the place of residence of Eystein's successor, Halfdan the Mild. He was buried at Borre, and therefore most scholars agree that his residence must have been at the farmstead which now bears the name Holtan, which is situated at Raet about 2.5 km north of Borre. The change of the name's ending follows a pattern common in Nor-

Definite identifications
Probable identifications
Possible identifications

0   10 m

Figure 20.1 *The various places and areas that with varying degrees of certainty can be associated with the place-names given in* Ynglingatal *(see also Skre, this vol. Ch. 18:Fig. 18.2). *Þótni, Toten in the Opplands, is of no significance in this context, and has been omitted for that reason. For* Holtar, raðar broddi *and* Geirstöðum *respectively, two, three, and two alternatives are given.* Geirstöðum *must correspond to one of the two alternatives given for it; therefore, its location close to Skiringssal can be considered secure. It is uncertain how far to the north-east the area of* Vestmar *extended. Green areas are wood, and yellow areas cultivated in modern times, for the most part corresponding to the Viking-age situation. Map, Anne Engesveen and Julie K. Øhre Askjem.*

wegian place-names (Rygh 1898:10–11). It is a fact, though, that there are today six other farms with the name Holtan in Vestfold (in the parishes Sande, Botne, Stokke, Sandar, Tjølling and Lardal, respectively; cf. Stylegar, this vol. Ch. 5:Fig. 5.11). Munch (1850:108) considered Holtan in Tjølling to be a possible candidate; this possibility can hardly be excluded. However, Halfdan the Mild's place of burial (Borre) does make it most likely that his place of residence (Holtar) referred to in *Ynglingatal* was the place which today is Holtan at Raet near Borre (Fig. 20.1).

Munch (1850:108) was sure that Olaf Geirstad-Elf's place of burial *Geirstöðum* is the farm of Gjerstad in Tjølling. An alternative view was first put forward by Sørensen (1902), when he proposed that the man interred in the Gokstad ship was Olaf, and suggested Gokstad's neighbouring farm, Gjekstad, as the *Geirstöðum* of the poem (Skre, this vol. Ch. 2:36–7).

These two farms are the only candidates in Vestfold. On a purely linguistic basis, it is impossible to determine which of them the poem refers to, and therefore both stand as equally plausible candidates. Both farms are situated within the area that the poem identifies as Olaf's kingdom, *Vestmar ok Grenlands fylki* (Fig. 20.1).

For Olaf's great-grandfather, Eystein Fart, the poem only gives his place of burial. *Ynglingatal* says that he is at rest "on Ra's shore, where, snow-cold, at the home of the Gautish king, the Vadla stream meets the bay" (Jónsson 1912b:13; Skre, this vol. Ch. 19:438). The "Gautish king" probably refers to Eystein himself, and the expression is likely to reflect his family's background in Sweden (Åkerlund 1939:75). This passage thus gives no clues as to the location of the burial place. Snorri says that it is at Borre, and many have accepted Snorri's account. However there is no *Vöðlu straumr* there.

Brøgger (1924–1926:93–4) tried to solve the riddle by suggesting that the name *Vöðlu straumr* denoted the sea current in the Oslofjord between Borre and the island of Bastøy, but his reasoning is not convincing. One problem with his suggestion is that the name means "the ford-stream"; however, the channel by Bastøy is much too deep to wade across. Moreover, *raðar broddi* means "at the point of Raet", not "on the edge of Raet", as Brøgger and several others have interpreted it. The cemetery at Borre is situated well down the eastern slope of Raet, right down by the shore, and Raet does not come to any sort of point there. That occurs first c. 6 km to the north, where the northern end of Raet runs down into the fjord. No outstanding funerary monuments are known there.

However, the situation at the southern end of Raet (Mølen) is quite different (Fig. 20.1). There Raet takes the form of a pebble ridge some 1.5 km long. The western end of the ridge runs into the sea, and the formation corresponds very well with the description "the point of Raet" (Løken 1977:79–82). There is also one of the most striking cemeteries in Norway, with hundreds of cairns, the four largest of which are from 25 to 35 m in diameter (Skre, this vol. Ch. 19:435). However, there is no *Vöðlu straumr* there either, or any watercourse that might have borne such a name.

All of the requisite features, however, do occur at another site, namely on the opposite side of the Oslofjord to Borre. The morainic ridge of Raet runs right across Østfold too (Koht 1955:24). Looked at from the north-west, Raet first crosses the island of Jeløy, and then runs under the sea in the channel between Jeløy and the mainland, at the site where the town of Moss grew up from the 16th century (Fig. 20.1). This channel was probably navigable in the Viking Period, but land-lift and sedimentation changed that; only an artificial canal excavated in the 1850s keeps it open nowadays.

Where Raet crosses the channel between Jeløy and Moss is now known as *Værla* or *Vedelen* (Bugge 1910:65). This name is probably a modernized form of *vaðill*, meaning "ford" or "wading place" (NSL; Skre, this vol. Ch. 19:433). Here, at its narrowest point, the channel has an intermittently powerful tidal current, and this could very fittingly be called *Vöðlu straumr*, "the current in (or beside) the wading place". Raet forms a conspicuous ridge on either side of the channel, and a barrow here could properly be said to be situated "on the point of Raet". No such barrow is known here nowadays. Since the growth of Moss in the post-medieval era, and especially from the 18th century onwards, the area has been densely covered with urban settlement. A barrow would have had little chance of surviving into the period when such monuments were recorded.

Of the three most credible candidates for identification as the site of Eystein's burial mound, Mølen, Borre and Moss, it is thus Moss alone that offers a place-name which can be connected with *Vöðlu straumr*. Unlike the other two sites there is no known barrow there, but this is readily explicable by the major landworks at this place over several centuries. I would consequently regard the shores of the Moss channel as the most likely location of Eystein's burial mound, but it is impossible to prove this conclusively.

When looking for a geographic pattern in the places and areas associated with the final six Yngling generations in *Ynglingatal*, the location categories based on the king's relationship to each site (Tab. 20.1), must be taken into consideration. The places where the kings died offer the least information about where they had their power-bases and areas of authority; however, the other three location categories are much more informative in this regard.

Taking this into consideration, a distinct pattern emerges (Fig. 20.1). The places mentioned in the poem cluster into two areas, one around Borre and

one around Skiringssal. Amongst the seven places (Tab. 20.1) that are mentioned in the poem, the areas around Borre (one definite: *á Borrói;* two probable: *Holtar, á raðar broddi;* one possible: *á raðar broddi)* and Skiringssal (three definite: *Skereið í Skíringssal, Vestmar, Geirstöðum* [one of the two possible]; two possible: *Holtar, á raðar broddi)* stand out very clearly. The Moss channel should be counted as part of the Borre area. At that time, the sea was the most important artery of communication and thus it linked the two sides of the fjord.

Besides this grouping into two areas, there is another pattern than can be seen. No two Ynglings are associated with exactly the same place in the poem. How are these two patterns to be explained?

The grouping of the Yngling sites in the areas around Borre and Skiringssal probably – as Munch (1850:108) and a number of scholars following him have pointed out – reflects the fact these two areas were central power-bases of the 8th- and 9th-century kings in Vestfold (Fig. 20.1). But why, then, are the various kings each associated with different locations within those areas? First one must consider how much weight should be attached to the royal genealogies of this period as historical source material. It is perfectly clear that the genealogies are *constructions* rather than factual lists of kinship (Krag 1991:174–82), produced with specific purposes and in specific circumstances (Dumville 1977). Genealogies were usually produced in connexion with an individual's assuming power; the genealogies played a key role in those situations. They were meant to document the legitimacy of the individual's claim on the kingship by listing his royal forefathers (Dumville 1977:73). This purpose, therefore, could easily be allowed to override factual biological kinship. A number of genealogies known from manuscript sources can be shown, with varying degrees of clarity, to have been constructed. The possibilities for investigating the relationship between geneaologies and factual kinship are better in anthropological studies. Such studies show that complicated genealogies "… may be accurately transmitted, but bear no relation to biologico-historical facts because it seeks to explain a phenomenon other than descent from father to son or because it seeks to assert a claim which is not historical in kind" (Dumville 1977:74).

This ancient approach to history should *not* be regarded as a form of manipulation or exploitation of history to achieve certain ends. It runs more deeply than such a purely pragmatic matter. It is a question of the role of history in preliterate society. History is formulated on the basis of contemporary circumstances; therefore, history is subject to more or less constant reformulation as political alliances, conquests and other significant changes take place. The scope for *creating* genealogy, however, is limited to a time that lies beyond people's memory. Concerning the most recent generations, genealogy must fairly accurately reflect known facts. That horizon's depth varies from society to society – Dumville (1977:87) suggests that 4–5 generations is normal.

The above assessment of *Ynglingatal* as a source (Skre, this vol. Chs. 18 and 19) agrees with these considerations. The five "Norwegian" generations of Ynglings preceding Rögnvald may have been reasonably historical – as far as the individuals are concerned, anyway. However one must allow for some creativity here too, concerning the biological basis for linking these individuals genealogically. The poem itself is silent on the nature of relationships, although it is implicit in this genre that kinship relationships are those portrayed. "Son of" is probably the least accurate term to describe an Yngling's relationship to his predecessor; "heir of" or "successor" would be most accurate. Since this is not an institutional kingship but rather a charismatic, power-based petty kingship, one can also assume that "successor" could have a broad range of meaning, possibly as broad as "just as important as the one before".

This kingship's nature may explain why the "Norwegian" Ynglings are associated with so many places. The succession was not necessarily one of fathers and sons, but rather of petty kings, each of whom might have won his position in a different way. Likely, each had some sort of kinship with his predecessor. A number of candidates probably vied to succeed a deceased king; the victor triumphed by either dint of force or by virtue of chieftainly support, or by both. A victor could come from other parts of the region than his predecessor.

This general understanding of how genealogies were developed allows for a hypothesis concerning the composition of *Ynglingatal*. The poem is usually described as a panegyric for Rögnvald Lord of the Heaths, and indeed that is what it is. But as described above, genealogies serve a special function, i.e. they help to legitimize a new king's claim to power. Is it therefore possible that *Ynglingatal* was produced for such a reason when Rögnvald succeeded his predecessor Olaf Geirstad-Elf as king?

One particular feature of the poem renders such a hypothesis credible. That there were precisely five generations before Rögnvald associated with Vestfold and Viken might have been of special significance when Rögnvald arrived as king. Indeed, in another law-region later, in the Gulathing Law (Ch. 266), which was probably written down in the second half of the 12th century, property had to have passed through five generations in inheritance before it became *odal*-property. Elsewhere, a listing of the inheritance of farms through five generations is found on two runestones, one each from the Swedish regions Hälsingland and Småland. Brink (2002a:103–5) interpreted these stones to represent the commissioners', the sixth heirs', claim to *odal*-rights over the farms in

question. The same number of royal generations is counted by Óttarr in his poem *Hyndluljóð* as the basis for his claim to royal rank (Brink 2002a:104–5). Therefore, it is credible that *Ynglingatal*, by placing five generations of Rögnvald's ancestors in the region where he himself probably lived, legitimized Rögnvald's claim to power, and perhaps also his *odal*-rights to land. His ancestors' possessions and status were documented by identifying their burial mounds (Skre 1997), as the poem does in several cases. Looked at in this light, *Ynglingatal* is as much a poem of inheritance as a panegyric.

Kaupang and Skiringssal AD 800–900: between the Ynglings and the Danes

It was pointed out above that *Ynglingatal* associates the final six Yngling generations with two areas within Viken, Skiringssal in southern Vestfold and the area around Borre further to the north including the Moss channel on the other side of the fjord. The chronological pattern within these connexions is striking. The first two generations can be associated with Skiringssal, but *Ynglingatal* and other sources give the impression that the connexion between the Ynglings and Skiringssal came to an end in the time of Eystein Fart (Skre, this vol. Ch. 19:440) around the date of Kaupang's founding. In the next two generations Halfdan the Mild can be associated with the Borre area with reasonable certainty, while Gudrød Hunter-King cannot be securely associated with any place. After that, Olaf Geirstad-Elf is associated with the Skiringssal area (Tab. 20.1). In what follows, it will be investigated whether this pattern can be linked to information from other sources, and whether on that basis it is possible to develop a hypothesis explaining the movements of the Yngling kings.

The removal of the Ynglings from Skiringssal to the Borre area can broadly be correlated with the period around the foundation of Kaupang and the Danish military expedition of 813, both of which marked the strengthening presence of the king of the Danes in Skiringssal and Viken. Because of the lack of precise chronological information, it is difficult to demonstrate any direct connexion between these events and the removal of the Ynglings. But the significance of Skiringssal for both the Ynglings and the Danish king certainly indicates such a link. How these events might have unfolded is unclear, however. Conceivably the Ynglings were driven out before or at the time of the foundation of Kaupang. But Kaupang might equally have been established by agreement and collaboration between the king of the Danes and the ruling Yngling, presumably Eystein. Or it could possibly have been the Danish king's military campaign to Vestfold in 813 that first marked a break in an alliance between him and the royal kindred of Skiringssal and eventually led to the king of the Danes establishing his own men there.

Although the chronology cannot be clarified further, it seems likely that the move of the Ynglings from Skiringssal to the Borre area was related to a greater level of involvement in Viken by the Danish king, represented by Kaupang's founding and the expedition of 813. The probably Danish origin of the Oseberg ship, buried in the barrow of a woman about 30 years old some 36 km north of Skiringssal, may be further evidence of a greater Danish presence. The dendrochronological analysis which dated the burial to AD 834 (Bonde and Christensen 1993a, 1993b) also revealed that the tree-ring pattern in the Oseberg ship's timbers corresponds somewhat better with the Danish master curve than with the so called "Oslo-fjord curve", which covers Østfold and Vestfold (Niels Bonde, pers. comm.). Consequently, it is more likely that the ship was built in present-day Denmark than in Viken. It would seem a realistic possibility that this ship, built some 10–15 years before it was buried (Bonde 1994:143), came first with the young woman from her home, possibly in Denmark, as part of her dowry when she was married to a Vestfold chieftain or king, and then went with her into the grave.

The return of the Ynglings to the Skiringssal area in the person of Olaf Geirstad-Elf two generations after Eystein Fart might have been linked to the weakening of the influence of the king of the Danes. The first part of stanza 35, which treats of Olaf, goes (Jónsson 1912b:13; Krag 1991:141; Hines)(as shown above).

This stanza shows that around the year 900, Rögnvald considered himself and his predecessors to have been ruling in a part of *Norway* rather than in some part of the Danish king's realm. This is certainly not to be taken as an indication that the entry in the Royal Frankish Annals for AD 813 was either in error or inaccurate when it reported that the king of the Danes ruled in Vestfold. But it is probably to be taken as evidence that in Rögnvald's time this Danish overlordship was no longer a reality – not in the area Rögnvald was in, in any event. Consequently, the skald reformulated history on the basis of contemporary reality and his immediate intention (to legitimize Rögnvald's claim to power and land), and so made all the Ynglings after Halfdan Whiteleg "Norwegian" by associating the whole kin-branch with Norway.

Such a reading of stanza 35 is perfectly congruent with the pattern of places and areas associated with the final two Yngling generations (Tab. 20.1, Fig. 20.1). After two generations that were not connected with Skiringssal, the poem connects Rögnvald's closest predecessor, Olaf, with the area. And in the next generation, possibly in the context of Rögnvald's succession to Olaf, the land of the final six generations of Ynglings is described as part of Norway. Could the return of the Ynglings to Skiringssal indicate that the overlordship of the king of the Danes came to an end at that time?

Ok niðkvísl	Og ættegrenen	And the kin-branch
I Nóregi	i Norge	in Norway
þróttar Þrós	etter styrkens sterkning	with the strength of the Mighty
of þróazk hafði;	trivdes hadde;	had thriven.

"And Odin's mighty family branch had grown mighty in Norway".

Much less is known about the Danish kingdom at the end of the 9th century than at its beginning. This is due to the fact that the Royal Frankish Annals do not go beyond 829, and *Vita Anskarii* only covers the period down to the 860s. In most of the 10th century there are only scattered pieces of information about who held power in south-west Scandinavia. There are several points, however, that imply that the Danish kingdom, which appears to have been unified under a single king in the period of Godfred and again under Horik I (d. 854), saw unstable government in the second half of the 9th century and was at times divided into a number of areas ruled by rival factions within the royal family (Krag 1995:89; Jensen 2004:282–4). This instability would appear to have continued right down to the time of Gorm the Old (died c. 958). In the context of this weakening of the Danish kingdom after the middle of the 9th century it seems probable that the Danish king's control over Viken, including Kaupang and Skiringssal, would have diminished and perhaps even completely evaporated.

The archaeological evidence from Kaupang may also imply that contact with the south diminished towards the end of the 9th century, although these changes elude a precise dating. The imported finds from the first century of Kaupang show a clear preponderance of goods from the south, from the western Continent. Around the year 900 a change occurred, and British and eastern goods (from the Baltic coastlands) became more strongly represented. This holds both for imported items found in burials (Stylegar, this vol. Ch. 5:84–5) and, as future volumes in this series will demonstrate, also for the imported finds from the settlement area of Kaupang (Graham-Campbell, in prep.; Hårdh, in prep.; Wamers, in prep.). Communication with the areas from which most of the 9th-century imported material came was by sea-routes and along the coasts which the king of the Danes ruled. Many of the imported goods probably lay in harbours in the Danish king's territory before they came to Skiringssal. Amongst the finds from Kaupang, the predominance of imports from the western Continent through most of the 9th century may therefore indicate that Danish rule in Vestfold was not merely an episode of the very early 9th century but rather continued until the middle or even the end of that century. The changes that appear in the imported material around the year 900 may have been connected with the weakening of the hold the king of the Danes had over Viken.

The archaeological evidence may thus corroborate the impression gained from *Ynglingatal*, namely that the Danes strengthened their authority over Skiringssal in the decades immediately around AD 800. Towards AD 900 there appears to have been a weakening or collapse of the dominance of the Danish king in Viken. These changes may correspond to the movement of the Ynglings to the Borre area sometime around AD 800, and their probable return in the late 9th century, when Olaf Geirstad-Elf might have resumed the Ynglings' lordship over Skiringssal.

All the same, the dating of both the archaeological material and the lives of the individual Yngling kings is relatively uncertain. Nor is it possible from contemporary documentary sources to date the weakening of the rule of the Danes in Viken any more precisely than to sometime after the mid-9th century. The connexions that have been proposed above between the geographical details in *Ynglingatal*, the historical sources for the kingdom of the Danes, and the archaeological evidence from Kaupang, have therefore to remain hypothetical.

Kaupang and Skiringssal after AD 900

Ynglingatal was composed around AD 900 or a little earlier, and therefore tells nothing about what happened to the Ynglings or Skiringssal after that date. Nor are any other documentary sources very informative about subsequent events. The picture of what happened at Skiringssal after c. AD 900 must therefore rely almost entirely on the archaeological evidence.

The hall at Huseby probably went out of use sometime in the first half of the 10th century. The number of burials in the cemeteries around Kaupang and along the roadway up to the hall indicates that the first 30–50 years of the 10th century were the period in which the urban site had its largest population (Stylegar, this vol. Ch. 5:86). This image is only partly confirmed by finds from the settlement site itself (Pilø, this vol. Chs. 8:177–8 and 10:200–3). Indeed, there are finds there from the first half of the 10th century, and even a little material from the decade or three following that, but the quantities are very much lower than in the 9th century. This could show that activity there changed such that fewer objects came into the ground in the town. Conceivably permanent occupation there had come to an end, and the site functioned only as a market site, but this is not consistent with the increase in the number of graves in the 10th century. Nor does it appear that the cemeteries were taken into use by new groups, as the burial practices at all of the sites show continuity, which implies that the same groups used them throughout their functioning periods.

With the information now available, it would appear unlikely that Kaupang developed from a town into a market site around the year 900. It is more likely that permanent occupation at Kaupang continued until c. 930 at least, and possibly 20–30 years beyond that. In considering this issue, the evidence of the number of burials and continuity in burial practice must carry considerable weight. The reduction in the quantity of finds from the urban area in the 10th century could be explained by a series of mundane circumstances, such as the types and amount of dress accessories worn by the population, the types of craftwork that were practised there, the places where the settlement's waste was dumped, and so on. But given that no intact stratified deposits post-dating c. AD 840/850 have been excavated in the settlement area, except for fill in pits, it is difficult to test whether the reduction in the quantity of finds can be explained in any such ways. The above suggestion about the end date of the permanent occupation at Kaupang must therefore also remain a hypothesis.

With the inferred break in the connexion between Skiringssal and the king of the Danes around AD 900, Kaupang's position on an important political border presumably also ended. The town now lay – according to the implications of the proposition that Olaf Geirstad-Elf returned to Skiringssal – within a central-place complex that was once more the seat of a lineage of petty kings, probably one of several within Viken. While Kaupang's economic life initially was apparently rooted in the opportunities for trade that its border location created, after the weakening of the connexion with the Danish kingdom it must have found some other basis. The relative quantity of non-Scandinavian imports to Scandinavian artefacts falls in the 10th century, and there is a reduction in the proportion of imported goods coming from the western parts of the Continent (Stylegar, this vol. Ch. 5:84–5). This may indicate that long-distance trade became less significant in Kaupang's economic life, and that more of the trade goods came from the western part of the main Scandinavian Peninsula. Judging from the number of finds, the links with Britain and Ireland and the Baltic were, however, maintained to a degree.

What effect might the macro-political history of the 10th century have had on Skiringssal? As has been noted, there is little evidence that Harald Fairhair's Norwegian kingdom ruled in Viken. But as the 10th century progressed, the growing Norwegian kingship also advanced into Viken. However, this did not amount to stable authority. Therefore, the term *Nóreg* in stanza 35 of *Ynglingatal* should be understood as a geographical rather than a political term.

In the course of the 10th century the Danish interest in Viken increased again. Shortly before the mid-10th century a new Danish royal dynasty assumed power in the person of Gorm the Old. Gorm and his son Harald Bluetooth had ambitions in Viken and

Norway. It was inscribed on Harald's memorial stone at Jelling in central Jutland that he "won for himself all of Denmark and Norway". The fact that activity at Kaupang ended in the era of the Jelling dynasty may be connected to the fact that Viken was becoming an increasingly contested region where two strengthening kingdoms, the Norwegian and the Danish, competed. This situation would have adversely affected the scope for trade. However, because archaeological and written sources say nothing about this matter, these connexions cannot be explored further.

It is possible to say something about another key reason why Kaupang and Skiringssal lost their importance, namely the conversion of the region to Christianity, which appears to have happened around AD 950. Until then the number of pagan burials in Vestfold was very large, whereas from the second half of the 10th century there are only a handful. This was most likely due to a general conversion in the region. The same near absence of post-950 graves is found in the rest of Viken and westwards to Agder and Rogaland. Generally, conversion in the rest of Norway did not take place until the very late 10th century, or a few decades into the 11th. Conversion in the Opplands, for example, occurred in the early 11th century (Skre 1998a).

The Christian conversion removed much of the reason for Skiringssal's existence. For example, the annual pagan sacrificial festivals, that brought lots of people to the town, would no longer be held. The sacred character of the site, which constituted an essential element in the ideological framework that provided secure trading conditions in Kaupang, was gone. After the conversion of Viken, trading expeditions to Kaupang from areas where the population was still predominantly non-Christian, such as the Opplands, would have been largely impractical.

It was not until the 11th century that a new, strong royal authority was established in the south-east of Norway. As a consequence of this, early in that century most of the Opplands were converted to the Christian religion. The integration of Viken, the Opplands and the rest of Norway into one political and religious unit, again favoured the establishment of towns. In Viken, the towns of Oslo, Sarpsborg and Tønsberg were founded. Skien could also have become a town in the 11th century, but due to limited excavations the character of the 10th and 11th century settlement there is uncertain. In the kingdom of Denmark the general conversion and the strengthening of royal control occurred rather contemporaneously as in Norway. There too, many new towns grew up in the 11th century.

The 11th century towns of Norway and Denmark had many of the same activities as those towns founded two centuries earlier. But trade and production in them were of an even more local and regional character than in the earlier towns. The new towns were also connected with the king. Compared to the earlier towns, it made a considerable difference to the social, political and economic life of the town that the king and his administration, eventually that of the Church as well, moved into the towns. To begin with, the towns were now the places in which the income in kind that the king and the Church obtained from their lands and other sources was exchanged. In addition, the 11th- and 12th-century consolidation of the kingdoms and the Church resulted in an increasing number of people being engaged in their administration, households and other activities. This growth took place in the towns, and therefore changed the social composition of the urban population.

The 11th- and 12th-century concentration of royal and ecclesiastical administration in the towns meant that they came to house the central juridical, economic and political functions of the surrounding areas. At the beginning of the Viking Period, those administrative functions were much more limited in extent, and were restricted to the king's retinue, and to central-place complexes which, with the exception of Skiringssal, were entirely rural in character. At Skiringssal the juridical and administrative activities were not located solely at Kaupang; it was probably only those who governed the internal affairs of the town who operated there. Those administrative services that were provided for the surrounding region were divided between two other elements within the complex, the hall and the *thing* site.

The new towns thus had greater local and regional significance than the earlier towns, comparable to that of the old central places. The location of some of the new towns illustrates this parallel, as they were established well inside the kingdom's territory and not in border zones as the earlier towns. This can also be seen in the archaeological material from them: it mainly reflects local trade and production and to a much lesser extent long distance trade. Still, some of the new Norwegian towns – Oslo, Bergen and Trondheim – had both a local and regional function as well as a border zone function, as they were major ports for people and goods coming into the kingdom.

In this way the new towns accommodated new social and political functions while a few of them continued to play the border-zone role of the 9th-century towns. In achieving a greater local and regional significance, the new towns appropriated the economic, social and political functions of the old central places like Skiringssal, all of which lost significance around the turn of the first millennium at the latest.

Abbreviations

ABJ   Jon Gunnar Jørgensen (ed.) 1997: *Aslak Bolts Jordebok.* Riksarkivet. Oslo.

AEW   Jan de Vries 1962: *Altnordisches etymologisches Wörterbuch,* 2 Aufl. Brill. Leiden.

Aks.   Accession number, KHM.

B   Eldre Borgartings kristenrett. In: *Norges gamle Love indtil 1387,* vol. I:337–372. Christiania.

C   Museum number, KHM.

DEO   Niels Åge Nielsen 1976: *Dansk etymologisk ordbog,* 3rd ed. Gyldendal København.

DN   Diplomatarium Norvegicum. *Oldbreve til Kundskab om Norges indre og ydre Forhold, Sprog, Slægter, Sæder, Lovgivning og Rettergang i Middelalderen,* vol. I-XXII. 1847–1995. Kristiania/Oslo. [NB! Number (e.g. DN I:543) always indicates the document *number,* not page.]

E   Eldre Eidsivatings Kristenrett. In: *NGL,* vol. I:375–406.

G   Eldre Gulatingslov. In: *NGL,* vol. I:3–118.

Ka.   Reference to Catalogue of Kaupang graves in Stylegar, this vol. Ch. 5:103–28.

KHM   Kulturhistorisk Museum, Universitetet i Oslo.

KLNM   *Kulturhistorisk Leksikon for Nordisk Middelalder fra vikingtid til reformasjonstid,* vol. 1–22. 1956–1978. København.

NGL   *Norges gamle Love indtil 1387,* vol. I–IV. Christiania 1846–95.

NO   Leiv Heggstad, Finn Hødnebø and Erik Simensen 1997: *Norrøn ordbok,* 4th ed. Det norske samlaget. Oslo.

NRJ   H.J. Huitfeldt-Kaas and A.O. Johnsen (eds.) 1885–1906: *Norske Regnskaber og Jordebøger fra det 16de Aarhundrede (1514–1570),* vol. 1–4. Kjeldeskriftfondet. Christiania.

NSL   Jørn Sandnes and Ola Stemshaug (eds.) 1990: *Norsk stadnamnleksikon,* 3rd ed. Det Norske Samlaget. Oslo.

RB   H. J. Huitfeldt (ed.) 1879: *Biskop Eysteins Jordebok (Den röde Bog). Fortegnelse over det geistlige gods i Oslo Bispedømme omkring Aar 1400.* Christiania.

SEO   Elof Hellquist 1948: *Svensk etymologisk ordbok,* 3rd ed. Gleerup. Lund.

TopArk   Topografisk Arkiv, Kulturhistorisk Museum, Universitetet i Oslo.

UMK   University Coin Cabinet, KHM, find number.

References

NB:

* *Icelanders are listed by their second name.*
* *Sagas, hagiographies etc. are generally not listed, except when specific editions are referred to.*

Aalto, M. and H. Heinäjoki-Majander 1997: Archaeobotany and palaeoenvironment of the Viking Age town of Staraja Ladoga, Russia. In: U. Miller and H. Clarke (eds.): *Environment and Vikings: Scientific methods and techniques*. Birka Studies, vol. 4:13–30. The Birka Project. Stockholm and Rixensart.

Acsádi, György and János Nemeskéri 1970: *History of human life span and mortality*. Budapest.

Adderley, W. Paul, Alberts, Ian A. Simpson and Timothy J. Wess 2004: Calcium-iron-phosphate features in archaeological sediments: characterization through microfocus synchrotoron X-ray scattering analyses. *Journal of Archaeological Science*, vol. 31:1215–24.

Adolfsen, Erik 2000: *Maktforholdene på tingene i Norge ca. 900–ca. 1200*. Unpublished thesis in History, University of Bergen.

Alkarp, Magnus and Neil Price 2005: Tempel av guld eller kyrka av trä? *Fornvännen*, vol. 100:261–72.

Allison, E., A. Hall and H. Kenward 1999: *Technical report. Living conditions and resource exploitation at the Early Christian rath at Deer Park Farms, Co. Antrim, N. Ireland: evidence from plants and invertebrates. Part 1: Text*. Unpublished report, Environmental Archaeology Unit Report 99/8. University of York. York.

Almond, Richard 2003: *Medieval hunting*. Stroud.

Amorosi, T. 1991: Icelandic archaeofauna. A preliminary review. *Acta Archaeologica*, vol. 61:272–84.

Ambrosiani, Björn 1986: [Review of Blindheim et al. 1981.] *Norwegian Archaeological Review*, vol. 16:1:53–4.

– 1992: What is Birka? In: Björn Ambrosiani and Helen Clarke: *Early Investigations and Future Plans*. Birka Studies, vol. 1:11–22. Stockholm.

– 1995: Excavations at Birka 1990: Interim Report. In: Björn Ambrosiani and Helen Clarke (eds.): *Excavations in the Black Earth 1990*. Birka Studies, vol. 2:19–39. Stockholm.

– (ed.) 2001a: *Excavations in the Black Earth 1990–1995. Eastern Connections Part One: The Falcon Motif*. Birka Studies, vol. 5. Stockholm.

– 2001b: The Birka falcon. In: B. Ambrosiani (ed.): *Eastern connections, part one: The falcon motif*. Birka Studies, vol. 5:11–27. Stockholm.

– (ed.) 2004: *Excavations in the Black Earth 1990–1995. Eastern Connections Part Two: Numismatics and Metrology*. Birka Studies, vol. 6. Stockholm.

Ambrosiani, Björn and Helen Clarke (eds.) 1992: *Early Investigations and Future Plans*. Birka Studies, vol. 1. Stockholm.

– 1995a: The Birka ash layers – an interdisciplinary problem. *Pact*, vol. 50:331–36.

– (eds.) 1995b: *Excavations in the Black Earth 1990*. Birka Studies, vol. 2. Stockholm.

Ambrosiani, Björn and Bo G. Erikson 1992: *Birka. Vikingastaden*, vol. 3. Stockholm.

– 1996: *Birka. Vikingastaden*, vol. 5. Stockholm.

Andersen, Even Ballangrud 2004: *Vikingtidens sverdtyper. Deres sosiale og symbolske betydning*. Unpublished master thesis in Archaeology, University of Oslo.

Andersen, Harald 1960: Hovedstaden i Riget. *Fra Nationalmuseets Arbejdsmark*, 1960:13–35. København.

Andersen, Harald H. 1991: Dendrokronologisk datering af Mammengraven. In: M. Iversen (ed.): *Mammen. Grav, kunst og samfund i vikingetid*. Jysk Arkæologisk Selskabs Skrifter, vol. 28:43–44. Højbjerg.

Andersen, Per Sveaas 1969: *Vikingtid og rikssamling*. Norsk Lektorlags faglig-pedagogiske skrifter, vol. 9. Oslo.

– 1977: *Samlingen av Norge og kristningen av landet 800–1130*. Universitetsforlaget. Bergen, Oslo, Tromsø.

Andersen, Steen W. 1995: Lejre – skibssætninger, vikingegrave og Grydehøj. *Aarbøger for Nordisk Oldkyndighed og Historie*, 1993:7–137.

Andersson, Eva 2003: *Tools for Textile Production from Birka and Hedeby*. Birka Studies, vol. 8. The Birka Project. Stockholm.

Andersson, Hans 1979: *Urbaniseringsprocessen i det medeltida Sverige. En forskningsöversikt*. Medeltidsstaden, vol. 7. Stockholm.

– 2003: Urbanisation. In: Knut Helle (ed.): *The Cam-*

bridge History of Scandinavia, pp. 312–42. Cambridge.

Andersson, Hans and Margareta Biörnstad 1976: *Projektprogram.* Medeltidsstaden, vol. 1. Stockholm.

Andersson, Hans and Lars Redin 1980: *Stadsarkeologi i Mellansverige. Läge, problem, möjligheter.* Medeltidsstaden, vol. 19. Stockholm.

Andersson, Thorsten 1975: Om ortnamnssuffixet *-str-.* *Namn och bygd,* vol. 63:143–163.

Andrén, Anders 1989: Dörrar till förgångna myter. En tolkning av de gotländska billedstenarna. In: Anders Andrén (ed.): *Medeltidens födelse,* pp. 287–319. Lund.

— 1998: En centraort utan textbelegg? – Uppåkra som ett historiskt-arkeologiskt problem. In: Lars Larsson and Birgitta Hårdh (eds.): *Centrala platser – Centrala frågor.* Uppåkrastudier, vol. 1:137–46. Lund.

— 2002: Platsernas betydelse. Norrön ritual och kultplatskontinuitet. In: Kristina Jennbert, Catharina Raudvere and Anders Andrén (eds.): *Plats och praxis. Studier av nordisk förkristen ritual.* Vägar til Midgård, vol. 2:299–342. Lund.

Andrén, Anders, Kristina Jennbert and Catharina Raudvere (eds.) 2004: *Ordning mot kaos. Studier av nordisk förkristen kosmologi.* Vägar til Midgård, vol. 4. Lund.

Andrews, G., J.C. Barrett and J.S.C. Lewis 2000: Interpretation not Record: The Practice of Archaeology. *Antiquity,* vol. 74:525–30.

Arbman, Holger 1940–1943: *Die Gräber.* Birka, vol. I. Stockholm.

Arendt, Martin Friedrich 1810: Extrait des Procès-verbaux des Sèances de l'Academie celtique. *Memoires l'Academie Celtique,* vol. V:520. Paris.

Arents, Ute 1992. *Die Wikingerzeitlichen Grabfunde aus Haithabu (Kr. Schleswig-Flensburg).* Department of prehistory, Kiel University.

Arrhenius, Birgit 1997: Granater som regalier. In: Johan Callmer and Erik Rosengren (eds.): *"…gick Grendel att söka det höga huset…". Arkeologiska källor till aristokratiska miljöer i Skandinavien under yngre järnålder,* pp. 39–46. Halmstad.

Arrhenius, Birgit and Helena Fennö Muying 2003: Iron Artefacts. In: Gerd Stamsø Munch, Olav Sverre Johansen and Else Roesdahl (eds.): *Borg in Lofoten. A Chieftain's farm in North Norway.* Lofotr, Vikingmuséet i Borg, Arkeologisk Skriftserie, vol. 1:167–97. Tapir Academic press. Trondheim.

Artelius, Tore 1996: *Långfärd och återkomst – skeppet i bronsålderns gravar.* Kungsbacka.

Arwidsson, Greta 1954: *Die Gräberfunde von Valsgärde. 2, Valsgärde 8.* Acta Musei antiquitatum septentrionalium Regiæ Universitatis Upsaliensis, vol. 4. København.

— 1989: Verschiedene Smuckgegenstände. In: Greta Arwidsson (ed.): *Systematische Analysen der Gräberfunde.* Birka, vol. II:3:55–62. Stockholm.

Askeladden: *http://159.162.103.56/info/om.jsp*

Aurousseau, P., P. Curmi and L. M. Bresson 1985: Microscopy of the cambic horizon. In: Lowell A. Douglas and Michael L. Thompson (eds.): *Soil Micromorphology and Soil Classification,* pp. 49–62. Soil Science Society

of America. Madison.

Bagøien, Anne Aure 1976: *Groper fra eldre jernalder på Oddernes. Et forsøk på rekonstruksjon av gropenes funksjon og kulturelle sammenheng.* Unpublished thesis in Archaeology, University of Oslo.

Baillie, Michael G.L. and Jonathan R. Pilcher 1973: A simple cross-dating program for tree-ring research. *Tree-Ring Bulletin,* vol. 33: 7–14.

Banning, E.B. 2002: *Archaeological survey.* Manuals in archaeoloigcal method, theory and technique, Kluwer Academic. New York.

Barnes, I., K. M. Dobney and J. P. Young 1998: The molecular palaeoecology of British geese species: A progress report on the identification of archaeological goose remains using DNA analysis. *International Journal of Osteoarchaeology,* vol. 8:280–7.

Barnes, I., J. P. W. Young and K. M. Dobney 2000: DNA-based identification of goose species from two archaeological sites in Lincolnshire. *Journal of Archaeological Science,* vol. 27:91–100.

Barnes, Michael 1974: Tingsted, Vesterhavsøyene. *KLNM,* vol. 19:382–7.

Barrett, J. H. 1997: Fish trade in Norse Orkney and Caithness: A zooarchaeological approach. *Antiquity,* vol. 71:616–38.

Barrett, J., R. Beukens, I. Simpson, P. Ashmore, S. Poaps and J. Huntley 2000: What was the Viking Age and when did it happen? A view from Orkney. *Norwegian Archaeological Review,* vol. 33:1–39.

Barrett, J., A. Hall, C. Johnstone, H. Kenward, T. O'Connor and S. Ashby 2004a: *Plant and Animal Remains from Viking Age Deposits at Kaupang, Norway.* Unpublished report, Centre for Human Palaeoecology Report 2004/10, Department of Archaeology, University of York.

Barrett, J. H., A. M. Locker and C. M. Roberts 2004b: 'Dark Age Economics' revisited: The English fish bone evidence AD 600–1600. *Antiquity,* vol. 78:618–36.

Barrett, J. H., R. A. Nicholson and R. Cerón-Carrasco 1999: Archaeo-ichthyological evidence for long-term socioeconomic trends in northern Scotland: 3500 BC to AD 1500. *Journal of Archaeological Science,* vol. 26:353–88.

Barrett, J. H. and M. P. Richards 2004: Identity, gender, religion and economy: New isotope and radiocarbon evidence for marine resource intensification in early historic Orkney, Scotland. *European Journal of Archaeology,* vol. 7:249–71.

Bartholin, Thomas S. 1993: Dendrochronology in building investigations in Sweden. In: Ola Storsletten and Terje Thun (eds.): *Dendrochronology and the Investigation of Buildings. Proceedings of an International Seminar at the Academy of Science and Letters, Oslo 1st–2nd November 1991.* Riksantikvarens Rapporter, vol. 22: 14–17. Oslo.

— 2001: Dendrochronological dating of medieval Norwegian Ships from Bergen. *The Bryggen Papers: Ships and Commodities, Supplementary Series,* vol. 7: 51–3.

Bately, Janet 2007: Commentary. In: Janet Bately and

Anton Eglert (eds.): *Ohthere's Voyage. A late 9th-century account of voyages along the coasts of Norway and Denmark and its cultural context.* Maritime Culture of the North 1. The Viking Ship Museum. Roskilde.

Bately, Janet and Anton Englert (eds.) 2007: *Ohthere's Voyage. A late 9th-century account of voyages along the coasts of Norway and Denmark and its cultural context.* Maritime Culture of the North, vol. 1. The Viking Ship Museum. Roskilde.

Baug, Irene 2003: *Innberetning fra metallsøk på Kaupang søndre og nordre, gnr. 1012 og 1029, Larvik k., Vestfold, i oktober 2002.* Unpublished report, KHM archive.

– 2004: *Innberetning fra undersøkelser i havneområdet på Kaupang. Kaupang, nordre og søndre, gnr. 1012 og 1029, Larvik kommune, Vestfold.* Unpublished report, KHM archive.

– in prep.: *Soapstone Artefacts from Kaupang.* To appear in the Kaupang Excavation Project Publication Series.

Behre, Karl-Ernst 1983: *Ernährung und Umwelt der Wikingerzeitlichen Siedlung Haithabu. Botanische Untersuchungen der Nutz- und Wildpflanzenreste.* Die Ausgrabungen in Haithabu, vol. 9. Karl Wachholtz. Neumünster.

– 1984: Zur geschichte der bierwürzen nach fruchtfunden und schriftlichen quellen. In: van W. Zeist and W. A. Casparie (eds.): *Plants and Ancient Man,* pp. 115–22. Balkema. Rotterdam.

– 2002: Landscape Development and Occupation History Along the Southern North Sea Coast. In: Gerold Wefer, Wolfgang H. Berger, Karl-Ernst Behre and Eystein Jansen (eds.): *Climate Development and History of the North Atlantic Realm,* pp. 299–312. Springer-Verlag. Berlin.

Bencard, Morgens and Lise Bender Jørgensen 1990: Excavation and stratigraphy. In: Morgens Bencard, Lise Bender Jørgensen and Helge Brinch Madsen (eds.): *Ribe Excavations 1970–76,* vol. 4:15–167. Sydjysk Universitetsforlag. Esbjerg.

Bendixen, Kirsten 1981: Sceattas and other coin finds. In: Mogens Bencard (ed.): *Ribe Excavations 1970–76,* vol. I:63–101. Sydjysk Universitetsforlag. Esbjerg.

Benediktsson, Jakob 1974: Tingsted, Island. *KLNM,* vol. 19:381–2.

Bennike, Pia 1994: An anthropological study of the skeletal remains of vikings from Langeland. In: O. Grøn, A. Hedeager Krag and P. Bennike, *Vikingetidsgravpladser på Langeland,* pp. 166–197. Rudkøbing.

Berg, Arne 1990: *Norske Tømmerhus i frå mellomalderen,* vol. 2. Oslo.

– 1992: Sannsynleg røykomnstove i Gamlebyen, Oslo. In: Jan-Erik Augustsson (ed.): *Medeltida husbyggande.* Lund studies in medieval archaeology, vol. 9:17–27. Stockholm.

Berg, Gösta 1935: *Sledges and wheeled vehicles. Ethnological studies from the view-point of Sweden.* Stockholm.

Berg, Lorens 1909: Om jordegodsets fordeling i Brunla len (det senere Larvik Grevskab) omkring 1650 og 1700. *Historisk Tidsskrift,* vol. 20:175–203.

– (ed.) 1915: *Tjølling. En bygdebok.* Kristiania.

Bergqvist, Johanna 1999: Spår av religion i Uppåkra under 1000 år. In: Birgitta Hårdh (ed.): *Fynden i centrum. Keramik, glas och metall från Uppåkra.* Lund.

Bergstøl, Jostein 2005: Kultsted, verksted eller bosted? In: Lil Gustafson, Tom Heibren and Jes Martens (eds.): *De gåtefulle kokegroper.* KHM Varia, vol. 58:145–154. Oslo.

Biddle, Martin 1976: Towns. In: David M. Wilson (ed.): *The Archaeology of Anlo-Saxon England,* pp. 99–150. London.

Binns, Richard 2000: *Undersøkelser med fluxgate gradiometer på Kaupang, Tjølling, Vestfold.* Kaupang Excavation Project Archive.

Bintliff, John 1993: Why Indiana Jones is Smarter Than the Post-Processualists. *Norwegian Archaeological Review,* vol. 26:91–100.

Birkedahl, Peter and Erik Johansen 1995: The Sebbersund Boat-graves. In: O. Crumlin-Pedersen and B. Munch Thye (eds.): *The Ship as Symbol in Prehistoric and Medieval Scandinavia.* Publications from the National Museum in Archaeology and History, vol. 1:160–164. København.

Bjerrum, L. 1971: *Kvikkleireskred.* Norges geotekniske institutt. Publikasjon 89:1–14.

Bjorvand, Harald, Fredrik Otto Lindeman 2000: *Våre arveord. Etymologisk ordbok.* Oslo.

Bjørkvik, Halvard 1998: Gardane som overlevde. In: Halvard Bjørkvik, Jon Bojer Godal and Terje Thun: *Hus for hus. Tillegg og tidfesting.* Norske Tømmerhus i frå mellomalderen, vol. 6:198–215. Oslo

Blackburn, Mark in prep.: *Coin Finds from Kaupang.* To appear in the Kaupang Excavation Project Publication Series.

Blair, John 1988: *Minsters and Parish Churches. The Local Church in Transition 950–1200.* Oxford University Commitee for Archaeology, Monograph, vol. 17. Oxford.

Blindheim, Charlotte 1947: Drakt og smykker. Studier i jernalderens drakthistorie i Norden. *Viking,* vol. 11:1–139. Oslo.

– 1951: *Kaupang-undersøkelsene.* Tjølling historielag, vol. 1:1–17. Tjølling.

– 1960: Kaupangundersøkelsen etter 10 år. *Viking,* vol. 24:43–68.

– 1969: Kaupangundersøkelsen avsluttet. *Viking,* vol. 33:5–39.

– 1974: Gjennem jerntider (ca. 500 f. Kr.–ca. 1000 e. Kr.). In: J. W. Krohn-Holm (ed.): *Tjølling bygdebok,* vol. I:67–126. Tjølling.

– 1976a: A collection of Celtic (?) bronze objects found at Kaupang (Skiringssal, Vestfold, Norway). In: B. Almqvist and D. Greene (eds.): *Proceedings of the Seventh Viking Congress, Dublin 1973,* pp. 9–27. Dublin.

– 1976b: Kaupang in Skiringssal. General background and the identification of the place. In: Gunnar Svahnström (ed.): *Häuser und Höfe der handelstreibenden Bevölkerung im Ostseegebiet und im Norden vor 1500. Beiträge zur Geschichte und Soziologie des Woh-*

nens. Acta Visbyensia, vol. 5:73–82. Gotlands Fornsal. Visby.

— 1977: Den første Kaupangundersøkelse, 1867. Antikvar Nicolay Nicolaysen som feltarkeolog. En etterprøving. *Viking,* vol. 40:11–27. Oslo.

— 1984: From Uppland in Sweden to the Upplands of Eastern Norway? *Festskrift til Thorleif Sjøvold på 70-årsdagen.* Universitetets Oldsaksamling Skrifter, Ny rekke, vol. 5:43–56. Oslo.

— 1997: Vestfold i Vikingetiden – dansk eller norsk territorium? Tore Frost (ed.): *Gokstadhøvdingen og hans tid,* pp. 81–91. Sandefjordmuseene. Sandefjord.

Blindheim, Charlotte, Birgit Heyerdahl-Larsen and Roar L. Tollnes 1981: *Kaupang-funnene. Bind 1.* Norske Old-funn, vol. XI. Universitetets Oldsaksamling, Universitetet i Oslo.

Blindheim, Charlotte and Birgit Heyerdahl-Larsen 1995: *Kaupang-funnene. Bind 2. Gravplassene i Bikjholbergene/Lamøya. Undersøkelsene 1950–57. Del A. Gravskikk.* Norske Oldfunn, vol. XVI. Institutt for arkeologi, kunsthistorie og numismatikk, Oldsaksamlingen, Universitetet i Oslo.

Blindheim, Charlotte, Birgit Heyerdahl-Larsen and Anne Stine Ingstad 1999: *Kaupang-funnene. B. 1999. IIB. Gravplassene i Bikjholbergene/Lamøya. Undersøkelsene 1950–1957. Del B. Oldsaksformer.* Norske Oldfunn, vol. XIX. UKM, Universitetet i Oslo.

Blindheim, Charlotte and Roar L. Tollnes 1972: *Kaupang. Vikingenes handelsplass.* Oslo.

Bond, J. M. 1996: Burnt offerings: Animal bone in Anglo-Saxon cremations. *World Archaeology,* vol. 28:76–88.

Bonde, Niels 1994: De norske vikingeskibsgraves alder. Et vellykket norsk-dansk forskningsprojekt. *Nationalmuseets Arbejdsmark,* 1994:128–148.

— 1997: Dendrochronological Dating of the Viking Age Ship Burials at Oseberg, Gokstad and Tune, Norway. In: Anthony Sinclair, Elisabeth Slater and John Gowlett (eds.): *Archaeological Sciences 1995. Proceedings of a conference on the application of scientific techniques to the study of archaeology.* Oxbow Monograph, vol. 64:195–200

Bonde, Niels, Arne Emil Christensen 1993a: Dendrokronologisk datering av tømmer fra gravkamrene i Oseberg, Gokstad og Tune. *Universitetets Oldsaksamling Årbok,* 1991/1992:153–60.

— 1993b: Dendrochronological dating of the Viking Age ship burials at Oseberg, Gokstad and Tune, Norway. *Antiquity,* vol. 67:575–583.

Botond, Stefan 2002: *Vikingatida ryttargraver i Småland. Studier utifrån fyre exempel och en jämförande analys av valda delar av Sverige och Skandinavien.* Department of archaeology, Stockholm University.

Bourdillon, J. and J. Coy 1980: The animal bones. In: P. Holdsworth (ed.): *Excavations at Melbourne Street, Southampton, 1971–1976,* pp. 79–121. Council for British Archaeology. York.

Bowden, M. (ed.) 1999: *Unravelling the Landscape. An Inquisitive Approach to Archaeology.* Royal Commision on the Historical Monuments of England.

von Brandt, A. 1984: *Fish Catching Methods of the World.* Fishing News Books. Farnham.

Brendalsmo, Arne Jan 2003: Tjølling kirke. Om en basilika, en kaupang og en storgård. In: Ingvar Skarvang (ed.): *Tjølling kirke. Veien, sannheten og livet i bygda gjennom 850 år,* pp. 22–38. Larvik.

Brendalsmo, Arne Jan and Rolf Sørensen 1995: Kvader i sentrum. *Hikuin,* vol. 22:77–94.

Bresson, L. M. and C. Zambaux 1990: Micromorphological study of compaction induced by mechanical stress for a dystrochreptic fragiudalf. In: L. A. Douglas (ed.): *Soil Micromorphology: A Basic and Applied Science,* pp. 33–40. Elsevier. Amsterdam.

Bridges, E. M. 1997: *World Soils,* 3rd edition. Cambridge University Press. Cambridge.

Brink, Stefan 1979: Bodlanden i Järvsö socken. In: Stefan Brink and Eva Brylle (eds.): *Uppsalastudier i namnforskning.* Ortnamn och samhälle, vol. 5:7–49. Seminariet för nordisk ortnamnsforskning, Uppsala universitet.

— 1983: När bildades våra äldsta bebyggelsenamn? *Ortnamnssällskapets i Uppsala årsskrift,* pp. 5–17.

— 1984: Absolut datering av bebyggelsenamn. In: Vibeke Dalberg (ed.): *Bebyggelsers og bebyggelsesnavnes alder.* NORNA-rapporter, vol. 26:18–66. Uppsala.

— 1988: Denotationsförändringar bland våra äldsta bebyggelsenamnstyper. In: Peter Slotte (ed.): *Denotationsbyte i ortnamn.* NORNA-rapporter, vol. 37:63–81. Uppsala.

— 1990: *Sockenbildning och sockennamn. Studier i äldre territoriell indelning i Norden.* Acta Academiae Regiae Gustavi Adolphi 57. Studier till en svensk ortnamnsatlas 14. Almqvist & Wiksell Int. Uppsala.

— 1991: Iakttagelser rörande namnen på -*hem* i Sverige. In: Gulbrand Alhaug, Kristoffer Kruken, Helge Salvesen (eds.): *Heiderskrift til Nils Hallan på 65-årsdagen 13. desember 1991,* pp. 66–80. Novus. Oslo.

— 1996a: The onomasticon and the role of analogy in name formation. *Namn och bygd,* vol. 84:61–84.

— 1996b: Political and social structures in Early Scandinavia. A Settlement-historical Pre-study of the Central Place. *Tor,* vol. 28:1996:235–81.

— 1998: Land, bygd, distrikt och centralort i Sydsverige. In: Lars Larsson and Birgitta Hårdh (eds.): *Centrala platser – Centrala frågor.* Uppåkrastudier, vol. 1:297–326. Lund.

— 1999a: Fornskadinavisk religion – förhistorisk samhälle. En bosetningshistorisk studie av centralorter i Norden. In: Ulf Drobin, Jens Peter Schjødt, Gro Steinsland and Preben Meulengracht Sørensen (eds.): *Religion och samhälle i det förkristna Norden. Ett symposium,* pp. 11–55. Odense.

— 1999b: Nordens husabyar – unga eller gamla? In: Ingrid Fuglestvedt, Terje Gansum and Arnfrid Opedal (eds.): *Et hus med mange rom. Vennebok til Bjørn Myhre på 60-årsdagen,* AmS-rapport, vol. 11AB:283–91. Arkeologisk museum i Stavanger: Stavanger.

– 2000: Husby. *Reallexikon der Germanischen Altertums-kunde*, vol. 15:274–278.

– 2001: Mythologizing Landscape. Place and space of Cult and Myth. In: Michael Stausberg, Olof Sundqvist, Astrid van Nahl and Anders Hultgård (eds.): *Kontinuitäten und Brüche in der Religionsgeschichte.* Ergänzungsbände zum Reallexikon der germanischen Altertumskunde, vol. 31:76–112. Berlin, New York.

– 2002a: Law and legal custom in Viking Age Scandinavia. In: Judith Jesch (ed.): *The Scandinavians from the Vendel period to the tenth century. An ethnographic perspective,* pp. 87–117. San Marino.

– 2002b: Sociolinguistic perspectives and language contact in Proto-Nordic. In: Oskar Bandle, Ernst Håkon Jahr (eds.): *The Nordic Languages. An International Handbook of the History of the North Germanic Languages*, vol. 1:685–690. de Gruyter. Berlin and New York.

Brochier, J. E. 2002: Les sédiments anthropiques: méthodes d'étude et perspectives. In: J. C. Miskovsky (ed.): *Géologie de la Préhistoire: Méthodes, Techniques, Applications*, pp. 453–77. Géopré Éditions. Paris.

Bronk Ramsey, Christopher 2001: Development of the Radiocarbon Program OxCal. *Radiocarbon*, vol. 43(2A):355–63

Brunstedt, Solveig 1996: *Alsnu Kungsgård. Forskningsprojekt Hovudgården.* Riksantikvarieämbetet, UV Stockholm, Rapport 1996:71/11/1 (2).

Brøgger, Anton Wilhelm 1915: Tjøling i hedens tid. In: Lorens Berg (ed.): *Tjølling. En bygdebok*, pp. 1–28. Kristiania.

– 1916: *Borrefundet og Vestfoldkongernes graver.* Kristiania.

– 1921: *Ertog og øre. Den gamle norske vegt.* Kristiania.

– 1922: Rolvsøyætten. Et arkeologisk bidrag til vikingetidens historie. *Bergens Museums Aarbok 1920–21. Hist.-antikv. Række*, vol. 1:1–42.

– 1924–26: Vestfold. Fra småkongedømme til rikssamling. *Vestfoldminne*, vol. 1:11–34, vol. 2:88–107, vol. 3:157–192.

Brøgger, Anton Wilhelm, Hjalmar Falk and Haakon Schetelig 1917: *Osebergfundet,* vol. I. Kristiania.

Brøndsted, Johannes 1936: Danish Inhumation Graves of the Viking Age. A Survey. *Acta Archaeologica,* vol. 7:81–228. København.

Bråthen, Alf 1982: *Dendrokronologisk serie från västra Sverige 831–1975.* Riksantikvarieämbetet och statens historiska museer Rapport 1982:1. Stockholm.

Braathen, Helge 1989: *Rytterregraver.* Universitetets Oldsaksamlings Varia, vol. 19. Oslo.

Bucht, Torsten 1951: Ortnamn innehållande lunger, lung. *Namn och bygd*, vol. 39:1–21.

Buckland, P. C. , J. P. Sadler and D. N. Smith 1993: An insect's eye view of the Norse farm. In: C. E. Batey, J. Jesch and C. D. Morris (eds.): *Caithness, Orkney and the North Atlantic in the Viking Age*, pp. 506–27. Edinburgh University Press. Edinburgh.

Buckland, P., R. Engelmark, J. Linderholm and P. Wagner 2001: *Environmental Archaeological Investigation of Samples from the Kaupang 2000 Excavations.* Unpublished report, University of Umeå, Environmental Archaeology Lab Report, vol. 2001–017. Umeå.

Bugge, Alexander 1909: Vestfold og Ynglingeætten. *Historisk tidsskrift*, vol. 20:433–54.

– 1910: *Norges Historie. I binds anden del. Tidsrummet ca 800–1030.* Kristiania.

– 1915: Skiringssal. In: Lorens Berg (ed.): *Tjølling. En bygdebok*, pp. 29–47. Kristiania.

– 1925: *Den norske trælasthandels historie,* vol. I–II, Skien.

Bugge, Sophus 1871: Om Skæreid i Skiringssal. *Historisk Tidsskrift*, vol. 1:385–388.

– 1910: *Der Runenstein von Rök in Östergötland, Schweden. Nach dem Tode des Verfassers hg. von der K. Akademie der schönen Wissenschaften, Geschichte und Altertumskunde durch Magnus Olsen unter Mitwirkung und mit Beiträgenvon Axel Olrik und Erik Brate.* Stockholm.

Bukholm, Kristine M. 2001: *Characterization of Viking-age black earth in the Kaupang investigations, Larvik, Southeastern Norway.* MSc-thesis, Department of Soil and Water Sciences, Agricultural University of Norway.

Bull, Edvard 1933: Byer i Norge i middelalderen. In: Edvard Bull and Sverre Steen (eds.): *Byer og bybebyggelse.* Nordisk Kultur, vol. 18:73–94. Stockholm, Oslo, København.

Bullock, P., N. Fedoroff, A. Jongerious, G. Stoops, T. Tursina and U. Babel 1985: *Handbook for Thin Section Description.* Waine Research Publications. Wolverhampton.

Burenhult, Göran 2000: *Arkeologi i Norden,* vol. 2. Stockholm.

Bø, Olav 1962: *Falcon catching in Norway. With emphasis on the post-reformation period.* Studia Norvegica, vol. 2. Oslo.

Bøe, Johannes 1940: *Norse Antiquities in Ireland.* Viking Antiquities in Great Britain and Ireland, vol. 3. Oslo.

Bøgh-Andersen, Susanne 1999: *Vendel- och vikingatida stekspett: ej blott för köket, ett redskap med anor från Homeros' tid.* Department of archaeology, Lund University.

Callmer, Johan 1977: *Trade beads and bead trade in Scandinavia ca. 800–1000 A.D.* Acta archaeologica Lundensia. Series in 4°, vol. 11. Institute of Archaeology, University of Lund.

– 1982: Production site and market area. *Meddelanden från Lunds universitets historiska museum*, 1981–1982:135–65.

– 1991: Platser med anknytning till handel och hantverk i yngre järnålder. Exempel från södra Sverige. In: Peder Mortensen and Birgit M. Rasmussen (eds.): *Høvdingesamfund og kongemagt. Fra stamme til stat i Danmark*, vol. 2. Jysk Arkæologisk Selskabs Skrifter XXII:2:29–47. Århus.

– 1994: Urbanization in Scandinavia and the Baltic Region c. AD 700–1100: Trading Places, Centres and Early Urban Sites. In: Björn Ambrosiani and Helen Clark (eds.): *Development around the Baltic and the*

North Sea in the Viking Age. Birka Studies, vol. 3:50–90. Stockholm.

– 1995: Hantverksproduktion, samhällsförändringar och bebyggelse. Iakttagelser från östra Sydskandinavien ca. 600–1100 e.Kr. In: Heid Gjøstein Resi (ed.): *Produksjon og samfunn. Om erverv, spesialisering og bosetning i Norden i 1. årtusen e.Kr.* Universitetets Oldsaksamling Varia, vol. 30:39–72. Oslo.

– 1998:Handelsplatser och kustplatser och deras förhållande till lokala politiska system. In: Lars Larsson and Birgitta Hårdh (eds.): *Centrala platser – Centrala frågor.* Uppåkrastudier, vol. 1:27–37. Lund.

– 2001: Extinguished solar systems and black holes: traces of estates in the Scandinavian Late Iron Age. In: Birgitta Hårdh (ed.): *Centrum och sammanhang,* Uppåkrastudier, vol. 3:109–38. Lund.

– 2002: North European trading centres and the Early Medieval craftsman. Craftsmen at Åhus, north-eastern Scania, Sweden ca. AD 750–850+. In: Birgitta Hårdh and Lars Larsson (eds.): *Central Places an the Migration and Merovingian Periods.* Uppåkrastudier, vol. 6:125–57. Lund.

Callmer, Johan and Erik Rosengren (eds.) 1997: *"...gick Grendel att söka det höga huset...". Arkeologiska källor till aristokratiska miljöer i Skandinavien under yngre järnålder.* Halmstad.

Campbell, E. 2000: The raw, the cooked and the burnt: Interpretations of food and animals in the Hebridean Iron Age. *Archaeological Dialogues,* vol. 7:184–98.

Canti, Matthew G. 2003: Aspects of the chemical and microscopic characteristics of plant ashes found in archaeological soils. *Catena,* vol. 54:339–61.

Capelle, Torsten 2004: Schiffssetzungen. *Reallexikon der Germanischen Altertumskunde,* vol. 27:78–81. Berlin.

Carlsson, Anders 1988: *Vikingatida ringspännen från Gotland.* Stockholm Studies in Archaeology, vol. 8. Stockholm.

– 1989. Granby-Hyppinge i Orkesta. Arkeologiska iakttagelser kring ett gårdskomplex från järnålder, vikingatid och tidig medeltid i Uppland. In: Mats Burström (ed.): *Mänsklighet genom millennier. En vänbok till Åke Hyenstrand,* pp. 43–54. RAÄ. Stockholm.

– 1997: Birkas kungsgård Adelsö och Svearnas Fornsigtuna – två aristokratiska miljöer i Mälardalen. In: Johan Callmer and Erik Rosengren (eds.): *"...gick Grendel att söka det höga huset...". Arkeologiska källor till aristokratiska miljöer i Skandinavien under yngre järnålder,* pp. 83–88. Halmstad.

Carlsson, Dan 1999: *Ridanäs. Vikingahamnen i Fröjel.* Visby.

– 2000: *Fröjel Discovery Programme 2000. Rapport 2.* (http://www.hgo.se/frojel/Reports00/svrapp2_00.htm)

von Carnap Bornheim, Claus and Volker Hilberg in press: Recent archaeological research in Haithabu. In: Joachim Henning (ed.): *The Heirs of the Roman West.* Post-Roman Towns, Trade and Settlement in Europe and Byzantium, vol. 1. de Gruyter. Berlin, New York.

Carver, Martin 1998: *Sutton Hoo. Burial ground of kings?* London.

Cerón-Carrasco, R. 2005: *Of Fish and Men, De Iasg agus Dhaoine: Aspects of the utilization of marine resources as recovered from selected Hebridean archaeological sites.* BAR Archaeological Reports 400:2005. Oxford.

Chadwick, Adrian 1997: Archaeology at the Edge of Chaos. *Assemblage, vol. 3.* (http://www.assemblage.group.shef.ac.uk/3/3chad.htm)

Christensen, Kjeld 1993: Can oak chronologies from Northern Jutland and Western Sweden be applied to dendrochronological dating of Norwegian oak timber? In Ola Storsletten and Terje Thun (eds.): *Dendrochronology and the Investigation of Buildings. Proceedings of an International Seminar at the Academy of Science and Letters, Oslo 1st–2nd November 1991.* Riksantikvarens Rapporter, vol. 22: 52–8. Oslo.

– 1996: Norsk eg. Dendrochronologi til lands og til vands. *Foreningen til norske fortidsminnesmerkers bevaring. Årbok,* 1996: 133–44.

Christensen, Kjeld and Kent Havemann 1992: Modern oak chronologies from Norway, *Dendrochronologia,* vol. 10:137–46.

– 1998: Dendrochronology of oak (*Quercus* sp.) in Norway. In: Lotte Selsing and Kerstin Griffin (eds.): *Dendrokronologi i Norge.* AmS-Varia, vol. 32:59–60, Stavanger.

Christensen, Kjeld and Knud J. Krogh 1987: Jelling-høiene dateret. *Nationalmuseets Arbejdsmark,* 1987:223–231. København.

Christensen, Peter Birkedahl and Erik Johansen 1992: En handelsplads fra yngre jernalder og vikingetid ved Sebbersund. *Aarbøger for Nordisk Oldkyndighed og Historie,* 1991:199–229.

Christensen, Tom 1991: *Lejre. Syn og segn.* Roskilde.

Christiansen, Inger 1975: Vetter. *KLNM,* vol. 19:678–9.

Christiansen, Per R. 1989: *Fra tåkefylt oldtid til kommunalt sjølstyre. Bygdehistoria fram til 1837.* Frostaboka, vol. 3. Frosta.

Christie, Håkon 1969: Østnorske basilikaer. *Kirkespeilet,* 1969:111–123.

– 2001: The *stofa* in Nordic Building Tradition. *Collegium Medievale,* vol. 15:127–40.

Christie, Sigrid and Håkon Christie 1959: *Østfold,* vol. 1. Norges kirker. Riksantikvaren. Oslo.

Christophersen, Axel 1991: Ports and trade in Norway during the transition to historical time. In: Ole Crumlin-Pedersen (ed.): *Aspects of Maritime Scandinavia AD 200–1200,* pp. 159–70. Roskilde.

Christophersen, Axel and Sæbjørg Walaker Nordeide 1994: *Kaupangen ved Nidelva. 1000 års byhistorie belyst gjennom de arkeologiske undersøkelsene på folkebibliotekstomten i Trondheim 1973–1985.* Riksantikvarens skrifter, vol. 7. Riksantikvaren. Oslo.

Cinthio, Erik 1975: Köping och stad i det tidigmedeltida Skåne. *Ale,* 1975:1–10.

Clark, John 1995: Horseshoes. In: J. Clark (ed.): *The medieval horse and its equipment.* Medieval finds from excavations in London, vol. 5:75–123. London.

Clarke, David L. (ed.) 1972: *Models in archaeology.* London.

Clarke, Helen, Björn Ambrosiani 1995: *Towns in the Viking age*, 2nd revised edition. Leicester University Press. London and New York.

Costamagno, S., I. Thery-Parisot, J.-P. Brugal and R. Guibert 2005: Taphonomic consequences of the use of bones as fuel: experimental data and archaeological applications. In: T. P. O'Connor (ed.): *Biosphere to Lithosphere: New studies in vertebrate taphonomy*, pp. 52–63. Oxbow Books. Oxford.

Courty, Marie-Agnes, Paul Goldberg and Richard Macphail 1989: *Soils and Micromorphology in Archaeology*. Cambridge University Press. Cambridge.

Crabtree, P. J. 1989: *West Stow, Suffolk: Early Anglo-Saxon animal husbandry*. Suffolk County Planning Dept., East Anglian Archaeology Report, vol. 47.

– 1994: Animal exploitation in East Anglian villages. In: J. Rackham (ed.): *Environment and Economy in Anglo-Saxon England*. Council for British Archaeology Research Report, vol. 89:40–54. York.

– 1996: Production and consumption in an early complex society: Animal use in Middle Saxon East Anglia. *World Archaeology*, vol. 28:58–75.

Crawford, Barbara E. 2001: The Historical and Archaeological Background to the Papa Stour Project. *Collegium Medievale*, vol. 15:13–35.

Crumlin-Pedersen, Ole 1997: *Viking-Age Ships and Shipbuilding in Hedeby/Haithabu and Schleswig*. Ships and Boats of the North, vol. 2. Schleswig and Roskilde.

Dalton, George 1977: Aboriginal Economies in Stateless Societies. In: Timothy K. Earle and Jonathon E. Ericson (eds.): *Exchange Systems in Prehistory*, pp. 191–212. New York, San Francisco, London.

Damell, David 1991a: Sammanfattning. In: Bibbi Andersson, David Damell and Jan Norrman (eds.): *Fornsigtuna. En kungsgårds historia*, pp. 121–5. Upplands-Bro.

– 1991b: Historiska notiser. In: Bibbi Andersson, David Damell and Jan Norrman (eds.): *Fornsigtuna. En kungsgårds historia*, pp. 30–1. Upplands-Bro.

Davidson, Donald. A., Stephen P. Carter and Timothy A. Quine 1992: An evaluation of micromorphology as an aid to archaeological interpretation. *Geoarchaeology: An International Journal*, vol. 7:55–65.

Deckers, Jozef A., Freddy O. Nachtergaele and Otto C. Spaargaren (eds.) 1998: *World Reference Base for Soil Resources – Introduction*. Acco. Leuven/Amersfoort.

Dillmann, Francois-Xavier 1997: Kring de rituella gästabuden i fornskandinavisk religion. In: Anders Hultgård (ed.): *Uppsalakulten och Adam av Bremen*, pp. 51–73. Nora.

Dobat, Andres S. Minos 2004: Die Neufund eines Wikingerzeitlichen Krummsielbeschlagfragments aus dem Landesteil Schleswig. *Archäologisches Korrespondenzblatt*, vol. 34:277–92.

– 2005a: Tidlige tegn. *Skalk*, 2005:5:15–17.

– 2005b: Maritime Cultural Landscapes – Recovering the Trajectories of Communication across the Baltic. *Quaestiones Medii Aevi Novae*, vol. 10:53–90.

Dobney, K., A.R. Hall, H.K. Kenward and A. Milles 1992: A working classification of sample types for environmental archaeology. *Circaea*, vol. 9:24–6.

Dommasnes, Liv Helga 1982: Late Iron Age in Western Norway. Female Roles and Ranks as Deduced from an Analysis of Burial Customs. *Norwegian Archaeological Review*, vol. 15:70–84.

von den Driesch, A. 1976: *A Guide to the Measurement of Animal Bones from Archaeological Sites*. Peabody Museum Bulletin, vol. 1. Cambridge.

Driessen, Paul, Jozef A. Deckers, Otto C. Spaargaren and Freddy O. Nachtergaele, (eds.) 2001: *Lecture notes on the major soils of the world*. World Soil Resources Reports, vol. 94. Food and Agriculture Organization of the United Nations. Rome.

Duczo, Wladyslaw (ed.) 1993: *Arkeologi och miljögeologi i Gamla Uppsala, studier och rapporter*. Uppsala.

– 1997: Gamla Uppsala – svearnas maktcentrum i äldre och nyare forskning. In: Johan Callmer and Erik Rosengren: *"...gick Grendel att söka det höga huset...". Arkeologiska källor till aristokratiska miljöer i Skandinavien under yngre järnålder*, pp. 71–81. Halmstad.

Dumville, David N. 1997: Kingship, Genealogies and Regnal Lists. In: Peter H. Sawyer and Ian N. Wood (eds.): *Early medieval kingship*, pp. 72–104. Leeds.

Düwel, Klaus 2001: *Runenkunde*. 3., vollständig neu bearbeitete Auflage. Weimar.

Eisenschmidt, Silke 1994: *Kammergräber der Wikingerzeit in Altdänemark*. Bonn.

Eithun, Bjørn, Magnus Rindal, Tor Ulset 1994: *Den eldre Gulatingslova*. Oslo.

Ekrem, Inger 1998: *Nytt lys over Historia Norwegiæ*. Bergen.

Ekrem, Inger and Lars Boje Mortensen (eds.) 2003: *Historia Norwegie*. Translated by Peter Fischer. København.

Ekroll, Øystein 1997: *Med kleber og kalk. Norsk steinbygging i mellomalderen*. Oslo

Ellmers, Detlev 1985: Loading and Unloading Ships using a Horse and Cart, standing in the Water. The Archaeological Evidence. In: Asbjørn E. Herteig (ed.): *Conference on Waterfront Archaeology in North European Towns No. 2. Bergen 1983*, pp. 25–30. Historisk Museum. Bergen.

Elster, Elisabeth and Ola Storsletten 1989: *Tjølling kirke*. Norges kirker, Vestfold. Unpublished manuscript, Riksantikvaren archive. Oslo.

Emanuelsson, Anders 2005: *Kyrkojorden och dess ursprung. Oslo biskopsdöme perioden ca 1000–ca 1400*. Göteborg.

Engesveen, Anne 2002: *Grevskapskartene over Tjølling. Rektifisering og analyser*. Unpublished thesis, Høgskolen i Ålesund.

– 2005: *På vei mellom levende og døde. En analyse av forholdet mellom veier og graver i Vestfold i vikingtid*. Unpublished master thesis in Archaeology, University of Oslo.

Enghoff, I. B. 1996: A medieval herring industry in Denmark and the importance of herring in eastern Denmark. *Archaeofauna*, vol. 5:43–7.

– 1999: Fishing in the Baltic region from the 5th century BC to the 16th century AD: Evidence from fish bones. *Archaeofauna*, vol. 8:41–85.

– 2000: Fishing in the southern North Sea region from the 1st to the 16th century AD: Evidence from fish bones. *Archaeofauna*, vol. 9:59–132.

– in prep. a: *Pattedyr og fugle fra markedspladsen i Ribe, ASR 9 Posthuset.*

– in prep. b: *Fiskeknogler fra markedspladsen i Ribe, ASR 9 Posthuset.*

Erbersdobler, K. 1968: *Vergleichende morphologische Untersuchungen an einzelknochen des postkranielen Skeletts in mitteleuropa vorkommender mittelgrosser Hühnervögel.* Munich.

Ericson, P. G. P. 1987: Exploitation of seabirds in central Sweden during Late Iron Age – conclusions drawn from the bird remains at Birka. In: H. Burenhult, A. Carlsson, A. Hyenstrand and T. Sjøvold (eds.): *Theoretical Approaches to Artefacts, Settlement and Society: Studies in honour of Mats P. Malmer.* British Archaeological Reports International Series, vol. 366(ii):445–53. Oxford.

Eyrbyggja saga: Einar Ól. Sveinsson and Matthías Þórðarson (eds.) 1935: *Eyrbyggja saga.* Íslenzk Fornrit, vol. 4. Reykjavík.

Fabech, Charlotte 1991: Samfundsorganisation, religiøse ceremonier og regional variation. I: Charlotte Fabech and Jytte Ringtved (eds.): *Samfundsorganisation og Regional Variation. Norden i romersk jernalder og folkevandringstid*, pp. 283–303. Århus.

– 1997: Slöinge i perspektiv. In: Johan Callmer and Erik Rosengren: *"...gick Grendel att söka det höga huset...". Arkeologiska källor till aristokratiska miljöer i Skandinavien under yngre järnålder*, pp. 145–60. Halmstad.

– 1998: Kult og samfund i yngre jernalder – Ravlunda som eksempel. In: Lars Larsson and Birgitta Hårdh (eds.): *Centrala platser – Centrala frågor.* Uppåkrastudier, vol. 1:147–63. Lund.

Fagrskinna: Finnur Jónsson (ed.) 1902–3: *Fagrskinna. Nóregs Kononga Tal.* Møller. København.

Falk, Hjalmar and Alf Torp 1903–1906: *Etymologisk ordbog over det norske og det danske sprog.* Kristiania.

Fell, C. E. 1984: Ohthere's Account. In: Niels Lund (ed.): *Two Voyagers at the Court of King Alfred*, pp. 18–22. William Sessions Limited. York.

Feltham, M. J. and M. Marquiss 1989: The use of first vertebrae in separating, and estimating the size of, trout (*Salmo trutta*) and salmon (*Salmo salar*) in bone remains. *Journal of Zoology, London*, vol. 219:113–22.

Fet, Tryggve M. 1989: Bygninger og bygningsdetaljer. In: Erik Schia (ed.): *Hus og gjerder.* De arkeologiske utgravninger i Gamlebyen, Oslo, vol. 6:15–92. Øvre Ervik.

Feveile, Claus 2003: Ribe. *Reallexikon der Germanischen Altertumskunde*, vol. 24:550–4. Berlin.

– (ed.) 2006a: *Det ældste Ribe. Udgravninger på nordsiden af Ribe Å 1984–2000.* Ribe Studier, vol. 1.1. Jysk Arkæologisk Selskab. Højbjerg.

– (ed.) 2006b: *Det ældste Ribe. Udgravninger på nordsiden af Ribe Å 1984–2000.* Ribe Studier, vol. 1.2. Jysk Arkæologisk Selskab. Højbjerg.

Feveile, Claus and Stig Jensen 1993: Sceattasfundene fra Ribe – nogle arkæologiske kendsgerninger. *Nordisk Numismatisk Unions Medlemsblad*, 1993:5:74–80.

– 2000: Ribe in the 8th and 9th Century. A Contribution to the Archaeological Chronology of North Western Europe. *Acta Archaeologica*, vol. 71:9–24.

Fidjestøl, Bjarne 1994: (Review of) *Ynglingatal* og *Ynglingesaga. Maal og minne*, 1994:191–9.

FitzPatrick, E. A. 1993: *Soil Microscopy and Micromorphology.* John Wiley and Sons. Chichester.

Forseth, Lars 1993: *Vikingtid i Østfold og Vestfold. En kildekritisk granskning av regionale forskjeller i gravfunnene.* Unpublished master thesis in Archaeology, University of Oslo.

Forsström, Margit 2001: Hans Andersson och projektet medeltidsstaden. In: Anders Andrén, Lars Ersgård and Jes Wienberg (eds.): *Från stad till land*, pp. 19–21. Stockholm.

Fossier, R. 1999: Rural economy and country life. In: T. Reuter (ed.): *The New Cambridge Medieval History: Volume III c. 900-c.1024*, pp. 27–63. Cambridge University Press. Cambridge.

Frankovich, R., H. Patterson and G. Barker (eds.) 2000: *Extracting Meaning from Ploughsoil Assemblages. The Archaeology of Mediterranean Landscapes*, vol. 5. Oxbow books. Oxford.

Fries, Sigurd 1980: Det gamla Skíringssalr i Vestfold. In: Olav Ahlbäck, Lars Huldén and Kurt Zilliacus (eds.): *Festskrift till Carl-Eric Thors 8.6.1980.* Studier i nordisk filologi, vol. 62:93–100. Svenska Litteratursällskapet i Finland. Helsingfors.

Fritzner, Johan 1883: Þing eðr þjóðarmál (Hávamál 114). *Arkiv for nordisk filologi*, vol. 1:22–32.

– 1886–1896: *Ordbog over Det gamle norske Sprog*, Omarb., forøget og forbedret Udg., vol. 1–3. Kristiania.

Fuglesang, Signe Horn 1993: Viking Art. In: Phillip Pulsiano and Kirsten Wolf (eds.): *Medieval Scandinavia: an encyclopaedia*, pp. 694–700. New York and London.

Fægri, Knut and Johannes Iversen 1950: *Textbook of modern pollen-analysis*, 1st edition. Munksgaard, København.

– 1989: *Textbook of pollen-analysis*, 4th edition. John Wiley & Sons, Chichester.

Gansum, Terje 1995: *Lamøya. En arkeologisk registrering av gravminner. Utført i tidsrommet 03–12.04 1995.* Unpublished survey report. Tønsberg.

– 2002: *Hulveger – fragmenter av fortidens ferdsel.* Tønsberg.

– 2004: *Hauger som konstruksjoner – arkeologiske forventninger gjennom 200 år.* Department of archaeology, Gothenburg University.

Gansum, Terje and Terje Østigård 1999: En haug med ritualer – Haugar og rikssamlingen. *Vestfoldminne*, 1998/1999:74–99.

Gaut, Bjarne 2001a: *Innberetning om arkeologisk overvåking i forbindelse med utskifting av spillvannsrør ved Søndre*

Kaupang, gnr. 1012/7 og 1012/2, Larvik kommune, Vest-fold. Unpublished report, KHM archive.

– 2001b: *Innberetning om arkeologiske undersøkelser i for-bindelse med utvidelse av gang og sykkelvei langs FV154 (Kaupangveien) ved Kaupang Søndre, gnr. 1012, Larvik kommune, Vestfold.* Unpublished report, KHM archive.

– 2004: *Rapport. Glassfunnene fra Huseby.* Unpublished report, KHM archive.

– 2006: A pseudo-cameo brooch-inlay from Kaupang, Southeast Norway. *Archäologisches Korrespondenzblatt,* vol. 35:4:545–558.

– in prep. a: *Vessel glass and evidence for glassworking at Kaupang.* To appear in the Kaupang Excavation Project Publication Series.

– in prep. b: *Manors, Missionaries, and Markets: Conti-nental perspectives on Viking-age production and ex-change.* To appear in the Kaupang Excavation Project Publication Series.

Gé, Thierry, Marie-Agnès Courty, Wendy Matthews and Julia Wattez 1993: Sedimentary formation processes of occupation surfaces. In: P. Goldberg, D. T. Nash and M. D. Petraglia (eds.): *Formation Processes in Archaeologi-cal Context,* pp. 149–63. Prehistory Press. Madison.

Geake, Helen 1992: Burial practice in seventh- and eighth-century England. In: Martin Carver (ed.): *The age of Sutton Hoo. The seventh century in North-western Europe,* pp. 83–94. Woodbridge.

Geibig, Alfred 1991: *Beiträge zur morphologischen Entwick-lung des Schwertes im Mittelalter. Eine Analyse des Fundmaterials vom ausgehenden 8. bis zum 12. Jah-hundert aus Sammlungen der Bundesrepublik Deutsch-land.* Offa-Bücher , vol. 52. Neumünster.

Geijer, Agnes 1938: *Die Textilfunde aus den Gräbern.* Birka, vol. 3. Stockholm.

Geraghty, Siobhán 1996: *Viking Dublin: Botanical Evidence from Fishamble Street.* Royal Irish Academy. Dublin.

Gifford-Gonzalez, Diane P., David B. Damrosch, Debra R. Damrosch, John Pryor and Robert L. Thunen 1985: The third dimension in site structure: an experiment in trampling and vertical dispersal. *American Antiquity,* vol. 50:803–18.

Gjerpe, Lars Erik 2001: Kult, politikk, fyll, vold og koke-gropfeltet på Hov. *Primitive Tider,* 2001:5–17.

– 2005a: Gården Gulli og gravfeltet Id. nr. 13144. In: Lars Erik Gjerpe (ed.): *Gravfeltet på Gulli.* KHM Varia, vol. 60:11–18. Oslo.

– 2005b: Gravene – en kort gjennomgang. In: Lars Erik Gjerpe (ed.): *Gravfeltet på Gulli.* KHM Varia, vol. 60:24–27. Oslo.

– 2005c: *Gravfeltet på Gulli.* E18-prosjektet i Vestfold, vol. 1. KHM Varia, vol. 60. Oslo.

Gjessing, Gustav Antonoi 1873: *Undersøgelse af Kongesaga-enes Fremvæxt,* vol. I. Christiania.

Gjessing, Gutorm 1934: *Studier i norsk merovingertid.* Skrifter utgitt av det Norske Videnskapsakademi i Oslo. II Hist.-Fil. Klasse, 1934:2. Oslo.

Graham-Campbell, James in prep.: *Western and Eastern Influences on Brooches and Pins from the Kaupang*

Excavations. To appear in the Kaupang Excavation Project Publication Series.

Grant, A. 1982: The use of tooth wear as a guide to the age of domestic animals. In: B. Wilson, C. Grigson and S. Payne (eds.): *Ageing and Sexing Animal Bones from Archaeological Sites.* British Archaeological Reports British Series, vol. 109:91–108. Oxford.

Greve, Mogens, Ragnhild Sperstad and Åge A. Nyborg 1999: *Retningslinjer for beskrivelse av jordprofil. Versjon 1.0.* Norsk institutt for jord- og skogkartlegging, rap-port 37/99. Ås.

Grieg, Sigurd 1923: Gravpladsene i Lille Guldkronen og paa Berg. *Oldtiden,* vol. X:1:1–58. Oslo.

– 1943: *Vestfolds oldtidsminner.* Oslo.

– 1947: *Gjermundbufunnet. En høvdingegrav fra 900-årene fra Ringerike.* Norske Oldfunn, vol. VIII. Oslo.

Griffin, K. 1988: Plant remains. In: Erik Schia (ed.): *"Mindets Tomt" – "Søndre Felt": Animal bones, moss-, plant-, insect- and parasite remains.* De Arkeologiske Utgravninger i Gamlebyen, Oslo, vol. 5:15–108. Alvheim & Eide. Øvre Ervik.

Grigson, C. 1982: Sex and age determination of some bones and teeth of domestic cattle: A review of the literature. In: B. Wilson, C. Grigson and S. Payne (eds.): *Ageing and Sexing Animal Bones from Archaeological Sites.* British Archaeological Reports British Series, vol. 109:7–24. Oxford.

Grove, Jean M. 2002: Climatic change in Northern Europe over the last two thousand years and its possible influ-ence on human activity. In: Gerold Wefer, Wolfgang H. Berger, Karl-Ernst Behre and Eystein Jansen (eds.): *Climate Development and History of the North Atlantic Realm,* pp. 313–26. Springer Verlag. Berlin.

Grundtvig, Nicolai Frederik Severin 1819: Sciringesheal. *Danne-Virke. Et Tids-Skrift,* vol. 4:187–92.

Gräslund, Anne-Sofie 1980: *The Burial Customs. A study of the graves on Björkö.* Birka, vol. IV. Stockholm.

– 1984: Schellen. In: Greta Arwidsson (ed.): *Systematische Analysen der Grabfunde.* Birka, vol. II:1:119–124. Stockholm.

– 1997: Adams Uppsala – och arkeologins. In: Anders Hultgård (ed.): *Uppsalakulten och Adam av Bremen,* pp. 101–115. Nora.

– 2004: Dogs in graves – a question of symbolism? In: B. Santello Frizell (ed.): *Pecus. Man and animal in Antiquity. Proceedings of the conference at the Swedish Institute in Rome, September 9–12, 2002,* pp. 167–176. Rome.

Gräslund, Bo 1993: Folkvandringstidens Uppsala. Namn, myter arkeologi och historia. *Kärnhuset i riksäpplet. Upplands fornminnesförening och hembygdsförbunds årsbok,* 1993:173–208. Uppsala.

Grøn, Ole, Anne Hedeager Krag and Pia Bennike 1994: *Vikingetidsgravpladser på Langeland.* Rudkøbing.

Grønvik, Ottar 1983: Runeinnskriften på Rök-steinen. *Maal og minne,* 1983:101–149.

– 2003: *Der Rökstein. Über die religiöse Bestimmung und das weltliche Schicksal eines Helden aus der frühen*

Wikingerzeit. Osloer Beiträge zur Germanistik, vol. 33. Frankfurt am Main.

Gudesen, Hans Gude 1980: *Merovingertiden i Øst-Norge. Kronologi, kulturmønster og tradisjonsforløp.* Universitetets oldsaksamling, Varia, vol. 2. Oslo.

Gullbekk, Svein H. 2003: *Pengevesenets fremvekst og fall i Norge i middelalderen.* Acta Humaniora, vol. 157. Oslo.

Gustafson, Lil 1993: Kvinnene i langhauger. *Kvinner i arkelogi i Norge,* vol. 16:47–70.

– 2005: Om kokegroper i Norge. Forskningshistorie og eksempler. In: Lil Gustafson, Tom Heibren and Jes Martens (eds.): *De gåtefulle kokegroper.* KHM Varia, vol. 58:103–34. Oslo.

Gustafson, Lil, Tom Heibren and Jes Martens (eds.) 2005: *De gåtefulle kokegroper.* KHM Varia, vol. 58. Oslo.

Gustin, Ingrid 1999: Vikter och varuutbyte i Uppåkra. In: Birgitta Hårdh (ed.): *Fynden i centrum.* Uppåkrastudier, vol. 2:243–269. Lund.

– 2004: *Mellan gåva och marknad. Handel, tillit och materiell kultur under vikingatid.* Lund Studies in Medieval Archaeology, vol. 34. Almqvist & Wiksell. Malmö.

Guttman, Dea Sidenius 2004: *Myth behind the Material – Viking Age Pendants from the High Status Settlement of Tissø (Denmark).* Unpublished manuscript.

Hafsten, Ulf 1956: *Pollen-analytic investigations on the late Quaternary development in the inner Oslofjord area.* Universitetet i Bergen, Årbok 1956. Naturvitenskapelig rekke, vol. 8:1–161.

Hafsten, Ulf, Kari E. Henningsmoen and Helge I. Høeg 1979: Innvandringen av gran til Norge. In: Reidar Nydal, Sverre Westin, Ulf Hafsten and Steinar Gulliksen (eds.): *Fortiden i søkelyset,* pp. 171–98. Trondheim.

Hakbijl, Tom 2002: The traditional, historical and prehistoric use of ashes as an insecticide, with an experimental study on the insecticidal efficacy of washed ash. *Environmental Archaeology,* vol. 7:13–22.

Hagland, Jan Ragnar and Jørn Sandnes 1994: *Frostatingslova.* Oslo.

Hall, A. and H. Kenward 2004: Setting people in their environment: plant and animal remains from Anglo-Scandinavian York. In: R. A. Hall (ed.): *Aspects of Anglo-Scandinavian York,* pp. 372–426. Council for British Archaeology. York.

Hall, A., H. Kenward and J. Carrott 2004: *Technical Report: plant and invertebrate remains from medieval deposits at various sites in Aberdeen. Part I: Text.* Unpublished report, Centre for Human Palaeoecology Report 2004/06. University of York. York.

Hall, Richard 1984: *The Viking Dig.* The Bodley Head. London.

– 1994: *English Heritage book of Viking Age York.* B.T.Batsford/English Heritage. London.

Halvorsen, Eyvind Fjeld 1987: East Norway in the Sagas. In: James E. Knirk (ed.): *Proceedings of the Tenth Viking Congress.* Universitetets Oldsaksamlings Skrifter, vol. 9:55–67. Oslo.

– 1997: De gamle østlandske kristenrettene. In: Audun Dybdahl and Jørn Sandnes (eds.): *Nordiske middelalderlover. Tekst og kontekst,* pp. 59–68. Trondheim.

Hansen, Henrik Jarl 1990: Dankirke. Jernalderboplads og rigdomscenter. Oversigt over udgravningerne 1965–70. *Kuml,* 1988–9:201–48.

Hansson, A.-M. and J. H. Dickson 1997: Plant remains in sediment from the Björkö Strait outside the black earth at the Viking Age town of Birka, Central Eastern Sweden. In: U. Miller and H. Clarke (eds.): *Environment and Vikings: Scientific methods and techniques.* Birka Studies, vol. 4:205–16. The Birka Project. Stockholm.

Harland, J. F., J. H. Barrett, J. Carrott, K. Dobney and D. Jaques 2003: The York System: An integrated zooarchaeological database for research and teaching. *Internet Archaeology,* vol. 13: http://intarch.ac.uk/journal/issue13/harland_index.html.

Harris, E.C. 1989: *Principles of Archaeological Stratigraphy,* 2nd edition. Academic Press. London.

Haselgrove, C., M. Millett and I. Smith (eds.) 1985: *Archaeology from the Ploughsoil: Studies in the Collection and Interpretation of Field Survey Data.* J.R.Collis. Sheffield.

Hasle, Grete R. and Erik E. Syvertsen 1996: Marine diatoms. In: Carmelo R. Thomas (ed.): *Identifying Marine Phytoplankto,* pp. 5–386. Academic Press Inc., San Diego.

Hatting, T. 1990: Cats from Viking Age Odense. *Journal of Danish Archaeology,* vol. 9:179–93.

– 1991: The archaeozoology. In: M. Bencard, L. B. Jørgensen and H. B. Madsen (eds.): *Ribe Excavations 1970–1976,* vol. 3:43–57. Sydjysk Universitetsforlag. Esbjerg.

Hauksbók. Published 1892–96 by Det Kongelige Nordiske Oldskrift-selskab. København.

Hed Jakobsson, Anna 2003: *Smältdeglars härskare och Jerusalems tillskyndare. Berättelser om vikingatid och tidig medeltid.* Stockholm Studies in Archaeology, vol. 25. Stockholm.

Hedeager, Lotte 1999: Sacred tophography. Depositions of wealth in the cultural landscape. In: Anders Gustafsson and Håkan Karlsson (eds.): *Glyfer och arkeologiska rum. En vänbok till Jarl Nordbladh,* pp. 229–52. Göteborg.

– 2001: Asgard reconstructed? Gudme – a 'Central Place' in the North. In: Mayke de Jong, Frans Theuws and Carine van Rhijn (eds.): *Topographies of power in the early middle ages,* pp. 467–507. Leiden.

– 2004: Dyr og andre mennesker – mennesker og andre dyr. Dyreornamentikens trancendentale realitet. In: Anders Andrén, Kristina Jennbert and Catharina Raudvere (eds.): *Ordning mot kaos. Studier av nordisk förkristen kosmologi.* Vägar til Midgård, vol. 4:219–252. Lund.

Hedeager Krag, Anne 1994: Dragtudviklingen fra 8.–10. årh. e.Kr. i Sydskandinavien – med udgangspunkt i skålformede spænder. *Lag,* vol. 5:7–114. Højbjerg.

Hedeager Madsen (Krag), Anne 1990: Women's dress in the Viking Period in Denmark, based on the tortoise brooches and textile remains. In: P. Walton and J.P. Wild (eds.): *Textiles in Northern Archaeology*, pp. 101–106. NESAT III Textile Symposium in York. London.

Hedges, R. E. M. 2002: Bone diagenesis: an overview of processes. *Archaeometry*, vol. 44:319–28.

Hedlund, Gunnar 1993: Utgrävningen 1992. In: Wladyslaw Duczko (ed.): *Arkeologi och milögeologi i Gamla Uppsala, studier och rapporter*, pp. 64–9. Uppsala.

Hedman, Anders 1989: Gård och samhälle under yngsta järnålder – utgångspunkter för en reviderad bebyggelsesarkeologi. In: Mats Buström (ed.): *Mänsklighet genom millennier. En vänbok till Åke Hyenstrand,* pp. 93–9. RAÄ. Stockholm.

– 1991: Platåhusen. In: Bibbi Andersson, David Damell and Jan Norrman (eds.): *Fornsigtuna. En kungsgårds historia*, pp. 58–74. Upplands-Bro.

Heibreen, Tom 2005: Kokegroper og beslektede teknologier – noen etnografiske eksempler. In: Lil Gustafson, Tom Heibren and Jes Martens (eds.): *De gåtefulle kokegroper.* KHM Varia, vol. 58:9–22. Oslo.

Helgason, Jón 1953: *Litteraturhistorie. Norge og Island*. Nordisk Kultur, vol. 8:B. Stockholm.

Helgen, Geir 1975: Fra de lange knivers tid. *Nicolay,* vol. 19:3–7.

Hellberg, Lars 1967: *Kumlabygdens ortnamn och äldre bebyggelse*. Kumlabygden. Forntid – nutid – framtid, vol. 3. Kumla bokhandel. Kumla.

– 1986: "Ingefreds sten" och häradsindelningen på Öland. In: Hans-Peter Naumann, Oskar Bandle, Stefan Sonderegger and Magnus von Platen (eds.): *Festschrift für Oskar Bandle. Zum 60. Geburtstag am 11. Januar 1986*. Beträge zur nordischen Philologie, vol. 15:19–29. Helbing & Lichtenhahn. Basel and Frankfurt am Main.

Helle, Knut 1974: *Norge blir en stat 1130–1319*. Bergen, Oslo, Tromsø.

– 1980: *Handelsplass – by. Handelsplats – stad – omland. Symposium om det medeltida stadsväsendet i Mellansverige.* Medeltidsstaden, vol. 18:16–23. Stockholm.

– 2001: *Gulatinget og Gulatingslova*. Leikanger.

Helle, Knut and Arnved Nedkvitne 1977: Sentrumsdannelser og byutvikling i norsk middelalder. In: Grethe Authén Blom (ed.): *Middelaldersteder.* Urbaniseringsprosesser i Norden, vol. 1:189–286. Oslo – Bergen – Tromsø.

Henningsmoen, Kari E. 1974: Tjølling – formet av naturens krefter. *Tjølling bygdebok,* vol. 1:13–38.

– 1979: En karbon-datert strandforskyvningskurve fra søndre Vestfold. In: Reidar Nydal, Stig Westin, Ulf Hafsten and Steinar Gulliksen (eds.): *Fortiden i søkelyset,* pp. 239–47. Trondheim,

– 1980: Trekk fra floraen i Vestfold. In: Vilhelm Møller (ed.): *Bygd og By i Norge – Vestfold,* pp. 163–75. Gyldendal norsk forlag. Oslo.

Henriksen, Mogens Bo 1999: Bål i lange baner. Om brugen af kokegruber i yngre bronsealder og ældre jernalder. *Fynske Minder,* 1999:93–128.

– (ed.) 2000: *Detektorfund – Hvad skal vi med dem? Dokumentation og registrering af bopladser med detektorfund fra jernalder og middelalder.* Skrifter fra Odense bys museer, vol. 5. Odense.

Hernæs, Per and Per Holck 1984: C22541a-g. Et gammelt funn tolkes på ny. *Nicolay,* vol. 43:31–9.

Herrmann, Joachim 1982: *Wikinger und Slawen. Zur Frühgeschichte der Ostseevölker*. Berlin.

Herschend, Frands 1993: The Origin of the Hall in Southern Scandinavia. *Tor,* vol. 25:175–99.

– 1995: Hus på Helgö. *Fornvännen,* vol. 90:221–8.

Herteig, Asbjørn E. 1969: *Kongers havn og handels sete. Fra de arkeologiske undersøkelser på Bryggen i Bergen 1955–68*. Aschehoug. Oslo.

Hinchliffe, J. and R.T. Schadla-Hall (eds.) 1980: *The Past under the Plough.* Directorate of Ancient Monuments and Historic Buildings Occasional Papers, vol. 3. Department of the Environment. London.

Hodder, Ian 1997: 'Always Momentary, Fluid and Flexible': Towards a Reflexive Excavation Methodology. *Antiquity,* vol. 71:690–700.

Hodges, Richard 1982: *Dark age economics. The origins of towns and trade A.D. 600–1000*. New York.

Hoel, Kåre 1986: Huseby-garders gamle navn. Huseby – Tesal, Huseby – Odinssal, Huseby – Skiringssal. *Årsmelding 1985 fra Institutt for namnegransking*, pp. 119–32. Oslo.

Hofseth, Ellen Høigård 1999: Historien bak handelskvinnen på Kaupang. Kvinnegraver fra vikingtid langs Vestfoldkysten. *Viking,* vol. 62:101–129.

Holand, Ingegerd 2003a: Pottery. In: Gerd Stamsø Munch, Olav Sverre Johansen and Else Roesdahl (eds.): *Borg in Lofoten. A Chieftain's farm in North Norway*. Lofotr, Vikingmuséet i Borg, Arkeologisk Skriftserie, vol. 1:199–212.. Tapir Academic press. Trondheim.

– 2003b: Glass vessels. In: Gerd Stamsø Munch, Olav Sverre Johansen and Else Roesdahl (eds.): *Borg in Lofoten. A Chieftain's farm in North Norway*. Lofotr, Vikingmuséet i Borg, Arkeologisk Skriftserie, vol. 1:211–30. Tapir Academic press. Trondheim.

Holand, Ingegerd and John S.R. Hood 2003: Graves below Borg I:1. In: Gerd Stamsø Munch, Olav Sverre Johansen and Else Roesdahl (eds.): *Borg in Lofoten. A Chieftain's farm in North Norway*. Lofotr, Vikingmuséet i Borg, Arkeologisk Skriftserie, vol. 1:103–4. Tapir Academic press. Trondheim.

Holck, Per 1986: *Cremated bones. A medical-anthropological study of an archaeological material on cremation burials.* Ph.D thesis, Anathomical Institute, University of Oslo.

– 1996: *Cremated Bones. A Medical-Anthropological Study of an Archaeological Material on Cremation Burials,* 2nd revised edition. Anathomical Institute, University of Oslo.

Hollstein, Ernst 1980: *Mitteleuropäische Eichenchronologie.* Mainz am Rhein.

Holm, Gösta 1991: *De nordiska anger-namnen*. Skrifter utg. av Norske videnskaps-akademi. II, Hist.-filos. klasse, N.S., vol. 18. Lund University Press. Lund.

Holm, P. 1986: The slave trade of Dublin, ninth to twelfth

centuries. *Peritia,* vol. 5:317–45.

Holmboe, J. 1927: Nytteplanter og ugræs i Osebergfundet. In: A. W. Brøgger and H. Schetelig (eds.): *Oseberg-fundet,* vol. V:1–78. Kristiania.

Holmqvist, Wilhelm (ed.) 1961: *Excavations at Helgö,* vol. I. Stockholm.

Holmquist Olausson, Lena 1993: *Aspects on Birka. Investigations and Surveys 1976–1989.* Theses and Papers in Archaeology, B:3. Stockholm.

Holtsmark, Anne 1970: Skaldediktning. *KLNM,* vol. 15:386–90.

Hougen, Bjørn 1924: *Grav og gravplass. Eldre jernalders gravplass i Østfold og Vestfold.* Kristiania.

– 1940: Osebergfunnets billedvev. *Viking,* vol. 4:85–124.

Hougen, Ellen Karine 1993: *Kaupang-funnene bd. IIIB. Bosetningsområdets keramikk.* Norske Oldfunn, vol. XIV. Institutt for arkeologi, kunsthistorie og numismatikk, Oldsaksamlingen, Universitetet i Oslo.

Hovda, Per 1971: Til norske elvenamn. *Namn och bygd,* vol. 59:124–148.

Hreinsson, Vidhar (ed.) 1997: *The Complete Sagas of the Icelanders,* vol. 5. Reykjavík.

http://www.kaupang.uio.no (2001–2002).

http://vannstand.statkart.no/ read 10.09.05

http://www.grida.no/climate/ipcc_tar/wg1/424.htm read 15.06.05

Hufthammer, A. K. 2000: Kosthold hos overklassen og hus vanlige husholdninger i middelalderen. En sammenligning mellom animalosteologisk material fra Trondheim og Oslo. In: Audun Dybdahl (ed.): *Osteologisk Materiale som Historisk Kilde,* pp. 163–87. Tapir Akademisk Forlag. Trondheim.

– 2003: Med kjøtt og fisk på menyen. In: O. Skevik (ed.): *Middelalder-Gården i Trøndelag,* pp. 182–96. Stiklestad Nasjonale Kultursenter.

Hufthammer, A. K. and O. F. Bratbak 2000: *Bones from the year 2000 excavation at the Kaupang Tjølling site.* Unpublished report, Museum of Zoology, University of Bergen.

Hultén, Eric 1971: *Atlas över växternas utbredning i Norden,* Stockholm.

Hunt, W. J. Jr. and J. Brandon 1990: Using Agricultural Grain Cleaners to Mechanically Screen Earth. *Journal of Field Archaeology,* vol. 17:116–21.

Hägg, Inga 1984: Die Tracht. In: Greta Arwidsson (ed.): *Systematische Analysen der Gräberfunde.* Birka, vol. II:2:51–72. Stockholm.

Høeg, Ove Arbo 1956: Growth-Ring Research in Norway, *Tree-Ring Bulletin* vol. 21: 2–15.

Hårdh, Birgitta 1996: *Silver in the Viking Age. A regional-economic Study.* Acta Archaeologica Lundensia, vol. 25. Almqvist & Wiksell. Lund.

– 1998: Preliminära notiser kring detektorfynden från Uppåkra. In: Lars Larsson and Birgitta Hårdh (eds.): *Centrala platser – Centrala frågor.* Uppåkrastudier, vol. 1:113–127. Lund

– (ed.) 2001: *Uppåkra. centrum och sammanhang.* Uppåkrastudier, vol. 3. Lund.

– in prep. a: *Hacksilver and Ingots from Kaupang.* To appear in the Kaupang Excavation Project Publication Series.

– in prep. b: *Scandinavian Metalwork from Kaupang.* To appear in the Kaupang Excavation Project Publication Series.

Hårdh, Birgitta and Lars Larsson (eds.) 2002: *Central Places in the Migration and Merovingian Periods. Papers from the 52nd Sachsensymposium.* Uppåkrastudier, vol. 6. Lund.

Haavaldsen, Per 1977: *Rapport om vegetasjonsmerker i Sandefjord, Tjølling, Hedrum og Brunlanes kommuner, Vestfold.* Unpublished report, KHM archive.

– 1980: *Trekk av eldre jernalder i Søndre Vestfold.* Unpublished master thesis in Archaeology, University of Oslo.

Ilkjær, Jørgen 2000: *Illerup Ådal – et arkæologisk tryllespejl.* Moesgård.

– 2002: Den bevidste ødelæggelse i krigsbytteofringerne. In: Kristina Jennbert, Catharina Raudvere and Anders Andrén (eds.): *Plats och praxis. Studier av nordisk förkristen ritual.* Vägar til Midgård, vol. 2:203–214. Lund.

– 2003: Danske krigsbytteofringer. In: Lars Jørgensen, Birger Storgaard and Lone G. Thomsen (eds.): *Sejrens triumf – Norden i skyggen af det romerske imperium,* pp. 44–64. København.

Indrebø Gustav 1935: *Fjordung. Granskingar i eldre norsk organisasjons-soge.* Bergens museums aarbok. Historisk-antikvarisk rekke, 1935:1. Bergen.

Indrebø, Gustav and Oluf Kolsrud 1924: *Lærde brev fraa og til P.A. Munch.* vol. I. Oslo.

Ingstad, Anne Stine 1992: Osebergdronningen – hvem var hun? In: A. E. Christensen, A. S. Ingstad and B. Myhre, *Osebergdronningens grav. Vår arkeologiske nasjonalskatt i nytt lys,* pp. 224–256. Oslo.

– 1999: Tekstilene. In: Charlotte Blindheim, Birgit Heyerdahl-Larsen and Anne Stine Ingstad 1999: *Kaupang-funnene. B. 1999. IIB. Gravplassene i Bikjholbergene/Lamøya. Undersøkelsene 1950–1957. Del B. Oldsaks-former.* Norske Oldfunn XIX:217–272. Universitetets Kulturhistoriske Museer. Oslo.

Iversen, Frode 2004: *Eiendom, makt og statsdannelse. Kongsgårder og gods i Hordaland i yngre jernalder og middelalder.* Unpublished PhD thesis in Archaeology, University of Bergen.

Iversen, Johannes 1944: *Viscum, Hedera* and *Ilex* as climate indicators. A contribution to the study of the Postglacial temperature climate. *Geologiska Föreningen Stockholm, Förhandlingar,* vol. 66:463.

Iversen, Mette and Ulf Näsman 1991: Mammengravens indhold. In: M. Iversen, U. Näsman and J. Vellev (eds.): *Mammen. Grav, kunst og samfund i vikingetid,* pp. 45–66. Højbjerg.

Iversen, Tore 1997: *Trelldommen. Norsk slaveri i middelalderen.* Historisk Institutt Universitetet i Bergen Skrifter, vol. 1. Bergen.

Jahnsen, Astri 1974: Faste oldtidsminner i Tjølling. In: Jan W. Krohn-Holm (ed.): *Tjølling bygdebok,* vol. I:524–41.

Tjølling.

Jankuhn, Herbert 1960: Archäologische zur frühen Falkenbeize im Norden. In: Wolfgang Krause (ed.): *Indogermanica. Festschrift für Wolfgang Krause*, pp. 31–37. Heidelberg.

– 1986: *Haithabu. Ein Handelsplatz der Wikingerzeit.* Neumünster.

Jansson, Ingmar 1985*: Ovala spännbucklor. En studie av vikingatida standardsmycken med utgångspunkt från Björkö-fynden.* Aun, vol. 7. Uppsala.

Jansson, Sven B.F. 1984: *Runinskrifter i Sverige.* Värnamo.

Jansson, Valter 1951: *Nordiska vin-namn. En ortnamnstyp och dess historia.* Skrifter utg. av Gustav Adolfs Akademien, vol. 24. Lundequistska bokhandeln. Uppsala and København.

Jenkins, D. A. 1994: Interpretation of interglacial cave sediments from a hominid site in North Wales: translocation of Ca-Fe-phosphates. In: A. J. Ringrose-Voase and G. S. Humphreys (eds.): *Soil Micromorphology: Studies in Management and Genesis*, pp. 293–305. Elsevier. Amsterdam.

Jensen, Jørgen 2004: *Danmarks Oldtid. Yngre Jernalder og Vikingetid 400 e.Kr–1050 e.Kr.* København.

Jensen, Stig 1991a: *Ribes vikinger.* Den antikvariske samling. Ribe.

– 1991b: Dankirke – Ribe. Fra handelsgård til handelsplads. In: Peder Mortensen and Birgit M. Rasmussen (eds.): *Høvdingesamfund og kongemagt.* Fra stamme til stat i Danmark, vol. 2:73–88. Jysk Arkæologisk Selskabs Skrifter, vol. XXII:2. Århus.

Jensenius, Jørgen 2001: *Trekirkene før stavkirkene. En undersøkelse av planlegging og design av kirker før ca år 1100.* Oslo.

Jesch, Judith 1998: Murder and treachery in the Viking Age. In: Timothy S. Haskett (ed.): *Crime and Punishment in the Middle Ages,* pp. 63–85. Victoria.

Johansen, Jannie Schnedler 2004: *Kremasjon – inhumasjon, kriger eller bonde? En studie av vikingtidens gravskikk i Rogaland og Vestfold.* Unpublished master thesis in Archaeology, University of Oslo.

Johansen, Olav Sverre, Karsten Kristiansen and Gerd Stamsø Munch 2003: Soapstone artefacts and whetstones. In: Gerd Stamsø Munch, Olav Sverre Johansen and Else Roesdahl (eds.): *Borg in Lofoten. A Chieftain's farm in North Norway.* Lofotr, Vikingmuséet i Borg, Arkeologisk Skriftserie, vol. 1:141–58. Tapir Academic press. Trondheim.

Johnsen, Oscar Albert 1929: *Tønsbergs historie.* Bind I: Middelalderen. Oslo.

Jónsson, Finnur 1900–1901: *Heimskringla IV. Fortolkning til versene.* København.

– 1911 (ed.): *Snorri Sturluson: Heimskringla, Nóregs konunga sögur.* København.

– 1912a: *Den norsk-islandske Skjaldedigtning, vol. I, A. Tekst etter handskrifterne.* København og Kristiania.

– 1912b: *Den norsk-islandske Skjaldedigtning, vol. I, B. Rettet tekst.* København, Kristiania.

– 1930 (ed.): *Íslendingabók.* Dansk-islandsk Forbunds-fond. København.

Jordforsk 1997: *Veileder for prioritering av arealer for tilskudd til endret jordarbeiding,* 3. ed. Landbruksdepartmentet. Oslo.

Jørgensen, Lars 1998: En storgård fra vikingetid ved Tissø, Sjælland – en foreløbig præsentasjon. In: Lars Larsson and Birgitta Hårdh (eds.): *Centrala platser – Centrala frågor.* Uppåkrastudier, vol. 1:233–48. Lund.

– 2001: From tribute to the estate system, 3rd–12th century. In: Birgit Arrhenius (ed.): *Kings and Regionality. Transactions from the 49th Sachsensymposium 1998 in Uppsala*, pp. 73–82. Stockholm.

– 2002: Kongsgård – kultsted – marked. Overvejelser omkring Tissøkompleksets struktur og funktion. In: Kristina Jennbert, Anders Andrén and Catharina Raudverre (eds.): *Plats och praxis. Studier av nordisk förkristen ritual.* Vägar til Midgård, vol. 2:215–47. Lund.

– 2003: Manor an Market at Lake Tissø in the sixth to Eleventh Centuries. The Danish 'Productive' Sites. In: Tim Pestell and Katharina Ulmschneider (eds.): *Markets in early Medieval Europe. Trading and 'productive' sites, 650–850*, pp. 175–207. Windgather Press. Bollington.

Jørgensen, Lars, Josefine F. Bican, Lone G. Thomsen, Xenia P. Jensen 2004: Stormænd, købmænd og håndverkere ved Tissø i det 6–11 årh. *Fra Holbæk Amt,* 2003:50–65.

Kaennel, Michèle and Fritz H. Schweingruber (eds.) 1995: *Multilingual Glossary of Dendrochronology.* Berne.

Karlsson, S. and A.-M. Robertsson 1997: Human impact in the Lake Mälaren region, south-central Sweden during the Viking Age (AD 750–1050): A survey of biostratigraphical evidence. In: U. Miller and H. Clarke (eds.): *Environment and Vikings: Scientific methods and techniques.* Birka Studies, vol. 4:47–72. The Birka Project. Stockholm.

Kaul, Flemming 2003: Mosen – porten til den anden verden. In: Lars Jørgensen, Birger Storgaard and Lone G. Thomsen (eds.): *Sejrens triumf – Norden i skyggen af det romerske imperium*, pp. 18–43. København.

Kenward, H. K. 1978: The analysis of archaeological insect assemblages: a new approach. *The Archaeology of York*, vol. 19/1:1–68.

– 1988: Insect remains. In: Erik Schia (ed.): *"Mindets Tomt" – "Søndre Felt": Animal bones, moss-, plant-, insect- and parasite remains.* De Arkeologiske Utgravninger i Gamlebyen, Oslo, vol. 5:115–40. Alvheim & Eide. Øvre Ervik.

– 1992: Rapid recording of archaeological insect remains – a reconsideration. *Circaea*, vol. 9:81–8.

– 1997: Synanthropic decomposer insects and the size, remoteness and longevity of archaeological occupation sites: applying concepts from biogeography to past 'islands' of human occupation. *Quaternary Proceedings*, vol. 5:135–52.

– 2005: Insects and other invertebrate remains. In: M. Iversen, D. Robinson, J. Hjermind and C. Christensen (eds.): *Viborg Søndersø 1018-1030.* Jysk Arkæologisk Selskabs skrifter, vol. 52:215–37. Århus.

Kenward, H. K. and E. P. Allison 1994: A preliminary view of the insect assemblages from the early Christian rath site at Deer Park Farms, Northern Ireland. In: D. J. Rackham (ed.): *Environment and economy in Anglo-Saxon England*, pp. 89–107. Council for British Archaeology. York.

Kenward, H. K., C. Engleman, A. Robertson and F. Large 1986: Rapid scanning of urban archaeological deposits for insect remains. *Circaea*, vol. 3:163–72.

Kenward, H. K. and A. R. Hall 1995: *Biological Evidence from Anglo-Scandinavian Deposits at 16–22 Coppergate*. Council for British Archaeology. York.

– 1997: Enhancing bioarchaeological interpretation using indicator groups: stable manure as a paradigm. *Journal of Archaeological Science*, vol. 24:663–73.

Kenward, H. K., A. R. Hall and A. K. G. Jones 1980: A tested set of techniques for the extraction of plant and animal macrofossils from waterlogged archaeological deposits. *Science and Archaeology*, vol. 22:3–15.

Kenward, H. K., M. Hill, D. Jaques, A. Kroupa and F. Large 2000: Coleoptera analysis. In: A. Crone (ed.): *The history of a Scottish lowland crannog: excavations at Buiston, Ayrshire 1989–90*. Scottish Trust for Archaeological Research Monograph, vol. 4:230–47. Edinburgh.

Kenward, H. and F. Large 1998: Recording the preservational condition of archaeological insect fossils. *Environmental Archaeology*, vol. 2:49–60.

Kenward, H. K. and D. Williams 1979: Biological evidence from the Roman warehouses in Coney Street. *The Archaeology of York*, vol. 14/2.

Kilger, Christoph in prep. a: *Kaupang form Afar: Aspects on Interpretation of Dirhem Finds dating from the End of the 8th until the Beginning of the 10th Century*. To appear in the Kaupang Excavation Project Publication Series.

– in prep. b: *(W)holy Objects and Fragments – Perspectives on the Use of Silver in Kaupang and around the North Sea during the Early Viking Age*. To appear in the Kaupang Excavation Project Publication Series.

Kirchhefer, Andreas J. 1999: *Dendroclimatology on Scots pine (Pinus sylvestris L.) in northern Norway*. DR. scient. thesis. University of Tromsø.

Kivikoski, Ella 1963: *Kvarnbacken. Ein Gräberfeld der jüngeren Eisenzeit auf Åland*. Helsinki.

Kjellmark, Knut 1906: Ett graffält från den yngre järnåldern i Ås i Jämtland. *Ymer*, vol. 25:1905:351–371.

Kjær, Albert 1909a: Hvad var Skíringssalr? *Historisk Tidsskrift*, vol. 20:267–283.

– 1909b: Aflsuttende svar til hr. S. A. Sørensen. *Historisk Tidsskrift*, vol. 20:425–30.

Kleiminger, Hans Ulrich 1993: Gravformer og gravskik i vikingetidens Danmark. *Lag*, vol. 4:77–177. Højbjerg.

Kloet, G. S. and W. D. Hincks 1964–1977: *A check list of British Insects*, 2nd edition. Royal Entomological Society. London.

Knudsen, Trygve and Per Sveaas Andersen 1971: *Lærde brev fraa og til P.A. Munch*, vol. 3. Oslo.

Koht, Halvdan 1921 [1919]: Upphave til dei gamle norske byane. In: Halvdan Koht: *Innhogg og utsyn i norsk historie*, pp. 20–33. Krsitiania.

– 1955: *Harald Hårfagre og rikssamlinga*. Oslo.

Kovacs, Gabriella, forthcoming: *Geoarchaeological Investigation of the Százhalombatta-Földvár Bronze Age Tell Settlement in Hungary*. PhD thesis, University of Cambridge. Cambridge.

Kraft, Jens 1822: *Topographisk-statistisk Beskrivelse over Jarlsbergs og Laurvigs Amt*. Topographisk-Statistisk Beskrivelse over Kongeriget Norge, vol. 2. Christiania.

– 1840: *Det Søndenfjeldske Norge*. Topographisk-statistisk Beskrivelse over Kongeriget Norge. Anden omarbeidede udgave, vol. 2. Christiania.

Krag, Claus 1990: Vestfold som utgangspunkt for den norske rikssamlingen. *Collegium Medievale*, vol. 3:1990:2:179–95.

– 1991: *Ynglingatal og Ynglingesaga. En studie i historiske kilder*. Studia humaniora, vol. 2. Universitetsforlaget. Oslo.

– 1995: *Vikingtid og rikssamling 800–1130*. Aschehougs Norges historie, vol. 2. Oslo.

Krahe, Hans 1964: *Unsere ältesten Flussnamen*. Harrassowitz. Weisbaden.

Kristensen, Steinar 2001a: *Innberetning fra overvåking og utgraving av sjakt på Leif Kaupangs eiendom, Nordre Kaupang (gnr. 1029/14), Larvik kommune, Vestfold fylke*. Unpublished report, KHM archive.

– 2001b: *Innberetning fra overvåking og utgraving på Kaupang Nordre, gnr. 1029, bnr. 1, Larvik kommune, Vestfold*. Unpublished report, KHM archive.

– 2003a: *Innberetning fra arkeologisk overvåking av gravearbeider i forbindelse med nye vann- og avløpsledninger. Kaupang, Larvik kommune, Vestfold fylkeskommune, gnr./bnr. 1012/23, 48, 59*. Unpublished report, KHM archive.

– 2003b: *Innberetning fra arkeologisk overvåking av gravearbeider i forbindelse med nye vann- og avløpsledninger. Kaupang, Larvik kommune, Vestfold fylkeskommune, gnr./bnr. 1012/52*. Unpublished report, KHM archive.

– 2003c: *Innberetning fra arkeologisk overvåking av gravearbeider i forbindelse med nye vann- og avløpsledninger. Kaupang, Larvik kommune, Vestfold fylkeskommune, gnr./bnr. 1012/72*. Unpublished report, KHM archive.

– 2003d: *Innberetning fra arkeologisk overvåking av gravearbeider i forbindelse med nye vann- og avløpsledninger. Kaupang, Larvik kommune, Vestfold fylkeskommune, gnr./bnr. 1029/5*. Unpublished report, KHM archive.

– 2005: *Kaupangregistreringen vår 2005, Larvik kommune, Vestfold fylke*. Unpublished report, KHM archive.

Krivogorskaya, Y., S. Perdikaris and T. H. McGovern 2005: Fish bones and fishermen: The potential of zooarchaeology in the Westfjords. *Archaeologica Islandica*, vol. 4:31–50.

Krohn-Holm, Jan W. 1970: *Tjølling bygdebok*, vol. II. Tjølling.

– 1974: *Tjølling bygdebok*, vol. I. Tjølling.

– 1982: *Hedrum bygdebok*, vol. I. Hedrum.

Lamm, Kristina 1999: Helgö. *Reallexikon der Germanischen Altertumskunde*, vol. 14:286–91. Berlin, New York.

Larsen, Jan Henning 1982: Hedrum i jernalderen. In: Jan W. Krohn-Holm (ed.): *Hedrum bygdebok,* vol. I:66–115. Larvik.

– 1984: Graver fra sen hedensk tid i Aust-Agder. *Universitetets Oldsaksamlings årbok,* 1982/1983:173–181.

– 1986: Noen akvareller av fornminner fra søndre Vestfold. *Viking,* vol. 44:81–95.

Larsen, Kari Ch. 1995: *Ytre Moa. Et gårdsanlegg fra vikingtid i Årdal, Sogn. En studie av byggeskikk og gårdsstruktur.* Unpublished thesis, Universitetet i Bergen.

Larsson, Annika 2005: *Påtning – vikingarnas stickning.* Unpublished thesis, Institutionen för bildpedagogik, Konstfack. Stockholm.

Larsson, Lars, Karl-Magnus Lenntorp 2004: The Enigmatic House. In: Lars Larsson (ed.): *Continuity for Centuries.* Uppåkrastudier, vol. 10:3–48. Lund.

Larsson, Lars (ed.) 2004: *Continuity for Centuries.* Uppåkrastudier, vol. 10. Lund.

Larsson, Lars and Birgitta Hårdh (eds.) 1998: *Centrala platser – Centrala frågor.* Uppåkrastudier, vol. 1. Lund.

– (eds.) 2002: *Central Places in the Migration and Merovingian Periods.* Uppåkrastudier, vol. 6. Lund.

– (eds.) 2003: *Centrality – Regionality.* Uppåkrastudier, vol. 7. Lund.

Lewis, Helen 1998: *The Characterisation and Interpretation of Ancient Tillage Practices through Soil Micromorphology: a Methodological Study.* PhD thesis, University of Cambridge. Cambridge.

Lewis, Helen and Karen Milek, forthcoming: *Bone diagenesis in wet environments: micromorphological and microprobe studies of bone diagenesis products.*

Lia, Øystein 2001: *Det rituelle rom. En fortolkende analyse av vikingtidens graver og landskap på Kaupang.* Unpublished master thesis in Archaeology, University of Oslo.

– 2005: *Rapport fra utgravningene av en yngre jernalders hallbygning på Huseby, Tjølling i Vestfold fylke, 2000 og 2001.* Unpublished report, KHM archive.

Lid, Johannes 1994. *Norsk flora.* Det norske samlaget. Oslo.

Lidén, Hans-Emil 1974: Eidsvoll kirke. Fra romansk til nyromansk. In: Fridtjov Birkeli, Arne Odd Johnsen and Einar Molland (eds.): *Oslo bispedømme 900 år,* pp. 207–218. Oslo.

– 1981: Middelalderens steinarkitektur i Norge. In: Knut Berg, Peter Anker, Per Palme and Stephan Tschudi-Madsen: *Norges Kunsthistorie,* vol. 2:7–125. Oslo.

– 2005: *Nicolay Nicolaysen.* Oslo.

Lie, R. W. 1988: Animal Bones. In: Erik Schia (ed.): *"Mindets Tomt" – "Søndre Felt": Animal bones, moss-, plant-, insect- and parasite remains.* De Arkeologiske Utgravninger i Gamlebyen, Oslo, vol. 5:153–96. Alvheim & Eide. Øvre Ervik.

– 1989: *Dyr i Byen – En Osteologisk Analyse.* Fortiden i Trondheim Bygrunn: Folkebibliotekstomten Meddelelser, vol. 18. Riksantikvaren, Utgravningskontoret for Trondheim.

Liestøl, Aslak 1953: The Hanging Bowl, a Liturgical and Domestic Vessel. *Acta Archaeologica,* vol. 24:163–170.

– 1960: *Norges innskrifter med de yngre runer,* vol. V. Oslo.

– 1973: Runenstäbe ais Haithabu – Hedeby. In: Kurt Schietzel (ed.): *Das archaeologische Fundmaterial II. Berichte über die ausgrabungen in Haithabu,* vol. 6:96–119. Neumünster.

Lindh, J. 1991: Aspects of sea-level changes, fishing, and fish processing in Tønsberg in the Middle Ages. In: G. L. Good, R. H. Jones and M. W. Ponsford (eds.): *Waterfront Archaeology: Proceedings of the third international conference on waterfront archaeology held at Bristol 23–26 September 1988,* pp. 67–75. Council for British Archaeology. York.

Lindner, Kurt 1973: *Beiträge zu Vogelfang und Falknerei im Altertum.* Berlin.

Lindquist, Sven-Olof (ed.) 1985: *Society and trade in the Baltic during the Viking Age.* Visby.

Lindroth, C. H. 1986: The Carabidae (Coleoptera) of Fennoscandia and Denmark. *Fauna Entomologica Scandinavica,* vol. 15 (2). Brill/Scandinavian Science Press. Leiden and København.

Ljunggren, Karl Gustav 1937: Køping, køpinge och kaupangr. *Namn och bygd,* vol. 25:1937:99–129.

Ljungkvist, John 2000: Den förhistoriska bebyggelsen i Gamla Uppsala. *Fornvännen,* vol. 95:145–163.

– 2005: Uppsala högars datering och några konsekvenser av en omdatering til tidiga vendeltiden. *Fornvännen,* vol. 100:245–259.

– 2006: *En hiar atti rikR. Om elit, struktur och ekonomi kring Uppsala och Mälaren under yngre järnålder.* Uppsala.

Lorra, Susanna and Andreas Karthage 2003: *The geophysical Exploration of the Kaupang Site by Means of Ground Penetrating Radar. Report on Field Survey and Results.* Allied Assoiates Office Germany. Borken.

Lucas, Gavin 2001: *Critical Approaches to Fieldwork. Contemporary and Historical Archaeological Practice.* Routledge. London and New York.

Lund, Allan A. (ed.) 1988: *P. Cornelius Tacitus Germania, interpretiert, herausgegeben, übertragen, kommentiert und mit einer Bibliographie versehen von Allan A. Lund Wissenschaftliche Kommentare zu greichischen und lateinischen Schriftstellern.* Winter. Heidelberg

Lund, Claus 1984: Indledning. In: Karsten Friis-Jensen and Claus Lund (eds.): *Skjoldungernes saga,* pp. 9–42. København.

Lund, Julie 2004: Våben i vand. Om deponeringer i vikingetiden. *Kuml,* 2004:197–220.

Lund, Niels (ed.) 1983: *Ottar og Wulfstan. To rejsebeskrivelser fra vikingetiden.* Roskilde.

Lundekvam, Helge 2002: *ERONOR/USLENO-Empirical erosion models for Norwegian conditions. Documentation.* Report 6/2002. Norwegian University of Life Sciences.

Lundqvist, Lars 1996: Slöinge – en stormansgård från järnåldern. In: Lars Lundqvist, Karin Lindeblad, Ann-Lili Nielsen and Lars Ersgård: *Slöinge och Borg. Stormans-*

gårdar i öst och väst. Linköping.

– 1997: Central Places and Central Areas in the Late Iron Age. In: Hans Andersson, Peter Carelli and Lars Ersgård (eds.): *Visions of the Past,* pp. 179–97. Stockholm.

– 2003: *Slöinge 1992–1996. Undersökningar av en boplats från yngre jernålder.* Slöingeprojektet, vol. 2. Gotarc Serie C. Arkeologiska Skrifter 42. Göteborgs Universitet. Göteborg.

Lyman, R. L. 1994: *Vertebrate Taphonomy.* Cambridge University Press. Cambridge.

Lyngstrøm, Henriette 1995: Ketting – en vikingetidsgravplads med ryttergrave. *Aarbøger for Nordisk Oldkyndighed og Historie,* 1993:143–179.

Løken, Trond 1974: *Gravminner i Østfold og Vestfold. Et forsøk på en typologisk-kronologisk analyse og en religionshistorisk tolkning.* Unpublished master thesis in Archaeology, University of Oslo.

– 1977: Mølen – et arkeologisk dateringsproblem og en historisk identifikasjonsmulighet. *Universitetets Oldsaksamling Årbok,* 1975/1976:67–86.

Låg, Jul 1945: Weathering of syenite in Kjose, Vestfold. *Norsk geologisk tidsskrift,* vol. 25:216–24.

Macklin, M. G., C. Bonsall, F. M. Davies and M. R. Robinson 2000: Human-environment interactions during the Holocene: New data and interpretations from the Oban area, Argyll, Scotland. *The Holocene,* vol. 10:109–21.

Macphail, Richard I., Marie Agnes Courty and Anne Gebhardt 1990: Soil micromorphological evidence of early agriculture in north-west Europe. *World Archaeology,* vol. 22(1):53–69.

Maixner, Birgit 2004: Die tierverzierte Metallarbeiten der Wikingerzeit aus Birka unter besonderer Berücksichtigung des Borrestils. In: Michael Müller-Wille (ed.): *Zwischen Tier und Kreuz. Untersuchen zur wikingerzeitlichen Ornamentik im Ostseeraum.* Studien zur Siedlungsgeschichte und Archäologie der Ostseegebiete, vol. 4:9–203. Neumünster.

Mangerud, Jan, Sven T. Andersen, Bjørn E. Berglund and Joachim J. Donner 1974: Quaternary stratigraphy of Norden, a proposal for terminology and classification. *Boreas,* vol. 3:109–28.

Marstrander, Sverre 1973: "… menneskebenrad i siddende stilling…" *Honos Ella Kivikoski.* Finska Fornminnesföreningens Tidskrift, vol. 75:137–145.

– 1976: Gravrøysene på Mølen. Med et tillegg av Bjørg Elisabeth Alfsen. *Viking,* vol. 39:11–59.

Martens, Irmelin 1969: Gravfeltet på By i Løten, Hedmark. *Universitetets Oldsaksamling Årbok,* 1965–1966:11–148.

Martens, Jes 2005: Kokegruber i syd og nord – samme sag? In: Lil Gustafson, Tom Heibreen and Jes Martens (eds.): *De gåtefulle kokegroper.* KHM Varia, vol. 58:37–56. Oslo.

Matthews, Wendy 1992: *The Micromorphology of Occupational Sequences and the Use of Space in a Sumerian City.* PhD thesis, University of Cambridge. Cambridge.

– 1995: Micromorphological characterisation and interpretation of occupation deposits and microstrati-

graphic sequences at Abu Salabikh, Southern Iraq. In: Anthony J. Barham and Richard I. Macphail (eds.): *Archaeological Sediments and Soils: Analysis, Interpretation, and Management,* pp. 41–74. Institute of Archaeology. London.

Mauss, Marcel 1954 [1925]: *The gift. Forms and functions of exchange in archaic societies.* London.

McCormick, F. 1997: The animal bones. In: M. F. Hurley, O. M. B. Scully and S. W. J. McCutcheon (eds.): *Late Viking Age and Medieval Waterford Excavations 1986–1992,* pp. 819–53. Waterford.

– 2005: *Feeding Dublin and other Viking towns: The zooarchaeological evidence.* Unpublished paper, presented at the XV Viking Congress, 18–24 August, 2005. Cork.

McGrail, Sean 1985: Early Landing Places. In: Asbjørn E. Herteig (ed.): *Conference on Waterfront Arhcaeology in North European Towns No. 2. Bergen 1983,* pp. 12–18. Historisk Museum. Bergen.

Melefors, Evert 1984: *Ling* och *graun* – växtbeteckningar i ortnamn på Gotland. In: Lars-Erik Edlund, Birger Liljestrand and Sigurd Fries (eds.): *Florilegium Nordicum. En bukett språk- och namnstudier tillägnade Sigurd Fries den 22 april 1984,* pp. 176–190. Umeå Studies in the Humanities 61. Almqvist & Wiksell Int. Umeå.

Melsom, Charlotte 2003: *Rangler i vikingtidsgraver fra Vestfold.* Unpublished master thesis in Archaeology, University of Oslo.

Meulengracht Sørensen, Preben 1991: Håkon den Gode og guderne. In: Peder Mortensen and Birgit M. Rasmussen (eds.): *Høvdingesamfund og kongemagt. Fra stamme til stat i Danmark,* vol. 2:235–44. Jysk Arkæologisk Selskabs Skrifter, vol. XXII:2. Århus.

– 2003: The Hall in Norse literature. In: Gerd Stamsø Munch, Olav Sverre Johansen and Else Roesdahl (eds.): *Borg in Lofoten. A Chieftain's farm in North Norway.* Lofotr, Vikingmuséet i Borg, Arkeologisk Skriftserie, vol. 1: 265–72. Tapir Academic press. Trondheim.

Michaelsen, Karsten Kjer 1993: På Sydøstfyn. In: Per O. Thomsen, Benno Blæsild, Nils Hardt, Karsten Kjer Michaelsen: *Lundeborg. En handelsplads fra jernalderen,* pp. 47–67. Svendborg.

Middleton, Neil 2005: Early medieval port customs, tolls and controls on foreign trade. *Early Medieval Europe,* vol. 13:313–58.

Mikkelsen, Egil 1999: Handel – misjon – religionsmøter. Impulser fra buddhisme, islam og kristendom i Norden 500–100 e.Kr. *Viking,* vol. 65:91–136.

Milek, Karen B. 2004: Aðalstræti, Reykjavík 2001: Geoarchaeological report on the deposits within the house and the soils immediately pre- and post-dating its occupation. In: Howell M. Roberts (ed.): *Excavations at Aðalstræti, 2003,* pp. 74–114. Fornleifastofnun Íslands. Reykjavík.

– 2006: *Houses and Households in Early Icelandic Society: Geoarchaeology and the Interpretation of Social Space.* PhD thesis, University of Cambridge. Cambridge.

Milek, Karen B. and Charles A. I. French forthcoming:

Natural site formation processes and the dramatic alteration of stratigraphy at the Viking Age trading centre of Kaupang, Norway.

Miller, Urve and Helen Clarke (eds.) 1997: *Environment and Vikings.* Birka Studies, vol. 4. Stockholm and Rixensart.

Moberg, Eva 1992: *Vikingtidssverdene. Hjemlig produserte eller importerte. Med utgangspunkt i et lokalt sverdmateriale fra Sogn og Fjordane.* Unpublished master thesis in Archaeology, Bergen University.

Moberg, Lennart 1988: Attmar. *Namn och bygd,* vol. 76:5–17.

Moreland, John 2000a: Concepts of the Early Medieval Economy. In: Inger Lyse Hansen and Chris Wickham (eds.): *The Long Eighth Century. Production, Distribution and Demand,* pp. 1–34. Leiden, Boston, Köln.

– 2000b: The Significance of Production in Eighth-century England. In: Inger Lyse Hansen and Chris Wickham (eds.): *The Long Eighth Century. Production, Distribution and Demand,* pp. 69–104. Leiden, Boston, Köln.

– 2004: Objects, identities and cosmological authetication. *Archaeological Dialogues,* vol. 10:144–9.

Mortensen, Lars Boje 2003: Introduction. In: Inger Ekrem and Lars Boje Mortensen (eds.): *Historia Norwegie,* pp. 8–47. København

Mortensen, Peder and Birgit M. Rasmussen (eds.) 1988: *Jernalderens stammesamfund. Fra stamme til stat i Danmark,* vol. 1. Jysk Arkæologisk Selskabs Skrifter, vol. XXII:1. Århus.

– (eds.) 1991: *Høvdingesamfund og kongemagt. Fra stamme til stat i Danmark,* vol. 2. Jysk Arkæologisk Selskabs Skrifter, vol. XXII:2. Århus.

Munch, Gerd Stamsø 2003: Jet, amber, bronze, silver and gold artefacts. In: Gerd Stamsø Munch, Olav Sverre Johansen and Else Roesdahl (eds.): *Borg in Lofoten. A Chieftain's farm in North Norway.* Lofotr, Vikingmuséet i Borg, Arkeologisk Skriftserie, vol. 1:241–52. Tapir Academic press. Trondheim.

Munch, Gerd Stamsø, Olav Sverre Johansen and Else Roesdahl (eds.) 2003: *Borg in Lofoten. A Chieftain's farm in North Norway.* Lofotr, Vikingmuséet i Borg, Arkeologisk Skriftserie, vol. 1. Tapir Academic press. Trondheim.

Munch, Peter Andreas 1837: Om Beliggenheden af det gamle Grenmar og andre Steder, som i Oldskrifterne forbindes demed. *Annaler for Nordisk Oldkyndighed,* 1836–37:62–79.

– 1849: *Historisk-geographisk Beskrivelse over Kongeriget Norge (Noregsveldi) i Middelalderen.* Moss.

– 1850: Om den gamle vestfoldske Søhandelsplads i Skiringssal og de vestfoldske Konger av Ynglinge-Ætten. *Norsk Tidsskrift for Videnskab og Literatur,* vol. 4:101–88.

– 1852: *Det norske Folks Historie,* vol. 1. Christiania.

– 1874: *Samlede afhandlinger,* vol. II. Christiania.

– 1967 [1854]: *Norrøne gude- og heltesagn,* 5th revised edition by Anne Holtsmark. Oslo.

Munthe, Gerhard 1847: *Norske Stedsnavnes rette Skrivemaade. En Fortegnelse, forsaavidt Land-districterne angaaer oversamtlige Rigets Amter, Fogderier, Thinglage, Præstegjelde ogKirkesogne samt endeel af de vigtigste Gaarde. Uddragen af den af Captain Munthe efter off. Foranstaltning gjennemgaaende fulstændige Udg. af den nye Matricul.* Christiania.

Murphy, C. P. 1986: *Thin Section Preparation of Soils and Sediments.* AB Academic Publishers. Berkhampstead.

Muus, B. J. and P. Dahlstrøm 1974: *Collins Guide to the Sea Fishes of Britain and North-Western Europe.* Collins. London.

Myhre, Bjørn 1980: *Gårdsanlegget på Ullandhaug,* vol. I. Stavanger

– 1992a: Diskusjonen om Ynglingeættens gravplasser. In: Arne Emil Christensen, Anne Stine Ingstad and Bjørn Myhre: *Osebergdronningens grav,* pp. 35–50. Oslo.

– 1992b: Borre – et merovingertidssentrum i Øst-Norge. In: Egil Mikkelsen and Jan Henning Larsen (eds.): *Økonomiske og politiske sentra i Norgen ca 400–1000 e. Kr.* Universitetets Oldsaksamlings Skrifter Ny Rekke, vol. 13:155–179.

– 1992c: Ynglingeætten i Vestfold. In: Arne Emil Christensen, Anne Stine Ingstad and Bjørn Myhre: *Osebergdronningens grav,* pp. 258–66. Oslo.

– 1992d: Kronologispørsmålet. In: Arne Emil Christensen, Anne Stine Ingstad and Bjørn Myhre: *Osebergdronningens grav,* pp. 267–71. Oslo.

– 1992e: Kildeproblem ved bruk av arkeologisk materiale. In: Arne Emil Christensen, Anne Stine Ingstad and Bjørn Myhre: *Osebergdronningens grav,* pp. 279–85. Oslo.

Myhre, Bjørn and Terje Gansum 2003: *Skipshaugen 900 e.Kr. Borrefunnet 1852–2002.* Midgard forlag. Tønsberg.

Müller, Inger-Helene Vibe 1971: *Østnorske basilika-anlegg. En sammenligning.* Unpublished master thesis in History of Art, University of Oslo.

Müller-Wille, Michael 1970: *Bestattung im Boot.* Offa, vol. 25/26.

– 1972: Zwei wikingerzeitliche Prachtschwerter aus der Umgebung von Haithabu. *Offa,* vol. 29:47–89.

– 1976: *Das Bootkammergrab von Haithabu.* Berichte über die ausgrabungen in Haithabu, vol. 8. Neumünster.

– 1977: Krieger und Reiter im Spiegel früh- und hochmittelalterlicher Funde Schleswig-Holsteins. *Offa,* vol. 34:40–74.

– 1987: *Das wikingerzeitliche Gräberfeld von Thumby-Bienebek (Kr. Rendsburg-Eckernförde), Teil 2.* Offa-Bücher, vol. 62.

– 2001: Tierstile des 8.–12. Jahrhunderts im Norden Europas. Dendrochronologie und kunsthistorische Einordnung. In: M. Müller-Wille and L. O. Larsson (eds.): *Tiere – Menschen – Götter. Wikingerzeitliche Kunststile und ihre neuzeitliche Rezeption,* pp. 215–250. Göttingen.

– 2002: Offerplatser på kontinenten. Några exempel från förkristen tid. In: Kristina Jennbert, Catharina Raudvere and Anders Andrén (eds.): *Plats och praxis. Studier av nordisk förkristen ritual.* Vägar til Midgård, vol.

2:135–66. Lund.

Narmo, Lars Erik 1996: "Kokekameratene på Leikvin". Kult og kokegroper. *Viking*, vol. 59:79–100.

Naumann, Hans-Peter 1987: Warenpreise und Wertverhältnisse im alten Norden. In: Klaus Düwel, Herbert Jahnkuhn, Harald Siems and Dieter Timpe (eds.): *Untersuchungen zu Handel und Verkehr der vor- und frühgeschichtlichen Zeit im Mittel- und Nordeuropa. Teil IV: Der Handel der Karolinger- und Wikingerzeit*, pp. 374–89. Göttingen.

Nedkvitne, A. 1976: Handelssjøfarten mellom Norge og England i Høymiddelalderen. *Sjøfartshistorisk Årbok*, 1976:7–254.

– 1993: Trade. In: P. Pulsiano (ed.): *Medieval Scandinavia*, pp. 649–53. Garland Publishing, Inc. London.

Neikter, Jacob Fredrik 1802: *Observationum Historico-Geographicarum Particula*. Uppsala.

Nicholson, R. A. 1995: Out of the frying pan into the fire: what value are burnt fish bones to archaeology? *Archaeofauna*, vol. 4:47–64.

– 1996: Bone degradation, burial medium and species representation: Debunking the myths, an experiment-based approach. *Journal of Archaeological Science*, vol. 23:513–34.

Nicolaysen, Nicolay 1853: Om Borrefundet i 1852. *Foreningen til norske fortidsminnesmerkers bevaring, Aarsberetning*, 1852:25–30.

– 1861: Reiseberetning, indsendt til det akademiske Kollegium. *Foreningen til norske fortidsminnesmerkers bevaring, Aarsberetning*, 1860:5–36.

– 1862–1866: *Norske fornlevninger. En oplysende fortegnelse over Norges fortidslevninger, ældre en reformationen og henførte til hver sit sted*. Kristiania.

– 1863: Indberetning til Kirkedepartementet om min antikvariske virksomhed fra 1 April 1862 til 1 April 1863. *Foreningen til norske fortidsminnesmerkers bevaring, Aarsberetning*, 1862:1–4.

– 1868: Tillæg til "Norske Fornlevninger" [Innberetning om utgravningene på Nordre og Søndre Kaupang]. *Foreningen til norske fortidsminnesmerkers bevaring, Aarsberetning*, 1867:77–91, Plansje III no 26, Plansje IV and VI.

– 1882: *Langskibet fra Gokstad ved Sandefjord*. Kristiania.

– 1888: Udgravninger i 1887. *Foreningen til norske Fortidsmindesmerkers Bevaring Aarsberetning*, 1887:25–44.

– 1894a: Antikvariske notiser. *Foreningen til norske Fortidsmindesmerkers Bevaring Aarsberetning*, 1893:173–182.

– 1894b: [Tale ved foreningens femtiårsjubileum 1894]. *Foreningen til norske fortidsminnesmerkers bevaring 1844–1894*, pp. 3–14. Kristiania.

Nielsen, Axel E. 1991: Trampling the archaeological record: an experimental study. *American Antiquity*, vol. 56:483–503.

Nielsen, Jens N. 2004: Sebbersund – tidlige kirker ved Limfjorden. In: Niels Lund (ed.): *Kristendommen i Danmark før 1050. Et symposium i Roskilde den 5.–7. februar 2003*, pp. 103–122. Roskilde.

Nielsen, Poul Otto, Klavs Randsborg and Henrik Thrane (eds.) 1994: *The Archaeology of Gudme and Lundeborg. Papers presented at a conference at Svendborg, October 1991*. Arkæologiske Studier, vol. 10. Akademisk forlag. København.

NIJOS 1993: Jordtypekart, målestokk 1:5000; *CH 024-1, CH 024-2, CH 025-3, CH 025-4*. Institute of Land Inventory. Ås.

Nordberg, Andreas 2002: Vertikalt placerade vapen i vikingatida gravar. *Fornvännen*, vol. 97:15–24. Stockholm.

– 2003: Om namnet Skiringssalr. *Fornvännen*, vol. 98:265–269.

Nordman, Ann-Marie 1989: *De arkeologiske undersøkelsene i Storgaten 18 og Conradis gate 5/7, Tønsberg 1987 og 1988*. Arkeologiske rapporter fra Tønsberg, vol. 1. Tønsberg.

Norr, Svante 1998: *To Rede and to Rown. Expressions of Early Scandinavian Kingship i Written Sources*. Uppsala.

– 1999: *Innberetning om prøvegravning på Huseby-terrassen høsten 1999*. Unpublished report, KHM archive.

Norr, Svante and Anneli Sundkvist 1995: Valsgärde Re-Visited. *Tor*, 1995:2:395–417.

– 1997: Boplatsundersökningarna i Valsgärde 1994–1996. *Rapport från utgrävningarna i Valsgärde*, pp. 1–41. SIV, Institutionen för Arkeologi och Antik historia, Uppsala Universitet.

Nyborg, Ebbe 1986: Kirke – sognedannelse – bebyggelse. *Hikuin*, vol. 12:17–44.

Nyborg, Åge A. and Eivind Solbakken 2003: *Klassifikasjonssystem for jordsmonn i Norge. Feltguide basert på WRB*. NIJOS dokument, vol. 6/03.

Näsman, Ulf 1991: Det syvende århundre – et mørkt tidsrum i ny belysning. In: Peder Mortensen and Birgit M. Rasmussen (eds.) 1991: *Høvdingesamfund og kongemagt. Fra stamme til stat i Danmark*, vol. 2:165–178. Jysk Arkæologisk Selskabs Skrifter, vol. XXII:2. Århus.

– 2003: Beads of amber, carnelian, glass, jet, rock-crystal and stone. In: Gerd Stamsø Munch, Olav Sverre Johansen and Else Roesdahl (eds.): *Borg in Lofoten. A Chieftain's farm in North Norway*. Lofotr, Vikingmuséet i Borg, Arkeologisk Skriftserie, vol. 1:231–40. Tapir Academic press. Trondheim.

Näsström, Brit-Mari 2002: I livets skeden. Om passageriter i fornskandinavisk religion. In: Kristina Jennbert, Catharina Raudvere and Anders Andrén (eds.): *Plats och praxis. Studier av nordisk förkristen ritual*. Vägar til Midgård, vol. 2:69–85. Lund.

Nørgård Jørgensen, Anne 1999: *Waffen und Gräber. Typologische und chronologische Studien zu skandinavischen Waffengräbern 520/30 bis 900 n. Chr*. København.

O'Connor, T. P. 1989: Bones from Anglo-Scandinavian levels at 16–22 Coppergate. *The Archaeology of York*, vol. 15/3:137–207.

– 1991: Bones from 46–54 Fishergate. *The Archaeology of York*, vol. 15/4:209–98.

– 2001: On the interpretation of animal bone assemblages from Wics. In: D. Hill and R. Cowie (eds.): *Wics: The early medieval trading centres of Northern Europe*, pp. 54–60. Sheffield Academic Press. Sheffield.

– 2004: Animal bones from Anglo-Scandinavian York. In: R. A. Hall, D. W. Rollason, M. Blackburn, D. N. Parsons, G. Fellows-Jensen, A. R. Hall, H. K. Kenward, T. P. O'Connor, D. Tweddle, A. J. Mainman and N. S. H. Rogers (eds.): *Aspects of Anglo-Scandinavian York*. Council for British Archaeology, Archaeology of York 8/4:427–45. York.

Odelman, Eva 1986: *Boken om Ansgar*. Stockholm.

Olausson, Michael (ed.) 2000: *En bok om Husbyar*. Riksantikvarieämbetet, Stockholm.

Olesen, Odleiv, John Dehls, Hilmar Bungum, Fridtjof Riis, Erik Hicks, Conrad Lindholm, Lars H. Blikra, Willy Fjeldskaar, Lars Olsen, Oddvar Longva, Jan I. Faleide, Lars Bockmann, Leif Rise, David Roberts, Alvar Braathen and Harald Brekke 2000: *Neotectonics in Norway, Final Report*. Norges geologiske undersøkelse, Report 2000.002.

Ólsen, Björn Magnússon 1910: Om ordet seyðir. *Aarbøger for Nordisk Oldkyndighed og Historie*, 1909:318–31.

Olsen, Knut S. and Arne Løwe 1984: *Sandefjord 1813 III, kvartærgeologisk kart, 1:50 000*. Norges geologiske undersøkelse.

Olsen, Magnus 1926: *Ættegård og helligdom. Norske stednavn sosialt og religionshistorisk belyst*. Inst. for Sammenlignende Kulturforskning. Serie A. Forelesninger 9a. Aschehoug & Co. Oslo.

Olsen, Olaf 1972: Sankt Mikkel i Slagelse. *Nationalmuseets Arbejdsmark*, 1972:131–52.

– 1975: Vi. *KLNM*, vol. 19:684–5.

Olsen, Ole Mikal 2004: Medieval fishing tackle from Bergen. In: Ingvild Øye (ed.): *Medieval Fishing Tackle from Bergen and Borgund*. The Bryggen Papers Main Series, vol. 5:11–106, Fagbokforlaget. Bergen.

Oggins, Robin S. 2004: *The kings and their hawks. Falconry in Medieval England*. New Haven.

Opedal, Arnfrid 1998: *De glemte skipsgravene. Makt og myter på Avaldsnes*. AmS-Småtrykk, vol. 47. Stavanger.

Orme, Nicholas 1984: *From childhood to chivalry*. London.

Ormåsen, Else G. 1977: *Foraminiferfauna og lithostratigrafi i kvartære sedimenter fra Larvik-Porsgrunn området*. Unpublished master thesis, Institutt for geologi, Universitetet i Oslo.

Orosius: Janet Bately (ed.) 1980: *The English Orosius*. Early English text society. Supplementary series 6. Oxford University Press for the Early English text society. Oxford.

Pallister, D.M. (ed.) 2000: *The Cambridge Urban History of Britain. Volume I: 600–1540*. Cambridge.

Palmer, Ben 2003: The Hinterlands of Three Southern English Emporia: Some Common Themes. In: Tim Pestell and Katharina Ulmschneider (eds.): *Markets in Early Medieval Europe. Trading and 'Productive' Sites, 650–850*, pp. 48–60. Bollington.

Pamp, Bengt 1974: *Ortnamnen i Sverige*. 3rd ed. Lundastudier i nordisk språkvetenskap. Serie B:2. Student-

litteratur. Lund.

Paulsen, Peter 1956: *Axt und Kreuz in Nord- und Ost-Europa*. Bonn.

Paulsson, Jonas 1999: Metalldetektering och Uppåkra. Att förhålla sig til detektormatrial. In: Birgitta Hårdh (ed.): *Fynden i sentrum. Keramik, glas och metal från Uppåkra*. Uppåkrastudier, vol. 2:41–58. Lund.

Payne, S. 1987: Reference codes for wear states in the mandibular cheek teeth of sheep and goats. *Journal of Archaeological Science*, vol. 14:609–14.

Payne, S. and G. Bull 1988: Components of variation in measurements of pig bones and teeth, and the use of measurements to distinguish wild from domestic pig remains. *Archaeozoologia*, vol. 2:27–66.

Pedersen, Anne 1997a: Søllested – nye oplysninger om et velkendt fund. *Aarbøger for Nordisk Oldkyndighed og Historie*, 1996:37–111.

– 1997b: Weapons and riding gear in burials – evidence of military and social rank in 10th century Denmark? In: A. Nørgård Jørgensen and B. L. Clausen (eds.): *Military aspects of Scandinavian society in a European perspective AD 1–1300*, pp. 123–135. København.

Pedersen, Ellen Anne 1989: *Jernalderbosetningen på Hadeland. En arkeologisk-geografisk analyse*. Universitetets Oldsaksamling Varia, vol. 17. Oslo.

Pedersen, Unn 2000: *Vektlodd – sikre vitnesbyrd om handelsvirksomet? Vektloddenes funksjoner i vikingtid, en analyse av vektloddmaterialet fra Kaupang og sørøst-Norge*. Unpublished master thesis in Archaeology, University of Oslo.

– in prep. a: *Weights and Balances from Kaupang*. To appear in the Kaupang Excavation Project Publication Series.

– in prep. b: *In the Melting pot: Metal Workers in Action in Early Viking-age Kaupang*. To appear in the Kaupang Excavation Project Publication Series.

Perdikaris, S. 1999: From chiefly provisioning to commercial fishery: Long-term economic change in Arctic Norway. *World Archaeology*, vol. 30:388–402.

Petersen, Jan 1919: *De norske vikingesverd. En typologisk-kronologisk studie over vikingetidens vaaben*. Videnskapsselskapet i Kristiania. Skrifter, II, Hist.-filos. klasse 1919:1. Kristiania.

– 1920: Universitetets Oldsaksamlings tilvekst 1916. *Oldtiden*, vol. VIII:161–192. Kristiania.

– 1928: *Vikingetidens smykker*. Stavanger museums skrifter, vol. 2. Stavanger.

– 1951: *Vikingetidens redskaper*. Skrifter utgitt av Det norske videnskaps-akademi i Oslo. II. Hist.-filos. klasse 1951:4. Oslo.

Petersen, Johannes S. 1978: Structure of the Larvikite-Lardalite Complex, Oslo Region, Norway, and its Evolution. *Geologische Rundschau*, vol. 67:330–40.

Pettersen, Gunnar I. 2000: Handel og priser i Norge i middelalderen. *Collegium Medievale*, vol. 13:203–28.

Pilø, Lars: 1989: Early Soapstone Vessels in Norway. *Acta Archaeologica*, vol. 60:87–100.

– 1999a: *Innberetning fra måling av kulturlagsdybde i bo-*

setningsområdet på Kaupang søndre og nordre, gnr. 1012 og 1929, Larvik. K., Vestfold. Unpublished report, KHM archive.

– 1999b: *Innberetning fra åkervandring på Kaupang søndre og nordre, gnr. 1012 og 1029, Larvik k., Vestfold, i april 1999*. Unpublished report, KHM archive.

– 1999c: *Innberetning fra åkervandring på Kaupang søndre og nordre, gnr. 1012 og 1029, Larvik k., Vestfold, i september 1999*. Unpublished report, KHM archive.

– 1999d: *Innberetning fra åkerregistrering på Huseby østre &vestre, gnr 1032/20–21, Larvik kommune, Vestfold, april 1999*. Unpublished report, KHM archive.

– 2001: *Innberetning fra metallsøk på Kaupang søndre og nordre, gnr. 1012 og 1029, Larvik k., Vestfold, i oktober 2001*. Unpublished report, KHM archive.

– 2005: *Bosted – urgård – enkeltgård. En analyse av premissene i den norske bosetningshistoriske forskningstradisjon på bakgrunn av bebyggelsesarkeologisk feltarbeid på Hedemarken*. Oslo Arkeologiske Serie, vol. 3. Institutt for arkeologi, kunsthistorie og konservering, Universitetet i Oslo.

– in prep.: *The Pottery from Kaupang*. To appear in the Kaupang Excavation Project Publication Series.

Pilø, Lars, Irene Baug, Steinar Kristensen, Unn Pedersen and Liliane Tarrou 2003: *Innberetning fra hovedundersøkelsen på Kaupang, gnr. 1012, Larvik k., Vestfold, 2000–2002*. Unpublished report, KHM archive.

Pilø, Lars, Unn Pedersen, Katrine Stene and Vanja Tørhaug 2000: *Innberetning fra undersøkelse av traséer for sykkel-/gangvei og avløp i bosetningsområdet på Kaupang, gnr. 1010/1029, Larvik kommune, Vestfold*. Unpublished report, KHM archive.

Polanyi, Karl 1944: *The great transformation*. New York.

Price, Neil S. 2002: *The Viking way. Religion and war in Late Iron Age Scandinavia*. Aun, vol. 31. Uppsala.

Prummel, W. 1983: *Excavations at Dorestad 2, Early Medieval Dorestad an Archaeozoological Study*. ROB. Amersfoort.

Ramskou, Thorkild 1950: Viking Age cremation graves in Denmark. A survey. *Acta Archaeologica*, vol. 21:137–182. København.

– 1976: *Lindholm Høje Gravpladsen*. Nordiske Fortidsminder Ser. B in quarto, vol. 2. København.

Ramus, Jonas 1719: *Norriges kongers historie*. København.

Randsborg, Klavs 1980 *The Viking Age in Denmark. The formation of a state*. London.

Rask, Rasmus K. 1815: Ottars og Ulfstens korte Rejseberetninger med dansk Oversættelse, kritiske Anmærkninger og andre Oplysninger. *Skandinavisk Literaturselskabs Skrifter*, 1815.

Rau, Reinhold (ed.) 1955: *Quellen der karolingischen Reichsgeschichte, erster Teil*. Berlin.

Ravn, Mads 2003: *Death Ritual and Germanic Social Structure (c. AD 200–600)*. BAR International Series, vol. 1164. Oxford.

Reichstein, H. and H. Pieper 1986: *Untersuchungen an Skelettresten van Vogeln aus Haithabu (Ausgrabung 1966–1969)*. Ausgrabungen in Haithabu, vol. 22. Karl Wachholz. Neumünster.

Reichstein, H. and M. Tiessen 1974: *Untersuchungen an Tierknochenfunden (1963–1964)*. Ausgrabungen in Haithabu, vol. 7. Karl Wachholz. Neumünster.

Reitan, Gaute 2005: Fra kokegroper til halshogging på Faret – bruk og gjenbruk av et kultsted gjennom 1600 år. In: Lil Gustafson, Tom Heibren and Jes Martens (eds.): *De gåtefulle kokegroper*. KHM Varia, vol. 58:177–88. Oslo.

Rentzel, Philippe and Gesa-Britt Narten 2000: Zur Entstehung von Gehniveaus in sandig-lehmigen Ablagerungen – Experimente und archäologische Befunde. *Jahresberichte der Archäologischen Bodenforschung Basel-Stadt*, 1999:107–27.

Resi, Heid Gjøstein in prep. a; *Whetstones from Kaupang*. To appear in the Kaupang Excavation Project Publication Series.

– in prep. b: *Finds of Jet, Amber and Gemstones from Kaupang*. To appear in the Kaupang Excavation Project Publication Series.

Reynolds, Susan 1977: *An introduction to the History of English Medieval Towns*. Oxford.

– 1992: The writing of Medieval Urban History in England. *Theoretische Geschiedens*, vol. 19:43–57.

Richards, Julian D., Marcus Jecock, Lizzie Richmond, and Catherine Tuck 1995: The Viking barrow cemetery at Heath Wood, Ingleby, Derbyshire. *Medieval Archaeology*, vol. 39:51–70.

Rick, J.W. 1976: Downslope movement and archaeological intrasite spatial analysis. *American Antiquity*, vol. 41:133–44.

Ridderspore, Mats 1998: Ravlunda och Uppåkra. Två exempel på försvunna storgårdar? In: Lars Larsson and Birgitta Hårdh (eds.): *Centrala platser – Centrala frågor*. Uppåkrastudier, vol. 1:165–77. Lund.

Riisøy, Anne Irene 2003: Komparativt blikk på "verdslig" rett i Eldre Borgartings kristenrett. In: Jón Viðar Sigurðsson and Per G. Norseng (eds.): *Over grenser. Østfold og Viken i yngre jernalder og middelalder*, pp. 155–177. Oslo.

– 2005: Kristenrettene og sosialhistorien. In: Steinar Imsen (ed.): *Den kirkehistoriske utfordring*, pp. 59–74. Trondheim.

Rindal, Magnus 1997: Ny utgåve av dei norske lovene frå mellomalderen? In: Audun Dybdahl and Jørn Sandnes (eds.): *Nordiske middelalderlover. Tekst og kontekst*, pp. 23–32. Trondheim.

Ringsted, Nils 2005: Karsvik platåhus – ett märkligt fornminne! *Brommaboken*, 2005. Bromma Hembygdsförenings Årsskrift. Bromma.

Risbøl, Ole 1994: Socialøkonomiske aspekter ved vikingetidens klæberstenshandel i Sydskandinavien. *Lag*, vol. 5:115–161. Højbjerg.

– 2005: Kokegroper i røyk og damp – et kokegropfelt i gårds- og landskapsperspektiv. In: Lil Gustafson, Tom Heibren and Jes Martens (eds.): *De gåtefulle kokegroper*. KHM Varia, vol. 58:155–66. Oslo.

Rispling, Gert 2004: Catalogue and Comments on the Islamic Coins from the Excavations 1990–1995. In:

Björn Ambrosiani (ed.): *Eastern Connections. Part Two: Numismatics and Metrology.* Birka Studies, vol. 6:26–60. The Birka Project. Stockholm.

Rispling, Gert, Mark Blackburn and Kenneth Jonsson, in prep.: *Catalogue of the Coins Found at Kaupang.* To appear in the Kaupang Excavation Project Publication Series.

Rives, James 1999: *Tacitus Germania.* Clarendons ancient history series. Clarendon. Oxford 1999.

Robberstad, Knut 1969: *Gulatingslovi.* Oslo.

Roberts, Howell M. 2003: *Excavations at Gásir 2003 – A Preliminary Statement.* Fornleifastofnun Íslands. Reykjavík.

Robinson, D. 1991: Plant remains from the late Iron Age/Early Viking Age settlement at Gammel Lejre. *Journal of Danish Archaeology,* vol. 10:191–8.

Roesdahl, Else 1977: *Fyrkat. En Jysk Vikingeborg II. Oldsagerne og Gravpladsen.* København.

– 1983: Fra vikingegrav til Valhal i 900-årenes Danmark. In: Torben Kisbye and Else Roesdahl (eds.): *Beretning fra andet tværfaglige vikingesymposium,* pp. 39–49. Århus.

– 1992: *The Vikings.* London

Rosenqvist. Ivan T. 1958: En stokkebro i Båsmyr på Freberg i Sandar, Vestfold. Den geologiske aldersbestemmelse. *Viking,* vol. 21/22:122–25.

– 1960: Marine clays and quick clays slides. In: O. Holtedahl (ed.): *Geology of Norway.* Norges geologiske undersøkelse, vol. 208:1–540.

af Rosenschöld, Viktoria Munck 2005: *Tidiga toner. Vikingatida musikinstrument och ljudredskap från Järrestad, Uppåkra och Löddeköpinge.* ARK 341, CD-uppsats, Lunds universitet.

Round, Frank E., Richard M. Crawford and David G. Mann 1990: *The Diatoms.* Cambridge University Press.

Rowley-Conwy, P. 1995: Wild or Domestic? On the evidence for the earliest domestic cattle and pigs in south Scandinavia and Iberia. *International Journal of Osteoarchaeology,* vol. 5:115–26.

Rundkvist, Martin 2003: *Barshalder 1. A cemetery in Grötlingbo and Fide parishes, Gotland, Sweden, c. AD 1–1100. Excavations and finds 1826–1971.* Stockholm.

Rygh, Karl 1910: *Arkæologiske undersøgelser 1910.* Det Kgl. norske videnskabers selskabs skrifter, 1910:6. Trondhjem.

Rygh, Oluf 1877: Om den yngre jernalder i Norge. *Aarbøger for Nordisk Oldkyndighed og Historie,* 1877:101–194.

– 1885: *Norske Oldsager. Ordnede og forklarede.* Christiania.

– 1896: Norske Fjordnavne. In: C.R. Unger (ed.): *Sproglig-Historiske Studier tilegnede Professor C. R. Unger,* pp. 30–86. Aschehoug. Kristiania.

– 1897–1936: *Norske Gaardnavne. Oplysninger samlede til Brug ved Matrikelens Revision,* vol. 1–19. Kristiania – Oslo.

– 1898: *Norske Gaardnavne. Forord og indledning.* Kristiania.

– 1901: *Gamle Personnavne i Norske Stedsnavne.* H. Aschehoug & co. Kristiania.

Ryste, Bengta 2005: *Edemetalldepotene fra folkevandringstid og vikingtid i Norge. Gull og sølv i kontekst.* Unpublished master thesis in Archaeology, University of Oslo.

Sandnes, Jørn 1969: Fylkeskirkene i Trøndelag i middelalderen. En del notater og detaljmateriale. *Årbok for Trøndelag,* 1969.

– 1973: Datering av navneklasser ved landskyldmetoden. *Maal og minne,* 1973:12–28.

– 1974: Tingsted, Norge. *KLNM,* vol. 18:379–81.

– 1994: (Review of) Ynglingatal og Ynglingesaga. *Historisk Tidsskrift,* vol. 73:2:229–231.

– 1998: Uppsala, Bjørkøy og Rosenborg. Oppkalling og mønsterstyrt navngiving i Skandinavia. *Namn och bygd,* vol. 86:81–90.

Sandvik, Gudmund 1965: *Prestegard og prestelønn.* Oslo.

Sanke, M. 2001: Gelbe Irdenware. In: Hartwig Lüdtke and Kurt Schietzel (eds.): *Handbuch zur mittelalterlichen Keramik in Nordeuropa,* vol. 1:271–428. Wachholtz Verlag. Neumünster.

Sapp, Christopher D. 2000: Dating Ynglingatal – Chronological Metrical Developments in Kviðuháttr. *Skandinavistik,* vol. 30:2:85–98.

Sawyer, Peter 1982: *Kings and Vikings.* London, New York.

– 1986: Early Fairs and Markets in England and Scandinavia. In: B. L. Anderson and A. J. H. Latham (eds.): *The Market in History,* pp. 59–77. London.

– 1991: Konger og kongemakt. In: Peder Mortensen and Birgit M. Rasmussen (eds.): *Høvdingesamfund og kongemagt. Fra stamme til stat i Danmark,* vol. 2:277–88. Jysk Arkæologisk Selskabs Skrifter, vol. XXII:2. Århus.

Schetelig, Haakon 1912: *Vestlandske grave fra jernalderen.* Bergen.

– 1917: Graven, In: A. W. Brøgger, H. Falk and H. Schetelig (eds.): *Osebergfundet,* vol. 1:209–278. Kristiania.

Schia, Erik 1987: Bebyggelsesrester og datering. In: Erik Schia (ed.): *"Søndre felt". Stratigrafi, bebyggelsesrester og daterende funngrupper.* De arkeologiske utgravninger i Gamlebyen, Oslo, vol. 3:41–168. Øvre Ervik.

– 1988: *"Mindets Tomt" – "Søndre Felt": Animal bones, moss-, plant-, insect- and parasite remains.* De Arkeologiske Utgravninger i Gamlebyen, Oslo, vol. 5. Alvheim & Eide. Øvre Ervik.

Schietzel, Kurt 1981: *Stand der siedlungsarchäologischen Forschung in Haithabu. Ergebnisse und Probleme.* Berichte über die Ausgrabungen in Haithabu, vol. 16. Wachholtz Verlag. Neumünster.

– 1984a: Die Baubefunde in Haithabu. In: Herbert Jankuhn, Kurt Schietzel and Hans Reichstein: *Handelsplätze des frühen und hohen Mittelalters,* pp. 135–158. Weinheim.

– 1984b: Hausrath in Haithabu. In: Herbert Jankuhn, Kurt Schietzel and Hans Reichstein: *Handelsplätze des frühen und hohen Mittelalters,* pp. 304–311. Weinheim.

– 1984c: Hafenanlagen von Haithabu. In: Herbert Jankuhn, Kurt Schietzel and Hans Reichstein (eds.): *Handelsplätze des frühen und hohen Mittelalters. Archäologische und naturwissenschaftliche Unter-*

suchungen an ländlichen und frühstädtischen Siedlungen im deutschen Küstengebiet vom 5. Jahrhundert v.Chr. bis zum 11. Jahrhundert n.Chr., vol. 2:184–91. Weinheim.

Schiffer, Michael B. 1996: *Formation Processes of the Archaeological Record.* University of Utah Press. Salt Lake City.

Schledermann, Helmuth 1974: Tingsted. *KLNM*, vol. 18:373–6.

Schmidt, Tom 2000a: *Norske gårdnavn på -by og -bø med personnavnforled.* Acta Humaniora, vol. 87. Unipub. Oslo.

– 2000b: Marked, torg og kaupang – språklige vitnemål om handel i middelalderen. *Collegium Medievale*, vol. 13:79–102.

Schmölcke, U. 2004: *Nutztierhaltung, Jagd und Fischfang: Zur Nahrungsmittelwirtschaft des frühgeschichtlichen Handelsplatzes von Groß Strömkendorf, Landkreis Nordwestmecklenburg.* Archäologisches Landsmuseum Mecklenburg-Vorpommern. Lübstorf.

Schofield, A.J. (ed.) 1991: *Interpreting Artefact Scatters: Contributions to Ploughzone Archaeology.* Oxbow books. Oxford.

Schou Jørgensen, Mogens 1998: Den berømte bro. *Skalk,* 1998:5:5–11.

Schultze, Joachim 2005: Zur Frage der Entwiklung des zentralen Siedlungskernes von Haithabu. In: Claus Dobiat (ed.): *Reliquiae Gentium. Festschrift für Horst Wolfgang Böhme zum 65. Gebrutsdag,* vol. I:359–373. Rahden/Westfalen.

Schøning, Gerhard 1771: *Riigets ældste Historie fra dets Begyndelse til Harald Haarfagers Tiider.* Norges Riiges Historie, vol. I. Mumme og Faber. Sorøe

Seip, Didrik Arup 1957: Borgarting, Borgartingsloven. *KLNM*, vol. 2:148–50.

Sedov, Valentin V. 1982: Ostslawen, Balten und Esten. In: J. Herrmann (ed.): *Wikinger und Slawen. Zur Frühgeschichte der Ostseevolker.* Berlin.

Sellevold, Berit J., Ulla Lund Hansen and Jørgen Balslev Jørgensen 1984: *Iron Age Man in Denmark.* Det Kongelige nordiske oldskriftselskab. København.

Serjeantson, D. 1988: Archaeological and ethnographic evidence for seabird exploitation in Scotland. *Archaeozoologia*, vol. 2:209–24.

– 1998: Birds: A seasonal resource. *Environmental Archaeology*, vol. 3:23–34.

– 2001: The great auk and the gannet: A prehistoric perspective on the extinction of the great auk. *International Journal of Osteoarchaeology*, vol. 11:43–55.

Shipman, P., G. F. Foster and M. Schoeninger 1984: Burnt bones and teeth: an experimental study of colour, morphology, crystal structure and shrinkage. *Journal of Archaeological Science*, vol. 11:307–25.

Shott, M. 1995: Reliability of Archaeological Records on Cultivated Surfaces: A Michigan Case Study. *Journal of Field Archaeology*, vol. 19:475–90.

Silver, I. A. 1969: The ageing of domestic animals. In: D. Brothwell and E. S. Higgs (eds.): *Science in Archaeology.*

A survey of progress and research, pp. 283–302. Thames & Hudson. London.

Silvegren, Ulla W. 1999: Mynten från Uppåkra. In: Birgitta Hårdh (ed.): *Fynden i centrum.* Uppåkrastudier, vol. 2:95–112. Lund.

Simonsson, Henry 1969: *Studier rörande vikingatida vapen- och ryttargravar, med utgångspunkt i det västmanländska materialet.* Department of archaeology, Uppsala University.

Simpson, Ian A., Sophia Perdikaris, Gordon Cook, John L. Campbell and William J. Teesdale 2000: Cultural sediment analyses and transitions in early fishing activity at Langenesværet, Vesterålen, northern Norway. *Geoarchaeology,* vol. 15:743–63.

Simpson, Linzi 1999: *Temple Bar West: Director's Findings.* Temple Bar Properties. Dublin.

Sindbæk, Søren 2003: Varægiske vinterruter. Slædetransport i Rusland og spørgsmålet om den tidlige vikingetids orientalske import i Nordeuropa. *Fornvännen*, vol. 98:179–193. Stockholm.

– 2005: *Ruter og rutinisering. Vikingetidens fjernhandel i Nordeuropa.* Multivers. København.

– in press: Too many towns. *Antiquity.*

Sjøkartverket 2003: *Vannstandsmålinger ved Helgeroa og Nevlunghavn, 1927 til 2003, og vannstandsprofil for Helgeroa.* (Daniel Hareide, e-mail 09.12.2003).

Sjøvold, Thorleif 1944: Studier i Vestfolds vikingtid. *Universitetets Oldsaksamling Årbok,* 1941–1942:5–102.

– 1974: *The Iron Age settlement of Arctic Norway. A study in the expansion of European Iron Age culture within the Arctic Circle,* vol. 2. Oslo.

Skibsted Klæsøe, Iben 1999: Vikingetidens kronologi – en nybearbejdning af det arkæologiske materiale. *Aarbøger for Nordisk Oldkyndighed og Historie,* 1997:89–142.

Skjoldunge saga = Karsten Friis-Jensen and Claus Lund (eds.): *Skjoldungernes saga.* Gad. København.

Skre, Dagfinn 1983: Kirkene ved Gildesvollen. *Hemgrenda,* 1983:3–8.

– 1988: *Gård og kirke, bygd og sogn. Organiseringsmodeller og organiseringsenheter i middelalderens kirkebygging i Sør-Gudbrandsdalen.* Riksantikvarens rapporter, vol. 16. Øvre Ervik.

– 1995: Kirken før sognet. Den tidligste kirkeordningen i Norge. In: Hans-Emil Lidén (ed.): *Møtet mellom hedendom og kristendom i Norge,* pp. 170–233. Oslo.

– 1997: Haug og grav. Hva betyr gravhaugene? In: Ann Christensson, Else Mundal and Ingvild Øye (eds.): *Middelalderens symboler.* Kulturtekster, vol. 11:37–52. Senter for europeiske kulturstudier. Bergen.

– 1998a: Missionary activity in Early Medieval Norway. Strategy, Organisation and the Course of Events. *Scandinavian Journal of History,* vol. 23:1–19.

– 1998b: *Herredømmet. Bosetning og besittelse på Romerike 200–1350 e.Kr.* Acta Humaniora, vol. 32. Oslo.

– 1998c: *Innberetning fra åkerregistrering og sondering etter bryggekonstruksjoner våren 1998 i svartjorden på Kaupang, nordre og søndre, gnr. 1012 og 1029, Larvik kommune, Vestfold*. Unpublished report, KHM archive.

– 1999: Tverrfaglighet i bosetningshistorisk forskning. Gleder og besværligheter. *Collegium Medievale*, vol. 11:1998:33–47.

– 2005: Dype er arkivenes gjemmer... Om noen gamle tegninger av fortidsminner i søndre Vestfold nylig gjenfunnet i Nationalmuseet, København. *Viking*, vol. 68:165–94.

– in prep.: *Viking-age Urbanism*. To appear in the Kaupang Excavation Project Publication Series.

Skre, Dagfinn and Frans-Arne Stylegar 2004: *Kaupang. Vikingbyen*. KHM, Universitetet i Oslo.

Skullerud, Anne E. 2003: *Rapport om arkeologisk undersøkelse av bosetningsspor på Tjølling kikegård 1038/1 i Larvik kommune, Vestfold*. Unpublished report, KHM archive.

Skaarup, J. 1976: *Stengade II. En langelandsk gravplads med grave fra romersk jernalder og vikingtid*. Rudkøbing.

Smedberg, Gunnar 1973: *Nordens första kyrkor. En kyrkorättslig studie*. Bibliotheca Theologiae Practicae, vol. 32. Lund

Smith, A. J. E. 1978: *The Moss Flora of Britain and Ireland*. Cambridge University Press. Cambridge.

Snow, D. W. and C. M. Perrins 1998: *The Birds of the Western Palearctic Concise Edition Volume 1: Non-passerines*. Oxford University Press. Oxford.

Sode, Torben and Claus Feveile 2002: Segmenterede metalfolierede glasperler og blæste hule glasperler med metalbelægning fra markedspladsen i Ribe. *By, marsk og geest, Kulturhistorisk årbog for Ribe-egnen*, vol. 14:5–14.

Sogner, Sølvi Bauge 1961: Herred, Norge. *KLNM*, vol. 6:492–494.

Solberg, Bergljot 1984: *Norwegian spearheads from the Merovingian and Viking periods*. Department of archaeology, Bergen University.

– 2000: *Jernalderen i Norge*. Cappelen. Oslo.

Speed, Greg and Penelope Walton Rogers 2004: A Burial of a Viking Woman at Adwick-le-Street, South Yorkshire. *Medieval Archaeology*, vol, 48:51–90.

Stalsberg, Anne 1982: Hver mann har ei hauk på hånd .... – ei heller falk på sverd. *DKNVS Årshefte 1981, Arkeologisk serie*, 1982:8:46–65. Trondheim.

Stein, Frauke 1967: *Adelsgräber des achten Jahrhunderts in Deutschland*. Germanische Denkmäler der Völkerwanderungszeit, Serie A:9. Berlin.

Steinnes, Asgaut 1955: *Husebyar*. Oslo.

Steinsland, Gro 1991: *Det hellige bryllup og norrøn kongeideologi*. Oslo.

– 2005: *Norrøn religion. Myter, riter, samfunn*. Pax. Oslo.

Stene, Katrine 2005: Kokegropene på Våle prestegård – klassisk beliggenhet for et kokegropfelt? In: Lil Gustafson, Tom Heibren and Jes Martens (eds.): *De gåtefulle kokegroper*. KHM Varia, vol. 58:167–76. Oslo.

Stephansen, Niels Seierløv 1970 [1800–1825]: Niels Seierløv Stephansens kallsbok. *Vestfoldminne*, 1970:5–80.

Steuer, Heiko 1984: Soziale Gliederung der Bevölkerung von Haithabu anhand der Gräberfelder. In: H. Jankuhn, K. Schietzel and H. Reichstein (eds.): *Archäolo-*

gische und naturwissenschaftliche Untersuchungen an ländlichen und frühstädtischen Siedlungen in deutschen Küstengebiet von 5. Jahrhundert v. Chr. bis zum 11. Jahrhundert n. Chr. 2. Handelsplätze des frühen und hohen Mittelalters, pp. 273–292. Weinheim.

– 1987: Gewichtsgeldwirtschaften im frühgeschichtlichen Europa – Feinwaagen und Gewichte als Quellen zur Währungsgeschichte. In: Klaus Düwel (ed.): *Der Handel der Karolinger- und Wikingerzeit. Untersuchungen zu Handel und Verkehr der vor- und frühgeschichtlichen Zeit in Mittel- und Nordeuropa*, vol. IV: 405–527. Vandenhoeck & Ruprecht. Göttingen.

– 1989: Archaeology and History: Proposals to the Social Structure of the Merovingian Kingdom. In: Klavs Randsborg (ed.): *The Birth of Europe: Archaeology and Social Development in the First Millenium A. D*, pp. 100–22. Roma.

– 2000: Hufeisen. *Reallexikon der germanischen Altertumskunde*, vol. 15:92–197. Berlin.

Stjernquist, Berta 1998: The Basic Perception of the Religious Activities at Cult-Sites such as Springs, Lakes and Rivers. In: Lars Larsson and Berta Stjernquist (eds.): *The World-view of prehistoric man*, pp. 157–78. Stockholm.

– 1999: Glass from the Uppåkra settlement. A Preliminary Study of Finds and Problems. In: Birgitta Hårdh (ed.): *Fynden i centrum*. Uppåkrastudier, vol. 2:67–94. Lund.

Stockmarr, Jens 1971: Tablets with spores used in absolute pollen-analysis. *Pollen et Spores*, vol. 13:612–21.

Stoops, Georges 2003: *Guidelines for Analysis and Description of Soil and Regolith Thin Sections*. Soil Science Society of America. Madison, WI.

Storm, Gustav 1901: Skiringssal og Sandefjord. *Historisk Tidsskrift*, vol. 16:214–237.

Strömberg, M. 1968: Ett gravfält från sen järnålder i Råga Hörstad i Skåne. *Antikvariskt arkiv*, vol. 35. Stockholm.

Stuiver, Minze, Paula J. Reimer and Thomas F. Braziunas, 1998: High-precision radiocarbon age calibration for terrestrial and marine samples. *Radiocarbon*, vol. 40: 1127–1151.

Sturluson, Snorri [1838–1839]: *Norske Kongers Sagaer*, vol. I–III. Translated by Jacob Aall. Christiania.

Stylegar, Frans-Arne 2003a: Grav, gård og gods i vikingtid. In: Ellen Anne Pedersen, Frans-Arne Stylegar and Per G. Norseng: *Øst for Folden*. Østfolds historie, vol. 1:336–377. Oslo.

– 2003b: Rolvsøy. *Reallexikon der Germanischen Altertumskunde*, vol. 25:202–206. Berlin.

– 2005a: Kammergraver fra vikingtiden i Vestfold. *Fornvännen*, vol. 100:161–177. Stockholm.

– 2005b: Stormenn og bønder – sverd og øks. Våpengravene i Rogalands vikingtid. *Frá haug ok heidni*, 2005:1:30–37. Stavanger.

– 2005c: "Vestfolds siste hedning". En branngrav fra 1000-årene fra Gipø på Nøtterøy. *Njotarøy*, 2005:12–14. Nøtterøy.

– 2006: Skeidfoler og blothester. Hingstekamp og døderitualer i yngre jernalder. In: H. Glørstad, B. Skar and D. Skre (eds.): *Historien i forhistorien. Festskrift til Einar Østmo på 60-årsdagen.* KHM Skrifter, vol. 4:207–220. Oslo.

— in prep. a: *Vikingtidens kvinnegraver i Øst-Norge: Smykkemote og draktskikk.*

— in prep. b: *Regionale tradisjoner i branngravskikken i østnorsk vikingtid.*

Stylegar, Frans-Arne and Oliver Grimm 2003: Da südnor-wegische Spangereid – Ein Beitrag zur Diskussion archäologischer Zentralplätze und norwegischer ringformiger Anlagen. *Offa*, vol. 59/60:81–124.

Stylegar, Frans-Arne and Per G. Norseng 2003: Mot historisk tid. In: Ellen Anne Pedersen, Frans-Arne Stylegar and Per G. Norseng: *Øst for Folden.* Østfolds historie, vol. 1:278–512. Oslo.

Ståhl, Harry 1976: *Ortnamn och ortnamnsforskning*, 2nd ed. AWE Geber. Stockholm.

Sundqvist, Ma 1993: Utgrävning pågår! Om storhögarna i Husby-Långhundra. In: *Långhundraleden – en seglats i tid och rum. 50 bidrag om den gamla vattenleden från Trälhavet till Uppsala genom årtusendena / sammanställda av redaktionsgruppen inom Arbetsgruppen Långhundraleden*, pp. 153–157. Uppsala.

Sundqvist, Olof 2002: *Freyr's offspring. Rulers and religion in ancient Svea society.* Uppsala.

— 2004: Uppsala och Asgård. Makt, offer och kosmos i forntida Skandinavien. In: Anders Andrén, Kristina Jennbert and Catharina Raudvere (eds.): *Ordning mot kaos. Studier av nordisk förkristen kosmologi.* Vägar til Midgård, vol. 4:145–79. Lund.

Svanberg, Fredrik 2003: *Death rituals in South-East Scandinavia AD 800–1000.* Decolonizing the Viking Age, vol. 2. Acta Archaeologica Lundensia Series in 4°:24. Lund.

Söderberg, Bengt 2005: *Aristokratiskt rum och gränsöverskridande. Järrestad och sydöstra Skåne mellan region och rike 600–1100.* Lund.

Sørensen, Palle Østergaard 1994: Gudmehallerne. Kongelig byggeri fra jernalderen. *Nationalmuseets Arbejdsmark*, 1994:25–39

Sørensen, Rolf 1999: En 14C datert og dendrokronologisk kalibrert strandforskyvningskurve for søndre Østfold, Sørøst-Norge. *AmS-Raport*, vol. 12A:227–42.

— 2002: *Rapport om feltarbeide på og omkring Kaupang i 2002.* Unpublished report, Institutt for jord- og vannfag, Norges landbrukshøgskole. Ås.

Sørensen, Rolf, Sivert Bakkelid and Bjørn Torp 1987: *Landhevning. Nasjonalatlas for Norge.* Kartblad 2.3.3. Målestokk 1:5 mill. Statens kartverk. Hønefoss.

Sørensen, Søren Anton 1900: *Det gamle Skiringssal 1. Stedets Beliggenhed.* Kristiania.

— 1902: *Er "Kongshaugen" hvori Vikingeskibet blev fundet Kong Olaf Geirstad-Alfs Haug? Svar til Prof. G. Storm.* Kristiania.

— 1909a: Om Skiringssal. *Historisk Tidsskrift*, vol. 20:358–97.

— 1909b: Bemerkninger til hr. A. Kjærs "afsluttende svar". *Historisk Tidsskrift*, vol. 20:431–2.

Sørheim, Helge 1989: Ildsteder. In: Erik Schia (ed.): *Hus og gjerder.* De arkeologiske utgravningene i Gamlebyen, Oslo, vol. 6:93–154. Øvre Ervik.

— 1997: En høvdings gård – en høvdings grav. En båtgrav fra Egge i Steinkjer, Nord-Trøndelag. *Gunneria*, vol. 72. Trondheim.

— 2004: Borgund and the Borgundfjord fisheries. In: Ingvild Øye (ed.): *Medieval Fishing Tackle from Bergen and Borgund.* The Bryggen Papers Main Series, vol. 5:107–33. Fagbokforlaget. Bergen.

— 2005: Fra hall til stove. In: Mari Høgestøl, Lotte Selsing, Trond Løken, Arne Johan Nærøy and Lisbeth Prøsch-Danielsen (eds.): *Konstruksjonsspor og byggeskikk.* AmS-Varia, vol. 43:155–64. Stavanger.

Sørheim, Helge, Morten Bertheussen, Henriette Hafsaas, Sverre Bakkevig and Catinka Borgarp 2004: Hus, åker, groper, graver og gripedyr. Litt om de foreløpige resultatene fra Søra Bråde 2. *Frá haug ok heidni*, 2004:4:3–19. Stavanger.

Tansøy, Birgit 2001: *Fisket på Kaupang i vikingtid.* Unpublished master thesis in Archaeology, University of Oslo.

Tegnér, Mimmi 1999: Uppåkra under sen vikingatid. In: Birgitta Hårdh (ed.): *Fynden i centrum.* Uppåkrastudier, vol. 2:225–41. Lund.

Theuws, Frands 2004: Exchange, rfeligion, identity and central places in the early middle Ages. *Archaeological Dialogues*, vol. 10:121–38.

Thomsen, Per O. 1993: Handelspladsen ved Lundeborg. In: Per O. Thomsen, Benno Blæsild, Nils Hardt and Karsten Kjer Michaelsen: *Lundeborg. En handelsplads fra jernalderen*, pp. 68–101. Svendborg.

Thordeman, Bengt 1920: *Alsnö hus. Ett svenskt medeltidspalats i sitt konsthistorika sammanhang.* Stockholm.

Thorvildsen, Knud 1957: *Ladby-skibet.* Nordiske fortidsminder, vol. 6:1. København.

Thun, Terje 2002: *Dendrochronological constructions of Norwegian conifer chronologies providing dating of historical material.* Trondheim.

— 2005: Norwegian conifer chronologies constructed to date historical timber. *Dendrochronologia*, vol. 23:63–74.

Thörn, Raimond 2005: Kokgropsrelationer. In: Lil Gustafson, Tom Heibren, Jes Martens (eds.): *De gåtefulle kokegroper.* KHM Varia, vol. 58:67–76. Oslo.

Tollnes, Roar L. 1969: Bygningsrester fra Kaupang. *Viking*, vol. 33:41–96.

— 1976: Kaupang in Skiringssal. The Building-remains and the structure of the settlement. *Häuser und Höfe der handeltreibenden Bevölkerung im Ostseegebiet und im Norden vor 1500. Visbysymposiet för historiska vetenskaper 1974.* Acta Visbyensia, vol. V:73–82.

— 1998: *Kaupang-funnene III A. Undersøkelser i bosetningsområdet 1956–1974. Hus og konstruksjoner.* Norske Oldfunn, vol. XVIII. Institutt for arkeologi, kunsthistorie og numismatikk, Universitetet i Oslo.

Tonning, Christer 2001: *Innberetning om graving av prøve-*

ruter på Nordre Kaupang (gnr. 1029/5), Larvik kommune, Vestfold. Unpublished report, KHM archive.

Tornbjerg, Sven Åge 1998: Toftegård – en fundrig gård fra sen jernalder og vikingetid. In: Lars Larsson and Birgitta Hårdh (eds.): *Centrala platser – Centrala frågor.* Uppåkrastudier, vol. 1:217–232. Lund.

Trotzig, Gustaf 1984: Gefässe aus Kupfer und seinen Legierungen. In: Greta Arwidsson (ed.): *Systematische Analysen der Gräberfunde.* Birka, vol. II:1:219–230. Stockholm.

Tutin, T. G., V. H. Heywood, N. A. Burges, D. M. Moore, D. H. Valentine, S. M. Walters and D. A. Webb 1964–80: *Flora Europaea,* vol. 1–5. Cambridge University Press. Cambridge.

Tyrberg, T. 2002: The archaeological record of domesticated and tamed birds in Sweden. *Acta Zoologica Cracoviensia,* vol. 45:215–31.

Underwood, Richard 1999: *Anglo-Saxon weapons and warfare.* Stroud.

Verhulst, Adriaan 2000: Roman cities, emporia and new towns. In: Inger Lyse Hansen and Chris Wickham (eds.): *The Long Eighth Century. Production, Distribution and Demand,* pp. 105–20. Leiden, Boston, Köln.

– 2002: *The Carolingian Economy.* Cambridge University Press. Cambridge.

Vikstrand, Per 2001: *Gudernas platser. Förkristna sakrala ortnamn i mälarlandskapen.* Uppsala.

– 2004a: Skúta and Vendil. Two Place Names in Ynglingatal. In: Astrid van Nahl, Lennart Elmevik and Stefan Brink (eds.): *Namenwelten. Orts und Personnamen in historischer Sicht,* pp. 372–387. Berlin.

– 2004b: Berget, lunden och åkern. In: Anders Andrén, Kristina Jennbert and Catharina Raudvere (eds.): *Ordning mot kaos. Studier av nordisk förkristen kosmologi.* Vägar til Midgård, vol. 4:317–41. Lund.

Villa, Paola and Jean Courtin 1983: The interpretation of stratified sites: a view from underground. *Journal of Archaeological Science,* vol. 10:267–81.

Visted, Kristoffer and Hilmar Stigum 1971: *Vår gamle bondekultur,* 3rd edition, vol. 1. Oslo.

Vollan, O. 1974: Torskefiske. *KLNM,* vol. 18:506–9.

Voss, Olfert 1991: Hørninggraven. In: M. Iversen, U. Näsman and J. Vellev (eds.): *Mammen. Grav, kunst og samfund i vikingetid,* pp. 189–203. Højbjerg.

Vretemark, Maria 1983: *Jakt med dresserad rovfågel i Sverige under yngre järnålder.*
http://users.cybercity.dk/~ccc12787/

de Vries, Jan 1970: *Altgermanische Religionsgeschichte,* vol. I. Berlin.

Wallace, Patric F. 1992: *The Viking Age Buildings of Dublin.* Medieval Dublin Excavations 1962–81, Ser. A, vol. 1. Royal Irish Academy, National Museum of Ireland. Dublin.

Wallin, Anette 1995: *Fyrfota färdmedel till dödsriket? Problematiken kring de gotländska så kallade ryttargravarna.* Department of archaeology, University College of Gotland.

Wamers, Egon 1985: *Insularer Metallschmuck in wikinger-*

zeitlichen Gräbern Nordeuropas. Offa-Bücher, vol. 56.

– 1994: König im Grenzland. Neue Analyse des Bootkammergrabes von Haiðaby. *Acta Archaeologica,* vol. 65:1–56.

– in prep.: *Continental and Insular Metalwork from Kaupang.* To appear in the Kaupang Excavation Project Publication Series.

Wandsnider, L. and E. Camilli 1992: The Character of Surface Archaeological Deposits and Its Influence on Survey Accuracy. *Journal of Field Archaeology,* vol. 19:169–88.

Watt, Margrethe 1991: Sorte Muld. Høvdingsæde og kultcentrum fra Bornholms yngre jernalder. In: Peder Mortensen and Birgit M. Rasmussen (eds.): *Høvdingesamfund og kongemagt.* Fra stamme til stat i Danmark, vol. 2:89–107. Jysk Arkæologisk Selskabs Skrifter, vol. XXII:2. Århus.

Wegraeus, Erik: Die Pfeilspitzen von Birka. In: Greta Arwidsson (ed.): *Systematische Analysen der Gräberfunde.* Birka, vol. II:221–34. Stockholm.

Wessén, Elias 1921: Linköping och lionga þing. *Namn och bygd,* vol. 9:27–44.

– 1958: *Runstenen vid Röks kyrka.* Stockholm.

Westerdahl, Christer and Frans-Arne Stylegar 2004: Husebyene i Norden. *Viking,* vol. 67:101–38.

Wheeler, A. and A. K. G. Jones 1989: *Fishes.* Cambridge University Press. Cambridge.

Whitehead, P. J. P., M. L. Bauchot, J. C. Hureau, J. Nielsen and E. Tortonese 1986: *Fishes of the North-eastern Atlantic and the Mediterranean,* vol. 2. United Nations Educational, Scientific and Cultural Organization. Paris.

Widmark, Gun 1997: Tolkning som sosial konstruktion. Rökstenens inskrift. In: Staffan Nyström (ed.): *Runor och ABC.* Stockholm.

Wienberg, Jes 2001: Churches and Centrality. Basilicas and Hall-Churches in Medieval Scandinavia and Livonia. In: Muntis Auns (ed.): *Lübeck Style? Novgorod Style?* pp. 269–303. Riga.

Wigh, Bengt 2001: *Animal Husbandry in the Viking Age Town of Birka and its Hinterland.* Birka Studies, vol. 7. The Birka Project. Stockholm.

Wiker, Gry 2000: *Metallsøking på Kaupang Nordre 1029/1 og Kaupang Søndre 1012/7, Larvik kommune, Vestfold fylke.* Unpublished report, KHM archive.

– 2001: *Utgravningsrapport for 2000 og 2001 fra forskningsgravningen i bosetningsområdet på Kaupang, gnr. 1012/1029, Larvik, Vestfold.* Unpublished report, KHM archive.

Zachrisson, Inger 2006: Väskan från Röstahammaren i Ås och gravfältets etniska tillhörighet. *Fornvännen,* vol. 101:19–28. Stockholm.

Zachrisson, Torun 1998: *Gård, gräns och gravfält, sammanhang kring ädelmetalldepåer och runstenar från vikingatid och tidigmedeltid i Uppland och Gästrikland.* Stockholm.

Zetterholm, Delmar Olof 1936: Hå 'årfäste'. In: V. Jansson (ed.): *Ordgeografi och språkhistoria. Bidrag från Nordi-*

ska seminariet vid Uppsala universitet. Nordiska texter och undersökningar, vol. 9:34–73. Gebers. Stockholm and København.

Ziefwert, Susanne 1992: *Ryttargravar på Gotland. Ett försök till analys av vikingatida fyndmiljøer*. Department of archaeology, Stockholm University.

Zimmermann, W. Haio 1998: Pfosten, Ständer und Schwelle und der Übergang vom Pfosten- zum Ständerbau – Eine Studie zu Innovation und Beharrung im Hausbau. Zu Konstruktion und Haltbarkeit prähistorischer bis neuzeitlicher Holtzbauten von den Nord- und Ostseeländern bis zu den Alpen. *Probleme der Küstenforschung im südlichen Nordseegebiet*, vol. 25:9–241. Niedersächsisches Institut für historische Küstenforschung, Wilhelmshafen. Isensee Verlag. Oldenburg.

Zong, Yongqiang 1997: Implications of *Paralia sulcata* abundance in Scottish isolation basins. *Diatom Research,* vol. 12:125–50.

Østmo, Mari 2005: *Tilhørighet i tid og rom. Om konstruksjon av kollektiv identitet og bygdefelleskap i jernalderen.* Unpublished master thesis in Archaeology, University of Oslo.

Øye, Ingvild in prep.: *Textile Tools from Kaupang.* To appear in the Kaupang Excavation Project Publication Series.

Åkerlund, Walter 1939: *Studier i Ynglingatal.* Lund.

Åkerström-Hougen, Gunilla 1981: Falconry as a motif in early Swedish art. Its historical and art historical significance. In: R. Zeitler (ed.): *Les pays du Nord et Byzance,* pp. 263–293. Uppsala.

List of Authors

Steve Ashby

Department of Archaeology,
University of York,
The King's Manor, York, YO1 7EP,
United Kingdom.
spa105@york.ac.uk

James Barrett

Department of Archaeology,
University of York,
The King's Manor, York, YO1 7EP,
United Kingdom.
jhb5@york.ac.uk

Niels Bonde

Nationalmuseet,
Frederiksholms Kanal 12,
DK-1220 København K,
Danmark.
niels.bonde@natmus.dk

Stefan Brink

Chair in Scandinavian Studies,
King's College, University of Aberdeen,
Aberdeen AB24 3FX,
UK Scotland.
s.brink@abdn.ac.uk

Kristine M. Bukholm

Department of Plant and Environmental
Sciences,
Norwegian University of Life Sciences,
P.O.Box 5003, NO-1432 Ås,
Norway.

Charles A. I. French

Department of Archaeology,
University of Cambridge,
Downing Street, Cambridge, CB2 3DZ,
United Kingdom.
caif2@cam.ac.uk

Allan Hall

Department of Archaeology,
University of York,
The King's Manor, York, YO1 7EP,
United Kingdom.
biol8@york.ac.uk

Kari E. Henningsmoen

Department of Geosciences
University of Oslo,
P.O.Box 1047 Blindern, NO-0316 Oslo,
Norway.

Helge I. Høeg

University Museum of Cultural History
P.O.Box 6762 St. Olavs plass, NO-0130 Oslo
Norway.
helge@hoeg.no

Cluny Johnstone

Department of Archaeology,
University of York,
The King's Manor, York, YO1 7EP,
United Kingdom.
@york.ac.uk

Harry Kenward

Department of Archaeology,
University of York,
The King's Manor, York, YO1 7EP,
United Kingdom.
hkk1@york.ac.uk

Karen B. Milek

Department of Archaeology,
University of Cambridge,
Downing Street,
Cambridge, CB2 3DZ,
United Kingdom.
kbm20@cam.ac.uk

Terry O'Connor

Department of Archaeology,
University of York,
The King's Manor, York, YO1 7EP,
United Kingdom.
tpoc1@york.ac.uk

Lars Pilø

University of Oslo,
Institute of Archaeology,
Conservation and Historic Studies,
P.O.Box 1008 Blindern, NO-0315 Oslo,
Norway.
l.h.pilo@iakh.uio.no

Unn Pedersen

University of Oslo,
Institute of Archaeology, Conservation
and Historic Studies,
P.O.Box 1008 Blindern, NO-0315 Oslo,
Norway.
unn.pedersen@iakh.uio.no

Dagfinn Skre

University of Oslo,
Institute of Archaeology, Conservation
and Historic Studies, P.O.Box 1008 Blindern,
NO-0315 Oslo, Norway.
dagfinn.skre@iakh.uio.no

Bjørg Stabell

Department of Geosciences,
University of Oslo,
P.O.Box 1047 Blindern, NO-0316 Oslo,
Norway.
bjorg.stabell@geo.uio.no

Frans-Arne Stylegar

Vest-Agder County Comcil,
Serviceboks 517, NO-4605 Kristiansand,
Norway.
fransarne.stylegar@vaf.no

Rolf Sørensen

Department of Plant and
Environmental Sciences,
Norwegian University of Life Sciences,
P.O.Box 5003, NO-1432 Ås,
Norway.
rolf.sorensen@umb.no

Members of the Kaupang Excavation Project Council 2000-2006

Björn Ambrosiani
Riksantikvarieämbetet
birkproj@raa.se

Reidar Bertelsen
University of Tromsø
reidarb@sv.uit.no

Anne-Merethe Lie Solberg
The Anders Jahre Humanitarian Foundation
post@ajhs.no

Øivind Lunde
Nidaros Domkirkes Restaureringsarbeider
oeivind.lunde@kirken.no

Richard Hall
York Archaeological Trust
rhall@yorkarchaeology.co.uk

Lotte Hedeager
University of Oslo
lotte.hedeager@iakh.uio.no

Hans Hjerpekjøn
Vestfold University College
hjerpekj@online.no

Even Hovdhaugen
University of Oslo
even.hovdhaugen@iln.uio.no

Halvard Kausland
Vestfold County Council
halvard.kausland@vestfold-f.kommune.no

Marie Kürstein
Vestfold County Council
marie.kurstein@c2i.net

Egil Mikkelsen
University of Oslo
egil.mikkelsen@khm.uio.no

Bjørn Myhre
Arkeologisk museum i Stavanger
bmy@ark.museum.no

Kaare R. Norum, Council President
University of Oslo
k.r.norum@basalmed.uio.no

Øyvind Riise Jenssen
The Municipality of Larvik
oyvind-r.jenssen@larvik.kommune.no

Else Roesdahl
University of Århus
marker@moes.hum.au.dk

Bjarne Rogan
University of Oslo
bjarne.rogan@iks.uio.no

Patric Wallace
National Museum of Ireland
pfwallace@museum.ie

Ingvild Øye
University of Bergen
ingvild.oye@bmu.uib.no

Members of the Kaupang Excavation Project Advisory Committee 2000-2002

Peter Birkedahl
Landsbyen Himmerland
pb@rorbak.dk

Ulf Bodin
Statens Historiska Museer
ulf.bodin@historiska.se

Axel Christophersen
NTNU, Vitenskapsmuseet
axel.christophersen@vm.ntnu.no

Claus Feveile
Den antikvariske Samling, Ribe
cf@asr-ribe.dk

Frands Herschend
University of Uppsala
frands.herschend@arkeologi.uu.se

Lars Jørgensen
Nationalmuseet
lars.joergensen@natmus.dk

Lars Larsson
University of Lund
lars.larsson@ark.lu.se

Trond Løken
Arkeologisk Museum i Stavanger
trond.loeken@ark.museum.no

Sæbjørg Nordeide
University of Bergen
sabjorg.nordeide@cms.uib.no

Brit Solli
University of Oslo
brit.solli@khm.uio.no

Kenneth Svensson
Arkeologikonsult
kenneth.svensson@telia.com

Roar L. Tollnes
rtollnes@frisurf.no

Haio Zimmermann
Niedersächsisches Institut für historische
Küstenforschung
zimmermann@nihk.de